THE
Jeffersonian Cyclopedia

VOLUME TWO

THE
Jeffersonian Cyclopedia

A COMPREHENSIVE COLLECTION OF THE
VIEWS OF

THOMAS JEFFERSON

Classified and Arranged in Alphabetical Order
Under Nine Thousand Titles

RELATING TO GOVERNMENT, POLITICS, LAW,
EDUCATION, POLITICAL ECONOMY, FINANCE,
SCIENCE, ART, LITERATURE, RELIGIOUS
FREEDOM, MORALS, ETC.

EDITED BY
JOHN P. FOLEY

WITH AN INTRODUCTION BY
JULIAN P. BOYD

VOLUME TWO

"I have sworn upon the altar of God eternal hostility against
every form of tyranny over the mind of man."—*Thomas Jefferson*

NEW YORK / RUSSELL & RUSSELL

FIRST PUBLISHED IN 1900

REISSUED, 1967, WITH AN INTRODUCTION BY JULIAN P. BOYD

AND PUBLISHED BY RUSSELL & RUSSELL

A DIVISION OF ATHENEUM HOUSE, INC.

THE SPECIAL CONTENTS OF THIS BOOK ARE

COPYRIGHT © 1967, BY JULIAN P. BOYD

L. C. CATALOG CARD NO.: 67–15473

PRINTED IN THE UNITED STATES OF AMERICA

4580. LEGISLATURES, Credentials.—
The Legislature shall form one house only for
the verification of their credentials.—Notes
for a Va. Constitution. Ford ed., vi, 521.
(1794.)

4581. LEGISLATURES, Despotism and.
—All the powers of government, legislative,
executive, and judiciary, result to the legislative body. The concentrating these in the
same hands is precisely the definition of despotic government. It will be no alleviation
that these powers will be exercised by a plurality of hands, and not by a single one. One
hundred and seventy-three despots would
surely be as oppressive as one. Let those
who doubt it turn their eyes on the republic
of Venice.—Notes on Virginia. viii, 361.
Ford ed., iii, 223. (1782.)

**4582. LEGISLATURES, Dissolution by
George III.—**One of the articles of impeachment against Trestlain and the other Judges of
Westminster Hall, in the reign of Richard the
Second, for which they suffered death, as
traitors to their country, was, that they had
advised the king that he might dissolve his Parliament at any time; and succeeding kings have
adopted the opinion of these unjust Judges.
Since the reign of the Second William, however,
under which the British constitution was settled
on its free and ancient principles, neither his
Majesty, nor his ancestors, have exercised such
a power of dissolution in the Island of Great
Britain *; and when his Majesty was petitioned,
by the united voice of his people there, to dissolve the present Parliament, who had become
obnoxious to them, his Ministers were heard to
declare, in open Parliament, that his Majesty
possessed no such power by the constitution.
But how different their language, and his practice, here! To declare, as their duty required,
the known rights of their country, to oppose the
usurpations of every foreign judicature, to disregard the imperious mandates of a minister or
governor, have been the avowed causes of dissolving Houses of Representatives in America.
But if such powers be really invested in his
Majesty, can he suppose they are there placed to
awe the members from such purposes as these?
When the representative body have lost the confidence of their constituents, when they have notoriously made sale of their most valuable rights,
when they have assumed to themselves powers
which the people never put into their hands,
then, indeed, their continuing in office becomes
dangerous to the State, and calls for an exercise
of the power of dissolution. Such being the
causes for which the representative body should,
and should not be dissolved, will it not appear
strange to an unbiased observer, that that of
Great Britain was not dissolved, while those
of the Colonies have repeatedly incurred that
sentence?—Rights of British America. i,
137. Ford ed., i, 441. (1774.)

4583. —— ——. Your Majesty, or your
governors, have carried this power [to dissolve

* "Since this period the King has several times
dissolved the parliament a few weeks before its expiration, merely as an assertion of right."—Note by
Jefferson.
"On further inquiry, I find two instances of dissolutions before the Parliament would, of itself, have
been at an end: viz., the Parliament called to meet
August 24, 1698, was dissolved by King William, December 19, 1700, and a new one called to meet February 6, 1701, which was also dissolved, November 11,
1701, and a new one met December 30, 1701."—Note
by Jefferson.

legislatures] beyond every limit known, or provided for, by the laws. After dissolving one
House of Representatives, they have refused to
call another, so that, for a great length of time,
the legislature provided by the laws has been
out of existence. From the nature of things,
every society must at all times possess within
itself the sovereign powers of legislation. The
feelings of humanity revolt against the supposition of a state so situated as that it may
not, in any emergency, provide against dangers which, perhaps, threaten immediate ruin.
While those bodies are in existence to whom the
people have delegated the powers of legislation,
they alone possess and may exercise those
powers. But when they are dissolved by the
lopping off of one or more of their branches,
the power reverts to the people, who may exercise it to unlimited extent, either assembling
together in person, sending deputies, or in any
other way they may think proper. * We forbear to trace consequences further; the dangers
are conspicuous with which this practice is
replete.—Rights of British America. i, 137.
Ford ed., i, 442. (1774.)

4584. —— ——. When the representative
body have lost the confidence of their constituents, when they have notoriously made sale of
their most valuable rights, when they have assumed to themselves powers which the people
never put into their hands, then, indeed, their
continuing in office becomes dangerous to the
State, and calls for an exercise of the power
of dissolution.—Rights of British America.
i, 137. Ford ed., i, 442. (1774.)

4585. —— ——. By one act they [Parlia-
ment] have suspended the powers of one American legislature, and by another have declared
they may legislate for us themselves in all
cases whatsoever. These two acts alone form
a basis broad enough whereon to erect a despotism of unlimited extent.—Declaration on
Taking up Arms. Ford ed., i, 469. (July
1775.)

4586. —— ——. He [George III.] has
endeavored to pervert the exercise of the kingly
office in Virginia into a detestable and insupportable tyranny * * * by dissolving legislative assemblies, repeatedly and continually, for
opposing with manly firmness his invasions on
the rights of the people.—Proposed Virginia
Constitution. ii, 10. (June 1776.)

4587. —— ——. He [George III.] has
dissolved Representative houses repeatedly and
continually † for opposing with manly firmness
his invasions on the rights of the people.—
Declaration of Independence as Drawn by
Jefferson.

4588. LEGISLATURES, Division of.—
The Legislature shall be separated by lot into
two chambers, which shall be called [a and w] ‡
on the first day of their session in every week;
which separation shall be effected by presenting to the representatives from each county
separately a number of lots equal to their own
number, if it be an even one or to the next
even number above, if their number be odd,

* A note in Jefferson's pamphlet copy of the
"Rights," &c., reads: "Insert 'and the frame of
government, thus dissolved, should the people take
upon them to lay the throne of your Majesty pros-
trate, or to discontinue their connection with the
British empire, none will be so bold as to decide
against the right or the efficacy of such avulsion'."
—Editor.
† Congress struck out "and continually".—Editor.
‡ The brackets and enclosures are Jefferson's.—
Editor.

one half of which lots shall be distinctively marked for the one chamber and the other half for the other, and each member shall be, for that week, of the chamber whose lot he draws. Members not present at the first drawing for the week shall draw on their first attendance after.—Notes for a Constitution. Ford ed., vi, 521. (1794.)

4589. —— ——. Each chamber shall appoint a speaker for the session, and it shall be weekly decided by lot between the two speakers, of which chamber each shall be for the ensuing week; and the chamber to which he is allotted shall have one the less in the lots presented to his colleagues for that week. —Notes for a Constitution. Ford ed., vi, 521. (1794.)

4590. —— ——. Our legislatures are composed of two houses, the Senate and Representatives, elected in different modes, and for different periods, and in some States, with a qualified veto in the Executive chief. But to avoid all temptation to superior pretensions of the one over the other house, and the possibility of either erecting itself into a privileged order, might it not be better to choose at the same time and in the same mode, a body sufficiently numerous to be divided by lot into two separate houses, acting as independently as the two houses in England, or in our governments, and to shuffle their names together and redistribute them by lot, once a week for a fortnight? This would equally give the benefit of time and separate deliberation, guard against an absolute passage by acclamation. derange cabals, intrigues, and the count of noses, disarm the ascendency which a popular demagogue might at any time obtain over either house, and render impossible all disputes between the two houses, which often form such obstacles to business.—To M. Coray. vii, 321. (M., 1823.)

4591. —— ——In the structure of our legislatures. we think experience has proved the benefit of subjecting questions to two separate bodies of deliberants; but in constituting these, natural right has been mistaken, some making one of these bodies. and some both, the representatives of property instead of persons; whereas the double deliberation might be as well obtained without any violation of true principle. either by requiring a greater age in one of the bodies, or by electing a proper number of representatives of persons, dividing them by lots into two chambers, and renewing the division at frequent intervals, in order to break up all cabals.—To John Cartwright. vii, 357. (M., 1824.)

4592. LEGISLATURES, Election of members.—So many [representatives] only shall be deemed elected as there are units actually v ting on that particular election, adding one for any fraction of votes exceeding the half unit. Nor shall more be deemed elected than the number last apportioned. If a county has not a half unit of votes, the Legislature shall incorporate its votes with those of some adjoining county.—Notes for a Va. Constitution. Ford ed., vi, 520. (1794.)

4593. —— ——. Every elector may vote for as many representatives as were apportioned by the Legislature to his county at the last establishment of the unit.—Notes for a Va. Constitution. Ford ed., vi, 520. (1794.)

4594. —— ——. There are parts of the new constitution of Spain in which you would expect, of course, that we should not concur. * * * One of these is the aristocracy, *quater sublimata*, of her legislators; for the ultimate electors of these will themselves have been three times sifted from the mass of the people, and may choose from the nation at large persons never named by any of the electoral bodies.—To Chevalier de Onis. vi, 342. (M., 1814.)

4595. —— ——. Let every man who fights or pays, exercise his just and equal right in the election of the legislature.—To Samuel Kerchival. vii, 11. Ford ed., x, 39. (M., 1816.)

4596. LEGISLATURES, Freedom of action.—The House of Representatives, when met, shall be free to act according to their own judgment and conscience.—Proposed Va. Constitution. Ford ed., ii, 15. (June 1776.)

4597. LEGISLATURES, Interregnum of.—He [George III.] has refused for a long time after such dissolutions [of representative houses] to cause others to be elected, whereby the legislative powers, incapable of annihilation, have returned to the people at large for their exercise, the State remaining, in the meantime, exposed to all the dangers of invasion from without and convulsions within. —Declaration of Independence as Drawn by Jefferson.

4598. LEGISLATURES, Officers of.— The General Assembly shall have power to appoint the speakers of their respective houses, treasurer, auditors, attorney general, register, all general offices of the military, their own clerks and serjeants, and no other officers, except where, in other parts of this constitution, such appointment is expressly given them.—Proposed Va. Constitution. viii, 446. Ford ed., iii, 325. (1783.)

4599. LEGISLATURES, The people and. —The people are not qualified to legislate. With us, therefore, they only choose the legislators.—To L'Abbé Arnond. iii, 89. Ford ed., v, 103. (P., 1789.)

4600. LEGISLATURES, Powers of.— Our legislators are not sufficiently apprized of the rightful limits of their power; that their true office is to declare and enforce only our natural rights and duties, and to take none of them from us.—To F. W. Gilmer. vii, 3. Ford ed., x, 32. (M., 1816.)

4601. LEGISLATURES, Privileges.— The members [of the General Assembly], during the attendance on the General Assembly, and for so long a time before and after as shall be necessary for travelling to and from the same, shall be privileged from all personal restraint and assault, and shall have no other privilege whatsoever.—Proposed Constitution for Virginia. viii, 444. Ford ed., iii, 324. (1783.)

4602. —— ——. The Legislature shall form one house only for * * * what relates to their privileges.—Notes for a Va. Constitution. vi, 521. (1794.)

4603. LEGISLATURES, Qualifications of Members.—Any member of the * * * Assembly accepting any office of profit under this State, or the United States, or any of them, shall thereby vacate his seat, but shall be capable of being reelected.—Proposed Va. Constitution. viii, 445. Ford ed., iii, 325. (1783.)

4604. —— ——. Of this General Assembly, the treasurer, attorney general, register, ministers of the gospel, officers of the regular armies of this State, or of the United States, persons receiving salaries or emoluments from any power foreign to our confederacy, those who are not resident in the county for which they are chosen delegates, or districts for which they are chosen senators, those who are not qualified, as electors, persons who shall have committed treason, felony, or such other crime as would subject them to infamous punishment, or shall have been convicted by due course of law of bribery or corruption, in endeavoring to procure an election to the said assembly, shall be incapable of being members. All others, not herein elsewhere excluded, who may elect, shall be capable of being elected thereto.—Proposed Constitution for Virginia. viii, 445. Ford ed., iii, 324. (1783.)

4605. LEGISLATURES, Size of.—Is it meant to confine the legislative body to their present numbers, that they may be the cheaper bargain whenever they shall become worth a purchase?—Rights of British America. i, 136. Ford ed., i, 441. (1774.)

4606. —— ——. Twelve hundred men in one room are too many.—To Thomas Paine. iii, 71. (P., 1789.)

4607. —— ——. The [National] Assembly [of France] proceeds slowly in the forming their constitution. The original vice of their numbers causes this, as well as a tumultuous manner of doing business.—To John Jay. iii, 115. (P., 1789.)

4608. —— ——. Render the [Virginia] legislature a desirable station by lessening the number of representatives (say to 100) and lengthening somewhat their term, and proportion them equally among the electors.—To Archibald Stuart. iii, 315. Ford ed., v, 410. (Pa., 1791.)

4609. —— ——. Reduce the legislature to a convenient number for full, but orderly discussion.—To Samuel Kerchival. vii, 11. Ford ed., x, 39. (M., 1816.)

4610. LEGISLATURES, Slothful.—The sloth of the [French National] Assembly (unavoidable from their number) has done the

most sensible injury to the public cause. The patience of a people who have less of that quality than any other nation in the world, is worn threadbare.—To John Jay. iii, 115. (P., Sep. 1789.)

4611. LEGISLATURES, Suspension of. —The act passed in the seventh year of the reign of George III., having been a peculiar attempt, must ever require peculiar mention. It is entitled, "An Act for Suspending the Legislature of New York". One free and independent legislature hereby takes upon itself to suspend the powers of another, free and independent as itself; thus exhibiting a phenomenon unknown in nature, the creator and creature of its own power.—Rights of British America. i, 131. Ford ed., i, 435. (1774.)

4612. —— ——. The proposition [of Lord North] is altogether unsatisfactory * * * because they (Parliament) do not renounce the power of suspending our own legislatures. —Reply to Lord North's Proposition. Ford ed., i, 480. (July 1775.)

4613. —— ——. He [George III.] has endeavored to pervert the exercise of the kingly office in Virginia into a detestable and unsupportable tyranny * * * by combining with others to subject us to a foreign jurisdiction, giving his assent to their pretended acts of legislation * * * for suspending our own legislatures, and declaring themselves invested with power to legislate for us in all cases whatsoever.—Proposed Va. Constitution. Ford ed., ii, 11. (June 1776.)

4614. LEGISLATURES, Two chambers. —The purpose of establishing different houses of legislation is to introduce the influence of different interests or different principles. Thus in Great Britain, it is said, their constitution relies on the House of Commons for honesty, and the Lords for wisdom; which would be a rational reliance, if honesty were to be bought with money, and if wisdom were hereditary. In some of the American States, the delegates and senators are so chosen, as that the first represent the persons, and the second the property of the State. But with us, wealth and wisdom have equal chance for admission into both houses. We do not, therefore, derive from the separation of our legislature into two houses, those benefits which a proper complication of principles is capable of producing, and those which alone can compensate the evils which may be produced by their dissensions.—Notes on Virginia. viii, 361. Ford ed., iii, 223. (1782.)

4615. —— ——. For good legislation two houses are necessary.—To Marquis Lafayette. iii, 20. Ford ed., v, 92. (P., 1789.)

4616. —— ——. I find my countrymen * * * thinking with the National Assembly [of France] in all points except that of a single house of legislation. They think their own experience has so decidedly proved the necessity of two Houses to prevent the tyranny of one that they fear that this single error will shipwreck your new constitution. I am myself persuaded that theory and practice are not at variance in this instance, and that you will find it necessary hereafter to add another branch.—To DUKE DE LA ROCHEFOUCAULD. iii, 136. (N. Y., 1790.)

4617. LEGISLATURES, Tyranny of.— The executive in our governments is not the sole, it is scarcely the principal object of my jealousy. The tyranny of the Legislatures is the most formidable dread at present, and will be for many years.—To JAMES MADISON. iii, 5. FORD ED., v, 83. (P., 1789.)

4618. LEGISLATURES, Unit of representation.—The Legislature shall provide that returns be made to themselves periodically of the qualified voters in every county, by their name and qualification; and from the whole number of qualified voters * * * such an unit of representation shall be * * * taken as will keep the number of representatives within the limits of 150 and 300, allowing to every county a representative for every unit and fraction of more than half an unit it contains.—NOTES FOR A VA. CONSTITUTION. FORD ED., vi, 520. (1794.)

4619. LEGISLATURES, Usurpation of power.—He has combined with others to subject us to a jurisdiction foreign to our constitutions and unacknowledged by our laws, giving his assent to their acts of pretended legislation for * * * suspending our own legislatures and declaring themselves invested with power to legislate for us in all cases whatsoever.—DECLARATION OF INDEPENDENCE AS DRAWN BY JEFFERSON.

4620. LEGISLATURES, Vacancies.— Vacancies in the House of Representatives, by death or disqualification, shall be filled by the electors, under a warrant from the Speaker of the said house.—PROPOSED VA. CONSTITUTION. FORD ED., ii, 14. (June 1776.)

4621. LEGISLATURES, Virginia.— Legislation shall be exercised by two separate houses, to wit, a House of Representatives, and a House of Senators, which shall be called the General Assembly of Virginia.— PROPOSED VA. CONSTITUTION. FORD ED., ii, 13. (June 1776.)

4622. ———— ————. The House of Representatives shall be composed of persons chosen by the people annually on the first day of October, and shall meet in General Assembly on the first day of November following, and so, from time to time, on their own adjournments, or at any time when summoned by the Administrator, and shall continue sitting so long as they shall think the public service requires.—PROPOSED VA. CONSTITUTION. FORD ED., ii, 14. (June 1776.)

4623. ———— ————. The Senate shall consist of not less than [15]* nor more than [50] members, who shall be appointed by the House of Representatives. One-third of them shall be removed out of office by lot at the end of the first [three] years, and their places

* The brackets and figures within them are Jefferson's.—EDITOR.

be supplied by a new appointment; one other third shall be removed by lot, in like manner, at the end of the second [three] years and their places be supplied by a new appointment; after which one-third shall be removed annually at the end of every [three] years according to seniority. When once removed, they shall be forever incapable of being reappointed to that House. Their qualifications shall be an oath of fidelity to the State, and of duty in their office, the being [31] years of age at the least, and the having given no bribe, directly or indirectly, to obtain their appointment. While in the senatorial office, they shall be incapable of holding any public pension, or post of profit, either themselves, or by others for their use.—PROPOSED VA. CONSTITUTION. FORD ED., ii, 15. (June 1776.)

4624. L'ENFANT (Major), Dismissal of. —It having been found impracticable to employ Major L'Enfant about the Federal city, in that degree of subordination which was lawful and proper, he has been notified that his services are at an end. It is now proper that he should receive the reward of his past services; and the wish that he should have no just cause of discontent, suggests that it should be liberal. The President thinks of two thousand five hundred, or three thousand dollars; but leaves the determination to you. *—To MESSRS. JOHNSON, CARROLL AND STEWART. iii, 336. (Pa., 1792.)

4625. LETHARGY, Fatal to liberty.— Lethargy is the forerunner of death to the public liberty.—To W. S. SMITH. ii, 318. FORD ED., iv, 467. (P., 1787.)

4626. LETTERS, Answering.—Instead of writing ten or twelve letters a day, which I have been in the habit of doing as a thing in course, I put off answering my letters now farmer-like, till a rainy day, and then find them sometimes postponed by other necessary occupations.—To JOHN ADAMS. iv, 103. FORD ED., vi, 505. (M., April 1794.)

4627. LETTERS, Distorted.—Every word which goes from me, whether verbally or in writing, becomes the subject of so much malignant distortion, and perverted construction, that I am obliged to caution my friends against admitting the possibility of my letters getting into the public papers or a copy of them to be taken under any degree of confidence.—To EDWARD DOWSE. iv, 477. (W., 1803.)

4628. LETTERS, Gleams of light.—Your letters * * * serve, like gleams of light, to cheer a dreary scene; where envy, hatred, malice, revenge, and all the worst passions of men, are marshalled to make one another as miserable as possible.—To MARTHA JEFFERSON RANDOLPH. D. L. J. 248. (Pa., Feb. 1798.)

4629. LETTERS, Private.—I have generally great aversion to the insertion of my letters in the public papers; because of my passion for quiet retirement, and never to be exhibited in scenes on the public stage.—To JOHN ADAMS. vii, 254. (M., 1822.)

4630. LETTERS, Sanctity of.—I should wish never to put pen to paper; and the more

* L'Enfant was a French engineer who was employed in laying out the City of Washington.—EDITOR

because of the treacherous practice some people have of publishing one's letters without leave. Lord Mansfield declared it a breach of trust, and punishable at law. I think it should be a penitentiary felony.—To JOHN ADAMS. vii, 244. FORD ED., x, 216. (M., 1822.)

4631. LETTERS, Unanswered.—The constant pressure of business has forced me to follow the practice of not answering letters which do not necessarily require it.—To ROBERT WILLIAMS. v, 209. FORD ED., ix, 166. (W., 1807.)

4632. LETTER-WRITING, Dangers of. —The abuse of confidence by publishing my letters has cost me more than all other pains, and makes me afraid to put pen to paper in a letter of sentiment.—To C. HAMMOND. vii, 217. (M., 1821.)

4633. ——— ———. I sometimes expressly desire that my letter may not be published; but this is so like requesting a man not to steal or cheat, that I am ashamed of it after I have done it.—To NATHANIEL MACON. vii, 223. FORD ED., x, 193. (M., 1821.)

4634. LETTER-WRITING, Drudgery of.—From sunrise to one or two o'clock, and often from dinner to dark, I am drudging at the writing table. And all this to answer letters into which neither interest nor inclination on my part enters; and often from persons whose names I have never before heard. Yet, writing civilly, it is hard to refuse them civil answers. This is the burthen of my life, a very grievous one indeed, and one which I must get rid of. Delaplaine lately requested me to give him a line on the subject of his book; meaning, as I well knew, to publish it. This I constantly refuse; but in this instance yielded, that in saying a word for him I might say two for myself. I expressed in it freely my sufferings from this source; hoping it would have the effect of an indirect appeal to the discretion of those, strangers and others, who, in the most friendly dispositions, oppress me with their concerns, their pursuits, their projects, inventions and speculations, political, moral, religious, mechanical, mathematical, historical, &c., &c. I hope the appeal will bring me relief, and that I shall be left to exercise and enjoy correspondence with the friends I love, and on subjects which they, or my own inclinations present.— To JOHN ADAMS. vii, 54. FORD ED., x, 71. (M., 1817.)

4635. LETTER-WRITING, Relief from. —It occurs then, that my condition of existence, truly stated in that letter, if better known, might check the kind indiscretions which are so heavily oppressing the departing hours of life. Such a relief [from letter-writers] would, to me, be an ineffable blessing. But yours, * * * equally interesting and affecting, should accompany that to which it is an answer. The two, taken together, would excite a joint interest, and place before our fellow-citizens the present condition of two ancient servants, who having faithfully performed their forty or fifty campaigns, *stipendiis omnibus expletus*, have a reasonable claim to repose from all disturbance in the sanctuary of invalids and superannuates. —To JOHN ADAMS. vii, 254. FORD ED., x, 218. (M., 1822.)

4636. LETTER-WRITING, Voluminous.—I do not know how far you may suffer, as I do, under the persecution of letters, of which every mail brings me a fresh load. They are letters of enquiry, for the most part, always of good will, sometimes from friends whom I

esteem, but much oftener from persons whose names are unknown to me, but written kindly and civilly, and to which, therefore, civility requires answers. * * * I happened to turn to my letter-list some time ago, and a curiosity was excited to count those received in a single year. It was the year before the last. I found the number to be one thousand two hundred and sixty-seven, many of them requiring answers of elaborate research, and all to be answered with due attention and consideration. Take an average of this number for a week or a day, and I will repeat the question * * * is this life? At best, it is but the life of a mill-horse, who sees no end to his circle but in death. To such a life, that of a cabbage is paradise.—To JOHN ADAMS. vii, 254. FORD ED., x, 218. (M., 1822.)

4637. LETTER-WRITING vs. READING.—The drudgery of letter writing often denies me the leisure of reading a single page in a week.—To EZRA STILES. vii, 127. (M., 1819.)

4638. LEWIS AND CLARK EXPEDITION, Jefferson suggests.—The river Missouri, and the Indians inhabiting it, are not as well known as is rendered desirable by their connection with the Mississippi, and consequently with us. It is, however, understood, that the country on that river is inhabited by numerous tribes, who furnish great supplies of furs and peltry to the trade of another nation, carried on in a high latitude, through an infinite number of portages and lakes, shut up by ice through a long season. The commerce on that line could bear no competition with that of the Missouri, traversing a moderate climate, offering, according to the best accounts, a continued navigation from its source, and possibly with a single portage, from the Western Ocean, and finding to the Atlantic a choice of channels through the Illinois or Wabash, the Lakes and Hudson, through the Ohio and Susquehanna, or Potomac or James rivers, and through the Tennessee and Savannah rivers. An intelligent officer, with ten or twelve chosen men, fit for the enterprise, and willing to undertake it, taken from our posts, where they may be spared without inconvenience, might explore the whole line, even to the Western Ocean; have conferences with the natives on the subject of commercial intercourse; get admission among them for our traders, as others are admitted; agree on convenient deposits for an interchange of articles; and return with the information required, in the course of two summers. Their arms and accoutrements, some instruments of observation, and light and cheap presents for the Indians, would be all the apparatus they could carry, and with an expectation of a soldier's portion of land on their return, would constitute the whole expense. Their pay would be going on, whether here or there. While other civilized nations have encountered great expense to enlarge the boundaries of knowledge, by undertaking voyages of discovery, and for other literary purposes, in various parts and directions, our nation seems to owe to the same object, as well as to its own interests, to explore this, the only line of easy communication across the continent, and so directly traversing our own part of it. The interests of commerce place the principal object within the constitutional powers and care of Congress, and that it should incidentally advance the geographical knowledge of our continent, cannot be but an additional gratification. The nation claiming the territory, regarding this as a literary pursuit, which it is in the habit of permitting within its Dominions, would not be disposed to view it with jealousy, even if the expiring state of its interests there did not render it a matter of indifference. The appropriation of two thousand five hundred dollars " for the purpose of extending the external commerce of the United States ', while understood and considered by the Executive as giving the legislative sanction, would cover the undertaking from notice, and prevent the obstructions which interested individuals might otherwise previously prepare in its way.—CONFIDENTIAL MESSAGE. viii, 243. FORD ED., viii, 201. (Jan. 1803.)

4639. LEWIS AND CLARK EXPEDITION, Preparations.—I had long deemed it incumbent on the authorities of our country to have the great western wilderness beyond the Mississippi explored, to make known its geography, its natural productions, its general character and inhabitants. Two attempts which I had myself made formerly, before the country was ours, the one from west to east, the other from east to west, had both proved abortive. When called to the administration of the general government, I made this an object of early attention, and proposed it to Congress. They voted a sum of five thousand dollars for its execution, and I placed Captain Lewis at the head of the enterprise. No man within the range of my acquaintance united so many of the qualifications necessary for its successful direction. But he had not received such an astronomical education as might enable him to give us the geography of the country with the precision desired. The Missouri and Columbia, which were to constitute the tract of his journey, were rivers which varied little in their progressive latitudes, but changed their longitudes rapidly and at every step. To qualify him for making these observations, so important to the value of the enterprise, I encouraged him to apply himself to this particular object, and gave him letters to Doctor Patterson and Mr. Ellicott, requesting them to instruct him in the necessary processes. Those for the longitude would, of course, be founded on the lunar distances. But as these require essentially the aid of a time-keeper, it occurred to me that during a journey of two, three, or four years, exposed to so many accidents as himself and the instrument would be, we might expect with certainty that it would become deranged, and in a desert country where it could not be repaired. I thought it then highly important that some means of observation should be furnished him which should be practicable and competent to ascertain his longitudes in that event. The equatorial occurred to myself as the most promising substitute. I observed only that Ramsden, in his explanation of its uses, and particularly that of finding the longitude at land, still required his observer to have the aid of a time-keeper. But this cannot be necessary, for the margin of the equatorial circle of this instrument being divided into time by hours, minutes and seconds, supplies the main functions of the time-keeper, and for measuring merely the interval of the observations, is such as not to be neglected. A portable pendulum for counting, by an assistant, would fully answer that purpose. I suggested my fears to several of our best astronomical friends, and my wishes that other processes should be furnished him, if any could be, which might guard us ultimately from disappointment. Several other methods were proposed, but all requiring the use of a time-keeper. That of the equatorial being recommended by none, and other duties refusing me time for protracted consultations, I relinquished the idea for that occasion. But, if a sound one, it should not be neglected. Those deserts are yet to be explored, and their geography given to the world and ourselves with a correctness worthy of the science of the age. The acquisition of the country before Captain Lewis's departure facilitated our enterprise, but his time-keeper failed early in his journey. His dependence, then, was on the compass and log-line, with the correction of latitudes only ; and the longitudes of the different points of the Missouri, of the Stony Mountains, the Columbia and Pacific, at its mouth, remain yet to be obtained by future enterprise.—To —— ——. vii, 224. (M., 1821.) See LATITUDE AND LONGITUDE.

4640. —— ——. In the journey you are about to undertake * * * should you reach the Pacific Ocean * * * and be * * * without money * * * your resource * * * can only be the credit of the United States ; for which purpose I hereby authorize you to draw on the Secretaries of State, of the Treasury, of War, and of the Navy of the United States, according as you may find your drafts will be most negotiable, for the purpose of obtaining money or necessaries for yourself and men ; and I solemnly pledge the faith of the United States that these drafts shall be paid punctually * * * And to give more entire satisfaction and confidence to those who may be disposed to aid you, I, Thomas Jefferson, President of the United States of America, have written this letter of general credit for you with my own hand, and signed it with my name.—To CAPTAIN MERIWETHER LEWIS. iv, 492. (W., July 4, 1803.)

4641. LEWIS AND CLARK EXPEDITION, Success.—The expedition of Messrs. Lewis and Clark, for exploring the river Missouri, and the best communication from that to the Pacific ocean, has had all the success which could have been expected. They have traced the Missouri nearly to its source, descended the Columbia to the Pacific ocean, ascertained with accuracy the geography of that interesting communication across our continent, learned the character of the country, of its commerce, and inhabitants ; and it is but justice to say that Messrs. Lewis and Clark, and their brave companions, have by this arduous service deserved well of their country.—SIXTH ANNUAL MESSAGE. viii, 66. FORD ED., viii, 492. (Dec. 1806.)

4642. LEVEES, Presidential.—Edmund Randolph tells James Madison and myself a curious fact which he had from Lear. When the President went to New York, he resisted for three weeks the efforts to introduce levees. At length he yielded, and left it to Humphreys and some others to settle the forms. Accordingly, an antechamber and presence room were provided, and when those who were to pay their court were assembled, the President set out, preceded by Humphreys. After passing through the antechamber, the door of the inner room was thrown open, and Humphreys entered first, calling out with a loud voice, " the President of the United States ". The President was so much disconcerted with it, that he did not recover from it the whole time of the levee, and when the company was gone, he said to Humphreys, " Well, you have taken me in once, but by God you shall never take me in a second time ".—THE ANAS. ix, 132. FORD ED., i, 216. (1793.)

4643. LEVEES, Washington's explanation.—President Washington [in conversation with me] went lengthily into the late attacks on him for levees, &c., and explained how he had been led into them by the persons he consulted at New York ; and that if he could but know what the sense of the public was, he would most cheerfully conform to it.—THE ANAS. ix, 132. FORD ED., i, 216. (Feb. 1793.) See CEREMONY, ETIQUETTE and FORMS.

4644. LIANCOURT (Duke de), Appeal for.—I wish the present government would permit M. de Liancourt's return. He is an honest man, sincerely attached to his country, and very desirous of being permitted to live retired in the bosom of his family. My sincere affection for his connections at Rocheguyon * * * would render it a peculiar felicity to me to be any ways instrumental in having him restored to them. I have no means, however, unless you can interpose without giving offence.—To JAMES MONROE. FORD ED., vii, 88. (M., 1796.)

4645. LIANCOURT (Duke de), Patriot. —The bearer hereof is the Duke de Liancourt, one of the principal noblemen of France, and one of the richest. All this he has lost in the revolutions of his country, retaining only his virtue and good sense, which he possesses in a high degree. He was President of the National Assembly of France in its earliest stage, and forced to fly from the proscriptions of Marat.— To MR. HITE. iv, 145. (M., 1796.)

4646. LIBELS, Federal cognizance.— Libels, falsehood, and defamation, equally with heresy and false religion, are withheld from the cognizance of Federal tribunals.— KENTUCKY RESOLUTIONS. ix, 466. FORD ED., vii, 295. (1798.)

4647. LIBELS, Guarding against.—I have seen in the New York papers a calumny which I suppose will run through the Union, that I had written by Doctor Logan letters to Merlin and Talleyrand. On retiring from the Secretary of State's office, I determined to drop all correspondence with France, knowing the base calumnies which would be built on the most innocent correspondence. I have not, therefore, written a single letter to that country, within that period except to Mr. Short on his own affairs merely which are under my direction, and once or twice to Colonel Monroe. By Logan, I did not write even a letter to Mr. Short, nor to any other person whatever. I thought this notice of the matter due to my friends, though I do not go into the newspapers with a formal declaration of it.—To AARON BURR. FORD ED., vii, 259. (M., Nov. 1798.)

4648. LIBELS, Jefferson and.—At this moment my name is running through all the city [Philadelphia] as detected in a criminal correspondence with the French Directory, and fixed upon me by the documents from our Envoys, now before the two Houses. The detection of this by the publication of the papers, should they be published, will not relieve all the effects of the lie, and should they not be published, they may keep it up as long and as successfully as they did and do that of my being involved in Blount's conspiracy.—To JAMES MONROE. FORD ED., vii, 233. (Pa., April 1798.)

4649. ——— ———. Party passions are indeed high. Nobody has more reasons to know it than myself. I receive daily bitter proofs of it from people who never saw me, nor know anything of me but through " Porcupine "

[William Cobbett] and Fenno.—To JAMES LEWIS, JR. iv, 241. FORD ED., vii, 250. (Pa., May 1798.)

4650. ——— ———. Our very long intimacy as fellow laborers in the same cause, the recent expressions of mutual confidence which had preceded your mission [to France], the interesting course which that had taken, and particularly and personally as it regarded yourself, made me anxious to hear from you * * * . I was the more so, too, as I had myself, during the whole of your absence, as well as since your return, been a constant butt for every shaft of calumny which malice and falsehood could form, and the presses, public speakers, or private letters disseminate. One of these, too, was of a nature to touch yourself; as if, wanting confidence in your efforts, I had been capable of usurping powers committed to you, and authorizing negotiations private and collateral to yours. The real truth is, that though Doctor Logan, the pretended missionary, about four or five days before he sailed for Hamburg, told me he was going there, and thence to Paris, and asked and received from me a certificate of his citizenship, character, and circumstances of life, merely as a protection, should he be molested on his journey, in the present turbulent and suspicious state of Europe, yet I had been led to consider his object as relative to his private affairs; and though, from an intimacy of some standing, he knew well enough my wishes for peace and my political sentiments in general, he nevertheless received then no particular declaration of them, no authority to communicate them to any mortal, nor to speak to any one in my name, or in anybody's name, on that, or on any other subject whatever; nor did I write by him a scrip of a pen to any person whatever. This he has himself honestly and publicly declared since his return; and from his well-known character and every other circumstance, every candid man must perceive that his enterprise was dictated by his own enthusiasm, without consultation or communication with any one; that he acted in Paris on his own ground; and made his own way. Yet to give some color to his proceedings, which might implicate the republicans in general, and myself particularly, they have not been ashamed to bring forward a supposititious paper, drawn by one of their own party in the name of Logan, and falsely pretended to have been presented by him to the government of France; counting that the bare mention of my name therein, would connect that in the eye of the public with this transaction.—To ELBRIDGE GERRY. iv, 266. FORD ED., vii, 325. (Pa., Jan. 1799.)

4651. ——— ———. It is hardly necessary for me to declare to you, on everything sacred, that the part they assigned to me was entirely a calumny. Logan called on me four or five days before his departure, and asked and received a certificate (in my private capacity) of his citizenship and circumstances of life, merely as a protection, should he be molested in the present turbulent state of Europe. I have given such to an hundred others, and they have been much more frequently asked and obtained by tories than whigs. I did not write a scrip of a pen by him to any person. From long acquaintance he knew my wishes for peace, and my political sentiments generally, but he received no particular declaration of them nor one word of authority to speak in my name, or anybody's name on that or any other subject. It was an enterprise founded in the enthusiasm of his own character. He went on his own ground, and made his own way. His object was virtuous, and the effect meritorious.—To EDMUND PENDLETON. iv, 276. FORD ED., vii, 338. (Pa., 1799.)

4652. LIBELS, Jurisdiction over.—Nor does the [my] opinion of the unconstitutionality, and consequent nullity of that law, [Sedition] remove all restraint from the overwhelming torrent of slander, which is confounding all vice and virtue, all truth and falsehood, in the United States. The power to do that is fully possessed by the several State Legislatures. It was reserved to them, and was denied to the General Government, by the Constitution, according to our construction of it. While we deny that Congress have a right to control the freedom of the press, we have ever asserted the right of the States, and their exclusive right, to do so. They have accordingly, all of them, made provisions for punishing slander, which those who have time and inclination, resort to for the vindication of their characters.—To MRS. JOHN ADAMS. iv, 561. FORD ED., viii, 311. (M., 1804.)

4653. LIBELS, Newspaper.—Printers shall be liable to legal prosecution for printing and publishing false facts, injurious to the party prosecuting; but they shall be under no other restraint.—FRENCH CHARTER OF RIGHTS. iii, 47. FORD ED., v, 102. (P., 1789.)

4654. —— ——. In those States where they do not admit even the truth of allegations to protect the printer, they have gone too far.—To MRS. JOHN ADAMS. iv, 561. FORD ED., viii, 311. (M., 1804.)

4655. —— ——. No inference is here intended, that the laws, provided by the States against false and defamatory publications, should not be enforced; he who has time, renders a service to public morals and public tranquillity, in reforming these abuses by the salutary coercions of the law.—SECOND INAUGURAL ADDRESS. viii, 44. FORD ED., viii, 346. (1805.)

4656. —— ——. We have received from your [Massachusetts] presses a very malevolent and incendiary denunciation of the administration, bottomed on absolute falsehood from beginning to end. The author would merit exemplary punishment for so flagitious a libel, were not the torment of his own abominable temper punishment sufficient for even as base a crime as this.—To LEVI LINCOLN. v, 264. (W., March 1808.)

4657. —— ——. Mr. Wagner's malignity, like that of the rest of his tribe of brother printers, who deal out calumnies for federal readers, gives me no pain. When a printer cooks up a falsehood, it is as easy to put it into the mouth of a Mr. Fox, as of a smaller man, and safer in that of a dead than a living one.—To THOMAS LAW. v, 555. FORD ED., ix, 291. (M., 1811.)

4658. LIBELS, Prosecutions for.—While a full range is proper for actions by individuals, either private or public, for slanders affecting them, I would wish much to see the experiment tried of getting along without public prosecutions for libels. I believe we can do it. Patience and well doing, instead of punishment, if it can be found sufficiently efficacious, would be a happy change in the instruments of government.—To LEVI LINCOLN. FORD ED., viii, 139. (March 1802.)

4659. LIBELS, Punishment for.—I might have filled the courts of the United States with actions for slanders, and have ruined, perhaps many persons who are not innocent. But this would be no equivalent for the loss of character. I leave them, therefore, to the reproof of their own consciences. If these do not condemn them, there will yet come a day when the false witness will meet a Judge who has not slept over his slanders.—To URIAH M'GREGORY. iv, 333. (M., 1800.)

4660. LIBELS, Sedition law and.—Mr. Randolph has proposed an inquiry [in Congress] into certain prosecutions at common law in Connecticut, for libels on the government, and not only himself but others have stated them with such affected caution, and such hints at the same time, as to leave on every mind the impression that they had been instituted either by my direction, or with my acquiescence, at least. This has not been denied by my friends, because probably the fact is unknown to them. I shall state it for their satisfaction, and leave it to be disposed of as they think best. I had observed in a newspaper some dark hints of a prosecution in Connecticut, but so obscurely hinted that I paid little attention to it. Some considerable time after, it was again mentioned, so that I understood that some prosecution was going on in the federal court there, for calumnies uttered from the pulpit against me by a clergyman. I immediately wrote to Mr. Granger, who, I think, was in Connecticut at the time, stating that I had laid it down as a law to myself, to take no notice of the thousand calumnies issued against me, but to trust my character to my own conduct, and the good sense and candor of my fellow citizens; that I had found no reason to be dissatisfied with that course, and I was unwilling it should be broke through by others as to any matter concerning me; and I, therefore, requested him to direct the district attorney to dismiss the prosecution. Some time after this, I heard of subpœnas being served on General Lee, David M. Randolph, and others, as witnesses to attend the trial. I then for the first time conjectured the subject of the libel. I immediately wrote to Mr. Granger, to require an immediate dismission of the prosecution. The answer of Mr. Huntington, the district attorney, was that these subpœnas had been issued by the defendant without his knowledge, that it had been his intention to dismiss all the prosecutions at the first meeting of the court, and to accompany it with an avowal of his opinion, that they could not be maintained, because the federal court had no jurisdiction over libels. This was accordingly done. I did not till then know that there were other prosecutions of the same nature, nor do I now know what were their subjects. But all went off together; and I afterwards saw in the hands of Mr. Granger, a letter written by the clergyman, disavowing any personal ill will towards me, and solemnly declaring he had never uttered the words charged. I think Mr. Granger either showed me, or said there were affidavits of at least half a dozen respectable men, who were present at the sermon and swore no such expressions were uttered, and as many equally respectable men who swore the contrary. But the clergyman expressed his gratification at the dismission of the prosecution. * * * Certain it is, that the prosecutions had been instituted, and had made considerable progress, without my knowledge, that they were disapproved by me as soon as known, and directed to be discontinued. The attorney did it on the same ground on which I had acted myself in the cases of Duane, Callendar and others; to wit, that the Sedition law was unconstitutional and null, and that my obligation to execute what was law, involved that of not suffering rights secured by valid laws to be prostrated by what was no law.—To WILSON C. NICHOLAS. v, 452. FORD ED., ix, 253. (M., 1809.)

4661. LIBELS, Voltaire and.—I send you Voltaire's legacy to the King of Prussia,—a libel which will do much more injury to Voltaire than to the King. Many of the traits in the character of the latter to which the former gives a turn satirical and malicious, are real virtues.— To JAMES MONROE. FORD ED., iv, 44. (P., 1785.)

4662. LIBERTY, America and.—The last hope of human liberty in this world rests on us. We ought, for so dear a stake, to sacrifice every attachment and every enmity.—To WILLIAM DUANE. v, 577. FORD ED., ix, 313. (M., 1811.)

4663. ——— ———. When we reflect that the eyes of the virtuous all over the earth are turned with anxiety on us, as the only depositories of the sacred fire of liberty, and that our falling into anarchy would decide forever the destinies of mankind, and seal the political heresy that man is incapable of self-government, the only contest between divided friends should be who will dare farthest into the ranks of the common enemy.—To JOHN HOLLINS. v, 597. (M., 1811.) See 296.

4664. LIBERTY, Attachment to.—Our attachment to no nation on earth should supplant our attachment to liberty.—DECLARATION ON TAKING UP ARMS. FORD ED., i, 470. (1775.)

4665. LIBERTY, Blood and.—The tree of liberty must be refreshed from time to time with the blood of patriots and tyrants. It is its natural manure.—To W. S. SMITH. ii, 319. FORD ED., iv, 467. (P., 1787.)

4666. ——— ———. A warm zealot for the attainment and enjoyment by all mankind of as much liberty, as each may exercise without injury to the equal liberty of his fellow citizens. I have lamented that in France the

endeavors to obtain this should have been attended with the effusion of so much blood.— To M. DE MEUNIER. FORD ED., vii, 13. (M., April 1795.)

4667. LIBERTY, Concern for.—Affectionate concern for the liberty of my fellow citizens will cease but with life to animate my breast.—REPLY TO ADDRESS. v, 262. (1808.)

4668. LIBERTY, Contagious.—The disease of liberty is catching.—To MARQUIS LAFAYETTE. vii, 194. FORD ED., x, 179. (M., 1820.)

4669. LIBERTY, Degeneracy and.—It astonishes me to find such a change wrought in the opinions of our countrymen since I left them, as that three-fourths of them should be contented to live under a system which leaves to their governors the power of taking from them the trial by jury in civil cases, freedom of religion, freedom of the press, freedom of commerce, the *habeas corpus* laws, and of yoking them with a standing army. This is a degeneracy in the principles of liberty to which I had given four centuries instead of four years.—To WILLIAM STEPHENS SMITH. FORD ED., v, 3. (P., Feb. 1788.)

4670. LIBERTY, Degrees of.—I would rather be exposed to the inconveniences attending too much liberty than to those attending too small a degree of it.—To ARCHIBALD STUART. iii, 314. FORD ED., v, 409. (Pa., 1791.)

4671. LIBERTY, Despotism and.—The agitations of the public mind advance its powers, and at every vibration between the points of liberty and despotism, something will be gained for the former.—To THOMAS COOPER. iv, 452. FORD ED., viii, 177. (W., Nov. 1802.)

4672. LIBERTY, European.—Heaven send that the glorious example of France may be but the beginning of the history of European liberty, and that you may live many years in health and happiness to see at length that heaven did not make man in its wrath.— To LA DUCHESSE D'AUVILLE. iii, 135. FORD ED., v, 154. (N.Y., April 1790.)

4673. ——— ———. God send that all the nations who join in attacking the liberties of France may end in the attainment of their own.—To JOEL BARLOW. iii, 451. FORD ED., vi, 88. (Pa., 1792.)

4674. LIBERTY, First of all.—Postpone to the great object of Liberty every smaller motive and passion.—To THE PRESIDENT OF CONGRESS. FORD ED., ii, 298. (Wg., 1780.)

4675. LIBERTY, France and.—The atrocious proceedings of France towards this country, had well nigh destroyed its liberties. The Anglomen and monocrats had so artfully confounded the cause of France with that of freedom, that both went down in the same scale.—To T. LOMAX. iv, 301. FORD ED., vii, 374. (M., March 1799.)

4676. ——— ———. May you see France reestablished in that temperate portion of liberty which does not infer either anarchy or licentiousness, in that high degree of prosperity which would be the consequence of such a government, in that, in short, which the constitution of 1789 would have insured it, if wisdom could have stayed at that point the fervid but imprudent zeal of men, who did not know the character of their own countrymen.—To MADAME DE STAEL. vi, 120. (May 1813.)

4677. LIBERTY, Free Press and.—The functionaries of every government have propensities to command at will the liberty and property of their constituents. There is no safe deposit for these but with the people themselves; nor can they be safe with them without information. Where the press is free, and every man able to read, all is safe.—To CHARLES YANCEY. vi, 517. FORD ED., x, 4. (M., 1816.)

4678. LIBERTY, French Revolution and.—The success of the French Revolution will ensure the progress of liberty in Europe, and its preservation here.—To EDMUND PENDLETON. FORD ED., v, 358. (Pa., 1791.)

4679. —— ——. The liberty of the whole earth was depending on the issue of the contest, and was ever such a prize won with so little innocent blood?—To WILLIAM SHORT. iii, 502. FORD ED., vi, 154. (Pa., 1793.)

4680. —— ——. I continue eternally attached to the principles of your [French] Revolution. I hope it will end in the establishment of some firm government, friendly to liberty, and capable of maintaining it. If it does, the world will become inevitably free. —To J. P. BRISSOT DE WARVILLE. FORD ED., vi, 249. (Pa., 1793.)

4681. LIBERTY, Gift of God.—All men * * * are endowed by their Creator with inherent* and inalienable rights. Among these * * * [is] liberty.—DECLARATION OF INDEPENDENCE AS DRAWN BY JEFFERSON.

4682. —— ——. Can the liberties of a nation be thought secure when we have removed their only firm basis, a conviction in the minds of the people that these liberties are the gift of God?—NOTES ON VIRGINIA. viii, 404. FORD ED., iii, 267. (1782.)

4683. LIBERTY, Government and.—The natural progress of things is for liberty to yield and government to gain ground.—To EDWARD CARRINGTON. ii, 404. FORD ED., v, 20. (P., 1788.)

4684. —— ——. The policy of the American government is to leave their citizens free, neither restraining nor aiding them in their pursuits.—To M. L'HOMMANDE. ii, 236. (P., 1787.)

4685. —— ——. The freedom and happiness of man * * * are the sole objects of all legitimate government.—To GENERAL KOSCIUSKO. v, 50. (M., 1810.)

* Congress struck out "inherent" and inserted "certain".—EDITOR.

4686. LIBERTY, Happiness and.—It is our glory that we first put the ball of liberty into motion, and our happiness that, being foremost, we had no bad examples to follow.—To TENCH COXE. FORD ED., vii, 22. (M., 1795.)

4687. LIBERTY, Kosciusko and.—General Kosciusko is as pure a son of liberty as I have ever known, and of that liberty which is to go to all, and not to the few or the rich alone.—To HORATIO GATES. iv, 212. FORD ED., vii, 204. (Pa., 1798.)

4688. LIBERTY, Life and.—The God who gave us life, gave us liberty at the same time: the hand of force may destroy, but it cannot disjoin them.*—RIGHTS OF BRITISH AMERICA. i, 142. FORD ED., i, 447. (1774.)

4689. LIBERTY, Light and.—Light and liberty go together.—To TENCH COXE. FORD ED., vii, 22. (M., 1795.)

4690. —— ——. I will not believe our labors are lost. I shall not die without a hope that light and liberty are on steady advance.— To JOHN ADAMS. vii, 217. (M., 1821.)

4691. LIBERTY, Love of.—The commotions in Massachusetts† are a proof that the people love liberty, and I could not wish them less than they have.—To EZRA STILES. ii, 77. (P., 1786.)

4692. LIBERTY, Napoleon and.—If the hero [Napoleon] who has saved you from a combination of enemies, shall also be the means of giving you as great a portion of liberty as the opinions, habits and character of the nation are prepared for, progressive preparation may fit you for progressive portions of that first of blessings, and you may in time attain what we erred in supposing could be hastily seized and maintained, in the present state of political information among your citizens at large.—To M. CABANIS. iv, 496. (W., 1803.)

4693. LIBERTY, Natural.—Under the law of nature, we are all born free.—LEGAL ARGUMENT. FORD ED., i, 380. (1770.)

4694. LIBERTY, No easy road to.— We are not to expect to be translated from despotism to liberty in a feather bed.—To MARQUIS DE LAFAYETTE. iii, 132. FORD ED., v, 152. (N.Y., 1790.)

4695. —— ——. The ground of liberty is to be gained by inches and we must be contented to secure what we can get, from time to time, and eternally press forward for what is yet to get. It takes time to persuade men to do even what is for their own good.—To REV. CHARLES CLAY. iii, 126. FORD ED., v, 142. (M., 1790.)

4696. LIBERTY, Order and.—Possessing ourselves the combined blessing of liberty and order, we wish the same to other countries.—To M. CORAY. vii, 318. (M., 1823.)

* "Ab eo libertas, a quo spiritus," was the motto on one of Jefferson's seals.—EDITOR.
† Shays's Rebellion.—EDITOR.

— **LIBERTY, Personal.**—See PERSONAL LIBERTY.

4697. LIBERTY, Preservation of.—We do then most solemnly, before God and the world declare that, regardless of every consequence, 'at the risk of every distress, the arms we have been compelled to assume we will use with the perseverance, exerting to their utmost energies all those powers which our Creator hath given us, to preserve that liberty which He committed to us in sacred deposit and to protect from every hostile hand our lives and our properties.—DECLARATION ON TAKING UP ARMS. FORD ED., i, 474. (July 1775.)

4698. —— ——. I am convinced that, on the good sense of the people, we may rely with the most security for the preservation of a due degree of liberty.—To JAMES MADISON. FORD ED., iv, 480. (P., 1787.)

4699. —— ——. The people are the only sure reliance for the preservation of our liberty.—To JAMES MADISON. ii, 332. (1787.)

4700. —— ——. The preservation of the holy fire is confided to us by the world, and the sparks which will emanate from it will ever serve to rekindle it in other quarters of the globe, *Numinibus secundis.*—To REV. MR. KNOX. v, 503. (M., 1810.)

4701. LIBERTY, Preparation for.—A full measure of liberty is not now perhaps to be expected by your nation, nor am I confident they are prepared to preserve it. More than a generation will be requisite, under the administration of reasonable laws favoring the progress of knowledge in the general mass of the people, and their habituation to an independent security of person and property, before they will be capable of estimating the value of freedom, and the necessity of a sacred adherence to the principles on which it rests for preservation. Instead of that liberty which takes root and growth in the progress of reason, if recovered by mere force or accident, it becomes, with an unprepared people, a tyranny still, of the many, the few, or the one.—To MARQUIS LAFAYETTE. vi, 421. FORD ED., ix, 505. (M., Feb. 1815.)

4702. LIBERTY, The Press and.—Our liberty cannot be guarded but by the freedom of the press, nor that be limited without danger of losing it.—To JOHN JAY. FORD ED., iv, 186. (P., 1786.) See PRESS and NEWSPAPERS.

4703. LIBERTY, Progress of.—I cordially wish well to the progress of liberty in all nations, and would forever give it the weight of our countenance.—To T. LOMAX. iv, 301. FORD ED., vii, 374. (M., March 1799.)

4704. LIBERTY, Resistance and.—What country can preserve its liberties if its rulers are not warned from time to time that the people preserve the spirit of resistance?—To W. S. SMITH. ii, 318. FORD ED., iv, 467. (P., 1787.) See REBELLION.

4705. LIBERTY, Restricted.—I had hoped that Geneva was familiarized to such a degree of liberty, that they might without difficulty or danger fill up the measure to its *maximum;* a term, which, though in the insulated man, bounded only by his natural powers, must, in society, be so far restricted as to protect himself against the evil passions of his associates, and consequently, them against him.—To M. D'IVERNOIS. iv, 114. FORD ED., vii, 4. (M., Feb. 1795.)

4706. LIBERTY, Royalty and.—The public liberty may be more certainly secured by abolishing an office [royalty] which all experience hath shown to be inveterately inimical thereto.—PROPOSED VA. CONSTITUTION. FORD ED., ii, 12. (June 1776.)

4707. —— ——. It is impossible for you to conceive what is passing in our conclave, and it is evident that one or two at least, under pretence of avoiding war on the one side, have no great antipathy to run foul of it on the other, and to make a part in the confederacy of princes against human liberty. —To JAMES MADISON. iii, 563. FORD ED., vI, 261. (Pa., May 1793.)

4708. —— ——. I am not for * * * joining in the confederacy of kings to war against the principles of liberty.—To ELBRIDGE GERRY. iv, 268. FORD ED., vii, 328. (Pa., 1799.)

4709. LIBERTY, Sacred.—For promoting the public happiness, those persons whom nature has endowed with genius and virtue should be rendered by liberal education worthy to receive, and able to guard the sacred deposit of the rights and liberties of their fellow citizens; and they should be called to that charge without regard to wealth, birth, or other accidental condition or circumstance.—DIFFUSION OF KNOWLEDGE BILL. FORD ED., ii, 221. (1779.)

4710. —— ——. The most sacred cause that ever man was engaged in.*—OPINION ON THE "LITTLE SARAH". ix, 155. FORD ED., vi, 344. (1793.)

4711. LIBERTY, Safeguards of.—I disapproved from the first moment [in the new Constitution] the want of a bill of rights, to guard liberty against the legislative as well as the executive branches of the government. —To F. HOPKINSON. ii, 586. FORD ED., v, 76. (P., March 1789.)

4712. —— ——. To insure the safety of the public liberty, its depository should be subject to be changed with the greatest ease possible, and without suspending or disturbing for a moment the movements of the machine of government.—To M. DESTUTT TRACY. v, 569. FORD. ED., ix, 308. (M., 1811.)

4713. LIBERTY, Science and virtue.—Liberty is the great parent of science and of virtue; and a nation will be great in both in proportion as it is free.—To DR. WILLARD. iii, 17. (P., 1789.)

* Jefferson was referring to the first French Republic.—EDITOR.

4714. ——— ———. The general spread of the light of science has already laid open to every view the palpable truth, that the mass of mankind has not been born with saddles on their backs, nor a favored few booted and spurred, ready to ride them legitimately, by the grace of God.—To ROGER C. WEIGHTMAN. vii, 451. FORD ED., x, 391. (M., 1826.)

4715. LIBERTY, Sea of.—The boisterous sea of liberty is never without a wave.—To RICHARD RUSH. vii, 182. (M., 1820.)

4716. LIBERTY, Security for.—We agree particularly in the necessity of some * * * better security for civil liberty.—To JOHN TAYLOR. iv, 259. FORD ED., vii, 309. (M., 1798.)

4717. ——— ———. Since, by the choice of my constituents, I have entered on a second term of administration, I embrace the opportunity to give this public assurance, * * * that I will zealously cooperate with you in every measure which may tend to secure the liberty, property, and personal safety of our fellow citizens, and to consolidate the republican forms and principles of our government. —FIFTH ANNUAL MESSAGE. viii, 53. FORD ED., viii, 396. (Dec. 1805.)

4718. LIBERTY, Subversion of.—The moderation and virtue of a single character have probably prevented this Revolution from being closed, as most others have been, by a subversion of that liberty it was intended to establish.—To GENERAL WASHINGTON. i, 335. FORD ED., iii, 467. (A., 1784.)

4719. LIBERTY, Universal.—The ball of liberty is now so well in motion that it will roll round the globe.—To TENCH COXE. FORD ED., vii, 22. (M., 1795.)

4720. ——— ———. I sincerely pray that all the members of the human family may, in the time prescribed by the Father of us all, find themselves securely established in the enjoyment of *. * * liberty.—REPLY TO ADDRESS. viii, 119. (1807.)

4721. ——— ———. That we should wish to see the people of other countries free, is as natural, and at least as justifiable, as that one king should wish to see the kings of other countries maintained in their despotism.—To ALBERT GALLATIN. vii, 78. FORD ED., x, 90. (M., 1817.)

4722. LIBERTY vs. WEALTH.—What a cruel reflection that a rich country cannot long be a free one.—TRAVELS IN FRANCE. ix, 319. (1787.)

4723. LIBRARY, Circulating.—Nothing would do more extensive good at small expense than the establishment of a small circulating library in every county.—To JOHN WYCHE. v, 448. (M., 1809.)

4724. LIBERTY, Founding.—There shall be paid out of the treasury [of Virginia] every year the sum of two thousand pounds, to be laid out in such books and maps as may be proper to be preserved in a public library;

which library shall be established at the town of Richmond.—PUBLIC LIBRARY BILL. FORD ED., ii, 236. (1799.)

4725. LIBRARY, Free.—No person shall remove any book or map out of the library; * * * but the same [may] be made useful by indulging the researches of the learned and curious, within the said library, without fee or reward.—PUBLIC LIBRARY BILL. FORD ED., ii, 236. (1799.)

4726. LIBRARY, Jefferson's.—You know my collection, its condition and extent. I have been fifty years making it, and have spared no pains, opportunity or expense, to make it what it is. While residing in Paris, I devoted every afternoon I was disengaged, for a summer or two, in examining all the principal book stores, turning over every book with my own hand, and putting by everything which related to America, and indeed whatever was rare and valuable in every science. Besides this, I had standing orders during the whole time I was in Europe, on its principal book-marts, particularly Amsterdam, Frankfort, Madrid and London, for such works relating to America as could not be found in Paris. So that in that department particularly, such a collection was made as probably can never again be effected, because it is hardly probable that the same opportunities, the same time, industry, perseverance and expense, with some knowledge of the bibliography of the subject, would again happen to be in concurrence. During the same period, and after my return to America, I was led to procure, also, whatever related to the duties of those in the high concerns of the nation. So that the collection, which I suppose is of between nine and ten thousand volumes, while it includes what is chiefly valuable in science and literature generally, extends more particularly to whatever belongs to the American Statesman. In the diplomatic and parliamentary branches, it is particularly full.—To S. H. SMITH. vi, 383. FORD ED., ix, 486. (M., Sep. 1814.)

4727. LIBRARY, Sale to Congress.—It is long since I have been sensible it ought not to continue private property, and had provided that at my death, Congress should have the refusal of it at their own price. But the loss they have now incurred, makes the present the proper moment for their accommodation, without regard to the small remnant of time and the barren use of my enjoying it. I ask of your friendship, therefore, to make for me the tender of it to the Library Committee of Congress, not knowing myself of whom the Committee consists. Nearly the whole are well bound, abundance of them elegantly, and of the choicest editions existing. They may be valued by persons named by themselves, and the payment made convenient to the public. * * * I do not know that it contains any branch of science which Congress would wish to exclude from their collection; there is, in fact, no subject to which a member of Congress may not have occasion to refer. But such a wish would not correspond with my views of preventing its dismemberment. My desire is either to place it in their hands entire, or to preserve it so here.*—To S. H. SMITH. vi, 384. FORD ED., ix, 486. (M., Sep. 1814.) See 1133.

4728. ——— ———. The arrangement [of the library at Monticello] is as follows: 1. Ancient

——————
* Jefferson's library was purchased by the United States Government for the use of Congress. The price paid was $23,950.—EDITOR.

History. 2. Modern do. 3. Physics. 4. Nat. Hist. proper. 5. Technical Arts. 6. Ethics. 7. Jurisprudence. 8. Mathematics. 9. Gardening, architecture, sculpture, painting, music, poetry. 10. Oratory. 11. Criticism. 12. Polygraphical.—To JAMES OGILVIE. FORD ED., viii, 418. (W., 1806.)

4729. LIES, Circulating.—There is an enemy somewhere endeavoring to sow discord among us. Instead of listening first, then doubting, and lastly believing anile tales handed round without an atom of evidence, if my friends will address themselves to me directly, as you have done, they shall be informed with frankness and thankfulness.—To WILLIAM DUANE. iv, 590. FORD ED., viii, 431. (W., 1806.)

4730. LIES, Fearless of.—The man who fears no truths has nothing to fear from lies. —To DR. GEORGE LOGAN. FORD ED., x, 27. (M., 1816.)

4731. LIES, Folly of.—It is of great importance to set a resolution, not to be shaken, never to tell an untruth. There is no vice so mean, so pitiful, so contemptible; and he who permits himself to tell a lie once, finds it much easier to do it a second and third time, till at length it becomes habitual; he tells lies without attending to it, and truths without the world's believing him. This falsehood of the tongue leads to that of the heart, and in time depraves all its good dispositions.—To PETER CARR. i, 396. (P., 1785.)

4732. LIES, Newspaper.—There was an enthusiasm towards us all over Europe at the moment of the peace. The torrent of lies published unremittingly in every day's London papers first made an impression and produced a coolness. The republication of these lies in most of the papers of Europe (done probably by authority of the governments to discourage emigrations), carried them home to the belief of every mind. They supposed everything in America was anarchy, tumult and civil war. The reception of the Marquis Lafayette gave a check to these ideas.—To JAMES MADISON. i, 413. (P., 1785.)

4733. —— ——. It has been so impossible to contradict all their lies, that I have determined to contradict none; for while I should be engaged with one, they would publish twenty new ones. Thirty years of public life have enabled most of those who read newspapers to judge of one for themselves.— To JAMES MONROE. FORD ED., vii, 448. (Ep., May 1800.)

4734. LIES, Political.—Were I to buy off every federal lie by a sacrifice of two or three thousand dollars, a very few such purchases would make me as bankrupt in reputation as in fortune. To buy off one lie is to give a premium for the invention of others. From the moment I was proposed for my present office, the volumes of calumny and falsehood issued to the public, rendered impracticable every idea of going into the work of finding and proving. I determined, therefore, to go

straight forward in what was right, and to rest my character with my countrymen not on depositions and affidavits, but on what they should themselves witness, the course of my life. I have had no reason to be dissatisfied with the confidence reposed in the public; on the contrary, great encouragement to persevere in it to the end.—To WILLIAM A. BURWELL. FORD ED., ix, 229. (W., 1808.)

4735. —— ——. Many of the [federal] lies would have required only a simple denial, but I saw that even that would have led to the infallible inference, that whatever I had not denied was to be presumed true. I have, therefore, never done even this, but to such of my friends as happen to converse on these subjects, and I have never believed that my character could hang upon every twopenny lie of our common enemies.—To WILLIAM A. BURWELL. FORD ED., ix, 230. (W., 1808.)

4736. —— ——. The federalists, instead of lying me down, have lied themselves down. —To WILLIAM A. BURWELL. FORD ED., ix, 230. (W., 1808.)

4737. LIES, Useless.—I consider it always useless to read lies.—To DE WITT CLINTON. iv, 520. (W., 1803.)

4738. LIFE, Art of.—The art of life is the art of avoiding pain; and he is the best pilot who steers clearest of the rocks and shoals with which it is beset.—To MRS. COSWAY. ii, 37. FORD ED., iv, 317. (P., 1786.)

4739. LIFE, Chronicles of.—Fifteen volumes of anecdotes and incidents, within the compass of my own time and cognizance, written by a man of genius, of taste, of point, an acquaintance, the measure and traverses of whose mind I know, could not fail to turn the scale in favor of life during their perusal.—To JOHN ADAMS. vii, 27. (M., 1816.)

4740. LIFE, City.—A city life offers * * * more means of dissipating time, but more frequent also and more painful objects of vice and wretchedness. New York, for example, like London seems to be a *cloacina* of all the depravities of human nature. Philadelphia doubtless has its share. Here [Virginia], on the contrary, crime is scarcely heard of, breaches of order rare, and our societies, if not refined, are rational, moral and affectionate at least.—To WILLIAM SHORT. vii, 310. (M., 1823.)

4741. LIFE, Declining.—I endeavor to beguile the wearisomeness of declining life by the delights of classical reading and of mathematical truths, and by the consolations of a sound philosophy, equally indifferent to hope and fear.—To W. SHORT. vii, 140. FORD ED., x, 145. (M., 1819.)

4742. LIFE, Enjoyment of.—I sincerely pray that all the members of the human family may, in the time prescribed by the Father of us all, find themselves securely established in the enjoyment of life, liberty and happiness.— REPLY TO ADDRESS. viii, 119. (1807.)

4743. LIFE, Government and.—The care of human life and happiness, and not their destruction, is the first and only legitimate object of good government.—R. TO A. MARYLAND CITIZENS. viii, 165. (1809.)

4744. LIFE, Happiness and.—The Giver of life * * * gave it for happiness and not for wretchedness.—TO JAMES MONROE. i, 319. FORD ED., iii, 59. (M., 1782.)

4745. LIFE, Individual.—In a government bottomed on the will of all, the life * * * of every individual citizen becomes interesting to all.—FIFTH ANNUAL MESSAGE. viii, 50. FORD ED., viii, 392. (1805.)

4746. LIFE, Jefferson's habits of.—I am retired to Monticello, where, in the bosom of my family, and surrounded by my books, I enjoy a repose to which I have been long a stranger. My mornings are devoted to correspondence. From breakfast to dinner, I am in my shops, my garden, or on horseback among my farms; from dinner to dark, I give to society and recreation with my neighbors and friends; and from candle light to early bed-time, I read. My health is perfect; and my strength considerably reinforced by the activity of the course I pursue; perhaps it is as great as usually falls to the lot of near sixty-seven years of age. I talk of ploughs and harrows, of seeding and harvesting, with my neighbors, and of politics, too, if they choose, with as little reserve as the rest of my fellow citizens, and feel, at length, the blessing of being free to say and do what I please, without being responsible for it to any mortal. A part of my occupation, and by no means the least pleasing, is the direction of the studies of such young men as ask it. They place themselves in the neighboring village, and have the use of my library and counsel, and make a part of my society.—TO GENERAL KOSCIUSKO. v, 508. (M., 1810.)

4747. ——— ———. My present course of life admits less reading than I wish. From breakfast, or noon at latest, to dinner, I am mostly on horseback, attending to my farm or other concerns, which I find healthful to my body, mind and affairs; and the few hours I can pass in my cabinet, are devoured by correspondences; not those with my intimate friends, with whom I delight to interchange sentiments, but with others, who, writing to me on concerns of their own in which I have had an agency, or from motives of mere respect and approbation, are entitled to be answered with respect and a return of good will. My hope is that this obstacle to the delights of retirement, will wear away with the oblivion which follows that, and that I may at length be indulged in those studious pursuits, from which nothing but revolutionary duties would ever have called me.—TO DR. BENJAMIN RUSH. v, 558. FORD ED., ix, 294. (M., 1811.)

4748. ——— ———. I am on horseback three or four hours of every day; visit three or four times a year a possession I have ninety miles distant, performing the winter journey on horseback. I walk little, however, a single mile being too much for me, and I live in the midst of my grandchildren, one of whom has lately promoted me to be a great grandfather.—TO JOHN ADAMS. vi, 37. FORD ED., ix, 334. (M., 1812.)

4749. ——— ———. I have for fifty years bathed my feet in cold water every morning,

and having been remarkably exempted from colds (not having had one in every seven years of my life on an average), I have supposed it might be ascribed to that practice.—TO MR. MAURY. vi, 472. (M., 1815.)

4750. ——— ———. The request of the history of my physical habits would have puzzled me not a little, had it not been for the model with which you accompanied it, of Doctor Rush's answer to a similar inquiry. I live so much like other people, that I might refer to ordinary life as the history of my own. * * * I have lived temperately, eating little animal food, and that not as an aliment, so much as a condiment for the vegetables which constitute my principal diet. I double, however, the Doctor's glass and a half of wine, and even treble it with a friend; but halve its effects by drinking the weak wines only. The ardent wines I cannot drink, nor do I use ardent spirits in any form. Malt liquors and cider are my table drinks, and my breakfast is of tea and coffee. I have been blest with organs of digestion which accept and concoct, without ever murmuring, whatever the palate chooses to consign to them, and I have not yet lost a tooth by age. I was a hard student until I entered on the business of life, the duties of which leave no idle time to those disposed to fulfil them; and now, retired, and at the age of seventy-six, I am again a hard student. Indeed, my fondness for reading and study revolts me from the drudgery of letter writing. And a stiff wrist, the consequence of an early dislocation, makes writing both slow and painful. I am not so regular in my sleep as the Doctor says he was, devoting to it from five to eight hours, according as my company or the book I am reading interests me; and I never go to bed without an hour, or half hour's previous reading of something moral, whereon to ruminate in the intervals of sleep. But whether I retire to bed early or late, I rise with the sun. I use spectacles at night, but not necessarily in the day, unless in reading small print. My hearing is distinct in particular conversation, but confused when several voices cross each other, which unfits me for the society of the table. I have been more fortunate than my friend in the article of health. So free from catarrhs that I have not had one (in the breast, I mean) on an average of eight or ten years through life. I ascribe this exemption partly to the habit of bathing my feet in cold water every morning, for sixty years past. A fever of more than twenty-four hours I have not had above two or three times in my life. A periodical headache has afflicted me occasionally, once, perhaps, in six or eight years, for two or three weeks at a time, which now seems to have left me; and except on a late occasion of indisposition, I enjoy good health; too feeble, indeed, to walk much, but riding without fatigue six or eight miles a day, and sometimes thirty or forty. I may end these egotisms, therefore, as I began, by saying that my life has been so much like that of other people, that I might say with Horace, to every one *" nomine mutato, de te fabula narratur "*.—TO DOCTOR VINE UTLEY. vii, 116. FORD ED., x, 125. (M., 1819.)

4751. LIFE, Liberty and.—The God who gave us life gave us liberty at the same time; the hand of force may destroy, but cannot disjoin them.*—RIGHTS OF BRITISH AMERICA. i, 142. FORD ED., i, 447. (1774.)

* *"Ab eo libertas, a quo spiritus,"* was the motto on one of Jefferson's seals.—EDITOR.

4752. LIFE, Order and.—The life of a citizen is never to be endangered, but as the last melancholy effort for the maintenance of order and obedience to the laws.*—Circular Letter to State Governors. v, 414. Ford ed., ix, 238. (W., 1809.)

4753. LIFE, Outdoor.—During the pleasant season, I am always out of doors, employed, not passing more time at my writing table than will dispatch my current business. But when the weather becomes cold, I shall go out but little.—To Joel Barlow. v, 476. Ford ed., ix, 263. (M., 1809.)

4754. LIFE, Pledge of.—And for the support of this Declaration,† we mutually pledge to each other our lives, our fortunes, and our sacred honor.—Declaration of Independence as Drawn by Jefferson.

4755. —— ——. It is from the supporters of regular government only that the pledge of life, fortune and honor is worthy of confidence.—R. to A. Philadelphia Citizens. viii, 145. (1809.)

— LIFE, Private.—See Private Life.

4756. LIFE, Prolonged.—My health has been always so uniformly firm, that I have for some years dreaded nothing so much as the living too long. I think, however, that a flaw has appeared which ensures me against that, without cutting short any of the period during which I could expect to remain capable of being useful. It will probably give me as many years as I wish, and without pain or debility. Should this be the case, my most anxious prayers will have been ·fulfilled by Heaven. * * * My florid health is calculated to keep my friends as well as foes quiet, as they should be.—To Dr. Benjamin Rush. iv, 426. Ford ed., viii, 128. (W., 1801.)

4757. —— ——. The most undesirable of all things is long life; and there is nothing I have ever so much dreaded.—To Dr. Benjamin Waterhouse. Ford ed., x, 336. (M., 1825.)

4758. LIFE, Reliving.—You ask, if I would agree to live my seventy or rather seventy-three years over again? To which I say, yea. I think with you, that it is a good world on the whole; that it has been framed on a principle of benevolence, and more pleasure than pain dealt out to us. There are, indeed, (who might say nay) gloomy and hypochondriac minds, inhabitants of diseased bodies, disgusted with the present, and despairing of the future; always counting that the worst will happen, because it may happen. To these I say, how much pain have cost us the evils which have never happened! My temperament is sanguine. I steer my bark with Hope in the head, leaving Fear in the stern. My hopes, indeed, sometimes fail; but not offener than the forebodings of the gloomy. There are, I acknowledge, even in the happiest life, some terrible convulsions, heavy set-offs against the opposite page of ·the account.—To John Adams. vi, 575. (M., April 1816.)

4759. —— ——. Putting to myself your question, would I agree to live my seventy-

* The letter was in reference to the employment of the militia to enforce the Embargo law.—Editor.
† Congress inserted after " Declaration " the words, " with a firm reliance on the protection of Divine Providence ".—Editor.

three years over again forever? I hesitate to say. With Chew's limitations from twenty-five to sixty, I would say yes; and I might go further back, but not come lower down. For, at the latter period, with most of us, the powers of life are sensibly on the wane; sight becomes dim, hearing dull, memory constantly enlarging its frightful blank and parting with all we have ever seen or known, spirits evaporate, bodily debility creeps on palsying every limb, and so faculty after faculty quits us, and where, then, is life? If, in its full vigor, of good as well as evil, your friend Vassall could doubt its value, it must be purely a negative quantity when its evils alone remain. Yet I do not go into his opinion entirely. I do not agree that an age of pleasure is no compensation for a moment of pain. I think, with you, that life is a fair matter of account, and the balance often, nay generally, in its favor. It is not indeed easy, by calculation of intensity and time, to apply a common measure, or to fix the par between pleasure and pain; yet it exists, and is measurable.—To John Adams. vii, 26. (M., Aug. 1816.)

4760. —— ——. You tell me my granddaughter repeated to you an expression of mine, that I should be willing to go again over the scenes of past life. I should not be unwilling, without, however wishing it; and why not? I have enjoyed a greater share of health than falls to the lot of most men; my spirits have never failed me except under those paroxysms of grief which you, as well as myself, have experienced in every form, and with good health and good spirits, the pleasures surely outweigh the pains of life. Why not, then, taste them again, fat and lean together? Were I indeed permitted to cut off from the train the last seven years, the balance would be much in favor of treading the ground over again. Being at that period in the neighborhood of our warm springs and well in health, I wished to be better, and tried them. They destroyed, in a great measure, my internal organism, and I have never since had a moment of perfect health.—To John Adams. vii, 421. Ford ed., x, 347. (M., 1825.)

4761. LIFE, Right to.—We hold these truths to be self-evident: that all men are created equal; that they are endowed by their Creator with inherent* and inalienable rights; that among these are life, liberty and the pursuit of happiness.—Declaration of Independence as Drawn by Jefferson.

4762. LIFE, Security of.—In no portion of the earth were life, liberty and property ever so securely held; and it is with infinite satisfaction that withdrawing from the active scenes of life, I see the sacred design of these blessings committed to those who are sensible of their value and determined to defend them.—R. to A. Virginia Assembly. viii, 148. (1809.)

4763. LIFE, Social.—Life is of no value but as it brings us gratifications. Among the most valuable of these is rational society. It informs the mind, sweetens the temper, cheers our spirits, and promotes health.—To James Madison. Ford ed., iii, 406. (A., 1784.)

4764. LIFE, Sunshine in.—Thanks to a benevolent arrangement of things, the greater

* Congress struck out " inherent and " and inserted " certain ".—Editor.

part of life is sunshine.—To Mrs. Cosway. ii, 39. Ford ed., iv, 319. (P., 1786.)

4765. LIFE, Worthy.—I cannot be insensible to the partiality which has induced several persons to think my life worthy of remembrance. And towards none more than yourself, who give me so much credit, more than I am entitled to, as to what has been effected for the safeguard of our republican Constitution. Numerous and able coadjutors have participated in these efforts, and merit equal notice. My life, in fact, has been so much like that of others, that their history is my history with a mere difference of feature.—To Mr. Spafford. vii, 118. (M., 1819.)

4766. LIFE IN PARIS.—I often wish myself among my lazy and hospitable countrymen, as I am here [Paris] burning the candle of life without present pleasure, or future object. A dozen or twenty years ago, this scene would have amused me, but I am past the age for changing habits.—To Mrs. Trist. Ford ed., iv, 330. (P., 1786.)

4767. LINCOLN (Levi), Bar.—The pure integrity, unimpeachable conduct, talents and republican firmness of Lincoln* leave him now entirely without a rival. He is not thought an able common lawyer. But there is not and never was an abler one in the New England States. Their system is *sui generis* in which the Common law is little attended to. Lincoln is one of the ablest in their system, and it is among them he is to exercise the great portion of his duties. Nothing is more material than to complete the reformation of the government by this appointment which may truly be said to be putting the keystone into the arch.—To Attorney General Rodney. v, 547. (1810.)

4768. LINCOLN (Levi), Bench.—I was overjoyed when I heard you were appointed to the Supreme Bench of national justice, and as much mortified when I heard you had declined it. You are too young to be entitled to withdraw your services from your country. You cannot yet number the *quadraginta stipendia* of the veteran.—To Levi Lincoln. vi, 8. (M., Aug. 1811.)

4769. LINCOLN (Levi), Congress.—There is good reason to believe that Levi Lincoln will be elected to Congress in Massachusetts. He will be a host in himself; being undoubtedly the ablest and most respectable man of the Eastern States.—To James Madison. Ford ed., vii, 457. (M., Sep. 1800.)

4770. LITERARY MEN, Relief of.—The efforts for the relief of literary men, made by a society of private citizens, are truly laudable; but they are * * * but a palliation of an evil, the cure of which calls for all the wisdom and the means of the nation.—To David Williams. v, 512. (W., 1803.)

4771. LITERATURE, Growth of.—Literature is not yet a distinct profession with us. Now and then a strong mind arises, and at its intervals of leisure from business, emits a flash of light. But the first object of young societies is bread and covering; science is but secondary and subsequent.—To J. Evelyn Denison. vii, 418. (M., 1825.)

* Levi Lincoln, of Massachusetts, who was Attorney General in Jefferson's first Cabinet. The extract is from a letter urging his appointment to the Supreme Court Bench to succeed Judge Cushing. Lincoln was nominated and confirmed, but declined. John Quincy Adams was then nominated, but he declined. The vacancy was then filled by the appointment of Judge Story.—Editor.

4772. LITTLEPAGE (Lewis), Polish Office-holder.—Littlepage has succeeded well in Poland. He has some office, it is said, worth five hundred guineas a year. To Dr. Currie. ii, 219. (P., 1787.)

4773. LITTLEPAGE (Lewis), Russian army officer.—Littlepage, who was in Paris as a secret agent for the King of Poland, rather overreached himself. He wanted more money. The King furnished it more than once. Still he wanted more, and thought to obtain a high bid by saying he was called for in America, and asking leave to go there. Contrary to his expectation, he received leave; but he went to Warsaw instead of America, and thence to join the Russian army.—To James Madison. ii, 444. Ford ed., v, 44. (P., 1788.)

4774. LIVINGSTON (Edward), Friendship for.—I receive Mr. Livingston's question through you with kindness, and answer it without hesitation. He may be assured I have not a spark of unfriendly feeling towards him. In all the earlier scenes of life, we thought and acted together. We differed in opinion afterwards on a single point. Each maintained his opinion, as he had a right, and acted on it as he ought. But why brood over a single difference, and forget all our previous harmonies?—To President Monroe. Ford ed., x, 298. (M., 1824.)

4775. LIVINGSTON (Edward), Louisiana Code.—Your work [Louisiana Code] will certainly arrange your name with the sages of antiquity.—To Edward Livingston. vii, 403. (M., 1825.)

4776. LIVINGSTON (Edward), Restoration.—It was with great pleasure I learned that the good people of New Orleans had restored you again to the councils of our country. I did not doubt the aid it would bring to the remains of our old school in Congress, in which your early labors had been so useful.—To Edward Livingston. vii, 342. Ford ed., x, 299. (M., 1824.)

4777. LIVINGSTON (Robert R.), Chancellor.—A part of your [letter] gave me that kind of concern which I fear I am destined often to meet. Men possessing minds of the first order, and who have had opportunities of being known, and of acquiring the general confidence, do not abound in any country beyond the wants of the country. In your case, however, it is a subject of regret rather than of complaint, as you are in fact serving the public in a very important station. *—To Robert R. Livingston. Ford ed., vii, 492. (W., Feb. 1801.)

4778. LIVINGSTON (Robert R.), French Mission.—It has occurred to me that possibly you might be willing to undertake the mission as Minister Plenipotentiary to France. If so, I shall most gladly avail the public of your services in that office. Though I am sensible of the advantages derived from your talent to your particular State, yet I cannot suppress the desire of adding them to the mass to be employed on the broader scale of the nation at large.—To Robert R. Livingston. iv, 360. Ford ed., vii, 499. (W., 1801.)

4779. ——— ———. You will find Chancellor Livingston, named to the Senate the day after I came into office as our Minister Plenipotentiary to France, * * * an able and honor-

* Chancellor of New York.

able man. He is, unfortunately, so deaf that he will have to transact all his business by writing.—To WILLIAM SHORT. iv, 415. FORD ED., viii, 99. (W., 1801.)

4780. LOANS, Corruption and.— [Among] the reasons against [a new loan] is the apprehension that the [Hamilton] head of the [Treasury] department means to provide idle money to be lodged in the banks, ready for the corruption of the next legislature, as it is believed the late ones were corrupted, by gratifying particular members with vast discounts for objects of speculation.— LOAN OPINION. vii, 636. FORD ED., vi, 506. (1793.)

4781. LOANS, Economy vs.—I learn with great satisfaction that wholesome economies have been found, sufficient to relieve us from the ruinous necessity of adding annually to our debt by new loans. The deviser of so salutary a relief deserves truly well of his country.—To SAMUEL SMITH. vii, 284. FORD ED., x, 251. (M., 1823.)

4782. LOANS, Instructions respecting. —I would take the liberty of suggesting the insertion of some such clause as the following into the instructions: " The agents to be employed shall never open a loan for more than one million of dollars at a time, nor open a new loan till the preceding one has been filled, and expressly approved by the President of the United States." A new man, alighting on the exchange of Amsterdam, with powers to borrow twelve millions of dollars, will be immediately beset with bankers and brokers, who will pour into his ear, from the most unsuspected quarters, such informations and suspicions as may lead him exactly into their snares. So wonderfully dexterous are they in wrapping up and complicating their propositions, that they will make it evident, even to a clear-headed man (not in the habit of this business), that two and two make five. The agent, therefore, should be guarded, even against himself. by putting it out of his power to extend the effect of any erroneous calculation beyond one million of dollars. Were he able, under a delusive calculation, to commit such a sum as twelve millions of dollars, what would be said of the government? Our bankers told me themselves that they would not choose, in the conduct of this great loan, to open for more than two or three millions of florins at a time, and certainly never for more than five. By contracting for only one million of dollars at a time, the agent will have frequent occasions of trying to better the terms. I dare say that this caution, though not expressed in the instructions, is intended by the Secretary of the Treasury to be carried into their execution. But, perhaps, it will be desirable for the President, that his sense of it also should be expressed in writing.—OPINION ON FOREIGN DEBT. vii, 507. FORD ED., v, 233. (1790.)

4783. LOANS, Limited.—Of the modes which are within the limits of right, that of raising within the year its whole expenses by taxation, might be beyond the abilities of our citizens to bear. It is, moreover, generally desirable that the public contribution should be as uniform as practicable from year to year. that our habits of industry and expense may become adapted to them; and that they may be duly digested and incorporated with our annual economy. There remains, then, for us but the method of limited anticipation, the laying taxes for a term of years within that of our right, which may be sold for a present sum equal to the expenses of the year; in other words, to obtain a loan equal to the expenses of the year, laying a tax adequate to its interest, and to such a surplus as will reimburse. by growing instalments, the whole principle within the term. This is, in fact, what has been called raising money on the sale of annuities for years. In this way a new loan, and of course a new tax, is requisite every year during the continuance of the war; and should that be so long as to produce an accumulation of tax beyond our ability, in time of war the resource would be an enactment of the taxes requisite to ensure good terms, by securing the lender, with a suspension of the payment of instalments of principal and perhaps of interest also, until the restoration of peace. This method of anticipating our taxes, or of borrowing on annuities for years. insures repayment to the lender, guards the rights of posterity, prevents a perpetual alienation of the public contributions, and consequent destitution of every resource even for the ordinary support of government.—To J. W. EPPES. vi, 198. FORD ED., ix, 398. (P.F., Sep. 1813.)

4784. LOANS, Negotiation of.—Dumas has been in the habit of sending his letters open to me, to be forwarded to Mr. Jay. During my absence they passed through Mr. Short's hands, who made extracts from them, by which I see he has been recommending himself and me for the money negotiations in Holland. It might be thought, perhaps, that I have encouraged him in this. Be assured that no such idea ever entered my head. On the contrary, it is a business which would be the most disagreeable to me of all others, and for which I am the most unfit person living. I do not understand bargaining. nor possess the dexterity requisite for the purpose. On the other hand, Mr. Adams, whom I expressly and sincerely recommend. stands already on ground for that business which I could not gain in years. Pray set me to rights in the minds of those who may have supposed me privy to this proposition.—To JAMES MADISON. ii, 154. FORD ED., iv, 393. (P., 1787.)

4785. LOANS, Power to negotiate.— Though much an enemy to the system of borrowing, yet I feel strongly the necessity of preserving the power to borrow. Without this we might be overwhelmed by another nation, merely by the force of its credit.—To THE TREASURY COMMISSIONERS. ii, 353. (P., 1788.)

4786. ——— ———. I wish it were possible to obtain a single amendment to our Constitution. I would be willing to depend on that alone for the reduction of the administration of our government to the genuine principles of its Constitution; I mean an additional article, taking from the Federal Government the power of borrowing. I now deny their power of making paper money, or anything else, a legal tender. I know that to pay all proper expenses within the year, would, in case of war, be hard on us. But not so hard as ten wars instead of one. For wars could be reduced in that proportion; besides that the State governments would be free to lend *their credit* in borrowing quotas.—To JOHN TAYLOR. iv, 260. FORD ED., vii, 310. (M., Nov. 1798.)

4787. LOANS, Redeeming taxes for.— Our government has not, as yet, begun to act on the rule of loans and taxation going hand in hand. Had any loan taken place in my time, I should have strongly urged a redeeming tax. For the loan which has been made since the last session of Congress, we should now set the example of appropriating some particular tax, sufficient to pay the interest annually, and the principal within a fixed term, less than nineteen years. I hope yourself and your committee will render the immortal service of introducing this practice.— To JOHN W. EPPES. vi, 138. FORD ED., ix, 391. (M., June 1813.) See GENERATIONS.

4788. LOANS, Treasury Notes vs.— The question will be asked and ought to be looked at, what is to be the resource if loans cannot be obtained? There is but one, *" Carthago delenda est"*. Bank paper must be suppressed, and the circulating medium must be restored to the nation to whom it belongs. It is the only fund on which they can rely for loans; it is the only resource which can never fail them, and it is an abundant one for every necessary purpose. Treasury bills, bottomed on taxes, bearing or not bearing interest, as may be found necessary, thrown into circulation will take the place of so much gold and silver, which last, when crowded, will find an efflux into other countries, and thus keep the *quantum* of medium at its salutary level.—To J. W. EPPES. vi, 199. FORD ED., ix, 399. (Sep. 1813.)

4789. LOANS, Unauthorized.— The manœuvre of opening a loan of three millions of florins, has, on the whole, been useful to the United States, and though unauthorized, I think should be confirmed.—OPINION ON FOREIGN DEBT. vii, 507. FORD ED., v, 232. (1790.)

— LOCKE (John).— See GOVERNMENT, WORKS ON.

4790. LOGAN (George), France and.— That your efforts did much towards preventing declared war with France, I am satisfied. Of those with England, I am not equally informed. —To DR. GEORGE LOGAN. vi, 215. FORD ED., ix, 421. (M., Oct. 1813.)

4791. —— ——. Dr. Logan, about a fortnight ago, sailed for Hamburg. Though for a twelvemonth past he had been intending to go to Europe as soon as he could get money

enough to carry him there, yet when he had accomplished this, and fixed a time for going, he very unwisely made a mystery of it; so that his disappearance without notice excited conversation. This was seized by the war hawks, and given out as a secret mission from the Jacobins here to solicit an army from France, instruct them as to their landing, &c. This extravagance produced a real panic among the citizens; and happening just when Bache published Talleyrand's letter, Harper * * * gravely announced to the House of Representatives, that there existed a traitorous correspondence between the Jacobins here and the French Directory; that he had got hold of some threads and clews of it, and would soon be able to develop the whole. This increased the alarm; their libellists immediately set to work, directly and indirectly to implicate whom they pleased. " Porcupine " gave me a principal share in it, as I am told, for I never read his papers. —To JAMES MADISON. iv, 250. FORD ED., vii, 273. (Pa., June 1798.)

4792. LOGAN (Mingo Chief), Murder of.— In the spring of the year 1774, a robbery and murder were committed on an inhabitant of the frontier of Virginia, by two Indians of the Shawnee tribe. The neighboring whites, according to their custom, undertook to punish this outrage in a summary way. Col. [Michael] Cresap, a man infamous for the many murders he had committed on those much injured people, collected a party and proceeded down the Kanawha in quest of vengeance. Unfortunately a canoe of women and children, with one man only, was seen coming from the opposite shore, unarmed, and unsuspecting a hostile attack from the whites. Cresap and his party concealed themselves on the bank of the river, and the moment the canoe reached the shore, singled out their objects, and at one fire, killed every person in it. This happened to be the family of Logan, who had long been distinguished as a friend of the whites. This unworthy return provoked his vengeance. He accordingly signalized himself in the war which ensued. In the autumn of the same year a decisive battle was fought at the mouth of the Great Kanawha between the collected forces of the Shawnees, Mingoes and Delawares, and a detachment of the Virginia militia. The Indians were defeated and sued for peace. Logan, however, disdained to be seen among the suppliants. But lest the sincerity of a treaty should be distrusted, from which so distinguished a chief absented himself, he sent, by a messenger, the following speech * to be delivered to Lord Dunmore * * * .—NOTES ON VIRGINIA. viii, 308. FORD ED., iii, 156. (1782.)

4793. LOGAN (Mingo Chief), Speech of.— I may challenge the whole orations of Demosthenes and Cicero, and of any other eminent orator, if Europe has furnished more eminent, to produce a single passage, superior to the speech of Logan.—NOTES ON VIRGINIA. viii, 308. FORD ED., iii, 155. (1782.)

— LOGARITHMS.— See MOUNTAINS.

* The speech referred to is the celebrated one beginning, " I appeal to any white man to say, if he ever entered Logan's cabin hungry, and he gave him not to eat ", &c. Jefferson cited it among other proofs in refutation of the theories of Count de Buffon, Raynal and others, respecting the degeneracy of animals in America, not even excepting man. Luther Martin, of Maryland, a son-in-law of Cresap, severely attacked Jefferson in defence of the memory of his relative, and questioned the authenticity of Logan's speech. Jefferson made a careful investigation of the whole case, and proved the speech to be genuine.—EDITOR.

4794. LONDON, Beauty.—The city of London, though handsomer than Paris, is not so handsome as Philadelphia.—To JOHN PAGE. i, 549. FORD ED., iv, 214. (P., 1786.)

4795. LONDON, Burning of.—She [England] may burn New York * * * by her ships and congreve rockets, in which case we must burn the city of London by hired incendiaries, of which her starving manufacturers will furnish abundance. A people in such desperation as to demand of their government *aut panem, aut furcam,* either bread or the gallows, will not reject the same alternative when offered by a foreign hand. Hunger will make them brave every risk for bread.—To GENERAL KOSCIUSKO. vi, 68. FORD ED.,ix, 362. (June 1812.)

4796. LONDON, Splendor of shops.—The splendor of the shops is all that is worth looking at in London.—To MADAME DE CORNY. ii, 161. (P., 1787.)

— LONGITUDE.—See LATITUDE AND LONGITUDE.

— LOOMING.—See MIRAGE.

4797. LOTTERY, Unadvisable.—Having myself made it a rule never to engage in a lottery or any other adventure of mere chance, I can, with the less candor or effect, urge it on others, however laudable or desirable its object may be.—To HUGH L. WHITE. v, 521. .(M., 1810.) See 2005.

4798. LOUISIANA, Acquisition of.—Congress witnessed, at their last session, the extraordinary agitation produced in the public mind by the suspension of our right of deposit at the port of New Orleans, no assignment of another place having been made according to treaty.* They were sensible that the continuance of that privation would be more injurious to our nation than any consequences which could flow from any mode of redress, but reposing just confidence in the good faith of the government whose officer had committed the wrong, friendly and reasonable representations were resorted to, and the right of deposit was restored. Previous, however, to this period, we had not been unaware of the danger to which our peace would be perpetually .exposed while so important a key to the commerce of the western country remained under foreign power. Difficulties, too, were presenting themselves to the navigation of other streams, which, arising within territories, pass through those adjacent. Propositions had, therefore, been authorized for obtaining, on fair conditions, the sovereignty of New Orleans, and of other possessions in that quarter interesting to our quiet,

* Spain, on October 1, 1800, ceded all Louisiana to France, but the transaction was kept so secret that it did not become known in the United States until the spring of 1802. In October of that year, the Spanish Intendant at New Orleans issued an order, in violation of treaty stipulations, depriving the United States of the right of deposit at that port. This act so inflamed the Western people that they threatened to march on New Orleans and settle the question by force of arms. The federalists clamored for war. In this perilous condition of affairs, Congress, in secret session, placed two million dollars at the disposal of the President, to be used as he saw fit, and left him free to deal with the situation. He immediately sent James Monroe as Minister Plenipotentiary to Paris, joining with him in a high Commission Robert R. Livingston, Minister to France. The purchase of Louisiana was negotiated by them.—EDITOR.

to such extent as was deemed practicable;. and the provisional appropriation of two millions of dollars, to be applied and accounted for by the President of the United States, intended as part of the price, was considered as conveying the sanction of Congress to the acquisition proposed. The enlightened Government of France saw, with just discernment, the importance to both nations of such liberal arrangements as might best and permanently promote the peace, friendship, and interests of both; and the property and sovereignty of all Louisiana, which had been restored to them, have on certain conditions been transferred to the United States by instruments bearing date the 30th of April last. When these shall have received the constitutional sanction of the Senate, they will without delay be communicated to the Representatives also, for the exercise of their functions, as to those conditions which are within the powers vested by the Constitution in Congress. While the property and sovereignty of the Mississippi and its waters secure an independent outlet for the produce of the Western States, and an uncontrolled navigation through their whole course, free from collision with other powers and the dangers to our peace from that source, the fertility of the country, its climate and extent, promise in due season important aids to our treasury, an ample provision for our posterity, and a wide-spread field for the blessings of freedom and equal laws. With the wisdom of Congress it will rest to take those ulterior measures which may be necessary for the immediate occupation and temporary government of the country; for its incorporation into our Union; for rendering the change of government a blessing to our newly-adopted brethren; for securing to them the rights of conscience and of property; for confirming to the Indian inhabitants their occupancy and self-government, establishing friendly and commercial relations with them, and for ascertaining the geography of the country acquired.—THIRD ANNUAL MESSAGE. viii, 23. FORD ED., viii, 267. (October 17, 1803.)

4799. ——— ———. The acquisition of Louisiana is a subject of mutual congratulation, as it interests every man of the nation.—To GENERAL HORATIO GATES. iv, 494. FORD ED., viii, 249. (W., 1803.)

4800. ——— ———. This acquisition is seen by our constituents in all its importance, and they do justice to all those who have been instrumental towards it.—To JAMES MONROE. FORD ED., viii, 287. (W., Jan. 1804.)

4801. ——— ———. On this important acquisition, so favorable to the immediate interests of our western citizens, so auspicious to the peace and security of the nation in general, which adds to our country territories so extensive and fertile, and to our citizens new brethren to partake of the blessings of freedom and self government, I offer to Congress and the country, my sincere congratulations.—SPECIAL MESSAGE. viii, 33- (Jan. 1804.)

4802. —— ——. Whatever may be the merit or demerit of that acquisition, I divide it with my colleagues, to whose councils I was indebted for a course of administration which, notwithstanding this late coalition of clay and brass, will, I hope, continue to receive the approbation of our country.—To HENRY DEARBORN. vii, 215. FORD ED., x, 192. (M., 1821.)

4803. LOUISIANA, Area of United States doubled.—The territory acquired, as it includes all the waters of the Missouri and Mississippi, has more than doubled the area of the United States, and the new part is not inferior to the old in soil, climate, productions and important communications.—To GENERAL HORATIO GATES. iv, 494. FORD ED., viii, 249. (W., 1803.)

4804. LOUISIANA, Bonaparte and.—I very early saw that Louisiana was indeed a speck in our horizon which was to burst in a tornado; and the public are unapprized how near this catastrophe was. Nothing but a frank and friendly development of causes and effects on our part, and good sense enough in Bonaparte to see that the train was unavoidable, and would change the face of the world, saved us from that storm. I did not expect he would yield till a war took place between France and England, and my hope was to palliate and endure, if Messrs. Ross, Morris, &c. did not force a premature rupture, until that event. I believed the event not very distant, but acknowledge it came on sooner than I had expected. Whether, however, the good sense of Bonaparte might not see the course predicted to be necessary and unavoidable, even before a war should be imminent, was a chance which we thought it our duty to try; but the immediate prospect of rupture brought the case to immediate decision. The *dénouement* has been happy; and I confess I look to this duplication of area for the extending a government so free and economical as ours, as a great achievement to the mass of happiness which is to ensue.—To DR. JOSEPH PRIESTLEY. iv, 525. FORD ED., viii, 294. (W., Jan. 1804.)

4805. LOUISIANA, The Constitution and.—There is no constitutional difficulty as to the acquisition of territory, and whether, when acquired, it may be taken into the Union by the Constitution as it now stands, will become a question of expediency. I think it will be safer not to permit the enlargement of the Union but by amendment of the Constitution.—To ALBERT GALLATIN. FORD ED., viii, 241. (Jan. 1803.)

4806. —— ——. There is a difficulty in this acquisition which presents a handle to the malcontents among us, though they have not yet discovered it. Our confederation is certainly confined to the limits established by the Revolution. The General Government has no powers but such as the Constitution has given it; and it has not given it a power of holding foreign territory, and still less of incorporating it into the Union. An amendment of the Constitution seems necessary for

this. In the meantime, we must ratify and pay our money, as we have treated, for a thing beyond the Constitution, and rely on the nation to sanction an act done for its great good, without its previous authority.— To JOHN DICKINSON. FORD ED., viii, 262. (M., Aug. 1803.)

4807. —— ——. The Constitution has made no provision for our holding foreign territory, still less for incorporating foreign nations into our Union. The Executive in seizing the fugitive occurrence [Louisiana purchase] which so much advances the good of their country, have done an act beyond the Constitution. The Legislature in casting behind them metaphysical subtleties, and risking themselves like faithful servants, must ratify and pay for it, and throw themselves on their country for doing for them unauthorized, what we know they would have done for themselves had they been in a situation to do it. It is the case of a guardian, investing the money of his ward in purchasing an important adjacent territory; and saying to him when of age, I did this for your good; I pretend to no right to bind you: you may disavow me, and I must get out of the scrape as I can: I thought it my duty to risk myself for you. But we shall not be disavowed by the nation, and their act of indemnity will confirm and not weaken the Constitution, by more strongly marking out its lines.—To JOHN C. BRECKENRIDGE. iv, 500. FORD ED., viii, 244. (M., Aug. 12, 1803.)

4808. LOUISIANA, Constitutional amendments.—

The province of Louisiana is incorporated with the United States, and made part thereof. The rights of occupancy in the soil, and of self-government are confirmed to the Indian inhabitants, as they now exist. Preemption only of the portions rightfully occupied by them, and a succession to the occupancy of such as they may abandon, with the full rights of possession as well as of property and sovereignty in whatever is not or shall cease to be so rightfully occupied by them shall belong to the United States. The Legislature of the Union shall have authority to exchange the right of occupancy in portions where the United States have full right for lands possessed by Indians within the United States on the east side

Louisiana, as ceded by France to the United States is made a part of the United States. Its white inhabitants shall be citizens, and stand, as to their rights and obligations on the same footing with other citizens of the United States in analogous situations. Save only that as to the portion thereof lying north of an east and west line drawn through the mouth of the Arkansas river, no new State shall be established, nor any grants of land made, other than to Indians in exchange for equivalent portions of land occupied by them, until authorized by further subsequent amendment to the Constitution shall be made for these purposes.

Florida, also, whenever it may be right-of the Mississippi: to exchange lands on the east side of the river for those of the white inhabitants on the west side thereof and above the latitude of 31 degrees: to maintain in any part of the province such military posts as may be requisite for peace or safety: to exercise police over all persons therein, not being Indian inhabitants: to work salt springs, or mines of coal, metals and other minerals within the possession of the United States or in any others with the consent of the possessors; to regulate trade and intercourse between the Indian inhabitants and all other persons; to explore and ascertain the geography of the province, its productions and other interesting circumstances; to open roads and navigation therein where necessary for beneficial communication; and to establish agencies and factories therein for the cultivation of commerce, peace and good understanding w i t h the Indians residing there. The Legislature shall have no authority to dispose of the lands of the province otherwise than as hereinbefore permitted, until a new amendment of the Constitution shall give that authority. Except as to that portion thereof which lies south of the latitude of 31 degrees; which whenever they deem expedient, they may erect into a territorial government, either separate or as making part with one on the eastern side of the river, vesting the inhabitants t h e r e o f with all the rights possessed by other territorial citizens of the United States.

DRAFTS OF AN AMENDMENT TO THE CONSTITUTION. iv, 503. FORD ED., viii, 241. (July 1803.)

fully obtained, shall become a part of the United States. Its white inhabitants shall thereupon be citizens, and shall stand, as to their rights and obligations, on the same footing with other citizens of the United States, in analogous situations.—

4809. —— ——. I wrote you on the 12th instant, on the subject of Louisiana, and the constitutional provision which might be necessary for it. A letter received yesterday shows that nothing must be said on that subject, which may give a pretext for retracting; but that we should do, *sub silentio*, what shall be found necessary. Be so good as to consider that part of my letter as confidential.—To JOHN C. BRECKENRIDGE. FORD ED., viii, 244. (Aug. 18 1803.)

4810. —— ——. Further reflection on the amendment to the Constitution necessary in the case of Louisiana, satisfies me it will be better to give general powers, with specified exceptions.—To JAMES MADISON. iv, 503. FORD ED., viii, 246. (M., Aug. 1803.)

4811. —— ——. On further consideration as to the amendment to our Constitution respecting Louisiana, I have thought it better, instead of enumerating the powers which Congress may exercise, to give them the same powers they have as to other portions of the Union generally, and to enumerate the special exceptions. * * * The less that is said about any constitutional difficulty, the better; and * * * it will be desirable for Congress to do what is necessary, *in silence*. —To LEVI LINCOLN. iv, 504. FORD ED., viii, 246. (M., Aug. 1803.)

4812. —— ——. Whatever Congress shall think it necessary to do, should be done with as little debate as possible, and particularly so far as respects the constitutional difficulty. I am aware of the force of the observations you make on the power given by the Constitution to Congress, to admit new States into the Union, without restraining the subject to the territory then constituting the United States. But when I consider that the limits of the United States are precisely fixed by the treaty of 1783, that the Constitution expressly declares itself to be made for the United States, I cannot help believing that the intention was to permit Congress to admit into the Union new States, which should be formed out of the territory for which, and under whose authority alone, they were then acting. I do not believe it was meant that they might receive England, Ireland, Holland, &c., into it, which would be the case on your construction. When an instrument admits two constructions, the one safe, the other dangerous; the one precise, the other indefinite. I prefer that which is safe and precise. I had rather ask an enlargement of power from the nation, where it is found necessary, than to assume it by a construction which would make our powers boundless. Our peculiar security is in the possession of a written Constitution. Let us not make it a blank paper by construction. I say the same as to the opinion of those who consider the grant of the treaty making power as boundless. If it is, then we have no Constitution. If it has bounds, they can be no others than the definitions of the powers which that instrument gives. It specifies and delineates the operations permitted to the Federal Government, and gives all the powers necessary to carry these into execution. Whatever of these enumerated objects is proper for a law, Congress may make the law; whatever is proper to be executed by way of a treaty, the President and Senate may enter into the treaty; whatever is to be done by a judicial sentence, the judges may pass the sentence. Nothing is more likely than that their enumeration of powers is defective. This is the ordinary case of all human works. Let us go on, then, perfecting it, by adding, by way of amendment to the Constitution, those powers which time and trial show are still wanting. But it has been taken too much for granted, that by this rigorous construction the treaty power would be reduced to nothing. I had occasion once to examine its effect on the French treaty, made by the old Congress, and found that out of thirty odd articles which that contained, there were one, two or three only which could not now be stipulated under our present Constitution. I confess, then, I thought it important, in the present case, to set an example against broad construction, by appealing for new power to the people. If, however, our friends shall think differently, certainly I shall acquiesce with satisfaction; confiding, that the good sense of our country will correct the evil of construction whenever it shall produce ill effects.—To WILSON C. NICHOLAS. iv, 505. FORD ED., viii, 247. (M., Sep. 1803.)

4813. LOUISIANA, Defence of.—What would you think of raising a force for the defence of New Orleans in this manner? Give a bounty of 50 acres of land, to be delivered immediately, to every able-bodied man who will immediately settle on it, and hold himself in readiness to perform two years' military service (on the usual pay) if called on within the first seven years of his residence? The lands to be chosen by himself of any of those in the Orleans Territory, * * * each to have his choice in the order of his arrival on the spot, a proclamation to be issued to this effect to engage as many as will go on, and present themselves to the officer there; and, moreover, recruiting officers to be sent into different parts of the Union to raise and conduct settlers at the public expense? When settled there, to be well trained as militia by officers living among them? *—CIRCULAR LETTER TO CABINET OFFICERS. FORD ED., viii, 425. (Feb. 1806.)

4814. ——— ———. Satisfied that New Orleans must fall a prey to any power which shall attack it, in spite of any means we now possess, I see no security for it but in planting on the spot the force which is to defend it. I therefore suggest to some members of the Senate to add to the volunteer bill now before them, as an amendment, some such section as that enclosed, which is on the principles of what we agreed on last year, except the omission of the two years' service. If, by giving one hundred miles square of that country, we can secure the rest, and at

* Jefferson framed a bill on this subject. See FORD ED., viii, 425.—EDITOR.

the same time create an American majority before Orleans becomes a State, it will be the best bargain ever made.—To ALBERT GALLATIN. v, 36. (W., Jan. 1807.)

4815. ——— ———. I propose to the members of Congress in conversation, the enlisting thirty thousand volunteers, Americans by birth, to be carried at the public expense, and settled immediately on a bounty of one hundred and sixty acres of land each, on the west side of the Mississippi, on the condition of giving two years of military service, if that country should be attacked within seven years. The defence of the country would thus be placed on the spot, and the additional number would entitle the Territory to become a State, would make the majority American, and make it an American instead of a French State. This would not sweeten the pill to the French; but in making the acquisition we had some view to our own good as well as theirs, and I believe the greatest good of both will be promoted by whatever will amalgamate us together.—To JOHN DICKINSON. v, 30. FORD ED., ix, 9. (W., 1807.)

4816. LOUISIANA, Expansion and.—I know that the acquisition of Louisiana has been disapproved by some, from a candid apprehension that the enlargement of our territory would endanger its Union. But who can limit the extent to which the federative principle may operate effectively? The larger our association, the less will it be shaken by local passions; and, in any view, is it not better that the opposite bank of the Mississippi should be settled by our own brethren and children, than by strangers of another family? With which shall we be most likely to live in harmony and friendly intercourse?—SECOND INAUGURAL ADDRESS. viii, 41. FORD ED., viii, 344. (1805.) See TERRITORY.

4817. LOUISIANA, Federalist opposition.—The opposition caught it as a plank in a shipwreck, hoping it would tack the western people to them. They raised the cry of war, were intriguing in all quarters to exasperate the western inhabitants to arm and go down on their own authority and possess themselves of New Orleans, and in the meantime were daily reiterating, in new shapes, inflammatory resolutions for the adoption of the House [of Representatives].—To ROBERT R. LIVINGSTON. iv, 460. FORD ED., viii, 209. (W., Feb. 1803.)

4818. ——— ———. These grumblers [the opposition], too, are very uneasy lest the administration should share some little credit for the acquisition, the whole of which they ascribe to the accident of war. They would be cruelly mortified could they see our files from May, 1801 [April 1801 in Ford edition], the first organization of the administration, but more especially from April, 1802. They would see, that though we could not say when war would arise, yet we said with energy what would take place when it should arise. We did not, by our intrigues, produce the war; but we availed ourselves of it when it happened. The other party saw the case now existing, on which our representations were predicted, and the wisdom of timely sacrifice. But when these people make the war give us everything, they authorize us to ask what the war gave us in their day? They had a war. What did they make it bring us? Instead of making our neutrality the ground of gain to their country, they were for plunging into the war. And if they were now in place, they would now be at war against the atheists and disorganizers of France. They were for making their country an appendage to England. We are friendly, cordially and conscientiously friendly to England. We are not hostile to France. We will be rigorously just and sincerely friendly to both. I do not believe we shall have as much to swallow from them as our predecessors had.—To GENERAL HORATIO GATES. iv, 495. FORD ED., viii, 250. (W., July 1803.)

4819. —— ——. These federalists [who are raising objections against the vast extent of our boundaries] see in this acquisition [Louisiana] the formation of a new confederacy, embracing all the waters of the Mississippi, on both sides of it, and a separation of its eastern waters from us. These combinations depend on so many circumstances which we cannot foresee, that I place little reliance on them. We have seldom seen neighborhood produce affection among nations. The reverse is almost the universal truth. Besides, if it should become the great interest of those nations to separate from this, if their happiness should depend on it so strongly as to induce them to go through that convulsion, why should the Atlantic States dread it? But especially why should we, their present inhabitants, take side in such a question? When I view the Atlantic States, procuring for those on the Eastern waters of the Mississippi friendly instead of hostile neighbors on its western waters, I do not view it as an Englishman would the procuring future blessings for the French nation, with whom he has no relations of blood or affection. The future inhabitants of the Atlantic and Mississippi States will be our sons. We leave them in distinct but bordering establishments. We think we see their happiness in their union, and we wish it. Events may prove it otherwise; and if they see their interest in separation, why should we take side with our Atlantic rather than our Mississippi descendants. It is the elder and the younger son differing. God bless them both, and keep them in union, if it be for their good, but separate them, if it be better.—To JOHN C. BRECKENRIDGE. iv, 499. FORD ED., viii, 243. (M., Aug. 1803.)

4820. —— ——. Objections are raising to the eastward against the vast extent of our boundaries, and propositions are made to exchange Louisiana, or a part of it, for the Floridas. But * * * we shall get the Floridas without, and I would not give one inch of the waters of the Mississippi to any nation, because I see in a light very impor-

tant to our peace the exclusive right to its navigation, and the admission of no nation into it, but as into the Potomac or Delaware, with our consent and under our police.—To JOHN C. BRECKENRIDGE. iv, 499. FORD ED., viii, 243. (M., Aug. 1803.)

4821. —— ——. Some inflexible federalists have still ventured to brave the public opinion. It will fix their character with the world and with posterity, who, not descending to the other points of difference between us, will judge them by this fact, so palpable as to speak for itself in all times and places. —To DUPONT DE NEMOURS. iv, 508. (W., 1803.)

4822. —— ——. The federalists spoke and voted against it, but they are now so reduced in their numbers as to be nothing.—To ROBERT R. LIVINGSTON. iv, 510. FORD ED., viii, 278. (W., Nov. 1803.)

4823. —— ——. The federal leaders have had the imprudence to oppose it pertinaciously, which has given an occasion to a great proportion of their quondam honest adherents to abandon them, and join the republican standard. They feel themselves now irretrievably lost.—To JAMES MONROE. FORD ED., viii, 287. (W., Jan. 1804.)

4824. LOUISIANA, French possession of.—The exchange, which is to give us new neighbors in Louisiana (probably the present French armies when disbanded), has opened us to a combination of enemies on that side where we are most vulnerable.—To THOMAS PINCKNEY. iv, 177. FORD ED., vii, 129. (Pa., May 1797.)

4825. —— ——. There is considerable reason to apprehend that Spain cedes Louisiana and the Floridas to France. It is a policy very unwise in both, and very ominous to us. —To JAMES MONROE. FORD ED., viii, 58. (W., May 1801.)

4826. —— ——. The cession of Louisiana and the Floridas by Spain to France, works most sorely on the United States. On this subject the Secretary of State has written to you fully, yet I cannot forbear recurring to it personally, so deep is the impression it makes on my mind. It completely reverses all the political relations of the United States, and will form a new epoch in our political course. Of all nations of any consideration, France is the one, which hitherto, has offered the fewest points on which we could have any conflict of right, and the most points of a communion of interests. From these causes, we have ever looked to her as our *natural* friend, as one with which we never could have an occasion of difference. Her growth, therefore, we viewed as our own, her misfortunes ours. There is on the globe one single spot, the possessor of which is our natural and habitual enemy. It is New Orleans, through which the produce of three-eighths of our territory must pass to market, and from its fertility it will ere long yield more than half of our whole produce, and contain more than half of our inhabitants.

France, placing herself in that door, assumes to us the attitude of defiance. Spain might have retained it quietly for years. Her pacific dispositions, her feeble state, would induce her to increase our facilities there, so that her possession of the place would be hardly felt by us, and it would not, perhaps, be very long before some circumstance might arise, which might make the cession of it to us the price of something of more worth to her. Not so can it ever be in the hands of France. The impetuosity of her temper, the energy and restlessness of her character, placed in a point of eternal friction with us, and our character, which, though quiet and loving peace and the pursuit of wealth, is high-minded, despising wealth in competition with insult or injury, enterprising and energetic as any nation on earth; these circumstances render it impossible that France and the United States can continue long friends, when they meet in so irritable a position. They, as well as we, must be blind if they do not see this; and we must be very improvident if we do not begin to make arrangements on that hypothesis. The day that France takes possession of New Orleans, fixes the sentence which is to restrain her forever within her low-water mark. It seals the union of two nations, who, in conjunction, can maintain exclusive possession of the ocean. From that moment, we must marry ourselves to the British fleet and nation. We must turn all our attention to a maritime force, for which our resources place us on very high ground; and having formed and cemented together a power which may render reinforcement of her settlements here impossible to France, make the first cannon, which shall be fired in Europe, the signal for tearing up any settlement she may have made, and for holding the two continents of America in sequestration for the common purposes of the united British and American nations. This is not a state of things we seek or desire. It is one which this measure, if adopted by France, forces on us, as necessarily as any other cause, by the laws of nature, brings on its necessary effect. It is not from a fear of France that we deprecate this measure proposed by her. For, however greater her force is than ours, compared in the abstract, it is nothing in comparison of ours, when to be exerted on our soil. But it is from a sincere love of peace, and a firm persuasion that bound to France by the interests and the strong sympathies still existing in the minds of our citizens, and holding relative positions which ensure their continuance, we are secure of a long course of peace. Whereas, the change of friends, which will be rendered necessary if France changes that position, embarks us necessarily as a belligerent power in the first war of Europe. In that case, France will have held possession of New Orleans during the interval of a peace, long or short, at the end of which it will be wrested from her. Will this short-lived possession have been an equivalent to her for the transfer of such a weight into the scale of her enemy? Will not the amalgamation of a young, thri-

ving, nation continue to that enemy the health and force which are at present so evidently on the decline? And will a few years' possession of New Orleans add equally to the strength of France? She may say she needs Louisiana for the supply of her West Indies. She does not need it in time of peace, and in war she could not depend on them, because they would be so easily intercepted. I should suppose that all these considerations might, in some proper form, be brought into view of the government of France. Though stated by us, it ought not to give offence; because we do not bring them forward as a menace, but as consequences not controllable by us, but inevitable from the course of things. We mention them, not as things which we desire by any means, but as things we deprecate; and we beseech a friend to look forward and to prevent them for our common interests. If France considers Louisiana, however, as indispensable for her views, she might perhaps be willing to look about for arrangements which might reconcile it to our interests. If anything could do this, it would be the ceding to us the island of New Orleans and the Floridas. This would certainly, in a great degree, remove the causes of jarring and irritation between us, and perhaps for such a length of time, as might produce other means of making the measure permanently conciliatory to our interests and friendships. It would, at any rate, relieve us from the necessity of taking immediate measures for countervailing such an operation by arrangements in another quarter. But still we should consider New Orleans and the Floridas as no equivalent for the risk of a quarrel with France, produced by her vicinage.—To ROBERT R. LIVINGSTON. iv, 431. FORD ED., viii, 144. (April 1802.)

4827. ———. I believe * * * that this measure will cost France, and perhaps not very long hence, a war which will annihilate her on the ocean, and place that element under the despotism of two nations, which I am not reconciled to the more because my own would be one of them. Add to this the exclusive appropriation of both continents of America as a consequence. I wish the present order of things to continue, and with a view to this I value highly a state of friendship between France and us. You know, too well how sincere I have ever been in these dispositions to doubt them. You know, too, how much I value peace, and how unwillingly I should see any event take place which would render war a necessary resource; and that all our movements should change their character and object. I am thus open with you, because I trust that you will have it in your power to impress on that government considerations, in the scale against which the possession of Louisiana is nothing. In Europe, nothing but Europe is seen, or supposed to have any right in the affairs of nations; but this little event, of France's possessing herself of Louisiana, which is thrown in as nothing, as a mere make-weight in the general settlement of accounts,—this speck which now appears as an almost invisible point in the horizon, is the embryo of a tornado which will burst on the countries on both sides of the Atlantic, and involve in its effects their highest destinies. That it may yet be avoided is my sincere prayer; and if you can be the means of informing the wisdom of Bonaparte of all its consequences, you will have deserved well of both countries. Peace and abstinence from European interferences are our objects, and so will continue while the present order of things in America remains uninterrupted.— To DUPONT DE NEMOURS. iv, 435. . (W.. April 1802.)

4828. —— ——. Whatever power, other than ourselves, holds the country east of the Mississippi becomes our natural enemy. Will such a possession do France as much good, as such an enemy may do her harm? And how long would it be hers, were such an enemy, situated at its door, added to Great Britain? I confess, it appears to me as essential to France to keep at peace with us, as it is to us to keep at peace with her; and that, if this cannot be secured without some compromise as to the territory in question, it will be useful for both to make some sacrifices to effect the compromise.—To DUPONT DE NEMOURS. iv, 458. FORD ED., viii, 207. (W., Feb. 1803.)

4829. LOUISIANA, Government for.— With respect to the territory acquired, I do not think it will be a separate government, as you imagine. I presume the island of New Orleans, and the settled country on the opposite bank, will be annexed to the Mississippi territory. We shall certainly endeavor to introduce the American laws there, and that cannot be done but by amalgamating the people with such a body of Americans as may take the lead in legislation and government. Of course, they will be under the Governor of Mississippi. The rest of the territory will probably be locked up from American settlement, and under the self-government of the native occupants.—To GENERAL HORATIO GATES. FORD ED., viii, 250. (W., July 1803.)

4830. —— ——. I thought I perceived in you the other day a dread of the job of preparing a constitution for the new acquisition. With more boldness than wisdom I, therefore, determined to prepare a canvas, give it a few daubs of outline, and send it to you to fill up. * * * In communicating it to you I must do it in confidence that you will never let any person know that I have put pen to paper on the subject. * * * My time does not permit me to go into explanation of the enclosed by letter. I will only observe as to a single feature of the Legislature, that the idea of an Assembly of Notables came into my head while writing, as a thing more familiar and pleasing to the French, than a legislation of judges. True it removes their dependence from the judges to the Executive; but this is what they are used to and would prefer. Should Congress reject the nomination of judges for four years, and make them during good behavior, as is probable, then, should

the judges take a kink in their heads in favor of leaving the present laws of Louisiana unaltered, that evil will continue for their lives, unamended by us, and become so inveterate that we may never be able to introduce the uniformity of law so desirable. The making the same persons so directly judges and legislators is more against principle, than to make the same persons executive, and the elector of the legislative members. The former, too, are placed above all responsibility; the latter is under a perpetual control if he goes wrong. The judges have to act on nine out of ten of the laws which are made; the governor not on one in ten. But strike it out, and insert the judges if you think it better, as it was a sudden conceit to which I am not attached.—To JOHN BRECKENRIDGE. FORD ED., viii, 279. (W., Nov. 1803.)

4831. —— ——. Without looking at the old Territorial Ordinance, I had imagined it best to found a government for the territory or territories of *lower* Louisiana on that basis. But on examining it, I find it will not do at all; that it would turn all their laws topsy-turvy. Still, I believe it best to appoint a governor and three judges, with legislative powers; only providing that the judges shall form the laws, and the governor have a negative only, subject further to the negative of a national legislature. The existing laws of the country being now in force, the new legislature will, of course, introduce the trial by jury in *criminal* cases, first; the *habeas corpus*, the freedom of the press, freedom of religion, &c., as soon as can be, and in general draw their laws, and organizations to the mould of ours by degrees, as they find practicable, without exciting too much discontent. In proportion as we find the people there riper for receiving these first principles of freedom, Congress may from session to session, confirm their enjoyment of them.— To ALBERT GALLATIN. FORD ED., viii, 275. (Nov. 1803.)

4832. —— ——. Although it is acknowledged that our new fellow citizens are as yet as incapable of self-government as children, yet some [in Congress] cannot bring themselves to suspend its principles for a single moment. The temporary or territorial government of that country, therefore, will encounter great difficulty [in Congress].—To DE WITT CLINTON. FORD ED., viii, 283. (W., Dec. 1803.)

4833. —— ——. Our policy will be to form New Orleans, and the country on both sides of it on the Gulf of Mexico, into a State; and, as to all above that, to transplant our Indians into it, constituting them a Marechausée to prevent emigrants crossing the river, until we shall have filled up all the vacant country on this side. This will secure both Spain and us as to the mines of Mexico, for half a century, and we may safely trust the provisions for that time to the men who shall live in it.—To DUPONT DE NEMOURS. iv, 509. (W., 1803.)

4834. —— ——. The inhabited part of Louisiana, from Point Coupee to the sea, will of course be immediately a territorial government, and soon a State. But above that, the best use we can make of the country for some time, will be to give establishments in it to the Indians on the East side of the Mississippi, in exchange for their present country, and open land offices in the last, and thus make this acquisition the means of filling up the eastern side, instead of drawing off its population. When we shall be full on this side, we may lay off a range of States on the western bank from the head to the mouth, and so, range after range, advancing compactly as we multiply.—To John C. Breckenridge. iv, 500. Ford ed., viii, 244. (M., Aug. 1803.)

4835. —— ——. In order to lessen the causes of appeal to the Convention, I sincerely wish that Congress at the next session may give to the Orleans Territory a legislature to be chosen by the people, as this will be advancing them quite as fast as the rules of our government will admit; and the evils which may arise from the irregularities which such a legislature may run into, will not be so serious as leaving them the pretext of calling in a foreign umpire between them and us.—To James Madison. Ford ed., viii, 314. (M., Aug. 1804.)

4836. —— ——. We are now at work on a * * * government for Louisiana. It will probably be a small improvement of our former territorial governments, or first grade of government. The act proposes to give them an assembly of Notables, selected by the Governor from the principal characters of the territory. This will, I think, be a better legislature than the former territorial one, and will not be a greater departure from sound principle.—To Thomas McKean. Ford ed., viii, 293. (Jan. 1804.)

4837. —— ——. The Legislative Council for the Territory of New Orleans, * * * to be appointed by me, * * * ought to be composed of men of integrity, of understanding, of clear property and influence among the people, well acquainted with the laws, customs, and habits of the country, and drawn from the different parts of the Territory, whose population is considerable.*—To Governor Claiborne. iv, 551. (W., July 1804.) See Claiborne.

4838. —— ——. I am so much impressed with the expediency of putting a termination to the right of France to patronize the rights of Louisiana, which will cease with their complete adoption as citizens of the United States, that I hope to see that take place on the meeting of Congress.—To James Madison. iv, 557. Ford ed., viii, 315. (M., Aug. 1804.)

4839. —— ——. It is but too true that great discontents exist in the Territory of

* Jefferson requested Governor Claiborne to send him the names of proper persons for the council.—Editor.

Orleans. Those of the French inhabitants have for their sources, 1, the prohibition of importing slaves. This may be partly removed by Congress permitting them to receive slaves from the other States, which, by dividing that evil, would lessen its danger; 2, the administration of justice in our forms, principles, and language, with all of which they are unacquainted, and are the more abhorrent, because of the enormous expense, greatly exaggerated by the corruption of bankrupt and greedy lawyers, who have gone there from the United States and engrossed the practice; 3, the call on them by the land commissioners to produce the titles of their lands. The object of this is really to record and secure their rights. But as many of them hold on rights so ancient that the title papers are lost, they expect the land is to be taken from them whenever they cannot produce a regular deduction of title in writing. In this they will be undeceived by the final result, which will evince to them a liberal disposition of the government towards them.—To John Dickinson. v, 29. Ford ed., ix, 8. (W., 1807.)

4840. LOUISIANA, Mission to France respecting.—The urgency of the case, as well as the public spirit, induced us to make a more solemn appeal to the justice and judgment of our neighbors, by sending a Minister Extraordinary to impress them with the necessity of some arrangement. Mr. Monroe has been selected. His good dispositions cannot be doubted. Multiplied conversations with him, and views of the subject taken in all the shapes in which it can present itself, have possessed him with our estimates of everything relating to it, with a minuteness which no written communication to Mr. Livingston could ever have attained. These will prepare them to meet and decide on every form of proposition which can occur, without awaiting new instructions from hence, which might draw to an indefinite length a discussion where circumstances imperiously oblige us to a prompt decision. For the occlusion of the Mississippi is a state of things in which we cannot exist. He goes, therefore, joined with Chancellor Livingston, to aid in the issue of a crisis the most important the United States have ever met since their Independence, and which is to decide their future character and career.—To Dupont de Nemours. iv, 456. Ford ed., viii, 204. (W., Feb. 1803.) See Monroe.

4841. —— ——. The future destinies of our country hang on the event of this negotiation, and I am sure they could not be placed in more able or more zealous hands. On our parts we shall be satisfied that what you do not effect, cannot be effected.—To Robert R. Livingston. iv, 461. Ford ed., viii, 210. (W., Feb. 1803.)

4842. —— ——. It may be said, if this object be so all-important to us, why do we not offer such a sum as to ensure its purchase? The answer is simple. We are an agricultural people, poor in money, and owing great debts. These will be falling due by instalments for fifteen years to come, and require from us the practice of a rigorous economy to accomplish their payment; and it is our principle to pay to a moment whatever we have engaged, and never to engage what we cannot, and mean not faithfully to pay. We have calculated our resources, and find the sum to be moderate which they would enable us to pay, and we know from late trials that little can be added to it by borrowing.—To DUPONT DE NEMOURS. iv, 458. FORD ED., viii, 206. (W., Feb. 1803.)

4843. —— ——. The country, too, which we wish to purchase, except the portion already granted, and which must be confirmed to the private holders, is a barren sand, six hundred miles from east to west, and from thirty to forty and fifty miles from north to south, formed by deposition of the sands by the Gulf Stream in its circular course round the Mexican Gulf, and which being spent after performing a semicircle, has made from its last depositions the sand bank of East Florida. In West Florida, indeed, there are on the borders of the rivers some rich bottoms, formed by the mud brought from the upper country. These bottoms are all possessed by individuals. But the spaces between river and river are mere banks of sand; and in East Florida there are neither rivers, nor consequently any bottoms. We cannot, then, make anything by a sale of the lands to individuals. So that it is peace alone which makes it an object with us, and which ought to make the cession of it desirable to France. —To DUPONT DE NEMOURS. iv, 458. FORD ED., viii, 206. (W., Feb. 1803.)

4844. —— ——. You see with what frankness I communicate with you on this subject; that I hide nothing from you, and that I am endeavoring to turn our private friendship to the good of our respective countries. And can private friendship ever answer a nobler end than by keeping two nations at peace, who, if this new position which one of them is taking were rendered innocent, have more points of common interest, and fewer of collision, than any two on earth; who become natural friends, instead of natural enemies, which this change of position would make them.—To DUPONT DE NEMOURS. iv, 459. FORD ED., viii, 207. (W., Feb. 1803.)

4845. —— ——. The measure was moreover proposed from another cause. We must know at once whether we can acquire New Orleans or not. We are satisfied nothing else will secure us against a war at no distant period; and we cannot press this reason without beginning those arrangements which will be necessary if war is hereafter to result. For this purpose it was necessary that the negotiators should be fully possessed of every idea we have on the subject, so as to meet the propositions of the opposite party, in whatever form they may be offered; and give them a shape admissible by us without being obliged to wait new instructions hence. With this view, we have joined Mr. Monroe

with yourself at Paris, and to Mr. Pinckney at Madrid, although we believe it will be hardly necessary for him to go to this last place. Should we fail in this object of the mission, a further one will be superadded for the other side of the channel.—To ROBERT R. LIVINGSTON. iv, 461. FORD ED., viii, 209. (W., Feb. 1803.)

4846. LOUISIANA, Mississippi navigation secured.—The acquisition of New Orleans would of itself have been a great thing, as it would have ensured to our western brethren the means of exporting their produce; but that of Louisiana is inappreciable, because, giving us the sole dominion of the Mississippi, it excludes those bickerings with foreign powers, which we know of a certainty would have put us at war with France immediately; and it secures to us the course of a peaceful nation.—To JOHN DICKINSON. FORD ED., viii, 261. (M., Aug. 1803.)

4847. —— ——. The acquisition of Louisiana, although more immediately beneficial to the western States, by securing for their produce a certain market, not subject to interruptions by officers over whom we have no control, yet is also deeply interesting to the maritime portion of our country, inasmuch as by giving the exclusive navigation of the Mississippi, it avoids the burthens and sufferings of a war, which conflicting interests on that river would inevitably have produced at no distant period. It opens, too, a fertile region for the future establishments in the progress of that multiplication so rapidly taking place in all parts.—R. TO A. TENNESSEE LEGISLATURE. viii, 115. (1803.)

— LOUISIANA, Monroe and.—See MONROE.

— LOUISIANA, New Orleans entrepot. —See NEW ORLEANS.

4848. LOUISIANA, Payment for.—We shall not avail ourselves of the three months' delay after possession of the province, allowed by the treaty for the delivery of the stock, but shall deliver it the moment that possession is known here, which will be on the eighteenth day after it has taken place.— To ROBERT R. LIVINGSTON. iv, 512. FORD ED., viii, 279. (W., Nov. 1803.)

4849. —— ——. When we contemplate the ordinary annual augmentation of imposts from increasing population and wealth, the augmentation of the same revenue by its extension to the new acquisition, and the economies which may still be introduced into our public expenditures, I cannot but hope that Congress in reviewing their resources will find means to meet the intermediate interests of this additional debt without recurring to new taxes, and applying to this object only the ordinary progression of our revenue.— THIRD ANNUAL MESSAGE. viii, 27. FORD ED., viii, 271. (Oct. 1803.)

4850. —— ——. [The acquisition] was so far from being thought, by any party, a breach of neutrality, that the British minister congratulated Mr. King on the acquisition, and declared that the King had learned it with great pleasure; and when Baring, the British banker, asked leave of the minister to purchase the debt and furnish the money to France, the minister declared to him, that so far from throwing obstacles in the way, if there were any difficulty in the payment of the money, it was the interest of Great Britain to aid it.—To W. A. BURWELL. v, 20. FORD ED.; viii, 469. (M., Sep. 1806.)

4851. LOUISIANA, Possession by Great Britain.—I am so deeply impressed with the magnitude of the dangers which will attend our government, if Louisiana and the Floridas be added to the British empire, that, in my opinion, we ought to make ourselves parties in the *general war* expected to take place, should this be the only means of preventing the calamity. But I think we should defer this step as long as possible; because war is so full of chances, which may relieve us from the necessity of interfering; and if necessary, still the later we interfere, the better we shall be prepared. It is often indeed more easy to prevent the capture of a place than to retake it. Should it be so in the case in question, the difference between the two operations of preventing and retaking, will not be so costly as two, three, or four years more of war. So that I am for preserving neutrality as long, and entering into the war as late, as possible.—OFFICIAL OPINION. vii, 509. FORD ED., v, 238. (August 1790.)

4852. ——— ———. It is said that Arnold is at Detroit reviewing the militia there. Other symptoms indicate a general design on all Louisiana and the two Floridas. What a tremendous position would success in these two objects place us in! Embraced from the St. Croix to the St. Mary's on one side by their possessions, on the other by their fleet, we need not hesitate to say that they would soon find means to unite to them all the territory covered by the ramifications of the Mississippi.—To JAMES MONROE. FORD ED., v, 199. (N.Y., July 1790.)

4853. LOUISIANA, Questions of boundary.—I suppose Monroe will touch on the limits of Louisiana only incidentally, inasmuch as its extension to Perdido curtails Florida, and renders it of less worth. * * * I am satisfied our right to the Perdido is substantial, and can be opposed by a quibble on form only; and our right westwardly to the bay of St. Bernard, may be strongly maintained.—To JAMES MADISON. iv, 502. FORD ED., viii, 245. (M., Aug. 1803.)

4854. ——— ———. We did not collect the sense of our brethren the other day by regular questions, but as far as I could understand from what was said, it appeared to be,—1. That an acknowledgment of our right to the Perdido, is a *sine qua non*, and no price to be given for it. 2. No absolute and perpetual relinquishment of right is to be made of the country east of the Rio Bravo del Norte, even in exchange for Florida. (I am not quite sure that this was the opinion of all.) It would be better to lengthen the term of years to any definite degree than to

cede in perpetuity. 3. That a country may be laid off within which no further settlement shall be made by either party for a given time, say thirty years. This country to be from the North river eastwardly towards the Rio Colorado, or even to, but not beyond the Mexican or Sabine river. To whatever river it be extended, it might from its source run northwest, as the most eligible direction; but a due north line would produce no restraint that we should feel in twenty years. This relinquishment, and two millions of dollars, to be the price of all the Floridas east of the Perdido, or to be apportioned to whatever part they will cede. But on entering into conferences, both parties should agree that, during their continuance, neither should strengthen their situation between the Iberville, Mississippi, and Perdido, nor interrupt the navigation of the rivers therein. If they will not give such an order instantly, they should be told that we have for peace's sake only, forborne till they could have time to give such an order, but that as soon as we receive notice of their refusal to give the order, we shall enter into the exercise of our right of navigating the Mobile, and protect it, and increase our force there *pari passu* with them.—To JAMES MADISON. iv, 550. FORD ED., viii, 309. (July 1804.)

4855. ——— ———. In conversation with Mr. Gallatin as to what might be deemed the result of our conference, he seemed to have understood the former opinion as not changed, to wit, that for the Floridas east of the Perdido might be given not only the two millions of dollars and a margin to remain unsettled, but an absolute relinquishment from the North river to the Bay of St. Bernard and Colorado river. This, however, I think should be the last part of the price yielded, and only for an entire cession of the Floridas, not for a part only.—To JAMES MADISON. FORD ED., viii, 313. (1804.)

4856. LOUISIANA, Spain and acquisition.—At this moment a little cloud hovers in the horizon. The government of Spain has protested against the right of France to transfer; and it is possible she may refuse possession, and that this may bring on acts of force. But against such neighbors as France there, and the United States here, what she can expect from so gross a compound of folly and false faith, is not to be sought in the book of wisdom. She is afraid of her enemies in Mexico; but not more than we are.—To DUPONT DE NEMOURS. iv, 509. (W., Nov. 1803.)

4857. ——— ———. Spain entered with us a protestation against our ratification of the treaty, grounded, first, on the assertion that the First Consul had not executed the conditions of the treaties of cession; and, secondly, that he had broken a solemn promise not to alienate the country to any nation. We answered, that these were private questions between France and Spain, which they must settle together; that we derived our title from the First Consul, and did not doubt his guarantee of it.—To ROBERT R. LIVINGSTON. iv, 511. FORD ED., viii, 278. (W., Nov. 1803.) See SPAIN.

4858. LOUISIANA, Taking possession of.—We * * * [have] sent off orders to the Governor of the Mississippi Territory and

General Wilkinson to move down with the troops at hand to New Orleans, to receive the possession from M. Laussat. If he is heartily disposed to carry the order of the [First] Consul into execution, he can probably command a volunteer force at New Orleans, and will have the aid of ours also, if he desires it, to take the possession, and deliver it to us. If he is not so disposed, *we* shall take the possession, and it will rest with the government of France, by adopting the act as their own, and obtaining the confirmation of Spain, to supply the non-execution of their stipulation to deliver, and to entitle themselves to the complete execution of our part of the agreements.—To ROBERT R. LIVINGSTON. iv, 511. FORD ED., viii, 279. (W., Nov. 1803.)

4859. —— ——. I think it possible that Spain, recollecting our former eagerness for the island of New Orleans, may imagine she can, by a free delivery of that, redeem the residue of Louisiana; and that she may withhold the peaceable cession of it. In that case no doubt force must be used.—To JAMES MADISON. FORD ED., viii, 263. (M., Sep. 1803.)

4860. LOUISIANA, Treaty ratified.— This treaty [Louisiana] must, of course, be laid before both Houses [of Congress], because both have important functions to exercise respecting it. They, I presume, will see their duty to their country in ratifying and paying for it, so as to secure a good which would otherwise probably be never again in their power. But, I suppose, they must then appeal to *the nation* for an additional article to the Constitution, approving and confirming an act which the nation had not previously authorized.—To JOHN C. BRECKENRIDGE. iv, 500. FORD ED., viii, 244. (M., Aug. 1803.)

4861. —— ——. Your treaty has obtained nearly a general approbation. * * * The question on its ratification in the Senate was decided by twenty-four against seven, which was ten more than enough. The vote in the House of Representatives for making provision for its execution was carried by eighty-nine against twenty-three, which was a majority of sixty-six, and the necessary bills are going through the Houses by greater majorities.—To ROBERT R. LIVINGSTON. iv, 510. FORD ED., viii, 278. (W., Nov. 1803.)

4862. —— ——. You will observe in the enclosed letter from Monroe a hint to do without delay what we are bound to do [regarding the treaty]. There is reason, in the opinion of our ministers, to believe, that if the thing were to do over again, it could not be obtained, and that if we give the least opening, they will declare the treaty void. A warning amounting to that has been given them, and an unusual kind of letter written by their minister to our Secretary of State, direct.—To WILSON C. NICHOLAS. iv, 505. FORD ED., viii, 247. (M., Sep. 1803.)

4863. —— ——. M. Pichon, according to instructions from his government, proposed to have added to the ratification a protestation against any failure in time or other circumstances of execution, on our part. He was told, that in that case we should annex a counter protestation, which would leave the thing exactly where it was; that this transaction had been conducted, from the commencement of the negotiation to this stage of it, with a frankness and sincerity honorable to both nations, and comfortable to the heart of an honest man to review; that to annex to this last chapter of the transaction such an evidence of mutual distrust, was to change its aspect dishonorably for us both, and, contrary to truth, as to us; for that we had not the smallest doubt that France would punctually execute its part; and I assured M. Pichon that I had more confidence in the word of the First Consul than in all the parchment we could sign. He saw that we had ratified the treaty; that both branches had passed, by great majorities, one of the bills for execution, and would soon pass the other two; that no circumstances remained that could leave a doubt of our punctual performance; and like an able and honest minister (which he is in the highest degree), he undertook to do what he knew his employers would do themselves, were they here spectators of all the existing circumstances, and exchanged the ratifications purely and simply; so that this instrument goes to the world as an evidence of the candor and confidence of the nations in each other, which will have the best effects.—To ROBERT R. LIVINGSTON. iv, 510. FORD ED., viii, 278. (W., Nov. 1803.)

4864. —— ——. The treaty which has so happily sealed the friendship of our two countries has been received here with general acclamation.—To DUPONT DE NEMOURS. iv, 508. (W., 1803.)

4865. —— ——. For myself and my country, I thank you for the aids you have given in it; and I congratulate you on having lived to give those aids in a transaction replete with blessings to unborn millions of men, and which will mark the face of a portion on the globe so extensive as that which now composes the United States of America.—To DUPONT DE NEMOURS. iv, 509. (W., 1803.)

4866. —— ——. It is not true that the Louisiana treaty was antedated, lest Great Britain should consider our supplying her enemies with money as a breach of neutrality. After the very words of the treaty were finally agreed to, it took some time, perhaps some days, to make out all the copies in the very splendid manner of Bonaparte's treaties. Whether the 30th of April, 1803, the date expressed, was the day of the actual compact, or that on which it was signed, our memories do not enable us to say. If the former, then it is strictly conformable to the day of the compact; if the latter, then it was postdated, instead of being antedated.*—To W. A. BURWELL. v, 20. FORD ED., viii, 469. (M., Sep. 1806.)

* This antedating of the treaty was one of the charges made by John Randolph against the administration of Jefferson.—EDITOR.

4867. LOUIS XVI., Character of.—He had not a wish but for the good of the nation; and for that object, no personal sacrifice would ever have cost him a moment's regret; but his mind was weakness itself, his constitution timid, his judgment null, and without sufficient firmness even to stand by the faith of his word. His Queen, too, haughty, and bearing no contradiction, had an absolute ascendency over him; and around her were rallied the King's brother, D'Artois, the court generally, and the aristocratic part of his ministers, particularly Breteuil, Broglio, Vauguyon, Foulon, Luzerne, men whose principles of government were those of the age of Louis XIV. Against this host, the good counsels of Necker, Montmorin, St. Priest, although in unison with the wishes of the King himself, were of little avail. The resolutions of the morning, formed under their advice, would be reversed in the evening, by the influence of the Queen and Court.—Autobiography. i, 88. Ford ed., i, 121. (1821.)

4868. —— ——. The King is a good man. To Edward Carrington. ii, 99. Ford ed., iv, 359. (P., 1787.)

4869. —— ——. Under a good and a young King, as the present, I think good may be made of the Assemblée des Notables.—To La Comtesse de Tesse. ii, 133. (N., March 1787.)

4870. —— ——. The model of royal excellence.—To Count de Montmorin. iii, 137. (N.Y., 1790.)

4871. —— ——. The King loves business, economy, order, and justice, and wishes sincerely the good of his people; but he is irascible, rude, very limited in his understanding, and religious, bordering on bigotry. He * * *, loves his Queen, and is too much governed by her. * * * Unhappily the King shows a propensity for the pleasures of the table. That for drink has increased lately, or, at least, it has become more known.—To James Madison. ii, 153. Ford ed., iv, 393. (P., 1787.)

4872. LOUIS XVI., Execution.—We have just received the news of the decapitation of the King of France. Should the present foment in Europe not produce republics everywhere, it will at least soften the monarchical governments by rendering monarchs amenable to punishment like other criminals, and doing away that rage of insolence and oppression, the inviolability of the King's person.—To —— ——. iii, 527. (Pa., March 1793.)

4873. —— ——. It is certain that the ladies of this city [Philadelphia], of the first circle, are open-mouthed against the murderers of a sovereign, and they generally speak those sentiments which the more cautious husband smothers.—To James Madison. iii, 520. Ford ed., vi, 193. (1793.)

4874. —— ——. The death of the King of France has not produced as open condemnations from the monocrats as I expected.—To James Madison. iii, 519. Ford ed., vi, 192. (March 1793.)

4875. —— ——. The deed which closed the mortal course of these sovereigns [Louis XVI. and Marie Antoinette], I shall neither approve nor condemn. I am not prepared to say that the first magistrate of a nation cannot commit treason against his country, or is unamenable to its punishment; nor yet, that where there is no written law, no regulated tribunal, there is not a law in our hearts, and a power

in our hands, given for righteous employment in maintaining right and redressing wrong. Of those who judged the King, many thought him wilfully criminal; many that his existence would keep the nation in perpetual conflict with the horde of kings who would war against a regeneration which might come home to themselves, and that it were better that one should die than all. I should not have voted with this portion of the legislature. I should have shut up the Queen in a convent, putting harm out of her power, and placed the King in his station, investing him with limited powers, which, I verily believe, he would have honestly exercised according to the measure of his understanding. In this way no void would have been created, courting the usurpation of a military adventurer, nor occasion given for those enormities which demoralized the nations of the world, and destroyed and are yet to destroy millions and millions of its inhabitants.—Autobiography. i, 101. Ford ed., i, 141. (1821.)

4876. LOUIS XVI., Friend to America. —Our best and greatest friend.—To Marquis de la Luzerne. iii, 141. (N.Y., 1790.)

4877. LOUIS XVI., Good qualities.—The King's dispositions are solidly good. He is capable of great sacrifices. All he wants to induce him to do a thing, is to be assured it will be for the good of the nation.—To Mr. Cutting. ii, 439. (P., 1788.)

4878. LOUIS XVI., Habits.—The King, long in the habit of drowning his cares in wine, plunges deeper and deeper. The Queen cries, but sins on.—To John Adams. ii, 258. (P., 1787.)

4879. —— ——. The King goes for nothing. He hunts one half the day, is drunk the other, and signs whatever he is bid [by the Queen].—To John Jay. ii, 294. (P., 1787.)

4880. LOUIS XVI., Honesty.—The King is the honestest man in his kingdom, and the most regular and economical. He has no foible which will enlist him against the good of his people; and whatever constitution will promote this, he will befriend. But he will not befriend it obstinately: he has given repeated proofs of a readiness to sacrifice his opinion to the wish of the nation. I believe he will consider the opinion of the States General, as the best evidence of what will please and profit the nation, and will conform to it.—To Mr. Cutting. ii, 470. (P., Aug. 1788.)

4881. —— ——. He is an honest, unambitious man, who desires neither money nor power for himself.—To John Jay. iii, 28. (P., 1789.)

4882. —— ——. The King is honest, and wishes the good of his people; but the expediency of an hereditary aristocracy is too difficult a question for him. On the contrary, his prejudices, his habits and his connections, decide him in his heart to support it.—To John Jay. iii, 51. (P., 1789.)

4883. —— ——. The King has an honest heart.—To James Monroe. Ford ed., iv, 39. (P., 1785.)

4884. LOUIS XVI., Revenues.—It is urged principally against the King that his revenue is one hundred and thirty millions more than that of his predecessor was, and yet he demands one hundred and twenty millions further.—To John Adams. ii, 258. (P., 1787.)

4885. LOUIS XVI., Sincerity.—I have not a single doubt of the sincerity of the King.—To Mr. Mason. iii, 72. (P., July 1789.) See Marie Antoinette and Revolution (French).

4886. LOUIS XVIII., Restoration of.—I have received some information from an eye-witness of what passed on the occasion of the second return of Louis XVIiI. The Emperor Alexander, it seems, was solidly opposed to this. In the consultation of the allied sovereigns and their representatives with the executive council at Paris, he insisted that the Bourbons were too incapable and unworthy of being placed at the head of the nation; declared he would support any other choice they should freely make, and continued to urge most strenuously that some other choice should be made. The debates ran high and warm, and broke off after midnight, every one retaining his own opinion. He lodged * * * at Talleyrand's. When they returned into council the next day, his host had overcome his firmness. Louis XVIII. was accepted, and through the management of Talleyrand, accepted without any capitulation, although the sovereigns would have consented that he should be first required to subscribe and swear to the constitution prepared, before permission to enter the kingdom. It would seem as if Talleyrand had been afraid to admit the smallest interval of time, lest a change of mind would bring back Bonaparte on them. But I observe that the friends of a limited monarchy there consider the popular representation as much improved by the late alteration, and confident it will in the end produce a fixed government in which an elective body, fairly representative of the people, will be an efficient element.—To John Adams. vii, 82. (P.F., 1817.)

4887. LUXURIES, The Republic and.—I own it to be my opinion, that good will arise from the destruction of our credit [in Europe]. I see nothing else which can restrain our disposition to luxury, and to the change of those manners which alone can preserve republican government.—To Archibald Stuart. i, 518. Ford ed., iv, 188. (1786.)

4888. LUXURIES, Taxation of.—The * * * revenue, on the consumption of foreign articles, is paid cheerfully by those who can afford to add foreign luxuries to domestic comforts.—Second Inaugural Address. viii, 41. Ford ed., viii, 343. (1805.)

4889. ———— ————. The great mass of the articles on which impost is paid is foreign luxuries, purchased by those only who are rich enough to afford themselves the use of them.—Sixth Annual Message. viii, 68. Ford ed., viii, 494. (Dec. 1806.)

4890. ———— ————. The government which steps out of the ranks of the ordinary articles of consumption to select and lay under disproportionate burthens a particular one, because it is a comfort, pleasing to the taste, or necessary to health, and will therefore be bought, is, in that particular, a tyranny.—To Samuel Smith. vii, 285. Ford ed., x, 252. (M., 1819.) See Taxation.

— LYNCH-LAW.—See Law.

4891. LUZERNE (Marquis de la), Disappointments.—We have, for some time, expected that the Chevalier de la Luzerne would obtain a promotion in the diplomatic line by being appointed to some of the courts where this country keeps an ambassador. But none of the vacancies taking place, I think the present disposition is to require his return to his station in America. He told me himself lately that he should return in the Spring. I have never pressed this matter on the court, though I knew it to be desirable and desired on our part; because, if the compulsion on him to return had been the work of Congress, he would have returned in such ill temper with them, as to disappoint them in the good they expected from it. He would forever have laid at their door his failure of promotion. I did not press it for another reason, which is, that I have great reason to believe that the character of the Count de Moustier, who would go, were the Chevalier to be otherwise provided for, would give the most perfect satisfaction in America.—To James Madison. ii, 106. Ford ed., iv, 364. (P., 1787.)

4892. LUZERNE (Marquis de la), Secret marriage.—The Marquis de la Luzerne had been for many years married to his brother's wife's sister, secretly. She was ugly and deformed, but sensible, amiable, and rather rich. When he was named ambassador to London, with ten thousand guineas a year, the marriage was avowed, and he relinquished his cross of Malta, from which he derived a handsome revenue for life, and which was very open to advancement. She stayed here [Paris] and not long after died. His real affection for her, which was great and unfeigned, and perhaps the loss of his order for so short-lived a satisfaction, has thrown him almost into a state of despondency.—To James Madison. ii, 445. Ford ed., v, 44. (P., 1788.)

4893. LUZERNE (Marquis de la), Tribute to.—This government is now formed, organized, and in action; and it considers among its earliest duties, and assuredly among its most cordial, to testify to you the regret which the people and government of the United States felt at your removal from among them; a very general and sincere regret, and tempered only by the consolation of your personal advancement, which accompanied it. You will receive, Sir, by order of the President of the United States, as soon as they can be prepared, a medal and chain of gold, of which he desires your acceptance in token of their esteem, and of the sensibility with which they will ever recall your recollection of their memory. But as this compliment may, hereafter, be rendered to other missions, from which yours was distinguished by eminent circumstances, the President of the United States wishes to pay you the distinct tribute of an express acknowledgment of your services, and our sense of them. You came to us, Sir, through all the perils which encompassed us on all sides. You found us struggling and suffering under difficulties, as singular and trying as our situation was new and unprecedented. Your magnanimous nation had taken side with us in the conflict, and yourself became the centre of our common councils, the link which connected our common operations. In that position you labored without ceasing, until all our labors were crowned with glory to your nation, freedom to ours, and benefit to both. During the whole, we are constant evidence of your zeal, your abilities and your good faith. We desire to convey this testimony of it home to your breast, and to that of your sovereign, our best and greatest friend, and this I do, Sir, in the name, and by the express instruction of the President of the United States.—To Marquis de la Luzerne. iii, 141. (N.Y., April 30, 1790.)

4894. LYON (Matthew), Prosecution of.—You will have seen the disgusting proceedings in the case of Lyon. If they would have accepted even of a commitment to the serjeant, it might have been had. But to get rid of his vote was the most material object. These proceedings must degrade the General Government, and lead the people to lean more on their State governments, which have been sunk under the early popularity of the former.—To James Madison. iv, 211. Ford ed., vii, 202. (Pa., Feb. 1798.)

4895. MACDONOUGH (Commodore), Victory of.—The success of Macdonough [in the battle of Lake Champlain] has been happily timed to dispel the gloom of your present meeting, and to open the present session of Congress with hope and good humor.—To James Monroe. Ford ed., ix, 488. (M., 1814.)

4896. ———— ————. I congratulate you on the destruction of a second hostile fleet on the Lakes by Macdonough. * * * While our enemies cannot but feel shame for their barbarous achievements at Washington, they will be stung to the soul by these repeated victories over them on that element on which they wish the world to think them invincible. We have dissipated that error. They must now feel a conviction themselves that we can beat them gun to gun, ship to ship, and fleet to fleet, and that their early successes on the land have been either purchased from traitors, or obtained from raw men entrusted of necessity with commands for which no experience had qualified them, and that every day is adding that experience to unquestioned bravery.—To President Madison. vi, 386. (M., 1814.)

4897. MACE, Design for.—I send you a design for a Mace by Dr. Thornton, whose taste and inspiration are both good. But I am not satisfied with the introduction of the rattlesnake into the design. There is in man as well as brutes, an antipathy to the snake, which renders it a disgusting object wherever it is presented. I would myself rather adopt the Roman staves and axe, trite as it is; or perhaps a sword, sheathed in a roll of parchment (that is to say an imitation in metal of a roll of parchment), written over, in the raised Gothic letters of the law, with that part of the Constitution which establishes the House of Representatives, for that house, or the Senate. For the Senate, however, if you have that same disgust for the snake, I am sure you will yourself imagine some better substitute; or perhaps you will find that disgust overbalanced by stronger considerations in favor of the emblem. —To Governor Henry Lee. Ford ed., vi, 320. (Pa., 1793.)

4898. MACON (Nathaniel) Confidence in.—Some enemy whom we know not, is sowing tares among us. Between you and myself nothing but opportunities of explanation can be necessary to defeat those endeavors. At least on my part my confidence in you is so unqualified that nothing further is necessary for my satisfaction. I must, therefore, ask a conversation with you.—To Nathaniel Macon. Ford ed., viii, 439. (W., 1806.)

4899. ———— ————. While such men as yourself and your worthy colleagues of the legislature, and such characters as compose the executive administration, are watching for us all,

I slumber without fear, and review in my dreams the visions of antiquity. *—To Nathaniel Macon. vii, 111. Ford ed., x, 120. (M., 1819.)

— MADEIRA, Climate of.—See Climate.

4900. MADISON (James), Ability of.— Mr. Madison came into the House [Legislature of Virginia] in 1776, a new member and young; which circumstances, concurring with his extreme modesty, prevented his venturing himself in debate before his removal to the Council of State, in November, '77. From thence he went to Congress, then consisting of few members. Trained in these successive schools, he acquired a habit of self-possession, which placed at ready command the rich resources of his luminous and discriminating mind, and of his extensive information, and rendered him the first of every assembly afterwards, of which he became a member. Never wandering from his subject into vain declamation, but pursuing it closely, in language pure, classical and copious, soothing always the feelings of his adversaries by civilities and softness of expression, he rose to the eminent station which he held in the great National Convention of 1787: and in that of Virginia which followed, he sustained the new Constitution in all its parts, bearing off the palm against the logic of George Mason, and the fervid declamation of Mr. [Patrick] Henry. With these consummate powers, were united a pure and spotless virtue, which no calumny has ever attempted to sully. Of the powers and polish of his pen, and of the wisdom of his administration in the highest office of the nation, I need say nothing. They have spoken, and will forever speak for themselves.—Autobiography. i, 41. Ford ed., i, 56. (1821.)

4901. MADISON (James), Administration of.—I leave everything in the hands of men so able to take care of them, that if we are destined to meet misfortunes, it will be because no human wisdom could avert them.—To Dupont de Nemours. v, 433. (W., 1809.)

4902. ———— ————. If peace can be preserved, I hope and trust you will have a smooth administration. I know no government which would be so embarrassing in war as ours. This would proceed very much from the lying and licentious character of our papers; but much, also, from the wonderful credulity of the members of Congress in the floating lies of the day. And in this no experience seems to correct them. I have never seen a Congress during the last eight years, a majority of which I would not implicitly have relied on in any question, could their minds have been purged of all errors of fact. The evil, too, increases greatly with the protraction of the session, and I apprehend, in case of war, their session would have a tendency to become permanent.—To President Madison. v, 437. (W., March 1809.)

4903. ———— ————. Any services which I could have rendered will be more than supplied by the wisdom and virtues of my successor. —Reply to Address. v, 473. (M., 1809.)

* Nathaniel Macon was Speaker of the House of Representatives from 1801 to 1806, and subsequently United States Senator from North Carolina. John Randolph of Roanoke made him one of the legatees of his estate, and said of him in his will, "he is the best, the purest, and wisest man I ever knew".— Editor.

4904. —— ——. Mr. Madison is my successor. This ensures to us a wise and honest administration.—To BARON HUMBOLDT. v, 435. (W., 1809.)

4905. —— ——. I do not take the trouble of forming opinions on what is passing among [my successors], because I have such entire confidence in their integrity and wisdom as to be satisfied all is going right, and that every one is best in the station confided to him.—To DAVID HOWELL. v, 555. (M., 1810.)

4906. —— ——. Anxious, in my retirement, to enjoy undisturbed repose, my knowledge of my successor and late coadjutors, and my entire confidence in their wisdom and integrity, were assurances to me that I might sleep in security with such watchmen at the helm, and that whatever difficulties and dangers should assail our course, they would do what could be done to avoid or surmount them. In this confidence I envelop myself, and hope to slumber on to my last sleep. And should difficulties occur which they cannot avert, if we follow them in phalanx, we shall surmount them without danger.—To WILLIAM DUANE. v, 533. (M., 1810.)

4907. —— ——. If you will except the bringing into power and importance those who were enemies to himself as well as to the principles of republican government, I do not recollect a single measure of the President which I have not approved. Of those under him, and of some very near him, there have been many acts of which we have all disapproved, and he more than we.—To THOMAS LEIPER. vi, 465. FORD ED., ix, 521. (M., 1815.)

4908. MADISON (James), Confidence in.—In all cases I am satisfied you are doing what is for the best, as far as the means put into your hands will enable you, and this thought quiets me under every occurrence.—To PRESIDENT MADISON. vi, 114. FORD ED., ix, 384. (M., May 1813.)

— **MADISON (James), Election contest.** —See HENRY (PATRICK).

4909. MADISON (James), Federal Convention debates.—In a society of members, between whom and yourself are great mutual esteem and respect, a most anxious desire is expressed that you would publish your debates of the [Federal] Convention. That these measures of the army, navy and direct tax will bring about a revolution of public sentiment is thought certain, and that the Constitution will then receive a different explanation. Could those debates be ready to appear critically, their effect would be decisive. I beg of you to turn this subject in your mind. The arguments against it will be personal; those in favor of it moral; and something is required from you as a set off against the sin of your retirement.— To JAMES MADISON. iv, 263. FORD ED., vii, 318. (Pa., Jan. 1799.)

4910. MADISON (James), Hamilton and.—Hamilton is really a Colossus to the anti-republican party. * * * When he comes forward, there is nobody but yourself who can meet him.—To JAMES MADISON. iv, 121. FORD ED., vii, 32. (M., 1795.)

4911. —— ——. You will see in Fenno two numbers of a paper signed " Marcellus ". They promise much mischief, and are ascribed, without any difference of opinion, to [Alexander] Hamilton. You must take your pen against this champion. You know the ingenuity of his talents; and there is not a person but yourself who can foil him. For heaven's sake, then, take up your pen, and do not desert the public cause altogether.—To JAMES MADISON. iv, 231. FORD ED., vii, 231. (Pa., April 1798.)

4912. —— ——. Let me pray and beseech you to set apart a certain portion of every post day to write what may be proper for the public. Send it to me while here [Philadelphia], and when I go away I will let you know to whom you may send, so that your name will be sacredly secret. You can render such incalculable services in this way, as to lessen the effect of our loss of your presence here.—To JAMES MADISON. iv, 281. FORD ED., vii, 344. (Pa., Feb. 1799.)

4913. MADISON (James), Jefferson and administration of.—The unwarrantable ideas often expressed in the newspapers, and by persons who ought to know better, that I intermeddle in the Executive councils, and the indecent expressions, sometimes, of a hope that Mr. Madison will pursue the principles of my administration. expressions so disrespectful to his known abilities and dispositions, have rendered it improper in me to hazard suggestions to him, on occasions even where ideas might occur to me, that might accidentally escape him —To JAMES MONROE. vi, 123. (M., 1813.)

— **MADISON (James), Jefferson, Presidency and.**—See PRESIDENT.

4914. MADISON (James), Jefferson's bequest to.—I give to my friend, James Madison, of Montpelier, my gold-mounted walking-staff of animal horn, as a token of the cordial and affectionate friendship, which, for nearly now an half-century, has united us in the same principles and pursuits of what we have deemed for the greatest good of our country.—JEFFERSON'S WILL. ix, 514. FORD ED., x, 395. (March 1826.)

4915. MADISON (James), Jefferson's friendship for.—My friendship for Mr. Madison, my confidence in his wisdom and virtue, and my approbation of all his measures, and especially of his taking up at length the gauntlet against England, is known to all with whom I have ever conversed or corresponded on these measures.—To THOMAS LEIPER. vi, 465. FORD ED., ix, 521. (M., 1815.)

4916. —— ——. The friendship which has subsisted between us, now half a century, and the harmony of our political principles and pursuits, have been sources of constant happiness to me through that long period. And if I remove beyond the reach of attentions to the University, or beyond the bourne of life itself, as I soon must, it is a comfort to leave that institution under your care, and an assurance that it will not be wanting. It has also been a great solace to me, to believe that you are engaged in vindicating to posterity the course we have pursued for preserving to them, in all their purity, the blessings of self-government, which we had assisted, too, in acquiring for them. If ever the earth has beheld a system of administration conducted with a single and steadfast eye to the general interest and happiness of those committed to it, one which, protected by truth, can never know reproach. it is that to which our lives have been devoted. To myself you have been a pillar of support through life. Take care of me when dead, and be assured that I shall leave with you my last affections.*—To JAMES MADISON. vii, 434. FORD ED., x, 377. (M., February 1826.)

4917. MADISON (James), John Adams and.—Charles Lee consulted a member from Virginia to know whether [John] Marshall would be agreeable [as Minister to France]. He named you, as more likely to give satisfaction. The answer was, " nobody of Mr. Madison's way of thinking will be appointed ".—To JAMES MADISON. iv, 179. FORD ED., vii, 132. (Pa., June 1797.)

4918. MADISON (James), Judgment of.—There is no sounder judgment than his. To J. W. EPPES. FORD ED., ix, 484. (M., 1814.)

— MADISON (James), Marbury vs.— See MARBURY vs. MADISON.

— MADISON (James), Monroe and.— See MONROE.

4919. MADISON (James), Opinions of. —No man weighs more maturely than Mr. Madison before he takes a side on any question.—To PEREGRINE FITZHUGH. iv, 170. (M., 1797.)

4920. MADISON (James), Opposition to.—With respect to the opposition threatened, although it may give some pain, no injury of consequence is to be apprehended. Duane flying off from the government, may, for a little while, throw confusion into our ranks as John Randolph did. But, after a moment of time to reflect and rally, and to see where he is, we shall stand our ground with firmness. A few malcontents will follow him, as they did John Randolph, and perhaps he may carry off some well-meaning Anti-Snyderites of Pennsylvania. The federalists will sing hosannas, and the world will thus know of a truth what they are. This new minority will perhaps bring forward their new favorite, who seems already to have betrayed symptoms of consent. They will blast him in the bud. which will be no misfortune. They will sound the tocsin against the ancient dominion, and anti-dominionism may become their rallying point. And it is better that all this should happen two than six years hence.—To PRESIDENT MADISON. FORD ED., ix, 321. (M., April 1811.)

4921. MADISON (James), Pure principles of.—I know them both [Mr. Madison and Mr. Monroe] to be of principles as truly republican as any men living.—To THOMAS RITCHIE. vii, 191. FORD ED., x, 170. (M., 1820.)

4922. MADISON (James), Reelection as President.—I have known Mr. Madison from 1779, when he first came into the public councils, and from three and thirty years' trial, I can say conscientiously that I do not know in the world a man of purer integrity, more dispassionate, disinterested, and devoted to genuine republicanism ; nor could I, in the whole scope of America and Europe, point out an ab'er head. He may be illy seconded by others, betrayed by the Hulls and Arnolds of our country, for such there are in every country, and with sorrow and suffering we know it. But what man can do will be done by Mr. Madison. I hope, therefore, there will be no difference among republicans as to his reelection; we shall know his

* The quotation is from the last letter written by Jefferson to Madison.—EDITOR.

value when we have to give him up, and to look at large for his successor.—To THOMAS C. FLOURNEY. vi, 82. (M., Oct. 1812.)

4923. MADISON (James), Removal of Armstrong.—If our operations have suffered or languished from any want of injury in the present head [of the War Department] which directs them, I have so much confidence in the wisdom and conscientious integrity of Mr. Madison, as to be satisfied, that however torturing to his feelings, he will fulfil his duty to the public and to his own reputation, by making the necessary change.—To WILLIAM DUANE. vi, 81. FORD ED., ix, 369. (M., Oct. 1812.)

4924. MADISON (James), Republicanism of.—Our enemies may try their cajoleries with my successor. They will find him as immovable in his republican principles as him whom they have honored with their peculiar enmity.—To DR. E. GRIFFITH. v, 451. (M., 1809.)

4925. MADISON (James), Services to Jefferson.—Mr. Madison is entitled to his full share of all the measures of my administration. Our principles were the same, and we never differed sensibly in the application of them.—To W. C. NICHOLAS. FORD ED., ix, 252. (M., 1809.)

4926. MADISON (James), Statesmanship.—Our ship is sound, the crew alert at their posts, and our ablest steersman at its helm.—To JOHN MELISH. v, 573. (M., 1811.)

4927. MADISON (James), University of Virginia and.—I do not entertain your apprehensions for the happiness of our brother Madison in a state of retirement. Such a mind as his, fraught with information and with matter for reflection, can never know *ennui*. Besides, there will always be work enough cut out for him to continue his active usefulness to his country. For example, he and Monroe (the President) are now here (Monticello) on the work of a collegiate institution to be established in our neighborhood, of which they and myself are three of six visitors. This, if it succeeds, will raise up children for Mr. Madison to employ his attention through life.—To JOHN ADAMS. vii, 62. (M., 1817.)

4928. MADISON (James), Wisdom of. —My successor, to the purest principles of republican patriotism, adds a wisdom and foresight second to no man on earth.—To GENERAL KOSCIUSKO. v, 508. (M., 1810.)

— MAGNETIC NEEDLE.—See LATITUDE AND LONGITUDE.

4929. MAILS, Expediting.—The President has desired me to confer with you on the proposition I made the other day, of endeavoring to move the posts at the rate of one hundred miles a day. It is believed to be practicable here, because it is practiced in every other country. * * * I am anxious that the thing should be begun by way of experiment, for a short distance, because I believe it will so increase the income of the post-office as to show we may go through with it.—To COLONEL PICKERING. iii, 344. (Pa., 1792.)

4930. MAINE, English encroachments. —The English encroachments on the province of Maine become serious. They have seized vessels, too, on our coast of Passamaquoddy, thereby displaying a pretension to the exclusive jurisdiction to the Bay of Fundy, which separates Nova Scotia and Maine, and belongs as much to us as them.—To MARQUIS DE LAFAYETTE. ii, 21. (P., 1786.)

4931. MAINE, Independence of.—If I do not contemplate this subject [the Missouri question] with pleasure, I do sincerely [contemplate] that of the independence of Maine, and the wise choice they have made of General King in the agency of their affairs.—To MARK LANGDON HILL. vii, 155. (M., 1820.)

4932. MAJORITY, Abuses by.—The majority, oppressing an individual, is guilty of a crime; abuses its strength, and, by acting on the law of the strongest, breaks up the foundations of society.—To DUPONT DE NEMOURS. vi, 591. FORD ED., x, 24. (P.F., 1816.)

4933. MAJORITY, Dissent from.—It is true that dissentients have a right to go over to the minority, and to act with them. But I do not believe your mind has contemplated that course; that it has deliberately viewed the strange company into which it may be led, step by step, unintended and unperceived by itself. The example of John Randolph is a caution to all honest and prudent men, to sacrifice a little of self-confidence, and to go with their friends, although they may sometimes think they are going wrong. * * * As far as my good will may go (for I can no longer act), I shall adhere to my government, Executive and Legislative, and, as long as they are republican, I shall go with their measures whether I think them right or wrong; because I know they are honest, and are wiser and better informed than I am. In doing this, however, I shall not give up the friendship of those who differ from me, and who have equal right with myself to shape their own course.—To WILLIAM DUANE. v, 592. FORD ED., ix, 316. (M., 1811.)

4934. MAJORITY, Force vs.—Absolute acquiescence in the decisions of the majority, —the vital principle of republics, from which is no appeal but to force, the vital principle and immediate parent of despotism, I deem [one of the] essential principles of our government and, consequently, [one] which ought to shape its administration.—FIRST INAUGURAL ADDRESS. viii, 4. FORD ED., viii, 4. (1801.)

4935. MAJORITY, Generations and.—This corporeal globe, and everything upon it, belong to its present corporeal inhabitants, during their generation. They alone have a right to direct what is the concern of themselves alone, and to declare the law of that direction; and this declaration can only be made by their majority.—To SAMUEL KERCHIVAL. vii, 16. FORD ED., x, 44. (M., 1816.)

4936. ———. A generation may bind itself as long as its majority continues in life; when that has disappeared, another majority is in place, holds all the rights and powers

their predecessors once held, and may change their laws and institutions to suit themselves.—To JOHN CARTWRIGHT. vii, 359. M., 1824.) See GENERATIONS.

4937. MAJORITY, Law of.—Where the law of the majority ceases to be acknowledged, there government ends; the law of the strongest takes its place, and life and property are his who can take them.—R. TO A. ANNAPOLIS CITIZENS. viii, 150. (1809.)

4938. ———. The *lex majoris partis* [is] founded in common law as well as common right.—NOTES ON VIRGINIA. viii, 367. FORD ED., iii, 229. (1782.)

4939. MAJORITY, Natural law.—The *lex majoris partis* is the natural law of every assembly of men, whose numbers are not fixed by any other law.—NOTES ON VIRGINIA. viii, 367. FORD ED., iii, 230. (1782.)

4940. ———. The law of the *majority* is the natural law of every society of men.—OFFICAL OPINION. vii, 496. FORD ED., v, 206. 1790.)

4941. ———. The *lex majoris partis* is a fundamental law of nature, by which alone self-government can be exercised by a society.—To JOHN BRECKENRIDGE. FORD ED., vii, 417. (Pa., 1800.)

4942. MAJORITY, Oppressive.—I have seen with deep concern the afflicting oppression under which the republican citizens of Connecticut suffer from an unjust majority. The truths expressed in your letter have been long exposed to the nation through the channel of the public papers, and are the more readily believed because most of the States during the momentary ascendancy of kindred majorities in them, have seen the same spirit of oppression prevail.—To THOMAS SEYMOUR. v, 43. FORD ED., ix, 29. (W., 1807.)

4943. MAJORITY, Reasonable.—Bear in mind this sacred principle. that though the will of the majority is in all cases to prevail. that will, to be rightful, must be reasonable; that the minority possess their equal rights, which equal laws must protect, and to violate would be oppression.—FIRST INAUGURAL ADDRESS. viii, 2. FORD ED., viii, 2. (March 1801.)

4944. MAJORITY, Representatives of.—Our Executive and Legislative authorities are the choice of the nation, and possess the nation's confidence. They are chosen because they possess it, and the recent elections prove it has not been abated by the attacks which have for some time been kept up against them. If the measures which have been pursued are approved by the majority, it is the duty of the minority to acquiesce and conform.—To WILLIAM DUANE. v, 592. FORD ED., ix, 315. (M., 1811.)

4945. MAJORITY, Respect for.—The measures of the fair majority * * * ought always to be respected.—To PRESIDENT WASHINGTON. iii, 461. FORD ED., vi, 103. (M., 1792.)

4946. MAJORITY, Slender.—After another election our majority will be two to one in the Senate, and it would· not be for the public good to have it greater.—To JOEL BARLOW. iv, 437. FORD ED., viii, 149. (W., May 1802.)

4947. —— ——. The first principle of republicanism is that the *lex majoris partis* is the fundamental law of every society of individuals of equal rights; to consider the will of the society enounced by the majority of a single vote as sacred as if unanimous, is the first of all lessons in importance, yet the last which is thoroughly learnt. This law once disregarded, no other remains but that of force, which ends necessarily in military despotism. This has been the history of the French Revolution.—To F. H. ALEXANDER VON HUMBOLDT. vii, 75. FORD ED., x, 89. (M., 1817.)

4948. MAJORITY, Submission to.—If we are faithful to our country, if we acquiesce, with good will, in the decisions of the majority, and the nation moves in mass in the same direction, although it may not be that which every individual thinks best, we have nothing to fear from any quarter.—R. TO A. VIRGINIA BAPTISTS. viii, 139. (1808.)

4949. —— ——. I readily suppose my opinion wrong, when opposed by the majority.—To JAMES MADISON. ii, 447. FORD ED., v, 48. (P., 1788.)

4950. —— ——. The fundamental law of every society is the *lex majoris partis,* to which we are bound to submit.—To DAVID HUMPHREYS. iii, 13. FORD ED., v, 90. (P., 1789.)

4951. MAJORITY, Will of.—The will of the majority honestly expressed should give law.—ANAS. ix, 131. FORD ED., i, 215. (1793.)

4952. —— ——. It is my principle that the will of the majority should always prevail.—To JAMES MADISON. ii, 332. FORD ED., iv, 479. (P., 1787.)

4953. —— ——. It accords with our principles to acknowledge any government to be rightful which is formed by the will of the nation substantially declared.—To GOUVERNEUR MORRIS. iii, 489. (1792.)

4954. —— ——. We are sensible of the duty and expediency of submitting our opinions to the will of the majority, and can wait with patience till they get right, if they happen to be at any time wrong.—To JOHN BRECKENRIDGE. FORD ED., vii, 418. (Pa., Jan. 1800.)

4955. —— ——. The fundamental principle of the government is that the will of the majority is to prevail.—To DR. WILLIAM EUSTIS. v, 411. FORD ED., ix, 236. (W., Jan. 1809.)

4956. MALESHERBES (C. G. de la M.), Eminence.—He is unquestionably the first character in the kingdom for integrity, patriotism, knowledge and experience in business.—To JOHN JAY. ii, 157. (P., 1787.)

4957. MALESHERBES (C. G. de la M.), Integrity.—I am particularly happy at the reentry of Malesherbes into the Council. His knowledge, his integrity, render his value inappreciable, and the greater to me, because, while he had no views of office, we had established together the most unreserved intimacy.—To JAMES MADISON. ii, 153. FORD ED., iv, 392. (P., 1787.)

4958. —— ——. No man's recommendation merits more reliance than that of M. de Malesherbes.—To —— ——. v, 381. (W., 1808.)

4959. MALICE, Escape from.—If *you* meant to escape malice, you should have confined yourself within the sleepy line of regular duty.—To JAMES STEPTOE. i, 324. FORD ED., iii, 63. (1782.)

4960. MALICE, Political.—You certainly acted wisely in taking no notice of what the malice of Pickering could say of you. Were such things to be answered, our lives would be wasted in the filth of fendings and provings, instead of being employed in promoting the happiness and prosperity of our fellow citizens. The tenor of your life is the proper and sufficient answer.—To JOHN ADAMS. vii, 62. (M., 1817.)

4961. MALICE, Virtue and.—There is no act, however virtuous, for which ingenuity may not find some bad motive.—To EDWARD DOWSE. iv, 477. (W., 1803.)

4962. —— ——. Malice will always find bad motives for good actions. Shall we therefore never do good?—To PRESIDENT MADISON. v, 524. (M., 1810.)

4963. MAN, A curious animal.—Man is in all his shapes a curious animal.—To MR. VOLNEY. iv, 159. (M., 1797.)

4964. MAN, Destructive.—In the whole animal kingdom I recollect no family but man, steadily and systematically employed in the destruction of itself. Nor does what is called civilization produce any other effect, than to teach him to pursue the principle of the *bellum omnium in omnia* on a greater scale, and instead of the little contest between tribe and tribe, to comprehend all the quarters of the earth in the same work of destruction. If to this we add, that as to other animals, the lions and tigers are mere lambs compared with man as a destroyer, we must conclude that nature has been able to find in man alone a sufficient barrier against the too great multiplication of other animals and of man himself, an equilibrating power against the fecundity of generation. While in making these observations, my situation points my attention to the warfare of man in the physical world, yours may present him as equally warring in the moral one.—To JAMES MADISON. iv, 156. FORD ED., vii, 99. (1797.)

4965. —— ——. The greatest honor of a man is in doing good to his fellow men, not in destroying them.—ADDRESS TO INDIANS. viii, 208. (1807.)

4966. —— ——. The Great Spirit did not make men that they might destroy one another, but doing to each other all the good in their power, and thus filling the land with happiness instead of misery and murder.—INDIAN ADDRESS. viii, 228. (1809.)

4967. MAN, Freedom and happiness of.—The freedom and happiness of man * * * are the sole objects of all legitimate government.—To GENERAL KOSCIUSKO. v, 509. (M., 1810.)

— **MAN, Future generations and.**—See GENERATIONS.

4968. MAN, Goodness in.—I am not yet decided to drop Lownes, on account of his being a good man, and I like much to be in the hands of good men. There is great pleasure in unlimited confidence.—To JAMES MADISON. FORD ED., vii, 62. (M., 1796.)

4969. MAN, Honesty of.—Men are disposed to live honestly, if the means of doing so are open to them.—To M. DE MARBOIS. vii, 77. (M., 1817.)

4970. —— ——. In truth man is not made to be trusted for life, if secured against all liability to account.—To M. CORAY. vii, 322. (M., 1823.)

4971. MAN, Madness of.—What a Bedlamite is man!—To JOHN ADAMS. vii, 200. FORD ED., x, 186. (M., 1821.)

4972. MAN, Political equality of.—All men are created equal.—DECLARATION OF INDEPENDENCE AS DRAWN BY JEFFERSON.

4973. MAN, A rational animal.—Man is a rational animal, endowed by nature with rights, and with an innate sense of justice.—To WILLIAM JOHNSON. vii, 291. FORD ED., x, 227. (M., 1823.)

— **MAN, Rights of.**—See RIGHTS OF MAN.

4974. MAN, Schoolboy through life.—The bulk of mankind are schoolboys through life.—NOTES ON A MONEY UNIT. i, 163. (1784.)

4975. MANKIND, Government of.—Men. enjoying in ease and security, the full fruits of their own industry, enlisted by all their interests on the side of law and order, habituated to think for themselves, and to follow their reason as their guide, * * * [are] more easily and safely governed than with minds nourished in error, and vitiated and debased, as in Europe. by ignorance, indigence, and oppression.—To WILLIAM JOHNSON. vii, 292. FORD ED., x, 227. (M., 1823.)

4976. MANKIND, Improvement of.—The energies of the nation, as depends on me, shall be reserved for the improvement of the condition of man, not wasted in his destruction.—REPLY TO ADDRESS. iv, 388. (W., 1801.)

4977. —— ——. Although a soldier yourself, I am sure you contemplate the peaceable employment of man in the improvement of his condition, with more pleasure than his murders, raperies and devastations.—To GENERAL KOSCIUSKO. vi, 69. FORD ED., ix, 363. (M., June 1812.)

4978. —— ——. That every man shall be made virtuous, by any process whatever, is, indeed, no more to be expected, than that every tree shall be made to bear fruit, and every plant nourishment. The brier and bramble can never become the vine and olive; but their asperities may be softened by culture, and their properties improved to usefulness in the order and economy of the world. And I do hope that, in the present spirit of extending to the great mass of mankind the blessings of instruction, I see a prospect of great advancement in the happiness of the human race; and that this may proceed to an indefinite, although not to an infinite degree.—To C. C. BLATCHLY. vii. 263. (M., 1822.)

4979. MANKIND, Love for.—Loving mankind in my individual relations with them, I pray to be permitted to depart in their peace.—To SPENCER ROANE. vii, 136. FORD ED., x, 142. (P.F., 1819.)

4980. MANKIND, Relations with.—During a long life, as much devoted to study as a faithful transaction of the trusts committed to me would permit, no subject has occupied more of my consideration than our relations with all the beings around us, our duties to them, and our future prospects. After reading and hearing everything which probably can be suggested respecting them, I have formed the best judgment I could as to the course they prescribe, and in the due observance of that course, I have no recollections which give me uneasiness.—To WILLIAM CANBY. vi, 210. (M., 1813.)

4981. —— ——. We must endeavor to forget our former love for them, and hold them as we hold the rest of mankind, enemies in War, in Peace friends.—DECLARATION OF INDEPENDENCE AS DRAWN BY JEFFERSON.

4982. MANNERS, American vs. French.—I am much pleased with the people of this country. The roughness of the human mind is so thoroughly rubbed off with them that it seems as if one might glide through a whole life among them without a jostle. Perhaps, too, their manners may be the best calculated for happiness to a people in their situation, but I am convinced they fall far short of effecting a happiness so temperate, so uniform and so lasting as is generally enjoyed with us.—To MRS. TRIST. i, 394. (P., 1785.)

4983. —— ——. Nourish peace with their [the French] persons, but war against their manners. Every step we take towards the adoption of their manners is a step to perfect misery.—To MRS. TRIST. i, 395. (P., 1785.)

4984. MANNERS, Institutions and.—Time indeed changes manners and notions and so far we must expect institutions to bend to them.—To SPENCER ROANE. vii, 211. FORD ED., x, 188. (M., 1821.)

4985. MANNERS, National.—The manners of every nation are the standard of orthodoxy within itself. But these standards being arbitrary, reasonable people in all allow free toleration for the manners, as for the religion of others.—To JEAN BAPTISTE SAY. vi, 433. (M., 1815.)

4986. MANSFIELD (Lord), Able and eloquent.—A man of the clearest head, and most seducing eloquence.—To PHILIP MAZZEI. FORD ED., iv, 115. (P., 1785.)

4987. MANSFIELD (Lord), Decisions of.—I hold it essential, in America, to forbid that any English decision which has happened since the accession of Lord Mansfield to the bench, should ever be cited in a court; because, though there have come many good ones from him, yet there is so much poison instilled into a great part of them, that it is better to proscribe the whole.—To MR. CUTTING. ii, 487. (P., 1788.)

4988. —— ——. The object of former judges has been to render the law more and more certain; that of this personage to render it more incertain under pretence of rendering it more reasonable.—To PHILIP MAZZEI. FORD ED., iv, 115. (P., 1785.)

4989. MANUFACTURES, Agriculture, commerce and.—I trust the good sense of our country will see that its greatest prosperity depends on a due balance between agriculture, manufactures and commerce.—To THOMAS LEIPER. v, 417. FORD ED., ix, 239. (W., 1809.)

4990. —— ——. An equilibrium of agriculture, manufactures and commerce, is certainly become essential to our independence. Manufactures sufficient for our own consumption, of what we raise the raw material (and no more). Commerce sufficient to carry the surplus produce of agriculture, beyond our own consumption, to a market for exchanging it for articles we cannot raise (and no more). These are the true limits of manufactures and commerce. To go beyond them is to increase our dependence on foreign nations, and our liability to war. These three important branches of human industry will then grow together, and be really handmaids to each other.—To JAMES JAY. v, 440. (M., April 1809.) See AGRICULTURE and COMMERCE.

4991. MANUFACTURES, British prohibition of.—By an act passed in the fifth year of the reign of his late Majesty, King George II., an American subject is forbidden to make a hat for himself, of the fur which he has taken perhaps on his own soil; an instance of despotism to which no parallel can be produced in the most arbitrary ages of British history.—RIGHTS OF BRITISH AMERICA. i, 129. FORD ED., i, 434. (1774.)

4992. —— ——. By an act passed in the twenty-third year of King George II., the iron which we make, we are forbidden to manufacture; and, heavy as that article is, and necessary in every branch of husbandry, besides commission and insurance, we are to pay freight for it to Great Britain, and freight for it back again, for the purpose of supporting, not men, but machines in the island of Great Britain.—RIGHTS OF BRITISH AMERICA. i, 129. FORD ED., i, 434. (1774.) See TRADE.

—— MANUFACTURES, Centralization and.—See 1159.

4993. MANUFACTURES, The Colonies and.—I think nothing can bring the security of our continent and its cause into danger, if we can support the credit of our paper. To do that, I apprehend, one of two steps must be taken. Either to procure free trade by alliance with some naval power able to protect it; or, if we find there is no prospect of that, to shut our ports totally, to all the world, and turn our Colonies into manufactories. The former would be most eligible, because most conformable to the habits and wishes of our people.—To BENJAMIN FRANKLIN. i, 205. FORD ED., ii, 132. (1777.)

4994. —— ——. During the present contest we have manufactured within our families the most necessary articles of clothing. Those of cotton will bear some comparison with the same kinds of manufacture in Europe; but those of wool, flax and hemp are very coarse, unsightly, and unpleasant; and such is our attachment to agriculture, and such our preference for foreign manufactures, that as wise or unwise, our people will certainly return as soon as they can, to the raising raw materials, and exchanging them for finer manufactures than they are able to execute themselves.—NOTES ON VIRGINIA. viii, 404. FORD ED., iii, 268. (1782.)

4995. MANUFACTURES, Cotton.—Great advances are making in the establishment of manufactures. Those of cotton will, I think, be so far proceeded on, that we shall never again have to recur to the importation of cotton goods for our own use.—To WILLIAM LYMAN. v, 280. (W., 1808.)

4996. —— ——. I am much pleased to find our progress in manufactures to be so great. That of cotton is peculiarly interesting, because we raise the raw material in such abundance, and because it may, to a great degree, supply our deficiencies both in wool and linen.—To J. DORSEY. v, 235. (W., 1808.)

4997. MANUFACTURES, The Embargo and.—The Embargo * * * promises lasting good by promoting among ourselves the establishment of manufactures hitherto sought abroad, at the risk of collisions no longer regulated by the laws of reason or morality.—R. TO A. PHILADELPHIA DEMOCRATIC-REPUBLICANS. viii, 128. (1808.)

4998. —— ——. The suspension of our foreign commerce, produced by the injustice of the belligerent powers, and the consequent losses and sacrifices of our citizens, are subjects of just concern. The situation into which we have thus been forced, has impelled us to apply a portion of our industry and capital to internal manufactures and improvements. The extent of this conversion is daily increasing, and little doubt remains that the establishments formed and forming will, under the auspices of cheaper materials and subsistence, the freedom of labor from taxation with us, and of protecting duties and prohibitions, become permanent.—EIGHTH ANNUAL MESSAGE. viii, 109. FORD ED., ix, 223. (1808.)

4999. —— ——. As a countervail to our short-lived sacrifices [by the Embargo], when these shall no longer be felt, we shall permanently retain the benefit they have prompted, of fabricating for our own use the materials of our own growth, heretofore carried to the work-houses of Europe, to be wrought and returned to us.—R. TO A. BALTIMORE TAMMANY SOCIETY. viii, 170. (1809.)

5000. —— ——. It is true that the Embargo laws have not had all the effect in bringing the powers of Europe to a sense of justice which a more faithful observance of them might have produced. Yet they have had the important effects of saving our seamen and property, of giving time to prepare for defence; and they will produce the further inestimable advantage of turning the attention and enterprise of our fellow citizens, and the patronage of our State Legislatures to the establishment of useful manufactures in our country. They will have hastened the day when an equilibrium between the occupations of agriculture, manufactures, and commerce, shall simplify our foreign concerns to the exchange only of that surplus which we cannot consume for those articles of reasonable comfort or convenience which we cannot produce.—R. TO A. PENNA. DEMOCRATIC-REPUBLICANS. viii, 163. (1809.)

5001. —— ——. Amidst the pressure of evils with which the belligerent edicts [Berlin decrees, Orders of Council, &c.], have afflicted us, some permanent good will arise; the spring given to manufactures will have durable effects. Knowing most of my own State, I can affirm with confidence that were free intercourse opened again to-morrow, she would never again import one-half of the coarse goods which she has done down to the date of the edicts. These will be made in our families. For finer goods we must resort to the larger manufactories established in the towns.—TO DAVID HUMPHREYS. v, 415. FORD ED., ix, 226. (W., 1809.)

5002. —— ——. The interruption of our commerce with England, produced by our Embargo and Non-Intercourse law, and the general indignation excited by her bare-faced attempts to make us accessories and tributaries to her usurpation on the high seas, have generated in this country an universal spirit for manufacturing for ourselves, and of reducing to a minimum the number of articles for which we are dependent on her. The advantages, too, of lessening the occasions of risking our peace on the ocean, and of planting the consumer in our own soil by the side of the grower of produce, are so palpable, that no temporary suspension of injuries on

her part, or agreements founded on that, will now prevent our continuing in what we have begun. The spirit of manufacturing has taken deep root among us, and its foundations are laid in too great expense to be abandoned.— TO DUPONT DE NEMOURS. v, 456. (M., June 1809.)

5003. —— ——. Nothing more salutary for us has ever happened than the British obstructions to our demands for their manufactures. Restore free intercourse when they will, their commerce with us will have totally changed its form, and the articles we shall in future want from them will not exceed their own consumption of our produce.—TO JOHN ADAMS. vi, 36. FORD ED., ix, 333. (M., Jan. 1812.)

5004. MANUFACTURES, Encouragement of.—The present aspect of our foreign relations has encouraged here a general spirit of encouragement to domestic manufactures. The Merino breed of sheep is well established with us, and fine samples of cloth are sent to us from the North. Considerable manufactures of cotton are also commencing. Philadelphia, particularly, is becoming more manufacturing than commercial.—TO MR. MAURY. v, 214. (W., Nov. 1807.)

5005. —— ——. My idea is that we should encourage home manufactures to the extent of our own consumption of everything of which we raise the raw material.—TO DAVID HUMPHREYS. v, 416. FORD ED., ix, 226. (W., 1809.)

5006. —— ——. Every syllable uttered in my name becomes a text for the federalists to torment the public mind on by their paraphrases and perversions. I have lately inculcated the encouragement of manufactures to the extent of our own consumption at least, in all articles of which we raise the raw material. On this the federal papers and meetings have sounded the alarm of Chinese policy, destruction of commerce, &c.; that is to say, the iron which we make must not be wrought here into plows, axes, hoes, &c., in order that the ship-owner may have the profit of carrying it to Europe, and bringing it back in a manufactured form, as if after manufacturing our own raw materials for our own use, there would not be a surplus produce sufficient to employ a due proportion of navigation in carrying it to market and exchanging it for those articles of which we have not the raw material. Yet this absurd hue and cry has contributed much to federalize New England. Their doctrine goes to the sacrificing agriculture and manufactures to commerce; to the calling off our people from the interior country to the sea shore to turn merchants, and to convert this great agricultural country into a city of Amsterdam. But I trust the good sense of our country will see that its greatest prosperity depends on a due balance between agriculture, manufactures and commerce, and not in this protuberant navigation which has kept us in hot water from the commencement of our government, and is now engaging us in war. —To THOMAS LEIPER. v, 417. FORD ED., ix, 239. (W., Jan. 1809.)

5007. —— ——. The government of the United States, at a very early period, when establishing its tariff on foreign importations, were very much guided in their selection of objects by a desire to encourage manufactures within themselves.—To —— ——. vii, 220. (M., 1821.)

5008. MANUFACTURES, Fear of British competition.—I much fear the effect on our infant establishments of the policy avowed by Mr. Brougham. Individual British merchants may lose by their late immense importations; but British commerce and manufactures, in the mass, will gain by beating down the competition of ours, in our own markets. Against this policy, our protecting duties are as nothing, our patriotism less.—To WILLIAM SAMPSON. FORD ED., x, 74. (M., 1817.)

5009. MANUFACTURES, Fostering.— Enough of 'the non-importation law should be reserved * * * to support those manufacturing establishments which the British Orders [of Council] and our interests forced us to make.—To PRESIDENT MADISON. v, 442. FORD ED., ix, 251. (M., April 1809.)

5010. MANUFACTURES, Great Britain and American.—Radically hostile to our navigation and commerce, and fearing its rivalry, Great Britain will completely crush it, and force us to resort to agriculture, not aware that we shall resort to manufactures also, and render her conquests over our navigation and commerce useless, at least, if not injurious, to herself in the end, and perhaps salutary to us, as removing out of our way the chief causes and provocations to war.—To HENRY DEARBORN. v, 530. FORD ED., ix, 278. (M., 1810.)

5011. MANUFACTURES,   Home.— There can be no question, in a mind truly American, whether it is best to send our citizens and property into certain captivity, and then wage war for their recovery, or to keep them at home, and to turn seriously to that policy which plants the manufacturer and the husbandman side by side, and establishes at the door of every one that exchange of mutual labors and comforts, which we have hitherto sought in distant regions, and under perpetual risk of broils with them.—R. TO A. OF NEW YORK TAMMANY SOCIETY. viii, 127. (Feb. 1808.)

5012. —— ——. I see with satisfaction * * * that our citizens * * * are preparing to provide for themselves those comforts and conveniences of life, for which it would be unwise evermore to recur to distant countries.—R. TO A. NEW HAMPSHIRE LEGISLATURE. viii, 131. (1808.)

5013. —— ——. I have not formerly been an advocate for great manufactories. I doubted whether our labor, employed in agriculture, and aided by the spontaneous ener-

gies of the earth, would not procure us more than we could make ourselves of other necessaries. But other considerations entering into the question, have settled my doubts.—To JOHN MELISH. vi, 94. FORD ED., ix, 373. (M., Jan. 1813.)

5014. —— ——. If the piracies of France and England are to be adopted as the law of nations, or should become their practice, it will oblige us to manufacture at home all the material comforts. This may furnish a reason to check imports until necessary manufactures are established among us. This offers the advantage. too, of placing the consumer of our produce near the producer.—To WILLIAM SHORT. vi, 128. (M., 1813.)

5015. —— ——. We are become manufacturers to a degree incredible to those who do not see it, and who only consider the short period of time during which we have been driven to them by the suicidal policy of England.—To JEAN BAPTISTE SAY. vi, 431. (M., March 1815.)

5016. —— ——. The prohibiting duties we lay on all articles of foreign manufacture which prudence requires us to establish at home, with the patriotic determination of every good citizen to use no foreign article which can be made within ourselves, without regard to difference of price, secures us against a relapse into foreign dependency.—To JEAN BAPTISTE SAY. vi, 431. (M., March 1815.)

5017. —— ——. It is our business to manufacture for ourselves whatever we can, to keep our markets open for what we can spare or want.—To THOMAS LEIPER. vi, 465. FORD ED., ix, 520. (M., 1815.) See MARKETS.

5018. —— ——. No one has been more sensible than myself of the advantages of placing the consumer by the side of the producer, nor more disposed to promote it by example.—To MRS. K. D. MORGAN. FORD ED., viii, 473. (M., 1822.) See PROTECTION and TARIFF.

5019. MANUFACTURES, Homespun.— Homespun is become the spirit of the times. I think it an useful one, and, therefore, that it is a duty to encourage it by example. The best fine cloth made in the United States is, I am told, at the manufacture of Colonel Humphreys in your neighborhood [New Haven]. Could I get the favor of you to procure me there as much of his best as would make me a coat? I should prefer a deep blue, but, if not to be had, then a black.—To ABRAHAM BISHOP. FORD ED., ix, 225. (W., 1808.)

5020. MANUFACTURES, Household.— There is no manufacture of wire or of cotton cards, or if any, it is not worth notice. No manufacture of stocking-weaving, consequently none for making the machine; none of cotton cloths of any kind for sale; though in almost every family some is manufactured for the use of the family, which is always good in quality, and often tolerably fine. In the same way, they make excellent stockings of cotton, weaving it in like manner, carried on principally in the family way. Among the poor, the wife weaves generally, and the rich either have a weaver among their servants, or employ their poor neighbors.—To Thomas Digges. ii, 412. Ford ed., v, 28. (P., 1788.)

5021. —— ——. The checks which the commercial regulations of Europe have given to the sale of our produce, has produced a very considerable degree of domestic manufacture, which, so far as it is in the household way, will doubtless continue; and so far as it is more public, will depend on the continuance or discontinuance of this policy of Europe.—To C. W. F. Dumas. Ford ed., vi, 70. (Pa., 1792.)

5022. —— ——. I shall be glad to hear * * * any improvements in the arts applicable to * * * household manufacture. —To Tench Coxe. iv, 105. Ford ed., vi, 509. (M., May 1794.)

5023. —— ——. The mass of *household* manufacture, unseen by the public eye, and so much greater than what is seen, is such at present, that let our intercourse with England be opened when it may, not one-half the amount of what we have heretofore taken from her will ever again be demanded. The great call from the country has hitherto been of coarse goods. These are now made in our families, and the advantage is too sensible ever to be relinquished. It is one of those obvious improvements in our condition which needed only to be forced on our attention, never again to be abandoned.—To Dupont de Nemours. v, 456. (M., June 1809.)

5024. —— ——. We are going greatly into manufactures; but the mass of them are household manufactures of the coarse articles worn by the laborers and farmers of the family. These I verily believe we shall succeed in making to the whole extent of our necessities. But the attempts at fine goods will probably be abortive. They are undertaken by company establishments, and chiefly in the towns; will have but little success and short continuance in a country where the charms of agriculture attract every being who can engage in it. Our revenue will be less than it would be were we to continue to import instead of manufacturing our coarse goods. But the increase of population and production will keep pace with that of manufactures, and maintain the quantum of exports at the present level at least; and the imports need be equivalent to them, and consequently the revenue on them be undiminished.—To Dupont de Nemours. v, 583. Ford ed., ix, 317. (M., 1811.)

5025. —— ——. The economy and thriftiness resulting from our household manufactures are such that they will never again be laid aside.—To John Adams. vi, 36. Ford ed., ix, 333. (M., Jan. 1812.)

5026. —— ——. Our manufacturers are now very nearly on a footing with those of England. She has not a single improvement which we do not possess, and many of them better adapted by ourselves to our ordinary use. We have reduced the large and expensive machinery for most things to the compass of a private family, and every family of any size is now getting machines on a small scale for their household purposes. Quoting myself as an example, and I am much behind many others in this business, my household manufactures are just getting into operation on the scale of a carding machine costing $60 only, which may be worked by a girl of twelve years old, a spinning machine, which may be had for $10, carrying six spindles for wool, to be worked by a girl also, another which can be made for $25, carrying twelve spindles for cotton, and a loom, with a flying shuttle, weaving its twenty yards a day. I need 2,000 yards of linen, cotton, and woollen yearly, to clothe my family, which this machinery, costing $150 only, and worked by two women and two girls, will more than furnish.—To General Kosciusko. vi, 68. Ford ed., ix, 362. (M., June 1812.)

5027. —— ——. I have hitherto myself depended entirely on foreign manufactures; but I have now thirty-five spindles agoing, a hand carding machine, and looms with the flying shuttle, for the supply of my own farms, which will never be relinquished in my time. The continuance of the war will fix the habit generally, and out of the evils of impressment and of the Orders of Council, a great blessing for us will grow.—To John Melish. vi, 94. Ford ed., ix, 373. (M., Jan. 1813.)

5028. —— ——. Small spinning jennies of from half a dozen to twenty spindles, will soon make their way into the humblest cottages, as well as the richest houses [in the South]; and nothing is more certain, than that the coarse and middling clothing for our families, will forever hereafter continue to be made within ourselves.—To John Melish. vi, 94. Ford ed., ix, 373. (M., Jan. 1813.)

5029. —— ——. Household manufacture is taking deep root with us. I have a carding machine, two spinning machines, and looms with the flying shuttle in full operation for clothing my own family; and I verily believe that by the next winter this State will not need a yard of imported coarse or middling cloth. I think we have already a sheep for every inhabitant, which will suffice for clothing; and one-third more, which a single year will add, will furnish blanketing.—To James Ronaldson. vi, 92. Ford ed., ix, 371. (M., Jan. 1813.)

5030. —— ——. The specimens of Mrs. Mason's skill in manufactures excite the admiration of all. They prove she is really a more dangerous adversary to our British foes than all our generals. These attack the hostile armies only; she the source of their subsistence. What these do counts nothing, because they take one day and lose another: what she does counts double, because what she takes from the enemy is added to us. I hope, too, she will have more followers than our generals, but few rivals, I fear. These specimens exceed anything I saw during the Revolutionary war: although our ladies of that day turned their whole efforts to these objects, and with great praise and success.—To John T. Mason. Ford ed., ix, 473. (M., 1814.)

5031. —— ——. I presume, like the rest of us in the country, you are in the habit of household manufacture, and that you will not, like too many, abandon it on the return of peace, to enrich our late enemy, and to nourish foreign agents in our bosom, whose baneful influence and intrigues cost us so much embarrassment and dissension.—To George Fleming. vi, 506. (M., Dec. 1815.)

5032. —— ——. The interruption of our intercourse with England has rendered us one essential service in planting, radically and firmly, coarse manufactures among us. I make in my family two thousand yards of cloth a year, which I formerly bought from England, and it only employs a few women, children and invalids, who could do little on the farm. The State generally does the same, and allowing ten yards to a person, this amounts to ten millions of yards; and if we are about the medium degree of manufacturers in the whole Union, as I believe we are, the whole will amount to one hundred millions of yards a year, which will soon reimburse us the expenses of the war.—To Mr. Maury. vi, 471. (M., 1815.)

5033. MANUFACTURES, Independence, prosperity and.—The risk of hanging our prosperity on the fluctuating counsels and caprices of others renders it wise in us to turn seriously to manufactures, and if Europe will not let us carry our provisions to their manufactures, we must endeavor to bring their manufactures to our provisions.—To David Humphreys. Ford ed., v, 344. (Pa., 1791.)

5034. MANUFACTURES, Jefferson's views in 1782.—The political economists of Europe have established it as a principle, that every State should endeavor to manufacture for itself; and this principle, like many others, we transfer to America, without calculating the difference of circumstance which should often produce a difference of result. In Europe, the lands are either cultivated, or locked up against the cultivator. Manufacture must, therefore, be resorted to of necessity, not of choice, to support the surplus of their people. But we have an immensity of land courting the industry of the husbandman. Is it best then that all our citizens should be employed in its improvement, or that one half of them should be called off from that to exercise manufactures and handicrafts for the other? Those who labor in the earth are the chosen people of God, if ever He had a chosen people, whose breasts He has made His peculiar deposit for substantial and genuine virtue. It is the focus in which He keeps alive that sacred fire, which otherwise might escape from the face of the earth. Corruption of morals in the mass of cultivators is a phenomenon of which no age nor nation has furnished an example. It is the mark set on those, who, not looking up to heaven, to their own soil and industry, as does the husbandman, for their subsistence, depend for it on casualities and caprice of customers. Dependence begets subservience and venality, suffocates the germ of virtue, and prepares fit tools for the designs of ambition. This, the natural progress and consequence of the arts, has sometimes perhaps been retarded by accidental circumstances; but, generally speaking, the proportion which the aggregate of the other classes of citizens bears in any State to that of its husbandmen, is the proportion of its unsound to its healthy parts, and is a good barometer whereby to measure its degree of corruption. While we have land to labor, then, let us never wish to see our citizens occupied at a work bench, or twirling a distaff. Carpenters, masons, smiths, are wanting in husbandry; but, for the general operations of manufacture, let our workshops remain in Europe. It is better to carry provisions and materials to workmen there, than bring them to the provisions and materials, and with them their manners and principles. The loss by the transportation of commodities across the Atlantic will be made up in happiness and permanence of government. The mobs of great cities add just so much to the support of pure government, as sores do to the strength of the human body. It is the manners and spirit of a people which preserve a republic in vigor. A degeneracy in these is a canker which soon eats to the heart of its laws and constitution.—Notes on Virginia. viii, 405. Ford ed., iii, 268. (1782.)

5035. MANUFACTURES, Jefferson's views in 1816.—You tell me I am quoted by those who wish to continue our dependence on England for manufactures. There was a time when I might have been so quoted with more candor, but within the thirty years which have since elapsed, how are circumstances changed! We were then in peace. Our independent place among nations was acknowledged. A commerce which offered the raw material in exchange for the same material after receiving the last touch of industry, was worthy of welcome to all nations. It was expected that those especially to whom manufacturing industry was important, would cherish the friendship of such customers by every favor, by every inducement, and, particularly, cultivate their peace by every act of justice and friendship. Under this prospect the question seemed legitimate, whether, with such an immensity of unimproved land, courting the hand of husbandry, the industry of agriculture, or that of manufactures, would add most to the national wealth? And the doubt was entertained on this consideration chiefly, that to the labor of the husbandman a vast addition is made by the spontaneous energies of the earth on which it is employed; for one grain of wheat committed to the earth, she renders twenty, thirty, and even fifty-fold, whereas to the labor of the manufacturer nothing is added. Pounds of flax, in his hands, yield, on the contrary, but pennyweights of lace. This exchange, too, laborious as it might seem, what a field did it promise for the occupations of the ocean; what a nursery for that class of citizens who were to exercise and maintain our equal rights on that element? This was the state of things in 1785, when the "Notes on Virginia" were first printed; when, the ocean being open to all nations, and their common right in it acknowledged and exercised under regulations sanctioned by the assent and usage of all, it was thought that the doubt might claim some consideration. But who, in 1785, could foresee the rapid depravity which was to render the close of that century the disgrace of the history of man? Who could have imagined that the two most distinguished in the rank of nations, for science and civilization, would have suddenly descended from that honorable eminence, and setting at defiance all those moral laws established by the Author of nature between nation and nation, as between man and man, would cover earth and sea with robberies and piracies, merely because strong enough to do it with temporal impunity; and that under this disbandment of nations from social order, we should have been despoiled of a thousand ships, and have thousands of our citizens reduced to Algerine slavery? Yet all this has taken place. One of these nations [Great Britain] interdicted to our vessels all harbors of the globe without having first proceeded to some one of hers, there paid a tribute proportioned to the cargo, and obtained her license to proceed to the port of destination. The other [France] declared them to be lawful prize if they had touched at the port, or been visited by a ship of the enemy nation. Thus were we completely excluded from the ocean. Compare this state of things with that of 1785, and say whether an opinion founded in the circumstances of that day can be fairly applied to those of the present? We have experienced what we did not then believe, that there exists both profligacy and power enough to exclude us from the field of interchange with other nations; that to be independent for the comforts of life we must fabricate them ourselves. We must now place the manufacturer by the side of the agriculturist. The former question is suppressed, or rather assumes a new form. Shall we make our own comforts, or go without them, at the will of a foreign nation? He, therefore, who is now against domestic manufacture, must be for reducing us either to dependence on that foreign nation, or to be clothed in skins, and to live, like wild beasts, in dens and caverns. I am not one of these; experience has taught me that manufactures are now as necessary to our independence as to our comfort; and if those who quote me as of a different opinion, will keep pace with me in purchasing nothing foreign where an equivalent of domestic fabric can be obtained, with-

out regard to difference of price, it will not be our fault if we do not soon have a supply at home equal to our demand, and wrest that weapon of distress from the hand which has wielded it. If it shall be proposed to go beyond our own supply, the question of 1785 will then recur, Will our *surplus* labor be then most beneficially employed in the culture of the earth, or in the fabrications of art? We have time yet for consideration, before that question will press upon us; and the maxim to be applied will depend on the circumstances which shall then exist; for in so complicated a science as political economy, no one axiom can be laid down as wise and expedient for all times and circumstances, and for their contraries. Inattention to this is what has called for this explanation, which reflection would have rendered unnecessary with the candid, while nothing will do with those who use the former opinion only as a stalking horse to cover their disloyal propensities to keep us in eternal vassalage to a foreign and unfriendly people.*—To Benjamin Austin. vi, 521. Ford ed., x, 8. (M., Jan. 1816.)

5036. MANUFACTURES, Labor and.—
In general, it is impossible that manufactures should succeed in America from the high price of labor. This is occasioned by the great demand of labor for agriculture. A manufacturer, going from Europe, will turn to labor of other kinds if he finds more to be got by it, and he finds some employment so profitable that he can soon lay up money enough to buy fifty acres of land, to the culture of which he is irresistibly tempted by the independence in which that places him, and the desire of having a wife and family around him. If any manufactures can succeed there, it will be that of cotton.—To Thomas Digges. ii, 412. Ford ed., v, 27. (P., 1788.)

5037. MANUFACTURES, Machinery and.—The endeavors which Dr. Wallace informed you we were making in the line of manufactures are very humble indeed. We have not as yet got beyond the clothing of our laborers. We hope, indeed, soon to begin finer fabrics, and for higher uses. But these will probably be confined to cotton and wool. * * * I have lately seen the improvement of the loom by Janes, the most beautiful machine I have ever seen. * * * I am endeavoring to procure this improvement. These cares are certainly more pleasant than those of the state.—To John T. Mason. Ford ed., ix, 475. (M., 1814.)

5038. MANUFACTURES, National defence and.—The endeavors of five years, aided with some internal manufacturers, have

* Mr. Austin asked Jefferson's permission to publish the letter containing the foregoing extract. Jefferson wrote in reply: "I am, in general, extremely unwilling to be carried into the newspapers, no matter what the subject; the whole pack of the Essex [Junto] Kennel would open upon me. With respect, however, to so much of my letter * * * as relates to manufactures, I have less repugnance, because there is, perhaps, a degree of duty to avow a change of opinion called for by a change of circumstance, and especially on a point now becoming peculiarly interesting."—Editor.

not yet found a tolerable supply of arms. To make these within ourselves, then, as well as the other implements of war, is as necessary as to make our bread within ourselves.—To SPEAKER HOUSE OF DELEGATES. FORD ED., ii, 267. (Wg., 1779.)

5039. —— ——. I suppose that the establishing a manufacture of arms [in Virginia] to go hand in hand with the purchase of them from hence [France] is at present opposed by good reasons. This alone would make us independent for an article essential to our preservation, and workmen could probably be either got here, or drawn from England to be embarked hence.—To GOVERNOR HENRY. FORD ED., iv, 48. (P., 1785.)

5040. MANUFACTURES, Navigation vs.—Some jealousy of this spirit of manufacture seems excited among commercial men. It would have been as just when we first began to make our own plows and hoes. They have certainly lost the profit of bringing these from a foreign country. * * * I do not think it fair in the shipowners to say we ought not to make our own axes, nails, &c., here, that they may have the benefit of carrying the iron to Europe. and bringing back the axes, nails, &c. Our agriculture will still afford surplus produce enough to employ a due proportion of navigation.—To DAVID HUMPHREYS. v, 415. FORD ED., ix, 226. (W., 1809.)

5041. MANUFACTURES, Protection of.—To protect the manufactures adapted to our circumstances * * * [is one of] the landmarks by which we are to guide ourselves in all our proceedings.—SECOND ANNUAL MESSAGE. viii, 21. FORD ED., viii, 187. (1802.) See PROTECTION and TARIFF.

5042. MANUFACTURES, Rivalry in foreign markets.—We hope to remove the British fully and finally from our continent. And what they will feel more, for they value their colonies only for the bales of cloth they take from them, we have established manufactures, not only sufficient to supersede our demand from them, but to rivalize them in foreign markets.—To MADAME DE TESSE. vi, 273. FORD ED., ix, 440. (Dec. 1813.)

5043. MANUFACTURES, Rooted.—Our domestic manufactures * * * have taken such deep root * * * [that they] never again can be shaken.—To MARQUIS LAFAYETTE. vi, 427. FORD ED., ix, 511. (M., 1815.)

5044. —— ——. We owe to the past follies and wrongs of the British the incalculable advantage of being made independent of them for every material manufacture. These have taken such root in our private families especially, that nothing now can ever extirpate them.—To W. H. CRAWFORD. vi, 420. FORD ED., ix, 504. (M., Feb. 1815.)

5045. MANUFACTURES, State aid to. —The House of Delegates of Virginia seemed disposed to adventure £2,500 for the establishing a woollen manufactory in Virginia, but the Senate did not concur. By their returning to the subject, however, at a subsequent session, and wishing more specific propositions, it is probable they might be induced to concur, if they saw a certain provision that their money would not be paid for nothing. Some unsuccessful experiments heretofore may have suggested this caution. Suppose the propositions brought into some such shape as this: The undertaker is to contribute £1,000, the State £2,500, viz.: the undertaker having laid out his £1,000 'n the necessary implements to be brought from Europe, and these being landed in Virginia as a security that he will proceed. let the State pay for the first necessary purpose then to occur £1,000.

Let it pay him a stipend of £100 a year for the first three years.......................................   £300

Let it give him a bounty (suppose one-third) on every yard of woollen cloth equal to good plains, which he shall weave for five years, not exceeding £250 a year (20,000 yards) the four first years, and £200 the fifth............   1,200

£2,500

To every workman whom he shall import, let them give, after he shall have worked in the manufactory five years, warrants for — acres of land, and pay the expenses of survey, patents, &c. (This last article is to meet the proposition of the undertaker. I do not like it, because it tends to draw off the manufacturer from his trade. I should better like a premium to him on his continuance in it; as, for instance, that he should be free from State taxes as long as he should carry on his trade.)

The President's intervention seems necessary till the contracts shall be concluded. It is presumed he would not like to be embarrassed afterwards with the details of superintendence. Suppose, in his answer to the Governor of Virginia, he should say that the undertaker being in Europe, more specific propositions cannot be obtained from him in time to be laid before this assembly; that in order to secure to the State the benefits of the establishment, and yet guard them against an unproductive grant of money, he thinks some plan like the preceding one might be proposed to the undertaker. That as it is not known whether he would accept it exactly in that form, it might disappoint the views of the State were they to prescribe that or any other form rigorously, consequently that a discretionary power must be given to a certain extent. That he would willingly cooperate with their Executive in effecting the contract. and certainly would not conclude it on any terms worse for the State than those before explained, and that the contracts being once concluded. his distance and other occupations would oblige him to leave the execution open to the Executive of the State.—OFFICIAL OPINION. vii, 460. (1790.)

5046. MANUFACTURES, Tariff on foreign.—Where a nation imposes high duties on our productions, or prohibits them altogether, it may be proper for us to do the same by theirs; first burdening or excluding those productions which they bring here. in competition with our own of the same kind; selecting next, such manufactures as we take from them in greatest quantity, and which, at the same time, we could the soonest furnish to ourselves, or obtain from other countries; imposing on them duties lighter at first. but heavier and heavier, afterwards, as other channels of supply open. Such duties, having the effect of indirect encouragement to domestic manufactures of the same kind, may induce the manufacturer to come himself into these States, where cheaper subsistence, equal laws, and a vent of his wares, free of duty, may ensure him the highest profits from his skill and industry. And here, it would be in the power of the State governments to cooperate essentially, by opening the resources of encouragement which are under their control, extending them liberally to artists in those particular branches of manufacture for which their soil, climate, population and other circumstances have matured them, and fostering the precious efforts and progress of *household* manufacture, by some patronage suited to the nature of its objects, guided by the local informations they possess, and guarded against abuse by their presence and attentions. The oppressions on our agriculture, in foreign ports, would thus be made the occasion of relieving it from a dependence on the councils and conduct of others, and of promoting arts, manufactures and population at home.—Foreign Commerce Report. vii. 648. Ford ed., vi, 481. (Dec. 1793.) See Duties, Protection and Tariff.

5047. MANUFACTURES, Virginia.— In Virginia we do little in the fine way, but in coarse and middling goods a great deal. Every family in the country is a manufactory within itself, and is very generally able to make within itself all the stouter and middling stuffs for its own clothing and household use. We consider a sheep for every person in the family as sufficient to clothe it, in addition to the cotton, hemp and flax which we raise ourselves. For fine stuff we shall depend on your northern manufactories. Of these, that is to say, of company establishments we have none. We use little machinery. The spinning jenny, and loom with the flying shuttle, can be managed in a family; but nothing more complicated.—To John Adams. vi, 36. Ford ed., ix, 332. (M., Jan. 1812.)

5048. ——— ———. For fine goods there are numerous establishments at work in the large cities, and many more daily growing up; and of merinos we have some thousands, and these multiplying fast. We consider a sheep for every person as sufficient for their woollen clothing, and this State and all to the north have fully that, and those to the south and west will soon be up to it. In other articles. we are equally advanced, so that nothing is more certain than that, come peace when it will, we shall never again go to England for a shilling where we have gone for a dollar's worth. Instead of applying to her manufacturers there, they must starve or come here to be employed.—To General Kosciusko. vi, 69. Ford ed., ix, 363. (M., June 1812.)

— MAPLE SUGAR.—See Sugar.

5049. MARBURY vs. MADISON, Case of.—I observe that the case of *Marbury vs. Madison* has been cited [in the trial of Aaron Burr], and I think it material to stop at the threshold the citing that case as authority and to have it denied to be law. 1. Because the

judges in the outset, disclaimed all cognizance of the case, although they then went on to say what would have been their opinion, had they had cognizance of it. This, then, was confessedly an extra-judicial opinion, and, as such of no authority. 2. Because, had it been judicially pronounced, it would have been against law; for to a commission, a deed, a bond, *delivery* is essential to give validity. Until, therefore, the commission is delivered out of the hands of the Executive and his agents, it is not his deed. He may withhold or cancel it at pleasure, as he might his private deed in the same situation. The Constitution intended that the three great branches of the government should be coordinate, and independent of each other. As to acts, therefore, which are to be done by either, it has given no control to another branch. A judge, I presume, cannot sit on a bench without a commission, or a record of a commission; and the Constitution having given to the Judiciary branch no means of compelling the Executive either to *deliver* a commission, or to make a record of it, shows that it did not intend to give the Judiciary that control over the Executive, but that it should remain in the power of the latter to do it or not. Where different branches have to act in their respective lines, finally and without appeal, under any law, they may give to it different and opposite constructions. Thus, in the case of William Smith, the House of Representatives determined he was a citizen; and in the case of William Duane (precisely the same in every material circumstance), the judges determined he was no citizen. In the cases of Callender and some others, the judges determined the Sedition Act was valid under the Constitution, and exercised their regular powers of sentencing them to fine and imprisonment. But the Executive determined that the Sedition Act was a nullity under the Constitution, and exercised his regular power of prohibiting the execution of the sentence, or rather of executing the real law, which protected the acts of the defendants. From these different constructions of the same act by different branches, less mischief arises than from giving to any one of them a control over the others. The Executive and Senate act on the construction, that until delivery from the Executive department, a commission is in their possession, and within their rightful power; and in cases of commissions not revocable at will, where, after the Senate's approbation and the President's signing and sealing, new information of the unfitness of the person has come to hand before the *delivery* of the commission, new nominations have been made and approved, and new commissions have issued. On this construction I have hitherto acted; on this I shall ever act, and maintain it with the powers of the government, against any control which may be attempted by the judges, in subversion of the independence of the Executive and Senate within their peculiar department. I presume, therefore, that in a case where our decision is by the Constitution the supreme one, and that which can be carried into effect, it is the constitutionally authoritative one, and that that by the judges was *coram non judice,* and unauthoritative, because it cannot be carried into effect. I have long wished for a proper occasion to have the gratuitous opinion in *Marbury vs. Madison* brought before the public, and denounced as not law; and I think the present a fortunate one, because it occupies such a place in the public attention. I should be glad, therefore, if, in noticing that case, you could take occasion to express the determination of the Executive, that the doctrines of that case were given extra-judicially and against law, and that their reverse will be the rule of action with the Executive.—To GEORGE HAY. v, 84. FORD ED., ix, 53. (W., June 1807.)

5050. MARIE ANTOINETTE, Character.—This angel, as gaudily painted in the rhapsodies of the Rhetor Burke, with some smartness of fancy, but no good sense, was proud, disdainful of restraint, indignant at all obstacles to her will, eager in the pursuit of pleasure, and firm enough to hold to her desires, or perish in their wreck.—AUTOBIOGRAPHY. i, 101. FORD ED., i, 140. (1821.)

5051. ———— ————. She is capricious like her brother, and governed by him; devoted to pleasure and expense; and not remarkable for any other vices or virtues.—To JAMES MADISON. ii, 154. FORD ED., iv, 393. (P., 1787.)

5052. ———— ————. It may be asked what is the Queen disposed to do in the present situation of things? Whatever rage, pride and fear can dictate in a breast which never knew the presence of one moral restraint.—To JOHN JAY. iii, 118. (P., Sep. 1789.)

5053. MARIE ANTOINETTE, Extravagance.—Nor should we wonder at * * * [the] pressure [for a fixed constitution in 1788-9] when we consider the monstrous abuses of power under which * * * [the French] people were ground to powder; when we pass in review * * * the enormous expenses of the Queen, the princes and the Court.—AUTOBIOGRAPHY. i, 86. FORD ED., i, 118. (1821.)

5054. MARIE ANTOINETTE, Gambling.—Her inordinate gambling and dissipations, with those of the Count d'Artois and others of her clique, had been a sensible item in the exhaustion of the treasury.—AUTOBIOGRAPHY. i, 101. FORD ED., i, 140. (1821.)

5055. MARIE ANTOINETTE, Reform. —The exhaustion of the treasury called into action the reforming hand of the nation; and her opposition to it, her inflexible perverseness and dauntless spirit, led herself to the guillotine, drew the King on with her, and plunged the world into crimes and calamities which will forever stain the pages of modern history.—AUTOBIOGRAPHY. i, 101. FORD ED., i, 140. (1821.)

5056. MARIE ANTOINETTE, The Revolution and.—I have ever believed, that had there been no Queen, there would have been no Revolution. No force would have been provoked, nor exercised. The King would have gone hand in hand with the wisdom of his sounder counsellors, who, guided by the increased lights of the age, wished only, with the

same pace, to advance the principles of their social constitution.—AUTOBIOGRAPHY. i, 101. FORD ED., i, 140. (1821.)

5057. MARINE HOSPITALS, Establishment of.—With respect to marine hospitals, I presume you know that such establishments have been made by the General Government in the several States, that a portion of seamen's wages is drawn for their support, and the Government furnishes what is deficient. Mr. Gallatin is attentive to them, and they will grow with our growth.—To JAMES RONALDSON. vi, 92. FORD ED., ix, 371. (M., Jan. 1813.)

—— **MARINE LEAGUE.**—See 1335.

5058. MARITIME LAW, Violation of. —A statement of the conduct of Great Britain towards this country, so far as respects the violations of the Maritime Law of nations [must be laid before Congress]. Here it would be necessary to state each distinct principle violated, and to quote the cases of violation, and to conclude with a view of her vice-admiralty courts, their venality and rascality, in order to show that however for conveniences (and not of right) the court of the captor is admitted to exercise the jurisdiction, yet that in so palpable an abuse of that trust, some remedy must be applied.—To CAESAR A. RODNEY. v, 200. FORD ED., ix, 144. (W., Oct. 1807.)

5059. MARKETS, Access to.—It is not to the moderation and justice of others we are to trust for fair and equal access to market with our productions, or for our due share in the transportation of them; but to our own means of independence, and the firm will to use them.—FOREIGN COMMERCE REPORT. vii, 650. FORD ED., vi, 483. (Dec. 1793.)

5060. MARKETS, British.—It is but too true, that Great Britain furnishes markets for three-fourths of the exports of the eight northernmost States,—a truth not proper to be spoken of, but which should influence our proceedings with them.—To JAMES MONROE. i, 406. FORD ED., iv, 85. (P., 1785.)

5061. MARKETS, Exclusion from.—Let them [the British] not think to exclude us from going to other markets to dispose of those commodities which they cannot use, nor to supply those wants which they cannot supply.—RIGHTS OF BRITISH AMERICA. i, 142. FORD ED., i, 446. (1774.)

5062. ———— ————. Besides the duties * * * [the acts of Parliament] impose on our articles of export and import they prohibit our going to any markets northward of Cape Finisterre, in the Kingdom of Spain, for the sale of commodities which great Britain will not take from us, and for the purchase of others, with which she cannot supply us; and that, for no other than the arbitrary purpose of purchasing for themselves, by a sacrifice of our rights and interests, certain privileges in their commerce with an allied State, who, in confidence, that their exclusive trade with America will be continued, while the principles and power of the British Parliament be the same, have indulged themselves in every exorbitance which their avarice could dictate or our necessity extort; have raised their commodities called for in America, to the double and treble of what they sold for, before such exclusive privileges were given them, and of what better commodities of the same kind would cost us elsewhere; and, at the same time, give us much less for what we carry thither, than might be had at more convenient ports.—RIGHTS OF BRITISH AMERICA. i, 128. FORD ED., i, 433. (1774.)

5063. —— ——. These acts [of Parliament] prohibit us from carrying, in quest of other purchasers, the surplus of our tobaccos, remaining after the consumption of Great Britain is supplied; so that we must leave them with the British merchant for whatever he will please to allow us, to be by him re-shipped to foreign markets, where he will reap the benefits of making sale of them for full value.—RIGHTS OF BRITISH AMERICA. i, 129. FORD ED., i, 433. (1774.)

5064. MARKETS, Extension of.—The mass of our countrymen being interested in agriculture, I hope I do not err in supposing that in a time of profound peace, as the present, to enable them to adopt their productions to the market, to point out markets for them, and endeavor to obtain favorable terms of reception, is within the line of my duty.—To JOHN JAY. ii, 139. FORD ED., iv, 378. (1787.)

5065. MARKETS, Fish oil.—The duty on whale oil [in the British markets] amounts to a prohibition. This duty was originally laid on all foreign fish oil with a view to favor the British and American fisheries. When we became independent, and of course foreign to Great Britain, we became subject to the foreign duty. No duty, therefore, which France may think proper to lay on this article, can drive it to the English market. It could only oblige the inhabitants of Nantucket to abandon their fishery. But the poverty of their soil, offering them no other resource, they must quit their country, and either establish themselves in Nova Scotia, where, as British fishermen, they may participate of the British premium in addition to the ordinary price of their whale oil, or they must accept the conditions which this government offers for the establishment they have proposed at Dunkirk. Your Excellency will judge what conditions may counterbalance in their minds the circumstances of the vicinity of Nova Scotia, sameness of language, laws, religion, customs and kindred. Remaining in their native country, to which they are most singularly attached, excluded from commerce with England, taught to look to France as the only country from which they can derive sustenance, they will in case of war become useful rovers against its enemies. Their position, their poverty, their courage, their address, and their hatred will render them formidable scourges on the British commerce.—To COUNT DE MONTMORIN. ii, 312. (P., 1787.)

5066. —— ——. You have heard of the *Arret* of September 28th [1788] excluding foreign whale oils from the ports of this country [France]. I have obtained the promise of an explanatory *Arret* to declare that that of September 28th was not meant to extend to us. Orders are accordingly given in the ports to receive ours, and the *Arret* will soon be published. This places us on a better footing than ever, as it gives us a monopoly of this market in conjunction with the French fishermen.—To THOMAS PAINE. ii, 549. (P., 1788.)

5067. —— ——. You recollect well the *Arret* of December 29th, 1787, in favor of our commerce, and which, among other things, gave free admission to our whale oil, under a duty of about two louis a ton. In consequence of the English treaty, their oils flowed in and overstocked the market. The light duty they were liable to under the treaty, still lessened by false estimates and aided by the high premiums of the British government, enabled them to undersell the French and American oils. This produced an outcry of the Dunkirk fishery. It was proposed to exclude all European oils, which would not infringe the British treaty. I could not but encourage this idea, because it would give to the French and American fisheries a monopoly of the French market. The *Arret* was so drawn up; but, in the very moment of passing it, they struck out the word *European*, so that our oils became involved. * * * As soon as it was known to me I wrote to Monsieur de Montmorin, and had conferences with him and the other ministers. * * * An immediate order was given for the present admission of our oils. * * * It was observed that if our States would prohibit all foreign oils from being imported into them, it would be a great safeguard, and an encouragement to them to continue the admission.—To JOHN ADAMS. ii, 538. (P., 1788.)

5068. —— ——. The *Arret* of September 28th [1788], to comprehend us with the English, in the exclusion of whale oil from their ports * * * would be a sentence of banishment to the inhabitants of Nantucket, and there is no doubt they would have removed to Nova Scotia or England, in preference to any other part of the world.—To WILLIAM CARMICHAEL. ii, 551. (P., 1788.)

5069. —— ——. This branch of commerce [whale oils] * * * will be on a better footing than ever as enjoying jointly with the French oil, a monopoly of the French markets.—To JOHN JAY. ii, 513. (P., 1788.)

5070. —— ——. The English began [in 1787] to deluge the markets of France with their whale oils; and they were enabled, by the great premiums given by their government, to undersell the French fisherman, aided by feebler premiums, and the American, aided by his poverty alone. Nor is it certain that these speculations were not made at the risk of the British government, to suppress the French and American fishermen in their only market. Some remedy seemed necessary. Perhaps it would not have been a bad one to subject, by a general law, the merchandise of every nation, and of every nature, to pay additional duties in the ports of France, exactly equal to the premiums and drawbacks given on the same merchandise by their own government. This might not only counteract the effect of premiums in the instance of whale oils, but attack the whole British system of bounties and drawbacks, five-eighths of our whale oil, and two-thirds of our salted fish, they take from us one-fourth of our tobacco, three-fourths of our live stock, * * * a considerable and growing portion of our rice, great supplies, occasionally, of other grain; in 1789, which, indeed, was extraordinary, four millions of bushels of wheat, and upwards of a million of bushels of rye and barley * * * and nearly the whole carried in our own vessels. They are a free market now, and will, in time, be a valuable one for ships and ship timber, potash and peltry.—REPORT ON THE FISHERIES. vii, 551. (1791.)

5071. —— ——. France is the only country which can take our surplus, and they take principally of the common oil; as the habit is but commencing with them of a just value to spermaceti whale. Some of this, however, finds its vent there. There was, indeed, a particular interest perpetually soliciting the exclusion of our oils from their markets. The late government there saw well that what we should lose thereby would be gained by others, not by themselves. And we are to hope that the present government, as wise and friendly, will also view us, not as rivals, but as cooperators against a common rival (England). Friendly arrangements with them, and accommodation to mutual interest, rendered easier by friendly dispositions existing on both sides, may long secure to us this important resource for our seamen. Nor is it the interest of the fisherman alone which calls for the cultivation of friendly arrangements with that nation; besides by the aid of which they make London the centre of commerce for the earth. A less general remedy, but an effectual one, was to prohibit the oils of all *European* nations; the treaty with England requiring only that she should be treated as well as the most favored *European* nation. But the remedy adopted was to prohibit all oils, without exception.—To COUNT DE MONTMORIN. ii, 520. (P., 1788.)

5072. —— ——. England is the market for the greatest part of our spermaceti oil. They impose on all our oils a duty of eighteen pounds five shillings sterling the ton. which, as to the common kind, is a prohibition, * * * and as to the spermaceti, gives a preference of theirs over ours to that amount, so as to leave, in the end, but a scanty benefit to the fishermen; and, not long since, by a change of construction, without any change of law, it was made to exclude our oils from their ports, when carried in our vessels. On some change of circumstance, it was construed back again to the reception of our oils,

on paying always, however. the same duty of eighteen pounds five shillings. This serves to show that the tenure by which we hold the admission of this commodity in their markets, is as precarious as it is hard. Nor can it be announced that there is any disposition on their part to arrange this or any other commercial matter to mutual convenience.—REPORT ON THE FISHERIES. vii, 552. (1791.)

5073. MARKETS, Fisheries.—Agriculture has too many markets to be allowed to take away those of the fisheries.—REPORT ON THE FISHERIES. vii, 544. (1791.)

5074. MARKETS, Foreign.—We have hitherto respected the indecision of Spain [with respect to the navigation of the Mississippi], * * * because our western citizens have had vent at home for their productions. A surplus of production begins now to demand foreign markets. Whenever they shall say, " We cannot, we will not, be longer shut up ", the United States will be reduced to the following dilemma: 1. To force them to acquiescence. 2. To separate from them rather than take part in a war against Spain. 3. Or to preserve them in our Union, by joining them in the war. * * * The third is the alternative we must adopt.—INSTRUCTIONS TO WILLIAM CARMICHAEL. ix, 412. FORD ED., v, 226. (1790.)

5075. —— ——. Our commerce is certainly of a character to entitle it to favor in most countries. The commodities we offer are either necessaries of life, or materials for manufacture, or convenient subjects of revenue; and we take in exchange, either manufactures, when they have received the last finish of art and industry, or mere luxuries. Such customers may reasonably expect welcome and friendly treatment at every market. Customers, too, whose demands, increasing with their wealth and population, must very shortly give full employment to the whole industry of any nation whatever, in any line of supply they may get into the habit of calling for from it.—FOREIGN COMMERCE REPORT. vii, 646. FORD ED., vi, 479. (Dec. 1793.)

5076. MARKETS, Fostering.—The way to encourage purchasers is to multiply their means of payment.—To COUNT DE MONTMORIN. ii, 529. (P., 1788.)

5077. MARKETS, French.—No two countries are better calculated for the exchanges of commerce. France wants rice, tobacco, potash, furs, and ship-timber. We want wines, brandies, oils, and manufactures.—To COUNT DE VERGENNES. i, 390. (P., 1785.)

5078. —— ——. If American produce can be brought into the ports of France, the articles of exchange for it will be taken in those ports; and the only means of drawing it hither is to let the merchant see that he can dispose of it on better terms here than anywhere else. If the market price of this country does not in itself offer this superiority, it may be worthy of consideration, whether it should be obtained by such abatements of duties, and even by such other encouragements as the importance of the article may justify. Should some loss attend this in the beginning, it can be discontinued when the trade shall be well established in this channel.—To MARQUIS LAFAYETTE. i, 597. FORD ED., iv, 256. (P., 1786.)

5079. —— ——. I have laid my shoulder to the opening the markets of France to our produce, and rendering its transportation a nursery for our seamen.—To GENERAL WASHINGTON. ii, 536. FORD ED., v, 58. (P., 1788.)

5080. —— ——. I very much fear that France will experience a famine this summer. The effects of this admit of no calculation. Grain is the thing for us now to cultivate. The demand will be immense, and the price high. I think cases were shown us that to sell it before the spring is an immense sacrifice. I fear we shall experience a want of vessels to carry our produce to Europe. In this case the tobacco will be left, because bread is more essential to them.—To T. M. RANDOLPH. FORD ED., vi, 241. (Pa., May 1793.)

5081. **MARKETS, French Asiatic.**—Article 13 of the *Arret* gives us the privileges and advantages of native subjects in all the French possessions in Asia, and in the *scales leading thereto.* This expression means at present the Isles of France and Bourbon, and will include the Cape of Good Hope, should any future event put it into the hands of France. It was with a view to this that I proposed the expression, because we were then in hourly expectation of a war, and it was suspected that France would take possession of that place. It will, in no case, be considered as including anything westward of the Cape of Good Hope. I must observe further, on this article, that it will only become valuable on the suppression of their East India Company; because as long as their monopoly continues, even native subjects cannot enter their Asiatic ports for the purposes of commerce. It is considered, however, as certain that this company will be immediately suppressed.—To JOHN JAY. ii, 343. (P., 1787.)

5082. **MARKETS, Fur.**—The fur trade is an object of desire in this country [France]. London is at present their market for furs. They pay for them there in ready money. Could they draw their furs into their own ports from the United States they would pay us for them in productions. Nor should we lose by the change of market, since, though the French pay the London merchants in cash, those merchants pay us with manufactures. A very wealthy and well connected company is proposing here to associate themselves with an American company, each to possess half the interest, and to carry on the fur trade between the two countries. The company here expect to make the principal part of the advances; they also are soliciting considerable indulgences from this government from which the part of the company

on our side of the water will reap half the advantage. As no exclusive idea enters into this scheme, it appears to me worthy of encouragement. It is hoped the government here will interest themselves for its success. If they do, one of two things may happen : either the English will be afraid to stop the vessels of a company consisting partly of French subjects, and patronized by the Court; in which case the commerce will be laid open generally; or if they stop the vessels, the French company, which is strongly connected with men in power, will complain in form to their government, who may thus be interested as principals in the rectification of this abuse. As yet, however, the proposition has not taken such a form as to assure us that it will be prosecuted to this length.— To JOHN JAY. FORD ED., iv, 231. (P., 1786.)

5083. **MARKETS, Home.**—There can be no question, in a mind truly American, whether it is best to send our citizens and property into certain captivity, and then wage war for their recovery, or to keep them at home, and to turn seriously to that policy which plants the manufacturer and the husbandman side by side, and establishes at the door of every one that exchange of mutual labors and comforts, which we have hitherto sought in distant regions, and under perpetual risk of broils with them.—R. TO A. N. Y. TAMMANY SOCIETY. viii, 127. (Feb. 1808.)

5084. —— ——. The advantages * * * of planting the consumer in our own soil by the side of the grower of produce. are so palpable, that no temporary suspension of injuries on England's part, or agreements founded on that, will now prevent our continuing in what we have begun [manufacturing].—To DUPONT DE NEMOURS. v, 456. (M., June 1809.)

5085. —— ——. The bringing our countrymen to a sound comparative estimate of the vast value of internal commerce, and the disproportionate importance of what is foreign. is the most salutary effort which can be made for the prosperity of these States. which are entirely misled from their true interests by the infection of English prejudices, and illicit attachments to English interests and connections.—To DR. THOMAS COOPER. vi, 294. (M., 1814.)

5086. **MARKETS, Land.**—The long succession of years of stunted crops, of reduced prices, the general prostration of the farming business, under levies for the support of manufacturers, &c., with the calamitous fluctuations of value in our proper medium. have kept agriculture in a state of abject depression, which has peopled the Western States by silently breaking up those on the Atlantic, and glutted the land market, while it drew off its bidders. In such a state of things, property has lost its character of being a resource for debts. Highland in Bedford, which, in the days of our plethory. sold readily for from fifty to one hundred dollars the acre (and such sales were many then), would not now sell for more than from ten to twenty dollars, or one-quarter or one-fifth of its former price.—To JAMES MADISON. vii, 434. FORD ED., x, 377. (M., February 1826.)

5087. MARKETS, Monopolized.—It is contrary to the spirit of trade, and to the dispositions of merchants, to carry a commodity to any market where but one person is allowed to buy it, and where, of course, that person fixes its price, which the seller must receive, or reexport his commodity, at the loss of his voyage thither. Experience accordingly shows, that they carry it to other markets, and that they take in exchange the merchandise of the place where they deliver it.—To COUNT DE VERGENNES. i, 386. (P., 1785.)

5088. MARKETS, Necessity and.—We must accept bread from our enemies if our friends cannot furnish it.—To COUNT DE MONTMORIN. ii, 523. (P., 1788.)

5089. MARKETS, Neutrality and.—If the new government wears the front which I hope it will. I see no impossibility in the availing ourselves of the wars of others to open up the other parts [West India Islands] of America to our commerce as the price of our neutrality.—To GENERAL WASHINGTON. ii, 533. FORD ED., v, 57. (P., 1788.)

5090. MARKETS, Reciprocity and.—It were to be wished that some positively favorable stipulations respecting our grain, flour and fish, could be obtained, even on our giving reciprocal advantages to some other commodities of Spain, say her wines and brandies. But if we quit the ground of the *most favored* nation, as to certain articles for our convenience, Spain may insist on doing the same for other articles for her convenience. * * * If we grant favor to the wines and brandies of Spain, then Portugal and France will demand the same; and in order to create an equivalent, Portugal may lay a duty on our fish and grain, and France, a prohibition on our whale oils, the removal of which will be proposed as an equivalent. This much, however, as to grain and flour, may be attempted. There has, not long since, been a considerable duty laid on them in Spain. This was while a treaty on the subject of commerce was pending between us and Spain, as that Court considers the matter. It is not generally thought right to change the state of things pending a treaty concerning them. On this consideration, and on the motive of cultivating our friendship, perhaps the Commissioners may induce them to restore this commodity to the footing on which it was on opening the conferences with Mr. Gardoqui, on the 26th day of July, 1785. If Spain says, " do the same by your tonnage on our vessels ", the answer may be, that our tonnage affects Spain very little, and other nations very much; whereas the duty on flour in Spain affects us very much, and other na-

tions very little. Consequently, there would be no equality in reciprocal relinquishment, as there had been none in the reciprocal innovation; and Spain, by insisting on this, would, in fact, only be aiding the interests of her rival nations, to whom we should be forced to extend the same indulgence. At the time of opening the conferences, too, we had as yet not erected any system; our government itself being not yet erected. Innovation then was unavoidable on our part. if it be innovation to establish a system. We did it on fair and general ground, on ground favorable to Spain. But they had a system and, therefore, innovation was avoidable on their part.—MISSISSIPPI RIVER INSTRUCTIONS. vii, 590. FORD ED., v, 479. (March 1792.)

5091. MARKETS, Salted provisions.—I wish that you could obtain the free introduction of our salted provisions into France. Nothing would be so generally pleasing from the Chesapeake to New Hampshire.—To WILLIAM SHORT. FORD ED., v, 168. (N.Y., 1790.)

5092. ———— ————. It gives great satisfaction that the *Arret du Conseil* of December, 1787, stands a chance of being saved. It is, in truth, the sheet-anchor of our connection with France, which will be much loosened when that is lost. This *Arret* saved, a free importation of salted meats into France, and of provisions of all kinds into her colonies, will bind our interests to that country more than to all the world besides.—To WILLIAM SHORT. iii, 225. (Pa., 1791.)

5093. MARKETS, Speculation and.—I think the best rule is, never to sell on a rising market. Wait till it begins to fall. Then, indeed, one will lose a penny or two, but with a rising market you never know what you are to lose.—To FRANCIS EPPES. FORD ED., vi, 163. (Pa., 1793.)

5094. MARKETS, Steady.—Sudden vicissitudes of opening and shutting ports do little injury to merchants settled on the opposite [British] coast, watching for the opening, like the return of a tide, and ready to enter with it. But they ruin the adventurer whose distance requires six months' notice.—To COUNT DE MONTMORIN. ii, 525. (P., 1788.)

5095. ———— ————. A regular course of trade is not quitted in an instant, nor constant customers deserted for accidental ones.—To MARQUIS DE LAFAYETTE. iii, 68. (P., 1789.)

5096. MARKETS, Sugar.—Evidence grows upon us that the United States may not only supply themselves with sugar for their own consumption, but be great exporters.—To T. M. RANDOLPH. FORD ED., v, 325. (Pa., 1791.)

5097. MARKETS, Tobacco.—While the navigating and provision States, who are the majority, can keep open all the markets, or at least sufficient ones for their objects, the cries of the tobacco makers, who are the minority, and not at all in favor, will hardly be listened to. It is truly the fable of the monkey pulling the nuts out of the fire with the cat's paw; and it shows that George Mason s proposition in the [Federal] Convention was wise, that on laws regulating commerce, two-thirds of the votes should be required to pass them.—To JAMES MADISON. iv, 323. FORD ED., vii, 432. (Pa., March 1800.) See TOBACCO.

5098. MARKETS, Wheat and flour.— We can sell them [the Portuguese] the flour ready manufactured for much less than the wheat of which it is made. In carrying to them wheat, we carry also the bran, which does not pay its own freight. In attempting to save and transport wheat to them, much is lost by the weavil, and much spoiled by heat in the hold of the vessel. This loss must be laid on the wheat which gets safe to market, where it is paid for by the consumer. Now, this is much more than the cost of manufacturing it with us, which would prevent that loss. * * * Let them buy of us as much wheat as will make a hundred weight of flour. They will find that they have paid more for the wheat than we should have asked for the flour, besides having lost the labor of their mills in grinding it. The obliging us, therefore, to carry it to them in the form of wheat, is a useless loss to both parties.—To JOHN ADAMS. i, 492. (P., 1785.)

5099. ——— ———. It seems that so far from giving new liberties to our corn trade, Portugal contemplates the prohibition of it, by giving that trade exclusively to Naples. What would she say should we give her wine trade exclusive to France and Spain? * * * Can a wise statesman seriously think of risking such a prospect as this?—To DAVID HUMPHREYS. iii, 488. (Pa., 1792.)

5100. ——— ———. I must forever repeat that, instead of excluding our wheat, Portugal will open her ports to our flour.—To DAVID HUMPHREYS. FORD ED., vi, 205. (Pa., 1793.)

5101. MARQUE, Letters of.—The Administrator shall not possess the prerogative * * * of issuing letters of marque, or reprisal.—PROPOSED VA. CONSTITUTION. FORD ED., ii, 19. (June 1776.)

5102. ——— ———. Our delegates [to Congress] inform us that we might now obtain letters of marque for want of which our people [in Virginia] have long and exceedingly suffered. I have taken the liberty of desiring them to apply for fifty.—To THE PRESIDENT OF CONGRESS. FORD ED., ii, 241. (1799.)

5103. ——— ———. I have to-day consulted the other gentlemen [of the Cabinet] on the question whether letters of marque were to be considered as written within our interdict. We are unanimously of opinion they are not. We consider them as essentially *merchant vessels;* that commerce is their main object, and arms merely incidental and defensive.—To ALBERT GALLATIN. v, 123. FORD ED., ix, 104. (W., July 1807.)

5104. MARRIAGE, Congratulations on. —It is customary in America to " wish joy " to a new married couple, and this is generally done by those present in the moment after the ceremony. A friend of mine, however, always delayed the wish of joy till one year after the ceremony, because he observed they had *by that time* need *of it.* I am entitled fully then to express the wish to you as you must now have been married at least three years. I have no doubt, however, that you have found real joy in the possession of a good wife, and the endearments of a child. —To PHILIP MAZZEI. FORD ED., viii, 15. (W., 1801.)

5105. MARRIAGE, Happiness in.—I * * * give you my sincere congratulations on your marriage. Your own dispositions, and the inherent comforts of that state, will insure you a great addition of happiness.— To JAMES MONROE. i, 590. FORD ED., iv, 250. (P., 1786.)

5106. ——— ———. The happiness of your life now depends on the continuing to please a single person. To this all other objects must be secondary, even your love for me, were it possible that could ever be an obstacle. But this it never can be. Neither of you can ever have a more faithful friend than myself, nor one on whom you can count for more sacrifices. My own is become a secondary object to the happiness of you both. Cherish, then, for me, my dear child, the affection of your husband, and continue to love me as you have done, and to render my life a blessing by the prospect it may hold up to me of seeing you happy.—To MARTHA JEFFERSON RANDOLPH. D. L. J., 180. (N. Y., 1790.)

5107. ——— ———. I have one daughter married to a man of science, sense, virtue. and competence; in whom indeed I have nothing more to wish. * * * If the other shall be as fortunate, * * * I shall imagine myself as blessed as the most blessed of the patriarchs.—To MRS. CHURCH. FORD ED., vi, 455. (G., 1793.)

5108. MARRIAGE, Harmony in.—Harmony in the married state is the very first object to be aimed at. Nothing can preserve affections uninterrupted but a firm resolution never to differ in will, and a determination in each to consider the love of the other as of more value than any object whatever on which a wish had been fixed. How light in fact is the sacrifice of any other wish when weighed against the affections of one with whom we are to pass our whole life! And though opposition in a single instance will hardly of itself produce alienation, yet every one has their pouch into which all these little oppositions are put; while that is filling the alienation is insensibly going on, and when filled it is complete.—To MARY JEFFERSON EPPES. D. L. J., 246. (Pa., 1798.)

5109. MARRIAGE, Motherhood and.— It [motherhood] is undoubtedly the key-

stone of the arch of matrimonial happiness.—
To MARTHA JEFFERSON RANDOLPH. D. L. J.,
192. (Pa., 1791.)

5110. MARRIAGE, Youthful.—I sincerely sympathize with you on the step which your brother has taken without consulting you, and wonder indeed how it could be done, with any attention in the agents, to the laws of the land. I fear he will hardly persevere in the second plan of life adopted for him, as matrimony illy agrees with study, especially in the first stages of both. However, you will readily perceive that, the thing being done, there is now but one question, that is what is to be done to make the best of it, in respect both to his and your happiness? A step of this kind indicates no vice, nor other foible than of following too hastily the movements of a warm heart. It admits, therefore, of the continuance of cordial affection, and calls perhaps more indispensably for your care and protection. To conciliate the affection of all parties, and to banish all suspicion of discontent, will conduce most to your own happiness also.—To JAMES MONROE. FORD ED., v, 317. (Pa., 1791.)

5111. MARRIAGE WITH ROYALTY.—Our young Republic * * * should prevent its citizens from becoming so established in wealth and power, as to be thought worthy of alliance by marriage with the nieces, sisters, &c., of kings.—To COLONEL HUMPHREYS. ii, 253. (P., 1787.)

5112. MARSHALL (John), Crafty.—A crafty chief judge, who sophisticates the law to his mind, by the turn of his own reasoning.—To THOMAS RITCHIE. vii, 192. FORD ED., x, 171. (M., 1820.)

5113. MARSHALL (John), Hamilton and.—I learn that [Alexander] Hamilton has expressed the strongest desire that Marshall shall come into Congress from Richmond, declaring that there is no man in Virginia whom he wishes so much to see there; and I am told that Marshall has expressed half a mind to come. Hence I conclude that Hamilton has plied him well with flattery and solicitation, and I think nothing better could be done than to make him a judge.—To JAMES MADISON. FORD ED., vi, 95. (Pa., 1792.)

5114. MARSHALL (John), Marbury vs. Madison Case.—His twistifications in the case of Marbury, in that of Burr, and the Yazoo case show how dexterously he can reconcile law to his personal biases.—To PRESIDENT MADISON. FORD ED., ix, 276. (M., 1810.)

5115. MARSHALL (John), Mischief-maker.—Though Marshall will be able to embarrass the republican party in the Assembly a good deal, yet upon the whole, his having gone into it will be of service. He has been hitherto able to do more mischief acting under the mask of republicanism than he will be able to do throwing it plainly off. His lax lounging manners have made him popular with the bulk of the people of Richmond, and a profound hypocrisy with many thinking men of our country. But having come forth in the full plenitude of his English principles, the latter will see that it is high time to make him known. —To JAMES MADISON. FORD ED., vii, 37. (Nov. 1795.)

5116. MARSHALL (John), Moot cases and.—The practice of Judge Marshall, of travelling out of his case to prescribe what the law would be in a moot case not before the court, is very irregular and very censurable.— To WILLIAM JOHNSON. vii, 295. FORD ED., x, 230. (M., 1823.)

5117. MARSHALL (John), Sophistry of.—The rancorous hatred which Marshall bears to the government of his country, and * * * the cunning and sophistry within which he is able to enshroud himself.—To PRESIDENT MADISON. FORD ED., ix, 275. (M., 1810.) See HISTORY, JUDICIARY, MAZZEI, and SUPREME COURT.

5118. MARTIAL LAW, Recourse to.— There are extreme cases where the laws become inadequate even to their own preservation, and where the universal resource is a dictator, or martial law.—To DR. JAMES BROWN. v, 379. FORD ED., ix, 211. (W., 1808.)

5119. MARTIN (Luther), Burr and.— Shall we move to commit Luther Martin as *particeps criminis* with Burr? Graybell will fix upon him misprision of treason at least. And at any rate, his evidence will put down this unprincipled and impudent federal bull-dog, and add another proof that the most clamorous defenders of Burr are all his accomplices. It will explain why Luther Martin flew so hastily to the " aid of his honorable friend ", abandoning his clients and their property during a session of a principal court in Maryland, now filled, as I am told, with the clamors and ruin of his clients.—To GEORGE HAY. v, 99. FORD ED., ix. 58. (W., June 1807.) See LOGAN.

5120. MASON (George), Ability of.— George Mason [was] a man of the first order of wisdom among those who acted on the theatre of the Revolution, of expansive mind, profound judgment, cogent in argument, learned in the lore of our former constitution, and earnest for the republican change on democratic principles.* His elocution was neither flowing or smooth ; but his language was strong, his manner most impressive, and strengthened by a dash of biting cynicism when provocation made it seasonable.—AUTOBIOGRAPHY. i, 40. FORD ED., i, 56. (1821.)

5121. MASON (George), Virginia Constitution and.—What are George Mason's sentiments as to the amendment of our Constitution? What amendment would he approve? Is he determined to sleep on, or will he rouse and be active?—To JAMES MADISON. FORD ED., iii, 347. (A., Dec. 1783.)

5122. ——— ———. That George Mason was the author of the Bill of Rights and of the Constitution founded on it, the evidence of the day established fully in my mind.—To HENRY LEE. vii, 407. FORD ED., x, 342. (M., 1825.)

5123. ——— ———. The fact is unquestionable, that the Bill of Rights and the Constitution of Virginia were drawn originally by George Mason, one of our really great men, and of the first order of greatness.—To A. B. WOODWARD. vii, 405. FORD ED., x, 341. (M., 1825.)

5124. MASON (J. M.), Red-hot Federalist.—I do not know Dr. [John M.] Mason

* George Mason was one of the signers of the Declaration. " Mason," said James Madison, " possessed the greatest talents for debate of any man I have ever seen or heard speak."—EDITOR.

personally, but by character well. He is the most red-hot federalist, famous, or rather infamous for the lying and slandering which he vomited from the pulpit in the political harangues with which he polluted the place. I was honored with much of it. He is a man who can prove everything if you will take his word for proof. Such evidence of Hamilton's being a republican he may bring; but Mr. Adams, Edmund Randolph, and myself, could repeat an explicit declaration of Hamilton's against which Dr. Mason's proofs would weigh nothing.—To JOEL BARLOW. v, 495. FORD ED., ix, 269. (M., 1810.)

5125. MASON (J. T.), Meteoric.—John Thompson Mason is a meteor whose path cannot be calculated. All the powers of his mind seem at present to be concentrated in one single object, the producing a convention to new model the [State] Constitution.—To JAMES MADISON. FORD ED., iii, 318. (T., May 1783.)

5126. MASSACHUSETTS, Apostasy.—Oh Massachusetts! how have I lamented the degradation of your apostasy! Massachusetts, with whom I went in pride in 1776, whose vote was my vote on every public question, and whose principles were then the standard of whatever was free or fearless. But she was then under the counsels of the two Adamses; while Strong, her present leader, was promoting petitions for submission to British power and British usurpation. While under her present counsels, she must be contented to be nothing; as having a vote, indeed, to be counted, but not respected. But should the State, once more, buckle on her republican harness, we shall receive her again as a sister, and recollect her wanderings among the crimes only of the parricide party, which would have basely sold what their fathers so bravely won from the same enemy. Let us look forward, then, to the act of repentance, which, by dismissing her venal traitors, shall be the signal of return to the bosom, and to the principles of her brethren; and, if her late humiliation can just give her modesty enough to suppose that her southern brethren are somewhat on a par with her in wisdom, in information, in patriotism, in bravery, and even in honesty, although not in psalm-singing, she will more justly estimate her own relative *momentum* in the Union. With her ancient principles, she would really be great, if she did not think herself the whole.—To GENERAL DEARBORN. vi, 451. (M., March 1815.)

5127. MASSACHUSETTS, Defection of.—Some apprehend danger from the defection of Massachusetts. It is a disagreeable circumstance but not a dangerous one. If they become neutral, we are sufficient for one enemy without them, and in fact we get no aid from them now. If their administration determines to join the enemy, their force will be annihilated by equality of division among themselves. Their federalists will then call in the English army, the republicans ours, and it will only be a transfer of the scene of war from Canada to Massachusetts; and we can get ten men to go to Massachusetts for one who will go to Canada. Every one, too, must know that we can at any moment make peace with England at the expense of the navigation and fisheries of Massachusetts. But it will not come to this. Their own people will put down these factionists as soon as they see the real object of their opposition; and of this Vermont, New Hampshire, and even Connecticut itself, furnish proofs.—To WILLIAM SHORT. vi, 402. (M., Nov. 1814.)

— MASSACHUSETTS, Federal Constitution and.—See CONSTITUTION (FEDERAL).

5128. MASSACHUSETTS, Federalism in.—Massachusetts still lags; because most deeply involved in the parricide crimes and treasons of the war. But her gangrene is contracting, the sound flesh advancing on it, and all there will be well.—To MARQUIS DE LAFAYETTE. vii, 66. FORD ED., x, 83. (M., 1817.)

5129. MASSACHUSETTS, Justice to.—So far as either facts or opinions have been truly quoted from me, they have never been meant to intercept the just fame of Massachusetts for the promptitude and perseverance of her early resistance. We willingly cede to her the laud of having been (although not exclusively) "the cradle of sound principles", and, if some of us believe she has deflected from them in her course, we retain full confidence in her ultimate return to them.—To SAMUEL A. WELLS. i, 117. FORD ED., x, 129. (M., 1819.)

5130. MASSACHUSETTS, Patriotism of People.—The progression of sentiment in the great body of our fellow citizens of Massachusetts, and the increasing support of their opinion, I have seen with satisfaction, and was ever confident I should see; persuaded that an enlightened people, whenever they should view impartially the course we have pursued, could never wish that our measures should have been reversed; could never desire that the expenses of the government should have been increased, taxes multiplied, debt accumulated, wars undertaken, and the tomahawk and scalping knife left in the hands of our neighbors, rather than the hoe and plough. In whatever tended to strengthen the republican features of our Constitution, we could not fail to expect from Massachusetts, the cradle of our Revolutionary principles, an ultimate concurrence; and cultivating the peace of nations, with justice and prudence, we yet were always confident that, whenever our rights would have to be vindicated against the aggression of foreign foes, or the machinations of internal conspirators, the people of Massachusetts, so prominent in the military achievements which placed our country in the right of self-government, would never be found wanting in their duty to the calls of their country, or the requisitions of their government. —R. TO A. MASSACHUSETTS LEGISLATURE. viii, 116. (Feb. 1807.)

5131. MASSACHUSETTS, Republicanism in.—I sincerely congratulate you on the triumph of republicanism in Massachusetts. The hydra of federalism has now lost all its heads but two [Connecticut and Delaware].—To MR. BIDWELL. v, 14. (W., 1806.)

5132. ———. I tender to yourself, to Mr. Lincoln, and to your State, my sincere congratulations on the happy event of the election of a republican Executive to preside over its councils. The * * * just respect with which all the States have ever looked to Massachusetts, could leave none of them without anxiety, while she was in a state of alienation from her family and friends.—To JAMES SULLIVAN. v, 100. FORD ED., ix, 75. (W., June 1807.)

5133. ———. Of the return of Massachusetts to sound principles I never had a doubt. The body of her citizens has never been otherwise than republican. Her would-be dukes and lords, indeed, have been itching for coronets; her lawyers for robes of ermine, her priests for lawn sleeves, and for a religious establishment which might give them wealth, power, and independence of personal merit. But her citizens, who were to supply with the sweat of their brow the treasures on which these drones were to riot, could never have seen anything to long for in the oppressions and pauperism of England. After the shackles of aristocracy of the bar and priesthood have been burst by Connecticut, we cannot doubt the return of Massachusetts to the bosom of the republican family.—To Samuel A. Wells. Ford ed., x, 133. (M., 1819.)

5134. MASSACHUSETTS, Saddled by. —We are completely under the saddle of Massachusetts and Connecticut, and they ride us very hard, cruelly insulting our feelings, as well as exhausting our strength and subsistence. Their natural friends, the three other eastern States, join them from a sort of family pride, and they have the art to divide certain other parts of the Union, so as to make use of them to govern the whole.—To John Taylor. iv, 245. Ford ed., vii, 263. (Pa., June 1798.)

5135. MASSACHUSETTS, Selfishness of.—Could the people of Massachusetts emerge from the deceptions under which they are kept by their clergy, lawyers, and English presses, our salvation would be sure and easy. Without that, I believe it will be effected; but it will be uphill work. Nor can we expect ever their cordial cooperation, because they will not be satisfied longer than while we are sacrificing everything to navigation and a navy.— To Edmund Pendleton. Ford ed., vii, 376. (M., 1799.)

5136. MASSACHUSETTS, The Union and.—The conduct of Massachusetts, which is the subject of your address to Mr. Quincy is serious, as embarrassing the operations of the war, and jeopardizing its issue; and is still more so, as an example of contumacy against the Constitution. One method of proving their purpose would be to call a convention of their State, and to require them to declare themselves members of the Union, and obedient to its determinations, or not members, and let them go. Put this question solemnly to their people, and their answer cannot be doubtful. One half of them are republicans, and would cling to the Union from principle. Of the other half, the dispassionate part would consider, first, that they do not raise bread sufficient for their own subsistence, and must look to Europe for the deficiency if excluded from our ports, which vital interests would force us to do. Secondly, that they are navigating people without a stick of timber for the hull of a ship, nor a pound of anything to export in it, which would be admitted at any market. Thirdly, that they are also a manufacturing people, and left by the exclusive system of Europe without a market but ours. Fourthly, that as rivals of England in manufactures, in commerce, in navigation, and fisheries, they would meet her competition in everp point. Fifthly, that England would feel no scruples in making the abandonment and ruin of such a rival the price of a treaty with the producing States; whose interest too it would be to nourish a navigation beyond the Atlantic, rather than a hostile one at our own door. And sixthly, that in case of war with the Union, which occurrences between coterminous nations frequently produce, it would be a contest of one against fifteen. The remaining portion of the federal moiety of the State would, I believe, brave all these obstacles, because they are monarchists in principle, bearing deadly hatred to their republican fellow citizens, impatient under the ascendency of republican principles, devoted in their attachment to England, and preferring to be placed under her despotism, if they cannot hold the helm of government here. I see, in their separation, no evil but the example, and I believe that the effect of that would be corrected by an early and humiliating return to the Union, after losing much of the population of their country, insufficient in its own resources to feed her numerous inhabitants, and inferior in all its allurements to the more inviting soils, climates, and governments of the other States. Whether a dispassionate discussion before the public, of the advantages and disadvantages of separation to both parties, would be the best medicine of this dialytic fever, or to consider it as a sacrilege ever to touch the question, may be doubted. I am, myself, generally disposed to indulge, and to follow reason; and believe that in no case would it be safer than in the present. Their refractory course, however, will not be unpunished by the indignation of their co-States, their loss of influence with them, the censures of history, and the stain on the character of their State.—To James Martin. vi, 213. Ford ed., ix, 420. (M., Sep. 1813.) See Federalists, Hartford Convention, and Parties.

5137. MASTODON, Bones of.—Of the bones you sent me, I reserved a very few for myself. I got Dr. Wistar to select from the rest every piece which could be interesting to the Philosophical Society [of Philadelphia]. and sent the residue to the National Institute of France. These have enabled them to decide that the animal was neither a mammoth nor an elephant, but of a distinct kind, to which they have given the name of Mastodont, from the protuberance of its teeth. These, from their forms, and the immense mass of their jaws, satisfy me this animal must have been arboriverous. Nature seems not to have provided other food sufficient for him, and the limb of a tree would be no more to him than a bough of a cotton tree to a horse.—To General William Clarke. v, 467. (M., 1809.) See Paleontology.

5138. MATCHES, Phosphoric.—I should have sent you a specimen of the phosphoric matches, but that I am told Mr. Rittenhouse has had some of them. They are a beautiful discovery and very useful, especially to heads which, like yours and mine, cannot at all times be got to sleep. The convenience of lighting a candle without getting out of bed, of sealing letters without calling a servant, of kindling a fire without flint, steel, punk, &c., is of value. —To Charles Thomson. Ford ed., iv, 14. (1784.)

5139. MATERIALISM, Views on.—I consider [Dugald] Stewart and [Destutt] Tracy as the ablest metaphysicians living; by which I mean investigators of the thinking faculty of man. Stewart seems to have given its natural history from facts and observations; Tracy its modes of action and deduction, which he calls Logic, and Ideology; and Cabanis, in his *Physique et Morale de l'Homme*, has investigated anatomically, and most ingeniously, the particular organs in the human structure which may most probably exercise that faculty. And they ask, why may not the mode of action called thought, have been given to a material organ of peculiar structure, as that of magnetism is to the needle, or of elasticity to the spring by a particular manipulation of the steel. They observe that on ignition of the needle or spring, their magnetism and elasticity cease. So on dissolution of the material organ by death, its action of thought may cease a.so, and that nobody supposes that the magnetism or elasticity retires to hold a substantive and distinct existence. These were qualities only of particular conformations of matter; change the conformation, and its qualities change also. Mr. Locke and other materialists have charged with blasphemy the spiritualists who have denied the Creator the power of endowing certain forms of matter with the faculty of thought. These, however, are speculations and subtleties in which, for my own part, I have little indulged myself. When I meet with a proposition beyond finite comprehension, I abandon it as I do a weight which human strength cannot lift, and I think ignorance in these cases is truly the softest pillow on which I can lay my head. Were it necessary, however, to form an opinion, I confess I should, with Mr. Locke, prefer swallowing one incomprehensibility rather than two. It requires one effort only to admit the single incomprehensibility of matter endowed with thought, and two to believe, first that of an existence called spirit, of which we have neither evidence nor idea, and then, secondly, how that spirit, which has neither extension nor solidity, can put material organs into motion. These are things which you and I may perhaps know ere long. We have so lived as to fear neither horn of the dilemma.—To JOHN ADAMS. vii, 153. (M., 1820.)

5140. —— ——. The crowd of scepticisms in your puzzling letter on matter, spirit, motion, &c., kept me from sleep. I read it and laid it down; read it, and laid it down, again and again; and to give rest to my mind, I was obliged to recur ultimately to my habitual anodyne, "I feel, therefore I exist". I feel bodies which are not myself: there are other existences then. I call them *matter*. I feel them changing place. This gives me *motion*. Where there is an absence of matter, I call it *void*, or *nothing*, or *immaterial space*. On the basis of sensation, of matter, and motion, we may erect the fabric of all the certainties we can have or need. I can conceive *thought* to be an action of a particular organization of matter, formed for that purpose by its creator, as well as that *attraction* is an action of matter, or *magnetism* of loadstone. When he who denies to the Creator the power of endowing matter with the mode of action called *thinking*, shall show how He could endow the sun with the mode of action called *attraction*, which reins the planets in the track of their orbits, or how an absence of matter can have a will, and by that will put matter into motion, then the materialist may be lawfully required to explain the process by which matter exercises the faculty of thinking. When once we quit the basis of sensation, all is in the wind. To talk of *immaterial* ex'stences, is to talk of *nothings*. To say that the human soul, angels, God, are immaterial, is to say, they are nothings. or that there is no God, no angels, no soul. I cannot reason otherwise; but I believe I am supported in my creed of materialism by the Lockes, the Tracys, and the Stewarts.—To JOHN ADAMS. vii, 175. (M., 1820.)

5141. MATHEMATICS, Favorite study. —Having to conduct my grandson through his course of mathematics, I have resumed that study with great avidity. It was ever my favorite one. We have no theories there, no uncertainties remain on the mind: all is demonstration and satisfaction. I have forgotten

much, and recover it with more difficulty than when in the vigor of my mind I originally acquired it.—To BENJAMIN RUSH. vi, 3. FORD ED., ix, 328. (P.F., 1811.)

5142. MAZZEI (Philip), Book by.— Mazzei will print soon two or three volumes 8vo., of *Recherches Historiques* and *Politiques sur les Etats d'Amerique*, which are sensible.—To M. OTTO. ii, 95. (P., 1787.)

5143. MAZZEI (Philip), Consulship and.—An alarming paragraph in your letter says Mazzei is coming to Annapolis. I tremble at the idea. I know he will be worse to me than a return of my double quotidian headache. There is a resolution, reported to Congress by a committee, that they will never appoint to the office of minister, chargé des affaires, consul. agent, &c., any but natives. To this I think there will not be a dissenting voice; and it will be taken up among the first things. Could you not, by making him acquainted with this, divert him from coming here? A consulate is his object, in which he will assuredly fail. But his coming will be attended with evil. He is the violent enemy of Franklin, having been some time at Paris, and, from my knowledge of the man, I am sure he will have employed himself in collecting on the spot facts true or false to impeach him. You know there are people here who, on the first idea of this, will take him to their bosom, and turn all Congress topsy-turvy. For God's sake, then, save us from this confusion if you can.—To JAMES MADISON. FORD ED., iii, 425. (A., 1784.)

5144. MAZZEI (Philip), Jefferson's letter to.—[Respecting] the letter to Mazzei imputed to me in the papers, the general substance is mine, though the diction has been considerably varied in the course of its translations from English into Italian, from Italian into French, and from French into English. I first met with it at Bladensburg, and for a moment conceived I must take the field of the public papers. I could not disavow it wholly, because the greatest part of it was mine, in substance though not in form. I could not avow it as it stood, because the form was not mine, and, in one place, the substance very materially falsified. This, then, would render explanations necessary; nay, it would render proofs of the whole necessary, and draw me at length into a publication of all (even the secret) transactions of the administration [of Washington] whi'e I was of it; and embroil me personally with every member of the Executive. with the Judiciary, and with others still. I soon decided in my own mind, to be entirely silent. I consulted with several friends at Phil adelphia, who, every one of them, were clearly against my avowing or disavowing, and some of them conjured me most earnestly to let nothing provoke me to it. I corrected, in conversation with them, a substantial misrepresentation in the copy published. The original has a sentiment *like* this (for I have it not before me). " they are endeavoring to submit us to the substance, as they already have to the *forms* of the British government"; meaning by *forms*, the birth-days, levees, processions to parliament, inauguration pomposities, &c. But the copy published says, " as they have already submitted us to the *form* of the British ", &c., making me express hostility to the form of our government. that is to say. to the Constitution itself. For this is really the difference of the word *form*, used in the singular or plural, in that phrase, in the English language. Now, it would be impossible for me to explain this publicly, without bringing on a personal difference between General Washington and myself, which nothing before the publication of this letter has ever done. It would embroil me also with all those with whom his character is still popular, that is to say, nine-tenths of the people of the United States; and what good would be obtained by avowing the letter with the necessary explanations? Very little indeed, in my opinion, to counterbalance a good deal of harm. From my silence in this instance, it can never be inferred that I am afraid to own the general sentiments of the letter. If I am subject to either imputation, it is to that of avowing such sentiments too frankly both in private and public, often when there is no necessity for it, merely because I disdain everything like duplicity. Still, however, I am open to conviction. Think for me. * * * advise me what to do, and confer with Colonel Monroe.—To JAMES MADISON. iv, 193. FORD ED., vii 164. (M., Aug. 1797.)

5145. ——— ———. The letter to Mazzei has been a precious theme of crimination for federal malice. It was a long letter of business in which was inserted a single paragraph only of political information as to the state of our country. In this information there was not one word which would not then have been, or would not now be approved by every republican in the United States, looking back to those times, as you will see by a faithful copy now enclosed of the whole of what that letter said on the subject of the United States, or of its government. This paragraph, extracted and translated, got into a Paris paper at a time when the persons in power there were laboring under very general disfavor, and their friends were eager to catch even at straws to buoy them up. To them, therefore, I have always imputed the interpolation of an entire paragraph additional to mine, which makes me charge my own country with ingratitude and injustice to France. There was not a word in my letter respecting France, or any of the proceedings or relations between this country and that. Yet this interpolated paragraph has been the burden of federal calumny, has been constantly quoted by them, made the subject of unceasing and virulent abuse, and is still quoted, * * * as if it were genuine, and really written by me. And even Judge Marshall makes history descend from its dignity, and the ermine from its sanctity, to exaggerate, to record and to sanction this forgery. In the very last note of his book [*Life of Washington*] he says, "a letter from Mr. Jefferson to Mr. Mazzei, an Italian, was published in Florence, and republished in the *Moniteur*, with very severe strictures on the conduct of the United States". And instead of the letter itself, he copies what he says are the remarks of the editor, which are an exaggerated commentary on the fabricated paragraph itself, and silently leaves to his reader to make the ready inference that these were the sentiments of the letter. Proof is the duty of the affirmative side. A negative cannot be positively proved. But, in defect of impossible proof of what was not in the original letter, I have its press-copy still in my possession. It has been shown to several and is open to anyone who wishes to see it. I have presumed only that the interpolation was done in Paris. But I never saw the letter in either its Italian or French dress, and it may have been done here, with the commentary handed down to posterity by the Judge. The genuine paragraph, retranslated through Italian and French into English, as it appeared here in a federal paper, besides the mutilated hue

which these translations and retranslations of it produced generally, gave a mistranslation of a single word, which entirely perverted its meaning, and made it a pliant and fertile text of misrepresentation of my political principles. The original, speaking of an Anglican, monarchical and aristocratical party, which had sprung up since he had left us, states their object to be "to draw over us the substance, as they had already done the *forms* of the British Government". Now the "forms" here meant, were the levees, birthdays, the pompous cavalcade to the State house on the meeting of Congress, the formal speech from the throne, the procession of Congress in a body to reecho the speech in an answer, &c., &c. But the translator here, by substituting *form*, in the singular number, for *forms* in the plural, made it mean the frame or organization of our government, or its form of legislative, executive and judiciary authorities, coordinate and independent; to which *form* it was to be inferred that I was an enemy. In this sense they always quoted it, and in this sense Mr. Pickering still quotes it and countenances the inference.—To MARTIN VAN BUREN. vii, 365. FORD ED., x, 308. (1824.)

5146. **MAZZEI (Philip), King of Poland and.**—The King of Poland sent an ancient Secretary here [Paris], * * * to look out for a correspondent, a mere letter writer for him. A happy hazard threw Mazzei in his way, * * * and he is appointed. He has no diplomatic character whatever, but is to receive eight thousand livres a year, as an intelligencer. I hope this employment may have some permanence. The danger is that he will overact his part.—To JAMES MADISON. ii, 444. FORD ED., v, 44. (P., 1788.)

5147. **MAZZEI (Philip), Worth of.**—An intimacy of forty years had proved to me his great worth, and a friendship which had begun in personal acquaintance, was maintained after separation, without abatement by a constant interchange of letters. His esteem, too, in this country was very general; his early and zealous cooperation in the establishment of our Independence having acquired for him here a great degree of favor.—To GIOVANNI CARMIGIANI. FORD ED., x, 49. (M., 1816.)

5148. ——— ———. Your letter brought me the first information of the death of my ancient friend Mazzei, which I learn with sincere regret. He had some peculiarities (and who of us has not?), but he was of solid worth; honest, able, zealous in sound principles, moral and political, constant in friendship, and punctual in all his undertakings. He was greatly esteemed in this country, and some one has inserted in our papers an account of his death, with a handsome and just eulogy of him, and a proposition to publish his life.—To THOMAS APPLETON. FORD ED., x, 46. (M., 1816.)

— **MEASURES, Standard of.**—See STANDARD OF MEASURES.

— **MECKLENBURG DECLARATION.** —See DECLARATION OF INDEPENDENCE.

5149. **MEDICINAL SPRINGS, France.** —I stayed at Aix [France] long enough to prove the inefficiency of the waters.—To JOHN JAY. ii, 138. FORD ED., iv, 376. (1787.)

5150. **MEDICINAL SPRINGS, Virginian.**—We [in Virginia] have taken too little pains to ascertain the properties of our different mineral waters, the cases in which they are respectively remedial, the proper process in their use, and other circumstances necessary to give us their full value.—To Miss Wright. vii, 408. (M., 1825.)

5151. MEDICINE, Molière and.—Medical science was demolished here [France] by the blows of Molière, and in a nation so addicted to ridicule, I question if ever it rises under the weight while his comedies continue to be acted. It furnished the most striking proof I have ever seen in my life of the injury which ridicule is capable of doing.—To Dr. James Currie. Ford ed., iv, 132. (P., 1786.)

5152. MEDICINE, Surgery vs.—While surgery is seated in the temple of the exact sciences, medicine has scarcely entered its threshold. Her theories have passed in such rapid succession as to prove the insufficiency of all, and their fatal errors are recorded in the necrology of man.—To Dr. Crawford. vi, 32. (M., 1812.)

5153. MEDICINE, Theories of.—Theories and systems of medicine have been in perpetual change from the days of the good Hippocrates to the days of the good Rush, but which of them is the true one? The present, to be sure, as long as it is the present, but to yield its place in turn to the next novelty, which is then to become the true system, and is to mark the vast advance of medicine since the days of Hippocrates. Our situation is certainly benefited by the discovery of some new and very valuable medicines; and substituting those for some of his with the treasure of facts, and of sound observations recorded by him (mixed to be sure with anilities of his day), we shall have nearly the present sum of the healing art.—To John Brazier. vii, 132. (P. F., 1819.)

5154. —— ——. In his theory of bleeding and mercury I was ever opposed to my friend Rush, whom I greatly loved. He did much harm, in the sincerest persuasion that he was preserving life and happiness to all around him.—To Thomas Cooper. vi, 390. (M., 1814.)

5155. MEDICINE, Views on Science of. —We know from what we see and feel, that the animal body is, in its organs and functions, subject to derangement, inducing pain, and tending to its destruction. In this disordered state, we observe nature providing for the reestablishment of order, by exciting some salutary evacuation of the morbific matter, or by some other operation which escapes our imperfect senses and researches. She brings on a crisis, by stools, vomiting, sweat, urine, expectoration, bleeding, &c., which, for the most part, ends in the restoration of healthy action. Experience has taught us, also, that there are certain substances, by which, applied to the living body, internally or externally, we can at will produce these small evacuations, and thus do, in a short time, what nature would do but slowly, and do effectually, what perhaps she would not have strength to accomplish. * * * So far, I bow to the utility of medicine. It goes to the well-defined forms of disease, and happily, to those the most frequent. But the disorders of the animal body, and the symptoms indicating them, are as various as the elements of which the body is composed. The combinations, too, of these symptoms are so infinitely diversified, that many associations of them appear too rarely to establish a definite disease: and to an unknown disease, there cannot be a known remedy. Here, then, the

judicious, the moral, the humane physician should stop. Having been so often a witness to the salutary efforts which nature makes to reestablish the disordered functions, he should rather trust to their action, than hazard the interruption of that, and a greater derangement of the system, by conjectural experiments on a machine so complicated and so unknown as the human body, and a subject so sacred as human life. Or, if the appearance of doing something be necessary to keep alive the hope and spirits of the patient, it should be of the most innocent character. One of the most successful physicians I have ever known, has assured me, that he used more bread pills, drops of colored water, and powders of hickory ashes, than of all other medicines put together. It was certainly a pious fraud. But the adventurous physician goes on, and substitutes presumption for knowledge. From the scanty field of what is known, he launches into the boundless region of what is unknown. He establishes for his guide some fanciful theory of corpuscular attraction, of chemical agency, of mechanical powers, of stimuli, of irritability accumulated or exhausted, of depletion by the lancet and repletion by mercury, or some other ingenious dream, which lets him into all nature's secrets at short hand. On the principle which he thus assumes, he forms his table of nosology, arrays his diseases into families, and extends his curative treatment, by analogy, to all the cases he has thus arbitrarily marshalled together. I have lived myself to see the disciples of Hoffman, Boerhaave, Stahl, Cullen, Brown, succeed one another like the shifting figures of a magic lantern, and their fancies, like the dresses of the annual doll-babies from Paris, becoming from their novelty, the vogue of the day, and yielding to the next novelty their ephemeral favor. The patient, treated on the fashionable theory, sometimes gets well in spite of the medicine. The medicine, therefore, restored him, and the young doctor receives new courage to proceed in his bold experiments on the lives of his fellow creatures. I believe we may safely affirm, that the inexperienced and presumptuous band of medical tyros let loose upon the world, destroys more of human life in one year, than all the Robinhoods, Cartouches, and Macheaths in a century. It is in this part of medicine that I wish to see a reform, an abandonment of hypothesis for sober facts, the first degree of value set on clinical observation, and the lowest on visionary theories. I would wish the young practitioner, especially, to have deeply impressed on his mind, the real limits of his art, and that when the state of his patient gets beyond these, his office is to be a watchful, but quiet spectator of the operations of nature, giving them fair play by a well-regulated regimen, and by all the aid they can derive from the excitement of good spirits and hope in the patient. I have no doubt, that some diseases not yet understood may in time be transferred to the table of those known. But, were I a physician, I would rather leave the transfer to the slow hand of accident, than hasten it by guilty experiments on those who put their lives into my hands. The only sure foundations of medicine are, an intimate knowledge of the human body, and observation on the effects of medicinal substances on that. The anatomical and clinical schools, therefore, are those in which the young physician should be formed. If he enters with innocence that of the theory of medicine, it is scarcely possible he should come out untainted with error. His mind must be strong indeed, if, rising above juvenile credulity, it can maintain a wise infidelity against the authority of his instructors, and the bewitching delusions of their theories. You see that I estimate justly that portion of instruction which our medical students derive from your labors; and, associating with it one of the chairs which my old and able friend, Dr. Rush, so honorably fills, I consider them as the two fundamental pillars of the edifice. Indeed, I have such an opinion of the talents of the professors in the other branches which constitute the school of medicine with you, as to hope and believe, that it is from this side of the Atlantic, that Europe, which has taught us so many other things, will at length be led into sound principles in this branch of science, the most important of all others, being that to which we commit the care of health and life.

I dare say, that by this time, you are sufficiently sensible that old heads as well as young, may sometimes be charged with ignorance and presumption. The natural course of the human mind is certainly from credulity to skepticism; and this is perhaps the most favorable apology I can make for venturing so far out of my depth, and to one, too, to whom the strong as well as the weak points of this science are so familiar. But having stumbled on the subject in my way, I wished to give a confession of my faith to a friend; and the rather, as I had perhaps, at times, to him as well as others, expressed my skepticism in medicine, without defining its extent or foundation. At any rate, it has permitted me, for a moment, to abstract myself from the dry and dreary waste of politics, into which I have been impressed by the times on which I happened, and to indulge in the rich fields of nature, where alone I should have served as a volunteer, if left to my natural inclinations and partialities.—To Dr. Caspar Wistar. v, 105. Ford ed., ix, 81. (W., June 1807.)

5156. MEDITERRANEAN TRADE, Reestablishment of.—It rests with Congress to decide between war, tribute, and ransom, as the means of reestablishing our Mediterranean commerce. If war, they will consider how far our own resources shall be called forth, and how far they will enable the Executive to engage. in the forms of the Constitution, the co-operation of other powers. If tribute or ransom, it will rest with them to limit and provide the amount; and with the Executive, observing the same constitutional forms, to take arrangements for employing it to the best advantage.—Report on Mediterranean Trade. vii, 526. (1790.)

— MEDIUM, Circulating.—See Money.

5157. MEMORY, Decay of.—Of all the faculties of the human mind that of memory is the first which suffers decay from age. * * * It was my earliest monition to retire from public business.—To Mr. Latrobe. vi, 74. (M., 1812.)

5158. MERCER (John Francis), Politics of.—Our old friend, Mercer, broke off from us some time ago; at first professing to disdain joining the federalists, yet, from the habit of voting together. becoming soon identified with them. Without carrying over with him one single person, he is now in a state of as perfect obscurity as if his name had never been known. Mr. J. Randolph is in the same track, and will end in the same way.—To James Monroe. v, 9. Ford ed., viii, 447. (W., May 1806.)

5159. MERCHANTS, Anglomaniac.—I join in your reprobation of our merchants, priests and lawyers, for their adherence to England and monarchy, in preference to their own country and its Constitution. But merchants have no country. The mere spot they stand on does not constitute so strong an attachment as that from which they draw their gains.—To Horatio G. Spafford. vi, 334. (M., 1814.)

5160. MERCHANTS, Education of.—For the merchant I should not say that the [classical] Languages are a necessary. Ethics, mathematics, geography, political economy, history, seem to constitute the immediate foundations of his calling.—To John Brazier. vii, 133. (P.F., 1819.)

5161. MERCHANTS, Freedom of Commerce and.—The merchants will manage commerce the better, the more they are left free to manage for themselves.—To Gideon Granger. iv, 331. Ford ed., vii, 452. (M., 1800.)

5162. MERCHANTS, Natural Republicans.—A merchant is naturally a republican, and can be otherwise only from a vitiated state of things.—To Albert Gallatin. Ford ed., viii, 252. (1803.)

5163. MERCHANTS, Patriotism of.—Merchants are the least virtuous citizens and possess the least of the *amor patriæ.*—To M. de Meunier. ix, 288. Ford ed., iv, 143. (P., 1786.)

5164. MERCHANTS, Peace and.—Some of our merchants have been milking the cow; yet the great mass of them have become deranged. They are daily falling down by bankruptcies, and on the whole, the condition of our commerce is far less firm and really prosperous, than it would have been by the regular operations and steady advances which a state of peace would have occasioned. Were a war to take place, and throw our agriculture into equal convulsions with our commerce, our business would be done at both ends.—To Horatio Gates. iv, 213. Ford ed., vii, 204. (Pa., 1798.)

5165. MERCHANTS, Protection of.—Where a nation refuses permission to our merchants and factors to reside within certain parts of their dominions, we may, if it should be thought expedient, refuse residence to theirs in any and every part of ours, or modify their transactions.—Foreign Commerce Report. vii, 649. Ford ed., vi, 482. (Dec. 1793.)

5166. MERCHANTS, Selfish.—Ministers and merchants love nobody.—To John Langdon. i, 429. (P., 1785.)

5167. —— ——. The merchants here [France] are endeavoring to exclude us from their islands. [West Indies].—To John Langdon. i, 429. (P., 1785.)

5168. MERCIER (James), Rescued from slavery.—In Mr. Barclay's letter (from Morocco) is this paragraph: " There is a young man now under my care who has been a slave some time with the Arabs in the desert." His name is James Mercier, born at the town of

Suffolk, Nansemond County, Virginia. The King sent him after the first audience, and I shall take him to Spain. On Mr. Barclay's return to Spain, he shall find there a letter from me to forward this young man to his own country, for the expenses of which I will make myself responsible.—To GOVERNOR HENRY. i, 601. (P., 1786.)

5169. MERIT, Relief of distressed.—I do not know that I can proffer you any reward for this favor [to my friend], other than the sublime pleasure of relieving distressed merit, a pleasure which can be properly felt by the virtuous alone.—To THOMAS ADAMS. FORD ED., i, 382. (1770.)

5170. MERRY (A.), Character.—With respect to Merry [British Minister] he appears so reasonable and good a man, that I should be sorry to lose him as long as there remains a possibility of reclaiming him to the exercise of his own dispositions. If his wife perseveres, she must eat her soup at home, and we shall endeavor to draw him into society as if she did not exist. It is unfortunate that the good understanding of nations should hang on the caprice of an individual, who ostensibly has nothing to do with them.—To JAMES MONROE. FORD ED., viii, 292. (W., Jan. 1804.)

5171. MERRY (A.), Social claims of.—Mr. Merry is with us, and we believe him to be personally as desirable a character as could have been sent us. But he is unluckily associated with one of an opposite in every point. She has already disturbed our harmony extremely. He began by claiming the first visit from the national ministers. He corrected himself in this. But a pretension to take precedence at dinners, &c., over all others is persevered in. We have told him that the principle of society, as well as of government, with us, is the equality of the individuals composing it; that no man here would come to a dinner, where he was to be marked with inferiority to any other; that we might as well attempt to force our principle of equality at St. James's as he his principle of precedence here. I had been in the habit, when I invited female company (having no lady in my family) to ask one of the ladies of the four Secretaries to come and take care of my company; and as she was to do the honors of the table I handed her to dinner myself. That Mr. Merry might not construe this as giving them a precedence over Mrs. Merry, I have discontinued it. And here, as well as in private houses, the pele-mele practice is adhered to. They have got Yrujo to take a zealous part in the claim of precedence. It has excited generally emotions of great contempt and indignation (in which the members of the Legislature participate sensibly), that the agents of foreign nations should assume to dictate to us what shall be the laws of our society. The consequence will be that Mr. and Mrs. Merry will put themselves into Coventry, and that he will lose the best half of his usefulness to his nation, that derived from a perfectly familiar and private intercourse with the Secretaries and myself. The latter, be assured, is a virago, and in the short course of a few weeks has established a degree of dislike among all classes which one would have thought impossible in so short a time. Thornton has entered into their ideas. At this we wonder, because he is a plain man, a sensible one, and too candid to be suspected of wishing to bring on their recall, and his own substitution. To counterwork their misrepresentations, it would be as well their government should understand as much of these things as can be communicated with decency, that they may know the spirit in which their letters are written.—To JAMES MONROE. FORD ED., viii, 290. (W., Jan. 1804.)

— MESMERISM.—See FRANKLIN (BENJAMIN).

— MESSAGES TO CONGRESS.—See CONGRESS.

5172. METAPHYSICS, Views on.—The relations between the physical and moral faculties of man have ever been a subject of great interest to the inquisitive mind * * *. That thought may be a faculty of our material organization has been believed in the gross; and though the *modus operandi* of nature, in this, as in most other cases, can never be developed and demonstrated to beings limited as we are, yet I feel confident you will have conducted us as far on the road as we can go, and have lodged us within reconnoitering distance of the citadel itself.—To M. CABANIS. iv, 496. (W., 1803.)

5173. ——. The science of the human mind is curious, but is one on which I have not indulged myself in much speculation. The times in which I have lived, and the scenes in which I have been engaged, have required me to keep the mind too much in action to have leisure to study minutely its laws of action.—To EZRA STILES. vii, 127. (M., 1819.)

5174. METEORIC STONES, Origin.—[With respect] to the stone in your possession, supposed meteoric, its descent from the atmosphere presents so much difficulty as to require careful examination. But I do not know that the most effectual examination could be made by the members of the national Legislature, to whom you have thought of exhibiting it. * * * I should think that an inquiry by some of our scientific societies, * * * would be likely to be directed * * * with such knowledge of the subject, as would inspire a general confidence. We certainly are not to deny whatever we cannot account for. A thousand phenomena present themselves daily which we cannot explain, but where facts are suggested, bearing no analogy with the laws of nature as yet known to us, their verity needs proofs proportioned to their difficulty. A cautious mind will weigh well the opposition of the phenomenon to everything hitherto observed, the strength of the testimony by which it is supported, and the errors and misconceptions to which even our senses are liable. It may be very difficult to explain how the stone you possess came into the position in which it was found, but is it easier to explain how it got into the clouds from whence it is supposed to have fallen? The actual fact, however, is the thing to be established, and this I hope will be done by those whose situations and qualifications enable them to do it.—To DANIEL SALMON. v, 245. (W., 1808.)

5175. METEOROLOGY, Slow progress in.—Of all the departments of science no one seems to have been less advanced for the last hundred years than that of meteorology. The new chemistry, indeed, has given us a new principle of the generation of rain, by proving water to be a composition of different gases, and has aided our theory of meteoric lights. Electricy stands where Dr. Franklin's early discoveries placed it, except with its new modification of galvanism. But the phenomena of snow, hail, halo, aurora borealis, haze, looming,

&c., are as yet very imperfectly understood. I am myself an empiric in natural philosophy, suffering my faith to go no further than my facts. I am pleased, however, to see the efforts of hypothetical speculation, because by the collisions of different hypotheses, truth may be elicited and science advanced in the end. This skeptical disposition does not permit me to say whether your hypothesis for looming and floating volumes of warm air occasionally perceived, may or may not be confirmed by future observations. More facts are yet wanting to furnish a solution on which we may rest with confidence. I even doubt as yet whether the looming at sea and on land is governed by the same laws.—To GEORGE F. HOPKINS. vii, 259. (M., 1822.) See CLIMATE.

— **METROPOTAMIA, Proposed State of.**—See WESTERN TERRITORY.

5176. MEXICO, Interesting.—Mexico is one of the most interesting countries of ur hemisphere, and merits every attention.—To DR. BARTON. v, 470. (M., 1809.)

— **MICHIGANIA, Proposed State of.**— See WESTERN TERRITORY.

5177. MILITIA, Bravery.—Ill armed and untried militia, who never before saw the face of an enemy, have, at times during the course of this war [of the Revolution] given occasions of exultation to our enemies, but they afforded us, while at Warwick, a little satisfaction in the same way. Six or eight hundred of their picked men of light infantry, with General Arnold at their head, having crossed the [James] river from Warwick, fled from a patrol of sixteen horse, every man into his boat as he could, some pushing North, some South as their fears drove them.—To GENERAL WASHINGTON. i, 306. FORD ED., iii, 33. (R., 1781.)

5178. —— ——. Our militia are heroes when they have heroes to lead them on.—To W. H. CRAWFORD. vi, 420. FORD ED., ix, 504. (M., 1815.)

5179. MILITIA, Classification.—You will consider whether it would not be expedient, for a state of peace as well as of war, so to organize or class the militia, as would enable us, on any sudden emergency, to call for the services of the younger portions, unencumbered with the old and those having families. Upwards of three hundred thousand able bodied men, between the ages of eighteen and twenty-six years, which the last census shows we may now count within our limits, will furnish a competent number for offence or defence in any point where they may be wanted, and give time for raising regular forces after the necessity of them shall become certain; and the reducing to the early period of life all its active service, cannot but be desirable to our younger citizens, of the present as well as future times, inasmuch as it engages to them in more advanced age a quiet and undisturbed repose in the bosom of their families. I cannot, then, but earnestly recommend to your early consideration the expediency of so modifying our militia system as, by a separation of the more active part from that which is less so, we

may draw from it, when necessary, an efficient corps, fit for real and active service, and to be called to it in regular rotation.— FIFTH ANNUAL MESSAGE. viii, 49. FORD ED., viii, 392. (Dec. 1805.)

5180. —— ——. A militia of young men will hold on until regulars can be raised, and will be the nursery which will furnish them. —To WILLIAM A. BURWELL. FORD ED., viii, 416. (W., 1806.)

5181. —— ——. A militia can never be used for distant service on any other plan; and Bonaparte will conquer the world, if they do not learn his secret of composing armies of young men only, whose enthusiasm and health enable them to surmount all obstacles. —To MR. BIDWELL. v, 16. (W., 1806.)

5182. —— ——. Convinced that a militia of all ages promiscuously are entirely useless for distant service, and that we never shall be safe until we have a selected corps for a year's distant service at least, the classification of our militia is now the most essential thing the United States have to do. Whether, on Bonaparte's plan of making a class for every year between certain periods, or that recommended in my message, I do not know, but I rather incline to his. The idea is not new, as you may remember we adopted it once in Virginia during the Revolution, but abandoned it too soon. It is the real secret of Bonaparte's success.—To JAMES MADISON. v, 76. FORD ED., ix, 49. (M., May 1807.)

5183. —— ——. The session before the last I proposed to the Legislature the classification of the militia, so that those in the prime of life only, and unburthened with families, should ever be called into distant service; and that every man should receive a stand of arms the first year he entered the militia. * * * It will prevail in time.— To MR. COXE. v, 58. (W., 1807.)

5184. —— ——. Against great land armies we cannot attempt defence but by equal armies. For these we must depend on a classified militia, which will give us the service of the class from twenty to twenty-six, in the nature of conscripts, comprising a body of about 250,000, to be specially trained. This measure, attempted at a former session, was pressed at the last, and might, I think, have been carried by a small majority. But considering that great innovations should not be forced on a slender majority, and seeing that the general opinion is sensibly rallying to it, it was thought better to let it lie over to the next session, when, I trust, it will be passed.—To GENERAL ARMSTRONG. v, 281. FORD ED., ix, 194. (W., May 1808.)

5185. —— ——. In the beginning of our government we were willing to introduce the least coercion possible on the will of the citizen. Hence a system of military duty was established too indulgent to his indolence. This [war] is the first opportunity we have had of trying it, and it has completely failed; an issue foreseen by many, and for which remedies have been proposed. That óf classing the militia according to age, and allotting each age to the particular kind of service to which it was competent, was proposed to Congress in 1805, and subsequently; and, on the last trial, was lost, I believe, by a single vote. Had it prevailed, what has now happened would not have happened. Instead of burning our Capitol, we should have possessed theirs in Montreal and Quebec. We must now adopt it, and all will be safe.—To THOMAS COOPER. vi, 379. (M., 1814.)

5186. MILITIA, Comfort of.—The soldiers themselves will thank you, when separated from domestic accommodation, they find themselves, through your attention to their comfort, provided with conveniences which will administer to their first wants.— LETTER TO COUNTY LIEUTENANTS. FORD ED., ii, 428. (R., 1781.)

5187. MILITIA, Commissions in.—The Executive, apprehending they have no authority to grant brevet commissions, refer to the General Assembly the expedience of authorizing them to give to this gentleman* a Lieutenant Colonel's commission by way of brevet.—To SPEAKER OF HOUSE OF DELEGATES. FORD ED., ii, 266. (Wg., 1779.)

5188. MILITIA, Compulsory service in.—We must train and classify the whole of our male citizens, and make military instruction a regular part of collegiate education. We can never be safe till this is done.—To JAMES MONROE. vi, 131. (M., 1813.)

5189. ———— ————. I think the truth must now be obvious that our people are too happy at home to enter into regular service, and that we cannot be defended but by making every citizen a soldier, as the Greeks and Romans who had no standing armies; and that in doing this all must be marshalled, classed by their ages, and every service ascribed to its competent class.— To J. W. EPPES. FORD ED., ix, 484. (M., 1814.)

5190. MILITIA, Crimes and punishments.—Any officer or soldier, guilty of mutiny, desertion, disobedience of command, absence from duty or quarters, neglect of guard, or cowardice, shall be punished at the discretion of a courtmartial by degrading, cashiering, drumming out of the army, whipping not exceeding twenty lashes, fine not exceeding two months, or imprisonment not exceeding one month.—INVASION BILL. FORD ED., ii, 127. (1777.)

5191. MILITIA, Defects in organization.—Congress have had too much experience of the radical defects and inconveniences of militia service to need my enumerating them.—To THE PRESIDENT OF CONGRESS. FORD ED., ii, 277. (Wg., 1779.)

5192. MILITIA, Distant service.—Militia do well for hasty enterprises, but cannot

* M. Le Mair, a Frenchman, who had purchased arms in Europe for Virginia and requested a brevet-commission as a reward for his services. Jefferson was then Governor of Virginia.—EDITOR.

be relied on for lengthy service, and out of their own country.—To NORTH CAROLINA ASSEMBLY. FORD ED., ii, 480. (R., 1781.)

5193. ———— ————. We hope it will be the last time we shall have occasion to require our militia to go out of their own country, as we think it most advisable to put that distant, disagreeable service on our regulars, * * * and to employ our militia on service in our own country.—To COLONEL ABRAHAM PENN. FORD ED., iii, 29. (R., 1781.)

5194. ———— ————. I am sensible it is much more practicable to carry on a war with militia within our own country [State] than out of it.—To MAJOR GENERAL GREENE. FORD ED., iii, 2. (R., 1781.)

5195. ———— ————. The law of a former session of Congress, for keeping a body of 100,000 militia in readiness for service at a moment's warning, is still in force. * * * When called into action, it will not be for a lounging, but for an active, and perhaps distant, service.*—To THE GOVERNOR OF OHIO. v, 51. FORD ED., ix, 34. (W., March 1807.)

5196. ———— ————. If the marching of the militia into an enemy's country be once ceded as unconstitutional (which I hope it never will be), then will [the British] force [in Canada], as now strengthened, bid us permanent defiance.—To JAMES MONROE. vi, 131. (M., June 1813.)

5197. ———— ————. Abolish, by a declaratory law, the doubts which abstract scruples in some, and cowardice and treachery in others, have conjured up about passing imaginary lines, and limiting, at the same time, the services of the militia to the *contiguous* provinces of the enemy.—To PRESIDENT MADISON. vi, 391. FORD ED., ix, 489. (M., Oct. 1814.)

— MILITIA, Draft law.—See DRAFT.

5198. MILITIA, Employment of.—I must desire that, so far as the agency of the militia be employed, it may be with the utmost discretion, and with no act of force beyond what shall be necessary to maintain obedience to the laws, using neither deeds nor words unnecessarily offensive.—To CHARLES SIMMS. v, 418. (W., Jan. 1809.)

5199. MILITIA, Enrolment.—For making provision against invasions and insurrections, and laying the burthen equally upon all * * * the commanding officer of every county * * * shall enroll under some captain such persons * * * as ought to make a part of the militia, who together with those before enrolled, and not yet formed into tenths * * * shall by such captain * * * be divided into equal parts. as nearly as may be, each part to be distinguished by fair and equal lot by numbers from one to ten, and when so distinguished, to be added to and make part of the militia of the county. Where any person * * * shall not attend,

* The Governors of Kentucky, Tennessee and Mississippi Territory were also urged to furnish volunteers.—EDITOR.

or shall refuse to draw for himself, the captain shall cause his lot to be drawn for him. —INVASION BILL. FORD ED., ii, 123. (1777.)

5200. MILITIA, Equalization of duty. —As militia duty becomes heavy, it becomes our duty to divide it equally.—To GENERAL NELSON. FORD ED., ii, 464. (R., 1781.)

5201. —— ——. Where any county shall have sent but half the quota called for, they have performed but half their tour, and ought to be called on again. Where any county has furnished their full complement, they have performed their full tour, and it would be unjust to call on them again till we have gone through the counties. Militia becoming burthensome, it is our duty to divide it as equally as we can.—To COLONEL JAMES INNES. FORD ED., ii, 465. (R., 1781.)

5202. —— ——. The spirit of disobedience * * * in your county must be subdued. Laws made by common consent must not be trampled on by individuals. It is very much [to] the [public] good to force the unworthy into their due share of contributions to the public support, otherwise the burthen on [the worthy] will become oppressive indeed.—To COLONEL VANMETER. FORD ED., iii, 24. (R., 1781.)

5203. MILITIA, Expensive.—Whether it be practicable to raise and maintain a sufficient number of regulars to carry on the war, is a question. That it would be burthensome is undoubted, yet perhaps it is as certain that no possible mode of carrying it on can be so expensive to the public, so distressing and disgusting to individuals, as the militia.— TO THE HOUSE OF DELEGATES. FORD ED., ii, 474. (R., 1781.)

5204. MILITIA, Improving.—We should at every session [of Congress] continue to amend the defects * * * in the laws for regulating the militia, until they are sufficiently perfect. Nor should we now or at any time separate, until we can say we have done everything for the militia which we could do were an enemy at our door.—FIRST ANNUAL MESSAGE. viii, 12. FORD ED., viii, 121. (Dec. 1801.)

5205. —— ——. Uncertain as we must ever be of the particular point in our circumference where an enemy may choose to invade us, the only force which can be ready at every point and competent to oppose them, is the body of neighboring citizens as formed into a militia. On these, collected from the parts most convenient, in numbers proportioned to the invading foe, it is best to rely, not only to meet the first attack, but if it threatens to be permanent, to maintain the defence until regulars may be engaged to relieve them.—FIRST ANNUAL MESSAGE. viii, 11. FORD ED., viii, 121. (Dec. 1801.)

5206. —— ——. Considering that our regular troops are employed for local purposes, and that the militia is our general reliance for great and sudden emergencies, you will doubtless think this institution worthy

of a review, and give it those improvements of which you find it susceptible.—SECOND ANNUAL MESSAGE. viii, 19. FORD ED., viii, 185. (Dec. 1802.)

5207. —— ——. In compliance with a request of the House of Representatives, as well as with a sense of what is necessary, I take the liberty of urging on you the importance and indispensable necessity of vigorous exertions, on the part of the State governments, to carry into effect the militia system adopted by the national Legislature, agreeable to the powers reserved to the States respectively, by the Constitution of the United States, and in a manner the best calculated to ensure such a degree of military discipline, and knowledge of tactics, as will under the auspices of a benign Providence, render the militia a sure and permanent bulwark of national defence.—To ——. iv, 469. (W., Feb. 1803.)

5208. —— ——. It is incumbent on us at every meeting, to revise the condition of the militia, and to ask ourselves if it is prepared to repel a powerful enemy at every point of our territories exposed to invasion. Some of the States have paid a laudable attention to this object; but every degree of neglect is to be found among others. Congress alone have power to produce a uniform state of preparation in this great organ of defence; the interests which they so deeply feel in their own and their country's security will present this as among the most important objects of their deliberation.—ANNUAL MESSAGE. viii, 108. FORD ED., ix, 223. (1808.)

5209. MILITIA, Maintenance of.—[The maintenance of] a well-disciplined militia, our best reliance in peace and for the first moments of war, till regulars may relieve them, I deem [one of the] essential principles of our government and, consequently [one] which ought to shape its administration.—FIRST INAUGURAL ADDRESS. viii, 4. FORD ED., viii, 4. (1803.)

5210. MILITIA, Menial labor.—A militia of freemen cannot easily be induced to labor in works of that kind [building forts]. —To THE HOUSE OF DELEGATES. FORD ED., iii, 36. (R., 1781.)

5211. MILITIA, Mutiny.—The precedent of a * * * mutiny would be so mischievous as to induce us to believe that an accommodation to their present temper [would be] most prudent.—To MAJOR-GENERAL STEUBEN. FORD ED., ii, 466. (R., Feb. 1781.)

5212. —— ——. The best way, perhaps, is not to go against the mutineers [militiamen] when embodied, which would bring on, perhaps, an open rebellion, or bloodshed most certainly; but, when they shall have dispersed, to go and take them out of their beds, singly and without noise; or, if they be not found, the first time, to go again and again, so that they may never be able to remain in quiet at home. This is what I must recommend to you and, therefore, furnish the bearers with the commissions as you desire.—To COLONEL VANMETER. FORD ED., iii, 25. (R., 1781.)

5213. MILITIA, Naval.—I send you a copy of the marine regulations of France. There are things in it which may become interesting to us; particularly, what relates to the establishment of a marine militia, and their classification.—To JOHN JAY. ii, 91. (P., 1787.)

5214. —— ——. I wish to consult you on a plan of a regular naval militia, to be composed of all our sea-faring citizens, to enable us to man a fleet speedily by supplying voluntary enlistments by calls on that militia.— To ROBERT SMITH. FORD ED., viii, 381. (W., Oct. 1805.)

5215. —— ——. I think it will be necessary to erect our sea-faring men into a naval militia, and subject them to tours of duty in whatever port they may be.—To GENERAL SMITH. v, 147. (W., July 1807.)

5216. —— ——. It is * * * material that the seaport towns should have artillery-militia duly trained * * * .—To W. H. CABELL. v, 191. (M., 1807.)

5217. —— ——. I think our *naval militia* plan, both as to name and structure, better for us than the English plan of Sea-fencibles. —To ROBERT SMITH. v, 234. (1808.)

5218. MILITIA, Officers.—Any officer resigning his commission on being called into duty by the Governor, or his commanding officer, shall be ordered into the ranks, and shall moreover suffer punishment as for disobedience of command.—INVASION BILL. FORD ED., ii, 125. (1777.)

5219. —— ——. Much will depend on the proper choice of officers.—INVASION CIRCULAR-LETTER. FORD ED., ii, 398. (R., 1781.)

5220. —— ——. The good of the service requires that the field officers at least be experienced in the service. For this reason, these will be provided for at the rendezvous. I beg that this may not be considered by the militia field officers [as arising] from want of respect to them. We know and confide in their zeal; but it cannot be disreputable to them to be less knowing in the art of war than those who have greater experience in it; and being less knowing, I am quite sure the spirit of patriotism, with which they are animated, will lead them to wish that measure to be adopted which will most promote the public safety, however it may tend to keep them from the post in which they would wish to appear in defence of their country.*—To COUNTY LIEUTENANTS. FORD ED., ii, 398. (R., 1781.)

5221. —— ——. I enclose you a charge against * * * [three militia officers], as having become members of an organized company, calling themselves the Tar Company, avowing their object to be the tarring and feathering citizens of some description. Although in some cases the animadversions of the law may be properly relied on to prevent what is unlawful, yet with those clothed with authority from the Executive, and being a part of the Executive, other preventives are expedient. These officers should be warned that the Executive cannot tamely look on and see its officers threaten to become the violators instead of the protectors of the rights of our citizens.—To HENRY DEARBORN. v, 383. (1808.)

5222. MILITIA, Payment of Ohio.—If we suffer the question of paying the [Ohio] militia embodied to be thrown on their Legislature, it will excite acrimonious debate in that body, and they will spread the same dissatisfaction among their constituents, and finally it will be forced back on us through Congress. Would it not, therefore, be better to say to Mr. Kirker, that the General Government is fully aware that emergencies which appertain to them will sometimes arise so suddenly as not to give time for consulting them, before the State must get into action; that the expenses in such cases, incurred on reasonable grounds, will be met by the General Government; and that in the present case [Burr's Conspiracy], although it appears there was no real ground for embodying the militia, and that more certain measures for ascertaining the truth should have been taken before embodying them. yet an unwillingness to damp the public spirit of our countrymen, and the justice due to the individuals who came forward in defence of their country, and could not know the grounds on which they were called, have determined us to consider the call as justifiable, and to defray the expenses.—To GENERAL DEARBORN. v, 206. FORD ED., ix, 22. (W., Oct. 1807.)

5223. MILITIA, Public property and. —Be pleased to give the same notice to the militia as formerly, that no man will be ever discharged till he shall have returned whatever public arms or accoutrements he shall have received.—To BRIGADIER-GENERAL NELSON. FORD ED., ii, 396. (R., 1781.)

5224. MILITIA, Regular army and.—I am for relying for internal defence on our militia solely, till actual invasion.—To ELBRIDGE GERRY. iv, 268. FORD ED., vii, 328. (Pa., 1799.)

5225. —— ——. None but an armed nation can dispense with a standing army. To keep ours armed and disciplined, is therefore at all times important.—To ——. iv, 469. (W., 1803.)

5226. MILITIA, Security in.—For a people who are free, and who mean to remain so, a well organized and armed militia is their best security.—EIGHTH ANNUAL MESSAGE. viii, 108. FORD ED., ix, 223. (Nov. 1808.)

5227. MILITIA, Slaves and.—Slaves are by the law excluded from the militia, and

* From a letter calling out the militia of several counties of Virginia when the State was invaded by the British forces.—EDITOR.

wisely as to that part of a soldier's duty which consists in exercise of arms. But whether male slaves might not under proper regulations be subjected to the routine of duty as pioneers, and to other military labors, can only be determined by the wisdom of the Legislature.—To THE VA. HOUSE OF DELE-GATES. FORD ED., iii, 36. (R., 1781.)

5228. MILITIA, Standing fire.—The scene of military operations has been hitherto so distant from these States that their militia are strangers to the actual presence of danger. Habit alone will enable them to view this with familiarity, to face it without dismay; a habit which must be purchased by calamity, but cannot be purchased too dear.—To THE PRESIDENT OF CONGRESS. FORD ED., ii, 335. (R., 1780.)

5229. MILITIA, Subsistence of.—The present [British] invasion [of Virginia] having rendered it necessary to call into the field a large body of militia, the providing them with subsistence, and the means of transportation becomes an arduous task in the unorganized state of our military system. To effect this we are obliged to vest the heads of the Commissary's and Quartermaster's departments with such powers as, if abused, will be most afflicting to the people. Major General Steuben, taught by experience on similar occasions, has pressed on us the necessity of calling to the superintendence of these officers some gentleman of distinguished character and abilities, who, while he prescribes to them such rules as will effectually produce the object of their appointment, will yet stand between them and the people as a guard from oppression. * * * Under the exigency we have taken the liberty of casting our eyes on yourself as most likely to fulfill our wishes and. therefore, solicit your undertaking this charge.—To COLONEL RICHARD MEADE. FORD ED., ii, 400. (R., 1781.)

5230. MILITIA, Washington on use of.—In conversation with the President, and speaking about General [Nathaniel] Greene, he said that he and General Greene had always differed in opinion about the manner of using militia. Greene always placed them in his front; himself was of opinion they should always be used as a reserve to improve any advantage, for which purpose they were the *finest fellows* in the world. He said he was on the ground of the battle of Guilford, with a person who was in the action, and who explained the whole of it to him. That General Greene's front was behind a fence at the edge of a large field, through which the enemy were obliged to pass to get at them; and that in their passage through this, they must have been torn all to pieces, if troops had been posted there who would have stood their ground; and that the retreat from that position was · through a thicket. perfectly secure. Instead of this, he posted the North Carolina militia there, who only gave one fire and fell back, so that the whole benefit of their position was lost. He thinks that the regulars, with their field pieces,

would have hardly let a single man get through that field.—THE ANAS. ix, 146. FORD ED., i, 232. (1793.) See ARMY and WAR.

5231. MILITIA FOR LOUISIANA.—The spirit of this country is totally adverse to a large military force. I have tried for two sessions to prevail on the Legislature to let me plant thirty thousand well chosen volunteers on donation lands on the west side of the Mississippi, as a militia always at hand for the defence of New Orleans; but I have not yet succeeded.—To MR. CHANDLER PRICE. v, 47. (W., 1807.)

5232. —— ——. The defence of Orleans against a land army can never be provided for, according to the principles of the Constitution, till we can get a sufficient militia there—To ALBERT GALLATIN. v, 215. FORD ED., ix, 167. (Nov. 1807.)

5233. —— ——. A measure has now twice failed, which I have warmly urged, the immediate settlement by donation lands, of such a body of militia in the Territories of Orleans and Mississippi, as will be adequate to the defence of New Orleans.—To GENERAL ARMSTRONG. v, 281. (W., May 1808.)

5234. MIND, Body and.—If this period [youth] be suffered to pass in idleness, the mind becomes lethargic and impotent, as would the body it inhabits if unexercised during the same time. The sympathy between body and mind during their rise, progress and decline, is too strict and obvious to endanger our being misled while we reason from the one to the other.—NOTES ON VIRGINIA. viii, 390. FORD ED., iii, 253. (1782.)

5235. MIND, Freedom of.—Almighty God hath created the mind free, and manifested His supreme will that free it shall remain by making it altogether insusceptible of restraint.—STATUTE OF RELIGIOUS FREEDOM. viii, 454. FORD ED., ii, 227. (1779.)

5236. MIND, Influencing.—All attempts to influence [the mind] by temporal punishments, or burthens, or by civil incapacitations, tend only to beget habits of hypocrisy and meanness, and are a departure from the plan of the Holy Author of our religion, who being Lord both of body and mind. yet choose not to propagate it by coercions on either, as was in his Almighty power to do, but to exalt it by its influence on reason alone.—STATUTE OF RELIGIOUS FREEDOM. viii, 454. FORD ED., ii, 238. (1779.)

5237. MIND, Qualities of.—I estimate the qualities of the mind; 1, good humor; 2, integrity; 3, industry; 4, science. The preference of the first to the second quality may not at first be acquiesced in; but certainly we had all rather associate with a good-humored, light-principled man, than with an ill-tempered rigorist in morality.—To DR. BENJAMIN RUSH. v, 225. (W., 1808.)

5238. MINERALOGISTS IN AMERICA.—I have never known in the United

States but one eminent mineralogist, who could have been engaged on hire. This was a Mr. Goudon from France, who came over to Philadelphia six or seven years ago.—To GOVERNOR NICHOLAS. vi, 588. (P.F., 1816.)

5239. MINERALOGY, Utility.—To learn * * * the ordinary arrangement of the different strata of minerals in the earth, to know from their habitual collocations and proximities, where we find one mineral; whether another, for which we are seeking, may be expected to be in its neighborhood, is useful. But the dreams about the modes of creation, enquiries whether our globe has been formed by the agency of fire or water, how many millions of years it has cost Vulcan or Neptune to produce what the fiat of the Creator would effect by a single act of will, is too idle to be worth a single hour of any man's life.—To DR. JOHN P. EMMETT. vii, 443. (M., 1826.)

5240. MINES, Federal Government and.—I am afraid we know too little as yet of the lead mines to establish a permanent system. I verily believe that of leasing will be far the best for the United States. But it will take time to find out what rent may be reserved, so as to enable the lessee to compete with those who work mines in their own right, and yet have an encouraging profit for themselves. Having on the spot two such men as Lewis and Bates, in whose integrity and prudence unlimited confidence may be placed, would it not be best to confide to them the whole business of leasing and regulating the management of our interests, recommending to them short leases, at first, till themselves shall become thoroughly acquainted with the subject, and shall be able to reduce the management to a system, which the government may then approve and adhere to? I think one article of it should be that the rent shall be paid in metal, not in mineral, so that we may have nothing to do with works which will always be mismanaged, and reduce our concern to a simple rent. We shall lose more by ill-managed smelting works than the digging the ore is worth. Then, it would be better that our ore remained in the earth than in a storehouse, and consequently we give nine-tenths of the ore for nothing. These thoughts are merely for your consideration.—To ALBERT GALLATIN. v, 210. (Nov. 1807.)

5241. —— ——. It is not merely a question about the terms we have to consider, but the expediency of working them.—To ALBERT GALLATIN. v, 290. (M., 1808.)

5242. —— ——. I received your favor covering an offer * * * of an iron mine to the public, and I thank you for * * * making the communication * * *. But having always observed that public works are much less advantageously managed than they are by private hands, I have thought it better for the public to go to market for whatever it wants which is to be found there; for there competition brings it down to the minimum of value. I have no doubt we can buy brass cannon at market cheaper than we could make iron ones. I think it material, too, not to abstract the high executive officers from those functions which nobody else is charged to carry on, and to employ them in superintending works which are going on abundantly in private hands. Our predecessors went on different principles; they bought iron mines, and sought for copper ones. We own a mine at Harper's Ferry of the finest iron ever put into a cannon, which we are afraid to attempt to work. We have rented it

heretofore, but it is now without a tenant.—To MR. BIBB. v, 326. (M., July 1808.)

5243. MINES, Silver.—I enclose for your information the account of a silver mine to fill your treasury.—To ALBERT GALLATIN. v, 245. (1808.)

5244. —— ——. With respect to the silver mine on the Platte, 1700 miles from St. Louis, I will observe that in the present state of things between us and Spain, we could not propose to make an establishment at that distance from all support. It is interesting, however, that the knowledge of its position should be preserved, which can be done either by confiding it to the government, who will certainly never make use of it without an honorable compensation for the discovery to yourself or your representatives, or by placing it wherever you think safest.—To ANTHONY G. BETTAY. v, 246. (W., 1808.)

5245. MINES, Virginia lead.—We take the liberty of recommending the lead mines to you as an object of vast importance. We great an extent. Considered as, perhaps, the think it impossible they can be worked to too sole means of supporting the American cause, they are inestimable. As an article of commerce to our Colony, too, they will be valuable; and even the wagonage, if done either by the Colony or individuals belonging to it, will carry to it no trifling sum of money.*—To GOVERNOR PATRICK HENRY. FORD ED., ii, 67. (July 1776.)

5246. MINISTERS (Foreign), Appointment and grade.—The Constitution having declared that the President shall *nominate* and, by and with the advice and consent of the Senate, shall *appoint*, ambassadors, other public ministers, and consuls, the President desired my opinion whether the Senate has a right to negative the *grade* he may think it expedient to use in a foreign mission as well as the *person* to be appointed. I think the Senate has no right to negative the *grade*. The Constitution has divided the powers of government into three branches, Legislative, Executive and Judiciary, lodging each with a distinct magistracy. The Legislative it has given completely to the Senate and House of Representatives. It has declared that the Executive powers shall be vested in the President, submitting only special articles of it to a negative by the Senate, and it has vested the Judiciary power in the courts of justice, with certain exceptions also in favor of the Senate. The transaction of business with foreign nations is Executive altogether. It belongs, then, to the head of that department, except as to such portions of it as are specially submitted to the Senate. Exceptions are to be construed strictly. The Constitution itself indeed has taken care to circumscribe this one within very strict limits; for it gives the *nomination* of the foreign agents to the President, the *appointments* to him and the Senate jointly, and the *commissioning* to the President. This analysis calls our attention to the strict import of each term. To *nominate* must be to *propose*. Appointment seems that act of the will which constitutes or makes the agent, and the *commission* is the public evidence of it. But there are still other acts previous to these not specially enumerated in the Constitution, to wit: 1st. The destination of a mission to the particular country where the public service calls for it, and 2nd,

* A note in the FORD EDITION says this paper was evidently intended to be signed by the whole Virginia delegation.—EDITOR.

the character or grade to be employed in it. The natural order of all these is first, destination; second, grade; third, nomination; fourth, appointment; fifth, commission. If *appointment* does not comprehend the neighbor ng acts *nomination* or *commission* (and the Con:titution says it shall not, by giving them exclusively to the President), still less can it pretend to comprehend those previous and more remote, of *destination* and *grade*. The Constitut:on, analyzing the three last, shows they do not comprehend the two first. The fourth is the only one it submits to the Senate. Shaping it into a right to say that " A or B is unfit to be appointed ". Now, this cannot comprehend a right to say that A or B is indeed fit to be appointed, but the grade fixed on is not the fit one to employ, or, " our connections with the country of his destination are not such as to call for any mission ". The Senate is not supposed by the Constitution to be acquainted with the concerns of the Executive Department. It was not* intended that these should be communicated to them, nor can they, therefore, be qualified to judge of the necessity which calls for a mission to any particular place, or of the particular grade, more or less marked, which special and secret circumstances may call for. All this is left to the President. They are only to see that no unfit person be employed. It may be objected that the Senate may by continual negatives on the *person*, do what amounts to a negative on the *grade*, and so, indirectly, defeat this right of the President. But this would be a breach of trust; an abuse of the power confided to the Senate, of which that body cannot be supposed capable. So the President has power to convoke the Legislature, and the Senate might defeat that power by refusing to come. This equally amounts to a negative on the power of convoking. Yet nobody will say they possess such a negative, or would be capable of usurping it by such oblique means. If the Constitution had meant to give the Senate a negative on the grade, or destination, as well as on the person, it would have said so in direct terms, and not left it to be effected by a sidewind. It could never mean to give them the use of one power through the abuse of another.—OPINION ON POWERS OF THE SENATE. vii, 465. FORD ED., v, 161. (1790.)

5247. —— ——. The Secretary of State recapitulated [to a committee of the Senate] the circumstances which justified the President's having continued the grade of Minister Plenipotentiary [at The Hague]; but added, that whenever the biennial bill should come on, each House would have a constitutional right to review the establishment again, and whenever it should appear that either House thought any part of it might be reduced, on giving to the Executive time to avail themselves of the first convenient occasion to reduce it, the Executive could not but do it; but that it would be extremely injurious * * * to do it so abruptly as to occasion the recall of ministers, or unfriendly sensations in any of those countries with which our commerce is interesting.—THE ANAS. ix, 422. FORD ED., i, 172. (January 1792.)

5248. —— ——. After mature consideration and consultation, I am of opinion that the

* In one of the two editions of JEFFERSON'S WRITINGS, quoted in this work, " not " is omitted. The MS. copy of the opinion which, with the other papers of Jefferson, is preserved in the Department of State, was examined in order to verify the text. Jefferson wrote " it was *not* intended".—EDITOR.

Constitution has made the President the sole competent judge to what places circumstances render it expedient that ambassadors, or other public ministers, should be sent, and of what grade they should be; and that it has ascribed to the Senate no executive act but the single one of giving or withholding their consent to the person nominated. I think it my duty, therefore, to protest, and do protest against the validity of any resolutions of the Senate asserting or implying any right in that House to exercise a..y executive authority, but the single one before mentioned.—PARAGRAPH FOR PRESIDENT'S MESSAGE. FORD ED., v, 415. (1792.)

5249. MINISTERS (Foreign), Exchange of.—I doubt whether it be honorable for us to keep anybody at London unless they keep some person at New York.—To W. S. SMITH. ii, 284. (P., 1787.)

5250. —— ——. The President * * * authorized Mr. Gouverneur Morris to enter into conference with the British ministers in order to discover their sentiments on the exchange of a minister. The letters of Mr. Morris * * * [to the President] state the communications, oral and written, which have passed between him and the ministers; and from these the Secretary of State draws the following inference: That * * * their Secretary for Foreign Affairs is disposed to exchange a minister, but meets with opposition in his Cabinet, so as to render the issue uncertain. The Secretary of State is of opinion that Mr. Morris's letters remove any doubts which might have been entertained as to the intentions and dispositions of the British Cabinet; that it would be dishonorable to the United States, useless and even injurious, to renew the propositions for * * * the exchange of a minister, and that this subject should now remain dormant, till it shall be brought forward earnestly by them.—OFFICIAL REPORT. vii, 517. FORD ED., v, 261. (December 1790.)

5251. —— ——. You have placed the British proposition of exchanging a minister on proper ground. It must certainly come from them, and come in unequivocal form. With those who respect their own dignity so much. ours must not be counted at naught. On their own proposal formally, to exchange a minister we sent them one. They have taken no notice of that, and talk of agreeing to exchange one now, as if the idea were new. Besides, what they are saying to you, they are talking to us through Quebec; but so informally, that they may disavow it when they please.—To GOUVERNEUR MORRIS. iii, 182. FORD ED., v, 224. (N. Y., Aug. 1790.)

5252. MINISTERS (Foreign). Extraordinary expenses.—With respect to the extraordinary expenses which you may be under the necessity of incurring at the coronation, I am not authorized to give any advice. * * * I should certainly suppose that the representative of the United States at Madrid, was to do as the representatives of other sovere'gnties do, and that it would be viewed as the compliment of our nation and not of its minister. If this be the true point of view, it proves at whose expense it should be.—To WILLIAM CARMICHAEL. FORD ED., v, 125. (P., 1789.)

5253. MINISTERS (Foreign), Outfit of.—When Congress made their first appointments of ministers to be resident in Europe, I have understood (for I was not then in Congress) that they allowed them all their expenses, and a fixed sum over and above for their time. Among their expenses was necessarily understood their outfit. Afterwards they thought proper to give them fixed salaries of eleven thousand one hundred and eleven dollars and one-ninth a year; and again by a resolution of May the 6th and 8th, 1784, the "salaries" of their ministers at foreign courts were reduced to nine thousand dollars, to take place on the 1st of August ensuing. On the 7th of May, I was appointed in addition to Mr. Adams and Dr. Franklin, for the negotiation of treaties of commerce; but this appointment being temporary, for two years only, and not as of a resident minister, the article of outfit did not come into question. I asked an advance of six months' salary, that I might be in cash to meet the first expenses, which was ordered. The year following I was appointed to succeed Dr. Franklin at this court [France]. This was the first appointment of a minister resident, since the original ones, under which all expenses were to be paid. So much of the ancient regulation as respected annual expenses had been altered to a sum certain; so much of it as respected first expenses, or outfit, remained unaltered; and I might, therefore, expect that the actual expenses for outfit were to be paid. When I prepared my account for settlement with Mr. Barclay, I began a detail of the articles of clothing, carriage, horses, and household furniture. I found they were numerous, minute, and incapable from their nature of being vouched; and often entered in my memorandum book under a general head only, so that I could not specify them. I found they would exceed a year's salary. Supposing, therefore, that mine being the first case, Congress would make a precedent of it, and prefer a sum fixed for the outfit as well as the salary, I have charged it in my account at a year's salary; presuming that there can be no question that an outfit is a reasonable charge. It is the usage here (and I suppose at all courts), that a minister resident shall establish his house in the first instant. If this is to be done out of his salary, he will be a twelvemonth, at least, without a copper to live on. It is the universal practice, therefore, of all nations to allow the outfit as a separate article from the salary. I have enquired here into the usual amount of it. I find that sometimes the sovereign pays the actual cost. This is particularly the case of the Sardinian ambassador now coming here, who is to provide a service of plate, and every article of furniture and other matters of first expense, to be paid for by his court. In other instances, they give a service of plate, and a fixed sum for all other articles, which fixed sum is in no case lower than a year's salary. I desire no service of plate, having no ambition for splendor. My furniture, carriage and apparel are all plain, yet they have cost me more than a year's salary. I suppose that in every country, and in every condition of life, a year's expense would be found a moderate measure for the furniture of a man's house. It is not more certain to me that the sun will rise tomorrow, than that our government must allow the outfit on their future appointment of foreign ministers; and it would be hard on me so to stand between the discontinuance of a former rule, and institution of a future one, as to have the benefit of neither.—To JOHN JAY. ii, 401. (P., 1788.)

5254. —— ——. The outfit given to ministers resident to enable them to furnish their house, but given by no nation to a temporary minister, who is never expected to take a house or to entertain, but considered on the footing of a *voyageur*, our predecessors gave to their extraordinary ministers by the wholesale. In the beginning of our administration, among other articles of reformation in expense, it was determined not to give an outfit to ministers extraordinary, and not to incur the expense with any minister of sending a frigate to carry or bring him. The Boston happened to be going to the Mediterranean, and was permitted, therefore, to take up Mr. Livingston, and touch in a port of France. A frigate was denied to Charles Pinckney, and has been refused to Mr. King for his return. Mr. Madison's friendship and mine to you being so well known, the public will have eagle eyes to watch if we grant you any indulgences out of the general rule; and on the other hand, the example set in your case [as Minister Extraordinary to France] will be more cogent on future ones, and produce greater approbation to our conduct. The allowance, therefore, will be in this, and all similar cases, all the expenses of your journey and voyage, taking a ship's cabin to yourself, nine thousand dollars a year from your leaving home till the proceedings of your mission are terminated, and then the quarter's salary for the expenses of your return, as prescribed by law.—To JAMES MONROE. iv, 455. FORD ED., viii, 191. (W., 1803.)

5255. MINISTERS (Foreign), **Privileges.**—Legal provision should be made for protecting and vindicating those privileges and immunities to which foreign ministers, and others attending on Congress are entitled by the law of nations.—CONGRESS RESOLUTION. FORD ED., iii, 463. (April 1784.)

5256. —— ——. Foreign ministers are not bound to an acquaintance with the laws of the land. They are privileged by their ignorance of them. They are bound by the laws of natural justice only.—To WILLIAM SHORT. FORD ED., v, 246. (M., 1790.)

5257. —— ——. Every person, diplomatic *in his own right,* is entitled to the privileges of the law of nations, in his own right. Among these is the receipt of all packages unopened and unexamined by the country which receives him. The usage of nations has established that this shall liberate whatever is imported *bonâ fide* for his own use, from paying duty. A government may control the number of diplomatic characters it will receive; but if it receives them it cannot control their rights while *bonâ fide* exercised. Thus Dr. Franklin, Mr. Adams, Colonel Humphreys and myself, all residing at Paris at the same time, had all of us our importation duty free. Great Britain had an ambassador and a minister plenipotentiary there, and an ambassador extra for several years; all three had their entries free. In most countries this privilege is permanent. Great Britain is niggardly, and allows it only on the first arrival. But in this, as she treats us only as *she does* the most favored nations, so we should treat her as *we do* the most favored nations. If these principles are correct, Mr. Foster is duty free.—To ALBERT GALLATIN. iv, 588. (W., 1805.)

5258. MINISTERS (Foreign), Reception of.—The Secretary of State has the honor to inform the Minister of France that the President will receive his letters of credence to-day at half after two: that this will be done in a room of private audience, without any ceremony whatever, or other person present than the Secretary of State, this being the usage which will be observed. As the Secretary of State will be with the President before that hour on business, the Minister will find him there.—To JEAN BAPTISTE TERNANT. FORD ED., v, 370. (Pa., 1791.)

5259. —— ——. The reception of the minister at all * * * (in favor of which Colonel Hamilton has given his opinion, though reluctantly, as he confessed), is an acknowledgment of the legitimacy of their [the French] government.—OPINION ON FRENCH TREATIES. vii, 616. FORD ED., vi, 223. (1793.)

5260. —— ——. It has been said without contradiction, and the people have been made to believe, that the refusal of the French to receive our Envoys was contrary to the law of nations, and a sufficient cause of war; whereas, every one who has ever read a book on the law of nations knows, that it is an unquestionable right in every power to refuse any minister who is personally disagreeable.—To EDMUND PENDLETON. iv, 289. FORD ED., vii, 359. (Pa., 1799.)

5261. —— ——. The Constitution has made the Executive the organ for managing our intercourse with foreign nations. It authorizes him to appoint and receive ambassadors, other public ministers, and consuls. The term minister being applicable to other agents as well as diplomatic, the constant practice of the government, considered as a commentary, established this broad meaning; and the public interest approves it; because it would be extravagant to employ a diplomatic minister for a business which a mere rider would execute. The Executive being thus charged with the foreign intercourse, no law has undertaken to prescribe its secific duties.—To ALBERT GALLATIN. iv, 520. (1804.)

5262. MINISTERS (Foreign), Rejection.—The public interest certainly made the rejection of Chevalier de Onis expedient, and as that is a motive which it is not pleasant always to avow, I think it fortunate that the contending claims of Charles and Ferdinand furnished such plausible embarrassment to the question of right; for, on our principles, I presume, the right of the Junta to send a minister could not be denied.—To PRESIDENT MADISON. v, 480. (M., Nov. 1809.)

5263. MINISTERS (Foreign), Revolutions and.—Whenever the scene [Paris during Revolution] became personally dangerous to you, it was proper you should leave it, as well from personal as public motives. But what degree of danger should be awaited, to what distance or place you should retire, are circumstances which must rest with your own discretion, it being impossible to prescribe them from hence.—To GOUVERNEUR MORRIS. iii, 489. FORD ED., vi, 131. (Pa., Nov. 1792.)

5264. MINISTERS (Foreign), Rotation in.—I think it possible that it will be established into a maxim of the new government to discontinue its foreign servants after a certain time of absence from their own country, because they lose in time that sufficient degree of intimacy with its circumstances which alone can enable them to know and pursue its interests. Seven years have been talked of.—To WILLIAM SHORT. FORD ED., v, 244. (M., 1790.)

5265. MINISTERS (Foreign), Salaries.—You have doubtless heard of the complaints of our foreign ministers as to the incompetency of their salaries. I believe it would be better

were they somewhat enlarged. Yet a moment's reflection will satisfy you that a man may live in any country on any scale he pleases, and more easily in that [France] than this, because there the grades are more distinctly marked. From the ambassador there a certain degree of representation is expected. But the lower grades of Envoy, Minister, Resident, Chargé, have been introduced to accommodate both the sovereign and missionary as to the scale of expense. I can assure you from my own knowledge of the ground, that these latter grades are left free in the opinion of the place to adopt any style they please, and that it does not lessen their estimation or their usefulness. When I was at Paris, two-thirds of the diplomatic men of the second and third orders entertained nobody. Yet they were as much invited out and honored as those of the same grades who entertained. * * * This procures one some sunshine friends who like to eat of your good things, but has no effect on the men of real business, the only men of real use to you, in a place where every man is estimated at what he really is.—To GENERAL JOHN ARMSTRONG. FORD ED., viii, 302. (W., 1804.)

—— MINISTERS (Foreign), Secretaries of Legation and.—See SUMTER.

5266. MINISTERS (Foreign), Verbal communications.—Verbal communications are very insecure; for it is only necessary to deny them or to change their terms, in order to do away their effect at any time. Those in writing have many and obvious advantages, and ought to be preferred.—To THOMAS PINCKNEY. iv, 63. FORD ED., vi, 416. (Pa., 1793.) See DIPLOMATIC ESTABLISHMENT.

5267. MINISTERS (Imperial).—What are their [Kings] ministers but a committee, badly chosen?—To BENJAMIN HAWKINS. ii, 221. FORD ED., iv, 426. (P., 1787.)

5268. MINISTERS (Imperial), Politic.—Ministers and merchants love nobody. The merchants here [France] are endeavoring to exclude us from their [West India] islands. The ministers will be governed in it by political motives, and will do it, or not do it, as these shall appear to dictate, without love or hatred to anybody.—To JOHN LANGDON. i, 429. (P., 1785.)

5269. MINISTERS (Religious), Fearless of.—You judge truly that I am not afraid of the priests. They have tried upon me all their various batteries, of pious whining, hypocritical canting, lying and slandering, without being able to give me one moment of pain.—To HORATIO GATES SPAFFORD. FORD ED., x, 13. (M., 1816.)

5270. MINISTERS (Religious), French.—The Curés throughout the [French] Kingdom form the mass of the clergy. They are the only part favorably known to the people, because solely charged with the duties of baptism, burial, confession, visitation of the sick, instruction of the children, and aiding the poor. They are themselves of the people, and united with them. The carriages and equipage only of the higher clergy, not their persons, are known to the people, and are in detestation with them.—To JAMES MADISON. iii, 58. (P., 1789.)

5271. —— ——. Nor should we wonder at * * * [the] pressure [for a fixed constitution in 1788-9] when we consider the monstrous abuses of power under which * * * the

[French] people were ground to powder; when we pass in review * * * the riches, luxury, indolence and immorality of the clergy.—Auto-biography. i, 86. Ford ed., i, 118. (1821.)

5272. MINISTERS (Religious), Hostility to Jefferson.—The delusion into which the X. Y. Z. plot shows it possible to push the people; the successful experiment made under the prevalence of that delusion on the clause of the Constitution, which, while it secured the freedom of the press, covered also the freedom of religion, had given to the clergy a very favorite hope of obtaining an establishment of a particular form of Christianity through the United States; and as every sect believes its own form the true one, every one, perhaps hoped for his own, but especially the Episcopalians and Congregationalists. The returning good sense of our country threatens abortion to their hopes, and they believe that any portion of power confided to me, will be exercised in opposition to their schemes. And they believe rightly; for I have sworn upon the altar of God eternal hostility against every form of tyranny over the mind of man. But this is all they have to fear from me; and enough, too, in their opinion. And this is the cause of their printing lying pamphlets against me, forging conversations for me with Mazzei, Bishop Madison, &c., which are absolute falsehoods without a circumstance of truth to rest on; falsehoods, too, of which I acquiet Mazzei and Bishop Madison for they are men of truth. But enough of this. It is more than I have before committed to paper on the subject of all the lies that have been preached and printed against me.—To Dr. Benjamin Rush. iv, 336. Ford ed., vii, 460. (M., Sep. 1800.)

5273. MINISTERS (Religious), Liberty and.—In every country and in every age, the priest has been hostile to liberty. He is always in alliance with the despot, abetting his abuses in return for protection to his own.—To Horatio G. Spafford. vi, 334. (M., 1814.)

5274. MINISTERS (Religious), New England.—The sway of the clergy in New England is indeed formidable. No mind beyond mediocrity dares there to develop itself. If it does, they excite against it the public opinion which they command, and by little, but incessant and tearing persecutions, drive it from among them. Their present emigrations to the Western country are real flights from persecution, religious and political, but the abandonment of the country by those who wish to enjoy freedom of opinion leaves the despotism over the residue more intense, more oppressive.— To Horatio Gates Spafford. Ford ed., x, 13. (M., 1816.)

5275. —— ——. The advocate of religious freedom is to expect neither peace nor forgiveness from the New England clergy.—To Levi Lincoln. iv, 427. Ford ed., viii, 129. (1802.) See Church, Church and State, Clergy, and Religion.

5276. MINORITY, Censorship by.—A respectable minority [in Congress] is useful as censors. The present one is not respectable, being the bitterest remains of the cup of federalism, rendered desperate and furious by despair.—To Joel Barlow. iv, 437. Ford ed., viii, 149. (W., May 1802.)

5277. MINORITY, Equal rights of.— Bear in mind this sacred principle that * * * the minority possess their equal rights, which

equal laws must protect, and to violate which would be oppression.—First Inaugural Address. viii, 2. Ford ed., viii, 2. (1801.)

5278. MINORITY, Sacrifices to.—The minorities [against the new Constitution] in most of the accepting States have been very respectable; so much so as to render it prudent, were it not otherwise reasonable, to make some sacrifice to them.—To General Washington. ii, 533. Ford ed., v, 56. (P., 1788.)

5279. —— ——. The minorities [against the new Constitution] are too respectable, not to be entitled to some sacrifice of opinion; especially when a great proportion of them would be contented with a bill of rights.—To James Madison. ii, 506. Ford ed., v, 53. (P., Nov. 1788.)

5280. MINT, Establishment of.—The propositions* under consideration [by Congress] suppose that the coinage is to be carried on in a foreign country, and that the implements are to remain the property of the undertaker; which conditions, in the opinion [of the Secretary of State] render them inadmissible, for these reasons: Coinage is peculiarly an attribute of sovereignty. To transfer its exercise into another country, is to submit it to another sovereign. Its transportation across the ocean, besides the ordinary dangers of the sea, would expose it to acts of piracy, by the crews to whom it would be confided, as well as by others apprized of its passage. In time of war, it would offer to the enterprises of an enemy what have been emphatically called the sinews of war. If the war were with the nation within whose territory the coinage is, the first act of war, or reprisal, might be to arrest this operation, with the implements and materials coined and uncoined, to be used at their discretion. The reputation and principles of the present undertaker are safeguards against the abuses of a coinage, carried on in a foreign country, where no checks could be provided by the proper sovereign, no regulations established, no police, no guard exercised; in short, none of the numerous cautions hitherto thought essential at every mint; but in hands less entitled to confidence, these will become dangers. We may be secured, indeed, by proper experiments as to the purity of the coin delivered us according to contract, but we cannot be secured against that which, though less pure, shall be struck in the general die, and protected against the vigilance of Government, till it shall have entered into circulation. We lose the opportunity of calling in and recoining the clipped money in circulation, or we double our risk by a double transportation. We lose, in like manner, the resource of coining up our household plate in the instant of great distress. We lose the means of forming artists to continue the works, when the common accidents of mortality shall have deprived us of those who began them. In fine, the carrying on a coin-

*The question was referred to Jefferson by the House of Representatives.—Editor.

age in a foreign country, as far as the Secretary knows, is without example; and general example is weighty authority. He is, therefore, of opinion, on the whole, that a mint, whenever established, should be established at home.—COINAGE REPORT. vii, 463. (April 1790.)

5281. MIRAGE AT MONTICELLO.— The elevation and particular situation at Monticello afford an opportunity of seeing a phenomenon which is rare at land, though frequent at sea. The seamen call it *looming*. Philosophy is as yet in the rear of the seamen, for so far from having accounted for it, she has not given it a name. Its principal effect is to make distant objects appear larger, in opposition to the general law of vision, by which they are diminished. I know an instance, at Yorktown, from whence the water prospect eastwardly is without termination, wherein a canoe with three men, at a great distance was taken for a ship with its three masts. I am little acquainted with the phenomenon as it shows itself at sea; but at Monticello it is familiar. There is a solitary mountain about forty miles off in the South, whose natural shape, as presented to view there, is a regular cone; but by the effect of looming, it sometimes subsides almost totally in the horizon; sometimes it rises more acute and more elevated; sometimes it is hemispherical; and sometimes its sides are perpendicular, its top flat, and as broad as its base. In short, it assumes at times the most whimsical shapes, and all these perhaps successively in the same morning. The Blue Ridge of mountains comes into view, in the north-east, at about one hundred miles distance, and approaching in a direct line, passes by within twenty miles, and goes off to the south-west. This phenomenon begins to show itself on these mountains at about fifty miles distance, and continues beyond that as far as they are seen. I remark no particular state, either in the weight, moisture, or heat of the atmosphere, necessary to produce this. The only constant circumstances are its appearance in the morning only, and on objects at least forty or fifty miles distant. In this latter circumstance, if not in both, it differs from the looming on the water. Refraction will not account for the metamorphosis. That only changes the proportions of length and breadth, base and altitude, preserving the general outlines. Thus it may make a circle appear elliptical, raise or depress a cone, but by none of its laws, as yet developed, will it make a circle appear a square, or a cone a sphere.—NOTES ON VIRGINIA. viii, 327. FORD ED., iii, 186. (1782.)

5282. MIRANDA EXPEDITION, Jefferson's knowledge of.— That the expedition of Miranda was countenanced by me, is an absolute falsehood, let it have gone from whom it might; and I am satisfied it is equally so as to Mr. Madison. To know as much of it as we could was our duty, but not to encourage it.—To WILLIAM DUANE. iv, 592. FORD ED., viii, 433. (W., 1806.)

5283. ⸺ ⸺. Your predecessor, soured on a question of etiquette against the administration of this country, wished to impute wrong to them in all their actions, even where he did not believe it himself. In this spirit, he wished it to be believed that we were in unjustifiable cooperation in Miranda's expedition. I solemnly, and on my personal truth and honor, declare to you. that this was entirely without foundation, and that there was neither cooperation, nor connivance on our part. He informed

us he was about to attempt the liberation of his native country from bondage, and intimated a hope of our aid, or connivance at least. He was at once informed, that although we had great cause of complaint against Spain, and even of war, yet whenever we should think proper to act as her enemy, it should be openly and above board, and that our hostility should never be exercised by such petty means. We had no suspicion that he expected to engage men here, but merely to purchase military stores. Against this there was no law, nor consequently any authority for us to interpose obstacles. On the other hand, we deemed it improper to betray his voluntary communication to the agents of Spain. Although his measures were many days in preparation at New York, we never had the least intimation or suspicion of his engaging men in his enterprise, until he was gone; and. I presume, the secrecy of his proceeding kept them equally unknown to the Marquis Yrujo at Philadelphia, and the Spanish consul at New York, since neither of them gave us any information of the enlistment of men, until it was too late for any measures taken at Washington to prevent their departure. The officer in the customs, who participated in the transaction with Miranda, we immediately removed, and should have had him and others further punished, had it not been for the protection given them by private citizens at New York, in opposition to the government, who, by their impudent falsehoods and calumnies, were able to overbear the minds of the jurors.—To DON VALENTINE DE FORONDA. v, 474. FORD ED., ix, 25c. (M., Oct. 1809.)

5284. MIRANDA EXPEDITION, Prosecutions.— On the prosecution of Ogden and Smith for participation in Miranda's expedition, the defendants and their friends have contrived to make it a government question, in which they mean to have the Administration and the judge tried as the culprits instead of themselves. Swartwout, the marshal to whom, in his duel with Clinton, Smith was second, and his bosom friend, summoned a panel of jurors, the greater part of which were of the bitterest federalists. His letter, too, covering to a friend a copy of Aristides,* and affirming that every fact in it was true as Holy Writ [was considered in Cabinet]. Determined unanimously that he be removed.—THE ANAS. FORD ED., i, 316. (May 1806.)

5285. MISFORTUNE, Pleasure and.— Pleasure is always before us; but misfortune is at our side; while running after that, this arrests us.—To MRS. COSWAY. ii, 37. FORD ED., iv, 317. (P., 1786.)

5286. MISFORTUNE, Solace in.— I most cordially sympathize in your losses. It is a situation in which a man needs the aid of all his wisdom and philosophy. But as it is better to turn from the contemplation of our misfortunes to the resources we possess of extricating ourselves, you will, of course, have found solace in your vigor of mind, health of body. talents, habits of business, in the consideration that you have time yet to retrieve everything, and a knowledge that the very activity necessary for this, is a state of greater happiness than the unoccupied one to which you had a thought of retiring.—To DR. CURRIE. ii, 218. (P., 1787.)

5287. MISSIONARIES, Foreign.— I do not know that it is a duty to disturb by missionaries the religion and peace of other

* W. P. Van Ness, who wrote a pamphlet in favor of Burr.—EDITOR.

countries, who may think themselves bound to extinguish by fire and fagot the heresies to which we give the name of conversions, and quote our own example for it.—To Mr. Me-gear. vii, 287. (M., 1823.)

5288. MISSISSIPPI RIVER NAVIGA-TION, Absolute cession.—The navigation of the Mississippi we must have. This is all we are as yet ready to receive.—To Archibald Stuart. i, 518. Ford ed., iv, 189. (P., Jan. 1786.)

5289. ——— ———. A cession of the navigation of the Mississippi, with such privileges as to make it useful, and free from future chicane, can be no longer dispensed with on our part.— To William Short. iii, 223. Ford ed., v, 299. (Pa., 1791.)

5290. MISSISSIPPI RIVER NAVIGA-TION, Congress and.—The affair of the Mississippi, by showing that Congress is capable of hesitating on a question, which proposes a clear sacrifice of the western to the maritime States, will with difficulty be obliterated. The proposition of my going to Madrid to try to recover there the ground which has been lost at New York, by the concession of the vote of seven States, I should think desperate.—To James Madison. ii, 153. Ford ed., iv, 392. (P., 1787.)

5291. ——— ———. I was pleased to see the vote of Congress, of September the 16th, on the subject of the Mississippi, as I had before seen, with great uneasiness, the pursuits of other principles, which I could never reconcile to my own ideas of probity or wisdom, and from which, and my knowledge of the character of our western settlers, I saw that the loss of that country was a necessary consequence. I wish this return to true policy may be in time to prevent evil.—To James Madison. ii, 563. Ford ed., v, 63. (P., 1789.)

5292. MISSISSIPPI RIVER NAVIGA-TION, Law of nature and.—But our right is built on ground still broader and more un-questionable, to wit: On the law of nature and nations. If we appeal to this, as we feel it written in the heart of man, what sentiment is written in deeper characters than that the ocean is free to all men, and their rivers to all their inhabitants? Is there a man, savage or civilized, unbiased by habit, who does not feel and attest this truth? Accordingly, in all tracts of country united under the same political society, we find this natural right universally acknowledged and protected by laying the navigable rivers open to all their inhabitants. When their rivers enter the limits of another society, if the right of the upper inhabitants to descend the stream is in any case obstructed, it is an act of force by a stronger society against a weaker, condemned by the judgment of mankind. The late case of Antwerp and the Scheldt was a striking proof of a general union of sentiment on this point; as it is believed that Amsterdam had scarcely an advocate out of Holland, and even there its pretensions were advocated on the ground of treaties, and not of natural right. * * * The Commissioners will be able perhaps to find, either in the practice or the pretensions of Spain as to the Douro, Tagus, and Guadiana, some acknowledgments of this principle on the part of that nation. This sentiment of right in favor of the upper inhabitants must become stronger in the pro-portion which their extent of country bears to the lower. The United States hold 600,000

square miles of habitable territory on the Mis-sissippi and its branches, and this river and its branches afford many thousands of miles of navigable waters penetrating this territory in all its parts. The inhabitable grounds of Spain below our boundary, and bordering on the river, which alone can pretend any fear of being incommoded by our use of the river, are not the thousandth part of that extent. This vast portion of the territory of the United States has no other outlet for its productions, and these productions are of the bulkiest kind. And in truth, their passage down the river may not only be innocent as to the Spanish subjects on the river, but cannot fail to enrich them far beyond their present condition. The real in-terests then of all the inhabitants, upper and lower, concur in fact with their rights. If we appeal to the law of nature and nations, as ex-pressed by writers on the subject, it is agreed by them, that, were the river, where it passes between Florida and Louisiana, the exclusive right of Spain, still an innocent passage along it is a natural right in those inhabiting its bor-ders above. It would indeed be what those writers call an imperfect right, because the modification of its exercise depends in a con-siderable degree on the conveniency of the nation through which they are to pass. But it is still a right as real as any other right, however well-defined; and were it to be refused, or to be so shackled by regulations, not neces-sary for the peace or safety of its inhabitants, as to render its use impracticable to us, it would then be an injury, of which we should be entitled to demand redress. The right of the upper inhabitants to use this navigation is the counterpart to that of those possessing the shore below, and founded in the same natural relations with the soil and water. And the line at which their rights meet is to be advanced or withdrawn, so as to equalize the inconve niences resulting to each party from the ex-ercise of the right by the other. This estimate is to be fairly made, with a mutual disposition to make equal sacrifices, and the numbers on each side are to have their due weight in the es-timate. Spain holds so very small a tract of habitable land on either side below our bound-ary, that it may in fact be considered as a strait of the sea; for though it is eighty leagues from our boundary to the mouth of the river, yet it is only here and there, in spots and slips, that the land rises above the level of the water in times of inundation. There are, then, and ever must be, so few inhabitants on her part of the river, that the freest use of its naviga-tion may be admitted to us without their an-noyance.—Mississippi River Instructions. vii, 577. Ford ed., v, 467. (1792.)

5293. MISSISSIPPI RIVER NAVIGA-TION, Sectional opposition.—It is true, there were characters whose stations entitled them to credit, and who, from geographical prejudices, did not themselves wish the naviga-tion of the Mississippi to be restored to us, and who believe, perhaps, as is common with mankind, that their opinion was the general opinion. But the sentiments of the great mass of the Union were decidedly otherwise then, and the very persons to whom M. Gardoqui alluded, have now come over to the opinion heartily, that the navigation of the Mississippi, in full and unrestrained freedom, is indispensably necessary, and must be obtained by any means it may call for.—To William Carmichael. iii, 246. (Pa., 1791.)

5294. MISSISSIPPI RIVER NAVIGA-TION, Spain and.—In the course of the

Revolutionary War, in which the thirteen colonies, Spain and France, were opposed to Great Britain, Spain took possess on of several posts held by the British in Florida. It is unnecessary to inquire whether the possession of half a dozen posts scattered through a country of seven or eight hundred miles extent, could be considered as the possession and conquest of that country. If it was, it gave still but an inchoate right, as was before explained, which could not be perfected but by the relinquishment of the former possession at the close of the war; but certainly it could not be cons dered as a conquest *of the river,* even against Great Britain, since the possession of the shores, to wit, of the island of New Orleans on the one side, and Louisiana on the other, having undergone no change, the right in the water would remain the same, if considered in its relation to them; and if considered as a distinct right, independent of the shores, then no naval victories obtained by Spain over Great Britain, in the course of the war, gave her the color of conquest over any water which the British fleet could enter. Still less can she be considered as having conquered the river, as against the United States, with whom she was not at war. We had a common right of navigation in the part of the river between Florida, the island of New Orleans, and the western bank, and nothing which passed between Spain and Great Britain, either during the war or at its conclusion, could lessen that right. Accordingly, at the treaty of November, 1782, Great Britain confirmed the rights of the United States to the navigation of the river, from its source to its mouth, and in January, 1783, completed the right of Spain to the territory of Florida, by an absolute relinquishment of all her rights in it. This relinquishment could not include the navigation held by the United States in their own right, because this right existed in themselves only, and was not in Great Britain. If it added anything to the rights of Spain respecting the river between the eastern and western banks, it could only be that portion of right which Great Britain had retained to herself in the treaty with the United States, held seven weeks before, to wit, a right of using it in common with the United States. So that as by the treaty of 1763, the United States had obtained a common right of navigating the whole river from its source to its mouth, so by the treaty of 1782, that common right was confirmed to them by the only power who could pretend claims against them, founded on the state of war; nor has that common right been transferred to Spain by either conquest or cession.—MISSISSIPPI RIVER INSTRUCTIONS. vii, 576. FORD ED., v, 466. (1792.)

5295. MISSISSIPPI RIVER NAVIGATION, Treaty of Paris and.—The war of 1755-1763, was carried on jointly by Great Britain and the Thirteen Colonies, now the United States of America, against France and Spain. At the peace which was negotiated by our common magistrate, a right was secured to the subjects of Great Britain (the common designation of all those under his government) to navigate the Mississippi in its whole breadth and length, from its source to the sea, and expressly that part which is between the Island of New Orleans and the right bank of the river, as well as the passage both in and out of its mouth; and that the vessels should not be stopped, visited, or subjected to the payment of any duty whatsoever. These are the words of the treaty, article VII. Florida was at the same time ceded by Spain, and its extent westwardly

was fixed to the Lakes Pontchartrain and Maurepas, and the River Mississippi; and Spain received soon after from France a cession of the island of New Orleans, and all the country she held westward of the Mississippi, subject. of course, to our right of navigating between that country and the island previously granted to us by France. This right was not parcelled out to us in severalty, that is to say, to each the exclusive navigation of so much of the river as was adjacent to our several shores, in which way it would have been useless to all; but it was placed on that footing, on which alone it could be worth anything, to wit: as a right to all to navigate the whole length of the river in common. The import of the terms, and the reason of the thing, prove it was a right of common in the whole, and not a several right to each of a particular part. To which may be added the evidence of the stipulation itself, that we should navigate between New Orleans and the western bank, which, being adjacent to none of our States, could be held by us only as a right of common. Such was the nature of our right to navigate the Mississippi, as far as established by the Treaty of Paris.—MISSISSIPPI RIVER INSTRUCTIONS. vii, 575. FORD ED., v, 466. (1792.)

5296. MISSISSIPPI RIVER NAVIGATION, Western people and.—The difficulty on which the negotiation with Spain hangs is a *sine qua non* with us. It would be to deceive them and ourselves, to suppose that an amity can be preserved while this right is withheld. Such a supposition would argue not only an ignorance of the people to whom this is most interesting, but an ignorance of the nature of man, or an inattention to it. Those who see but half way into our true interest will think that that concurs with the views of the other party. But those who see it in all its extent, will be sensible that our true interest will be best promoted, by making all the just claims of our fellow citizens, wherever situated, our own, by urging and enforcing them with the weight of our whole influence, and by exercising in this, as in every other instance, a just government in their concerns, and making common cause even where our separate interest would seem opposed to theirs. No other conduct can attach us together; and on this attachment depends our happiness.—To JAMES MONROE. i, 605. FORD ED., iv, 262. (P., 1786.)

5297. ———— ————. If they declare themselves a separate people, we are incapable of a single effort to retain them. Our citizens can never be induced, either as militia or as soldiers, to go there to cut the throats of their own brothers and sons, or rather, to be themselves the subjects, instead of the perpetrators of the parricide. Nor would that country requite the cost of being retained against the will of its inhab.tants, could it be done. But it cannot be done. They are able already to rescue the navigation of the Mississippi out of the hands of Spain, and to add New Orleans to their own territory. They will be joined by the inhabitants of Louisiana. This will bring on a war between them and Spain; and that will produce the question with us, whether it will not be worth our while to become parties with them in the war, in order to reunite them with us, and thus correct our error? And were I to permit my forebodings to go one step further, I should predict that the inhabitants of the United States would force their rulers to take the affirmative of that question.—To JAMES MADISON. ii, 106. FORD ED., iv, 363. (P., 1787.)

5298. —— ——. I never had any interest westward of the Alleghany; and I never will have any. But I have had great opportunities of knowing the character of the people who inhabit that country; and I will venture to say, that the act which abandons the navigation of the Mississippi is an act of separation between the eastern and western country. It is a relinquishment of five parts out of eight of the territory of the United States; an abandonment of the fairest subject for the payment of our public debts, and the chaining those debts on our necks, *in perpetuum.*—To JAMES MADISON. ii, 105. FORD ED., iv, 363. (P., 1787.)

5299. —— ——. The navigation of the Mississippi was perhaps the strongest trial to which the justice of the Federal Government could be put. If ever they thought wrong about it, I trust they have got to rights. I should think it proper for the Western country to defer pushing their right to that navigation to extremity as long as they can do without it tolerably; but that the moment it becomes absolutely necessary for them, it will become the duty of the maritime States to push it to every extremity to which they would their own right of navigating the Chesapeake, the Delaware, the Hudson, or any other water.—To JOHN BROWN. ii, 395. FORD ED., v, 17. (P., May 1788.)

5300. —·—— ——. It is impossible to answer for the forbearance of our western citizens. We endeavor to quiet them with the expectation of an attainment of their rights by peaceable means. But should they, in a moment of impatience, hazard others, there is no saying how far we may be led; for neither themselves nor their rights will be ever abandoned by us.— To WILLIAM CARMICHAEL. iii, 173. FORD ED., v, 217. (N.Y., 1790.)

5301. —— ——. The navigation of the Mississippi is necessary to us. More than half the territory of the United States is on the waters of that river. Two hundred thousand of our citizens are settled on them, of whom forty thousand bear arms. These have no other outlet for their tobacco, rice, corn, hemp, lumber, house timber, ship timber. We have hitherto respected the indecision of Spain, because we wish peace;—because our western citizens have had vent at home for their productions. A surplus of production begins now to demand foreign markets. Whenever they shall say, " We cannot, we will not, be longer shut up ", the United States will be reduced to the following dilemma: 1. To force them to acquiescence. 2. To separate from them, rather than take part in a war against Spain. 3. Or to preserve them in our Union, by joining them in the war. The 1st is neither in our principles, nor in our power. 2. A multitude of reasons decide against the second. It may suffice to speak but one: were we to give up half our territory rather than engage in a just war to preserve it, we should not keep the other half long. The third is the alternative we must adopt.— INSTRUCTIONS TO WILLIAM CARMICHAEL. ix, 412. FORD ED., v, 225. (1790.) See LOUISIANA and NEW ORLEANS.

5302. MISSISSIPPI TERRITORY, Government of.—As to the people you are to govern, we are apprised that they are divided into two adverse parties, the one composed of the richer and better informed, attached to the first grade of government, the other of the body of the people, not a very homogeneous mass, advocates for the second grade which they possess in fact. Our love of freedom, and the

value we set on self-government dispose us to prefer the principles of the second grade, and they are strengthened by knowing they are [faded in MS.] by the will of the majority. While cooperation with that plan, therefore, is essentially to be observed, your best endeavors should be exerted to bring over those opposed to it by every means soothing and conciliatory. The happiness of society depends so much on preventing party spirit from infecting the common intercourse of life, that nothing should be spared to harmonize and amalgamate the two parties in social circles.—To WILLIAM C. CLAIBORNE. FORD ED., viii, 71. (W., July 1801.) See LOUISIANA.

5303. MISSOURI, Admission of.—I rejoice that * * * Missouri is at length a member of our Union. Whether the question it excited is dead, or only sleepeth, I do not know. I see only that it has given resurrection to the Hartford Convention men. They have had the address, by playing on the honest feelings of our former friends, to seduce them from their kindred spirits, and to borrow their weight into the Federal scale. Desperate of regaining power under political distinctions, they have adroitly wriggled into its seat under the auspices of morality, and are again in the ascendency from which their sins had hurled them. * * * I still believe that the Western extension of our Confederacy will insure its duration, by overruling local factions, which might shake a smaller association.—To HENRY DEARBORN. vii, 215. FORD ED., x, 191. (M., 1821.)

5304. MISSOURI QUESTION, A breaker.—The banks, bankrupt law, manufactures, Spanish treaty, are nothing. These are occurrences which, like waves in a storm, will pass under the ship. But the Missouri question is a breaker on which we lose the Missouri country by revolt, and what more, God only knows. From the battle of Bunker's Hill to the treaty of Paris, we never had so ominous a question. * * * I thank God that I shall not live to witness its issue.*—To JOHN ADAMS. vii, 148. FORD ED., x, 151. (M., December 1819.)

5305. MISSOURI QUESTION, Federalists and.—Nothing has ever presented so threatening an aspect as what is called the Missouri question. The federalists, completely put down and despairing of ever rising again under the old divisions of Whig and Tory, devised a new one of slave-holding and non-slave-holding States, which, while it had a semblance of being moral, was at the same time geographical, and calculated to give them ascendency by debauching their old opponents to a coalition with them. Moral the question certainly is not, because the re-

* Mr. Adams replied as follows: " The Missouri question, I hope, will follow the other waves under the ship, and do no harm. I know it is high treason to express a doubt of the perpetual duration of our vast American empire, and our free institution; and I say as devoutly as father Paul, *esto perpetua,* but I am sometimes Cassandra enough to dream, that another Hamilton, and another Burr, might rend this mighty fabric in twain, or perhaps into a leash; and a few more choice spirits of the same stamp, might produce as many nations in North America as there are in Europe."—EDITOR.

moval of slaves from one State to another, no more than their removal from one country to another, would never make a slave of one human being who would not be so without it. Indeed, if there were any morality in the question it is on the other side; because by spreading them over a larger surface their happiness would be increased, and the burden for their future liberation lightened by bringing a greater number of shoulders under it. However, it served to throw dust into the eyes of the people and to fanaticize them, while to the knowing ones it gave a geographical and preponderant line of the Potomac and Ohio, throwing fourteen States to the North and East, and ten to the South and West. With these, therefore, it is merely a question of power; but with this geographical minority it is a question of existence. For if Congress once goes out of the Constitution to arrogate a right of regulating the condition of the inhabitants of the States, its majority may, and probably will, next declare that the condition of all men within the United States shall be that of freedom; in which case all the whites south of the Potomac and Ohio must evacuate their States, and most fortunate those who can do it first. And so far this crisis seems to be advancing.—To ALBERT GALLATIN. FORD ED., x, 177. (M., Dec. 1820.)

5306. MISSOURI QUESTION, Geographical line.—I am so completely withdrawn from all attention to public matters, that nothing less could arouse me than the definition of a geographical line, which on an abstract principle is to become the line of separation of these States, and to render desperate the hope that man ever enjoys the two blessings of peace and self-government. The question sleeps for the present, but is not dead.—To H. NELSON. vii, 151. FORD ED., x, 156. (M., March 1820.)

5307. ——. I congratulate you on the sleep of the Missouri question. I wish I could say in its death, but of this I despair. The idea of a geographical line once suggested will brood in the minds of all those who prefer the gratification of their ungovernable passions to the peace and union of their country.—To MARK LANGDON HILL. vii, 155. (M., April 1820.)

5308. ——. This momentous question, like a fire bell in the night, awakened and filled me with terror. I considered it at once as the knell of the Union. It is hushed, indeed, for the moment. But this is a reprieve only, not a final sentence. A geographical line, coinciding with a marked principle, moral and political, once conceived and held up to the angry passions of men, will never be obliterated; and every new irritation will mark it deeper and deeper.—To JOHN HOLMES. vii, 159. FORD ED., x, 157. (M., April 1820.)

5309. MISSOURI QUESTION, A Party trick.—The Missouri question is a mere party trick. The leaders of federalism, defeated in their schemes of obtaining power by rallying partisans to the principle of monarchism, a principle of personal not of local division, have changed their tack, and thrown out another barrel to the whale. They are taking advantage of the virtuous feelings of the people to effect a division of parties by a geographical line; they expect that this will insure them, on local principles, the majority they could never obtain on principles of federalism; but they are still putting their shoulder to the wrong wheel; they are wasting Jeremiads on the miseries of slavery, as if we were advocates for it. Sincerity in their declamations should direct their efforts to the true point of difficulty, and unite their counsels with ours in devising some reasonable and practicable plan of getting rid of it. Some of these leaders, if they could attain the power, their ambition would rather use it to keep the Union together, but others have ever had in view its separation. If they push it to that, they will find the line of separation very different from their 36° of latitude, and as manufacturing and navigating States, they will have quarreled with their bread and butter, and I fear not that after a little trial they will think better of it and return to the embraces of their natural and best friends. But this scheme of party I leave to those who are to live under its consequences. We who have gone before have performed an honest duty, by putting in the power of successors a state of happiness which no nation ever before had within their choice. If that choice is to throw it away, the dead will have neither the power nor the right to control them.—To CHARLES PINCKNEY. vii, 180. FORD ED., x, 162. (M., 1820.)

5310. MISSOURI QUESTION, Portentous.—The Missouri question is the most portentous one which ever yet threatened our Union. In the gloomiest moment of the Revolutionary war I never had any apprehensions equal to what I feel from this source.—To HUGH NELSON. FORD ED., x, 156. (M., Feb. 1820.)

5311. ——. Last and most portentous of all is the Missouri question. It is smeared over for the present; but its geographical demarcation is indelible. What it is to become I see not.—To SPENCER ROANE. vii, 212. FORD ED., x, 189. (M., 1821.)

5312. MISSOURI QUESTION, Presidential politics.—The boisterous sea of liberty is never without a wave, and that from Missouri is now rolling towards us, but we shall ride over it as we have over all others. It is not a moral question, but one merely of power. Its object is to raise a geographical principle for the choice of a President, and the noise will be kept up till that is effected.—To MARQUIS LAFAYETTE. vii, 194. FORD ED., x, 180. (M., 1820.)

5313. ——. Nothing disturbs us so much as the dissension lately produced by what is called the Missouri question; a question having just enough of the semblance of morality to throw dust into the eyes of the people and to fanaticize; while with the knowing ones it is simply a question of power.—To D. B. Warden. Ford ed., x, 172. (M., Dec. 1820.)

5314. MISSOURI QUESTION, Separation.—The Missouri question aroused and filled me with alarm. The old schism of federal and republican threatened nothing, because it existed in every State, and united them together by the fraternism of party. But the coincidence of a marked principle, moral and political, with a geographical line, once conceived, I feared would never more be obliterated from the mind; that it would be recurring on every occasion and renewing irritations, until it would kindle such mutual and mortal hatred, as to render separation preferable to eternal discord. I have been among the most sanguine in believing that our Union would be of long duration. I now doubt it much, and see the event at no great distance, and the direct consequence of this question; not by the line which has been so confidently counted on; the laws of nature control this; but by the Potomac, Ohio and Missouri, or more probably, the Mississippi upwards to our northern boundary. My only comfort and confidence is, that I shall not live to see this; and I envy not the present generation the glory of throwing away the fruits of their fathers' sacrifices of life and fortune, and of rendering desperate the experiment which was to decide ultimately whether man is capable of self-government. This treason against human hope, will signalize their epoch in future history, as the counterpart of the medal of their predecessors.—To William Short. vii, 158. (M., April 1820.)

5315. —— ——. Should the schism [on the Missouri question] be pushed to separation it will be for a short term only; two or three years' trial will bring them back, like quarrelling lovers to renewed embraces, and increased affections. The experiment of separation would soon prove to both that they had mutually miscalculated their best interests. And even were the parties in Congress to secede in a passion, the soberer people would call a convention and cement again the severance attempted by the insanity of their functionaries. With this consoling view, my greatest grief would be for the fatal effect of such an event on the hopes and happiness of the world. We exist, and are quoted, as standing proofs that a government, so modelled as to rest continually on the will of the whole society, is a practicable government. Were we to break to pieces, it would damp the hopes and the efforts of the good, and give triumph to those of the bad through the whole enslaved world. As members, therefore, of the universal society of mankind, and standing in high and responsible relation with them, it is our sacred duty to suppress passion among ourselves, and not to blast the confidence we have inspired of proof that a government of reason is better than one of force.—To Richard Rush. vii, 182. (M., 1820.)

5316. MISSOURI QUESTION, Slavery extension.—All know that permitting the slaves of the south to spread into the west will not add one being to that unfortunate condition, that it will increase the happiness of those existing, and by spreading them over a larger surface, will dilute the evil everywhere, and facilitate the means of getting finally rid of it, an event more anxiously wished by those on whom it presses than by the noisy pretenders to exclusive humanity. In the meantime, it is a ladder for rivals climbing to power.—To M. de Lafayette. vii, 194. Ford ed., x, 180. (M., 1820.)

5317. —— ——. A hideous evil, the magnitude of which is seen, and at a distance only, by the one party, and more sorely felt and sincerely deplored by the other, from the difficulty of the cure, divides us at this moment too angrily. The attempt by one party to prohibit willing States from sharing the evil, is thought by the other to render desperate, by accumulation, the hope of its final eradication. If a little time, however, is given to both parties to cool, and to dispel their visionary fears, they will see that concurring in sentiment as to the evil, moral and political, the duty and interest of both is to concur also in devising a practicable process of cure. Should time not be given, and the schism be pushed to separation, it will be for a short term only; two or three years' trial will bring them back, like quarrelling lovers to renewed embraces, and increased affections. The experiment of separation would soon prove to both that they had mutually miscalculated their best interests.— To Richard Rush. vii, 182. (M., October 1820.)

5318. —— ——. Our anxieties in this quarter [the South] are all concentrated in the question, what does the Holy Alliance in and out of Congress mean to do with us on the Missouri question? And this, by-the-bye, is but the name of the case, it is only the John Doe or Richard Roe of the ejectment. The real question, as seen in the States afflicted with this unfortunate population, is, are our slaves to be presented with freedom and a dagger? For if Congress has the power to regulate the conditions of the inhabitants of the States, within the States, it will be but another exercise of that power, to declare that all shall be free. Are we then to see again Athenian and Lacedemonian confederacies? To wage another Peloponnesian war to settle the ascendency between them? Or is this the tocsin of merely a servile war? That remains to be seen; but not, I hope, by you or me.—To John Adams. vii, 200. Ford ed., x, 186. (M., January 1821.)

5319. MOBS, Government and.—The mobs of great cities add just so much to the support of pure government, as sores do to the strength of the human body.—Notes on Virginia. viii, 406. Ford ed., iii, 269. (1782.)

5320. MOBS, Imaginary.—It is in the London newspapers only that exist those mobs and riots, which are fabricated to deter strangers from going to America. Your person will be sacredly safe and free from insult.—To MRS. SPROWLE. FORD ED., iv, 66. (P., 1785.)

5321. MOBS, Revolutionary.—For sometime mobs of ten, twenty and thirty thousand people collected daily, surrounded the Parliament House [in Paris], huzzaed the members, even entered the doors and examined into their conduct, took the horses out of the carriages of those who did well, and drew them home. The government thought it prudent to prevent these, drew some regiments into the neighborhood, multiplied the guards, had the streets constantly patrolled by strong parties, suspended privileged places, forbade all clubs, &c. The mobs have ceased; perhaps this may be partly owing to the absence of parliament.—To JOHN ADAMS. ii, 258. (P., Aug. 1787.) See BASTILE.

5322. MODERATION, Political.—A moderate conduct throughout, which may not revolt our new friends [the federalists], and which may give them tenets with us, must be observed.—To JOHN PAGE. iv, 378. (W., March 1801.)

5323. MODESTY, American.—There is modesty often which does itself injury. Our countrymen possess this. They do not know their own superiority.—To WILLIAM RUTLEDGE. ii, 350. FORD ED., v, 5. (P., 1788.)

5324. MONARCHY, Advocates for.—I know there are some among us who would now establish a monarchy. But they are inconsiderable in number and weight of character.—To JAMES MADISON. iii, 5. FORD ED., v, 83. (P., 1789.)

5325. ——— ———. It cannot be denied that we have among us a sect who believe that the English constitution contains whatever is perfect in human institutions; that the members of this sect have, many of them, names and offices which stand high in the estimation of our countrymen. I still rely that the great mass of our community is untainted with these heresies, as its head. On this I build my hope that we have not labored in vain, and that our experiment will still prove that men can be governed by reason.—To GEORGE MASON. iii, 209. FORD ED., v, 275. (Pa., 1791.)

5326. ——— ———. We have some names of note here who have apostatized from the true faith; but they are few indeed, and the body of our citizens pure and insusceptible of taint in their republicanism. Mr. Paine's answer to Burke will be a refreshing shower to their minds.—To BENJAMIN VAUGHAN. FORD ED., v, 334. (Pa., 1791.)

5327. ——— ———. There are high names* here in favor of [monarchy], but the publications in Bache's paper have drawn forth pretty generally expressions of the public sentiment on the subject, and I thank God to find they are, to a man, firm as a rock in their republicanism. I much fear that the honestest man of the party will fall a victim to his imprudence on this occasion, while another of them, from the mere caution of holding his tongue, and buttoning

* At this point a series of cipher figures is written on the margin, which, when translated, reads: "Adams, Jay, Hamilton, Knox. Many of the Cincinnati. The second says nothing. The third is open. Both are dangerous. They pant after union with England as the power which is to support their projects. and are most determined Anti-gallicans. It is prognosticated that our republic is to end with the president's life. But I believe they will find themselves all head and no body."—NOTE IN FORD EDITION.

himself up, will gain what the other loses.—To WILLIAM SHORT. FORD ED., v, 361. (Pa., 1791.)

5328. ——— ———. The ultimate object of all this increase of public debt, establishment of a paper money system, corruption of Congress, etc., is, it is charged, to prepare the way for a change from the present republican form of government to that of a monarchy, of which the English constitution is to be the model. That this was contemplated in the [Federal] Convention is no secret, because its partisans have made none of it. To effect it then was impracticable, but they are still eager after their object, and are predisposing everything for its ultimate attainment. So many of them have got into the Legislature, that, aided by the corrupt squadron of paper dealers, who are at their devotion, they make a majority in both houses. The republican party, who wish to preserve the government in its present form, are fewer in number. They are fewer even when joined by the two, three, or half dozen anti-federalists, who, though they dare not avow it, are still opposed to any General Government; but, being less so to a republican than a monarchical one, they naturally join those whom they think pursuing the lesser evil.—To PRESIDENT WASHINGTON. iii, 361. FORD ED., vi, 3. (Pa., May 1792.)

5329. ——— ———. While you [in France] are exterminating the monster aristocracy, and pulling out the teeth and fangs of its associate, monarchy, a contrary tendency is discovered in some here. A sect has shown itself among us, who declare they espoused our new Constitution not as a good and sufficient thing in itself, but only as a step to an English constitution, the only thing good and sufficient in itself, in their eyes. It is happy for us that these are preachers without followers, and that our people are firm and constant in their republican purity. You will wonder to be told that it is from the Eastward chiefly that these champions for a King, lords and commons, come. They get some important associates from New York, and are puffed up by a tribe of Agioteurs which have been hatched in a bed of corruption made up after the model of their beloved England. Too many of these stock-jobbers and king-jobbers have come into our Legislature, or rather too many of our Legislature have become stock-jobbers and king-jobbers. However, the voice of the people is beginning to make itself heard, and will probably cleanse their seats at the ensuing election. —To GENERAL LAFAYETTE. iii, 450. FORD ED., vi, 78. (Pa., 1792.)

5330. ——— ———. He [President Washington] said that as to the idea of transforming this government into a monarchy he did not believe there were ten men in the United States whose opinions were worth attention, who entertained such a thought. I told him there were many more than he imagined. I recalled to his memory a dispute at his own table * * * between General Schuyler, on one side, and Pinckney and myself on the other, wherein the former maintained the position, that hereditary descent was as likely to produce good magistrates as election. I told him, that though the people were sound, there was a numerous sect who had monarchy in contemplation; that the Secretary of the Treasury was one of these; that I had heard him say that this Constitution was a shilly-shally thing of mere milk and water, which could not last, and was only good as a step to something better. That when we reflected, that he had endeavored in the convention, to make an English constitution out of it, and when failing in that, we saw all his measures tending to bring it to the same thing, it was natural for us to be jealous; and particularly, when we saw that these measures had established corruption in the Legislature, where there was a squadron devoted to the nod of the Treasury, doing whatever he had directed, and ready to do what he should direct. That if the equilibrium of the three great bodies, Legislative, Executive, and Judiciary, could be preserved, if the Legislature could be kept independent, I should never fear the result of such a government; but that I could not but be uneasy when I saw that the Executive had swallowed up the Legislative branch. He said, that as to that interested spirit in the Legislature, it was what could not be avoided in any government, unless we were to exclude particular descriptions of men, such as the holders of the funds from all office. I told him, there was great difference between the little accidental schemes of self-interest, which would take place in every body of men, and influence their votes, and a regular system for forming a corps of interested persons who should be steadily at the orders of the Treasury.—THE ANAS. ix, 121. FORD ED., i, 204. (Oct. 1792.)

5331. —— ——. In the course of our [members of the Cabinet] conversation Knox, stickling for parade, got into great warmth and swore that our government must either be entirely new modeled or it would be knocked to pieces in less than ten years, and that, as it is at present, he would not give a copper for it; that it is the President's character, and not the written Constitution, which keeps it together.— THE ANAS. ix, 139. FORD ED., i, 222. (Feb. 1793.)

5332. —— ——. The aspect of our politics has wonderfully changed since you left us. In place of that noble love of liberty, and republican government which carried us triumphantly through the war, an Anglican, monarchical, aristocratical party has sprung up, whose avowed object is to draw over us the substance, as they have already done the forms of the British government. The mass of our citizens, however, remain true to their republican principles; the whole landed interest is republican, and so is a great mass of talents. Against us are the Executive, the Judiciary, two out of three branches of the Legislature, all the officers of the Government, all who want to be officers, all timid men who prefer the calm of despotism to the boisterous sea of liberty. British merchants and Americans trading on British capitals. speculators and holders in the banks and public funds, a contrivance invented for the purposes of corruption, and for assimilating us in all things to the rotten as well as the sound parts of the British model. It would give you a fever were I to name to you the apostates who have gone over to these heresies, men who were Samsons in the field and Solomons in the council, but who have had their heads shorn by * * * England. In short, we are likely to preserve the liberty we have obtained only by unremitting labors and perils. But we shall preserve it; and our mass of weight and wealth on the good side is so great, as to leave no danger that force will ever be attempted against us. We have only to awake and snap the Lilliputian cords with which they have been entangling us during the first sleep which succeeded our labors.—To PHILIP MAZZEI. iv, 139. FORD ED., vii, 75. (M., April 1796.) See MAZZEI.

5333. —— ——. It would seem that changes in the principles of our government are to be pushed till they accomplish a monarchy peaceably, or force a resistance which, with the aid of an army, may end in monarchy. Still, I hope that this will be peaceably prevented by the eyes of the people being opened, and the consequent effect of the elective principle.—To CHARLES PINCKNEY. FORD ED., vii, 398. (M., Oct. 1799.)

5334. —— ——. I know, indeed, that there are monarchists among us. One character of these is in theory only, and perfectly acquiescent in our form of government as it is, and not entertaining a thought of destroying it merely on their theoretic opinions. A second class, at the head of which is our quondam colleague [in the cabinet, Hamilton], are ardent for introduction of monarchy, eager for armies, making more noise for a great naval establishment than better patriots, who wish it on a rational scale only, commensurate to our wants and our means. This last class ought to be tolerated but not trusted.—To GENERAL HENRY KNOX. iv, 386. FORD ED., viii, 36. (W., March 1801.)

5335. MONARCHY, Colonists and.—I believe you may be assured, that an idea or desire of returning to anything like their [the Colonists'] ancient government, never entered into their heads.*—To DAVID HARTLEY. ii, 165. (P., 1787.)

5336. —— ——. I am satisfied that the King of England believes the mass of our people to be tired of their independence, and desirous of returning under his government, and that the same opinion prevails in the ministry and nation. They have hired their newswriters to repeat this lie in their gazettes so long, that they have become the dupes of it themselves.—To JOHN JAY. ii, 305. (P., 1787.)

5337. MONARCHY, Evils of.—If anybody thinks that kings, nobles or priests are good conservators of the public happiness, send him here [France]. It is the best school in the universe to cure him of that folly. He will see here, with his own eyes, that these descriptions of men are an abandoned confederacy against the happiness of the mass of the people. The omnipotence of their effect cannot be better proved than in this country particularly, where, notwithstading the finest soil upon earth, the finest climate under heaven, and a people of the most benevolent, the most gay and amiable character of which the human form is susceptible; where such a people, I say, surrounded by so many blessings from nature, are loaded with misery, by kings, nobles and priests, and by them alone.—To GEORGE WYTHE. ii, 7. FORD ED., iv, 268. (P., 1786.)

5338. —— ——. I am astonished at some people's considering a kingly government as a refuge [from the evils of the Confederation]. Advise such to read the fable of the frogs who solicited Jupiter for a king. If that does not put them to rights send them to Europe to see something of the trappings of monarchy, and I will undertake that every man shall go back thoroughly cured. If all the evils which can arise among us from the republican form of government from this day to the day of judgment could be put into a scale against what this country [France] suffers from its monarchical form in a week, or England in a month, the latter would predominate. Consider the

* David Hartley was the British agent in Paris.— EDITOR.

contents of the Red Book in England, or the Almanac Royale of France, and say what a people gain by monarchy. No race of kings has ever presented above one man of common sense in twenty generations. The best they can do is to leave things to their ministers, and what are their ministers but a committee, badly chosen? If the king ever meddles it is to do harm.—To BENJAMIN HAWKINS. ii, 220. FORD ED., iv, 426. (P., Aug. 1787.)

5339. ——— ———. I hear there are people among you who think the experience of our governments has already proved that republican government will not answer. Send those gentry here to count the blessings of monarchy. A king's sister, for instance, stopped on the road, and on a hostile journey, is sufficient cause for him to march immediately twenty thousand men to revenge this insult.—To JOSEPH JONES. ii, 249. FORD ED., iv, 438. (P., 1787.)

5340. ——— ———. There is scarcely an evil known in the European countries which may not be traced to their king, as its source, nor a good which is not derived from the small fibres of republicanism existing among them.— To GENERAL WASHINGTON. ii, 375. FORD ED., v, 8. (P., 1788.)

5341. MONARCHY, The Federal Convention and.—The want of some authority which should procure justice to the public creditors, and an observance of treaties with foreign nations, produced * * * the call of a convention of the States at Annapolis. Although, at this meeting, a difference of opinion was evident on the question of a republican or kingly government, yet, so generally through the States was the sentiment in favor of the former, that the friends of the latter confined themselves to a course of obstruction only, and delay, to everything proposed. They hoped, that nothing being done, and all things going from bad to worse, a kingly government might be usurped, and submitted to by the people, as better than anarchy and wars, internal and external, the certain consequences of the present want of a general government. The effect of their manœuvres, with the defective attendance of deputies from the States, resulted in the measure of calling a more general convention, to be held at Philadelphia. At this, the same party exhibited the same practices, and with the same views of preventing a government of concord, which they foresaw would be republican, and of forcing through anarchy their way to monarchy. But the mass of that convention was too honest, too wise, and too steady, to be baffled or misled by their manœuvres. One of these was a form of government proposed by Colonel Hamilton, which would have been in fact a compromise between the two parties of royalism and republicanism. According to this, the Executive and one branch of the Legislature were to be during good behavior, i. e. for life, and the governors of the States were to be named by these two prominent organs. This, however, was rejected; on which Hamilton left the Convention, as desperate, and never returned again, until near its conclusion. These opinions and efforts, secret or avowed, of the advocates for monarchy, had begotten great jealousy through the States generally; and this jealousy it was which excited the strong opposition to the conventional Constitution; a jealousy which yielded at last only to a general determination to establish certain amendments as barriers against a government either monarchical or consolidated.*—THE ANAS. ix, 89. FORD ED., i, 158. (1818.)

5342. MONARCHY, French Revolution and.—The failure of the French Revolution would have been a powerful argument with those who wish to introduce a king, lords, and commons here, a sect which is all head and no body.—To EDMUND PENDLETON. FORD ED., v, 358. (Pa., 1791.)

5343. ——— ———. President Washington added that he considered France as the sheet anchor of this country and its friendship as a first object. There are in the United States some characters of opposite principles; some of them are high in office, others possessing great wealth, and all of them hostile to France, and fondly looking to England as the staff of their hope. * * * They * * * have espoused [the Constitution] only as a stepping-stone to monarchy, and have endeavored to approximate it to that in its administration in order to render its final transition more easy. The successes of republicanism in France have given the coup de grace to their prospects, and I hope to their projects.—To WILLIAM SHORT. iii, 503. FORD ED., vi, 155. (Pa., 1793.)

5344. MONARCHY, Hamilton and.— [Alexander] Hamilton's financial system had then [1790] passed. It had two objects. First, as a puzzle, to exclude popular understanding and inquiry. Secondly, as a machine for the corruption of the Legislature; for he avowed the opinion, that man could be governed by one of two motives only, force or interest.† Force, he observed, in this country was out of the question; and the interests, therefore, of the members must be laid hold of, to keep the Legislature in unison with the Executive. And with grief and shame it must be acknowledged that his machine was not without effect; that even in this, the birth of our government, some members were found sordid enough to bend their duty to their interests, and to look after personal, rather than public good. * * * [The measures of Hamilton's financial system, —the Funding and United States Bank Acts,

* Jefferson added: "In what passed through the whole period of these conventions, I have gone on the information of those who were members of them, being myself absent on my mission to France." A note in the FORD EDITION reads: "No evidence whatever has been found to confirm Jefferson's account of this Convention * * *."—EDITOR.

† The subjoined extracts from Hamilton's Works set forth his principles of government in this respect:
"A vast majority of mankind is naturally biased by the motives of self-interest."—Hamilton's Works, ii, 10.
"The safest reliance of every government is on men's interests. This is a principle of human nature on which all political speculation, to be just, must be founded."—Hamilton's Works. ii, 298.
"We may preach until we are tired of the theme the necessity of disinterestedness in republics, without making a single proselyte."—Hamilton's Works. ii, 197.
"A small knowledge of human nature will convince us that with far the greatest part of mankind interest is the governing principle, and that almost every man is more or less under its influence. Motives of public virtue may for a time, or in particular instances, actuate men to the observance of a conduct purely disinterested, but they are not sufficient of themselves to produce a conformity to the refined dictates of social duty. Few men are capable of making a continual sacrifice of all views of profit, interest, or advantage, to the common good. It is in vain to exclaim against the depravity of human nature on this account; the fact is so, and we must in a great measure change the constitution of man before we can make it otherwise. No institution not built on the presumptive truth of these maxims can succeed."—Hamilton's Works. ii, 140.—EDITOR.

&c.,] added to the number of votaries to the Treasury, and made its Chief the master of every vote in the Legislature, which might give to the government the direction suited to his political views. I know well, and so must be understood, that' nothing like a majority in Congress had yielded to this corruption. Far from it. But a division, not very unequal, had already taken place in the honest part of that body, between the parties styled republican and federal. The latter being monarchists in principle, adhered to Hamilton of course, as their leader in that principle, and this mercenary phalanx added to them, ensured him always a majority in both Houses; so that the whole action of the Legislature was now under the direction of the Treasury. * * * By this combination, legislative expositions were given to the Constitution, and all the administrative laws were shaped on the model of England, and so passed. * * * Here then was the real ground of the opposition which was made to the course of administration. Its object was to preserve the Legislature pure and independent of the Executive, to restrain the administration to republican forms and principles, and not permit the Constitution to be construed into a monarchy, and to be warped in practice into all the principles and pollutions of their favorite English model. Nor was this an opposition to General Washington. He was true to the republican charge confided to him; and has solemnly and repeatedly protested to me, in our conversations that he would lose the last drop of his blood in support of it; and he did this the oftener, and with the more earnestness, because he knew my suspicions of Hamilton's designs against it, and wished to quiet them. For he was not aware of the drift, or of the effect of Hamilton's schemes. Unversed in financial projects, and calculations and budgets, his approbation of them was bottomed on his confidence in the man.—THE ANAS. ix, 91. FORD ED., i, 160, 164, 165. (1818.)

5345. —— ——. Hamilton was not only a monarchist, but for a monarchy bottomed on corruption. In proof of this, I will relate an anecdote, for the truth of which I attest the God who made me. Before the President [Washington] set out on his southern tour in April, 1791, he addressed a letter of the fourth of that month, from Mount Vernon, to the Secretaries of State, Treasury, and War, desiring that if any serious and important cases should arise during his absence, they would consult and act on them. And he requested that the Vice-President should also be consulted. This was the only occasion on which that officer was ever requested to take part in a cabinet question. Some occasion for consultation arising, I invited those gentlemen (and the Attorney-General as well as I remember), to dine with me, in order to confer on the subject. After the cloth was removed, and our question agreed and dismissed, conversation began on other matters, and, by some circumstance, was led to the British Constitution, on which Mr. Adams observed, " Purge that constitution of its corruption, and give to its popular branch equality of representation, and it would be the most perfect constitution ever devised by the wit of man ". Hamilton paused and said, " purge it of its corruption, and give to its popular branch equality of representation, and it would become an *impracticable* government; as it stands at present, with all its supposed defects, it is the most perfect government which ever existed ". And this was assuredly the exact line which separated the political

creeds of these two gentlemen. The one was for two hereditary branches and an honest elective one; the other for an hereditary King, with a House of Lords and Commons corrupted to his will, and standing between him and the people. THE ANAS. ix, 96. FORD ED., i, 165. (1818.)

5346. —— ——. Hamilton frankly avowed that he considered the British constitution, with all the corruptions of its administration, as the most perfect model of government which had ever been devised by the wit of man; professing however, at the same time, that the spirit of this country was so fundamentally republican that it would be visionary to think of introducing monarchy here, and that, therefore, it was the duty of its administrators to conduct it on the principles their constituents had elected.—To MARTIN VAN BUREN. vii, 371. FORD ED., x, 314. (M., 1824.)

5347. —— ——. Harper takes great pains to prove that Hamilton was no monarchist, by exaggerating his own intimacy with him, and the impossibility, if he was so, that he should not at some time have betrayed it to him. This may pass with uninformed readers, but not with those who have had it from Hamilton's own mouth. I am one of those, and but one of many. At my own table, in presence of Mr. Adams, Knox, Randolph and myself, in a dispute between Mr. Adams and himself, he avowed his preference of monarchy over every other government, and his opinion that the English was the most perfect model of government ever devised by the wit of man, Mr. Adams agreeing, " if its corruptions were done away "; while Hamilton insisted that " with these corruptions it was perfect, and without them it would be an impracticable government ". —To WILLIAM SHORT. vii, 389. FORD ED., x, 330. (M., 1825.)

5348. MONARCHY, Imitation of.— When on my return from Europe, I joined the government in March, 1790, at New York, I was much astonished, indeed, at the mimicry I found established of royal forms and ceremonies, and more alarmed at the unexpected phenomenon, by the monarchical sentiments I heard expressed and openly maintained in every company, executive and judiciary (General Washington alone excepted), and by a great part of the Legislature, save only some members who had been of the old Congress, and a very few of recent introduction. I took occasion, at various times, of expressing to General Washington my disappointment at these symptoms of a change of principle, and that I thought them encouraged by the forms and ceremonies which I found prevailing, not at all in character with the simplicity of republican government, and looking as if wishfully to those of European courts. His general explanations to me were, that when he arrived at New York to enter on the executive administration of the new government, he observed to those who were to assist him, that placed as he was in an office entirely new to him, unacquainted with the forms and ceremonies of other governments, still less apprised of those which might be properly established here, and himself perfectly indifferent to all forms, he wished them to consider and prescribe what they should be; and the task being assigned particularly to General Knox, a man of parade, and to Colonel Humphreys, who had resided sometime at a foreign court. They, he said, were the authors of the present regulations, and that others were proposed so highly strained that he absolutely rejected them. Attentive to the difference of opinion prevailing on this subject, when the term of his second election arrived, he called the heads of Departments together, observed to them the situation in which he had been at the commencement of the government, the advice he had taken and the course he had observed in compliance with it; that a proper occasion had now arrived of revising that course, of correcting it in any particulars not approved in experience; and he desired us to consult together, agree on any changes we should think for the better, and that he should willingly conform to what we should advise. We met at my office. Hamilton and myself agreed at once that there was too much ceremony for the character of our government, and particularly that the parade of the installation at New York ought not to be copied on the present occasion, that the President should desire the Chief Justice to attend him at his chambers, that he should administer the oath of office to him in the presence of the higher officers of the government, and that the certificate of the fact should be delivered to the Secretary of State to be recorded. Randolph and Knox differed from us, the latter vehemently; they thought it not advisable to change any of the established forms, and we authorized Randolph to report our opinions to the President. As these opinions were divided, and no positive advice given as to any change, no change was made.—To MARTIN VAN BUREN. vii, 367. FORD ED., x, 310. (M., 1824.)

5349. ———— ————. The forms which I had censured in my letter to Mazzei were perfectly understood by General Washington, and were those which he himself but barely tolerated. He had furnished me a proper occasion for proposing their reformation, and my opinion not prevailing, he knew I could not have meant any part of the censure for him.—To MARTIN VAN BUREN. vii, 368. FORD ED., x, 311. (M., 1824.)

5350. MONARCHY, Inimical to.—I was much an enemy to monarchies before I came to Europe. I am ten thousand times more so, since I have seen what they are.—To GENERAL WASHINGTON. ii, 375. FORD ED., v, 8. (P., 1788.)

5351. MONARCHY, Preference for.—I returned from the mission [to France] in the first year of the new government * * * and proceeded to New York to enter on the office of Secretary of State. Here, certainly, I found a state of things which, of all I had ever contemplated, I the least expected. I had left France in the first year of her Revolution, in the fervor of natural rights, and zeal for reformation. My conscientious devotion to these rights could not be heightened, but it had been aroused and excited by daily exercise. The President received me cordially, and my colleagues and the circle of principal citizens, apparently, with welcome. The courtesies of dinner parties given me, as a stranger newly arrived among them, placed me at once in their familiar society. But I cannot describe the wonder and mortification with which the table conversations filled me. Politics was the chief topic, and a preference of kingly, over republican, government was evidently the favorite sentiment. An apostate I could not be, nor yet a hypocrite; and I found myself, for the most part the only advocate on the republican side of the question, unless among the guests there chanced to be some member of that party

from the Legislative Houses.—THE ANAS. ix, 91. FORD ED., i, 159. (1818.)

5352. ———— ————. When I arrived at New York in 1790, to take a part in the administration, being fresh from the French Revolution, while in its first and pure stage, and consequently somewhat whetted up in my own republican principles, I found a state of things, in the general society of the place, which I could not have supposed possible. Being a stranger there, I was feasted from table to table, at large set dinners, the parties generally from twenty to thirty. The revolution I had left, and that we had just gone through in the recent change of our own government, being the common topics of conversation, I was astonished to find the general prevalence of monarchical sentiments, insomuch that in maintaining those of republicanism, I had always the whole company on my hands, never scarcely finding among them a single coadvocate in that argument, unless some old member of Congress happened to be present. The furthest that any one would go, in support of the republican features of our new government, would be to say, "the present Constitution is well as a beginning and may be allowed a fair trial; but it is, in fact, only a stepping stone to something better". Among their writers, [Joseph] Dennie, the editor of the "Portfolio", who was a kind of oracle with them, and styled "the Addison of America", openly avowed his preference of monarchy over all other forms of government, prided himself on the avowal, and maintained it by argument freely and without reserve in his publications. I do not myself know that the Essex Junta, of Boston, were monarchists, but I have always heard it so said, and never doubted. These are but detached items from a great mass of proofs then fully before the public. * * * They are now disavowed by the party. But, had it not been for the firm and determined stand then made by a counter party, no man can say what our government would have been at this day. Monarchy, to be sure, is now defeated, and they wish it should be forgotten that it was ever advocated. They see that it is desperate, and treat its imputation to them as a calumny; and I verily believe that none of them have it now in direct aim. Yet the spirit is not done away. The same party takes now what they deem the next best ground, the consolidation of the government; the giving to the Federal member of the Government, by unlimited constructions of the Constitution, a control over all the functions of the States, and the concentration of all power ultimately at Washington.—To WILLIAM SHORT. vii, 390. FORD ED., x, 332. (M., 1825.)

5353. MONARCHY, Throwing off.—With respect to the State of Virginia in particular, the people seem to have laid aside the monarchical, and taken up the republican form of government with as much ease as would have attended their throwing off an old and putting on a new suit of clothes. Not a single throe has attended this important transformation. A half-dozen aristocratical gentlemen, agonizing under the loss of preeminence, have sometimes ventured their sarcasms on our political metamorphosis. They have been thought fitter objects of pity than of punishment.—To BENJAMIN FRANKLIN. i, 204. FORD ED., ii, 131. (August 1777.)

5354. MONARCHY, Washington and.—I am satisfied that General Washington had not a wish to perpetuate his authority; but he who supposes it was practicable, had he wished it, knows nothing of the spirit of America, either of the people or of those who possessed their confidence. There was, indeed, a cabal of the officers of the army who proposed to establish a monarchy and to propose it to General Washington. He frowned indignantly at the proposition (according to the information which got abroad), and Rufus King and some few civil characters, chiefly (indeed, I believe, to a man) north of Maryland, who joined in this intrigue. But they never dared openly to avow it, knowing that the spirit which had produced a change in the form of government was alive to the preservation of it.—Notes on Marshall's Life of Washington. ix, 478. Ford ed., ix, 262.

5355. ——— ———. The next effort was (on suggestion of the same individuals, in the moment of their separation), the establishment of an hereditary order, under the name of the Cincinnati, ready prepared, by that distinction, to be engrafted into the future form of government, and placing General Washington still at their head. The General wrote to me on this subject, while I was in Congress at Annapolis. * * *[*] He afterwards called on me at that place, on his way to a meeting of the society, and after a whole evening of consultation, he left that place fully determined to use all his endeavors for its total suppression. But he found it so firmly riveted in the affections of the members that, strengthened as they happened to be by an adventitious occurrence of the moment [the arrival of the badges of the Order from France], he could effect no more than the abolition of its hereditary principle.* He called again on his return.† and explained to me fully the opposition which had been made, the effect of the occurrence from France, and the difficulty with which its duration had been limited to the lives of the present members.—The Anas. ix, 89. Ford ed., i, 157. (1818.) See Cincinnati Society.

5356. MONARCHY vs. REPUBLIC, —With all the defects of our Constitution, whether general or particular, the comparison of our governments with those of Europe, is like a comparison of heaven and hell. England, like the earth, may be allowed to take the intermediate station.—To J. Jones. ii, 249. (P., 1787.)

5357. ——— ———. We were educated in royalism; no wonder if some of us retain that idolatry still. Our young people are educated in republicanism; an apostasy from that to royalism, is unprecedented and impossible.— To James Madison. iii, 5. Ford ed., v, 83. (P., 1789.)

5358. MONEY, Circulating Medium.— The increase of circulating medium * * * according to my ideas of paper money, is clearly a demerit [in the bill providing for the establishment of a national bank.]—National Bank Opinion. vii, 558. Ford ed., v, 287. (1791.)

5359. ——— ———. The adequate price of a thing depends on the capital and labor nec-

* This is an error. The abolition of the hereditary principle was proposed, but never adopted.—Note in Ford Edition.
† This cannot be so, as Washington did not leave Philadelphia till after May 16th, and Jefferson left Annapolis for France on May 11th.—Note in Ford Edition.

essary to produce it. In the term *capital,* I mean to include science, because capital as well as labor has been employed to acquire it. Two things requiring the same capital and labor, should be of the same price. If a gallon of wine requires for its production the same capital and labor with a bushel of wheat, they should be expressed by the same price, derived from the application of a common measure to them. The comparative prices of things being thus to be estimated and expressed by a common measure, we may proceed to observe that were a country so insulated as to have no commercial interchange with any other, to confine the interchange of all its wants and supplies within itself, the amount of circulating medium, as a common measure for adjusting these exchanges, would be quite immaterial. If their circulation, for instance, were a million of dollars, and the annual produce of their industry equivalent to ten millions of bushels of wheat, the price of a bushel of wheat might be one dollar. If, then, by a progressive coinage, their medium should be doubled, the price of a bushel of wheat might become progressively two dollars. and without inconvenience. Whatever be the proportion of the circulating medium to the value of the annual produce of industry, it may be considered as the representative of that industry. In the first case, a bushel of wheat will be represented by one dollar; in the second, by two dollars. This is well explained by Hume, and seems to be admitted by Adam Smith. But where a nation is in a full course of interchange of wants and supplies with all others, the proportion of its medium to its produce is no longer indifferent.—To J. W. Eppes. vi, 233. Ford ed., ix, 406. (M., 1813.)

5360. ——— ———. One of the great advantages of specie as a medium is, that being of universal value, it will keep itself at a general level, flowing out from where it is too high into parts where it is lower. Whereas, if the medium be of local value only, as paper money, if too little, indeed, gold and silver will flow in to supply the deficiency; but if too much, it accumulates, banishes the gold and silver not locked up in vaults and hoards. and depreciates itself; that is to say, its proportion to the annual produce of industry being raised, more of it is required to represent any particular article of produce than in the other countries. This is agreed to by [Adam] Smith, the principal advocate for a paper circulation; but advocating it on the sole condition that it be strictly regulated. He admits, nevertheless, that "the commerce and industry of a country cannot be so secure when suspended on the Dædalian wings of paper money, as on the solid ground of gold and silver; and that in time of war, the insecurity is greatly increased, and great confusion possible where the circulation is for the greater part in paper". But in a country where loans are uncertain. and a specie circulation the only sure resource for them, the preference of that circulation assumes a far different degree of importance.—To J. W. EPPES. vi, 233. FORD ED., ix, 407. (M., Nov. 1813.)

5361. —— ——. The only advantage which [Adam] Smith proposes by substituting paper in the room of gold and silver money, B. 2. c. 2. 434, is "to replace an expensive instrument with one much less costly, and *sometimes* equally convenient"; that is to say, page 437, "to allow the gold and silver to be sent abroad and converted into foreign goods", and to substitute paper as being a cheaper measure. But this makes no addition to the stock or capital of the nation. The coin sent was worth as much, while in the country, as the goods imported and taking its place. It is only, then, a change of form in a part of the national capital, from that of gold and silver to other goods. He admits, too, that while a part of the goods received in exchange for the coin exported may be materials, tools and provisions for the employment of an additional industry, a part, also, may be taken back in foreign wines, silks, &c., to be consumed by idle people who produce nothing; and so far the substitution promotes prodigality, increases expense and corruption, without increasing production. So far also, then, it lessens the capital of the nation. What may be the amount which the conversion of the part exchanged for productive goods may add to the former productive mass, it is not easy to ascertain, because, as he says, page 441, "it is impossible to determine what is the proportion which the circulating money of any country bears to the whole value of the annual produce. It has been computed by different authors, from a fifth to a thirtieth of that value". In the United States it must be less than in any other part of the commercial world; because the great mass of their inhabitants being in responsible circumstances, the great mass of their exchanges in the country is effected on credit, in their merchants' ledger, who supplies all their wants through the year, and at the end of it receives the produce of their farms, or other articles of their industry. It is a fact that a farmer with a revenue of ten thousand dollars a year, may obtain all his supplies from his merchant, and liquidate them at the end of the year by the sale of his produce to him, without the intervention of a single dollar of cash. This, then, is merely barter, and in this way of barter a great portion of the annual produce of the United States is exchanged without the intermediation of cash. We might safely, then, state our medium at the minimum of one-thirtieth. —To J. W. EPPES. vi, 234. FORD ED., ix, 407. (M., Nov. 1813.)

5362. —— ——. But what is one-thirtieth of the value of the annual produce of the industry of the United States? Or what is the whole value of the annual produce of the United States? An able writer and competent judge of the subject, in 1799, on as good grounds as probably could be taken, estimated it, on the then population of four and a half millions of inhabitants, to be thirty-

seven and a half millions sterling, or one hundred and sixty-eight and three-fourths millions of dollars. According to the same estimate for our present population, it will be three hundred millions of dollars, one-thirtieth of which, Smith's minimum, would be ten millions, and one-fifth, his maximum, would be sixty millions for the quantum of circulation. But suppose that instead of our needing the least circulating medium of any nation, from the circumstance before mentioned, we should place ourselves in the middle term of the calculation, to wit: at thirty-five millions. One-fifth of this, at the least, Smith thinks, should be retained in specie, which would leave twenty-eight millions of specie to be exported in exchange for other commodities; and if fifteen millions of that should be returned in productive goods, and not in articles of prodigality, that would be the amount of capital which this operation would add to the existing mass. But to what mass? Not that of the three hundred millions, which is only its gross annual produce, but to that capital of which the three hundred millions are but the annual produce. But this being gross, we may infer from it the value of the capital by considering that the rent of lands is generally fixed at one-third of the gross produce, and is deemed its net profit, and twenty times that its fee simple value. The profits on landed capital may, with accuracy enough for our purpose, be supposed to be on a par with those of other capital. This would give us, then, for the United States, a capital of two thousand millions, all in active employment, and exclusive of unimproved lands lying in a great degree dormant. Of this, fifteen millions would be the hundred and thirty-third part. And it is for this petty addition to the capital of the nation, this minimum of one dollar, added to one hundred and thirty-three and a third or three-fourths per cent., that we are to give up our gold and silver medium, its intrinsic solidity, its universal value, and its saving powers in time of war, and to substitute for it paper, with all its train of evils, moral, political, and physical, which I will not pretend to enumerate. There is another authority to which we may appeal for the proper quantity of circulating medium for the United States. The old Congress, when we were estimated at about two millions of people, on a long and able discussion, June 22, 1775, decided the sufficient quantity to be two millions of dollars, which sum they then emitted,* According to this, it should be eight millions, now that we are eight millions of people. This differs little from Smith's minimum of ten millions, and strengthens our respect for that estimate.—To J. W. EPPES. vi, 234. FORD ED., ix, 408. (M., Nov. 1813.) See BANKS and DEBT.

5363. —— ——. Specie is the most perfect medium because it will preserve its own level;

* Within five months after this, they were compelled by the necessities of the war, to abandon the idea of emitting only an adequate circulation, and to make their necessities the sole measure of their emissions.—NOTE BY JEFFERSON.

because, having intrinsic and universal value, it can never die in our hands, and it is the surest resource of reliance in time of war.—To J. W. Eppes. vi, 246. Ford ed., ix, 416. (M., Nov. 1813.)

5364. —— ——. It would be best that our medium should be so proportioned to our produce, as to be on a par with that of the countries with which we trade, and whose medium is in a sound state.—To J. W. Eppes. vi, 246. Ford ed., ix, 416. (M., Nov. 1813.)

5365. —— ——. Instead of yielding to the cries of scarcity of medium set up by speculators, projectors and commercial gamblers, no endeavors should be spared to begin the work of reducing it by such gradual means as may give time to private fortunes to preserve their poise, and settle down with the subsiding medium.—To J. W. Eppes. vi, 246. Ford ed., ix, 417. (M., Nov. 1813.)

5366. —— ——. We are already at ten or twenty times the due quantity of medium; insomuch, that no man knows what his property is now worth, because it is bloating while he is calculating; and still less what it will be worth when the medium shall be relieved from its present dropsical state.—To J. W. Eppes. vi, 246. Ford ed., ix, 417. (M., Nov. 1813.)

5367. —— ——. This State [Virginia] is in a condition of unparalleled distress. The sudden reduction of the circulating medium from a plethora to all but annihilation is producing an entire revolution of fortune. In other places I have known lands sold by the sheriff for one year's rent; beyond the mountains we hear of good slaves selling for one hundred dollars, good horses for five dollars, and the sheriffs generally the purchasers. Our produce is now selling at market for one-third of its price before this commercial catastrophe, say flour at three and a quarter and three and a half dollars the barrel. We should have less right to expect relief from our legislators if they had been the establishers of the unwise system of banks. A remedy to a certain degree was practicable, that of reducing the quantum of circulation gradually to a level with that of the countries with which we have commerce, and an eternal abjuration of paper. * * * I fear local insurrections against these horrible sacrifices of property.—To H. Nelson. vii, 151. Ford ed., x, 156. (M., 1820.) See National Currency and Paper Money.

5368. MONEY, Clipped.—The Legislatures should cooperate with Congress in providing that no money be received or paid at their treasuries, or by any of their officers, or any bank, but on actual weight; in making it criminal, in a high degree, to diminish their own coins and, in some smaller degree, to offer them in payment when diminished.—Notes on a Money Unit. i, 169. Ford ed., iii, 453. (1784.)

5369. MONEY, Coinage.—The Administrator [Governor] shall not possess the pre-

rogative * * * of coining moneys, or regulating their values.—Proposed Va. Constitution. Ford ed., ii, 19. (June 1776.)

5370. —— ——. For rendering the half penny pieces of copper coin of this Commonwealth of more convenient value, and by that means introducing them into more general circulation; Be it enacted by the General Assembly of the Commonwealth of Virginia that * * * the said pieces of copper coin shall pass in all payments for one penny each of current money of Virginia. Provided * * * that no person shall be obliged to take above one shilling of * * * copper coin in any one payment of twenty shillings, or under, nor more than two shillings and six pence * * * in any one payment of a greater sum than twenty shillings.—Copper Coinage Bill. Ford ed., ii, 118. (1776.)

5371. —— ——. It is difficult to familiarize a new coin to the people; it is more difficult to familiarize them to a new coin with an old name.—Notes on a Money Unit. i, 165. Ford ed., iii, 449. (1784.) See Dollar.

5372. —— ——. A great deal of small change is useful in a State, and tends to reduce the price of small articles.—Notes on a Money Unit. i, 166. Ford ed., iii, 450. (1784.)

5373. —— ——. I think it my duty to inform Congress that a Swiss, of the name of Drost, established in Paris, has invented a method of striking the two faces and the edge of a coin, at one stroke. By this, and other simplifications of the process of coinage, he is enabled to coin from twenty-five to thirty thousand pieces a day, with the assistance of only two persons, the pieces of metal being first prepared. I send you by Colonel Franks three coins of gold, silver and copper, which you will perceive to be perfect medals; and I can assure you, from having seen him coin many, that every piece is as perfect as these. There has certainly never yet been seen any coin, in any country, comparable to this. The best workmen in this way, acknowledge that his is like a new art. Coin should always be made in the highest perfection possible, because it is a great guard against the danger of false coinage. This man would be willing to furnish his implements to Congress, and if they please, he will go over and instruct a person to carry on the work; nor do I believe he would ask anything unreasonable. It would be very desirable, that in the institution of a new coinage, we could set out on so perfect a plan as this, and the more so as while the work is so exquisitely done, it is done cheaper.—To John Jay. ii, 89. (P., Jan. 1787.)

5374. —— ——. Coinage is peculiarly an attribute of sovereignty. To transfer its exercise into another country, is to submit it to another sovereign.—Coinage Report. vii, 463. (April 1790.)

5375. —— ——. The carrying on a coinage in a foreign country, as far as the Secretary [of State] knows, is without example; and general experience is weighty authority.—COINAGE REPORT. vii, 464. (April 1790.)

5376. ——— ———. Perfection in the engraving is among the greatest safeguards against counterfeits, because engravers of the first class are few, and elevated by their rank in their art, and far above the base and dangerous business of counterfeiting.—COINAGE REPORT. vii, 463. (April 1790.)

5377. ——— ———. As to the question on whom the expense of coinage is to fall, I have been so little able to make up an opinion satisfactory to myself, as to be ready to concur in either decision.—To ALEXANDER HAMILTON. iii, 330. (1792.)

5378. MONEY, Foreign.—The quantity of fine silver which shall constitute the Unit being settled, and the proportion of the value of gold to that of silver; a table should be formed * * * classing the several foreign coins according to their fineness, declaring the worth of a pennyweight or grain in each class, and that they shall be lawful tenders at those rates, if not clipped or otherwise diminished; and, where diminished, offering their value for them at the mint, deducting the expense of recoinage.—NOTES ON A MONEY UNIT. i, 169. FORD ED., iii, 453. (1784.) See GOLD and SILVER.

5379. ——— ———. Most of the gold and silver coins of Europe pass in the several States of America according to the quantity of pure metal they contain.—M. DU RIVAL. ii, 52. (P., 1786.)

5380. ——— ———. A bill has passed the Representatives giving three years longer currency to foreign coins. * * * The effect of stopping the currency of gold and silver is to force bank paper through all the States. However, I presume the State Legislatures will exercise their acknowledged right of regulating the value of foreign coins, when not regulated by Congress, and their exclusive right of declaring them a tender.—To JAMES MONROE. FORD ED., vii, 183. (Pa., Dec. 1797.)

5381. ——— ———. By the Constitution Congress may regulate the value of foreign coin; but if they do not do it, the old power revives to the State, the Constitution only forbidding them to make anything but gold and silver a tender in payment of debts.—To JOHN TAYLOR. FORD ED., vii, 182. (Pa., 1797.)

5382. ——— ———. A bill has passed the Representatives to suspend for three years the law arresting the currency of foreign coins. The Senate proposed an amendment, continuing the currency of the foreign gold only. * * * The object of opposing the bill is to make the French crowns a subject of speculation (for it seems they fell on the President's proclamation to a dollar in most of the States) and to force bank paper (for want of other medium) through all the States generally.—To JAMES MADISON. iv, 205. FORD ED., vii, 189. (Pa., 1798.)

5383. MONEY, Legal tender.—I deny the power of the General Government of making paper money, or anything else, a legal tender.—To JOHN TAYLOR. iv, 260. FORD ED., vii, 310. (M., 1798.)

— **MONEY, Loaning.**—See TRADE.

5384. MONEY, Morality and.—Money, and not morality, is the principle of commercial nations.—To JOHN LANGDON. v, 513. (1810.)

5385. MONEY, National rights and.—Money is the agent by which modern nations will recover their rights.—To COMTE DE MOUSTIER. ii, 389. FORD ED., v, 12. (P., 1788.)

— **MONEY, Prices and.**—See PAPER MONEY.

5386. MONEY, Scarcity of.—An unparalleled want of money here, and stoppage of discount at all the banks, oblige the merchants to slacken the price of wheat and flour; but it is only temporary.—To GEORGE GILMER. FORD ED., vi, 202. (Pa., 1793.)

5387. MONEY, Standard.—I believe all the countries in Europe determine their standard of money in gold as well as silver. Thus, the laws of England direct that a pound Troy of gold, of twenty-two carats fine, shall be cut into forty-four and a half guineas, each of which shall be worth twenty-one and a half shillings, that is, into 956 3-4 shillings. This establishes the shilling at 5.518 grains of *pure* gold. They direct that a pound of silver, consisting of 11 1-10 ounces of pure silver and 9-10 of an ounce alloy, shall be cut into sixty-two shillings. This establishes the shilling at 85.93 grains of pure silver, and, consequently, the proportion of gold to silver as 85.93 to 5.518, or as 15.57 to 1. If this be the true proportion between the value of gold and silver at the general market of Europe, then the value of the shilling, depending on two standards, is the same, whether a payment be made in gold or in silver. But if the proportion of the general market at Europe be as fifteen to one, then the Englishman who owes a pound weight of gold at Amsterdam, if he sends the pound of gold to pay it, sends 1043.72 shillings; if he sends fifteen pounds of silver, he sends only 1030.5 shillings; if he pays half in gold and half in silver, he pays only 1037.11 shillings. And this medium between the two standards of gold and silver, we must consider as furnishing the true medium value of the shilling. If the parliament should now order the pound of gold (of one-twelfth alloy as before) to be put into a thousand shillings instead of nine hundred and fifty-six and three-fourths, leaving the silver as it is, the medium or true value of the shilling would suffer a change of half the difference; and in the case before stated, to pay a debt of a pound weight of gold, at Amsterdam, if he sent the pound weight of gold, he would send 1090.9 shillings; if he sent fifteen pounds of silver, he would send 1030.5 shillings; if half in gold and half in silver, he would send 1060.7 shillings; which shows that this parliamentary operation would reduce the value of the shilling in the proportion of 1060.7 to 1037.11.—To J. SARSFIELD. iii, 18. (P., April 1789.)

5388. —— ——. Now this is exactly the effect of the late change in the quantity of gold contained in your louis. Your *marc d'argent fin* is cut into 53.45 livres (fifty-three livres and nine sous), the *marc de l'or fin* was cut, heretofore, by law, into 784.6 livres (seven hundred and eighty-four livres and twelve sous); gold was to silver then as 14.63 to 1. And if this was different from the proportion at the markets of Europe, the true value of your livre stood half way between the two standards. By the ordinance of October the 30th, 1785, the *marc* of pure gold has been cut into 828.6 livres. If your standard had been in gold alone, this would have reduced the value of your livre in the proportion of 828.6 to 784.6. But as you had a standard of silver as well as gold, the true standard is the medium between the two; consequently the value of the livre is reduced only one-half the difference, that is as 806.6 to 784.6, which is very nearly three per cent. Commerce, however, has made a difference of four per cent., the average value of the pound sterling, formerly twenty-four livres, being now twenty-five livres. Perhaps some other circumstance has occasioned an addition of one per cent. to the change of your standard.—To J. SARSFIELD. iii, 19. (P., April 1789.)

5389. —— ——. To trade on equal terms, the common measure of values should be as nearly as possible on a par with that of its corresponding nations, whose medium is in a sound state; that is to say, not in an accidental state of excess or deficiency. Now, one of the great advantages of specie as a medium is, that being of universal value, it will keep itself at a general level, flowing out from where it is too high into parts where it is lower. Whereas, if the medium be of local value only, as paper money, if too little, indeed, gold and silver will flow in to supply the deficiency; but if too much, it accumulates, banishes the gold and silver not locked up in vaults and hoards, and depreciates itself; that is to say, its proportion to the annual produce of industry being raised, more of it is required to represent any particular article of produce than in the other countries. This is agreed by [Adam] Smith, (B. 2. c. 2. 437.) the principal advocate for a paper circulation; but advocating it on the sole condition that it be strictly regulated. He admits, nevertheless, that " the commerce and industry of a country cannot be so secure when suspended on the Dædalian wings of paper money, as on the solid ground of gold and silver; and that in time of war, the insecurity is greatly increased, and great confusion possible where the circulation is for the greater part in paper ". (B. 2. c. 2. 484.) But in a country where loans are uncertain, and a specie circulation the only sure re-

source for them, the preference of that circulation assumes a far different degree of importance.—To J. W. EPPES. vi, 233. FORD ED., ix, 407. (M., Nov. 1813.)

5390. —— ——. Our dropsical medium is long since divested of the quality of a medium of value; nor can I find any other. In most countries a fixed quantity of wheat is perhaps the best permanent standard. But here the blockade of our whole coast, preventing all access to a market, has depressed the price of that, and exalted that of other things, in opposite directions, and, combined with the effects of the paper deluge, leaves really no common measure of values to be resorted to.—To M. CORREA. vi, 406. (M., 1814.)

5391. —— ——. We have no metallic measure of values at present, while we are overwhelmed with bank paper. The depreciation of this swells nominal prices, without furnishing any stable index of real value.—To JEAN BAPTISTE SAY. vi, 434. (M., March 1815.)

5392. —— ——. We are now without any common measure of the value of property, and private fortunes are up or down at the will of the worst of our citizens. Yet there is no hope of relief from the Legislatures who have immediate control over this subject. As little seems to be known of the principles of political economy as if nothing had ever been written or practiced on the subject, or as was known in old times, when the Jews had their rulers under the hammer. It is an evil, therefore, which we must make up our minds to meet and to endure as those of hurricanes, earthquakes and other casualties.—To ALBERT GALLATIN. vi, 499. (M., Oct. 1815.)

5393. —— ——. The flood with which the banks are deluging us of nominal money has placed us completely without any certain measure of value, and, by interpolating a false measure, is deceiving and ruining multitudes of our citizens.—To ALBERT GALLATIN. FORD ED., x, 116. (M., 1818.)

5394. —— ——. There is one evil which awakens me at times, because it jostles me at every turn. It is that we have now no measure of value. I am asked eighteen dollars for a yard of broadcloth, which, when we had dollars, I used to get for eighteen shillings; from this I can only understand that a dollar is now worth but two inches of broadcloth, but broadcloth is no standard of measure or value. I do not know, therefore, whereabouts I stand in the scale of property, nor what to ask, or what to give for it. I saw, indeed, the like machinery in action in the years '80 and '81, and without dissatisfaction; because in wearing out, it was working out our salvation. But I see nothing in this renewal of the game of *" Robin's Alive "* but a general demoralization of the nation, a filching from industry its honest earnings, wherewith to build up palaces, and raise gambling stock for swindlers and shavers, who are to close, too, their career of piracies by fraudulent bankruptcies.—To NATHANIEL MACON. vii, 111. FORD ED., x, 121. (M., 1819.)

5395. —— ——. The evils of this deluge of paper money are not to be removed, until our citizens ·are generally and radically instructed in their cause and consequences, and silence by their authority the interested clamors and sophistry of speculating, shaving, and banking institutions. Till then we must be content to return, *quoad hoc*, to the savage state, to recur to barter in the exchange of our property, for want of a stable, common measure of value, that now in use being less fixed than the beads and wampum of the Indian, and to deliver up our citizens, their property and their labor, passive victims to the swindling tricks of bankers and mountebankers.—To JOHN ADAMS. vii, 115. (M., 1819.) See BANKS, DOLLAR, NATIONAL CURRENCY, and PAPER MONEY.

5396. MONEY, Unit of.—The plan reported by the Financier [Robert Morris] is worthy of his sound judgment. It admits, however, of objection in the size of the Unit. He proposes that this shall be the 1440th part of a dollar; so that it will require 1440 of his units to make the one before proposed. He was led to adopt this by a mathematical attention to our old currencies, all of which this Unit will measure without leaving a fraction. But as our object is to get rid of those currencies, the advantage derived from this coincidence will soon be past, whereas the inconveniences of this Unit will forever remain, if they do not altogether prevent its introduction. It is defective in two of the three requisites of a Money Unit. 1. It is inconvenient in its application to the ordinary money transactions. Ten thousand dollars will require eight figures to express them, to wit, 14,400,000 units. A horse or bullock of eighty dollars' value, will require a notation of six figures, to wit, 115,200 units. As a money of account, this will be laborious, even when facilitated by the aid of decimal arithmetic: as a common measure of the value of property, it will be too minute to be comprehended by the people. The French are subjected to very laborious calculations, the livre being their ordinary money of account, and this but between 1-5th and 1-6th of a dollar; but what will be our labors, should our money of account be 1-1440th of a dollar? 2. It is neither equal, nor near to any of the known coins in value.—NOTES ON A MONEY UNIT. i, 166. FORD ED., iii, 450. (1784.) See DOLLAR.

5397. —— ——. I concur with you in thinking that the Unit must stand on both metals.—To ALEXANDER HAMILTON. iii, 330. (Feb. 1792.)

5398. MONEY, War and.—Money is the nerve of war.—To ALBERT GALLATIN. vi, 498. (M., 1815.)

5399. MONEY BILLS, Origination.— Bills for levying money shall be originated

and amended by the Representatives only.— PROPOSED VA. CONSTITUTION. FORD ED., ii, 17. (June 1776.)

5400. —— ——. The Senate and the House of Representatives [of Virginia] shall each * * * have power to originate and amend bills; save only that bills for levying money shall be originated and amended by the representatives only: the assent of both houses shall be requisite to pass a law.— PROPOSED VA. CONSTITUTION. FORD ED., ii, 17. (June 1776.)

5401. MONEY BILLS, Parliament and. —By the law and usage of the British parliament, all those are understood to be money bills which raise money in any way, or which dispose of it, and which regulate those circumstances of matter, method and time, which attend as of consequence on the right of giving and disposing. Again, the law and customs of their Parliament, which include the usage as to " money bills ", are a part of the law of their land; our ancestors adopted their system of law in the general, making from time to time such alterations as local diversities required; but that part of their law, which relates to the matter now in question, was never altered by our Legislature, in any period of its history; but on the contrary, the two Houses of Assembly, both under our regal and republican governments, have ever done business on the constant admission that the law of Parliament was their law.— CONGRESS REPORT. FORD ED., ii, 136. (1777.)

5402. —— ——. The right of levying money, in whatever way, being * * * exercised by the Commons, as their exclusive office, it follows, as a necessary consequence, that they may also exclusively direct its application. *"Cujus est dare, ejus est disponere"*, is an elementary principle both of law and of reason. That he who gives, may direct the application of the gift: or, in other words, may dispose of it; that if he may give absolutely, he may also carve out the conditions, limitations, purposes, and measure of the gift, seems as evidently true as that the greater power contains the lesser.—CONGRESS REPORT. FORD ED., ii, 139. (1778.)

5403. —— ——. In 1701, the Lords having amended a bill, " for stating and examining the public accounts ", by inserting a clause for allowing a particular debt, the Commons disagreed to the amendment; and declared for a reason, " that the disposition, as well as granting of money by act of Parliament, hath ever been in the House of Commons; and, that the amendment relating to the disposal of money does entrench upon that right ". And, to a bill of the same nature the year following, the Lords having proposed an amendment, and declared, " that their right in gaming, limiting, and disposing of public aids, being the main hinge of the controversy, they thought it of the highest concern that it should be cleared and settled ". They then go on to prove the usage by precedents, and declarations, and from these conclude, "that the limitation, disposition, and manner of account belong only to them".—Congress Report. Ford ed., ii, 140. (1778.)

5404. MONEY BILLS, Virginia Constitution and.—Had those who framed the [Virginia] Constitution, as soon as they had completed that work, been asked, man by man, what a money bill was, it is supposed that, man by man, they would have referred for answer to the well known laws and usages of Parliament, or would have formed their answer on the Parliamentary idea of that term. Its import, at this day, must be the same as it was then. And it would be as unreasonable, now, to send us to seek its definition in the subsequent proceedings of that body, as it would have been for them, at that day, to have referred us to such proceedings before they had come into existence. The meaning of the term must be supposed complete at the time they use it; and to be sought for in those resources only which existed at the time. Constructions, which do not result from the words of the legislator, but lie hidden in his breast, till called forth, *ex post facto*, by subsequent occasions, are dangerous, and not to be justified by ordinary emergencies.—Congress Report. Ford ed., ii, 138. (1778.)

5405. MONEY (Continental), Depreciation of.—Previous to the Revolution, most of the States were in the habit, whenever they had occasion for more money than could be raised immediately by taxes, to issue paper notes or bills, in the name of the State, wherein they promised to pay to the bearer the sum named in the note or bill. In some of the States no time of payment was fixed, nor tax laid to enable payment. In these, the bills depreciated. But others of the States named in the bill the day when it should be paid, laid taxes to bring in money for that purpose, and paid the bills punctually, on or before the day named. In these States, paper money was in as high estimation as gold and silver. On the commencement of the late Revolution, Congress had no money. The external commerce of the States being suppressed, the farmer could not sell his produce, and, of course, could not pay a tax. Congress had no resource then but in paper money. Not being able to lay a tax for its redemption, they could only promise that taxes should be laid for that purpose, so as to redeem the bills by a certain day. They did not foresee the long continuance of the war, the almost total suppression of their exports, and other events, which rendered the performance of their engagement impossible. The paper money continued for a twelve-month equal to gold and silver. But the quantities which they were obliged to emit for the purpose of the war, exceeded what had been the usual quantity of the circulating medium. It began, therefore, to become cheaper, or, as we expressed it, it depreciated, as gold and silver would have done, had they been thrown into circulation in equal quantities. But not having, like them, an intrinsic

value, its depreciation was more rapid and greater than could ever have happened with them. In two years, it had fallen to two dollars of paper money for one of silver; in three years, to four for one; in nine months more, it fell to ten for one; and in the six months following, that is to say, by September, 1779, it had fallen to twenty for one. Congress, alarmed at the consequences which were to be apprehended should they lose this resource altogether, thought it necessary to make a vigorous effort to stop its further depreciation. They, therefore, determined, in the first place, that their emissions should not exceed two hundred millions of dollars, to which term they were then nearly arrived; and though they knew that twenty dollars of what they were then issuing would buy no more for their army than one silver dollar would buy, yet they thought it would be worth while to submit to the sacrifice of nineteen out of twenty dollars, if they could thereby stop further depreciation. They, therefore, published an address to their constituents, in which they renewed their original declarations, that this paper money should be redeemed at dollar for dollar. They proved the ability of the States to do this, and that their liberty would be cheaply bought at that price. The declaration was ineffectual. No man received the money at a better rate; on the contrary, in six months more, that is, by March, 1780, it had fallen to forty for one. Congress then tried an experiment of a different kind. Considering their former offers to redeem this money at par, as relinquished by the general refusal to take it but in progressive depreciation, they required the whole to be brought in, declared it should be redeemed at its present value, of forty for one, and that they would give to the holders new bills, reduced in their denomination to the sum of gold or silver, which was actually to be paid for them. This would reduce the nominal sum of the mass in circulation to the present worth of that mass, which was five millions; a sum not too great for the circulation of the States, and which, they therefore hoped, would not depreciate further, as they continued firm in their purpose of emitting no more. This effort was as unavailing as the former. Very little of the money was brought in. It continued to circulate and to depreciate till the end of 1780, when it had fallen to seventy-five for one, and the money circulated from the French army, being, by that time, sensible in all the States north of the Potomac, the paper ceased its circulation altogether in those States. In Virginia and North Carolina it continued a year longer, within which time it fell to one thousand for one, and then expired, as it had done in the other States, without a single groan. Not a murmur was heard on this occasion among the people. On the contrary, universal congratulations took place on their seeing this gigantic mass, whose dissolution had threatened convulsions which should shake their infant confederacy to its centre, quietly interred in its grave. Foreigners, indeed, who do not, like the natives, feel indulgence for its memory, as of a being which vindicated their liberties, and fallen in the moment of victory, have been loud, and still are loud in their complaints. A few of them have reason; but the most noisy are not the best of them. They are persons who have become bankrupt by unskilful attempts at commerce with America. That they may have some pretext to offer to their creditors, they have bought up great masses of this dead money in America, where it is to be had at five thousand for one, and they show the certificates of their paper possessions, as if they had all died in their hands, and had been the cause of their bankruptcy. Justice will be done to all, by paying to all persons what this money actually cost them, with an interest of six per cent. from the time they received it. If difficulties present themselves in the ascertaining the epoch of the receipt, it has been thought better that the State should lose, by admitting easy proofs, than that individuals, and especially foreigners, should, by being held to such as would be difficult, perhaps impossible.—To M. DE MEUNIER. ix, 248. FORD ED., iv, 153. (P., 1786.)

5406. MONEY (Continental), Redemption of.—It will be asked, how will the two masses of Continental and State money have cost the people of the United States seventy-two millions of dollars, when they are to be redeemed, now, with about six millions? I answer, that the difference, being sixty-six millions, has been lost on the paper bills, separately, by the successive holders of them. Every one, through whose hands a bill passed, lost on that bill what it lost in value, during the time it was in his hands. This was a real tax on him; and, in this way, the people of the United States actually contributed those sixty-six millions of dollars, during the war, and by a mode of taxation the most oppressive of all, because the most unequal of all.—To M. DE MEUNIER. ix, 260. FORD ED., iv, 165. (P., 1786.)

5407. —— ——. The soldier, victualer, or other person who received forty dollars for a service, at the close of the year 1779, received in fact, no more than he who received one dollar for the same service, in the year 1775, or 1776; because, in those years, the paper money was at par with silver; whereas, by the close of 1799, forty paper dollars were worth but one of silver, and would buy no more of the necessaries of life. —To M. DE MEUNIER. ix, 259. FORD ED., iv, 163. (P., 1786.)

5408. —— ——. As to the paper money in your hands, the States have not yet been able to take final arrangements for its redemption. But, as soon as they get their finances into some order, they will assuredly pay for what it was worth in silver at the time you received it, with interest.—To M. DULER. ii, 64. (P., 1786.) See ASSUMPTION OF STATE DEBTS.

— **MONEY (Metallic) Alloy in.**—See DOLLAR.

5409. MONEY (Metallic) Gold and silver ratio.—The proportion between the values of gold and silver is a mercantile problem altogether. It would be inaccurate to fix it by the popular exchanges of a half Joe for eight dollars, a Louis for four French crowns, or five Louis for twenty-three dollars. The first of these, would be to adopt* the Spanish proportion between gold and silver; the second, the French; the third, a mere popular barter, wherein convenience is consulted more than accuracy. The legal proportion in Spain is 16 for 1; in England 15 1-2 for 1; in France, 15 for 1. * * * Just principles will lead us to disregard legal proportions altogether; to enquire into the market price of gold, in the several countries with which we shall principally be connected in commerce, and to take an average from them. Perhaps we might, with safety, lean to a proportion somewhat above par for gold, considering our neighborhood, and commerce with the sources of the coins, and the tendency which the high price of gold in Spain has, to draw thither all that of their mines, leaving silver principally for our and other markets. It is not impossible that 15 for 1, may be found an eligible proportion. I state it, however, as a conjecture only.—NOTES ON A MONEY UNIT. i, 168. FORD ED., iii, 452. (1784.)

5410. —— ——. I observed * * * that the true proportion or value between gold and silver was a mercantile problem altogether and that, perhaps, fifteen for one might be found an eligible proportion. The Financier [Robert Morris] is so good as to inform me that this would be higher than the market would justify. Confident of his better information on this subject, I recede from that idea.†—SUPPLEMENTARY EXPLANATIONS. i, 171. FORD ED., iii, 454. (1784.)

5411. —— ——. There are particular public papers here [Paris] which collect and publish with a good deal of accuracy the facts connected with political arithmetic. In one of these I have just read the following table of the proportion between the value of gold and silver in several countries: Germany 1. to 14 11-71. Spain 1. to 14 3-10. Holland 1. to 14 3-4. England 1. to 15 1-2. France 1. to 14 42-100. Savoy 1. to 14 3-5. Russia 1. to 15. The average is 1. to 14 5-8.—To JAMES MONROE. FORD ED., iv, 45. (P., 1785.)

5412. —— ——. I concur with you * * * in the proportion you establish between the value of the two metals.—To ALEXANDER HAMILTON. iii, 330. (Feb. 1792.) See DOLLAR.

* In the FORD EDITION the text reads, "would be *about* the Spanish proportion".—EDITOR.

† Jefferson appends this note: "In a newspaper, which frequently gives good details in political economy, I find under the Hamburg head, that the present market price of gold and silver is, in England, 15.5 for 1; in Russia, 15; in Holland, 14.75; in Savoy, 14.6; in France, 14.42; in Spain, 14.3; in Germany, 14.155; the average of which is 14.675 or 14 5-8. I would still incline to give a little more than the market price for gold, because of its superior convenience in transportation."—EDITOR.

5413. MONEY (Metallic), Payments in.
—As the laws authorize the payment of a
given number of dollars to you, and as your
duties place you in London, I suppose we are
to pay you *the dollars* there, or other money
of equal value, estimated by the par of the
metals. Such has, accordingly, been the practice ever since the close of the war.—To
THOMAS PINCKNEY. iii, 526. (Pa., 1793.) See
BANKS, DOLLAR, MONEY, NATIONAL CUR-
RENCY, and PAPER MONEY.

**5414. MONEY (Metallic) vs. PAPER
MONEY.**—Sober thinkers cannot prefer a paper medium at 13 per cent. interest to gold
and silver for nothing.—To JAMES MADISON.
FORD ED., v, 350. (Pa., 1791.)

5415. —— ——. Experience has proved
to us that a dollar of silver disappears for
every dollar of paper emitted.—To JAMES
MONROE. iii, 268. FORD ED., v, 353. (Pa.,
July, 1791.)

5416. —— ——. Admit none but a *metallic
circulation* that will take its proper level with
the like circulation in other countries.—To
CHARLES PINCKNEY. vii, 180. FORD ED., x,
162. (M., 1820.) See MONEY.

5417. MONOPOLY, Abolish.—It is better to abolish monopolies in all cases, than
not to do it in any.—To JAMES MADISON. ii,
446. FORD ED., v, 46. (P., 1788.)

5418. MONOPOLY, Banking.—The bill
for establishing a National Bank undertakes
* * * , to form the subscribers into a corporation [and] * * * to give them the sole
and exclusive right of banking under the
national authority; and so far is against the
laws of *Monopoly.*—NATIONAL BANK OPIN-
ION. vii, 555. FORD ED., v, 285. (1791.) See
BANKS, NATIONAL CURRENCY and PAPER
MONEY.

5419. —— ——. These foreign and false
citizens * * * are advancing fast to a
monopoly of our banks and public funds,
thereby placing our finances under their control.—To ELBRIDGE GERRY. iv, 172. FORD ED.,
vii, 121. (Pa., 1797.)

5420. MONOPOLY, Colonies and.—The
monopoly of our [the Colonies] trade * * *
brings greater loss to us and benefit to them
than the amount of our proportional contributions to the common defence [of the em-
pire].—ADDRESS TO GOVERNOR DUNMORE.
FORD ED., i, 457. (1775.)

5421. —— ——. The Congress stated the
lowest terms they thought possible to be accepted, in order to convince the world they
were not unreasonable. They gave up the
monopoly and regulation of trade, and all
acts of Parliament prior to 1764, leaving to
British generosity to render these, at some
future time, as easy to America as the interest of Britain would admit.—To JOHN
RANDOLPH. i, 201. FORD ED., i, 483. (M.,
1775.)

5422. —— ——. It is not just that the
Colonies should be required to oblige themselves to other contributions while Great
Britain possesses a monopoly of their trade.
This does of itself lay them under heavy
contribution. To demand, therefore, an additional contribution in the form of a tax,
is to demand the double of their equal proportion. If we are to contribute equally with
the other parts of the empire, let us equally
with them enjoy free commerce with the
whole world. But while the restrictions on
our trade shut to us the resources of wealth,
is it just we should bear all other burthens
equally with those to whom every resource
is open?—REPLY TO LORD NORTH'S PROPO-
SITION. FORD ED., i, 479. (July 1775.) See
COLONIES.

5423. MONOPOLY, Commerce and.—By
a declaration of rights, I mean one which
shall stipulate * * * freedom of commerce
against monopolies.—To A. DONALD. ii, 355.
(P., 1788.)

5424. —— ——. The British have wished
a monopoly of commerce * * * with us,
and they have in fact obtained it.—To EL-
BRIDGE GERRY. iv, 172. FORD ED., vii, 121.
(Pa., 1797.) See COMMERCE and FREE TRADE.

5425. —— ——. Nor should we wonder
at * * * [the] pressure [for a fixed constitution in 1788-9] when we consider the
monstrous abuses of power under which
* * * [the French] people were ground
to powder; when we pass in review the
* * * shackles on commerce by monopolies.—AUTOBIOGRAPHY. i, 86. FORD ED., i, 118.
(1821.)

5426. MONOPOLY, Corporations.—Nor
should we wonder at the pressure [for a fixed
constitution in France in 1788-9], when we
consider the monstrous abuses of power under which this people were ground to powder,
* * * the shackles * * * ; on industry
by guilds and corporations * * * .—AU-
TOBIOGRAPHY. i, 86. FORD ED., i, 118. (1821.)
See INCORPORATION.

5427. MONOPOLY, Farmers General.—
The true obstacle to this proposition has penetrated, in various ways, through the veil
which covers it. The influence of the
Farmers General has been heretofore found
sufficient to shake a minister in his office.
Monsieur de Calonne's continuance or dismission has been thought, for some time, to
be on a poise. Were he to shift this great
weight, therefore, out of his own scale into
that of his adversaries, it would decide their
preponderance. The joint interests of France
and America would be insufficient counter-
poise in his favor.—REPORT TO CONGRESS. ix,
242. FORD ED., iv, 129. (P., 1785.)

5428. —— ——. As to the article of
tobacco, which had become an important
branch of remittance to almost all the States,
I had the honor of communicating to you my
proposition to the Court to abolish the monopoly of it in their farm; that the Count de
Vergennes was, I thought, thoroughly sensible of the expediency of this proposition,
and disposed to befriend it; that the renewal

of the lease of the farms had been consequently suspended six months and was still in suspense, but that so powerful were the Farmers General and so tottering the tenure of the Minister of Finance in his office, that I despaired of preventing the renewal of the farm at that time. Things were in this state when the Marquis de Lafayette * * * proposed to me a conference with some persons well acquainted with the commercial system of this country. We met. They proposed the endeavoring to have a committee appointed to inquire into the subject. The proposition was made to the Count de Vergennes, who befriended it, and had the Marquis de Lafayette named a member of the committee. He became, of course, the active and truly zealous member for the liberty of commerce; others, though well-disposed, not choosing to oppose the farm openly. * * * The committee showed an early and decisive conviction that the measure taken by the farm to put the purchase of their tobaccos into monopoly on that side of the water, as the sale of them was on this, tended to the annihilation of commerce between the two countries. Various palliatives were proposed from time to time. I confess that I met them all with indifference; my object being a radical cure of the evils by discontinuing the farm, and not a mere assuagement of it for the present moment, which, rendering it more bearable, might lessen the necessity of removing it totally, and perhaps prevent that removal.—To JOHN JAY. FORD ED., iv, 232. (P., 1786.)

5429. —— ——. The Count de Vergennes said that the difficulty of changing so ancient an institution [Farmers General] was immense; that the King draws from it a revenue of 29 millions of livres; that an interruption of this revenue at least, if not a diminution, would attend a change; that their finances were not in a condition to bear even an interruption, and in short that no minister could venture to take upon himself so hazardous an operation. This was only saying explicitly what I had long been sensible of, that the Comptroller General's continuance in office was too much on a poise to permit him to shift this weight out of his own scale into that of his adversaries; and that we must be contented to await the completion of the public expectation that there will be a change in this office, which change may give us another chance for effecting this desirable reformation.—To JOHN JAY. FORD ED., iv, 234. (P., 1786.)

5430. —— ——. The only question agitated [at the next meeting of the committee] was how best to relieve the trade under its double monopoly. The committee found themselves supported by the presence and sentiments of the Count de Vergennes. They, therefore, resolved that the contract with Mr. Morris, if executed on his part, ought not to be annulled here, but that no similar one should ever be made hereafter; that, so long as it continued, the Farmers should be obliged to purchase from twelve to fifteen

thousand hhds. of tobacco a year, over and above what they should receive from Mr. Morris, from such merchants as should bring it in French or American vessels, on the same conditions contracted with Mr. Morris; providing, however, that where the cargo shall not be assorted, the prices shall be $38, $36 and $34 for the 1st, 2d and 3d qualities of whichsoever the cargo may consist. In case of dispute about the quality, specimens are to be sent to the council, who will appoint persons to examine and decide on it. This is indeed the least bad of all the palliatives which have been proposed; but it contains the seeds of perpetual trouble. It is easy to foresee that the Farmers will multiply the difficulties and vexations on those who shall propose to sell to them by force, and that these will be making perpetual complaints, so that both parties will be kept on the fret. If, without fatiguing the friendly dispositions of the ministry, this should give them just so much trouble as may induce them to look to the demolition of the monopoly as a desirable point of rest, it may produce permanent as well as temporary good.—To JOHN JAY. FORD ED., iv, 235. (P., 1786.)

5431. —— ——. The body [Farmers General] to which this monopoly [tobacco] was given, was not mercantile. Their object is to simplify as much as possible the administration of their affairs. They sell for cash; they purchase, therefore, with cash. Their interest, their principles and their practice, seem opposed to the general interest of the kingdom, which would require that this capital article should be laid open to a free exchange for the productions of this country. So far does the spirit of simplifying their operations govern this body, that relinquishing the advantages to be derived from a competition of sellers, they contracted some time ago with a single person (Mr. Morris), for three years' supplies of American tobacco, to be paid for in cash. They obliged themselves too, expressly, to employ no other person to purchase in America, during that term. In consequence of this, the mercantile houses of France, concerned in sending her productions to be exchanged for tobacco, cut off, for three years, from the hope of selling these tobaccos in France, were of necessity to abandon that commerce. In consequence of this, too, a single individual, constituted sole purchaser of so great a proportion of the tobaccos made, had the price in his own power. A great reduction in it took place, and that, not only on the quantity he bought, but on the whole quantity made. The loss to the States producing the article did not go to cheapening it for their friends here. Their price was fixed. What was gained on their consumption was to enrich the person purchasing it; the rest, the monopolists and merchants of other countries.—To COUNT DE MONTMORIN. ii, 186. (P., 1787.)

5432. MONOPOLY, Indian trade.— Colonel McGillivray, with a company of British merchants, having hitherto enjoyed a monopoly of the commerce of the Creek nation, with a right of importing their goods duty free, and considering these privileges as the principal sources of his power over that nation, is unwilling to enter into treaty with us, unless they can be continued to him. And the question is how this may be done consistently with our laws, and so as to avoid just complaints from those of our citizens who would wish to participate of the trade? Our citizens, at this time, are not permitted to trade in that nation. The nation has a right to give us their peace, and to withhold their commerce, to place it under whatever monopolies or regulations they please. If they insist that only Colonel McGillivray and his company shall be permitted to trade among them, we have no right to say the contrary. We shall even gain some advantage in substituting citizens of the United States instead of British subjects, as associates of Colonel McGillivray, and excluding both British subjects and Spaniards from the country. Suppose, then, it be expressly stipulated by treaty, that no person be permitted to trade in the Creek country, without a license from the President, but that a fixed number shall be permitted to trade there at all, and that the goods imported for and sent to the Creek nation, shall be duty free. It may further be either expressed that the person licensed shall be approved by the leader or leaders of the nation, or without this, it may be understood between the President and McGillivray that the stipulated number of licenses shall be sent to him blank, to fill up.—OPINION ON INDIAN TRADE. vii, 504. FORD ED., v, 215. (1790.)

5433. ———— ————. The enclosed reclamations of Girod and Choate against the claims of Bapstropp to a monopoly of the Indian commerce, supposed to be under the protection of the 3rd article of the Louisiana Convention, as well as some other claims to abusive grants, will probably force us to meet that question. * * * Congress has [extended] about twenty particular laws * * * to Louisiana. Among these is the act concerning intercourse with the Indians, which establishes a system of intercourse with them admitting no monopoly. That class of rights, therefore, is now taken from under the treaty, and placed under the principles of our laws.—To JAMES MADISON. FORD ED., viii, 313. (July 1804.)

5434. MONOPOLY, Of influence.—The British have wished a monopoly of influence with us, and they have, in fact, obtained it.—To ELBRIDGE GERRY. iv, 172. FORD ED., vii, 121. (Pa., 1797.)

5435. MONOPOLY, Inventions and.—I like the declaration of rights as far as it goes, but I should have been for going further. For instance, the following alterations and additions would have pleased me. * * * . Article. 9. Monopolies may be allowed to persons for their own productions in literature, and their own inventions in the arts, for a term not exceeding — years, but for no longer term, and for no other purpose.—To JAMES MADISON. iii, 101. FORD ED., v, 113. (P., Aug. 1789.)

5436. ———— ————. To embarrass society with monopolies for every utensil existing, and in all the details of life, would be more injurious to them than had the supposed inventors never existed; because the natural understanding of its members would have suggested the same things or others as good. —To OLIVER EVANS. v, 75. (M., 1807.) See INVENTIONS and PATENTS.

5437. MONOPOLY, Of the judiciary.— It is the self-appointment [of the county courts] I wish to correct; to find some means of breaking up a cabal, when such a one gets possession of the bench. When this takes place, it becomes the most afflicting of tyrannies, because its powers are so various, and exercised on everything most immediately around us. And how many instances have you and I known of these monopolies of county administration? I know a county in which a particular family (a numerous one) got possession of the bench, and for a whole generation never admitted a man on it who was not of its clan or connection. I know a county now of one thousand and five hundred militia, of which sixty are federalists. Its court is of thirty members, of whom twenty are federalists (every third man of the sect). There are large and populous districts in it without a justice, because without a federalist for appointment; the militia are as disproportionably under federal officers. * * * The remaining one thousand four hundred and forty, free, fighting and paying citizens, are governed by men neither of their choice or confidence, and without a hope of relief. They are certainly excluded from the blessings of a free government for life, and indefinitely, for aught the Constitution has provided. This solecism may be called anything but republican.—To JOHN TAYLOR. vii, 18. FORD ED., x, 52. (M., 1816.)

5438. MONOPOLY, Land.—The property of France is absolutely concentrated in a very few hands, having revenues of from half a million of guineas a year downwards. These employ the flower of the country as servants, some of them having as many as two hundred domestics, not laboring. They employ also a great number of manufacturers, and tradesmen, and lastly the class of laboring husbandmen. But after all, there comes the most numerous of all the classes, that is, the poor who cannot find work. I asked myself what could be the reason that so many should be permitted to beg who are willing to work, in a country where there is a very considerable proportion of uncultivated lands? Those lands are undisturbed only for the sake of game. It should seem then that it must be because of the enormous wealth of the proprietors which places them above attention to the increase of their revenues by permitting these lands to be labored.—To REV. JAMES MADISON. FORD ED., vii, 35. (P., 1785.)

5439. MONOPOLY, Limited.—I sincerely rejoice at the acceptance of the new Constitution by nine States. It is a good canvas, on which some strokes only want retouching. What these are, I think are sufficiently manifested by the general voice from north to south, which calls for a bill of rights. It seems pretty generally understood that this should go to * * * monopolies. * * * The saying there shall be no monopolies, lessens the incitements to ingenuity, which is spurred on by the hope of a monopoly for a limited time, as of fourteen years; but the benefit of even limited monopolies is too doubtful to be opposed to that of their general suppression.—To JAMES MADISON. ii, 445. FORD ED., v, 45. (P., July 1788.)

5440. MONOPOLY, Military.—Nor should we wonder at the pressure [for a fixed constitution in 1788-9], when we consider the monstrous abuses of power under which * * * the [French] people were ground to powder, when we pass in review the * * * monopoly of military honors by the noblesse * * *.—AUTOBIOGRAPHY. i, 86. FORD ED., i, 118. (1821.)

5441. MONOPOLY, Of office.—When it is considered that during the late administration, those who were not of a particular sect of politics were excluded from all office; when, by a steady pursuit of this measure, nearly the whole offices of the United States were monopolized by that sect; when the public sentiment at length declared itself, and burst open the doors of honor and confidence to those whose opinions they more approved, was it to be imagined that this monopoly of office was still to be continued in the hands of the minority? Does it violate their *equal rights* to assert some rights in the majority also? Is it *political intolerance* to claim a proportionate share in the direction of the public affairs? Can they not *harmonize* in society unless they have everything in their own hands? —To THE NEW HAVEN COMMITTEE. iv, 404. FORD ED., viii, 69. (W., July 1801.)

5442. MONOPOLY, Restrict.—I do not like [in the new Federal Constitution] the omission of a bill of rights, providing clearly and without the aid of sophisms for * * * restriction of monopolies.—To JAMES MADISON. ii, 329. FORD ED., iv, 476. (P., December 1787.)

5443. MONOPOLY, Special privileges. —Monopolizing compensations are among the most fatal abuses which some governments practice from false economy.—OPINION ON STEVENS CASE. ix, 474. (1804.)

5444. MONOPOLY, Suppress.—A company had silently and by unfair means obtained a monopoly for the making and selling spermaceti candles [in France]. As soon as we* discovered it, we solicited its suppression which is effected by a clause in the *Arret.*—To JOHN JAY. ii, 342. (P., 1787.)

* An acknowledgment of Lafayette's assistance.— EDITOR.

5445. MONOPOLY, Tobacco.—The abolition of the monopoly of our tobacco in the hands of the Farmers General will be pushed by us with all our force. But it is so interwoven with the very foundations of their system of finance that it is of doubtful event.— To JAMES MONROE. FORD ED., iv, 20. (P., Dec. 1784.)

5446. ——— ———. The monopoly of the purchase of tobacco in France discourages both the French and American merchant from bringing it here, and from taking in exchange the manufactures and productions of France. It is contrary to the spirit of trade, and to the dispositions of merchants, to carry a commodity to any market where but one person is allowed to buy it, and where, of course, that person fixes its price which the seller must receive, or reexport his commodity, at the loss of his voyage thither. Experience accordingly shows that they carry it to other markets, and that they take in exchange the merchandise of the place where they deliver it. I am misinformed, if France has not been furnished from a neighboring nation with considerable quantities of tobacco since the peace, and been obliged to pay there in coin, what might have been paid here (France) in manufactures, had the French and American merchants brought the tobacco originally here. I suppose, too, that the purchases made by the Farmers General in America are paid for chiefly in coin, which coin is also remitted directly hence to England, and makes an important part of the balance supposed to be in favor of that nation against this. Should the Farmers General, by themselves, or by the company to whom they may commit the procuring these tobaccos from America, require, for the satisfaction of government on this head, the exportation of a proportion of merchandise in exchange for them, it would be an unpromising expedient. It would only commit the exports, as well as imports, between France and America, to a monopoly which, being secure against rivals in the sale of the merchandise of France, would not be likely to sell at such moderate prices as might encourage its consumption there, and enable it to bear a competition with similar articles from other countries. I am persuaded this exportation of coin may be prevented, and that of commodities effected, by leaving both operations to the French and American merchants, instead of the Farmers General. They will import a sufficient quantity of tobacco, if they are allowed a perfect freedom in the sale; and they will receive in payment, wines, oils, brandies, and manufactures, instead of coin; forcing each other, by their competition, to bring tobaccos of the best quality; to give to the French manufacturer the full worth of his merchandise, and to sell to the American consumer at the lowest price they can afford; thus encouraging him to use, in preference, the merchandise of this country.—To COUNT DE VERGENNES. i, 386. (P., 1785.)

5447. ——— ———. If, by a simplification of the collection of the King's duty on tobacco, the cost of that collection can be reduced even to five per cent., or a million and a half, instead of twenty-five millions; the price to the consumer will be reduced from three to two livres the pound. * * * The price, being thus reduced one-third, would be brought within the reach of a new and numerous circle of the people, who cannot, at present, afford themselves this luxury. The consumption, then, would probably increase, and perhaps, in the same if not a greater proportion with the reduction of the price; that is to say, from twenty-four to thirty-six millions of pounds; and the King, continuing to receive twenty-five sous on the pound, as at present, would receive forty-five instead of thirty millions of livres, while his subjects would pay but two livres for an object which has heretofore cost them three. Or if, in event, the consumption were not to be increased, he would levy only forty-eight millions on his people, where seventy-two millions are now levied, and would leave twenty-four millions in their pockets, either to remain there, or to be levied in some other form, should the state of revenue require it. It will enable his subjects, also, to dispose of between nine and ten millions worth of their produce and manufactures, instead of sending nearly that sum annually, in coin, to enrich a neighboring nation.—To COUNT DE VERGENNES. i, 388. (P., 1785.)

5448. ——— ———. I have heard two objections made to the suppression of this monopoly. 1. That it might increase the importation of tobacco in contraband. 2. That it would lessen the abilities of the Farmers General to make occasional loans of money to the public treasury. * * * With respect to the first * * * I may observe that contraband does not increase on lessening the temptations to it. It is now encouraged by those who engage in it being able to sell for sixty sous what cost but fourteen, leaving a gain of forty-six sous. When the price shall be reduced from sixty to forty sous, the gain will be but twenty-six, that is to say, a little more than one-half of what it is at present. It does not seem a natural consequence then, that contraband should be increased by reducing its gain nearly one-half. As to the second objection, if we suppose (for elucidation and without presuming to fix) the proportion of the farm on tobacco, at one-eighth of the whole mass farmed, the abilities of the Farmers General to lend will be reduced one-eighth, that is, they can hereafter lend only seven millions, where heretofore they have lent eight. It is to be considered, then, whether this eighth (or other proportion, whatever it be) is worth the annual sacrifice of twenty-four millions, or if a much smaller sacrifice to other moneyed men, will not produce the same loans of money in the ordinary way.—To COUNT DE VERGENNES. i, 389. (P., 1785.)

5449. ——— ———. While the advantages of an increase of revenue to the crown, a diminution of impost on the people, and a payment in merchandise, instead of money, are conjectured as likely to result to France from a suppression of the monopoly on tobacco, we have also reason to hope some advantages on our part * * * . I do not expect this advantage will be by any augmentation of price. The other markets of Europe have too much influence on this article to admit any sensible augmentation of price to take place. But the advantage I principally expect is an increase of consumption. This will give us a vent for so much more, and, of consequence, find employment for so many more cultivators of the earth; and, in whatever proportion it increases this production for us, in the same proportion will it procure additional vent for the merchandise of France, and employment for the hands that produce it. I expect, too, that by bringing our merchants here, they would procure a number of commodities in exchange, better in kind and cheaper in price. ——To THE COUNT DE VERGENNES. i, 390. (P., 1785.)

5450. ——— ———. I observed [to the Count de Vergennes] that France paid us two millions of livres for tobacco; that for such portions of it as were bought in London, they sent the money directly there, and for what they bought in the United States, the money was still remitted to London by bills of exchange; whereas, if they would permit our merchants to sell this article freely, they would bring it here, and take the returns on the spot in merchandise, not money. The Count observed that my proposition contained what was doubtless useful, but that the king received on this article, at present, a revenue of twenty-eight millions, which was so considerable as to render them fearful of tampering with it; that the collection of this revenue by way of Farm was of very ancient date, and that it was always hazardous to alter arrangements of long standing, and of such infinite combinations with the fiscal system. I answered, that the simplicity of the mode of collection proposed for this article, withdrew it from all fear of deranging other parts of their system; that I supposed they would confine the importation to some of their principal ports, probably not more than five or six; that a single collector in each of these was the only new officer requisite; that he could get rich himself on six livres a hogshead, and would receive the whole revenue, and pay it into the treasury, at short hand.—CONFERENCE WITH COUNT DE VERGENNES. ix, 232. FORD ED., iv, 119. (1785.)

5451. ——— ———. I have received the propositions of Messrs. Ross, Pleasants, &c., for furnishing tobacco to the Farmers General; but Mr. Morris had, in the meantime, obtained the contract. I have been fully sensible of the baneful influence on the commerce of France and America, which this double monopoly will have. I have struck at its root here, and spared no pains to have the farm itself demolished, but it has been in vain. The persons interested in it are too powerful to be opposed, even by the interest of the whole country.—To GOVERNOR PATRICK HENRY. i, 515. FORD ED., iv, 137. (P., 1786.)

5452. ——— ———. Till I see all hope of removing the evil [the tobacco monopoly in France] by the roots desperate, I cannot propose to prune its branches.—To JOHN PAGE. i, 549. FORD ED., iv, 213. (P., 1786.)

5453. ——— ———. Morris's contract for sixty thousand hogsheads of tobacco has been concluded with the Farmers General. I have been for some time occupied in endeavoring to destroy the root of the evils which the tobacco trade encounters in this country, by making the ministers sensible that merchants will not bring a commodity to a market, where but one person is allowed to buy it; and that so long as that single purchaser is obliged to go to foreign markets for it, he must pay for it in coin, and not in commodities. These truths have made their way to the minds of the ministry, insomuch as to have delayed the execution of the new lease of the Farms six months. It is renewed, however, for three years, but so as not to render impossible a reformation of this great evil. They are sensible of the evil, but it is so interwoven with their fiscal system, that they find it hazardous to disentangle. The temporary distress, too, of the revenue, they are not prepared to meet. My hopes, therefore, are weak, though not quite desperate. When they become so, it will remain to look about for the best palliative this monopoly can bear. My present idea is that it will be found in a prohibition to the Farmers General to purchase tobacco anywhere but in France.—To JAMES ROSS. i, 560. FORD ED., iv, 216. (P., 1786.)

5454. —— ——. I consider [the suppression of the tobacco monopoly in France] as the most effectual means of procuring the full value of our produce, of diverting our demands for manufactures from Great Britain to this country to a certain amount, and of thus producing some equilibrium in our commerce which, at present, lies all in the British scale. It would cement an union with our friends, and lessen the torrent of wealth we are pouring into the laps of our enemies.—To T. PLEASANTS. i, 563. (P., 1786.)

5455. —— ——. I think that so long as the monopoly in the sale [of tobacco] is kept up, it is of no consequence to us how they modify the pill for their own internal relief; but, on the contrary, the worse it remains, the more necessary it will render a reformation. Any palliative would take from us all those arguments and friends that would be satisfied with accommodation. The Marquis de Lafayette, though differing from me in opinion on this point, has, however, adhered to my principle of absolute liberty or nothing.—To COL. MONROE. i, 568. FORD ED., iv, 225. (P., 1786.)

5456. —— ——. Some symptoms make me suspect that my proceedings to reduce the abusive administration of tobacco by the Farmers General have indisposed towards me a powerful person in Philadelphia, who was profiting from that abuse. An expression in the enclosed letter of M. de Calonnes would seem to imply that I had asked the abolition of Mr. Morris's contract. I never did. On the contrary, I always observed to them that it would be unjust to annul that contract. I was led to this by principles both of justice and interest. Of interest, because that contract would keep up the price of tobacco here to thirty-four, thirty-six and thirty-eight livres, from which it will fall when it shall no longer have that support. However, I have done what was right, and I will not so far wound my privilege of doing that, without regard to any man's interest, as to enter into any explanation of this paragraph with him. Yet I esteem him highly, and suppose that hitherto he had esteemed me. —To JAMES MONROE. ii, 70. (P., 1786.)

5457. —— ——. I shall certainly press for something to be done by way of antidote to the monopoly under which tobacco is placed in France.—To JOSEPH FENWICK. ii, 182. (P., 1787.)

5458. —— ——. Of these eighty millions [of American exports to Europe], thirty are constituted by the single article of tobacco. Could the whole of this be brought into the ports of France, to satisfy its own demands, and the residue to be revended to other nations, it would be a powerful link of commercial connection. But we are far from this.

Even her own consumption, supposed to be nine millions, under the administration of the monopoly to which it is farmed, enters little, as an article of exchange, into the commerce of the two nations. When this article was first put into Farm, perhaps it did not injure the commercial interests of the kingdom; because nothing but British manufactures were then allowed to be given in return for American tobaccos. The laying the trade open, then, to all the subjects of France, would not have relieved her from a payment in money. Circumstances are changed; yet the old institution remains.—To COUNT DE MONTMORIN. ii, 186. (P., 1787.)

5459. —— ——. The effect of this operation was vitally felt by every farmer in America, concerned in the culture of this plant. At the end of the year, he found he had lost a fourth or a third of his revenue; the State, the same proportion of its subjects of exchange with other nations. The manufacturers of this country [France], too, were either not to go there at all, or go through the channel of a new monopoly, which, freed from the control of competition in prices and qualities, was not likely to extend their consumption. It became necessary to relieve the two countries from the fatal effects of this double monopoly.—To COUNT DE MONTMORIN. ii, 187. (P., 1787.)

5460. —— ——. The governments have nothing to do, but not to hinder their merchants from making the exchange.—To COUNT DE MONTMORIN. ii, 189. (P., 1787.)

5461. MONOPOLY, Western trade.— The Ohio and its branches, which head up against the Potomac, afford the shortest water communication by five hundred miles of any which can ever be got between the western waters and Atlantic; and, of course, promise us almost a monopoly of the Western and Indian trade.—To JAMES MADISON. FORD ED., iii, 402. (A., Feb. 1784.)

5462. MONOPOLY, Whale oil.—My endeavors for emancipating the tobacco trade have been less successful [than have been those with respect to whale oil]. I still continue to stir, however, this and all other articles.—To MR. OTTO. i, 559. (P., 1786.)

5463. —— ——. On the subject of the whale fishery, I enclose you some observations I drew up for the ministry here, in order to obtain a correction of their *Arret* of September last, whereby they had involved our oils with the English, in a general exclusion from their ports. They will accordingly correct this, so that our oils will participate with theirs, in the monopoly of their markets.—To GENERAL WASHINGTON. ii, 538. FORD ED., v, 60. (P., 1788.)

5464. —— ——. I have obtained the promise of an explanatory *Arret* to declare that that of September 28 [1788], was not meant to extend to us. Orders are accordingly given in the ports to receive our [oils]. This places us on a better footing than ever, as it gives us a monopoly of this market in conjunction with the French fishermen.—To THOMAS PAINE. ii, 549. (P., 1788.)

5465. MONROE DOCTRINE, Jefferson and.—The question presented by the letters*

* The letters were those of Mr. Rush, our minister at the Court of St. James's, in which he communi-

you have sent me, is the most momentous which has been offered to my contemplation since that of Independence. That made us a nation, this sets our compass and points the course which we are to steer through the ocean of time opening on us. And never could we embark on it under circumstances more auspicious. Our first and fundamental maxim should be, never to entangle ourselves in the broils of Europe. Our second, never to suffer Europe to intermeddle with cis-Atlantic affairs. America, North and South, has a set of interests distinct from those of Europe, and peculiarly her own. She should therefore have a system of her own, separate and apart from that of Europe. While the last is laboring to become the domicile of despotism, our endeavor should surely be, to make our hemisphere that of freedom. One nation, most of all, could disturb us in this pursuit: she now offers to lead, aid, and accompany us in it. By acceding to her proposition, we detach her from the bands, bring her mighty weight into the scale of free government, and emancipate a continent at one stroke, which might otherwise linger long in doubt and difficulty. Great Britain is the nation which can do us the most harm of any one, or all on earth; and with her on our side we need not fear the whole world. With her, then, we should most sedulously cherish a cordial friendship; and nothing would tend more to knit our affections than to be fighting once more, side by side in the same cause. Not that I would purchase even her amity at the price of taking part in her wars. But the war in which the present proposition might engage us, should that be its consequence, is not her war, but ours. Its object is to introduce and establish the American system, of keeping out of our land all foreign powers, of never permitting those of Europe to intermeddle with the affairs of our nations. It is to maintain our own principle, not to depart from it. And if, to facilitate this, we can effect a division in the body of the European powers, and draw over to our side its most powerful member, surely we should do it. But I am clearly of Mr. Canning's opinion, that, it will prevent instead of provoke war. With Great Britain withdrawn from their scale and shifted into that of our two continents, all Europe combined would not undertake such a war. For how would they propose to get at either enemy without superior fleets? Nor is the occasion to be slighted which this proposition offers, of declaring our protest against the atrocious violations of the rights of nations, by the interference of any one in the internal affairs of another, so flagitiously begun by Bonaparte, and now continued by the equally

cated to President Monroe the proposition of Mr. Canning that the United States and England should issue a joint declaration announcing that, while the two governments desired for themselves no portion of the Spanish-American colonies, then in revolt against Spain, they would not view with indifference any foreign intervention in their affairs, or their acquisition by a third power. The declaration was intended to be a warning to the allied powers, Russia, Prussia and Austria, the members of the Holy Alliance.—EDITOR.

lawless Alliance, calling itself Holy. But we have first to ask ourselves a question. Do we wish to acquire to our own confederacy any one or more of the Spanish provinces? I candidly confess, that I have ever looked on Cuba as the most interesting addition which could ever be made to our system of States. The control which, with Florida Point, this island would give us over the Gulf of Mexico, and the countries and isthmus bordering on it, as well as all those whose waters flow into it, would fill up the measure of our political well-being. Yet, as I am sensible that this can never be obtained, even with her own consent, but by war; and its independence, which is our second interest (and especially its independence of England), can be secured without it. I have no hesitation in abandoning my first wish to future chances, and accepting its independence, with peace and the friendship of England, rather than its association, at the expense of war and her enmity. I could honestly, therefore, join in the declaration proposed, that we aim not at the acquisition of any of those possessions, that we will not stand in the way of any amicable arrangement between them and the mother country; but that we will oppose, with all our means, the forcible interposition of any other power, as auxiliary, stipendiary, or under any other form or pretext, and most especially, their transfer to any power by conquest, cession, or acquisition in any other way.* I should

* The subjoined extract from President Monroe's Message to Congress on Dec. 2d, 1823, embodies the Monroe Doctrine:

" In the wars of European powers, in matters relating to themselves, we have never taken any part, nor does it comport with our policy so to do. It is only when our rights are invaded or seriously menaced that we resent injuries or make preparations for our defence. With the movements on this hemisphere we are, of necessity, more immediately connected, and by causes which must be obvious to all enlightened and impartial observers. The political system of the allied powers [the Holy Alliance] is essentially different in this respect from that of America. This difference proceeds from that which exists in their respective governments. And to the defence of our own, which has been achieved by the loss of so much blood and treasure, and matured by the wisdom of their most enlightened citizens, and under which we have enjoyed unexampled felicity, this whole Nation is devoted. We owe it, therefore, to candor and to the amicable relations existing between the United States and those powers to declare that we should consider any attempt on their part to extend their system to any portion of this hemisphere as dangerous to our peace and safety. With the existing colonies or dependencies of any European power we have not interfered, and shall not interfere. But with the Governments who have declared their independence and maintained it we have, on great consideration and on just principles, acknowledged, we could not view any interposition for the purpose of oppressing them, or controlling in any other manner their destiny, by any European power, in any other light than as the manifestation of an unfriendly disposition towards the United States. Our policy in regard to Europe, which was adopted at an early stage of the wars which have so long agitated that quarter of the globe, nevertheless remains the same, which is not to interfere in the internal concerns of any of its powers; to consider the Government de facto as the legitimate Government for us; to cultivate friendly relations with it, and to preserve those relations by a frank, firm, and manly policy; meeting in all instances the just claims of every power, submitting to injuries from none. But in regard to these continents, circumstances are eminently and conspicuously different. It is impossible that the allied powers should extend think it, therefore, advisable, that the Executive should encourage the British government to a continuance in the dispositions expressed in these letters, by an assurance of his concurrence with them as far as his authority goes; and that as it may lead to war, the declaration of which requires an act of Congress, the case shall be laid before them for consideration at their first meeting, and under the reasonable aspect in which it is seen by himself. I have been so long weaned from political subjects, and have so long ceased to take any interest in them, that I am sensible I am not qualified to offer opinions on them worthy of any attention. But the question now proposed involves consequences so lasting, and effects so decisive of our future destinies, as to rekindle all the interest I have heretofore felt on such occasions, and to induce me to the hazard of opinions, which will prove only my wish to contribute still my mite towards anything which may be useful to our country.*—To PRESIDENT MONROE. vii, 315. FORD ED., x, 277. (M., October 1823.) See POLICY.

5466. MONROE (James), Ability.— Many points in Monroe's character would render him the most valuable acquisition the republican interest in this Legislature [Congress] could make.—To JOHN TAYLOR. FORD ED., vii, 322. (Pa., Jan. 1799.)

5467. ———. I clearly think with you on the competence of Monroe to embrace great views of action. The decision of his character, his enterprise, firmness, industry, and unceasing vigilance, would, I believe, secure, as I am sure they would merit, the public confidence, and give us all the success which our means can accomplish.—To WILLIAM DUANE. vi, 81. FORD ED., ix, 368. (M., Oct. 1812.)

5468. MONROE (James), Book by.— Your book * * * works irresistibly. It would be very gratifying to you to hear the unqualified eulogies both on the matter and manner by all who are not hostile to it from principle.—To JAMES MONROE. FORD ED., vii, 183. (Pa., Dec. 1797.)

5469. ——— ———. Monroe's book is considered as masterly by all those who are not opposed in principle, and it is deemed unanswerable. An answer, however, is commenced in Fenno's paper, under the signature of " Scipio " [Uriah Tracy]. The real author is not yet

their political system to any portion of either continent without endangering our peace and happiness; nor can any one believe that our Southern brethren, if left to themselves, would adopt it of their own accord. It is equally impossible, therefore, that we should behold such interposition, in any form, with indifference."—EDITOR.

* Morse, in his *Life of Jefferson* (p. 235), says : " It is curious to note that in the course of this business (navigation of Mississippi), there was already a faint foreshadowing of that principle, which many years afterwards was christened with the name of Monroe. For a brief time it was thought, not without reason, that so soon as hostilities should break out between England and Spain, the former power would seize upon the North American possessions of the latter. Jefferson wrote to Gouverneur Morris : ' We wish you, therefore, to intimate to them (the British ministry) that we cannot be indifferent to enterprises of this kind. That we should contemplate a change of neighbors with extreme uneasiness. That a due balance on our borders is not less desirable to us than a balance of power in Europe has always appeared to them'."—EDITOR.

conjectured.—To JAMES MADISON. iv, 206. FORD ED., vii, 190. (Pa., Jan. 1798.)

5470. MONROE (James), British treaty and.— You complain of the manner in which the [British] treaty was received. But what was that manner? I cannot suppose you to have given a moment's credit to the stuff which was crowded in all sorts of forms into the public papers, or to the thousand speeches they put into my mouth, not a word of which I had ever uttered. I was not insensible at the time of the views to mischief, with which these lies were fabricated. But my confidence was firm, that neither yourself nor the British government, equally outraged by them, would believe me capable of making the editors of newspapers the confidants of my speeches or opinions. The fact was this. The treaty was communicated to us by Mr. Erskine on the day Congress was to rise. Two of the senators enquired of me in the evening, whether it was my purpose to detain them on account of the treaty. My answer was, " that it was not; that the treaty containing no provision against the impressment of our seamen, and being accompanied by a kind of protestation of the British ministers, which would leave that government free to consider it as a treaty or no treaty, according to their own convenience, I should not give them the trouble of deliberating on it ". This was substantially, and almost verbally, what I said whenever spoken to about it, and I never failed when the occasion would admit of it, to justify yourself and Mr. Pinckney, by expressing my conviction, that it was all that could be obtained from the British government; that you had told their commissioners that your government could not be pledged to ratify, because it was contrary to their instructions; of course, that it should be considered but as a *projet*; and in this light I stated it publicly in my message to Congress on the opening of the session. Not a single article of the treaty was ever made known beyond the members of the administration, nor would an article of it be known at this day, but for its publication in the newspapers, as communicated by somebody from beyond the water, as we have always understood. But as to myself, I can solemnly protest, as the most sacred of truths, that I never, one instant, lost sight of your reputation and favorable standing with your country, and never omitted to justify your failure to attain our wish, as one which was probably unattainable. Reviewing, therefore, this whole subject, I cannot doubt you will become sensible, that your impressions have been without just ground.—To JAMES MONROE. v, 254. FORD ED., ix, 179. (W., March 1808.) See IMPRESSMENT.

5471. MONROE (James), Confidence in.— I have had, and still have, such entire confidence in the late and present Presidents, that I willingly put both soul and body into their pockets.—To NATHANIEL MACON. vii, 111. FORD ED., x, 120. (M., 1819.)

5472. MONROE (James), Defence of.— I should be glad to see the defence of Monroe's conduct which you possess, though no paper of that title is necessary to me. He was appointed to an office during pleasure merely to get him out of the Senate, and with an intention to seize the first pretext for exercising the pleasure of recalling him. * * * I think with you it will be best to publish nothing concerning Colonel Monroe till his return, that he may accommodate the complexion of his publication to times and circumstances.—To JOHN EDWARDS. iv, 164. FORD ED., vii, 112. (M., Jan. 1797.)

5473. —— ——. I understand that the opposite party admit that there is nothing in your conduct which can be blamed, except the divulging secrets; and this, I think, might be answered by a few sentences, discussing the question whether an ambassador is the representative of his country or of the President.—To JAMES MONROE. FORD ED., vii, 197. (Pa., Feb. 1798.)

5474. MONROE (James), Diplomatic expenses.—Although it is not pleasant to fall short in returning civilities, yet necessity has rendered this so familiar in Europe as not to lessen respect for the person whose circumstances do not permit a return of hospitalities. I see by your letters the pain which this situation gives you, and I can estimate its acuteness from the generosity of your nature. But, my dear friend, calculate with mathematical rigor the pain annexed to each branch of the dilemma, and pursue that which brings the least. To give up entertainment, and to live with the most rigorous economy till you have cleared yourself of every demand is a pain for a definite time only; but to return here with accumulated encumbrances on you, will fill your life with torture. We wish to do everything for you which law and rule will permit. But more than this would injure you as much as us. Believing that the mission to Spain will enable you to suspend expense greatly in London, and to apply your salary during your absence to the clearing off your debt, you will be instructed to proceed there as soon as you shall have regulated certain points of neutral right for us with England, or as soon as you find nothing in that way can be done.—To JAMES MONROE. FORD ED., viii, 288. (W., Jan. 1804.)

5475. MONROE (James), Distaste for law.—You wish not to engage in the drudgery of the bar. You have two asylums from that. Either to accept a seat in the Council, or in the Judiciary department. The latter, however, would require a little previous drudgery at the bar to qualify you to discharge your duty with satisfaction to yourself. Neither of these would be inconsistent with a continued residence at Albemarle. It, is but twelve hours' drive in a sulky from Charlottesville to Richmond, keeping a fresh horse always at the half-way, which would be a small annual expense.—To JAMES MONROE. ii, 71. (P., 1786.)

5476. MONROE (James), English mission.—I perceive that painful impressions have been made on your mind during your late mission, of which I had never entertained a suspicion. I must, therefore, examine the grounds, because explanations between reasonable men can never but do good. 1. You consider the mission of Mr. Pinkney as an associate, to have been in some way injurious to you. Were I to take that measure on myself, I might say in its justification, that it has been the regular and habitual practice of the United States to do this, under every form in which their government has existed. I need not recapitulate the multiplied instances, because you will readily recollect them. I went as an adjunct to Dr. Franklin, and Mr. Adams, yourself as an adjunct first to Mr. Livingston, and then to Mr. Pinkney, and I really believe there has scarcely been a great occasion which has not produced an extraordinary mission. Still, however, it is well known that I was strongly opposed to it in the case of which you complain. A committee of the Senate called on me with two resolutions of that body, on the subject of impressment and spoliations by Great Britain, and requesting that I would demand satisfaction. After delivering the resolutions, the committee entered into free conversation, and observed that although the Senate could not, in form, recommend any extraordinary mission, yet that as individuals, there was but one sentiment among them on the measure, and they pressed it. I was so much averse to it, and gave them so hard an answer, that they felt it, and spoke of it. But it did not end here. The members of the other House took up the subject, and set upon me individually, and these the best friends to you, as well as myself, and represented the responsibility which a failure to obtain redress would throw on us both, pursuing a conduct in opposition to the opinion of nearly every member of the Legislature. I found it necessary, at length, to yield my own opinion to the general sense of the national council, and it really seemed to produce a jubilee among them; not from any want of confidence in you, but from a belief in the effect which an extraordinary mission would have on the British mind, by demonstrating the degree of importance which this country attached to the rights which we considered as infracted.—To JAMES MONROE. v, 253. FORD ED., ix, 178. (W., March 1808.)

5477. MONROE (James), Friendship for.—I have ever viewed Mr. Madison and yourself as two principal pillars of my happiness. Were either to be withdrawn, I should consider it as among the greatest calamities which could assail my future peace of mind. I have great confidence that the candor and high understanding of both will guard me against this misfortune, the bare possibility of which has so far weighed on my mind, that I could not be easy without unburthening it.*—To JAMES MONROE. v, 248. FORD ED., ix, 178. (W., Feb. 1808.)

5478. MONROE (James), Leaves Congress.—I look forward with anxiety to the approaching moment of your departure from Congress. Besides the interest of the Confederacy and of the State, I have a personal interest in it. I know not to whom I may venture confidential communications after you are gone.—To JAMES MONROE. i, 607. FORD ED., iv, 265. (P., 1786.)

5479. —— ——. I regret your departure [from Congress]. I feel, too, the want of a person there to whose discretion I can trust confidential communications, and on whose friendship I can rely against the designs of malevolence.—To JAMES MONROE. ii, 70. (P., 1786.)

5480. MONROE (James), Louisiana purchase.—I find our opposition is very willing to pluck feathers from Monroe [on the acquisition of Louisiana], although not fond of sticking them into Livingston's coat. The truth is, both have a just portion of merit; and were it necessary or proper, it could be shown that each has rendered peculiar services, and of important value.—To GENERAL HORATIO GATES. iv, 495. FORD ED., viii, 249. (W., July 1803.) See LOUISIANA.

5481. MONROE (James), Madison and.—I had * * * a frank conversation with Colonel Monroe. * * * I reminded him that in the letter I wrote to him while in Eu-

* From a letter concerning the Presidential contest and his neutrality in the struggle for the nomination.—EDITOR.

rope, proposing the government of Orleans, I also suggested that of Louisiana, if fears for health should be opposed to the other. I said something on the importance of the post, its advantages, &c.—expressed my regret at the curtain which seemed to be drawn between him and his best friends, and my wish to see his talents and integrity engaged in the service of his country again, and that his going into any post would be a signal of reconciliation, on which the body of republicans, who lamented his absence from the public service, would again rally to him. * * * The sum of his answers was, that to accept of that office was incompatible with the respect he owed himself; that he never would act in any office where he should be subordinate to anybody but the President himself, or which did not place his responsibility substantially with the President and the nation; that at your accession to the chair, he would have accepted a place in the cabinet, and would have exerted his endeavors most faithfully in support of your fame and measures; that he is not unready to serve the public, and especially in the case of any difficult crisis in our affairs; that he is satisfied that such is the deadly hatred of both France and England, and such their self-reproach and dread at the spectacle of such a government as ours, that they will spare nothing to destroy it; that nothing but a firm union among the whole body of republicans can save it, and, therefore, that no schism should be indulged on any ground; that in his present situation, he is sincere in his anxieties for the success of the Administration, and in his support of it as far as the limited sphere of his action or influence extends; that his influence to this end had been used with those with whom the world had ascribed to him an interest he did not possess, until, whatever it was, it was lost (he particularly named J. Randolph, who, he said, had plans of his own, on which he took no advice); and that he was now pursuing what he believed his properest occupation, devoting his whole time and faculties to the liberation of his pecuniary embarrassments, which, three years of close attention, he hoped, would effect. In order to know more exactly what were the kinds of employ he would accept, I adverted to the information of the papers, * * * that General Hampton was dead, but observed that the military life in our present state, offered nothing which could operate on the principle of patriotism; he said he would sooner be shot than take a command under Wilkinson. * * * On the whole, I conclude he would accept a place in the cabinet, or a military command dependent on the Executive alone, and I rather suppose a diplomatic mission, because it would fall within the scope of his views, and not because he said so, for no allusion was made to anything of that kind in our conversation. Everything from him breathed the purest patriotism, involving, however, a close attention to his own honor and grade. He expressed himself with the utmost devotion to the interests of our own country, and I am satisfied he will pursue them with honor and zeal in any character in which he shall be willing to act.—To President Madison. v, 481. Ford ed., ix, 265. (M., Nov. 1809.)

5482. MONROE (James), Mission to France.—The fever into which the western mind is thrown by the affair at New Orleans [suspension of right of deposit], stimulated by the mercantile and generally the federal interests. threatens to overbear our peace. In this situation we are obliged to call on you for a temporary sacrifice of yourself, to prevent this greatest of evils in the present prosperous tide of our affairs. I shall to-morrow nominate you to the Senate for an extraordinary mission to France, and the circumstances are such as to render it impossible to decline; because the whole public hope will be vested on you.—To James Monroe. Ford ed., viii, 188. (W., Jan. 10, 1803.)

5483. —— ——. You possess the unlimited confidence of the Administration, and of the western people; and generally of the republicans everywhere; and were you to refuse to go, no other man can be found who does this. * * * All eyes, all hopes, are now fixed on you; and were you to decline, the chagrin would be universal, and would shake under your feet the high ground on which you stand with the public. Indeed, I know nothing which would produce such a shock, for on the event of this mission depend the future destinies of this republic. If we cannot, by a purchase of the country, ensure to ourselves a course of perpetual peace and friendship with all nations, then, as war cannot be distant, it behooves us immediately to be preparing for that course, without, however, hastening it; and it may be necessary (on your failure on the continent) to cross the channel. We shall get entangled in European politics, and figuring more, be much less happy and prosperous. This can only be prevented by a successful issue to your present mission. I am sensible after the measures you have taken for getting into a different line of business, that it will be a great sacrifice on your part, and presents from the season and other circumstances serious difficulties. But some men are born for the public. Nature by fitting them for the service of the human race on a broad scale, has stamped them with the evidences of her destination and their duty.—To James Monroe. vi, 454. Ford ed., iv, 190. (W., Jan. 1803.) See Louisiana.

5484. MONROE (James), Orleans governorship.—When mentioning your going to New Orleans [as Governor], and that the salary there would not increase the ease of your situation, I meant to have added that the only considerations which might make it eligible to you were the facility of getting there the richest land in the world, the extraordinary profitableness of its culture, and that the removal of your slaves there might immediately put you under way.—To James Monroe. Ford ed., viii, 290. (W., Jan. 1804.)

5485. —— ——. I wish you were here at present, to take your choice of the two governments of Orleans and Louisiana, in either of which I could now place you; and I verily believe it would be to your advantage to be just that much withdrawn from the focus of the ensuing contest, until its event should be known. —To James Monroe. v, 11. Ford ed., viii, 448. (W., May 1806.)

5486. —— ——. The government of New Orleans is still without such a head as I wish. The salary of five thousand dollars is too small; but I am assured the Orleans Legislature would make it adequate, would you accept it. It is the second office in the United States in importance, and I am still in hopes you will accept it. It is impossible to let you stay at home while the public has so much need of talents.—To James Monroe. v, 54. Ford ed., ix, 37. (W., March 1807.)

5487. MONROE (James), President.— Nor is the election of Monroe an inefficient circumstance in our felicities. Four and twenty years, which he will accomplish, of administration in republican forms and principles, will so consecrate them in the eyes of the people as to secure them against the danger of change.—To Marquis Lafayette. vii, 67. Ford ed., x, 84. (M., 1817.)

5488. —— ——. I had had great hopes that while in your present office you would break up the degrading practice of considering the President's house as a general tavern, and economize sufficiently to come out of it clear of difficulties. I learn the contrary with great regret.—To James Monroe. Ford ed., x, 246. (M., 1823.)

5489. MONROE (James), Presidential contest.—I had intended to have written you to counteract the wicked efforts which the federal papers are making to sow tares between you and me, as if I were lending a hand to measures unfriendly to any views which our country might entertain respecting you. But I have not done it, because I have before assured you that a sense of duty, as well as of delicacy, would prevent me from ever expressing a sentiment on the subject, and that I think you know me well enough to be assured I shall conscientiously observe the line of conduct I profess.—To James Monroe. v, 82. (W., May 1807.)

5490. —— ——. I cannot, indeed, judge what falsehoods may have been written or told you; and that, under such forms as to command belief. But you will soon find that so inveterate is the rancor of party spirit among us, that nothing ought to be credited but what we hear with our own ears. If you are less on your guard than we are here, at this moment, the designs of the mischief-makers will not fail to be accomplished, and brethren and friends will be made strangers and enemies to each other, without ever having said or thought a thing amiss of each other. I presume that the most insidious falsehoods are daily carried to you, as they are brought to me, to engage us in the passions of our informers, and stated so positively and plausibly as to make even *doubt* a rudeness to the narrator; who, imposed on himself, has no other than the friendly view of putting us on our guard. My answer is, invariably, that my knowledge of your character is better testimony to me of a negative, than an affirmative which my informant did not hear *from yourself*, with his own ears. In fact, when you shall have been a little longer among us,* you will find that little is to be believed which interests the prevailing passions, and happens beyond the limits of our own senses. Let us not, then, my dear friend, embark our happiness and our affections on the ocean of slander, of falsehood and of malice, on which our credulous friends are floating. If you have been made to believe that I ever did, said, or thought a thing unfriendly to your fame and feelings, you do me injury as causeless as it is afflicting to me.—To James Monroe. v, 255. Ford ed., ix, 180. (W., March 1808.)

5491. —— ——. In the present contest in which you are concerned, I feel no passion, I take no part, I express no sentiment. Whichever of my friends is called to the supreme cares of the nation, I know that they will be wisely and faithfully administered, and as far as my individual conduct can influence, they shall be cordially supported. For myself I have nothing further to ask of the world, than

* Monroe had just returned from Europe.—Editor.

to preserve in retirement so much of their esteem as I may have fairly earned, and to be permitted to pass in tranquillity, in the bosom of my family and friends, the days which yet remain for me. Having reached the harbor myself, I shall view with anxiety (but certainly not with a wish to be in their place) those who are still buffeting the storm, uncertain of their fate.—To James Monroe. v, 255. Ford ed., ix, 181. (W., March 1808.) See Madison.

5492. MONROE (James), Purity of.—He is a man whose soul might be turned wrong side outwards, without discovering a blemish to the world.—To W. T. Franklin. i, 555. (P., 1786.)

5493. MONROE (James), Randolph and.—One popular paper is endeavoring to maintain equivocal ground; approving the administration in all its proceedings, and Mr. [John] Randolph in all those which have heretofore merited approbation, carefully avoiding to mention his late aberration. The ultimate view of this paper is friendly to you; and the editor, with more judgment than him who assumes to be at the head of your friends, sees that the ground of opposition to the administration is not that on which it would be advantageous to you to be planted. The great body of your friends are among the firmest adherents to the administration; and in their support of you, will suffer Mr. Randolph to have no communications with them. * * * But it is unfortunate for you to be embarrassed with such a *soi-disant* friend. You must not commit yourself to him.—To James Monroe. v, 10. Ford ed., viii, 448. (W., May 1806.)

5494. MONROE (James), Recall from France.—I should not wonder if Monroe were * * * recalled [from France], under the idea of his being of the partisans of France, whom the President [Washington] considers as the partisans of *war and confusion,* * * * and as disposed to excite them to hostile measures, or at least to unfriendly sentiments; a most infatuated blindness to the true character of the sentiments entertained in favor of France.—To W. B. Giles. iv, 127. Ford ed., vii, 44. (M., Dec. 1795.)

5495. MONROE (James), Republicanism of.—I know them both [Mr. Madison and Mr. Monroe] to be of principles as truly republican as any men living.—To Thomas Ritchie. vii, 191. Ford ed., x, 170. (M., 1820.)

5496. MONROE (James), Secretary of State.—Although I may not have been among the first, I am certainly with the sincerest, who congratulate you on your entrance into the national councils. Your value there has never been unduly estimated by those whom personal feelings did not misguide.—To James Monroe. v, 597. Ford ed., ix, 323. (M., May 1811.)

5497. MONROE (James), Selection of a home.—On my return from the South of France, I shall send you * * * a plan of your house. I wish to heaven you may continue in the disposition to fix it in Albemarle. Short will establish himself there, and perhaps Madison may be tempted to do so. This will be society enough, and it will be the great sweetener of our lives. Without society, and a society to our taste, men are never contented. The one here supposed, we can regulate to our minds, and we may extend our regulations to the sumptuary department so as to set a good example to a country which needs it, and to preserve our own happiness clear of embarrassment. * * * I am in hopes that Mrs. Monroe will have, in her domestic cares, occupation and pleasure sufficient to fill her time and insure her against the *tedium vitæ;* that she will find that the distractions of a town and the waste of life under these can bear no comparison with the tranquil happiness of domestic life. If her own experience has not yet taught her this truth, she has in its favor the testimony of one who has gone through the various scenes of business, of bustle, of office, of rambling and of quiet retirement and who can assure her that the latter is the one point upon which the mind can settle at rest. Though not clear of inquietudes, because no earthly situation is so, they are fewer in number and mixed with more objects of contentment than in any other mode of life.—To JAMES MONROE. ii, 71. (P., 1786.)

5498. —— ——. I had entertained hopes of your settling in my neighborhood; but these were determined by your desiring a plan of a house for Richmond. However reluctantly I relinquish this prospect, I shall not the less readily obey your commands by sending you a plan.—To JAMES MONROE. i, 564. FORD ED., iv, 220. (P., 1786.)

5499. MONROE (James), Slanderous attack on.—I have reason to believe they are preparing a batch of small stuff, such as refusing to drink General Washington's health, speaking ill of him, and the government, withdrawing civilities from those attached to him, countenancing Paine, to which they add connivance at the equipment of privateers by Americans. * * * We are of opinion here that Dr. Edward's certificate * * * should be reserved to repel these slanders—To JAMES MONROE. FORD ED., vii, 232. (Pa., April 1798.)

5500. —— ——. I have had a consultation with Mr. Dawson on the matter respecting Skipwith. We have neither of us the least hesitation, on a view of the ground, to pronounce against your coming forward in it at all. Your name would be the watchword of party at this moment, and the question would give opportunities of slander, personal hatred, and injustice, the effect of which on the justice of the case cannot be calculated. Let it, therefore, come forward in Skipwith's name, without your appearing even to know of it. * * * I do not think "Scipio" worth your notice. * * * Your narrative and letters, wherever they are read, produce irresistible conviction, and cannot be attacked but by a contradiction of facts, on which they do not venture.—To JAMES MONROE. FORD ED., vii, 232. (Pa., April 1798.)

5501. —— ——. You will have seen, among numerous addresses [to the President] and answers, one from Lancaster in Pennsylvania, and its answer; the latter travelling out of the topics of the address altogether, to mention you in a most injurious manner. Your feelings have no doubt been much irritated by it, as in truth it had all the characters necessary to produce irritation. What notice you should take of it, is difficult to say. But there is one step in which two or three with whom I have spoken concur with me, that feeble as the hand is from which this shaft is thrown, yet with a great mass of our citizens, strangers to the leading traits of the character from which it came, it will have considerable effect; and that in order to replace yourself on the high ground you are entitled to, it is absolutely necessary

that you should reappear on the public theatre, and take an independent stand, from which you can be seen and known to your fellow citizens. The House of Representatives appears the only place which can answer this end, as the proceedings of the other House are too obscure. Cabell has said he would give way to you, should you choose to come in, and I really think it would be expedient for yourself as well as the public, that you should not wait until another election, but come to the next session. No interval should be admitted between this last attack of enmity and your reappearance with the approving voice of your constituents, and your taking a commanding attitude. * * * If this be done, I should think it best that you take no notice at all of the answer.—To JAMES MONROE. iv, 242. FORD ED., vii, 257. (Pa., May 1798.)

5502. MONTESQUIEU (Baron), Author.—The history of Montesquieu's "Spirit of Laws" is well known. He had been a great reader, and had commonplaced everything he read. At length he wished to undertake some work into which he could bring his whole commonplace book in a digested form. He fixed on the subject of his "Spirit of Laws", and wrote the book. He consulted his friend Helvetius about publishing it, who strongly dissuaded it. He published it, however, and the world did not confirm Helvetius's opinion.— To WILLIAM DUANE. v, 535. (M., 1810.)

5503. —— ——. Every man who reflects as he reads, has considered it as a book of paradoxes; having, indeed, much of truth and sound principle, but abounding also with inconsistencies, apocryphal facts and false inferences.—To WILLIAM DUANE. v, 535. (M., 1810.)

5504. —— ——. I had, with the world, deemed Montesquieu's work of much merit; but saw in it, with every thinking man, so much of paradox, of false principle and misapplied fact, as to render its value equivocal on the whole. Williams and others had nibbled only at its errors. A radical correction of them, therefore, was a great desideratum. This want is now supplied, and with a depth of thought, precision of idea, of language and of logic, which will force conviction even to every mind. I declare to you, in the spirit of truth and sincerity, that I consider it the most precious gift the present age has received. But what would it have been, had the author, or would the author, take up the whole scheme of Montesquieu's work, and following the correct analysis he has here developed, fill up all its parts according to his sound views of them. Montesquieu's celebrity would be but a small portion of that which would immortalize the author.—To M. DESTUTT TRACY. v, 566. FORD ED., ix, 305. (M., 1811.)

5505. MONTESQUIEU (Baron), Monarchist.—I am glad to hear of everything which reduces Montesquieu to his just level, as his predilection for monarchy, and the English monarchy in particular, has done mischief everywhere.—To WILLIAM DUANE. v, 539. (M., 1810.)

5506. MONTICELLO, Beauties of.—And our own dear Monticello: where has nature spread so rich a mantle under the eye? Mountains, forests, rocks, rivers! With what majesty do we there ride above the storms! How sublime to look down into the workhouse of nature, to see her clouds, hail, snow, rain, thunder, all fabricated at our feet! And the

Monticello

The home of Thomas Jefferson

glorious sun when rising, as if out of a distant water, just gilding the tops of the mountains, and giving life to all nature!*—To Mrs. Cosway. ii, 35. Ford ed., iv, 315. (P., 1786.) See Mirage.

5507. MONTICELLO, Guests at.—You know our practice of placing our guests at their ease, by showing them we are so ourselves and that we follow our necessary vocations, instead of fatiguing them by hanging unremittingly on their shoulders.—To Francis W. Gilmer. vii, 5. (1816.)

5508. MONTICELLO, Recollections of. —All my wishes end, where I hope my days will end, at Monticello. Too many scenes of happiness mingle themselves with all the recollections of my native woods and fields, to suffer them to be supplanted in my affection by any other.—To Dr. George Gilmer. ii, 243. Ford ed., iv, 436. (P., 1787.)

5509. MONTMORIN (Count), Honest. —I am pleased with Montmorin. His honesty proceeds from the heart as well as the head, and therefore may be more securely counted on.—To James Madison. ii, 153. Ford ed., iv, 393. (P., 1787.)

5510. MONTMORIN (Count), Modest.— I am extremely pleased with his modesty, the simplicity of his manners, and his dispositions towards us. I promise myself a great deal of satisfaction in doing business with him.—To Marquis de Lafayette. ii, 131. (P., 1787.)

5511. MONTMORIN (Count), Weak but worthy.—Montmorin is weak, though a most worthy character. He is indolent and inattentive, too, in the extreme.—To James Madison. ii, 444. Ford ed., v, 43. (P., 1788.)

— **MOON.**—See Latitude and Longitude.

5512. MORAL LAW, Evidence of.— Man has been subjected by his Creator to the moral law, of which his feelings, or conscience as it is sometimes called, are the evidence with which his Creator has furnished him.—Opinion on French Treaties. vii, 613. Ford ed., vi, 220. (1793.)

5513. MORAL LAW, Nations and.— The moral duties which exist between individual and individual in a state of nature, accompany them into a state of society, and the aggregate of the duties of all the individuals composing the society constitutes the duties of that society towards any other; so that between society and society the same moral duties exist as did between the individuals composing them while in an unassociated state, their Maker not having released them from those duties on

---

* With the cares and delights of his family, his books and his farm, he mingled the gratification of his devotion to the Fine Arts, particularly architecture. He superintended [in 1781–2] the construction of his elegant mansion, which had been commenced some years before, and was already in a habitable condition. The plan of the building was entirely original in this country. He had drawn it himself from books, with a view to improve the architecture of his countrymen, by introducing an example of the tastes and arts of Europe. The original design of the structure, which was executed before his travels in Europe had supplied him with any models, is allowed by European travelers to have been infinitely superior, in taste and convenience, to that of any other house in America. The fame of the Monticellean philosopher having already spread over Europe, his hospitable seat was made the resort of scientific adventurers, and of dignified travelers from many parts of that continent. — Rayner's *Life of Jefferson*, p. 221.

their forming themselves into a nation.—Opinion on French Treaties. vii, 613. Ford ed., vi, 220. (1793.)

5514. MORAL SENSE, Innate.—I think it is lost time to attend lectures on moral philosophy. He who made us would have been a pitiful bungler, if He had made the rules of our moral conduct a matter of science. For one man of science, there are thousands who are not. What would have become of them? Man was destined for society. His morality, therefore, was to be formed to this object. He was endowed with a sense of right and wrong, merely relative to this. This sense is as much a part of his nature, as the sense of hearing, seeing, feeling; it is the true foundation of morality, and not the το καλον, truth, &c., as fanciful writers have imagined. The moral sense, or conscience, is as much a part of man as his leg or arm. It is given to all human beings in a stronger or weaker degree, as force of members is given them in a greater or less degree. It may be strengthened by exercise, as may any particular limb of the body. This sense is submitted, indeed, in some degree, to the guidance of reason; but it is a small stock which is required for this; even a less one than what we call common sense. State a moral case to a plowman and a professor. The former will decide it as well and often better than the latter, because he has not been led astray by artificial rules. In this branch, therefore, read good books, because they will encourage as well as direct your feelings. The writings of Sterne, particularly, form the best course of morality that ever was written. Lose no occasion of exercising your dispositions to be grateful, to be generous, to be charitable, to be humane, to be true, just, firm, orderly, courageous, &c. Consider every act of this kind as an exercise which will strengthen your moral faculties, and increase your worth.—To Peter Carr. ii, 238. Ford ed., iv, 428. (P., 1787.)

5515. ——— ———. I sincerely believe in the general existence of a moral instinct. I think it the brighest gem with which the human character is studded, and the want of it as more degrading than the most hideous of the bodily deformities.—To Thomas Law. vi, 351. (M., 1814.)

5516. ——— ———. I believe * * * that the moral sense is as much a part of our constitution as that of feeling, seeing, or hearing; as a wise Creator must have seen to be necessary in an animal destined to live in society.— To John Adams. vii, 39. (M., 1816.)

5517. ——— ———. The moral sense [is] the first excellence of well-organized man.—To John Adams. vii, 275. (M., 1823.)

5518. MORAL SENSE, Utility and.— Some have argued against the existence of a moral sense, by saying that if nature had given us such a sense, impelling us to virtuous actions, and warning us against those which are vicious, then nature would also have designated, by some particular earmarks, the two sets of actions which are, in themselves, the one virtuous and the other vicious. Whereas, we find, in fact, that the same actions are deemed virtuous in one country and vicious in another. The answer is that nature has constituted *utility* to man the standard and test of virtue. Men living in different countries, under different circumstances, different habits and regimens, may have different utilities; the same act, therefore, may be useful, and consequently virtuous in one country which is injurious and vicious in another differently circumstanced.—To THOMAS LAW. vi, 351. (M., 1814.)

5519. MORAL SENSE, Want of.—The Creator would, indeed, have been a bungling artist, had He intended man for a social animal, without planting in him social dispositions. It is true that they are not planted in every man, because there is no rule without exceptions; but it is false reasoning which converts exceptions into the general rule. Some men are born without the organs of sight, or of hearing, or without hands. Yet it would be wrong to say that man is born without these faculties, and sight, hearing, and hands may with truth enter into the general definition of man. The want or imperfection of the moral sense in some men, like the want or imperfection of the senses of sight and hearing in others, is no proof that it is a general characteristic of the species.—To THOMAS LAW. vi, 350. (M., 1814.)

5520. —— ——. When the moral sense is wanting, we endeavor to supply the defect by education, by appeals to reason and calculation, by presenting to the being so unhappily conformed, other motives to do good and to eschew evil, such as the love, or the hatred, or the rejection of those among whom he lives, and whose society is necessary to his happiness and even existence; demonstrations by sound calculation that honesty promotes interest in the long run; the rewards and penalties established by the laws; and ultimately the prospects of a future state of retribution for the evil as well as the good done while here. These are the correctives which are supplied by education, and which exercise the functions of the moralist, the preacher, and legislator; and they lead into a course of correct action all those whose depravity is not too profound to be eradicated.— To THOMAS LAW. vi, 350. (M., 1814.)

5521. MORALITY, Code of.—I know but one code of morality for men, whether acting singly or collectively. He who says I will be a rogue when I act in company with a hundred others, but an honest man when I act alone, will be believed in the former assertion, but not in the latter. I would say with the poet, " *hic niger est, hunc tu Romane cavato* ". If the morality of one man produces a just line of conduct in him, acting individually, why should not the morality of one hundred men produce a just line of conduct in them, acting together?—To JAMES MADISON. iii, 99. FORD ED., v, 111. (P., 1789.)

5522. —— ——. I never did, or countenanced, in public life, a single act inconsistent with the strictest good faith; having never believed there was one code of morality for a public, and another for a private man.—To DON VALENTINE DE FERONDA. v, 475. FORD ED., ix, 260. (M., 1809.)

5523. MORALITY, Foundations of.—It is really curious that on a question so fundamental, such a variety of opinions should have prevailed among men, and those, too, of the most exemplary virtue and first order of understanding. It shows how necessary was the care of the Creator in making the moral principle so much a part of our constitution as that no errors of reasoning or of speculation might lead us astray from its observance in practice. Of all the theories on this question, the most whimsical seems to have been that of Wollaston, who considers *truth* as the foundation of morality. The thief who steals your guinea does wrong only inasmuch as he acts a lie in using your guinea as if it were his own. Truth is certainly a branch of morality, and a very important one to society. But presented as its foundation, it is as if a tree taken up by the roots, had its stem reversed in the air, and one of its branches planted in the ground.—To THOMAS LAW. vi, 348. (M., 1814.)

5524. —— ——. Some have made the *love of God* the foundation of morality. This, too, is but a branch of our moral duties, which are generally divided into duties to God and duties to man. If we did a good act merely from the love of God and a belief that it is pleasing to Him, whence arises the morality of the atheist? It is idle to say, as some do, that no such Being exists. We have the same evidence of the fact as of most of those we act on, to wit their own affirmations, and their reasonings in support of them. I have observed, indeed, generally that while in Protestant countries the defections from the Platonic Christianity of the priests is to Deism, in Catholic countries they are to Atheism. Diderot, D'Alembert, D'Holbach, Condorcet, are known to have been among the most virtuous of men. Their virtue, then, must have had some other foundation than the love of God.—To THOMAS LAW. vi, 348. (M., 1814.)

5525. —— ——. The *To καλον* of others is founded in a different faculty, that of taste, which is not even a branch of morality. We have, indeed, an innate sense of what we call *the beautiful*, but that is exercised chiefly on subjects addressed to the fancy, whether through the eye in visible forms, as landscape, animal figure, dress, drapery, architecture, the composition of colors, &c., or to the imagination directly, as imagery, style, or measure in prose or poetry, or whatever constitutes the domain of criticism or taste, a faculty entirely distinct from the moral one.—To THOMAS LAW. vi, 349. (M., 1814.)

5526. —— ——. Self-interest, or rather self-love, or *egoism*, has been more plausibly substituted as the basis of morality. But I consider our relations with others as constituting the boundaries of morality. With ourselves we stand on the ground of identity, not of relation, which last, requiring two subjects, excludes self-love confined to a single one. To ourselves, in strict language, we can owe no duties, obligation requiring also two parties. Self-love, therefore, is no part of morality. Indeed it is exactly its counterpart. It is the sole antagonist of virtue, leading us constantly by our propensities to self-gratification in violation of our moral duties to others. Accordingly, it is against this enemy that are erected the batteries of moralists and religionists, as the only obstacle to the practice of morality. Take from man his selfish propensities, and he can have nothing to seduce him from the practice of virtue. Or subdue those propensities by education, instruction, or restraint, and virtue remains without a competitor.—To THOMAS LAW. vi, 349. (M., 1814.)

5527. —— ——. Egoism in a broader sense, has been thus presented as the source of moral action. It has been said that we feed the hungry, clothe the naked, bind up the wounds of the man beaten by thieves, pour oil and wine into them, set him on our own beast and bring him to the inn, because we receive ourselves pleasure from these acts. So Helvetius, one of the best men on earth, and the most ingenious advocate of this principle, after defining " interest " to mean not merely that which is pecuniary, but whatever may procure us pleasure, or withdraw us from pain (*De l'Esprit* 2, 1), says (ib. 2, 2), "the humane man is he to whom the sight of misfortune is insupportable, and who to rescue himself from this spectacle, is forced to succor the unfortunate object". This, indeed, is true. But it is one step short of the ultimate question. These good acts give us pleasure, but how happens it that they give us pleasure? Because nature hath implanted in our breasts a love of others, a sense of duty to them, a moral instinct, in short, which prompts us irresistibly to feel and to succor their distresses, and protests against the language of Helvetius (ib. 2, 5), "what other motive than self-interest could determine a man to generous actions? It is as impossible for him to love what is good for the sake of good, as to love evil for the sake of evil".—To Thomas Law. vi, 349. (M., 1814.)

5528. —— ——. God has formed us moral agents. Not that, in the perfection of His state, He can feel pain or pleasure in anything we may do; He is far above our power; but that we may promote the happiness of those with whom He has placed us in society, by acting honestly towards all, benevolently to those who fall within our way, respecting sacredly their rights, bodily and mental, and cherishing especially their freedom of conscience, as we value our own.—To Miles King. vi, 388. (M., 1814.)

5529. MORALITY, Religion and.— Reading, reflection and time have convinced me that the interests of society require the observation of those moral precepts only in which all religions agree (for all forbid us to steal, murder, plunder, or bear false witness), and that we should not intermeddle with the particular dogmas in which all religions differ, and which are totally unconnected with morality. In all of them we see good men, and as many in one as another. The varieties in the structure and action of the human mind as in those of the body, are the work of our Creator, against which it cannot be a religious duty to erect the standard of uniformity. The practice of morality being necessary for the well-being of society, he has taken care to impress its precepts so indelibly on our hearts that they shall not be effaced by the subtleties of our brain. We all agree in the obligation of the moral precepts of Jesus, and nowhere will they be found delivered in greater purity than in His discourses. It is, then, a matter of principle with me to avoid disturbing the tranquillity of others by the expression of any opinion on the innocent questions on which we schismatize.—To James Fishback. v, 471. (M., 1809.)

5530. —— ——. In that branch of religion which regards the moralities of life, and the duties of a social being, which teaches us to love our neighbors as ourselves, and to do good to all men, I am sure that you and I do not differ.—To Ezra Stiles. vii, 127. (M., 1819.)

5531. MORALITY, Sublimest system of.—There never was a more pure and sublime system of morality delivered to man than is to be found in the four Evangelists.—To Samuel Greenhow. vi, 309. (M., 1814.)

5532. —— ——. I know nothing more moral, more sublime, more worthy of your preservation than David's description of the good man, in 15th Psalm.—To Isaac Englebrecht. vii, 337. (M., 1824.)

5533. MORALITY (National), Abandonment of.—It was not expected in this

age, that nations so honorably distinguished by their advances in science and civilization, would suddenly cast away the esteem they had merited from the world, and, revolting from the empire of morality, assume a character in history, which all the tears of their posterity will never wash from its pages.—Reply to Address. viii, 128. (1808.)

5534. —— ——. It has been peculiarly unfortunate for us, personally, that the portion in the history of mankind, at which we were called to take a share in the direction of their affairs, was such an one as history has never before presented. At any other period, the even-handed justice we have observed towards all nations, the efforts we have made to merit their esteem by every act which candor or liberality could exercise, would have preserved our peace, and secured the unqualified confidence of all other nations in our faith and probity. But the hurricane which is now blasting the world, physical and moral, has prostrated all the mounds of reason as well as right. All those calculations which, at any other period, would have been deemed honorable, of the existence of a moral sense in man, individually or associated, of the connection which the laws of nature have established between his duties and his interests, of a regard for honest fame and the esteem of our fellow men, have been a matter of reproach on us, as evidences of imbecility. As if it could be a folly for an honest man to suppose that another could be honest also, when it is their interest to be so. And when is this state of things to end? The death of Bonaparte would, to be sure, remove the first and chiefest apostle of the desolation of men and morals, and might withdraw the scourge of the land. But what is to restore order and safety on the ocean? The death of George III.? Not at all. He is only stupid; and his ministers, however weak and profligate in morals, are ephemeral. But his nation is permanent, and it is that which is the tyrant of the ocean. The principle that force is right, is become the principle of the nation itself. They would not permit an honest minister, were accident to bring such an one into power, to relax their system of lawless piracy. These were the difficulties when I was with you. I know they are not lessened, and I pity you.—To Caesar A. Rodney. v, 500. Ford ed., ix, 271. (M., Feb. 1810.)

5535. MORALITY (National), Extinction of.—There are three epochs in history, signalized by the total extinction of national morality. The first was of the successors of Alexander, not omitting himself. The next, the successors of the first Cæsar. The third, our own age. This was begun by the partition of Poland, followed by that of the treaty of Pilnitz; next the conflagration of Copenhagen; then the enormities of Bonaparte, partitioning the earth at his will, and devastating it with fire and sword; now the conspiracy of Kings, the successors of Bonaparte, blasphemously calling themselves the Holy Alliance, and treading in the footsteps of their incarcerated leader; not yet indeed usurping the government of other nations, avowedly and in detail, but controlling by their armies the forms in which they will permit them to be governed; and reserving, *in petto*, the order and extent of the usurpations further meditated.—Autobiography. i, 102. Ford ed., i, 141. (1821.)

5536. MORALITY (National), Governments and.—Your ideas of the moral obligations of governments are perfectly correct. The man who is dishonest as a statesman would be a dishonest man in any station. It is strangely absurd to suppose that a million of human beings, collected together, are not under the same moral laws which bind each of them separately.—To GEORGE LOGAN. FORD ED., x, 68. (P.F., Nov. 1816.)

5537. —— ——. Moral duties are as obligatory on nations as on individuals.*—THE ANAS. FORD ED., i, 332. (1808.)

5538. MORALITY (National), Progress in.—The eighteenth century certainly witnessed the sciences and arts, manners and morals, advanced to a higher degree than the world had ever before seen. And might we not go back to the era of the Borgias, by which time the barbarous ages had reduced national morality to its lowest point of depravity, and observe that the arts and sciences, rising from that point, advanced gradually through all the sixteenth, seventeenth and eighteenth centuries, softening and correcting the manners and morals of man?—To JOHN ADAMS. vi, 523. (M., 1816.)

5539. —— ——. With some exceptions only, through the seventeenth and eighteenth centuries, morality occupied an honorable chapter in the political code of nations. You must have observed while in Europe, as I thought I did, that those who administered the governments of the greater powers at least, had a respect to faith, and considered the dignity of their government as involved in its integrity. A wound indeed was inflicted on this character of honor in the eighteenth century by the partition of Poland. But this was the atrocity of a barbarous government chiefly, in conjunction with a smaller one still scrambling to become great, while one only of those already great, and having character to lose, descended to the baseness of an accomplice in the crime. France, England, Spain, shared in it only inasmuch as they stood aloof and permitted its perpetration. How, then, has it happened that these nations, France especially, and England, so great, so dignified, so distinguished by science and the arts, plunged all at once into all the depths of human enormity, threw off suddenly and openly all the restraints of morality, all sensation to character, and unblushingly avowed and acted on the principle that power was right? Can this sudden apostasy from national rectitude be accounted for? The treaty of Pilnitz seems to have begun it, suggested perhaps by the baneful precedent of Poland. Was it from the terror of monarchs, alarmed at the light returning on them from the west, and kindling a volcano under their thrones? Was it a combination to extinguish that light, and to bring back, as their best auxiliaries, those enumerated by you, the Sorbonne, the Inquisition, the *Index Expurgatorius*, and the knights of Loyola? Whatever it was, the close of the new century saw the moral world thrown back again to the age of the Borgias, to the point from which it had departed three hundred years before. France, after crushing and punishing the conspiracy of Pilnitz, went deeper herself and deeper into the crimes she had been chastising. I say France and not Bonaparte; for, although he was the head and mouth, the nation furnished the hands which executed his enormities. England, although in opposition, kept full pace with France, not indeed by the manly force of her own arms, but by oppressing the weak and bribing the strong. At

* Reply, rejecting the proposal of a person entrusted with the British minister's dispatches, to turn them over to the United States government for a reward.—EDITOR.

length the whole choir joined and divided the weaker nations among them.—To JOHN ADAMS. vi, 524. (M., Jan. 1816.)

5540. MORALITY (National), United States and.—Let us hope that our new [Federal] government will * * * show that they mean to proscribe no virtue from the canons of their conduct with other nations.—To JAMES MADISON. iii, 100. FORD ED., v, 112. (P., 1789.)

5541. —— ——. We are firmly convinced, and we act on that conviction, that with nations, as with individuals, our interests soundly calculated, will ever be found inseparable from our moral duties; and history bears witness to the fact, that a just nation is taken on its word, when recourse is had to armaments and wars to bridle others.—SECOND INAUGURAL ADDRESS. viii, 40. FORD ED., viii, 343. (1805.)

5542. —— ——. It is a great consolation to me that our government, as it cherishes most its duties to its own citizens, so is it the most exact in its moral conduct towards other nations. I do not believe that in the four Administrations which have taken place, there has been a single instance of departure from good faith towards other nations. We may sometimes have mistaken our rights, or made an erroneous estimate of the actions of others, but no voluntary wrong can be imputed to us.—To GEORGE LOGAN. FORD ED., x, 68. (P.F., Nov. 1816.)

5543. —— ——. It is of great consequence to us, and merits every possible endeavor, to maintain in Europe a correct opinion of our political morality.—To PRESIDENT MONROE. FORD ED., x, 123. (M., 1819.)

5544. MORALS, Preservation of.—The pursuits of agriculture are * * * the best preservative of morals.—To J. BLAIR. ii, 248. (P., 1787.)

5545. —— —— We wish to preserve the morals of our citizens from being vitiated by courses of lawless plunder and murder.—To GEORGE HAMMOND. iii, 559. FORD ED., vi, 253. (Pa., 1793.)

5546. MORALS, Science and.—I fear, from the experience of the last twenty-five years, that morals do not of necessity advance hand in hand with the sciences.—To M. CORREA. vi, 480. (M., 1815.)

5547. MOREAU (General J. Victor), Esteem for.—No one entertains a more cordial esteem for General Moreau's character than I do, and although our relations with France have rendered it a duty in me not to seek any public manifestation of it, yet were accident to bring us together, I could not be so much wanting to my sentiments and those of my constituents individually, as to omit a cordial manifestation of it.—To WILLIAM SHORT. v, 212. (W., Nov. 1807.)

5548. MOREAU (General J. Victor), Reception of.—I confess that the enclosed letter from General Turreau excites in me both jealousy and offence in undertaking, and without apology, to say in what manner to receive and treat Moreau within our own country. Had Turreau been here longer he would have known that the national authority pays honors to no foreigners. That the State authorities, municipalities and individuals, are free to render whatever they please, voluntarily, and free from restraint by us; and he ought to know that no part of the criminal sentence of another country can have any effect here. The style of that government in the Spanish business, was calculated to excite indignation; but it was a case in which that might have done injury. But the present is a case which would justify some notice in order to let them understand we are not of those powers who will receive and execute mandates. I think the answer should show independence as well as friendship.—To JAMES MADISON. iv, 584. FORD ED., viii, 376. (M., Aug. 1805.)

5549. MORGAN (George), Exposure of Burr.—Your situation and the knowledge you already possess would probably put it in your power to trace the footsteps of this enterprise [Burr's conspiracy] on the public peace with more effect than any other with whom I could communicate. Whatever zeal you might think proper to use in this pursuit, would be used in fulfilment of the duties of a good citizen, and any communications you may be so good as to make to me on the subject shall be thankfully received, and so made use of as not to commit you any further than yourself may think proper to express. A knowledge of the persons who may reject, as well as of those who may accept parricide propositions will be peculiarly useful.—To GEORGE MORGAN. FORD ED., viii, 473. (M., Sep. 1806.)

5550. ———— ————. Yours was the very first intimation I had of Burr's plot, for which it is but justice to say you have deserved well of your country.—To COLONEL GEORGE MORGAN. v. 57. (W., 1807.)

5551. ———— ————. Colonel Morgan first gave us notice of the mad project of that day, which if suffered to proceed, might have brought afflicting consequences on persons whose subsequent lives have proved their integrity and loyalty to their country.—To MRS. K. D. MORGAN. FORD ED., viii, 473. (M., 1822.)

5552. MORGAN (George), Land grant.—Spain has granted to Colonel Morgan, of New Jersey, a vast tract of land on the western side of the Mississippi with the monopoly of the navigation of that river. He is inviting settlers and they swarm to him. Even the settlement of Kentucky is likely to be much weakened by emigrations to Morgan's grant.—To WILLIAM SHORT. ii, 574. FORD ED., v, 71. (P., 1789.)

5553. MOROCCO, Brig Betsey.—The Court of Madrid has obtained the delivery of the crew of the brig Betsey, taken by the Emperor of Morocco. The Emperor had treated them kindly, new clothed them, and delivered them to the Spanish minister, who sent them to Cadiz. This is the only American vessel ever taken by the Barbary States.—To JAMES MADISON. i, 413. (P., 1785.)

5554. MOROCCO, Proofs of friendship.—The Emperor [of Morocco] continues to give proofs of his desire to be in friendship with us, or, in other words, of receiving us into the number of his tributaries. Nothing further need be feared from him.—To JAMES MADISON. i, 413. (P., 1785.)

5555. MOROCCO, Treaty.—The treaty with Morocco * * * is signed before this time: for which we are much indebted to Spain.—To DAVID HUMPHREYS. ii, 10. (P., 1786.)

5556. MOROCCO, Tribute or war.—The Emperor of Morocco * * * is ready to receive us into the number of his tributaries. What will be the amount of tribute remains yet to be known, * * * but it will surely be more than a free people ought to pay to a power owning only four or five frigates, under twenty-two guns. He has not a port into which a larger vessel can enter. The Algerines possess fifteen or twenty frigates, from that size up to fifty guns. Disinclination on their part has lately broken off a treaty between Spain and them, whereon they were to have received a million of dollars, besides great presents in naval stores. What sum they intend we shall pay, I cannot say. Then follow Tunis and Tripoli. You will probably find the tribute to all these powers make such a proportion of the Federal taxes, as that every man will feel them sensibly when he pays those taxes. The question is whether their peace or war will be cheaper? But it is a question which should be addressed to our honor, as well as our avarice. Nor does it respect us as to these pirates only, but as to the nations of Europe. If we wish our commerce to be free and uninsulted, we must let these nations see that we have an energy which at present they disbelieve. The low opinion they entertain of our powers cannot fail to involve us soon in a naval war.—To JOHN PAGE. i, 401. (P., 1785.)

5557. MORRIS (Gouverneur), Monarchist.—Gouverneur Morris, a high flying monarchy man, shutting his eyes and his faith to every fact against his wishes, and believing everything he desires to be true, has kept the President's [Washington's] mind constantly poisoned with his forebodings [respecting the French Revolution].—THE ANAS. ix, 111. FORD ED., i, 188. (1792.)

5558. MORRIS (Gouverneur), Opposition to.—The opposition to Gouverneur Morris was upon the following principles: 1. His general character, being such that we would not confide in it. 2. His known attachment to monarchy, and contempt of republican government; and 3, his present employment abroad being a news vender of back-lands and certificates. We took the yeas and nays on his appointment and eleven voted against it.—To ARCHIBALD STUART. FORD ED., v, 454. (Pa. 1792.)

5559. ———— ————. The nomination of Mr. Morris was so extremely unpopular, and so little relished by several of the Senate, that every effort was used to negative it. Those whose personal objections to Mr. Morris overruled their deference to the President, finding themselves in a minority, joined with another small party who were against all foreign appointments, and endeavored with them to put down the whole system rather than let this article pass. This plan was defeated, and Mr. Morris passed by a vote of 16 against 11.—To WILLIAM SHORT. iii, 329. FORD ED., v, 434. (Pa., 1792.)

5560. MORRIS (Gouverneur), Services in England.—President Washington's letter of January 22d [1790], authorized Mr. Morris to enter into conference with the British ministers in order to discover their sentiments on [certain] subjects. * * * The Secretary of State is of opinion that Mr. Morris's letters [to the President] remove any doubts which might have been entertained as to the intentions and dispositions of the British cabinet; * * * that Mr. Morris should be informed that he has fulfilled the object of his agency to the satisfaction of the President.—OFFICIAL REPORT. vii, 517. FORD ED., v, 261. (December 1790.)

5561. MORTMAIN, Laws of.—The bill for establishing a National Bank undertakes * * * to form the subscribers into a corporation and enables them in their corporate capacities to receive grants of land, and, so far, is against the laws of Mortmain. Though the Constitution controls the laws of Mortmain so far as to permit Congress itself to hold land for certain purposes, yet not so far as to permit them to communicate a similar right to other corporate bodies.—NATIONAL BANK OPINION. vii, 555. FORD ED., v, 284. (1791.)

5562. MOTTOES, Beauty of.—I shall omit the word *agisos*, according to the license you allow me, because I think the beauty of a motto is to condense much matter in as few words as possible.*—To GEORGE WYTHE. ii, 6. FORD ED., iv, 267. (P., 1786.)

5563. MOUNTAINS, Altitude of.—I examined, with great satisfaction, your barometrical estimate of the heights of our mountains; and with the more, as they corroborated conjectures on this subject which I had made before. My estimates had made them a little higher than yours (I speak of the Blue Ridge). Measuring with a very nice instrument the angle subtended vertically by the highest mountain of the Blue Ridge opposite to my own house, a distance of about eighteen miles southwestward, I made the highest about two thousand feet, as well as I remember. * * * I do not remember from what principles I estimated the Peaks of Otter at four thousand feet; but some late observations of Judge Tucker's coincided very nearly with my estimate. Your measures confirm another opinion of mine, that the Blue Ridge, on its south side, is the highest ridge in our country compared with its base.—To JONATHAN WILLIAMS. iv, 146. FORD ED., vii, 85. (M., 1796.)

5564. MOUNTAINS, Barometrical measurement.—The method of estimating heights [of mountains] by the barometer, is convenient and useful, as being ready, and furnishing an approximation to truth. Of what degree of accuracy it is susceptible we know not as yet; no certain theory being established for ascertaining the density and weight of that portion of the column of atmosphere contiguous to the mountain; from the weight of which, nevertheless, we are to infer the height of the mountain. The most plausible seems to be that which supposes the mercury of barometer divided into horizontal lamina of equal *thickness*; and a similar column of the atmosphere into lamina of equal *weights*. The former divisions give a set of arithmetical, the latter of geometrical progressionals, which being the character of logarithms and their numbers, the tables of these furnish ready computations, needing, however, the corrections which the state of the thermometer calls for. It is probable that in taking heights in the vicinity of each other in this way, there may be no considerable error, because the passage between them may be quick and repeated. The height of a mountain from its base, thus taken, merits, therefore, a very different degree of credit from that of its height above the level of the sea, where that is distant. According, for example, to the theory above mentioned, the height of Monticello from its base is 580 feet, and its base 610 feet 8 inches, above the level of the ocean; the former, from

* Jefferson proposed this motto for the Coat of Arms of Virginia: "Rex est qui regem non habet." The mottoes on his own seals were: "Ab eo libertas, a quo spiritus", and "Rebellion to tyrants is obedience to God".—EDITOR.

other facts, I believe to be near the truth; but a knowledge of the different falls of water from hence to the tide-water at Richmond, a distance of seventy-five miles, enables us to say that the whole descent to that place is but 170 or 180 feet. From thence to the ocean may be a distance of one hundred miles; it is all tide-water, and through a level country. I know not what to conjecture as the amount of descent, but certainly not 435 feet, as that theory would suppose, nor the quarter part of it. I do not know by what rule General Williams made his computations. He reckons the foot of the Blue Ridge, twenty miles from here, but 100 feet above the tide-water at Richmond. We know the descent, as before observed, to be at least 170 feet from hence, to which is to be added that from the Blue Ridge to this place, a very hilly country, with constant and great waterfalls. His estimate, therefore, must be much below truth. Results so different prove that for distant comparisons of height, the barometer is not to be relied on according to any theory yet known. While, therefore, we give a good degree of credit to the results of operations between the summit of a mountain and its base, we must give less to those between its summit and the level of the ocean.—To CAPT. A. PARTRIDGE. vi, 495. (M., 1815.)

5565. MOUNTAINS, Trigonometrical measurement.—I thank you for * * * the corrections of Colonel Williams's altitudes of the mountains of Virginia, * * * and especially for the very able extract on barometrical measures. The precision of the calculations, and soundness of the principles on which they are founded, furnish, I am satisfied, a great approximation towards truth, and raise that method of estimating heights to a considerable degree of rivalship with the trigonometrical. The last is not without some sources of inaccuracy. The admeasurement of the base is liable to errors which can be rendered insensible only by such degrees of care as have been exhibited by the mathematicians who have been employed in measuring degrees on the surface of the earth. * * * No two men can differ on a principle of trigonometry. Not so on the theories of barometrical mensuration. On these have been great differences of opinion, and among characters of just celebrity. * * * In 1776, I observed the height of the mercury at the base and summit of the mountain I live on, and by Nettleton's tables, estimated the height at 512.17 feet, and called it about 500 feet in the *Notes on Virginia*. But calculating it since on the same observations, according to Bongour's method with De Luc's improvements, the result was 579.5 feet; and lately I measured the same height trigonometrically, with the aid of a base line of 1,175 feet in a vertical plane with the summit, and at the distance of about 1500 yards from the axis of the mountain, and made it 599.35 feet. I consider this as testing the advance of the barometrical process towards truth by the adoption of the logarithmic ratio of heights and densities; and continued observations and experiments will continue to advance it still more. But the first character of a common measure of things being that of invariability, I can never suppose that a substance so heterogeneous and variable as the atmospheric fluid, changing daily and hourly its weight and dimensions to the amount, sometimes, of one-tenth of the whole, can be applied as a standard of measure to anything, with as much mathematical exactness, as a trigonometrical process. It is still, however, a resource of great value for these purposes, because its use is so easy, in comparison with the other, and especially where the grounds are unfavorable for a base; and its results are so near the truth as to answer all the common purposes of information. Indeed, I should in all cases, prefer the use of both, to warn us against gross error, and to put us, when that is suspected on a repetition of our process.*—To Capt. A. Partridge. vi, 510. (M., 1816.)

5566. MOURNING, Official.—No one would more willingly than myself pay the just tribute due to the services of Captain [John] Barry, by writing a letter of condolence to his widow, as you suggest. But when one undertakes to administer justice, it must be with an even hand, and by rule; what is done for one, must be done for every one in equal degree. To what a train of attentions would this draw a President. How difficult it would be to draw the line between that degree of merit entitled to such a testimonial of it, and that not so entitled? If drawn in a particular case differently from what the friends of the deceased would judge right, what offence would it give, and of the most tender kind? How much offence would be given by accidental inattentions, or want of information? The first step into such an undertaking ought to be well weighed. On the death of Dr. Franklin, the King and Convention of France went into mourning. So did the House of Representatives of the United States. The Senate refused. I proposed to General Washington that the Executive department should wear mourning. He declined it. because he said he should not know where to draw the line, if he once began that ceremony. Mr. Adams was then Vice-President, and I thought General Washington had his eye on him, whom he certainly did not love. I told him the world had drawn so broad a line between himself and Dr. Franklin, on the one side, and the residue of mankind, on the other, that we might wear mourning for them, and the question still remain new and undecided as to all others. He thought it best, however, to avoid it. On these considerations alone, however well affected to the merit of Commodore Barry, I think it prudent not to engage myself in a practice which may become embarrassing.—To Dr. Benjamin Rush. iv, 507. Ford ed., viii, 264. (W., 1803.)

5567. MOUSTIER (Count), Attachment for.—Fortune seems to have arranged among her destinies that I should never continue for any time with a person whose manners and principles had excited my warm attachment. While I resided in France, you resided in America. While I was crossing over to America, you were crossing back to France; when I am come to reside with our government, your residence is transferred to Berlin. Of all this, Fortune is the mistress, but she cannot change my affections, nor lessen the regrets I feel at their perpetual disappointment.—To Count Moustier. iii, 199. (Pa., 1790.)

5568. MOUSTIER (Count), Character of.—You will find him open, communicative, candid, simple in his manners, and a declared enemy to ostentation and luxury. He goes with a resolution to add no aliment to it by his example, unless he finds that the dispositions of our countrymen require it indispensably.—To John Jay. ii, 293. (P., 1787.)

5569. —— ——. De Moustier is remarkably communicative. With adroitness he may

be pumped of anything. His openness is from character, not from affectation. An intimacy with him may, on this account, be politically valuable.—To James Madison. Ford ed., iv, 461. (P., 1787.)

5570. MOUSTIER (Count), Medal for.—The President, in a letter to the King, has expressed his sense of your merit, and his entire approbation of your conduct while here, and has charged me to convey to yourself the same sentiments on his part. Had you returned to your station with us, you would have received new and continued marks of the esteem inspired by the general worth of your character, as well as by the particular dispositions you manifested towards this country. * * * As a testimony of these sentiments, we ask your acceptance of a medal and chain of gold.*—To Count Moustier. iii, 216. (Pa., 1791.)

5571. MOUSTIER (Count), Minister to America.—The count Moustier is nominated Minister Plenipotentiary to America, and a frigate is ordered to Cherbourg to carry him over.—To John Jay. ii, 274. (P., Sept. 1787.)

5572. MOUSTIER (Count), Recall.—We had before understood * * * that the conduct of the Count Moustier was politically and morally offensive. It was delicate for me to speak on the subject to the Count de Montmorin. The invaluable mediation of * * * the Marquis de Lafayette was, therefore, resorted to, and the subject explained, though not pressed. Later intelligence showing the necessity of pressing it, it has been represented through the same medium to the Count de Montmorin, that recent information proved to us, that his minister's conduct had rendered him personally odious in America, and might even influence the dispositions of the two nations; that his recall was become a matter of mutual concern; that we had understood he was instructed to remind the new government of their debt to this country, and that he was in the purpose of doing it in very harsh terms; that this could not increase their desire of hastening payment, and might wound their affections; that, therefore, it was much to be desired that his discretion should not be trusted to, as to the form in which the demand should be made, but that the letter should be written here, and he instructed to add nothing but his signature; nor was his private conduct omitted. The Count de Montmorin was sensibly impressed. * * * It had been decided, on the request of the Marquis de la Luzerne, that Otto should go to London; that they would send a person [Colonel Ternant] to America as Chargé des Affaires in place of Otto, and that if the President (General Washington) approved of him, he should be afterwards made minister. * * * Ternant will see that his predecessor is recalled for unconciliatory deportment, and that he will owe his own promotion to the approbation of the President.—To John Jay. ii, 571. (P., 1789.)

5573. MOUSTIER (Count), Unostentatious.—He is a great enemy to formality, etiquette, ostentation and luxury. He goes with the best dispositions to cultivate society, without poisoning it by ill example. He is sensible, disposed to view things favorably, and being well acquainted with the constitution of England, her manners and language, is the

---

* Captain Partridge was an Engineer officer at West Point.—Editor.

* De Moustier was appointed minister to Berlin.—Editor.

better prepared for his station with us.—To JAMES MADISON. ii, 292. FORD ED., iv, 460. (P., 1787.) See ETIQUETTE.

5574. MURDER, Child.—By the stat. 21. Jac. 1. c. 27. and Act. Ass. 1170. c. 12. concealment by the mother of the death of a bastard child is made murder. In justification of this, it is said, that shame is a feeling which operates so strongly on the mind, as frequently to induce the mother of such a child to murder it, in order to conceal her disgrace. The act of concealment, therefore, proves she was influenced by shame, and that influence produces a presumption that she murdered the child. The effect of this law, then is, to make what, in its nature, is only presumptive evidence of a murder conclusive of that fact. To this I answer, 1. So many children die before or soon after birth, that to presume all those murdered who are found dead, is a presumption which will lead us oftener wrong than right, and consequently would shed more blood than it would save. 2. If the child were born dead, the mother would naturally choose rather to conceal it, in hopes of still keeping a good character in the neighborhood. So that the act of concealment is far from proving the guilt of murder on the mother. 3. If shame be a powerful affection of the mind, is not parental love also? Is it not the strongest affection known? Is it not greater even than that of self-preservation? While we draw presumptions from shame, one affection of the mind, against the life of the prisoner, should we not give some weight to presumptions from parental love, an affection at least as strong, in favor of life? If concealment of the fact is a presumptive evidence of murder, so strong as to overbalance all other evidence that may possibly be produced to take away the presumption, why not trust the force of this incontestable presumption to the jury, who are, in a regular course, to hear presumptive, as well as positive testimony? If the presumption arising from the act of concealment, may be destroyed by proof, positive or circumstantial, to the contrary, why should the legislature preclude that contrary proof? Objection. The crime is difficult to prove, being usually committed in secret. Answer. But circumstantial proof will do; for example, marks of violence, the behavior, countenance, &c., of the prisoner, &c. And if conclusive proof be difficult to be obtained, shall we, therefore, fasten irremovably upon equivocal proof? Can we change the nature of what is contestable, and make it incontestable? Can we make that conclusive which God and nature have made inconclusive? Solon made no law against parricide, supposing it impossible that any one could be guilty of it; and the Persians from the same opinion, adjudged all who killed their reputed parents to be bastards; and although parental be yet stronger than filial affection, we admit saticide proved on the most equivocal testimony, whilst they rejected all proof of an act certainly not more repugnant to nature, as of a thing impossible, unprovable.—NOTE TO CRIMES BILL. i, 149. FORD ED., ii, 206. (1778.)

5575. MURDER, Of colonists.—The proposition [of Lord North] is altogether unsatisfactory * * * because it does not propose to repeal the several acts of Parliament * * * exempting, by mock trial, the murderers of colonists from punishment.—REPLY TO LORD NORTH'S PROPOSITION. FORD ED., i, 480. (July 1775.)

5576. ——— ———. He has combined with others to subject us to a jurisdiction foreign to our constitutions and unacknowledged by our laws, giving his assent to their acts of pretended legislation, for quartering large bodies of armed troops among us; for protecting them by a mock trial from punishment for any murders which they should commit on the inhabitants of these States.—DECLARATION OF INDEPENDENCE AS DRAWN BY JEFFERSON.

5577. MURDER, Degrees of.—Manslaughter is the killing a man with design, but in a sudden gust of passion, and where the killer has not had time to cool. The first offence is not punished capitally, but the second is. This is the law of England and of all the American States; and is not now a new proposition. Those laws have supposed that a man, whose passions have so much dominion over him, as to lead him to repeated acts of murder, is unsafe to society; that it is better he should be put to death by the law, than others more innocent than himself, on the movements of his impetuous passions.—To M. DE MEUNIER. ix, 263. FORD ED., iv, 169. (P., 1786.)

5578. ——— ———. In 1796, our Legislature passed the law for amending the penal laws of the Commonwealth. [Virginia.] * * * Instead of the settled distinctions of murder and manslaughter, preserved in my bill, they introduced the new terms of murder in the first and second degrees.*—AUTOBIOGRAPHY. i, 47. FORD ED., i, 65. (1821.)

5579. MURDER, Excusable.—Excusable homicides are in some cases not quite unblamable. These should subject the party to marks of contrition; viz., the killing of a man in defence of property; so also in defence of one's person, which is a species of excusable homicide; because, although cases may happen where these are also commendable, yet most frequently they are done on too slight appearance of danger; as in return for a blow, kick, fillip, &c., or on a person's getting into a house, not *animo furandi*, but perhaps *veneris causa*, &c. Excusable homicides are by misadventure, or in self-defence.—NOTE TO CRIMES BILL. i, 152. FORD ED., ii, 209. (1779.)

5580. MURDER, Indian.—I wish Governor Harrison may be able to have the murder of the Kaskaskian by the Kickapoo settled in the Indian way. * * * Both the Indians and our own people need some example of punishment for the murder of an Indian.—To HENRY DEARBORN. v, 162. (M., 1807.)

5581. ——— ———. When a murder has been committed on one of our stragglers, the murderer should be demanded. If not delivered, give time, and still press the demand. We find it difficult, with our regular government, to take and punish a murderer of an Indian. Indeed, I believe we have never been able to do it in a single instance. They have their difficulties also, and require time. In fact, it is a case where indulgence on both sides is just and necessary, to prevent the two nations from being perpetually committed in war, by the acts of the most vagabond and ungovernable of their members. When the refusal to deliver

* The clause of Jefferson's bill read as follows: "And where persons, meaning to commit a trespass only, or larceny, or other unlawful deed, and doing an act from which involuntary homicide hath ensued, have heretofore been adjudged guilty of manslaughter, or of murder, by transferring such their unlawful intention to an act, much more penal than they could have in probable contemplation; no such case shall hereafter be deemed manslaughter, unless manslaughter was intended, nor murder, unless murder was intended."—EDITOR.

the murderer is permanent, and proceeds from the want of will, and not of ability we should then interdict all trade and intercourse with them till they give us complete satisfaction.—To MERIWETHER LEWIS. v, 350. (M., 1808.)

5582. —— ——. If we had to go to war [with the Indians] for every hunter or trader killed, and murderer refused, we should have had general and constant war. The process to be followed, in my opinion, when a murder has been committed, is first to demand the murderer, and not regarding a first refusal to deliver, give time and press it. If perseveringly refused, recall all traders, and interdict commerce with them, until he be delivered.—To HENRY DEARBORN. v, 348. (M., Aug. 1808.)

5583. MURDER, Punishment for.—As there was but one white man murdered by the Indians, I should be averse to the execution of more than one of them, selecting the most guilty and worst character. Nothing but extreme criminality should induce the execution of a second, and nothing beyond that. Their idea is that justice allows only man for man, that all beyond that is new aggression, which must be expiated by a new sacrifice of an equivalent number of our people.—To MERIWETHER LEWIS. v, 354. (M., 1808.)

5584. —— ——. There is the more reason for moderation, as we know we cannot punish any murder which shall be committed by us on them. Even if the murderer can be taken, our juries have never yet convicted the murderer of an Indian.—To MERIWETHER LEWIS. v, 354. (M., 1808.)

5585. MURDER, Self.—Suicide is by law punishable by forfeiture of chattels. This bill (revising the Virginia Code) exempts it from forfeiture. The suicide injures the State less than he who leaves it with his effects. If the latter then be not punished, the former should not. As to the example, we need not fear its influence. Men are too much attached to life, to exhibit frequent instances of depriving themselves of it. At any rate, the quasi-punishment of confiscation will not prevent it. For if one be found who can calmly determine to renounce life, who is so weary of his existence here, as rather to make experiment of what is beyond the grave, can we suppose him, in such a state of mind, susceptible of influence from the losses to his family from confiscation? That men in general, too, disapprove of this severity, is apparent from the constant practice of juries finding the suicide in a state of insanity; because they have no other way of saving the forfeiture. Let it then be done away.—NOTE TO CRIMES BILL. i, 152. FORD ED., ii, 210. (1779.)

5586. MUSEUMS, Maintenance of.—Nobody can desire more ardently than myself, to concur in whatever may promote useful science, and I view no science with more partiality than Natural History. But I have ever believed that in this, as in most other cases, abortive attempts retard rather than promote this object. To be really useful we must keep pace with the state of society, and not dishearten it by attempts at what its population, means, or occupations will fail in attempting. In the particular enterprises for museums, we have seen the populous and wealthy cities of Boston and New York unable to found or maintain an institution. The feeble condition of that in each of these places sufficiently proves this. In Philadelphia alone, has this attempt succeeded to a good degree. It has

been owing there to a measure of zeal and perseverance in an individual rarely equal.ed; to a population, crowded, wealthy, and more than usually addicted to the pursuit of knowledge. And, with all this, the institution does not maintain itself.—To MR. DE LA COSTE. v, 79. (W., 1807.)

5587. MUSIC, Domestic bands.—The bounds of an American fortune will not admit the indulgence of a domestic band of musicians, yet I have thought that a passion for music might be reconciled with that economy which we are obliged to observe. I retain, for instance, among my domestic servants a gardener, a weaver, a cabinet-maker, and a stone-cutter, to which I would add a *vigneron*. In a country where, like yours [France], music is cultivated and practiced by every class of men, I suppose there might be found persons of these trades who could perform on the French horn, clarinet, or hautboy, and bassoon, so that one might have a band of two French horns, two clarionets, two hautboys, and a bassoon, without enlarging his domestic expenses. A certainty of employment for a half dozen years, and at the end of that time, to find them, if they chose, a conveyance to their own country, might induce them to come here on reasonable wages. Without meaning to give you trouble, perhaps it might be practicable for you * * * to find out such men disposed to come to America. Sobriety and good nature would be desirable parts of their characters. If you think such a plan practicable, and will be so kind as to inform me what will be necessary to be done on my part, I will take care that it shall be done. To ——. i, 209. FORD ED., ii, 159. (Wg., 1778.)

5588. MUSIC, Ear for.—Music is invaluable where a person has an ear. Where they have not, it should not be attempted.—To N. BURWELL. vii, 103. FORD ED., x, 105. (M., 1818.)

5589. MUSIC, Enjoyment of.—Music is an enjoyment [in France] the deprivation of which with us, cannot be calculated. I am almost ready to say, it is the only thing which from my heart I envy them, and which, in spite of all the authority of the Decalogue, I do covet.—To MR. BELLINI. i, 445. (P., 1785.)

5590. MUSIC, Foot-bass.—I have lately examined a foot-bass, newly invented by the celebrated Krumfoltz. It is precisely a pianoforte, about ten feet long, eighteen inches broad, and nine inches deep. It is of one octave only, from fa to fa. The part where the keys are projects at the side in order to lengthen the levers of the keys. It is placed on the floor, on the harpsichord or other pianoforte, is set over it, the foot acting in concert on that, while the fingers play on this. There are three unison chords to every note, of strong brass wire, and the lowest have wire wrapped on them as the lowest in the pianoforte. The chords give a fine, clear, deep tone almost like the pipe of an organ.—To FRANCIS HOPKINSON. ii, 75. (P., 1786.)

5591. MUSIC, Harmonica.—I am very much pleased with your project on the harmonica, and the prospect of your succeeding in the application of keys to it. It will be the greatest present which has been made to the musical world this century, not excepting the piano-forte. If its tone approaches that given by the finger as nearly only as the harpsichord does that of the harp, it will be very valuable. —To FRANCIS HOPKINSON. ii, 75. (P., 1786.)

5592. MUSIC, Harpsichord.—I applaud much your perseverance in improving this instrument [harpsichord], and benefiting mankind almost in spite of their teeth.—To Francis Hopkinson. i, 440. (P., 1785.)

5593. MUSIC, Keeping time.—Monsieur Renaudin's invention for determining the true time of the musical movements, Largo, Adagio, &c. * * * has been examined by the [Paris] Academy of Music, who are so well satisfied of its utility, that they have ordered all music which shall be printed here, in future, to have the movements numbered in correspondence with this plexi-chronometer. * * * The instrument is useful, but still it may be greatly simplified. I got him to make me one, and having fixed a pendulum vibrating seconds, I tried by that the vibrations of his pendulum, according to the several movements. I find the pendulum regulated to

Largo			52	
Adagio			60	times
Andante	vibrates		70	in a
Allegro			95	minute
Presto			135	

Every one, therefore, may make a chronometer adapted to his instrument. For a harpsichord, the following occurs to me: In the wall of your chamber, over the instrument, drive five little brads, as 1, 2, 3, 4, 5, in the following manner. Take a string with a bob to it, of such length, as that hung on No. 1, it shall vibrate fifty-two times in a minute. Then proceed by trial to drive number No. 2, at such a distance, that drawing the loop of the string to that, the part remaining between 1 and the bob, shall vibrate sixty times in a minute. Fix the third for seventy vibrations, &c.; the chord always hanging over No. 1, as the centre of vibration. A person, playing on the violin, may fix this on his music stand. A pendulum, thrown into vibration, will continue in motion long enough to give you the time of your piece.—To Francis Hopkinson. i, 504. (P., 1786.)

5594. MUSIC, Negroes and.—In music the blacks are more generally gifted than the whites, with accurate ears for tune and time, and they have been found capable of imagining a small catch.* Whether they will be equal to the composition of a more extensive run of melody, or of complicated harmony, is yet to be proved.—Notes on Virginia. viii, 383. Ford ed., iii, 246. (1782.)

5595. MUSIC, Passion for.—If there is a gratification which I envy any people in this world, it is to your country [France] its music. This is the favorite passion of my soul, and fortune has cast my lot in a country where it is in a state of deplorable barbarism.—To ——. i, 209. Ford ed., ii, 158. (Wg., 1778.)

5596. MUSIC, Piano.—I wrote [you] for a Clavichord. I have since seen a Forte-piano and am charmed with it. Send me this instrument then instead of the Clavichord: let the case be of fine mahogany, solid, not veneered, the compass from Double G. to F. in alt, a plenty of spare strings; and the workmanship

* The instrument proper to them is the banjer (corrupted by the negroes into "banjo") which they brought hither from Africa, which is the original of the guitar, its chords being precisely the four lower chords of the guitar.—Note by Jefferson.

of the whole very handsome and worthy the acceptance of a lady for whom I intend it.—To Thomas Adams. Ford ed., i, 395. (M., 1771.)

5597. —— ——. I had almost decided, on Piccini's advice, to get a piano-forte for my daughter; but your last letter may pause me, till I see its effect.—To Francis Hopkinson. i, 440. (P., 1785.)

5598. MUSIC, Quilling.—I do not altogether despair of making something of your method of quilling, though, as yet, the prospect is not favorable.—To Francis Hopkinson. i, 440. (P., 1785.)

5599. —— ——. I mentioned to Piccini the improvement [quilling] with which I am entrusted. He plays on the piano-forte, and therefore did not feel himself personally interested.—To Francis Hopkinson. i, 440. (P., 1785.)

5600. MUSKETS, Improved.—An improvement is made here [France] in the construction of muskets, which it may be interesting to Congress to know, should they at any time propose to procure any. It consists in the making every part of them so exactly alike, that what belongs to any one, may be used for every other musket in the magazine. * * * As yet, the inventor has only completed the lock of the musket, on this plan. * * * He presented me the parts of fifty locks taken to pieces, and arranged in compartments. I put several together myself, taking pieces at hazard as they came to hand, and they fitted in the most perfect manner.—To John Jay. i, 411. (P., 1785.)

— NAIL-MAKING.—See Jefferson (Thomas.)

5601. NAMES, Authority of great.—It is surely time for men to think for themselves, and to throw off the authority of names so artificially magnified.—To William Short. vii, 165. (M., 1820.)

5602. NAMES, Bestowal of.—I agree with you entirely in condemning the mania of giving names to objects of any kind after persons still living. Death alone can seal the title of any man to this honor, by putting it out of his power to forfeit it.—To Dr. Benjamin Rush. iv, 335. Ford ed., vii, 459. (M., 1800.)

5603. —— ——. There is one * * * mode of recording merit, which I have often thought might be introduced, so as to gratify the living by praising the dead. In giving, for instance, a commission of Chief Justice to Bushrod Washington, it should be in consideration of his integrity, and science in the laws, and of the services rendered to our country by his illustrious relation, &c. A commission to a descendant of Dr. Franklin, besides being in consideration of the proper qualifications of the person, should add that of the great services rendered by his illustrious ancestor, Benjamin Franklin, by the advancement of science, by inventions useful to man, &c.—To Dr. Benjamin Rush. iv, 335. Ford ed., vii, 459. (M., 1800.)

5604. —— ——. I am sensible of the mark of esteem manifested by the name you have given to your son. Tell him from me, that he must consider as essentially belonging to it, to love his friends and wish no ill to his enemies.—To David Campbell. v, 499. (M., 1810.)

5605. NAMES, Opinions and.—If * * * opinions are sound ‸ * * they will prevail by their own weight without the aid of names.—To Samuel Kerchival. vii, 35. Ford ed., x, 45. (M., 1816.)

5606. NAMES, Political party.—The appellation of aristocrats and democrats is the true one expressing the essence of all [parties].—To H. Lee. vii, 376. Ford ed., x, 318. (M., 1824.)

5607. NAMES, Property in.—I am not sure that we ought to change all our names. During the regal government, sometimes, indeed, they were given through adulation; but often also as the reward of the merit of the times, sometimes for services rendered the colony. Perhaps, too, a name when given, should be deemed a sacred property.—To Dr. Benjamin Rush. iv, 335. Ford ed., vii, 459. (M., 1800.)

5608. NASSAU, Fame of.—Nassau is a village the whole rents of which would not amount to more than a hundred or two guineas. Yet it gives the title of Prince to the house of Orange to which it belongs.—Travels in Holland. ix, 383. (1787.)

5609. NATION (United States), Building the.—The interests of the States ought to be made joint in every possible instance, in order to cultivate the idea of our being one nation, and to multiply the instances in which the people shall look up to Congress as their head.—To James Monroe. i, 347. Ford ed., iv, 52. (P., 1785.)

5610. ——— ———. It is, indeed, an animating thought that, while we are securing the rights of ourselves and posterity, we are pointing out the way to struggling nations who wish, like us, to emerge from their tyrannies also.—Reply to Address. iii, 128. Ford ed., v, 147. (1790.)

5611. NATION (United States), Conscience of.—It is true that nations are to be judges for themselves since no one nation has a right to sit in judgment over another. But the tribunal of our consciences remains, and that also of the opinion of the world. These will revise the sentence we pass in our own case, and as we respect these, we must see that in judging ourselves we have honestly done the part of impartial and rigorous judges.—Opinion on French Treaties. vii, 614. Ford ed., vi, 221. (1793.)

5612. NATION (United States), Foreign policy.—Unmeddling with the affairs of other nations, we presume not to prescribe or censure their course.—To Madame de Stael. v, 133. (W., 1807.)

5613. ——— ———. We wish the happiness and prosperity of every nation.—To Madame de Stael. vi, 482. (M., 1815.)

5614. NATION (United States), Liberality.—I am in all cases for a liberal conduct towards other nations, believing that the practice of the same friendly feelings and generous dispositions, which attach individuals in private life, will attach societies on the larger scale, which are composed of individuals.—To Albert Gallatin. Ford ed., viii, 222. (M., 1803.)

5615. NATION (United States), Objects of.—Peace with all nations, and the right which that gives us with respect to all nations, are our object.—To C. W. F. Dumas. iii, 535. (Pa., 1793.)

5616. ——— ———. I hope the United States will ever place themselves among [the number of] peaceable nations.—To Robert R. Livingston. iv, 411. Ford ed., viii, 91. (M., Sep. 1801.)

5617. NATION (United States), Supremacy.—Not in our day, but at no distant one, we may shake a rod over the heads of all, which may make the stoutest of them tremble. But I hope our wisdom will grow with our power, and teach us, that the less we use our power the greater it will be.—To Thomas Leiper. vi, 465. Ford ed., ix, 520. (M., 1815.) See Policy.

5618. ——— ———. The day is not distant, when we may formally require a meridian of partition through the ocean which separates the two hemispheres, on the hither side of which no European gun shall ever be heard, nor an American on the other; and when, during the rage of the eternal wars of Europe, the lion and the lamb, within our regions, shall lie down together in peace.—To William Short. vii, 168. (M., 1820.)

— NATIONAL CAPITAL.—See Washington City.

5619. NATIONAL CURRENCY, Bank paper and.—The question will be asked and ought to be looked at, what is to be the resource if loans cannot be obtained? There is but one, "*Carthago delenda est*". Bank paper must be suppressed, and the circulating medium must be restored to the nation to whom it belongs. It is the only fund on which they can rely for loans; it is the only resource which can never fail them and it is an abundant one for every necessary purpose. Treasury bills, bottomed on taxes, bearing or not bearing interest, as may be found necessary, thrown into circulation will take the place of so much gold and silver, which last, when crowded, will find an efflux into other countries, and thus keep the quantum of medium at its salutary level. Let banks continue if they please, but let them discount for cash alone or for treasury notes. They discount for cash alone in every other country on earth except Great Britain, and her too often unfortunate copyist, the United States. If taken in time, they may be rectified by degrees, and without injustice, but if let alone till the alternative forces itself on us, of submitting to the enemy for want of funds, or the suppression of bank paper, either by law or by convulsion, we cannot foresee how it will end.—To J. W. Eppes. vi, 199. Ford ed., ix, 399. (P.F., Sep. 1813.)

5620. ——— ———. Put down the banks, and if this country could not be carried through the longest war against her most powerful enemy, without ever knowing the want of a dollar, without dependence on the traitorous classes of her citizens, without bearing hard on the resources of the people, or loading the public with an indefinite burthen of debt, I know nothing of my countrymen. Not by any novel project, not by any charlatanerie, but by ordinary and well-experienced means; by the total prohibition of all private paper at all times, by reasonable taxes in war aided by the necessary emissions of public paper of circulating size, this bottomed on special taxes, redeemable annually as this special tax comes in, and finally within a moderate period.—To ALBERT GALLATIN. vi, 498. (M., Oct. 1815.)

5621. NATIONAL CURRENCY, Bank suspensions and.—The failure of our banks * * * restores to us a fund which ought never to have been surrendered by the nation, and which now, prudently used, will carry us through all the fiscal difficulties of the war.—To PRESIDENT MADISON. vi, 386. (M., Sep. 1814.)

5622. NATIONAL CURRENCY, Borrowing fund.—I am sorry to see our loans begin at so exorbitant an interest. And yet, even at that you will soon be at the bottom of the loan-bag. We are an agricultural nation. Such an one employs its sparings in the purchase or improvement of land or stocks. The lendable money among them is chiefly that of orphans and wards in the hands of executors and guardians, and that which the former lays by till he has enough for the purchase in view. In such a nation there is one, and only one, resource for loans, sufficient to carry them through the expense of a war; and that will always be sufficient, and in the power of an honest government, punctual in the preservation of its faith. The fund I mean, is *the mass of circulating coin*. Every one knows, that although not literally, it is nearly true, that every paper dollar emitted banishes a silver one from the circulation. A nation, therefore, making its purchases and payments with bills fitted for circulation, thrusts an equal sum of coin out of circulation. This is equivalent to borrowing that sum, and yet the vendor, receiving in payment a medium as effectual as coin for his purchases or payments, has no claim to interest. And so the nation may continue to issue its bills as far as its wants require, and the limits of the circulation will admit. Those limits are understood to extend with us at present, to two hundred millions of dollars, a greater sum than would be necessary for any war. But this, the only resource which the government could command with certainty, the States have unfortunately fooled away, nay corruptly alienated to swindlers and shavers, under the cover of private banks. Say, too, as an additional evil, that the disposal funds of individuals, to this great amount, have thus been withdrawn from improvement and useful enterprise, and employed in the useless, usu-

rious and demoralizing practices of bank directors and their accomplices. In the year 1775, our State [Virginia] availed itself of this fund by issuing a paper money, bottomed on a specific tax for its redemption, and, to insure its credit, bearing an interest of five per cent. Within a very short time, not a bill of this emission was to be found in circulation. It was locked up in the chests of executors, guardians, widows, farmers, &c. We then issued bills bottomed on a redeeming tax, but bearing no interest. These were readily received, and never depreciated a single farthing. In the Revolutionary war, the old Congress and the States issued bills without interest, and without a tax. They occupied the channels of circulation very freely, till those channels were overflowed by an excess beyond all the calls of circulation. But, although we have so improvidently suffered the field of circulating medium to be filched from us by private individuals, yet I think we may recover it in part, and even in the whole, if the States will cooperate with us. If Treasury bills are emitted on a tax appropriated for their redemption in fifteen years, and (to ensure preference in the first moments of competition) bearing an interest of six per cent. there is no one who would not take them in preference to the bank paper now afloat, on a principle of patriotism as well as interest; and they would be withdrawn from circulation into private hoards to a considerable amount. Their credit once established, others might be emitted, bottomed also on a tax, but not bearing interest, and if even their credit faltered, open public loans, on which these bills alone should be received as specie. These, operating as a sinking fund, would reduce the quantity in circulation, so as to maintain that in an equilibrium with specie. It is not easy to estimate the obstacles which, in the beginning, we should encounter in ousting the banks from their possession of the circulation; but a steady and judicious alternation of emissions and loans, would reduce them in time. But while this is going on, another measure should be pressed, to recover ultimately our right to the circulation. The States should be applied to, to transfer the right of issuing circulating paper to Congress exclusively, *in perpetuum,* if possible, but during the war at least, with a saving of charter rights. I believe that every State west and south of the Connecticut River, except Delaware, would immediately do it; and the others would follow in time. Congress would, of course, begin by obliging unchartered banks to wind up their affairs within a short time, and the others as their charters expired, forbidding the subsequent circulation of their paper. This, they would supply with their own, bottomed, every emission, on an adequate tax, and bearing or not bearing interest, as the state of the public pulse should indicate. Even in the non-complying States, these bills would make their way, and supplant the unfunded paper of their banks, by their solidity, by the universality of their currency, and by their receivability for customs and taxes. It would be in their power, too, to curtail those banks to the amount of their actual specie, by gathering up their paper, and running it constantly on them. The national paper might thus take place even in the non-complying States. In this way, I am not without a hope, that this great, this sole resource for loans in an agricultural country, might yet be recovered for the use of the nation during war; and, if obtained *in perpetuum,* it would always be sufficient to carry us through any war; provided, that in the interval between war and war, all the outstanding paper should be called in, coin be permitted to flow in again, and to hold the field of circulation until another war should require its yielding place again to the national medium.—To JOHN WAYLES EPPES. vi, 139. FORD ED., ix, 391. (M., June 1813.)

5623. ——— ———. I like well your idea of issuing treasury notes bearing interest, because I am persuaded they would soon be withdrawn from circulation and locked up in vaults in private hoards. It would put it in the power of every man to lend his $100 or $1000, though not able to go forward on the great scale, and be the most advantageous way of obtaining a loan.—To THOMAS LAW. FORD ED., ix, 433. (M., Nov. 1813.)

5624. ——— ———. The circulating fund is the only one we can ever command with certainty. It is sufficient for all our wants; and the impossibility of even defending the country without its aid as a borrowing fund, renders it indispensable that the nation should take and keep it in their own hands, as their exclusive resource.— To PRESIDENT MADISON. vi, 393. FORD ED., ix, 491. (M., Oct. 1814.)

5625. ——— ———. Although a century of British experience has proved to what a wonderful extent the funding on specific redeeming taxes enables a nation to anticipate in war the resources of peace, and although the other nations of Europe have tried and trodden every path of force or folly in fruitless quest of the same object, yet *we* still expect to find in juggling tricks and banking dreams, that money can be made out of nothing, and in sufficient quantities to meet the expenses of a heavy war by sea and land. It is said, indeed, that money cannot be borrowed from our merchants as from those of England. But it can be borrowed from our people. They will give you all the necessaries of war they produce, if, instead of the bankrupt trash they are now obliged to receive for want of any other, you will give them a paper promise funded on a specific pledge, and of a size for common circulation. But you say the merchants will not take this paper. What the people take the merchants must take, or sell nothing. All these doubts and fears prove only the extent of the dominion which the banking institutions have obtained over the minds of our citizens, and especially of those inhabiting cities or other banking places; and this

dominion must be broken, or it will break us. But * * * we must make up our minds to suffer yet longer before we can get right. The misfortune is, that in the meantime, we shall plunge ourselves in unextinguishable debt, and entail on our posterity an inheritance of eternal taxes, which will bring our government and people into the condition of those of England, a nation of pikes and gudgeons, the latter bred merely as food for the former.—To JAMES MONROE. vi, 409. FORD ED., ix, 497. (M., Jan. 1815.)

5626. NATIONAL CURRENCY, Circulating medium.—If I have used any expression restraining the emissions of treasury notes to a *sufficient* medium, * * * I have done it inadvertently, and under the impression then possessing me, that the war would be very short. A *sufficient* medium would not, on the principles of any writer, exceed thirty millions of dollars, and of those of some not ten millions. Our experience has proved it may be run up to two or three hundred millions, without more than doubling what would be the prices of things under a *sufficient* medium, or say a metallic one, which would always keep itself at the *sufficient* point; and, if they rise to this term, and the descent from it be gradual, it would not produce sensible revolutions in private fortunes. I shall be able to explain my views more definitely by the use of numbers. Suppose we require, to carry on the war, an annual loan of twenty millions, then I propose that, in the first year, you shall lay a tax of two millions, and emit twenty millions of treasury notes, of a size proper for circulation, and bearing no interest, to the redemption of which the proceeds of that tax shall be inviolably pledged and applied, by recalling annually their amount of the identical bills funded on them. The second year, lay another tax of two millions, and emit twenty millions more. The third year the same, and so on, until you have reached the maximum of taxes which ought to be imposed. Let me suppose this maximum to be one dollar a head, or ten millions of dollars, merely as an exemplification more familiar than would be the algebraical symbols x or y. You would reach this in five years. The sixth year, then, still emit twenty millions of treasury notes, and continue all the taxes two years longer. The seventh year, twenty millions more, and continue the whole taxes another two years; and so on. Observe, that although you emit twenty millions of dollars a year, you call in ten millions, and, consequently, add but ten millions annually to the circulation. It would be in thirty years, then, *primâ facie,* that you would reach the present circulation of three hundred millions, or the ultimate term to which we might venture. But observe, also, that in that time we shall have become thirty millions of people, to whom three hundred millions of dollars would be no more than one hundred millions to us now; which sum would probably not have raised prices more than fifty per cent. on what may be deemed the standard, or metallic prices. This increased population and consumption, while it would be increasing the proceeds of the redemption tax, and lessening the balance annually thrown into circulation, would also absorb, without saturation, more of the surplus medium, and enable us to push the same process to a much higher term, to one which we might safely call indefinite, because extending so far beyond the limits, either in time or expense, of any supposable war. All we should have to do would be, when the war should be ended, to leave the gradual extinction of these notes to the operation of the taxes pledged for their redemption; not to suffer a dollar of paper to be emitted either by public or private authority, but let the metallic medium flow back into the channels of circulation, and occupy them until another war should oblige us to recur, for its support, to the same resource, and the same process, on the circulating medium.—To PRESIDENT MADISON. vi, 392. FORD ED., ix, 489. (M., Oct. 1814.)

5627. ——— ———. The government is now issuing Treasury notes for circulation, bottomed on solid funds and bearing interest. The banking confederacy (and the merchants bound to them by their debts) will endeavor to crush the credit of these notes; but the country is eager for them, as something they can trust to, and as soon as a convenient quantity of them can get into circulation the bank notes die.—To JEAN BAPTISTE SAY. vi, 434. (M., 1815.)

5628. ——— ———. The war, had it proceeded, would have upset our government; and a new one, whenever tried, will do it. And so it must be while our money, the nerve of war, is much or little, real or imaginary, as our bitterest enemies choose to make it.— To ALBERT GALLATIN. vi, 498. (M., Oct. 1815.)

5629. NATIONAL CURRENCY, Congressional control.—From the establishment of the United States Bank, to this day, I have preached against this system, and have been sensible no cure could be hoped but in the catastrophe now happening. The remedy was to let banks drop gradually at the expiration of their charters, and for the State governments to relinquish the power of establishing others. This would not, as it should not, have given the power of establishing them to Congress. But Congress could then have issued treasury notes payable within a fixed period, and founded on a specific tax, the proceeds of which. as they came in, should be exchangeable for the notes of that particular emission only. This depended, it is true, on the will of the State Legislatures, and would have brought on us the phalanx of paper interest. But that interest is now defunct.—To THOMAS COOPER. vi, 381. (M., Sep. 1814.)

5630. ——— ———. To give readier credit to their bills, without obliging themselves to give cash for them on demand. let their collectors be instructed to do so, when they have cash; thus, in some measure, performing the

functions of a bank, as to their own notes.— To THOMAS COOPER. vi, 382. (M., Sep. 1814.)

5631. NATIONAL CURRENCY, Redemption.—Treasury notes of small as well as high denomination, bottomed on a tax which would redeem them in ten years, would place at our disposal the whole circulating medium of the United States; a fund of credit sufficient to carry us through any probable length of war. A small issue of such paper is now commencing. It will immediately supersede the bank paper; nobody receiving that now but for the purposes of the day, and never in payments which are to lie by for any time. In fact, all the banks having declared they will not give cash in exchange for their own notes, these circulate merely because there is no other medium of exchange. As soon as the treasury notes get into circulation, the others will cease to hold any competition with them. I trust that another year will confirm this experiment, and restore this fund to the public, who ought never more to permit its being filched from them by private speculators and disorganizers of the circulation.—To W. H. CRAWFORD. vi, 419. FORD ED., ix, 503. (M., Feb. 1815.)

5632. ——— ———. The third great measure necessary to ensure us permanent prosperity, should ensure resources of money by the suppression of all paper circulation during peace, and licensing that of the nation alone during war. The metallic medium of which we should be possessed at the commencement of a war, would be a sufficient fund for all the loans we should need through its continuance; and if the national bills issued, be bottomed (as is indispensable) on pledges of specific taxes for their redemption within certain and moderate epochs, and be of proper denominations for circulation, no interest on them would be necessary or just, because they would answer to every one the purposes of the metallic money withdrawn and replaced by them.—To WILLIAM H. CRAWFORD. vii, 8. FORD ED., x, 36. (M., 1816.) See BANKS, DOLLAR, MONEY, and PAPER MONEY.

— NATIONAL UNIVERSITY.—See UNIVERSITY.

5633. NATIONS, Constitutions for.— Such indeed are the different circumstances, prejudices, and habits of different nations, that the constitution of no one would be reconcilable to any other in every point.—To M. CORAY. vii, 320. (M., 1823.)

5634. NATIONS, Dictation to.—The presumption of dictating to an independent nation the form of its government, is so arrogant, so atrocious, that indignation, as well as moral sentiment, enlists all our partialities and prayers in favor of one, and our equal execrations against the other.—To JAMES MONROE. vii, 287. FORD ED., x, 257. (M., 1823.)

5635. NATIONS, European.—The European societies * * * under pretence of governing, have divided their nations into two classes, wolves and sheep.—To EDWARD CARRINGTON. ii, 100. FORD ED., iv, 360. (P., 1787.)

5636. ——— ———. The European are nations of eternal war. All their energies are expended in the destruction of the labor, property, and lives of their people.—To PRESIDENT MONROE. vii, 288. FORD ED., x, 257. (M., 1823.)

5637. NATIONS, Extinction of.—I shall not wonder to see the scenes of ancient Rome and Carthage renewed in our day; and if not pursued to the same issue, it may be because the republic of modern powers will not permit the extinction of any one of its members.—To C. W. F. DUMAS. i, 553. (P., 1786.)

5638. NATIONS, Good faith.—A character of good faith is of as much value to a nation as to an individual.—THE ANAS. FORD ED., i, 332. (1808.)

5639. NATIONS, Government of.—I think, with others, that nations are to be governed according to their own interest, but I am convinced that it is their interest, in the long run to be grateful, faithful to their engagements, even in the worst of circumstances, and honorable and generous always.—To M. DE LAFAYETTE. iii, 132. FORD ED., v, 152. (N.Y., 1790.)

5640. NATIONS, History and.—Wars and contentions, indeed, fill the pages of history with more matter. But more blest is that nation whose silent course of happiness furnishes nothing for history to say. This is what I ambition for my own country.—To COUNT DIODATI. v, 62. (W., 1807.)

5641. NATIONS, Ignorant.—If a nation expects to be ignorant and free, in a state of civilization, it expects what never was and never will be.—To CHARLES YANCEY. vi, 517. FORD ED., x, 4. (M., 1816.)

5642. NATIONS, Interest of.—The interests of a nation, when well understood, will be found to coincide with their moral duties.—PARAGRAPH FOR PRESIDENT'S MESSAGE. FORD ED., vi, 119. (1792.)

5643. NATIONS, Jefferson's prayer for all.—I wish that all nations may recover and retain their independence; that those which are overgrown may not advance beyond safe measures of power, that a salutary balance may be ever maintained among nations, and that our peace, commerce and friendship, may be sought and cultivated by all.—To THOMAS LEIPER. vi, 464. FORD ED., ix, 520. (M., 1815.)

5644. ——— ———. Notwithstanding all the French and British atrocities, which will forever disgrace the present era of history, their shameless prostration of all the laws of morality which constitute the security, the peace and comfort of man—notwithstanding the waste of human life, and measure of human suffering which they have inflicted on the world—nations hitherto in slavery have desired through all this bloody mist a glimmering of their own rights. have dared to open their eyes, and to see that their own power will suffice for their emancipation. Their tyrants must now give them more moderate forms of government, and they seem now to be sensible of this themselves. Instead of the parricide treason of Bonaparte in employing the means confided to him as a republican magistrate to the overthrow of that republic, and establishment of a military despotism in himself and his descendants, to the subversion of the neighboring governments, and erection of thrones for his brothers, his sisters and sycophants, had he honestly employed that power in the establishment and support of the freedom of his own country, there is not a nation in Europe which would not at this day have had a more rational government, one in which the will of the people should have had a moderating and salutary influence. The work will now be longer, will swell more rivers with blood, produce more sufferings and more crimes. But it will be consummated; and that it may be will be the theme of my constant prayers while I shall remain on the earth beneath, or in the heavens above.—To WILLIAM BENTLEY. vi, 503. (M., 1815.)

5645. NATIONS, Just and unjust.—A just nation is taken on its word, when recourse is had to armaments and wars to bridle others.—SECOND INAUGURAL ADDRESS. viii, 40. FORD ED., viii, 343. (1805.)

5646. ——— ———. No nation, however powerful, any more than an individual, can be unjust with impunity. Sooner or later public opinion, an instrument merely moral in the beginning, will find occasion physically to inflict its sentences on the unjust.—To JAMES MADISON. FORD ED., viii, 300. (M., 1804.)

5647. NATIONS, Justice and.—No nation can answer for perfect exactitude of proceedings in all their inferior courts. It suffices to provide a supreme judicature, where all error and partiality will be ultimately corrected.—To GEORGE HAMMOND. iii, 414. FORD ED., vi, 55. (Pa., 1792.)

5648. NATIONS, Liberal.—A nation, by establishing a character of liberality and magnanimity, gains in the friendship and respect of others more than the worth of mere money.—SPECIAL MESSAGE. viii, 56. (1806.)

5649. NATIONS, Manners of.—It is difficult to determine on the standard by which the manners of a nation may be tried, whether *catholic* or *particular*. It is more difficult for a native to bring to that standard the manners of his own nation, familiarized to him by habit.—NOTES ON VIRGINIA. viii, 403. FORD ED., iii, 266. (1782.)

5650. NATIONS, Money and rights of. —Money is the agent by which modern nations will recover their rights.—To COMTE DE MOUSTIER. ii, 389. FORD ED., v, 12. (P., 1788.)

5651. NATIONS, Morality.—A nation, as a society, forms a moral person, and every member of it is personally responsible for his society.—To George Hammond. iii, 419. Ford ed., vi, 59. (Pa., 1792.) See Morality (National).

5652. ——— ———. The moral obligations constitute a law for nations as well as individuals.—R. to A. N. Y. Tammany Society. viii, 127. (1808.)

5653. NATIONS, Natural rights of.— In no case are the laws of a nation changed, of natural right, by their passage from one to another domination. The soil, the inhabitants, their property, and the laws by which they are protected go together. Their laws are subject to be changed only in the ease, and extent which their new legislature shall will.—Batture Case. viii, 528. (1812.)

5654. NATIONS, Neighboring.—We have seldom seen neighborhood produce affection among nations. The reverse is almost the universal truth.—To John C. Breckenridge. iv, 499. Ford ed., viii, 243. (M., 1803.)

5655. NATIONS, Oppressed.—That we should wish to see the people of other countries free, is as natural, and at least as justifiable, as that one King should wish to see the Kings of other countries maintained in their despotism.—To Albert Gallatin. vii, 78. Ford ed., x, 90. (M., 1817.)

5656. NATIONS, Peculiarities of.—In reading the travels of a Frenchman through the United States what he remarks as peculiarities in us, prove to us the contrary peculiarities of the French. We have the accounts of Barbary from European and American travellers. It would be more amusing if Melli Melli would give us his observations on the United States. If, with the fables and follies of the Hindoos, so justly pointed out to us by yourself and other travellers, we could compare the contrast of those which an Hindoo traveller would imagine he found among us, it might enlarge our instruction. It would be curious to see what parallel among us he would select for his Veeshni.—To Nathaniel Greene. vi, 72. (M., 1812.)

5657. NATIONS, Political conditions in.—The condition of different descriptions of inhabitants in any country is a matter of municipal arrangement, of which no foreign country has a right to take notice. All its inhabitants are as men to them.—To Samuel Kerchival. vii, 37. Ford ed., x, 46. (M., 1816.)

5658. NATIONS, Representation and.—The [representative principle] has taken deep root in the European mind, and will have its growth; their despots,* sensible of this, are already offering this modification of their governments, as if of their own accord. In-

*In consenting to the newspaper publication of this extract, Jefferson directed that "despots" be changed to "rulers".—Editor.

stead of the parricide treason of Bonaparte, in perverting the means confided to him as a republican magistrate, to the subversion of that republic and erection of a military despotism for himself and his family, had he used it honestly for the establishment and support of a free government in his own country, France would now have been in freedom and rest; and her example operating in a contrary direction, every nation in Europe would have had a government over which the will of the people would have had some control. His atrocious egotism has checked the salutary progress of principle, and deluged it with rivers of blood which are not yet run out. To the vast sum of devastation and of human misery, of which he has been the guilty cause, much is still to be added. But the object is fixed in the eye of nations, and they will press on to its accomplishment and to the general amelioration of the condition of man. What a germ have we planted, and how faithfully should we cherish the parent tree at home!—To Benjamin Austin. vi, 520. Ford ed., x, 8. (M., 1816.)

5659. NATIONS, Revolution.—When subjects are able to maintain themselves in the field, they are then an independent power as to all neutral nations, are entitled to all commerce, and to protection within their limits.—To James Monroe. vi, 550. Ford ed., x, 19. (M., 1816.)

5660. NATIONS, Standing of.—The just standing of all nations is the health and security of all.—To James Maury. vi, 52. Ford ed., ix, 349. (M., 1812.)

5661. NATIONS, Unity of large.—The laws of nature render a large country unconquerable if they adhere firmly together, and to their purpose.—To H. Innes. Ford ed., vi, 266. (Pa., 1793.)

5662. ——— ———. Without union of action and effort in all its parts, no nation can be happy or safe.—To James Sullivan. v, 100. Ford ed., ix, 75. (W., 1807.)

5663. ——— ———. A nation united can never be conquered. We have seen what the ignorant, bigoted and unarmed Spaniards could do against the disciplined veterans of their invaders. * * * The oppressors may cut off heads after heads, but like those of the Hydra they multiply at every stroke. The recruits within a nation's own limits are prompt and without number; while those of their invaders from a distance are slow, limited, and must come to an end.—To John Adams. vi, 525. (M., 1816.)

5664. NATIONS, Young.—The first object of young societies is bread and covering; science is but secondary and subsequent.—To J. Evelyn Denison. vii, 418. (M., 1825.)

5665. NATIONS (American), Coalition of.—Nothing is so important as that America shall separate herself from the systems of Europe, and establish one of her own. Our circumstances, our pursuits, our interests, are distinct, the principles of our policy should be so also. All entanglements with that quarter of the globe should be avoided if we mean that peace and justice shall be the polar stars of the American societies. * * * [This] would be a leading principle with me, had I longer to live.—To J. CORREA DE SERRA. vii, 184. FORD ED., x, 162. (M., Oct. 1820.)

5666. NATURAL BRIDGE, Description.—The Natural Bridge, the most sublime of Nature's works, * * * is on the ascent of a hill which seems to have been cloven through its length by some great convulsion. The fissure, just at the Bridge, is, by some admeasurements, 270 feet deep, by others only 205. It is about 45 feet wide at the bottom and 90 feet at the top; this of course determines the length of the bridge, and its height from the water. Its breadth in the middle is about 60 feet, but more at the ends, and the thickness of the mass, at the summit of the arch, about forty feet. A part of this thickness is constituted by a coat of earth, which gives growth to many large trees. The residue, with the hill on both sides, is one solid rock of limestone. The arch approaches the semi-elliptical form; but the larger axis of the ellipsis, which would be the chord of the arch, is many times longer than the semi-axis which gives its height. Looking down from this height about a minute, gave me a violent headache. If the view from the top be painful and intolerable, that from below is delightful in an equal extreme. It is impossible for the emotions arising from the sublime to be felt beyond what they are here; so beautiful an arch, so elevated, so light, and springing as it were up to heaven, the rapture of the spectator is really indescribable! The fissure continuing narrow, deep and straight, for a considerable distance above and below the Bridge, opens a short but very pleasing view of the North Mountain on one side and the Blue Ridge on the other, at the distance each of them of about five miles.—NOTES ON VIRGINIA. viii, 269. FORD ED., iii, 109. (1782.)

5667. NATURAL BRIDGE, Greatest curiosity.—The greatest of our curiosities, the Natural Bridge.—To REV. CHAS. CLAY. iii, 125. FORD ED., v, 142. (M., 1790.)

5668. NATURAL BRIDGE, Hermitage near.—I sometimes think of building a little hermitage at the Natural Bridge (for it is my property) and of passing there a part of the year at least.—To WILLIAM CARMICHAEL. ii, 80. FORD ED., iv, 345. (P., 1786.)

5669. NATURAL HISTORY, American animals.—I really doubt whether the flat-horned elk exists in America. * * * I have seen the daim, the cerf, the chevreuil of Europe. But the animal we call elk, and which may be distinguished as the round-horned elk, is very different from them. * * * I suspect that you will find that the moose, the round-horned elk, and the American deer are species not existing in Europe. The moose is perhaps of a new class.—To COMTE DE BUFFON. ii, 286. FORD ED., iv, 458. (P., 1787.)

5670. NATURAL HISTORY, Anatomy and.—The systems of Cuvier and Blumenbach, and especially that of Blumenbach, are liable to the objection of going too much into the province of anatomy. It may be said, indeed, that anatomy is a part of natural history. In the broad sense of the word, it certainly is. In that sense, however, it would comprehend all the natural sciences, every created thing being a subject of natural history in extenso. * * * As soon as the structure of any natural production is destroyed by art, it ceases to be a subject of natural history, and enters into the domain ascribed to chemistry, to pharmacy, to anatomy, &c. Linnæus's method was liable to this objection so far as it required the aid of anatomical dissection, as of the heart, for instance, to ascertain the place of any animal, or of a chemical process for that of a mineral substance. It would certainly be better to adopt as much as possible such exterior and visible characteristics as every traveler is competent to observe, to ascertain and to relate.—To DR. JOHN MANNERS. vi, 321. (M., 1814.) See ANATOMY.

5671. NATURAL HISTORY, Buffon and.—You must not presume too strongly that your comb-footed bird is known to M. de Buffon. He did not know our panther. I gave him the striped skin of one I bought in Philadelphia, and it presents him a new species which will appear in his next volume.—To FRANCIS HOPKINSON. ii, 74. (P., 1786.)

5672. ———. I have convinced M. de Buffon that our deer is not a chevreuil, and would you believe that many letters to different acquaintances in Virginia, where this animal is so common, have never enabled me to present him with a large pair of their horns, a blue and a red skin stuffed, to show him their colors at different seasons. He has never seen the horns of what we call the elk. This would decide whether it be an elk or a deer.*—To FRANCIS HOPKINSON. ii, 74. (P., 1786.)

5673. ———. I have made a particular acquaintance with Monsieur de Buffon, and have a great desire to give him the best idea I can of our elk. You could not oblige me more than by sending me the horns, skeleton and skin of an elk, were it possible to procure them. * * * Everything of this kind is precious here [France].—To ARCHIBALD STUART. i, 518. FORD ED., iv, 189. (P., 1786.) See BUFFON.

5674. NATURAL HISTORY, Costly specimens.—You ask if you shall say anything to Sullivan about the bill. No; only that it is paid. I have received letters from him explaining the matter. It was really for the skin and bones of the moose, as I had conjectured. It was my fault that I had not given him a rough idea of the expense I would be willing to incur for them. He made the acquisition an object of a regular campaign, and that, too, of a winter one. The troops he employed sallied forth, as he writes me, in the month of March—much snow—a herd attacked—one killed—in the wilderness—a road to cut twenty miles—to be drawn by hand from the frontiers to his house—bones to be cleaned, &c., &c. In fine, he puts himself to an infinitude of trouble, more than I meant. He did it cheerfully, and I feel myself really under obligations to him. That the tragedy might not want a proper catastrophe, the box, bones, and all are lost; so that this chapter of natural history will still remain a blank. But I have

* " The venerable Buffon was indebted to Jefferson for torrents of information concerning nature in America, as well as for many valuable specimens. Buffon wrote to Jefferson, ' I should have consulted you, sir, before publishing my natural history, and then I should have been sure of my facts '."—PARTON'S *Life of Jefferson.*

written to him not to send me another.—To
W. S. SMITH. ii, 284. (P., 1787.)

**5675. NATURAL HISTORY, Elk and
deer.**—In my conversations with the Count
de Buffon on the subjects of natural history,
I find him absolutely unacquainted with our
elk and our deer. He has hitherto believed
that our deer never had horns more than a
foot long; and has, therefore, classed them
with the roe buck which, I am sure, you know
them to be different from. * * * Will you
take the trouble to procure for me the largest
pair of buck's horns you can, and a large skin
of each color, that is to say, a red and a blue?
If it were possible to take these from a buck
just killed, to leave all the bones of the head
in the skin, with the horns on, to leave the
bones of the legs in the skin also, and the hoofs
to it, so that, having only made an incision
all along the belly and neck, to take the animal
out at, we could, by sewing up that incision,
and stuffing the skin, present the true size and
form of the animal; it would be a most precious
present.—To A. CARY. i, 507. (P., 1786.)

5676. —— ——. You give me hopes of
being able to procure for me some of the big
bones. * * * A specimen of each of the
several species of bones now to be found, is
to me the most desirable object in natural history. And there is no expense of package or
of safe transportation which I will not gladly
reimburse to procure them safely. Elk horns
of very extraordinary size, or anything else
uncommon, would be very acceptable.—To
JAMES STEPTOE. i, 323. FORD ED., iii, 62.
(1782.)

**5677. NATURAL HISTORY, Export-
ing deer.**—Our deer have been often sent to
England and Scotland. Do you know (with
certainty) whether they have ever bred with
the red deer of those countries?—To A. CARY.
i, 508. (P., 1786.)

**5678. NATURAL HISTORY, Far
West.**—Any observations of your own on
the subject of the big bones or their history,
or anything else in the western country, will
come acceptably to me, because I know you
see the works of nature in the great, and not
merely in detail. Descriptions of animals,
vegetables, minerals or other curious things;
notes as to the Indians' information of the
country between the Mississippi and the waters
of the South Sea, &c., &c., will strike your mind
as worthy being communicated.—To JAMES
STEPTOE. i, 323. FORD ED., iii, 63. (1782.)

**5679. NATURAL HISTORY, French
deer.**—I have examined some of the red deer
of this country [France] at the distance of
about sixty yards, and I find no other difference
between them and ours than a shade or two in
the color.—To A. CARY. i, 507. (P., 1786.)

**5680. NATURAL HISTORY, Grouse
and pheasant.**—In the King's cabinet of
Natural History, of which Monsieur de Buffon
has the superintendence, I observed that they
had neither our grouse nor our pheasant.
* * * Pray buy the male and female of
each, employ some apothecary's boy to prepare
them, and send them to me.—To F. HOPKIN-
SON. i, 506. (P., 1786.) See BIRDS.

**5681. NATURAL HISTORY, Import-
ing Useful Animals.**—A fellow passenger
with me from Boston to England, promised to
send to you, in my name, some hares, rabbits,
pheasants, and partridges, by the return of the
ship, which was to go to Virginia, and the

captain promised to take great care of them.
My friend procured the animals, and the ship
changing her destination, he kept them in
hopes of finding some other conveyance, till
they all perished. I do not despair, however,
of finding some opportunity still of sending a
colony of useful animals.—To A. CARY. i,
508. (P., 1786.)

**5682. NATURAL HISTORY, Nomen-
clature.**—The uniting all nations under one
language in natural history had been happily
effected by Linnæus, and can scarcely be
hoped for a second time. Nothing, indeed,
is so desperate as to make all mankind agree
in giving up a language they possess, for one
which they have to learn. * * * Disciples
of Linnæus, of Blumenbach, and of Cuvier,
exclusively possessing their own nomenclatures,
can no longer communicate intelligibly with one
another.—To DR. JOHN MANNERS. vi, 321.
(M., 1814.)

5683. —— ——. To disturb Linnæus's
system was unfortunate. The new system attempted in botany, by Jussieu, in mineralogy,
by Haüiy, are subjects of the same regret, and
so also the no-system of Buffon, the great advocate of individualism in opposition to classification. He would carry us back to the days
and to the confusion of Aristotle and Pliny,
give up the improvements of twenty centuries,
and cooperate with the neologists in rendering
the science of one generation useless to the
next by perpetual changes of its language.—
To DR. JOHN MANNERS. vi, 322. (M., 1814.)

**5684. NATURAL HISTORY, A pas-
sion.**—Natural History is my passion.—To
HARRY INNES. iii, 217. FORD ED., v, 294.
(Pa., 1791.)

**5685. NATURAL HISTORY, Weevil
fly.**—I do not think the natural history of the
weevil fly of Virginia has been yet sufficiently
detailed. What do you think of beginning to
turn your attention to this insect, in order to
give its history to the Philosophical Society?
It would require some Summers' observations.
* * * I long to be free for pursuits of this
kind instead of the detestable ones in which I
am now laboring without pleasure to myself,
or profit to others. In short, I long to be with
you at Monticello.—To T. M. RANDOLPH. FORD
ED., v, 325. (Pa., 1791.)

**5686. NATURAL HISTORY, Wild
sheep.**—I have never known to what family
you ascribed the Wild Sheep, or Fleecy Goat,
as Governor Lewis called it, or the *Potio-
trajos*, if its name must be Greek. He gave
me a skin, but I know he carried a more perfect one, with the horns on, to Mr. Peale;
and if I recollect well those horns, they, with
the fleece, would induce one to suspect it to
be the Lama, or at least a *Lamæ affinis*. I
will thank you to inform me what you determine it to be.—To DR. WISTAR. v, 218. (W.,
1807.)

— NATURAL LAW.—See MAJORITY.

5687. NATURAL RIGHTS, Abridging.
—All natural rights may be abridged or modi-
fied in their exercise by law.—OFFICIAL OPIN-
ION. vii, 498. FORD ED., v, 206. (1790.)

5688. —— ——. Laws abridging the natural right of the citizen, should be restrained
by rigorous constructions within their narrowest limits.—To ISAAC MCPHERSON. vi,
176. (M., 1813.) See DUTY (NATURAL).

5689. NATURAL RIGHTS, Authority over.—Our rulers can have * * * authority over such natural rights only as we have submitted to them.—NOTES ON VIRGINIA. viii, 400. FORD ED., iii, 263. (1782.)

5690. NATURAL RIGHTS, Choice of vocation.—Everyone has a natural right to choose that vocation in life which he thinks most likely to give him comfortable subsistence.—THOUGHTS ON LOTTERIES. ix, 505. FORD ED., x, 366. (M., Feb. 1826.)

5691. NATURAL RIGHTS, Equal Rights vs.—No man has a natural right to commit aggression on the equal rights of another; and this is all from which the laws ought to restrain him.—To F. W. GILMER. vii, 3. FORD ED., x, 32. (M., 1816.)

5692. NATURAL RIGHTS, Kings and.—These are our grievances, which we have thus laid before his Majesty, with that freedom of language and sentiment which becomes a free people, claiming their rights as derived from the laws of nature, and not as the gift of their Chief Magistrate.—RIGHTS OF BRITISH AMERICA. i, 141. FORD ED., i, 445. (1774.)

5693. NATURAL RIGHTS, Moral sense and.—Questions of natural right are triable by their conformity with the moral sense and reason of man.—OPINION ON FRENCH TREATIES. vii, 618. FORD ED., vi, 225. (1793.) See MORAL SENSE.

5694. NATURAL RIGHTS, Restoring.—I shall see with sincere satisfaction the progress of those sentiments which tend to restore to man all his natural rights.—R. TO A. DANBURY BAPTISTS. viii, 113. (1802.)

5695. NATURAL RIGHTS, Retention of.—The idea is quite unfounded that on entering into society we give up any natural rights.—To F. W. GILMER. vii, 3. FORD ED., x, 32. (M., 1816.)

5696. NATURAL RIGHTS, Self-government and.—Every man, and every body of men on earth, possesses the right of self-government. They receive it with their being from the hand of nature. Individuals exercise it by their single will; collections of men by that of their majority; for the law of the *majority* is the natural law of every society of men. When a certain description of men are to transact together a particular business, the times and places of their meeting and separating, depend on their own will; they make a part of the natural right of self-government. This, like all other natural rights, may be abridged or modified in its exercise by their own consent, or by the law of those who depute them, if they meet in the right of others; but as far as it is not abridged or modified, they retain it as a natural right, and may exercise them in what form they please, either exclusively by themselves, or in association with others, or by others altogether, as they shall agree.—OFFICIAL OPINION. vii, 496. FORD ED., v, 205. (1790.)

5797. NATURAL RIGHTS, Social duties and.—I am convinced man has no natural right in opposition to his social duties.—R. TO A. DANBURY BAPTISTS. viii, 113. (1802.) See RIGHTS.

— NATURAL SELECTION, Application to mankind.—See RACE.

5698. NATURALIZATION, Eligibility.—All persons who, by their own oath or affirmation, or by other testimony, shall give satisfactory proof to any court of record in this Colony that they propose to reside in the same seven years, at the least, and who shall subscribe the fundamental laws, shall be considered as residents, and entitled to all the rights of persons natural born.—PROPOSED VA. CONSTITUTION. FORD ED., ii, 26. (June 1776.)

5699. NATURALIZATION, Laws.—I cannot omit recommending a revisal of the laws on the subject of naturalization. Considering the ordinary chances of human life, a denial of citizenship under a residence of fourteen years is a denial to a great proportion of those who ask it, and controls a policy pursued from their first settlement by many of these States, and still believed of consequence to their prosperity. And shall we refuse the unhappy fugitives from distress that hospitality which the savages of the wilderness extended to our fathers arriving in this land? Shall oppressed humanity find no asylum on this globe? The Constitution, indeed, has wisely provided that, for admission to certain offices of important trust, a residence shall be required sufficient to develop character and design. But might not the general character and capabilities of a citizen be safely communicated to every one manifesting a *bonâ fide* purpose of embarking his life and fortunes permanently with us? with restrictions, perhaps, to guard against the fraudulent usurpation of our flag; an abuse which brings so much embarrassment and loss on the genuine citizen, and so much danger to the nation of being involved in war, that no endeavor should be spared to detect and suppress it.—FIRST ANNUAL MESSAGE. viii, 14. FORD ED., viii, 124. (Dec. 1801.) See CITIZENS and EXPATRIATION.

5700. NATURALIZATION, Non-recognition of.—The decrees of the British courts that British subjects adopted here since the peace, and carrying on commerce from hence, are still British subjects, and their cargoes British property, have shaken these quasi-citizens in their condition. The French adopt the same principle as to their cargoes when captured. * * * Is it worth our while to go to war to support the contrary doctrine? The British principle is clearly against the law of nations, but which way our interest lies is also worthy of consideration.—To JAMES MONROE. FORD ED., vii, 214. (Pa., March 1798.)

5701. NATURALIZATION, Obstructing.—He [George III.] has endeavored to pervert the exercise of the kingly office in

Virginia into a detestable and insupportable tyranny * * * by endeavoring to prevent the population of our country, and for that purpose obstructing the laws for naturalization of foreigners.—PROPOSED VA. CONSTITUTION. FORD ED., ii, 10. (June 1776.)

5702. NATURALIZATION, Power of. —The Administrator [of Virginia] shall not possess the prerogative * * * of making denizens.—PROPOSED VA. CONSTITUTION. FORD ED., ii, 19. (June 1776.)

5703. NATURE, Classifications.—Ray formed one classification on such lines of division as struck him most favorably; Klein adopted another; Brisson a third, and other naturalists other designations, till Linnæus appeared. Fortunately for science, he conceived in the three kingdoms of nature, modes of classification which obtained the approbation of the learned of all nations. This system was accordingly adopted by all, and united all in a general language. It offered the three great desiderata; First, of aiding the memory to retain a knowledge of the productions of nature. Secondly, of rallying all to the same names for the same objects, so that they could communicate understandingly on them. And, thirdly, of enabling them, when a subject was first presented, to trace it by its character up to the conventional name by which it was agreed to be called. This classification was indeed liable to the imperfection of bringing into the same group individuals which, though resembling in the characteristics adopted by the author for his classification, yet have strong marks of dissimilitude in other respects. But to this objection every mode of classification must be liable, because the plan of creation is inscrutable to our limited faculties. Nature has not arranged her productions on a single and direct line. They branch at every step, and in every direction, and he who attempts to reduce them into departments, is left to do it by the lines of his own fancy. The objection of bringing together what are disparata in nature, lies against the classifications of Blumenbach and of Cuvier, as well as that of Linnæus, and must forever lie against all.—To DR. JOHN MANNERS. vi, 320. (M., 1814.)

5704. NATURE, Love of.—There is not a sprig of grass that shoots uninteresting to me.—To MARTHA JEFFERSON RANDOLPH. D. L. J., 192. (Pa., 1790.)

5705. NATURE, Units in.—Nature has, in truth, produced units only through all her works. Classes, orders, genera, species, are not of her work. Her creation is of individuals. No two animals are exactly alike; no two plants, nor even two leaves or blades of grass; no two crystallizations. And if we may venture from what is within the cognizance of such organs as ours, to conclude on that beyond their powers, we must believe that no two particles of matter are of exact resemblance. This infinitude of units or individuals being far beyond the capacity of our memory, we are obliged, in aid of that, to distribute them into masses, throwing into each of these all the individuals which have a certain degree of resemblance; to subdivide these again into smaller groups, according to certain points of dissimilitude observable in them, and so on until we have formed what we call a system of classes, orders, genera, and species. In doing this, we fix arbitrarily on such characteristic resemblances and differences as seem to us most prominent and invariable in the several subjects, and most likely to take a strong hold in our memories.—To DR. JOHN MANNERS. vi, 319. (M., 1814.)

5706. NATURE AND FREEDOM.— Under the law of nature we are all born free. —LEGAL ARGUMENT. FORD ED., i, 380. (1770.)

5707. NAVIES, 'Equalization of.—I have read with great satisfaction your observations on the principles for equalizing the power of the different nations on the sea, and think them perfectly sound. Certainly it will be better to produce a balance on that element, by reducing the means of its great monopolizer [England], than by endeavoring to raise our own to an equality with theirs.— To TENCH COXE. v, 199. FORD ED., ix, 142. (M., Sep. 1807.) See NAVY.

5708. NAVIGATION, Coasting and carrying trade.—I like your convoy bill, because although it does not assume the maintenance of all our maritime rights, it assumes as much as it is our interest to maintain. Our coasting trade is the first and most important branch, never to be yielded but with our existence. Next to that is the carriage of our own productions in our own vessels, and bringing back the returns for our own consumption; so far I would protect it and force every part of the Union to join in the protection at the point of the bayonet. But though we have a right to the remaining branch of carrying for other nations, its advantages do not compensate its risks. Your bill first rallies us to the ground the Constitution ought to have taken, and to which we ought to return without delay; the moment is the most favorable possible, because the Eastern States, by declaring they will not protect that cabotage by war, and forcing us to abandon it, have released us from every future claim for its protection on that part. Your bill is excellent in another view: It presents still one other ground to which we can retire before we resort to war; it says to the belligerents, rather than go to war, we will retire from the brokerage of other nations, and will confine ourselves to the carriage and exchange of our own productions; but we will vindicate that in all its rights—if you touch it, it is war.—To MR. BURWELL. v, 505. (M., Feb. 1810.)

5709. NAVIGATION, Defensive value of.—Our navigation * * * as a resource of defence, [is] essential, [and] will admit neither neglect nor forbearance. The position and circumstances of the United States leave them nothing to fear on their landboard, and nothing to desire beyond their present rights. But on their seaboard, they are open to injury, and they have there, too, a commerce which must be protected. This can only be done by possessing a respectable body of citizen-seamen, and of artists and establishments in readiness for ship-building. * * * If we lose the seamen and artists whom [our navigation] now occupies, we lose the present means of marine defence, and time will be requisite to raise up others, when disgrace or losses shall bring home to our feelings the error of having abandoned them. —Foreign Commerce Report. vii, 647-8. Ford ed., vi, 480. (Dec. 1793.)

5710. NAVIGATION, Develop.—Our people are decided in the opinion that it is necessary for us to take a share in the occupation of the ocean, and their established habits induce them to require that the sea be kept open to them, and that that line of policy be pursued which will render the use of that element to them as great as possible. I think it a duty in those intrusted with the administration of their affairs to conform themselves to the decided choice of their constituents; and that therefore, we should, in every instance, preserve an equality of right to them in the transportation of commodities, in the right of fishing and in the other uses of the sea.—To John Jay. i, 404. Ford ed., iv, 88. (P., 1785.)

5711. NAVIGATION, Encourage.—Our people have a decided taste for navigation and commerce. They take this from their mother country; and their servants are in duty bound to calculate all their measures on this datum. We wish to do it by throwing open all the doors of commerce, and knocking off its shackles. But as this cannot be done for others, unless they will do it for us, and there is no great probability that Europe will do this, I suppose we shall be obliged to adopt a system which may shackle them in our ports, as they do us in theirs.—To Count Van Hogendorp. i, 465. Ford ed., iv, 105. (P., 1785.)

5712. NAVIGATION, English monopoly of.—The British say they will pocket our carrying trade as well as their own.—To John Page. i, 550. Ford ed., iv, 215. (P., 1786.)

5713. NAVIGATION, Freedom of.—I think, whatever sums we are obliged to pay for freedom of navigation in the European seas, should be levied on the European commerce with us by a separate impost, that these powers may see that they protect these enormities [Barbary piracies] for their own loss.—To General Greene. i, 509. (P., 1786.)

5714. ———. What sentiment is written in deeper characters on the heart of man than that the ocean is free to all men, and their rivers to all their inhabitants? Is there a man, savage or civilized, unbiased by habit, who does not feel and attest this truth? Accordingly, in all tracts of country united under the same political society, we find this natural right universally acknowledged and protected by laying the navigable rivers open to all their inhabitants. When their rivers enter the limits of another society, if the right of the upper inhabitants to descend the stream is in any case obstructed, it is an act of force by a stronger society against a weaker, condemned by the judgment of mankind. The late case of Antwerp and the Scheldt was a striking proof of a general

union of sentiment on this point; as it is believed that Amsterdam had scarcely an advocate out of Holland, and even there its pretensions were advocated on the ground of treaties, and not of natural right.—Mississippi River Instructions. vii, 577. Ford ed., v, 468. (March 1792.)

5715. NAVIGATION, French and English hostility.—The difference of sixty-two livres ten sols the hogshead established by the National Assembly [of France] on tobacco brought in their and our ships, is such an act of hostility against our navigation, as was not to have been expected from the friendship of that nation. It is as new in its nature as extravagant in its degree; since it is unexampled that any nation has endeavored to wrest from another the carriage of its own produce, except in the case of their colonies.—To William Short. iii, 274. Ford ed., v, 362. (Pa., 1791.)

5716. ——— ———. I apprehend that these two great nations [France and England] will think it their interest not to permit us to be navigators.—To Horatio Gates. iv, 213. Ford ed., vii, 205. (Pa., Feb. 1798.)

5717. ——— ———. Every appearance and consideration render it probable that, on the restoration of peace, both France and Britain will consider it their interest to exclude us from the ocean, by such peaceable means as are in their power. Should this take place, perhaps it may be thought just and politic to give to our *native capitalists* the monopoly of our internal commerce.—To James Madison. iv, 214. Ford ed., vii, 206. (Pa., Feb. 1798.)

5718. ——— ———. The countervailing acts of Great Britain, now laid before Congress, threaten, in the opinion of merchants, the entire loss of our navigation to England. It makes a difference, from the present state of things, of five hundred guineas on a vessel of three hundred and fifty tons.—To Horatio Gates. iv, 213. Ford ed., vii, 205. (Pa., Feb. 1798.)

5719. ——— ———. The [British] countervailing act * * * will, confessedly, put American bottoms out of employ in our trade with Great Britain.—To James Madison. iv, 214. Ford ed., vii, 206. (Pa., Feb. 1798.)

5720. ——— ———. I hope we shall rub through the war [between France and England], without engaging in it ourselves, and that when in a state of peace our Legislature and Executive will endeavor to provide peaceable means of obliging foreign nations to be just to us, and of making their injustice recoil on themselves.—To Peregrine Fitzhugh. iv, 216. Ford ed., vii, 209. (Pa., Feb. 1798.)

5721. NAVIGATION, Industrial value. —Our navigation * * * as a branch of industry * * * is valuable * * * . Its value, as a branch of industry, is enhanced by the dependence of so many other branches on it. In times of general peace it multiplies competitors for employment in transportation, and so keeps that at its proper level; and in times of war, that is to say, when those nations who may be our principal carriers, shall be at war with each other, if we have not within ourselves the means of transportation, our produce must be exported in belligerent vessels, at the increased expense of war-freight and insurance, and the articles which will not bear that, must perish on our hands.—FOREIGN COMMERCE REPORT. vii, 647. FORD ED., vi, 480. (Dec. 1793.)

5722. NAVIGATION, Jefferson's report on.—You may recollect that a report which I gave into Congress in 1793, and Mr. Madison's propositions of 1794, went directly to establish a navigation act on the British principle. On the last vote given on this (which was in Feb. 1794), from the three States of Massachusetts, Connecticut, and Rhode Island there were two votes for it, and twenty against it; and from the three States of Virginia, Kentucky, and North Carolina, wherein not a single top-mast vessel is, I believe, owned by a native citizen, there were twenty-five votes for and four against the measure. I very much suspect that were the same proposition now brought forward, the northern vote would be nearly the same, while the southern one, I am afraid, would be radically varied. The suggestion of their disinterested endeavors for placing our navigation on an independent footing, and forcing on them the British treaty, have not had a tendency to invite new offers of sacrifice, and especially under the prospect of a new rejection. You observe that the rejection would change the politics of New England. But it would afford no evidence which they have not already in the records of January and February, 1794. However, I will * * * sound the dispositions [of members of Congress] on that subject. If the proposition should be likely to obtain a reputable vote, it may do good. As to myself, I sincerely wish that the whole Union may accommodate their interests to each other, and play into their hands mutually as members of the same family, that the wealth and strength of any one part should be viewed as the wealth and strength of the whole.—To HUGH WILLIAMSON. FORD ED., vii, 200. (Pa., Feb. 1798.)

5723. NAVIGATION, Madness for.—We are running navigation mad.—To JOSEPH PRIESTLEY. iv, 311. FORD ED., vii, 406. (Pa., Jan. 1800.)

5724. NAVIGATION, Maintain.—To maintain commerce and navigation in all their lawful enterprises * * * [is one of] the landmarks by which we are to guide ourselves in all our proceedings.—SECOND ANNUAL MESSAGE. viii, 21. FORD ED., viii, 186. (Dec. 1802.)

5725. NAVIGATION, Mediterranean.—We must consider the Mediterranean as absolutely shut to us until we can open it with money. Whether this will be best expended

in buying or forcing a peace is for Congress to determine.—To MR. HAWKINS. ii, 4. (P., 1786.)

5726. NAVIGATION, Nurseries of.—We have three nurseries for forming seamen: 1. Our coasting trade, already on a safe footing. 2. Our fisheries, which in spite of natural advantages, give just cause of anxiety. 3. Our carrying trade, our only resource of indemnification for what we lose in the other. The produce of the United States, which is carried to foreign markets, is extremely bulky. That part of it which is now in the hands of foreigners, and which we may resume into our own, without touching the rights of those nations who have met us in fair arrangements by treaty, or the interests of those who, by their voluntary regulations, have paid so just and liberal a respect to our interests, as being measured back to them again, places both parties on as good ground, perhaps, as treaties could place them—the proportion, I say, of our carrying trade, which may be resumed without affecting either of these descriptions of nations, will find constant employment for ten thousand seamen, be worth two millions of dollars, annually, will go on augmenting with the population of the United States, secure to us a full indemnification for the seamen we lose, and be taken wholly from those who force us to this act of self-protection in navigation. * * * If regulations exactly the counterpart of those established against us, would be ineffectual, from a difference of circumstances, other regulations equivalent can give no reasonable ground of complaint to any nation. Admitting their right of keeping their markets to themselves, ours cannot be denied of keeping our carrying trade to ourselves. And if there be anything unfriendly in this, it was in the first example.—REPORT ON THE FISHERIES. vii, 553. (1791.)

5727. ——— ———. The loss of seamen, unnoticed, would be followed by other losses in a long train. If we have no seamen, our ships will be useless, consequently our ship-timber, iron and hemp; our shipbuilding will be at an end, ship carpenters go over to other nations, our young men have no call to the sea, our produce, carried in foreign bottoms, be saddled with war freight and insurance in times of war; and the history of the last hundred years shows, that the nation which is our carrier has three years of war for every four years of peace. We lose, during the same periods, the carriage for belligerent powers, which the neutrality of our flag would render an incalculable source of profit; we lose at this moment the carriage of our own produce to the annual amount of two millions of dollars, which, in the possible progress of the encroachment, may extend to five or six millions, the worth of the whole, with an increase in the proportion of the increase of our members. It is easier, as well as better, to stop this train at its entrance, than when it shall have ruined or banished whole classes of useful and industrious citizens. It will doubtless be thought expedient that the resumption suggested should take effect so gradually, as not to endanger the loss of produce for the want of transportation; but that, in order to create transportation. the whole plan should be developed, and made known at once, that the individuals who may be disposed to lay themselves out for the carrying business, may make their calculations on a full view of all the circumstances.—Report on the Fisheries. vii, 554. (1791.)

5728. NAVIGATION, Protection of.— The British attempt, without disguise, to possess themselves of the carriage of our produce, and to prohibit our own vessels from participating of it. This has raised a general indignation in America. The States see, however, that their constitutions have provided no means of counteracting it. They are, therefore, beginning to invest Congress with the absolute power of regulating their commerce, only reserving all revenue arising from it to the State in which it is levied. This will consolidate our federal building very much, and for this we shall be indebted to the British.—To Count Van Hogendorp. i. 465. Ford ed., iv, 104. (P., 1785.)

5729. ———. I think it essential to exclude the British from the carriage of American produce.—To James Monroe. Ford ed., iv, 41. (P., 1785.)

5730. ———. The determination of the British cabinet to make no equal treaty with us. confirms me in the opinion expressed in your letter that the United States must pass a navigation act against Great Britain, and load her manufactures with duties so as to give a preference to those of other countries; and I hope our Assemblies will wait no longer, but transfer such a power to Congress, at the sessions of this fall.—To John Adams. i, 486. (P., 1785.)

5731. ———. I hope we shall show [the British] we have sense and spirit enough * * * to exclude them from any share in the carriage of our commodities.—To David Humphreys. i, 560. (P., 1786.)

5732. ———. A bill which may be called the true navigation act for the United States, is before Congress, and will probably pass. I hope it will lay the foundation of a due share of navigation for us.—To John Coffin Jones. iii, 155. (N.Y., 1790.)

5733. ———. I participate fully of your indignation at the trammels imposed on our commerce with Great Britain. Some attempts have been made in Congress, and others are still making to meet their restrictions by effectual restrictions on our part. It was proposed to double the foreign tonnage for a certain time, and after that to prohibit the exportation of our commodities in the vessels of nations not in treaty with us. This has been rejected. It is now proposed to prohibit any nation from bringing or carrying in their vessels what may not be brought or carried in ours from or to the same ports; also to prohibit those from bringing to us anything not of their own produce. who prohibit us from carrying to them anything but our own produce. It is thought, however, that this cannot be carried. The fear is that it would irritate Great Britain were we to feel any irritation ourselves.—To Edward Rutledge. iii, 164. Ford ed., v, 196. (N.Y., 1790.)

5734. ———. Were the ocean, which is the common property of all, open to the industry of all, so that every person and vessel should be free to take employment wherever it could be found, the United States would certainly not set the example of appropriating to themselves, exclusively, any portion of the common stock of occupation. They would rely on the enterprise and activity of their citizens for a due participation of the benefits of the seafaring business, and for keeping the marine class of citizens equal to their object. But if particular nations grasp at undue shares, and, more especially, if they seize on the means of the United States, to convert them into aliment for their own strength, and withdraw them entirely from the support of those to whom they belong, defensive and protecting measures become necessary on the part of the nation whose marine resources are thus invaded; or it will be disarmed of its defence; its productions will lie at the mercy of the nation which has possessed itself exclusively of the means of carrying them, and its politics may be influenced by those who command its commerce. The carriage of our own commodities, if once established in another channel, cannot be resumed in the moment we may desire. If we lose the seamen and artists whom it now occupies, we lose the present means of marine defence, and time will be requisite to raise up others, when disgrace or losses shall bring home to our feelings the error of having abandoned them. The materials for maintaining our due share of navigation, are ours in abundance. And, as to the mode of using them, we have only to adopt the principles of those who put us on the defensive, or others equivalent and better fitted to our circumstances.—Foreign Commerce Report. vii, 647. Ford ed., vi, 481. (Dec. 1793.)

5735. ———. I have ever wished that all nations would adopt a navigation law against those who have one, which perhaps would be better than against all indiscriminately, and while in France I proposed it there.—To Tench Coxe. v, 199. Ford ed., ix, 142. (M., 1807.)

5736. ———. Among the laws of the late Congress, some were of note; a navigation act, particularly, applicable to those nations only who have navigation acts; pinching one of them especially, not only in the general way, but in the intercourse with her foreign possessions. This part may react on us, and it remains for trial which may bear longest. —To Albert Gallatin. vii, 78. Ford ed., x, 90. (M., 1817.)

5737. NAVIGATION, Protuberant.—I trust the good sense of our country will see that its greatest prosperity depends on a due balance between agriculture, manufactures and commerce, and not in this protuberant navigation which has kept us in hot water from the commencement of our government, and is now engaging us in war.—To THOMAS LEIPER. v, 417. FORD ED., ix, 239. (W., 1809.)

5738. NAVIGATION, Reciprocity and.—The following principles, being founded in reciprocity, appear perfectly just, and to offer no cause of complaint to any nation: Where a nation refuses to receive in our vessels any productions but our own, we may refuse to receive, in theirs, any but their own productions. Where a nation refuses to consider any vessel as ours which has not been built within our territories, we should refuse to consider as theirs, any vessel not built within their territories. Where a nation refuses to our vessels the carriage even of our own productions, to certain countries under their domination, we might refuse to theirs of every description, the carriage of the same productions to the same countries. But as justice and good neighborhood would dictate that those who have no part in imposing the restriction on us, should not be the victims of measures adopted to defeat its effect, it may be proper to confine the restriction to vessels owned or navigated by any subjects of the same dominant power, other than the inhabitants of the country to which the said productions are to be carried. And to prevent all inconvenience to the said inhabitants, and to our own, by too sudden a check on the means of transportation, we may continue to admit the vessels marked for future exclusion, on an advanced tonnage, and for such length of time only, as may be supposed necessary to provide against that inconvenience. The establishment of some of these principles by Great Britain, alone, has already lost us in our commerce with that country and its possessions, between eight and nine hundred vessels of near 40,000 tons burden, according to statements from official materials, in which they have confidence. This involves a proportional loss of seamen, shipwrights, and ship-building, and is too serious a loss to admit forbearance of some effectual remedy.—REPORT ON COMMERCE AND NAVIGATION. vii, 648. FORD ED., vi, 481. (Dec. 1793.)

5739. NAVIGATION, Reduction of British.—It has been proposed in Congress to pass a navigation act which will deeply strike at that of Great Britain. * * * Would it not be worth while to have the bill now enclosed, translated, printed and circulated among the members of the [French] National Assembly? If you think so, have it done at the public expense, with any little comment you may think necessary, concealing the quarter from whence it is distributed; or take any other method you think better, to see whether that Assembly will not pass a similar act? I shall send copies of it to Mr. Carmichael, at Madrid, and to Colonel Humphreys, appointed resident at Lisbon, with a desire for them to suggest similar acts there. The measure is just, perfectly innocent as to all other nations, and will effectually defeat the navigation act of Great Britain, and reduce her power on the ocean within safer limits.—To WILLIAM SHORT. iii, 225. (Pa., 1791.)

5740. ———. The navigation act, if it can be effected, will form a remarkable and memorable epoch in the history and freedom of the ocean. Mr. Short will press it at Paris, and Colonel Humphreys at Lisbon.—To WILLIAM CARMICHAEL. iii, 245. (Pa., 1791.)

5741. ———. The Navigation Act proposed in the late Congress, but which lies over to the next, * * * is perfectly innocent as to other nations, is strictly just as to the English, cannot be parried by them, and if adopted by other nations would inevitably defeat their navigation act, and reduce their power on the sea within safer limits. It is indeed extremely to be desired that other nations would adopt it. * * * Could France, Spain and Portugal agree to concur in such a measure, it would soon be fatally felt by the navy of England.—To DAVID HUMPHREYS. FORD ED., v, 302. (Pa., March 1791.)

5742. NAVIGATION, Retaliatory duties.—Where a nation refuses to our vessels the carriage even of our own productions, to certain countries under their domination, we might refuse to theirs of every description, the carriage of the same productions to the same countries. But as justice and good neighborhood would dictate that those who have no part in imposing the restriction on us, should not be the victims of measures adopted to defeat its effect, it may be proper to confine the restriction to vessels owned or navigated by any subjects of the same dominant power, other than the inhabitants of the country to which the said productions are to be carried. And to prevent all inconvenience to the said inhabitants, and to our own, by too sudden a check on the means of transportation, we may continue to admit the vessels marked for future exclusion, on an advanced tonnage, and for such length of time only, as may be supposed necessary to provide against that inconvenience.—FOREIGN COMMERCE REPORT. vii, 649. FORD ED., vi, 482. (Dec. 1793.)

— NAVIGATION, Subsidies.—See BOUNTIES.

5743. NAVIGATION, Sufficient.—It is essentially interesting to us to have shipping and seamen enough to carry our surplus produce to market; but beyond that I do not think we are bound to give it encouragement by drawbacks or other premiums.—To BENJAMIN STODDERT. v, 426. FORD ED., ix, 245. (W., 1809.) See COMMERCE, DUTIES, EMBARGO, FREE TRADE, PROTECTION and SHIPS.

5744. NAVY, Bravery of.—Our public ships have done wonders. They have saved our military reputation sacrificed on the shores of Canada.—To General Bailey. vi, 101. (M., Feb. 1813.)

5745. —— ——. No one has been more gratified than myself by the brilliant achievements of our little navy. They have deeply wounded the pride of our enemy, and been balm to ours, humiliated on the land where our real strength was felt to lie.—To President Madison. vi, 112. Ford ed., ix, 383. (M., May 1813.)

5746. —— ——. I sincerely congratulate you on the successes of our little navy; which must be more gratifying to you than to most men, as having been the early and constant advocate of wooden walls. If I have differed with you on this ground, it was not on the principle, but the time; supposing that we cannot build or maintain a navy, which will not immediately fall into the gulf which has swallowed not only the minor navies, but even those of the great second-rate powers of the sea. Whenever these can be resuscitated, and brought so near to a balance with England that we can turn the scale, then is my epoch for aiming at a navy. In the meantime, one competent to keep the Barbary States in order, is necessary; these being the only smaller powers disposed to quarrel with us.—To John Adams. vi, 122. (M., May 1813.)

5747. —— ——. At sea we have rescued our character; but the chief fruit of our victories there is to prove to those who have fleets, that the English are not invincible at sea, as Alexander has proved that Bonaparte is not invincible by land.—To Samuel Brown. vi, 165. (M., July 1813.)

5748. —— ——. I congratulate you on the brilliant affair of the Enterprise and Boxer. No heart is more rejoiced than mine at these mortifications of English pride, and lessons to Europe that the English are not invincible at sea. If these successes do not lead us too far into the navy mania, all will be well.—To William Duane. vi, 211. (M., Sep. 1813.)

5749. —— ——. Strange reverse of expectations that our land force should be under the wing of our little navy.—To William Duane. vi, 212. (M., Sep. 1813.)

5750. —— ——. On the water we have proved to the world the error of British invincibility, and shown that with equal force and well-trained officers, they can be beaten by other nations as brave as themselves.—To Don V. Toronda Coruna. vi, 275. (M., Dec. 1813.)

5751. —— ——. I * * * congratulate you on the destruction of a second hostile fleet on the Lakes by Macdonough. While our enemies cannot but feel shame for their barbarous achievements at Washington [burning of Capitol], they will be stung to the soul by these repeated victories over them on that element on which they wish the world to think them invincible. We have dissipated that error. They must now feel a conviction themselves that we can beat them gun to gun, ship to ship, and fleet to fleet, and that their early successes on the land have been either purchased from traitors, or obtained from raw men entrusted of necessity with commands for which no experience had qualified them, and that every day is adding that experience to unquestioned bravery.—To President Madison. vi, 386. (M., Sep. 1814.) See Capitol.

5752. —— ——. Frigates and seventy-fours are a sacrifice we must make, heavy as it is, to the prejudices of a part of our citizens. They have, indeed, rendered a great moral service, which has delighted me as much as any one in the United States. But they have had no physical effect sensible to the enemy; and now, while we must fortify them in our harbors, and keep armies to defend them, our *privateers* are bearding and blockading the enemy in their own seaports. —To James Monroe. vi, 409. Ford ed., ix, 498. (M., Jan. 1815.)

5753. —— ——. Through the whole period of the war, we have beaten the [British] single-handed at sea, and so thoroughly established our superiority over them with equal force, that they retire from that kind of contest, and never suffer their frigates to cruise singly. The Endymion would never have engaged the frigate President, but knowing herself blocked by three frigates and a razee, who, though somewhat slower sailers, would get up before she could be taken.—To Marquis de Lafayette. vi, 424. Ford ed., ix, 508. (M., 1815.)

5754. NAVY, Build a.—We ought to begin a naval power, if we mean to carry on our own commerce.—To James Monroe. Ford ed., iv, 10. (P., Nov. 1784.)

5755. —— ——. Tribute or war is the usual alternative of these [Barbary] pirates. * * * Why not begin a navy then and decide on war? We cannot begin in a better cause nor against a weaker foe.—To Horatio Gates. Ford ed., iv, 24. (P., Dec. 1784.)

5756. —— ——. It is proper and necessary that we should establish a small marine force.—To John Adams. i, 592. (P., 1786.)

— NAVY, Censure of officers.—See Porter.

— NAVY, Chesapeake.—See Chesapeake.

5757. NAVY, Coercion by a.—[A naval force] will arm the federal head with the safest of all the instruments of coercion over its delinquent members, and prevent it from using what would be less safe.—To John Adams. i, 592. (P., 1786.)

5758. —— ——. Every rational citizen must wish to see an effective instrument of coercion, and should fear to see it on any other element than the water.—To JAMES MONROE. i, 606. FORD ED., iv, 265. (P., 1786.)

5759. NAVY, Dockyards for.—Presuming it will be deemed expedient to expend annually a sum towards providing the naval defence which our situation may require, I cannot but recommend that the first appropriations for that purpose may go to the saving what we already possess. No cares, no attentions, can preserve vessels from rapid decay which lie in water and exposed to the sun. These decays require great and constant repairs, and will consume, if continued, a great portion of the money destined to naval purposes. To avoid this waste of our resources, it is proposed to add to our navy yard here [Washington] a dock, within which our vessels may be laid up dry and under cover from the sun. Under these circumstances experience proves that works of wood will remain scarcely at all affected by time. The great abundance of running water which this situation possesses, at heights far above the level of the tide, if employed as is practiced for lock navigation, furnishes the means of raising and laying up our vessels on a dry and sheltered bed.—SECOND ANNUAL MESSAGE. viii, 20. FORD ED., viii, 186. (Dec. 1802.)

5760. ———. The proposition for building lock-docks for the preservation of our navy, has local rivalries to contend against. Till these can be overruled or compromised, the measure can never be adopted. Yet there ought never to be another ship built until we can provide some method of preserving them through the long intervals of peace which I hope are to be the lot of our country.—To MR. COXE. v, 58. (W., 1807.)

5761. ———. While I was at Washington, in the administration of the government, Congress was much divided in opinion on the subject of a navy, a part of them wishing to go extensively into the preparation of a fleet, another part opposed to it, on the objection that the repairs and preservation of a ship, even idle in harbor, in ten or twelve years, amount to her original cost. It has been estimated in England, that if they could be sure of peace a dozen years it would be cheaper for them to burn their fleet, and build a new one when wanting, than to keep the old one in repair during that term. I learnt that, in Venice, there were then ships, lying on their original stocks, ready for launching at any moment, which had been so for eighty years, and were still in a state of perfect preservation; and that this was effected by disposing of them in docks pumped dry, and kept so by constant pumping. It occurred to me that this expense of constant pumping might be saved by combining a lock with the common wet dock, wherever there was a running stream of water, the bed of which, within a reasonable distance, was of sufficient height above the high-water level of the harbor. This was the case at the navy yard, on the Eastern Branch at Washington, the high-water line of which was seventy-eight feet lower than the ground on which the Capitol stands, and to which it was found that the water of the Tiber Creek could be brought for watering the city. My proposition then was as follows: Let a b be the high-water level of the harbor, and the vessel to be laid up draw eighteen feet of water. Make a chamber A twenty feet deep below

high-water and twenty feet high above it as c d e f, and at the upper end make another chamber, B,

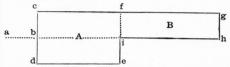

the bottom of which should be in the high-water level, and the tops twenty feet above that. g h is the water of the Tiber. When the vessel is to be introduced, open the gate at c b a. The tide water rises in tne chamber A to the level b i, and floats the vessel in with it. Shut the gate c b d and open that of f i. The water of the Tiber fills both chambers to the level c f g, and the vessel floats into the chamber B; then opening both gates c b d and f i, the water flows out, and the vessel settles down on the stays previously prepared at the bottom i h to receive her. The gate at g h must of course be closed, and the water of the feeding stream be diverted elsewhere. The chamber B is to have a roof over it of the construction of that over the meal market at Paris, except that that is hemispherical, this semi-cylindrical. For this construction see Delenne's Architecture, whose invention it was. The diameter of the dome of the meal market is considerably over one hundred feet. It will be seen at once that instead of making the chamber B of sufficient width and length for a single vessel only, it may be widened to whatever span the semi-circular framing of the roof can be trusted, and to whatever length you please, so as to admit two or more vessels in breadth, and as many in length as the localities render expedient. I had a model of this lock-dock made and exhibited in the President's house during the session of Congress at which it was proposed. But the advocates for a navy did not fancy it, and those opposed to the building of ships altogether, were equally indisposed to provide protection for them. Ridicule was also resorted to, the ordinary substitute for reason, when that fails, and the proposition was passed over. I then thought and still think the measure wise, to have a proper number of vessels always ready to be launched, with nothing unfinished about them except the planting their masts, which must of necessity be omitted, to be brought under a roof. Having no view in this proposition but to combine for the public a provision for defence, with economy in its preservation, I have thought no more of it since. And if any of my ideas anticipated yours, you are welcome to appropriate them to yourself, without objection on my part.—To LEWIS M. WISS. vii, 419. (M., 1825.)

5762. NAVY, Early history of.—I have racked my memory and ransacked my papers, to enable myself to answer the inquiries of your favor of Oct. the 15th; but to little purpose. My papers furnish me nothing, my memory, generalities only. I know that while I was in Europe, and anxious about the fate of our sea-faring men, for some of whom, then in captivity in Algiers, we were treating, and all were in like danger, I formed, undoubtedly, the opinion that our government, as soon as practicable, should provide a naval force sufficient to keep the Barbary States in order; and on this subject we communicated together; as you observe. When I returned to the United States and took part in the administration under General Washington, I constantly maintained that opinion; and in December, 1790, took advantage of a reference to me from the first Congress which met after I was in office, to report in favor of a force sufficient for the protection of our Mediterranean commerce; and I laid before them an accurate statement of the whole Barbary force, public and private. I think General Washington approved of building vessels of war to that extent. General Knox, I know, did. But what was Colonel Hamilton's opinion, I do not in the least remember. Your recollections on that subject are certainly corroborated by his known anxieties for a close connection with Great Britain, to which he might apprehend danger from collisions between their vessels and ours. Randolph was then Attorney-General; but his opinion on the question I also entirely forget. Some vessels of war were accordingly built and sent into the Mediterranean. The additions to these in your time, I need not note to you, who are well known to have ever been an advocate for the wooden walls of Themistocles. Some of those you added, were sold under an act of Congress passed while you were in office. I thought, afterwards, that the public safety might require some additional vessels of strength, to be prepared and in readiness for the first moment of a war, provided they could be preserved against the decay which is unavoidable if kept in the water, and clear of the expense of officers and men. With this view I proposed that they should be built in dry docks, above the level of the tide waters, and covered with roofs. I further advised that places for these docks should be selected where there was a command of water on a high level, as that of the Tiber at Washington, by which the vessels might be floated out, on the principle of a lock. But the majority of the Legislature was against any addition to the Navy, and the minority, although for it in judgment, voted against it on a principle of opposition. We are now, I understand, building vessels to remain on the stocks, under shelter, until wanted, when they will be launched and finished. On my plan they could be in service at an hour's notice. On this, the finishing, after launching, will be a work of time. This is all I recollect about the origin and progress of our navy. That of the late war, certainly raised our rank and character among nations. Yet a navy is a very expensive engine. It is admitted, that in ten or twelve years a vessel goes to entire decay; or, if kept in repair, costs as much as would build a new one: and that a nation who could count on twelve or fifteen years of peace, would gain by burning its navy and building a new one in time. Its extent, therefore, must be governed by circumstances. Since my proposition for a force adequate to the piracies of the Mediterranean, a similar necessity has arisen in our own seas for considerable addition to that force. Indeed, I wish we could have a convention with the naval powers of Europe, for them to keep down the pirates of the Mediterranean, and the slave ships on the coast of Africa, and for us to perform the same duties for the society of nations in our seas. In this way, those collisions would be avoided between the vessels of war of different nations, which beget wars and constitute the weightiest objection to navies. *—To JOHN ADAMS. vii, 264. FORD ED., x, 238. (M., 1822.)

— NAVY, Equalization of sea-power.— See NAVIES.

* Mr. Adams in the letter to which the quotation is a reply said that he "always believed the navy to be Jefferson's child".—EDITOR.

5763. NAVY, Europe and.—A maritime force is the only one by which we can act on Europe.—To GENERAL WASHINGTON. ii, 536. FORD ED., v, 58. (P., 1788.)

5764. NAVY, Expansion and.—Nothing should ever be accepted which would require a navy to defend it.—To PRESIDENT MADISON. v, 445. (M., April 1809.)

5765. NAVY, Future of.—Paul Jones is young enough to see the day * * * when we shall be able to fight the British ship to ship.—To E. CARRINGTON. ii, 405. FORD ED., v, 22. (P., 1788.)

5766. NAVY, Gunboats.—The obstacle, to naval enterprise which vessels of this construction offer for our seaport towns; their utility toward supporting within our waters the authority of the laws; the promptness with which they will be manned by the seamen and militia of the place the moment they are wanted; the facility of their assembling from different parts of the coast to any point where they are required in greater force than ordinary; the economy of their maintenance and preservation from decay when not in actual service; and the competence of our finances to this defensive provision, without any new burden, are considerations which will have due weight with Congress in deciding on the expediency of adding to their number from year to year, as experience shall test their ability, until all our important harbors, by these and auxiliary means, shall be ensured against insult and opposition to the laws.—FOURTH ANNUAL MESSAGE. viii, 38. FORD ED., viii, 331. (Nov. 1804.)

5767. ——— ———. The efficacy of gunboats for the defence of harbors, and of other smooth and enclosed waters, may be estimated in part from that of galleys, formerly much used, but less powerful, more costly in their construction and maintenance, and requiring more men. But the gunboat itself is believed to be in use with every modern maritime nation for the purpose of defence. In the Mediterranean, on which are several small powers, whose system like ours is peace and defence, few harbors are without this article of protection. Our own experience there of the effect of gunboats for harbor service is recent. Algiers is particularly known to have owed to a great provision of these vessels the safety of its city, since the epoch of their construction. Before that it had been repeatedly insulted and injured. The effect of gunboats at present in the neighborhood of Gibraltar, is well known, and how much they were used both in the attack and defence of that place during a former war. The extensive resort to them by the two greatest naval powers in the world, on an enterprise of invasion not long since in prospect, shows their confidence in their efficacy for the purpose for which they are suited. By the northern powers of Europe, whose seas are particularly adapted to them, they are still more used. The remarkable action between the Russian flotilla of gunboats and galleys, and a Turkish fleet of ships-of-the-line and frigates in the Liman Sea, 1788, will be readily recollected. The latter, commanded by their most celebrated admiral, were completely defeated, and several of their ships-of-the-line destroyed.—SPECIAL MESSAGE. viii, 80. FORD ED., ix, 24. (Feb. 1807.)

5768. ——— ———. Of these boats a proper proportion would be of the larger size, such as those heretofore built, capable of navigating any seas, and of reinforcing occasionally the strength of even the most distant port when menaced with danger. The residue would be confined to their own or the neighboring harbors, would be smaller, less furnished for accommodation, and consequently less costly. Of the number supposed necessary, seventy-three are built or building. and the hundred and twenty-seven still to be provided, would cost from five to six hundred thousand dollars. * * * At times when Europe as well as the United States shall be at peace, it would not be proposed that more than six or eight of these vessels should be kept afloat. When Europe is in war, treble that number might be necessary to be distributed among those particular harbors which foreign vessels of war are in the habit of frequenting, for the purpose of preserving order therein. But they would be manned, in ordinary, with only their complement for navigation, relying on the seamen and militia of the port if called into action on sudden emergency. It would be only when the United States should themselves be at war, that the whole number would be brought into actual service, and would be ready in the first moments of the war to co-operate with other means for covering at once the line of our seaports. At all times, those unemployed would be withdrawn into places not exposed to sudden enterprise, hauled up under sheds from the sun and weather, and kept in preservation with little expense for repairs or maintenance. It must be superfluous to observe, that this species of naval armament is proposed merely for defensive operation; that it can have but little effect toward protecting our commerce in the open seas even on our coast; and still less can it become an excitement to engage in offensive maritime war, toward which it would furnish no means.—SPECIAL MESSAGE. viii, 81. FORD ED., ix, 26. (Feb. 1807.)

5769. —— ——. I believe that gunboats are the only *water* defence which can be useful to us, and protect us from the ruinous folly of a navy.—To THOMAS PAINE. v, 189. FORD ED., ix, 137. (M., Sep. 1807.) See GUNBOATS.

5770. NAVY, Increase of.—The building some ships of the line instead of our most indifferent frigates is not to be lost sight of. That we should have a squadron properly composed to prevent the blockading our ports is indispensable. The Atlantic frontier from numbers, wealth, and exposure to potent enemies, have a proportionate right to be defended with the Western frontier, for whom we keep up 3.000 men. Bringing forward the measure, therefore, in a moderate form, placing it on the ground of comparative right, our nation which is a just one, will come into it, notwithstanding the repugnance of some on the subject being first presented.—To JACOB CROWNINSHIELD. FORD ED., viii, 453. (M., May 1806.)

5771. NAVY, Liberty and a.—A naval force can never endanger our liberties, nor occasion bloodshed; a land force would do both.—To JAMES MONROE. i, 606. FORD ED., iv, 265. (P., 1786.)

5772. —— ——. A public force on that element [the ocean] * * * can never be dangerous.—To COLONEL HUMPHREYS. ii, 10. (P., 1786.)

5773. —— ——. It is on the sea alone [that] we should think of ever having a force. —To E. CARRINGTON. ii, 405. FORD ED., v, 22. (P., 1788.)

5774. NAVY, Madness for.—We are running navigation mad, and commerce mad, and navy mad, which is worst of all.—To JOSEPH PRIESTLEY. iv, 311. FORD ED., vii, 406. (Pa., Jan. 1800.)

5775. NAVY, Mediterranean pirates and.—The promptitude and energy of Commodore Preble, the efficacious cooperation of Captains Rodgers and Campbell of the returning squadron, the proper decision of Captain Bainbridge that a vessel which had committed an open hostility was of right to be detained for inquiry and consideration, and the general zeal of the other officers and men, are honorable facts which I make known with pleasure. And to these I add what was indeed transacted in another quarter—the gallant enterprise of Captain Rodgers in destroying, on the coast of Tripoli, a corvette of that power, of twenty-two guns.—SPECIAL MESSAGE. viii, 32. (Dec. 1803.)

5776. —— ——. Reflecting with high satisfaction on the distinguished bravery displayed whenever occasion permitted in the late Mediterranean service, I think it would be an useful encouragement to make an opening for some present promotion, by enlarging our peace establishment of captains and lieutenants.—FIFTH ANNUAL MESSAGE. viii, 50. FORD ED., viii, 393. (1805.)

5777. NAVY, Midshipmen.—The places of midshipman are so much sought that (being limited) there is never a vacancy. Your son shall be set down for the second which shall happen; the first being anticipated. We are not long generally without vacancies happening. As soon as he can be appointed, you shall know it.—To THOMAS COOPER. iv, 453. FORD ED., viii, 178. (W., 1802.)

5778. NAVY, Militia and.—For the purpose of manning the gunboats in sudden attacks on our harbors, it is a matter for consideration, whether the seamen of the United States may not justly be formed into a special militia, to be called on for tours of duty in defence of the harbors where they shall happen to be; the ordinary militia furnishing that portion which may consist of landsmen.—SEVENTH ANNUAL MESSAGE. viii, 86. FORD ED., ix, 161. (Oct. 1807.) See MILITIA.

5779. NAVY, National respect and.—Were we possessed even of a small naval force what a bridle would it be in the mouths of the West Indian powers, and how respectfully would they demean themselves towards us. Be assured that the present disrespect of the nations of Europe for us will inevitably bring on insults which must involve us in war.—To JAMES MONROE. FORD ED., iv, 34. (P., 1785.)

5780. NAVY, Navigation and.—[Our navigation] will require a protecting force on the sea. Otherwise the smallest power in Europe, every one which possesses a single ship of the line, may dictate to us. and enforce their demands by captures on our commerce. Some naval force then is necessary if we mean to be commercial. Can we have a better occasion of beginning one? or find a foe* more certainly within our dimensions? The motives pleading for war rather than tribute are numerous and honorable, those opposing them are mean and short-sighted.—To James Monroe. Ford ed., iv, 32. (P., 1785.)

5781. —— ——. A naval force alone can countenance our people as carriers on the water.—To John Jay. i, 405. Ford ed., iv, 90. (P., 1785.) See Navigation.

5782. NAVY, Necessary.—A land army would be useless for offence, and not the best nor safest instrument of defence. For either of the sea purposes, the sea is the field on which we should meet an European enemy. On that element we should possess some power.—Notes on Virginia. viii, 413. Ford ed., iii, 279. (1782.)

5783. —— ——. A small naval force is sufficient for us, and a small one is necessary. —Notes on Virginia. viii, 414. Ford ed., iii, 280. (1782.)

5784. —— ——. The justest dispositions possible in ourselves, will not secure us against war. It would be necessary that all other nations were just also. Justice indeed, on our part, will save us from those wars which would have been produced by a contrary disposition. But how can we prevent those produced by the wrongs of other nations? By putting ourselves in a condition to punish them. Weakness provokes insult and injury, while a condition to punish, often prevents them. This reasoning leads to the necessity of some naval force; that being the only weapon by which we can reach an enemy. I think it to our interest to punish the first insult; because an insult unpunished is the parent of many others. We are not, at this moment, in a condition to do it, but we should put ourselves into it, as soon as possible. If a war with England should take place, it seems to me that the first thing necessary would be a resolution to abandon the carrying trade, because we cannot protect it. Foreign nations must, in that case, be invited to bring us what we want, and to take our productions in their own bottoms. This alone could prevent the loss of those productions to us, and the acquisition of them to our enemy. Our seamen might be employed in depredations on their trade. But how dreadfully we shall suffer on our coasts, if we have no force on the water, former experience has taught us. Indeed, I look forward with horror to the very possible case of war with an European power, and think there is no protection against them, but from the possession of some force on the sea. Our vicinity to their West India possessions, and to the fisheries, is a bridle which a small naval force, on our part, would hold in the mouths of the most powerful of these countries. I hope our land office will rid us of

*The Barbary powers.—Editor.

our debts, and that our first attention then, will be to the beginning a naval force of some sort. This alone can countenance our people as carriers on the water, and I suppose them to be determined to continue such.—To John Jay. i, 404. Ford ed., iv, 89. (P., 1785.)

5785. —— ——. A little navy [is] the only kind of force we ought to possess.—To Richard Henry Lee. Ford ed., iv, 70. (P., July 1785.)

5786. NAVY, Peace establishment.—The law providing for a naval peace establishment fixes the number of frigates which shall be kept in constant service in time of peace, and prescribes that they shall be manned by not more than two-thirds of their complement of seamen and ordinary seamen. Whether a frigate may be trusted to two-thirds only of her proper complement of men must depend on the nature of the service on which she is ordered. She may sometimes, for her safety, so as to ensure her object, require her fullest complement. * * * Congress will perhaps consider whether the best limitation on the Executive discretion * * * would not be by the number of seamen which may be employed in the whole service, rather than the number of vessels.—Fifth Annual Message. viii, 51. Ford ed., viii, 393. (Dec. 1805.)

5787. NAVY, Reduction.—The navy will be reduced to the legal establishment by the last of this month.—To Nathaniel Macon. iv, 397. (W., May 1801.)

5788. —— ——. The session of the first Congress, convened since republicanism has recovered its ascendency, * * * will pretty completely fulfil all the desires of the people. They have reduced the * * * navy to what is barely necessary.—To General Kosciusko. iv, 430. (W., April 1802.)

5789. NAVY, Secretary of.—I believe I shall have to advertise for a Secretary of the Navy. General Smith is performing the duties gratis, as he refuses both commission and salary, even his expenses, lest it should affect his seat in the House of Representatives.—To Gouverneur Morris. Ford ed., viii, 49. (W., May 1801.) See Lear.

5790. NAVY, Size of.—The actual habits of our countrymen attach them to commerce. They will exercise it for themselves. Wars, then, must sometimes be our lot; and all the wise can do, will be to avoid that half of them which would be produced by our own follies and our own acts of injustice; and to make for the other half the best preparations we can. Of what nature should these be? A land army would be useless for offence, and not the best nor safest instrument of defence. For either of these purposes, the sea is the field on which we should meet an European enemy. On that element it is necessary we should possess some power. To aim at such a navy as the greater nations of Europe possess, would be a foolish and wicked waste of the energies of our countrymen. It would be to pull on our own heads that load of military expense which makes the European laborer go supperless to bed, and moistens his bread with the sweat of his brows. It will be enough if we enable ourselves to prevent insults from those nations of Europe which are weak on the sea, because circumstances exist, which render even the stronger ones weak as to us. Providence has placed their richest and most defenceless possessions at our door; has obliged their most precious commerce to pass, as it were, in review before us. To protect this, or to assail, a small part only of their naval force will ever be risked across the Atlantic. The dangers to which the elements expose them here are too well known, and the greater dangers to which they would be exposed at home were any general calamity to involve their whole fleet. They can attack us by detachment only; and it will suffice to make ourselves equal to what they may detach. Even a smaller force than they may detach will be rendered equal or superior by the quickness with which any check may be repaired with us, while losses with them will be irreparable till too late. A small naval force, then, is sufficient for us, and a small one is necessary. * * * It should by no means be so great as we are able to make it.—NOTES ON VIRGINIA. viii, 413. FORD ED., iii, 279. (1782.)

5791. —— ——. I am for such a naval force only as may protect our coasts and harbors from such depredations as we have experienced; * * * * not for a navy, which by its own expenses and the eternal wars in which it will implicate us, will grind us with public burthens, and sink us under them.—To ELBRIDGE GERRY. iv, 268. FORD ED., vii, 328. (Pa., 1799.)

5792. —— ——. With respect to the extent to which our naval preparations should be carried, some difference of opinion may be expected to appear; but just attention to the circumstances of every part of the Union will doubtless reconcile all. A small force will probably continue to be wanted for actual service in the Mediterranean. Whatever annual sum beyond that you may think proper to apportionate to naval preparations, would perhaps be better employed in providing those articles which may be kept without waste or consumption, and be in readiness when any exigence calls them into use.—FIRST INAUGURAL MESSAGE. viii, 12. FORD ED., viii, 122. (Dec. 1801.)

5793. NAVY, Submarine boats.—I have ever looked to the submarine boat as most to be depended on for attaching the torpedoes, and * * * I am in hopes it is not abandoned as impracticable. I should wish to see a corps of young men trained to this service. It would belong to the engineers if at hand, but being nautical, I suppose we must have a corps of naval engineers, to practice and use them. I do not know whether we have authority to put any part of our existing naval establishment in a course of training, but it shall be the subject

of a consultation with the Secretary of the Navy.—To ROBERT FULTON. v, 165. FORD ED., ix, 125. (M., Aug. 1807.)

5794. —— ——. I wait [Colonel Fulton's] answer as to the submarine boat, before I make you the proposition in form. The very name of a corps of submarine engineers would be a defence.—To ROBERT SMITH. v, 172. (M., Aug. 1807.)

5795. NAVY DEPARTMENT, Bill to establish.—The bill for establishing a Department of Secretary of the Navy was tried yesterday [April 25th] on its passage to the third reading, and prevailed by 47 against 41.—To JAMES MADISON. iv, 237. FORD ED., vii, 244. (Pa., 1798.)

5796. NAVY YARDS, Location of.— From the federalists [in Virginia] I expect nothing on any principle of duty or patriotism; but I did suppose they would pay some attentions to the interests of Norfolk. Is it the interest of that place to strengthen the hue and cry against the policy of making the Eastern Branch [Washington] our great naval deposit? Is it their interest that this should be removed to New York or Boston, to one of which it must go if it leaves this? Is it their interest to scout a defence by gunboats in which they would share amply, in hopes of a navy which will not be built in our day, and would be no defence if built, or of forts which will never be built or maintained, and would be no defence if built? Yet such are the objects which they patronize in their papers. This is worthy of more consideration than they seem to have given it.—To WILSON C. NICHOLAS. FORD ED., viii, 338. (W., Dec. 1804.)

5797. NECESSITY, Law of.—A strict observance of the written law is * * * one of the high duties of a good citizen, but it is not the *highest*. The laws of necessity, of self-preservation, of saving our country when in danger, are of higher obligation. To lose our country by a scrupulous adherence to written law, would be to lose the law itself, with life, liberty, property, and all those who are enjoying them with us; thus absurdly sacrificing the end to the means.— To J. B. COLVIN. v, 542. FORD ED., ix, 279. (M., 1810.)

5798. NECKER (Jacques), Ambition of. —It is a tremendous cloud, indeed, which hovers over this nation, and he at the helm has neither the courage nor the skill necessary to weather it. Eloquence in a high degree, knowledge in matters of account and order, are distinguishing traits in his character. Ambition is his first passion, virtue his second. He has not discovered that sublime truth, that a bold, unequivocal virtue is the best handmaid even to ambition, and would carry him further, in the end, than the temporizing, wavering policy he pursues. His judgment is not of the first order, scarcely even of the second; his resolution frail; and upon the whole, it is rare to meet an instance of a person so much below the reputation he has obtained.—To JOHN JAY. iii, 52. (P., 1789.)

5799. NECKER (Jacques), Friend of liberty.—Though he has appeared to trim a little, he is still, in the main, a friend to public liberty.—To JOHN JAY. iii, 28. (P., 1789.)

5800. NECKER (Jacques), Praise of.— The grandson of M. Necker cannot fail of a hearty welcome in a country which so much respected him. To myself, who loved the virtues and honored the talents of the grandfather, the attentions I received in his natal house, and particular esteem for yourself, are additional titles to whatever service I can render him.— To Madame de Stael. v, 133. (W., 1807.)

5801. NECKER (Jacques), Unfriendly to America.— Necker never set any store by us, or the connection with us.—To John Jay. ii, 342. (P., 1787.)

5802. NEGROES, Amalgamation.— Their amalgamation with the other color produces a degradation to which no lover of his country, no lover of excellence in the human character can innocently consent.—To Edward Coles. Ford ed., ix, 478. (M., 1814.)

5803. NEGROES, Bravery.— They are at least as brave, and more adventuresome. But this may proceed from a want of forethought, which prevents their seeing a danger till it be present. When present, they do not go through it with more coolness or steadiness than the whites.—Notes on Virginia. viii, 381. Ford ed., iii, 245. (1782.)

5804. NEGROES, Colonization.— The bill reported by the revisors* of the whole [Virginia] code does not itself contain the proposition to emancipate all slaves born after the passing the act; but an amendment containing it was prepared, to be offered to the Legislature whenever the bill should be taken up, and further directing, that they should continue with their parents to a certain age, then to be brought up, at the public expense, to tillage, arts or sciences, according to their geniuses, till the females should be eighteen, and the males twenty-one years of age, when they should be colonized to such place as the circumstances of the time should render most proper, sending them out with arms, implements of household and of the handicraft arts, seeds, pairs of the useful domestic animals, &c., to declare them a free and independent people, and extend to them our alliance and protection, till they shall have acquired strength; and to send vessels at the same time to other parts of the world for an equal number of white inhabitants; to induce them to migrate hither, proper encouragements were to be proposed.—Notes on Virginia. viii, 380. Ford ed., iii, 243. (1782.)

5805. ———. This unfortunate difference of color, and perhaps of faculty, is a powerful obstacle to the emancipation of these people. Many of their advocates, while they wish to vindicate the liberty of human nature, are anxious also to preserve its dignity and beauty. Some of these, embarrassed by the question, " What further is to be done with them "? join themselves in opposition with those who are actuated by sordid avarice only. Among the Romans emancipation required but one effort. The slave, when made free, might mix with, without straining the blood of his master. But with us a second is necessary, unknown to history. When freed, he is to be removed beyond the reach of mixture.—Notes on Virginia. viii, 386. Ford ed., iii, 250. (1782.)

5806. ———. You ask my opinion on the proposition of Mrs. Mifflin, to take measures for procuring, on the coast of Africa, an establishment to which the people of color of these States might, from time to time, be colonized,

* Jefferson prepared the report and bill.—Editor.

under the auspices of different governments. Having long ago made up my mind on this subject, I have no hesitation in saying that I have ever thought it the most desirable measure which could be adopted, for gradually drawing off this part of our population, most advantageously for themselves as well as for us. Going from a country possessing all the useful arts, they might be the means of transplanting them among the inhabitants of Africa, and would thus carry back to the country of their origin, the seeds of civilization which might render their sojournment and sufferings here a blessing in the end to that country.—To John Lynch. v, 563. Ford ed., ix, 303. (M., 1811.)

5507. ———. Nothing is more to be wished than that the United States would themselves undertake to make such an establishment on the coast of Africa. Exclusive of motives of humanity, the commercial advantages to be derived from it might repay all its expenses. But for this, the national mind is not yet prepared. It may perhaps be doubted whether many of these people would voluntarily consent to such an exchange of situation, and very certain that few of those advanced to a certain age in habits of slavery, would be capable of self-government. This should not, however, discourage the experiment, nor the early trial of it.—To John Lynch. v, 565. Ford ed., ix, 304. (M., 1811.)

5808. ———. I received in the first year of my coming into the administration of the General Government, a letter from the Governor of Virginia (Colonel Monroe), consulting me, at the request of the Legislature of the State, on the means of procuring some such asylum, to which these people might be occasionally sent. I proposed to him the establishment of Sierra Leone, to which a private company in England had already colonized a number of negroes and particularly the fugitives from these States during the Revolutionary War; and at the same time suggested, if this could not be obtained, some of the Portuguese possessions in South America, as next most desirable. The subsequent Legislature approving these ideas, I wrote, the ensuing year, 1802, to Mr. King, our Minister in London, to endeavor to negotiate with the Sierra Leone company a reception of such of these people as might be colonized thither. He opened a correspondence with Mr. Wedderburne and Mr. Thornton, secretaries of the company, on the subject, and, in 1803, I received through Mr. King the result, which was that the colony was going on, but in a languishing condition; that the funds of the company were likely to fail, as they received no returns of profit to keep them up; that they were, therefore, in treaty with their government to take the establishment off their hands; but that in no event should they be willing to receive more of these people from the United States, as it was exactly that portion of their settlers which had gone from hence, which, by their idleness and turbulence, had kept the settlement in constant danger of dissolution, which could not have been prevented but for the aid of the maroon negroes from the West Indies, who were more industrious and orderly than the others, and supported the authority of the government and its laws. * * * The effort which I made with Portugal, to obtain an establishment for them within their claims in South America, proved also abortive.—To John Lynch. v, 564. Ford ed., ix, 303. (M., 1811.) See Colonization.

5809. NEGROES, Elevating.— Nobody wishes more ardently than I do to see a good system commenced for raising the condition both of their body and mind to what it ought to be, as fast as the imbecility of their present existence, and other circumstances which cannot be neglected, will admit.—To BENJAMIN BANNEKER. iii, 291. FORD ED., v, 377. (Pa., 1791.)

— NEGROES,   Emancipation.—See SLAVERY.

5810. NEGROES, Future of.—I have supposed the black man, in his present state, might not be in body and mind equal to the white man; but it would be hazardous to affirm, that, equally cultivated for a few generations, he would not become so.—To GENERAL CHASTELLUX. i, 341. FORD ED., iii, 138. (P., 1785.)

5811. NEGROES, Griefs.—Their griefs are transient. Those numberless afflictions, which render it doubtful whether Heaven has given life to us in mercy or in wrath, are less felt, and sooner forgotten with them.—NOTES ON VIRGINIA. viii, 382. FORD ED., iii, 245. (1782.)

5812. NEGROES, Improvement.—The improvement of the blacks in body and mind, in the first instance of their mixture with the whites, has been observed by every one, and proves that their inferiority is not the effect merely of their condition in life.—NOTES ON VIRGINIA. viii, 384. FORD ED., iii, 247. (1782.)

5813. —— ——. Bishop Grégoire wrote to me on the doubts I had expressed five or six and twenty years ago, in the Notes on Virginia, as to the grade of understanding of the negroes, and he sent me his book on the literature of the negroes. His credulity has made him gather up every story he could find of men of co or (without distinguishing whether black, or of what degree of mixture), however slight the mention, or light the authority on which they are quoted. The whole do not amount, in point of evidence, to what we know ourselves of Banneker. We know he had spherical trigonometry enough to make almanacs, but not without the suspicion of aid from Ellicot, who was his neighbor and friend, and never missed an opportunity of puffing him. I have a long letter from Banneker, which shows him to have had a mind of very common stature indeed. As to Bishop Grégoire, I wrote him a very soft answer. It was impossible for doubt to have been more tenderly or hesitatingly expressed than that was in the Notes on Virginia, and nothing was or is farther from my intentions, than to enlist myself as the champion of a fixed opinion, where I have only expressed a doubt. St. Domingo will, in time, throw light on the question.—To JOEL BARLOW. v, 475. FORD ED., ix, 261. (M., 1809.)

5814. NEGROES, Indians vs.—Comparing them by their faculties of memory, reason, and imagination, it appears to me that in memory they are equal to the whites; in reason much inferior, as I think one could scarcely be found capable of tracing and comprehending the investigations of Euclid; and that in imagination they are dull, tasteless, and anomalous. It would be unfair to follow them to Africa for this investigation. We will consider them here, on the same stage with the whites, and where the facts are not apocryphal on which a judgment is to be formed. It will be right to make great allowances for the difference of condition, of education, of conversation, of the sphere in which they move. Many millions of them have been brought to, and born in Amer-

ica. Most of them, indeed, have been confined to tillage, to their own homes, and their own society; yet many of them have been so situated that they might have availed themselves of the conversation of their masters; many of them have been brought up to the handicraft arts, and from that circumstance have always been associated with the whites. Some have been liberally educated, and all have lived in countries where the arts and sciences are cultivated to a considerable degree, and have had before their eyes samples of the best works from abroad. The Indians, with no advantages of this kind, will often carve figures on their pipes not destitute of design and merit. They will crayon out an animal, a plant, or a country, so as to prove the existence of a germ in their minds which only wants cultivation. They astonish you with strokes of the most sublime oratory; such as prove their reason and sentiment strong, their imagination glowing and elevated. But never yet could I find that a black had uttered a thought above the level of plain narration; never saw even an elementary trait of painting or sculpture.—NOTES ON VIRGINIA. viii, 382. FORD ED., iii, 245. (1782.)

5815. NEGROES, Industry.—An opinion is hazarded by some, but proved by none, that moral urgencies are not sufficient to induce the negro to labor; that nothing can do this but physical coercion. But this is a problem which the present age alone is prepared to solve by experiment. It would be a solecism to suppose a race of animals created, without sufficient foresight and energy to preserve their own existence. It is disproved, too, by the fact that they exist, and have existed through all the ages of history. We are not sufficiently acquainted with all the nations of Africa, to say that there may not be some in which habits of industry are established, and the arts practiced which are necessary to render life comfortable. The experiment now in progress in St. Domingo, those of Sierra Leone and Cape Mesurado, are but beginning. Your proposition has its aspects of promise also; and should it not fully answer to calculations in figures, it may yet, in its developments, lead to happy results.—To MISS FANNY WRIGHT. vii, 408. FORD ED., x, 344. (M., 1825.)

5816. NEGROES, Integrity.—Notwithstanding these considerations which must weaken their respect for the laws of property, we find among them numerous instances of the most rigid integrity, and as many as among their better instructed masters, of benevolence, gratitude, and unshaken fidelity.—NOTES ON VIRGINIA. viii, 386. FORD ED., iii, 249. (1782.) See SLAVERY.

5817. NEGROES, Literary.—Misery is often the parent of the most affecting touches in poetry. Among the blacks is misery enough, God knows, but no poetry. Love is the peculiar cestrum of the poet. Their love is ardent, but it kindles the senses only, not the imagination. Religion, indeed, has produced a Phyllis Wheatley;* but it could not produce a poet. The compositions published under her name are below the dignity of criticism. The heroes of the Dunciad are to her, as Hercules to the author of that poem.—NOTES ON VIRGINIA. viii, 383. FORD ED., iii, 246. (1782.)

5818. —— ——. Ignatius Sancho has approached nearer to merit in composition [than Phyllis Wheatley]: yet his letters do more honor to the heart than the head. They breathe the

* A collection of poems by Phyllis Wheatley was printed in London in 1773.—EDITOR.

purest effusions of friendship and general philanthropy, and show how great a degree of the latter may be compounded with strong religious zeal. He is often happy in the turn of his compliments, and his style is easy and familiar, except when he affects a Shandean fabrication of words. But his imagination is wild and extravagant, escapes incessantly from every restraint of reason and taste, and, in the course of its vagaries, leaves a tract of thought as incoherent and eccentric, as is the course of a meteor through the sky. His subjects should often have led him to a process of sober reasoning; yet we find him always substituting sentiment for demonstration. Upon the whole, though we admit him to the first place among those of his own color who have presented themselves to the public judgment, yet when we compare him with the writers of the race among whom he lived and particularly with the epistolary class in which he has taken his own stand, we are compelled to enroll him at the bottom of the column. This criticism supposes the letters published under his name to be genuine, and to have received amendment from no other hand; points which would not be of easy investigation.—NOTES ON VIRGINIA. viii. 383. FORD ED., iii, 247. (1782.)

5819. NEGROES, Music.—In music they are more generally gifted than the whites, with accurate ears for tune and time, and they have been found capable of imagining a small catch.* Whether they will be equal to the composition of a more extensive run of melody, or of complicated harmony, is yet to be proved.—NOTES ON VIRGINIA. viii, 383. FORD ED., iii, 246. (1782.)

5820. NEGROES, Natural History and. —The opinion that they are inferior in the faculties of reason and imagination, must be hazarded with great diffidence. To justify a general conclusion, requires many observations, even where the subject may be submitted to the anatomical knife, to optical glasses, to analysis by fire or by solvents. How much more then where it is a faculty, not a substance, we are examining; where it eludes the research of all the senses; where the conditions of its existence are various and variously combined; where the effects of those which are present or absent bid defiance to calculation; let me add, too, as a circumstance of great tenderness, where our conclusion would degrade a whole race of men from the rank in the scale of beings which their Creator may perhaps have given them. To our reproach it must be said, that though for a century and a half we have had under our eyes the races of black and of red men, they have never yet been viewed by us as subjects of natural history. I advance it, therefore, as a suspicion only, that the blacks, whether originally a distinct race, or made distinct by time and circumstances, are inferior to the whites in the endowments both of body and mind. It is not against experience to suppose that different species of the same genus, or varieties of the same species, may possess different qualifications. Will not a lover of natural history, then, one who views the gradations in all the races of animals with the eye of philosophy, excuse an effort to keep those in the department of man as distinct as nature has formed them?—NOTES ON VIRGINIA. viii, 386. FORD ED., iii, 249. (1782.)

* The instrument proper to them is the Banjer [corrupted by the negroes into "banjo"] which they brought hither from Africa, and which is the original of the guitar, its chords being precisely the four lower chords of the guitar.—NOTE BY JEFFERSON.

5821. NEGROES, Peculiarities.—To these objections, which are political, may be added others, which are physical and moral. Whether the black of the negro resides in the reticular membrane between the skin and scarf-skin, or in the scarf-skin itself; whether it proceeds from the color of the blood, the color of the bile, or from that of some other secretion, the difference is fixed in nature, and is as real as if its seat and cause were better known to us. And is this difference of no importance? Is it not the foundation of a greater or less share of beauty in the two races? Are not the fine mixtures of red and white, the expressions of every passion by greater or less suffusions of color in the one, preferable to that eternal monotony, which reigns in the countenances, that immovable veil of black which covers all the emotions of the other race? Add to these, flowing hair, a more elegant symmetry of form, their own judgment in favor of the whites, declared by their preference of them, as uniformly as is the preference of the Oranootan for the black woman over those of his own species. The circumstance of superior beauty, is thought worthy attention in the propagation of our horses, dogs, and other domestic animals; why not in that of man? Besides those of color, figure, and hair, there are other physical distinctions proving a difference of race. They have less hair on the face and body. They secrete less by the kidneys, and more by the glands of the skin, which gives them a very strong and disagreeable odor. This greater degree of transpiration renders them more tolerant of heat, and less of cold than the whites. Perhaps, too, a difference of structure in the pulmonary apparatus, which a late ingenious experimentalist (Crawford) has discovered to be the principal regulator of animal heat, may have disabled them from extricating, in the act of inspiration, so much of that fluid from the outer air, or obliged them in expiration, to part with more of it.—NOTES ON VIRGINIA. viii, 381. FORD ED., iii, 244. (1782.)

— NEGROES, Penal Colony for.—See COLONY, PENAL.

5822. NEGROES, Racial differences.— It will probably be asked, why not retain and incorporate the blacks into the State, and thus save the expense of supplying by importation of white settlers, the vacancies they will leave? Deep-rooted prejudices entertained by the whites; ten thousand recollections, by the blacks, of the injuries they have sustained; new provocations; the real distinctions which nature has made; and many other circumstances will divide us into parties, and produce convulsions, which will probably never end but in the extermination of the one or the other race.—NOTES ON VIRGINIA. viii, 380. FORD ED., iii, 244. (1782.)

5823. NEGROES, Rights of.—Be assured that no person living wishes more sincerely than I do, to see a complete refutation of the doubts I have myself entertained and expressed on the grade of understanding allotted to the negroes by nature, and to find that in this respect they are on a par with ourselves. My doubts were the result of personal observation on the limited sphere of my own State, where the opportunities for the development of their genius were not favorable, and those of exercising it still less so. I expressed them, therefore, with great hesitation; but whatever be their degree of talent it is no measure of their rights. Because Sir Isaac Newton was superior to others in understanding, he was not therefore lord of the person or property of others. On this subject they are gaining daily in the opinions of nations, and hopeful advances are making towards their reestablishment on an equal footing with the other colors of the human family. I pray you, therefore, to accept my thanks for the many instances you have enabled me to observe of respectable intelligence in that race of men, which cannot fail to have effect in hastening the day of their relief.—To HENRI GREGOIRE. v, 429. FORD ED., ix, 246. (W., 1809.)

5824. NEGROES, Sleep and amusements.—They seem to require less sleep. A black, after hard labor through the day, will be induced by the slightest amusements to sit up till midnight, or later, though knowing he must be out with the first dawn of the morning.—NOTES ON VIRGINIA. viii, 381. FORD ED., iii, 245. (1782.)

5825. ———. In general, their existence appears to participate more of sensation than reflection. To this must be ascribed their disposition to sleep when abstracted from their diversions, and unemployed in labor. An animal whose body is at rest, and who does not reflect, must be disposed to sleep of course.—NOTES ON VIRGINIA. viii, 382. FORD ED., iii, 245. (1782.)

5826. NEGROES, Talents.—Nobody wishes more than I do to see such proofs as you exhibit, that nature has given to our black brethren talents equal to those of the other colors of men, and that the appearance of a want of them is owing merely to the degraded condition of their existence, both in Africa and America. * * * I have taken the liberty of sending your Almanac to Monsieur de Condorcet, Secretary of the Academy of Sciences at Paris, and member of the Philanthropic Society, because I considered it as a document to which your color had a right for their justification against the doubts which have been entertained of them.—To BENJAMIN BANNEKER. iii, 291. FORD ED., v, 377. (Pa., 1791.) See BANNEKER.

5827. NELSON (Thomas), Governor of Virginia.—[Governor Jefferson's] office was now [June, 1781,] near expiring, the country [Virginia] under invasion by a powerful army, no services but military of any avail, unprepared by his line of life and education for the command of armies, he believed it right not to stand in the way of talents better fitted than his own to the circumstances under which the country was placed. He, therefore, himself proposed to his friends in the Legislature that General Nelson, who commanded the militia of the State, should be appointed Governor, as he was sensible that the union of the civil and military power in the same hands at this time, would greatly facilitate military measures. This appointment accordingly took place on the 12th of June, 1781.—INVASION OF VA. MEMORANDUM. ix, 223. (M., 1781.)

5828. NEOLOGY, American.—I am no friend to what is called *Purism*, but a zealous one to the *Neology* which has introduced these two words without the authority of any dictionary. I consider the one as destroying the nerve and beauty of language, while the other improves both, and adds to its copiousness. I have been not a little disappointed, and made suspicious of my own judgment, on seeing the Edinburgh Reviewers, the ablest critics of the age, set their faces against the introduction of new words into the English language; they are particularly apprehensive that the writers of the United States will adulterate it. Certainly so great growing a population, spread over such an extent of country, with such a variety of climates, of productions, of arts, must enlarge their language, to make it answer its purpose of expressing all ideas, the new as well as the old. The new circumstances under which we are placed, call for new words, new phrases, and for the transfer of old words to new objects. An American dialect will, therefore, be formed; so will a West-Indian and Asiatic, as a Scotch and an Irish are already formed. But whether will these adulterate, or enrich the English language? Has the beautiful poetry of Burns, or his Scottish dialect, disfigured it? Did the Athenians consider the Doric, the Ionian, the Aeolic, and other dialects as disfiguring or as beautifying their language? Did they fastidiously disavow Herodotus, Pindar, Theocritus, Sappho, Alcæus, as Grecian writers? On the contrary, they were sensible that the variety of dialects, still infinitely varied by poetical license, constituted the riches of their language, and made the Grecian Homer the first of poets, as he must ever remain, until a language equally ductile and copious shall again be spoken.—To JOHN WALDO. vi, 184. (M., 1813.)

5829. NEUTRALITY, Carrying trade and.—If war in Europe take place, I hope the new world will fatten on the follies of the old. If we can but establish the principles of the armed neutrality for ourselves, we must become carriers for all parties as far as we can raise vessels.—To E. RUTLEDGE. iii, 165. FORD ED., v, 197. (N.Y., 1790.)

5830. ———. A stoppage by some of the belligerent powers of one of our vessels going with grain to an unblockaded port, would be so unequivocal an infringement of the neutral rights, that we cannot conceive it will be attempted.—To THOMAS PINCKNEY. iii, 551. FORD ED., vi, 243. (Pa., May 1793.)

5831. ———. The rights of a neutral to carry on a commercial intercourse with every part of the dominions of a belligerent, permitted by the laws of the country (with the exception of blockaded ports and contraband of war), was believed to have been decided between Great Britain and the United States by the sentence of the commissioners mutually appointed to decide on that and other questions of difference between the two nations, and by the actual payment of damages awarded by them against Great Britain for the infraction of that right. When, therefore, it was perceived that the same principle was revived with others more novel, and extending the injury, instructions were given to the Minister Plenipotentiary of the United States at the court of London, and remonstrances duly made by him on the subject. These were followed by a partial and temporary suspension only, without the disavowal of the principle. He has, therefore, been instructed to urge this subject anew, to bring it more fully to the bar of reason, and to insist on the rights too evident and too important to be surrendered. SPECIAL MESSAGE. viii, 57. FORD ED., viii, 417. (Jan. 1806.)

5832. ———. To former violations of maritime rights, another is now added of very extensive effect. The government of that nation [Great Britain] has issued an order interdicting all trade by neutrals between ports not in amity with them; and being now at war with nearly every nation on the Atlantic and Mediterranean seas, our vessels are required to sacrifice their cargoes at the first port they touch, or to return home without the benefit of going to any other market. Under this new law of the ocean, our trade on the Mediterranean has been swept away by seizures and condemnations, and that in other seas is threatened with the same fate.—SEVENTH ANNUAL MESSAGE. viii, 84. FORD ED., ix, 156. (1807.) See NAVIGATION.

5833. NEUTRALITY, Contraband of war.—In our treaty with Prussia, we have gone ahead of other nations in doing away with restraints on the commerce of peaceful nations, by declaring that nothing shall be contraband. For, in truth, in the present improved state of the arts, when every country has such ample means of procuring arms within and without itself, the regulations of contraband answer no other end than to draw other nations into the war. However, as other nations have not given sanction to this improvement, we claim it, at present, with Prussia alone.—To THOMAS PINCKNEY. iii, 551. FORD ED., vi, 243. (Pa., May 1793.) See BELLIGERENTS and CONTRABAND OF WAR.

5834. NEUTRALITY, Duties.—We have seen with sincere concern the flames of war lighted up again in Europe, and nations with which we have the most friendly and useful relations engaged in mutual destruction. While we regret the miseries in which we see others involved, let us bow with gratitude to that kind Providence which, inspiring with wisdom and moderation our late legislative councils while placed under the urgency of the greatest wrongs, guarded us from hastily entering into the sanguinary contest, and left us only to look on and to pity its ravages. These will be heaviest on those immediately engaged. Yet the nations pursuing peace will not be exempt from all evil. In the course of this conflict [France and England], let it be our endeavor, as it is our interest and desire, to cultivate the friendship of the belligerent nations by every act of justice and of incessant kindness; to receive their armed vessels with hospitality from distresses of the sea, but to administer the means of annoyance to none; to establish in our harbors such a police as may maintain law and order; to restrain our citizens from embarking individually in a war in which their country takes no part; to punish severely those persons, citizen or alien, who shall usurp the cover of our flag for vessels not entitled to it, infecting thereby with suspicion those of real Americans, and committing us into controversies for the redress of wrongs not our own; to exact from every nation the observance, toward our vessels and citizens, of those principles and practices which all civilized people acknowledge; to merit the character of a just nation, and maintain that of an independent one, preferring every consequence to insult and habitual wrong. Congress will consider whether the existing laws enable us efficaciously to maintain this course with our citizens in all places, and with others while within the limits of our jurisdiction, and will give them the new modifications necessary for these objects. Some contraventions of right have already taken place, both within our jurisdictional limits and on the high seas. The friendly disposition of the governments from whose agents they have proceeded, as well as their wisdom and regard for justice, leave us in reasonable expectation that they will be rectified and prevented in future; and that no act will be countenanced by them which threatens to disturb our friendly intercourse. Separated by a wide ocean from the nations of Europe, and from the political interests which entangle them together, with productions and wants which render our commerce and friendship useful to them and theirs to us, it cannot be the interest of any to assail us, nor ours to disturb them.

We should be most unwise, indeed, were we to cast away the singular blessings of the position in which nature has placed us, the opportunity she has endowed us with of pursuing, at a distance from foreign contentions, the paths of industry, peace and happiness; of cultivating general friendship, and of bringing collisions of interest to the umpirage of reason rather than of force. How desirable, then, must it be, in a government like ours, to see its citizens adopt individually the views, the interests, and the conduct which their country should pursue, divesting themselves of those passions and partialities which tend to lessen useful friendships, and to embarrass and embroil us in the calamitous scenes of Europe. Confident that you will duly estimate the importance of neutral dispositions toward the observance of neutral conduct, that you will be sensible how much it is our duty to look on the bloody arena spread before us with commiseration indeed, but with no other wish than to see it closed, I am persuaded you will cordially cherish these dispositions in all discussions among yourselves, and in all communications with your constituents; and I anticipate with satisfaction the measures of wisdom which the great interests now committed to *you* will give you an opportunity of providing, and *myself* that of approving and carrying into execution with the fidelity I owe to my country.—THIRD ANNUAL MESSAGE. viii, 27. FORD ED., viii, 272. (Oct. 1803.)

5835. NEUTRALITY, Enemy goods.—Another source of complaint with Mr. Genet has been that the English take French goods out of American vessels, which he says is against the law of nations and ought to be prevented by us. On the contrary, we suppose it to have been long an established principle of the law of nations, that the goods of a friend are free in an enemy's vessel, and an enemy's goods lawful prize in the vessel of a friend. The inconvenience of this principle which subjects merchant vessels to be stopped at sea, searched, ransacked, led out of their course, has induced several nations latterly to stipulate against it by treaty, and to substitute another in its stead, that free bottoms shall make free goods, and enemy bottoms enemy goods; a rule equal to the other in point of loss and gain, but less oppressive to commerce. As far as it has been introduced, it depends on the treaties stipulating it, and forms exceptions, in special cases, to the general operation of the law of nations. We have introduced it into our treaties with France, Holland and Prussia; and French goods found by the two latter nations in American bottoms are not made prize of. It is our wish to establish it with other nations. But this requires their consent also, is a work of time, and in the meanwhile, they have a right to act on the general principle, without giving to us or to France cause of complaint. Nor do I see that France can lose by it on the whole. For though she loses *her* goods when found in our vessels by the nations with whom we have no treaties, yet she gains *our* goods, when found in the vessels of the same and all other nations; and we believe the latter mass to be greater than the former.—To GOUVERNEUR MORRIS. iv, 43. FORD ED., vi, 387. (Pa., Aug. 1793.)

5836. ———. It is to be lamented, indeed, that the general principle has operated so cruelly in the dreadful calamity which has lately happened in St. Domingo. The miserable fugitives, who, to save their lives, had taken asylum in our vessels, with such valuable and portable things as could be gathered in the moment out of the ashes of their houses and wrecks of their fortunes, have been plundered of these remains by the licensed sea rovers of their enemies. This has swelled, on this occasion, the disadvantages of the general principle, that " an enemy's goods are free prize in the vessels of a friend ". But it is one of those deplorable and unforeseen calamities to which they expose themselves who enter into a state of war, furnishing to us an awful lesson to avoid it by justice and moderation, and not a cause of encouragement to expose our own towns to the same burning and butcheries, nor of complaint because we do not.—To GOUVERNEUR MORRIS. iv, 44. FORD ED., vi, 387. (Pa., Aug. 1793.) See ENEMY GOODS.

5837. NEUTRALITY, Fraudulent use of flag.—As there appears * * * a probability of a very general war in Europe, you will be pleased to be particularly attentive to preserve for our vessels all the rights of neutrality, and to endeavor that our flag be not usurped by others to procure to themselves the benefits of our neutrality. This usurpation tends to commit us with foreign nations, to subject those vessels truly ours to rigorous scrutinies and delays, to distinguish them from counterfeits, and to take the business of transportation out of our hands.—To DAVID HUMPHREYS. iii, 533. FORD ED., vi, 205. (Pa., 1793.)

5838. —— ——. It will be necessary for all our public agents to exert themselves with vigilance for securing to our vessels all the rights of neutrality.—To C. W. F. DUMAS. iii, 535. (Pa., 1793.) See FLAG.

5839. NEUTRALITY, The Grange capture.—The capture of the British ship Grange, by the French frigate L'Embuscade, has been found to have taken place within the * * * jurisdiction of the United States * * * . The government, is, therefore, taking measures for the liberation of the crew and restitution of the ship and cargo.—To GEORGE HAMMOND. iii, 559. FORD ED., vi, 253. (Pa., May 1793.)

5840. —— ——. The government deems the capture [of the Grange] to have been unquestionably within its jurisdiction, and that according to the rules of neutrality and the protection it owes to all persons while within its limits, it is bound to see that the crew be liberated, and the vessel and cargo restored to their former owners. * * * I am, in consequence, charged by the President of the United States to express to you his expectation, and at the same time his confidence, that you will be pleased to take immediate and effectual measures for having the ship Grange and her cargo restored to the British owners, and the persons taken on board her set at liberty.—To JEAN BAPTISTE TERNANT. iii, 561. FORD ED., vi, 256. (Pa., May 15, 1793.)

5841. —— ——. In forming these determinations [respecting Grange, &c.,] the government of the United States has listened to nothing but the dictates of immutable justice; they consider the rigorous exercise of that virtue as the surest means of preserving perfect harmony between the United States and the powers at war.—To JEAN BAPTISTE TERNANT. iii, 562. FORD ED., vi, 257. (Pa., May 1793.)

5842. NEUTRALITY, Impartial.—Our conduct as a neutral nation is marked out in our treaties with France and Holland, two of the belligerent powers: and as the duties of neutrality require an *equal* conduct to both parties, we should, on that ground, act on the same

principles towards Great Britain.—To THOMAS PINCKNEY. iii, 551. FORD ED., vi, 243. (Pa., May 1793.)

5843. —— ——. A manly neutrality, claiming the liberal rights ascribed to that condition by the very powers at war, was the part we should have taken, and would, I believe, have given satisfaction to our allies. If anything prevents its being a mere English neutrality, it will be that the penchant of the President is not that way, and above all, the ardent spirit of our constituents.—To JAMES MADISON. iii, 557. FORD ED., vi, 251. (May 1793.)

5844. —— ——. The line is now drawn so clearly as to show on one side, 1. The fashionable circles of Philadelphia, New York, Boston and Charleston (natural aristocrats). 2. Merchants trading on British capital. 3. Paper men (all the old tories are found in some one of the three descriptions). On the other side are, 1. Merchants trading on their own capital. 2. Irish merchants. 3. Tradesmen, mechanics, farmers, and every other possible description of our citizens.—To JAMES MADISON. iii, 557. FORD ED., vi, 251. (May 1793.)

5845. —— ——. I trust that in the readiness with which the United States have attended to the redress of such wrongs as are committed by their citizens, or within their jurisdiction, you will see proofs of their justice and impartiality to all parties, and that it will ensure to their citizens pursuing their lawful business by sea or by land, in all parts of the world, a like efficacious interposition of the governing powers to protect them from injury, and redress it, where it has taken place. With such dispositions on both sides, vigilantly and faithfully carried into effect, we may hope that the blessings of peace, on the one part, will be as little impaired, and the evils of war on the other, as little aggravated, as the nature of things will permit; and that this should be so, is, we trust, the prayer of all.—To GEORGE HAMMOND. iii, 559. FORD ED., vi, 254. (Pa., 1793.)

5846. —— ——. The course intended to be pursued being that of a strict and impartial neutrality, decisions, rendered by the President on that principle, dissatisfy both parties, and draw complaints from both.—To GOUVERNEUR MORRIS. iii, 580. FORD ED., vi, 299. (Pa., June 1793.)

5847. —— ——. It will never be easy to convince me that by a firm yet just conduct in 1793, we might not have obtained such a respect for our neutral rights from Great Britain, as that her violations of them and use of our means to wage her wars, would not have furnished any pretence to the other party to do the same. War with both would have been avoided, commerce and navigation protected and enlarged. We shall now either be forced into a war, or have our commerce and navigation at least totally annihilated, and the produce of our farms for some years left to rot on our hands. A little time will unfold these things, and show which class of opinions would have been most friendly to the firmness of our government, and to the interests of those for whom it was made.—To DR. JOHN EDWARDS. iv, 165. FORD ED., vii, 113. (M., Jan. 1797.)

5848. —— ——. It is to be deplored that distant as we are from the storms and convulsions which agitate the European world, the pursuit of an honest neutrality, beyond the reach of reproach, has been insufficient to secure to us the certain enjoyments of peace with those whose interests as well as ours would be promoted by it.—R. TO A. NEW JERSEY LEGISLATURE. viii, 122. (1807.)

5849. —— ——. I verily believe that it will ever be in our power to keep so even a stand between England and France, as to inspire a wish in neither to throw us into the scale of his adversary. If we can do this for a dozen years only, we shall have little to fear from them.—To MR. COXE. v, 58. (W., 1807.)

5850. —— ——. Neither belligerent pretends to have been injured by us, or can say that we have in any instance departed from the most faithful neutrality.—R. TO A. VIRGINIA ASSEMBLY. viii, 148. (1809.)

5851. —— ——. A law respecting our conduct as a neutral between Spain and her contending colonies was passed [by the late Congress] by a majority of one only, I believe, and against the very general sentiment of our country. It is thought to strain our complaisance to Spain beyond her right or merit, and almost against the right of the other party, and certainly against the claims they have to our good wishes and neighborly relations. That we should wish to see the people of other countries free, is as natural, and, at least as justifiable, as that one king should wish to see the kings of other countries maintained in their despotism. Right to both parties, innocent favor to the juster cause, is our proper sentiment.—To ALBERT GALLATIN. vii, 78. FORD ED., x, 90. (M., 1817.)

5852. NEUTRALITY, Markets and.— If the new government wears the front which I hope it will, I see no impossibility in the availing ourselves of the wars of others to open the other parts of America [West Indies] to our commerce, as the price of our neutrality.—To GENERAL WASHINGTON. ii, 533. FORD ED., v, 57. (P., 1788.)

5853. —— ——. With England, I think we shall cut off the resource of impressing our seamen to fight her battles, and establish the inviolability of our flag in its commerce with her enemies. We shall thus become what we sincerely wish to be, honestly neutral, and truly useful to both belligerents. To the one, by keeping open market for the consumption of her manufactures, while they are excluded from all the other countries under the power of her enemy; to the other, by securing for her a safe carriage of all her productions, metropolitan or colonial, while her own means are restrained by her enemy, and may, therefore, be employed in other useful pursuits. We are certainly more useful friends to France and Spain as neutrals, than as allies.—To JAMES BOWDOIN. v, 18. (W., 1806.) See COMMERCE, MARKETS, and NAVIGATION.

5854. NEUTRALITY, Obligations of. —Where [treaties] are silent, the general principles of the law of nations must give the rule [of neutral obligation]. I mean the principles of that law as they have been liberalized in latter times by the refinement of manners and morals, and evidenced by the declarations, stipulations, and practice of every civilized nation.— To THOMAS PINCKNEY. iii, 551. FORD ED., vi, 243. (Pa., May 1793.)

5855. NEUTRALITY, Passage of troops.—It is well enough agreed in the laws of nations, that for a neutral power to give or refuse permission to the troops of either belligerent party to pass through their territory, is no breach of neutrality, provided the same refusal or permission be extended to the other party. If we give leave of passage then to the British troops, Spain will have no just cause of complaint against us, provided we extend the same leave to her when demanded. If we refuse (as indeed we have a right to do), and the troops should pass notwithstanding, of which there can be little doubt, we shall stand committed. For either we must enter immediately into the war, or pocket an acknowledged insult in the face of the world; and one insult pocketed soon produces another. There is, indeed, a middle course which I should be inclined to prefer; that is to avoid giving any answer. They will proceed notwithstanding, but to do this under our silence, will admit of palliation, and produce apologies, from military necessity; and will leave us free to pass it over without dishonor, or to make it a handle of quarrel hereafter, if we should have use for it as such. But, if we are obliged to give an answer, I think the occasion not such as should induce us to hazard that answer which might commit us to the war at so early a stage of it; and, therefore, that the passage should be permitted. If they should pass without having asked leave, I should be for expressing our dissatisfaction to the British court, and keeping alive an altercation on the subject, till events should decide whether it is most expedient to accept their apologies, or to profit of the aggression as a cause of war.— OFFICIAL OPINION. vii, 509. FORD ED., v, 239. (1790.)

5856. NEUTRALITY, Passports for vessels.—The proposition to permit all our vessels destined for any port in the French West India Islands to be stopped, unless furnished with passports from yourself, is so far beyond the powers of the Executive, that it will be unnecessary to enumerate the objections to which it would be liable.—To E. C. GENET. iv, 88. FORD ED., vi, 460. (Pa., Nov. 1793.)

5857. NEUTRALITY, Preserving.— Amidst the confusion of a general war which seems to be threatening that quarter of the globe [Europe], we hope to be permitted to preserve the line of neutrality.—To C. W. F. DUMAS. iii, 535. (Pa., March 1793.)

5858. —— ——. I wish we may be able to repress the spirit of the people within the limits of a fair neutrality.—To JAMES MONROE. iii, 548. FORD ED., vi, 238. (Pa., 1793.)

5859. —— ——. You may, on every occasion, give assurances [to the British government] which cannot go beyond the real desires of this country, to preserve a fair neutrality in the present war, on condition that the rights of neutral nations are respected in us, as they have been settled in *modern* times, either by the express declarations of the powers of Europe, or their adoption of them on particular occasions.—To THOMAS PINCKNEY. iii, 542. (Pa., April 1793.)

5860. —— ——. We shall be a little embarrassed occasionally till we feel ourselves firmly seated in the saddle of neutrality.—To GEORGE WYTHE. FORD ED., vi, 218. (Pa., April 1793.)

5861. —— ——. I fear that a fair neutrality will prove a disagreeable pill to our friends [the French], though necessary to keep out of the calamities of a war.—To JAMES MADISON. FORD ED., vi, 232. (Pa., April 1793.)

5862. —— ——. No country, perhaps, was ever so thoroughly against war as ours. These dispositions pervade every description of its citizens, whether in or out of office. They cannot, perhaps, suppress their affections, nor their wishes. But they will suppress the effects of them so as to preserve a fair neutrality. Indeed we shall be more useful as neutrals than as parties, by the protection which our flag will give to supplies of provisions. In this spirit let all your assurances be given to the government [of France].—To Gouverneur Morris. Ford ed., vi, 217. (Pa., April 1793.)

5863. —— ——. If we preserve even a sneaking neutrality, we shall be indebted for it to the President, and not to his counsellors.— To Colonel Monroe. iii, 548. Ford ed., vi, 239. (Pa., May 1793.)

5864. NEUTRALITY, Profitable.—The great harvest for [the profits of navigation] is when other nations are at war and our flag neutral.—Opinion on Ship Passports. vii, 625. (1793.)

5865. —— ——. Let us milk the cow while the Russian holds her by the horns and the Turk holds her by the tail.—To John Adams. vii, 245. Ford ed., x, 217. (M., 1822.)

5866. NEUTRALITY, Provisions not contraband.—This article* is so manifestly contrary to the law of nations, that nothing more would seem necessary than to observe that it is so. Reason and usage have established that when two nations go to war, those who choose to live in peace retain their natural right to pursue their agriculture, manufactures, and other ordinary vocations, to carry the produce of their industry for exchange to all nations, belligerent or neutral, as usual, to go and come freely, without injury or molestation, and, in short, that the war among others shall be, for them, as if it did not exist. One restriction on their natural rights has been submitted to by nations at peace; that is to say, that of not furnishing to either party implements merely of war, for the annoyance of the other, nor anything whatever to a place blockaded by its enemy. What these implements of war are, has been so often agreed and is so well understood, as to leave little question about them at this day. There does not exist, perhaps, a nation in our common hemisphere which has not made a particular enumeration of them, in some or all of their treaties, under the name of contraband. It suffices for the present occasion, to say, that corn flour and meal, are not of the class of contraband, and consequently remain articles of free commerce. A culture, which, like that of the soil, gives employment to such a proposition of mankind, could never be suspended by the whole earth, or interrupted for them, whenever any two nations should think proper to go to war.—To Thomas Pinckney. iv, 59. Ford ed., vi, 413. (Pa., Sep. 1793.)

5867. —— ——. The state of war existing between Great Britain and France, furnishes no legitimate right either to interrupt the agriculture of the United States, or the peaceable exchange of its produce with all nations; and

* Instructions to commanders of British war ships directing them to stop vessels carrying provisions to French ports, and send them to English ports where their cargoes may be purchased by that government, or released on security that they will be taken to the ports of some country in amity with Great Britain.—Editor.

consequently, the assumption of it will be as lawful hereafter as now, in peace as in war. No ground, acknowledged by the common reason of mankind, authorizes this act now, and unacknowledged ground may be taken at any time and all times. We see, then, a practice begun, to which no time, no circumstances prescribe any limits, and which strikes at the root of our agriculture, that branch of industry which gives food, clothing and comfort to the great mass of the inhabitants of these States. If any nation whatever has a right to shut up to our produce all the ports of the earth except her own, and those of her friends, she may shut up these also, and so confine us within our own limits. No nation can subscribe to such pretensions; no nation can agree, at the mere will or interest of another, to have its peaceable industry suspended, and its citizens reduced to idleness and want. The loss of our produce, destined for foreign markets, or that loss which would result from an arbitrary restraint of our markets, is a tax too serious for us to acquiesce in. It is not enough for a nation to say, we and our friends will buy your produce. We have a right to answer, that it suits us better to sell to their enemies as well as their friends. Our ships do not go to France to return empty. They go to exchange the surplus of our produce, which we can spare, for surpluses of other kinds, which they can spare, and we want; which they can furnish on better terms, and more to our mind, than Great Britain or her friends. We have a right to judge for ourselves what market best suits us, and they have none to forbid to us the enjoyment of the necessaries and comforts which we may obtain from any other independent country.—To Thomas Pinckney. iv, 60. Ford ed., vi, 413. (Pa., Sep. 1793.)

5868. —— ——. This act, too, tends directly to draw us from that state of peace in which we are wishing to remain. It is an essential character of neutrality to furnish no aids (not stipulated by treaty) to one party, which we are not equally ready to furnish to the other. If we permit corn to be sent to Great Britain and her friends, we are equally bound to permit it to France. To restrain it, would be a partiality which might lead to war with France; and, between restraining it ourselves, and permitting her enemies to restrain it unrightfully, is no difference. She would consider this as a mere pretext, of which she would not be the dupe; and on what honorable ground could we otherwise explain it? Thus we should see ourselves plunged, by this unauthorized act of Great Britain, into a war with which we meddle not, and which we wish to avoid, if justice to all parties, and from all parties, will enable us to avoid it. In the case where we found ourselves obliged, by treaty, to withhold from the enemies of France the right of arming in our ports, we thought ourselves in justice bound to withhold the same right from France also, and we did it. Were we to withhold from her supplies of provisions, we should, in like manner, be bound to withhold them from her enemies also; and thus shut to ourselves all the ports of Europe, where corn is in demand, or make ourselves parties in the war. This is a dilemma, which Great Britain has no right to force upon us, and for which no pretext can be found in any part of our conduct. She may, indeed, feel the desire of starving an enemy nation; but she can have no right of doing it at our loss, nor of making us the instruments of it.—To Thomas Pinckney. iv, 61. Ford ed., vi, 414. (Pa., Sep. 1793.)

5869. NEUTRALITY, Public vessels.—
The public ships of war of both nations [France
and England] enjoy a perfect equality in our
ports; first, in cases of urgent necessity; secondly, in cases of comfort or convenience; and
thirdly, in the time they choose to continue;
and all a friendly power. can ask from another is, to extend to her the same indulgences
which she extends to other friendly powers.—
To George Hammond. iv, 66. Ford ed., vi,
423. (Pa., 1793.) See Asylum.

5870. —— ——. The bringing vessels to,
of whatever nation, while within the limits of
the protection of the United States, will be
pointedly forbidden; the government being
firmly determined to enforce a peaceable de-
meanor among all the parties within those
limits, and to deal to all the same impartial
measure.—To the Governor of Virginia. iii,
564. (Pa., May 1793.)

5871. —— ——. Mr. Thornton's attempt
to justify his nation in using our ports as cruising stations on our friends and ourselves, renders the matter so serious as to call, I think, for
answer. That we ought, in courtesy and friendship, to extend to them all the rights of hospitality is certain; that they should not use our
hospitality to injure our friends or ourselves is
equally enjoined by morality and honor. After
the rigorous exertions we made in Genet's time
to prevent this abuse on his part, and the indulgences extended by Mr. Adams to the
British cruisers even after our pacification with
France, by ourselves also from an unwillingness
to change the course of things as the war was
near its close, I did not expect to hear from
that quarter charges of partiality.—To James
Madison. iv, 501. (M., Aug. 1803.)

5872. —— ——. I do not think the loan
of our navy yard any more contrary to neutrality than that of our ports. It is merely
admitting a ship to a proper station in our
waters.—To James Madison. Ford ed., viii,
475. (M., Sep. 1806.)

5873. —— ——. Several French vessels
of war, disabled from keeping the sea, * * *
put into the harbors of the United States to
avoid the danger of shipwreck. The minister
of their nation states that their crews are without resources for subsistence, and other necessaries, for the reimbursement of which he offers
bills on his government, the faith of which he
pledges for their punctual payment. The laws
of humanity make it a duty for nations, as
well as individuals, to succor those whom accident and distress have thrown upon them. By
doing this in the present case, to the extent of
mere *subsistence and necessaries*, and so as to
aid no military equipment, we shall keep within
the duties of rigorous neutrality, which never
can be in opposition to those of humanity. We
furnished, on a former occasion, to a distressed
crew of the other belligerent party, similar accommodations, and we have ourselves received
from both those powers, friendly and free supplies to the necessities of our vessels of war in
their Mediterranean ports. In fact, the governments of civilized nations generally are in
the practice of exercising these offices of humanity towards each other. Our government
having as yet made no regular provision for the
exchange of these offices of courtesy and humanity between nations, the honor, the interest, and the duty of our country require that we
should adopt any other mode by which it may
legally be done on the present occasion. It
is expected that we shall want a large sum of

money in Europe, for the purposes of the present negotiation with Spain, and besides this we
want annually large sums there, for the discharge of our installments of debt. Under
these circumstances, supported by the unanimous opinion of the heads of Departments,
* * * and firmly trusting that the government of France will feel itself peculiarly interested in the punctual discharge of the bills
drawn by their Minister, * * * I approve
of the Secretary of the treasury's taking the
bills of the Minister of France, to an amount
not exceeding sixty thousand dollars.—To Albert Gallatin. v, 35. (W., Jan. 1807.)

5874. —— ——. Armed vessels remaining within our jurisdiction in defiance of the
authority of the laws, must be viewed either as
rebels, or public enemies. The latter character'
it is most expedient to ascribe to them; the
laws of intercourse with persons of that description are fixed and known. If we relinquish
them we shall have a new code to settle with
those individual offenders, with whom self-respect forbids any intercourse but merely for
purposes of humanity.—To Governor W. H.
Cabell. v, 170. (M., 1807.)

5875. NEUTRALITY, Rights.—The
doctrine that the rights of nations remaining quietly under the exercise of moral and
social duties, are to give way to the convenience
of those who prefer plundering and murdering
one another, is a monstrous doctrine; and ought
to yield to the more rational law, that "the
wrongs which two nations endeavor to inflict
on each other, must not infringe on the rights
or conveniences of those remaining at peace".
—To Robert R. Livingston. iv, 410. Ford
ed., viii, 90. (M., 1801.)

5876. —— ——. It would indeed be advantageous to us to have neutral rights established on a broad ground; but no dependence
can be placed in any European coalition for
that. They have so many other bye-interests
of greater weight, that some one or other will
always be bought off. To be entangled with
them would be a much greater evil than a
temporary acquiescence in the false principles
which have prevailed.—To William Short.
iv, 414. Ford ed., viii, 98. (W., 1801.)

5877. —— ——. With respect to the
rights of neutrality, we have certainly a great
interest in their settlement. But this depends
exclusively on the will of two characters, Bonaparte and Alexander. The dispositions of the
former to have them placed on liberal grounds
are known. The interest of the latter should
insure the same disposition. The only thing
to be done is to bring the two characters together to treat on the subject. All the minor
maritime powers of Europe will of course concur with them. We have not failed to use such
means as we possess to induce these two
sovereigns to avail the world of its present situation to declare and enforce the laws of nature
and convenience on the seas. But the organization of the treaty-making power by our Constitution is too particular for us to commit the
nation in so great an operation with all the
European powers. With such a federal phalanx in the Senate, compact and vigilant for
opportunities to do mischief, the addition of a
very few other votes, misled by accidental or
imperfect views of the subject, would suffice to
commit us most dangerously. All we can do,
therefore, is to encourage others to declare and
guarantee neutral rights, by excluding all intercourse with any nation which infringes them,
and so leave a niche in their compact for us, if

our treaty-making power shall choose to occupy it.—To THOMAS PAINE. FORD ED., viii, 437. (W., March 1806.)

5878. —— ——. The license to four British vessels to sail to Lima proves that belligerents may, either by compact or force, conduct themselves towards one another as they please; but not that a neutral may, unless by some express permission of the belligerent.—To ALBERT GALLATIN. FORD ED., viii, 466. (M., Aug. 1806.)

5879. —— ——. It is all important that we should stand in terms of the strictest cordiality with France. In fact, we are to depend on her and Russia for the establishment of neutral rights by the treaty of peace, among which should be that of taking no persons by a belligerent out of a neutral ship, unless they be the *soldiers* of an enemy.—To JAMES BOWDOIN. v, 64. FORD ED., ix, 40. (W., April 1807.)

5880. —— ——. The instructions given to our ministers [to England] were framed in the sincerest spirit of amity and moderation. They accordingly proceeded, in conformity therewith, to propose arrangements which might embrace and settle all the points in difference between us, which might bring us to a mutual understanding on our neutral and national rights, and provide for a commercial intercourse on conditions of some equality. After long and fruitless endeavors to effect the purposes of their mission, and to obtain arrangements within the limits of their instructions, they concluded to sign such as could be obtained, and to send them for consideration, candidly declaring to the other negotiators, at the same time, that they were acting against their instructions, and that their government, therefore, could not be pledged for ratification. Some of the articles proposed might have been admitted on a principle of compromise, but others were too highly disadvantageous, and no sufficient provision was made against the principal source of the irritations and collisions which were constantly endangering the peace of the two nations. The question, therefore, whether a treaty should be accepted in that form could have admitted but of one decision, even had no declarations of the other party impaired our confidence in it. Still anxious not to close the door against friendly adjustment, new modifications were framed, and further concessions authorized than could before have been supposed necessary; and our ministers were instructed to resume their negotiations on these grounds. On this new reference to amicable discussion, we were reposing in confidence, when on the 22nd day of June last, by a formal order from the British admiral, the frigate Chesapeake, leaving her port for distant service, was attacked by one of those vessels which had been lying in our harbors under the indulgences of hospitality, was disabled from proceeding, had several of her crew killed, and four taken away.—SEVENTH ANNUAL MESSAGE. viii, 83. FORD ED., ix, 150. (Oct. 27, 1807.) See CHESAPEAKE.

5881. —— ——. The nations of the earth prostrated at the foot of power, the ocean submitted to the despotism of a single nation, the laws of nature and the usages which have hitherto regulated the intercourse of nations and interposed some restraint between power and right, now totally disregarded. Such is the state of things when the United States are left single-handed to maintain the rights of neutrals, and the principles of public right against a warring world.—R. TO A. NIAGARA REPUBLICANS. viii, 155. (1809.)

5882. —— ——. When two nations go to war, it does not abridge the rights of neutral nations but in the two articles of blockade and contraband of war.—To BENJAMIN STODDERT. v, 425. FORD ED., ix, 245. (W., 1809.) See ALEXANDER OF RUSSIA and EMBARGO.

5883. NEUTRALITY, Sale of arms.— The manufacture of arms is the occupation and livelihood of some of our citizens; and * * * it ought not to be expected that a war among other nations should produce such an internal derangement of the occupations of a nation at peace, as the suppression of a manufacture which is the support of some of its citizens; but * * * if they should export these arms to nations at war, they would be abandoned to the seizure and confiscation which the law of nations authorized to be made of them on the high seas.—To E. C. GENET. iv, 87. FORD ED., vi, 460. (Pa., Nov. 1793.) See BELLIGERENTS.

— NEUTRALITY, Sale of ships.—See BELLIGERENTS.

5884. NEUTRALITY, Treasury Department and.—Hamilton produced [at a cabinet meeting] the draft of a letter by himself to the collectors of the customs, giving them in charge to watch over all proceedings in their districts, contrary to the laws of neutrality, or tending to infract our peace with the belligerent powers, and particularly to observe if vessels pierced for guns should be built, and to inform *him* of it. This was objected to, 1. As setting up a system of espionage, destructive of the peace of society. 2. Transferring to the Treasury Department the conservation of the laws of neutrality and peace with foreign nations. 3. It was rather proposed to intimate to the judges that the laws respecting neutrality being now come into activity, they should charge the grand juries with the observance of them; these being constitutional and public informers, and the persons accused knowing of what they should do, and having an opportunity of justifying themselves. E. R. [Edmund Randolph] found a hair to split, which, as always happens, became the decision. Hamilton is to write to the collectors of the customs, who are to convey their information to the attorneys of the district to whom E. R. is to write to receive their information and proceed by indictment. The clause respecting the building vessels pierced for guns was omitted, for though three against one thought it would be a breach of neutrality, yet they thought we might defer giving a public opinion on it as yet.—To JAMES MADISON. iii, 556. FORD ED., vi, 250. (May 1793.)

5885. —— ——. I have been still reflecting on the draft of the letter from the Secretary of the Treasury to the custom house officers, instructing them to be on the watch as to all infractions or tendencies to infraction of the laws of neutrality by our citizens, and to communicate the same to him. When this paper was first communicated to me, though the whole of it struck me disagreeably. I did not in the first moment see clearly the improprieties but of the last clause. The more I have reflected, the more objectionable the whole appears. By this proposal the collectors of the customs are to be made an established corps of spies or informers against their fellow citizens, whose actions they are to watch in secret, inform against in secret to the Secretary of the Treasury, who is to communicate it to the President. If the action and evidence appear to justify a prosecution, a prosecution is to be set on foot on the *secret information* of a collector. If it will not justify it, then the only consequence is that the mind of government has been poisoned against a citizen, neither known nor suspecting it, and perhaps too distant to bring forward his justification. This will at least furnish the collector with a convenient weapon to keep down a rival, draw a cloud over an inconvenient censor, or satisfy mere malice and private enmity. The object of this new institution is to be to prevent infractions of the laws of neutrality, and preserve our peace with foreign nations; but I cannot possibly conceive how the superintendence of the laws of neutrality, or the preservation of our peace with foreign nations can be ascribed to the department of the Treasury, which I suppose to comprehend merely matters of revenue. It would be to add a new and a large field to a department already amply provided with business, patronage, and influence. It was urged as a reason that the collectors of the customs are in convenient positions for this espionage. They are in convenient positions, too, for building ships of war; but will that business be transplanted from its department, merely because it can be conveniently done in another? It seemed the desire that if this means was disapproved, some other equivalent might be adopted. Though we consider the acts of a foreigner making a captive within our limits, as an act of public hostility, and therefore to be turned over to the military rather than the civil power; yet the acts of our citizens infringing the laws of neutrality, or contemplating that, are offences against the ordinary laws and cognizable by them. Grand juries are the constitutional inquisitors and informers of the country; they are scattered everywhere, see everything, see it while they suppose themselves mere private persons, and not with the prejudiced eye of a permanent and systematic spy. Their information is on *oath*, is public, it is in the vicinage of the party charged, and can be at once refuted. These officers taken only occasionally from among the people, are familiar to them, the office respected, and the experience of centuries has shown that it is safely entrusted with our character, property and liberty. A grand juror cannot carry on systematic persecution against a neighbor whom he hates, because he is not permanent in the office. The judges generally, by a charge. instruct the grand jurors in the infractions of law which are to be noticed by them; and our judges are in the habit of printing their charges in the newspapers. The judges, having notice of the proclamation, will perceive that the occurrence of a foreign war has brought into activity the laws of neutrality, as a part of the law of the land. This new branch of the law they will know needs explanation to the grand juries more than any other. They will study and define the subjects to them and to the public. The public mind will by this be warned against the acts which may endanger our peace, foreign nations will see a much more respectable evidence of our *bonâ fide* intentions to preserve neutrality, and society will be relieved from the inquietude which must forever be excited by the knowledge of the existence of such a poison in it as secret accusation. It will be easy to suggest this matter to the attention of the judges, and that alone puts the whole machine into motion. The one is a familiar, impartial and precious instrument; the other, not popular in its present functions, will be odious in the new ones, and

the odium will reach the Executive, who will be considered as having planted a germ of private inquisition absolutely unknown to our laws.—To EDMUND RANDOLPH. iii, 553. FORD ED., vi, 245. (May 1793.)

5886. NEUTRALITY, Usurpation of jurisdiction.—The United States being at peace with both parties, will certainly not see with indifference its territory or jurisdiction violated by [France or England] either. and will proceed immediately to enquire into the facts and to do what these shall show ought to be done with exact impartiality.—To GEORGE HAMMOND. FORD ED., vi, 236. (Pa., May 1793.)

5887. ———— ————. It is the *right* of every nation to prohibit acts of sovereignty from being exercised by any other within its limits; and the *duty* of a neutral nation to prohibit such as would injure one of the warring powers.— To E. C. GENET. iii, 572. FORD ED., vi, 283. (Pa., June 1793.) See CONSULS, GENET, and PRIVATEERS.

5888. NEUTRALITY, Violations of.—Since our last meeting the aspect of our foreign relations has considerably changed. Our coasts have been infested and our harbors watched by private armed vessels, some of them without commissions, some with illegal commissions, others with those of legal form but committing piratical acts beyond the authority of their commissions. They have captured in the very entrance of our harbors, as well as on the high seas, not only the vessels of our friends coming to trade with us, but our own also. They have carried them off under pretence of legal adjudication, but not daring to approach a court of justice, they have plundered and sunk them by the way, or in obscure places where no evidence could arise against them; maltreated the crews, and abandoned them in boats in the open sea, or on desert shores without food or covering. These enormities appearing to be unreached by any control of their sovereigns, I found it necessary to equip a force to cruise within our own seas, to arrest all vessels of these descriptions found hovering on our coast within the limits of the Gulf Stream, and to bring the offenders in for trial as pirates. The same system of hovering on our coasts, and harbors under color of seeking enemies, has been also carried on by public armed ships, to the great annoyance and oppression of our commerce. New principles, too, have been interpolated into the law of nations, founded neither in justice, nor the usage, or acknowledgment of nations. According to these, a belligerent takes to itself a commerce with its own enemy, which it denies to a neutral on the ground of its aiding that enemy in the war. But reason revolts at such an inconsistency; and the neutral having equal right with the belligerent to decide the question, the interest of our constituents and the duty of maintaining the authority of reason, the only umpire between just nations, impose on us the obligation of providing an effectual and determined opposition to a doctrine so injurious to the rights of peaceable nations. Indeed, the confidence we ought to have in the justice of others, still countenances the hope that a sounder view of those rights will of itself induce from every belligerent a more correct observance of them.—FIFTH ANNUAL MESSAGE. viii, 47. FORD ED., viii, 389. (Dec. 1805.)

5889. NEUTRALITY PROCLAMATION, History of.—The public papers giving us reason to believe that the war is becoming nearly general in Europe, and that it has already involved nations with which we are in daily habits of commerce and friendship, the President has thought it proper to issue the Proclamation of which I enclose you a copy, in order to mark out to our citizens the line of conduct they are to pursue. That this intimation, however, might not work to their prejudice, by being produced against them as conclusive evidence of their knowledge of the existence of war and of the nations engaged in it, in any case where they might be drawn into courts of justice for acts done without that knowledge, it has been thought necessary to write to the representatives of the belligerent powers here, * * * reserving to our citizens those immunities to which they are entitled, till authentic information shall be given to our government by the parties at war, and be thus communicated, with due certainty, to our citizens. You will be pleased to present to the government where you reside this proceeding of the President, as a proof of the earnest desire of the United States to preserve peace and friendship with all the belligerent powers, and to express his expectation that they will in return extend a scrupulous and effectual protection to all our citizens, wheresoever they may need it, in pursuing their lawful and peaceable concerns with their subjects, or within their jurisdiction. You will, at the same time, assure them that the most exact reciprocation of this benefit shall be practiced by us towards their subjects, in the like cases.—To Messrs. Morris, Pinckney and Short. iii, 543. (Pa., April 26, 1793.)

5890. —— ——. I dare say you will have judged from the pusillanimity of the proclamation, from whose pen it came. A fear lest any affection [to France] should be discovered is distinguishable enough. This base fear will produce the very evil they wish to avoid. For our constituents, seeing that the government does not express their mind, perhaps rather leans the other way, are coming forward to express it themselves.—To James Madison. iii, 562. Ford ed., vi, 259. (Pa., May 1793.)

5891. —— ——. The proclamation as first proposed was to have been a declaration of neutrality. It was opposed on these grounds. 1. That a declaration of neutrality was a declaration there should be no war, to which the Executive was not competent. 2. That it would be better to hold back the declaration of neutrality, as a thing worth something to the powers at war; that they would bid for it, and we might reasonably ask a price, the *broadest privileges* of neutral nations. The first objection was so far respected as to avoid inserting the term *neutrality*, and the drawing the instrument was left to E. R. [Edmund Randolph]. —To James Madison. iii, 591. Ford ed., vi, 315. (1793.)

5892. —— ——. That there should be a proclamation was passed unanimously with the approbation or the acquiescence of all parties. Indeed, it was not expedient to oppose it altogether, lest it should prejudice what was the next question, the boldest and greatest that ever was hazarded, and which would have called for extremities had it prevailed.—To James Madison. iii, 591. Ford ed., vi, 316. (June 1793.)

5893. —— ——. You have most perfectly seized the *original* idea of the proclamation. When first proposed as a declaration of neutrality, it was opposed, first, because the Executive had no power to declare neutrality. Secondly, as such a declaration would be premature, and would lose us the benefit for which it might be bartered. It was urged that there was a strong impression in the minds of many that they were free to join in the hostilities on the side of France. Others were unapprised of the danger they would be exposed to in carrying contraband goods. It was, therefore, agreed that a proclamation should issue, declaring that we were in a state of peace with all the parties, admonishing the people to do nothing contravening it, and putting them on their guard as to contraband. On this ground it was accepted or acquiesced in by all [the cabinet], and E. R. [Edmund Randolph] who drew it, brought to me the draft, to let me see there was no such word as *neutrality* in it. Circumstances forbid other criticism. The public, however, soon took it up as a declaration of neutrality, and it came to be considered at length as such.—To James Monroe. iv, 17. Ford ed., vi, 346. (Pa., 1793.)

5894. —— ——. "On the declaration of war between France and England, the United States being at peace with both, their situation was so new and unexperienced by themselves, that their citizens were not, in the first instant, sensible of the new duties resulting therefrom, and of the laws it would impose *even on their dispositions* towards the belligerent powers. Some of them imagined (and chiefly their transient sea-faring citizens) that they were free to indulge those dispositions, to take side with either party, and enrich themselves by depredations on the commerce of the other, and were meditating enterprises of this nature, as was said. In this state of the public mind, and before it should take an erroneous direction difficult to be set right, and dangerous to themselves and their country, the President thought it expedient, by way of Proclamation, * to remind our fellow-citizens that we were in a state of peace with all the belligerent powers; that in that state it was our duty neither to aid nor injure any; to exhort and warn them against acts which might contravene this duty, and particularly those of positive hostility, for the punishment of which the laws would be appealed to, and to put them on their guard also as to the risks they would run if they should attempt to carry articles of contraband to any. Very soon afterwards we learnt that Genet was undertaking the fitting and arming vessels in that port [Charleston], enlisting men, foreigners and citizens, and giving them commissions to commit hostilities against nations at peace with us; that these vessels were taking and bringing prizes into our ports; that the consuls of France were assuming to hold courts of admiralty on them, to try, condemn and authorize their sale as legal prizes, and all this before Mr. Genet had presented himself or his credentials to the President, before he was received by him, without his consent or consultation, and directly in contravention of the state of peace existing and declared to exist in the President's proclamation, and which it was incumbent on him to preserve till the constitutional au-

* In sending this explanation of the intention of the proclamation to Madison, Jefferson wrote : " Having occasion to state it (the intention, &c.) in a paper which I am preparing, I have done it in the following [above quoted] terms. Edmund Randolph called on me just as I had finished so far [within the quotation marks], and he said it presented fairly his view of the matter. He recalled to my mind that I had, at the time, opposed its being made a declaration of neutrality, on the ground that the Executive was not the competent authority for that, and, therefore, that it was agreed the instrument should be drawn with great care."—Editor.

thority should otherwise declare. These proceedings became immediately, as was naturally to be expected, the subject of complaint by the representative here of that power against whom they would chiefly operate." This was the true sense of the proclamation in the view of the draftsman and of the two signers; but H. [Hamilton] had other views. The instrument was badly drawn, and made the President go out of his line to declare things which, though true, it was not his province to declare. The instrument was communicated to me after it was drawn, but I was busy, and only ran an eye over it to see that it was not made a declaration of neutrality, and gave it back again, without, I believe, changing a tittle.—To JAMES MADISON. iv, 29. FORD ED., vi, 368. (Aug. 1793.)

5895. —— ——. You will see a piece signed "Pacificus" [Alexander Hamilton] in defence of the proclamation. You will readily know the pen. I know it the more readily because it is an amplification only of the topics urged in discussing the question [in cabinet] when first proposed. The right of the *Executive* to declare that we are *not bound to execute the guarantee* [to France] was then advanced by him and denied by me. No other opinion was expressed on it. In this paper he repeats it, and even considers the proclamation as such a declaration; but if anybody intended it as such (except himself) they did not then say so. The passage beginning with the words, "the answer to this is," &c., is precisely the answer he gave at the time to my objection, that the Executive had no authority to issue a declaration of neutrality, nor to do more than declare the actual state of things to be that of peace. "For until the new government is acknowledged the treaties, &c., are, of course, suspended." This, also, is the sum of his arguments the same day on the great question which followed that of the proclamation, to wit, whether the Executive might not, and ought not to declare the [French] treaties suspended. * * * Upon the whole, my objections to the competence of the Executive to declare neutrality (that being understood to respect the future) were supposed to be got over by avoiding the use of that term. The declaration of the disposition of the United States can hardly be called illegal, though it was certainly officious and improper. The truth of the fact lent it some cover. My objections to the impolicy of a premature declaration were answered by such arguments as timidity would reasonably suggest. I now think it extremely possible that Hammond might have been instructed to have asked it, and to offer the *broadest neutral privileges*, as the price, which was exactly the price I wanted that we should contend for. But is it not a miserable thing that the three heresies I have quoted from this paper, should pass unnoticed and unanswered, as these certainly will, for none but mere bunglers and brawlers have for some time past taken the trouble to answer anything?—To JAMES MADISON. FORD ED., vi, 327. (June 1793.)

5896. —— ——. The real milk and water views of the proclamation appeared to me to have been truly given in a piece published in the papers soon after [it was issued], and which I knew to be E. R.'s [Edmund Randolph's] from its exact coincidence with what he has expressed.—To JAMES MADISON. FORD ED., vi, 328. (1793.)

— **NEW ENGLAND, Secession of.**—See SECESSION.

5897. NEW HAMPSHIRE, Opinion in.
—The public sentiment in New Hampshire is no longer progressive in any direction; * * * it is dead water.—To JAMES MADISON. FORD ED., vii, 343. (Pa., Feb. 1799.)

5898. NEW HAMPSHIRE, Republicanism in.—Although we have not yet got a majority into the fold of republicanism in your State, yet one long pull more will effect it, * * * unless it be true, as is sometimes said, that New Hampshire is but a satellite of Massachusetts. In this last State, the public sentiment seems to be under some influence additional to that of the clergy and lawyers. I suspect there must be a leaven of State pride at seeing itself deserted by the public opinion, and that their late popular song of "Rule New England" betrays one principle of their present variance from the Union. But I am in hopes they will in time discover that the shortest road to rule is to join the majority.—To JOHN LANGDON. FORD ED., viii, 161. (W., June 1802.)

— **NEW HAVEN, Remonstrance.**—See BISHOP.

5899. NEW JERSEY, Republicanism in.—Jersey is coming majestically round to the true principles.—To T. LOMAX. iv, 300. FORD ED., vii, 374. (M., March 1799.)

5900. NEW ORLEANS, Battle of.—I am glad we closed our war with the eclat of the action at New Orleans.—To MARQUIS LAFAYETTE. vi, 427. FORD ED., ix, 510. (M., 1815.)

5901. —— ——. Peace was indeed desirable; yet it would not have been as welcome without the successes of New Orleans. These last have established truths too important not to be valued; that the people of Louisiana are sincerely attached to the Union; that their city can be defended; that the Western States make its defence their peculiar concern; that the militia are brave; that their deadly aim countervails the manœuvring skill of the enemy; that we have officers of natural genius now starting forward from the mass; and that putting together all our conflicts, we can beat the British by sea and by land, with equal numbers.—To GENERAL DEARBORN. vi, 450. (M., 1815.)

5902. —— ——. The affair of New Orleans was fraught with useful lessons to ourselves, our enemies, and our friends, and will powerfully influence our future relations with the nations of Europe. It will show them we mean to take no part in their wars, and count no odds when engaged in our own.—To PRESIDENT MADISON. vi, 453. FORD ED., ix, 512. (M., 1815.)

5903. —— ——. It may be thought that useless blood was spilt at New Orleans, after the treaty of peace had been actually signed. I think it had many valuable uses. It proved the fidelity of the Orleanese to the United States. It proved that New Orleans can be defended both by land and water; that the Western country will fly to its relief (of which ourselves had doubted before); that our militia are heroes when they have heroes to lead them on; and that, when unembarrassed by field evolutions, which they do not understand, their skill in the fire-arm, and deadly aim, give them advantage over regulars.—To W. H. CRAWFORD. vi, 420. FORD ED., ix, 504. (M., 1815.) See FEDERALISTS.

— **NEW ORLEANS, Batture Case.**—See BATTURE.

5904. NEW ORLEANS, Right of deposit.—We state in general the necessity, not only of our having a port near the mouth of the river (without which we could make no use of the ·navigation at all) but of its being so well separated from the territories of Spain and her jurisdiction, as not to engender daily disputes and broils between us. It is certain, that if Spain were to retain any jurisdiction over our *entrepôt*, her officers would abuse that jurisdiction, and our people would abuse their privileges in it. Both parties must foresee this, and that it will end in war. Hence the necessity of a well-defined separation. Nature has decided what shall be the geography of that in the end, whatever it might be in the beginning, by cutting off from the adjacent countries of Florida and Louisiana, and enclosing between two of its channels, a long and narrow strip of land, called the Island of New Orleans. The idea of ceding this could not be hazarded to Spain, in the first step; it would be too disagreeable at first view; because this island, with its town, constitutes at present, their principal settlement in that part of their dominions, containing about ten thousand white inhabitants of every age and sex. Reason and events, however, may by little and little, familiarize them to it. That we have a right to some spot as an *entrepôt* for our commerce, may be at once affirmed. The expediency, too, may be expressed of so locating it as to cut off the source of future quarrels and wars. A disinterested eye, looking on a map, will remark how conveniently this tongue of land is formed for the purpose.—To WILLIAM SHORT. iii, 178. FORD ED., v, 219. (N.Y., 1790.)

5905. —— ——. Observe always, that to accept the navigation of the river without an *entrepôt* would be perfectly useless, and that an *entrepôt*, if trammelled, would be a certain instrument for bringing on war instead of preventing it.—To WILLIAM SHORT. iii, 228. FORD ED., v, 305. (Pa., 1791.)

5906. —— ——. To conclude the subject of navigation, each of the following conditions is to be considered by the· Commissioners [to Spain] as a *sine quâ non*. 1. That our right be acknowledged of navigating the Mississippi in its whole breadth and length, from its source to the sea, as established by the treaty of 1763. 2. That neither the vessels, cargoes, or the persons on board, be stopped, visited, or subjected to the payment of any duty whatsoever; or, if a visit must be permitted, that it be under such restrictions as to produce the least possible inconvenience. But it should be altogether avoided, if possible, as the parent of perpetual broils. 3. That such conveniences be allowed us ashore, as may render our right of navigation practicable and under such regulations as may *bonâ fide* respect the preservation of peace and order alone, and may not have in object to embarrass our navigation, or raise a revenue on it. *—MISSISSIPPI RIVER INSTRUCTIONS. vii, 585. FORD ED., v, 475. (1792.)

* " The right of navigation (of the Mississippi) was conceded by the treaty of 1795, and with it a right to the free use of the port of New Orleans upon reasonably satisfactory terms for a period of three years, and thereafterward until some equally convenient harbor should be allotted. The credit of this ultimate achievement was Mr. Jefferson's, none the less because the treaty was not signed until he had retired from office. It was really his statesmanship which had secured it, not only in spite of the natural repugnance of Spain, but also in spite of the obstacles in-

5907. NEW ORLEANS, Suspension of right.—The suspension of the right of deposit at New Orleans, ceded to us by our treaty with Spain, threw our whole country into such a ferment as imminently threatened its peace. This, however, was believed to be the act of the Intendant, unauthorized by his government. But it showed the necessity of making effectual arrangements to secure the peace of the two countries against the indiscreet acts of subordinate agents.—To DUPONT DE NEMOURS. iv, 456. FORD ED., viii, 204. (W., Feb. 1803.)

5908. —— ——. The government of Spain has instantly redressed the infraction of treaty by her Intendant at New Orleans. * * * By a reasonable and peaceable process we have obtained in four months, what would have cost us seven years of war, 100,000 human lives, 100 millions of additional debt, besides ten hundred millions lost by the want of market for our produce, or depredations on it in seeking markets, and the general demoralizing of our citizens which war occasions.—To JOHN BACON. FORD ED., viii, 229. (W., April 1803.) See LOUISIANA and MISSISSIPPI RIVER NAVIGATION.

5909. NEW YORK, Politics of.—I have been much pleased to see a dawn of change in the spirit of your State [New York]. The late elections have indicated something, which, at a distance, we do not understand. However, what with the English influence in the lower, and the Patroon influence in the upper part of your State, I presume little is to be hoped.—To AARON BURR. iv, 186. FORD ED., vii, 147. (Pa., June 1797.)

5910. —— ——. New York is coming majestically round to the true principles.—To T. LOMAX. iv, 300. FORD ED., vii, 374. (M., March 1799.)

5911. NEW YORK CITY, Depravity in.—New York, like London. seems to be a cloacina of all the depravities of human nature. —To WILLIAM SHORT. vii, 310. (M., 1823.)

5912. NEW YORK CITY, Washington's defence.—The maxim laid down by Congress to their generals was that not a foot of territory was to be ceded to their enemies where there was a possibility of defending it. In consequence of these views, and against his own judgment, General Washington was obliged to fortify and attempt to defend the city of New York. But that could not be defended without occupying the heights on Long Island which commanded the city of New York. He was, therefore, obliged to establish a strong detachment in Long Island to defend those heights. The moment that detachment was routed, which he had much expected, his first object was to withdraw them, and his second to evacuate New York. He did this, therefore. immediately, and without waiting any movement of the enemy. He brought off his whole baggage. stores, and other implements, without leaving a single article except the very heaviest of his cannon, and things of little value. I well remember his letter to Congress, wherein he expressed his wonder that the enemy had given him this leisure, as, from the heights they had got possession of, they might have compelled him to a very precipitate retreat. This was one of the instances where our commanding officers directly thrown in his way in the earlier stages by many persons in the United States, who privately gave the Spanish minister to understand that the country cared little about the Mississippi, and would not support the Secretary in his demands."— MORSE'S *Life of Jefferson.*

were obliged to conform to popular views, though they foresaw certain loss from it. Had he proposed at first to abandon New York, he might have been abandoned himself. An obedience to popular will cost us an army in Charleston in the year 1779.—Notes on M. Soules's Work. ix, 298. Ford ed., iv, 305. (P., 1786.)

5913. NEWS, Home.—But why has nobody else written to me? Is it that one is forgotten as soon as their back is turned? I have a better opinion of men. It must be either that they think that the details known to themselves are known to everybody, and so come to us through a thousand channels, or that we should set no value on them. Nothing can be more erroneous than both those opinions. We value those details, little and great, public and private, in proportion to our distance from our own country; and so far are they from getting to us through a thousand channels, that we hear no more of them or of our country here [Paris] than if we were among the dead.—To James Monroe. Ford ed., iv, 45. (P., 1785.)

5914. ————. It is unfortunate that most people think the occurrences passing daily under their eyes, are either known to all the world, or not worth being known. * * * I hope you will be so good as to continue your friendly information. The proceedings of our public bodies, the progress of the public mind on interesting questions, the casualities which happen among our private friends, and whatever is interesting to yourself and family, will always be anxiously received by me.—To John Page. i, 549. Ford ed., iv, 212. (P., 1786.)

5915. ————. I give you thanks for the details of small news contained in your letter. You know how precious that kind of information is to a person absent from his country, and how difficult it is to be procured. —To David Humphreys. iii, 13. Ford ed., v, 91. (P., 1789.)

5916. ————. If there is any news stirring in town or country, such as deaths, courtships, or marriages, in the circle of my acquaintance, let me know it.—To John Page. i, 183. Ford ed., i, 344. (F., 1762.)

5917. NEWS, Minor.—Details, political and literary, and even of the small history of our country, are the most pleasing communications possible.—To John Page. i, 402. (P., 1785.)

5918. ————. I pray you to write to me often. Do not turn politician too; but write me all the small news—the news about persons and about States; tell me who dies, that I may meet these disagreeable events in detail, and not all at once when I return (from France); who marry, who hang themselves because they cannot marry, &c.—To Mrs. Trist. i, 395. (P., 1785.)

5919. ————. It is more difficult here [Paris] to get small than great news, because most of our correspondents in writing letters to cross the Atlantic, think they must always tread in buskins, so that half one's friends might be dead without its being ever spoken of here.—To Dr. James Currie. Ford ed., iv, 131. (P., 1786.)

5920. ————. Nothing is so grateful to me, at this distance [Paris], as details, both great and small, of what is passing in my own country. * * * When one has been long absent from his neighborhood, the small news

of that is the most pleasing, and occupies his first attention.—To Archibald Stuart. i, 517. Ford ed., iv, 187. (P., 1786.)

5921. NEWS, Useful.—The details from my own country of the proceedings of the legislative, executive and judiciary bodies, and even those which respect individuals only, are the most pleasing treat we can receive at this distance [Paris], and the most useful, also.—To Joseph Jones. i, 354. (P., 1785.)

5922. NEWSPAPERS, Abuses by.— The abuses of the freedom of the press here have been carried to a length never before known or borne by any civilized nation.—To M. Pictet. iv, 463. (W., 1803.)

5923. NEWSPAPERS, Advertisements. —We have been trying to get another weekly or half weekly paper set up [in Philadelphia], excluding advertisements, so that it might go through the States, and furnish a whig vehicle of intelligence. We hoped at one time to have persuaded Freneau to set up here, but failed. In the meantime, Bache's paper [The Advertiser] the principles of which were always republican, improves in its matter. If we can persuade him to throw all his advertisements on one leaf, by tearing that off, the leaf containing intelligence may be sent, without overcharging the post, and be generally taken instead of Fenno's.—To T. M. Randolph. Ford ed., v, 336. (Pa., 1791.)

5924. NEWSPAPERS, Agitation by.— In the first moments of quietude which have succeeded the [Presidential] election, the printers seem to have aroused their lying faculties beyond their ordinary state, to re-agitate the public mind. What appointments to office have they detailed which had never been thought of, merely to found a text for their calumniating commentaries.—To Elbridge Gerry. iv, 392. Ford ed., viii, 43. (W., March 1801.)

5925. NEWSPAPERS, Attacks by.—I have been for some time used as the property of the newspapers, a fair mark for every man's dirt. Some, too, have indulged themselves in this exercise who would not have done it, had they known me otherwise than through these impure and injurious channels. It is hard treatment, and for a singular kind of offence, that of having obtained by the labors of a life the indulgent opinions of a part of one's fellow citizens. However, these moral evils must be submitted to, like the physical scourges of tempest, fire, &c.—To Peregrine Fitzhugh. iv, 216. Ford ed., vii, 208. (Pa., 1798.)

5926. ————. Were I to undertake to answer the calumnies of the newspapers, it would be more than all my own time and that of twenty aids could effect. For while I should be answering one, twenty new ones would be invented. * * * But this is an injury to which duty requires every one to submit whom the public think proper to call into its councils.—To Samuel Smith. iv, 255. Ford ed., vii, 279. (M., 1798.)

5927. —— ——. [I said to Colonel Burr] that as to the attack excited against him in the newspapers, I had noticed it but as the passing wind; that I had seen complaints that Cheetham, employed in publishing the laws, should be permitted to eat the public bread and abuse its second officer; * * * that these federal printers did not in the least intermit their abuse of me, though receiving emoluments from the government and that I have never thought it proper to interfere for myself, and consequently not in the case of the Vice-President.—The Anas. ix, 206. Ford ed., i, 302. (Jan. 1804.)

5928. —— ——. That tory printers should think it advantageous to identify me with that paper [The National Intelligencer], the Aurora, &c., in order to obtain ground for abusing me, is perhaps fair warfare. But that anyone who knows me should listen one moment to such an insinuation, is what I did not expect. I neither have, nor ever had, any more connection with those papers than our antipodes have; nor know what is to be in them until I see it in them, except proclamations and other documents sent for publication.—To Thomas Paine. iv, 582. Ford ed., viii, 361. (W., June 1805.)

5929. —— ——. I met the scurrilities of the newswriters without concern, while in pursuit of the great interests with which I was charged. But in my present retirement, no duty forbids my wish for quiet.—To J. B. Colvin. v, 544. Ford ed., ix, 282. (M., 1810.)

5930. NEWSPAPERS, Banks and.— Notwithstanding the magnitude of this calamity [bank failures], every newspaper almost is silent on it, Frenau's excepted, in which you will see it mentioned.—To Thomas Mann Randolph. Ford ed., v, 510. (April 1792.)

5931. NEWSPAPERS, Caricatures.— Our newspapers for the most part, present only the caricatures of disaffected minds.— To M. Pictet. iv, 463. (W., 1803.)

5932. NEWSPAPERS, Classics vs.—I read one or two newspapers a week, but with reluctance give even that time from Tacitus and Horace, and so much other more agreeable reading.—To David Howell. v, 555. (M., 1810.)

5933. —— ——. I have given up newspapers in exchange for Tacitus and Thucydides, for Newton and Euclid, and I find myself much the happier.—To John Adams. vi, 37. Ford ed., ix, 334. (M., 1812.)

5934. —— ——. I read but a single paper, and that hastily. I find Horace and Tacitus so much better writers than the champions of the gazettes, that I lay those down to take up these with great reluctance. —To James Monroe. vii, 287. Ford ed., x, 256. (M., 1823.)

5935. NEWSPAPERS, Defamation.— Defamation is becoming a necessary of life; insomuch, that a dish of tea in morning or

evening cannot be digested without this stimulant. Even those who do not believe these abominations, still read them with complacence to their auditors, and instead of the abhorrence and indignation which should fill a virtuous mind, betray a secret pleasure in the possibility that some may believe them, though they do not themselves.—To John Norvell. v. 93. Ford ed., ix, 74. (W., 1807.) See Calumny.

—— NEWSPAPERS, Editors of.—See Editors.

5936. NEWSPAPERS, English.—The English papers are so incessantly repeating their lies about the tumults, the anarchy, the bankruptcies, and distresses of America, that these ideas prevail very generally in Europe. —To James Monroe. i, 407. Ford ed., iv, 87. (P., 1785.)

5937. —— ——. The English papers— those infamous fountains of falsehood.—To F. Hopkinson. ii, 204. (P., 1787.)

5938. NEWSPAPERS, Falsehoods.— The press is impotent when it abandons itself to falsehood.—To Thomas Seymour. v, 44. Ford ed., ix, 30. (W., 1807.)

5939. —— ——. Nothing can now be believed which is seen in a newspaper.—To John Norvell. v, 92. Ford ed., ix, 73. (W., 1807.)

5940. —— ——. Truth itself becomes suspicious by being put into that polluted vehicle.—To John Norvell. v, 92. Ford ed., ix, 73. (W., 1807.)

5941. —— ——. The real extent of the misinformation [in the newspapers] is known only to those who are in situations to confront facts within their knowledge with the lies of the day.—To John Norvell. v, 92. Ford ed., ix, 73. (W., 1807.)

5942. —— ——. The man who never looks into a newspaper is better informed than he who reads them; inasmuch as he who knows nothing is nearer to truth than he whose mind is filled with falsehoods and errors. He who reads nothing will still learn the great facts, and the details are all false. —To John Norvell. v, 92. Ford ed., ix, 73. (W., 1807.)

5943. —— ——. These texts of truth relieve me from the floating falsehoods of the public papers.—To President Monroe. vii. 160. Ford ed., x, 158. (M., 1820.) See Lies.

5944. NEWSPAPERS, Freedom of.— Considering the great importance to the public liberty of the freedom of the press, and the difficulty of submitting it to very precise rules, the laws have thought it less mischievous to give greater scope to its freedom than to the restraint of it. The President has, therefore, no authority to prevent publications of the nature of those you complain of.* —To the Spanish Commissioners. iv, 21 Ford ed., vi, 350. (Pa., 1793.)

* Attacks on the King of Spain—Editor.

5945. —— ——. No experiment can be more interesting than that we are now trying, and which we trust will end in establishing the fact, that man may be governed by reason and truth. Our first object should therefore be, to leave open to him all the avenues to truth. The most effectual hitherto found, is the freedom of the press. It is, therefore, the first shut up by those who fear the investigation of their actions.—To JUDGE TYLER. iv, 548. (W., 1804.)

5946. —— ——. The liberty of speaking and writing guards our other liberties.— REPLY TO ADDRESS. viii, 129. (1808.)

5947. —— ——. Where the press is free, and every man able to read, all is safe.—To CHARLES YANCEY. vi, 517. FORD ED., x, 4. (M., 1816.)

5948. —— ——. The only security of all is in a free press. The force of public opinion cannot be resisted, when permitted freely to be expressed. The agitation it produces must be submitted to. It is necessary to keep the waters pure.—To MARQUIS DE LAFAYETTE. vii, 325. FORD ED., x, 280. (M., 1823.) See PRESS, FREEDOM OF.

5949. NEWSPAPERS, Friends of Liberty.—Within the pale of truth, the press is a noble institution, equally the friend of science and of civil liberty.—To THOMAS SEYMOUR. v, 44. FORD ED., ix, 30. (W., 1807.)

5950. NEWSPAPERS, Government and.—The basis of our governments being the opinion of the people, the very first object should be to keep that right; and were it left to me to decide whether we should have a government without newspapers or newspapers without a government, I should not hesitate a moment to prefer the latter.—To EDWARD CARRINGTON. ii, 100. FORD ED., iv, 359. (P., 1787.)

5951. NEWSPAPERS, And history.—I really look with commiseration over the great body of my fellow citizens, who, reading newspapers, live and die in the belief, that they have known something of what has been passing in the world in their time; whereas the accounts they have read in newspapers are just as true a history of any other period of the world as of the present, except that the real names of the day are affixed to their fables.—To JOHN NORVELL. v, 92. FORD ED., ix, 73. (W., 1807.)

5952. NEWSPAPERS, Indifference to. —A truth now and then projecting into the ocean of newspaper lies, serves like headlands to correct our course. Indeed, my scepticism as to everything I see in a newspaper, makes me indifferent whether I ever see one.—To JAMES MONROE. vi, 407. FORD ED., ix, 496. (M., 1815.)

5953. —— ——. I have almost ceased to read newspapers. Mine remain in our post office a week or ten days, sometimes, unasked for. I find more amusement in studies to which I was always attached, and from which I was dragged by the events of the times in which I have happened to live.—To THOMAS LEIPER. vi, 466. FORD ED., ix, 521. (M., 1815.)

5954. NEWSPAPERS, Licentiousness of.—During this course of administration [first term] and in order to disturb it, the artillery of the press has been levelled against us, charged with whatsoever its licentiousness could devise or dare. These abuses of an institution so important to freedom and science, are deeply to be regretted, inasmuch as they tend to lessen its usefulness, and to sap its safety; they might, indeed, have been corrected by the wholesome punishments reserved and provided by the laws of the several States against falsehood and defamation; but public duties more urgent press on the time of public servants, and the offenders have therefore been left to find their punishment in the public indignation. Nor was it uninteresting to the world, that an experiment should be fairly and fully made, whether freedom of discussion, unaided by power, is not sufficient for the propagation and protection of truth—whether a government, conducting itself in the true spirit of its Constitution, with zeal and purity, and doing no act which it would be unwilling the world should witness, can be written down by falsehood and defamation. The experiment has been tried; you have witnessed the scene; our fellow-citizens looked on, cool and collected; they saw the latent source from which these outrages proceeded; they gathered around their public functionaries, and when the Constitution called them to the decision by suffrage, they pronounced their verdict, honorable to those who had served them, and consolatory to the friend of man, who believes he may be intrusted with his own affairs. No inference is here intended, that the laws, provided by the States against false and defamatory publications, should not be enforced; he who has time, renders a service to public morals and public tranquillity, in reforming these abuses by the salutary coercions of the law; but the experiment is noted, to prove that, since truth and reason have maintained their ground against false opinions in league with false facts, the press, confined to truth, needs no other legal restraint; the public judgment will correct false reasonings and opinions, on a full hearing of all parties; and no other definite line can be drawn between the inestimable liberty of the press and its demoralizing licentiousness. If there be still improprieties which this rule would not restrain, its supplement must be sought in the censorship of public opinion.*—SECOND INAUGURAL ADDRESS. viii, 43. FORD ED., viii, 346. (1805.)

5955. NEWSPAPERS, And light.— Our citizens may be deceived for awhile, and have been deceived; but as long as the presses can be protected, we may trust to them for light.—To ARCHIBALD STUART. FORD ED., vii, 378. (M., 1789.)

* This was Jefferson's reply to the severe attacks. made on his first administration.—EDITOR.

5956. NEWSPAPERS, Mischief-makers.—The federal papers appear desirous of making mischief between us and England, by putting speeches into my mouth which I never uttered.—To Robert R. Livingston. v, 54. Ford ed., ix, 37. (W., 1807.)

5957. —— ——. That first of all human contrivances for generating war.—To Mr. Maury. vi, 469. (M., 1815.)

5958. NEWSPAPERS, Monarchical.—Fenno's [The United States Gazette] is a paper of pure toryism, disseminating the doctrines of monarchy, aristocracy, and the exclusion of the influence of the people. —To T. M. Randolph. Ford ed., v, 336. (Pa., 1791.)

5959. NEWSPAPERS, Official.—You have seen too much of the conduct of the press in countries where it is free, to consider the gazettes as evidence of the sentiments of any part of the government; you have seen them bestow on the government itself, in all its parts, its full share of inculpation.—To George Hammond. iii, 331. Ford ed., v, 436. (Pa., 1792.)

5960. NEWSPAPERS, Political bulldogs.—The malignity with which political enemies torture every sentence from me into meanings imagined by their own wickedness only, justify my expressing a solicitude, that this * * * communication may in nowise be permitted to find its way into the public papers. Not fearing these political bulldogs, I yet avoid putting myself in the way of being baited by them, and do not wish to volunteer away that portion of tranquillity, which a firm execution of my duties will permit me to enjoy.—To John Norvell. v, 93. Ford ed., ix, 75. (W., 1807.)

5961. NEWSPAPERS, Postoffice and.—The expense of French postage is so enormous, that I have been obliged to desire that my newspapers, from the different States, may be sent to the office for Foreign Affairs at New York; and I have requested of Mr. Jay to have them always packed in a box and sent as merchandise.—To R. Izard. i, 443. (P., 1785.)

5962. NEWSPAPERS, Power of.—Freneau's paper has saved our Constitution, which was galloping fast into monarchy, and has been checked by no means so powerfully as by that paper. It is well and universally known, that it has been that paper which has checked the career of the Monocrats.— The Anas. ix, 145. Ford ed., i, 231. (1793.)

5963. —— ——. These foreign and false citizens * * * possess our printing presses, a powerful engine in their government of us. —To Elbridge Gerry. iv, 173. Ford ed., vii, 122. (Pa., 1797.)

5964. —— ——. This paper [The Aurora] has unquestionably rendered incalculable services to republicanism through all its struggles with the federalists, and has been the rallying point for the orthodoxy of the whole Union. It was our comfort in the gloomiest days, and is still performing the office of a watchful sentinel.—To Dabney Carr. Ford ed., ix, 316. (M., 1811.)

5965. NEWSPAPERS, President and.—The Chief Magistrate cannot enter the arena of the newspapers.—To President Madison. v, 601. Ford ed., ix, 326. (M., July 1811.)

5966. NEWSPAPERS, Principles of.—A paper which shall be governed by the spirit of Mr. Madison's celebrated report [on the Virginia Resolutions] cannot be false to the rights of all classes.—To H. Lee. vii, 376. Ford ed., x, 318. (M., 1824.)

5967. NEWSPAPERS, Prosecution of.—The federalists having failed in destroying the freedom of the press by their gag-law, seem to have attacked it in an opposite direction; that is by pushing its licentiousness and its lying to such a degree of prostitution as to deprive it of all credit. And the fact is that so abandoned are the tory presses in this particular, that even the least informed of the people have learned that nothing in a newspaper is to be believed. This is a dangerous state of things, and the press ought to be restored to its credibility if possible. The restraints provided by the laws of the States are sufficient for this, if applied. And I have, therefore, long thought that a few prosecutions of the most prominent offenders would have a wholesome effect in restoring the integrity of the presses. Not a general prosecution, for that would look like persecution; but a selected one.—To Thomas McKean. Ford ed., viii, 218. (W., Feb. 1803.)

5968. NEWSPAPERS, Purifiers.—Newspapers serve to carry off noxious vapors and smoke.—To General Kosciusko. iv, 431. (W., April 1802.)

5969. NEWSPAPERS, Reading of.—Reading the newspapers but little and that little but as the romance of the day, a word of truth now and then comes like the drop of water on the tongue of Dives.—To President Madison. v, 442. Ford ed., ix, 251. (M., April 1809.)

5970. NEWSPAPERS, Reform by.—This formidable censor of the public functionaries, by arraigning them at the tribunal of public opinion, produces reform peaceably, which must otherwise be done by revolution. It is also the best instrument for enlightening the mind of man, and improving him as a rational, moral, and social being.—To M. Coray. vii, 324. (M., 1823.)

5971. NEWSPAPERS, Reformation of.—Perhaps an editor might begin a reformation [of his newspaper] in some such way as this: Divide his paper into four chapters, heading the first " Truths "; the second, " Probabilities "; third, " Possibilities "; fourth, " Lies ". The first chapter would be very short, as it would contain little more than authentic papers, and information from such sources, as the editor would be willing to risk his own reputation for their truth. The second would contain what, from a mature consideration of all circumstances, his judgment should conclude to be probably true. This, however, should rather contain too little than too much. The third and fourth should be professedly for those readers who would rather have lies for their money than the blank paper they would occupy.— To JOHN NORVELL. v, 92. FORD ED., ix, 74. (W., 1807.)

5972. NEWSPAPERS, Regulation of.— It is so difficult to draw a clear line of separation between the abuse and the wholesome use of the press, that as yet we have found it better to trust the public judgment, than the magistrate, with the discrimination between truth and falsehood.—To M. PICTET. iv, 463. (W., 1803.)

5973. NEWSPAPERS, Reliability of.— General facts may indeed be collected from the newspapers, such as that Europe is now at war, that Bonaparte has been a successful warrior, that he has subjugated a great portion of Europe to his will, &c., but no details can be relied on.—To JOHN NORVELL. v, 92. FORD ED., ix, 73. (W., 1807.)

5974. NEWSPAPERS, Responsibility for.— It is not he who prints, but he who pays for printing a slander, who is its real author. —To JOHN NORVELL. v, 93. FORD ED., ix, 74. (W., 1807.)

5975. NEWSPAPERS, Restraint on.— To your request of my opinion of the manner in which a newspaper should be conducted, so as to be most useful, I should answer: "By restraining it to true facts and sound principles only." Yet I fear such a paper would find few subscribers.—To JOHN NORVELL. v, 91. FORD ED., ix, 73. (W., 1807.)

5976. —— ——. The papers have lately advanced in boldness and flagitiousness beyond even themselves. Such daring and atrocious lies as fill the third and fourth columns of the third page of the United States Gazette of August 31st were never before. I believe, published with impunity in any country. However, I have from the beginning determined to submit myself as the subject on whom may be proved the impotency of a free press in a country like ours, against those who conduct themselves honestly and enter into no intrigue. I admit at the same time that restraining the press *to truth,* as the present laws do, is the only way of making it useful. But I have thought necessary first to prove it can never be dangerous.—To WILLIAM SHORT. v, 362. (M., Sep. 1808.)

5977. NEWSPAPERS, Rulers and.— It is the office of the rulers on both sides [United States and England] to rise above these vulgar vehicles of passion.—To MR. MAURY. vi, 469. (M., 1815.)

5978. NEWSPAPERS, Slanders in.— An editor [should] set his face against the demoralizing practice of feeding the public mind habitually on slander, and the depravity of taste which this nauseous aliment induces. —To JOHN NORVELL. v, 93. FORD ED., ix, 74. (W., 1807.) See LIBELS and SLANDER.

5979. NEWSPAPERS, Support of.— Bache's paper and also Carey's totter for want of subscriptions. We should really exert ourselves to procure them, for if these papers fall, republicanism will be entirely browbeaten.*—To JAMES MADISON. iv, 237. FORD ED., vii, 245. (Pa., 1798.) See CALLENDER and DUANE.

5980. —— ——. The engine is the press. Every man must lay his purse and his pen under contribution.—To JAMES MADISON. iv, 281. FORD ED., vii, 344. (Pa., 1799.)

5981. NEWSPAPERS, Suppression of. —It is a melancholy truth, that a suppression of the press could not more completely deprive the nation of its benefits, than is done by its abandoned prostitution to falsehood.— To JOHN NORVELL. v, 92. FORD ED., ix, 73. (W., 1807.)

5982. NEWSPAPERS, Torture by.— I confide them [opinions on government] to your honor, so to use them as to preserve me from the gridiron of the public papers.— To SAMUEL KERCHIVAL. vii, 17. FORD ED., x, 44. (M., 1816.)

5983. NEWSPAPERS, Uncertain.— Newspaper information is too uncertain ground for the government to act on.—To JAMES MADISON. FORD ED., viii, 81. (M., 1801.)

5984. NEWSPAPERS, Vulgar.— I deplore with you the putrid state into which our newspapers have passed, and the malignity, the vulgarity, and mendacious spirit of those who write for them. * * * These ordures are rapidly depraving the public taste, and lessening its relish for sound food. As vehicles of information, and a curb on our functionaries, they have rendered themselves useless, by forfeiting all title to belief. This has in a great degree been produced by the violence and malignity of party spirit.—To DR. WALTER JONES. vi, 284. FORD ED., ix, 446. (M., Jan. 1814.)

5985. NEWSPAPERS, Weaned from.— I have never seen a Philadelphia paper since I left it, till those you enclosed me; and I feel myself so thoroughly weaned from the interest I took in the proceedings there, while there, that I have never had a wish to see one, and believe that I never shall take another newspaper of any sort. I find my mind totally absorbed in my rural occupations.—To JAMES MADISON. iv, 103. FORD ED., vi, 503. (M., April 1794.)

5986. NEWSPAPERS, Writing for.— I have preserved through life a resolution, set

* Of the two hundred newspapers then (1800) in the United States all but about twenty were enlisted by preference or patronage on the Federal side.—ALEXANDER H. STEPHENS *History of the United States*, p. 386.

in a very early part of it, never to write in a public paper without subscribing my name.—To EDMUND RANDOLPH. iii, 470. FORD ED., vi, 112. (M., 1792.)

5987. —— ——. From a very early period of my life, I had laid it down as a rule of conduct, never to write a word for the public papers. From this, I have never departed in a single instance; and on a late occasion, when all the world seemed to be writing, besides a rigid adherence to my own rule, I can say with truth, that not a line for the press was ever communicated to me, by any other, except a single petition referred for my correction; which I did not correct, however, though the contrary, as I have heard, was said in a public place, by one person through error, through malice by another [General Henry Lee].—To PRESIDENT WASHINGTON. iv, 142. FORD ED., vii, 82. (M., June 1796.)

5988. —— ——. At a very early period of my life, I determined never to put a sentence into any newspaper. I have religiously adhered to the resolution through my life, and have great reason to be contented with it.—To SAMUEL SMITH. iv, 255. FORD ED., vii, 279. (M., 1798.)

5989. —— ——. I pray that my letter may not go out of your own hands, lest it should get into the newspapers, a bear-garden scene into which I have made it a point to enter on no provocation.—To URIAH M'GREGORY. iv, 334. (M., 1800.)

5990. —— ——. I never in my life, directly or indirectly, wrote one sentence for a newspaper.—THE ANAS. ix, 199. FORD ED., i, 285. (1800.)

5991. NICE, Climate.—I find the climate of Nice quite as delightful as it has been represented. Hieres is the only place in France, which may be compared with it. The climates are equal.—To WILLIAM SHORT. ii, 137. (Ne., 1787.)

5992. NICHOLAS (W. C.), Character.— I have ascertained that on Mr. Nicholas no impression unfavorable to you was made by * * * [the removal of Secretary Robert Smith], and that his friendship for you has never felt a moment's abatement. Indeed we might have been sure of this from his integrity, his good sense, and his sound judgment of men and things.—To PRESIDENT MADISON. FORD ED., ix, 378. (M., Feb. 1813.)

5993. NICHOLAS (W. C.), French mission.—A last effort at friendly settlement with Spain is proposed to be made at Paris, and under the auspices of France. For this purpose, General Armstrong and Mr. Bowdoin (both now at Paris) have been appointed joint commissioners; but such a cloud of dissatisfaction rests on General Armstrong in the minds of many persons, * * * that we have in contemplation to add a third commissioner, in order to give the necessary measure of public confidence to the commission. Of these two gentlemen, one being of Massachusetts and one of New York, it is thought the third should be a southern man; and the rather, as the interests to be negotiated are almost entirely southern and western. * * * My wish is

that you may be willing to undertake it.*—To WILSON C. NICHOLAS. v, 3. FORD ED., viii, 434. (W., March 1806.)

— NICHOLAS (W. C.), Leadership in Congress.—See CONGRESS.

— NIGHTINGALES, Jefferson's delight in.—See BIRDS.

5994. NON-IMPORTATION, Efficacy of.—The most eligible means of effecting * * * the reestablishment of the constitutional rights of our fellow-subjects, will be to put an immediate stop to all imports from Great Britain * * * and to all exports thereto, * * * and immediately to discontinue all commercial intercourse with every part of the British Empire which shall not, in like manner, break off their commerce with Great Britain.†—RESOLUTION OF ALBEMARLE COUNTY. FORD ED., i, 419. (July 26, 1774.)

5995. —— ——. These measures [nonintercourse] should be pursued until a repeal be obtained of the act for blocking up the harbor of Boston; of the acts prohibiting or restraining internal manufactures in America; of the acts imposing on any commodities duties to be paid in America; and of the act laying restrictions on the American trade; and, on such repeal, it will be reasonable to grant to our brethren of Great Britain such privileges in commerce as may amply compensate their fraternal assistance, past and future.—RESOLUTION OF ALBEMARLE COUNTY. FORD ED., i, 419. (July 26, 1774.)

5996. —— ——. The idea seems to gain credit that the naval powers, combined against France, will prohibit supplies even of provisions to that country. Should this be formally notified, I should suppose Congress would be called, because it is a justifiable cause of war, and as the Executive cannot decide the question of war on the affirmative side, neither ought it to do so on the negative side, by preventing the competent body from deliberating on the question. But I should hope that war would not be their choice. I think it will furnish us a happy opportunity of setting another example to the world, by showing that nations may be brought to justice by appeals to their interests as well as by appeals to arms. I should hope that Congress, instead of a denunciation of war, would instantly exclude from our ports all the manufactures, produce, vessels, and subjects of the nations committing this aggression, during the continuance of the aggression, and till full satisfaction is made for it. This would work well in many ways, safely in all, and introduce between nations another umpire than arms. It would relieve us, too, from the risks and the horrors of cutting throats.—To JAMES MADISON. iii, 519. FORD ED., vi, 192. (March 1793.)

5997. NON-IMPORTATION, Popular. —I have never known a measure more universally desired by the people than the passage of the non-importation bill.—To JAMES MADISON. iv, 107. FORD ED., vi, 511. (M., May 1794.)

5998. —— ——. I love Mr. Clarke's proposition of cutting off all communication with the nation [Great Britain] which has con-

* Mr. Nicholas was prevented from accepting by business considerations.—EDITOR.
† Albemarle was Jefferson's native county. The date of putting the regulations into effect was October 1, 1775.—EDITOR.

ducted itself so atrociously. This may bring on war. If it does we will meet it like men; but it may not bring on war, and then the experiment will have been a happy one.—To TENCH COXE. iv, 105. FORD ED., vi, 508. (M., May 1794.)

5999. NON-IMPORTATION, Principle of.—To yield the principle of the non-importation act would be yielding the only peaceable instrument for coercing all our rights.— THE ANAS. FORD ED., i, 322. (Feb. 1807.)

6000. NON-IMPORTATION vs. IMPRESSMENTS.—If [the British] keep up impressments, we must adhere to non-intercourse, manufacturer's and a navigation act.— To JAMES MADISON. v, 362. FORD ED., ix, 208. (M., Sep. 1808.)

6001. NON-INTERCOURSE, Unpopular.—Our affairs are certainly now at their ultimate point of crisis. I understand the Eastern republicans will agree to nothing which shall render non-intercourse effectual, and that in any question of that kind, the federalists will have a majority. There remains, then, only war or submission, and if we adopt the former, they will desert us.—To W. C. NICHOLAS. v, 488. (M., Dec. 1809.)

— NORFOLK.—See ALEXANDRIA.

6002. NORTH CAROLINA, Political conditions in.—North Carolina is at present in the most dangerous state. The lawyers all tories, the people substantially republican, but uninformed and deceived by the lawyers, who are elected of necessity because few other candidates. The medicine for that State must be very mild and secretly administered. But nothing should be spared to give them true information.—To P. N. NICHOLAS. iv, 328. FORD ED., vii, 440. (Pa., April 1800.)

— NORTH (Lord), Ability of.—See GEORGE III., CONTROL OF.

6003. NORTH (Lord), Hostile to America.—Lord North's hostility to us is notorious.—To BENJAMIN HARRISON. FORD ED., iii, 414. (A., March 1784.)

6004. NORTH (Lord), Proposition of.— I was under appointment to attend the General Congress; but knowing the importance of the answer to be given to the Conciliatory Proposition, and that our leading whig characters were then in Congress, I determined to attend on the Assembly, and, though a young member, to take on myself the carrying through an answer to the Proposition. The Assembly met the 1st of June. I drew and proposed the answer, and carried it through the House with very little alteration, against the opposition of our timid members who wished to speak a different language. This was finished before the 11th of June, because on that day, I set out from Williamsburg to Philadelphia, and was the bearer of an authenticated copy of this instrument to Congress. The effect it had in fortifying their minds, and in deciding their measures, renders its true date important; because only Pennsylvania had as yet answered the Proposition. Virginia was the second. It was known how Massachusetts would answer it; and the example of these three principal Colonies would determine the measures of all the others, and of course the fate of the Proposition. Congress received it, therefore, with much satisfaction. The Assembly of Virginia did not deliver the answer to Lord Dunmore till late in the session. They supposed it would bring on a dissolution of their body whenever they should deliver it to him; and they wished previously to get some important acts passed. For this reason they kept it up. I think Lord Dunmore did not quit the metropolis till he knew that the answer framed by the House was a rejection of the Proposition, though that answer was not yet communicated to him regularly.—NOTES ON M. SOULES'S WORK. ix, 302. FORD ED., iv, 309. (P., 1786.)

6005. ——— ———. On the receipt of Lord North's Proposition, in May or June, 1775, Lord Dunmore called the Assembly. Peyton Randolph, the President of Congress, and Speaker of the House of Burgesses, left the former body and came home to hold the Assembly, leaving in Congress the other delegates who were the ancient leaders of our House. He, therefore, asked me to prepare the answer to Lord North's Proposition, which I did. Mr. Nicholas, whose mind had as yet acquired no tone for that contest, combatted the answer from *alpha* to *omega,* and succeeded in diluting it in one or two small instances. It was firmly supported, however, in Committee of the Whole, by Peyton Randolph, who had brought with him the spirit of the body over which he had presided, and it was carried, with very little alteration, by strong majorities. I was the bearer of it myself to Congress, by whom, as it was the first answer given to the Proposition by any Legislature, it was received with peculiar satisfaction.— To WILLIAM WIRT. vi, 487. FORD ED., ix 475. (M., 1815.)

— NORTHWEST BOUNDARY.—See BOUNDARIES.

6006. NOTES ON VIRGINIA, History of.—Before I had left America, that is to say, in the year 1781, I had received a letter from M. de Marbois, of the French legation in Philadelphia, informing me that he had been instructed by his government to obtain such statistical accounts of the different States of our Union, as might be useful for their information; and addressing to me a number of queries relative to the State of Virginia. I had always made it a practice, whenever an opportunity occurred, of obtaining any information of our country which might be of use to me in any station, public or private, to commit it to writing. These memoranda were on loose papers, bundled up without order, and difficult of recurrence, when I had occasion for a particular one. I thought this a good occasion to embody their substance, which I did in the order of M. Marbois's queries, so as to answer his wish, and to arrange them for my own use. Some friends, to whom they were occasionally communicated, wished for copies; but their volume rendering this too laborious by hand, I proposed to get a few printed for their gratification. I was asked such a price, however, as exceeded the importance of the object. On my arrival at Paris, I found it could be done for a fourth of what I had been asked here. I, therefore, corrected and enlarged them, and had two hundred copies printed, under the title of " Notes on Virginia ". I gave a very few copies to some particular persons in Europe, and sent the rest to my friends in America. An European copy, by the death of the owner, got into the hands of a bookseller, who engaged its translation, and, when ready for the press, communicated his intentions and manuscript to me, suggesting that I should correct it without asking any other permission for the publication. I never had seen so wretched an attempt at translation. Interverted, abridged, mutilated, and often reversing the sense of the original, I found it a blotch of errors from beginning to end. I corrected some of the most material, and, in that form, it was printed in French. A London bookseller, on seeing the translation, requested me to permit him to print the English original. I thought it best to do so, to let the world see that it was not really so bad as the French translation had made it appear. And this is the true history of that publication.—AUTOBIOGRAPHY. i, 61. FORD ED., i, 85. (1821.)

6007. NOTES ON VIRGINIA, Principles in.—The experience of nearly forty years additional in the affairs of mankind has not altered a single principle [in the "Notes on Virginia"].—To JOHN MELISH. vi, 404. FORD ED., iii, 79. (M., 1814.)

6008. NOTES ON VIRGINIA, Slavery and.—I had two hundred copies [of my "Notes on Virginia"] printed, but do not put them out of my own hands, except two or three copies here and two which I shall send to America, to yourself and Colonel Monroe. * * * I beg you to peruse it carefully, because I ask your advice on it, and ask nobody's else. I wish to put it into the hands of the young men at the College [William and Mary,] as well on account of the political as the physical parts. But there are sentiments on some subjects which I apprehend might be displeasing to the country, perhaps to the Assembly, or to some who lead it. I do not wish to be exposed to their censure; nor do I know how far their influence, if exerted, might effect a misapplication of law to such a publication were it made. Communicate it, then, in confidence to those whose judgments and information you would pay respect to; and if you think it will give no offense, I will send a copy to each of the students of William and Mary College, and some others to my friends and to your disposal; otherwise I shall send over only a very few copies to particular friends in confidence and burn the rest. Answer me soon and without reserve. Do not view me as an author, and attached to what he has written. I am neither. They were at first intended only for Marbois. When I had enlarged them, I thought first of giving copies to three or four friends. I have since supposed they might set our young students into a useful train of thought, and in no event do I propose to admit them to go to the public at large.—To JAMES MADISON. FORD ED., iv, 46. (P., May 1785.)

6009. —— ——. I send you a copy of the "Notes on Virginia". * * * I have taken measures to prevent its publication. My reason is that I fear the terms in which I speak of slavery and of our [State] Constitution may produce an irritation, which will revolt the minds of our countrymen against reformation in these two articles, and thus do more harm than good.—To JAMES MONROE. i, 347. FORD ED., iv, 53. (P., 1785.)

6010. NOVA SCOTIA, Conciliation of.—Is it impossible to persuade our countrymen to make peace with the Nova Scotians? I am persuaded nothing is wanting but advances on our part; and that it is in our power to draw off the greatest proportion of that settlement, and thus to free ourselves from rivals [in the fisheries] who may become of consequence. We are at present cooperating with Great Britain, whose policy it is to give aliment to that bitter enmity between her States and ours, which may secure her against their ever joining

us. But would not the existence of a cordial friendship between us and them, be the best bridle we could possibly put into the mouth of England?—To JOHN ADAMS. i, 488. (P., 1785.)

—— NOVELS, Good and bad.—See FICTION.

6011. NULLIFICATION, British statutes.—We do not point out to his Majesty the injustice of these acts [of Parliament], with intent to rest on that principle the cause of their nullity; but to show that experience confirms the propriety of those political principles which exempt us from the jurisdiction of the British Parliament. The true ground on which we declare these acts void is, that the British Parliament has no right to exercise authority over us.—RIGHTS OF BRITISH AMERICA. i, 129. FORD ED., i, 434. (P.F., 1774.)

6012. NULLIFICATION, States and.—Every State has a natural right in cases not within the compact (*casus non foederis*), to nullify of their own authority all assumptions of power by others within their limits. Without this right they would be under the dominion, absolute and unlimited, of whosoever might exercise this right of judgment for them.—KENTUCKY RESOLUTIONS. ix, 469. FORD ED., vii, 301. (1798.)

6013. —— ——. Where powers are assumed which have not been delegated, a nullification of the act is the rightful remedy.—KENTUCKY RESOLUTIONS. ix, 469. FORD ED., vii, 301. (1798.)

6014. OATH, Against tyranny.—I have sworn upon the altar of God eternal hostility against every form of tyranny over the mind of man.—To DR. BENJAMIN RUSH. iv, 336. FORD ED., vii, 460. (M., 1800.)

6015. OATH OF OFFICE, Presidential.—I propose to take the oath or oaths of office as President of the United States, on Wednesday the 4th inst., at 12 o'clock, in the Senate chamber. May I hope the favor of your attendance to administer the oath? As the two Houses have notice of the hour, I presume a precise punctuality to it will be expected from me. I would pray you, in the meantime, to consider whether the oath prescribed in the Constitution be not the only one necessary to take? It seems to comprehend the substance of that prescribed by the act of Congress to all officers, and it may be questionable whether the Legislature can require any new oath from the President. I do not know what has been done in this heretofore; but I presume the oaths administered to my predecessors are recorded in the Secretary of State's office.—To JOHN MARSHALL. iv, 364. (W., March 2, 1801.)

6016. OBSCURITY, Happiness in.—He is happiest of whom the world says least, good or bad.—To JOHN ADAMS. FORD ED., iv, 297. (P., 1786.)

6017. OCCUPATIONS, Agricultural.—The class principally defective is that of Agriculture. It is the first in utility, and ought to be the first in respect. The same artificial means which have been used to produce a competition in learning, may be equally successful in restoring agriculture to its primary dignity in the eyes of men. It is a science of the very first order. It counts among its handmaids the most respectable sciences, such as Chemistry, Natural Philosophy, Mechanics,

Mathematics, generally, Natural History, Botany. In every college and university, a professorship of agriculture, and the class of its students, might be honored as the first. Young men closing their academical education with this, as the crown of all other sciences, fascinated with its solid charms, and at a time when they are to choose an occupation, instead of crowding the other classes, would return to the farms of their fathers, their own, or those of others, and replenish and invigorate a calling now languishing under contempt and oppression. The charitable schools, instead of storing their pupils with a love which the present state of society does not call for, converted into schools of agriculture, might restore them to that branch qualified to enrich and honor themselves, and to increase the productions of the nation instead of consuming them. An abolition of the useless offices, so much accumulated in all governments, might close this drain also from the labors of the field, and lessen the burthens imposed on them. By these, and the better means which will occur to others, the surcharge of the learned, might in time be drawn off to recruit the laboring class of citizens, the sum of industry be increased, and that of misery diminished.—To DAVID WILLIAMS. iv, 513. (W., 1803.)

6018. OCCUPATIONS, Choice of.— Every one has a natural right to choose that vocation in life which he thinks most likely to give him comfortable subsistence.—THOUGHTS ON LOTTERIES. ix, 505. FORD ED., x, 366. (M., Feb. 1826.)

6019. OCCUPATIONS, Governmental regulation.—The greatest evils of populous society have ever appeared to me to spring from the vicious distribution of its members among the occupations called for. I have no doubt that those nations are essentially right, which leave this to individual choice, as a better guide to an advantageous distribution than any other which could be devised. But when, by a blind concourse, particular occupations are ruinously overcharged, and others left in want of hands, the national authorities can do much towards restoring the equilibrium.—To DAVID WILLIAMS. iv, 512. (W., 1803.)

6020. OCCUPATIONS OF IMMIGRANTS.—Among the ancients, the redundance of population was sometimes checked by exposing infants. To the moderns, America has offered a more humane resource. Many, who cannot find employment in Europe, accordingly come here. Those who can labor, do well for the most part. Of the learned class of emigrants, a small proportion find employments analogous to their talents. But many fail, and return to complete their course of misery in the scenes where it began.—To DAVID WILLIAMS. iv, 514. (W., 1803.)

6021. OCEAN, American supremacy.— The day is within my time as well as yours, when we may say by what laws other nations shall treat us on the sea. And we will say it. —To WILLIAM SHORT. iv, 415. FORD ED., viii, 98. (W., 1801.) See NAVY.

6022. ———. The possession of Louisiana will cost France * * * a war which will annihilate her on the ocean, and place that element under the despotism of two nations, which I am not reconciled to the more because my own would be one of them. —To M. DUPONT DE NEMOURS. iv, 435. (W., April 1802.)

6023. OCEAN, Barrier of liberty.—I am happy in contemplating the peace, prosperity, liberty and safety of my country, and especially the wide ocean, the barrier of all these.—To MARQUIS LAFAYETTE. FORD ED., ix, 302. (M., 1811.)

6024. OCEAN, Claimed by England.—I despair of accommodation with [the British government], because I believe they are weak enough to intend seriously to claim the ocean as their conquest, and think to amuse us with embassies and negotiations, until the claim shall have been strengthened by time and exercise, and the moment arrive when they may boldly avow what hitherto they have only squinted at.—To PRESIDENT MADISON. v, 468. (M., Sep. 1809.)

6025. ——— ———. It has now been some years that I am perfectly satisfied that Great Britain's intentions have been to claim the ocean as her conquest, and prohibit any vessel from navigating it but on such a tribute as may enable her to keep up such a standing navy as will maintain her dominion over it. She has hauled in, or let herself out, been bold or hesitating, according to occurrences, but has in no situation done anything which might amount to a relinquishment of her intentions.—To HENRY DEARBORN. v, 529. FORD ED., ix, 278. (M., 1810.)

6026. ——— ———. It can no longer be doubted that Great Britain means to claim the ocean as her conquest, and to suffer not even a cock-boat, as they express it, to traverse it but on paying them a transit duty to support the very fleet which is to keep the nations under tribute, and to rivet the yoke around their necks. Although their government has never openly avowed this, yet their orders of council, in their original form, were founded on this principle, and I have observed for years past, that however ill success may at times have induced them to amuse by negotiation, they have never on any occasion dropped a word disclaiming this pretension, nor one which they would have to retract when they shall judge the times ripe for openly asserting it. * * * They do not wish war with us, but will meet it rather than relinquish their purpose.—To JOHN HOLLINS. v, 597. (M., May 1811.)

6027. ——— ———. The intention which the British now formally avow of taking possession of the ocean as their exclusive domain, and of suffering no commerce on it but through their ports, makes it the interest of all mankind to contribute their efforts to bring such usurpations to an end.—To CLEMENT CAINE. vi, 14. FORD ED., ix, 330. (M., Sep. 1811.)

6028. ——— ———. Ever since the rupture of the treaty of Amiens, the object of Great Britain has visibly been the permanent conquest of the ocean, and levying a tribute on every vessel she permits to sail on it, as the Barbary powers do on the Mediterranean, which they call their sea.—To WILLIAM SHORT. vi, 128. (M., June 1813.) See EMBARGO and IMPRESSMENT.

6029. OCEAN, Common birthright.—
The ocean, like the air, is the common birthright of mankind.—R. TO A. N. Y. TAMMANY SOCIETY. viii, 127. (1808.)

6030. OCEAN, Common property.—The ocean is the common property of all.—FOREIGN COMMERCE REPORT. vii, 647. FORD ED., vi, 481. (1793.)

6031. —— ——. Nature has not subjected the ocean to the jurisdiction of any particular nation, but has made it common to all for the purposes to which it is fitted.—To ROBERT R. LIVINGSTON. iv, 409. FORD ED., viii, 89. (M., Sep. 1801.)

6032. OCEAN, Dominion of.—I fear the dominion ·of the sea is the insanity of the nation itself.—To HENRY DEARBORN. v, 608. (P.F., Aug. 1811.)

6033. OCEAN, England's policy.—If the British ministry are changing their policy towards us, it is because their nation, or rather the city of London, which is the nation to them, is shaking as usual, by the late reverses in Spain. I have for some time been persuaded that the government of England was systematically decided to claim a dominion of the sea, and to levy contributions on all nations, by their licenses to navigate, in order to maintain that dominion to which their own resources are inadequate. The mobs of their cities are unprincipled enough to support this policy in prosperous times, but change with the tide of fortune, and the ministers to keep their places, change with them.—To PRESIDENT MADISON. v, 442. FORD ED., ix, 251. (M., April 1809.) See ENGLAND.

6034. OCEAN, English ascendency.—An English ascendency on the ocean is safer for us than that of France.—To JAMES MONROE. v, 12. FORD ED., viii, 450. (W., 1806.)

6035. OCEAN, Freedom of.—I join you * * * in a sense of the necessity of restoring freedom to the ocean. But I doubt, with you, whether the United States ought to join in an armed confederacy for that purpose; or rather I am satisfied they ought not. It ought to be the very first object of our pursuits to have nothing to do with the European interests and politics. Let them be free or slaves at will, navigators or agriculturists, swallowed into one government or divided into a thousand, we have nothing to fear from them in any form. * * * ·To take part in their conflicts would be to divert our energies from creation to destruction. Our commerce is so valuable to them that they will be glad to purchase it when the only price we ask is to do us justice. I believe we have in our own hands the means of peaceable coercion; and that the moment they see our government so united as that they can make use of it, they will for their own interest be disposed to do us justice. In this way you shall not be obliged by any

treaty of confederation to go to war for injuries done to others.—To DR. GEORGE LOGAN. FORD ED., viii, 23. (W., March 1801.) See NAVIGATION and SHIPS.

6036. OCEAN, Lawlessness on.—The sea has become a field of lawless and indiscriminate rapine and violence.—To ——. iv, 223. (Pa., 1798.)

6037. OCEAN, Piracy.—I sincerely wish the British orders may be repealed. If they are it will be because the nation will not otherwise let the ministers keep their places. Their object has unquestionably been fixed to establish the Algerine system, and to maintain their possession of the ocean by a system of piracy against all nations.—To COLONEL LARKIN SMITH. v, 441. (M., April 1809.) See BARBARY STATES, MOROCCO and PIRACY.

6038. OCEAN, Usurpation of.—The usurpation of the sea has become a national disease.—To W. A. BURWELL. v, 5. (P.F., Aug. 1811.)

6039. OFFICE, Appointment to.—I like as little as you do to have the gift of appointments. I hope Congress will not transfer the appointment of their consuls to their ministers.—To JOHN ADAMS. i, 502. (P., 1785.)

6040. —— ——. Every office becoming vacant, every appointment made, *me donne un ingrat, et cent ennemis.*—To JOHN DICKINSON. v, 31. FORD ED., ix, 10. (W., 1807.)

6041. —— ——. I know none but public motives in making appointments.—To JOSEPH B. VARNUM. v, 223. (W., 1807.)

6042. —— ——. I am thankful at all times for information on the subject of appointments, even when it comes too late to be used. It is more difficult and more painful than all the other duties of my office, and one in which I am sufficiently conscious that involuntary error must often be committed.—To JOSEPH B. VARNUM. v, 223. (W., 1807.)

6043. —— ——. My usage is to make the best appointment my information and judgment enable me to do, and then fold myself up in the mantle of conscience, and abide unmoved the peltings of the storm. And oh! for the day when I shall be withdrawn from it; when I shall have leisure to enjoy my family, my friends, my farm and books.—To DR. BENJAMIN RUSH. v, 225. (W., 1808.)

6044. —— ——. I shall make no new appointments which can be deferred until the 4th of March, thinking it fair to leave to my successor to select the agents for his own administration.—To DR. LOGAN. v, 404. (W., Dec. 1808.) See OFFICE-HOLDERS.

6045. OFFICE, Choice of.—It is not for an individual to choose his post. You are to marshal us as may be best for the public good.—To PRESIDENT WASHINGTON. iii, 125. FORD ED., v, 141. (Dec. 1789.)

6046. —— ——. A good citizen should take his stand where the public authority marshals him.—To La Duchesse D'Auville. iii, 135. Ford ed., v, 153. (N.Y., 1790.)

6047. —— ——. I never thought of questioning the free exercise of the right of my fellow citizens, to marshal those whom they call into their service according to their fitness, nor ever presumed that they were not the best judges of that.—To James Sullivan. iv, 168. Ford ed., vii, 116. (M., 1797.)

6048. —— ——. I profess so much of the Roman principle, as to deem it honorable for the general of yesterday to act as a corporal to-day, if his services can be useful to his country; holding that to be false pride, which postpones the public good to any private or personal considerations.—To William Duane. vi, 80. Ford ed., ix, 367. (M., Oct. 1812.)

6049. OFFICE, Claims to.—In appointments to public offices of mere profit, I have ever considered faithful service in either our first or second* revolution as giving preference of claim, and that appointments on that principle would gratify the public, and strengthen confidence so necessary to enable the Executive to direct the whole public force to the best advantage of the nation.— To John Page. v, 135. Ford ed., ix, 117. (W., July 1807.)

6050. OFFICE, Declination of.—Whether the State may command the political services of all its members to an indefinite extent, or, if these be among the rights never wholly ceded to the public power, is a question which I do not find expressly decided in England. Obiter dictums on the subject I have indeed met with, but the complexion of the times in which these have dropped would generally answer them; besides that, this species of authority is not acknowledged in our profession. In this country, however, since the present government has been established, the point has been settled by uniform, pointed and multiplied precedents. Offices of every kind, and given by every power, have been daily and hourly declined and resigned from the Declaration of Independence to this moment. The General Assembly has accepted these without discrimination of office, and without ever questioning them in point of right. If the difference between the office of a delegate and any other could ever have been supposed, yet in the case of Mr. Thompson Mason, who declined the office of delegate, and was permitted so to do by the House, that supposition has been proved to be groundless. But, indeed, no such distinction of offices can be admitted. Reason, and the opinions of the lawyers, putting all on a footing as to this question, and so giving to the delegate the aid of all the precedents of the refusal of other offices. The law then does not warrant the assumption of such a power by the State

* The political revolution of 1800.—Editor.

over its members. For if it does, where is that law? nor yet does reason. For though I will admit that this does subject every individual, if called on, to an equal tour of political duty, yet it never can go so far as to submit to it his whole existence. If we are made in some degree for others, yet in a greater, are we made for ourselves. It were contrary to feeling and, indeed, ridiculous to suppose that a man had less right in himself than one of his neighbors, or indeed, all of them put together. This would be slavery, and not that liberty which the bill of rights [of Virginia] has made inviolable, and for the preservation of which our government has been charged. Nothing could so completely divest us of that liberty as the establishment of the opinion, that the State has a *perpetual* right to the services of all its members. This, to men of certain ways of thinking, would be to annihilate the blessing of existence, and to contradict the Giver of life, who gave it for happiness and not for wretchedness. And certainly, to such it were better that they had never been born.—To James Monroe. i, 318. Ford ed., iii, 57. (M., 1782.)

6051. —— ——. Though I will admit that * * * reason does subject every individual, if called on, to an equal tour of political duty, yet it never can go so far as to submit to it his whole existence.—To James Monroe. i, 319. Ford ed., iii, 58. (M., 1782.)

6052. OFFICE, Desire for.—No man ever had less desire of entering into public offices than myself.—The Anas. ix, 102. Ford ed., i, 175. (1792.)

6053. OFFICE, Distribution.—Should distributive justice give preference to a successor of the same State with the deceased, I take the liberty of suggesting to you Mr. Hayward.—To President Washington. iii, 249. Ford ed., v, 322. (Pa., 1791.)

6054. OFFICE, A duty.—To my fellow-citizens the debt of service has been fully and faithfully paid. I acknowledge that such a debt exists, that a tour of duty, in whatever line he can be most useful to his country, is due from every individual. It is not easy perhaps to say of what length exactly this tour should be, but we may safely say of what length it should not be. Not of our whole life, for instance, for that would be to be born a slave,—not even of a very large portion of it. I have now been in the public service four and twenty years; one half of which has been spent in total occupation with their affairs, and absence from my own. I have served my tour then.—To James Madison. iii, 577. Ford ed., vi, 290. (June 1793.)

6055. —— ——. The duties of office are a corvée which must be undertaken on far other considerations than those of personal happiness.—To General Armstrong. vi, 103. (M., 1813.)

6056. OFFICE, Exclusion from.—The republicans have been excluded from all offices from the first origin of the division into republican and federalist. They have a reasonable claim to vacancies till they occupy their due share.—To Dr. B. S. Barton. iv, 353. Ford ed., vii, 489. (W., Feb. 1801.)

6057. ———. Exercising that discretion which the Constitution has confided to me in the choice of public agents, I have been sensible, on the one hand, of the justice due to those who have been systematically excluded from the service of their country, and attentive, on the other, to restore justice in such a way as might least affect the sympathies and the tranquillity of the public mind. —To William Judd. viii, 114. (Nov. 1802.)

6058. OFFICE, Good behavior.—In the office to which I have been called [Secretaryship of State] all was full, and I could not in any case think it just to turn out those in possession who have behaved well, merely to put others in.—To Francis Willis. Ford ed., v, 157. (N.Y., 1790.)

6059. ———. There are no offices in my gift [as Secretary of State] but of mere scribes in the office room at $800 and $500 a year. These I found all filled, and of long possession in the hands of those who held them, and I thought it would not be just to remove persons in possession, who had behaved well, to make places for others.—To Colonel Henry Lee. Ford ed., v, 163. (N. Y., 1790.)

6060. OFFICE, Happiness and.—Were happiness the only legitimate object, the public councils would be deserted. That corvée once performed, however, the independent happiness of domestic life may rightfully be sought and enjoyed.—To John T. Mason. Ford ed., ix, 476. (M., 1814.)

6061. OFFICE, Life appointments to. —Appointments in the nature of freehold render it difficult to undo what is done.—To James Madison. iv, 344. Ford ed., vii, 474. (W., Dec. 1800.)

6062. OFFICE, Motives for holding.—I have no motive to public service but the public satisfaction.—To President Washington. iii, 124. Ford ed., v, 140. (Dec. 1789.)

6063. OFFICE, Poisonous.—We have put down the great mass of offices which gave such patronage to the President. These had been so numerous, that presenting themselves to the public eye at all times and places, office began to be looked to as a resource for every man whose affairs were getting into derangement, or who was too indolent to pursue his profession, and for young men just entering into life. In short, it was poisoning the very source of industry, by presenting an easier resource for a livelihood, and was corrupting the principles of the great mass of those who passed a wishful eye on office. —To Thomas McKean. Ford ed., viii, 217. (W., Feb. 1803.)

6064. OFFICE, Poverty and.—There is not, and has not been, a single vacant office

at my disposal. Nor would I, as your friend, ever think of putting you into the petty clerkships in the several offices, where you would have to drudge through life for a miserable pittance, without a hope of bettering your situation.—To John Garland Jefferson. Ford ed., v, 180. (N.Y., 1790.)

6065. OFFICE, Private advantage.— Public employment contributes neither to advantage nor happiness. It is but honorable exile from one's family and affairs.—To Francis Willis. Ford ed., v, 157. (N.Y., 1790.)

6066. OFFICE, Profits in.—I love to see honest and honorable men at the helm, men who will not bend their politics to their purses, nor pursue measures by which they may profit, and then profit by their measures. —To Edward Rutledge. iv, 153. Ford ed., vii, 95. (M., 1796.)

6067. OFFICE, Refusing.—We find it of advantage to the public to ask of those to whom appointments are proposed, if they are not accepted, to say nothing of the offer, at least for a convenient time. The refusal cheapens the estimation of the public appointments, and renders them less acceptable to those to whom they are secondarily proposed. —To General John Armstrong. Ford ed., viii, 302. (W., 1804.)

6068. OFFICE, Sale of.—These exercises [by Parliament] of usurped power* have not been confined to instances alone in which themselves were interested, but they have also intermeddled with the regulation of the internal affairs of the Colonies. The act of the 9th of June for establishing a Post Office in America seems to have had little connection with British convenience, except that of accommodating his Majesty's ministers and favorites with the sale of an easy and lucrative office.—Rights of British America. i, 130. Ford ed., i, 434. (1774.)

6069. OFFICE, Seekers of.—Whenever a man has cast a longing eye on offices, a rottenness begins in his conduct.—To Tench Coxe. Ford ed., vii, 381. (M., 1799.)

6070. OFFICE, Solicitation.—With respect to the young gentlemen in the office of foreign affairs, their possession and your recommendation are the strongest titles. But I suppose the ordinance establishing my office allows but one assistant; and I should be wanting in candor to you and them, were I not to tell you that another candidate has been proposed to me, on ground that cannot but command respect.—To Chief Justice Jay. iii, 127. Ford ed., v, 144. (M., 1790.)

6071. OFFICE, Talents and.—Talents and science are sufficient motives with me in appointments to which they are fitted.—To President Washington. iii, 466. Ford ed., vi, 107. (M., 1792.)

6072. OFFICE, Training for.—For promoting the public happiness, those persons,

* Over manufactures, exports and imports, &c.—Editor.

whom nature has endowed with genius and virtue, should be rendered by liberal education worthy to receive, and able to guard the sacred deposit of the rights and liberties of their fellow citizens; and they should be called to that charge without regard to wealth, birth, or other accidental condition or circumstance.—DIFFUSION OF KNOWLEDGE BILL. FORD ED., ii, 221. (1779.)

6073. OFFICE, Unprincipled men and.—An unprincipled man, let his other fitnesses be what they will, ought never to be employed.—To DR. GILMER. iv, 5. FORD ED., vi, 325. (Pa., 1793.)

6074. OFFICE, Weariness of.—I must yet a little while bear up against my weariness of public office.—To T. M. RANDOLPH. FORD ED., v, 417. (Pa., Jan. 1792.)

6075. OFFICES, Administration of.—Nothing presents such difficulties of administration as offices.—To GIDEON GRANGER. FORD ED., viii, 44. (W., March 1801.)

6076. —— ——. To you I need not make the observation that of all the duties imposed on the executive head of a government, appointment to office is the most difficult and irksome.—To GEORGE CLINTON. FORD ED., viii, 52. (W., May 1801.)

6077. —— ——. The transaction of the great interests of our country costs us little trouble or difficulty. There the line is plain to men of some experience. But the task of appointment is a heavy one indeed. He on whom it falls may envy the lot of a Sisyphus or Ixion. Their agonies were of the body: this of the mind. Yet, like the office of hangman, it must be executed by some one. It has been assigned to me and made my duty. I make up my mind to it, therefore, and abandon all regard to consequences.—To LARKIN SMITH. FORD ED., viii, 336. (W., Nov. 1804.)

6078. OFFICES, Bestowal.—I have firmly refused to follow the counsels of those who have desired the giving offices to some of the [federal] leaders, in order to reconcile. I have given, and will give only to republicans, under existing circumstances.—To JAMES MONROE. iv, 368. FORD ED., viii, 10. (W., March 1801.)

6079. —— ——. The consolidation of our fellow citizens in general is the great object we ought to keep in view, and that being once obtained, while we associate with us in affairs. to a certain degree, the federal sect of republicans, we must strip of all the means of influence the Essex Junto, and their associate monocrats in every part of the Union. —To LEVI LINCOLN. iv, 398. FORD ED., viii, 66. (W., July 1801.)

6080. OFFICES, Burthens.—In a virtuous government, and more especially in times like these, public offices are, what they should be, burthens to those appointed to them, which it would be wrong to decline, though foreseen to bring with them intense labor,

and great private loss.—To RICHARD HENRY LEE. FORD ED., ii, 192. (Wg., 1779.)

6081. OFFICES, Charity and.—I did not think the public · offices confided to me to give away as charities.—To JAMES MONROE. iv, 446. FORD ED., viii, 166. (W., 1802.)

6082. OFFICES, Confirming power.—I have always considered the control of the Senate as meant to prevent any bias or favoritism in the President towards his own relations, his own religion, towards particular States, &c., and perhaps to keep very obnoxious persons out of offices of the first grade. But in all subordinate cases, I have ever thought that the selection made by the President ought to inspire a general confidence that it has been made on due enquiry and investigation of character, and that the Senate should interpose their negative only in those particular cases where something happens to be within their knowledge, against the character of the person, and unfitting him for the appointment.—To ALBERT GALLATIN. FORD ED., viii, 211. (1803.)

6083. OFFICES, Creation of.—The Administrator [of Virginia] shall not possess the prerogative * * * of erecting offices.— PROPOSED VA. CONSTITUTION. FORD ED., ii, 19. (June 1776.)

6084. —— ——. He has erected a multitude of new offices by a self-assumed power.* —DECLARATION OF INDEPENDENCE AS DRAWN BY JEFFERSON.

6085. —— ——. He has sent hither swarms of new officers to harass our people, and eat out their substance.—DECLARATION OF INDEPENDENCE AS DRAWN BY JEFFERSON.

6086. OFFICES, Difficult to fill.—The present situation of the President. unable to get the offices filled, really calls with uncommon obligation on those whom nature has fitted for them.—To EDWARD RUTLEDGE. iv, 124. FORD ED., vii, 40. (M., Nov. 1795.)

6087. —— ——. Should the [federalists] yield the election, I have reason to expect, in the outset, the greatest difficulties as to nominations. The late incumbents, running away from their offices and leaving them vacant, will prevent my filling them without the *previous* advice of the Senate. How this difficulty is to be got over I know not.—To JAMES MONROE. iv, 355. FORD ED., vii, 491. (W., Feb. 1801.)

6088. OFFICES, Factions and.—In appointments to office, the government refuses to know any difference between descriptions of republicans, all of whom are in principle, and cooperate with the government.—To WILLIAM SHORT. v, 362. (M., Sep. 1808.)

6089. OFFICES, Favoritism.—Mr. Nicholas's being a Virginian is a bar. It is essential that I be on my guard in appointing persons from that State.—To SAMUEL SMITH. FORD ED., viii, 29. (W., March 1801.)

* Congress struck out " by a self-assumed power ".
—EDITOR.

6090. OFFICES, Federal monarchists and.—Amiable monarchists are not safe subjects of republican confidence.—To LEVI LINCOLN. iv, 399. FORD ED., viii, 67. (W., 1801.)

6091. —— ——. I do not know that [the introducing republicans to some share in the offices] will be pushed further * * * except as to Essex [Junto] men. I must ask you to make out a list of those in office in your own State and the neighboring ones, and to furnish me with it. There is little of this spirit south of the Hudson. I understood that Jackson is a very determined one, though in private life amiable and honorable. * * * What will be the effect of his removal? How should it be timed? Who his successor? What place can General Lyman properly occupy?—To LEVI LINCOLN. iv, 399. FORD ED., viii, 67. (W., July 1801.)

6092. —— ——. I have spoken of the federalists as if they were a homogeneous body, but this is not the truth. Under that name lurks the heretical sect of monarchists. Afraid to wear their own name, they creep under the mantle of federalism, and the federalists, like sheep, permit the fox to take shelter among them, when pursued by the dogs. These men have no right to office. If a monarchist be in office anywhere, and it be known to the President, the oath he has taken to support the Constitution imperiously requires the instantaneous dismission of such officer; and I should hold the President criminal if he permitted such to remain. To appoint a monarchist to conduct the affairs of a republic, is like appointing an atheist to the priesthood. As to the real federalists, I take them to my bosom as brothers. I view them as honest men, friends to the present Constitution.*—FROM A NEWSPAPER LETTER. FORD ED., viii, 237. (June 1803.)

6093. OFFICES, Geographical equilibrium.—In our country, you know, talents alone are not to be the determining circumstance, but a geographical equilibrium is to a certain degree expected. The different parts in the Union expect to share the public appointments.—To HORATIO GATES. FORD ED., viii. 11. (W., March 1801.)

6094. —— ——. Virginia is greatly over her due proportion of appointments in the General Government; and though this has not been done by me, it would be imputed as blamed to me to add to her proportion. So that for all general offices persons to fill them must, for some time, be sought from other States, and only offices which are to be exercised within the State can be given to its own citizens.—To JOHN PAGE. FORD ED., viii, 133. (W., Feb. 1802.)

6095. —— ——. Mr. R[obert] S. S[mith, Attorney-General], has had a commission given to Eli Williams as commissioner of the

*An article in the New York Evening Post led Jefferson to write a letter, signed " Fair Play ", with a view to publication in New England. It was the second instance of Jefferson's departure from his rule of not writing for newpapers. The object was to provoke discussion.—EDITOR.

Western road. I am sorry he has gone out of Baltimore for the appointment, and also out of the ranks of Republicanism. It will furnish new matter for clamor.—To ALBERT GALLATIN. FORD ED., viii, 464. (M., Aug. 1806.)

6096. OFFICES, Gift of.— I dare say you have found that the solicitations for office are the most painful incidents to which an executive magistrate is exposed. The ordinary affairs of a nation offer little difficulty to a person of any experience; but the gift of office is the dreadful burthen which oppresses him.—To JAMES SULLIVAN. v, 252. (W., 1808.)

6097. —— ——. A person who wishes to make [the gift of office] an engine of self-elevation, may do wonders with it; but to one who wishes to use it conscientiously for the public good, without regard to the ties of blood or friendship, it creates enmities without number, many open, but more secret, and saps the happiness and peace of his life. —To JAMES SULLIVAN. v, 252. (W., 1808.)

6098. OFFICES, Importunity for.— When I retired from the government four years ago, it was extremely my wish to withdraw myself from all concern with public affairs, and to enjoy with my fellow citizens the protection of government, under the auspices and direction of those to whom it was so worthily committed. Solicitations from my friends, however, to aid them in their applications for office, drew from me an unwary compliance, till at length these became so numerous as to occupy a great portion of my time in writing letters to the President and heads of departments, and although these were attended to by them with great indulgence, yet I was sensible they could not fail of being very embarrassing. They kept me, at the same time, standing forever in the attitude of a suppliant before them, daily asking favors as humiliating and afflicting to my own mind, as they were unreasonable from their multitude. I was long sensible of putting an end to these unceasing importunities, when a change in the heads of the two departments to which they were chiefly addressed, presented me an opportunity. I come to a resolution, therefore, on that change, never to make another application. I have adhered to it strictly, and find that on its rigid observance, my own happiness and the friendship of the government too much depend, for me to swerve from it in future.—To THOMAS PAINE M'MATRON. vi, 108. (M., 1813.)

6099. OFFICES, Intolerance and.—Our gradual reformations seem to produce good effects everywhere except in Connecticut. Their late session of Legislature has been more intolerant than all others. We must meet them with equal intolerance. When they will give a share in the State offices, they shall be replaced in a share of the general offices. Till then, we must follow their example.—To LEVI LINCOLN. iv, 399. FORD ED., viii, 67. (W., July 1801.)

6100. —— ——. When I entered on office, after giving a very small participation in office to republicans by removal of a very few federalists, selected on the principle of their own intolerance while in office, I never meant to have touched another, but to leave to the ordinary accidents to make openings for republicans, but the vindictive, indecent and active opposition of some individuals has obliged me from time to time to disarm them of the influence of office.—To ANDREW ELLICOTT. FORD ED., viii, 479. (W., Nov. 1806.)

6101. OFFICES, Jefferson and.—I have solicited none, intrigued for none. Those which my country has thought proper to confide to me have been of their own mere motion, unasked by me.—To JAMES LYON. vi, 10. (M., 1811.)

6102. OFFICES, Labor and.—Considering the general tendency to multiply offices and dependencies, and to increase expense to the ultimate term of burden which the citizen can bear, it behooves us to avail ourselves of every occasion which presents itself for taking off the surcharge; that it may never be seen here that, after leaving to labor the smallest portion of its earnings on which it can subsist, government shall itself consume the residue of what it was instituted to guard.—FIRST ANNUAL MESSAGE. viii, 10. FORD ED., viii, 120. (Dec. 1801.)

6103. OFFICES, Local.—Where an office is local we never go out of the limits for the officer.—To CÆSAR A. RODNEY. FORD ED., viii, 498. (W., 1806.)

6104. OFFICES, Lopping off.—I had foreseen, years ago, that the first republican President who should come into office after all the places in the government had become exclusively occupied by federalists, would have a dreadful operation to perform. That the republicans would consent to a continuation of everything in federal hands, was not to be expected, because neither just nor politic. On him, then, was to devolve the office of an executioner, that of lopping off. I cannot say that it has worked harder than I expected.—To LEVI LINCOLN. iv, 406. FORD ED., viii, 83. (M., Aug. 1801.)

6105. OFFICES, Midnight appointments.—The nominations crowded in by Mr. Adams, after he knew he was not appointing for himself, I treat as mere nullities. His best friends do not disapprove of this.—To WILLIAM FINDLEY. FORD ED., viii, 28. (W., March 1801.)

6106. —— ——. In the class of removals, I do not rank the new appointments which Mr. Adams crowded in with whip and spur from the 12th of December, when the event of the election was known (and, consequently, that he was making appointments, not for himself, but his successor), until 9 o'clock of the night, at 12 o'clock of which he was to go out of office. This outrage on decency should not have its effect, except in the life appointments which are irremovable; but as to the others, I consider the nomina-

tions as nullities, and will not view the persons as even candidates for *their* office, much less as possessing it by any title meriting respect.—To GENERAL HENRY KNOX. iv, 386. FORD ED., vi , 36. (W., March 1801.)

6107. —— ——. Mr. Adams's last appointments, when he knew he was naming counsellors and aids for me and not for himself, I set aside as far as depends on me.—To ELBRIDGE GERRY. iv, 391. FORD ED., viii, 42. (W., March 1801.)

6108. —— ——. I consider as nullities all the appointments (of a removable character) crowded in by Mr. Adams, when he knew he was appointing counsellors and agents for his successor and not for himself.—To GIDEON GRANGER. FORD ED., viii, 44. (W., March 1801.)

6109. —— ——. I have not considered as candid, or even decorous, the crowding of appointments by Mr. Adams after he knew he was making them for his successor and not himself even to nine o'clock of the night at twelve of which he was to go out of office. I do not think I ought to permit that conduct to have any effect as to the offices removable in their nature.—To PIERREPONT EDWARDS. FORD ED., viii, 44. (W., March 1801.)

6110. —— ——. The last Congress established a Western Judiciary district in Virginia, comprehending chiefly the Western countries. Mr. Adams, who continued filling all the offices till nine o'clock of the night, at twelve of which he was to go out of office himself, took care to appoint for this district also. The judge, of course, stands till the laws shall be repealed, which we trust will be at the next Congress. But as to all others I made it immediately known that I should consider them as nullities, and appoint others.—To A. STUART iv, 393. FORD ED., viii, 46. (M., April 1801.)

6111. —— ——. If the will of the nation, manifested by their various elections, calls for an administration of government according with the opinions of those elected; if, for the fulfillment of that will, displacements are necessary, with whom can they so justly begin as with persons appointed in the last moments of an administration, not for its own aid, but to begin a career at the same time with their successors, by whom they had never been approved, and who could scarcely expect from them a cordial cooperation?—To THE NEW HAVEN COMMITTEE. iv, 404. FORD ED., viii, 69. (W., July 1801.)

6112. OFFICES, Multiplication of.—The multiplication of public offices, increase of expense beyond income, growth and entailment of a public debt, are indications soliciting the employment of the pruning knife.—To SPENCER ROANE. vii, 212. FORD ED., x. 188. (M., 1821.)

6113. OFFICES, Newspaper cajolery and.—I was not deluded by the eulogiums of the public papers in the first moments of change. If they could have continued to get all the loaves and fishes, that is, if I would have gone over to them, they would continue to eulogize. But I well knew that the moment that such removals should take place, as the justice of the preceding administration ought to have executed, their hue and cry would be set up, and they would take their old stand. I shall disregard that also.—To ELBRIDGE GERRY. iv, 391. FORD ED., viii, 41. (W., March 1801.)

6114. OFFICES, Nominations.—There is nothing I am so anxious about as good nominations, conscious that the merit as well as reputation of an administration depends as much on that as on its measures.—To A. STUART. iv, 394. FORD ED., viii, 47. (M., April 1801.)

6115. —— ——. My nominations are sometimes made on my own knowledge of the persons; sometimes on the information of others given either voluntarily, or at my request and in personal confidence. This I could not communicate without a breach of confidence, not I am sure, under the contemplation of the committee.* They are sensible the Constitution has made it my duty to nominate; and has not made it my duty to lay before them the evidences or reasons whereon my nominations are founded; and of the correctness of this opinion the established usage in the intercourse between the Senate and President is a proof. During nearly the whole of the time this Constitution has been in operation, I have been in situations of intimacy with this part of it, and may observe, from my knowledge, that it has not been the usage of the President to lay before the Senate, or a committee, the information on which he makes his nominations. In a single instance lately, I did make a communication of papers, but there were circumstances so peculiar in that case as to distinguish it from all others.—To URIAH TRACY. FORD ED., viii, 412. (1806.)

6116. —— ——. Nomination to office is an executive function. To give it to the Legislature, as we [in Virginia] do, is a violation of the principle of the separation of powers. It swerves the members from correctness, by temptations to intrigue for office themselves, and to a corrupt barter of votes; and destroys responsibility by dividing it among a multitude. By leaving nomination in its proper place, among executive functions, the principle of the distribution of power is preserved, and responsibility weighs with its force on a single head.—To SAMUEL KERCHIVAL. vii, 12. FORD ED., x, 40. (M., 1816.)

6117. OFFICES, Participation in.—It would have been to me a circumstance of great relief, had I found a moderate participation of office in the hands of the majority. I would gladly have left to time and accident to raise them to their just share. But their

* A committee of the Senate which had asked Jefferson concerning the characters and qualifications of certain persons nominated by him. This paper was not sent.—EDITOR.

total exclusion calls for prompter correctives.—To THE NEW HAVEN COMMITTEE. iv, 405. FORD ED., viii, 70. (W., July 1801.)

6118. —— ——. After so long and complete an exclusion from office as republicans have suffered, insomuch that every place is filled with their opponents, justice as well as principle requires that they should have some participation. I believe they will be contented with less than their just share for the sake of peace and conciliation.—To PIERCE BUTLER. FORD ED., viii, 82. (M., Aug. 1801.)

6119. —— ——. If a due participation of office is a matter of right, how are vacancies to be obtained? Those by death are few; by resignation, none. Can any other mode than that of removal be proposed?—To THE NEW HAVEN COMMITTEE. iv, 404. FORD ED., viii, 70. (W., July 1801.)

6120. —— ——. I still think our original idea as to office is best; that is, to depend, for the obtaining a just participation, on deaths, resignations, and delinquencies. This will least affect the tranquillity of the people, and prevent their giving in to the suggestion of our enemies, that ours has been a contest for office, not for principle. This is rather a slow operation, but it is sure if we pursue it steadily, which, however, has not been done with the undeviating resolution I could have wished.—To LEVI LINCOLN. iv, 451. FORD ED., viii, 176. (W., Oct. 1802.)

6121. —— ——. The present administration had a task imposed on it which was unavoidable, and could not fail to exert the bitterest hostility in those who opposed it. The preceding administration left ninety-nine out of every hundred in public office of the federal sect. Republicanism had been the mark on Cain which had rendered those who bore it exiles from all portion in the trusts and authorities of their country. This description of citizens called imperiously and justly for a restoration of right. It was intended, however, to have yielded to this in so moderate a degree as might conciliate those who had obtained exclusive possession; but as soon as they were touched, they endeavored to set fire to the four corners of the public fabric, and obliged us to deprive of the influence of office several who were using it with activity and vigilance to destroy the confidence of the people in their government, and thus to proceed in the drudgery of removal farther than would have been, had not their own hostile enterprises rendered it necessary in self-defence.—To BENJAMIN HAWKINS. iv, 466. FORD ED., viii, 212. (W., 1803.)

6122. —— ——. Whether a participation of office in proportion to numbers should be effected in each State separately, or in the whole States taken together, is difficult to decide, and has not yet been settled in my own mind. It is a question of vast complications.—To WILLIAM DUANE. FORD ED., viii. 258. (W., July 1803.)

6123. OFFICES, Perplexity over.—My position is painful enough between federalists who cry out on the first touch of their monopoly, and republicans who clamor for universal removal. A subdivision of the latter will increase the perplexity. I am proceeding with deliberation and enquiry to do what I think just to both descriptions and conciliatory to both.—To JOHN DICKINSON. FORD ED., viii, 76. (W., July 1801.)

6124. OFFICES, Policy respecting.— You know the moderation of our views in this business, and that we all concurred in them. We determined to proceed with deliberation. This produced impatience in the republicans, and a belief we meant to do nothing.—To LEVI LINCOLN. iv, 406. FORD ED., viii, 83. (M., Aug. 1801.)

6125. —— ——. All offices were in the hands of the federalists. The injustice of having totally excluded republicans was acknowledged by every man. To have removed one half, and to have placed good republicans in their stead, would have been rigorously just, when it was known that these composed a very great majority of the nation. Yet such was their moderation in most of the States, that they did not desire it. In these, therefore, no removals took place but for malversation. In the middle States, the contention had been higher, spirits were more sharpened and less accommodating. It was necessary in these to practice a different treatment, and to make a few changes to tranquilize the injured party.—To WILLIAM SHORT. iv, 414. FORD ED., viii, 97. (W., 1801.)

6126. OFFICES, Public opinion and.— Some States require a different regimen from others. What is done in one State very often shocks another, though where it is done it is wholesome. South of the Potomac, not a single removal has been asked. On the contrary, they are urgent that none shall be made. Accordingly, only one has been made, which was for malversation. They censure much the removals north of this. You see, therefore, what various tempers we have to harmonize.—To THOMAS McKEAN. FORD ED., viii, 78. (W., July 1801.)

6127. OFFICES, Qualifications.—I shall * * * return with joy to that state of things when the only questions concerning a candidate shall be: Is he honest? Is he capable? Is he faithful to the Constitution?—To THE NEW HAVEN COMMITTEE. iv, 405. FORD ED., viii, 70. (W., 1801.)

6128. OFFICES, Refusal.—For God's sake get us relieved from this dreadful drudgery of refusal.—To ALBERT GALLATIN. v, 398. (Dec. 1808.)

6129. OFFICES, Regeneration of.—We are proceeding gradually in the regeneration of offices, and introducing republicans to some share in them.—To LEVI LINCOLN. iv, 399. FORD ED., viii, 67. (W., July 1801.)

6130. OFFICES, Unconstitutional nominations.—The President cannot, before the 4th of March, make nominations [of Vermont officers] which will be good in law; because till that day, Vermont will not be a separate and integral member of the U. S., and it is only to integral members of the Union that his right of nomination is given by the Constitution.—REPORT ON ADMISSION OF VERMONT. FORD ED., v. 290. (1791.)

6131. OFFICES, Vacancies.—I think I have a preferable right to name agents for my own administration, at least to the vacancies falling after it was known that Mr. Adams was not naming for himself.—To A. STUART. iv, 393. FORD ED., viii, 46. (M., April 1801.)

6132. —— ——. The phrase in the Constitution is, "to fill up all vacancies that may happen during the recess of the Senate" This may mean "vacancies that may happen to be", or "may happen to fall"; it is, certainly, susceptible of both constructions, and we took the practice of our predecessors as the commentary established. This was done without deliberation; and we have not before taken an exact view of the precedents. They more than cover our cases, but I think some of them are not justifiable. We propose to take the subject into consideration, and to fix on such a rule of conduct, within the words of the Constitution, as may save the government from serious injury, and yet restrain the Executive within limits which might admit mischief. You will observe the cases of Reade and Putnam, where the persons nominated declining to accept, the vacancy remained unfilled, and had happened before the recess. It will be said these vacancies did not remain unfilled by the intention of the Executive, who had, by nomination, endeavored to fill them. So in our cases, they were not unfilled by the intention of the successor, but by the omission of the predecessor. Charles Lee informed me that wherever an office became vacant so short a time before Congress rose, as not to give an opportunity of enquiring for a proper character, they let it lie always till recess. * * * We must establish a correct and well digested rule of practice, to bind up our successors as well as ourselves. If we find that any of our cases go beyond the limits of such a rule, we must consider what will be the best way of preventing their being considered authoritative examples.—To WILSON C. NICHOLAS. FORD ED., viii, 131. (W., Jan. 1802.)

6133. —— ——. The mischievous law vacating, every four years, nearly all the executive offices of the government, saps the constitutional and salutary functions of the President, and introduces a principle of intrigue and corruption, which will soon leaven the mass, not only of senators, but of citizens. It is more baneful than the attempt which failed in the beginning of the government, to make all officers irremovable but with the consent of the Senate. This places, every four years, all appointments under their power, and even obliges them to act on every one nomination. It will keep in constant excitement all the hungry cormorants for office, render them, as well as those in place, sycophants to their Senators, engage these in eternal intrigue to turn out one and put in another, in cabals to swap work; and make of them what all executive directories become, mere sinks of corruption and faction. This must have been one of the midnight signatures of the President when he had not time to consider, or even to read the law; and the more fatal as being irrepealable but with the consent of the Senate, which will never be obtained.—To JAMES MADISON. vii, 190. FORD ED., x, 168. (P.F., 1820.)

6134. OFFICES, Women and.—The appointment of a woman to office is an innovation for which the public is not prepared, nor am I.—To ALBERT GALLATIN. FORD ED., ix. 7. (W., Jan. 1807.)

6135. OFFICE-HOLDERS, Appointments.—With regard to appointments, I have so much confidence in the justice and good sense of the federalists, that I have no doubt they will concur in the fairness of the position, that after they have been in the exclusive possession of all offices from the very first origin of party among us, to the 3d of March, at 9 o'clock in the night, no republican ever admitted, and this doctrine newly avowed, it is now perfectly just that the republicans should come in for the vacancies which may fall in, until something like an equilibrium in office be restored; after which *"Tros Tyriusque mihi nullo discrimine agetur."**—To DR. BENJAMIN RUSH. iv, 382. FORD ED., viii, 31. (W., March 1801.)

6136. —— ——. About appointments to offices the rule is simple enough. The federalists having been in exclusive possession of them from the first origin of the party among us, to the 3d of March, nine o'clock p. m. of the evening, at twelve of which Mr. Adams was to go out of office, their reason will acknowledge the justice of giving vacancies, as they happen, to those who have been so long excluded, till the same general proportion prevails in office which exists out of it.—To GIDEON GRANGER. FORD ED., viii. 44. (W., March 1801.)

6137. —— ——. Which appointment would be most respected by the public, for that circumstance is not only generally the best criterion of what is best, but the public respect can alone give strength to the government.—To ARCHIBALD STUART. FORD ED., viii, 47. (M., April 1801.)

6138. —— ——. There is nothing I am so anxious about as making the best possible appointments, and no case in which the best men are more liable to mislead us, by yielding to the solicitations of applicants.—To NATHANIEL MACON. iv, 396. FORD ED., viii, 52. (W., May 1801.)

* The Congress edition omits the Latin quotation. In the Ford edition, "habetur", not "agetur".— EDITOR.

6139. —— ——. The grounds on which one of the competitors stood, set aside of necessity all hesitation. Mr. Hall's having been a member of the Legislature, a Speaker of the Representatives, and a member of the Executive Council, were evidences of the respect of the State towards him, which our respect for the State could not neglect.—To J. F. MERCER. iv, 562. (W., 1804.)

6140. OFFICE-HOLDERS, Caucuses and.—The allegations against Pope, of New Bedford, are insufficient. Although meddling in political caucuses is no part of that freedom of personal suffrage which ought to be allowed him, yet his mere presence at a caucus does not necessarily involve an active and official influence in opposition to the government which employs him.—To ALBERT GALLATIN. FORD ED., viii, 499. (W., 1806.)

6141. OFFICE-HOLDERS, Charges against.—I have made it a rule not to give up letters of accusation, or copies of them, in any case.—To ALBERT GALLATIN. FORD ED., viii, 500. (W., 1806.)

6142. OFFICE-HOLDERS, Elections and.—Interferences with elections, whether of the State or General Government, by officers of the latter, should be deemed cause of removal; because the constitutional remedy by the elective principle becomes nothing, if it may be smothered by the enormous patronage of the General Government.—To THOMAS McKEAN. iv, 350. FORD ED., vii, 487. (W., 1801.)

6143. —— ——. To these means [deaths, resignations, and delinquencies] of obtaining a just share in the transaction of the public business, shall be added one other, to wit, removal for electioneering activity, or open and industrious opposition to the principles of the present government, Legislative and Executive. Every officer of the government may vote at elections according to his conscience; but we should betray the cause committed to our care, were we to permit the influence of official patronage to be used to overthrow that cause.—To LEVI LINCOLN. iv. 451. FORD ED., viii, 176. (W., Oct. 1802.)

6144. —— ——. I think it not amiss that it should be known that we are determined to remove officers who are active or open mouthed against the government, by which I mean the Legislature as well as the Executive.—To LEVI LINCOLN. iv, 452. FORD ED., viii, 176. (W., Oct. 1802.)

6145. —— ——. I have received two addresses from meetings of democratic republicans at Dover, praying the removal of Allen McLane. * * * If he has been active in electioneering in favor of those who wish to subvert the present order of things, it would be a serious circumstance. I do not mean as to giving his personal vote, in which he ought not to be controlled; but as to using his influence (which necessarily includes his official influence) to sway the votes of others.—To CÆSAR A. RODNEY. FORD ED., viii, 154. (W. 1802.)

6146. —— ——. I think the officers of the Federal Government are meddling too much with the public elections. Will it be best to admonish them privately or by proclamation?—To ALBERT GALLATIN. iv, 559. FORD ED., viii, 320. (M., Sep. 1804.)

6147. OFFICE-HOLDERS, Executive explanations and.—It has not been the custom, nor would it be expedient, for the Executive to enter into details for the rejection of candidates for offices or removal of those who possess them.—To MRS. SARAH MEASE. FORD ED., viii, 35. (W., March 1801.)

6148. —— ——. These letters [from you] all relating to office, fall within the general rule which even the very first week of my being engaged in the administration obliged me to establish, to wit, that of not answering letters on office specifically, but leaving the answer to be found in what is done or not done on them. You will readily conceive into what scrapes one would get by saying *no*, either with or without reason, by using a softer language which might excite false hope, or by saying *yes* prematurely. And to take away all offence from this silent answer, it is necessary to adhere to it in every case rigidly, as well with bosom friends as strangers.—To AARON BURR. FORD ED., viii, 102. (W., Nov. 1801.)

6149. —— ——. The circumstance of exhibiting our recommendations even to our friends, requires great consideration. Recommendations, when honestly written, should detail the bad as well as the good qualities of the person recommended. That gentlemen may do freely, if they know their letter is to be confined to the President or the head of a department; but if communicated further, it may bring on them troublesome quarrels. In General Washington's time, he resisted every effort to bring forth his recommendations. In Mr. Adams's time, I only know that the republicans knew nothing of them. * * * To Mr. Tracy, at any rate, no exhibition or information of recommendations ought to be communicated. He may be told that the President does not think it regular to communicate the grounds or reasons of his decision.—To ALBERT GALLATIN. FORD ED., viii, 210. (Feb. 1803.)

6150. —— ——. The address of the Ward Committee of Philadelphia on the subject of removals from office was received. I cannot answer it, because I have given no answers to the many others I have received from other quarters. * * * Although no person wishes more than I do to learn the opinions of respected *individuals,* because they enable me to examine, and often to correct my own, yet I am not satisfied that I ought to admit the addresses even of those bodies of men which are organized by the Constitution (the Houses of Legislature for instance) to influence the appointment to office for which the Constitution has chosen to rely on the independence and integrity of the Executive, controlled by the Senate, chosen both of them by the whole Union. Still less of those bodies whose organization is unknown to the Constitution. As revolutionary instruments (when nothing but revolution will cure the evils of the State) they are necessary and indispensable, and the right to use them is inalienable by the people; but to admit them as ordinary and habitual instruments as a part of the machinery of the Constitution, would be to change that machinery by introducing moving powers foreign to it, and to an extent depending solely on local views, and therefore incalculable. The opinions offered by *individuals,* and of right, are on a different ground; they are sanctioned by the Constitution; which has also prescribed, when they choose to act in bodies, the organization, objects and rights of those bodies. * * * This view of the subject forbids me, in my judgment, to give answers to addresses of this kind.*—To WILLIAM DUANE. FORD ED., viii, 255. (M., 1803.)

6151. —— ——. You complain that I did not answer your letters applying for office. But if you will reflect a moment you may judge whether this ought to be expected. To the successful applicant for an office the commission is the answer. To the unsuccessful multitude am I to go with every one into the reasons for not appointing him? Besides that this correspondence would literally engross my whole time, into what controversies would it lead me? Sensible of this dilemma, from the moment of coming into office I laid it down as a rule to leave the applicants to collect their answer from the facts. To entitle myself to the benefit of the rule in any case it must be observed in every one; and I never have departed from it in a single case, not even for my bosom friends. You observe that you are, or probably will be appointed an elector. I have no doubt you will do your duty with a conscientious regard to the public good, and to that only. Your decision in favor of another would not excite in my mind the slightest dissatisfaction towards you. On the contrary, I should honor the integrity of your choice. In the nominations I have to make, do the same justice to my motives. Had you hundreds to nominate, instead of one, be assured they would not compose for you a bed of roses. You would find yourself in most cases with one loaf and ten wanting bread. Nine must be disappointed, perhaps become secret, if not open enemies.—To LARKIN SMITH. FORD ED., viii, 336. (W., Nov. 1804.)

6152. OFFICE-HOLDERS, Freedom of opinion and.—Opinion, and the just maintenance of it, shall never be a crime in my view; nor bring injury on the individual.—To SAMUEL ADAMS. iv, 389. FORD ED., viii, 39. (W., March 1801.)

6153. —— ——. The right of opinion shall suffer no invasion from me. Those who have acted well have nothing to fear, however they may have differed from me in opinion;

* The letter containing this extract was not sent to Mr. Duane.—EDITOR.

those who have done ill, however, have nothing to hope; nor shall I fail to do justice lest it should be ascribed to that difference of opinion.—To ELBRIDGE GERRY. iv, 391. FORD ED., viii, 42. (W., March 1801.)

6154. OFFICE-HOLDERS, Half-breeds.—I never did the federalists an act of injustice, nor failed in any duty to them imposed by my office. Out of about six hundred officers, named by the President, there were six republicans only when I came into office, and these were chiefly half-breeds. Out of upwards of three hundred holding during pleasure, I removed about fifteen, or those who had signalized themselves by their own intolerance in office, because the public voice called for it imperiously, and it was just that the republicans should at length have some participation in the government. There never was another removal but for such delinquencies as removed the republicans equally. In this horrid drudgery I always felt myself as a public executioner, an office which no one who knows me, I hope, supposes very grateful to my feelings. It was considerably alleviated, however, by the industry of their newspapers in endeavoring to excite resentment enough to enable me to meet the operation. However, I hail the day which is to relieve me from being viewed as an official enemy. In private life, I never had above one or two; to the friendship of that situation I look with delight.—To WILLIAM SHORT. FORD ED., ix, 51. (W., May 1807.)

6155. OFFICE-HOLDERS, Malignant opposition.—Deaths, resignations, delinquencies, malignant and active opposition to the order of things established by the will of the nation, will, it is believed, within a moderate space of time, make room for a just participation in the management of the public affairs; and that being once effected, future changes at the helm will be viewed with tranquillity by those in subordinate station.—To WILLIAM JUDD. viii, 114. (1802.)

6156. OFFICE-HOLDERS, Matrimony and.—Mr. Remsen having decided definitely to resign his office of Chief clerk, I have considered with all the impartiality in my power the different grounds on which yourself and Mr. Taylor stand in competition for the succession. I understand that he was appointed a month before you, and that you came into actual service about a month before he did. These circumstances place you so equally, that I cannot derive from them any ground of preference. Yet obliged to decide one way or the other, I find in a comparison of your conditions a circumstance of considerable equity in his favor. He is a married man, with a family; yourself single. There can be no doubt but that $500 place a single man as much at his ease as $800 do a married one. On this single circumstance, then, I have thought myself bound to appoint Mr. Taylor chief clerk.—To JACOB BLACKWELL. FORD ED., v, 490. (Pa., 1792.)

6157. OFFICE-HOLDERS, Multiplication of.—I am not for a multiplication of

officers * * * merely to make partizans.—To ELBRIDGE GERRY. iv, 268. FORD ED., vii, 327. (Pa., 1799.)

6158. OFFICE-HOLDERS, Partizan.—A few examples of justice on officers who have perverted their functions to the oppression of their fellow citizens, must, in justice to those citizens, be made.—To SAMUEL ADAMS. iv, 389. FORD ED., viii, 39. (W., March 1801.)

6159. —— ——. Those whose misconduct in office ought to have produced their removal even by my predecessor, must not be protected by the delicacy due only to honest men.—To SAMUEL ADAMS. iv, 389. FORD ED., viii, 39. (W., March 1801.)

6160. —— ——. Officers who have been guilty of gross abuses of office, such as marshals packing juries, &c., I shall now remove, as my predecessor ought in justice to have done. The instances will be few, and governed by strict rule, and not party passion.—To ELBRIDGE GERRY. iv, 391. FORD ED., viii, 42. (W., March 1801.)

6161. —— ——. I have never removed a man merely because he was a federalist. I have never wished them to give a vote at an election, but according to their own wishes. But as no government could discharge its duties to the best advantage of its citizens, if its agents were in a regular course of thwarting instead of executing all its measures, and were employing the patronage and influence of their offices against the government and its measures, I have only requested they would be quiet, and they should be safe; that if their conscience urges them to take an active and zealous part in opposition, it ought also to urge them to retire from a post which they could not conscientiously conduct with fidelity to the trust reposed in them; and on failure to retire, I have removed them; that is to say, those who maintained an active and zealous opposition to the government.—To JOHN PAGE. v, 136. FORD ED., ix, 118. (W., July 1807.)

6162. —— ——. Our principles render federalists in office safe, if they do not employ their influence·in opposing the government, and only give their own vote according to their conscience. And this principle we act on as well with those put in office by others, as by ourselves.—To LEVI LINCOLN. v, 264. (W., March 1808.)

6163. OFFICE-HOLDERS, Recommendations.—Should I be placed in office, nothing would be more desirable to me than the recommendations of those in whom I have confidence, of persons fit for office; for if the good withhold their testimony, we shall be at the mercy of the bad.—To DR. B. S. BARTON. iv, 353. FORD ED., vii, 489. (W., Feb. 1801.)

6164. —— ——. It is so far from being improper to receive the communications you had in contemplation as to arrangements [respecting the offices] in your State, that I have been in the constant expectation you would find time to do me the favor of calling and making them, when we could in conversation explain them better than by writing, and I should with frankness and thankfulness enter into the explanations. The most valuable source of information we have is that of the members of the Legislature, and it is one to which I have resorted and shall resort with great freedom.—To CHARLES PINCKNEY. FORD ED., viii, 6. (W., March 1801.)

6165. —— ——. We want an attorney and marshal for the Western [Virginia] district. * * * Pray recommend [persons] to me; and let them be the most respectable and unexceptionable possible, and especially let them be republicans.—To A. STUART. iv, 393. FORD ED., viii, 46. (M., April 1801.)

6166. —— ——. In all cases, when an office becomes vacant in your State [North Carolina], as the distance would occasion a great delay were you to wait to be regularly consulted, I shall be much obliged to you to recommend the best characters.—To NATHANIEL MACON. iv, 396. FORD ED., viii, 52. (W., May 1801.)

6167. —— ——. Disposed myself to make as few changes in office as possible, to endeavor to restore harmony by avoiding everything harsh, and to remove only for malconduct, I have, nevertheless, been persuaded that circumstances in New York, and still more in the neighboring States on both sides, require something more. It is represented that the Collector, Naval Officer, and Supervisor ought all to be removed for the violence of their characters and conduct. The following arrangement was agreed on by Colonel Burr and some of your Senators and Representatives: David Gelston, Collector, Theodorus Bailey, Naval Officer, and M. L. Davis, Supervisor. Yet all did not agree in all the particulars, and I have since received letters expressly stating that Mr. Bailey has not readiness and habit enough of business for the office of Naval Officer, and some suggestions that Mr. Davis's standing in society, and other circumstances will render his not a respectable appointment to the important office of Supervisor. Unacquainted myself with these and the other characters in the State which might be proper for these offices, and forced to decide on the opinions of others, there is no one whose opinion would command with me greater respect than yours, if you would be so good as to advise me, which of these characters and what others would be fittest for these offices. Not only competent talents, but respectability in the public estimation are to be considered.—To GEORGE CLINTON. FORD ED., viii, 53. (W., May 1801.)

6168. —— ——. To exhibit recommendations would be to turn the Senate into a court of honor, or a court of slander, and to expose the character of every man nominated to an ordeal, without his own consent, subjecting the Senate to heats and waste of time.—To ALBERT GALLATIN. FORD ED., viii, 211. (1803.)

6169. —— ——. The friendship which has long subsisted between the President of the United States and myself gave me reason to expect, on my retirement from office, that I might often receive applications to interpose with him on behalf of persons desiring appointments. Such an abuse of his dispositions towards me would necessarily lead to the loss of them, and to the transforming me from the character of a friend to that of an unreasonable and troublesome solicitor. It, therefore, became necessary for me to lay down as a law for my future conduct never to interpose in any case, either with him or the heads of departments, in any application whatever for office.—CIRCULAR LETTER. FORD ED., ix, 248. (March 1809.)

6170. OFFICE-HOLDERS, Reduction.—Among those [officers] who are dependent on Executive discretion, I have begun the reduction of what was deemed necessary. The expense of diplomatic agency have been considerably diminished. The inspectors of internal revenue, who were found to obstruct the accountability of the institution, have been discontinued. Several agencies created by Executive authority, on salaries fixed by that also, have been suppressed, and should suggest the expediency of regulating that power by law, so as to subject its exercises to legislative inspection and sanction. Other reformations of the same kind will be pursued with that caution which is requisite in removing useless things, not to injure what is retained. But the great mass of public offices is established by law, and, therefore, by law alone can be abolished.—FIRST ANNUAL MESSAGE. viii, 10. FORD ED., viii, 120. (Dec. 1801.)

6171. —— ——. When we consider that this government is charged with the eternal and mutual relations only of these States; that the States themselves have principal care of our persons, our property, and our reputation, constituting the great field of human concerns, we may well doubt whether our organization is not too complicated, too expensive; whether offices and officers have not been multiplied unnecessarily, and sometimes injuriously to the service they were meant to promote. I will cause to be laid before you an essay towards a statement of those who, under public employment of various kinds, draw money from the treasury or from our citizens.—FIRST ANNUAL MESSAGE. viii, 9. FORD ED., viii, 120. (Dec. 1801.)

6172. —— ——. The session of the first Congress, convened since republicanism has recovered its ascendancy, * * * will pretty completely fulfil all the desires of the people. * * * They are disarming executive patronage and preponderance, by putting down one half the offices of the United States, which are no longer necessary.—To GENERAL KOSCIUSKO. iv, 430. (W., April 1802.)

6173. OFFICE-HOLDERS, Removals.— Some [removals] I know must be made. They must be as few as possible, done gradually, and bottomed on some malversation or inherent disqualification.—To JAMES MONROE. iv, 368. (W., March 1801.)

6174. —— ——. I believe with others, that deprivations of office, if made on the ground of political principles alone, would revolt our new converts, and give a body to leaders who now stand alone. Some, I know, must be made. They must be as few as possible, done gradually, and bottomed on some malversation or inherent disqualification. Where we shall draw the line between retaining all and none, is not yet settled, and it will not be till we get our administration together; and perhaps even then, we shall proceed *à tâtons,* balancing our measures according to the impression we perceive them to make.—To JAMES MONROE. iv, 368. FORD ED., viii, 10. (W., March 1801.)

6175. —— ——. That some ought to be removed from office, and that all ought not, all mankind will agree. But where to draw the line, perhaps no two will agree. Consequently, nothing like a general approbation on this subject can be looked for. Some principles have been the subject of conversation [in cabinet] but not of determination, *e. g.,* I. All appointments to *civil* offices *during pleasure,* made after the event of the election was certainly known to Mr. Adams, are considered as nullities. I do not view the persons appointed as even candidates for the office, but make others without noticing or notifying them. Mr. Adams's best friends have agreed this is right. 2. Officers who have been guilty of *official* malconduct are proper subjects of removal. 3. Good men, to whom there is no objection but a difference of political principle, practiced on only as far as the right of a private citizen will justify, are not proper subjects of removal except in the case of attorneys and marshals. The courts being so decidedly federal and irremovable, it is believed that republican attorneys and marshals, being the doors of entrance into the courts, are indispensably necessary as a shield to the republican part of our fellow citizens, which, I believe, is the main body of the people.—To WILLIAM B. GILES. iv, 380. FORD ED., viii, 25. (W., March 1801.)

6176. —— ——. As to removals from office, great differences of opinion exist. That some ought to be removed, all will agree. That all should, nobody will say. And no two will probably draw the same line between these two extremes; consequently nothing like general approbation can be expected. Malconduct is a just ground of removal: mere difference of political opinion is not. The temper of some States requires a stronger procedure; that of others would be more alienated even by a milder course. Taking into consideration all circumstances, we can only do in every case what to us seems best, and trust to the indulgence of our fellow citizens who may see the same matter in a different point of view. * * * Time, prudence, and patience will, perhaps, get us over this whole difficulty.—To WILLIAM FINDLEY. FORD ED., viii, 27. (W., March 1801.)

6177. —— ——. The great stumbling block will be removals, which, though made on those just principles only on which my predecessor ought to have removed the same persons, will nevertheless be ascribed to removal on party principles. 1st. I will expunge the effects of Mr. Adams's indecent conduct, in crowding nominations after he knew they were not for himself, till 9 o'clock of the night, at 12 o'clock of which he was to go out of office. So far as they are during pleasure, I shall not consider the persons named, as even candidates for the office, nor pay the respect of notifying them that I consider what was done as a nullity. 2d. Some removals must be made for misconduct. One of these is of the marshal in your city, who being an officer of justice, intrusted with the function of choosing impartial judges for the trial of his fellow citizens, placed at the awful tribunal of God and their country, selected judges who either avowed, or were known to him to be predetermined to condemn; and if the lives of the unfortunate persons were not cut short by the sword of the law, it was not for want of *his* good will. In another State, I have to perform the same act of justice on the dearest connection of my dearest friend, for similar conduct, in a case not capital. The same practice of packing juries, and prosecuting their fellow citizens with the bitterness of party hatred, will probably involve several other marshals and attorneys. Out of this line, I see but very few instances where past misconduct has been in a degree to call for notice. Of the thousands of officers, therefore, in the United States, a very few individuals only, probably not twenty, will be removed; and these only for doing what they ought not to have done. Two or three instances, indeed, where Mr. Adams removed men because they would not sign addresses, &c., to him, will be rectified—the persons restored. The whole world will say this is just. I know that in stopping thus short in the career of removal, I shall give great offence to many of my friends. That torrent has been pressing me heavily, and will require all my force to bear up against; but my maxim is, "*fiat justitia, ruat cœlum.*"—To DR. BENJAMIN RUSH. iv, 383. FORD ED., viii, 31. (W., March 1801.)

6178. —— ——. I am aware that the necessity of a few removals for legal oppressions, delinquencies, and other official malversations, may be misconstrued as done for political opinions, and produce hesitation in the coalition so much to be desired; but the extent of these will be too limited to make permanent impressions.—To GENERAL HENRY KNOX. iv, 386. FORD ED., viii, 36. (W., March 1801.)

6179. —— ——. No one will say that all should be removed, or that none should. Yet no two scarcely draw the same lines. * * * Persons who have perverted their offices to the oppression of their fellow citizens, as marshals packing juries, attorneys grinding their legal victims, intolerants removing those under them for opinion's sake, substitutes for honest men removed for their republican principles, will probably find few advocates even among their quondam party. But the freedom of opinion, and the reasonable maintenance of it, is not a crime, and ought not to occasion injury.—To GIDEON GRANGER. FORD ED., viii, 44. (W., March 1801.)

6180. —— ——. In Connecticut alone, a general sweep seems to be called for on principles of justice and policy. Their Legislature are removing every republican even from the commissions of the peace and the lowest offices. There, then, we will retaliate. Whilst the federalists are taking possession of all the State offices, exclusively, they ought not to expect we will leave them the exclusive possession of those at our disposal. The republicans have some rights and must be protected.—To WILSON C. NICHOLAS. FORD·ED., viii, 64. (W., June 1801.)

6181. —— ——. I am satisfied that the heaping of abuse on me, personally, has been with the design and hope of provoking me to make a general sweep of all federalists out of office. But as I have carried no passion into the execution of this disagreeable duty, I shall suffer none to be excited. The clamor which has been raised will not provoke me to remove one more, nor deter me from removing one less, than if not a word had been said on the subject.—To LEVI LINCOLN. iv, 407. FORD ED., viii, 84. (M., Aug. 1801.)

6182. —— ——. The removal of excrescences from the judiciary is the universal demand.—To LEVI LINCOLN. iv, 407. FORD ED., viii, 85. (M., Aug. 1801.)

6183. —— ——. Rigorous justice required that as the federalists had filled every office with their friends to the avowed exclusion of republicans, that the latter should be admitted to a participation of office, by the removal of some of the former. This was done to the extent of about twenty only out of some thousands, and no more was intended. But instead of their acknowledging its moderation, it has been a ground for their more active enmity. After a twelve months' trial I have at length been induced to remove three or four more of those most marked for their bitterness, and active zeal in slandering, and in electioneering. Whether we shall proceed any further, will depend on themselves. Those who are quiet, and take no part against that order of things which the public will has established, will be safe. Those who continue to clamor against it, to slander and oppose it, shall not be armed with its wealth and power for its own destruction. The late re-

movals have been intended merely as monitory, but such officers, as shall afterwards continue to bid us defiance, shall as certainly be removed, if the case shall become known. A neutral conduct is all I ever desired, and this the public have a right to expect.—To ELBRIDGE GERRY. FORD ED., viii, 169. (W., Aug. 1802.)

6184. —— ——. We laid down our line of proceedings on mature inquiry and consideration in 1801, and have not departed from it. Some removals, to wit, sixteen to the end of our first session of Congress were made on political principles alone, in very urgent cases; and we determined to make no more but for delinquency, or active and bitter opposition to the order of things which the public will had established. On this last ground nine were removed from the end of the first to the end of the second session of Congress; and one since that. So that sixteen only have been removed on the whole for political principles, that is to say, to make room for some participation for the republicans. * * * Pursuing our object of harmonizing all good people of every description, we shall steadily adhere to our rule, and it is with sincere pleasure I learn that it is approved by the more moderate part of our friends.—To MR. NICHOLSON. iv, 485. (W., May 1803.)

6185. —— ——. Many vacancies have been made by death and resignation, many by removal for malversation in office, and for open, active, and virulent abuse of official influence in opposition to the order of things established by the will of the nation. Such removals continue to be made on sufficient proof. The places have been steadily filled with republican characters until out of 316 officers in all the United States, subject to appointment and removal by me, 130 only are held by federalists. I do not include in this estimate the judiciary and military, because not removable but by established process, nor the officers of the internal revenue, because discontinued by law, nor postmasters, or any others not named by me. And this has been effected in little more than two years by means so moderate and just as cannot fail to be approved in future.*—To WILLIAM DUANE. FORD ED., viii, 258. (W., July 1803.)

6186. —— ——. I give full credit to the wisdom of the measures pursued by the Governor of Pennsylvania in removals from office. I have no doubt he followed the wish of the State; and *he* had no other to consult. But in the General Government each State is to be administered, not on its local principles, but on the principles of all the States formed into a general result. That I should administer the affairs of Massachusetts and Connecticut, for example, on federal principles, could not be approved. I dare say, too, that the extensive removals from office in Pennsylvania may have contributed to the great conversion which has been manifested among

* The letter containing this extract was not sent to Mr. Duane.—EDITOR.

its citizens. But I respect them too much to believe it has been the exclusive or even the principal motive. I presume the sound measures of their government, and of the General one, have weighed more in their estimation and conversation, than the consideration of the particular agents employed.—To WILLIAM DUANE. FORD ED., viii, 259. (M., July 1803.)

6187. —— ——. Although I know that it is best generally to assign no reason for a removal from office, yet there are also times when the declaration of a principle is advantageous. Such was the moment at which the New Haven letter appeared. It explained our principles to our friends, and they rallied to them. The public sentiment has taken a considerable stride since that, and seems to require that they should know again where we stand. I suggest, therefore, for your consideration, instead of the following passage in your letter to Bowen, "I think it due to candor at the same time to inform you, that I had for some time been determined to remove you from office, although a successor has not yet been appointed by the President, nor the precise time fixed for that purpose communicated to him", to substitute this, "I think it due to candor at the same time to inform you, that the President, considering that the patronage of public office should no longer be confided to one who uses it for active opposition to the national will, had, some time since, determined to place your office in other hands. But a successor not being yet fixed on, I am not able to name the precise time when it will take place". My own opinion is, that the declaration of this principle will meet the entire approbation of all moderate republicans, and will extort indulgence from the warmer ones. Seeing that we do not mean to leave arms in the hands of active enemies, they will care the less at our tolerance of the inactive.—To ALBERT GALLATIN. iv, 543. FORD ED., viii, 303. (May 1804.)

6188. —— ——. In the case of the removal proposed by the collector of Baltimore, I consider it as entirely out of my sphere, and resting solely with yourself. Were I to give an opinion on the subject, it would only be by observing that in the cases under my immediate care, I have never considered the length of time a person has continued in office, nor the money he has made in it, as entering at all into the reasons for a removal.—To ALBERT GALLATIN. FORD ED., viii, 499. (W., 1806.)

6189. OFFICE-HOLDERS, Tenure of.—
Should I be placed in office * * * no man who has conducted himself according to his duties would have anything to fear from me, as those who have done ill, would have nothing to hope, be their political principles what they might.—To DR. B. S. BARTON. iv, 353. FORD ED., vii, 489. (W., Feb. 1801.)

6190. OFFICE-HOLDERS, Useless.—
The suppression of useless offices * * * will probably produce some disagreeable altercations [in Congress].—To DR. BENJAMIN RUSH. iv, 426. FORD ED., viii, 128. (W., 1801.)

— OIL OF BENI.—See OLIVE, SUBSTITUTE FOR.

— OLD AGE.—See AGE.

6191. OLIVE, Adapted to America.—
The olive tree * * * would surely succeed in your country, and would be an infinite blessing after some fifteen or twenty years. The caper would also probably succeed, and would offer a very great and immediate profit.—To E. RUTLEDGE. ii, 180. FORD ED., iv, 410. (P., 1787.)

6192. OLIVE, Blessing to the poor.—
After bread, I know no blessing to the poor, in this world, equal to that of oil.—To RALPH IZARD. FORD ED., v, 128. (P., 1789.)

6193. OLIVE, Cultivation of.—The olive is a tree the least known in America, and yet the most worthy of being known. Of all the gifts of heaven to man, it is next to the most precious, if it be not the most precious. Perhaps it may claim a preference even to bread, because there is such an infinitude of vegetables, which it renders a proper and comfortable nourishment. In passing the Alps at the Col de Tende, where they are mere masses of rock, wherever there happens to be a little soil, there are a number of olive trees, and a village supported by them. Take away these trees, and the same ground in corn would not support a single family. A pound of oil which can be bought for three or four pence sterling, is equivalent to many pounds of flesh, by the quantity of vegetables it will prepare, and render fit and comfortable food. Without this tree, the country of Provence and territory of Genoa would not support one-half, perhaps not one-third, their present inhabitants. The nature of the soil is of little consequence if it be dry. The trees are planted from fifteen to twenty feet apart, and when tolerably good, will yield fifteen or twenty pounds of oil yearly, one with another. There are trees which yield much more. They begin to render good crops at twenty years old, and last till killed by cold, which happens at some time or other, even in their best positions in France. But they put out again from their roots. In Italy, I am told they have trees two hundred years old.—To WILLIAM DRAYTON. ii, 199. (P., 1787.)

6194. OLIVE, Heaven's gift.—The olive tree is assuredly the richest gift of heaven. I can scarcely except bread.—To GEORGE WYTHE. ii, 266. FORD ED., iv, 443. (P., 1787.)

6195. OLIVE, Importing trees.—I wish the cargo of olive plants * * * may arrive to you in good order. This is the object for the patriots of your country [South Carolina]; for that tree once established there will be the source of the greatest wealth and happiness. But to insure success, perseverance may be necessary. An essay or two may fail. I think, therefore, that an annual sum should be subscribed, and it need not be a great one.—To E. RUTLEDGE. iii, 110. (P., 1789.)

6196. —— ——. I have arrived at Baltimore from Marseilles forty olive trees of the best kind, and a box of seed, the latter to raise stocks, and the former, cuttings to enfraft on the stocks. I am ordering them on instantly to Charleston. * * * Another cargo is on its way from Bordeaux, so that I hope to secure the commencement of this culture, and from the best species. Sugar and oil will be no mean addition to the articles of our culture.— To PRESIDENT WASHINGTON. iii, 255. FORD ED., v, 327. (Pa., 1791.)

6197. —— ——. I have one hundred olive trees, and some caper plants from Marseilles, which I am sending on to Charleston where * * * they have already that number living of those I had before sent them.—To PRESIDENT WASHINGTON. iii, 357. FORD ED., v, 514. (Pa., 1792.)

6198. —— ——. It is now twenty-five years since I sent my southern fellow citizens two shipments (about 500 plants) of the olive tree of Aix, the finest olives in the world. If any of them still exist, it is merely as a curiosity in their gardens; not a single orchard of them has been planted.—To JAMES RONALDSON. vi, 92. FORD ED., ix, 371. (M., Jan. 1813.)

6199. OLIVE, Oil.—The oil of the olive is an article the consumption of which will always keep pace with its production. Raise it, and it begets its own demand. Little is carried to America because Europe has it not to spare. We, therefore, have not learned the use of it. But cover the Southern States with it, and every man will become a consumer of oil, within whose reach it can be brought in point of price.—To WILLIAM DRAYTON. ii, 200. (P., 1787.)

6200. OLIVE, Planting trees.—Were the owner of slaves to view it only as the means of bettering their condition, how much would he better that by planting one of those trees for every slave he possessed! Having been myself an eye-witness to the blessings which this tree sheds on the poor, I never had my wishes so kindled for the introduction of any article of new culture into our own country. —To WILLIAM DRAYTON. ii, 201. (P., 1787.)

6201. OLIVE, South Carolina and.—If the memory of those persons is held in great respect in South Carolina who introduced there the culture of rice, a plant which sows life and death with almost equal hand, what obligations would be due to him who should introduce the olive tree, and set the example of its culture!—To WILLIAM DRAYTON. ii, 200. (P., 1787.)

6202. —— ——. I am gratified by letters from South Carolina, which inform me that in consequence of the information I had given them on the subject of the olive tree, and the probability of its succeeding with them, several rich individuals propose to begin its culture there.—To M. DE BERTROUS. ii, 359. (P., 1788.)

6203. —— ——. This is the most interesting plant in the world for South Carolina and Georgia. You will see in various places [on your tour] that it gives being to whole villages in places where there is not soil enough to subsist a family by the means of any other culture. But consider it as the means of bettering the condition of your slaves in South Carolina. See in the poorer parts of France and Italy what a number of vegetables are rendered eatable by the aid of a little oil, which would otherwise be useless.—To WILLIAM RUTLEDGE. ii, 414. (P., 1788.)

6204. OLIVE, Substitute for.—I lately received from Colonel Few in New York, a bottle of the oil of Beni, believed to be a sesamum. I did not believe there existed so perfect a substitute for olive oil. Like that of

Florence, it has no taste, and is perhaps rather more limpid. A bushel of seed yields three gallons of oil; and Governor Milledge, of Georgia, says the plant will grow wherever the Palmi Christi will.—To ROBERT R. LIVINGSTON. v, 225. (W., 1808.)

6205. OPINION, Avowal of.—I never had an opinion in politics or religion which I was afraid to own.—To F. HOPKINSON. ii. 587. FORD ED., v, 78. (P., 1789.)

6206. —— ——. There is, perhaps, a degree of duty to avow a change of opinion called for by a change of circumstances.—To BENJAMIN AUSTIN. vi, 553. FORD ED., x, 11. (M., 1816.)

6207. OPINION, Coercion.—Subject opinion to coercion: whom will you make your inquisitors? Fallible men; governed by bad passions, by private as well as public reasons. And why subject it to coercion? To produce uniformity? But is uniformity of opinion desirable? No more than of face and stature.—NOTES ON VIRGINIA. viii, 401. FORD ED., iii, 264. (1782.)

6208. OPINION, Collisions of.—I wish to avoid all collisions of opinion with all mankind.—To CHARLES YANCEY. vi, 517. FORD ED., x, 4. (M., 1816.)

6209. OPINION, Compromise of.—Some [members of Congress] think that independence requires them to follow always their own opinion, without respect for that of others. This has never been my opinion, nor my practice, when I have been of that or any other body. Differing, on a particular question, from those whom I knew to be of the same political principles with myself, and with whom I generally thought and acted, a consciousness of the fallibility of the human mind, and of my own in particular, with a respect for the accumulated judgment of my friends, has induced me to suspect erroneous impressions in myself, to suppose my own opinion wrong, and to act with them on theirs. The want of this spirit of compromise, or of self-distrust, proudly, but falsely called independence, is what gives the federalists victories which they could never obtain, if these brethren could learn to respect the opinions of their friends more than of their enemies, and prevents many able and honest men from doing all the good they otherwise might do. These considerations * * * have often quieted my own conscience in voting and acting on the judgment of others against my own.—To WILLIAM DUANE. v, 591. FORD ED., ix, 315. (M., 1811.)

6210. OPINION, Differences of.—Even if we differ in principle more than I believe we do, you and I know too well the texture of the human mind, and the slipperiness of human reason, to consider differences of opinion otherwise than differences of form or feature.—To ELBRIDGE GERRY. iv, 273. FORD ED., vii, 335. (Pa., 1799.)

6211. —— ——. In every country where man is free to think and to speak, differences of opinion will arise from difference of perception, and the imperfection of reason; but these differences when permitted, as in this happy country, to purify themselves by free discussion, are but as passing clouds overspreading our land transiently, and leaving our horizon more bright and serene.—To BENJAMIN WARING. iv, 378. (W., March 1801.)

6212. —— ——. Every difference of opinion is not a difference of principle. We have called by different names brethren of the same principle. We are all republicans: we are all federalists.—FIRST INAUGURAL ADDRESS. viii, 2. FORD ED., viii, 3. (1801.)

6213. —— ——. I lament sincerely that unessential differences of opinion should ever have been deemed sufficient to interdict half the society from the rights and the blessings of self-government, to proscribe them as characters unworthy of every trust.—To THE NEW HAVEN COMMITTEE. iv, 405. FORD ED., viii, 70. (W., July 1801.)

6214. —— ——. I tolerate with the utmost latitude the right of others to differ from me in opinion without imputing to them criminality. I know too well the weakness and uncertainty of human reason to wonder at its different results.—To MRS. JOHN ADAMS. iv, 562. FORD ED., viii, 312. (M., 1804.)

6215. —— ——. That in a free government there should be differences of opinion as to public measures and the conduct of those who direct them, is to be expected. It is much, however, to be lamented, that these differences should be indulged at a crisis which calls for the undivided counsels and energies of our country, and in a form calculated to encourage our enemies in the refusal of justice, and to force their country into war as the only resource for obtaining it.—R. TO A. NEW LONDON REPUBLICANS. viii, 151. (1809.)

6216. —— ——. That differences of opinion should arise among men, on politics, on religion, and on every other topic of human inquiry, and that these should be freely expressed in a country where all our faculties are free, is to be expected. But these valuable privileges are much perverted when permitted to disturb the harmony of social intercourse, and to lessen the tolerance of opinion.—R. TO A. CITIZENS OF WASHINGTON. viii, 158. (1809.)

6217. —— ——. Some friends have left me by the way, seeking by a different political path, the same object, their country's good, which I pursued with the crowd along the common highway. It is a satisfaction to me that I was not the first to leave them.—To DAVID CAMPBELL. v, 499. (M., 1810.)

6218. —— ——. I have never thought that a difference in political, any more than in religious opinions, should disturb the friendly intercourse of society.—To DAVID CAMPBELL. v, 499. (M., 1810.)

6219. —— ——. With respect to impressions from any differences of political opinion, whether major or minor, * * * I have none. I left them all behind me on quitting Washington, where alone the state of things had, till then, required some attention to them. Nor was that the lightest part of the load I was there disburthened of; and could I permit myself to believe that with the change of circumstances a corresponding change had taken place in the minds of those who differed from me, and that I now stand in the peace and good will of my fellow-citizens generally, it would, indeed, be a sweetening ingredient in the last dregs of my life.—To JOHN NICHOLAS. vii, 143. FORD ED., x, 148. (M., 1819.)

6220. —— ——. Difference of opinion was never, with me, a motive of separation from a friend.—To PRESIDENT MONROE. FORD ED., x, 298. (M., 1824.)

6221. —— ——. Men, according to their constitutions and the circumstances in which they are placed, differ honestly in opinion. Some are whigs, liberals, democrats, call them what you please. Others are tories, serviles, aristocrats, &c.—To WILLIAM SHORT. vii, 391. FORD ED., x, 334. (M., 1825.)

6222. OPINION, Freedom of.—The will of the people is the only legitimate foundation of any government, and to protect its free expression should be our first object.—To BENJAMIN WARING. iv, 379. (W., March 1801.)

6223. —— ——. Opinion, and the just maintenance of it, shall never be a crime in my view; nor bring injury on the individual. —To SAMUEL ADAMS. iv, 389. FORD ED., viii, 39. (W., March 1801.)

6224. —— ——. The freedom of opinion, and the reasonable maintenance of it, is not a crime, and ought not to occasion injury.— To GIDEON GRANGER. FORD ED., viii, 44. (W., March 1801.)

6225. —— ——. The right of opinion shall suffer no invasion from me. Those [office-holders] who have acted well have nothing to fear, however they may have differed from me in opinion: those who have done ill, however, have nothing to hope; nor shall I fail to do justice lest it should be ascribed to that difference of opinion.—To ELBRIDGE GERRY. iv, 391. FORD ED., viii, 42. (W., March 1801.)

6226. —— ——. The legislative powers of government reach actions only and not opinions.—REPLY TO BAPTIST ADDRESS. viii, 113. (1802.)

6227. —— ——. Where thought is free in its range, we need never fear to hazard what is good in itself.—To MR. OGILVIE. v, 604. (M., 1811.)

6228. —— ——. Difference of opinion leads to enquiry, and enquiry to truth; and I am sure * * * we both value too much the freedom of opinion sanctioned by our Constitution, not to cherish its exercise even where in opposition to ourselves.—To Mr. Wendover. vi, 447. (M., 1815.)

6229. —— ——. The amendments [to the constitution of Massachusetts] of which we have as yet heard, prove the advance of liberalism * * * and encourage the hope that the human mind will some day get back to the freedom it enjoyed two thousand years ago.—To John Adams. vii, 199. Ford ed., x, 185. (M., 1821.)

6230. —— ——. I respect the right of free opinion too much to urge an uneasy pressure of [my own] opinion on [others]. Time and advancing science will ripen us all in its course, and reconcile all to wholesome and necessary changes.—To Samuel Kerchival. Ford ed., x, 320. (M., 1824.)

6231. OPINION, Government and.— Government is founded in opinion and confidence.—The Anas. ix, 121. Ford ed., i, 204. (1792.)

6232. OPINION, Individual.—I never submitted the whole system of my opinions to the creed of any party of men whatever, in religion, in philosophy, in politics, or in anything else, where I was capable of thinking for myself. Such an addiction is the last degradation of a free and moral agent. If I could not go to heaven but with a party, I would not go there at all.—To Francis Hopkinson. ii, 585. Ford ed., v, 76. (P., 1789.)

6233. OPINION, Legal.—On every question the lawyers are about equally divided, and were we to act but in cases where no contrary opinion of a lawyer can be had, we should never act.—To Albert Gallatin. v, 369. (M., 1808.)

6234. OPINION, Majority and.—I readily suppose my opinion wrong, when opposed by the majority.—To James Madison. ii, 447. Ford ed., v, 48. (P., 1788.)

6235. OPINION, Power of.—Opinion is power.—To John Adams. vi, 525. (M., 1816.)

6236. OPINION, Right of.—I may sometimes differ in opinion from some of my friends, from those whose views are as pure and sound as my own. I censure none, but do homage to every one's right of opinion.— To William Duane. v, 577. Ford ed., ix, 314. (M., 1811.)

6237. OPINION, Sacrifices of.—If we do not learn to sacrifice small differences of opinion, we can never act together. Every man cannot have his way in all things. If his own opinion prevails at some times, he should acquiesce on seeing that of others preponderate at other times. Without this mutual disposition we are disjointed individuals, but not a society.—To John Dickinson. Ford ed., viii, 76. (W., July 1801.)

6238. —— ——. I see too many proofs of the imperfection of human reason, to entertain wonder or intolerance at any difference of opinion on any subject; and acquiesce in that difference as easily as on a difference of feature or form; experience having long taught me the reasonableness of mutual sacrifices of opinion among those who are to act together for any common object, and the expediency of doing what good we can, when we cannot do all we would wish.—To John Randolph. iv, 518. Ford ed., viii, 282. (W., Dec. 1803.)

6239. —— ——. To the principles of union I sacrifice all minor differences of opinion. These, like differences of face, are a law of our nature, and should be viewed with the same tolerance.—To William Duane. v, 603. (M., 1811.)

6240. OPINION, Uniformity.—Suppose the State should take into head that there should be an uniformity of countenance. Men would be obliged to put an artificial bump or swelling here, a patch there, &c., but this would be merely hypocritical, or if the alternative was given of wearing a mask, ninety-nine one-hundredths must immediately mask. Would this add to the beauty of nature? Why otherwise in opinions?—Notes on Religion. Ford ed., ii, 95. (1776?)

6241. —— ——. Is uniformity of opinion desirable? No more than that of face and stature.—Notes on Virginia. viii, 401. Ford ed., iii, 264. (1782.)

6242. OPINION, War an —If we are forced into war [with France] we must give up differences of opinion, and unite as one man to defend our country.—To General Kosciusko. iv, 295. (Pa., 1799.)

6243. OPINION (Public), Administration and.—Ministers * * * cannot in any country be uninfluenced by the voice of the people.—To John Jay. ii, 46. (P., 1786.)

6244. OPINION (Public), Advantageous.—The advantage of public opinion is like that of the weather-gauge in a naval action.—To James Monroe. vi, 408. Ford ed., ix, 496. (M., 1815.)

6245. OPINION (Public), Attention to.—More attention should be paid to the general opinion.—To George Mason. iii, 209. Ford ed., v, 275. (Pa., 1791.)

6246. OPINION (Public), Censorship by.—Public opinion is a censor before which the most exalted tremble for their future as well as present fame.—To John Adams. vi, 524. (M., 1816.)

6247. —— ——. The public judgment will correct false reasonings and opinions, on a full hearing of all parties; and no other definite line can be drawn between the inestimable liberty of the press and its demoralizing licentiousness. If there be still improprieties which this rule would not restrain, its supplement must be sought in the censorship of public opinion.—Second Inaugural Address. viii, 44. Ford ed., viii, 346. (1805.)

6248. OPINION (Public), Changes in.—
When public opinion changes, it is with the rapidity of thought.—To CHARLES YANCEY. vi, 516. FORD ED., x, 3. (M., 1816.)

6249. OPINION (Public), Conforming to.—I think it a duty in those intrusted with the administration of their affairs to conform themselves to the decided choice of their constituents.—To JOHN JAY. i, 404. FORD ED., iv, 89. (P., 1785.)

6250. OPINION (Public), Degeneracy.
—It is the manners and spirit of a people which preserve a republic in vigor. A degeneracy in these is a canker which soon eats to the heart of its laws and constitution.—NOTES ON VIRGINIA. viii, 406. FORD ED., iii, 269. (1782.)

6251. OPINION (Public), Force of.—
The public mind [in France] is manifestly advancing on the abusive prerogatives of their governors, and bearing them down. No force in the government can withstand this in the long run.—To COMTE DE MOUSTIER. ii, 389. FORD ED., v, 12. (P., 1788.)

6252. —— ——. A King [Louis XVI.] with two hundred thousand men at his orders, is disarmed by force of public opinion and want of money.—To MADAME DE BREHAN. ii, 591. FORD ED., v, 79. (P., 1789.)

6253. —— ——. The good opinion of mankind, like the lever of Archimedes, with the given fulcrum, moves the world.—To M. CORREA. vi, 405. (M., 1814.)

6254. —— ——. The spirit of our people would oblige even a despot to govern us republicanly.—To SAMUEL KERCHIVAL. vii, 11. FORD ED., x, 39. (M., 1816.)

6255. —— ——. The force of public opinion cannot be resisted, when permitted freely to be expressed. The agitation it produces must be submitted to. It is necessary, to keep the waters pure.—To THE MARQUIS DE LAFAYETTE. vii, 325. FORD ED., x, 280. (M., 1823.)

6256. OPINION (Public), Indian.—I am convinced that those societies (as the Indians) which live without government, enjoy in their general mass an infinitely greater degree of happiness, than those who live under the European governments. Among the former, public opinion is in the place of law, and restrains morals as powerfully as laws ever did anywhere.—To EDWARD CARRINGTON. ii, 100. FORD ED., iv, 360. (P., 1787.)

6257. OPINION (Public), Inquisition of.—This country, which has given to the world the example of physical liberty, owes to it that of moral emancipation also, for as yet it is but nominal with us. The inquisition of public opinion overwhelms in practice the freedom asserted by the laws in theory.—To JOHN ADAMS. vii, 200. FORD ED., x, 185. (M., 1821.)

6258. OPINION (Public), Nourish.—
Secure self-government by the republicanism of our constitution, as well as by the spirit of the people; and nourish and perpetuate that spirit.—To SAMUEL KERCHIVAL. vii, 13. FORD ED., x, 41. (M., 1816.)

6259. OPINION (Public), Preserving.—
The basis of our governments being the opinion of the people, the very first object should be to keep that right.—To EDWARD CARRINGTON. ii, 100. FORD ED., iv, 359. (P., 1787.)

6260. OPINION (Public), Respect for.—
When, in the course of human events, it becomes necessary for one people to dissolve the political bands which have connected them with another, and to assume among the powers of the earth the separate and equal station to which the laws of nature and of nature's God entitle them, a decent respect to the opinions of mankind requires that they should declare the causes which impel them to the separation.—DECLARATION OF INDEPENDENCE AS DRAWN BY JEFFERSON.

6261. —— ——. There are certainly persons in all the departments who are driving too fast. Government being founded on opinion, the opinion of the public, even when it is wrong, ought to be respected to a certain degree.—To NICHOLAS LEWIS. FORD ED., v, 282. (Pa., 1791.)

6262. —— ——. We have believed we should afford England an opportunity of making reparation, as well from justice and the usage of nations, as a respect to the opinion of an impartial world, whose approbation and esteem are always of value.—To W. H. CABELL. v, 142. FORD ED., ix, 90. (W., July 1807.)

6263. —— ——. A regard for reputation, and the judgment of the world, may sometimes be felt where conscience is dormant.—To EDWARD LIVINGSTON. vii, 404. (M., 1825.)

6264. OPINION (Public), Revolution by.—A complete revolution in the French government has, within the space of two years, been effected by the mere force of public opinion, aided, indeed, by the want of money which the dissipations of the Court had brought on.—To DAVID HUMPHREYS. iii, 10. FORD ED., v, 86. (P., 1789.)

6265. OPINION (Public), Supremacy.—
Public opinion, that lord of the universe.—To WILLIAM SHORT. vii, 157. (M., 1820.)

6266. OPINION (Public), Wisdom of.—
It is rare that the public sentiment decides immorally or unwisely, and the individual who differs from it ought to distrust and examine well his own opinion.—To WILLIAM FINDLEY. FORD ED., viii, 27. (W., March 1801.)

6267. OPINIONS, Canvassing.—In canvassing my opinions you have done what every man has a right to do, and it is for the good of society that that right should be freely exercised.—To NOAH WEBSTER. iii, 201. FORD ED., v, 254. (Pa., 1790.)

6268. OPINIONS, Exchange of.—I shall be happy, at all times, in an intercommunication of sentiments with you, believing that the dispositions of the different parts of our country have been considerably misrepresented and misunderstood in each part, as to the other, and that nothing but good can result from an exchange of information and opinions between those whose circumstances and morals admit no doubt of the integrity of their views.—To ELBRIDGE GERRY. iv, 174. FORD ED., vii, 123. (Pa., 1797.)

6269. OPINIONS, Formation.—The opinions and belief of men depend not on their own will, but follow involuntarily the evidence proposed to their minds.—STATUTE OF RELIGIOUS FREEDOM. FORD ED., ii, 237. (1779.)

6270. OPINIONS, Government and.—The opinions of men are not the object of civil government, nor under its jurisdiction.—STATUTE OF RELIGIOUS FREEDOM. FORD ED., ii, 238. (1779.)

6271. OPINIONS, Moral facts.—Opinions constitute moral facts, as important as physical ones to the attention of the public functionary.—To RICHARD RUSH. vii, 183. (M., 1820.)

6272. OPINIONS, Propagation of.—To compel a man to furnish contributions of money for the propagation of opinions which he disbelieves and abhors, is sinful and tyrannical.—STATUTE OF RELIGIOUS FREEDOM. FORD ED., ii, 238. (1779.)

6273. OPINIONS, Revealing.—The sentiments of men are known not only by what they receive, but what they reject.—AUTOBIOGRAPHY. i, 19. FORD ED., i, 28. (1821.)

6274. OPINIONS, Social intercourse and.—Opinions, which are equally honest on both sides, should not affect personal esteem or social intercourse.—To JOHN ADAMS. vi, 146. (M., 1813.)

6275. OPINIONS, Strength of sound.—If * * * opinions are sound * * * they will prevail by their own weight, without the aid of names.—To SAMUEL KERCHIVAL. vii, 35. FORD ED., x, 45. (M., 1816.)

6276. OPINIONS, Vindication of.—My occupations do not permit me to undertake to vindicate all my opinions, nor have they importance enough to merit it.—To NOAH WEBSTER. iii, 203. FORD ED., v, 257. (Pa., 1790.)

6277. OPPOSITION, To Administrations.—A quondam colleague of yours, who had acquired some distinction and favor in the public eye, is throwing it away by endeavoring to obtain his end by rallying an opposition to the administration. This error has already ruined some among us, and will ruin others who do not perceive that it is the steady abuse of power in other governments which renders that of opposition always the popular party.—To ALBERT GALLATIN. FORD ED., x, 106. (M., 1818.)

6278. OPPOSITION, Continual.—In the Middle and Southern States, as great an union of sentiment has now taken place as is perhaps desirable. For as there will always be an opposition, I believe it had better be from avowed monarchists than republicans.—To ELBRIDGE GERRY. iv, 536. FORD ED., viii, 297. (W., March 1804.)

6279. OPPOSITION, Crushing.—I have removed those [officeholders] who maintained an active and zealous opposition to the government.—To JOHN PAGE. v, 136. FORD ED., ix, 119. (W., 1807.)

6280. OPPOSITION, Of enemies.—The clouds which have appeared for some time to be gathering around us, have given me anxiety lest an enemy, always on the watch, always prompt and firm, and acting in well-disciplined phalanx, should find an opening to dissipate hopes, with the loss of which I would wish that of life itself.—To WILLIAM DUANE. v, 603. (M., 1811.)

6281. OPPOSITION, Federal elements.—I have never dreamed that all opposition was to cease. The clergy who have missed their union with the State, the Anglomen, who have missed their union with England, and the political adventurers, who have lost the chance of swindling and plunder in the waste of public money, will never cease to bawl, on the breaking up of their sanctuary. But among the people, the schism is healed, and with tender treatment the wound will not reopen. Their quondam leaders have been astounded with the suddenness of the desertion; and their silence and appearance of acquiescence have proceeded not from a thought of joining us, but the uncertainty what ground to take.—To GIDEON GRANGER. iv, 395. FORD ED., viii, 48. (W., May 1801.)

6282. OPPOSITION, Federalist.—The federalists meant by crippling my rigging to leave me an unwieldy hulk at the mercy of the elements.—To THEODORE FOSTER. FORD ED., viii, 51. (W., May 1801.)

6283. ——— ———. Their rallying point is "war with France and Spain, and alliance with Great Britain"; and everything is wrong with them which checks their new ardor to be fighting for the liberties of mankind; on the sea always excepted. There, one nation is to monopolize all the liberties of the others.—To MR. BIDWELL. v, 15. (W., 1806.)

6284. ——— ———. I should suspect error where the federalists found no fault.—To MR. BIDWELL. v, 15. (W., 1806.)

6285. OPPOSITION, Fighting.—While duty required it, I met opposition with a firm and fearless step.—To SPENCER ROANE. vii, 136. FORD ED., x, 142. (P.F., 1819.)

6286. OPPOSITION, Malicious.—There is nothing against which human ingenuity will not be able to find something to say.—To GIDEON GRANGER. iv, 396. FORD ED., viii, 48. (W., 1801.)

6287. OPPRESSION, Colonies and.—A series of oppressions, begun at a distinguished period, and pursued unalterably through every change of ministers, too plainly prove a deliberate, systematical plan of reducing us to slavery.—RIGHTS OF BRITISH AMERICA. i, 130. FORD ED.. i, 435. (1774.)

6288. OPPRESSION, Nations and.—It is, indeed, an animating thought that, while we are securing the rights of ourselves and our posterity, we are pointing out the way to struggling nations who wish, like us, to emerge from their tyrannies also. Heaven help their struggles, and lead them, as it has done us, triumphantly through them.—REPLY TO ADDRESS. iii, 128. FORD ED., v, 147. (1790.)

6289. OPTICS, Laws of.—To distinct vision it is necessary not only that the visual angle should be sufficient for the powers of the human eye, but that there should be sufficient light also on the object of observation. In microscopic observations, the enlargement of the angle of vision may be more indulged, because auxiliary light may be concentrated on the object by concave mirrors. But in the case of the heavenly bodies we can have no such aid. The moon, for example, receives from the sun but a fixed quantity of light. In proportion as you magnify her surface, you spread that fixed quantity over a greater space, dilute it more, and render the object more dim. If you increase her magnitude infinitely, you dim her face infinitely also, and she becomes invisible. When under total eclipse, all the direct rays of the sun being intercepted, she is seen but faintly, and would not be seen at all but for the refraction of the solar rays in their passage through our atmosphere. In a night of extreme darkness, a house or a mountain is not seen, as not having light enough to impress the limited sensibility of our eye. I do suppose in fact that Herschel has availed himself of the properties of the parabolic mirror to the point beyond which its effect would be countervailed by the diminution of light on the object. I barely suggest this element, not presented to view in your letter, as one which must enter into the estimate of the improved telescope you propose.—To THOMAS SKIDMAN. vii, 259. (M., 1822.)

6290. ORATORY, Art in.—In a republican nation, whose citizens are to be led by reason and persuasion, and not by force, the art of reasoning becomes of first importance. In this line antiquity has left us the finest models for imitation; and he who studies and imitates them most nearly, will nearest approach the perfection of the art. Among these I should consider the speeches of Livy, Sallust and Tacitus as preeminent specimens of logic, taste, and that sententious brevity which, using not a word to spare, leave not a moment for inattention to the hearer. Amplification is the vice of modern oratory. It is an insult to an assembly of reasonable men, disgusting and revolting instead of persuading. Speeches measured by the hour die with the hour.—To DAVID HARDING. vii, 347. (M., 1824.)

6291. ORATORY, Models for.—The models for that oratory which is to produce the greatest effect by securing the attention of hearers and readers, are to be found in Livy, Tacitus, Sallust, and most assuredly not in Cicero. I doubt if there is a man in the world who can now read one of his orations through but as a piece of task work.—To J. W. EPPES. v, 490. FORD ED., ix, 267. (M., 1810.)

6292. ORATORY, Modern and Ancient.—The short, the nervous, the unanswerable speech of Carnot, in 1803, on the proposition to declare Bonaparte consul for life,—this creed of republicanism should be well translated, and placed in the hands and heart of every friend to the rights of self-government.—To ABRAHAM SMALL. vi, 347. (M., 1814.)

6293. —— ——. The finest thing, in my opinion, which the English language has produced, is the defence of Eugene Aram, spoken by himself at the bar of the York assizes. in 1759.—To ABRAHAM SMALL. vi, 347. (M., 1814.)

6294. —— ——. I consider the speeches of Aram and Carnot, and that of Logan, as worthily standing in a line with those of Scipio and Hannibal in Livy, and of Cato and Cæsar in Sallust.—To ABRAHAM SMALL. vi, 347. (M., 1814.)

6295. ORATORY, Scathing.—Lord Chatham's reply to Horace Walpole, on the Seamen's bill, in the House of Commons, in 1740, is one of the severest which history has recorded.—To ABRAHAM SMALL. vi, 346. (M., 1814.)

6296. ORDER, Liberty and.—Possessing ourselves the combined blessing of liberty and order, we wish the same to other countries. —To M. CORAY. vii, 318. (M., 1823.)

6297. ORDER, Maintenance of.—The life of the citizen is never to be endangered, but as the last melancholy effort for the maintenance of order and obedience to the laws.*—To THE GOVERNORS OF THE STATES. v, 414. FORD ED., ix, 238. (W., 1809.)

6298. ORDER, Preservation of.—Every man being at his ease, feels an interest in the preservation of order. and comes forth to preserve it at the first call of the magistrate. —To M. PICTET. iv, 463. (W., 1803.)

6299. ORDERS IN COUNCIL, Repeal of.—The British ministry has been driven from its Algerine system, not by any remaining morality in the people, but by their unsteadiness under severe trial. But whencesoever it comes, I rejoice in it as the triumph of our forbearing and yet persevering system. It will lighten your anxieties, take from cabal its most fertile ground of war, will give us peace during your time, and by the complete extinguishment of our public debt, open upon us the noblest application of revenue that has ever been exhibited by any nation.—To PRESIDENT MADISON. v, 443. (M.. April 1809.) See BERLIN DECREES and EMBARGO.

— OREGON.—See LEWIS AND CLARK EXPEDITION.

6300. ORLEANS (Duke of), Unprincipled.—The Duke d'Orleans is as unprincipled as his followers; sunk in debaucheries of the lowest kind, and incapable of quitting them for business; not a fool, yet not head enough to conduct anything.—To JOHN JAY. iii, 95. (P., 1789.)

* From a letter in regard to the employment of the militia.—EDITOR.

6301. ORLEANS (Duke of), Vicious.—
He is a man of moderate understanding, of no principle, absorbed in low vice, and incapable of extracting himself from the filth of that, to direct anything else. His name and his money, therefore, are mere tools in the hands of those who are duping him. Mirabeau is their chief.—To James Madison. iii, 98. Ford ed., v, 109. (P., 1789.)

6302. OSSIAN, Poems of.—These pieces have been and will, I think, during my life, continue to be to me the sources of daily and exalted pleasures. The tender and the sublime emotions of the mind were never before so wrought up by the human hand. I am not ashamed to own that I think this rude bard of the North the greatest poet that has ever existed. Merely for the pleasure of reading his works, I am become desirous of learning the language in which he sung, and of possessing his songs in their original form.—To Charles McPherson. i, 195. Ford ed., i, 413. (A., 1773.)

6303. ——— ———. If not ancient, it is equal to the best morsels of antiquity.—To Marquis Lafayette. vii, 326. Ford ed., x, 282. (M., 1823.)

6304. OSTENTATION, Good deeds and.
—What is proposed, though but an act of duty, may be perverted into one of ostentation, but malice will always find bad motives for good actions. Shall we therefore never do good?—To President Madison. v, 524. (M., 1810.)

— OUTACITE, Indian Chief.—See Indians.

— PACIFIC, Exploration of the.—See Lewis and Clark Expedition.

6305. PAGE (John), Jefferson and.—It had given me much pain, that the zeal of our respective friends should ever have placed you and me in the situation of competitors.* I was comforted, however, with the reflection, that it was their competition, not ours, and that the difference of the numbers which decided between us, was too insignificant to give to you a pain, or me a pleasure, had our dispositions towards each other been such as to admit those sensations.—To John Page. i, 210. Ford ed., ii, 187. (1779.)

6306. PAGE (John), Tribute to.—I have known Mr. Page from the time we were boys and classmates together, and love him as a brother, but I have always known him the worst judge of men existing. He has fallen a sacrifice to the ease with which he gives his confidence to those who deserve it not. * * * I am very anxious to do something useful for him; and so universally is he esteemed in this country [Virginia], that no man's promotion would be more generally approved. He has but an enemy in the world.—To Albert Gallatin. Ford ed., viii, 85. (M., 1801.)

6307. PAIN, Pleasure vs.—We have no rose without its thorn; no pleasure without alloy. It is the law of our existence; and we must acquiesce. It is the condition annexed to all our pleasures, not by us who receive, but by Him who gives them.—To Mrs. Cosway. ii, 41. Ford ed., iv, 321. (P., 1786.)

6308. ——— ———. I do not agree that an age of pleasure is no compensation for a mo-

* For the governorship of Virginia. On the first vote, the figures were: Jefferson, 55; Nelson, 32; and Page, 38. The second vote resulted: Jefferson, 67, Page 61.—Editor.

ment of pain.—To John Adams. vii, 26. (M., 1816.)

6309. PAIN, Security against.—The most effectual means of being secure against pain is to retire within ourselves and to suffice for our own happiness. Those which depend on ourselves are the only pleasures a wise man will count on; for nothing is ours which another may deprive us of. Hence the inestimable value of intellectual pleasures. Ever in our power, always leading us to something new, never cloying, we ride serene and sublime above the concerns of this mortal world, contemplating truth and nature, matter and motion, the laws which bind up their existence, and that Eternal Being who made and bound them up by those laws.—To Mrs. Cosway. ii, 37. Ford ed., iv, 317. (P., 1786.)

6310. PAINE (Thomas), Common Sense.—Paine's Common Sense electrified us.—Autobiography. i, 91. Ford ed., i, 127. (1821.)

6311. PAINE (Thomas), Correspondence.—I have been in daily intention of answering your letters, fully and confidentially; but you know, such a correspondence between you and me cannot pass through the post, nor even by the couriers of ambassadors.—To Thomas Paine. ii, 545. (P., 1788.)

6312. PAINE (Thomas), Gunboats.—The model of a contrivance for making one gunboat do nearly double execution has all the ingenuity and simplicity which generally mark your inventions. I am not nautical enough to judge whether two guns may be too heavy for the bow of a gunboat, or whether any other objection will countervail the advantage it offers, and which I see visibly enough. I send it to the Secretary of the Navy, within whose department it lies to try and to judge it.—To Thomas Paine. v, 189. Ford ed., ix, 136. (M., 1807.)

6313. PAINE (Thomas), Honors to.—You expressed a wish to get a passage to this country in a public vessel. Mr. Dawson is charged with orders to the captain of the Maryland, a sloop of war, to receive and accommodate you.—To Thomas Paine. iv, 371. Ford ed., viii, 18. (W., March 1801.)

6314. ——— ———. I am in hopes you will [on your return from France] find us returned generally to sentiments worthy of former times. In these it will be your glory to have steadily labored, and with as much effect as any man living.—To Thomas Paine. iv, 371. Ford ed., viii, 19. (W., March 1801.)

6315. PAINE (Thomas), Iron bridge.—Mr. Paine (Common Sense) is in Paris on his way to England. He has brought the model of an iron bridge, with which he supposes a single arch of four hundred feet, may be made.—To B. Vaughan. ii, 166. (P., 1787.)

6316. ——— ———. I feel myself interested in your bridge, and it is with great pleasure that I learn that the execution of the arch of experiment exceeds your expectation. In your former letter, you mention that instead of arranging your tubes and bolts as ordinates to the chord of the arch, you had reverted to your first idea, of arranging them in the direction of the radii. I am sure it will gain both in beauty and strength. It is true that the divergence of those radii recurs as a difficulty, in getting the rails upon the bolts; but I thought this removed by the answer you first gave me, when I suggested that difficulty, to wit, that you should place the rails first, and drive the bolts through them, and not, as I had imagined, place the bolts first, and put the rails on them. I must doubt whether what you now suggest, will be as good as your first idea; to wit, to have every rail split into two pieces longitudinally, so that there shall be but the halves of the holes in each, and then to clamp the two halves together. The solidity of this method cannot be equal to that of the solid rail, and it increases the suspicious part of the whole machine, which, in a first experiment, ought to be rendered as few as possible. But of all this, the practical iron men are much better judges than we theorists. You hesitate between the catenary and portion of a circle. I have lately received from Italy, a treatise on the equilibrium of arches by the Abbé Mascheroni. * * * I find that the conclusions of his demonstrations are that every part of the catenary is in perfect equilibrium. It is a great point, then, in a new experiment, to adopt the sole arch, where the pressure will be equally borne by every point of it. If any one point is pushed with accumulated pressure, it will introduce a danger foreign to the essential part of the plan. The difficulty you suggest is, that the rails being all in catenaries, the tubes must be of different lengths, as these approach nearer, or recede farther from each other, and therefore, you recur to the portions of concentric circles, which are equi-distant in all their parts. But I would rather propose that you make your middle rail an exact catenary, and the interior and exterior rails parallels to that. It is true they will not be exact catenaries, but they will depart very little from it; much less than portions of circles will.—To THOMAS PAINE. ii, 546. (P., 1788.)

6317. —— ——. To say another word about the catenary arch, without caring about mathematical demonstrations, its nature proves it to be in equilibrio in every point. It is the arch formed by a string fixed at both ends, and swaying loose in all the intermediate points. Thus at liberty, they must finally take that position, wherein every one will be equally pressed; for if any one was more pressed than the neighboring point, it would give way, from the flexibility of the matter of the string.—To THOMAS PAINE. ii, 547. (P., 1788.)

6318. —— ——. Mr. Paine, the author of "Common Sense", has invented an iron bridge, which promises to be cheaper by a great deal than stone, and to admit of a much greater arch. He supposes it may be ventured for an arch of five hundred feet. He has obtained a patent for it in England, and is now executing the first experiment with an arch of between ninety and one hundred feet.—To DR. WILLARD. iii, 16. (P., 1789.)

6319. —— ——. I congratulate you sincerely on the success of your bridge. I was sure of it before from theory; yet one likes to be assured from practice also.—To THOMAS PAINE. iii, 40. (P., 1789.)

6320. PAINE (Thomas), Planing Machine.—How has your planing machine answered? Has it been tried and persevered in by any workmen?—To THOMAS PAINE. iv, 582. FORD ED., viii, 360. (W., 1805.)

6321. PAINE (Thomas), Republicanism.—A host of writers have risen in favor of Paine, and prove that in this quarter [Philadelphia], at least, the spirit of republicanism is sound. The contrary spirit of the high officers

of government is more understood than I expected.—To JAMES MONROE. iii, 268. FORD ED., v, 352. (Pa., 1791.)

6322. —— ——. Would you believe it possible that, in this country, there should be high and important characters who need your lessons in republicanism, and who do not heed them? It is but too true that we have a sect preaching up and panting after an English constitution of king, lords, and commons, and whose heads are itching for crowns, coronets, and mitres. But our people * * * are firm and unanimous in their principles of republicanism, and there is no better proof of it than that they love what you write and read it with delight. The printers season every newspaper with extracts from your last, as they did before from your first part of the Rights of Man.—To THOMAS PAINE. FORD ED., vi, 87. (Pa., June 1792.)

6323. PAINE (Thomas), Respect for.—You have certainly misconceived what you deem shyness. Of that I have not had a thought towards you, but on the contrary have openly maintained in conversation the duty of showing our respect to you, and of defying federal calumny in this as in other cases, by doing what is right. As to fearing it, if I ever could have been weak enough for that, they have taken care to cure me of it thoroughly.—To THOMAS PAINE. FORD ED., viii, 189. (W., 1803.)

6324. PAINE (Thomas), Rewards to.—The Assembly of New York have made Paine, the author of "Common Sense", a present of a farm. Could you prevail on our Assembly to do something for him? I think their quota of what ought to be given him would be 2000 guineas, or an inheritance within 100 guineas a year. It would be peculiarly magnanimous in them to do it; because it would show that no particular and smaller passion has suppressed the grateful impressions which his services have made on our minds.—To JAMES MADISON. FORD ED., iii, 499. (Pa., May 1784.)

6325. —— ——. I still hope something will be done for Paine. He richly deserves it; and it will give a character of littleness to our State if they suffer themselves to be restrained from the compensation due for his services by the paltry consideration that he opposed our right to the Western country. Who was there out of Virginia who did not oppose it? Place this circumstance in one scale, and the effect of his writings produced in uniting us in independence in the other, and say which preponderates. Have we gained more by his advocacy of independence than we lost by his opposition to our territorial right? Pay him the balance only.—To JAMES MADISON. FORD ED., iv, 17. (P., Dec. 1784.)

6326. PAINE (Thomas), Rights of Man.—The "Rights of Man" would bring England itself to reason and revolution, if it was permitted to be read there. However, the same things will be said in milder forms, will make their way among the people, and you must reform at last.—To BENJAMIN VAUGHAN. FORD ED., v, 334. (Pa., 1791.)

6327. —— ——. The "Rights of Man" has been much read in America with avidity and pleasure. A writer under the signature of "Publicola" has attacked it. A host of champions entered the arena immediately in your defence. The discussion excited the public attention, recalled it to the "Defence of the American Constitutions", and the "Discourses on Davila ", which it had kindly passed over without censure in the moment, and very general expressions of their sense have been now drawn forth ; and I thank God that they appear firm in their republicanism, notwithstanding the contrary hopes and assertions of a sect here, high in names, but small in numbers. These had flattered themselves that the silence of the people under the " Defence " and " Davila " was a symptom of their conversion to the doctrine of king, lords, and commons. They are checked at least by your pamphlet, and the people confirmed in their good old faith.—To THOMAS PAINE. iii, 278. FORD ED., v, 367. (Pa., 1791.)

6328. PAINE (Thomas), Thinker.— Paine thought more than he read.—To JOHN CARTWRIGHT. vii, 355. (M., 1824.)

6329. PALEONTOLOGY, Bones.— General Clark has employed ten laborers several weeks at the Big-bone Lick, and has shipped the result * * * for this place [Washington]. He has sent, 1st, of the Mammoth, as he calls it, frontals, jaw-bones, tusks, teeth, ribs, a thigh, and a leg, and some bones of the paw ; 2d, of what he calls the Elephant, a jaw-bone, tusks, teeth, ribs ; 3d, of something of the Buffalo species, a head and some other bones unknown. My intention, in having this research thoroughly made, was to procure for the [Philosophical] Society as complete a supplement to what is already possessed as that lick can furnish at this day, and to serve them first with whatever they wish to possess of it. There are a tusk and a femur which General Clark procured particularly at my request, for a special kind of Cabinet I have at Monticello. But the great mass of the collection are mere duplicates of what you possess at Philadelphia, of which I would wish to make a donation to the National Institute of France, which I believe has scarcely any specimens of the remains of these animals. But how make the selection without the danger of sending away something which might be useful to our own Society? Indeed, my friend, you must give a week to this object, * * * examine these bones, and set apart what you would wish for the Society.— To DR. WISTAR. v, 219. (W., 1807.)

6330. PALEONTOLOGY, Mammoth.— It is well known, that on the Ohio, and in many parts of America further north, tusks, grinders, and skeletons of unparalleled magnitude, are found in great numbers, some lying on the surface of the earth, and some a little below it. A Mr. Stanley, taken prisoner near the mouth of the Tennessee, relates, that after being transferred through several tribes, from one to another, he was at length carried over the mountains west of the Missouri to a river which runs westwardly ; that these bones abounded there, and that the natives described to him the animal to which they belonged as still existing in the northern parts of their country ; from which description he judged it to be an elephant. Bones of the same kind have been lately found, some feet below the surface of the earth, in salines opened on the North Holston, a branch of the Tennessee, about the latitude of 36½° north. From the accounts published in Europe, I suppose it to be decided that these are of the same kind with those found in Siberia. * * * It is remarkable that the tusks and skeletons have been ascribed by the naturalists of Europe to the elephant, while the grinders have been given to the hippopotamus, or river horse. Yet it is acknowledged, that the tusks and skeletons are much larger than those of the elephant, and

the grinders many times greater than those of the hippopotamus, and essentially different in form. * * * We must agree, then, that these remains belong to each other, that they are of one and the same animal, that this was not a hippopotamus, because the hippopotamus had no tusks, nor such a frame, and because the grinders differ in their size as well as in the number and form of their points. That this was not an elephant, I think ascertained by proofs equally decisive. * * * I have never heard an instance, and suppose there has been none, of the grinder of an elephant being found in America. From the known temperature and constitution of the elephant, he could never have existed in those regions where the remains of the mammoth have been found. The elephant is a native only of the torrid zone and its vicinities. * * * No bones of the mammoth, have ever been found farther south than the salines of Holston, and they have been found as far north as the Arctic circle. * * * For my own part, I find it easier to believe that an animal may have existed, resembling the elephant in his tusks, and general anatomy, while his nature was in other respects extremely different. From the 30th degree of south latitude to the 30th degree of north, are nearly the limits which nature has fixed for the existence and multiplication of the elephant known to us. Proceeding thence northwardly to 36½° degrees, we enter those assigned to the mammoth. The farther we advance north, the more their vestiges multiply as far as the earth has been explored in that direction ; and it is as probable as otherwise, that this progression continues to the pole itself, if land extends so far. The centre of the frozen zone, then, may be the acme of their vigor, as that of the torrid is of the elephant. Thus nature seems to have drawn a belt of separation between these two tremendous animals, whose breadth, indeed, is not precisely known, though at present we may suppose it about 6½ degrees of latitude ; to have assigned to the elephant the regions south of these confines, and those north to the mammoth, founding the constitution of the one in the extreme of heat, and that of the other in the extreme of cold. * * * But to whatever animal we ascribe these remains, it is certain that such a one has existed in America, and that it has been the largest of all terrestrial beings.—NOTES ON VIRGINIA. viii, 286. FORD ED., iii, 134. (1782.)

6331. ——— ———. I have heard of the discovery of some large bones, supposed to be of the mammoth, at about thirty or forty miles distant from you ; and among the bones found, are said to be some which we have never been able to procure. The first interesting question is, whether they are the bones of the mammoth? The second, what are the particular bones, and could I possibly procure them? * * * If they are to be bought I will gladly pay for them whatever you shall agree to as reasonable.—To ROBERT R. LIVINGSTON. iv, 337. FORD ED., vii, 463. (W., 1800.)

— PANAMA CANAL.—See CANAL.

6332. PANICS, Evils of.— Buildings and other improvements are suspended. Workmen turned adrift. Country produce is not to be sold at any price ; because even substantial merchants, who never meddled with paper, cannot tell how many of their debtors have meddled and may fail ; consequently they are afraid to make any new money arrangements till they shall know how they stand.—To T. M. RANDOLPH. FORD ED., v, 509. (Pa., April 1792.)

6333. PANICS, Financial.—I learn with real concern the calamities which are fallen on New York, and which must fall on Philadelphia also. No man of reflection who had ever attended to the South Sea bubble, in England, or that of Law in France, and who applied the lessons of the past to the present time, could fail to foresee the issue though he might not calculate the moment at which it would happen. The evidences of the public debt are solid and sacred. I presume there is not a man in the United States who would not part with his last shilling to pay them. But all that stuff called scrip, of whatever description, was folly or roguery, and under a resemblance to genuine public paper, it buoyed itself up to a par with that. It has given a severe lesson; yet such is the public gullibility in the hands of cunning and unprincipled men, that it is doomed by nature to receive these lessons once in an age at least. Happy if they now come about and get back into the tract of plain unsophisticated common sense which they ought never to have been decoyed from.—To Francis Eppes. Ford ed., v, 507. (Pa., April 1792.) See Banks.

6334. PANICS, Losses by.—It is computed there is a dead loss at New York of about five millions of dollars, which is reckoned the value of all the buildings of the city: so that if the whole town had been burned to the ground it would have been just the measure of the present calamity, supposing goods to have been saved. In Boston, the dead loss is about a million of dollars. * * * It is conjectured that the loss in Philadelphia will be about equal to that of Boston.—To T. M. Randolph. Ford ed., v, 509. (1792.)

6335. —— ——. The losses on this occasion would support a war such as we now have on hand, five or six years. Thus you will see that the calamity has been greater in proportion than that of the South Sea in England, or Law in France.—To William Short. Ford ed., v, 510. (Pa., April 1792.)

6336. PANICS, Paper money and.—At length our paper bubble is burst. The failure of Duer, in New York, soon brought on others, and these still more, like nine pins knocking one another down, till at that place the bankruptcy is become general. Every man concerned in paper being broke, and most of the tradesmen and farmers, who had been laying down money, having been tempted by these speculators to lend it to them at an interest of from 3 to 6 per cent. a month, have lost the whole.—To T. M. Randolph. Ford ed., v, 509. (Pa., 1792.) See Paper Money.

6337. —— ——. The paper debt of the United States is scarcely at par. Bank stock is at 25 per cent. It was once upwards of 300 per cent.—To William Short. Ford ed., v, 510. (Pa., April 1792.)

6338. PANICS, Stocks and.—What a loss you would have suffered if we had laid out your paper for bank stock? * * * Though it would have been improper for me to have given at any time, an opinion on the subject of stocks to Mr. Brown, or any man dealing in them, yet I have been unable to refrain from interposing for you on the present occasion. I found that your stock stood so as not to charge Donald & Co. I know Brown to be a good man, but to have dealt in paper, I did not know how far he was engaged. I knew that good men might sometimes avail themselves of the property of others in their power, to help themselves out of a present difficulty in

an honest but delusive confidence that they will be able to repay; that the best men and those whose transactions stand all in an advantageous form, may fail by the failure of others. Under the impulse, therefore, of the general panic, I ventured to enter a caveat in the treasury office against permitting the transfer of any stock standing in your name, or in any other for your use. This was on the 19th of April. I knew your stock had not been transferred before March 31, and that from that time to this, Mr. Brown had not been in Virginia, so as to give me a reasonable confidence that it had not been transferred between the 1st and 19th inst. If so, it is safe. But it would be still safer invested in Ned Carter's lands at five dollars the acre.—To William Short. Ford ed., v, 510. (Pa., April 1792.) See Speculation.

6339. PAPER AND CIVILIZATION.—This article, the creature of art, and but latterly so comparatively, is now interwoven so much into the conveniences and occupations of men, as to have become one of the necessaries of civilized life.—To Robert R. Livingston. Ford ed., vii, 445. (Pa., 1800.)

6340. PAPER MONEY, Abuses.—Paper is liable to be abused, has been, is, and forever will be abused, in every country in which it is permitted.—To J. W. Eppes. vi, 246. Ford ed., ix, 416. (M., Nov. 1813.)

6341. —— ——. Paper is already at a term of abuse in these States, which has never been reached by any other nation, France excepted, whose dreadful catastrophe should be a warning against the instrument which produced it.—To J. W. Eppes. vi, 246. Ford ed., ix, 416. (M., Nov. 1813.)

6342. PAPER MONEY, A cheat.—Paper money was a cheat. Tobacco was the counter-cheat. Everyone is justifiable in rejecting both except so far as his contracts bind him.—To Francis Eppes. Ford ed., v, 212. (N.Y., 1790.)

6343. PAPER MONEY, Continental.—When I speak comparatively of the paper emission of the old Congress and the present banks, let it not be imagined that I cover them under the same mantle. The object of the former was a holy one; for if ever there was a holy war it was that which saved our liberties and gave us independence. The object of the latter is to enrich swindlers at the expense of the honest and industrious part of the nation.—To J. W. Eppes. vi, 246. Ford ed., ix, 416. (M., Nov. 1813.)

6344. —— ——. The errors of that day* cannot be recalled. The evils they have engendered are now upon us, and the question is how we are to get out of them? Shall we build an altar to the old money of the Revolution, which ruined individuals but saved the Republic, and burn on that all the bank charters, present and future, and their notes with them? For these are to ruin both Republic and individuals. This cannot be done. The mania is too strong. It has seized, by its delusions and corruptions, all

* When the United States Bank was founded.— Editor.

the members of our governments, general, special and individual.—To JOHN ADAMS. vi, 305. (M., Jan. 1814.)

6345. PAPER MONEY, Contraction.—I have been endeavoring to persuade a friend in our Legislature to try and save this State [Virginia] from the general ruin by timely interference. I propose to him, first, to prohibit instantly, all foreign paper. Secondly, to give our banks six months to call in all their five-dollar bills (the lowest we allow); another six months to call in their ten-dollar notes, and six months more to call in all below fifty dollars. This would produce so gradual a diminution of medium, as not to shock contracts already made—would leave finally, bills of such size as would be called for only in transactions between merchant and merchant, and ensure a metallic circulation for those of the mass of citizens. But it will not be done. You might as well, with the sailors, whistle to the wind, as suggest precautions against having too much money. We must bend, then, before the gale, and try to hold fast ourselves by some plank of the wreck. God send us all a safe deliverance.— To JOHN ADAMS. vi, 306. (M., Jan. 1814.)

6346. —— ——. I had been in hopes that good old Virginia, not yet so far embarked as her northern sisters, would have set the example this winter, of beginning the process of cure, by passing a law that, after a certain time, suppose of six months, no bank bill of less than ten dollars should be permitted. That after some reasonable term, there should be none less than twenty dollars, and so on, until those only should be left in circulation whose size would be above the common transactions of any but merchants. This would ensure us an ordinary circulation of metallic money, and would reduce the quantum of paper within the bounds of moderate mischief. And it is the only way in which the reduction can be made without a shock to private fortunes. A sudden stop to this trash, either by law or its own worthlessness, would produce confusion and ruin. Yet this will happen by its own extinction if left to itself. Whereas, by a salutary interposition of the Legislature, it may be withdrawn insensibly and safely. Such a mode of doing it, too, would give less alarm to the bankholders, the discreet part of whom must wish to see themselves secured by circumscription. It might be asked what we should do for change? The banks must provide it, first to pay off their five-dollar bills, next their ten-dollar bills and so on, and they ought to provide it to lessen the evils of their institution. But I now give up all hope. After producing the same revolutions in private fortunes as the old Continental paper did, it will die like that, adding a total incapacity to raise resources for the war.—To JOSEPH C. CABELL. vi, 300. (M., Jan. 1814.)

6347. —— ——. Let us be allured by no projects of banks, public or private, or ephemeral expedients, which, enabling us to gasp and flounder a little longer, only in-

crease, by protracting the agonies of death.— To JAMES MONROE. vi, 395. FORD ED., ix, 492. (M., 1814.)

6348. —— ——. Different persons, doubtless, will devise different schemes of relief. One would be to suppress instantly the currency of all paper not issued under the authority of our own State or of the General Government; to interdict after a few months the circulation of all bills of five dollars and under; after a few months more, all of ten dollars and under; after other terms, those of twenty, fifty, and so on to one hundred dollars, which last, if any must be left in circulation, should be the lowest denomination. These might be a convenience in mercantile transactions and transmissions, and would be excluded by their size from ordinary circulation. But the disease may be too pressing to await such a remedy. With the Legislature I cheerfully leave it to apply this medicine, or no medicine at all. I am sure their intentions are faithful; and embarked in the same bottom, I am willing to swim or sink with my fellow citizens. If the latter is their choice, I will go down with them without a murmur. But my exhortation would rather be "not to give up the ship".—To CHARLES YANCEY. vi, 516. FORD ED., x, 3. (M., Jan. 1816.)

6349. —— ——. That in the present state of the circulation the banks should resume payments in specie, would require their vaults to be like the widow's cruse. The thing to be aimed at is, that the excesses of their emissions should be withdrawn gradually, but as speedily, too, as is practicable, without so much alarm as to bring on the crisis dreaded.—To CHARLES YANCEY. vi, 516. FORD ED., x, 3. (M., Jan. 1816.)

6350. PAPER MONEY, Convenience of. —There is, indeed, a convenience in paper; its easy transmission from one place to another. But this may be mainly supplied by bills of exchange, so as to prevent any great displacement of actual coin. Two places trading together balance their dealings, for the most part, by their mutual supplies, and the debtor individuals of either may, instead of cash, remit the bills of those who are creditor in the same dealings; or may obtain them through some third place with which both have dealings. The cases would be rare where such bills could not be obtained, either directly or circuitously, and too unimportant to the nation to overweigh the train of evils flowing from paper circulation.—To J. W. EPPES. vi, 237. FORD ED., ix, 409. (M., Nov. 1813.)

6351. PAPER MONEY, A deluge of.—I told the President [Washington] that a system had there [the Treasury Department] been contrived, for deluging the States with paper money instead of gold and silver, for withdrawing our citizens from the pursuits of commerce, manufactures, buildings, and other branches of useful industry, to occupy themselves and their capitals in a species of gambling, destructive of morality, and which had introduced its poison into the government itself.—THE ANAS. ix, 104. FORD ED., i, 177. (Feb. 1792.)

6352. PAPER MONEY, Depreciation.— The first symptom of the depreciation of our present paper money, was that of silver dollars selling at six shillings, which had before been worth but five shillings and nine pence. The Assembly thereupon raised them by law to six shillings.—NOTES ON VIRGINIA. viii, 410. FORD ED., iii, 275. (1782.)

6353. ———— ————. The acknowledged depreciation of the paper circulation of England, with the known laws of its rapid progression to bankruptcy, will leave that nation shortly without revenue.—To CLEMENT CAINE. vi, 14. FORD ED., ix, 330. (M., Sep. 1811.)

6354. ———— ————. The rapid rise in the nominal price of land and labor (while war and blockade should produce a fall) proves the progressive state of the depreciation of our medium.—To THOMAS LAW. FORD ED., ix, 433. (M., 1813.)

6355. PAPER MONEY, Economy of.— The trifling economy of paper, as a cheaper medium, or its convenience for transmission, weighs nothing in opposition to the advantages of the precious metals.—To J. W. EPPES. vi, 246. FORD ED., ix, 416. (M., Nov. 1813.)

6356. PAPER MONEY, English assignats.— England is emitting assignats also, that is to say exchequer bills, to the amount of five millions English, or one hundred and twenty-five millions French; and these are not founded on land as the French assignats are, but on pins, thread, buckles, hops, and whatever else you will pawn in the exchequer of double the estimated value. But we all know that five millions of such stuff forced for sale on the market of London, where there will be neither cash nor credit, will not pay storage. This paper must rest, then, ultimately on the credit of the nation as the rest of their public paper does, and will sink with that.—To JAMES MONROE. iv, 7. FORD ED., vi, 322. (Pa., June 1793.)

6357. ———— ————. England, too, is issuing her paper, not founded, like the assignats, on land, but on pawns of thread, ribbons, buckles, &c. They will soon learn the science of depreciation, and their whole paper system vanish into nothing, on which it is bottomed. —To DR. GILMER. iv, 6. FORD ED., vi, 325. (Pa., 1793.)

6358. ———— ————. The English are trying to stop the torrent of bankruptcies by an emission of five millions of exchequer bills, loaned on the pawn-broking plan, consequently much inferior to the assignats in value. But the paper will sink to an immediate level with their other public paper, and consequently can only complete the ruin of those who take it from the government at par, and on a pledge of pins, buckles, &c., of double value, which will not sell so as to

pay storage in a country where there is no specie, and we may say no paper of confidence. Every letter which comes expresses a firm belief that the whole paper system will now vanish into that nothing on which it is bottomed. For even the public faith is nothing, as the mass of paper bottomed on it is known to be beyond its possible redemption. I hope this will be a wholesome lesson to our future Legislature.—To JAMES MADISON. iv, 8. FORD ED., vi, 326. (June 1793.)

6359. PAPER MONEY, Evils of.— Stock dealers and banking companies, by the aid of a paper system, are enriching themselves to the ruin of our country, and swaying the government by their possession of the printing presses, which their wealth commands, and by other means, not always honorable to the character of our countrymen.—To ARTHUR CAMPBELL. iv, 197. FORD ED., vii, 170. (M., 1797.)

6360. PAPER MONEY, Farmers and.— The redundancy of paper in the cities is palpably a tax on the distant farmer.—To JAMES MADISON. FORD ED., vi, 404. (Pa., 1793.)

6361. PAPER MONEY, Fluctuations in.— The long succession of years of stunted crops, of reduced prices, the general prostration of the farming business, under levies for the support of manufactures, &c., with the calamitous fluctuations of value in our paper medium, have kept agriculture in a state of abject depression, which has peopled the Western States by silently breaking up those on the Atlantic, and glutted the land market, while it drew off its bidders. In such a state of things, property has lost its character of being a resource for debts. Highland, in Bedford, which, in the days of our plethory, sold readily for from fifty to one hundred dollars the acre (and such sales were many then), would not now sell for more than from ten to twenty dollars, or one-quarter to one-fifth of its former price.—To JAMES MADISON. vii, 434. FORD ED., x, 377. (M., February 1826.)

6362. PAPER MONEY, Gambling in.— What do you think of this scrippomany? Ships are lying idle at the wharves, buildings are stopped, capital withdrawn from commerce, manufactures, arts and agriculture, to be employed in gambling, and the tide of prosperity almost unparalleled in any country, is arrested in its course, and suppressed by the rage of getting rich in a day. No mortal can tell where this will stop; for the spirit of gaming, when once it has seized a subject, is incurable. The tailor who has made thousands in one day, though he has lost them the next, can never again be content with the slow and moderate earnings of his needle. Nothing can exceed the public felicity, if our papers are to be believed, because our papers are under the orders of the scripmen. I imagine, however, we shall hear that all our cash has quitted the extremities of the nation, and accumulated here [Philadelphia] ; that produce and property fall to half price there, and the same things rise to double price here ; that the cash accumulated and stagnated here, as soon as the bank paper gets out, will find its vent into foreign countries ; and instead of this solid medium, which we might have kept for nothing, we shall have a paper one, for the use of which we are to pay these gamesters fifteen per cent. per annum, as they say.—To E. RUTLEDGE. iii, 285. FORD ED.. v, 375. (Pa., 1791.)

6363. ————. Our public credit is good, but the abundance of paper has produced a spirit of gambling in the funds, which has laid up our ships at the wharves, as too slow instruments of profit, and has even disarmed the hand of the tailor of his needle and thimble. They say the evil will cure itself. I wish it may ; but I have rarely seen a gamester cured, even by the disasters of his vocation.—To GOUVERNEUR MORRIS. iii, 290. (Pa., 1791.) See SPECULATION.

6364. **PAPER MONEY, Manufactures.** —New schemes are on foot for bringing more paper to market by encouraging great manufacturing companies to form, and their actions, or paper-shares, to be transferable as bank stock.—To JAMES MONROE. FORD ED., v, 320. (Pa., 1791.)

6365. **PAPER MONEY, Mississippi scheme.**—The Mississippi scheme, it is well known, ended in France in the bankruptcy of the public treasury, the crash of thousands and thousands of private fortunes, and scenes of desolation and distress equal to those of an invading army, burning and laying waste all before it.—To J. W. EPPES. vi. 239. FORD ED., ix, 411. (M., Nov. 1813.)

6366. **PAPER MONEY, Perilous.**—Paper money would be perilous even to the paper men.—To JOHN TAYLOR. iv, 259. FORD ED., vii, 310. (M., 1798.)

6367. **PAPER MONEY, Plan to reduce.** —The plethora of circulating medium which raised the prices of everything to several times their ordinary and standard value, in which state of things many and heavy debts were contracted ; and the sudden withdrawing too great a proportion of that medium, and reduction of prices far below that standard, constitute the disease under which we are now laboring, and which must end in a general revolution of property, if some remedy is not applied. That remedy is clearly a gradual reduction of the medium to its standard level, that is to say, to the level which a metallic medium will always find for itself, so as to be in *equilibrio* with that of the nations with which we have commerce. To effect this : Let the whole of the present paper medium be suspended in its circulation after a certain and not distant day. Ascertain by proper inquiry the greatest sum of it which has at any one time been in actual circulation. Take a certain term of years for its gradual reduction. Suppose it to be five years ; then let the solvent banks issue 5-6 of that amount in new notes, to be attested by a public officer. as a security that neither more nor less is issued, and to be given out in exchange

for the suspended notes, and the surplus in discount. Let 1-5 of these notes bear on their face that the bank will discharge them with specie at the end of one year : another 5th at the end of two years : a third 5th at the end of three years ; and so of the 4th and 5th. They will be sure to be brought in at their respective periods of redemption. Make it a high offense to receive or pass within this State a note of any other. There is little doubt that our banks will agree readily to this operation : if they refuse, declare their charters forfeited by their former irregularities, and give summary process against them for the suspended notes. The Bank of the United States will probably concur also ; if not, shut their doors and join the other States in respectful, but firm applications to Congress, to concur in constituting a tribunal (a special convention, *e. g.*) for settling amicably the question of their right to institute a bank, and that also of the States to do the same. A stay-law for the suspension of executions, and their discharge at five annual instalments, should be accommodated to these measures. Interdict forever, to both the State and National Governments, the power of establishing any paper bank ; for without this interdiction. we shall have the same ebbs and flows of medium, and the same revolutions of property to go through every twenty or thirty years. In this way the value of property, keeping pace nearly with the sum of circulating medium, will descend gradually to its proper level, at the rate of about 1-5 every year, the sacrifices of what shall be sold for payment of the first instalments of debts will be moderate, and time will be given for economy and industry to come in aid of those subsequent. Certainly no nation ever before abandoned to the avarice and jugglings of private individuals to regulate according to their own interests, the quantum of circulating medium for the nation ; to inflate, by deluges of paper, the nominal prices of property. and then to buy up that property at 1s. in the pound, having first withdrawn the floating medium which might endanger a competition in purchase. Yet this is what has been done, and will be done, unless stayed by the protecting hand of the Legislature. The evil has been produced by the error of their sanction of this ruinous machinery of banks ; and justice. wisdom, duty, all require that they should interpose and arrest it before the schemes of plunder and spoliation desolate the country. It is believed that Harpies are already hoarding their money to commence these scenes on the separation of the Legislature ; and we know that lands have been already sold under the hammer for less than a year's rent.—To W. C. RIVES. vii, 145. FORD ED., x, 150. (M., Nov. 1819.)

6368. **PAPER MONEY, Poverty.**—Paper is poverty. It is only the ghost of money, and not money itself.—To E. CARRINGTON. ii, 405. FORD ED., v, 21. (P., 1788.)

6369. **PAPER MONEY, Prices and.**— All the imported commodities are raised about fifty per cent. by the depreciation of the money. Tobacco shares the rise, because it has no competition abroad. Wheat has been extravagantly high from other causes. When these cease, it must fall to its ancient nominal price, notwithstanding the depreciation of that. because it must contend at market with foreign wheats. Lands have risen within the notice of the papers, and as far out as that can influence. They have not risen at all here [Virginia]. On the contrary, they are lower than they were twenty years ago.—To JAMES MONROE. iv, 141. FORD ED., vii, 80. (M., June 1796.) See PRICE.

6370. PAPER MONEY, Private property and.—Money is leaving the remoter parts of the Union, and flowing to this place [Philadelphia] to purchase paper; and here, a paper medium supplying its place, it is shipped off in exchange for luxuries. The value of property is necessarily falling in the places left bare of money. In Virginia, for instance, property has fallen 25 per cent. in the last twelve months.—To WILLIAM SHORT. iii. 343. FORD ED., v, 459. (Pa., March 1792.)

6371. —— ——. That paper money has some advantages, is admitted. But that its abuses also are inevitable, and, by breaking up the measure of value, makes a lottery of all private property, cannot be denied. Shall we ever be able to put a constitutional veto on it?—To DR. JOSEPHUS B. STUART. vii, 65. (M., May 1817.)

6372. PAPER MONEY, Redeeming taxes.—M. Say will be surprised to find, that forty years after the development of sound financial principles by Adam Smith and the Economists, and a dozen years after he has given them to us in a corrected, terse, and lucid form, there should be so much ignorance of them in our country; that instead of funding issues of paper on the hypothecation of specific redeeming taxes (the only method of anticipating, in a time of war, the resources of times of peace, tested by the experience of nations), we are trusting to the tricks of jugglers on the cards, to the illusions of banking schemes for the resources of the war, and for the cure of colic to inflations of more wind.—To M. CORREA. vi, 406. (M., 1814.)

6373. PAPER MONEY, Ruin by.—Not Quixotic enough to attempt to reason Bedlam to rights, my anxieties are turned to the most practicable means of withdrawing us from the ruin into which we have run. Two hundred millions of paper in the hands of the people (and less cannot be from the employment of a banking capital known to exceed one hundred millions), is a fearful tax to fall at haphazard on their heads. The debt which purchased our Independence was but of eighty millions, of which twenty years of taxation had, in 1889, paid but the one-half. And what have we purchased with this tax of two hundred millions which we are to pay, by wholesale, but usury, swindling, and new forms of demoralization?—To CHARLES YANCEY. vi, 515. FORD ED., x, 2. (M., Jan. 1816.)

6374. PAPER MONEY, Silver for.—It is said that our paper is as good as silver, because we may have silver for it at the bank where it issues. This is not true. One, two, or three persons might have it; but a general application would soon exhaust their vaults, and leave a ruinous proportion of their paper in its intrinsic worthless form. It is a fallacious pretence, for another reason. The inhabitants

of the banking cities might obtain cash for their paper, as far as the cash of the vaults would hold out, but distance puts it out of the power of the country to do this. A farmer having a note of a Boston or Charleston bank, distant hundreds of miles, has no means of calling for the cash. And while these calls are impracticable for the country, the banks have no fear of their being made from the towns; because their inhabitants are mostly on their books, and there on sufferance only, and during good behavior.—To J. W. EPPES. vi, 243. FORD ED., ix, 414. (M., Nov. 1813.)

6375. PAPER MONEY, Specie and.—The unlimited emission of bank paper has banished all Great Britain's specie, and is now, by a depreciation acknowledged by her own statesmen, carrying her rapidly to bankruptcy, as it did France, as it did us, and will do us again, and every country permitting paper money to be circulated, other than that by public authority, rigorously limited to the just measure for circulation.—To JOHN W. EPPES. vi, 142. FORD ED., ix, 394. (M., June 1813.)

6376. —— ——. Revolutionary history has warned us of the probable moment when this baseless trash is to receive its fiat. Whenever so much of the precious metals shall have returned into the circulation as that every one can get some in exchange for his produce, paper, as in the Revolutionary war, will experience at once an universal rejection. When public opinion changes, it is with the rapidity of thought. Confidence is already on the totter, and every one now handles this paper as if playing at "Robin's Alive".—To CHARLES YANCEY. vi, 516. FORD ED., x, 3. (M., Jan. 1816.)

6377. PAPER MONEY, Treasury notes vs.—Even with the flood of private paper by which we were deluged, would the treasury have ventured its credit in bills of circulating size, as of fives or ten dollars, &c., they would have been greedily received by the people in preference to bank paper. But unhappily the towns of America were considered as the nation of America, the dispositions of the inhabitants of the former as those of the latter, and the treasury, for want of confidence in the country, delivered itself bound hand and foot to bold and bankrupt adventurers and pretenders to be moneyholders, whom it could have crushed at any moment. Even the last half-bold, half-timid threat of the Treasury showed at once that these jugglers were at the feet of the government. For it never was, and is not, any confidence in their frothy bubbles, but the want of all other medium, which induced, or now induces, the *country* people to take their paper; and at this moment, when nothing else is to be had, no man will receive it but to pass it away instantly, none for distant purposes.—To ALBERT GALLATIN. vi, 498. (M., Oct. 1815.) See NATIONAL CURRENCY.

6378. PAPER MONEY, Tricks with.—We are now taught to believe that legerdemain tricks upon paper can produce as solid wealth as hard labor in the earth. It is vain for common sense to urge that *nothing* can produce but *nothing;* that it is an idle dream to believe in a philosopher's stone which is to turn everything into gold, and to redeem man from the original sentence of his Maker, "in the sweat of his brow shall he eat his bread".—To CHARLES YANCEY.   vi, 515. FORD ED., x, 2.   (M., Jan. 1816.)

6379. PAPER MONEY, War and.—If this war continues, bank circulation must be suppressed, or the government shaken to its foundation by the weight of taxes, and impracticability to raise funds on them.—To J. W. EPPES.   vi, 204.   FORD ED., ix, 402.   (P.F., Sep. 1813.) See BANKS, DOLLAR, MONEY, and NATIONAL CURRENCY.

6380. PAPERS, Communication of.— With respect to [Executive] papers, there is certainly a public and a private side to our offices. To the former belong grants of land, patents for inventions, certain commissions, proclamations, and other papers patent in their nature. To the other belong mere executive proceedings. All nations have found it necessary, that for the advantageous conduct of their affairs, some of these proceedings, at least, should remain known to their executive functionary only. He, of course, from the nature of the case, must be the sole judge of which of them the public interests will permit publication. Hence, under our Constitution, in requests of papers, from the Legislative to the Executive branch, an exception is carefully expressed, as to those which he may deem the public welfare may require not to be disclosed. —To GEORGE HAY.   v, 97.   FORD ED., ix, 57. (W., 1807.)

6381. PAPERS, Confidential.—Understanding that it is thought important that a letter of Nov. 12, 1806, from General Wilkinson to myself, should be produced in evidence on the charges against Burr, * * * I send you a copy of it, omitting only certain passages, * * * entirely confidential, given for my information in the discharge of my executive functions, and which my duties and the public interest forbid me to make public.—To GEORGE HAY.   v, 190.   FORD ED., ix, 63.   (M., Sep. 1807.)

6382. ——— ———. You are certainly free to make use of any of the papers we put into Mr. Hay's hands, with a single reservation: to wit, some of them are expressed to be confidential, and others are of that kind which I always consider as confidential, conveying censure on particular individuals, and therefore never communicate them beyond the immediate executive circle.—To GENERAL WILKINSON.   v, 198.   FORD FD., ix, 141.   (M., 1807.)

6383. ——— ———. Papers containing censures on particular individuals. * * * I always deem confidential, and therefore cannot communicate, but for regularly official purposes, without a breach of trust.—To GEORGE HAY. v, 198.   FORD ED., ix, 141.   (M., 1807.)

6384. PAPERS, Executive.—Reserving the necessary right of the President of the United States to decide, independently of all other authority, what papers, coming to him as President, the public interests permit to be communicated, and to whom, I assure you of my readiness, under that restriction, voluntarily

to furnish on all occasions, whatever the purposes of justice may require.—To GEORGE HAY. v, 94.   FORD ED., ix, 55.   (W., June 1807.)

6385. ——— ———. When the request goes to "copies of the orders issued in relation to Colonel Burr, to the officers at Orleans, Natchez, &c., by the Secretaries of the War and Navy Departments", it seems to cover a correspondence of many months, with such a variety of officers, civil and military, all over the United States, as would amount to laying open the whole executive books. I have desired the Secretary of War to examine his official communications; and on a view of these, we may be able to judge, what can and ought to be done, towards a compliance with the request. If the defendant alleges that there was any particular order, which, as a cause, produced any particular act on his part, then he must know what this order was, can specify it, and a prompt answer can be given.—To GEORGE HAY.   v, 95. FORD ED., ix, 55.   (W., June 1807.)

6386. PAPERS, Retention of.—I enclose you a copy of [General] Armstrong's letter, covering the papers sent to Congress. The date was blank, as in the copy; the letter was so immaterial that I had really forgotten it altogether when I spoke with you. I feel myself much indebted to you for having given me this private opportunity of showing that I have kept back nothing material. That the federalists and a few others should by their vote make such a charge on me, is never unexpected. But how can any join in it who call themselves friends? The President sends papers to the House, which he thinks the public interest requires they should see. They immediately pass a vote, implying irresistibly their belief that he is capable of having kept back other papers which the same interest requires they should see. They pretend to no direct proof of this. It must, then, be founded in presumption: and on what act of my life or of my administration is such a presumption founded? What interest can I have in leading the Legislature to act on false grounds? My wish is certainly to take that course with the public affairs which the body of the Legislature would prefer. It is said, indeed, that such a vote is to satisfy the federalists and their partisans. But were I to send twenty letters, they would say. "You have kept back the twenty-first; send us that". If I sent one hundred, they would say, "There were one hundred and one": and how could I prove the negative? Their malice can be cured by no conduct: it ought, therefore, to be disregarded, instead of countenancing their imputations by the sanction of a vote. Indeed I should consider such a vote as a charge, in the face of the nation calling for a serious and public defence of myself.*—To JOSEPH B. VARNUM.   v, 249.   (W., Feb. 1808.)

6387. PARASITES, Government and.— I think we have more machinery of government than is necessary, too many parasites living on the labor of the industrious.—To WILLIAM LUDLOW.   vii, 378.   (M., 1824.)

6388. PARDONS, Abolition of.—Nor shall there be power anywhere to pardon crimes or to remit fines or punishments.—PROPOSED VA. CONSTITUTION.   FORD ED., ii, 17.   (June 1776.)

6389. PARDONS, Conditions of.—I have made it a rule to grant no pardon in any criminal case but on the recommendation of the

---

* Mr. Varnum was then Speaker of the House of Representatives.—EDITOR.

judges who sat on the trial, and the district attorney, or two of them. I believe it a sound rule, and not to be departed from but in extraordinary cases.—To ALBERT GALLATIN. FORD ED., viii, 465. (M., 1806.)

6390. ——— ———. In all cases I have referred petitions [for pardons] to the judges and prosecuting attorney, who having heard all the circumstances of the case, are the best judges whether any of them were of such a nature as ought to obtain for the criminal a remission or abridgment of the punishment.— To GEORGE BLAKE. v, 113. (W., 1807.)

6391. ——— ———. The Legislature having made stripes a regular part of the punishment [for robbing the mails], the pardoning them cannot be a thing of course, as that would be to repeal the law. Extraordinary and singular considerations are necessary to entitle the criminal to that remission.—To E. RANDOLPH. v, 406. (W., 1808.)

6392. PARDONS, Imprudent.—It would be against every rule of prudence for me to undertake to revise the verdict of a jury on *ex parte* affidavits and recommendations.—To GEORGE BLAKE. v, 371. (W., 1808.)

6393. PARDONS, Proper.—The power of pardon, committed to Executive discretion, [can] never be more properly exercised than where citizens [are] suffering without the authority of law, or, which [is] equivalent, under a law unauthorized by the Constitution, and therefore null.—To SPENCER ROANE. vii, 135. FORD ED., x, 141. (P.F., 1819.)

6394. PARDONS FOR COUNTERFEITERS.—Pardons for counterfeiting bank paper are yielded with much less facility than others. —To GEORGE BLAKE. v, 113. (W., 1807.)

6395. PARDONS OF INDIANS.—As the case of the five Alabamas, under prosecution for the murder of a white man, may not admit delay, if a conviction takes place, I have thought it necessary to recommend to you in that case to select the leader, or most guilty, for execution, and to reprieve the others; * * * letting them return to their friends, with whom you will of course take just merit for this clemency. Our wish * * * [is] merely to make them sensible by the just punishment of one. that our citizens are not to be murdered or robbed with impunity.—To Governor CLAIBORNE. v, 345. (M., 1808.)

6396. PARDONS BY LAW.—The " privilege of clergy ", originally allowed to the clergy, is now extended to every man, and even to women. It is a right of exemption from capital punishment, for the first offence in most cases. It is, then, a pardon by the law. In other cases, the Executive gives the pardon. But when laws are made as mild as they should be, both those pardons are absurd. The principle of Beccaria is sound. Let the legislators be merciful, but the executors of the law inexorable.—To M. DE MEUNIER. ix, 263. FORD ED., iv, 168. (P., 1786.)

6397. PARIS, Bois de Boulogne.—The Bois de Boulogne invites you earnestly to come and survey its beautiful verdure, to retire to its umbrage from the heats of the season. I was through it to-day, as I am every day.—To MADAME DE CORNY. ii, 161. (P., 1787.)

6398. PARIS, Evils of.—From what I have seen in Paris, I know not one good purpose on earth which can be effected by a young

gentleman coming here. He may learn indeed to speak the language, but put this in the scale amongst other things he will learn and evils he is sure to acquire, and it will be found too light. I have always disapproved of a European education for our youth from theory; I now do it from inspection.—To CHARLES THOMSON. FORD ED., iv, 15. (P., 1784.)

6399. PARK (Mungo), Work on Africa. —I fear Park's work on Africa will throw cold water on the hopes of the friends of freedom.—To DR. BENJAMIN RUSH. iv, 336. FORD ED., vii, 461. (M., 1800.)

6400. PARLIAMENT, Dignity of.—The dignity of Parliament, it seems, can brook no opposition to its power. Strange, that a set of men, who have made sale of their virtue to the Minister, should yet talk of retaining dignity.—To DR. WILLIAM SMALL. i, 199. FORD ED., i, 454. (1775.)

6401. PARLIAMENT, Executive Power of.—A new executive power, unheard of till then [the date of the Boston Port Bill, 14. G. 3.]. that of a British Parliament.—RIGHTS OF BRITISH AMERICA. i, 133. FORD ED., i, 438. (1774.)

6402. PARLIAMENT, Injuries by.— [During] the reigns which preceded his Majesty's [George III.] the violations of our rights were less alarming, because repeated at more distant intervals, than that rapid and bold succession of injuries, which is likely to distinguish the present from all other periods of American history. Scarcely have our minds been able to emerge from the astonishment into which one stroke of Parliamentary thunder has involved us, before another more heavy and more alarming is fallen on us.—RIGHTS OF BRITISH AMERICA. i, 130. FORD ED., i, 435. (1774.)

6403. PARLIAMENT, Jurisdiction of. —The British Parliament has no right to exercise authority over us.—RIGHTS OF BRITISH AMERICA. i, 130. FORD ED., i, 434. (1774.)

6404. ——— ———. He [George III.] has endeavored to pervert the exercise of the kingly office in Virginia into a detestable and insupportable tyranny * * * by combining with others to subject us to a foreign jurisdiction, giving his assent to their pretended acts of legislation.—PROPOSED VA. CONSTITUTION. FORD ED., ii, 10. (June 1776.)

6405. ——— ———. He has combined with others to subject us to a jurisdiction foreign to our constitutions and unacknowledged by our laws, giving his assent to their acts of pretended legislation. * * * declaring themselves invested with power to legislate for us in all cases whatsoever.—DECLARATION OF INDEPENDENCE AS DRAWN BY JEFFERSON.

6406. PARLIAMENT, Misgovernment by.—Not only the principles of common sense, but the feelings of human nature, must be surrendered up before his Majesty's subjects here, can be persuaded to believe that they hold their political existence at the will of a British Parliament. Shall these governments be dissolved, their property annihilated, and their people reduced to a state of nature, at the imperious breath of a body of men whom they never saw, in whom they never confided, and over whom they have no powers of punishment or removal, let their crimes against the American public be ever so great? Can any one reason be assigned why one hundred and sixty thousand electors in the Island of Great Britain should give law to four millions in the States of America, every individual of whom is equal to every individual of them, in virtue, in understanding, and in bodily strength? Were this to be admitted, instead of being a free people, as we have hitherto supposed, and mean to continue ourselves, we should suddenly be found the slaves, not of one, but of one hundred and sixty thousand tyrants, distinguished, too, from all others by this singular circumstance, that they are removed from the reach of fear, the only restraining motive which may hold the hand of a tyrant.—RIGHTS OF BRITISH AMERICA. i, 131. FORD ED., i, 436. (1774.)

6407. PARLIAMENT, Purchase of favor.—Congress are of opinion that the proposition * * * [of Lord North] is unreasonable and insidious: unreasonable because, if we declare we accede to it, we declare without reservation we will purchase the favor of parliament not knowing at the same time at what price they will please to estimate their favor. It is insidious because any individual Colonies, having bid and bidden again till they find the avidity of the seller unattainable by all their powers, are then to return into opposition, divided from their sister Colonies whom the minister will have previously detached by a grant of easier terms, or by an artful procrastination of a definitive answer.—REPLY TO LORD NORTH'S PROPOSITION. FORD ED., i, 478. (July 1775.)

6408. PARLIAMENT, Repudiation of. —A body of men foreign to our constitutions, and unacknowledged by our laws.—RIGHTS OF BRITISH AMERICA. i, 134. FORD ED., i, 439. (1774.)

6409. —— ——. Rather than submit to the rights of legislating for us, assumed by the British Parliament, * * * I would lend my hand to sink the whole Island in the ocean.— To JOHN RANDOLPH. i, 201. FORD ED., i, 484. (M., 1775.)

6410. —— ——. We utterly dissolve all political connection which may heretofore have subsisted between us and the people or parliament of Great Britain.*—DECLARATION OF INDEPENDENCE AS DRAWN BY JEFFERSON.

6411. PARLIAMENT, Submission to.— In constituting indeed our several forms of government, we had adopted one common king, thereby laying a foundation for perpetual league and amity with them; but that submission to their parliament was no part of our constitution, nor ever in idea, if history may be credited. † —DECLARATION OF INDEPENDENCE AS DRAWN BY JEFFERSON.

6412. PARLIAMENT, Tyranny of.— History has informed us that bodies of men as well as individuals are susceptible of the spirit of tyranny. A view of these acts of Parliament for regulation, as it has been affectedly called, of the American trade, if all other evidences were removed out of the case, would undeniably evince the truth of this observation.— RIGHTS OF BRITISH AMERICA. i, 128. FORD ED., i, 433. (1774.)

6413. PARLIAMENTARY LAW, Compilation of.—I do not mention the Parliamentary Manual published for the use of the Senate of the United States because it was a mere compilation into which nothing entered of my own but the arrangement and a few observations necessary to explain that and some of the cases. —To JOHN W. CAMPBELL. v, 466. FORD ED., ix, 258. (M., 1809.)

* Struck out by the Congress.—EDITOR.
† Congress struck out this passage.—EDITOR.

6414. PARLIAMENTARY LAW, Study of.—It seems probable that I will be called on to preside in a legislative chamber. It is now so long since I have acted in the legislative line, that I am entirely rusty in the Parliamentary rules of procedure. I know they have been more studied and are better known by you than by any man in America, perhaps by any man living. I am in hopes that while inquiring into the subject you made notes on it. If any such remain in your hands, however informal, in books or in scraps of paper, and you will be so good as to trust me with them a little while, they shall be most faithfully returned.—To GEORGE WYTHE. iv, 163. FORD ED., vii, 110. (M., 1797.)

6415. PARTIES, Amalgamation of.— What do you think of the state of parties at this time [1822]? An opinion prevails that there is no longer any distinction, that the republicans and federalists are completely amalgamated, but it is not so. The amalgamation is of name only, not of principle. All, indeed, call themselves by the name of republicans, because that of the federalists was extinguished in the battle of New Orleans. But the truth is that finding that monarchy is a desperate wish in this country, they rally to the point which they think next best, a consolidated government. Their aim is now, therefore, to break down the rights reserved by the Constitution to the States as a bulwark against that consolidation, the fear of which produced the whole of the opposition to the Constitution at its birth. Hence new republicans in Congress, preaching the doctrines of the old federalists, and the new nicknames of " Ultras " and " Radicals ". But, I trust, they will fail under the new, as the old name, and that the friends of the real Constitution and Union will prevail against consolidation, as they have done against monarchism. I scarcely know myself which is most to be deprecated, a consolidation, or dissolution of the States. The horrors of both are beyond the reach of human foresight.—To WILLIAM JOHNSON. FORD ED., x, 225. (M., Oct. 1822.)

6416. —— ——. You are told, indeed, that there are no longer parties among us; that they are all now amalgamated; the lion and the lamb lie down together in peace. Do not believe a word of it. The same parties exist now as ever did. No longer, indeed, under the name of republicans and federalists. The latter name was extinguished in the battle of Orleans. Those who wore it, finding monarchism a desperate wish in this country, are rallying to what they deem the next best point, a consolidated government. Although this is not yet avowed (as that of monarchy, you know, never was), it exists decidedly, and is the true key to the debates in Congress, wherein you see many calling themselves republicans, and preaching the rankest doctrines of the old federalists.*—To ALBERT GALLATIN. FORD ED., x, 235. (M., Oct. 1822.)

6417. —— ——. You will be told that parties are now all amalgamated; the wolf now dwells with the lamb, and the leopard lies down with the kid. It is true that federalism has changed its name and hidden itself among us. Since the Hartford convention it is deemed even by themselves a name of reproach. In some degree, too, they have varied their object. To monarchize this nation they see is impossible; the next best thing in their view is to consolidate it into one government as a *premier pas* to monarchy. The party is now as strong

* Gallatin was then in Europe.—EDITOR.

as it ever has been since 1800; and though mixed with us are to be known by their rallying together on every question of power in a general government. The judges, as before, are at their head, and are their entering wedge. Young men are more easily seduced into this principle than the old one of monarchy.—To ALBERT GALLATIN. FORD ED., x, 262. (M., Aug. 1823.)

6418. —— ——. [It is] an amalgamation of name but not of principle. Tories are tories still, by whatever name they may be called.—To MARTIN VAN BUREN. vii, 373. FORD ED., x, 316. (M., 1824.)

6419. —— ——. I am no believer in the amalgamation of parties, nor do I consider it as either desirable or useful for the public; but only that, like religious differences, a difference in politics should never be permitted to enter into social intercourse, or to disturb its friendships, its charities, or justice. In that form, they are censors of the conduct of each other, and useful watchmen for the public.—To H. LEE. vii, 376. FORD ED., x, 317. (M., 1824.)

6420. —— ——. There is really no amalgamation [of parties]. The parties exist now as heretofore. The one, indeed, has thrown off its old name, and has not yet assumed a new one, although obviously consolidationists. And among those in the offices of every denomination I believe it to be a bare minority.—To WILLIAM SHORT. vii, 392. FORD ED., x, 335. (M., January 1825.)

6421. **PARTIES, Birth of.**—At the formation of our government, many had formed their political opinions on European writings and practices, believing the experience of old countries, and especially of England, abusive as it was, to be a safer guide than mere theory. The doctrines of Europe were, that men in numerous associations cannot be restrained within the limits of order and justice, but by forces physical and moral, wielded over them by authorities independent of their will. Hence their organization of kings, hereditary nobles, and priests. Still further to constrain the brute force of the people, they deem it necessary to keep them down by hard labor, poverty and ignorance, and to take from them, as from bees, so much of their earnings, as that unremitting labor shall be necessary to obtain a sufficient surplus barely to sustain a scanty and miserable life. And these earnings they apply to maintain their privileged orders in splendor and idleness, to fascinate the eyes of the people, and excite in them an humble adoration and submission, as to an order of superior beings. Although few among us had gone all these lengths of opinion, yet many had advanced, some more, some less, on the way. And in the convention which formed our government, they endeavored to draw the cords of power as tight as they could obtain them, to lessen the dependence of the general functionaries on their constituents, to subject to them those of the States, and to weaken their means of maintaining the steady equilibrium which the majority of the convention had deemed salutary for both branches, general and local. To recover, therefore, in practice the powers which the nation had refused, and to warp to their own wishes those actually given, was the steady object of the Federal party. Ours, on the contrary, was to maintain the will of the majority of the convention, and of the people themselves. We believed, with them, that man was a rational animal, endowed by nature with rights, and with an innate sense of justice; and that he could be restrained from wrong and protected in right, by moderate powers, confided to persons of his own choice, and held to their duties by dependence on his own will. We believed that the complicated organization of kings, nobles, and priests, was not the wisest nor best to effect the happiness of associated man; that wisdom and virtue were not hereditary; that the trappings of such a machinery, consumed by their expense, those earnings of industry, they were meant to protect, and, by the inequalities they produced, exposed liberty to sufferance. We believed that men, enjoying in ease and security the full fruits of their own industry, enlisted by all their interests on the side of law and order, habituated to think for themselves, and to follow their reason as their guide, would be more easily and safely governed, than with minds nourished in error, and vitiated and debased, as in Europe, by ignorance, indigence and oppression. The cherishment of the people then was our principle, the fear and distrust of them, that of the other party. Composed, as we were, of the landed and laboring interests of the country, we could not be less anxious for a government of law and order than were the inhabitants of the cities, the strongholds of federalism. And whether our efforts to save the principles and form of our Constitution have not been salutary, let the present republican freedom, order and prosperity of our country determine.—To WILLIAM JOHNSON. vii, 290. FORD ED., x, 226. (M., June, 1823.)

6422. **PARTIES, History.**—Let me implore you to finish your history of parties, leaving the time of publication to the state of things you may deem proper, but taking especial care that we do not lose it altogether. We have been too careless of our future reputation, while our tories will omit nothing to place us in the wrong. Besides the five-volumed libel which represents us as struggling for office, and not at all to prevent our government from being administered into a monarchy, the Life of Hamilton is in the hands of a man who, to the bitterness of the priest, adds the rancor of the fiercest federalism. Mr. Adams's papers, too, and his biography will descend, of course, to his son whose pen, you know, is pointed, and his prejudices not in our favor. And, doubtless, other things are in preparation, unknown to us. On our part, we are depending on truth to make itself known, while history is taking a contrary set which may become too inveterate for correction. Mr. Madison will probably leave something, but, I believe, only particular passages of our history, and these chiefly confined to the period between the dissolution of the old and commencement of the new government, which is peculiarly within his knowledge. After he joined us in the administration, he had no leisure to write. This, too, was my case. But although I had not time to prepare anything express, my letters (all preserved) will furnish the daily occurrences and views from my return from Europe in 1790, till I retired finally from office. These will command more conviction than anything I could have written after my retirement; no day having ever passed during that period without a letter to somebody. Written, too, in the moment, and in the warmth and freshness of fact and feeling, they will carry internal evidence that what they breathe is genuine. Selections from these, after my death, may come out successively as the maturity of circumstances may render their appearance seasonable. But multiplied testimony, multiplied views will be necessary to give solid establishment to truth. Much is known to one which is not known to another, and no one knows everything. It is the sum of individual knowledge which is to make up the whole truth, and to give its correct current through future time. Then, do not * * * withhold your stock of information; and I would moreover recommend that you trust it not to a single copy, nor to a single depository. Leave it not in the power of any one person, under the distempered view of an unlucky moment, to deprive us of the weight of your testimony, and to purchase, by its destruction, the favor of any party or person.—To WILLIAM JOHNSON. vii, 277. FORD ED., x, 247. (M., 1823.)

6423. —— ——. Our opponents are far ahead of us in preparations for placing their cause favorably before posterity. Yet I hope even from some of them the escape of precious truths, in angry explosions or effusions of vanity, which will betray the genuine monarchism of their principles. They do not themselves believe what they endeavor to inculcate, that we were an opposition party, not on principle, but merely seeking for office.—To WILLIAM JOHNSON. vii, 290. FORD ED., x, 226. (M., 1823.)

6424. PARTIES, Independent of.—If I could not go to heaven but with a party, I would not go there at all.—To FRANCIS HOPKINSON. ii, 585. FORD ED., v, 76. (P., 1789.)

6425. PARTIES, Jay's Treaty and.—You well know how strong a character of division had been impressed on the Senate by the British treaty. Common error, common censure, and common efforts of defence had formed the treaty majority into a common band, which feared to separate even on other subjects. Towards the close of the last Congress, however, it had been hoped that their ties began to loosen, and their phalanx to separate a little. This hope was blasted at the very opening of the present session, by the nature of the appeal which the President made to the nation: the occasion for which had confessedly sprung from the fatal British treaty. This circumstance rallied them again to their standard, and hitherto we have had pretty regular treaty votes on all questions of principle. And, indeed, I fear, that as long as the same individuals remain, so long we shall see traces of the same division.—To AARON BURR. iv, 184. FORD ED., vii, 145. (Pa., June 1797.)

6426. PARTIES, Motives.—That each party endeavors to get into the administration of the government, and exclude the other from power, is true, and may be stated as a motive of action: but this is only secondary; the primary motive being a real and radical difference of political principle. I sincerely wish our differences were but personally who should govern, and that the principles of our Constitution were those of both parties. Unfortunately, it is otherwise; and the question of preference between monarchy and republicanism, which has so long divided mankind elsewhere, threatens a permanent division here.—To JOHN MELISH. vi, 95. FORD ED., ix, 374. (M., Jan. 1813.)

6427. PARTIES, Names.—The appellation of aristocrats and democrats is the true one expressing the essence of all [political parties].—To H. LEE. vii, 376. FORD ED., x, 318. (M., 1824.)

6428. PARTIES, Natural division.—The division into whig and tory is founded in the nature of men; the weakly and nerveless,

the rich and the corrupt, seeing more safety and accessibility in a strong executive; the healthy, firm, and virtuous, feeling confidence in their physical and moral resources, and willing to part with only so much power as is necessary for their good government; and, therefore, to retain the rest in the hands of the many, the division will substantially be into whig and tory, as in England formerly.—To JOEL BARLOW. iv, 438. FORD ED., viii, 150. (W., May 1802.)

6429. —— ——. I consider the party division of whig and tory the most wholesome which can exist in any government, and well worthy of being nourished, to keep out those of a more dangerous character.—To WILLIAM T. BARRY. vii, 255. (M., 1822.)

6430. —— ——. The parties of whig and tory are those of nature. They exist in all countries, whether called by these names, or by those of aristocrats and democrats, *coté droite* and *coté gauche*, ultras and radicals, serviles and liberals. The sickly, weakly, timid man fears the people, and is a tory by nature. The healthy, strong and bold, cherishes them, and is formed a whig by nature.—To MARQUIS LAFAYETTE. vii, 325. FORD ED., x, 281. (M., 1823.)

6431. —— ——. Men by their constitutions are naturally divided into two parties: 1. Those who fear and distrust the people, and wish to draw all powers from them into the hands of the higher classes. 2. Those who identify themselves with the people, have confidence in them, cherish and consider them as the most honest and safe, although not the most wise depository of the public interests. In every country these two parties exist, and in every one where they are free to think, speak and write, they will declare themselves. Call them, therefore, liberals and serviles, Jacobins and ultras, whigs and tories, republicans and federalists, aristocrats and democrats, or by whatever name you please, they are the same parties still, and pursue the same object. The last appellation of aristocrats and democrats is the true one expressing the essence of all.—To H. LEE. vii, 376. FORD ED., x, 317. (M., 1824.)

6432. —— ——. The division of whig and tory, or, according to our denominations, of republican and federal, is the most salutary of all divisions, and ought, therefore, to be fostered, instead of being amalgamated; for, take away this, and some more dangerous principle of division will take its place.—To WILLIAM SHORT. vii, 392. FORD ED., x, 335. (M., 1825.)

6433. PARTIES, Opposite.—In every free and deliberating society, there must, from the nature of man, be opposite parties, and violent dissensions and discords; and one of these, for the most part, must prevail over the other for a longer or shorter time.—To JOHN TAYLOR. iv, 246. FORD ED., vii, 264. (Pa., 1798.)

6434. —— ——. Wherever there are men, there will be parties; and wherever there are free men they will make themselves heard. Those of firm health and spirits are unwilling to cede more of their liberty than is necessary to preserve order; those of feeble constitutions will wish to see one strong arm able to protect them from the many. These are the whigs and tories of nature. These mutual jealousies produce mutual security; and while the laws shall be obeyed, all will be safe. He alone is your enemy who disobeys them.—JEFFERSON'S MSS. FORD ED., viii, 1. (1801?)

6435. —— ——. Men have differed in opinion, and been divided into parties by these opinions, from the first origin of societies, and in all governments where they have been permitted freely to think and to speak. The same political parties which now agitate the United States, have existed through all time. Whether the power of the people or that of the αριϛοι should prevail, were questions which kept the States of Greece and Rome in eternal convulsions, as they now schismatize every people whose minds and mouths are not shut up by the gag of a despot. And in fact, the terms of whig and tory belong to natural as well as to civil history. They denote the temper and constitution of mind of different individuals.— To JOHN ADAMS. vi, 143. (M., 1813.)

6436. —— ——. To me it appears that there have been differences of opinion and party differences, from the first establishment of government to the present day, and on the same question which now divides our own country; that these will continue through all future time; that every one takes his side in favor of the many, or of the few, according to his constitution, and the circumstances in which he is placed; that opinions which are equally honest on both sides, should not affect personal esteem or social intercourse; that as we judge between the Claudii and the Gracchi, the Wentworths and the Hampdens of past ages, so of those among us whose names may happen to be remembered for awhile, the next generations will judge favorably or unfavorably, according to the complexion of individual minds, and the side they shall themselves have taken; that nothing new can be added by you or me in support of the conflicting opinions on government; and that wisdom and duty dictate a humble resignation to the verdict of our future peers. —To JOHN ADAMS. vi, 145. (M., 1813.)

6437. —— ——. To come to our own country, and to the times when you and I became first acquainted, we well remember the violent parties which agitated the old Congress, and their bitter contests. There you and I were together, and the Jays, and the Dickinsons, and other anti-independents, were arrayed against us. They cherished the monarchy of England, and we the rights of our countrymen. When our present government was in the mew, passing from Confederation to Union, how bitter was the schism between the " Feds " and the " Antis ". Here you and I were together again. For although, for a moment, separated by the Atlantic from the scene of action, I favored the opinion that nine States should confirm the Constitution, in order to secure it, and the others hold off until certain amendments, deemed favorable to freedom, should be made. I rallied in the first instant to the wiser proposition of Massachusetts, that all should confirm, and then all instruct their delegates to urge those amendments. The amendments were made, and all were reconciled to the government. But as soon as it was put into motion, the line of division was again drawn. We broke into two parties, each wishing to give the government a different direction; the one to strengthen the most popular branch, the other the more permanent branches, and to extend their permanence.—To JOHN ADAMS. vi, 143. (M., 1813.)

6438. —— ——. Here you and I separated for the first time, and as we had been longer than most others on the public theatre, and our names were more familiar to our countrymen, the party which considered you as thinking with them, placed your name at their head; the other, for the same reason, selected mine. But neither decency nor inclination permitted us to become the advocates of ourselves, or to take part personally in the violent contests which followed. We suffered ourselves, as you so well expressed it, to be passive subjects of public discussion. And these discussions, whether relating to men, measures or opinions, were conducted by the parties with an animosity, a bitterness and an indecency which had never been exceeded. All the resources of reason and of wrath were exhausted by each party in support of its own, and to prostrate the adversary opinions; one was upbraided with receiving the anti-federalists, the other the old tories and refugees, into their bosom. Of this acrimony, the public papers of the day exhibit ample testimony, in the debates of Congress, of State Legislatures, of stump-orators, in addresses, answers, and newspaper essays; and to these, without question, may be added the private correspondences of individuals; and the less guarded in these, because not meant for the public eye, not restrained by the respect due to that, but poured forth from the overflowings of the heart into the bosom of a friend, as a momentary easement of our feelings.—To JOHN ADAMS. vi, 144. (1813.)

6439. PARTIES, Principles and.—Were parties here divided merely by a greediness for office, as in England, to take a part with either would be unworthy of a reasonable or moral man. But where the principle of difference is as substantial, and as strongly pronounced as between the republicans and the monocrats of our country, I hold it as honorable to take a firm and decided part, and as immoral to pursue a middle line, as between the parties of honest men and rogues, into which every country is divided.—To WILLIAM B. GILES. iv, 126. FORD ED., vii, 43. (M., Dec. 1795.)

6440. —— ——. What in fact is the difference of principle between the two parties? The one desires to preserve an entire independence of the Executive and Legislative on each other, and the dependence of both on the same source—the free election of the people. The other party wishes to lessen the dependence of the Executive, and of one branch of the Legislature on the people, some by making them hold for life, some hereditary, and some even for giving the Executive an influence by patronage or corruption over the remaining popular branch, so as to reduce the elective franchise to its minimum.—To J. F. MERCER. iv, 563. (W., 1804.)

6441. —— ——. It is indeed of little consequence who governs us, if they sincerely and zealously cherish the principles of union and republicanism.—To HENRY DEARBORN. vii, 215. FORD ED., x, 192. (M., 1821.)

6442. PARTIES, Public welfare and.— Both of our political parties, at least the honest part of them, agree conscientiously in the same object—the public good; but they differ essentially in what they deem the means of promoting that good. One side believes it best done by one composition of the governing powers; the other, by a different one. One fears most the ignorance of the people; the other, the selfishness of rulers independent of them. Which is right, time and experience will prove. We think that one side of this experiment has been long enough tried, and proved not to promote the good of the many; and that the other has not been fairly and sufficiently tried. Our opponents think the reverse. With whichever opinion the body of the nation concurs, that must prevail.—To Mrs. John Adams. iv, 562. Ford ed., viii, 312. (M., 1804.)

6443. PARTIES, Republican vs. Monarchical.—Where a Constitution, like ours, wears a mixed aspect of monarchy and republicanism, its citizens will naturally divide into two classes of sentiment according to their tone of body or mind. Their habits, connections and callings induce them to wish to strengthen either the monarchical or the republican features of the Constitution. Some will consider it as an elective monarchy, which had better be made hereditary, and, therefore, endeavor to lead towards that all the forms and principles of its administration. Others will view it as an energetic republic, turning in all its points on the pivot of free and frequent elections. The great body of our native citizens are unquestionably of the republican sentiment. Foreign education, and foreign conventions of interest, have produced some exceptions in every part of the Union, North and South, and perhaps other circumstances in your quarter, better known to you, may have thrown into the scale of exceptions a greater number of the rich. Still there, I believe, and here [the South] I am sure, the great mass is republican. Nor do any of the forms in which the public disposition has been pronounced in the last half dozen years, evince the contrary. All of them, when traced to their true source, have only been evidences of the preponderant popularity of a particular great character. That influence once withdrawn, and our countrymen left to the operation of their own unbiased good sense, I have no doubt we shall see a pretty rapid return of general harmony, and our citizens moving in phalanx in the paths of regular liberty, order, and a sacrosanct adherence to the Constitution. Thus I think it will be, if war with France can be avoided. But if that untoward event comes athwart us in our present point of deviation, nobody, I believe, can foresee into what port it will drive us.— To James Sullivan. iv, 168. Ford ed., vii, 117. (M., Feb. 1797.)

6444. ———. The toryism with which we struggled in 1777 differed but in name from the federalism of 1799, with which we struggled also; and the Anglicism of 1808, against which we are now struggling, is but the same thing still in another form. It is a longing for a king and an English king rather than any other. This is the true source of their sorrows and wailings.—To John Langdon. v, 512. (M., 1810.)

6445. PARTIES, Washington's relations to.—You expected to discover the difference of our party principles in General Washington's valedictory, and my inaugural address. Not at all. General Washington did not harbor one principle of federalism. He was neither an Angloman, a monarchist, nor a separatist. He sincerely wished the people to have as much self-government as they were competent to exercise themselves. The only point on which he and I ever differed in opinion, was, that I had more confidence than he had in the natural integrity and discretion of the people, and in the safety and extent to which they might trust themselves with a control of their government. He has asseverated to me a thousand times his determination that the existing government should have a fair trial, and that in support of it he would spend the last drop of his blood. He did this the more repeatedly, because he knew General Hamilton's political bias, and my apprehensions from it. It is a mere calumny, therefore, in the monarchists, to associate General Washington with their principles. But that may have happened in this case which has been often seen in ordinary cases, that, by oft repeating an untruth, men come to believe it themselves. It is a mere artifice in this party to bolster themselves up on the revered name of that first of our worthies.—To John Melish. vi, 97. Ford ed., ix, 376. (M., Jan. 1813.) See Federalists, Hartford Convention, Monarchists, Republicanism and Republicans.

6446. PASSIONS, Control.—We must keep the passions of men on our side, even when we are persuading them to do what they ought to do.—To M. de Meunier. ix, 272. Ford ed., iv, 177. (P., 1786.)

6447. PASSIONS, Suppress.—It is our sacred duty to suppress passion among ourselves, and not to blast the confidence we have inspired of proof that a government of reason is better than one of force.—To Richard Rush. vii, 183. (M., 1820.)

6448. PATENTS, Benefits of.—In the arts, and especially in the mechanical arts, many ingenious improvements are made in consequence of the patent-right giving exclusive use of them for fourteen years.—To M. Pictet. iv, 462. (W., 1803.)

6449. PATENTS, Combinations in.—If we have a right to use three things separately, I see nothing in reason, or in the patent law, which forbids our using them all together. A man has a right to use a saw, an axe, a plane separately; may he not combine their uses on the same piece of wood? He has a right to use his knife to cut his meat, a fork to hold it; may a patentee take from him the right to continue their use on the same subject? Such a law, instead of enlarging our conveniences, as was intended, would most fearfully abridge them, and crowd us by monopolies out of the use of the things we have.—To Oliver Evans. vi, 298. (M., 1814.)

6450. PATENTS, Duration of.—Certainly an inventor ought to be allowed a right to the benefit of his invention for some certain time. It is equally certain it ought not to be perpetual; for to embarrass society with monopolies for every utensil existing, and in all the details of life, would be more injurious to them than had the supposed inventors never existed; because the natural understanding of its members would have suggested the same things or others as good. How long the term should be, is the difficult question. Our legislators have copied the English estimate of the term, perhaps without sufficiently considering how much longer, in a country so much more sparsely settled, it takes for an invention to become known, and used to an extent profitable to the inventor. Nobody wishes more than I do that ingenuity should receive a liberal encouragement.—To Oliver Evans. v, 75. (M., 1807.)

6451. PATENTS, Frivolous.—The abuse of frivolous patents is likely to cause more inconvenience than is countervailed by those really useful. We know not to what uses we may apply implements which were in our hands before the birth of our government, and even the discovery of America.—To Dr. Thomas Cooper. vi, 295. (M., 1814.)

6452. PATENTS, Granting of.—Considering the exclusive right to invention as given not of natural right, but for the benefit of society, I know well the difficulty of drawing a line between the things which are worth to the public the embarrassment of an exclusive patent, and those which are not. As a member of the patent board for several years, while the law authorized a board to grant or refuse patents, I saw with what slow progress a system of general rules could be matured. Some, however, were established by that board. One of these was, that a machine of which we were possessed, might be applied to every man to any use of which it is susceptible, and that this right ought not to be taken from him and given to a monopolist, because the first perhaps had occasion to apply it. Thus a screw for crushing plaster might be employed for crushing corncobs. And a chain-pump for raising water might be used for raising wheat; this being merely a change of application. Another rule was that a change of material should not give title to a patent. * * * A third was that a mere change of form should give no right to a patent. * * * But there were still abundance of cases which could not be brought under rule, until they should have presented themselves under all their aspects; and these investigations occupying more time of the members of the board than they could spare from higher duties, the whole was turned over to the judiciary, to be matured into a system, under which every one might know when his actions were safe and lawful. Instead of refusing a patent in the first instance, as the board was authorized to do, the patent now issues of course, subject to be declared void on such principles as should be established by the courts of law. This business, however, is but little analogous to their course of reading, since we might in vain turn over all the lubberly volumes of the law to find a single ray which would lighten the path of the mechanic or the mathematician. It is more within the information of a board of academical professors, and a previous refusal of patent would better guard our citizens against harassment by lawsuits. But England had given it to her judges, and the usual predominancy of her examples carried it to ours.—To ISAAC McPHERSON. vi, 181. (M., 1813.)

— **PATENTS, Inventors and.**—See INVENTIONS and INVENTORS, RIGHTS OF.

6453. PATENTS, Law of.—I found it more difficult than I had on first view imagined, to draw the clause you wish to have introduced in the inclosed bill.* Will you make the first trial against the patentee conclusive against all others who might be interested to contest his patent? If you do he will always have a conclusive suit brought against himself at once. Or will you give every one a right to bring actions separately. If you do, besides running him down with the expenses and vexations of lawsuits, you will be sure to find some jury in the long run, who from motives of partiality or ignorance, will find a verdict against him, though a hundred should have been before found in his favor. I really believe that less evil will follow from leaving him to bring suits against those who invade his right.—To HUGH WILLIAMSON. FORD ED., v, 392. (1791.)

* Jefferson's bill "to Promote the Progress of the Useful Arts" was introduced into the House of Representatives by Mr. White on Feb. 7, 1791. No action was taken upon it, however; but in the next Congress it was passed after many minor alterations had been made.—EDITOR.

6454. PATENTS, Monopoly and.—If a new application of our old machines be a ground of monopoly, the patent law will take from us much more good than it will give.—To OLIVER EVANS. vi, 298. (M., 1814.)

6455. PATENTS, Regulation of.—A rule has occurred to me, which I think, would * * * go far towards securing the citizen against the vexation of frivolous patents. It is to consider the invention of any new mechanical power, or of any new combination of the mechanical powers already known, as entitled to an exclusive grant; but that the purchaser of the right to use the invention should be free to apply it to every purpose of which it is susceptible.—To THOMAS COOPER. vi, 372. (M., 1814.)

6456. PATENTS, Scope of.—[You say] that your patent is for your improvement in the manufacture of flour by the application of certain principles, and of such machinery as will carry those principles into operation, whether of the improved elevator, improved hopper-boy, or (without being confined to them) of any machinery known and free to the public. I can conceive how a machine may improve the manufacture of flour; but not how a *principle* abstracted from any machine can do it. It must then be the machine, and the principle of that machine, which is secured to you by your patent. Recurring now to the words of your definition, do they mean that, while all are free to use the old string of buckets, and Archimedes's screw for the purposes to which they have been formerly applied, you alone have the exclusive right to apply them to the manufacture of flour? that no one has a right to apply his old machines to all the purposes of which they are susceptible? that every one, for instance, who can apply the hoe, the spade, or the axe, to any purpose to which they have not been before applied, may have a patent for the exclusive right to that application? and may exclude all others, under penalties, from so using their hoe, spade, or axe? If this be the meaning, [it is] my opinion that the Legislature never meant by the patent law to sweep away so extensively the rights of their constituents [and thus] to environ everything they touch with snares.—To OLIVER EVANS. vi, 297. (M., 1814.)

6457. PATERNALISM, Condemned.—Having always observed that public works are much less advantageously managed than the same are by private hands, I have thought it better for the public to go to market for whatever it wants which is to be found there; for there competition brings it down to the minimum of value. * * * I think it material, too, not to abstract the high executive officers from those functions which nobody else is charged to carry on, and to employ them in superintending works which are going on abundantly in private hands. Our predecessors went on different principles; they bought iron mines, and sought for copper ones. We own a mine at Harper's Ferry of the finest iron ever put into a cannon, which we are afraid to attempt to work. We have rented it heretofore, but it is now without a tenant.—To MR. BIBB. v. 326. (M., 1808.)

6458. PATERNALISM, Private enterprise vs.—Private enterprise manages * * * much better [than the government] all the con-

cerns to which it is equal.—SIXTH ANNUAL
MESSAGE. viii, 68. FORD ED., viii, 494.
(1806.)

6459. PATIENCE, Abuse of.—When
patience has begotten false estimates of its
motives, when wrongs are pressed because it is
believed they will be borne, resistance becomes
morality.—To MADAME DE STAEL. v, 133. (W.,
1807.)

6460. PATRIOTISM, Cherish.—Let the
love of our country soar above all minor
passions.—To JOHN HOLLINS. v, 597. (M.,
1811.)

6461. ——— ———. The first object of my
heart is my country. In that is embarked my
family, my fortune, and my own existence.
I have not one farthing of interest, nor one
fibre of attachment out of it, nor a single
motive of preference of any one nation to
another, but in proportion as they are more
or less friendly to us.—To ELBRIDGE GERRY.
iv, 269. FORD ED., vii, 329. (Pa., 1799.)

6462. PATRIOTISM, Disinterested.—
The man who loves his country on its own
account, and not merely for its trappings of
interest or power, can never be divorced from
it, can never refuse to come forward when
he finds that she is engaged in dangers which
he has the means of warding off.—To EL-
BRIDGE GERRY. iv, 188. FORD ED., vii, 151.
(Pa., June 1797.)

6463. ——— ———. Let us deserve well of
our country by making her interests the end
of all our plans, and not our own pomp,
patronage, and irresponsiblity.—To ALBERT
GALLATIN. iv, 429. FORD ED., viii, 141. (W.,
1802.)

6464. PATRIOTISM, Inspirations to.—
I sincerely wish you may find it convenient to
come to Europe. * * * It will make you
adore your own country, its soil, its climate,
its equality, liberty, laws, people and manners.
* * * While we shall see multiplied instances of Europeans going to live in America, I will venture to say, no man now living
will ever see an instance of an American removing to settle in Europe, and continuing
there. Come, then, and see the proofs of this,
and on your return add your testimony to
that of every thinking American, in order to
satisfy our countrymen how much it is their
interest to preserve, uninfected by contagion,
those peculiarities in their government and
manners, to which they are indebted for those
blessings.—To JAMES MONROE. i, 352. FORD
ED., iv, 59. (P., 1785.)

6465. PATRIOTISM, Sacrifices for.—
To preserve the peace of our fellow citizens,
promote their prosperity and happiness, reunite opinion, cultivate a spirit of candor,
moderation, charity and forbearance toward
one another, are objects calling for the efforts and sacrifices of every good man and
patriot. Our religion enjoins it; our happiness demands it; and no sacrifice is requisite but of passions hostile to both.—To
RHODE ISLAND ASSEMBLY. iv, 397. (W.,
1801.)

6466. PATRONAGE, Advantages of.—
Those who have once got an ascendancy, and
possessed themselves of all the resources of
the nation, their revenues and offices, have
immense means for retaining their advantage.
—To JOHN TAYLOR. iv, 246. FORD ED., vii,
263. (Pa., June 1798.)

6467. PATRONAGE, Corruption and.—
Bad men will sometimes get in [the Pres-
idency], and with such an immense patronage,
may make great progress in corrupting the
public mind and principles. This is a subject with which wisdom and patriotism should
be occupied.—To MOSES ROBINSON. iv, 380.
(W., 1801.)

6468. PATRONAGE, Curtailing.—They
[first republican Congress] * * * are disarming executive patronage and preponderance, by putting down one-half the offices of
the United States, which are no longer necessary.—To GENERAL KOSCIUSKO. iv, 430.
(W., April 1802.) See OFFICES and OFFICE-
HOLDERS.

6469. PATRONAGE, Distribution of.—
I am sensible of the necessity as well as justice of dispersing employments over the whole
of the United States. But this is difficult as
to the smaller offices, which require to be
filled immediately as they become vacant and
are not worth coming for from the distant
States. Hence they will unavoidably get into
the sole occupation of the vicinities of the
seat of government,—a reason the more for
removing that seat to the true centre.—To
COLONEL HENRY LEE. FORD ED., v, 163.
(N.Y., 1790.)

6470. PATRONAGE, Elections and.—
The elective principle becomes nothing, if it
may be smothered by the enormous patronage
of the General Government.—To GOVERNOR
THOMAS M'KEAN. iv, 350. FORD ED., vii,
487. (W., 1801.)

6471. PATRONAGE, Necessity for.—
The safety of the government absolutely required that its direction in its higher departments should be taken into friendly hands.
Its safety did not even admit that the whole
of its immense patronage should be left at
the command of its enemies to be exercised
secretly or openly to reestablish the tyrannical
and dilapidating system of the preceding administration, and their deleterious principles
of government.—To ELBRIDGE GERRY. FORD
ED., viii, 169. (W., 1802.)

6472. PATRONAGE, Partizans and.—
Every officer of the government may vote at
elections according to his conscience; but we
should betray the cause committed to our
care, were we to permit the influence of official patronage to be used to overthrow that
cause.—To LEVI LINCOLN. iv, 451. FORD ED.,
viii, 176. (W., 1802.)

6473. PATRONAGE, For personal ends.
—A person who wishes to make [the bestowal
of office] an engine of self-elevation, may
do wonders with it; but to one who wishes to

use it conscientiously for the public good, without regard to the ties of blood or friendship, it creates enmities without number, many open, but more secret, and saps the happiness and peace of his life.—To JAMES SULLIVAN. v, 252. (W., 1808.)

6474. PATRONAGE, Use of.—The patronage of public office should no longer be confided to one who uses it for active opposition to the national will.—To ALBERT GALLATIN. iv, 544. FORD ED., viii, 304. (1804.)

6475. —— ——. No government [can] discharge its duties to the best advantage of its citizens, if its agents [are] in a regular course of thwarting instead of executing all its measures, and [are] employing the patronage and influence of their offices against the government and its measures.—To JOHN PAGE. v, 136. FORD ED., ix, 118. (W., July 1807.)

6476. PATRONAGE vs. PATRIOTISM.—Let us deserve well of our country by making her interests the end of all our plans, and not our own pomp, patronage, and irresponsibility.—To ALBERT GALLATIN. iv, 429. FORD ED., viii, 141. (W., 1802.)

6477. PAUPERS, No American.—We have no paupers, the old and crippled among us, who possess nothing and have no families to take care of them, being too few to merit notice as a separate section of society, or to affect a general estimate. The great mass of our population is of laborers; our rich who can live without labor, either manual or professional, being few, and of moderate wealth. Most of the laboring class possess property, cultivate their own lands, have families, and from the demand for their labor are enabled to exact from the rich and the competent such prices as enable them to be fed abundantly, clothed above mere decency, to labor moderately and raise their families.—To THOMAS COOPER. vi, 377. (M., 1814.)

6478. PEACE, America and.—Twenty years of peace, and the prosperity so visibly flowing from it, have but strengthened our attachment to it, and the blessings it brings, and we do not despair of being always a peaceable nation.—To M. CABANIS. iv, 497. (W., 1803.)

6479. PEACE, Blessings of.—Wars and contentions, indeed, fill the pages of history with more matter. But more blessed is that nation whose silent course of happiness furnishes nothing for history to say. This is what I ambition for my own country.—To COMTE DIODATI. v, 62. (W., 1807.)

6480. PEACE, Bread and.—Were I in Europe, *pax et panis* [peace and a loaf] would certainly be my motto.—To COMTE DIODATI. v, 62. (W., 1807.)

6481. PEACE, Cherishing.—I believe that through all America there has been but a single sentiment on the subject of peace and war, which was in favor of the former. The Executive here has cherished it with equal and unanimous desire. We have differed, perhaps, as to the tone of conduct exactly adapted to the securing it.—To JAMES MONROE. iv, 6. FORD ED., vi, 321. (Pa., June 1793.)

6482. —— ——. Having seen the people of all other nations bowed down to the earth under the wars and prodigalities of their rulers, I have cherished their opposites, peace, economy, and riddance of public debt, believing that these were the high road to public as well as private prosperity and happiness.—To HENRY MIDDLETON. vi, 90. (M., Jan. 1813.)

6483. PEACE, Cultivate.—Young as we are, and with such a country before us to fill with people and with happiness, we should point in that direction the whole generative force of nature, wasting none of it in efforts of * * * destruction.—NOTES ON VIRGINIA. viii, 412. FORD ED., iii, 278. (1782.)

6484. —— ——. It should be our endeavor to cultivate the peace and friendship of every nation, even of that which has injured us most, when we shall have carried our point against her.—NOTES ON VIRGINIA. viii, 412. FORD ED., iii, 279. (1782.)

6485. —— ——. I am decidedly of opinion we should take no part in European quarrels, but cultivate peace and commerce with all.—To GENERAL WASHINGTON. ii, 533. FORD ED., v, 57. (P., 1788.)

6486. —— ——. We wish to cultivate peace and friendship with all nations, believing that course most conducive to the welfare of our own.—To SIR JOHN SINCLAIR. vii, 24. (M., 1816.)

6487. PEACE, The Deity and.—I bless the Almighty Being, Who, in gathering together the waters under the heavens into one place, divided the dry land of your hemisphere from the dry lands of ours. and said, at least be there peace.—To EARL OF BUCHAN. iv, 493. (W., 1803.)

6488. PEACE, Desire for.—The power of making war often prevents it, and in our case would give efficacy to our desire of peace.—To GENERAL WASHINGTON. ii, 533. FORD ED., v, 57. (P., Dec. 1788.)

6489. —— ——. The bravery exhibited by our citizens on that element [the ocean] will, I trust, be a testimony to the world that it is not the want of that virtue which makes us seek their peace, but a conscientious desire to direct the energies of our nation to the multiplication of the human race, and not to its destruction.—FIRST ANNUAL MESSAGE. viii, 8. FORD ED., viii, 118. (1801.)

6490. PEACE, With England.—I am glad of the pacification of Ghent, and shall still be more so, if, by a reasonable arrangement against impressment, they will make it truly a treaty of peace, and not a mere truce, as we must all consider it, until the principle of the war is settled.—To GENERAL DEARBORN. vi, 450. (M., March 1815.)

6491. —— ——. The United States and Great Britain ought to wish for peace and cordial friendship; we, because you can do us more harm than any other nation; and you, because we can do you more good than any other nation.—To SIR JOHN SINCLAIR. vii, 22. (M., 1816.)

6492. —— ——. .I reciprocate congratulations with you sincerely on the restoration of peace between our two nations. * * * Let both parties now count soberly the value of mutual friendship.—To SIR JOHN SINCLAIR. vii, 22. (M., 1816.)

6493. PEACE, European wars and.— Till our treaty with England be fully executed, it is desirable to us that all the world should be in peace. That done, their wars would do us little harm.—To SAMUEL OS-GOOD. i, 450. (P., 1785.)

6494. PEACE, Faith, honor and.—I hope some means will turn up of reconciling our faith and honor with peace.—To JOHN ADAMS. iv, 104. FORD ED., vi, 505. (M., April 1794.)

6495. —— ——. I wish for peace, if it can be preserved, *salvê fide et honore.*—To JAMES MONROE. FORD ED., vi, 504. (M., 1794.)

6496. PEACE, With France.—The agents of the two people[United States and France] are either great bunglers or great rascals, when they cannot preserve that peace which is the universal wish of both.—To JAMES MONROE. iv, 20. FORD ED., vi, 349. (Pa., 1793.)

6497. —— ——. [My assailant] says I am "for peace; but it is only with France". He has told half the truth. He would have told the whole, if he had added England. I am for peace with both countries.—To SAMUEL SMITH. iv, 254. FORD ED., vii, 277. (M., 1798.)

6498. PEACE, Happiness and prosperity.—Always a friend to peace, and believing it to promote eminently the happiness and prosperity of nations, I am ever unwilling that it should be disturbed, until greater and more important interests call for an appeal to force.—To GENERAL SHEE. v, 33. (W., 1807.)

6499. —— ——. All the energies of the European nations are expended in the destruction of the labor, property and lives of their people. On our part, never had a people so favorable a chance of trying the opposite system, of peace and fraternity with mankind, and the direction of all our means and faculties to the purposes of improvement instead of destruction.—To PRESIDENT MONROE. vii, 288. FORD ED., x, 257. (M., 1823.)

6500. PEACE, Importance of.—Peace is our most important interest, and a recovery from debt.—To WILLIAM SHORT. iv, 414. FORD ED., viii, 98. (W., 1801.)

6501. PEACE, Independence and.— Peace is the most important of all things for us, except the preserving an erect and independent attitude.—To ROBERT R. LIVINGSTON. iv, 448. FORD ED., viii, 173. (W., Oct. 1802.)

6502. PEACE, A landmark.—To cultivate peace * * * [is one of] the landmarks by which we are to guide ourselves in all our proceedings.—SECOND ANNUAL MESSAGE. viii, 21. FORD ED., viii, 186. (Dec. 1802.)

6503. PEACE, Love of.—I love peace, and am anxious that we should give the world still another useful lesson, by showing to them other modes of punishing injuries than by war, which is as much a punishment to the punisher as to the sufferer.—To TENCH COXE. iv, 105. FORD ED., vi, 508. (M., May 1794.)

6504. PEACE, With mankind.—I do not recall these recollections [of conflicts with the federal monarchists] with pleasure, but rather wish to forget them, nor did I ever permit them to affect social intercourse. And now, least of all, am I disposed to do so. Peace and good will with all mankind is my sincere wish.—To WILLIAM SHORT. vii, 392. FORD ED., x, 335. (M., 1825.)

6505. PEACE, Markets and.—I hope France, England and Spain will all see it their interest to let us make bread for them in peace, and to give us a good price for it.— To COLONEL M. LEWIS. iii, 163. (N.Y., 1790.)

6506. PEACE, National reputation and. —I am so far from believing that our reputation will be tarnished by our not having mixed in the mad contests of the rest of the world, that, setting aside the ravings of pepper-pot politicians, of whom there are enough in every age and country, I believe it will place us high in the scale of wisdom, to have preserved our country tranquil and prosperous during a contest which prostrated the honor, power, independence, laws and property of every country on the other side of the Atlantic. Which of them have better preserved their honor? Has Spain, has Portugal, Italy, Switzerland, Holland, Prussia, Austria, the other German powers, Sweden, Denmark, or even Russia? And would we accept of the infamy of France or England in exchange for our honest reputation, or of the result of their enormities, despotism to the one, and bankruptcy and prostration to the other, in exchange for the prosperity, the freedom and independence, which we have preserved safely through the wreck?—To J. W. EPPES. vi, 15. (M., Sep. 1811.)

6507. PEACE, Our object.—Peace with all nations, and the right which that gives us with respect to all nations, are our object.— To C. W. F. DUMAS. iii, 535. (Pa., 1793.)

6508. PEACE, Passion for.—Peace is our passion.—To SIR JOHN SINCLAIR. iv, 491. (W., 1803.)

6509. PEACE, Pipe of.—I have joined with you sincerely in smoking the pipe of peace; it is a good old custom handed down by your ancestors, and as such I respect and join in it with reverence. I hope we shall long continue to smoke in friendship together.—To BROTHER JOHN BAPTIST DE COIGNE. viii, 172. (1781.)

6510. PEACE, A Polar star.—Peace and justice [should] be the polar stars of the American Societies.—To J. CORREA. vii, 184. FORD ED., x, 164. (M., 1820.)

6511. PEACE, A policy of.—Determined as we are to avoid, if possible, wasting the energies of our people in war and destruction, we shall avoid implicating ourselves with the powers of Europe, even in support of principles which we mean to pursue. They have so many other interests different from ours, that we must avoid being entangled in them. We believe we can enforce those principles, as to ourselves, by peaceable means, now that we are likely to have our public councils detached from foreign views. —To THOMAS PAINE. iv, 370. FORD ED., viii, 18. (W., March 1801.)

6512. ——— ———. I hope that peace and amity with all nations will long be the character of our land, and that its prosperity under the Charter will react on the mind of Europe, and profit her by the example.—To EARL OF BUCHAN. iv, 494. (W., 1803.)

6513. ——— ———. We ask for peace and justice from all nations.—To JAMES MONROE. v, 12. FORD ED., viii, 450. (W., May 1806.)

6514. ——— ———. The desire to preserve our country from the calamities and ravages of war, by cultivating a disposition, and pursuing a conduct, conciliatory and friendly to all nations, has been sincerely entertained and faithfully followed. It was dictated by the principles of humanity, the precepts of the gospel, and the general wish of our country. —REPLY TO ADDRESS. viii, 118. (1807.)

6515. PEACE, Politics and.—We have great need of peace in Europe, that foreign affairs may no longer bear so heavily on ours. We have great need for the ensuing twelve months to be left to ourselves. The enemies of our Constitution are preparing a fearful operation, and the dissensions in this State [Pennsylvania] are too likely to bring things to the situation they wish, when our Bonaparte, surrounded by his comrades in arms, may step in to give us political salvation in his way. It behooves our citizens to be on their guard, to be firm in their principles, and full of confidence in themselves. We are able to preserve our self-government if we will but think so.—To T. M. RANDOLPH. iv, 319. FORD ED., vii, 422. (Pa., Feb. 1800.)

6516. PEACE, Prayers for.—I pray for peace, as best for all the world, best for us, and best for me, who have already lived to see three wars, and now pant for nothing more than to be permitted to depart in peace. —To THOMAS LEIPER. vi, 466. FORD ED., ix, 522. (M., 1815.)

6517. PEACE, Preserving.—My hope of preserving peace for our country is not founded in the greater principles of non-resistance under every wrong, but in the belief that a just and friendly conduct on our part will produce justice and friendship from others.—To EARL OF BUCHAN. iv, 494. (W., 1803.)

6518. ——— ———. If nations go to war for every degree of injury, there would never be peace on earth.—To MADAME DE STAEL. v, 133. (W., 1807.)

6519. ——— ———. To preserve and secure peace has been the constant aim of my administration.—R. TO A. BALTIMORE BAPTISTS. viii, 137. (1808.)

6520. PEACE, A principle of government.—Peace, commerce and honest friendship with all nations, entangling alliances with none, * * * I deem [one of the] essential principles of our government and, consequently, [one] which ought to shape its administration.—FIRST INAUGURAL ADDRESS. viii, 4. FORD ED., viii, 4. (1801.)

6521. ——— ———. Peace has been our principle, peace is our interest, and peace has saved to the world this only plant of free and rational government now existing in it. * * * However, therefore, we may have been reproached for pursuing our Quaker system, time will affix the stamp of wisdom on it, and the happiness and prosperity of our citizens will attest its merit. And this, I believe, is the only legitimate object of government, and the first duty of governors, and not the slaughter of men and devastation of the countries placed under their care, in pursuit of a fantastic honor, unallied to virtue or happiness; or in gratification of the angry passions, or the pride of administrators, excited by personal incidents, in which their citizens have no concern.—To GENERAL KOSCIUSKO. v, 585. (M., 1811.)

6522. PEACE, And profit.—Peace and profit will, I hope, be our lot.—To BENJAMIN VAUGHAN. iii, 159. (N.Y., 1790.)

6523. PEACE, Prosperity and.—Our desire is to pursue ourselves the path of peace as the only one leading surely to prosperity. —To GEORGE HAMMOND. iii, 559. FORD ED., vi, 253. (Pa., 1793.)

6524. ——— ———. I have ever cherished the same spirit with all nations, from a consciousness that peace, prosperity, liberty and morals, have an intimate connection.—To DR. GEORGE LOGAN. vi, 215. FORD ED., ix, 421. (M., 1813.)

6525. PEACE, Public welfare and.—We wish to cultivate peace and friendship with all nations, believing that course most conducive to the welfare of our own.—To RUFUS KING. iv, 444. FORD ED., viii, 164. (W., 1802.)

6526. PEACE, Pursuit of.—From the moment which sealed our peace and independence, our nation has wisely pursued the paths of peace and justice. During the period in which I have been charged with its concerns, no effort has been spared to exempt us from the wrongs and the rapacity of foreign nations, and * * * I feel assured that no American will hesitate to rally round the standard of his insulted country, in defence of that freedom and independence achieved by the wisdom of sages, and consecrated by the blood of heroes.—R. TO A. GEORGETOWN REPUBLICANS. viii, 159. (1809.)

6527. —— ——. Do what is right, leaving the people of Europe to act their follies and crimes among themselves, while we pursue in good faith the paths of peace and prosperity.—To PRESIDENT MONROE. vii, 290. FORD ED., x, 259. (M., 1823.)

6528. PEACE, Securing.—Whatever enables us to go to war, secures our peace.—To JAMES MONROE. FORD ED., v, 198. (N.Y., 1790.)

6529. PEACE, Wisdom of.—Peace and friendship with all mankind is our wisest policy; and I wish we may be permitted to pursue it.—To C. W. F. DUMAS. i, 553. (P., 1786.)

6530. PEACE, Wishes for.—That peace, safety, and concord may be the portion of our native land, and be long enjoyed by our fellow-citizens, is the most ardent wish of my heart, and if I can be instrumental in procuring or preserving them, I shall think I have not lived in vain.—To BENJAMIN WARING. iv, 378. (W., March 1801.)

6531. —— ——. It is impossible that any other man should wish peace as much as I do; although duty may control that wish.— To JOEL BARLOW. v, 216. FORD ED., ix, 168. (W., Dec. 1807.) See ALLIANCES.

6532. PEACE vs. WAR.—I value peace, and I should unwillingly see any event take place which would render war a necessary resource.—To M. DUPONT DE NEMOURS. iv, 435. (W., April 1802.)

6533. —— ——. I hope we shall prove how much happier for man the Quaker policy is, and that the life of the feeder, is better than that of the fighter; and it is some consolation that the desolation by these maniacs [European kings] of one part of the earth is the means of improving it in other parts.—To JOHN ADAMS. vii, 245. FORD ED., x, 217. (M., 1822.)

— **PELISIPIA, Proposed State of.**—See WESTERN TERRITORY.

6534. PENDLETON (Edmund), Address of.—Your patriarchal address to your country is running through all the republican papers, and has a very great effect on the people. It is short, simple, and presents things in a view they readily comprehend. The character and circumstances, too, of the writer leave them without doubts of his motives.—To EDMUND PENDLETON. iv, 274. FORD ED., vii, 336. (Pa., 1799.)

6535. PENDLETON (Edmund), Perseverance.—Mr. Pendleton * * * 'was the ablest man in debate I have ever met with. He had not, indeed, the poetical fancy of Mr. Henry, his sublime imagination, his lofty and overwhelming diction; but he was cool, smooth and persuasive; his language flowing, chaste and embellished; his conceptions quick, acute and full of resource; never vanquished: for if he lost the main battle, he returned upon you, and regained so much of it as to make it a drawn one, by dexterous manœuvres, skirmishes in detail, and the recovery of small advantages which, little singly, were important altogether. You never knew when you were clear of him, but were harassed by his perseverance, until the patience was worn down of all who had less of it than himself. Add to this, that he was one of the most virtuous and benevolent of men, the kindest friend, the most amiable and pleasant of companions, which insured a favorable reception to whatever came from him.—AUTOBIOGRAPHY. i, 37. FORD ED., i. 50. (1821.)

6536. PENDULUM, Advantages of.— The great and decisive superiority of the pendulum, as a standard of measure, is its accessibility to all men, at all times, and in all places. —To DR. ROBERT PATTERSON. vi, 20. (M., 1811.)

6537. PENDULUM, Construction of.—I have a curiosity to try the length of a pendulum vibrating seconds here. * * * The bob should be spherical, of lead, and its radius, I presume, about one inch. * * * The suspending rod should be such as not to be affected by heat or cold, nor yet so heavy as to affect too sensibly the centre of oscillation. Would not a rod of wood not larger than a large wire answer this double view? * * * Iron has been found but about six times as strong as wood while its specific gravity is eight times as great. * * * A rod of white oak not larger than a seine twine, would probably support a spherical bob of lead of one inch radius.—To DR. ROBERT PATTERSON. vi, 26. (M., 1811.)

6538. PENDULUM, Experiments with. —I had taken no notice of the precaution of making the experiment of the pendulum on the sea-shore, because the highest mountain in the United States would not add 1-5000 part to the length of the earth's radius, nor 1-128 of an inch to the length of the pendulum. The highest part of the Andes, indeed, might add about 1-1000 to the earth's radius, and 1-25 of an inch to the pendulum. As it has been thought worth mention, I will insert it also.—To DAVID RITTENHOUSE. iii, 149. (N.Y., 1790.)

— **PENNSYLVANIA, Boundary line.**— See BOUNDARIES.

6539. PENNSYLVANIA, Electoral influence.—In Pennsylvania, the election has been triumphantly carried by the republicans; their antagonists having got but two out of eleven members [of Congress], and the vote of this State can generally turn the balance.—To T. M. RANDOLPH. iii, 491. FORD ED., vi, 134. (Pa., 1792.)

6540. PENNSYLVANIA, Patriotism.— I shall always be thankful for any information * * * which may enable me to understand the differences of opinion and interest which seem to be springing up in Pennsylvania, and to be subjects of uneasiness. If that State splits it will let us down into the abyss. I hope so much from the patriotism of all, that they will make all smaller interests give way to the greater importance of the general welfare.—To WILLIAM DUANE. FORD ED., viii, 54. (W., May 1801.)

6541. PENNSYLVANIA, Religious freedom.—The laws of Pennsylvania set us the first example of the wholesome and happy effects of religious freedom.—To M. DUFIEF. vi, 341. (M., 1814.)

6542. —— ——. The cradle of toleration and freedom of religion.—To DR. THOMAS COOPER. vii, 266. FORD ED., x, 242. (M., 1822.)

6543. PENNSYLVANIA, Republicanism.—Pennsylvania is coming majestically round to the true principles.—To T. LOMAX. iv, 300. FORD ED., vii, 374. (M., March 1799.)

6544. —— ——. In the electoral election [1808] Pennsylvania really spoke in a voice of thunder to the monarchists of our country, and while that State continues so firm, with the solid mass of republicanism to the South and West, such efforts as we have lately seen in the anti-republican portion of our country cannot ultimately affect our security.—To DR. E. GRIFFITH. v, 450. (M., 1809.)

6545. PENNSYLVANIA, Virginia and.—With respect to your State particularly, we shall take very great pleasure in cultivating every disposition to harmony and mutual aid. That policy would be very unsound which should build our interest or happiness on anything inconsistent with yours.—To THE PRESIDENT OF PENNSYLVANIA. FORD ED., iii, 17. (R., 1781.)

6546. —— ——. The permanence of our Union hanging on the harmony of Pennsylvania and Virginia, I hope that will continue as long as our government continues to be a blessing to mankind.—To THOMAS LEIPER. FORD ED., x, 299. (M., 1824.)

6547. PENSACOLA, Capture of.—The capture of Pensacola, which furnished so much speculation for European news-writers (who imagine that our political code, like theirs, had no chapter of morality), was nothing here. In the first moment, indeed there was a general outcry of condemnation of what appeared to be a wrongful aggression. But this was quieted at once by information that it had been taken without orders, and would be instantly restored. * * * This manifestation of the will of our citizens to countenance no injustice towards a foreign nation filled me with comfort as to our future course.—To ALBERT GALLATIN. FORD ED., x, 115. (M., Nov. 1818.)

6548. PENSIONS, Prodigalities of.—Nor should we wonder at * * * [the] pressure [for a fixed constitution in 1788-9] when we consider the monstrous abuses of power under which * * * [the French] people were ground to powder; when we pass in review * * * the prodigalities of pensions.—AUTOBIOGRAPHY. i, 86. FORD ED., i, 118. (1821.)

6549. PENSIONS, Public.—Every person * * * qualified to elect [to the House of Representatives of Virginia] shall be capable of being elected [to the House of Representatives]. * * * During his continuance in the said office, he shall hold no public pension * * * .—PROPOSED VA. CONSTITUTION. FORD ED., ii, 15. (June 1776.)

6550. —— ——. While in the senatorial office they [the members] shall be incapable of holding any public pension.—PROPOSED VA. CONSTITUTION. FORD ED., ii, 16. (June 1776.)

6551. PENSIONS, Taxes and.—We do not mean that our people shall be burthened with oppressive taxes to provide sinecures for the idle or the wicked, under color of providing for a civil list.—REPLY TO LORD NORTH'S PROPOSITION. FORD ED., i, 480. (July 1775.)

6552. PEOPLE, Administration of law and.—That people will be happiest whose laws are best, and are best administered.—DIFFUSION OF KNOWLEDGE BILL. FORD ED., ii, 221. (1779.)

6553. PEOPLE, American vs. British.—Our country is getting into a ferment against yours, or rather has caught it from yours. God knows how this will end; but assuredly in one extreme or the other. There can be no medium between those who have loved so much.—To DR. PRICE. i, 378. FORD ED., iv, 84. (P., 1785.)

6554. PEOPLE, American and European.—If all the sovereigns of Europe were to set themselves to work to emancipate the minds of their subjects from their present ignorance and prejudices, and that, as zealously as they now endeavor the contrary, a thousand years would not place them on that high ground on which our common people are now setting out. Ours could not have been so fairly put into the hands of their own common sense, had they not been separated from their parent stock, and kept from contamination, either from them, or the other people of the old world, by the intervention of so wide an ocean.—To GEORGE WYTHE. ii, 7. FORD ED., iv, 268. (P., 1786.)

6555. PEOPLE, American and French.—There is an affection between the two peoples [the Americans and French] which disposes them to favor one another.—To COUNT DE VERGENNES. i, 390. (P., 1785.)

6556. PEOPLE, Animosities.—The animosities of sovereigns are temporary and may be allayed; but those which seize the whole body of a people, and of a people, too, who dictate their own measures, produce calamities of long duration.—To C. W. F. DUMAS. i, 553. (P., 1786.)

6557. PEOPLE, Ascendency of.—Lay down true principles and adhere to them inflexibly. Do not be frightened into their surrender by the alarms of the timid, or the croakings of wealth against the ascendency of the people. If experience be called for, appeal to that of our fifteen or twenty governments for forty years, and show me where the people have done half the mischief in these forty years, that a single despot would have done in a single year; or show half the riots and rebellions, the crimes and the punishments, which have taken place in any single nation, under kingly government, during the same period.—To SAMUEL KERCHIVAL. vii, 11. FORD ED., x, 39. (M., 1816.)

6558. PEOPLE, Authority of.—I consider the people who constitute a society or nation as the source of all authority in that nation; as free to transact their common concerns by any agents they think proper; to change these agents individually, or the organization of them in form or function whenever they please; that all the acts done by these agents under the authority of the nation, are the acts of the nation, are obligatory on them, and enure to their use, and can in no wise be annulled or affected by any change in the form of the government, or of the persons administering it.—OPINION ON FRENCH TREATIES. vii, 612. FORD ED., vi, 220. (April 1793.)

6559. —— ——. Leave no authority existing not responsible to the people.—To ISAAC H. TIFFANY. vii, 32. (M., 1816.)

6560. —— ——. All authority belongs to the people.—To SPENCER ROANE. vii, 213. FORD ED., x, 190. (M., 1821.)

6561. PEOPLE, Blood of.—On this side of the Atlantic [Europe] the blood of the people is become an inheritance, and those who fatten on it will not relinquish it easily. —To E. RUTLEDGE. ii, 435. FORD ED., v, 42. (P., 1788.)

6562. PEOPLE, Cities and.—When the people get piled upon one another in large cities, as in Europe, they will become corrupt as in Europe.*—To JAMES MADISON. ii, 332. FORD ED., iv, 479. (P., 1787.)

6563. PEOPLE, City and country.—The inhabitants of the commercial cities are as different in sentiment and character from the country people as any two distinct nations, and are clamorous against the order of things [republicanism] established by the agricultural interest.—To M. PICTET. iv, 463. (W., 1803.)

6564. PEOPLE, Confidence in.—My confidence * * * in my countrymen generally leaves me without much fear for the future. —To JAMES FISHBACK. v, 470. (M., 1809.)

6565. PEOPLE, Control by.—Unless the mass retains sufficient control over those intrusted with the powers of their government, these will be perverted to their own oppression, and to the perpetuation of wealth and power in the individuals and their families selected for the trust. Whether our Constitution has hit on the exact degree of control necessary, is yet under experiment; and it is a most encouraging reflection that distance and other difficulties securing us against the brigand governments of Europe, in the safe enjoyment of our farms and firesides, the experiment stands a better chance of being satisfactorily made here than on any occasion yet presented by history.—To MR. VANDER KEMP. vi, 45. (M., 1812.)

6566. —— ——. I know no safe depositary of the ultimate powers of the society but the people themselves; and if we think them not enlightened enough to exercise their control with a wholesome discretion, the

* In the Congress edition " When we get piled upon one another in large cities, as in Europe, we shall become as corrupt as in Europe, and go to eating one another as they do there. "—EDITOR.

remedy is not to take it from them, but to inform their discretion by education. This is the true corrective of abuses of constitutional power.—To WILLIAM C. JARVIS. vii, 179. FORD ED., x, 161. (M., 1820.)

6567. PEOPLE, Corruption and.—A germ of corruption indeed has been transferred from our dear mother country, and has already borne fruit, but its blight is begun from the breath of the people.—To J. P. BRISSOT DE WARVILLE. FORD ED., vi, 249. (Pa., 1793.)

6568. PEOPLE, Deception of.—The spirit of 1776 is not dead. It has only been slumbering. The body of the American people is substantially republican. But their virtuous feelings have been played on by some fact with more fiction; they have been the dupes of artful manœuvres, and made for a moment to be willing instruments in forging chains for themselves. But time and truth have dissipated the delusion, and opened their eyes.—To T. LOMAX. iv, 300. FORD ED., vii, 373. (M., March 1799.)

6569. —— ——. Our citizens may be deceived for awhile, and have been deceived; but as long as the presses can be protected, we may trust to them for light.—To ARCHIBALD STUART. FORD ED., vii, 378. (M., 1799.)

6570. —— ——. The lesson we have had will probably be useful to the people at large, by showing to them how capable they are of being made the instruments of their own bondage.—To JOHN DICKINSON. iv, 424. (W., 1801.)

6571. PEOPLE, Duty of rulers.—To inform the minds of the people, and to follow their will, is the chief duty of those placed at their head.—To M. DUMAS. ii, 297. (P., 1787.)

6572. PEOPLE, Enforcement of rights. —The spirit of the times may alter, will alter. Our rulers will become corrupt, our people careless. * * * They will be forgotten, and their rights disregarded. They will forget themselves, but in the sole faculty of making money, and will never think of uniting to effect a due respect for their rights.— NOTES ON VIRGINIA. viii, 402. FORD ED., iii, 266. (1782.)

6573. PEOPLE, English.—For the achievement of this happy event [peace] we call for and confide in the good offices of our fellow-subjects beyond the Atlantic. Of their friendly dispositions we do not cease to hope; aware, as they must be, that they have nothing more to expect from the same common enemy, than the humble favor of being last devoured.—DECLARATION ON TAKING UP ARMS. FORD ED., i, 475. (July 1775.)

6574. —— ——. Nor have we been wanting in attentions to our British brethren. We have warned them from time to time of attempts by their legislature to extend an unwarrantable jurisdiction over these our States. We have reminded them of the circumstances .

of our emigration and settlement here, no one of which could warrant so strange a pretension; that these were effected at the expense of our own blood and treasure, unassisted by the wealth or strength of Great Britain; that in constituting, indeed, our several forms of government, we had adopted one common king, thereby laying a foundation for perpetual league and amity with them; but that submission to their parliament was no part of our constitution, nor ever in idea, if history may be credited; and we have appealed to their native justice and magnanimity as well as to the ties of our common kindred to disavow these usurpations which were likely to interrupt our connection and correspondence. They, too, have been deaf to the voice of justice and of consanguinity, and when occasions have been given them, by the regular course of their laws, of removing from their councils the disturbers of our harmony, they have, by their free elections, reestablished them in power. At this very time, too, they are permitting their chief Magistrate to send over not only soldiers of our common blood, but Scotch and foreign mercenaries, to invade and destroy us. These facts have given the last stab to agonizing affection, and manly spirit bids us to renounce forever these unfeeling brethren. We must endeavor to forget our former love for them, to hold them as we hold the rest of mankind, enemies in war, in peace, friends. We might have been a free and a great people together; but a communication of grandeur and of freedom, it seems, is below their dignity. Be it so, since they will have it. The road to happiness and to glory is open to us, too. We will tread it apart from them, and acquiesce in the necessity which denounces our eternal separation.*—DECLARATION OF INDEPENDENCE AS DRAWN BY JEFFERSON.

6575. —— ——. The spirit of hostility to us has always existed in the mind of the King, but it has now extended itself through the whole mass of the people, and the majority of the public councils. In a country, where the voice of the people influences so much the measures of administration, and where it coincides with the private temper of the King, there is no pronouncing on future events. It is true they have nothing to gain, and much to lose by a war with us; but interest is not the strongest passion in the human breast.—To JAMES ROSS. i, 561. FORD ED., iv, 217. (P., 1786.)

6576. —— ——. The people of England, I think, are less oppressed than the people in France. But it needs but half an eye to see, when among them, that the foundation is laid in their

* Congress changed the passage as follows. "Nor have we been wanting in attentions to our British brethren. We have warned them, from time to time, of attempts by their legislature to extend an unwarrantable jurisdiction over us. We have reminded them of the circumstances of our emigration and settlement here. We have appealed to their native justice and magnanimity, and we have conjured them, by the ties of our common kindred, to disavow these usurpations, which would inevitably interrupt our connection and correspondence. They, too, have been deaf to the voice of justice and of consanguinity. We must, therefore, acquiesce in the necessity, which denounces our separation, and hold them, as we hold the rest of mankind, Enemies in War, in Peace, Friends."—EDITOR.

dispositions for the establishment of a despotism. Nobility, wealth and pomp are the objects of their admiration. They are by no means the free-minded people we suppose them in America. Their learned men, too, are few in number, and are less learned, and infinitely less emancipated from prejudices than are those of this country [France].—To GEORGE WYTHE. ii, 8. FORD ED., iv, 269. (P., 1786.)

6577. —— ——. England presents the singular phenomenon of a nation, the individuals of which are as faithful to their private engagements and duties, as honorable, as worthy, as those of any nation on earth, and whose government is yet the most unprincipled at this day known.—To JOHN LANGDON. v, 514. (M., 1810.)

6578. —— ——. The English people are individually as respectable as those of other nations,—it is her government which is so corrupt, and which has destroyed the nation.—To WILLIAM DUANE. v, 552. FORD ED., ix, 287. (M., 1810.)

6579. —— ——. I should be glad to see their farmers and mechanics come here, but I hope their nobles, priests and merchants will be kept at home to be moralized by the discipline of the new government.—To WILLIAM DUANE. v, 552. FORD ED., ix, 287. (M., 1810.)

6580. —— ——. The English have been a wise, a virtuous and truly estimable people. But commerce and a corrupt government have rotted them to the core. Every generous, nay, every just sentiment, is absorbed in the thirst for gold. I speak of their cities, which we may certainly pronounce to be ripe for despotism, and fitted for no other government. Whether the leaven of the agricultural body is sufficient to regenerate the residuary mass, and maintain it in a sound state, under any reformation of government, may still be doubted.—To MR. OGILVIE. v, 604. (M., 1811.)

6581. —— ——. The individuals of the [British] nation I have ever honored and esteemed, the basis of their character being essentially worthy; but I consider their government as the most flagitious which has existed since the days of Philip of Macedon, whom they make their model.—To JOHN ADAMS. vii, 46. (P.F., 1816.)

6582. PEOPLE, Errors of.—The people are the only censors of their governors; and even their errors will tend to keep these to the true principles of their institution. To punish these errors too severely would be to suppress the only safeguard of the public liberty.—To EDWARD CARRINGTON. ii, 99. FORD ED., iv, 359. (P., 1787.)

6583. PEOPLE, European.—Behold me at length on the vaunted scene of Europe! * * * You are, perhaps, curious to know how this new scene has struck a savage of the mountains of America. Not advantageously, I assure you. I find the general fate of humanity here most deplorable. The truth of Voltaire's observation offers itself perpetually, that every man here must be either the hammer or the anvil. It is a true picture of that country to which they say we shall pass hereafter, and where we are to see God and His angels in splendor, and crowds of the damned trampled under their feet. While the great mass of the people are thus suffering under physical and moral oppression, I have endeavored to examine more nearly the condition of the great, to appreciate the true value of the circumstances in their situation which dazzle the bulk of spectators, and, especially, to compare it with that degree of happiness which is enjoyed in America, by every class of people. Intrigues of love occupy the younger, and those of ambition, the elder part of the great. Conjugal love having no existence among them, domestic happiness, of which that is the basis, is utterly unknown. In lieu of this, are substituted pursuits which nourish and invigorate all our bad passions, and which offer only moments of ecstacy amidst days and months of restlessness and torment. Much, very much inferior, this, to the tranquil, permanent felicity with which domestic society in America blesses most of its inhabitants; leaving them to follow steadily those pursuits which health and reason approve, and rendering truly delicious the intervals of those pursuits.—To Mr. Bellini. i, 444. (P., 1785.)

6584. PEOPLE, Freedom and.—I am not among those who fear the people. They, and not the rich, are our dependence for continued freedom.—To Samuel Kerchival. vii, 14. Ford ed., x, 41. (M., 1816.)

6585. PEOPLE, French.—I do love this people with all my heart, and think that with a better religion, a better form of government and their present governors, their condition and country would be most enviable.—To Mrs. John Adams. Ford ed., iv, 61. (P., 1785.)

6586. —— ——. It is difficult to conceive how so good a people, with so good a King, so well-disposed rulers in general, so genial a climate, so fertile a soil, should be rendered so ineffectual for producing human happiness by one single curse,—that of a bad form of government. But it is a fact. In spite of the mildness of their governors, the people are ground to powder by the vices of the form of government. Of twenty millions of people supposed to be in France, I am of opinion there are nineteen millions more wretched, more accursed in every circumstance of human existence than the most conspicuously wretched individual of the whole United States.—To Mrs. Trist. i, 394. (P., 1785.)

6587. —— ——. Two peoples whose interests, whose principles, whose habits of attachment, founded on fellowship in war and mutual kindnesses, have so many points of union, cannot but be easily kept together.—To M. Odit. iv, 123. (M., Oct. 1795.)

6588. —— ——. The body of the people of * * * [France] love us cordially.—To John Langdon. i, 429. (P., 1785.)

6589. —— ——. In science the mass of the people [of France] are two centuries behind ours; their literati a dozen years before us. Books, really good, acquire just reputation in that time, and so become known to us, and communicate to us all their advances in knowledge. Is not this delay compensated by our being placed out of the reach of that swarm of nonsensical publications which issues daily from a thousand presses, and perishes in the issuing?—To Mr. Bellini. i, 444. (P., 1785.)

6590. —— ——. Certain it is that they [the farming classes in South of France] are less happy and less virtuous in villages, than they would be insulated with their families on the grounds they cultivate.—Travels in France. ix, 313. (1787.)

6591. —— ——. I cannot leave this great and good country without expressing my sense of its preeminence of character among the nations of the earth. A more benevolent people I have never known, nor greater warmth and devotedness in their select friendships. Their kindness and accommodation to strangers is unparalleled, and the hospitality of Paris is beyond anything I had conceived to be practicable in a large city. Their eminence, too, in science, the communicative dispositions of their scientific men, the politeness of the general manners, the ease and vivacity of their conversation, give a charm to their society, to be found nowhere else. In a comparison of this with other countries, we have the proof of primacy, which was given to Themistocles after the battle of Salamis. Every general voted to himself the first reward of valor, and the second to Themistocles. So, ask the travelled inhabitant of any nation, in what country on earth would you rather live? Certainly, in my own, where are all my friends, my relations, and the earliest and sweetest affections and recollections of my life. Which would be your second choice? France.—Autobiography. i, 107. Ford ed., i, 148. (1821.)

6592. PEOPLE, Frugality and happiness.—Kindly separated by nature and a wide ocean from the exterminating havoc of one quarter of the globe; too high-minded to endure the degradations of the others; possessing a chosen country, with room enough for our descendants to the hundredth and thousandth generation; entertaining a due sense of our equal right to the use of our own faculties, to the acquisitions of our own industry, to honor and confidence from our fellow-citizens, resulting, not from birth, but from our actions, and their sense of them; enlightened by a benign religion, professed, indeed, and practiced in various forms, yet all of them inculcating honesty, truth, temperance, gratitude and the love of man; acknowledging and adoring an overruling Providence, which, by all its dispensations, proves that it delights in the happiness of man here and his greater happiness hereafter,—with all these blessings, what more is necessary to make us a happy and prosperous people? Still one thing more, fellow-citizens—a wise and frugal government, which shall restrain men from injuring one another, which shall leave them otherwise free to regulate their own pursuits of industry and improvement, and shall not take from the mouth of labor the bread it has earned. This is the sum of good government, and this is necessary to close the circle of our felicities.—First Inaugural Address. viii, 3. Ford ed., viii, 3. (1801.)

6593. PEOPLE, Government and.—Every government degenerates when trusted to the rulers of the people alone. The people themselves, therefore, are its only safe depositaries. And to render even them safe, their minds must be improved to a certain degree.—Notes on Virginia. viii, 390. Ford ed., iii, 254. (1782.)

6594. —— ——. A tractable people may be governed in large bodies; but, in proportion as they depart from this character, the extent of their government must be less.—To JAMES MADISON. ii, 66. FORD ED., iv, 333. (P., 1786.)

6595. —— ——. The government which can wield the arm of the people must be the strongest possible.—To MR. WEAVER. v, 89. (W., 1807.)

6596. —— ——. No government can continue good, but under the control of the people.—To JOHN ADAMS. vii, 149. FORD ED., x, 153. (M., 1819.)

6597. PEOPLE, Imposing upon.—As little [as to shut up the press] is it necessary to impose on the people's senses, or dazzle their minds by pomp, splendor, or forms. Instead of this artificial, how much surer is that real respect, which results from the use of their reason, and the habit of bringing everything to the test of common sense.—To JUDGE TYLER. iv, 548. (W., 1804.)

6598. PEOPLE, Independent of all.— Independence can be trusted nowhere but with the people in mass. They are inherently independent of all but moral law.—To SPENCER ROANE. vii, 134. FORD ED., x, 141. (P. F., 1819.)

6599. PEOPLE, Industry.—The rights [of the people] to the exercise and fruits of their own industry can never be protected against the selfishness of rulers not subject to their control at short periods.—To ISAAC H. TIFFANY. vii. 32. (M., 1816.)

6600. —— ——. No other depositaries of power [than the people themselves] have ever yet been found, which did not end in converting to their own profit the earnings of those committed to their charge.—To SAMUEL KERCHIVAL. vii, 36. FORD ED., x, 45. (M., 1816.) See INDUSTRY.

6601. PEOPLE, Judgment of.—The firmness with which the people have withstood the late abuses of the press, the discernment they have manifested between truth and falsehood, show that they may safely be trusted to hear everything true and false, and to form a correct judgment between them.—To JUDGE TYLER. iv, 549. (W., 1804.) See NEWSPAPERS.

6602. PEOPLE, Legislative powers.— While those bodies are in existence to whom the people have delegated the powers of legislation, they alone possess, and may exercise, those powers. But when they are dissolved by the lopping off of one or more of their branches, the power reverts to the people, who may exercise it to unlimited extent, either assembling together in person, sending deputies, or in any other way they may think proper.—RIGHTS OF BRITISH AMERICA. i, 138. FORD ED., i, 443. (1774.)

6603. PEOPLE, Liberty and the.—The people are the only sure reliance for the preservation of our liberty.—To JAMES MADISON. ii, 332. (P., 1787.)

6604. PEOPLE, New England.—The adventurous genius and intrepidity of those peo-

ple [New Englanders] is amazing. They are now intent on burning Boston as a hive which gives cover to [British] regulars; and none are more bent upon it than the very people who come out of it, and whose prosperity lies there.—To FRANCIS EPPES. FORD ED., i, 461. (Pa., July 4, 1775.)

6605. PEOPLE, Oppressed.—To constrain the brute force of the people, the European governments deem it necessary to keep them down by hard labor, poverty and ignorance, and to take from them, as from bees, so much of their earnings, as that unremitting labor shall be necessary to obtain a sufficient surplus barely to sustain a scanty and miserable life. And these earnings they apply to maintain their privileged orders in splendor and idleness, to fascinate the eyes of the people, and excite in them an humble adoration and submission, as to an order of superior beings.—To WILLIAM JOHNSON. vii, 291. FORD ED., x, 226. (M., 1823.)

6606. PEOPLE, Participation in government.—We think in America that it is necessary to introduce the people into every department of government, as far as they are capable of exercising it; and that this is the only way to ensure a long-continued and honest administration of its powers.—To M. L'ABBÉ ARNOND. iii, 81. FORD ED., v, 103. (P., 1789.)

6607. —— ——. The people are not qualified to exercise themselves the executive department, but they are qualified to name the person who shall exercise it. With us, therefore, they choose this officer every four years.—To L'ABBÉ ARNOND. iii, 81. FORD ED., v, 103. (P., 1789.)

6608. —— ——. The people are not qualified to legislate. With us, therefore, they only choose the legislators.—To M. L'ABBÉ ARNOND. iii, 81. FORD ED., v, 103. (P., 1789.)

6609. —— ——. Were I called upon to decide whether the people had best be omitted in the Legislative or Judiciary department, I would say it is better to leave them out of the Legislative. The execution of the laws is more important than the making them. However, it is best to have the people in all the three departments where that is possible. —To M. L'ABBÉ ARNOND. iii, 82. FORD ED., v, 104. (P., 1789.)

6610. —— ——. The people, being the only safe depositary of power, should exercise in person every function which their qualifications enable them to exercise, consistently with the order and security of society.—To DR. WALTER JONES. vi, 285. FORD ED., ix, 447. (M., 1814.)

6611. PEOPLE, Prussian.—The transition from ease and opulence to extreme poverty is remarkable on crossing the line between the Dutch and Prussian territories. The soil and climate are the same; the governments alone differ. With the poverty, the fear also of slaves is visible in the faces of the Prussian subjects. —TRAVELS IN PRUSSIA. ix, 378. (1787.)

6612. PEOPLE, Reasonable.—It is a blessing that our people are reasonable; that they are kept so well informed of the state of things as to judge for themselves, to see the true sources of their difficulties, and to maintain their confidence undiminished in the wisdom and integrity of their functionaries.—To Cæsar A. Rodney. v, 501. Ford ed., ix, 272. (M., 1810.)

6613. PEOPLE, Representation.—I look for our safety to the broad representation of the people [in Congress]. It will be more difficult for corrupt views to lay hold of so large a mass.—To T. M. Randolph. Ford ed., v, 455. (Pa., 1792.)

6614. PEOPLE, Representation and taxation.—Preserve inviolate the fundamental principle, that the people are not to be taxed but by representatives chosen immediately by themselves.—To James Madison. ii, 328. Ford ed., iv, 475. (P., 1787.)

6615. PEOPLE, Republic.—It is the manners and spirit of a people which preserve a republic in vigor. A degeneracy in these is a canker which soon eats to the heart of its laws and constitution.—Notes on Virginia. viii, 406. Ford ed., iii, 269. (1782.)

6616. PEOPLE, Respect for.—My visit to Philadelphia will be merely out of respect to the public, and to the new President.—To Mr. Volney. iv, 159. (M., Jan. 1797.)

6617. PEOPLE, Rights of.—Their rights * * * [are] derived from the laws of nature, and [are] not the gift of their Chief Magistrate.—Rights of British America. i, 141. Ford ed., i, 446. (1774.)

6618. —— ——. The people of every country are the only safe guardians of their own rights, and are the only instruments which can be used for their destruction. And certainly they would never consent to be so used were they not deceived. To avoid this they should be instructed to a certain degree.—To John Wyche. v, 448. (M., 1809.)

6619. —— ——. The people, especially when moderately instructed, are the only safe, because the only honest, depositaries of the public rights, and should, therefore, be introduced into the administration of them in every function to which they are sufficient. They will err sometimes and accidentally, but never designedly, and with a systematic and persevering purpose of overthrowing the free principles of the government.—To M. Coray. vii, 319. (M., 1823.)

6620. PEOPLE, Roman.—The letters of Cicero breathe the purest effusions of an exalted patriot, while the parricide Cæsar is lost in odious contrast. When the enthusiasm, however, kindled by Cicero's pen and principles, subsides into cool reflection, I ask myself, what was that government, which the virtues of Cicero were so zealous to restore, and the ambition of Cæsar to subvert? And if Cæsar had been as virtuous as he was daring and sagacious, what could he, even in the plenitude of his usurped power, have done to lead his fellow citizens into good government? I do not say to *restore* it, because they never had it, from the rape of the Sabines to the ravages of the Cæsars. If their people, indeed, had been, like ourselves, enlightened, peaceable and really free, the answer would be obvious. "Restore independence to all your foreign conquests, relieve Italy from the government of the rabble of Rome, consult it as a nation entitled to self-government, and do its will". But steeped in corruption, vice and venality, as the whole nation was (and nobody had done more than Cæsar to corrupt it), what could even Cicero, Cato, Brutus have done, had it been referred to them to establish a good government for their country? They had no ideas of government themselves, but of their degenerate Senate, nor the people of liberty, but of the factious opposition of their Tribunes. They had afterwards their Tituses, their Trajans and Antoninuses, who had the will to make them happy, and the power to mould their government into a good and permanent form. But it would seem as if they could not. see their way clearly to do it. No government can continue good, but under the control of the people; and their people were so demoralized and depraved, as to be incapable of exercising a wholesome control. Their reformation then was to be taken up *ab incunabulis*. Their minds were to be informed by education what is right and what wrong; to be encouraged in habits of virtue and deterred from those of vice by the dread of punishments proportioned, indeed, but irremissible; in all cases, to follow truth as the only safe guide, and to eschew error, which bewilders us in one false consequence after another, in endless succession. These are the inculcations necessary to render the people a sure basis for the structure of order and good government. But this would have been an operation of a generation or two, at least, within which period would have succeeded many Neros and Commoduses, who would have quashed the whole process. I confess, then, I can neither see what Cicero, Cato and Brutus, united and uncontrolled, could have devised to lead their people into good government, nor how this enigma can be solved, nor how further shown why it has been the fate of that delightful country never to have known, to this day, and through a course of five and twenty hundred years, the history of which we possess, one single day of free and rational government. Your intimacy with their history, ancient, middle and modern, your familiarity with the improvements in the science of government at this time, will enable you, if anybody, to go back with our principles and opinions to the times of Cicero, Cato and Brutus, and tell us by what process these great and virtuous men could have led so unenlightened and vitiated a people into freedom and good government.*—To John Adams. vii, 148. Ford ed., x, 152. (M., 1819.)

6621. PEOPLE, Self-government.—The panic into which the people were artfully thrown in 1798, the frenzy which was excited in them by their enemies against their apparent readiness to abandon all the principles established for their own protection, seemed for awhile to countenance the opinions of those who say they cannot be trusted

* "I never could discover," wrote Mr. Adams in reply, "that they possessed much virtue, or real liberty. Their Patricians were in general griping usurers, and tyrannical creditors in all ages. Pride, strength, and courage, were all the virtues that composed their national characters."—Editor.

with their own government. But I never doubted their rallying; and they did rally much sooner than I expected. On the whole, that experiment on their credulity has confirmed my confidence in their ultimate good sense and virtue.—To JUDGE TYLER. iv, 549. (W., 1804.)

6622. —— ——. To open the doors of truth, and to fortify the habit of testing everything by reason, are the most effectual manacles we can rivet on the hands of our successors to prevent their manacling the people with their own consent.—To JUDGE TYLER. iv, 549. (W., 1804.)

6623. PEOPLE, Spirit of.—Cherish the spirit of our people and keep alive their attention. Do not be too severe upon their errors, but reclaim them by enlightening them. If once they become inattentive to the public affairs, you and I and Congress and assemblies, judges and governors shall all become wolves.—To EDWARD CARRINGTON. ii, 100. FORD ED., iv, 360. (P., 1787.)

6624. PEOPLE, Supreme.—He [George III.] is no more than the chief officer of the people, appointed by the laws, and circumscribed with definite powers, to assist in working the great machine of government, erected for their use, and, consequently. subject to their superintendence.—RIGHTS OF BRITISH AMERICA. i, 125. FORD ED., i, 429. (1774.)

6625. PEOPLE, A united.—Spain, under all her disadvantages, physical and mental, is an encouraging example of the impossibility of subduing a people acting with an undivided will. She proves, too, another truth not less valuable, that a people having no king to sell them for a mess of pottage for himself, no shackles to restrain their powers of self-defence, find resources within themselves equal to every trial. This we did during the Revolutionary war. and this we can do again, let who will attack us, if we act heartily with one another. This is my creed. To the principles of union I sacrifice all minor differences of opinion. These, like differences of face, are a law of our nature, and should be viewed with the same tolerance.—To WILLIAM DUANE. v, 603. (M., July 1811.)

6626. PEOPLE, A well-informed.— Whenever the people are well-informed they can be trusted with their own government.— To DR. PRICE. ii, 553. (P., 1789.)

6627. —— ——. Whenever the people are well-informed * * * and things get so far wrong as to attract their notice, they may be relied on to set them to rights.— To DR. PRICE. ii, 553. (P., 1789.)

6628. PEOPLE, The western.—That our fellow citizens of the West would need only to be informed of criminal machinations [by Aaron Burr] against the public safety to crush them at once, I never entertained a doubt.—To GOVERNOR H. D. TIFFIN. v, 37. FORD ED., ix, 21. (W., 1807.)

6629. —— ——. They are freer from prejudices than we are, and bolder in grasping at truth. The time is not distant. though neither you nor I shall see it, when we shal' be but a secondary people to them. Our greediness for wealth, and fantastical expense, have degraded. and will degrade, the minds of our maritime citizens. These are the peculiar vices of commerce.—To JOHN ADAMS. vii, 103. FORD ED., x, 107. (M., 1818.)

6630. —— ——. The bait of local interests, artfully prepared for their palate, has decoyed them [the Western people] from their kindred attachments to alliances alien to them.—To C. W. GOOCH. vii, 430. (M., 1826.)

6631. PEOPLE, Will of.—It accords with our principles to acknowledge any government to be rightful, which is formed by the will of the people substantially declared. —To GOUVERNEUR MORRIS. iii, 489. FORD ED., vi, 131. (Pa., Nov. 1792.)

6632. —— ——. The will of the people is the only legitimate foundation of any government, and to protect its free expression should be our first object.—To BENJAMIN WARING. iv, 379. (W., March 1801.)

6633. PEOPLE, Wisdom of.—Our people in a body are wise, because they are under the unrestrained and unperverted operation of their own understandings.—To DR. JOSEPH PRIESTLEY. iv, 440. FORD ED.. viii, 158. (W., 1802.)

6634. PERCEVAL (Spencer), Ministry. —I am glad of the reestablishment of a Perceval ministry. * The opposition would have recruited our minority by half-way offers.—To PRESIDENT MADISON. vi, 77. (M., Aug. 1812.)

6635. PERPETUAL MOTION, Delusion of.—I am very thankful to you for the description of Redhefer's machine. I had never been able to form an idea of what his principle of deception was. He is the first of the inventors of perpetual motion within my knowledge, who has had the cunning to put his visitors on a false pursuit, by amusing them with a sham machinery whose loose and vibratory motion might impose on them the belief that it is the real source of the motion they see. To this device he is indebted for a more extensive delusion than I have before witnessed on this point. We are full of it as far as this State, and I know not how much farther. In Richmond, they have done me the honor to quote me as having said that it was a possible thing. A poor Frenchman who called on me the other day, with another invention of perpetual motion, assured me that Dr. Franklin, many years ago, expressed his opinion to him that it was not impossible. Without entering into contest on this abuse of the Doctor's name, I gave him the answer I had given to others be-

* Spencer Perceval, who succeeded the Duke of Portland as Premier, was assassinated in the lobby of the House of Commons on May 11, 1812, three months before this letter was written, by John Bellingham, an English merchant, who was engaged in business at Archangel, and who had been unable to obtain redress from the Russian Government for some alleged injury. The murderer was hanged.— EDITOR.

fore, that the Almighty himself could not construct a machine of perpetual motion while the laws exist which he has prescribed for the government of matter in our system; that the equilibrium established by him between cause and effect must be suspended to effect that purpose.—To DR. ROBERT PATTERSON. vi, 83. (M., 1812.)

6636. PERPETUAL MOTION, Friction and.—The diminution of friction is certainly one of the most desirable reformations in mechanics. Could we get rid of it altogether we should have perpetual motion. I was afraid that using a fluid for a fulcrum, the pivot (for so we may call them) must be of such a diameter as to lose what had been gained. I shall be glad to hear the event of any other experiments you may make on this subject.— To ROBERT R. LIVINGSTON. FORD ED., v, 277. (Pa., 1791.)

6637. PERSONAL LIBERTY, Children of slaves.—The reducing the mother to servitude was a violation of the law of nature, surely, then, the same law cannot prescribe a continuance of the violation to her issue, and that, too, without end, for if it extends to any, it must to every degree of descendants.—LEGAL ARGUMENT. FORD ED., i, 376. (1770.)

6638. —— ——. That the bondage of the mother does not under the law of nature, infer that of her issue, as included in her, is further obvious from this consideration, that by the same reason, the bondage of the father would infer that of his issue; for he may with equal, and some anatomists say with greater reason, be said to include all his posterity.—LEGAL ARGUMENT. FORD ED., i, 377. (1770.)

6639. PERSONAL LIBERTY, Inconsistent laws.—If it be a law of nature that the child shall follow the condition of the parent, it would introduce a very perplexing dilemma; as where the one parent is free and the other a slave. Here the child is to be a slave, says this law, by inheritance of the father's bondage; but it is also to be free, says the same law, by inheritance of its mother's freedom. This contradiction proves it to be no law of nature.—LEGAL ARGUMENT. FORD ED., i, 377. (1770.)

6640. PERSONAL LIBERTY, Invasion of.—There are rights which it is useless to surrender to the government, and which governments have yet always been found to invade. [Among] these is * * * the right of personal freedom.—To DAVID HUMPHREYS. iii, 13. FORD ED., v, 89. (P., 1789.)

6641. PERSONAL LIBERTY, Lettres de cachet.—Nor should we wonder at * * * [the] pressure [for a fixed constitution in 1788-9] when we consider the monstrous abuses of power under which * * * [the French] people were ground to powder; when we pass in review the shackles * * * on the freedom * * * of the person by Lettres de Cachet.—AUTOBIOGRAPHY. i, 86. FORD ED., i, 118. (1821.)

6642. PERSONAL LIBERTY, Natural. —Under the law of nature, all men are born free, every one comes into the world with a right to his own person, which includes the liberty of moving and using it at his own will. This is what is called personal liberty, and is given him by the Author of nature, because necessary for his own sustenance.— LEGAL ARGUMENT. FORD ED., i, 376. (1770.)

6643. PERSONAL LIBERTY, Preservation of.—If we are made in some degree for others, yet in a greater are we made for ourselves. It were contrary to feeling, and indeed ridiculous to suppose that a man had less rights in himself than one of his neighbors, or indeed all of them put together. This would be slavery, and not that liberty which the bill of rights has made inviolable, and for the preservation of which our government has been charged.—To JAMES MONROE. i, 319. FORD ED., iii, 58. (M., 1782.)

6644. PERSONAL LIBERTY, In private life.—I feel at length [in my retirement from public life] the blessing of being free to say and do what I please, without being responsible for it to any mortal.—To GEN. KOSCIUSKO. v, 50. (M., 1810.)

6645. PERSONAL LIBERTY, Universal.—In a government bottomed on the will of all, the * * * liberty of every individual citizen becomes interesting to all.— FIFTH ANNUAL MESSAGE. viii, 50. FORD ED., viii, 392. (1805.)

— PERSONAL RIGHTS.—See RIGHTS.

6646. PETITION, Right of.—The people have a right to petition, but not to use that right to cover calumniating insinuations. —To JAMES MADISON. v, 367. FORD ED., ix, 209. (M., 1808.)

6647. PETITIONS, The Executive and. —In my report on How's case, where I state that it should go to the President, it will become a question with the House [of Representatives] whether they shall refer it to the President themselves, or give it back to the petitioner, and let him so address it, as he ought to have done at first. I think the latter proper, 1. because it is a case belonging purely to the Executive; 2, because the Legislature should never show itself in a matter with a foreign nation, but where the case is very serious and they mean to commit the nation on its issue; 3, because if they indulge individuals in handing through the Legislature their applications to the Executive, all applicants will be glad to avail themselves of the weight of so powerful a solicitor. Similar attempts have been repeatedly made by individuals to get the President to hand in their petitions to the Legislature, which he has constantly refused. It seems proper that every person should address himself directly to the department to which the Constitution has allotted his case; and that the proper answer to such from any other department is, " that it is not to us that the Constitution has assigned the transaction of this business ".—To JAMES MADISON. iii, 296. FORD ED., v, 391. (Pa., 1791.)

6648. —— ——. The Executive of the Union is, by the Constitution, made the channel of communication between *foreign* powers and the United States. But citizens, whether individually, or in bodies corporate, or associated, have a right to apply directly to any department of their government, whether Legislative, Executive, or Judiciary, the exercise of whose powers they have a right to claim; and neither of these can regularly offer its intervention in a case belonging to the other. The communication and recommendation by me to Congress of the memorial you * * * enclose me, would be an innovation, not authorized by the practice of our government, and, therefore, the less likely to add to its weight or effect.— To JAMES SULLIVAN. v, 203. (W., 1807.)

6649. —— ——. I cannot lay petitions before Congress consistently with my own opinion of propriety, because where the petitioners have a right to petition their immediate representatives in Congress directly, I have deemed it neither necessary nor proper for them to pass their petition through the intermediate channel of the Executive.—To JOSEPH B. VARNUM. v, 388. (W., 1808.)

6650. —— ——. I have never presumed to place myself between the Legislative Houses and those who have a constitutional right to address them directly.—To ANDREW GREGG. v, 431. (W., 1809.)

6651. PETITIONS, Punishment for.— He [George III.] has endeavored to pervert the exercise of the kingly office of Virginia into a detestable and insupportable tyranny * * * by answering our repeated petitions for redress with a repetition of injuries.—PROPOSED VA. CONSTITUTION. FORD ED., ii, 12. (June 1776.)

6652. PETITIONS, Rejected.—We [Virginia] have exhausted every mode of application which our invention could suggest as proper and promising. We have decently remonstrated with Parliament: they have added new injuries to the old. We have wearied our King with applications; he has not deigned to answer us. We have appealed to the native honour and justice of the British Nation: their efforts in our favor have been hitherto ineffectual. What, then, remains to be done? That we commit our injuries to the even-handed justice of the Being who doth no wrong, earnestly beseeching Him to illuminate the councils, and prosper the endeavors of those to whom America hath confided her hopes, that through their wise direction we may again see reunited the blessings of liberty, property, and harmony with Great Britain.—ADDRESS OF HOUSE OF BURGESSES TO LORD DUNMORE. FORD ED., i, 458. (1775.)

6653. PETITIONS, Repetition of injury and.—In every stage of these oppressions we have petitioned for redress, in the most humble terms; Our repeated petitions have been answered only by repeated injuries.—DECLARATION OF INDEPENDENCE AS DRAWN BY JEFFERSON.

6654. PETITIONS, Unanswered.—Our complaints were either not heard at all, or were answered with new and accumulated injuries.—REPLY TO LORD NORTH'S PROPOSITION. FORD ED., i, 481. (July 1775.)

6655. PETITIONS, Vain.—We have supplicated our king at various times in terms almost disgraceful to freedom; we have reasoned, we have remonstrated with parliament in the most mild and decent language; we have even proceeded to break off our commercial intercourse with our fellow-subjects, as the last peaceful admonition that our attachment to no nation on earth should supplant our attachment to liberty. And here we had well hoped was the ultimate step of the controversy. But subsequent events have shown how vain was even this last remain of confidence in the moderation of the British ministry.—DECLARATION ON TAKING UP ARMS. FORD ED., i, 470. (July 1775.)

6656. PEYROUSE EXPEDITION, Objects of.—You have, doubtless, seen in the papers, that this court [France] was sending two vessels into the South Sea, under the conduct of a Captain Peyrouse. They give out that the object is merely for the improvement of our knowledge of the geography of that part of the globe. And certain it is, that they carry men of eminence in different branches of science. Their loading, however, as detailed in conversations, and some other circumstances, appeared to me to indicate some other design; perhaps that of colonizing on the Western coast of America; or, it may be, only to establish one or more factories there, for the fur trade. Perhaps we may be little interested in either of these objects. But we are interested in another, that is, to know whether they are perfectly weaned from the desire of possessing continental colonies in America. Events might arise, which would render it very desirable for Congress to be satisfied they have no such wish. If they would desire a colony on the western side of America, I should not be quite satisfied that they would refuse one which should offer itself on the eastern side. Captain Paul Jones being at L'Orient, within a day's journey of Brest, where Captain Peyrouse's vessels lay, I desired him, if he could not satisfy himself at L'Orient of the nature of this equipment, to go to Brest for that purpose; conducting himself so as to excite no suspicion that we attended at all to this expedition. His discretion can be relied on.—To JOHN JAY. i, 382. (P., 1785.)

6657. —— ——. The circumstances are obvious which indicate an intention to settle factories and not colonies, at least for the present.—To JOHN JAY. i, 454. (P., 1785.)

6658. —— ——. The Gazette of France announces the arrival of Peyrouse at Brazil, that he was to touch at Otaheite, and proceed to California, and still further northwardly. * * * The presumption is, that they will make an establishment of some sort, on the northwest coast of America.—To JOHN JAY. i, 602. (P., 1786.)

6659. PHILADELPHIA, Injuries by war.—I sincerely congratulate you on the recovery of Philadelphia and wish it may be found uninjured by the enemy. How far the interests of literature may have suffered by the injury, or removal of the Orrery (as it is miscalled), the public libraries, your papers and implements, are doubts which still excite anxiety.—To David Rittenhouse. i, 210. Ford ed., ii, 162. (M., July 1778.)

6660. PHILOSOPHY, Ancient.—The moral principles inculcated by the most esteemed of the sects of ancient philosophy, or of their individuals; particularly, Pythagoras, Socrates, Epicurus, Cicero, Epictetus, Seneca and Antoninus, related chiefly to ourselves, and the government of those passions which, unrestrained, would disturb our tranquillity of mind. In this branch of philosophy they were really great. In developing our duties to others, they were short and defective. They embraced, indeed, the circles of kindred and friends, and inculcated patriotism, or the love of our country in the aggregate, as a primary obligation; towards our neighbors and countrymen they taught justice, but scarcely viewed them as within the circle of benevolence. Still less have they inculcated peace, charity, and love to our fellow men, or embraced with benevolence the whole family of mankind.—Syllabus of the Doctrines of Jesus. iv, 480. Ford ed., viii, 224. (1803.)

6661. PHILOSOPHY, Epicureanism.— I am Epicurean. I consider the genuine (not the imputed) doctrines of Epicurus as containing everything rational in moral philosophy which Greece and Rome have left us. Epictetus, indeed, has given us what was good of the Stoics; all beyond, of their dogmas being hypocrisy and grimace. Their great crime was in their calumnies of Epicurus and misrepresentations of his doctrines; in which we lament to see the candid character of Cicero engaging as an accomplice.—To William Short. vii, 138. Ford ed., x, 143. (M., 1819.)

— PHILOSOPHY, Platonic.—See Plato.

6662. PHILOSOPHY, Seneca.—Seneca is, indeed, a fine moralist, disfiguring his work at times with some Stoicisms, and affecting too much of antithesis and point, yet giving us on the whole a great deal of sound and practical morality.—To William Short. vii, 139. Ford ed., x, 144. (M., 1819.)

6663. PHILOSOPHY, Socratic.—Of Socrates we have nothing genuine but in the Memorabilia of Xenophon; for Plato makes him one of his collocutors, merely to cover his own whimsies under the mantle of his name; a liberty of which we are told Socrates himself complained.—To William Short. vii, 139. Ford ed., x, 144. (M., 1819.)

6664. PHILOSOPHY, War against.—I still dare to use the word philosophy, notwithstanding the war waged against it by bigotry and despotism.—To Dr. Hugh Williamson. iv, 347. Ford ed., vii, 481. (W., Jan. 1801.)

6665. PICKERING (Timothy), Jefferson and.—I could not have believed that for so many years, and to such a period of advanced age, Mr. Pickering could have nourished passions so vehement and viperous. It appears that for thirty years past, he has been industriously collecting materials for vituperating the characters he had marked for his hatred; some of whom, certainly, if enmities towards him had ever existed, had forgotten them all, or buried them in the grave with themselves. As to myself, there never had been anything personal between us, nothing but the general opposition of party sentiment; and our personal intercourse

had been that of urbanity, as himself says. But it seems he has been all this time brooding over an enmity which I had never felt, and that with respect to myself, as well as others, he has been writing far and near, and in every direction, to get hold of original letters, where he could, copies, where he could not, certificates and journals, catching at every gossiping story he could hear of in any quarter, supplying by suspicions what he could find nowhere else, and then arguing on this motley farrago as if established on gospel evidence. * * * He arraigns me on two grounds, my actions and my motives. The very actions, however, which he arraigns, have been such as the great majority of my fellow citizens have approved. The approbation of Mr. Pickering and of those who thought with him, I had no right to expect. My motives he chooses to ascribe to hypocrisy, to ambition, and a passion for popularity. Of these the world must judge between us. It is no office of his or mine. To that tribunal I have ever submitted my actions and motives, without ransacking the Union for certificates, letters, journals and gossiping tales to justify myself and weary them. * * * If no action is to be deemed virtuous for which malice can imagine a sinister motive, then there never was a virtuous action; no, not even in the life of our Saviour himself. But He has taught us to judge the tree by its fruit and to leave motives to Him who can alone see into them. * * * I leave to its fate the libel of Mr. Pickering, with the thousands of others like it, to which I have given no other answer than a steady course of similar action * * *.— To Martin Van Buren. vii, 362. Ford ed., x, 305. (M., 1824.) See Declaration of Independence.

6666. PICKERING (Timothy), Josiah Quincy and.—The termination of Mr. Rose's mission, *re infecta,* put it in my power to communicate to Congress yesterday, everything respecting our relations with England and France, which will effectually put down Mr. Pickering, and his worthy coadjutor Mr. [Josiah] Quincy. Their tempers are so much alike, and really their persons, as to induce a supposition that they are related.—To Levi Lincoln. v, 264. (W., March 1808.)

6667. PIERS, Power to build.—You know my doubts, or rather convictions, about the unconstitutionality of the act for building piers in the Delaware, and the fears that it will lead to a bottomless expense, and to the greatest abuses. There is, however, one intention of which the act is susceptible, and which will bring it within the Constitution; and we ought always to presume that the real intention which is alone consistent with the Constitution. Although the power to regulate commerce does not give a power to build piers, wharves, open ports, clear the beds of rivers, dig canals, build warehouses, build manufacturing machines, set up manufactories, cultivate the earth, to all of which the power would go if it went to the first, yet a power to provide and maintain a navy is a power to provide receptacles for it, and places to cover and preserve it. In choosing the places where this money should be laid out, I should be much disposed, as far as contracts will permit, to confine it to such place or places as the ships of war may lie at, and be protected from ice; and I should be for stating this in a message to Congress, in order to prevent the effect of the present example. This act has been built on the exercise of the power of building light houses, as a regulation of commerce. But I well remember the opposition, on this very ground, to the first act for building a lighthouse. The utility of the thing has sanctioned the infraction. But if, on that infraction, we build a second, and on that second a third, &c., any one of the powers in the Constitution may be made to comprehend every power of government.—To ALBERT GALLATIN. iv, 449. FORD ED., viii, 174. (Oct. 1802.)

6668. —— ——. The act of Congress of 1789, c. 9, assumes on the General Government the maintenance and repair of all lighthouses, beacons, buoys, and public piers then existing, and provides for the building a new lighthouse. This was done under the authority given by the Constitution " to regulate commerce ", and was contested at the time as not within the meaning of its terms, and yielded to only on the urgent necessity of the case. The act of 1802, c. 20, f. 8, for repairing and erecting public piers in the Delaware, does not take any new ground— it is in strict conformity with the act of 1789. While we pursue, then, the construction of the Legislature, that the repairing and erecting lighthouses, beacons, buoys, and piers, is authorized as belonging to the regulation of commerce, we must take care not to go ahead of them, and strain the meaning of the terms still further to the clearing out the channels of all the rivers, &c., of the United States. The removing a sunken vessel is not the repairing of a pier. How far the authority " to levy taxes to provide for the common defence ", and that " for providing and maintaining a navy ", may authorize the removing obstructions in a river or harbor, is a question not involved in the present case.—To ALBERT GALLATIN. iv, 478. (April 1803.)

6669. PIKE (General Z. M.), Death of. —He died in the arms of victory gained over the enemies of his country. * * * [He was] an honest and zealous patriot who lived and died for his country.—To BARON VON HUMBOLDT. vi, 270. FORD ED., ix, 432. (1813.)

6670. PIKE (General Z. M.), Expedition.—On the transfer of Louisiana by France to the United States, according to its boundaries when possessed by France, the government of the United States considered itself as entitled as far west as the Rio Norte; but understanding soon afterwards that Spain, on the contrary, claimed eastwardly to the river Sabine, it has carefully abstained from doing any act in the intermediate country, which might disturb the existing state of things, until these opposing claims should be explained and accommodated amicably. But that the Red River and all its waters belonged to France, that she made several settlements on that river, and held them as a part of Louisiana until she delivered that country to Spain, and that Spain, on the contrary, had never made a single settlement on the river are circumstances so well known, and so susceptible of proof, that it was not supposed that Spain would seriously contest the facts ; or the right established by them. Hence our government took measures for exploring that river, as it did that of the Missouri, by sending Mr. Freeman to proceed from the mouth upwards, and Lieutenant Pike from the source downwards merely to acquire its geography, and so far enlarge the boundaries of science. For the day must be very distant when it will be either the interest or the wish of the United States to extend settlements into the interior of that country. Lieutenant Pike's orders were accordingly strictly confined to the waters of the Red river, and from his known observance of orders, I am persuaded that it must have been, as he himself declares, by miss-

ing his way that he got on the waters of the Rio Norte, instead of those of the Red river. That your Excellency should excuse this involuntary error, and indeed misfortune, was expected from the liberality of your character; and the kindnesses you have shown him are an honorable example of those offices of good neighborhood on your part, which it will be so agreeable to us to cultivate. * * * To the same liberal sentiment Lieutenant Pike must appeal for the restoration of his papers. You must have seen in them no trace of unfriendly views towards your nation, no symptoms of any other design than that of extending geographical knowledge ; and it is not in the nineteenth century, nor through the agency of your Excellency, that science expects to encounter obstacles.*—To GENERAL HENRY DEARBORN. v, 110. FORD ED., ix, 85. (W., 1807.)

6671. PIKE (General Z. M.), Mission.— I think that the truth as to Pike's mission might be so simply stated as to need no argument to show that (even during the suspension of our claims to the eastern border of the Rio Norte) his getting on it was a mere error, which ought to have called for the setting him right, instead of forcing him through the interior country.— To JAMES MADISON. v, 294. FORD ED., x, 195. (M., May 1808.)

6672. PINCKNEY (Charles), Political ambition.—There is here a great sense of the inadequacy of C. Pinckney to the office he is in. His continuance is made a subject of standing reproach to myself personally, by whom the appointment was made before I had collected the administration. He declared at the time that nothing would induce him to continue so as not to be here at the ensuing Presidential election. I am persuaded he expected to be proposed at it as V. P. After he got to Europe his letters asked only a continuance of two years ; but he now does not drop the least hint of a voluntary return. Pray, avail yourself of his vanity, his expectations, his fears, and whatever will weigh with him to induce him to ask leave to return, and obtain from him to be the bearer of the letter yourself. You will render us in this the most acceptable service possible. His enemies here are perpetually dragging his character in the dirt, and charging it on the administration. He does, or ought to know this, and to feel the necessity of coming home to vindicate himself, if he looks to anything further in the career of honor.—To JAMES MONROE. FORD ED., viii, 289. (W., Jan. 1804.)

6673. PINCKNEY (Thomas), Character.—An honest, sensible man, and good republican.—To JOEL BARLOW. iii, 451. FORD ED., vi, 88. (Pa., 1792.)

6674. PINCKNEY (Thomas), Minister. —Your nomination as Minister to London gave general satisfaction.—To THOMAS PINCKNEY. iii, 321. FORD ED., v, 423. (Pa., Jan. 1792.)

6675. PINCKNEY (Thomas), Vice-Presidency.—The federalists will run Mr. Pinckney for the Vice-Presidency. They regard his southern position rather than his principles. To JAMES MONROE. iv, 149. FORD ED., vii, 89. (M., July 1796.)

6676. PITT (William), Friend of America.—Pitt is rather well disposed to us.—To GOVERNOR BENJ. HARRISON. FORD ED., iii, 414. (A., March 1784.)

* Draft of letter to be sent to Spanish governor.— EDITOR.

6677. PLANTS, Useful.—The greatest service which can be rendered any country is to add an useful plant to its culture; especially, a bread grain; next in value to bread is oil.—JEFFERSON'S MSS. i, 176. (M., 1821.)

6678. PLATO, Teachings of.—No writer, ancient or modern, has bewildered the world with more *ignes fatui*, than this renowned philosopher, in ethics, in politics, and physics.—TO WILLIAM SHORT. vii, 165. (M., 1820.)

6679. PLATO, Whimsies.—Plato * * * used the name of Socrates to cover the whimsies of his own brain.—SYLLABUS OF THE DOCTRINES OF JESUS. iv, 481. (1803.)

6680. PLATO'S REPUBLIC.—I amused myself [recently] with reading Plato's Republic. I am wrong, however, in calling it amusement, for it was the heaviest task-work I ever went through. I had occasionally before taken up some of his other works, but scarcely ever had patience to get through a whole dialogue. While wading through the whimsies, the puerilities, and unintelligible jargon of this work, I laid it down often to ask myself how it could have been that the world should have so long consented to give reputation to such nonsense as this? How the soi-disant Christian world, indeed, should have done it, is a piece of historical curiosity. But how could the Roman good sense do it? And particularly, how could Cicero bestow such eulogies on Plato? Although Cicero did not wield the dense logic of Demosthenes, yet he was able, learned, laborious, practiced in the business of the world, and honest. He could not be the dupe of mere style, of which he was himself the first master in the world. With the moderns, I think, it is rather a matter of fashion and authority. Education is chiefly in the hands of persons who, from their profession, have an interest in the reputation and the dreams of Plato. They give the tone while at school, and few in after years have occasion to revise their college opinions. But fashion and authority apart, and bringing Plato to the test of reason, take from him his sophisms, futilities and incomprehensibilities, and what remains? In truth, he is one of the race of genuine Sophists, who has escaped the oblivion of his brethren, first, by the eloquence of his diction, but chiefly, by the adoption and incorporation of his whimsies into the body of artificial Christianity. His foggy mind is forever presenting the semblances of objects which, half seen through a mist, can be defined neither in form nor dimensions. * * * Socrates had reason, indeed, to complain of the misrepresentations of Plato; for in truth, his dialogues are libels on Socrates.—TO JOHN ADAMS. vi, 354. FORD ED., ix, 462. (M., 1814.)

6681. —— ——. It is fortunate for us, that Platonic republicanism has not obtained the same favor as Platonic Christianity; or we should now have been all living men, women and children pell mell together, like beasts of the field or forest.—TO JOHN ADAMS. vi, 355. (1814.)

6682. PLEASURE, Bait of.—Do not bite at the bait of pleasure till you know there is no hook beneath it.—TO MRS. COSWAY. ii, 37. FORD ED., iv, 317. (P., 1786.)

6683. PLEASURE AND PAIN.—We have no rose without its thorn: no pleasure without alloy. It is the law of Existence; and we must acquiesce. It is the condition annexed to all our pleasures, not by us who receive, but by Him who gives them.—TO MRS. COSWAY. ii, 41. FORD ED., iv, 321. (P., 1786.)

6684. —— ——. I do not agree that an age of pleasure is no compensation for a moment of pain.—TO JOHN ADAMS. vii, 26. (M., 1816.)

6685. POETRY, Judging.—It is not for a stranger to decide on the merits of poetry in a language foreign to him.—TO M. HILLIARD D'AUBERTEUIL. ii, 103. (P., 1787.)

6686. —— ——. To my own mortification, * * * of all men living, I am the last who should undertake to decide as to the merits of poetry. In earlier life I was fond of it, and easily pleased. But as age and cares advanced, the powers of fancy have declined. Every year seems to have plucked a feather from her wings, till she can no longer waft one to those sublime heights to which it is necessary to accompany the poet. So much has my relish for poetry deserted me that, at present, I cannot read even Virgil with pleasure. I am consequently utterly incapable to decide on the merits of poetry. The very feelings to which it is addressed are among those I have lost. So that the blind man might as well undertake to [faded in MS.] a painting, or the deaf a musical composition. *—TO JOHN D. BURKE. FORD ED., viii, 65. (W., 1801.)

6687. POLAND, Partition of.—The history of Poland gives a lesson which all our countrymen should study; the example of a country erased from the map of the world by the dissensions of its own citizens. The papers of every day read them the counter lesson of the impossibility of subduing a people acting with an undivided will. Spain, under all her disadvantages, physical and mental, is an encouraging example of this.—TO WILLIAM DUANE. v, 603. (M., July 1811.)

6688. —— ——. The partition of Poland * * * was the atrocity of a barbarous government chiefly, in conjunction with a smaller one still scrambling to become great, while one only of those already great, and having character to lose, descended to the baseness of an accomplice in the crime.—TO JOHN ADAMS. vi, 524. (M., 1816.)

6689. POLICY (American), Balance of power.—We especially ought to pray that the powers of Europe may be so poised and counterpoised among themselves, that their own safety may require the presence of all their force at home, leaving the other quarters of the globe in undisturbed tranquillity.—TO DR. CRAWFORD. vi, 33. (1812.)

6690. POLICY (American), Coalition of American nations.—From many conversations with him [M. Correa †] I hope he sees, and will promote in his new situation [in Brazil] the advantages of a cordial fraternization among all the American nations, and the importance of their coalescing in an American system of policy, totally independent of and unconnected with that of Europe. The day is not distant, when we may formally require a meridian of partition through the ocean which separates the two hemispheres, on the hither side of which no European gun shall ever be heard, nor an American on the other; and when, during the rage of the eternal wars of Europe, the lion

* Mr. Burke had sent Jefferson a copy of the Columbiad.—EDITOR.

† Portuguese Minister at Washington.—EDITOR.

and the lamb, within our regions, shall lie down together in peace. * * * I wish to see this coalition begun.—To WILLIAM SHORT. vii, 168. (1820.)

6691. —— ——. I wish to see this coalition begun. I am earnest for an agreement with the maritime powers of Europe, assigning them the task of keeping down the piracies of their seas and the cannibalism of the African coasts, and to us, the suppression of the same enormities within our seas; and for this purpose, I should rejoice to see the fleets of Brazil and the United States riding together as brethren of the same family, and pursuing the same object. And indeed it would be of happy augury to begin at once this concert of action here, on the invitation of either to the other government, while the way might be preparing for withdrawing our cruisers from Europe, and preventing naval collisions there which daily endanger our peace.—To WILLIAM SHORT. vii, 169. (M., 1820.)

6692. POLICY (American), Coercion of Europe.—We think that peaceable means may be devised of keeping nations in the path of justice towards us, by making justice their interest and injuries to react on themselves. Our distance enables us to pursue a course which the crowded situation of Europe renders, perhaps, impracticable there.—To M. CABANIS. iv, 497. (W., 1803.)

6693. POLICY (American), Detachment from Europe.—We cannot too distinctly detach ourselves from the European system, which is essentially belligerent, nor too sedulously cultivate an American system, essentially pacific.—To PRESIDENT MADISON. vi, 453. FORD ED., ix, 513. (M., March 1815.)

6694. POLICY (American), European politics and.—The politics of Europe render it indispensably necessary that, with respect to everything external, we be one nation only, firmly hooped together.—To JAMES MADISON. i, 531. FORD ED., iv, 192. (P., February 1786.)

6695. POLICY (American), European quarrels.—I am decidedly of opinion we should take no part in European quarrels, but cultivate peace and commerce with all.—To GENERAL WASHINGTON. ii, 533. FORD ED., v, 57. (P., 1788.)

6696. —— ——. At such a distance from Europe, and with such a distance between us, we hope to meddle little in its quarrels or combinations. Its peace and its commerce are what we shall court.—To M. DE PINTO. iii. 174. (N.Y., 1790.)

6697. POLICY (American), European system and.—The European nations constitute a separate division of the globe; their localities make them part of a distinct system; they have a set of interests of their own in which it is our business never to engage ourselves.—To BARON VON HUMBOLDT. vi, 268. FORD ED., ix, 431. (Dec. 1813.)

6698. POLICY (American), France and England.—We owe gratitude to France, justice to England, good will to all, and subservience to none.—To ARTHUR CAMPBELL. iv, 198. FORD ED., vii, 170. (M., 1797.)

6699. —— ——. It is our unquestionable interest and duty to conduct ourselves with such sincere friendship and impartiality towards both France and England, as that each may see unequivocally, what is unquestionably true, that we may be very possibly driven into her scale by unjust conduct in the other.—To JAMES MADISON. iv, 557. FORD ED., viii, 315. (M., Aug. 1804.)

6700. POLICY (American), Freedom of the ocean.—That the persons of our citizens shall be safe in freely traversing the ocean, that the transportation of our own produce, in our own vessels, to the markets of our choice, and the return to us of the articles we want for our own use, shall be unmolested. I hold to be fundamental, and the gauntlet that must be forever hurled at him who questions it.—To JOHN ADAMS. vi, 459. (M., June 1815.)

6701. POLICY (American), Great Britain and.—With respect to the English government, or policy, as concerning themselves or other nations, we wish not to intermeddle in word or deed, and that it be not understood that our government permits itself to entertain either a will or opinion on the subject.—To THOMAS PINCKNEY. iii, 442. FORD ED., vi, 75. (Pa., 1792.)

6702. POLICY (American), Gulf of Mexico.—We begin to broach the idea that we consider the Gulf Stream as of our waters, in which hostilities and cruising are to be frowned on for the present, and prohibited so soon as either consent or force will permit us. We shall never permit another privateer to cruise within it, and shall forbid our harbors to national cruisers. This is essential for our tranquillity and commerce.—To JAMES MONROE. v, 12. FORD ED., viii, 450. (W., May 1806.)

6703. POLICY (American), Internal resources.—The promotion of the arts and sciences * * * becomes peculiarly interesting to us, at this time, when the total demoralization of the governments of Europe, has rendered it safest, by cherishing internal resources, to lessen the occasions of intercourse with them.—To DR. JOHN L. E. W. SHECUT. vi, 153. (M., 1813.)

6704. POLICY (American), A just.—Let it be our endeavor * * * to merit the character of a just nation.—THIRD ANNUAL MESSAGE. viii, 28. FORD ED., viii, 272. (1803.)

6705. POLICY (American), Markets.—Our object is to feed and theirs to fight.—To JAMES MONROE. FORD ED., v, 198. (N. Y., 1790.)

6706. POLICY (American), Mid-Atlantic meridian.—When our strength will permit us to give the law of our hemisphere, it should be that the meridian of the mid-Atlantic should be the line of demarcation between war and peace, on this side of which no act of hostility should be committed, and the lion and the lamb lie down in peace together.—To Dr. Crawford. vi, 33. (M., Jan. 1812.)

6707. POLICY (American), Peace and friendship.—Peace and friendship with all mankind is our wisest policy. and I wish we may be permitted to pursue it.—To C. W. F. Dumas. i, 553. (1786.)

6708. —— ——. Peace with all nations, and the right which that gives us with respect to all nations, are our object.—To C. W. F. Dumas. iii, 535. (Pa., 1793.)

6709. —— ——. Peace, justice, and liberal intercourse with all the nations of the world, will, I hope, characterize this commonwealth.—Reply to Address. iv, 388. (W., 1801.)

6710. —— ——. Separated by a wide ocean from the nations of Europe, and from the political interests which entangle them together, with productions and wants which render our commerce and friendship useful to them and theirs to us, it cannot be the interest of any to assail us, nor ours to disturb them. We should be most unwise, indeed were we to cast away the singular blessings of the position in which nature has placed us, the opportunity she has endowed us with of pursuing at a distance from foreign contentions, the paths of industry, peace and happiness; of cultivating general friendship, and of bringing collisions of interest to the umpirage of reason rather than of force.—Third Annual Message. viii, 29. Ford ed., viii, 273. (Oct. 1803.)

6711. POLICY (American), Peace and justice.—We ask for peace and justice from all nations.—To James Monroe. ii, 12. Ford ed., viii, 450. (W., May 1806.)

6712. POLICY (American), Peopling the continent.—Our Confederacy must be viewed as the nest from which all America, North and South, is to be peopled.—To Archibald Stuart. i, 518. Ford ed., iv, 188. (P., Jan. 1786.)

6713. POLICY (American), Principles.—On the question you propose [James Monroe], whether we can, in any form, take a bolder attitude than formerly in favor of liberty, I can give you but commonplace ideas. They will be but the widow's mite, and offered only because requested. The matter which now embroils Europe, the presumption of dictating to an independent nation the form of its government, is so arrogant, so atrocious, that indignation, as well as moral sentiment, enlists all our partialities and prayers in favor of one, and our equal execrations against the other. I do not know. indeed, whether all nations do not owe to one another a bold and open declaration of their sympathies with the one party, and their detestation of the conduct of the other. But farther than this we are bound to go; and indeed, for the sake of the world, we ought not to increase the jealousies, or draw on ourselves the power of this formidable confederacy [The Holy Alliance], I have ever deemed it fundamental for the United States never to take active part in the quarrels of Europe. Their political interests are entirely distinct from ours. Their mutual jealousies, their balance of power, their complicated alliances, their forms and principles of government, are all foreign to us. They are nations of eternal war. All their energies are expended in the destruction of the labor, property and lives of their people. On our part, never had a people so favorable a chance of trying the opposite system, of peace and fraternity with mankind, and the direction of all our means and faculties to the purposes of improvement instead of destruction. With Europe we have few occasions of collision, and these, with a little prudence and forbearance, may be generally accommodated. Of the brethren of our own hemisphere, none is yet, or for an age to come will be, in a shape, condition, or disposition to war against us. And the foothold which the nations of Europe had in either America, is slipping from under them, so that we shall soon be rid of their neighborhood. Cuba alone seems at present to hold up a speck of war to us. Its possession by Great Britain would indeed be a great calamity to us. Could we induce her to join us in guaranteeing its independence against all the world, *except* Spain, it would be nearly as valuable to us as if it were our own.* But should she take it, I would not immediately go to war for it; because the first war on other accounts will give it to us; or the island will give itself to us, when able to do so. While no duty, therefore, calls on us to take part in the present war of Europe, and a golden harvest offers itself in reward for doing nothing. peace and neutrality seem to be our duty and interest. We may gratify ourselves, indeed, with a neutrality as partial to Spain as would be justifiable without giving cause of war to her adversary; we might and ought to avail ourselves of the happy occasion of procuring and cementing a cordial reconciliation with her, by giving assurance of every friendly office which neutrality admits, and especially, against all apprehension of our intermeddling in the quarrel with her colonies. And I expect daily and confidently to hear of a spark kindled in France. which will employ her at home, and relieve Spain from all further apprehension of danger. That England is playing false with Spain cannot be doubted. Her government is looking one way and rowing another. * * * You will do what is right, leaving the people of Europe to act their follies and crimes among themselves, while we pursue in good faith the paths of peace and prosperity.—To President Monroe. vii, 287. Ford ed., x, 257. (M., June 1823.)

* See note under Cuba.—Editor..

6714. POLICY (American), Resistance to wrong.—We believe that the just standing of all nations is the health and security of all. We consider the overwhelming power of England on the ocean, and of France on the land, as destructive of the prosperity and happiness of the world, and wish both to be reduced only to the necessity of observing moral duties. We believe no more in Bonaparte's fighting for the liberty of the seas, than in Great Britain fighting for the liberties of mankind. The object of both is the same. to draw to themselves the power, the wealth and the resources of other nations. We resist the enterprises of England first, because they first come vitally home to us. And our feelings repel the logic of bearing the lash of George III. for fear of that of Bonaparte at some future day. When the wrongs of France shall reach us with equal effect, we shall resist them also. But one at a time is enough; and having offered a choice to the champions, England first takes up the gauntlet.—To JAMES MAURY. vi, 52. FORD ED., ix, 349. (M., April 1812.)

6715. POLICY (American), A system of.—America has a hemisphere to itself. It must have its separate system of interests, which must not be subordinated to those of Europe.—To BARON VON HUMBOLDT. vi, 268. FORD ED., ix, 431. (Dec. 1813.)

6716. —— ——. Distance, and difference of pursuits, of interests, of connections and other circumstances, prescribe to us a different system, having no object in common with Europe, but a peaceful interchange of mutual comforts for mutual wants.—To MADAME DE STAEL. vi, 481. (M., 1815.)

6717. —— ——. Nothing is so important as that America shall separate herself from the systems of Europe, and establish one of her own. Our circumstances, our pursuits, our interests, are distinct; the principles of our policy should be so also. All entanglements with that quarter of the globe should be avoided if we mean that peace and justice shall be the polar stars of the American Societies. * * * This would be a leading principle with me, had I longer to live. * * * —To J. CORREA. vii, 184. FORD ED., x, 164. (M., 1820.)

6718. —— ——. Our first and fundamental maxim should be never to entangle ourselves in the broils of Europe. Our second, never to suffer Europe to intermeddle with cis-Atlantic affairs. America, North and South, has a set of interests distinct from those of Europe, and peculiarly her own. She should therefore have a system of her own, separate and apart from that of Europe. While the last is laboring to become the domicil of despotism, our endeavor should surely be, to make our hemisphere that of freedom.—To PRESIDENT MONROE. vii, 315. FORD ED., x, 277. (M., 1823.)

6719. POLICY (American), Wars of Europe.—The insulated state in which nature has placed the American continent, should so far avail it that no spark of war kindled in the other quarters of the globe should be wafted across the wide oceans which separate us from them. And it will be so. In fifty years more the United States alone will contain fifty millions of inhabitants, and fifty years are soon gone over. The peace of 1763 is within that period. I was then twenty years old, and of course remember well all the transactions of the war preceding it. And you will live to see the period equally ahead of us; and the numbers which will then be spread over the other parts of the American hemisphere, catching long before that the principles of our portion of it, and concurring with us in the maintenance of the same system. * * * I am anticipating events of which you will be the bearer to me in the Elysian fields fifty years hence.—To BARON VON HUMBOLDT. vi, 268. FORD ED., ix, 431. (Dec. 1813.)

6720. —— ——. Your exhortations to avoid taking any part in the war * * * in Europe were a confirmation of the policy I had myself pursued, and which I thought and still think should be the governing canon of our republic.—To MADAME DE STAEL. vi, 481. (M., July 1815.)

6721. —— ——. I hope no American patriot will ever lose sight of the essential policy of interdicting in the seas and territories of both Americas, the ferocious and sanguinary contests of Europe.—To WILLIAM SHORT. vii, 168. (M., 1820.)

6722. POLITENESS, European.—With repect to what are termed polite manners, without sacrificing too much the sincerity of language, I would wish my countrymen to adopt just so much of European politeness, as to be ready to make all those little sacrifices of self, which really render European manners amiable, and relieve society from the disagreeable scenes to which rudeness often subjects it. Here (France). it seems that a man might pass a life without encountering a single rudeness.—To MR. BELLINI. i, 445. (P., 1785.)

6723. POLITENESS, Good humor and. —I have mentioned good humor as one of the preservatives of our peace and tranquillity. It is among the most effectual, and its effect is so well imitated and aided, artificially, by politeness, that this also becomes an acquisition of first rate value. In truth, politeness is artificial good humor; it covers the natural want of it, and ends by rendering habitual a substitute nearly equivalent to the real virtue. It is the practice of sacrificing to those whom we meet in society, all the little conveniences and preferences which will gratify them, and deprive us of nothing worth a moment's consideration; it is the giving a pleasing and flattering turn to our expressions, which will conciliate others, and make them pleased with us as well as themselves. How cheap a price for the good will of another! When this is in return for a rude thing said by another, it brings him to his senses, it mortifies and corrects him in the most salutary way, and places him at the feet of your good nature, in the eyes of the company.—To THOMAS JEFFERSON RANDOLPH. v, 389. FORD ED., ix, 231. (W., 1808.)

— POLITICAL ECONOMY.—See ECONOMY (POLITICAL).

6724. POLITICS, Bigotry in.—What an effort of bigotry in politics * * * have we gone through! The barbarians really flattered themselves they should be able to bring back the times of Vandalism, when ignorance put everything into the hands of power and priestcraft. All advances in science were proscribed as innovations. They pretended to praise and encourage education, but it was to be the education of our ancestors. We were to look backwards, not forwards, for improvement; the President himself [John Adams] declaring in one of his answers to addresses, that we were never to expect to go beyond them in real science.— To Dr. Joseph Priestley. iv, 373. Ford ed., viii, 21. (W., 1801.)

6725. POLITICS, Commercial influence.—The system of alarm and jealousy which has been so powerfully played off in England, has been mimicked here, not entirely without success. The most long-sighted politician could not, seven years ago, have imagined that the people of this wide-extended country could have been enveloped in such delusion, and made so much afraid of themselves and their own power, as to surrender it spontaneously to those who are manœuvring them into a form of government, the principal branches of which may be beyond their control. The commerce of England, however, has spread its roots over the whole face of our country. This is the real source of all the obliquities of the public mind.—To A. H. Rowan. iv, 256. Ford ed., vii, 280. (M., 1798.)

6726. POLITICS, Conversations on.— Political conversations I really dislike, and therefore avoid where I can without affectation. But when urged by others, I have never conceived that having been in public life requires me to belie my sentiments, or even to conceal them. When I am led by conversation to express them, I do it with the same independence here which I have practiced everywhere, and which is inseparable from my nature.—To President Washington. iv, 142. Ford ed., vii, 83. (M., 1796.)

6727. POLITICS, Destructive of happiness.—Politics and party hatreds destroy the happiness of every being here. They seem, like salamanders, to consider fire as their element. —To Martha Jefferson Randolph. D. L. J., 249. (Pa., May 1798.)

6728. POLITICS, Differences in.—I never suffered a political to become a personal difference.—To Timothy Pickering. vii, 210. (M., 1821.)

6729. POLITICS, Dislike of.—It is a relief to be withdrawn from the torment of the scenes amidst which we are. Spectators of the heats and tumults of conflicting parties, we cannot help participating of their feelings. * * * .—To Martha Jefferson Randolph. Ford ed., v. 487. (Pa., March 1792.)

6730. POLITICS, Divorce from.—In my retirement I shall certainly divorce myself from all part in political affairs. To get rid of them is the principal object of my retirement, and the first thing necessary to the happiness which it is in vain to look for in any other situation.—To Benjamin Stoddert. v, 427. Ford ed., ix, 246. (W., 1809.)

6731. POLITICS, A duty.—Politics is my duty.—To Harry Innes. Ford ed., v, 294. (Pa., 1791.)

6732. POLITICS, Estrangement from. —I think it is Montaigne who has said that ignorance is the softest pillow on which a man can rest his head. I am sure it is true as to everything political, and shall endeavor to estrange myself to everything of that character.—To Edmund Randolph. iv, 101. Ford ed., vi, 498. (M., Feb. 1794.)

6733. POLITICS, French furnace of.— The gay and thoughtless Paris is now become a furnace of politics. All the world is now politically mad. Men, women, children talk nothing else, and you know that naturally they talk much, loud and warm. Society is spoiled by it, at least for those who, like myself, are but lookers on.—To Mrs. William Bingham. Ford ed., v, 9. (P., 1788.)

6734. POLITICS, Hateful.—The ensuing year will be the longest of my life, and the last of such hateful labors. The next we will sow our cabbages together.—To Martha Jefferson Randolph. Ford ed., v, 488. (March 1792.)

6735. ———— ————. I am to thank you for forwarding M. d'Ivernois's book on the French Revolution. But it is on politics, a subject I never loved, and now hate.—To John Adams. Ford ed., vii, 56. (M., Feb. 1796.)

6736. POLITICS, Influencing.—I have made great progress into the MS., and still with the same pleasure. I have no doubt it must produce great effect. But that this may be the greatest possible, its coming out should be timed to the best advantage. It should come out just so many days before the meeting of Congress as will prevent suspicions of its coming with them, yet so as to be a new thing when they arrive, ready to get into their hands while yet unoccupied. * * * I will direct it to appear a fortnight before their meeting unless you order otherwise. It might as well be thrown into a churchyard, as come out now.—To James Madison. Ford ed., vi, 404. (Pa., 1793.)

6737. POLITICS, Knowledge of European.—I often doubt whether I should trouble Congress or my friends with * * * details of European politics. I know they do not excite that interest in America of which it is impossible for one to divest himself here. I know, too, that it is a maxim with us, and I think it a wise one, not to entangle ourselves with the affairs of Europe. Still, I think we should know them. The Turks have practiced the same maxim of not meddling in the complicated wrangles of this continent. But they have unwisely chosen to be ignorant of them also, and it is this total ignorance of Europe, its combinations, and its movements which exposes them to that annihilation possibly about taking place. While there are powers in Europe which fear our views, or have views on us, we should keep an eye on them, their connections and oppositions, that in a moment of need we may avail ourselves of their weakness with respect to others as well as ourselves, and calculate their designs and movements on all the circumstances under which they exist. Though I am persuaded, therefore, that these details are read by many with great indifference, yet I think it my duty to enter into them, and to run the risk of giving too much, rather than too little information.—To E. Carrington. ii, 334. Ford ed., iv, 482. (P., 1787.)

6738. POLITICS, Liberation from.—I shall be liberated from the hated occupations of politics, and remain in the bosom of my family, my farm, and my books.—To Mrs. Church. Ford ed., vi, 455. (G., 1793.)

6739. POLITICS, A maxim in.—The maxim of your letter " slow and sure " is not less a good one in agriculture than in politics. I sincerely wish it may extricate us from the event of a war, if this can be done saving our faith and our rights.—To President Washington. iv, 106. Ford ed., vi, 510. (M., May 1794.)

6740. POLITICS, Moral right and.—Political interest can never be separated in the long run from moral right.—To James Monroe. Ford ed., viii, 477. (W., 1806.)

6741. POLITICS, Neutrality in factional.—We must be neutral between the discordant republicans, but not between them and their common enemies.—To Robert Smith. Ford ed., viii, 318. (M., 1804.)

6742. POLITICS, Pamphlets on.—You will receive some pamphlets * * * on the acts of the last session. These I would wish you to distribute, not to sound men who have no occasion for them, but to such as have been misled, are candid, and will be open to the conviction of truth, and are of influence among their neighbors. It is the sick who need medicine, and not the well.—To Archibald Stuart. iv, 286. Ford ed., vii, 354. (Pa., 1799.)

6743. POLITICS, Partizan.—You have found on your return [from Europe] a higher style of political difference than you had left here. I fear this is inseparable from the different constitutions of the human mind, and that degree of freedom which permits unrestrained expression.—To Thomas Pinckney. iv, 176. Ford ed., vii, 128. (Pa., 1797.)

6744. POLITICS, Passions and.—You and I have formerly seen warm debates and high political passions. But gentlemen of different politics would then speak to each other, and separate the business of the Senate

from that of society. It is not so now. Men who have been intimate all their lives, cross the streets to avoid meeting, and turn their heads another way, lest they should be obliged to touch their hats. This may do for young men with whom passion is enjoyment; but it is afflicting to peaceable minds.—To Edward Rutledge. iv, 191. Ford ed., vii, 154. (Pa., June 1797.)

6745. POLITICS, Price of wheat and.—Wherever there was any considerable portion of federalism, it has been so much reinforced by those of whose politics the price of wheat is the sole principle, that federalists will be retained from many districts of Virginia.—To President Madison. v, 443. (M., April 1809.)

6746. POLITICS, Propriety and.—I have had a proposition to meet Mr. [Patrick] Henry this month, to confer on the subject of a convention, to the calling of which he is now become a convert; * * * but the impropriety of my entering into consultation on a measure in which I would take no part, is a permanent one.—To James Madison. iv, 118. Ford ed., vii, 11. (M., April 1795.)

6747. ——— ———. The question of a [constitutional] convention is become a party one with which I shall not intermeddle.—To Samuel Kerchival. Ford ed., x, 47. (M., 1816.)

6748. POLITICS, Pursuit of.—I am glad to find that among the various branches of science presenting themselves to your mind, you have fixed on that of politics as your principal pursuit. Your country will derive from this a more immediate and sensible benefit. She has much for you to do. For, though we may say with confidence, that the worst of the American constitutions is better than the best which ever existed before in any other country, and that they are wonderfully perfect for a first essay, yet every human essay must have defects. It will remain, therefore, to those now coming on the stage of public affairs, to perfect what has been so well begun by those going off it.—To T. M. Randolph, Jr. ii, 175. Ford ed., iv, 403. (P., 1787.)

6749. ——— ———. Having pursued your main studies [in France] about two years, and acquired a facility in speaking French, take a tour of four or five months through this country and Italy, return then to Virginia, and pass a year in Williamsburg under the care of Mr. Wythe; and you will be ready to enter on the public stage, with superior advantages.—To T. M. Randolph, Jr. ii, 176. Ford ed., iv, 405. (P., 1787.)

6750. POLITICS, Reformation of.—Politics, like religion, holds up the torches of martyrdom to the reformers of error.—To Mr. Ogilvie. v, 605. (M., 1811.)

6751. POLITICS, Retirement from.—I ought not to quit the port in which I am quietly moored to commit myself again to the stormy ocean of political or party contest.

to kindle new enmities, and lose old friends. No, tranquillity is the *summum bonum* of old age, and there is a time when it is a duty to leave the government of the world to the existing generation, and to repose one's self under their protecting hand. That time is come with me, and I welcome it.—To SAMUEL H. SMITH. FORD ED., x, 263. (M., Aug. 1823.) See RETIREMENT.

6752. POLITICS, Revolution in.— Things have so much changed their aspect, it is like a new world. Those who know us only from 1775 to 1793, can form no better idea of us now than of the inhabitants of the moon; I mean as to political matters.— To COLONEL HAWKINS. iv, 326. FORD ED., vii, 435. (Pa., March 1800.)

6753. POLITICS, Taxation and.—The purse of the people is the real seat of sensibility. It is to be drawn upon largely, and they will then listen to truths which could not excite them through any other organ.— To A. H. ROWAN. iv, 257. FORD ED., vii, 281. (M., 1798.)

6754. ———. Excessive taxation· * * * will carry reason and reflection to every man's door, and particularly in the hour of election.—To JOHN TAYLOR. iv, 259. FORD ED., vii, 310. (M., 1798.)

6755. POLITICS, Torment of.—It is a relief to be withdrawn from the torment of the scenes amidst which we are. Spectators of the heats and tumults of conflicting parties, we cannot help participating of their feelings.—To MARTHA JEFFERSON RANDOLPH. FORD ED., v, 487. (Pa., March 1792.)

6756. ——— ———. Politics is such a torment that I would advise every one I love not to mix with it.—To MARTHA JEFFERSON RANDOLPH. D. L. J., 262. (Pa., 1800.)

— POLYGRAPH.—See INVENTIONS.

— POLYPOTAMIA, Proposed State of. —See WESTERN TERRITORY.

6757. POOR, Care of.—The poor who have neither property, friends, nor strength to labor, are boarded in the houses of good farmers, to whom a stipulated sum is annually paid. To those who are able to help themselves a little, or have friends from whom they derive some succor, inadequate however to their full maintenance, supplementary aids are given which enable them to live comfortably in their own houses, or in the houses of their friends. * * * From Savannah to Portsmouth, you will seldom meet a beggar. In the larger towns, indeed, they sometimes present themselves. These are usually foreigners, who have never obtained a settlement in any parish. I never yet saw a native American begging in the streets or highways.—NOTES ON VIRGINIA. viii, 375. FORD ED., iii, 239. (1782.)

6758. POPE PIUS VI., Influence of.— A dispute has arisen between the Papal See and the King of Naples, which may in its progress enable us to estimate what degree of influence that See retains at the present day. The Kingdom of Naples, at an early period of its history, became feudatory to the See of Rome, and in acknowledgment thereof, has annually paid a hackney to the Pope in Rome, to which place it has always been sent by a splendid embassy. The hackney has been refused by the King this year, and the Pope, giving him three months to return to obedience, threatens, if he does not, to proceed seriously against him.—To JOHN JAY. ii, 454. (P., 1788.)

6759. POPULATION, America's capacity for.—The territory of the United States contains about a million of square miles, English. There is, in them, a greater proportion of fertile lands than in the British dominions in Europe. Suppose the territory of the United States, then, to attain an equal degree of population with the British European dominions, they will have an hundred millions of inhabitants. Let us extend our views to what may be the population of North and South America, supposing them divided at the narrowest part of the Isthmus of Panama. Between this line and that of 50° of north latitude, the northern continent contains about five millions of square miles, and south of this line of division the southern continent contains about seven millions of square miles. * * * Here are twelve millions of square miles which, at the rate of population before assumed, will nourish twelve hundred millions of inhabitants, a greater number than the present population of the whole globe is supposed to amount to. If those who propose medals for the resolution of questions, about which nobody makes any question, those who have invited discussion on the pretended problem, " whether the discovery of America was for the good of mankind"? if they, I say, would have viewed it only as doubling the numbers of mankind, and, of course, the quantum of existence and happiness, they might have saved the money and the reputation which their proposition has cost them.—To M. DE MEUNIER. ix, 275. FORD ED., iv, 179. (P., 1786.)

6760. POPULATION, Extension of.— The present population of the inhabited parts of the United States is of about ten to the square mile; and experience has shown us, that wherever we reach that, the inhabitants become uneasy, as too much compressed, and so go off in great numbers to search for vacant country. Within forty years their whole territory will be peopled at that rate. We may fix that, then, as the term beyond which the people of those States will not be restricted within their present limits; we may fix that population, too, as the limit which they will not exceed till the whole of those two continents are filled up to that mark, that is to say, till they shall contain one hundred and twenty millions of inhabitants.—To M. DE MEUNIER. ix, 275. FORD ED., iv, 180. (P., 1786.)

6761. ———. The soil of the country on the western side of the Mississippi, its climate and its vicinity to the United States, point it out as the first which will receive population from that nest. The present occupiers will just have force enough to repress and restrain the emigrations to a certain degree of consistence. —To M. DE MEUNIER. ix, 276. FORD ED., iv, 180. (P., 1786.)

6762. ——— ———. We have lately seen a single person go and decide on a settlement in Kentucky, many hundred miles from any white inhabitant, remove thither with his family and a few neighbors; and though perpetually harassed by the Indians, that settlement in the course of ten years has acquired thirty thousand inhabitants.—To M. DE MEUNIER. ix, 276. FORD ED., iv, 181. (P., 1786.)

6763. POPULATION, Growth of.—The census just now concluded, shows we have added to our population a third of what it was ten years ago. This will be a duplication in twenty-three or twenty-four years. If we can delay but for a few years the necessity of vindicating the laws of nature on the ocean, we shall be the more sure of doing it with effect.—To WILLIAM SHORT. iv, 415. FORD ED., viii, 98. (W., Oct. 1801.)

6764. ———— ————. Our growth is now so well established by regular enumerations through a course of forty years, and the same grounds of continuance so likely to endure for a much longer period, that, speaking in round numbers, we may safely call ourselves twenty millions in twenty years, and forty millions in forty years.—To SIR JOHN SINCLAIR. vii, 22. (M., 1816.) See EMIGRATION.

6765. POPULATION, Happiness and. —The increase of numbers during the last ten years, proceeding in a geometrical ratio, promises a duplication in a little more than twenty-two years. We contemplate this rapid growth, and the prospect it holds up to us, not with a view to the injuries it may enable us to do to others in some future day, but to the settlement of the extensive country still remaining vacant within our limits, to the multiplications of men susceptible of happiness, educated in the love of order, habituated to self-government, and valuing its blessings above all price.—FIRST ANNUAL MESSAGE. viii, 8. FORD ED., viii, 119. (1801.)

6766. POPULATION, Malefactors and. —The malefactors sent to America were not sufficient in number to merit enumeration as one class out of three which peopled America. It was at a late period of their history that this practice began. * * * I do not think the whole number sent would amount to two thousand, and being principally men, eaten up with disease, they married seldom and propagated little. I do not suppose that themselves and their descendants are at present four thousand, which is little more than one thousandth part of the whole inhabitants.—To M. DE MEUNIER. ix, 254. FORD ED., iv, 158. (P., 1786.)

6767. POPULATION, Preventing.—He has endeavored to prevent the population of these States; for that purpose, obstructing the laws for naturalization of foreigners; refusing to pass other laws to encourage their migrations hither, and raising the conditions of new appropriations of lands.—DECLARATION OF INDEPENDENCE AS DRAWN BY JEFFERSON.

6768. POPULATION, Theories of Malthus.—Malthus's work on Population is a work of sound logic, in which some of the opinions of Adam Smith, as well as of the Economists, are ably examined. * * * The differences of circumstances between this and the old countries of Europe, furnish differences of fact whereon to reason in questions of political economy, and will consequently produce sometimes a difference of result. There, for example, the quantity of food is fixed, or increasing in a slow and only arithmetical ratio, and the proportion is limited by the same ratio. Supernumerary births consequently add only to your mortality. Here the immense extent of uncultivated and fertile lands enables every one who will labor to marry young, and to raise a family of any size. Our food, then, may increase geometrically with our laborers, and our births, however multiplied, become effective. Again, there the best distri-

bution of labor is supposed to be that which places the manufacturing hands alongside of the agricultural; so that the one part shall feed both, and the other part furnish both with clothes and other comforts. Would that be best here? Egoism and first appearances say "yes". Or would it be better that all our laborers should be employed in agriculture? In this case a double or treble portion of fertile lands would be brought into culture; a double or treble creation of food be produced, and its surplus go to nourish the now perishing births of Europe, who in return would manufacture and send us in exchange our clothes and other comforts. Morality listens to this, and so invariably do the laws of nature create our duties and interests, that when they seem to be at variance, we ought to suspect some fallacy in our reasonings. In solving this question, too, we should allow just weight to the moral and physical preference of the agricultural, over the manufacturing, man.—To M. SAY. iv, 526. (W., Feb. 1804.) See MALTHUS.

6769. PORTER (David), Complaint against.—Mr. Madison * * * suggests the expediency of immediately taking up the case of Captain Porter, against whom Mr. Erskine [British minister] lodged a very serious complaint, for an act of violence committed on a British seaman in the Mediterranean. While Mr. Erskine was reminded of the mass of complaints we had against his government for similar violences, he was assured that contending against such irregularities ourselves, and requiring satisfaction for them, we did not mean to follow the example, and that on Captain Porter's return, it should be properly inquired into. The sooner this is done the better; because if Great Britain settles with us satisfactorily all our subsisting differences, and should require in return (to have an appearance of reciprocity of wrong as well as redress), a marked condemnation of Captain Porter, it would be embarrassing were that the only obstacle to a peaceable settlement, and the more so as we cannot but disavow his act. On the contrary, if we immediately look into it, we shall be more at liberty to be moderate in the censure of it, on the very ground of British example; and the case being once passed upon, we can more easily avoid the passing on it a second time, as against a settled principle. It is, therefore, to put it in our power to let Captain Porter off as easily as possible, as a valuable officer whom we all wish to favor, that I suggest to you the earliest attention to the inquiry, and the promptest settlement of it.—To ROBERT SMITH. v, 192. FORD ED., ix, 138. (M., Sep. 1807.)

6770. PORTUGAL, Commerce with.—I am in hopes Congress will send a minister to Lisbon. I know no country with which we are likely to cultivate a more useful commerce. I have pressed this in my private letters.—To JOHN ADAMS. i, 530. (P., 1786.)

6771. ———— ————. [In arranging the treaty of commerce] we wished much to have had some privileges in their American possessions; but this was not to be effected. The right to import flour into Portugal, though not conceded by the treaty, we are not without hopes of obtaining.—To WILLIAM CARMICHAEL. i, 551. (P., 1786.)

6772. ———— ————. While in London we entered into negotiations with the Chevalier Pinto, Ambassador of Portugal at that place. The only article of difficulty between us was a stipulation that our bread stuff should be received in Portugal in the form of flour as well as of grain. He approved of it himself, but observed that several Nobles, of great influence at their court, were the owners of wind-mills in the neighborhood of Lisbon which depended much for their profits on manufacturing our wheat, and that this stipulation would endanger the whole treaty. He signed it, however, and its fate was what he had candidly portended.—AUTOBIOGRAPHY. i, 64. FORD ED., i, 90. (1821.)

6773. PORTUGAL, Government of.— The government of Portugal is so peaceable and inoffensive that it has never any altercations with its friends. If their minister abroad writes them once a quarter that all is well, they desire no more.—To F. W. GILMER. vii, 5. FORD ED., x, 33. (M., 1816.)

6774. ———— ————. During six and thirty years that I have been in situations to attend to the conduct and characters of foreign nations, I have found the government of Portugal the most just, inoffensive, and unambitious of any one with which we had concern, without a single exception. I am sure that this is the character of ours also. Two such nations can never wish to quarrel with each other.—To J. CORREA. vii, 184. FORD ED., x, 164. (M., 1820.)

6775. POSTERITY, Judgment of.—It is fortunate for those in public trust, that posterity will judge them by their works, and not by the malignant vituperations and invectives of the Pickerings and Gardiners of their age.— To JOHN ADAMS. vii, 62. (M., 1817.)

6776. POSTERITY, Sacrifices for.—It is from posterity we are to expect remuneration for the sacrifices we are making for their service, of time, quiet and good will.—To JOSEPH C. CABELL. vii, 394. (M., 1825.)

6777. ———— ————. It has been a great solace to me to believe that you are engaged in vindicating to posterity the course we have pursued for preserving to them, in all their purity, the blessings of self-government, which we had assisted, too, in acquiring for them.— To JAMES MADISON. vii, 435. FORD ED., x, 378. (M., 1826.)

6778. POST OFFICE, Appointments.— A very early recommendation * * * [was] given to the Postmaster General to employ no printer, foreigner, or revolutionary tory in any of his offices.—To NATHANIEL MACON. iv, 397. (W., May 1801.)

6779. ———— ————. The true remedy for putting those [Post office] appointments into a wholesome state would be a law vesting them in the President, but without the intervention of the Senate. That intervention would make the matter worse. Every Senator would expect to dispose of all the post offices in his vicinage, or perhaps in his State. At present the President has some control over those appointments by his authority over the postmaster himself.— To PRESIDENT MADISON. FORD ED., ix, 460. (M., 1814.)

6780. POST OFFICE, Benefits of.—I wish the regulation of the post office, adopted by Congress * * * , could be put in practice. It was for the travel night and day, and to go their several stages three times a week. The speedy and frequent communication of intelligence is really of great consequence. So many falsehoods have been propagated that nothing now is believed unless coming from Congress or camp. Our people, merely for

want of intelligence which they may rely on, are becoming lethargic and insensible of the state they are in.—To JOHN ADAMS. FORD ED., ii, 130. (May 1777.)

6781. POST OFFICE, The Colonial.— [The] exercises of usurped power [by Parliament] have not been confined to instances alone in which themselves were interested; but they have also intermeddled with the regulation of the internal affairs of the Colonies.— RIGHTS OF BRITISH AMERICA. i, 130. FORD ED., i, 434. (1774.)

6782. ———— ————. The act of the 9th [year] of [Queen] Anne for establishing a post office in America, seems to have had little connection with British convenience, except that of accommodating his Majesty's ministers and favorites with the sale of a lucrative and easy office.— RIGHTS OF BRITISH AMERICA. i, 130. FORD ED., i, 434. (1774.)

6783. POST OFFICE, Expediting mails. —Congress have adopted the late improvement in the British post office, of sending their mails by the stages.—To WM. CARMICHAEL. i, 475. (P., 1785.)

6784. ———— ————. I opened to the President a proposition for doubling the velocity of the post riders, who now travel about fifty miles a day, and might, without difficulty, go one hundred, and for taking measures (by way-bills) to know where the delay is, when there is any. —THE ANAS. ix, 101. FORD ED., i, 174. (1792.)

6785. ———— ————. I am now on a plan with the Postmaster General to make the posts go from Philadelphia to Richmond in two days and a half instead of six, which I hope to persuade him is practicable.—To T. M. RANDOLPH. FORD ED., v, 456. (Pa., 1792.)

6786. POST OFFICE, Foreign mails.— The person at the head of the post office here says he proposed to Dr. Franklin a convention to facilitate the passage of letters through their office and ours, and that he delivered a draft of the convention proposed, that it might be sent to Congress. I think it possible he may be mistaken in this, as, on my mentioning it to Dr. Franklin, he did not recollect any such draft having been put into his hands. An answer, however, is expected by them. I mention it, that Congress may decide whether they will make any convention on the subject, and on what principle. The one proposed here was, that, for letters passing hence into America. the French postage should be collected by our post officers, and paid every six months, and for letters coming from America here, the American postage should be collected by the post officers here, and paid to us in like manner. A second plan, however, presents itself; that is, to suppose the sums to be thus collected, on each side, will be equal, or so nearly equal, that the balance will not pay for the trouble of keeping accounts. and for the little bickerings that the settlement of accounts and demands of the balances may occasion; and therefore, to make an exchange of postage. This would better secure our harmony; but I do not know that it would be agreed to here. If not, the other might then be agreed to.—To JOHN JAY. i, 410. (P., 1785.)

6787. POST OFFICE, Infidelities in foreign.—The infidelities of the post offices, both of England and France, are not unknown to you. The former are the most rascally, because they retain one's letters, not choosing to take the trouble of copying them. The latter, when they have taken copies, are so civil as to send the originals, resealed clumsily with a composition, on which they have previously taken the impression of the seal.—To R. Izard. i, 442. (P., 1785.)

6788. —— ——. Send your letters by the French packet. They come by that conveyance with certainty, having first undergone the ceremony of being opened and read in the post office, which I am told is done in every country in Europe.—To James Monroe. Ford ed., iv, 33. (P., 1785.)

6789. —— ——. All letters [are] opened which come either through the French or English channel, unless trusted to a messenger. I think I never received one through the post office which had not been. It is generally discoverable by the smokiness of the wax and faintness of the reimpression. Once they sent me a letter open, having forgotten to reseal it. —To Richard H. Lee. Ford ed., iv, 69. (P., 1785.)

6790. —— ——. [I wrote] on such things only as both the French and English post offices were welcome to see.—To James Monroe. i, 590. Ford ed., iv, 250. (P., 1786.)

6791. POST OFFICE, Newspaper postage.—I desired you * * * to send the newspapers notwithstanding the expense. I had then no idea of it. Some late instances have made me perfectly acquainted with it. I have, therefore been obliged * * * to have my newspapers from the different States, enclosed to the office for Foreign Affairs, and to desire Mr. Jay to pack the whole in a box, and send it * * * as merchandise. * * * In this way, they will cost me livres where they now cost me guineas.—To F. Hopkinson. i, 441. (P., 1785.)

6792. POST OFFICE, Patronage of.—[I said to President Washington] that I thought it would be advantageous to declare [that the Post office is included in the Department of State] for another reason, to wit, that the Department of Treasury possessed already such an influence as to swallow up the whole Executive powers, and that even the future Presidents (not supported by the weight of character which himself possessed) would not be able to make head against this Department. That in urging this measure I had certainly no personal interest, since, if I was supposed to have any appetite for power, yet as my career would certainly be exactly as short as his own, the intervening time was too short to be an object. My real wish was to avail the public of every occasion during the residue of the President's period, to place things on a safe footing.—The Anas. ix, 101. Ford ed., i, 174. (Feb. 1792.)

6793. POST OFFICE, Political spies in. —The interruption of letters is becoming so notorious, that I am forming a resolution of declining correspondence with my friends through the channels of the Post Office altogether.—To E. Randolph. iv, 192. Ford ed., vii, 156. (Pa., June 1797.)

6794. —— ——. The impression of my seal on wax (which shall be constant hereafter) will discover whether my letters are opened by the way. The nature of some of my communications furnishes ground of inquietude for their safe conveyance.—To James Madison. iv, 231. Ford ed., vii, 230. (Pa., April 1798.)

6795. —— ——. To avoid the suspicions and curiosity of the post office, which would

have been excited by seeing your name* and mine on the back of a letter, I have delayed acknowledging the receipt of your favor * * * till an occasion to write to an inhabitant of Wilmington gives me an opportunity of putting my letter under cover to him.—To Archibald Hamilton Rowan. iv, 256. Ford ed., vii, 280. (M., 1798.)

6796. —— ——. The infidelities of the post office and the circumstances of the times are against my writing fully and freely.—To John Taylor. iv, 259. Ford ed., vii, 309. (M., 1798.)

6797. —— ——. I shall follow your direction in conveying this [letter] by a private hand, though I know not as yet when one worthy of confidence will occur. * * * Did we ever expect to see the day, when, breathing nothing but sentiments of love, to our country and its freedom and happiness, our correspondence must be as secret as if we were hatching its destruction!—To Elbridge Gerry. iv, 273. Ford ed., vii, 335. (Pa., 1799.)

6798. —— ——. A want of confidence in the post office deters me from writing to my friends on the subject of politics.—To Robert R. Livingston. iv, 297. Ford ed., vii, 368. (Pa., 1799.)

6799. —— ——. From the commencement of the ensuing session [of Congress], I shall trust the post offices with nothing confidential, persuaded that during the ensuing twelve months they will lend their inquisitorial aid to furnish matter for newspapers.—To James Madison. iv, 307. Ford ed., vii, 400. (M., Nov. 1799.)

6800. —— ——. One of your electors * * * offers me a safe conveyance at a moment when the post offices will be peculiarly suspicious and prying. Your answer may come by post without danger, if directed in some other handwriting than your own.—To Robert R. Livingston. iv, 339. Ford ed., vii, 466. (W., Dec. 1800.)

6801. —— ——. Mr. Brown's departure for Virginia enables me to write confidentially what I could not have ventured by the post at this prying season.—To James Madison. iv, 342. Ford ed., vii, 470. (W., Dec. 1800.)

6802. —— ——. I shall neither frank nor subscribe my letter, because I do not choose to commit myself to the fidelity of the post office. For the same reason, I have avoided putting pen to paper through the whole summer, except on mere business, because I knew it was a prying season.—To Tench Coxe. iv, 345. Ford ed., vii, 474. (W., Dec. 1800.)

6803. —— ——. I dare not through the channel of the post hazard a word to you on the subject of the [Presidential] election. Indeed the interception and publication of my letters expose the republican cause, as well as myself personally, to such obloquy that I have come to a resolution never to write another sentence of politics in a letter.—To James Madison. Ford ed., vii, 484. (W., Feb. 1801.)

6804. —— ——. Several letters from you have not been acknowledged. By the post I dare not, * * *.—To James Monroe. iv, 354. Ford ed., vii, 490. (W., Feb. 1801.)

*Rowan was one of the leaders in the Irish Rebellion of 1798.—Editor.

6805. POST OFFICE, Reformed.—Your letters through the post will now come safely.—To ELBRIDGE GERRY. iv, 393. FORD ED., viii, 43. (W., March 1801.)

6806. —— ——. I trust that the post is become a safe channel to and from me. I have heard, indeed, of some extraordinary licences practiced in the post offices of your State, and there is nothing I desire so much as information of facts on that subject, to rectify the office.—To GIDEON GRANGER. FORD ED., viii, 44. (W., March 1801.)

6807. POST ROADS, Building.—Have you considered all the consequences of your proposition respecting post roads? I view it as a source of boundless patronage to the Executive, jobbing to members of Congress and their friends, and a bottomless abyss of public money. You will begin by appropriating only the surplus of the Post Office revenues; but the other revenues will soon be called into their aid, and it will be the source of eternal scramble among the members, who can get the most money wasted in their State; and they will always get most who are meanest. We have thought, hitherto, that the roads of a State could not be so well administered even by the State Legislature, as by the magistracy of the county, on the spot. How will it be when a member of New Hampshire is to mark out a road for Georgia? Does the power to *establish* post roads, given you by the Constitution, mean that you shall *make* the roads, or only *select* from those already made, those on which there shall be a post? If the term be equivocal (and I really do not think it so,) which is the safer construction? That which permits a majority of Congress to go cutting down mountains and bridging of rivers, or the other, which, if too restricted, may be referred to the States for amendment, securing still due measure and proportion among us, and providing some means of information to the members of Congress tantamount to that ocular inspection, which, even in our county determinations, the magistrate finds cannot be supplied by any other evidence? The fortification of harbors was liable to great objection. But national circumstances furnished some color. In this case there is none. The roads of America are the best in the world except those of France and England. But does the state of our population, the extent of our internal commerce, the want of sea and river navigation, call for such expense on roads here, or are our means adequate to it?—To JAMES MADISON. iv, 131. FORD ED., vii, 63. (M., March 1796.)

6808. POST ROADS, Expense.—I very much fear the road system will be urged. The mines of Peru would not supply the moneys which would be wasted on this object, nor the patience of any people stand the abuses which would be incontrollably committed under it.—To JAMES MADISON. iv, 344. FORD ED., vii, 472. (W., Dec. 1800.)

6809. POST ROADS, Jobbery.—The Roads bill will be a bottomless abyss for money, the most fruitful field for ——* and the richest provision for jobs to favorites that has ever yet been proposed.—To CÆSAR RODNEY. FORD ED., vii, 473. (W., Dec. 1800.)

6810. POSTS (Western), England's detention of.—England shows no dispositions to enter into friendly connections with us. On the contrary, her detention of our posts seems to be the speck which is to produce a storm.—To R. IZARD. i, 442. (P., 1785.)

6811. —— ——. The British garrisons were not withdrawn with all convenient speed, nor have ever yet been withdrawn from Machilimackinac, on Lake Michigan; Detroit, on the straits of Lake Erie and Huron; Fort Erie, on Lake Erie; Niagara, Oswego, on Lake Ontario; Oswegatchie, on the River St. Lawrence; Point Au-Fer, and Dutchman's Point, on Lake Champlain.—To GEORGE HAMMOND. FORD ED., vi, 468. (P., Dec. 1793.)

6812. POSTS (Western), France and.—The question * * * proposed [by you], "How far France considers herself as bound to insist on the delivery of the posts", would infallibly produce another, "How far we consider ourselves as guarantees of their American possessions, and bound to enter into any future war in which these may be attacked"? The words of the treaty of alliance seem to be without ambiguity on either head, yet I should be afraid to commit Congress by answering without authority. I will endeavor on my return [from London to Paris] to sound the opinion of the minister, if possible without exposing myself to the other question. Should anything forcible be meditated on these posts, it would possibly be thought prudent, previously, to ask the good offices of France to obtain their delivery. In this case, they would probably say, we must first execute the treaty on our part by repealing all acts which have contravened it. Now this measure, if there be any candor in the court of London, would suffice to obtain a delivery of the posts from them without the mediation of any third power. However, if this mediation should be finally needed, I see no reason to doubt our obtaining it, and still less to question its omnipotent influence on the British court.—To JOHN JAY. i, 539. FORD ED., iv, 200. (L., March 1786.)

6813. POSTS (Western), Indian murders.—Were the western posts in our possession, it cannot be doubted but there would be an end to the murders daily committed by the Indians on our Northwestern frontier, and to a great part of the expense of our armaments in that quarter.—To GEORGE HAMMOND. FORD ED., vi, 321. (1793.)

6814. POTATO, Nativity of.—You say in your "General Geography" the potato is a native of the United States. I presume you speak of the Irish potato. I have inquired much into the question, and think I can assure you that the plant is not a native of North America. Zimmerman, in his "Geographical Zoology", says it is a native of Guiana; and Clavigers, that the Mexicans got it from South America, *its native country*. The most probable account I have been able to collect is, that a vessel of Sir Walter Raleigh's, returning from Guiana, put into the west of Ireland in distress, having on board some potatoes which they called earth apples. That the season of the year, and circumstance of their being already sprouted, induced them to give them all out

* Illegible in MS.

there, and they were no more heard or thought of, till they had spread considerably into that island, whence they were carried over into England, and, therefore, called the Irish potato. From England they came to the United States bringing their name with them.—To MR. SPAFFORD. v, 445. (M., 1809.)

— **POTOMAC AND OHIO CANAL.**— See CANAL.

6815. POWER, Abridgment of.—The functionaries of public power rarely strengthen in their dispositions to abridge it.— To JOHN TAYLOR. vi, 608. FORD ED., x, 31. (M., 1816.)

6816. POWER, Abuses.—Education is the true corrective of abuses of constitutional power.—To WILLIAM C. JARVIS. vii, 179. FORD ED., x, 161. (M., 1820.)

6817. POWER, Depositaries of.—No other depositaries of power [than the people themselves] have ever yet been found, which did not end in converting to their own profit the earnings of those committed to their charge.—To SAMUEL KERCHIVAL. vii, 36. FORD ED., x, 45. (M., 1816.)

6818. ——— ———. I know no safe depositary of the ultimate powers of the society but the people themselves; and if we think them not enlightened enough to exercise their control with a wholesome discretion, the remedy is not to take it from them, but to inform their discretion by education.— To WILLIAM C. JARVIS. vii, 179. FORD ED., x, 161. (M., 1820.)

6819. POWER, Exercise of.—I have never been able to conceive how any rational being could propose happiness to himself from the exercise of power over others.—To M. DESTUTT TRACY. v, 569. FORD ED., ix, 308. (M., 1811.)

6820. ——— ———. An honest man can feel no pleasure in the exercise of power over his fellow citizens. And considering as the only offices of power those conferred by the people directly, that is to say, the Executive and Legislative functions of the General and State Governments, the common refusal of these, and multiplied resignations, are proofs sufficient that power is not alluring to pure minds, and is not with them, the primary principle of contest. This is my belief of it; it is that on which I have acted; and had it been a mere contest who should be permitted to administer the Government according to its genuine republican principles, there has never been a moment of my life in which I should have relinquished for it the enjoyments of my family, my farm, my friends and books.—To JOHN MELISH. vi, 96. FORD ED., ix, 376. (M., 1813.)

6821. ——— ———. In one sentiment of [your] speech I particularly concur,—" if we have a doubt relative to any power, we ought not to exercise it ".—To EDWARD LIVINGSTON. vii, 343. FORD ED., x, 300. (M., 1824.)

6822. POWER, Independent.—It should be remembered, as an axiom of eternal truth in politics, that whatever power in any government is independent, is absolute also; in theory only, at first, while the spirit of the people is up, but in practice, as fast as that relaxes. Independence can be trusted nowhere but with the people in mass. They are inherently independent of all but moral law.—To SPENCER ROANE. vii, 134. FORD ED., x, 141. (P.F., 1819.)

6823. POWER, Limitation.—In a free country every power is dangerous which is not bound up by general rules.—To PHILIP MAZZEI. FORD ED., iv, 116. (P., 1785.)

6824. POWER, Origin of.—Hume, the great apostle of toryism, says [in his History of England, c. 159] " the Commons established a principle, which is noble in itself, and seems specious, but is belied by all history and experience, *that the people are the origin of all just power*". And where else will this degenerate son of science, this traitor to his fellow men, find the origin of *just* power, if not in the majority of the society? Will it be in the minority? Or in an individual of that minority?—To JOHN CARTWRIGHT. vii, 356. (M., 1824.)

6825. ——— ———. All power is inherent in the people.—To JOHN CARTWRIGHT. vii, 357. (M., 1824.)

6826. POWER, Perpetuation of.—The principles of our Constitution are wisely opposed to all perpetuations of power, and to every practice which may lead to hereditary establishments.—REPLY TO ADDRESS. v, 473. (M., 1809.)

6827. POWER, Perversion of.—Even under the best forms [of government] those entrusted with power have perverted it into tyranny.—DIFFUSION OF KNOWLEDGE BILL. FORD ED., ii, 221. (1779.)

6828. POWER, Shifting.—I have never been so well pleased as when I could shift power from my own, on the shoulders of others.—To M. DESTUTT TRACY. v, 569. FORD ED., ix, 308. (M., 1811.)

6829. POWER, Use of.—I hope our wisdom will grow with our power, and teach us, that the less we use our power, the greater will it be.—To THOMAS LEIPER. vi, 465. FORD ED., ix, 520. (M., 1815.) See AUTHORITY.

6830. POWERS, Assumed.—I had rather ask an enlargement of power from the nation, where it is found necessary, than to assume it by a construction [of the Constitution] which would make our powers boundless.— To WILSON C. NICHOLAS. iv, 506. FORD ED., viii, 247. (M., 1803.)

6831. ——— ———. If, wherever the Constitution assumes a single power out of many which belong to the same subject, we should consider it as assuming the whole, it would vest the General Government with a mass of powers never contemplated. On the contrary, the assumption of particular powers seems an exclusion of all not assumed.—To JOSEPH C. CABELL. vi, 310. FORD ED., ix, 452. (M., 1814.)

6832. —— ——. If the three powers maintain their mutual independence on each other our Government may last long, but not so if either can assume the authorities of the other.—To WILLIAM C. JARVIS. vii, 179. FORD ED., x, 161. (M., 1820.)

6833. POWERS, Civil.—Civil powers alone have been given to the President of the United States, and no authority to direct the religious exercises of his constituents.—To REV. SAMUEL MILLAR. v, 237. FORD ED., ix, 175. (W., 1808.) See RELIGION.

6834. POWERS, Conflicting.—The peculiar happiness of our blessed system is, that in differences of opinion between these different sets of servants [in the three departments of the Federal Government], the appeal is to neither, but to their employers, peaceably assembled by their representatives in convention.—To SPENCER ROANE. vii, 214. FORD ED., x, 190. (M., 1821.)

6835. POWERS, Constitutional.—To keep in all things within the pale of our constitutional powers, * * * [is one of] the landmarks by which we are to guide ourselves in all our proceedings.—SECOND ANNUAL MESSAGE. viii, 21. FORD ED., viii, 187. (Dec. 1802.)

6836. POWERS, Constructive.—The States supposed that by their Tenth Amendment, they had secured themselves against constructive powers. They were not lessoned yet by Cohen's Case, nor aware of the slipperiness of the eels of the law. I ask for no straining of words against the General Government, nor yet against the States. I believe the States can best govern our home concerns, and the General Government our foreign ones. I wish, therefore, to see maintained that wholesome distribution of powers established by the Constitution for the limitation of both; and never to see all offices transferred to Washington, where, further withdrawn from the eyes of the people, they may more secretly be bought and sold as at market.—To WILLIAM JOHNSON. vii, 297. FORD ED., x, 232. (M., 1823.)

6837. POWERS, Control by the people. —Unless the mass retains sufficient control over those intrusted with the powers of their government, these will be perverted to their own oppression, and to the perpetuation of wealth and power in the individuals and their families selected for the trust.—To MR. VAN DER KEMP. vi, 45. (M., 1812.)

6838. POWERS, Delegated.—The Constitution of the United States * * * [has] delegated to Congress a power to punish treason, counterfeiting the securities and current coin of the United States, piracies, and felonies committed on the high seas, and offences against the law of nations, and no other crimes whatsoever; and it being true, as a general principle, and one of the amendments to the Constitution having also declared, that " the powers not delegated to the United States by the Constitution, nor prohibited by it to the States, are reserved to the States respectively, or to the people ", * * * the power to create, define, and punish * * * other crimes is reserved, and of right, appertains solely and exclusively to the respective States, each within its own territory.—KENTUCKY RESOLUTIONS. ix, 465. FORD ED., vii, 292. (1798.)

6839. —— ——. In case of an abuse of the delegated powers, the members of the General Government, being chosen by the people, a change by the people would be the constitutional remedy.—KENTUCKY RESOLUTIONS. ix, 469. FORD ED., vii, 301. (1798.)

6840. POWERS, Distribution of.—To preserve the republican form and principles of our Constitution, and cleave to the salutary distribution of powers, which that has established, * * * are the two sheet anchors of our Union. If driven from either, we shall be in danger of foundering.—To WILLIAM JOHNSON. vii, 298. FORD ED., x, 232. (M., 1823.)

6841. POWERS, Enlarging.—It [is] inconsistent with the principles of civil liberty, and contrary to the natural rights of the other members of the society, that any body of men therein should have authority to enlarge their own powers * * * without restraint.*—ALLOWANCE BILL. FORD ED., ii, 165. (1778.)

6842. —— ——. Nothing is more likely than that their [the framers of the Constitution] enumeration of powers is defective. This is the ordinary case of all human works. Let us go on, then, perfecting it by adding, by way of amendment, to the Constitution those forms which time and trial show are still wanting.—To WILSON C. NICHOLAS. iv, 506. FORD ED., viii, 248. (M., 1803.)

6843. POWERS, The enumerated.—To take a single step beyond the boundaries specifically drawn around the powers of Congress [in the enumerated powers] is to take possession of a boundless field of power, no longer susceptible of any definition.—NATIONAL BANK OPINION. vii, 556. FORD ED., v, 285. (1791.)

6844. —— ——. A little *difference* in the degree of *convenience* cannot constitute the necessity which the Constitution makes the ground for assuming any non-enumerated power.—NATIONAL BANK OPINION. vii, 559. FORD ED., v, 288. (1791.)

6845. —— ——. [By] the general phrase " to make all laws *necessary* and proper for carrying into execution the enumerated powers" * * * the Constitution allows only the means which are " *necessary* ", not those which are merely " convenient " for effecting the enumerated powers. If such a latitude of construction be allowed to this phrase as to

---

* A Bill in the Virginia Legislature providing for increased pay and allowances to members.—EDITOR.

give any non-enumerated power, it will go to every one, for there is not one which ingenuity may not torture into a *convenience* in some instance *or other,* to *some one* of so long a list of enumerated powers. It would swallow up all the delegated powers, and reduce the whole to one power. Therefore it was that the Constitution restrained them to the *necessary* means, that is to say, to those means without which the grant of power would be nugatory.—NATIONAL BANK OPINION. vii, 558. FORD ED., v, 287. (1791.) See MANUFACTURES.

6846. POWERS, Indestructible.—Legislative powers [are] incapable of annihilation.—DECLARATION OF INDEPENDENCE AS DRAWN BY JEFFERSON.

6847. POWERS, Nullification.—Where powers are assumed which have not been delegated, a nullification of the act is the rightful remedy.—KENTUCKY RESOLUTIONS. ix, 469. FORD ED., vii, 301. (1798.)

6848. POWERS, Organization.—Whenever any form of government becomes destructive of these ends [life, liberty and the pursuit of happiness], it is the right of the people to alter or to abolish it, and to institute new government, laying its foundation on such principles, and organizing its powers in such form, as to them shall seem most likely to effect their safety and happiness.—DECLARATION OF INDEPENDENCE AS DRAWN BY JEFFERSON.

6849. POWERS, Self-constituted.—I shall not undertake to draw the line of demarcation between private associations of laudable views and unimposing numbers, and those whose magnitude may rivalize and jeopardize the march of regular government. Yet such a line does exist. I have seen the days,—they were those which preceded the Revolution,—when even this last and perilous engine became necessary; but they were days which no man would wish to see a second time. That was the case where the regular authorities of the government had combined against the rights of the people, and no means of correction remained to them but to organize a collateral power, which, with their support, might rescue and secure their violated rights. But such is not the case with our government. We need hazard no collateral power, which, by a change of its original views, and assumption of others we know not how virtuous or how mischievous, would be ready organized and in force sufficient to shake the established foundations of society, and endanger its peace and the principles on which it is based. Is not the machine* now proposed of this gigantic stature?—To JEDEDIAH MORSE. vii, 234. FORD ED., x, 204. (M., 1822.)

* The " machine " was a society for the civilization of the Indians, to be composed of nearly all the officers of the Federal and State Governments, the clergy of all denominations, and as many citizens as would pay for membership. Jefferson commended the object, but condemned so vast an organization as unnecessary, dangerous and bad as a precedent.—EDITOR.

6850. ——— ———. Might we not as well appoint a committee for each department of the Government, to counsel and direct its head separately, as volunteer ourselves to counsel and direct the whole, in mass? And might we not do it as well for their foreign, their fiscal, and their military, as for their Indian affairs? And how many societies, auxiliary to the Government, may we expect to see spring up, in imitation of this, offering to associate themselves in this and that of its functions? In a word, why not take the Government out of its constitutional hands, associate them indeed with us, to preserve a semblance that the acts are theirs, but ensuring them to be our own by allowing them a minor vote only?—To JEDEDIAH MORSE. vii, 236. FORD ED., x, 206. (M., 1822.)

6851. POWERS, Separation of.—The principle of the Constitution is that of a separation of Legislative, Executive and Judiciary functions, except in cases specified. If this principle be not expressed in direct terms, it is clearly the spirit of the Constitution, and it ought to be so commented and acted on by every friend of free government.—To JAMES MADISON. iv, 161. FORD ED., vii, 108. (M., Jan. 1797.)

6852. POWERS, Undelegated.—Whenever the General Government assumes undelegated powers, its acts are unauthoritative, void, and of no force.—KENTUCKY RESOLUTIONS. ix, 464. FORD ED., vii, 291. (1798.)

6853. ——— ———. This Commonwealth [Kentucky] is determined, as it doubts not its co-States are, to submit to undelegated, and consequently unlimited powers in no man, or body of men on earth.—KENTUCKY RESOLUTIONS. ix, 469. FORD ED., vii, 301. (1798.)

6854. ——— ———. The power to regulate commerce does not give a power to build piers, wharves, open ports, clear the beds of rivers, dig canals, build warehouses, build manufacturing machines, set up manufactories, cultivate the earth, to all of which the power would go if it went to the first.—To ALBERT GALLATIN. iv, 449. FORD ED., viii, 174. (1802.)

6855. POWERS, Unlimited.—I have no idea of entering into the contest, whether it be expedient to delegate unlimited powers to our ordinary governors? My opinion is against that expediency; but my occupations do not permit me to undertake to vindicate all my opinions, nor have they importance enough to merit it.—To NOAH WEBSTER. iii, 203. FORD ED., v, 257. (Pa., 1790.) See BANK (U. S.). CONSTITUTIONALITY.

6856. PRADT (Abbe de), Writings of.—Of the character of M. de Pradt his political writings furnish a tolerable estimate, but not so full as you have favored me with. He is eloquent, and his pamphlet on colonies shows him ingenious. I was gratified by his *Recit Historique,* because, pretending, as all men do, to some character, and he to one of some distinction, I supposed he would not place before the world facts of glaring falsehood, on which so many living and distinguished witnesses could convict him.—To John Quincy Adams. vii, 87. (M., 1817.)

6857. PRAISE, Undeserved.—To give praise where it is not due might be well from the venal, but it would ill beseem those who are asserting the rights of human nature.—Rights of British America. i, 141. Ford ed., i, 446. (1774.)

6858. PRECEDENT, Oppression and.—For what oppression may not a precedent be found in this world of the *bellum omnium in omnia?*—Notes on Virginia. viii, 371. Ford ed., iii, 235. (1782.)

6859. PRECEDENT, Power and.—One precedent in favor of power is stronger than an hundred against it.—Notes on Virginia. viii, 367. Ford ed., iii, 230. (1782.)

6860. PREEMPTION, Right of.—If the country, instead of being altogether vacant, is thinly occupied by another nation, the right of the native forms an exception to that of the new comers; that is to say, these will only have a right against all other nations except the natives. Consequently, they have the exclusive privilege of acquiring the native right by purchase or other just means. This is called the right of preemption, and is become a principle of the law of nations, fundamental with respect to America. There are but two means of acquiring the native title. First, war; for even war may, sometimes, give a just title. Second, contracts, or treaty.—Opinion on Georgian Land Grants. vii, 467. Ford ed., v, 166. (1790.)

6861. PREROGATIVE, Barriers against.—The privilege of giving or withholding our moneys is an important barrier against the undue exertion of prerogative, which if left altogether without control may be exercised to our great oppression.—Reply to Lord North's Proposition. Ford ed., i, 477. (July 1775.)

6862. PRESBYTERIAN SPIRIT, Liberty and.—The Presbyterian spirit is known to be so congenial with friendly liberty, that the patriots, after the Restoration, finding that the humor of the people was running too strongly to exalt the prerogative of the crown, promoted the dissenting interest as a check and balance, and thus was produced the Toleration Act.—Notes on Religion. Ford ed., ii, 98. (1776?)

6863. PRESENTS, Declination of.—I return you my thanks for a bust of the Emperor Alexander [of Russia]. These are the more cordial, because of the value the bust derives from the great estimation in which its original is held by the world, and by none more than myself. It will constitute one of the most valued ornaments of the retreat I am preparing for myself at my native home. * * * I had laid it down as a law for my conduct while in office, and hitherto scrupulously observed, to accept of no present beyond a book, a pamphlet, or other curiosity of minor value; as well to avoid imputation on my motives of action, as to shut out a practice susceptible to such abuse. But my particular esteem for the character of the Emperor, places his image in my mind above the scope of law. I receive it, therefore, and shall cherish it with affection. It nourishes the contemplation of all the good placed in his

power, and of his disposition to do it.—To Mr. Harris. v, 6. (W., 1806.)

6864. ——— ———. Mr. Granger has sent me the very elegant ivory staff of which you wished my acceptance. The motives of your wish are honorable to me, and gratifying, as they evidence the approbation of my public conduct by a stranger who has not viewed it through the partialities of personal acquaintance. Be assured, Sir, that I am as grateful for the testimony, as if I could have accepted the token of it which you have so kindly offered. On coming into public office, I laid it down as a law of my conduct, while I should continue in it, to accept no present of any sensible pecuniary value. A pamphlet, a new book, or an article of new curiosity, have produced no hesitation, because below suspicion. But things of sensible value, however innocently offered in the first examples, may grow at length into abuse, for which I wish not to furnish a precedent. The kindness of the motives which led to this manifestation of your esteem, sufficiently assures me that you will approve of my desire, by a perseverance in the rule, to retain that consciousness of a disinterested administration of the public trusts, which is essential to perfect tranquillity of mind.—To Samuel Hawkins. v, 393. (W., Nov. 1808.)

6865. PRESENTS, Diplomatic.—As custom may have rendered some presents necessary in the beginning or progress of this business [negotiation of a treaty with the Emperor of Morocco] and before it is concluded, or even in a way to be concluded, we authorize you to conform to the custom, confiding in your discretion to hazard as little as possible before a certainty of the event. We trust to you also to procure the best information as to what persons, and in what form, these presents should be made, and to make them accordingly.—To Thomas Barclay. i, 421. (P., 1785.)

6866. PRESENTS, To Foreign Ministers.—It was proposed that the medal [to be given to recalled foreign ministers] should always contain 150 dollars' worth of gold; it was presumed the gentleman would always keep this. The chain was to contain 365 links always, but these were to be proportioned in value to the time the person had been here, making each link worth 3 dimes for every year of residence. No expense was to be bestowed on the making because it was expected they would turn the chain into money.—Note by Jefferson. Ford ed., vi, 263. (1793.)

6867. ——— ———. It has become necessary to determine on a present proper to be given to diplomatic characters on their taking leave of us; and it is concluded that a medal and chain of gold will be the most convenient. I have, therefore, to ask the favor of you to order the dies to be engraved with all the dispatch practicable. The medal must be of thirty lines diameter, with a loop on the edge to receive the chain. On one side, must be the arms of the United States, of which I send you a written description; * * * round them as a legend must be "The United States of America". The device of the other side we do not decide on. One suggestion has been a Columbia (a fine female figure) delivering the emblems of peace and commerce to a Mercury, and the date of our republic, to wit, 4th July, MDCCLXXVI.—To William Short. iii, 142. (N.Y., 1790.)

6868. PRESENTS, To Indians.—I hope we shall give the Indians a thorough drubbing this summer, and I should think it better perhaps afterwards to take up the plan of liberal and repeated presents to them. This would be much the cheapest in the end and would save all the blood which is now being spilt; in time, too, it would produce a spirit of peace and friendship between us. The expense of a single expedition would last very long for presents.—To PRESIDENT WASHINGTON. iii, 248. FORD ED., v, 321. (Pa., 1791.)

6869. —— ——. The giving medals and marks of distinction to the Indian chiefs * * * has been an ancient custom from time immemorial. The medals are considered as complimentary things, as marks of friendship to those who come to see us, or who do us good offices, conciliatory of their good will towards us, and not designed to produce a contrary disposition towards others. They confer no power, and seem to have taken their origin in the European practice, of giving medals or other marks of friendship to the negotiators of treaties and other diplomatic characters, or visitors of distinction. The British government, while it prevailed here, practiced the giving medals, gorgets, and bracelets to the savages, invariable.—To CARMICHAEL AND SHORT. iv, 15. FORD ED., vi, 336. (Pa., 1793.)

6870. PRESENTS, Public.—The bounties from one's country, expressions of its approbation, are honors which it would be arrogance to refuse, especially where flowing from the willing only.—To THOMAS RITCHIE. FORD ED., x, 382. (M., 1826.)

6871. PRESENTS, Tribute and.—We rely that you will be able to obtain an acknowledgment of our treaty with Morocco, giving very moderate presents. As the amount of these will be drawn into precedent, on future similar repetitions of them, it becomes important. Our distance, our seclusion from the ancient world, its politics and usages, our agricultural occupations and habits, our poverty, and lastly, our determination to prefer war in all cases, to tribute under any form, and to any people whatever, will furnish you with topics for opposing and refusing high or dishonorable pretensions.—To THOMAS BARCLAY. iii, 262. (Pa., 1791.)

— PRESIDENT, Administration and Cabinet.—See ADMINISTRATION and CABINET.

6872. PRESIDENT, Depositions by.—If the defendant supposes there are any facts within the knowledge of the heads of departments, or of myself, which can be useful for his defence, from a desire of doing anything our situation will permit in furtherance of justice, we shall be ready to give him the benefit of it, by way of deposition, through any persons whom the Court shall authorize to take our testimony at this place [Washington].—To GEORGE HAY. v, 97. FORD ED., ix, 57. (W., June 1807.)

6873. PRESIDENT, Direct vote for.—One part of the subject of one of your letters is of a nature which forbids my interference altogether. The amendment of the Constitution of which you speak, would be a remedy to a certain degree. So will a different amendment which I know will be proposed, to wit, to have no electors, but let the people vote directly, and the ticket which has a plurality of the votes of any State to be considered as receiving thereby the vote of the State.—To ALBERT GALLATIN. FORD ED., viii, 94. (M., Sep. 1801.)

6874. —— ——. The President is chosen by ourselves, directly in *practice*, for we vote for A as elector only on the condition he will vote for B.—To DUPONT DE NEMOURS. vi, 590. FORD ED., x, 23. (P.F., 1816.)

6875. PRESIDENT, Election of.—The bill for the election of the President and Vice-President has undergone much revolution. Marshall made a dexterous maneuver. He declares against the constitutionality of the Senate's bill, and proposed that the right of decision of their grand committee should be controllable by the *concurrent* vote of the two houses of Congress; but to stand good if not rejected by a concurrent vote. You will readily estimate the amount of this sort of control. The committee of the House of Representatives, however, took from the committee the right of giving any opinion, requiring them to report the facts only, and that the votes returned by the States should be counted, unless reported by a concurrent vote of both houses.—To E. LIVINGSTON. iv, 328. FORD ED., vii, 443. (Pa., April 1800.)

6876. —— ——. That great opposition is and will be made by federalists to this amendment [to the Constitution], is certain. They know that if it prevails, neither a President nor Vice-President can ever be made but by the fair vote of the majority of the nation, of which they are not. That either their opposition to the principle of discrimination now, or their advocation of it formerly was on party, not moral motives, they cannot deny. Consequently, they fix for themselves the place in the scale of moral rectitude to which they are entitled. I am a friend to the discriminating principle; and for a reason more than others have, inasmuch as the discriminated vote of my constituents will express unequivocally the verdict they wish to cast on my conduct.—To THOMAS MCKEAN. FORD ED., viii, 292. (W., Jan. 1804.)

6877. PRESIDENT, The judiciary and. —The interference of the Executive can rarely be proper where that of the Judiciary is so.—To GEORGE HAMMOND. FORD ED., vi, 298. (Pa., 1793.)

— PRESIDENT, Oath of office.—See WASHINGTON.

6878. PRESIDENT, Petitions to.—The right of our fellow citizens to represent to the public functionaries their opinion on proceedings interesting to them, is unquestionably a constitutional right, often useful, sometimes necessary, and will always be respectfully acknowledged by me.—To THE NEW HAVEN COMMITTEE. iv, 402. FORD ED., viii, 68. (W., 1801.)

6879. PRESIDENT, Polish Kings and. —The President seems a bad edition of a Polish King.—To JOHN ADAMS. ii, 316. (P., Nov. 1787.)

6880. —— ——. What we have lately read in the history of Holland, in the chapter on the Stadtholder.* would have sufficed to

* See " HOLLAND " in this volume.—EDITOR.

set me against a chief magistrate eligible for a long duration, if I had ever been disposed towards one; and what we have always read of the elections of Polish Kings should have forever excluded the idea of one continuable for life.—To W. S. SMITH. ii, 318. FORD ED., iv, 466. (P., 1787.) See CONSTITUTION (FEDERAL).

6881. PRESIDENT, Reelection.—I fear much the effects of the perpetual reeligibility of the President. But it is not thought of in America, and I have, therefore, no prospect of a change of that article [in the Constitution].—To WILLIAM STEPHENS SMITH. FORD ED., v, 3. (P., 1788.)

6882. —— ——. There is a strong feature in the new Constitution which I strongly dislike. That is the perpetual reeligibility of the President. Of this I expect no amendment at present because I do not see that anybody has objected to it on your side of the water. But it will be productive of cruel distress to our country, even in your day and mine. The importance to France and England, to have our government in the hands of a friend or a foe, will occasion their interference by money, and even by arms. Our President will be of much more consequence to them than a King of Poland. We must take care, however, that neither this, nor any other objection to the new form produces a schism in our Union.—To A. DONALD. ii, 355. (P., 1788.)

6883. —— ——. I dislike strongly [in the new Constitution] the perpetual reeligibility of the President. This, I fear, will make that an office for life, first, and then hereditary. * * * However, I shall hope that before there is danger of this change taking place in the office of President, the good sense and free spirit of our countrymen will make the changes necessary to prevent it.—To GENERAL WASHINGTON. ii, 375. FORD ED., v, 8. (P., 1788.)

6884. —— ——. Reeligibility makes the President an officer for life, and the disasters inseparable from an elective monarchy, render it preferable, if we cannot tread back that step, that we should go forward and take refuge in an hereditary one. Of the correction of this article [in the new Constitution], I entertain no present hope, because I find it has scarcely excited an objection in America. And if it does not take place ere long, it assuredly never will. The natural progress of things is for liberty to yield and government to gain ground. As yet our spirits are free. Our jealousy is only put to sleep by the unlimited confidence we all repose in the person to whom we all look as our President. After him inferior characters may perhaps succeed, and awaken us to the danger which his merit has led us into.—To E. CARRINGTON. ii, 404. FORD ED., v, 20. (P., 1788.)

6885. —— ——. The perpetual reeligibility of the same President will probably not be cured during the life of General Washington. His merit has blinded our country-

men to the danger of making so important an officer reeligible.—To WILLIAM CARMICHAEL. ii, 465. (P., Aug. 1788.)

6886. —— ——. The convention of Virginia annexed to their ratification of the new Constitution * * * propositions for specific alterations of the Constitution. Among these was one for rendering the President incapable of serving more than eight years in any term of sixteen. New York has followed the example of Virginia, * * * proposing amendments, * * * which concur as to the President, only proposing that he shall be incapable of being elected more than twice. But I own I should like better than either of these, what Luther Martin tells us was repeatedly voted and adhered to by the Federal Convention, and only altered about twelve days before their rising, when some members had gone off; to wit, that he should be elected for seven years, and incapable forever after.—To WILLIAM SHORT. ii, 480. FORD ED., v, 48. (P., 1788.)

6887. —— ——. I am glad to see that three States have at length considered the perpetual reeligibility of the President, as an article [of the new Constitution] which should be amended.—To JAMES MADISON. ii, 506. FORD ED., v, 53. (P., Nov. 1788.)

6888. —— ——. The general voice * * * has not authorized me to consider as a real defect [in the new Constitution] what I thought and still think one, the perpetual reeligibility of the President. But three States out of eleven, having declared against this, we must suppose we are wrong, according to the fundamental law of every society, the *lex majoris partis,* to which we are bound to submit. And should the majority change their opinion, and become sensible that this trait in their Constitution is wrong, I would wish it to remain uncorrected, as long as we can avail ourselves of the services of our great leader, whose talents and whose weight of character, I consider as peculiarly necessary to get the government so under way, as that it may afterwards be carried on by subordinate characters.—To DAVID HUMPHREYS. iii, 13. FORD ED., v, 90. (P., 1789.) See CONSTITUTION (FEDERAL).

6889. PRESIDENT, The senate and.— The transaction of business with foreign nations is Executive altogether. It belongs, then, to the head of that department, except as to such portions of it as are specially submitted to the Senate. Exceptions are to be construed strictly.—OPINION ON THE POWERS OF THE SENATE. vii, 465. FORD ED., v, 161. (1790.)

6890. —— ——. The Senate is not supposed by the Constitution to be acquainted with the concerns of the Executive department. It was not* intended that these should be communicated to them.—OPINION ON THE POWERS OF THE SENATE. vii, 466. FORD ED., v, 162. (1790.)

* " Not " is omitted in the FORD EDITION. It is in the original MS.—EDITOR.

6891. PRESIDENT, State executives and.—I have the honor to enclose you the draft of a letter to Governor Pinckney, and to observe, that I suppose it to be proper that there should, on fit occasions, be a direct correspondence between the President of the United States and the Governors of the States; and that it will probably be grateful to them to receive from the President, answers to the letters they address to him. The correspondence with them on ordinary business, may still be kept up by the Secretary of State, in his own name.—To PRESIDENT WASHINGTON. iii, 297. (1791.)

6892. PRESIDENT, State powers and.—As to the portions of power within each State assigned to the General Government, the President is as much the Executive of the State, as their particular governor is in relation to State powers.—To MR. GOODENOW. vii, 251. (M., 1822.)

6893. PRESIDENT, Subpœnas for.—As to our personal attendance at Richmond, I am persuaded the Court is sensible, that paramount duties to the nation at large control the obligation of compliance with their summons in [Burr's] case; as they would, should we receive a similar one, to attend the trials of Blennerhassett and others in the Mississippi Territory, those instituted at St. Louis and other places on the western waters, or at any place, other than the seat of government. To comply with such calls would leave the nation without an Executive branch, whose agency, nevertheless, is understood to be so constantly necessary, that it is the sole branch which the Constitution requires to be always in function. It could not then mean that it should be withdrawn from its station by any coordinate authority.—To GEORGE HAY. v, 97. FORD ED., ix, 57. (W., June 1807.)

6894. —— ——. I did not see till last night the opinion of the Judge [Marshall] on the *subpœna duces tecum* against the President. Considering the question there as *coram non judice,* I did not read his argument with much attention. Yet I saw readily enough, that, as is usual where an opinion is to be supported, right or wrong, he dwells much on smaller objections, and passes over those which are solid. Laying down the position generally, that all persons owe obedience to *subpœnas* he admits no exception unless it can be produced in his law books. But if the Constitution enjoins on a particular officer to be always engaged in a particular set of duties imposed on him, does not this supersede the general law, subjecting him to minor duties inconsistent with these? The Constitution enjoins his constant agency in the concerns of six millions of people. Is the law paramount to this, which calls on him on behalf of a single one? Let us apply the Judge's own doctrine to the case of himself and his brethren. The sheriff of Henrico summons him from the bench, to quell a riot somewhere in his county. The Federal judge is, by the general law, a part of the *posse* of the State sheriff. Would the judge abandon major duties to perform lesser ones? Again: the court of Orleans or Maine commands, by subpœnas, the attendance of all the judges of the Supreme Court. Would they abandon their

posts as judges, and the interests of millions committed to them, to serve the purposes of a single individual? The leading principle of our Constitution is the independence of the Legislature, Executive, and Judiciary of each other, and none are more jealous of this than the Judiciary. But would the Executive be independent of the Judiciary, if he were subject to the *commands* of the latter, and to imprisonment for disobedience; if the several courts could bandy him from pillar to post, keep him constantly trudging from north to south and east to west, and withdraw him entirely from his constitutional duties? The intention of the Constitution, that each branch should be independent of the others, is further manifested by the means it has furnished to each, to protect itself from enterprises of force attempted on them by the others, and to none has it given more effectual or diversified means than to the Executive. Again, because ministers can go into a court in London as witnesses, without interruption to their executive duties, it is inferred that they would go to a court one thousand or one thousand five hundred miles off, and that ours are to be dragged from Maine to Orleans by every criminal who will swear that their testimony " may be of use to him ". The Judge says, " *it is apparent* that the President's duties as Chief Magistrate do not demand his whole time, and are not unremitting ". If he alludes to our annual retirement from the seat of government. during the sickly season, he should be told that such arrangements are made for carrying on the public business, at and between the several stations we take, that it goes on as unremittingly there, as if we were at the seat of government. I pass more hours in public business at Monticello than I do here, every day; and it is much more laborious, because all must be done in writing.—To GEORGE HAY. v, 103. FORD ED., ix, 59. (W., June 1807.)

6895. —— ——. As I do not believe that the District Courts have a power of *commanding* the Executive government to abandon superior duties and attend on them, at whatever distance, I am unwilling, by any notice of the subpœna, to set a precedent which might sanction a proceeding so preposterous. I enclose you, therefore, a letter, public and for the court, covering substantially all they ought to desire.—To GEORGE HAY. v, 191. (M., Sep. 1807.)

6896. —— ——. The enclosed letter is written in a spirit of conciliation and with the desire to avoid conflicts of authority between the high branches of the government, which would discredit it equally at home and abroad. That Burr and his counsel should wish to [struck out " divert the public attention from him to this battle of giants was to be "] convert his trial into a contest between the Judiciary and Executive authorities, was to be expected. But that the Chief Justice should lend himself to it, and take the first step to bring it on, was not expected. Nor can it be now believed that his prudence or good sense will permit him to press it. But should he, contrary to expectation, proceed to issue any process which should involve any act of force to be committed on the persons of the Executive or heads of departments, I must desire you to give me instant notice, and by express if you find that can be quicker done than by post; and that, moreover, you will advise the marshal on his conduct, as he will be critically placed between us. His safest way will be to take no part in the exercise of any act of force ordered in this case. The powers given to the Executive by the Constitu-

Thomas Jefferson

Age about 78 years

From the painting by Thomas Sully. The last portrait painted of Jefferson. It hangs in the main corridor, Senate wing of the United States Capitol.

tion are sufficient to protect the other branches from Judiciary usurpation of preeminence, and every individual also from Judiciary vengeance and the marshal may be assured of its effective exercise to cover him. I hope, however, that the discretion of the Chief Justice will suffer this question to lie over for the present, and at the ensuing session of the Legislature he may have means provided for giving to individuals the benefit of the testimony of the Executive functionaries in proper cases, without breaking up the Government. Will not the associate judge assume to divide his court and procure a truce at least in so critical a conjuncture? * —DRAFT OF A LETTER TO GEORGE HAY. FORD ED., ix, 62. (1807.)

6897. PRESIDENCY, Burden.—I part with the powers entrusted to me by my country, as with a burden of heavy bearing.—R. TO A. CITIZENS OF WASHINGTON. viii, 158. (March 4, 1809.)

6898. PRESIDENCY, Corruption and. —I sincerely wish we could see our government so secured as to depend less on the character of the person in whose hands it is trusted. Bad men will sometimes get in, and with such an immense patronage, may make great progress in corrupting the public mind and principles. This is a subject with which wisdom and patriotism should be occupied.—To MOSES ROBINSON. iv, 380. (W., March 1801.)

6899. PRESIDENCY, Electoral college. —The contrivance in the Constitution for marking the votes works badly, because it does not enounce precisely the true expression of the public will.—To TENCH COXE. iv, 345. FORD ED., vii, 474. (W., Dec. 1800.)

6900. —— ——. I have ever considered the constitutional mode of election ultimately by the Legislature, voting by States, as the most dangerous blot in our Constitution, and one which some unlucky chance will some day hit, and give us a pope and anti-pope. I looked, therefore, with anxiety to the amendment proposed by Colonel Taylor at the last session of Congress, which I thought would be a good substitute, if on an equal division of the electors, after a second appeal to them, the ultimate decision between the two highest had been given by it to the Legislature, voting per capita. But the States are now so numerous that I despair of ever seeing another amendment to the Constitution, although the innovations of time will certainly call, and now already call, for some, and especially the smaller States are so numerous as to render desperate every hope of obtaining a sufficient number of them in favor of " Phocion's " proposition. Another general convention can alone relieve us. What, then, is the best palliative of the evil in the meantime? Another short question points to the answer. Would we rather the choice should be made by the Legislature voting in Congress by States, or in caucus per capita? The remedy is indeed bad, but the disease

* A note in the FORD EDITION says this letter may have never been sent.—EDITOR.

worse.—To GEORGE HAY. FORD ED., x, 264. (M., Aug. 1823.)

6901. PRESIDENCY, Expenses of.—I had hoped to keep the expenses of my office within the limits of its salary, so as to apply my private income entirely to the improvement and enlargement of my estate; but I have not been able to do it.—To REV. CHARLES CLAY. v, 27. FORD ED., ix, 6. (W., 1807.)

6902. PRESIDENCY, Jefferson, Adams and.—My letters inform me that Mr. Adams speaks of me with * * * satisfaction in the prospect of administering the government in concurrence with me. * * * If by that he meant the Executive Cabinet, both *duty* and *inclination* will shut that door to me. I cannot have a wish to see the scenes of 1793 revived as to myself, and to descend daily into the arena, like a gladiator, to suffer martyrdom in every conflict. As to duty, the Constitution will know me only as the member of a legislative body; and its principle is, that of a separation of Legislative, Executive, and Judiciary functions, except in cases specified. If this principle be not expressed in direct terms, yet it is clearly the spirit of the Constitution, and it ought to be so commented and acted on by every friend to free government.—To MR. MADISON. iv, 161. FORD ED., vii, 107. (January 1797.)

6903. —— ——. No arguments were wanting to reconcile me to a relinquishment of the first office, or *acquiescence under* the second. As to the first it was impossible that a more solid unwillingness, settled on full calculation, could have existed in any man's mind, short of the degree of absolute refusal. The only view on which I would have gone into it for awhile was to put our vessel on her republican tack, before she should be thrown too much to leeward of her true principles. As to the second, it is the only office in the world which I cannot decide in my own mind, whether I had rather have it or not have it. Pride does not enter into the estimate. For I think with the Romans of old, that the general of to-day should be a common soldier to-morrow if necessary.—To JAMES MADISON. iv, 155. FORD ED., vii, 98. (Jan. 1797.)

6904. —— ——. If Mr. Adams could be induced to administer the government on its true principles, quitting his bias for an English constitution, it would be worthy consideration whether it would not be for the public good, to come to a good understanding with him as to his future elections. He is the only sure barrier against Hamilton's getting in.—To JAMES MADISON. iv, 155. FORD ED., vii, 99. (Jan. 1797.)

6905. —— ——. As to Mr. Adams, particularly, I could have no feelings which would revolt at being placed in a secondary station to him. I am his junior in life, was his junior in Congress, his junior in the diplomatic line, his junior lately in the civil

government.—To JAMES MADISON. iv, 155.
FORD ED., vii, 99. (Jan. 1797.) See ADAMS,
JOHN.

6906. PRESIDENCY, Jefferson, Madison and.—I do not see in the minds of those
with whom I converse, a greater affliction
than the fear of your retirement; but this
must not be, unless to a more splendid and a
more efficacious post. There I should rejoice
to see you; I hope I may say, I shall rejoice
to see you. I have long had much in my
mind to say to you on that subject. But
double delicacies have kept me silent. I
ought perhaps to say, while I would not give
up my own retirement for the empire of the
universe, how I can justify wishing one
whose happiness I have so much at heart as
yours, to take the front of the battle which
is fighting for my security. This would be
easy enough to be done, but not at the heel
of a lengthy epistle.—To JAMES MADISON.
iv, 112. FORD ED., vi, 519. (M., Dec. 1794.)

6907. ——— ———. In my letter * * * I
expressed my hope of the only change of position I ever wished to see you make, and
I expressed it with entire sincerity, because
there is not another person in the United
States, who being placed at the helm of our
affairs, my mind would be so completely at
rest for the fortune of our political bark.
The wish, too, was pure, and unmixed with
anything respecting myself personally. For
as to myself, the subject had been thoroughly
weighed and decided on, and my retirement
from office had been meant from all office
high or low, without exception. I can say,
too, with truth, that the subject had not been
presented to my mind by any vanity of my
own. I know myself and my fellow citizens
too well to have ever thought of it. But the
idea was forced upon me by continual insinuations in the public papers, while I was
in office. As all these came from a hostile
quarter, I knew that their object was to
poison the public mind as to my motives,
when they were not able to charge me with
facts. But the idea being once presented to
me, my own quiet required that I should face
it and examine it. I did so thoroughly, and
had no difficulty to see that every reason which
had determined me to retire from the office
I then held, operated more strongly against
that which was insinuated to be my object.
I decided then on those general grounds
which could alone be present to my mind at
the time, that is to say, reputation, tranquillity, labor; for as to public duty, it could
not be a topic of consideration in my case.
If these general considerations were sufficient
to ground a firm resolution never to permit
myself to think of the office, or to be thought
of for it, the special ones which have
supervened on my retirement, still more insuperably bar the door to it. My health is
entirely broken down within the last eight
months; my age requires that I should place
my affairs in a clear state; these are sound
if taken care of, but capable of considerable
dangers if longer neglected; and above all
things, the delights I feel in the society of

my family, and the agricultural pursuits in
which I am so eagerly engaged. The little
spice of ambition which I had in my younger
days has long since evaporated, and I set
still less store by a posthumous than present
name. In stating to you the heads of reasons
which have produced my determination, I do
not mean an opening for future discussion,
or that I may be reasoned out of it. The
question is forever closed with me; my sole
object is to avail myself of the first opening
ever given me from a friendly quarter (and
I could not with decency do it before), of
preventing any division or loss of votes,
which might be fatal to the republican interest. If that has any chance of prevailing,
it must be by avoiding the loss of a single
vote, and by concentrating all its strength on
one object. Who this should be, is a question I can more freely discuss with anybody
than yourself. In this I feel painfully the
loss of Monroe. Had he been here, I should
have been at no loss for a channel through
which to make myself understood, if I have
been misunderstood by anybody through the
instrumentality of Mr. Fenno and his abettors.—To JAMES MADISON. iv, 116. FORD
ED., vii, 8. (M., April 1795.)

6908. ——— ———. I think our foreign affairs never wore so gloomy an aspect since
the year 1783. Let those come to the helm
who think they can steer clear of the difficulties. I have no confidence in myself for
the undertaking.—To JAMES MADISON. iv,
150. FORD ED., vii, 92. (M., Dec. 1796.)

6909. ——— ———. The honeymoon would
be as short in that case [election to the
Presidency] as in any other, and its moments
of ecstacy would be ransomed by years of
torment and hatred.—To EDWARD RUTLEDGE.
iv, 152. FORD ED., vii, 93. (M., Dec. 1796.)

6910. ——— ———. You, who know me,
know that my private gratifications would be
most indulged by that issue, which should
leave me most at home. If anything supersedes this propensity, it is merely the desire
to see this government brought back to its
republican principles.—To JAMES MONROE.
iv, 309. FORD ED., vii, 402. (Pa., Jan. 1800.)

6911. PRESIDENCY, Misery in.—The
second office of the* government is honorable
and easy; the first is but a splendid misery.—
To ELBRIDGE GERRY. iv, 171. FORD ED., vii,
120. (Pa., 1797.)

6912. PRESIDENCY, Reelection to.—I
sincerely regret that the unbounded calumnies of the federal party have obliged me to
throw myself on the verdict of my country
for trial, my great desire having been to retire, at the end of the present term, to a life
of tranquillity; and it was my decided purpose
when I entered into office. They force my
continuance. If we can keep the vessel of
State as steadily in her course for another
four years, my earthly purposes will be accomplished, and I shall be free to enjoy

* "This" government in FORD EDITION.—EDITOR.

* * * my family, my farm, and my books. —To ELBRIDGE GERRY. iv, 536. FORD ED., viii, 297. (W., March 1804.)

6913. PRESIDENCY, Reputation and. —No man will ever bring out of the presidency the reputation which carries him into it.—To EDWARD RUTLEDGE. iv, 152. FORD ED., vii, 93. (M., 1796.)

6914. —— ——. I have learned to expect that it will rarely fall to the lot of imperfect man to retire from this station with the reputation and the favor which bring him into it.—FIRST INAUGURAL ADDRESS. viii, 5. FORD ED., viii, 5. (1801.)

6915. PRESIDENCY, Tired of the.—I am tired of an office where I can do no more good than many others, who would be glad to be employed in it. To myself, personally, it brings nothing but unceasing drudgery and daily loss of friends. Every office becoming vacant, every appointment made, *me donne un ingrat, et cent ennemis.* My only consolation is in the belief that my fellow citizens at large will give me credit for good intentions.—To JOHN DICKINSON. v, 31. FORD ED., ix, 10. (W., Jan. 1807.)

6916. PRESIDENCY, Unattractive.—Neither the splendor, nor the power, nor the difficulties, nor the fame or defamation, as may happen, attached to the First Magistracy, have any attractions for me.—To JAMES SULLIVAN. iv, 168. FORD ED., vii, 117. (M., 1797.)

— PRESS (Copying).—See COPYING PRESS and INVENTIONS.

6917. PRESS (Freedom of the), Abolished.—The press, the only tocsin of a nation, is completely silenced in France.—To THOMAS COOPER. iv, 452. FORD ED., viii, 177. (W., Nov. 1802.)

6918. PRESS (Freedom of the), Abused. —The firmness with which the people have withstood the late abuses of the press, the discernment they have manifested between truth and falsehood, show that they may safely be trusted to hear everything true and false, and to form a correct judgment between them.—To JUDGE TYLER. iv, 549. (W., 1804.)

— PRESS (Freedom of the), Bill of Rights and.—See BILL OF RIGHTS.

6919. PRESS (Freedom of the), Control of.—While we deny that Congress have a right to control the freedom of the press, we have ever asserted the right of the States, and their exclusive right, to do so. They have accordingly. all of them, made provisions for punishing slander. * * * In general, the State laws appear to have made the presses responsible for slander as far as is consistent with its useful freedom. In those States where they do not admit even the truth of allegations to protect the printer, they have gone too far.—To MRS. JOHN ADAMS. iv, 561. FORD ED., viii, 311. (M., 1804.)

6920. PRESS (Freedom of the), The Constitution and.—It is true as a general principle, and is also expressly declared by one of the amendments to the Constitution, that " the powers not delegated to the United States by the Constitution, nor prohibited by it to the States, are reserved to the States respectively, or to the people; and * * * no power over the freedom of religion, freedom of speech, or freedom of the press being delegated to the United States by the Constitution, nor prohibited by it to the States, all lawful powers respecting the same did of right remain, and were reserved to the States or the people. * * * Thus was manifested their determination to retain to themselves the right of judging how far the licentiousness of speech, and of the press, may be abridged without lessening their useful freedom, and how far those abuses which cannot be separated from their use should be tolerated, rather than the use be destroyed. And thus also they guarded against all abridgment by the United States of the freedom of religious opinions and exercises, and retained to themselves the right of protecting the same, as this State [Kentucky], by a law passed on the general demand of its citizens, had already protected them from all human restraint or interference. * * * In addition to this general principle and express declaration, another and more special provision has been made by one of the amendments to the Constitution, which expressly declares, that " Congress shall make no law respecting an establishment of religion, or prohibiting the free exercise thereof, or abridging the freedom of speech, or of the press ", thereby guarding in the same sentence, and under the same words, the freedom of religion, of speech and of the press; insomuch, that whatever violates either, throws down the sanctuary which covers the others, and that libels, falsehood, and defamation, equally with heresy and false religion, are withheld from the cognizance of Federal tribunals. * * * Therefore, the act of Congress of the United States passed on the 14th day of July, 1798, intituled, " An Act in addition to the act intituled ' An Act for the punishment of certain crimes against the United States ' ", which does abridge the freedom of the press, is not law, but is altogether void, and of no force.—KENTUCKY RESOLUTIONS. ix, 465. FORD ED., vii, 294. (1798.)

6921. —— ——. I am for freedom of the press, and against all violations of the Constitution to silence by force and not by reason the complaints or criticisms, just or unjust, of our citizens against the conduct of their agents.—To ELBRIDGE GERRY. iv, 269. FORD ED., vii, 328. (Pa., 1799.)

6922. PRESS (Freedom of the), Government and.—No government ought to be without censors; and where the press is free, no one ever will.—To PRESIDENT WASHINGTON. iii, 467. FORD ED., vi, 108. (M., 1792.)

6923. —— ——. Conscious that there was not a *truth* on earth which I feared should be known, I have lent myself willingly as the subject of a great experiment, which was to prove that an administration, conducting itself with integrity and common understanding, cannot be battered down, even by the falsehoods of a licentious press, and consequently still less by the press, as restrained within the legal and wholesome limits of truth. This experiment was wanting for the world to demonstrate the falsehood of the pretext that freedom of the press is incompatible with orderly government. I have never, therefore, even contradicted the thousands of calumnies so industriously propagated against myself. But the fact being once established, that the press is impotent when it abandons itself to falsehood, I leave to others to restore it to its strength, by recalling it within the pale of truth. Within that, it is a noble institution, equally the friend of science and of civil liberty.—To THOMAS SEYMOUR. v, 43. FORD ED., ix, 30. (W., Feb. 1807.)

6924. PRESS (Freedom of the), Invasions of.—There are rights which it is useless to surrender to the government, and which governments have yet always been found to invade. [Among] are the rights of thinking and publishing our thoughts by * * * writing.—To DAVID HUMPHREYS. iii, 13. FORD ED., v, 89. (P., 1789.)

6925. PRESS (Freedom of the), Libels.—Printing presses shall be subject to no other restraint than liableness to legal prosecution for false facts printed and published.—PROPOSED CONSTITUTION FOR VIRGINIA. viii, 452. FORD ED., iii, 332. (1783.)

6926. ——— ———. Printing presses shall be free except as to false facts published maliciously, either to injure the reputation of another, whether followed by pecuniary damages or not, or to expose him to the punishment of the law.—NOTES FOR A CONSTITUTION. FORD ED., vi, 521. (1794.)

6927. PRESS (Freedom of the), Liberty and.—Our liberty depends on the freedom of the press, and that cannot be limited without being lost.—To DR. JAMES CURRIE. FORD ED., iv, 132. (P., 1786.)

6928. ——— ———. The liberty of speaking and writing guards our other liberties.—REPLY TO ADDRESS. viii, 129. (1808.)

6929. PRESS (Freedom of the), Mankind and.—The press is the best instrument for enlightening the mind of man, and improving him as a rational, moral, and social being.—To M. CORAY. vii, 324. (M., 1823.)

6930. PRESS (Freedom of the), Principle of government.—Freedom of the press I deem [one of the] essential principles of our government and, consequently, [one] which ought to shape its administration.—FIRST INAUGURAL ADDRESS. viii, 4. FORD ED., viii, 5. (1801.)

6931. ——— ———. There are certain principles in which the constitutions of our several States all agree, and which all cherish

as vitally essential to the protection of the life, liberty, property and safety of the citizen. [One is] Freedom of the Press, subject only to liability for personal injuries.—To M. CORAY. vii, 323. (M., 1823.)

6932. PRESS (Freedom of the), Private injury.—Printing presses shall be free, except so far as, by commission of private injury, cause may be given of private action.—PROPOSED VA. CONSTITUTION. FORD ED., ii, 27. (June 1776.)

6933. PRESS (Freedom of the), Reform through.—This formidable censor of the public functionaries, by arraigning them at the tribunal of public opinion, produces reform peaceably, which must otherwise be done by revolution.—To M. CORAY. vii, 324. (M., 1823.)

6934. PRESS (Freedom of the), Safety in.—Where the press is free, and every man able to read, all is safe.—To CHARLES YANCEY. vi, 517. FORD ED., x, 4. (M., 1816.)

6935. PRESS (Freedom of the), Security in.—The only security of all is in a free press. The force of public opinion cannot be resisted, when permitted freely to be expressed. The agitation it produces must be submitted to. It is necessary to keep the waters pure.—To MARQUIS LAFAYETTE. vii, 325. FORD ED., x, 280. (M., 1823.)

6936. PRESS (Freedom of the), Shackled.—Nor should we wonder at * * * [the] pressure [for a fixed constitution in 1788-9] when we consider the monstrous abuses of power under which * * * [the French] people were ground to powder; when we pass in review the shackles * * * on the freedom of the press by the Censure.—AUTOBIOGRAPHY. i, 86. FORD ED., i, 118. (1821.) See EDITORS, NEWSPAPERS, and PUBLICITY.

6937. PRICE, Basis of.—The adequate price of a thing depends on the capital and labor necessary to produce it. In the term *capital*, I mean to include science, because capital as well as labor has been employed to acquire it. Two things requiring the same capital and labor, should be of the same price. If a gallon of wine requires for its production the same capital and labor with a bushel of wheat, they should be expressed by the same price, derived from the application of a common measure to them.—To J. W. EPPES. vi, 233. FORD ED., ix, 406. (M., 1813.)

6938. PRICE OF WHEAT.—The average price of wheat on the continent of Europe, at the commencement of its present war with England, was about a French crown, of one hundred and ten cents, the bushel. With us it was one hundred cents, and consequently we could send it there in competition with their own. That ordinary price has now doubled with us, and more than doubled in England; and although a part of this augmentation may proceed from the war demand, yet from the extraordinary nominal rise in the prices of land and labor here, both of which have nearly doubled in that period, and are still rising with every new bank, it is evident that were a general peace to take place to-morrow, and time allowed for the reestablishment of commerce, justice and order, we could not raise wheat for much less than two dollars, while the continent of Europe, having no paper circulation, and that of its specie not being augmented, would raise it at their former price of one hundred and ten cents. It follows, then, that with our redundancy of paper, we cannot, after peace, send a bushel of wheat to Europe, unless extraordinary circumstances double its price in particular places, and that then the exporting countries of Europe could undersell us.—To J. W. Eppes. vi, 242. Ford ed., ix, 414. (M., Nov. 1813.)

6939. PRIESTLEY (Joseph), Author.— The papers of political arithmetic in your pamphlets * * * are the most precious gifts that can be made us; for we are running navigation mad, and commerce mad, and navy mad, which is worst of all. * * * From the "*Porcupines*" of our country you will receive no thanks; but the great mass of our nation will edify and thank you.—To Joseph Priestley. iv, 311. Ford ed., vii, 406. (Pa., Jan. 1800.) See Government, Works on.

6940. PRIESTLEY (Joseph), Dupont and.— I have a letter from Mr. Dupont [de Nemours], since his arrival at New York. * * * How much it would delight me if a visit from you at the same time, were to show us two such illustrious foreigners embracing each other in my country, as the asylum for whatever is great and good.—To Joseph Priestley. iv, 317. Ford ed., vii, 415. (Pa., 1800.)

6941. PRIESTLEY (Joseph), Persecuted.— How deeply have I been chagrined and mortified at the persecutions which fanaticism and monarchy have excited against you, even here. At first I believed it was merely a continuance of the English persecution. But I observe that on the demise of "*Porcupine*", and division of his inheritance between Fenno and Brown, the latter (though succeeding only to the *federal* portion of Porcupinism, not the *Anglican*, which is Fenno's part) serves up for the palate of his sect, dishes of abuse against you as high seasoned as "*Porcupine's*" were. You have sinned against church and king, and can, therefore, never be forgiven.—To Joseph Priestley. iv, 311. Ford ed., vii, 406. (Pa., Jan. 1800.)

6942. PRIESTLEY (Joseph), Revered. —I revered the character of no man living more than his.—To Thomas Cooper. v, 182. (M., 1807.)

6943. PRIESTLEY (Joseph), Services. —No man living had a more affectionate respect for Dr. Priestley. In religion, in politics in physics, no man has rendered more service.—To Thomas Cooper. v, 121. Ford ed., ix, 102. (W., 1807.)

6944. PRIESTLEY (Joseph), Welcome to.— Yours is one of the few lives precious to mankind, and for the continuance of which every thinking man is solicitous. Bigots may be an exception. What an effort, my dear sir, of bigotry in politics and religion have we gone through. The barbarians really flattered themselves they should be able to bring back the times of Vandalism, when ignorance put everything into the hands of power and priestcraft. All advances in science were proscribed as innovations. They pretended to praise and encourage education, but it was to be the education of our ancestors. We were to look backwards, not forwards, for improvement: the President himself [John Adams] declaring, in one of his answers to addresses, that we were

never to expect to go beyond them in real science. This was the real ground of all the attacks on you. * * * Our countrymen have recovered from the alarm into which art and industry had thrown them; science and honesty are replaced on their high ground; and you, as their great apostle, are on its pinnacle. It is with heartfelt satisfaction that, in the first moments of my public action, I can hail you with welcome to our land, tender to you the homage of its respect and esteem, cover you under the protection of those laws which were made for the wise and good like you, and disclaim the legitimacy of that libel on legislation, which under the form of a law was for some time placed among them.*—To Joseph Priestley. iv, 373. Ford ed., viii, 21. (W., March 1801.)

6945. PRIMOGENITURE, Abolition of law.— As the law of Descents, and the Criminal law fell, of course, within my portion [in the revision of the Virginia Code], I wished the Committee to settle the leading principles of these, as a guide for me in framing them; and, with respect to the first, I proposed to abolish the law of primogeniture, and to make real estate descendible in parcenary to the next of kin, as personal property is, by the statute of distribution. Mr. Pendleton wished to preserve the right of primogeniture, but seeing at once that that could not prevail, he proposed we should adopt the Hebrew principle, and give a double portion to the elder son. I observed that if the eldest son could eat twice as much, or do double work, it might be a natural evidence of his right to a double portion; but, being on a par in his powers and wants with his brothers and sisters, he should be on a par also in the partition of the patrimony; and such was the decision of the other members. †—Autobiography. i, 43. Ford ed., i, 59. (1821.)

6946. PRIMOGENITURE, Feudal and unnatural.— The abolition of primogeniture, and equal partition of inheritances, removed the feudal and unnatural distinctions which made one member of every family rich, and all the rest poor, substituting equal partition, the best of all Agrarian laws. ‡—Autobiography. i, 49. Ford ed., i, 69. (M., 1821.) See Entails.

* Jefferson wrote on the margin "Alien Law".—Editor.

† The preamble to this great law is as follows: "Whereas, the perpetuation of property in certain families, by means of gifts made to them in fee taille, is contrary to good policy, tends to deceive fair traders, who give credit on the visible possession of such estates, discourages the holders thereof from taking care and improving the same, and sometimes does injury to the morals of youth, by rendering them independent of, and disobedient to their parents; and whereas, the former method of docking such estates taille, by special act of Assembly, formed for every particular case, employed very much of the time of the Legislature, and the same, as well as the method of defeating such estates, when of small value, was burthensome to the public, and also to individuals. Be it therefore enacted."—Editor.

‡ It was an audacious move. From generation to generation lands and slaves—almost the only valuable kind of property in Virginia—had been handed down protected against creditors, even against the very extravagance of spendthrift owners; and it was largely by this means that the quasi-nobility of the colony had succeeded in establishing and maintaining itself. A great groan seemed to go up from all respectable society at the terrible suggestion of Jefferson, a suggestion daringly cast before an Assembly thickly sprinkled with influential delegates strongly bound by family ties and self-interest to defend the present system. * * * Thus was a great social revolution wrought in a few months by one man. * * * But his brilliant triumph cost him a price. That distinguished class, whose existence as

6947. PRINCIPLE, Departure from.—A departure from principle in one instance becomes a precedent for a second; that second for a third; and so on, till the bulk of the society is reduced to be mere automatons of misery, to have no sensibilities left but for sin and suffering. Then begins, indeed, the *bellum omnium in omnia,* which some philosophers observing to be so general in this world, have mistaken it for the natural, instead of the abusive state of man. And the forehorse of this frightful team is public debt. Taxation follows that, and in its train wretchedness and oppression.—To SAMUEL KERCHIVAL. vii, 14. FORD ED., x, 42. (M., 1816.)

6948. PRINCIPLE, Doubt and.—If doubtful, we should follow principle.—To SAMUEL KERCHIVAL. vii, 12. FORD ED., x, 40. (M., 1816.)

6949. PRINCIPLE, A guide.—Principle will in * * * most * * * cases open the way for us to correct conclusion.—To SAMUEL KERCHIVAL. vii, 36. FORD ED., x, 45. (M., 1816.)

6950. PRINCIPLE, Opinion and.— Every difference of opinion is not a difference of principle. We have called by different names brethren of the same principle. We are all republicans: we are all federalists.— FIRST INAUGURAL ADDRESS. viii, 2. FORD ED., viii, 3. (1801.)

6951. PRINCIPLE, Republican vs. Monarchical.—The contests of that day [1793-1800] were contests of principle, between the advocates of republican and those of kingly government, and had not the former made the efforts they did, our government would have been, even at this early day (1818) a very different thing from what the successful issue of those efforts have made it.—THE ANAS. ix, 88. FORD ED., i, 156. (1818.)

6952. PRINCIPLES, Adherence to.—An adherence to fundamental principles is the most likely way to save both time and disagreement [between legislative bodies]; and [as] a departure from them may at some time or other be drawn into precedent for dangerous innovations. * * * it is better for both Houses, and for those by whom they are entrusted, to correct error while new, and before it becomes inveterate by habit and custom.—CONFERENCE REPORT. FORD ED., ii, 135. (1777.)

6953. —— ——. I am happy in your approbation of the principles I avowed on entering on the government. Ingenious minds, availing themselves of the imperfections of language, have tortured the expressions out of their plain meaning in order to infer departures from them in practice. If revealed

a social caste had been forever destroyed, reviled the destroyer from this time forth with relentless animosity; and, even to the second and third generations, the descendants of many of these patrician families vindictively cursed the statesman who had placed them on a level with the rest of their countrymen.—MORSE'S *Life of Jefferson.*

language has not been able to guard itself against misinterpretations I could not expect it. But if an administration, " quadrating with the obvious import of my language, can conciliate the affections of my opposers ", I will merit that conciliation.—To THE REV. ISAAC STORY. iv, 423. FORD ED., viii, 107. (W., 1802.)

6954. —— ——. On taking this station [Presidency] on a former occasion, I declared the principles on which I believed it my duty to administer the affairs of our commonwealth. My conscience tells me that I have, on every occasion, acted up to that declaration, according to its obvious import, and to the understanding of every candid mind.— SECOND INAUGURAL ADDRESS. viii, 40. FORD ED., viii, 342. (1805.)

6955. —— ——. Continue to 'go straight forward, pursuing always that which is right, as the only clue which can lead us out of the labyrinth.—To CÆSAR A. RODNEY. v, 501. FORD ED., ix, 272. (M., 1810.)

6956. —— ——. Lay down true principles, and adhere to them inflexibly. Do not be frightened into their surrender by the alarms of the timid, or the croakings of wealth against the ascendency of the people. —To SAMUEL KERCHIVAL. vii, 11. FORD ED., x, 39. (M., 1816.)

6957. PRINCIPLES, Application of.— When principles are well understood their application is less embarrassing.—To GOUVERNEUR MORRIS. FORD ED., vi, 149. (Pa., 1792.)

6958. PRINCIPLES, Avowal of.—I know my own principles to be pure, and therefore am not ashamed of them. On the contrary, I wish them known, and therefore willingly express them to every one. They are the same I have acted on from the year 1775 to this day, and are the same. I am sure, with those of the great body of the American people. I only wish the real principles of those who censure mine were also known. —To SAMUEL SMITH. iv, 254. FORD ED., vii, 277. (M., 1798.)

6959. —— ——. I make no secret of my principles; on the contrary, I wish them known to avoid the imputation of those which are not mine.—To JEREMIAH MOOR. FORD ED., vii, 454. (M., Aug. 1800.)

6960. PRINCIPLES, Constitutional.— A part of the Union having held on to the principles of the Constitution, time has been given to the States to recover from the temporary frenzy into which they had been decoyed, to rally round the Constitution, and to rescue it from the destruction with which it had been threatened even at their own hands. —To GIDEON GRANGER. iv, 332. FORD ED., vii, 452. (M., 1800.)

6961. PRINCIPLES, Independence and. —The contest which began with us, which ushered in the dawn of our national existence and led us through various and trying scenes, was for everything dear to free-born man.

The principles on which we engaged, of which the charter of our independence is the record, were sanctioned by the laws of our being, and we but obeyed them in pursuing undeviatingly the course they called for. It issued finally in that inestimable state of freedom which alone can ensure to man the enjoyment of his equal rights.—R. TO A. GEORGETOWN REPUBLICANS. viii. 159. (1809.)

6962. PRINCIPLES, Jefferson's in 1799.—In confutation of * * * all future calumnies. by way of anticipation, I shall make to you a profession of my political faith: in confidence that you will consider every future imputation on me of a contrary complexion as bearing on its front the mark of falsity and calumny. I do then, with sincere zeal, wish an inviolable preservation of our Federal Constitution, according to the true sense in which it was adopted by the States: that in which it was advocated by its friends, and not that which its enemies apprehended, who therefore became its enemies; and I am opposed to the monarchizing its features by the forms of its administration, with a view to conciliate a first transition to a President and Senate for life, and from that to an hereditary tenure of these offices, and thus to worm out the elective principle. I am for preserving to the States the powers not yielded by them to the Union, and to the Legislature of the Union its constitutional share in the division of powers; and I am not for transferring all the powers of the States to the General Government, and all those of that Government to the Executive branch. I am for a government rigorously frugal and simple. applying all the possible savings of the public revenue to the discharge of the national debt; and not for a multiplication of officers and salaries merely to make partizans. and for increasing, by every device. the public debt, on the principle of its being a public blessing. I am for relying for internal defence on our militia solely, till actual invasion, and for such a naval force only as may protect our coasts and harbors from such depredations as we have experienced; and not for a standing army in time of peace, which may overawe the public sentiment; nor for a navy, which, by its own expenses and the eternal wars in which it will implicate us, will grind us with public burdens and sink us under them. I am for free commerce with all nations; political connection with none; and little or no diplomatic establishment. And I am not for linking ourselves by new treaties with the quarrels of Europe; entering that field of slaughter to preserve their balance, or joining in the confederacy of kings to war against the principles of liberty. I am for freedom of religion, and against all manœuvres to bring about a legal ascendency of one sect over another; for freedom of the press, and against all violations of the Constitution to silence by force and not by reason the complaints or criticisms, just or unjust, of our citizens against the conduct of their agents. And I am for encouraging the progress of science in all its branches; and not for raising a hue and cry against the sacred name of philosophy; for awing the human mind by stories of raw-head and bloody bones to a distrust of its own vision, and to repose implicitly on that of others; to go backwards instead of forwards to look for improvement; to believe that government, religion, morality, and every other science were in the highest perfection in the ages of the darkest ignorance, and that nothing can ever be devised more perfect than what was established by our forefathers. To these I will add, that I was a sincere well-wisher to the success of the French Revolution, and still wish it may end in the establishment of a free and well-ordered republic; but I have not been insensible under the atrocious depredations they have committed on our commerce. The first object of my heart is my country. In that is embarked my family, my fortune, and my own existence. I have not one farthing of interest, nor one fibre of attachment out of it, nor a single motive of preference of any one nation to another. but in proportion as they are more or less friendly to us. * * * These are my principles. They are unquestionably the principles of the great body of our fellow-citizens, and I know there is not one of them which is not yours also. In truth, we never differed but on one ground, the Funding System; and as, from the moment of its being adopted by the constituted authorities, I became religiously principled in the sacred discharge of it to the uttermost farthing, we are united now even on that single ground of difference.*—To ELBRIDGE GERRY. iv. 267. FORD ED., vii. 327. (Pa., January 1799.) See ADMINISTRATION; also INAUGURAL ADDRESSES, in APPENDIX.

6963. —— ——. In the maintenance of * * * [our] principles * * * I verily believe the future happiness of our country essentially depends.—To SPENCER ROANE. vii. 136. FORD ED., x, 143. (P.F., 1819.)

6964. PRINCIPLES, Not men.—Two facts are certainly as true as irreconcilable. The people of Massachusetts love economy and freedom, civil and religious. The present legislative and executive functionaries endeavor to practice economy. and to strengthen civil and religious freedom. Yet they are disapproved by the people of Massachusetts. It cannot be that these had rather give up principles than men. However the riddle is to be solved, our duty is plain, to administer their interests faithfully, and to overcome evil with good.—To JOHN BACON. FORD ED., viii, 228. (W., April 1803.)

6965. —— ——. If our fellow citizens * * * will sacrifice favoritism towards men for the preservation of principle, we

* Jefferson differed from the time-serving politician, because he staked his individual success upon the success of what he deemed intrinsically right principles. He differed even from the statesman who acts conscientiously upon every measure, inasmuch as, beyond devising specific measures, he set forth a broad faith or religion in statesmanship, making special measures only single blocks in the wide pavement of his road.—MORSE'S *Life of Jefferson.*

may hope that no divisions will again endanger a degeneracy in our government.—To RICHARD M. JOHNSON. v, 526. (1808.)

6966. PRINCIPLES, Political schism and.—We ought not to schismatize on either men or measures. Principles alone can justify that.—To WILLIAM DUANE. v, 577. FORD ED., ix, 313. (M., 1811.)

6967. PRINCIPLES, Practice and.— True wisdom does not lie in mere practice without principle.—To JOHN ADAMS. vii, 39. (M., 1816.)

6968. PRINCIPLES, Toleration of.—It is time enough, for the rightful purposes of civil government, for its officers to interfere when principles break out into overt acts against peace and good order.—STATUTE OF RELIGIOUS FREEDOM. FORD ED., ii, 239. (1779.)

6969. PRINTING, Preservative.—The art of printing secures us against the retrogradation of reason and information; the examples of its safe and wholesome guidance in government, which will be exhibited through the wide-spread regions of the American continent, will obliterate, in time, the impressions left by the abortive experiment of France.— To M. PAGANEL. v, 582. (M., 1811.)

6970. PRINTING, Progress in.—Among the arts which have made great progress among us is that of printing. Heretofore, we imported our books, and with them much political principle from England. We now print a great deal, and shall soon supply ourselves with most of the books of considerable demand. But the foundation of printing, you know, is the type-foundry, and a material essential to that is antimony. Unfortunately that mineral is not among those as yet found in the United States, and the difficulty and dearness of getting it from England, will force us to discontinue our type-founderies, and resort to her again for our books, unless some new source of supply can be found.—To DUPONT DE NEMOURS. v, 457. (M., June 1809.) See EDITORS, NEWSPAPERS and PRESS.

6971. PRINTING vs. BARBARISM.— We have seen, indeed, once within the records of history, a complete eclipse of the human mind continuing for centuries. And this, too, by swarms of the same northern barbarians, conquering and taking possession of the countries and governments of the civilized world. Should this be again attempted, should the same northern hordes, allured again by the corn, wine, and oil of the south, be able again to settle their swarms in the countries of their growth, the art of printing alone, and the vast dissemination of books, will maintain the mind where it is, and raise the conquering ruffians to the level of the conquered, instead of degrading these to that of their conquerors. And even should the cloud of barbarism and despotism again obscure the science and liberties of Europe, this country remains to preserve and restore light and liberty to them.—To JOHN ADAMS. vii, 218. (M., 1821.)

6972. PRISON, Breaking.—It is not only vain, but wicked, in a legislator to frame laws in opposition to the laws of nature, and to arm them with the terrors of death. This is truly creating crimes in order to punish them. The law of nature impels every one to escape from confinement; it should not, therefore, be subjected to punishment. Let the legislator restrain his criminal by walls, not by parchment. As to strangers breaking prison to enlarge an offender, they should, and may be fairly considered as accessories after the fact.—NOTE ON CRIMES BILL. i, 159. FORD ED., ii, 218. (1779.)

— PRISON, Plan of.—See ARCHITECTURE.

— PRISONERS OF WAR.—See WAR.

6973. PRIVACY, Indispensable.—A room to myself, if it be but a barrack, is indispensable. *—To JAMES MADISON. FORD ED., iii, 339. (M., 1783.)

6974. PRIVATE LIFE, Contentment.— I thank you * * * for your felicitations on my present quiet. The difference of my present and past situation is such as to leave me nothing to regret, but that my retirement has been postponed four years too long. The principles on which I calculated the value of life, are entirely in favor of my present course.—To JOHN ADAMS. iv, 103. FORD ED., vi, 504. (M., April 1794.)

6975. ———. As to the concerns of my own country, I leave them willingly and safely to those who will have a longer interest in cherishing them. My books, my family, my friends, and my farm, furnish more than enough to occupy me the remainder of my life, and of that tranquil occupation most analogous to my physical and moral constitution.—To M. ODIT. iv, 123. (M., Oct. 1795.)

6976. ———. My farm, my family, my books and my building, give me more pleasure than any public office would, and, especially, one which would keep me constantly from them.—To MR. VOLNEY. iv, 158. (M., 1797.)

6977. PRIVATE LIFE, Freedom of.—I am now a private man, free to express my feelings, and their expression will be estimated at neither more nor less than they weigh, to wit, the expressions of a private man. Your struggles for liberty keep alive the only sparks of sensation which public affairs now excite in me.—To M. ODIT. iv, 123. (M., Oct. 1795.)

6978. PRIVATE LIFE, Happiness.— The happiness of the domestic fireside is the first boon of heaven; and it is well it is so, since it is that which is the lot of the mass of mankind.—To GENERAL ARMSTRONG. vi, 103. (M., Feb. 1813.)

6979. PRIVATE LIFE, Independence of.—The independence of private life, under the protection of republican laws, will I hope yield me the happiness from which no slave is so remote as the minister of a commonwealth.—To MARQUIS LAFAYETTE. i, 312. FORD ED., iii, 49. (M., 1781.)

* From a letter requesting Madison to select a lodging for him.—EDITOR.

6980. PRIVATE LIFE, Public duty and.—You hope I have not abandoned entirely the service of our country. After five and twenty years' continual employment in it, I trust it will be thought I have fulfilled my tour, like a punctual soldier, and may claim my discharge. But I am glad of the sentiment from you, because it gives a hope you will practice what you preach, and come forward in aid of the public vessel. I will not admit your old excuse that you are in public service though at home. The campaigns which are fought in a man's own house are not to be counted. The present situation of the President, unable to get the offices filled, really calls with uncommon obligation on those whom nature has fitted for them.—To EDWARD RUTLEDGE. iv, 124. FORD ED., vii, 39. (M., Nov. 1795.)

6981. PRIVATE LIFE, Retirement to.—My first wish is a restoration of our just rights; my second, a return of the happy period, when, consistently with duty, I may withdraw myself totally from the public stage and pass the rest of my days in domestic ease and tranquillity, banishing every desire of ever hearing what passes in the world.—To JOHN RANDOLPH. i, 200. FORD ED., i, 482. (M., 1775.)

6982. —— ——. I have laid up my Rosinante in his stall, before his unfitness for the road shall expose him faultering to the world. —To MANN PAGE. iv, 119. FORD ED., vii, 24. (M., 1795.) See RETIREMENT.

6983. PRIVATE LIFE, Rural.—I am savage enough to prefer the woods, the wilds, and the independence of Monticello, to all the brilliant pleasures of this gay capital.— To BARON GEISMER. i, 427. (P., 1785.) See LIFE and MONTICELLO.

6984. PRIVATE LIFE vs. PUBLIC LIFE.—I had rather be shut up in a very modest cottage, with my books, my family and a few old friends, dining on simple bacon, and letting the world roll on as it liked, than to occupy the most splendid post which any human power can give.—To A. DONALD. ii, 356. (P., 1788.)

6985. —— ——. I ever preferred the pursuits of private life to those of public life.— ANAS. ix, 121. FORD ED., i, 203. (1792.)

6986. —— ——. The pomp, the turmoil, the bustle and splendor of office, have drawn but deeper sighs for the tranquil and irresponsible occupations of private life.—To THE INHABITANTS OF ALBEMARLE COUNTY, VA. v, 439. FORD ED., ix, 250. (M., April 1809.)

6987. PRIVATEERING, Abolition of.—If war should hereafter arise between the two contracting parties, * * * all merchants and traders, exchanging the products of different places, and thereby rendering the necessaries, conveniences, and comforts of human life more easy to obtain and more general, shall be allowed to pass free and unmolested; and neither of the contracting powers shall grant or issue any commission to any private armed vessels, empowering them to take or destroy such trading ships, or interrupt such commerce. *—TREATY INSTRUCTIONS. FORD ED., iii, 490. (May 1784.)

6988. —— ——. I am to acknowledge the receipt of your letter, proposing a stipulation for the abolition of the practice of privateering in times of war. The benevolence of this proposition is worthy of the nation [France] from which it comes, and our sentiments on it have been declared in the treaty to which you are pleased to refer, as well as in some others which have been proposed. There are in those treaties some other principles which would probably meet the approbation of your government, as flowing from the same desire to lessen the occasions and the calamities of war. On all these * * * we are ready to enter into negotiation with you, only proposing to take the whole into consideration at once.— To JEAN BAPTISTE TERNANT. iii, 477. FORD ED., vi, 122. (Pa., 1792.)

6989. —— ——. During the negotiations for peace [in 1783] with the British Commissioner David Hartley, our Commissioners had proposed, on the suggestion of Dr. Franklin, to insert an article exempting from capture by the public or private armed ships of either belligerent, when at war, all merchant vessels and their cargoes, employed merely in carrying on the commerce between nations. It was refused by England, and unwisely in my opinion. For, in the case of a war with us, their superior commerce places infinitely more at hazard on the ocean than ours; and, as hawks abound in proportion to game, so our privateers would swarm in proportion to the wealth exposed to their prize, while theirs would be few for want of subjects of capture. We [Adams, Franklin and Jefferson] inserted this article in our form, with a provision against the molestation of fishermen, husbandmen, citizens unarmed and following their occupations in unfortified places, for the humane treatment of prisoners of war, the abolition of contraband of war, which exposes merchant vessels to such vexations and ruinous detentions and abuses; and for the principle of free bottoms, free goods.—AUTOBIOGRAPHY. i, 62. FORD ED., i, 86. (1821.)

6990. PRIVATEERS, Advantages of.—Our ships of force will undoubtedly be blockaded by the enemy, and we shall have no means of annoying them at sea but by small, swift-sailing vessels; these will be better managed and more multiplied in the hands of individuals than of the government. In short, they are our true and only weapon in a war against Great Britain, when once Canada and Nova Scotia shall have been rescued from them. The opposition to them in Congress is merely partial. It is a part of the navy fever, and proceeds from the desire of securing men for the public ships by suppressing all other employments from them. But I do not apprehend that this ill-judged principle is that of a majority of Congress. I hope, on the contrary, they will spare no encouragement to that kind of enterprise. Our public ships, to be sure, have done wonders. They have saved our military reputation sacrificed on the shores of Canada; but in point of real injury and depredation on the enemy, our privateers without question have been most effectual. Both species of force have their peculiar value.—To GENERAL BAILEY. vi, 100. (M., Feb. 1813.)

* Instructions respecting the negotiation of commercial treaties with European nations.—EDITOR.

6991. PRIVATEERS, Commerce destroyers.—I hope we shall confine ourselves to the conquest of their possessions, and defence of our harbors, leaving the war on the ocean to our privateers. These will immediately swarm in every sea, and do more injury to British commerce than the regular fleets of all Europe would do.—To GENERAL KOSCIUSKO. vi, 68. FORD ED., ix, 362. (M., June 1812.)

6992. —— ——. Our privateers will eat out the vitals of British commerce.—To WILLIAM DUANE. vi, 76. FORD ED., ix, 366. (M., Aug. 1812.)

6993. —— ——. Every sea on the globe where England has any commerce, and where any port can be found to sell prizes, will be filled with our privateers.—To GENERAL KOSCIUSKO. vi, 77. (M., Aug. 1812.)

6994. PRIVATEERS, Encouragement of.—Privateers will find their own men and money. Let nothing be spared to encourage them. They are the dagger which strikes at the heart of the enemy, their commerce.—To JAMES MONROE. vi, 409. FORD ED., ix, 498. (M., 1815.)

6995. PRIVATEERS, Exclusion of.—Measures are taking for excluding, from all further asylum in our ports, vessels armed in them to cruise on nations with which we are at peace.—To GEORGE HAMMOND. iv, 56. FORD ED., vi, 408. (Pa., Sep. 1793.)

6996. PRIVATEERS, Fitting out foreign.—By our treaties with several of the belligerent powers, which are a part of the laws of our land, we have established a state of peace with them. But, without appealing to treaties, we are at peace with them all by the law of nature. For by nature's law, man is at peace with man, till some aggression is committed, which, by the same law, authorizes one to destroy another as his enemy. For our citizens, then, to commit murders and depredations on the members of nations at peace with us, or combine to do it, appeared to the Executive, and to those with whom they consulted, as much against the laws of the land, as to murder or rob, or combine to murder or rob its own citizens; and as much to require punishment, if done within their limits, where they have a territorial jurisdiction, or on the high seas, where they have a personal jurisdiction, that is to say, one which reaches their own citizens only, this being an appropriate part of each nation, on an element where all have a common jurisdiction. So say our laws, as we understand them ourselves. To them the appeal is made; and whether we have construed them well or ill, the constitutional judges will decide. Till that decision shall be obtained, the government of the United States must pursue what they think right with firmness, as is their duty.—To E. C. GENET. iii, 589. FORD ED., vi, 310. (Pa., June 1793.)

6997. —— ——. Besides taking efficacious measures to prevent the future fitting out of privateers in the ports of the United States, they will not give asylum therein to any which shall have been at any time so fitted out, and will cause restitution of all such prizes as shall be hereafter brought within their ports by any of the said privateers.—To E. C. GENET. iv, 27. FORD ED., vi, 366. (Pa., Aug. 1793.)

6998. PRIVATEERS, French.—Some privateers have been fitted out in Charleston by French citizens, with their own money, manned by themselves, and regularly commissioned by their nation. They have taken several prizes, and brought them into our ports. Some native citizens had joined them. These are arrested and under prosecution, and orders are sent to all the ports to prevent the equipping privateers by any persons foreign or native. So far is right. But the vessels so equipped at Charleston are ordered to leave the ports of the United States. This, I think, was not right. Hammond [British Minister] demanded further a surrender of the prizes they had taken. This is refused, on the principle that by the laws of war the property is transferred to the captors.—To JAMES MADISON. iii, 568. FORD ED., vi, 277. (June 1793.)

6999. —— ——. The arming and equipping vessels in the ports of the United States to cruise against nations with whom they are at peace, is incompatible with the territorial sovereignty of the United States. It makes them instrumental to the annoyance of those nations and thereby tends to compromit their peace.—To EDMOND CHARLES GENET. iii, 571. FORD ED., vi, 282. (Pa., June 1793.)

7000. PRIVATEERS, Gulf of Mexico and.—Our [the Cabinet's] general opinion is that as soundings on our coast cease at the beginning of the Gulf Stream, we ought to endeavor to assume all the waters within the Gulf Stream as our waters, so far as to exclude privateers from hovering within them.—THE ANAS. FORD ED., i, 308. (July 1805.)

7001. PRIVATEERS, Merchant vessels and.—Can it be necessary to say that a merchant vessel is not a privateer? That though she has arms to defend herself in time of war, in the course of her regular commerce, this no more makes her a privateer, than a husbandman following his plow, in time of war, with a knife or pistol in his pocket, is, thereby, made a soldier? The occupation of a privateer is attack and plunder, that of a merchant vessel is commerce and self-preservation.—To GOUVERNEUR MORRIS. iv, 41. FORD ED., vi, 385. (Pa., Aug. 1793.)

7002. PRIVATEERS, Prizes.—Encourage the privateers to burn all their prizes, and let the public pay for them. They will cheat us enormously. No matter; they will make the merchants of England feel, and squeal, and cry out for peace.—To JAMES MONROE. vi, 410. FORD ED., ix, 498. (M., 1815.)

7003. PRIVILEGES, Abolition of.—All pecuniary privileges and exemptions, enjoyed by any description of persons, are abolished.—FRENCH CHARTER OF RIGHTS. iii, 47. FORD ED., v, 102. (P., 1789.)

7004. PRIVILEGES, Unequal.—To unequal privileges among members of the same society the spirit of our nation is, with one accord, adverse.—REPLY TO ADDRESS. iv, 394. (W., 1801.) See EQUALITY, EQUAL RIGHTS, FAVORITISM and RIGHTS.

7005. PRIZES, Condemnation of.—The condemnation by the consul of France at Charleston, as legal prize, of a British vessel captured by a French frigate, is not, as you justly [observe], a judicial act warranted by the law of nations, nor by the stipulations existing between the United States and France. I observe further that it is not warranted by any law of the land. It is consequently a mere nullity; as such it can be respected in no court, can make no part in the title to the vessel, nor give to the purchaser any other security than what he would have had without it. In short, it is so absolutely nothing as to give no foundation of just concern to any person interested in the fate of the vessel. * * * The proceeding, indeed, * * * [if the information be correct], has been an act of disrespect towards the United States, to which its government cannot be inattentive. A just sense of our own rights and duties, and the obviousness of the principle are a security that no inconveniences will be permitted to arise from repetitions of it.—To GEORGE HAMMOND. iii, 558. FORD ED., vi, 252. (Pa., May 1793.)

7006. PRIZES, Consular jurisdiction.— No particular rules have been established by the President for the conduct of consuls with respect to prizes. In one particular case where a prize is brought into our ports by any of the *belligerent* parties, and is reclaimed of the Executive, the President has hitherto permitted the consul of the captor to hold the prize until his determination is known. But in all cases respecting a neutral nation, their vessels are placed exactly on the same footing with our own, entitled to the same remedy from our courts of justice, and the same protection from the Executive, as our own vessels in the same situation. The remedy in the courts of justice, the only one which they or our own can have access to, is slower than where it lies with the Executive, but it is more complete, as damages can be given by the Court but not by the Executive.—To MR. SODERSTROM. iv, 83. (G., Nov. 1793.)

7007. PRIZES, Restitution.—The restitution of the prizes [which French privateers might bring into the ports of the United States]. is understood to be inconsistent with the rules which govern such cases, and would, therefore, be unjustifiable towards the other party.—To GEORGE HAMMOND. iii, 573. FORD ED., vi, 286. (Pa., June 1793.)

7008. —— ——. Restitution of prizes has been made by the Executive of the United States only in the two cases: 1, of capture within their jurisdiction, by armed vessels, originally constituted such without the limits of the United States; or, 2, of capture, either within or without their jurisdiction, by armed vessels, originally constituted such within the limits of the United States. Such last have been called proscribed vessels.—To GEORGE HAMMOND. iv, 78. FORD ED., vi, 444. (G., Nov. 1793.)

7009. —— ——. Can prizes and the proceeds of them, taken after the date of the treaty [of peace] with France be restored by the Executive, or need an act of the Legislature? The Constitution has authorized the ordinary Legislature alone to declare war against any foreign nation. If they may enact a perfect, they may a qualified war, and appropriate the proceeds of it. In this state of things, they may modify the acts of war, and appropriate the proceeds of it. The act authorizing the capture of French armed vessels, and dividing and appropriating their proceeds, was of this kind. The Constitution has given to the President and Senate alone the power (with the consent of the foreign nation) of enacting peace. Their treaty for this purpose is an absolute repeal of the declaration of war, and of all laws authorizing or modifying war measures. The treaty with France had this effect. From the moment it was signed all the acts legalizing war measures ceased *ipso facto;* and all subsequent captures became unlawful.

Property wrongfully taken from a friend on the high sea is not thereby transferred to the captor. In whatever hands it is found, it remains the property of those from whom it was taken; and any person possessed of it, private or public, has a right to restore it. If it comes to the hands of the Executive, they may restore it. If into those of the Legislature (as by formal payment into the Treasury), they may restore it. Whoever, private or public, undertakes to restore it, takes on themselves the risk of proving that the goods were taken without authority of law, and consequently that the captor had no right to them. The Executive, charged with our exterior relations, seems bound, if satisfied of the fact, to do right to the foreign nation, and take on itself the risk of justification.—To JAMES MADISON. FORD ED., viii, 73. (W., July 1801.)

7010. PRIZES, Rules governing.—The doctrine as to the admission of prizes, maintained by the government from the commencement of the war between England and France. &c., to this day, has been this: The treaties give a right to armed vessels, with their prizes, to go where they please (consequently into our ports), and that these prizes shall not be detained, seized, nor adjudicated; but that the armed vessel may depart as *speedily as may be, with her prize,* to the place of her commission; and we are not to suffer their enemies to sell in our ports the prizes taken by their privateers. Before the British treaty, no stipulation stood in the way of permitting France to sell her prizes here; and we did permit it, but expressly as a favor, not a right. * * * These stipulations admit the prizes to put into our ports in cases of necessity, or perhaps of convenience, but no right to remain if disagreeable to us; and absolutely not to be sold.—To ALBERT GALLATIN. FORD ED., viii, 86. (M., Aug. 1801.) See PRIVATEERS and NEUTRALITY.

7011. PROCRASTINATION, Indolence and.—My acknowledgments have been delayed by a blamable spirit of procrastination, forever suggesting to our indolence that we need not do to-day what may be done to-morrow.— To THOMAS PINCKNEY. iv, 176. FORD ED., vii, 127. (Pa., 1797.)

7012. PRODUCTION, National.—In general, it is a truth that if every nation will employ itself in what it is fittest to produce, a greater quantity will be raised of the things contributing to human happiness, than if every nation attempts to raise everything it wants within itself.—To M. LASTEYRIE. v, 315. (W., 1808.)

7013. PROGRESS, Constant.—When I contemplate the immense advances in science and discoveries in the arts which have been made within the period of my life, I look forward with confidence to equal advances by the present generation, and have no doubt they will consequently be as much wiser than we have been as we than our fathers were, and they than the burners of witches.—To DR. BENJAMIN WATERHOUSE. vii. 101. FORD ED., x, 103. (M., 1818.)

7014. PROGRESS, Gothic idea of.—The Gothic idea that we were to look backwards instead of forwards for the improvement of the human mind, and to recur to the annals of our ancestors for what is most perfect in government, in religion and in learning, is worthy of those bigots in religion and government, by whom it has been recommended, and whose purposes it would answer. But it is not an idea which this country will endure.—To JOSEPH PRIESTLEY. iv, 318. FORD ED., vii, 415. (Pa., 1800.)

7015. PROGRESS, In government.—Laws and institutions must go hand in hand with the progress of the human mind. As that becomes more developed, more enlightened, as new discoveries are made, new truths disclosed, and manners and opinions change with the change of circumstances, institutions must advance also, and keep pace with the times. We might as well require a man to wear still the coat which fitted him when a boy, as civilized society to remain ever under the regimen of their barbarous ancestors. It is this preposterous idea which has lately deluged Europe in blood. Their monarchs, instead of wisely yielding to the general change of circumstances, of favoring progressive accommodation to progressive improvement, have clung to old abuses, entrenched themselves behind steady habits, and obliged their subjects to seek through blood and violence rash and ruinous innovations, which, had they been referred to the peaceful deliberations and collected wisdom of the nation, would have been put into acceptable and salutary forms. Let us follow no such examples, nor weakly believe that one generation is not as capable as another of taking care of itself, and of ordering its own affairs.—To SAMUEL KERCHIVAL. vii, 15. FORD ED., x, 42. (M., 1816.) See GENERATIONS.

7016. PROGRESS, Perseverance and.—In endeavors to improve our situation, we should never despair.—To JOHN QUINCY ADAMS. vii, 89. (M., 1817.)

7017. PROGRESS, In Science.—One of the questions, you know, on which our parties took different sides, was on the improvability of the human mind in science, in ethics, in government, &c. Those who advocated reformation of institutions, *pari passu* with the progress of science, maintained that no definite limits could be assigned to that progress. The enemies of reform, on the other hand, denied improvement, and advocated steady adherence to the principles, practices and institutions of our fathers, which they represented as the consummation of wisdom, and acme of excellence, beyond which the human mind could never advance. Although in the passage of your answer alluded to, you expressly disclaim the wish to influence the freedom of inquiry, you predict that that will produce nothing more worthy of transmission to posterity than the principles, institutions and systems of education received from their ancestors. I do not consider this as your deliberate opinion. You possess, yourself, too much science, not to see how much is still ahead of you, unexplained and unexplored. Your own consciousness must place you as far before our ancestors as in the rear of posterity.—To JOHN ADAMS. vi, 126. FORD ED., ix, 387. (M., 1813.)

7018. PROGRESS, Sluggish.—There is a snail-paced gait for the advance of new ideas on the general mind, under which we must acquiesce. A forty years' experience of popular assemblies has taught me, that you must give them time for every step you take. If too hard pushed, they balk, and the machine retrogrades.—To JOEL BARLOW. v, 217. FORD ED., ix, 169. (W., Dec. 1807.)

7019. PROGRESS, Time and.—Time indeed changes manners and notions, and so far we must expect institutions to bend to them.—To SPENCER ROANE. vii, 211. FORD ED., x, 188. (M., 1821.)

— PROHIBITION.—See WHISKY.

7020. PROPERTY, Acquisition of.—The political institutions of America, its various soils and climates opened a certain resource to the unfortunate and to the enterprising of every country, and insured to them the acquisition and free possession of property.—DECLARATION ON TAKING UP ARMS. FORD ED., i, 465. (July 1775.)

7021. PROPERTY, Of aliens.—Resolved, that no right be stipulated for aliens to hold real property within these States, this being utterly inadmissible by their several laws and policy; but when on the death of any person holding real estate within the territories of one of the contracting parties, such real estate would by their laws descend on a subject or citizen of the other, were he not disqualified by alienage, then he shall be allowed reasonable time to dispose of the same, and withdraw the proceeds without molestation.—COMMERCIAL TREATIES INSTRUCTIONS. FORD ED., iii, 492. (1784.)

7022. ——— ———. It is reasonable that every one who asks justice should do justice; and it is usual to consider the property of a foreigner, in any country, as a fund appropriated to the payment of what he owes in that country exclusively. It is a care which most nations take of their own citizens, not to let the property, which is to answer their demands, be withdrawn from its jurisdiction, and send them to seek it in foreign countries, and before foreign tribunals.—To GEORGE HAMMOND. iii, 395. FORD ED., vi, 37. (Pa., May 1792.)

7023. PROPERTY, Annihilation of.—They [Parliament] have interdicted all commerce to one of our principal towns, thereby annihilating its property in the hands of the holders.—DECLARATION ON TAKING UP ARMS. FORD ED., i, 468. (July 1775.)

7024. PROPERTY, Confiscation of.—[In Lord North's proposition] our adversaries still claim a right of demanding *ad libitum*, and of taxing us themselves to the full amount of their demand, if we do not comply with it. This leaves us without anything we can call property.—REPLY TO LORD NORTH'S PROPOSITION. FORD ED., i, 481. (July 1775.)

7025. ——— ———. He has incited treasonable insurrections of our fellow citizens, with the allurements of forfeiture and confiscation of our property.*—DECLARATION OF INDEPENDENCE AS DRAWN BY JEFFERSON.

7026. PROPERTY, Defence of.—In defence of our persons and properties under actual violation, we took up arms. When that violence shall be removed, when hostilities shall cease on the part of the aggressors, hostilities shall cease on our part also. —DECLARATION ON TAKING UP ARMS. FORD ED., i, 475. (July 1775.)

7027. PROPERTY, Depreciation.— Money is leaving the remoter parts of the Union, and flowing to this place [Philadelphia] to purchase paper; and here. a paper medium supplying its place, it is shipped off in exchange for luxuries. The value of property is necessarily falling in the places left bare of money. In Virginia, for instance, property has fallen 25 per cent. in the last twelve months.—To WILLIAM SHORT.   iii, 343. FORD ED., v, 459. (Pa., March 1792.)

7028. —— ——. The long succession of years of stunted crops, of reduced prices, the general prostration of the farming business, under levies for the support of manufacturers, &c., with the calamitous fluctuations of value in our paper medium, have kept agriculture in a state of abject depression, which has peopled the western States by silently breaking up those on the Atlantic, and glutted the land market, while it drew off its bidders. In such a state of things, property has lost its character of being a resource for debts. Highland in Bedford, which, in the days of our plethory, sold readily for from fifty to one hundred dollars the acre (and such sales were many then), would not now sell for more than from ten to twenty dollars, or one quarter to one-fifth of its former price.—To JAMES MADISON. vii, 434. FORD ED., x, 377. (M., February 1826.) See BANKS, MONEY and PAPER MONEY.

7029. PROPERTY, Descent of.—The descent of property of every kind to all the children, or to all the brothers and sisters, or other relations, in equal degree, is a politic measure, and a practicable one.—To REV. JAMES MADISON. FORD ED., vii, 35. (P., 1785.) See DESCENTS, ENTAIL and PRIMOGENITURE.

7030. PROPERTY, Division of.—I am conscious that an equal division of property is impracticable. But the consequences of this enormous inequality [in France] producing so much misery to the bulk of mankind, legislators cannot invent too many devices for subdividing property, only taking care to let their subdivisions go hand in hand with the natural affections of the human mind.—To REV. JAMES MADISON. FORD ED., vii, 35. (P., 1785.) See DESCENTS, ENTAIL and PRIMOGENITURE.

7031. PROPERTY, Equal rights and.— The true foundation of republican government is the equal right of every citizen, in his person and property, and in their management.—To SAMUEL KERCHIVAL.   vii, 11. FORD ED., x, 39. (M., 1816.)

7032. PROPERTY, Federal.—The property of the United States can never be questioned in any court, but in special cases in which, by some particular law, they delegate a special power, as to the boards of commissioners, and in some small fiscal cases. But a general jurisdiction over the national demesnes, being more than half the territory of the United States, has never been by them, and never ought to be, subjected to any tribunal.—BATTURE CASE.   viii, 521. (1812.)

7033. PROPERTY, Forfeited.—All forfeitures heretofore going to the king, shall go to the State; save only such as the legislature may hereafter abolish.—PROPOSED VA. CONSTITUTION. FORD ED., i, 27. (June 1776.)

7034. —— ——. In all cases of petty treason and murder, one-half of the lands and goods of the offender shall be forfeited to the next of kin to the person killed, and the other half descend and go to his representatives. Save only, where one shall slay the challenger in a duel, in which case, no part of his lands or goods shall be forfeited to the kindred of the party slain, but instead thereof, a moiety shall go to the Commonwealth.*—CRIMES BILL. i, 150. FORD ED., ii, 207. (1779.)

7035. PROPERTY, Free Press and.— The functionaries of every government have propensities to command at will the liberty and property of their constituents. There is no safe deposit for these but with the people themselves; nor can they be safe with them without information. Where the press is free, and every man able to read, all is safe. —To CHARLES YANCEY. vi, 517. FORD ED., x, 4. (M., 1816.)

7036. PROPERTY, Impressing.—In a country where means of payment are neither prompt, nor of the most desirable kind, impressing property for the public use has been found indispensable. We have no fears of complaint under your exercise of those powers.—To MAJOR-GENERAL LAFAYETTE. FORD ED., ii, 502. (R., 1781.)

7037. PROPERTY, Industry and.—Our wish is that * * * [there be] maintained that state of property, equal or unequal, which results to every man from his own industry, or that of his fathers.—SECOND INAUGURAL ADDRESS. viii, 44. FORD ED., viii, 347. (1805.)

7038. PROPERTY, Inequality of.— Another means of silently lessening the inequality of property [in France] is to exempt all from taxation below a certain point, and to tax the higher portions of property in geometrical progression as they rise. —To REV. JAMES MADISON. FORD ED., vii, 36. (P., 1785.)

* Struck out by Congress.—EDITOR.

* Quære, if the estates of both parties in a duel, should not be forfeited? The deceased is equally guilty with a suicide.—NOTE BY JEFFERSON.

7039. PROPERTY, Inventions as.—Inventions cannot in nature be a subject of property.—To ISAAC MCPHERSON. vi, 181. (M.. 1813.) See INVENTIONS and PATENTS.

7040. PROPERTY, Jurisdiction over.—The functions of the Executive are not competent to the decision of questions of property between individuals. They are ascribed to the Judiciary alone, and when either persons or property are taken into their custody, there is no power in this country that can take them out.—To EDMOND CHARLES GENET. iii, 586. FORD ED., vi, 312. (Pa., 1793.)

7041. PROPERTY, Laws of.—Whenever there is in any country, uncultivated lands and unemployed poor, it is clear that the laws of property have been so far extended as to violate natural right.—To REV. JAMES MADISON. FORD ED., vii, 36. (P., 1785.)

7042. PROPERTY, Life and.—They [Parliament] have deprived us of the inestimable privilege of trial by a jury of the vicinage in cases affecting both life and property.—DECLARATION ON TAKING UP ARMS. FORD ED., i, 468. (July 1775.)

7043. PROPERTY, Paper money and.—That paper money has some advantages, is admitted. But that its abuses also are inevitable, and, by breaking up the measure of value, makes a lottery of all private property, cannot be denied.—To DR. JOSEPHUS B. STUART. vii, 65. (M., May 1817.) See BANKS and PAPER MONEY.

7044. PROPERTY, Protection of.—The persons and property of our citizens are entitled to the protection of our government in all places where they may lawfully go.—OPINION ON SHIP PASSPORTS. vii, 624. (May 1793.)

7045. ——— ———. We give you [Choctaws] a copy of the law, made by our great Council, for punishing our people, who may encroach on your lands, or injure you otherwise. Carry it with you to your homes, and preserve it, as the shield which we spread over you, to protect your land, your property, and persons.—ADDRESS TO THE CHOCTAWS. viii, 192. (1803.)

7046. ——— ———. When once you [the Indians] have property, you will want laws and magistrates to protect your property and persons, and to punish those among you who commit crimes. You will find that our laws are good for this purpose.—ADDRESS TO DELAWARES. viii, 226. (1808.)

7047. ——— ———. We wish to see you [the Indians] possessed of property, and protecting it by regular laws.—INDIAN ADDRESS. viii, 234. (1809.)

7048. ——— ———. The first foundations of the social compact would be broken up, were we definitely to refuse to its members the protection of their persons and property, while in their lawful pursuits.—To JAMES MAURY. vi, 52. FORD ED., ix, 348. (M., 1812.)

7049. PROPERTY, Public office as.—The field of public office will not be perverted by me into a family property.—To DR. HORATIO TURPIN. v, 90. (W., 1807.) See RELATIONS.

7050. PROPERTY, Recovery of.—By nature's law, every man has a right to seize and retake by force. his own property. taken from him by another, by force or fraud. Nor is this natural right among the first which is taken into the hands of regular government, after it is instituted. It was long retained by our ancestors. It was a part of their common law, laid down in their books, recognized by all the authorities, and regulated as to circumstances of practice.—BATTURE CASE. viii, 584. (1812.)

7051. PROPERTY, Representation of.—In some of the American States, the delegates and Senators are so chosen as that the first represent the persons. and the second the property of the State. But with us [Virginia] wealth and wisdom have equal chance for admission into both houses.—NOTES ON VIRGINIA. viii, 361. FORD ED., iii, 223. (1782.)

7052. PROPERTY, Rescue of.—Nature has given to all men, individual or associated, the right of rescuing their own property wrongfully taken. In cases of forcible entry on individual possessions, special provisions, both of the common and civil law, have restrained the right of rescue by private force, and substituted the aid of the civil power. But no law has restrained the right of the nation itself from removing by its own arm, intruders on its possessions.—To GOVERNOR CLAIBORNE. v, 518. (M., 1810.)

7053. PROPERTY, Restitution.—Congress should immediately and earnestly recommend to the legislatures of the respective States to provide for the restitution of all estates, rights and properties which have been confiscated, belonging to British subjects; and also of the estates, rights and properties of persons resident in districts which were in the possession of his Britannic Majesty's arms at any time between the 30th day of November, 1782, and the 14th day of January, 1784, and who have not borne arms against the United States, and that persons of any other description shall have free liberty to go to any part or parts of any of the thirteen United States, and therein to remain twelve months unmolested in their endeavors to obtain the restitution of such of their estates, rights and properties as may have been confiscated.—REPORT ON PEACE TREATY. FORD ED., iii, 349. (Dec. 1783.)

7054. PROPERTY, Restoration.—I am not fond of encouraging an intercourse with the enemy for the recovery of property; however, I shall not forbid it while conducted on principles which are fair and general. If the British commander chooses to discriminate between the several species of property taken from the people; if he chooses to say he will restore all of one kind, and retain all of another, I am contented that individuals shall avail themselves of this discrimination; but no distinctions of persons must be admitted. The moment it is proposed that the same species of property shall be restored to one which is refused to another, let every application to him for restitution be prohibited. The principles by which his discrimination would be governed are but too obvious, and they are the reverse of what we should approve.—To COLONEL JOHN NICHOLAS. FORD ED., ii, 409. (1781.)

7055. —— ——. A right to take the side, which every man's conscience approves in a civil contest, is too precious a right, and too favorable to the preservation of liberty not to be protected by all its well informed friends. The Assembly of Virginia have given sanction to this right in several of their laws, discriminating honorably those who took side against us before the Declaration of Independence, from those who remained among us and strove to injure us by their treacheries. I sincerely wish that you, and every other to whom this distinction applies favorably, may find, in the Assembly of Virginia, the good effects of that justice and generosity which have dictated to them this discrimination. It is a sentiment which will gain strength in their breasts in proportion as they can forget the savage cruelties committed on them, and will, I hope, in the end induce them to restore the property itself wherever it is unsold, and the price received for it, where it has been actually sold.—To MRS. SPROWLE. FORD ED., iv, 66. (P., 1785.)

7056. PROPERTY, Right to.—A right to property is founded in our natural wants, in the means with which we are endowed to satisfy these wants, and the right to what we acquire by those means without violating the similar rights of other sensible beings. —To DUPONT DE NEMOURS. vi, 591. FORD ED., x, 24. (P.F., 1816.)

7057. PROPERTY, Sale under execution.—The immensity of this [Virginia] debt [to British creditors] was another reason for forbidding such a mass of property to be offered for sale under execution at once, as, from the small quantity of circulating money, it must have sold for little or nothing, whereby the creditor would have failed to receive his money, and the debtor would have lost his whole estate without being discharged of his debt.*—REPORT TO CONGRESS. ix, 241. FORD ED., iv, 127. (F., 1785.) See DEBTS DUE BRITISH.

—— **PROPERTY, At sea.**—See TREATIES.

7058. PROPERTY, Seizure in war.—It cannot be denied that a state of war directly permits a nation to seize the property of its enemies found within its own limits or taken in war and in whatever form it exists whether in action or possession.—To GEORGE HAMMOND. iii, 369. FORD ED., vi, 15. (Pa., 1792.)

* Report of Conference with Count de Vergennes, Foreign Minister of France, respecting commerce.— EDITOR.

7059. PROPERTY, Sequestration.—For securing to the citizens of the Commonwealth [of Virginia] an indemnification out of the property of British subjects here, * * * in case the sovereign of the latter should confiscate the property of the former in his dominions, as well as to prevent that accession of strength which the enemy might derive by withdrawing their property * * * hence * * * the lands, slaves, flocks, implements of industry * * * of British subjects, shall be sequestered.—BRITISH PROPERTY BILL. FORD ED., ii, 199. (1779.)

7060. PROPERTY, Slaves as.—The cession of that kind of property [Slaves], for so it is misnamed, is a bagatelle which would not cost me a second thought, if, in that way, a general emancipation and expatriation could be effected.—To JOHN HOLMES. vii, 159. FORD ED., x, 157. (M., 1820.)

7061. —— ——. Actual property has been lawfully vested in [negroes] and who can lawfully take it from the possessors?—To JARED SPARKS. vii, 333. FORD ED., x, 290. (M., 1824.)

7062. PROPERTY, Stable ownership.—By an universal law, indeed, whatever [property], whether fixed or movable, belongs to all men equally and in common, is the property for the moment of him who occupies it; but when he relinquishes the occupation, the property goes with it. Stable ownership is the gift of social law, and is given late in the progress of society.—To ISAAC McPHERSON. vi, 180. (M., 1813.)

7063. PROPERTY, Taxation.—I am principally afraid that commerce will be overloaded by the assumption [of the State debts], believing it would be better that property should be duly taxed.—To MR. RANDOLPH. iii, 185. (N.Y., 1790.) See TAXATION.

7064. PROPERTY, Unequal division.—The unequal division of property [in France] * * * occasions numberless instances of wretchedness and is to be observed all over Europe.—To REV. JAMES MADISON. FORD ED., vii, 35. (P., 1785.)

7065. PROPERTY, Untaxed.—The clergy and nobles [in France], by their privileges and influence, have kept their property in a great measure untaxed.—To DR. PRICE. ii, 556. (P., Jan. 1789.)

7066. PROPHECY, Conditional.—Who can withhold looking into futurity on events which are to change the face of the world, and the condition of man throughout it, without indulging himself in the effusions of the holy spirit of Delphos? I may do it the more safely, as to my vaticinations I always subjoin the proviso "that nothing unexpected happen to change the predicted course of events".—To WILLIAM SHORT. FORD ED., x, 249. (M., 1823.)

7067. PROPHECY, Fallacious.—Perhaps in that super-mundane region, we may be amused with seeing the fallacy of our own guesses.—To JOHN ADAMS. vii, 105. FORD ED., x, 109. (M., 1818.)

7068. PROPHET, Wabash.—With respect to the [Wabash] prophet, if those who are in danger from him would settle it in their own way, it would be their affair. But we should do nothing towards it. That kind of policy is not in the character of our government, and still less of the paternal spirit we wish to show towards that people. But could not [General] Harrison gain over the Prophet, who no doubt is a scoundrel, and only needs his price?—To General Dearborn. v, 163. (M., Aug. 1807.)

7069. PROSCRIPTION vs. JUST TRIAL.—To fill up the measure of irritation, a proscription of individuals has been substituted in the room of just trial. Can it be believed that a grateful people will suffer those to be consigned to execution whose sole crime has been the developing and asserting their rights? Had the Parliament possessed the power of reflection, they would have avoided a measure as impotent, as it was inflammatory.—To Dr. William Small. i, 199. Ford ed., i, 454. (May 1775.)

7070. PROSPERITY, American.—There is not a nation under the sun enjoying more present prosperity, nor with more in prospect.—To C. W. F. Dumas. iii, 260. (Pa., 1791.)

7071. PROSPERITY, Basis.—A prosperity built on the basis of agriculture is that which is most desirable to us, because to the efforts of labor it adds the efforts of a greater proportion of soil.—Circular to Consuls. iii, 431. (Pa., 1792.)

7072. PROSPERITY, Concern for.—Affectionate concerns for the prosperity of my fellow citizens will cease but with life to animate my breast.—Reply to Address. v, 262. (W., 1808.)

7073. PROSPERITY, Conditions of.—I trust the good sense of our country will see that its greatest prosperity depends on a due balance between agriculture, manufactures and commerce.—To Thomas Leiper. v, 417. Ford ed., ix, 239. (W., 1809.)

7074. PROSPERITY, Pillars of.—Agriculture, manufactures, commerce, and navigation, the four pillars of our prosperity, are the most thriving when left most free to individual enterprise.—First Annual Message. viii, 13. Ford ed., viii, 123. (Dec. 1801.)

7075. PROSPERITY, Stability of.—On the useful pursuits of peace alone, a stable prosperity can be founded.—R. to A. Pittsburg Republicans. viii, 142. (1808.)

7076. PROTECTION, Commerce and navigation.—We wish [to encourage navigation and commerce] by throwing open all the doors of commerce, and knocking off its shackles. But as this cannot be done for others, unless they will do it for us, and there is no probability that Europe will do this, I suppose we shall be obliged to adopt a system which may shackle them in our ports, as they do us in theirs.—To Count Van Hogendorp. i, 465. Ford ed., iv, 105. (P., 1785.) See Commerce and Navigation.

7077. ———. Should any nation, contrary to our wishes, suppose it may better find its advantage by continuing its system of prohibitions, duties and regulations, it behooves us to protect our citizens, their commerce and navigation, by counter prohibitions, duties and regulations, also. Free commerce and navigation are not to be given in exchange for restrictions and vexations; nor are they likely to produce a relaxation of them.—Foreign Commerce Report. vii. 647. Ford ed., vi, 480. (Dec. 1793.) See Duties and Free Trade.

7078. PROTECTION, Manufactures and.—To protect the manufactures adapted to our circumstances * * * [is one of] the landmarks by which we are to guide ourselves in all our proceedings.—Second Annual Message. viii, 21. Ford ed., viii, 187. (Dec. 1802.)

7079. ———. Little doubt remains that the [manufacturing] establishments formed and forming will, under the auspices of cheaper materials and subsistence, the freedom of labor from taxation with us, and of protecting duties and prohibitions, become permanent.—Eighth Annual Message. viii, 109. Ford ed., ix, 224. (Nov. 1808.) See Manufactures and Tariff.

7080. PROTECTION, Oppressive.—I do not mean to say that it may not be for the general interest to foster for awhile certain infant manufactures, until they are strong enough to stand against foreign rivals; but when evident that they will never be so, it is against right to make the other branches of industry support them.—To Samuel Smith. vii, 285. Ford ed., x, 252. (M., 1823.)

7081. PROTECTION, Petitions for.—I observe you [Congress] are loaded with petitions from the manufacturing, commercial and agricultural interests, each praying you to sacrifice the others to them. This proves the egoism of the whole and happily balances their cannibal appetites to eat one another. * * * I do not know whether it is any part of the petitions of the farmers that our citizens shall be restrained to eat nothing but bread, because that can be made here. But this is the common spirit of all their petitions.—To Hugh Nelson. Ford ed., x, 156. (M., 1820.)

7082. PROTECTION, Printing and.—None of these [books in foreign living languages] are printed here, and the duty on them becomes consequently not a protecting, but really a prohibitory one.—To ———. vii. 220. (M., 1821.) See Books.

7083. PROTESTANTS, French edict respecting.—The long expected edict for the Protestants at length appears here [Paris]. Its analysis is this: It is an acknowledgment (hitherto withheld by the laws,) that Protestants can beget children, and that they can die, and be offensive unless buried. It does not give them permission to think, to speak, or to worship. It enumerates the humiliations to which they shall remain subject, and the burthens to which they shall continue to be unjustly exposed. What are we to think of the condition of the human mind in a country where such a wretched thing as this has thrown the State into convulsions, and how must we bless our own situation in a country the most illiterate peasant of which is a Solon compared with the authors of this law?—To William Rutledge. ii, 350. Ford ed., v, 4. (P., Feb. 1788.)

7084. PROVIDENCE, An approving.—
We remark with special satisfaction those circumstances which, under the smiles of Providence, result from the skill, industry and order of our citizens, managing their own affairs in their own way and for their own use, unembarrassed by too much regulations, unoppressed by fiscal exactions.—Second Annual Message. viii, 15. Ford ed., viii, 182. (Dec. 1802.)

7085. PROVIDENCE, Goodness of.—
Providence in His goodness gave it [the yellow fever] an early termination * * * and lessened the number of victims which have usually fallen before it.—Fifth Annual Message. viii, 461. Ford ed., viii, 386. (Dec. 1805.)

7086. PROVIDENCE, Gratitude to.—
Let us bow with gratitude to that kind Providence which * * * guarded us from hastily entering into the sanguinary contest [between France and England].—Third Annual Message. viii, 28. Ford ed., viii, 272. (Oct. 1803.)

7087. PROVIDENCE, Human happiness and.—An overruling Providence * * * by all its dispensations proves that it delights in the happiness of man here and his greater happiness hereafter.—First Inaugural Address. viii, 3. Ford ed., viii, 4. (1801.)

7088. PROVIDENCE, A just.—You [General Washington] have persevered till these United States, aided by a magnanimous king and nation, have been enabled, under a just Providence, to close the war in freedom, safety, and independence. * * * We join you in commending the interests of our dearest country to the protection of Almighty God, beseeching Him to dispose the hearts and minds of its citizens to improve the opportunity afforded them of becoming a happy and respectable nation.*—Congress to Washington on Surrendering his Commission. (Dec. 23, 1783.)

7089. PROVIDENCE, Prayers to.—I pray that that Providence in whose hands are the nations of the earth, may continue towards ours His fostering care, and bestow on yourselves the blessings of His protection and favor.—R. to A. Massachusetts Legislature. viii, 117. (1807.)

* Thomas Mifflin, the President of Congress, read the reply of Congress to Washington's address on surrendering his commission. It was written by Jefferson, but is not included in the editions of his works.—Editor.

7090. PROVIDENCE, Slavery and.—
We must await with patience the workings of an overruling Providence, and hope that that is preparing the deliverance of these, our suffering brethren [Slaves].—To M. de Meunier. ix, 279. Ford ed., iv, 185. (P., 1786.) See Deity and God.

7091. PROVIDENCE, Supplicating.—I supplicate a protecting Providence to watch over your own and our country's freedom and welfare.—R. to A. N. Y. Tammany Society. viii, 127. (Feb. 1808.)

7092. ———— ————. I sincerely supplicate that overruling Providence which governs the destinies of men and nations, to dispense His choicest blessings on yourselves and our beloved country.—R. to A. Massachusetts Citizens. viii, 161. (1809.)

— PRUSSIA.—See Frederick The Great.

7093. PSALMS, Estimate of the.—I acknowledge all the merit of the hymn of Cleanthes to Jupiter, which you ascribe to it. It is as highly sublime as a chaste and correct imagination can permit itself to go. Yet in the contemplation of a Being so superlative, the hyperbolic flights of the Psalmist may often be followed, with approbation, even with rapture; and I have no hesitation in giving him the palm over all the hymnists of every language and of every time. Turn to the 148th psalm, in Brady and Tate's version. Have such conceptions been ever before expressed? Their version of the 15th psalm is more to be esteemed for its pithiness than its poetry. Even Sternhold, the leaden Sternhold, kindles, in a single instance, with the sublimity of his original, and expresses the majesty of God descending on the earth, in terms not unworthy of the subject:

" The Lord descended from above,
    And bowed the heav'ns most high,
    And underneath His feet He cast,
    The darkness of the sky.
    On Cherubim and Seraphim
    Full royally He rode;
    And on the wings of mighty winds
    Came flying all abroad."—Psalm XVIII.

* * * The best collection of these psalms is that of the Octagonian dissenters of Liverpool. * * * Indeed, bad is the best of the English versions; not a ray of poetical genius having ever been employed on them. And how much depends on this, may be seen by comparing Brady and Tate's 15th psalm with Blacklock's *Justum et tenacem propositi virum* of Horace. A translation of David in this style, or in that of Pompei's Cleanthes, might give us some idea of the merit of the original. The character, too, of the poetry of these hymns is singular to us; written in monostichs, each divided into strophe and anti-strophe, the sentiment of the first member responded with amplification or antithesis in the second.—To John Adams. vi, 220. (M., 1813.)

7094. PUBLIC CONFIDENCE, Abuse of.—In questions of power * * * let no more be heard of confidence in man, but bind him down from mischief by the chains of the Constitution.—Kentucky Resolutions. ix, 471. Ford ed., vii, 305. (1798.)

7095. PUBLIC CONFIDENCE, Acquirement of.—The energy of the government depending mainly on the confidence of the people in the Chief Magistrate, makes it his duty to spare nothing which can strengthen him with that confidence.—To DR. HORATIO TURPIN. v, 90. (W., 1807.)

7096. —— ——. In a government like ours, it is the duty of the Chief Magistrate, in order to enable himself to do all the good which his station requires, to endeavor, by all honorable means, to unite in himself the confidence of the whole people. This alone, in any case where the energy of the nation is required, can produce a union of the powers of the whole, and point them in a single direction, as if all constituted but one body and one mind; and this alone can render a weaker nation unconquerable by a stronger one. Towards acquiring the confidence of the people, the very first measure is to satisfy them of his disinterestedness, and that he is directing their affairs with a single eye to their good, and not to build up fortunes for himself and family.—To J. GARLAND JEFFERSON. v, 498. FORD ED., ix, 270. (M., 1810.)

7097. PUBLIC CONFIDENCE, Asked for.—Without pretensions to that high confidence you reposed in our first and greatest revolutionary character, * * * I ask so much confidence only as may give firmness and effect to the legal administration of your affairs.—FIRST INAUGURAL ADDRESS. viii, 5. FORD ED., viii, 5. (1801.)

7098. PUBLIC CONFIDENCE, Dangerous.—It would be a dangerous delusion were a confidence in the men of our choice to silence our fears for the safety of our rights.—KENTUCKY RESOLUTIONS. ix, 470. FORD ED., vii, 303. (1798.)

7099. PUBLIC CONFIDENCE, Despotism and.—Confidence is everywhere the parent of depotism—free government is founded in jealousy, and not in confidence.—KENTUCKY RESOLUTIONS. ix, 470. FORD ED., vii, 304. (1798.)

7100. PUBLIC CONFIDENCE, Lack of. —We do not find it easy to make commercial arrangements in Europe. There is a want of confidence in us.—To NATHANIEL GREENE. FORD ED., iv, 25. (P., 1785.)

7101. PUBLIC CONFIDENCE, Limits to.—Our Constitution has * * * fixed the limits to which, and no further, our confidence may go; and let the honest advocate of confidence read the Alien and Sedition Acts, and say if the Constitution has not been wise in fixing limits to the government it created, and whether we should be wise in destroying those limits.—KENTUCKY RESOLUTIONS. ix, 470. FORD ED., vii, 304. (1798.)

7102. —— ——. Is confidence or discretion, or is strict limit, the principle of our Constitution?—To JEDEDIAH MORSE. vii, 235. FORD ED., x, 205. (M., 1822.)

7103. PUBLIC CONFIDENCE, Perversion of.—What person, who remembers the times and tempers we have seen, would have believed that within so short a period, not only the jealous spirit of liberty which shaped every operation of our Revolution, but even

the common principles of English whigism would be scouted, and the tory principle of passive obedience under the new-fangled names of confidence and responsibility, become entirely triumphant? That the tories, whom in mercy we did not crumble to dust and ashes, could so have entwined us in their scorpion toils, that we cannot now move hand or foot?—To ROBERT R. LIVINGSTON. iv, 297. FORD ED., vii, 369. (Pa., Feb. 1799.)

7104. PUBLIC CONFIDENCE, Preserve.—Let nothing be spared of either reason or passion, to preserve the public confidence entire, as the only rock of our safety. —To CÆSAR A. RODNEY. v, 501. FORD ED., ix, 272. (M., 1810.)

7105. PUBLIC CONFIDENCE, Sacrifices and.—Bringing into office no desires of making it subservient to the advancement of my own private interests, it has been no sacrifice, by postponing them, to strengthen the confidence of my fellow citizens.—To HORATIO TURPIN. v, 90. (W., 1807.)

7106. PUBLIC CONFIDENCE, Wisdom and.—It is not wisdom alone, but public confidence in that wisdom, which can support an administration.—To PRESIDENT MONROE. FORD ED., x, 316. (M., 1824.)

— PUBLIC IMPROVEMENTS.—See INTERNAL IMPROVEMENTS.

— PUBLIC OFFICE.—See OFFICE and OFFICES.

7107. PUBLIC WORKS, Government and.—The New Orleans Canal Company ask specifically that we should loan them $50,000, or take the remaining fourth of their shares now on hand. This last measure is too much out of our policy of not embarking the public in enterprises better managed by individuals, and which might occupy as much of our time as those political duties for which the public functionaries are particularly instituted. Some money could be lent them, but only on an assurance that it would be employed so as to secure the public objects.— To GOVERNOR CLAIBORNE. v, 319. (W., July 1808.)

7108. PUBLICITY, Adams's administration and.—Reserve as to all their proceedings is the fundamental maxim of the Executive department.—To BENJAMIN HAWKINS. iv, 326. FORD ED., vii, 435. (Pa., March 1800.)

7109. PUBLICITY, Complete.—There is not a truth existing which I fear, or would wish unknown to the whole world.—To HENRY LEE. vii, 448. FORD ED., x, 389. (M., 1826.)

7110. PUBLICITY, Darkness and.— Ours, as you know, is a government which will not tolerate the being kept entirely in the dark.—To JAMES MONROE. v, 52. FORD ED., ix, 36. (W., 1807.) See CONVENTION (FEDERAL).

7111. PUBLICITY, Demanded.—The journals of Congress not being printed earlier, gives more uneasiness than I would wish ever to see produced by any act of that body, from whom alone, I know, our salvation can proceed. In our [Virginia] Assembly, even the best affected think it an indignity to freemen to be voted away, life and fortune, in the dark.—To JOHN ADAMS. FORD ED., ii, 130. (Wg., 1777.)

7112. PUBLICITY, Executive, Congress and.—I remember Mr. Gallatin expressed an opinion that our negotiations with England should not be laid before Congress at their meeting, but reserved to be communicated all together with the answer they should send us, whenever received. I am not of this opinion. I think, on the meeting of Congress, we should lay before them everything that has passed to that day, and place them on the same ground of information we are on ourselves.—To JAMES MADISON. v, 174. FORD ED., ix, 131. (M., 1807.)

7113. —— ——. I am desirous that nothing shall be omitted on my part which may add to your information on this subject [relations with France], or contribute to the correctness of the views which should be formed.—SPECIAL MESSAGE. viii, 102. FORD ED., ix. 187. (1808.)

7114. PUBLICITY, Executive support.—No ground of support for the Executive will ever be so sure as a complete knowledge of their proceedings by the people; and it is only in cases where the public good would be injured, and *because* it would be injured, that proceedings should be secret. In such cases it is the duty of the Executive to sacrifice their personal interests (which would be promoted by publicity) to the public interest.—To PRESIDENT WASHINGTON. iv, 89. FORD ED., vi, 461. (1793.)

7115. PUBLICITY, Expediency of.—If the negotiations with England are at an end, if not given to the public now, when are they to be given? and what moment can be so interesting? If anything amiss should happen from the concealment, where will the blame originate at least? It may be said, indeed, that the President *puts it in the power* of the Legislature to communicate these proceedings to *their constituents;* but is it more their duty to communicate them to their constituents, than it is the President's to communicate them to *his constituents?* And if they were desirous of communicating them, ought the President to restrain them by making the communication confidential? I think no harm can be done by the publication. because it is impossible England, after doing us an injury, should *declare war* against us, merely because we tell our constituents of it; and I think good may be done, because while it puts it in the power of the Legislature to adopt peaceable measures of doing ourselves justice, it prepares the minds of our constituents to go cheerfully into an acquiescence under these measures, by impressing them with a thorough and enlightened conviction that they are founded in right.—To PRESIDENT WASHINGTON. iv, 89. FORD ED., vi, 461. (Dec. 1793.)

7116. —— ——. On a severe review of the question, whether the British communication should carry any such mark of being confidential as to prevent the Legislature from publishing them, he is clearly of opinion they ought not. Will they be kept secret if secrecy be enjoined? Certainly not, and all the offence will be given (if it be possible any should be given) which would follow their complete publication. If they would be kept secret, from whom would it be? From our own constituents only, for Great Britain is possessed of every tittle. Why, then, keep it secret from them?—To PRESIDENT WASHINGTON. iv, 89. FORD ED., vi, 461. (Dec. 1793.)

7117. PUBLICITY, Full.—I hope that to preserve this weather-gauge of public opinion, and to counteract the slanders and falsehoods disseminated by the English papers, the government will make it a standing instruction to their ministers at foreign courts, to keep Europe truly informed of occurrences here, by publishing in their papers the naked truth always, whether favorable or unfavorable. For they will believe the good, if we candidly tell them the bad also.—To JAMES MONROE. vi, 408. FORD ED., ix, 497. (M., 1815.)

7118. PUBLICITY, The people and.—I have not been in the habit of mysterious reserve on any subject, nor of buttoning up my opinions within my own doublet. On the contrary. while in public service especially, I thought the public entitled to frankness, and intimately to know whom they employed.—To SAMUEL KERCHIVAL. vii, 9. FORD ED., x, 37. (M., 1816.)

7119. PUBLICITY, Preservation of order and.—The way to prevent these* irregular interpositions of the people is to give them full information of their affairs through the channel of the public papers, and to contrive that those papers should penetrate the whole mass of the people.—To EDWARD CARRINGTON. ii, 99. FORD ED., iv, 359. (P., 1787.)

7120. PUBLICITY, War intelligence.—When our constituents are called on for considerable exertions to relieve a part of their fellow-citizens, suffering from the hand of an enemy, it is desirable for those entrusted with the administration of their affairs to communicate without reserve what they have done to ward off the evil.†—To PRESIDENT WASHINGTON. FORD ED., v, 431. (1792.)

* Jefferson was discussing Shays's rebellion.—EDITOR.

† The extract is from the draft of a letter written by Jefferson for President Washington, to be sent by him to the Secretary of War, as an introduction to a report on Indian affairs. Hamilton doubted "whether 'our constituents' was a proper phrase to be used by the President in addressing a subordinate officer", and suggested instead of it, "the community". Washington adopted it. Hamilton also suggested that the close of the sentence after "desirable" be made to read, "to manifest that due pains have been taken by those entrusted with the administration of their affairs to avoid the evil". Washington made the change.—EDITOR.

7121. —— ——. A fair and honest narrative of the bad, is a voucher for the truth of the good. In this way the old Congress set an example to the world, for which the world amply repaid them, by giving unlimited credit to whatever was stamped with the name of Charles Thomson. It is known that this was never put to an untruth but once, and that where Congress was misled by the credulity of their General (Sullivan). The first misfortune of the Revolutionary war, induced a motion to suppress or garble the account of it. It was rejected with indignation. The whole truth was given in all its details, and there never was another attempt in that body to disguise it.—To MATTHEW CARR. vi, 133. (M., 1813.)

7122. PUNISHMENT, Excessive.—All excess of punishment is a crime.—REPORT ON SPANISH CONVENTION. iii, 354. FORD ED., v, 484. (1792.)

7123. QUAKERS, English attachments of.—An attempt has been made to get the Quakers to come forward with a petition [against war with France], to aid with the weight of their body the feeble band of peace. They have, with some effort, got a petition signed by a few of their society; the main body of their society refuse it. M'Lay's peace motion in the Assembly of Pennsylvania was rejected with an unanimity of the Quaker vote, and it seems to be well understood, that their attachment to England is stronger than to their principles or their country. The Revolutionary war was a proof of this.—To JAMES MADISON. iv, 227. FORD ED., vii, 226. (Pa., 1798.)

7124. —— ——. I sincerely wish the circulation of the letters of "Cerus and Amicus" among the Society of Friends may have the effect you expect, of abating their prejudices against the government of their country. But I apprehend their disease is too deeply seated; that identifying themselves with the mother Society in England, and taking from them implicitly their politics, their principles and passions, it will be long before they cease to be Englishmen in everything but the place of their birth, and to consider that, and not America, as their real country.—To MR. BALDWIN. v, 494. (M., 1810.)

7125. QUAKERS, Indian civilization and.—In this important work [Indian civilization,] I owe to your Society an acknowledgment that we have felt the benefits of their zealous cooperation, and approved its judicious direction towards producing among those people habits of industry, comfortable subsistence, and civilized usages, as preparatory to religious instruction and the cultivation of letters.—REPLY TO ADDRESS. viii, 118. (1807.)

7126. QUAKERS, Jefferson's administration and.—Conscious that the present administration has been essentially pacific, and that in all questions of importance it has been governed by the identical principles professed by the Society of Friends, it has been quite at a loss to conjecture the unknown cause of the opposition of the greater part, and bare neutrality of the rest. The hope, however, that prejudices would at length give way to facts, has never been entirely extinguished, and still may be realized in favor of another administration.—To MR. FRANKLIN. v, 303. (W., 1808.)

7127. —— ——. You observe very truly, that both the late and the present administration conducted the government on principles *professed* by the Friends. Our efforts to preserve peace, our measures as to the Indians, as to slavery, as to religious freedom, were all in consonance with their *profession*. Yet I never expected we should get a vote from them, and in this I was neither deceived nor disappointed. There is no riddle in this to those who do not suffer themselves to be duped by the *professions* of religious sectaries. The theory of American Quakerism is a very obvious one. The mother Society is in England. Its members are English by birth and residence, devoted to their own country, as good citizens ought to be. The Quakers of these States are colonies or filiations from the mother Society, to whom that Society sends its yearly lessons. On these, the filiated Societies model their opinions, their conduct, their passions and attachments. A Quaker is essentially an Englishman, in every part of the earth he is born or lives. The outrages of Great Britain on our navigation and commerce have kept us in perpetual bickerings with her. The Quakers have taken side against their own government, not on their *profession* of peace, for they saw that peace was our object also; but from devotion to the views of the mother Society. In 1797-'98, when an administration sought war with France, the Quakers were the most clamorous for war. Their principle of peace, as a secondary one, yielded to the primary one of adherence to the Friends in England, and what was patriotism in the original, became treason in the copy. On that occasion, they obliged their good old leader, Mr. Pemberton, to erase his name from a petition to Congress against war, which had been delivered to a representative of Pennsylvania, a member of the late and present administration; he accordingly permitted the old gentleman to erase his name. * * * I apply this to the Friends in general, not universally. I know individuals among them as good patriots as we have.—To SAMUEL KERCHIVAL. v, 492. (M., 1810.)

7128. QUAKERS, Oppression of.—The first settlers in this country [Virginia] were emigrants from England, of the English Church, just at a point of time when it was flushed with complete victory over the religions of all other persuasions. Possessed, as they became, of the powers of making, administering, and executing the laws, they showed equal intolerance in this country with their Presbyterian brethren, who had emigrated to the northern government. The poor Quakers were flying from persecution in England. They cast their eyes on these new countries as asylums of civil and religious freedom; but they found them free only for the reigning sect. Several acts of the Virginia Assembly of 1659, 1662, and 1693, had made it penal in parents to refuse to have their children baptized; had prohibited the unlawful assembling of Quakers; had made it penal for any master of a vessel to bring a Quaker into the State; had ordered those already here, and such as should come thereafter, to be imprisoned till they should abjure the country; provided a milder punishment for their first and second return, but death for the third; had inhibited all persons from suffering their meetings in or near their houses, entertaining them individually, or disposing of books which supported their tenets. If no capital execution took place here, as did in New England, it was not owing to the moderation of the church, or spirit of the legislature, as may be inferred from the law itself; but to historical circumstances which have not been handed down to us. The Anglicans retained full possession of the country about a century. Other opinions began then to creep in, and the great care of the government to support their own church, having begotten an equal degree of indolence in its clergy, two-thirds of the people had become dissenters at the commencement of the present Revolution. The laws, indeed, were still oppressive on them, but the spirit of the one party had subsided into moderation, and of the other had risen to a degree of determination which commanded respect.—NOTES ON VIRGINIA. viii, 398. FORD ED., iii, 261. (1786.)

7129. QUARANTINE, Uniform laws.— Many are the exercises of power preserved to the States, wherein a uniformity of proceeding would be advantageous to all. Such are quarantines, health laws, &c.—To JAMES SULLIVAN. v, 101. FORD ED., ix, 76. (W., 1807.)

7130. QUARRELS, Among friends. —The way to make friends quarrel is to put them in disputation under the public eye. An experience of near twenty years has taught me that few friendships stand this test; and that public assemblies, where every one is free to act and speak, are the most powerful looseners of the bands of private friendship.—To GENERAL WASHINGTON. i, 334. FORD ED., iii, 466. (A., 1784.)

7131. QUARRELS, Cowards and.—A coward is much more exposed to quarrels than a man of spirit.—To JAMES MONROE. FORD ED., iv, 34. (P., 1785.)

7132. QUARRELS, European.—I am decidedly of opinion we should take no part in European quarrels.—To GENERAL WASHINGTON. ii, 533. FORD ED., v, 57. (P., 1788.) See ALLIANCES.

7133. QUARRELS, Human nature and. —An association of men who will not quarrel with one another is a thing which never yet existed, from the greatest confederacy of nations down to a town meeting or a vestry.—To JOHN TAYLOR. iv, 247. FORD ED., vii, 265. (Pa., 1798.)

— QUEBEC, Expedition against.—See ARNOLD.

7134. QUIET, Love of.—I want to be quiet; and although some circumstances, now and then, excite me to notice them, I feel safe, and happier in leaving events to those whose turn it is to take care of them; and, in general, to let it be understood, that I meddle little or not at all with public affairs.—To JOSEPH C. CABELL. vi, 310. FORD ED., ix, 452. (M., 1814.)

— QUILLING.—See MUSIC.

7135. QUORUM, Constitution of.—Two-thirds of the members of either house shall be a quorum.—PROPOSED VA. CONSTITUTION. FORD ED., ii, 17. (June 1776.)

**7136. —— ——. Two-thirds of the members of the General Court, High Court of Chancery, or Court of Appeals, shall be a quorum * * *.—PROPOSED VA. CONSTITUTION. FORD ED., ii, 24. (June 1776.)

7137. —— ——. A majority of either house shall be a quorum, * * * but any smaller proportion which from time to time shall be thought expedient by the respective houses, shall be sufficient to call for, and to punish, their non-attending members, and to adjourn themselves for any time not exceeding one week.—PROPOSED CONSTITUTION FOR VIRGINIA. viii, 444. FORD ED., iii, 324. (1783.)

7138. QUORUM, Size of.—The Assembly exercises a power of determining the quorum of their own body which may legislate for us.* After the establishment of the new form they adhered to the *Lex majoris partis*, founded in common law as well as common right (Bro. abr. Corporations, 31, 34. Hakewell, 93.) It is the natural law of every assembly of men, whose numbers are not fixed by any other law. (Puff. Off. hom. 1, 2, c. 6, § 12.) They continued for some time to require the presence of a majority of their whole number to pass an act. But the British parliament fixes its own quorum; our former assemblies fixed their own quorum; and one precedent in favor of power is stronger than an hundred against it. The House of Delegates, therefore, have lately voted (June 4, 1781), that, during the present dangerous invasion, forty members shall be a house to proceed to business. They have been moved to this by the fear of not being able to collect a house. But this danger could not authorize them to call that a house which was none; and if they may fix it at one number, they may at another, till it loses its fundamental character of being a representative body. As this vote expires with the present invasion, it is probable the former rule will be permitted to revive; because at present no ill is meant. The power, however, of fixing their own quorum has been avowed, and a precedent set. From forty it may be reduced to four, and from four to one; from a house to a committee, from a committee to a chairman or speaker, and thus an oligarchy or monarchy be substituted under forms supposed to be regular. " *Omnia mala exempla ex bonis orta sunt; sed ubi imperium ad ignaros aut minus bonos pervenit, novum illud exemplum ab dignis et idoneis ad indignos et non indoneos fertur*". When, therefore, it is considered that there is no legal obstacle to the assumption by the Assembly of all the powers legislative, executive and judiciary, and that these may come to the hands of the smallest rag of delegation, surely the people will say, and their representatives, while yet they have honest representatives, will advise them to say, that they will not acknowledge as laws any acts not considered and assented to by the major part of their delegates.—NOTES ON VIRGINIA. viii, 367. FORD ED., iii, 229. (1782.)

7139. RACE, Improvement of human. —The passage you quote from Theognis, I think has an ethical rather than a political object. The whole piece is a moral *exhortation*, * * * and this passage particularly seems to be a reproof to man, who, while with his domestic animals he is curious to improve the race, by employing always the finest male, pays no attention to the improvement of his own race, but intermarries with the vicious, the ugly or the old, for considerations of wealth or ambition. It is in conformity with the principle adopted afterwards by the Pythagoreans, and expressed by Ocellus in another form * * * which, as literally as intelligibility will admit, may be thus translated, " concerning the interprocreation of men, how, and of whom it sha'l be, in a perfect manner, and according to the laws of modesty and sanctity, conjointly, this is what I think right. First, to lay it down that we do not commix for the sake of pleasure, but of the procreation of children. For the powers, the organs and desires for coition have not been given by God to man for the sake of pleasure, but for the procreation of the race. For as it were incongruous, for a mortal born to partake of divine life, the immortality of the race being

* Jefferson characterized this power as one of the defects of the first Virginia constitution.—EDITOR.

taken away, God fulfilled the purpose by making the generations uninterrupted and continuous. This, therefore, we are especially to lay down as a principle, that coition is not for the sake of p.easure ". But nature, not trusting to this moral and abstract motive, seems to have provided more securely for the perpetuation of the species, by making it the effect of the *oestrum* implanted in the constitution of both sexes. And not only has the commerce of love been indulged on this unhallowed impulse, but made subservient also to wealth and ambition by marriage, without regard to the beauty, the healthiness, the understanding, or virtue of the subject from which we are to breed. The selecting the best male for a harem of well chosen females also, which Theognis seems to recommend from the example of our sheep and asses, would doubtless improve the human. as it does the brute animal, and produce a race of veritable αριϛτοι. For experience proves that the moral and physical qualities of man, whether good or evil, are transmissible in a certain degree from father to son. But I suspect that the equal rights of man will rise up against this privileged Solomon and his harem, and oblige us to continue acquiescence under the "Αμαμρωϛις γενεος αϛτων" which Theognis complains of. and to content ourselves with the accidental aristoi produced by the fortuitous concourse of breeders.—To JOHN ADAMS. vi, 222. FORD ED., ix, 424. (M., 1813.)

7140. RACES, Mingling of.—In time, you [Indians] will be as we are; you will become one people with us. Your blood will mix with ours: and will spread with ours, over this great Island.—INDIAN ADDRESS. viii, 234. (1809.)

7141. RAINBOWS, Formation of.—An Abbé here [Paris] has shaken, if not destroyed, the theory of Dominis, Descartes and Newton, for explaining the phenomenon of the rainbow. According to that theory, you know, a cone of rays issuing from the sun, and falling on a cloud in the opposite part of the heavens, is reflected back in the form of a smaller cone. the apex of which is the eye of the observer; so that the eye of the observer must be in the axis of both cones, and equally distant from every part of the bow. But he observes that he has repeatedly seen bows, the one end of which has been very near to him, and the other at a very great distance. I have often seen the same thing myself. I recollect well to have seen the end of a rainbow between myself and a house, or between myself and a bank, not twenty yards distant; and this repeatedly. But I never saw, what he says he has seen, different rainbows at the same time intersecting each other. I never saw coexistent bows, which were not concentric also. Again, according to the theory, if the sun is in the horizon, the horizon intercepts the lower half of the bow; if above the horizon, that intercepts more than half, in proportion. So that, generally, the bow is less than a semi-circle, and never more. He says he has seen it more than a semi-circle. I have often seen the leg of the bow below my level. My situation at Monticello admits this, because there is a mountain there in the opposite direction of the afternoon's sun, the valley between which and Monticello, is five hundred feet deep. I have seen a leg of a rainbow plunge down on the river running through the valley. But I do not recollect to have remarked at any time that the bow was more than half a circle. It appears to me that these facts demolish the Newtonian hypothesis, but they do not support that in its

stead by the Abbé. He supposes a cloud between the sun and the observer, and that through some opening in that cloud, the rays pass, and form an iris on the opposite part of the heavens, just as a ray passing through a hole in the shutter of a darkened room, and falling on a prism there, forms the prismatic colors on the opposite wall. According to this, we might see bows of more than the half circle, as often as of less. A thousand other objections occur to this hypothesis. * * * The result is that we were wiser than we were, by having an error the less in our catalogue.—To REV. JAMES MADISON. ii, 430. (P., 1788.)

7142. RAINBOWS, Lunar.—I have twice seen bows formed by the moon. They were of the color of the common circle round the moon, and were very near, being within a few paces of me in both instances.—To WILLIAM DUNBAR. iv, 348. FORD ED., vii, 482. (W., Jan. 1801.)

7143. RAINBOWS AT MONTICELLO. —I remark a rainbow of a great portion of the circle observed by you when on the line of demarcation. I live in a situation which has given me an opportunity of seeing more than the semicircle often. I am on a hill five hundred feet perpendicularly high. On the east side it breaks down abruptly to the base, where a river passes through. A rainbow, therefore, about sunset, plunges one of its legs down to the river, five hundred feet below the level of the eye on the top of the hill.—To WILLIAM DUNBAR. iv, 348. FORD ED., vii, 482. (W., Jan. 1801.)

7144. RANDOLPH (Edmund), Indecisiveness.—Everything [in the cabinet] hangs upon the opinion of a single person [Edmund Randolph] and that the most indecisive one I ever had to do business with. He will always contrive to agree in principle with one but in conclusion with the other.—To JAMES MADISON. iii, 556. (1793.)

7145. RANDOLPH (Edmund), Principles and practice.—Though he mistakes his own political character in the aggregate, yet he gives it * * * in the detail [in his pamphlet entitled " Vindication "]. Thus, he supposes himself a man of no party (page 97); that his opinions not containing any systematic adherence to party, fall sometimes on one side and sometimes on the other (page 58). Yet he gives you these facts, which show that they fall generally on both sides, and are .complete inconsistencies. 1. He never gave an opinion in the cabinet against the rights of the people (page 97); yet he advised the denunciation of the popular [Democratic] societies (page 67). 2. He would not neglect the overtures of a commercial treaty with France (page 70); yet he always opposed it while Attorney General. and never seems to have proposed it while Secretary of State. 3. He concurs in resorting to the militia to quell the pretended insurrections in the west (page 81), and proposes an augmentation from twelve thousand five hundred to fifteen thousand, to march against men at their ploughs (page 80); yet on the 5th of August he is against their marching (pages 83, 101), and on the 25th of August he is for it (page 84). 4. He concurs in the measure of a mission extraordinary to London (as inferred from page 58), but objects to the men, to wit, Hamilton and Jay (page 58). 5. He was against granting commercial powers to Mr. Jay (page 58): yet he besieged the doors of the Senate to procure their advice to ratify. 6. He advises the President to a ratification on the merits of the [Jay] treaty (page 97), but to a suspension till the provision order is repealed (page 98). The fact is, that he has generally given his principles to the one party, and his practice to the other, the oyster to one, the shell to the other. Unfortunately, the shell was generally the lot of his friends, the French and republicans, and the oyster of their antagonists. Had he been firm to the principles he professes in the year 1793, the President would have been kept from an habitual concert with the British and anti-republican party. But at that time I do not know which Randolph feared most, a British fleet, or French disorganizers. Whether his conduct is to be ascribed to a superior view of things, an adherence to right without regard to party, as he pretends, or to an anxiety to trim between both, those who know his character and capacity will decide.—To WILLIAM B. GILES. iv, 125. FORD ED., vii, 40. (M., Dec. 1795.)

7146. —— ——. [Edmund Randolph's] narrative [in his pamphlet] is so straight and plain, that even those who did not know him will acquit him of the charge of bribery. Those who knew him had done it from the first.—To WILLIAM B. GILES. iv, 125. FORD ED., vii, 41. (M., Dec. 1795.)

7147. RANDOLPH (Edmund), Resignation.—The resignation, or rather the removal, of Randolph, you will have learned. His vindication bears hard on the Executive in the opinions of this quarter, and though it clears him in their judgment of the charge of bribery, it does not give them high ideas of his wisdom or steadiness.—To JAMES MONROE. FORD ED., vii, 59. (M., 1796.)

7148. RANDOLPH (John), Attacks on Jefferson.—That Mr. Randolph has openly attacked the Administration is sufficiently known. We were not disposed to join in league with Britain, under any belief that she is fighting for the liberties of mankind, and to enter into war with Spain, and consequently France. The House of Representatives were in the same sentiment when they rejected Mr. Randolph's resolutions for raising a body of regular troops for the western service. We are for a peaceable accommodation with all those nations, if it can be effected honorably. This, perhaps, is not the only ground of his alienation; but which side retains its orthodoxy, the vote of eighty-seven to eleven republicans may satisfy you.—To WILLIAM DUANE. iv, 591. FORD ED., viii, 432. (W., March 1806.)

7149. RANDOLPH (John), Defection.—The separation of a member of great talents and weight from the present course of things, scattered dismay for a time among those who had been used to see him with them. A little time, however, enabled them to rally to their own principles, and to resume their track under the guidance of their own good sense. As long as we pursue without deviation the principles we have always professed, I have no fear of deviation from them in the main body of republicans.—To CAESAR A. RODNEY. FORD ED., viii, 436. (W., March 1806.)

7150. —— ——. Unexpected and strange phenomena in the early part of the session, produced a momentary dismay within the walls of the House of Representatives. However the body of republicans soon discovered their true situation, rallied to their own principles, and moved on towards their object in a solid phalanx; insomuch that the session did most of the good which was in their power, and did it well. Republicanism may perhaps have lost a few of its anomalous members, but the steadiness of its great mass has considerably increased on the whole my confidence in the solidity and permanence of our government.—To JOHN TYLER. FORD ED., viii, 442. (W., April 1806.)

7151. —— ——. His course [in opposition to the administration] has excited considerable alarm. Timid men consider it as a proof of the weakness of our government, and that it is to be rent into pieces by demagogues, and to end in anarchy. I survey the scene with a different eye and draw a different augury from it. In a House of Representatives of a great mass of good sense, Mr. Randolph's popular eloquence gave him such advantages as to place him unrivalled as a leader of the House; and although not conciliatory to those whom he led, principles of duty and patriotism induced many of them to swallow humiliations he subjected them to, and to vote as was right, as long as he kept the path of right himself. The sudden defection of such a man could not but produce a momentary astonishment, and even dismay; but for a moment only. The good sense of the House rallied around its principles, and without any leader pursued steadily the business of the session, did it well, and by a strength of vote which has never before been seen. Upon all trying questions, exclusive of the federalists, the minority of republicans voting with him has been from four to six or eight, against from ninety to one hundred; and although he treats the federalists with ineffable contempt, yet, having declared eternal opposition to this administration, and consequently associated with them, in his votes, he will * * * end with them. The augury I draw from this is, that there is a steady, good sense in the Legislature, and in the body of the nation, joined with good intentions, which will lead them to discern and to pursue the public good under all circumstances which can arise, and that no *ignis fatuus* will be able to lead them long astray.—To JAMES MONROE. v, 9. FORD ED., viii, 447. (W., May 1806.)

7152. RANDOLPH (John), Florida purchase.—He speaks of secret communications between the Executive and members [of Congress], of backstairs' influence, &c. But he never spoke of this while he and Mr. Nicholson enjoyed it almost solely. But when he differed from the Executive in a leading measure, and the Executive, not submitting to him, expressed their sentiments to others, the very sentiments (to wit, the purchase of Florida) which he acknowledges they expressed to him, then he roars out upon the backstairs' influence.—To W. A. BURWELL. v, 21. FORD ED., viii, 470. (M., Sep. 1806.) See CONGRESS, LEADERSHIP.

7153. RANDOLPH (Peyton), Estimate of.—He was indeed a most excellent man; and none was ever more beloved and respected by his friends. Somewhat cold and coy towards strangers, but of the sweetest affability when ripened into acquaintance. Of Attic pleasantry in conversation, always good humored and conciliatory. With a sound and logical head, he was well read in the law; and his opinions, when consulted, were highly regarded, presenting always a learned and sound view of the subject, but generally, too, a listlessness to go into its thorough development; for being heavy and inert in body, he was rather too indolent and careless for business, which occasioned him to get a smaller proportion of it at the bar than his abilities would otherwise have commanded. Indeed, after his appointment as Attorney-General [of the King], he did not seem to court, nor scarcely to welcome business. In that office, he considered himself equally charged with the rights of the Colony as with those of the crown; and in criminal prosecutions, exaggerating nothing, he aimed at a candid and just state of the transaction, believing it more a duty to save an innocent than to convict a guilty man. Although not eloquent, his matter was so substantial that no man commanded more attention, which, joined with a sense of his great worth, gave him a weight in the House of Burgesses which few ever attained.—To JOSEPH DELAPLAINE. FORD ED., x, 59. (M., 1816.)

7154. RANDOLPH (Thomas Mann), Independence.—I am aware that in parts of the Union, and even with persons to whom Mr. Eppes and Mr. [T. M.] Randolph are unknown, and myself little known, it will be presumed, from their connection,* that what comes from them comes from me. No men on earth are more independent in their sentiments than they are, nor any one less disposed than I am to influence the opinions of others. We rarely speak of politics, or of the proceedings of the House, but merely historically, and I carefully avoid expressing an opinion on them in their presence, that we may all be at our ease. With other members [of Congress], I have believed that more unreserved communications would be advantageous to the public.—To JOHN RANDOLPH. D. L. J., 293. (W., Dec. 1803.)

7155. RANDOLPH (Thomas Mann), Tribute to.—A gentleman of genius, science, and honorable mind.† He filled a dignified station in the General Government, and the most dignified in his own State.—AUTOBIOGRAPHY. i, 108. FORD ED., i, 150. (1821.)

— RATIO OF APPORTIONMENT.—
See APPORTIONMENT.

7156. READING, Passion for.—My repugnance to the writing table becomes daily and hourly more deadly and insurmountable. In place of this has come on a canine appetite for reading. And I indulge in it, because I see in it a relief against the *tædium senectutis;* a lamp to lighten my path through the dreary wilderness of time before me, whose bourne I see not. Losing daily all interest in the things around us, something else is necessary to fill the void. With me it is reading, which occupies the mind without the labor of producing ideas from my own stock.—To JOHN ADAMS. vii, 104. FORD ED., x, 108. (M., 1818.)

7157. REASON, Action and.—Every one must act according to the dictates of his own reason.—To REV. SAMUEL MILLER. v, 237. FORD ED., ix, 175. (W., 1808.)

7158. REASON, Diverting.—Is reason to be forever amused with the crochets of physical sciences, in which she is indulged merely to divert her from solid speculations on the rights of man, and wrongs of his oppressors? It is impossible. The day of deliverance will come, although I shall not live to see it.—To M. PAGANEL. v, 582. (M., 1811.)

7159. REASON, Fallible.—I have learned to be less confident in the conclusions of human reason, and give more credit to the

* Sons-in-law of Jefferson.—EDITOR.
† He married Jefferson's eldest daughter.—EDITOR.

honesty of contrary opinions.—To EDWARD LIVINGSTON. vii, 342. FORD ED., x, 300. (M., 1824.)

7160. REASON, Government and.—I hope that we have not labored in vain and that our experiment will still prove that men can be governed by reason.—To GEORGE MASON. iii, 209. FORD ED., v, 275. (Pa., 1791.)

7161. REASON, Oracle.—Every man's own reason must be his oracle.—To DR. BENJAMIN RUSH. vi, 106. (M., 1813.)

7162. REASON, Power of.—Truth and reason are eternal. They have prevailed. And they will eternally prevail, however, in times and places they may be overborne for a while by violence, military, civil, or ecclesiastical.—To REV. MR. KNOX. v, 503. (M., 1810.)

7163. REASON, Seeking.—The public say from all quarters that they wish to hear *reason* and not *disgusting blackguardism.*—To JAMES MADISON. iv, 281. FORD ED., vii, 344. (Pa., 1799.)

7164. REASON, Surrender of.—Man once surrendering his reason, has no remaining guard against absurdities the most monstrous, and like a ship without rudder, is the sport of every wind.—To JAMES SMITH. vii, 270. (M., 1822.)

7165. REASON, Umpirage of.—We should be most unwise, indeed, were we to cast away the singular blessings of the position in which nature has placed us, the opportunity she has endowed us with * * * of cultivating general friendship, and of bringing collisions of interest to the umpirage of reason rather than of force.—THIRD ANNUAL MESSAGE. viii, 29. FORD ED., viii, 273. (1803.)

7166. ——. Every man's reason is his own rightful umpire. This principle, with that of acquiescence in the will of the majority, will preserve us free and prosperous as long as they are sacredly observed.—To JOHN F. WATSON. vi, 346. (M., 1814.)

7167. REASON vs. ERROR.—Reason and experiment have been indulged, and error has fled before them.—NOTES ON VIRGINIA. viii, 401. FORD ED., iii, 264. (1782.)

7168. ——. Reason and free inquiry are the only effectual agents against error.—NOTES ON VIRGINIA. viii, 400. FORD ED., iii, 263. (1782.)

7169. REASON vs. FORCE.—A government of reason is better than one of force.—To RICHARD RUSH. vii, 183. (M., 1820.)

7170. REBELLION, Bacon's.—I return you the manuscript history of Bacon's rebellion. * * * It is really a valuable morsel in the history of Virginia. That transaction is the more marked, as it was the only rebellion or insurrection * * * in the colony before the American Revolution.—To RUFUS KING. iv, 528. (W., 1804.)

7171. REBELLION, Freedom from.—We have had thirteen States independent eleven years. There has been one rebellion. That comes to one rebellion in a century and a half for each State. What country before ever existed a century and a half without a rebellion?—To W. S. Smith. ii, 318. Ford ed., iv, 467. (P., 1787.) See Government.

7172. REBELLION, Necessary.—I hold it that a little rebellion, now and then, is a good thing, and as necessary in the political world as storms are in the physical.—To James Madison. ii, 105. Ford ed., iv, 362. (P., 1787.)

7173. —— ——. A little rebellion now and then * * * is a medicine necessary for the sound health of government.—To James Madison. ii, 105. Ford ed., iv, 363. (P., 1787.)

— **REBELLION, Shays's.**—See Shays's Rebellion.

7174. REBELLION, Spirit of.—The spirit of resistance to government is so valuable on certain occasions, that I wish it to be always kept alive. It will often be exercised when wrong, but better so than not to be exercised at all.—To Mrs. John Adams. Ford ed., iv, 370. (P., 1787.)

7175. REBELLION, Remedy for.—What country can preserve its liberties if its rulers are not warned, from time to time, that the people preserve the spirit of resistance? Let them take arms. The remedy is to set them right as to facts, pardon and pacify them.—To W. S. Smith. ii, 318. Ford ed., iv, 467. (P., 1787.) See Publicity.

7176. REBELLION, Unsuccessful.—Unsuccessful rebellions generally establish the encroachments on the rights of the people which have produced them. An observation of this truth should render honest republican governors so mild in their punishment of rebellions, as not to discourage them too much.—To James Madison. ii, 105. Ford ed., iv, 362. (P., 1787.)

7177. REBELLION, Useful.—I like a little rebellion now and then. It is like a storm in the atmosphere.—To Mrs. John Adams. Ford ed., iv, 370. (P., 1787.)

— **RECEPTIONS, Presidential.**—See Ceremony, Etiquette, Formalities and Levees.

7178. RECIPROCITY, British.—It is with satisfaction I lay before you an act of the British Parliament anticipating this subject so far as to authorize a mutual abolition of the duties and countervailing duties permitted under the treaty of 1794. It shows on their part a spirit of justice and friendly accommodation which it is our duty and our interest to cultivate with all nations. Whether this would produce a due equality in the navigation between the two countries, is a subject for your consideration.—Second Annual Message. viii, 16. Ford ed., viii, 182. (Dec. 1802.)

7179. RECIPROCITY, Commerce and.—Free commerce and navigation are not to be given in exchange for restrictions and vexations; nor are they likely to produce any relaxation of them.—Foreign Commerce Report. vii, 647. Ford ed., vi. 480. (1793.)

7180. RECIPROCITY, French.—I have been laboring with the ministry to get the trade between France and the United States put on a better footing, by admitting a free importation and sale of our produce, assuring them that we should take their manufactures at whatever extent they would enable us to pay for them.—To Mr. Otto. i, 558. (P., 1786.)

7181. RECIPROCITY, Justice and.—On the restoration of peace in Europe, that portion of the general carrying trade which had fallen to our share during the war, was abridged by the returning competition of the belligerent powers. This was to be expected, and was just. But in addition we find in some parts of Europe monopolizing discriminations, which, in the form of duties, tend effectually to prohibit the carrying thither our own produce in our own vessels. From existing amities, and a spirit of justice, it is hoped that friendly discussion will produce a fair and adequate reciprocity. But should false calculations of interest defeat our hope, it rests with the Legislature to decide whether they will not meet inequalities abroad with countervailing inequalities at home. or provide for the evil in any other way.—Second Annual Message. viii, 16. Ford ed., viii, 182. (Dec. 1802.)

7182. RECIPROCITY, Modification of.—Where the circumstances of either party render it expedient to levy a revenue, by way of impost, on commerce, its freedom might be modified, in that particular. by mutual and equivalent measures, preserving it entire in all others.—Foreign Commerce Report. vii, 646. Ford ed., vi, 479. (Dec. 1793.)

— **RECORDS, Preservation of.**—See History, Records of.

7183. RECTITUDE, Contentment and.—Crooked schemes will end by overwhelming their authors and coadjutors in disgrace. and he alone who walks strict and upright, and who, in matters of opinion, will be contented that others should be as free as himself, and acquiesce when his opinion is fairly overruled, will attain his object in the end.—To Gideon Granger. iv, 543. Ford ed., viii, 300. (M., 1804.)

7184. RECTITUDE, Fame and.—Give up money, give up fame, give up science, give the earth itself and all it contains, rather than do an immoral act. And never suppose, that in any possible situation, or under any circumstances, it is best for you to do a dishonorable thing, however slightly so it may appear to you.* —To Peter Carr. i, 396. (P., 1785.)

— **REDEMPTIONERS.**—See Population.

7185. REFORM, Adequate.—The hole and the patch should be commensurate.—To James Madison. ii, 152. Ford ed., iv, 390. (P., 1787.)

7186. REFORM, Congress and.—The representatives of the people in Congress are alone competent to judge of the general disposition of the people and to what precise point of reformation they are ready to go.— To Mr. Rutherford. iii, 499. (Pa., 1792.)

* Peter Carr was the young nephew of Jefferson.— Editor.

7187. REFORM, Constitutional.—Happily for us that when we find our constitutions defective and insufficient to secure the happiness of our people, we can assemble with all the coolness of philosophers, and set them to rights, while every other nation on earth must have recourse to arms to amend. or to restore their constitutions.—To M. DUMAS. ii, 264. (P., 1787.)

7188. REFORM, In France.—Surely under such a mass of misrule and oppression [as existed in France in 1788] a people might justly press for a thorough reformation, and might even dismount their rough-shod riders and leave them to walk on their own legs.—AUTOBIOGRAPHY. i, 86. FORD ED., i, 119. (1821.)

7189. REFORM, Generations and.—The idea that institutions established for the use of the nation cannot be touched nor modified, even to make them answer their end. because of rights gratuitously supposed in those employed to manage them in trust for the public. may perhaps be a salutary provision against the abuses of a monarch. but is most absurd against the nation itself. Yet our lawyers and priests generally inculcate this doctrine, and suppose that preceding generations held the earth more freely than we do; had a right to impose laws on us. unalterable by ourselves, and that we, in like manner. can make laws and impose burthens on future generations, which they will have no right to alter; in fine, that the earth belongs to the dead and not to the living.—To GOVERNOR PLUMER. vii, 19. (M., 1816.) See GENERATIONS.

7190. REFORM, Government and.—Our citizens may be deceived for awhile, and have been deceived; but as long as the presses can be protected, we may trust to them for light; still more perhaps to the taxgatherers; for it is not worth the while of our anti-republicans to risk themselves on any change of government, but a very *expensive* one. Reduce every department to economy, and there will be no temptation to them to betray their constituents.—To ARCHIBALD STUART. FORD ED., vii, 378. (M., 1799.)

7191. REFORM, Gradual.—A forty years' experience of popular assemblies has taught me, that you must give them time for every step you take. If too hard pushed, they balk, and the machine retrogrades.—To JOEL BARLOW. v, 217. FORD ED., ix, 169. (W., 1807.)

7192. —— ——. Truth advances, and error recedes step by step only; and to do our fellow-men the most good in our power, we must lead where we can. follow where we cannot, and still go with them. watching always the favorable moment for helping them to another step.—To THOMAS COOPER. vi, 390. (M., 1814.)

7193. REFORM, Moderation in.—Things even salutary should not be crammed down the throats of dissenting brethren, es-

pecially when they may be put into a form to be willingly swallowed.*—To EDWARD LIVINGSTON. vii, 343. FORD ED., x, 301. (M., 1824.)

7194. REFORM, Necessity for.—I think moderate imperfections [in constitutions and laws] had better be borne with; because, when once known, we accommodate ourselves to them, and find practical means of correcting their ill effects. But I know also, that laws and institutions must go hand in hand with the progress of the human mind. As that becomes more developed, more enlightened, as new discoveries are made, new truths disclosed, and manners and opinions change with the change of circumstances, institutions must advance also, and keep pace with the times.—To SAMUEL KERCHIVAL. vii, 15. FORD ED., x, 42. (M., 1816.)

7195. REFORM, Peaceable.—Go on doing with your pen what in other times was done with the sword: show that reformation is more practicable by operation on the mind than on the body of man.—To THOMAS PAINE. FORD ED., vi, 88. (Pa., 1792.)

7196. —— ——. All [reforms] can be * * * [achieved] peaceably, by the people confining their choice of Representatives and Senators to persons attached to republican government and the principles of 1776, not office-hunters. but farmers, whose interests are entirely agricultural. Such men are the true representatives of the great American interest, and are alone to be relied on for expressing the proper American sentiments.—To ARTHUR CAMPBELL. iv, 198. FORD ED., vii, 170. (M., 1797.)

7197. REFORM, People and.—Whenever things get so far wrong as to attract their notice, the people, if well informed, may be relied on to set them to rights.—To DR. PRICE. ii, 553. (P., 1789.)

7198. —— ——. [Reformation] must be brought about by the people, using their elective rights with prudence and self-possession. and not suffering themselves to be duped by treacherous emissaries.—To ARTHUR CAMPBELL. iv, 198. FORD ED., vii, 170. (M., 1797.)

7199. REFORM, Persistent.—No good measure was ever proposed which, if duly pursued, failed to prevail in the end.—To EDWARD COLES. FORD ED., ix, 479. (M., 1814.)

7200. —— ——. In endeavors to improve our situation, we should never despair. —To JOHN QUINCY ADAMS. vii, 89. (M., 1817.)

7201. REFORM, Public money and.—I am sensible how far I should fall short of effecting all the reformation which reason would

* From the time when Jefferson began his great reforms in the Virginia House of Burgesses, the general tendency and large lines of his purposes and policy held with much steadiness in the noble direction of a perfect humanitarianism. To this day [1886] the multitude cherish and revere his memory, and in so doing pay a just debt of gratitude to a friend who not only served them, as many have done, but who honored and respected them, as very few have done.—MORSE'S *Life of Jefferson.*

suggest, and experience approve, were I free to
do whatever I thought best; but when we
reflect how difficult it is to move or inflect the
great machine of society, how impossible to
advance the notions of a whole people suddenly to ideal right, we see the wisdom of
Solon's remark, that no more good must be
attempted than the nation can bear, and that
all will be chiefly to reform the waste of public money, and thus drive away the vultures
who prey upon it and improve some little
upon old routines. Some new fences for securing constitutional rights may, with the aid
of a good Legislature, perhaps be attainable.
—To Dr. Walter Jones. iv, 392. (W.,
March 1801.)

7202. REFORM, Quixotic.—Don Quixote
undertook to redress the bodily wrongs of the
world, but the redressment of mental vagaries
would be an enterprise more than Quixotic.—
To Dr. Waterhouse. vii, 257. Ford ed., x,
220. (M., 1822.)

7203. REFORM, Retrenchment and.—
Levees are done away. The first communication to the next Congress will be, like all
subsequent ones, by message, to which no answer will be expected. The diplomatic establishment in Europe will be reduced to three
ministers. The compensations to collectors
depend on you [Congress], and not on me.
The army is undergoing a chaste reformation.
The navy will be reduced to the legal establishment by the last of this month. Agencies
in every department will be revised. We
shall push you to the uttermost in economi-
zing. A very early recommendation * * *
[was] to the Postmaster General to employ
no printer, foreigner, or revolutionary tory in
any of his offices.—To Nathaniel Macon.
iv. 396. Ford ed., viii, 52. (W., May 1801.)

7204. ———. The multiplication of
public offices, increase of expense beyond income, growth and entailment of a public debt,
are indications soliciting the employment of
the pruning knife.—To Spencer Roane. vii,
212. Ford ed., x, 188. (M., 1821.)

7205. REFORM, Suffrage and.—The
revolution of 1800 was as real a revolution in
the principles of our government as that of
1776 was in its form; not effected, indeed, by
the sword, as that, but by the rational and
peaceable instrument of reform, the suffrage
of the people. To Spencer Roane. vii, 133.
Ford ed., x. 140. (P.F., 1819.)

7206. REFORM, Timely.—It can never
be too often repeated that the time for fixing
every essential right, on a legal basis, is while
our rulers are honest and ourselves united.—
Notes on Virginia. viii, 402. Ford ed., iii,
266. (1782.)

7207. REFORMERS, Dangerous.—The
office of reformer of the superstitions of a
nation is ever dangerous.—To William
Short. vii, 167. (M., 1820.)

7208. REGENCIES, Peaceable.—Regencies are generally peaceable.—To Dr. Currie. ii, 544. (P., 1788.)

**7209. RELATIONS, Appointment to
office.**—The public will never be made to
believe that an appointment of a relative is
made on the ground of merit alone, uninfluenced by family views; nor can they ever
see with approbation offices the disposal of
which they entrust to their Presidents for public purposes, divided out as family property.
Mr. Adams degraded himself infinitely by his
conduct on this subject, as General Washington had done himself the greatest honor.
With two such examples to proceed by, I
should be doubly inexcusable to err. It is
true that this places the relations of the President in a worse situation than if he were a
stranger, but the public good, which cannot
be affected if its confidence be lost, requires
this sacrifice. Perhaps, too, it is compensated
by sharing in the public esteem.—To George
Jefferson. iv, 388. Ford ed., viii, 38. (W.,
March 1801.)

7210. ———. I am much concerned to
learn that any disagreeable impression was made
on your mind, by the circumstances which are
the subject of your letter. Permit me first to
explain the principles which I had laid down
for my own observance. In a government like
ours, it is the duty of the Chief Magistrate, in
order to enable himself to do all the good which
his station requires, to endeavor, by all honorable means, to unite in himself the confidence
of the whole people. This alone, in any case
where the energy of the nation is required, can
produce a union of the powers of the whole,
and point them in a single direction, as if all
constituted but one body and one mind, and this
alone can render a weaker nation unconquerable
by a stronger one. Towards acquiring the confidence of the people, the very first measure is
to satisfy them of his disinterestedness, and that
he is directing their affairs with a single eye
to their good, and not to build up fortunes for
himself and family, and especially, that the officers appointed to transact their business, are
appointed because they are the fittest men, and
not because they are his relations. So prone
are they to suspicion, that where a President ap-
points a relation of his own, however worthy,
they will believe that favor and not merit, was
the motive. I, therefore, laid it down as a law
of conduct for myself, never to give an appointment to a relation. Had I felt any hesitation in
adopting this rule, examples were not wanting
to admonish me what to do and what to avoid.
Still, the expression of your willingness to act
in any office for which you were qualified, could
not be imputed to you as blame. It would not
readily occur that a person qualified for office
ought to be rejected merely because he was
related to the President, and the then more recent examples favored the other opinion. In
this light I considered the case as presenting
itself to your mind, and that the application
might be perfectly justifiable on your part,
while, for reasons occurring to none perhaps,
but the person in my situation, the public interest might render it unadvisable. Of this,
however, be assured that I considered the
proposition as innocent on your part, and that
it never lessened my esteem for you, or the interest I felt in your welfare.—To J. Garland
Jefferson. v, 497. Ford ed., ix, 270. (M., 1810.)

7211. ———. I have never enquired
what number of sons, relations and friends of
Senators, Representatives, printers, or other useful partisans Colonel Hamilton has provided for

among the hundred clerks of his department, the thousand excisemen, custom house officers, loan officers, &c., &c., &c., appointed by him, or at his nod, and spread over the Union; nor could I ever have imagined that the man who has the shuffling of millions backwards and forwards from paper into money and money into paper, from Europe to America, and America to Europe, the dealing out of Treasury-secrets among his friends in what time and measure he pleases, and who never slips an occasion of making friends with his means, that such an one, I say, would have brought forward a charge against me for having appointed the poet, Freneau, translating clerk to my office, with a salary of 250 dollars a year.—To President Washington. iii, 464. Ford ed., vi, 105. (M., 1792.)

7212. RELATIONS, Recommending.— Does Mr. Lee go back to Bordeaux? If he does, I have not a wish to the contrary. If he does not, permit me to place my friend and kinsman G. J. [George Jefferson] on the list of candidates. No appointment can fall on an honester man, and his talents though not of the first order, are fully adequate to the station. His judgment is very sound, and his prudence consummate.—To President Madison. Ford ed., ix, 284. (M., 1810.)

7213. RELIGION, Compulsion.—Compulsion in religion is distinguished peculiarly from compulsion in every other thing. I may grow rich by art I am compelled to follow; I may recover health by medicines I am compelled to take against my own judgment; but I cannot be saved by a worship I disbelieve and abhor.—Notes on Religion. Ford ed., ii, 102. (1776?)

7214. RELIGION, Differences.—If thinking men would have the courage to think for themselves, and to speak what they think, it would be found they do not differ in religious opinions as much as is supposed.— To John Adams. vi, 191. Ford ed., ix, 410. (M., 1813.)

7215. RELIGION, Discussions concerning.—I not only write nothing on religion, but rarely permit myself to speak on it, and never but in a reasonable society.—To Charles Clas. vi, 412. (M., 1815.)

7216. RELIGION, Essence of.—The life and essence of religion consist in the internal persuasion or belief of the mind.— Notes on Religion. Ford ed., ii, 101. (1776?)

7217. RELIGION, Faith and.—No man has power to let another prescribe his faith. Faith is not faith without believing.—Notes on Religion. Ford ed., ii, 101. (1776?)

7218. RELIGION, Federal government and.—In matters of religion, I have considered that its free exercise is placed by the Constitution independent of the powers of the General Government. I have, therefore, undertaken, on no occasion, to prescribe the religious exercises suited to it; but have left them, as the Constitution found them, under the direction and discipline of State or church authorities acknowledged by the several religious societies.—Second Inaugural Address. viii, 42. Ford ed., viii, 344. (1805.)

7219. ——— ———. I consider the government of the United States as interdicted by the Constitution from intermeddling with religious institutions, their doctrines, discipline, or exercises. This results not only from the provision that no law shall be made respecting the establishment or free exercise of religion, but from that also which reserves to the States the powers not delegated to the United States. Certainly, no power to prescribe any religious exercise, or to assume any authority in religious discipline, has been delegated to the General Government. It must then rest with the States, as far as it can be in any human authority.—To Rev. Samuel Miller. v, 236. Ford ed., ix, 174. (W., 1808.)

7220. ——— ———. I do not believe it is for the interest of religion to invite the civil magistrate to direct its exercises, its discipline, or its doctrines; nor of the religious societies, that the General Government should be invested with the power of effecting any uniformity of time or matter among them.—To Rev. Samuel Miller. v, 237. Ford ed., ix, 175. (W., 1808.)

7221. RELIGION, Freedom of.—All persons shall have full and free liberty of religious opinion.—Proposed Va. Constitution. Ford ed., ii, 27. (June 1776.)

7222. ——— ———. From the dissensions among Sects themselves arise, necessarily, a right of choosing and necessity of deliberating to which we will conform. But if we choose for ourselves, we must allow others to choose also. This establishes religious liberty. —Notes on Religion. Ford ed., ii, 98. (1776?)

7223. ——— ———. If I be marching on with my utmost vigor in that way which according to the sacred geography leads to Jerusalem straight, why am I beaten and ill used by others because my hair is not of the right cut; because I have not been dressed right; because I eat flesh on the road; because I avoid certain by-ways which seem to lead into briars; because among several paths I take that which seems shortest and cleanest; because I avoid travellers less grave and keep company with others who are more sour and austere; or because I follow a guide crowned with a mitre and clothed in white? Yet these are the frivolous things which keep Christians at war.—Notes on Religion. Ford ed., ii, 100. (1776?)

7224. ——— ———. We [the Assembly of Virginia] * * * declare that the rights hereby asserted [in the Statute of Religious Freedom] are of the natural rights of mankind, and that if any act shall be hereafter passed to repeal the present [act], or to narrow its operations, such act will be an infringement of natural right.—Statute of Religious Freedom. viii, 456. Ford ed., ii, 239. (1779.)

7225. ——— ———. I do not like [in the Federal Constitution] the omission of a bill of rights, providing clearly and without the aid of sophisms for freedom of religion.—To JAMES MADISON. ii, 329. FORD ED., iv, 476. (P., Dec. 1787.)

7226. —— ——. Almighty God hath created the mind free, and manifested His supreme will that free it shall remain by making it altogether insusceptible of restraint. * * * All attempts to influence it by temporal punishments or burthens, or by civil incapacitations, tend only to beget habits of hypocrisy and meanness, and are a departure from the plan of the Holy Author of our religion, who, being Lord both of body and mind, yet chose not to propagate it by coercions on either, as was in his Almighty power to do, but to exalt it by its influence on reason alone.—STATUTE OF RELIGIOUS FREEDOM. viii, 454. FORD ED., ii, 237. (1779.)

7227. —— ——. By a declaration of rights I mean one which shall stipulate freedom of religion.—To A. DONALD. ii, 355. (P., 1788.)

7228. —— ——. I sincerely rejoice at the acceptance of our new Constitution by nine States. It is a good canvas, on which some strokes only want retouching. What these are, I think are sufficiently manifested by the general voice from north to south, which calls for a bill of rights. It seems pretty generally understood that this should go to * * * religion. * * * The declaration, that religious faith shall be unpunished, does not give impunity to criminal acts, dictated by religious error.—To JAMES MADISON. ii, 445. FORD ED., v, 45. (P., July 1788.)

7229. —— ——. One of the amendments to the Constitution * * * expressly declares, that "Congress shall make no law respecting an establishment of religion, or prohibiting the free exercise thereof, or abridging the freedom of speech, or of the press"; thereby guarding in the same sentence, and under the same words, the freedom of religion, of speech and of the press; insomuch, that whatever violates either, throws down the sanctuary which covers the others.—KENTUCKY RESOLUTIONS. ix, 466. FORD ED., vii, 295. (1798.)

7230. —— ——. I am for freedom of religion, and against all manœuvres to bring about a legal ascendancy of one sect over another.—To ELBRIDGE GERRY. iv, 268. FORD ED., vii, 328. (Pa., 1799.)

7231. —— ——. Freedom of religion I deem [one of the] essential principles of our government and, consequently, [one] which ought to shape its administration.—FIRST INAUGURAL ADDRESS. viii, 4. FORD ED., viii, 5. (1801.)

7232. —— ——. Among the most inestimable of our blessings is that * * * of liberty to worship our Creator in the way we think most agreeable to His will; a liberty deemed in other countries incompatible with good government and yet proved by our experience to be its best support.—R. TO A. OF BAPTISTS. viii, 119. (1807.)

7233. —— ——. We have solved * * * the great and interesting question whether freedom of religion is compatible with order in government, and obedience to the laws. And we have experienced the quiet as well as the comfort which results from leaving every one to profess freely and openly those principles of religion which are the inductions of his own reason, and the serious convictions of his own inquiries.—R. TO A. VIRGINIA BAPTISTS. viii, 139. (1808.)

7234. —— ——. Having ever been an advocate for the freedom of religious opinion and exercise, from no person, certainly, was an abridgment of these sacred rights to be apprehended less than from myself.—R. TO A. PITTSBURG METHODISTS. viii, 142. (1808.)

7235. —— ——. The Constitution has not placed our religious rights under the power of any public functionary.—R. TO A. PITTSBURG METHODISTS. viii, 142. (1808.)

7236. —— ——. There are certain principles in which the constitutions of our several States all agree, and which all cherish as vitally essential to the protection of the life, liberty, property and safety of the citizen. [One is] Freedom of Religion. restricted only from *acts* of trespass on that of others.—To M. CORAY. vii, 323. (M., 1823.) See VIRGINIA STATUTE OF RELIGIOUS FREEDOM, in APPENDIX.

7237. RELIGION, Government and.— Whatsoever is lawful in the Commonwealth. or permitted to the subject in the ordinary way, cannot be forbidden to him for religious uses; and whatsoever is prejudicial to the Commonwealth in their ordinary uses and, therefore, prohibited by the laws. ought not to be permitted to churches in their sacred rites. For instance, it is unlawful in the ordinary course of things, or in a private house, to murder a child. It should not be permitted any sect then to sacrifice children: it is ordinarily lawful (or temporarily lawful) to kill calves or lambs. They may, therefore, be religiously sacrificed, but if the good of the State required a temporary suspension of killing lambs, as during a siege, sacrifices of them may then be rightfully suspended also. This is the true extent of toleration.—NOTES ON RELIGION. FORD ED., ii, 102. (1776?)

7238. RELIGION, Growth of.—To me no information could be more welcome than that the minutes of the several religious societies should prove, of late. larger additions than have been usual, to their several associations.—R. TO A. NEW LONDON METHODISTS. viii, 147. (1809.)

7239. RELIGION, Honesty of life and. —I must ever believe that religion substantially good which produces an honest life. —To MILES KING. vi, 388. (M., 1814.)

7240. RELIGION, Interference with.— No man complains of his neighbor for ill management of his affairs, for an error in sowing his land, or marrying his daughter, for consuming his substance in taverns, pulling down, building, &c. In all these he has his liberty: but if he do not frequent the church, or there conform to ceremonies, there is an immediate uproar. The care of every man's soul belongs to himself. But what if he neglect the care of it? Well, what if he neglect the care of his health or estate, which more nearly relate to the State? Will the magistrate make a law that he shall not be poor or sick? Laws provide against injury from others, but not from ourselves. God Himself will not save men against their wills.—NOTES ON RELIGION. FORD ED., ii. 99. (1776?)

7241. RELIGION, Intermeddling with. —With the religion of other countries my own forbids intermeddling.—To SAMUEL GREENHOW. vi, 308. (M., 1814.)

7242. RELIGION, And law.—I consider * * * religion a supplement to law in the government of men.—To MR. WOODWARD. vii, 339. (M., 1824.)

7243. RELIGION, Opinions respecting. —It is a matter of principle with me to avoid disturbing the tranquillity of others by the expression of any opinion on the innocent questions on which we schismatize.—To JAMES FISHBACK. v, 471. (M., 1809.)

7244. RELIGION, Personal.—Neither of us knows the religious opinions of the other; that is a matter between our Maker and ourselves.—To THOMAS LEIPER. v, 417. FORD ED., ix, 238. (W., 1809.)

7245. ———. I have considered religion as a matter between every man and his Maker, in which no other, and far less the public had a right to intermeddle.—To RICHARD RUSH. FORD ED., ix, 385. (M., 1813.)

7246. ———. Religion is a subject on which I have ever been most scrupulously reserved. I have considered it as a matter between every man and his Maker, in which no other, and far less the public had a right to intermeddle.—To RICHARD RUSH. FORD ED., ix, 385. (M., 1813.)

7247. ———. I inquire after no man's religion, and trouble none with mine; nor is it given us in this life to know whether yours or mine, our friends' or our foes', is exactly the right.—To MILES KING. vi, 388. (M., 1814.)

7248. ———. Our particular principles of religion are a subject of accountability to our God alone.—To MILES KING. vi, 388. (M., 1814.)

7249. ———. I have ever thought religion a concern purely between our God and our consciences, for which we were accountable to Him, and not to the priests. I never told my own religion, nor scrutinized that of another. I never attempted to make a convert nor wished to change another's creed. I have ever judged of the religion of others by their lives * * * for it is in our lives,

and not from our words, that our religion must be read.—To MRS. M. HARRISON SMITH. vii, 28. (M., 1816.)

7250. ———. I do not wish to trouble the world with my creed, nor to be troubled for them. These accounts are to be settled only with Him who made us; and to Him we leave it, with charity for all others, of whom, also, He is the only rightful and competent judge.—To TIMOTHY PICKERING. vii, 211. (M., 1821.)

7251. ———. I am of a sect by myself, as far as I know.—To EZRA STILES. vii, 127. (M., 1819.)

7252. ———. One of our fan-coloring biographers, who paints small men as very great, enquired of me lately, with real affection, too, whether he might consider as authentic, the change in my religion much spoken of in some circles. Now this supposed that they knew what had been my religion before, taking for it the word of their priests, whom I certainly never made the confidants of my creed. My answer was, " say nothing of my religion. It is known to my God and myself alone. Its evidence before the world is to be sought in my life; if that has been *honest and dutiful* to society, the religion which has regulated it cannot be a bad one ".—To JOHN ADAMS. vii, 55. FORD ED., x, 73. (M., 1817.)

7253. RELIGION, Political sermons.— On one question I differ. * * * the right of discussing public affairs in the pulpit. * * * The mass of human concerns, moral and physical, is so vast, the field of knowledge requisite for man to conduct them to the best advantage is so extensive, that no human being can acquire the whole himself, and much less in that degree necessary for the instruction of others. It has of necessity, then, been distributed into different departments, each of which singly, may give occupation enough to the whole time and attention of a single individual. Thus we have teachers of languages, teachers of mathematics, of natural philosophy, of chemistry, of medicine, of law, of history, of government, &c. Religion, too, is a separate department, and happens to be the only one deemed requisite for all men, however high or low. Collections of men associate under the name of congregations, and employ a religious teacher of the particular set of opinions of which they happen to be, and contribute to make up a stipend as a compensation for the trouble of delivering them, at such periods as they agree on, lessons in the religion they profess. If they want instruction in other sciences or arts, they apply to other instructors; and this is generally the business of early life. But, I suppose, there is not a single instance of a single congregation which has employed their preacher for the mixed purposes of lecturing them *from the pulpit* in chemistry in medicine, in law, in the science and principles of government, or in anything but religion exclusively. Whenever, therefore, preachers, instead of a lesson in religion, put them off with a discourse on the Copernican system, on chemical affinities, on the construction of government, or the characters or conduct of those administering it, it is a breach of contract, depriving their audience of the kind of service for which they are salaried, and giving them, instead of it, what they did not want, or, if wanted, would rather seek from better sources in that particular art or science. In choosing our pastor, we look to his religious qualifications, without enquiring into his physical or political dogmas, with which we mean to have nothing to do. I am aware that arguments may be found, which may twist a thread of politics into the cord of religious duties. So may they for every other branch of human art or science. Thus, for example, it is a religious duty to obey the laws of our country; the teacher of religion, therefore, must instruct us in those laws, that we may know how to obey them. It is a religious duty to assist our sick neighbors; the preacher must, therefore, teach us medicine, that we may do it understandingly. It is a religious duty to preserve our health; our religious teacher, then, must tell us what dishes are wholesome, and give us recipes in cookery, that we may learn how to prepare them. And so, ingenuity, by generalizing more and more, may amalgamate all the branches of science into every one of them, and the physician who is paid to visit the sick, may give a sermon instead of medicine; and the merchant to whom money is sent for a hat, may send a handkerchief instead of it. But notwithstanding this possible confusion of all sciences into one, common sense draws the lines between them sufficiently distinct for the general purposes of life, and no one is at a loss to understand that a recipe in medicine or cookery, or a demonstration in geometry, is not a lesson in religion. I do not deny that a congregation may if they please, agree with their preacher that he shall instruct them in medicine also, or law, or politics. Then, lectures in these, from the pulpit, become not only a matter of right, but of duty also. But this must be with the consent of every individual; because the association being voluntary, the majority has no right to apply the contributions of the minority to purposes unspecified in the agreement of the congregation.—To MR. WENDOVER. vi, 445. (M., 1815.)

7254. —— ——. I agree, too, that on all other occasions, the preacher has the right, equally with every other citizen, to express his sentiments, in speaking or writing, on the subjects of medicine, law, politics, &c., his leisure time being his own, and his congregation not obliged to listen to his conversation or to read his writings.—To MR. WENDOVER. vi, 446. (M., 1815.)

7255. RELIGION, Public office and.— The proscribing any citizen as unworthy the public confidence, by laying upon him an incapacity of being called to offices of trust or emolument, unless he profess or renounce this

or that religious opinion, * * * tends to corrupt the principles of that very religion it is meant to encourage, by bribing with a monopoly of worldly honors and emoluments, those who will externally profess and conform to it.—STATUTE OF RELIGIOUS FREEDOM. viii, 455. FORD ED., ii, 238. (1779.)

7256. RELIGION, Public opinion and. —We ought with one heart and one hand to hew down the daring and dangerous efforts of those who would seduce the public opinion to substitute itself into that tyranny over religious faith which the laws have so justly abdicated. For this reason, were my opinions up to the standard of those who arrogate the right of questioning them, I would not countenance that arrogance by descending to an explanation.—To EDWARD DOWSE. iv. 478. (W., 1803.)

7257. RELIGION, Reason and.— Dispute as long as we will on religious tenets, our reason at last must ultimately decide, as it is the only oracle which God has given us to determine between what really comes from Him and the phantasms of a disordered or deluded imagination. When He means to make a personal revelation, He carries conviction of its authenticity to the reason He has bestowed as the umpire of truth. You believe you have been favored with such a special communication. Your reason, not mine, is to judge of this; and if it shall be His pleasure to favor me with a like admonition, I shall obey it with the same fidelity with which I would obey His known will in all cases.—To MILES KING. vi, 387. (M., 1814.)

7258. —— ——. Hitherto I have been under the guidance of that portion of reason which God has thought proper to deal out to me. I have followed it faithfully in all important cases, to such a degree at least as leaves me without uneasiness; and if on minor occasions I have erred from its dictates, I have trust in Him who made us what we are, and I know it was not His plan to make us always unerring.—To MILES KING. vi, 388. (M., 1814.)

7259. RELIGION, Schismatics.— It was the misfortune of mankind that during the darker centuries the Christian priests, following their ambition and avarice, combining with the magistrate to divide the spoils of the people, could establish the notion that schismatics might be ousted of their possessions and destroyed. This notion we have not yet cleared ourselves from. In this case no wonder the oppressed should rebel, and they will continue to rebel, and raise disturbance, until their civil rights are fully restored to them, and all partial distinctions, exclusions and incapacitations are removed.—NOTES ON RELIGION. FORD ED., ii, 103. (1776?)

7260. RELIGION, Toleration.— How far does the duty of toleration extend? 1. No church is bound by the duty of toleration to retain within her bosom obstinate offenders against her laws. 2. We have no right to prejudice another in his *civil* enjoyments because he is of another church. If any man err from the right way, it is his own misfortune, no injury to thee; nor therefore art thou to punish him in the things of this life because thou supposeth he will be miserable in that which is to come—on the contrary, according to the spirit of the gospel, charity, bounty, liberality are due him.—NOTES ON RELIGION. FORD ED., ii, 99. (1776?) See PRESBYTERIAN SPIRIT.

7261. ―― ――. Why have Christians been distinguished above all people who have ever lived, for persecutions? Is it because it is the genius of their religion? No, its genius is the reverse. It is the refusing *toleration* to those of a different opinion which has produced all the bustles and wars on account of religion.—NOTES ON RELIGION. FORD ED., ii, 103. (1776?)

7262. ―― ――. Three of our papers have presented us the copy of an act of the Legislature of New York, which if it has really passed, will carry us back to the times of the darkest bigotry and barbarism, to find a parallel. Its purport is, that all those who shall *hereafter* join in communion with the religious sect of Shaking Quakers, shall be deemed civilly dead, their marriages dissolved, and all their children and property taken out of their hands. This act being published nakedly in the papers, without the usual signatures, or any history of the circumstances of its passage, I am, not without a hope it may have been a mere abortive attempt. It contrasts singularly with a cotemporary vote of the Pennsylvania Legislature, who, on a proposition to make the belief in God a necessary qualification for office, rejected it by a great majority, although assuredly there was not a single atheist in their body. And you may remember to have heard that when the act for Religious Freedom was before the Virginia Assembly, a motion to insert the name of Jesus Christ before the phrase, " the author of our holy religion ", which stood in the bill, was rejected, although that was the creed of a great majority of them.—To AL-BERT GALLATIN. vii, 79. FORD ED., x, 91. (M., 1817.)

7263. RELIGION, Virginia laws respecting.—The present [1782] state of our [Virginia] laws on the subject of religion is this. The convention of May, 1776, in their declaration of rights, declared it to be a truth, and a natural right, that the exercise of religion should be free; but when they proceeded to form on that declaration the ordinance of government, instead of taking up every principle declared in the bill of rights, and guarding it by legislative sanction, they passed over that which asserted our religious rights, leaving them as they found them. The same convention, however, when they met as a member of the General Assembly in October, 1776, repealed all *acts of Parliament* which had rendered criminal the maintaining any opinions in matters of religion, the forbearing to repair to church, and the exercising any mode of worship: and suspended the laws giving salaries to the clergy, which suspension was made perpetual in October, 1779. Statutory oppressions in religion being thus wiped away, we remain at present under those only imposed by the common law, or by our own acts of Assembly. At the common law, *heresy* was a capital offence, punishable by burning. Its definition was left to the ecclesiastical judges, before whom the conviction was, till the statute of the 1 El. c. 1. circumscribed it, by declaring, that nothing should be deemed heresy, but what had been so determined by authority of the canonical Scriptures, or by one of the four first general councils, having for the grounds of their declaration the express and plain words of the Scriptures. Heresy, thus circumscribed, being an offence against the common law, our act of Assembly of October, 1777. c. 17, gives cognizance of it to the General Court, by declaring that the jurisdiction of that Court shall be general in all matters at the common law. The execution is by the writ *De hæretico comburendo*. By our act of Assembly of 1705, c. 30, if a person brought up in the Christian religion denies the being of a God, or the Trinity, or asserts that there are more gods than one, or denies the Christian religion to be true, or the Scriptures to be of divine authority, he is punishable on the first offence by incapacity to hold any office or employment, ecclesiastical, civil, or military: on the second, by disability to sue, to take any gift or legacy, to be guardian, executor, or administrator, and by three years' imprisonment, without bail. A father's right to the custody of his own children being founded in law on his right of guardianship, this being taken away, they may, of course, be severed from him, and put by the authority of a court, into more orthodox hands. This is a summary view of that religious slavery under which a people have been willing to remain, who have lavished their lives and fortunes for the establishment of their civil freedom. The error seems not sufficiently eradicated, that the operations of the mind, as well as the acts of the body, are subject to the coercion of the laws. But our rulers can have no authority over such natural rights, only as we have submitted to them. The rights of conscience we never submitted, we could not submit. We are answerable for them to our God. The legitimate powers of government extend to such acts only as are injurious to others. * But it does me no injury for my neighbor to say there are twenty gods, or no god. It neither picks my pocket nor breaks my legs. If it be said, his testimony in a court cannot be relied on, reject it then, and be the stigma on him. Constraint may make him worse by making him a hypocrite, but it will never make him a truer man. It may fix him obstinately in his errors, but will not cure them.—NOTES ON VIRGINIA. viii, 398. FORD ED., iii, 262. (1782.)

7264. REPARATION, Demand for.—It will be very difficult to answer Mr. Erskine's demand respecting the water casks in the tone proper for such a demand. I have heard of one who, having broken his cane over the head of another, demanded payment for his cane. This demand might well enough have made part of an offer to pay the damages

* Jefferson makes the following note from "Tertullianus ad Scapulam, cap. ii."

" Tamen humani juris et naturalis potestatis est, unicuique quod putaverit, colere; *nec alii obest, aut prodest, alterius religio.* Sed nec religionis est cogere religionem, quæ sponte suscipi debeat, non vi."—EDITOR. See CHURCH and CHURCH AND STATE.

done to the Chesapeake, and to deliver up the authors of the murders committed on board her.—To JAMES MADISON. v, 169. FORD ED., ix, 127. (M., Aug. 1807.) See CHESAPEAKE.

7265. REPARATION, War and.—Congress could not declare war without a demand of satisfaction.—To GENERAL SMITH. v, 146. (W., July 1807.) See INDEMNIFICATION.

7266. REPOSE, Evils of.—Your love of repose will lead, in its progress, to a suspension of healthy exercise, a relaxation of mind, an indifference to everything around you, and finally to a debility of body, and hebetude of mind, the farthest of all things from the happiness which the well-regulated indulgences of Epicurus ensure.—To WILLIAM SHORT. vii, 140. FORD ED., x, 145. (M., 1819.)

7267. REPRESENTATION, Apportionment and.—No invasions of the Constitution are fundamentally so dangerous as the tricks played on their own numbers, apportionment, and other circumstances respecting themselves, and affecting their legal qualifications to legislate for the Union.—OPINION ON APPORTIONMENT BILL. vii, 601. FORD ED., v, 500. (1792.) See APPORTIONMENT.

7268. REPRESENTATION, Aristocracy and.—It will be forever seen that of bodies of men even elected by the people, there will always be a greater proportion aristocratic than among their constituents.—To BENJAMIN HAWKINS. iv, 466. FORD ED., viii, 212. (W., 1803.)

7269. REPRESENTATION, Broad.—I look for our safety to the broad representation of the people [in Congress]. It will be more difficult for corrupt views to lay hold of so large a mass.—To T. M. RANDOLPH. FORD ED., v, 455. (Pa., 1792.)

— REPRESENTATION, In Congress.— See CONGRESS.

7270. REPRESENTATION, Democratic.—The full experiment of a government democratical, but representative, was and is still reserved for us. The idea (taken, indeed, from the little specimen formerly existing in the English constitution, but now lost) has been carried by us, more or less, into all our legislative and executive departments; but it has not yet, by any of us, been pushed into all the ramifications of the system, so far as to leave no authority existing not responsible to the people; whose rights, however, to the exercise and fruits of their own industry, can never be protected against the selfishness of rulers not subject to their control at short periods. The introduction of this new principle of representative democracy has rendered useless almost everything written before on the structure of government; and, in a great measure, relieves our regret, if the political writings of Aristotle, or of any other ancient, have been lost, or are unfaithfully rendered or explained to us.—To ISAAC H. TIFFANY. vii, 32. (M., 1816.)

7271. —— ——. My most earnest wish is to see the republican element of popular

control pushed to the maximum of its practicable exercise. I shall then believe that our Government may be pure and perpetual.— To ISAAC H. TIFFANY. vii, 32. (M., 1816.)

7272. REPRESENTATION, Deprivation of.—George III. in execution of the trust confided to him, has, within his own day, loaded the inhabitants of Great Britain with debts equal to the whole fee-simple value of their island, and, under pretext of governing it, has alienated its whole soil to creditors who could lend money to be lavished on priests, pensions, plunder and perpetual war. This would not have been so, had the people retained organized means of acting on their agents. In this example, then, let us read a lesson for ourselves, and not "go and do likewise".—To SAMUEL KERCHIVAL. vii, 36. FORD ED., x, 45. (M., 1816.) See DEBT, OPPRESSIVE ENGLISH.

7273. REPRESENTATION, Equal.— The French flatter themselves they shall form a better constitution than the English one. I think it will be better in some points—worse in others. It will be better in the article of representation, which will be more equal.— To DR. PRICE. ii, 557. (P., Jan. 1789.)

7274. —— ——. At the birth of our republic I committed my opinion [an equal representation] to the world in the draft of a constitution annexed to the "Notes on Virginia", in which a provision was inserted for a representation permanently equal. The infancy of the subject at that moment, and our inexperience of self-government, occasioned gross departures in that draft from genuine republican canons. In truth, the abuses of monarchy had so much filled all the space of political contemplation, that we imagined everything republican which was not monarchy. We had not yet penetrated to the mother principle, that "governments are republican only in proportion as they embody the will of their people, and execute it" Hence, our first constitutions had really no leading principles in them. But experience and reflection have but more and more confirmed me in the particular importance of the equal representation then proposed.—To SAMUEL KERCHIVAL. vii, 9. FORD ED., x, 37. (M., 1816.)

7275. —— ——. A government is republican in proportion as every member composing it has his equal voice in the direction of its concerns (not indeed in person, which would be impracticable beyond the limits of a city, or small township, but) by representatives chosen by himself, and responsible to him at short periods.—To SAMUEL KERCHIVAL. vii, 10. FORD ED., x, 38. (M., 1816.)

7276. —— ——. Let every man who fights or pays, exercise his just and equal right in the election of [members of the Legislature]. —To SAMUEL KERCHIVAL. vii, 11. FORD ED., x, 39. (M., 1816.)

7277. REPRESENTATION, Freedom and.—To us is committed [by the Constitution] the important task of proving by example that a government, if organized in all its parts on the representative principle, unadulterated by the infusion of spurious elements, if founded, not in the fears and follies of man, but on his reason, on his sense of right, on the predominance of the social over his dissocial passions, may be so free as to restrain him in no moral right, and so firm as to protect him from every moral wrong.—Reply to Vermont Address. iv, 418. (W., 1801.)

7278. REPRESENTATION, Government by.—Modern times have * * * discovered the only device by which the [equal] rights [of man] can be secured, to wit: government by the people, acting not in person, but by representatives chosen by themselves, that is to say, by every man of ripe years and sane mind, who either contributes by his purse or person to the support of his country.—To M. Coray. vii, 319. (M., 1823.)

7279. REPRESENTATION, Government without.—Shall these governments be dissolved, their property annihilated, and their people reduced to a state of nature, at the imperious breath of a body of men whom they never saw, in whom they never confided, and over whom they have no powers of punishment or removal, let their crimes against the American public be ever so great?—Rights of British America. i, 131. Ford ed., i, 436. (1774.)

7280. ———. Can any one reason be assigned why one hundred and sixty thousand electors in the Island of Great Britain should give law to four millions in the States of America, every individual of whom is equal to every individual of them, in virtue, in understanding, and in bodily strength? Were this to be admitted, instead of being a free people, as we have hitherto supposed, and mean to continue ourselves, we should suddenly be found the slaves not of one but of one hundred and sixty thousand tyrants, distinguished, too, from all others by the singular circumstances, that they are removed from the reach of fear, the only restraining motive which may hold the hand of a tyrant.—Rights of British America. i, 131. Ford ed., i. 436. (1774.)

7281. REPRESENTATION, Human happiness and.—A representative government, responsible at short intervals of election, * * * produces the greatest sum of happiness to mankind.—R. to A. Vermont Legislature. viii, 121. (1807.)

7282. REPRESENTATION, Imperfect.—The small and imperfect mixture of representative government in England, impeded as it is by other branches, aristocratical and hereditary, shows yet the power of the representative principle towards improving the condition of man.—To M. Coray. vii, 319. (M., 1823.)

7283. REPRESENTATION, Principles of.—In the structure of our Legislatures, we think experience has proved the benefit of subjecting questions to two separate bodies of deliberants; but in constituting these, natural right has been mistaken, some making one of these bodies, and some both, the representatives of property instead of persons; whereas the double deliberation might be as well obtained without any violation of true principle, either by requiring a greater age in one of the bodies, or by electing a proper number of representatives of persons, dividing them by lot into two chambers, and renewing the division at frequent intervals, in order to break up all cabals.—To John Cartwright. vii, 357. (M., 1824.)

7284. REPRESENTATION, Qualified.—Were our State a pure democracy, in which all its inhabitants should meet together to transact all their business, there would yet be excluded from their deliberations: 1. Infants, until arrived at age of discretion. 2. Women, who, to prevent depravation of morals and ambiguity of issue, could not mix promiscuously in the public meetings of men. 3. Slaves, from whom the unfortunate state of things with us takes away the rights of will and of property. Those, then, who have no will could be permitted to exercise none in the popular assembly; and, of course, could delegate none to an agent in a representative assembly. The business, in the first case, would be done by qualified citizens only.—To Samuel Kerchival. vii, 36. Ford ed., x, 46. (M., 1816.)

7285. REPRESENTATION, Right of.—Does his Majesty seriously wish, and publish it to the world, that his subjects should give up the glorious right of representation, with all the benefits derived from that, and submit themselves the absolute slaves of his sovereign will?—Rights of British America. i, 136. Ford ed., i, 441. (1774.)

7286. ——— ———. He [George III.] has endeavored to pervert the exercise of the kingly office in Virginia into a detestable and insupportable tyranny * * * by refusing to pass certain laws unless the persons to be benefited by them would relinquish the inestimable right of representation in the Legislature.—Proposed Va. Constitution. Ford ed., ii, 10. (June 1776.)

7287. ——— ———. He has refused to pass * * * laws for the accommodation of large districts of people, unless those people would relinquish the right of representation in the legislature, a right inestimable to them, and formidable to tyrants only.—Declaration of Independence as Drawn by Jefferson.

7288. REPRESENTATION, For slaves.—I have been told, that on the question of equal representation, our fellow-citizens in some sections of the State [Virginia] claim peremptorily a right of representation for their slaves. Principle will, in this, as in most other cases, open the way for us to correct conclusion. * * * It is true, that in the general Constitution, our State is allowed a larger representation on account of its slaves. But every one knows, that that Consituion was a matter of compromise; a capitulation between conflicting interests and opinion. In truth, the condition of different descriptions of inhabitants in any country is a matter of municipal arrangement, of which no foreign country has a right to take notice. All its inhabitants are men as to them. Thus, in the New England States, none have the powers of citizens but those whom they call *freemen;* and none are *freemen* until admitted by a vote of the freemen of the town. Yet, in the General Government, these non-freemen are counted in their quantum of representation and of taxation. So, slaves with us have no powers as citizens; yet, in representation in the General Government, they count in the proportion of three to five; and so also in taxation. Whether this is equal, is not here the question. It is a capitulation of discordant sentiments and circumstances, and is obligatory on that ground. But this view shows there is no inconsistency in claiming representation for them for the other States, and refusing it within our own.—To SAMUEL KERCHIVAL. vii, 36. FORD ED., x, 45. (M., 1816.)

7289. REPRESENTATION, Taxation and.—Preserve inviolate the fundamental principle that the people are not to be taxed but by representatives chosen immediately by themselves.—To JAMES MADISON. ii, 328. FORD ED., iv, 475. (P., 1787.)

7290. REPRISAL, Act of war.—Remonstrance and refusal of satisfaction ought to precede reprisal, and when reprisal follows it is considered as an act of war, and never yet failed to produce it in the case of a nation able to make war.—OPINION ON THE "LITTLE SARAH". vii, 628. FORD ED., vi, 259. (1793.)

7291. REPRISAL, Congress and.—If the case were important enough to require reprisal, and ripe for that step, Congress must be called on to take it; the right of reprisal being expressly lodged with them by the Constitution, and not with the Executive.—OPINION ON THE "LITTLE SARAH". vii, 628. FORD ED., vi, 259. (1793.)

7292. REPRISAL, Retaliation by.—The determination to take all our vessels bound to any other than her ports, amounting to all the war she can make (for we fear no invasion), it would be folly in us to let that war be all on one side only, and to make no effort towards indemnification and retaliation by reprisal.—To CLEMENT CAINE. vi, 14. FORD ED., ix, 330. (M., Sep. 1811.)

7293. REPUBLIC, Definition of.—It must be acknowledged that the term *republic* is of very vague application in every language. Witness the self-styled republics of Holland, Switzerland, Genoa, Venice, Poland. Were I to assign to this term a precise and definite idea, I would say, purely and simply, it means a government by its citizens in mass, acting directly and personally, according to rules established by the majority; and that every other government is more or less republican, in proportion as it has in its compo-

sition more or less of this ingredient of the direct action of the citizens. Such a government is evidently restrained to very narrow limits of space and population. I doubt if it would be practicable beyond the extent of a New England township.—To JOHN TAYLOR. vi, 605. FORD ED., x, 28. (M., 1816.)

7294. —— ——. The first shade from this pure element, which, like that of pure vital air, cannot sustain life of itself, would be where the powers of the government, being divided, should be exercised each by representatives chosen either *pro hoc vice,* or for such short terms as should render secure the duty of expressing the will of their constituents. This I should consider as the nearest approach to a pure republic, which is practicable on a large scale of country or population. And we have examples of it in some of our State constitutions, which, if not poisoned by priestcraft, would prove its excellence over all mixtures with other elements; and, with only equal doses of poison, would still be the best.—To JOHN TAYLOR. vi, 605. FORD ED., x, 29. (M., 1816.)

7295. —— ——. Other shades of republicanism may be found in other forms of government, where the executive, legislative and judiciary functions, and the different branches of the latter, are chosen by the people more or less directly, for longer terms of years, or for life, or made hereditary; or where there are mixtures of authorities, some dependent on, and others independent of the people. The further the departure from direct and constant control by the citizens, the less has the government the ingredient of republicanism; evidently none where the authorities are hereditary, as in France, Venice, &c., or self-chosen, as in Holland; and little, where for life, in proportion as the life continues in being after the act of election.—To JOHN TAYLOR. vi, 606. FORD ED., x, 29. (M., 1816.)

7296. —— ——. The purest republican feature in the government of our own State, is the House of Representatives. The Senate is equally so the first year, less the second, and so on. The Executive still less, because not chosen by the people directly. The judiciary seriously anti-republican, because for life; and the national arm wielded * * * by military leaders, irresponsible but to themselves. Add to this the vicious constitution of our county courts (to whom the justice, the executive administration, the taxation, police, the military appointments of the county, and nearly all our daily concerns are confided), self-appointed, self-continued, holding their authorities for life, and with an impossibility of breaking in on the perpetual succession of any faction once possessed of the bench. They are in truth, the executive, the judiciary, and the military of their respective counties, and the sum of the counties makes the State. And add, also, that one-half of our brethren who fight and pay taxes, are excluded, like helots, from the rights of representation, as if society were instituted for the soil, and not for the men inhabiting it; or one-half of these could dispose of the rights and the will of the other half, without their consent.*—To John Taylor. vi, 606. Ford ed., x, 29. (M., 1816.)

7297. —— ——. If, then, the control of the people over the organs of their government be the measure of its republicanism, and I confess I know no other measure, it must be agreed that our governments have much less of republicanism than ought to have been expected; in other words, that the people have less regular control over their agents than their rights and their interests require. And this I ascribe, not to any want of re-. publican dispositions in those who formed these constitutions, but to a submission of true principle to European authorities, to speculators on government, whose fears of the people have been inspired by the populace of their own great cities, and were unjustly entertained against the independent, the happy, and, therefore, orderly citizens of the United States. Much I apprehend that the golden moment is past for reforming these heresies. The functionaries of public power rarely strengthen in their dispositions to abridge it, and an unorganized call for timely amendment is likely to prevail against an organized opposition to it. We are told that things are going on well; why change them? " *Chi sta bene, non si muova*," said the Italian, " let him who stands well, stand still ". This is true; and I verily believe they would go on well with us under an absolute monarch, while our present character remains, of order, industry and love of peace, and restrained, as he would be, by the proper spirit of the people. But it is while it remains such, we should provide against the consequences of its deterioration. And let us rest in the hope that it will yet be done, and spare ourselves the pain of evils which may never happen.—To John Taylor. vi, 607. Ford ed., x, 30. (M., 1816.)

7298. —— ——. In the General Government, the House of Representatives is mainly republican; the Senate scarcely so at all, as not elected by the people directly, and so long secured even against those who do elect them; the Executive more republican than the Senate, from its shorter term, its election by the people, in *practice* (for they vote for A only on an assurance that he will vote for B) and because, in practice also, a principle of rotation seems to be in a course of establishment; the judiciary independent of the nation, their coercion by impeachment being found nugatory.—To John Taylor. vi, 607. Ford i.d., x, 30. (M., 1816.)

7299. —— ——. On this view of the import of the term *republic,* instead of saying, as has been said, " that it may mean anything or nothing ", we may say with truth and meaning, that governments are more or less republican, as they have more or less of the element of popular election and control in

*Jefferson here quotes from Sir William Jones's ode the lines beginning: " What constitutes a State? "—Editor.

their composition; and believing, as I do, that the mass of the citizens is the safest depositary of their own rights, and especially, that the evils flowing from the duperies of the people are less injurious than those from the egoism of their agents, I am a friend to that composition of government which has in it the most of this ingredient. And I sincerely believe * * * that banking establishments are more dangerous than standing armies; and that the principle of spending money to be paid by posterity, under the name of funding, is but swindling futurity on a large scale.—To John Taylor. vi, 608. Ford ed., x, 31. (M., 1816.)

7300. REPUBLIC, Essence of.—Action by the citizens in person, in affairs within their reach and competence, and in all others by representatives, chosen immediately, and removable by themselves, constitutes the essence of a republic.—To Dupont de Nemours. vi, 591. Ford ed., x, 24. (P.F., 1816.)

7301. REPUBLIC, First principle of.—The first principle of republicanism in that the *lex majoris partis* is the fundamental law of every society of individuals of equal right; to consider the will of the society enounced by the majority of a single vote, as sacred as if unanimous, is the first of all lessons of importance, yet the last which is thoroughly learnt. This law once disregarded, no other remains but that of force, which ends necessarily in military despotism.—To Baron Humboldt. vii, 75. Ford ed., x, 89. (M., 1817.)

7302. REPUBLIC (American), Establishment of.—In the great work which has been effected in America, no individual has a right to take any great share to himself. Our people in a body are wise, because they are under the unrestrained and unperverted operation of their own understanding. Those whom they have assigned to the direction of their affairs, have stood with a pretty even front. If any one of them was withdrawn, many others entirely equal, have been ready to fill his place with as good abilities. A nation, composed of such materials, and free in all its members from distressing wants, furnishes hopeful implements for the interesting experiment of self-government; and we feel that we are acting under obligations not confined to the limits of our own society. It is impossible not to be sensible that we are acting for all mankind; that circumstances denied to others, but indulged to us, have imposed on us the duty of proving what is the degree of freedom and self-government in which a society may venture to leave its individual members.—To Dr. Joseph Priestley. iv, 440. Ford ed., viii, 158. (W., 1802.)

7303. REPUBLIC (American), Maintenance of.—Whatever may be the fate of republicanism in France, we are able to preserve it inviolate here.—To John Breckenridge. Ford ed., vii, 418. (Pa., Jan. 1800.)

7304. REPUBLIC (American), A model.—The spirit of our citizens * * * will make this government in practice, what it is in principle, a model for the protection of man in a state of *freedom* and *order*.—To GENERAL KOSCIUSKO. iv, 295. (Pa., Feb. 1799.)

7305. REPUBLIC (American), Perils of.—I had sent to the President yesterday [May 22] drafts of a letter from him to the Provisory Executive Council of France, and one from myself to Mr. Ternant, both on the occasion of his recall. I called on him to-day [May 23]. He said there was an expression in one of them, which he had never before seen in any of our public communications, to wit, "our republic". The letter prepared for him to the Council, began thus: "The Citizen Ternant has delivered to me the letter wherein you inform me, that yielding, &c., you had determined to recall him from his mission, as your Minister Plenipotentiary to *our republic.*" He had underscored the words, *our republic.* He said that certainly ours was a republican government, but yet we had not used that style in this way; that if anybody wanted to change its form into a monarchy, he was sure it was only a few individuals, and that no man in the United States would set his face against it more than himself; but that this was not what he was afraid of; his fears were from another quarter; that there was more danger of anarchy being introduced. He adverted to a piece in Freneau's paper of yesterday, said he despised all their attacks on him personally, but that there never had been an act of the government, not meaning in the Executive line only, but in any line, which that paper had not abused. He had also marked the word republic thus V where it was applied to the French republic. He was evidently sore and warm, and I took his intention to be, that I should interpose in some way with Freneau, perhaps withdraw his appointment of translating clerk to my office. But I will not do it. His paper has saved the Constitution, which was galloping fast into monarchy, and has been checked by no means so powerfully as by that paper. It is well and universally known, that it has been that paper which has checked the career of the monocrats; and the President. not sensible of the designs of the party, has not with his usual good sense and *sang froid*, looked on the efforts and effects of this free press, and seen that, though some bad things have passed through it to the public, yet the good have preponderated immensely.—THE ANAS. ix, 144. FORD ED., i, 230. (May 1793.)

7306. REPUBLIC (American), Salvation of.—To save the Republic * * * is the first and supreme law.—AUTOBIOGRAPHY. i, 82. FORD ED., i, 114. (1821.)

7307. REPUBLIC (American), Stability of.—We can no longer say there is nothing new under the sun. For this whole chapter in the history of man is new. The great extent of our Republic is new. Its sparse habi-

tation is new. The mighty wave of public opinion which has rolled over it is new. But the most pleasing novelty is, its so quietly subsiding over such an extent of surface to its true level again. The order and good sense displayed in this recovery from delusion. and in the momentous crisis which lately arose [election of President], really bespeak a strength of character in our nation which augurs well for the duration of our Republic; and I am much better satisfied now of its stability than I was before it was tried.—To DR. JOSEPH PRIESTLEY. iv, 374. FORD ED., viii, 22. (W., March 1801.)

7308. ———— ————. We may still believe with security that the great body of the American people must for ages yet be substantially republican.—To ROBERT R. LIVINGSTON. iv, 297. FORD ED., vii, 369. (Pa., 1799.)

7309. ———— ————. The resistance which our Republic has opposed to a course of operation, for which it was not destined, shows a strength of body which affords the most flattering presage of duration. I hope we shall now be permitted to steer her in her natural course, and to show by the smoothness of her motion the skill with which she has been formed for it.—To GENERAL WARREN. iv, 375. (W., March 1801.)

7310. ———— ————. We are never permitted to despair of the Commonwealth.—To JAMES MADISON. ii, 331. (P., 1787.)

7311. ———— ————. The good citizen must never despair of the Commonwealth.—To NATHANIEL NILES. iv, 376. FORD ED., viii, 24. (W., 1801.)

7312. REPUBLIC (American), Triumphant.—The cause of republicanism, triumphing in Europe, can never fail to do so here in the long run.—To ARCHIBALD STUART. FORD ED., vii, 378. (M., May 1799.)

7313. REPUBLIC (American), Washington and.—I was happy to see that Randolph had, by accident, used the expression "our republic", in the [President's] speech. The President, however, made no objection to it. and so, as much as it had disconcerted him on a former occasion with me, it was now put into his own mouth to be pronounced to the two Houses of Legislature.*—THE ANAS. ix, 183. FORD ED., i, 270. (Nov. 1793.)

7314. REPUBLIC (English), France and.—Nothing can establish firmly the republican principles of our government but an establishment of them in England. France will be the apostle for this.—To E. RANDOLPH. iv. 192. FORD ED., vii, 156. (Pa.. June 1797.)

7315. REPUBLIC (English), Prospective.—If I could but see the French and Dutch at peace with the rest of their continent. I should have little doubt of dining with Piche-

* Edmund Randolph, Attorney General, had been selected to write the speech, or message, to Congress.—EDITOR.

gru in London, next autumn; for I believe I should be tempted to leave my clover for awhile, to go and hail the dawn of liberty and republicanism in that island.—To WILLIAM B. GILES. iv. 118. FORD ED., vii, 11. (M., April 1795.)

7316. REPUBLIC (French), America and.—I look with great anxiety for the firm establishment of the new government in France, being perfectly convinced that if it takes place there, it will spread sooner or later all over Europe. On the contrary, a check there would retard the revival of liberty in other countries. I consider the establishment and success of their government as necessary to stay up our own, and to prevent it from falling back to that kind of half-way house, the English constitution.—To GEORGE MASON. iii, 209. FORD ED., v, 274. (Pa., Feb. 1791.)

7317. REPUBLIC (French), Bonaparte and.—I fear our friends on the other side of the water, laboring in the same cause, have a great deal of crime and misery to wade through. My confidence has been placed in the head, not in the heart of Bonaparte. I hoped he would calculate truly the difference between the fame of a Washington and a Cromwell. Whatever his views may be, he has transferred the destinies of the republic from the civil to the military arm. Some will use this as a lesson against the practicability of republican government. I read it as a lesson against the danger of standing armies.—To SAMUEL ADAMS. iv, 321. FORD ED., vii, 425. (Pa., Feb. 1800.)

7318. REPUBLIC (French), Future.—France will yet attain representative government. You observe it makes the basis of every constitution which has been demanded or offered.—of that demanded by their Senate; of that offered by Bonaparte; and of that granted by Louis XVIII. The idea, then, is rooted, and will be established, although rivers of blood may yet flow between them and their object.—To JOHN ADAMS. vi, 525. (M., 1816.)

7319. REPUBLIC (French), Gratitude to.—I hope you have been sensible of the general interest which my countrymen take in all the successes of your republic. In this no one joins with more enthusiasm than myself, an enthusiasm kindled by our love of liberty, by my gratitude to your nation who helped us to acquire it, by my wishes to see it extended to all men, and first to those whom we love most.—To M. ODIT. iv, 123. (M., May 1795.)

7320. REPUBLIC (French), Sympathy with.—Be assured that the government and the citizens of the United States view with the most sincere pleasure every advance of France towards its happiness, an object essentially connected with its liberty, and they consider the union of principles and pursuits between our two countries as a link which binds still closer their interests and affections. The genuine and general effusions of joy which

you saw overspread our country, on their seeing the liberties of yours rise superior to foreign invasion and domestic trouble, have proved to you that our sympathies are great and sincere, and we earnestly wish on our part that these our natural* dispositions may be improved to mutual good, by establishing our commercial intercourse on principles as friendly to natural right and freedom, as are those of our government.—To JEAN BAPTISTE TERNANT. iii, 517. FORD ED., vi, 189. (Pa., Feb. 1793.)

7321. REPUBLIC (French), Washington and.—I have laid before the President of the United States your notification, * * * in the name of the Provisory Executive Council charged with the administration of your government, that the French nation has constituted itself into a Republic. The President receives with great satisfaction this attention of the Executive Council, and the desire they have manifested of making known to us the resolution entered into by the National Convention, even before a definitive regulation of their new establishment could take place.—To JEAN BAPTISTE TERNANT. iii, 516. FORD ED., vi, 189. (Pa., Feb. 1793.)

7322. REPUBLIC (French), Washington's cabinet and.—We met at the President's to examine by paragraphs the draft of a letter I had prepared to Gouverneur Morris on the conduct of Mr. Genet. There was no difference of opinion on any part of it, except on this expression, " An attempt to embroil both, to add still another nation to the enemies of his country, and to draw on both a reproach which, it is hoped, will never stain the history of either, that of *liberty warring on herself*". Hamilton moved to strike out these words, " that of liberty warring on herself". He urged generally that it would give offence to the combined powers; that it amounted to a declaration that they were warring on liberty; that we were not called on to declare that the cause of France was that of liberty; that he had at first been with them with all his heart, but that he had long since left them, and was not for encouraging the idea here, that the cause of France was the cause of liberty in general, or could have either connection or influence in our affairs. Knox, according to custom, jumped plump into all his opinions. The President, with a good deal of positiveness, declared in favor of the expression; that he considered the pursuit of France to be that of liberty, however they might sometimes fail of the best means of obtaining it; that he had never at any time entertained a doubt of their ultimate success, if they hung well together; and that as to their dissensions, there were such contradictory accounts given, that no one could tell what to believe. I observed that it had been supposed among us all along that the present letter might become public; that we had, therefore, three parties to attend to,—1st. France; 2d, her enemies; 3d, the people of

* Mutual in FORD EDITION.—EDITOR.

the United States; that as to the enemies of France, it ought not to offend them, because the passage objected to, only spoke of an attempt to make the United States, a *free nation,* war on France, a *free nation,* which would be liberty warring on herself, and, therefore, a true fact; that as to France, we were taking so harsh a measure (desiring her to recall her minister) that a precedent for it could scarcely be found; that we knew that minister would represent to his government that our Executive was hostile to liberty, leaning to monarchy, and would endeavor to parry the charges on himself, by rendering suspicious the source from which they flowed; that, therefore, it was essential to satisfy France, not only of our friendship to her, but our attachment to the general cause of liberty, and to hers in particular; that as to the people of the United States, we knew there were suspicions abroad that the Executive, in some of its parts, was tainted with a hankering after monarchy, an indisposition towards liberty, and towards the French cause; and that it was important, by an explicit declaration, to remove these suspicions, and restore the confidence of the people in their government. Randolph opposed the passage on nearly the same ground with Hamilton. He added, that he thought it had been agreed that this correspondence should contain no expressions which could give offence to either party. I replied that it had been my opinion in the beginning of the correspondence, that while we were censuring the conduct of the French minister, we should make the most cordial declarations of friendship to them; that in the first letter or two of the correspondence, I had inserted expressions of that kind, but that himself and the other two gentlemen had struck them out; that I thereupon conformed to their opinion in my subsequent letters, and had carefully avoided the insertion of a single term of friendship to the French nation, and the letters were as dry and husky as if written between the generals of two enemy nations; that on the present occasion, however, it had been agreed that such expressions ought to be inserted in the letter now under consideration, and I had accordingly charged it pretty well with them; that I had further thought it essential to satisfy the French and our own citizens of the light in which we viewed their cause, and of our fellow feeling for the general cause of liberty, and had ventured only four words on the subject; that there was not from beginning to end of the letter one other expression or word in favor of liberty, and I should think it singular, at least, if the single passage of that character should be struck out. The President again spoke. He came into the idea that attention was due to the parties who had been mentioned, France and the United States; that as to the former, thinking it certain their affairs would issue in a government of some sort—of considerable freedom—it was the only nation with whom our relations could be counted on; that as to the United

States, there could be no doubt of their universal attachment to the cause of France, and of the solidity of their republicanism. He declared his strong attachment to the expression, but finally left it to us to accommodate. It was struck out, of course, and the expressions of affection in the context were a good deal taken down.—THE ANAS. ix, 169. FORD ED., i, 259. (Aug. 1793.)

7323. REPUBLIC OF LETTERS, Dictatorship.—No republic is more real than that of letters, and I am the last in principles, as I am the least in pretensions to any dictatorship in it.—To NOAH WEBSTER. iii, 201. FORD ED., v, 254. (Pa., 1790.)

7324. REPUBLIC OF LETTERS, Wars and.—The republic of letters is unaffected by the wars of geographical divisions of the earth.—To DR. PATTERSON. vi, 11. (M., 1811.)

7325. REPUBLICANISM (Governmental), American.—The light from our West seems to have spread and illuminated the very engines employed to extinguish it. It has given them a glimmering of their rights and their power. The idea of representative government has taken root and growth among them. Their masters feel it, and are saving themselves by timely offers of this modification of their powers. Belgium, Prussia, Poland, Lombardy, &c., are now offered a representative organization; illusive, probably, at first, but it will grow into power in the end. Opinion is power, and that opinion will come. —To JOHN ADAMS. vi, 525. (M., 1816.)

7326. REPUBLICANISM (Governmental) Apostasy from.—An apostasy from republicanism to royalism is unprecedented and impossible.—To JAMES MADISON. iii, 5. FORD ED., v, 83. (P., 1789.)

7327. REPUBLICANISM (Governmental), Catholic principle of.—The catholic principle of republicanism is that every people may establish what form of government they please, and change it as they please, the will of the nation being the only thing essential.*—THE ANAS. ix, 129. FORD ED., i, 214. (1792.)

7328. REPUBLICANISM (Governmental), Extension of.—It is hoped that by a due poise and partition of powers between the General and particular governments, we have found the secret of extending the benign blessings of republicanism over still greater tracts of country than we possess, and that a subdivision may be avoided for ages, if not for ever.—To JAMES SULLIVAN. FORD ED., v, 369. (Pa., 1791.)

7329. REPUBLICANISM (Governmental), Happiness and.—I conscientiously believe that governments founded in republican principles are more friendly to the happiness of the people at large, and especially

* " I took the occasion," says Jefferson, "furnished by Pinckney's letter of Sep. 19, asking instructions how to conduct himself with respect to the French Revolution to lay down this principle."—EDITOR.

of a people so capable of self-government as ours.—To DAVID HOWELL. v, 554. (M., 1810.)

7330. REPUBLICANISM (Governmental), Majority rule.—A nation ceases to be republican * * * when the will of the majority ceases to be the law.—REPLY TO ADDRESS. v, 262. (W., 1808.)

7331. REPUBLICANISM (Governmental), Rights of man and.—The republican is the only form of government which is not eternally at open or secret war with the rights of mankind.—REPLY TO ADDRESS. iii, 128. FORD ED., v, 147. (1790.)

7332. REPUBLICANISM (Governmental), Schools of.—The best schools for republicanism are London, Versailles, Madrid, Vienna, Berlin, &c.—To GOVERNOR RUTLEDGE. ii, 234. (P., 1787.)

7333. REPUBLICANISM (Governmental), Union and.—It is, indeed, of little consequence who govern us, if they sincerely and zealously cherish the principles of Union and republicanism.—To GENERAL DEARBORN. vii, 215. FORD ED., x, 192. (M., 1821.)

7334. REPUBLICANISM (Partisan), Ardent and moderate.—I had always expected that when the republicans should have put down all things under their feet, they would schismatize among themselves. I always expected, too, that whatever names the parties might bear, the real division would be into moderate and ardent republicanism. In this division there is no great evil,—not even if the minority obtain the ascendency by the accession of federal votes to their candidate; because this gives us one shade only, instead of another, of republicanism. It is to be considered as apostasy only when they purchase the votes of federalists with a participation in honor and power.—To THOMAS COOPER. v, 121. FORD ED., ix, 102. (W., July 1807.)

7335. REPUBLICANISM (Partisan), Benefits of.—If we are left in peace, I have no doubt the wonderful turn in the public opinion now manifestly taking place and rapidly increasing, will * * * become so universal and so weighty, that friendship abroad and freedom at home will be firmly established by the influence and constitutional powers of the people at large.—To GENERAL KOSCIUSKO. iv, 295. (Pa., Feb. 1799.)

7336. REPUBLICANISM (Partisan), Corruption.—How long we can hold our ground I do not know. We are not incorruptible; on the contrary, corruption is making sensible though silent progress. Offices are as acceptable in Virginia as elsewhere, and whenever a man has cast a longing eye on them, a rottonness begins in his conduct.—To TENCH COXE. FORD ED., vii, 380. (M., May, 1799.)

7337. REPUBLICANISM (Partisan), Faith in.—The tide against our Constitution is unquestionably strong, but it will turn. Everything tells me so, and everything verifies the prediction.—To WILLIAM BRANCH GILES. FORD ED., vi, 516. (M., Dec. 1797.)

7338. REPUBLICANISM (Partisan), Fidelity to.—I have taken the liberty of referring him [Brissot de Warville] to you for a true state of republicanism here, as for the characters, objects, numbers and force of our parties. It is really interesting that these should be well understood in France, and particularly by their government. Particular circumstances have generated suspicions among them that we are swerving from our republicanism.—To DR. ENOCH EDWARDS. FORD ED., vi, 248. (Pa., 1793.)

7339. REPUBLICANISM (Partisan), Fortifying.—My great anxiety at present is, to avail ourselves of our ascendency to establish good principles and good practices: to fortify republicanism behind as many barriers as possible, that the outworks may give time to rally and save the citadel, should that be again in danger.—To JOHN DICKINSON. iv, 424. (W., 1801.)

7340. REPUBLICANISM (Partisan), The Judiciary and.—The revolution of 1800 was as real a revolution in the principles of our government as that of 1776 was in its form; not effected, indeed, by the sword, as that, but by the rational and peaceable instrument of reform, the suffrage of the people. The nation declared its will by dismissing functionaries of one principle, and electing those of another, in the two branches, Executive and Legislative, submitted to their election. Over the Judiciary department, the Constitution had deprived them of their control. That, therefore, has continued the reprobated system, and although new matter has been occasionally incorporated into the old, yet the leaven of the old mass seems to assimilate to itself the new, and after twenty years' confirmation of the federal system by the voice of the nation, declared through the medium of elections, we find the Judiciary on every occasion, still driving us into consolidation.—To SPENCER ROANE. vii, 133. FORD ED., x, 140. (P.F., 1819.) See CENTRALIZATION, JUDICIARY and SUPREME COURT.

7341. REPUBLICANISM (Partisan), Liberty and.—Under republicanism, our citizens generally are enjoying a very great degree of liberty and security in the most temperate manner.—To M. PICTET. iv, 463. (W., 1803.)

7342. REPUBLICANISM (Partisan), Missouri question and.—[The Missouri question] has given resurrection to the Hartford Convention men. They have had the address, by playing on the honest feelings of our former friends, to seduce them from their kindred spirits, and to borrow their weight into the federal scale. Desperate of regaining power under political distinctions, they have adroitly wriggled into its seat under the auspices of morality, and are again in the ascendency from which their sins had hurled them. It is, indeed, of little consequence who govern us if they sincerely and zealously cherish the principles of union and republicanism.—To HENRY DEARBORN. vii, 215. FORD ED., x, 191. (M., 1821.) See MISSOURI QUESTION and PARTIES.

7343. REPUBLICANISM (Partisan), Outlawed.—Republicanism had been the mark on Cain, which had rendered those who bore it exiles from all portion in the trusts and authorities of their country.—To BENJAMIN HAWKINS. iv, 466. FORD ED., viii, 212. (W., 1803.) See OFFICE and OFFICES.

7344. REPUBLICANISM (Partisan), The people and.—The people are essentially republican. They retain unadulterated the principles of '75, and those who are conscious of no change in themselves have nothing to fear in the long run.—To JAMES LEWIS, JR. iv, 241. FORD ED., vii, 250. (Pa., May 1798.)

7345. ———. The people through all the States are for republican forms, republican principles, simplicity, economy, religious and civil freedom.—To E. LIVINGSTON. iv, 328. FORD ED., vii, 443. (Pa., 1800.)

7346. REPUBLICANISM (Partisan), Preservation of.—Whether the surrender of our opponents, their reception into our camp, their assumption of our name, and apparent accession to our objects, may strengthen or weaken the genuine principles of republicanism, may be a good or an evil, is yet to be seen.—To WILLIAM T. BARRY. vii, 255. (M., 1822.)

7347. REPUBLICANISM (Partisan), Safety in.—So long as the pure principles of our revolution [of 1800] prevail, we are safe from everything which can assail us from without or within.—To MR. LAMBERT. v, 528. (M., 1810.)

7348. REPUBLICANISM (Partisan), Seceders from.—My opinion is that two or three years more will bring back to the fold of republicanism all our wandering brethren whom the cry of "wolf" scattered in 1798. Till that is done, let every man stand to his post, and hazard nothing by change. And when that is done, you and I may retire to that tranquillity which our years begin to call for, and review with satisfaction the efforts of the age we happened to be born in, crowned with complete success. In the hour of death, we shall have the consolation to see established in the land of our fathers the most wonderful work of wisdom and disinterested patriotism that has ever yet appeared on the globe.—To DE WITT CLINTON. iv, 521. (W., 1803.)

7349. REPUBLICANISM (Partisan), Ship of State and.—The time is coming when we shall fetch up the lee-way of our vessel. The changes in your House [of Representatives] I see, are going on for the better, and even the Augean herd over your heads are slowly purging off their impurities. Hold on, then, that we may not shipwreck in the meanwhile.—To JAMES MADISON. iv, 112. FORD ED., vi, 519. (M., Dec. 1794.)

7350. ———. The storm through which we have passed has been tremendous indeed. The tough sides of our Argosy have been thoroughly tried. Her strength has stood the waves into which she was steered, with a view to sink her. We shall put her on her republican tack, and she will now show by the beauty of her motion the skill of her builders.—To JOHN DICKINSON. iv, 365. FORD ED., viii, 7. (W., March 1801.)

7351. ———. The storm is over, and we are in port. The ship was not rigged for the service she was put on. We will show the smoothness of her motions on her republican tack.—To SAMUEL ADAMS. iv, 389. FORD ED., viii, 39. (W., March 1801.)

7352. REPUBLICANISM (Partisan), Sincerity in.—That I have acted through life on principles of sincere republicanism, I feel in every fibre of my constitution. And when men, who feel like myself, bear witness in my favor, my satisfaction is complete.—To REV. MR. KNOX. v, 502. (M., 1810.)

7353. REPUBLICANS, Aims of.—Surely we had in view to obtain the theory and practice of good government; and how any, who seemed so ardent in this pursuit, could as shamelessly have apostatized, and supposed we meant only to put our government into other hands, but not other forms, is indeed wonderful.—To JOHN DICKINSON. iv, 424. (W., 1801.)

7354. ———. The federalists wished for everything which would approach our new government to a monarchy. The republicans to preserve it essentially republican. This was the true origin of the division, and remains still the essential principle of difference between the two parties.—NOTES ON MARSHALL'S LIFE OF WASHINGTON. ix, 480. FORD ED., ix, 263. (M., 1809.) See FEDERALISTS and PARTIES.

7355. REPUBLICANS, Antagonistic to England.—The war between France and England has brought forward the republicans and monocrats in every State so openly, that their relative numbers are perfectly visible. It appears that the latter are as nothing.—To JAMES MADISON. iv, 9. FORD ED., vi, 326. (June 1793.) See FEDERALISTS.

7356. REPUBLICANS, Belief of.—[The Republicans] believed that men, enjoying in ease and security the full fruits of their own industry, enlisted by all their interests on the side of law and order, habituated to think for themselves, and to follow their reason as their guide, would be more easily and safely governed than with minds nourished in error, and vitiated and debased, as in Europe, by ignorance, indigence and oppression.—To WILLIAM JOHNSON. vii, 292. FORD ED., x, 227. (M., 1823.)

7357. REPUBLICANS, Defeated.—I had always hoped, that the popularity of the late President being once withdrawn from active effect, the natural feelings of the people towards liberty would restore the equilibrium between the Executive and Legislative departments, which had been destroyed by the superior weight and effect of that popularity; and that their natural feelings of moral obligation would discountenance the ungrateful predilection of the Executive in favor of Great Britain. But, unfortunately, the preceding measures had already alienated the nation which was the object of them, had excited reaction from them and this reaction has on the minds of our citizens an effect which supplies that of the Washington popularity. This effect was sensible on some of the late congressional elections, and this it is which has lessened the republican majority in Congress. When it will be reinforced, must depend on events, and these are so incalculable, that I consider the future character of our republic as in the air; indeed its future fortune will be in the air, if war is made on us by France, and if Louisiana becomes a Gallo-American colony.—To AARON BURR. iv, 185. FORD ED., vii, 147. (Pa., June 1797.) See FEDERALISTS.

7358. REPUBLICANS, Dividing.—Little squibs in certain papers had long ago apprised me of a design to sow tares between particular republican characters, but to divide those by lying tales whom truths cannot divide, is the hackneyed policy of the gossips of every society. Our business is to march straight forward to the object which has occupied us for eight and twenty years, without turning either to the right or left.—To DE WITT CLINTON. iv, 520. (W., 1803.)

7359. REPUBLICANS, Divisions among.—The operations of this session of Congress, when known among the people at large, will consolidate them. We shall now be so strong that we shall certainly split again; for freemen, thinking differently and speaking and acting as they think, will form into classes of sentiment, but it must be under another name. That of federalism is become so odious that no party can rise under it.—To JOEL BARLOW. iv, 437. FORD ED., viii, 150. (W., May 1802.)

7360. —— ——. I have for some time been satisfied a schism was taking place in Pennsylvania between the moderates and high-flyers. The same will take place in Congress whenever a proper head for the latter shall start up, and we must expect division of the same kind in other States as soon as the republicans shall be so strong as to fear no other enemy.—To ALBERT GALLATIN. FORD ED., viii, 222. (M., March 1803.)

7361. —— ——. I think it possibly may happen that we shall divide among ourselves whenever federalism is completely eradicated, yet I think it the duty of every republican to make great sacrifices of opinion to put off the evil day.—To JOSEPH SCOTT. FORD ED., viii, 305. (W., March 1804.)

7362. —— ——. The divisions among the republicans * * * are distressing, but they are not unexpected to me. From the moment I foresaw the entire prostration of federalism, I knew that at that epoch more distressing divisions would take its place. The opinions of men are as various as their faces, and they will always find some rallying principle or point at which those nearest to it will unite, reducing

themselves to two stations, under a common name for each. These stations, or camps, will be formed of very heterogeneous materials, combining from very different motives, and with very different views.—To WILSON C. NICHOLAS. FORD ED., viii, 348. (M., March 1805.)

7363. —— ——. I did believe my station in March, 1801, as painful as could be undertaken, having to meet in front all the terrible passions of federalism in the first moment of its defeat and mortification, and to grapple with it until completely subdued. But I consider that as less painful than to be placed between conflicting friends. There my way was clear and my mind made up. I never for a moment had to balance between two opinions. In the new divisions which are to arise the case will be very different. Even those who seem to coalesce will be like the image of clay and brass. However, under difficulties of this kind, I have ever found one, and only one rule, *to do what is right*, and generally we shall disentangle ourselves without almost perceiving how it happens.—To WILSON C. NICHOLAS. FORD ED., viii, 349. (M., March 1805.)

7364. —— ——. The duty of an upright Administration is to pursue its course steadily, to know nothing of these family dissensions, and to cherish the good principles of both parties. The war *ad internecionem* which we have waged against federalism, has filled our later times with strife and unhappiness. We have met it, with pain indeed, but with firmness, because we believed it the last convulsive effort of that hydra, which in earlier times had conquered in the field. But if any degeneracy of principle should ever render it necessary to give ascendancy to one of the rising sections over the other, I thank my God it will fall to some other to perform that operation. The only cordial I wish to carry into my retirement, is the undivided good will of all those with whom I have acted.—To DR. GEORGE LOGAN. iv, 575. FORD ED., viii, 353. (W., May 1805.)

7365. —— ——. I see with infinite pain the bloody schism which has taken place among our friends in Pennsylvania and New York, and will probably take place in other States. The main body of both sections mean well, but their good intentions will produce great public evil. The minority, whichever section shall be the minority, will end in coalition with the federalists, and some compromise of principle; because these will not sell their aid for nothing. Republicanism will thus lose, and royalism gain, some portion of that ground which we thought we had rescued to good government. I do not express my sense of our misfortunes from any idea that they are remediable. I know that the passions of men will take their course, that they are not to be controlled but by despotism, and that this melancholy truth is the pretext for despotism.—To DR. GEORGE LOGAN. iv, 575. FORD ED., viii, 352. (W., May 1805.)

7366. —— ——. I see with extreme concern the acrimonious dissensions into which our friends in Pennsylvania have fallen, but have long since made up my mind on the propriety of the General Government's taking no side in State quarrels. And with respect to myself particularly, after eight and thirty years of uniform action in harmony with those now constituting the republican party, without one single instant of alienation from them, it cannot be but my most earnest desire to carry into retirement with me their undivided approbation and esteem. I retain, therefore, a cordial friendship for both the sections now so unhappily dividing your State.—To THOMAS LEIB. FORD ED., viii, 353. (M., Aug. 1805.)

7367. —— ——. Of the unhappy effects of the schisms in Pennsylvania and New York, you see the fruit in the State lying between them, where the federalists have recovered a majority in one branch of the legislature, are very near it in the other, and as soon as they shall reach it, they place the executive and every office under it in federal hands. If the two sections of republicans were irreconcilable, still the minor one should not have coalesced with, and voted for federalists. If, on the contrary, they would keep themselves independent, and set up their own ticket, their whole body would come forward and vote, which would give them the benefit of that part of their force which kept back because it could not support federalists, and the federalists themselves, having no hope of bringing in men of their own, would have to choose between the two republican tickets that least disagreeable to themselves. This would only bring into the public councils the different shades of republicans so that the whole body should be represented.— To ANDREW ELLIOTT. FORD ED., viii, 479. (W., Nov. 1806.)

7368. —— ——. I determined from the first dawn of the first schism, never to take part in any schism of republicans, nor in distributing the public trusts ever to ask of which section a party was.—To ANDREW ELLICOTT. FORD ED., viii, 480. (W., Nov. 1806.)

7369. —— ——. I have long seen, and with very great regret, the schisms which have taken place among the republicans, and principally those of Pennsylvania and New York. As far as I have been able to judge, they have not been produced by any difference of political principle,—at least, any important difference, but by a difference of opinion as to persons. I determined from the first moment to take no part in them, and that the Government should know nothing of any such differences. Accordingly, it has never been attended to in any appointment, or refusal of appointment.—To JAMES GAMBLE. v, 204. FORD ED., ix, 129. (W., 1807.)

7370. —— ——. If we schismatize on either men or measures, if we do not act in phalanx, as when we rescued the country from the satellites of monarchy, I will not say our *party* (the term is false and degrading), but our *nation* will be undone. For the republicans are the *nation*. Their opponents are but a faction, weak in numbers, but powerful and profuse in the command of money, and backed by a nation [England], powerful also and profuse in the use of the same means; and the more profuse, in both cases, as the money they thus employ is not their own but their creditors, to be paid off by a bankruptcy, which whether it pays a dollar or a shilling in the pound, is of little concern with them. The last hope of human liberty in this world rests on us. We ought, for so dear a stake, to sacrifice every attachment and every enmity. Leave the President free to choose his own coadjutors, to pursue his own measures, and support him and them, even if we think we are wiser than they, honester than they are, or possessing more enlarged information of the state of things. If we move in mass, be it ever so circuitously, we shall attain our object; but if we break into squads, every one pursuing the path he thinks most direct, we become an easy conquest to those who can now barely hold us in check. I repeat again, that we ought not to schismatize on either men or measures. Principles alone can justify that. If we find our government in all its branches rushing headlong, like our predecessors, into the arms of monarchy, if we find them violating our dearest rights, the trial by jury, the freedom of the press, the freedom of opinion, civil or religious, or opening on our peace of mind or personal safety the sluices of terrorism; if we see them raising standing armies, when the absence of all other danger points to these as the sole objects on which they are to be employed, then, indeed, let us withdraw and call the nation to its tents. But, while our functionaries are wise, and honest, and vigilant, let us move compactly under their guidance, and we have nothing to fear. Things may here and there go a little wrong. It is not in our power to prevent it. But all will be right in the end, though not, perhaps, by the shortest means. You know that this union of republicans has been the constant theme of my exhortations, that I have ever refused to know any sub-divisions among them, to take part in any personal differences; and, therefore, you will not give to the present observations any other than general application. I may sometimes differ in opinion from some of my friends, from those whose views are as pure and sound as my own. I censure none, but do homage to everyone's right of opinion.— To WILLIAM DUANE. v, 576. FORD ED., ix, 313. (M., March 1811.)

7371. —— ——. The only contest between divided [political] friends should be who will dare farthest into the ranks of the common enemy.—To JOHN HOLLINS. v, 597. (M., 1811.)

7372. —— ——. The schism in Massachusetts, when brought to the crisis of principle, will be found to be exactly the same as in the Revolutionary war. The monarchists will be left alone, and will appear to be exactly the tories of the last war.—To THOMAS LETRE. vi. 79. (M., Aug. 1812.)

7373. REPUBLICANS, Early contests of.—The inconveniences of an inefficient government, driving the people as is usual, into the opposite extreme, the elections to the first Congress ran very much in favor of those who were known to favor a very strong government. Hence the anti-republicans appeared a considerable majority in both houses of Congress. They pressed forward the plan, therefore, of strengthening all the features of the government which gave it resemblance to an English constitution, of adopting the English forms and principles of administration, and of forming like them a moneyed interest, by means of a funding system, not calculated to pay the public debt, but to render it perpetual, and to make it an engine in the hands of the executive branch of government which, added to the great patronage it possessed in the disposal of public offices, might enable it to assume by degrees a kingly authority. The biennial period of Congress being too short to betray to the people, spread over this great continent, this train of things during the first Congress, little change was made in members to the second. But, in the meantime, two very distinct parties had formed in Congress; and before the third election, the people in general became apprised of the game which was playing for drawing over them a kind of government which they never had in contemplation. At the third election, therefore, a decided majority of republicans were sent to the lower House of Congress; and, as information spread still farther among the people, after the fourth election the anti-republican members have become a weak minority.—To C. D. EBELING. FORD ED., vii, 46. (1795.)

7374. —— ——. When Congress first met, the assemblage of facts presented in the President's [Adams's] speech [message], with the multiplied accounts of spoliations by the French West Indians, appeared by sundry votes on the address, to incline a majority to put themselves in a posture of war. Under this influence the address was formed, and its spirit would probably have been pursued by corresponding measures, had the events of Europe been of an ordinary train. But this has been so extraordinary, that numbers have gone over to those, who, from the first, feeling with sensibility the French insults, as they had felt those of England before, thought now as they thought then, that war measures should be avoided, and those of peace pursued. Their favorite engine, on the former occasion, was *commercial regulations* in preference to negotiations, to war preparations, and increase of debt. On the latter, as we have no commerce with France, the restriction of which could press on them, they wished for negotiation. Those of the opposite sentiment had, on the former occasion, preferred negotiation, but at the same time voted for great war preparations, and increase of debt; now also they were for negotiation, war preparations and debt. The parties have in debate mutually charged each other with inconsistency, and with being governed by an attachment to this or that of the belligerent nations, rather than the dictates of reason and pure Americanism. But, in truth, both have been consistent; the same men having voted for war measures who did before, and the same against them now who did before.—To EDWARD RUTLEDGE. iv, 190. FORD ED., vii, 152. (Pa., June 1797.)

7375. —— ——. The spirit of both the speech [message of the President] and the address [of Congress] has been so whittled down by Bonaparte's victories, victories on the Rhine, the Austrian peace, Irish insurgency, English bankruptcy, insubordination of the [British] fleet, &c., that Congress is rejecting, one by one, the measures brought in on the principles of their own address. But nothing less than such miraculous events, as have been pouring in on us from the first of our convening, could have assuaged the fermentation produced in men's minds. In consequence of these events, what was the majority at first, is by degrees become the minority, so that we may say that, in the Representatives, moderation will govern.—To E. RANDOLPH. iv, 192. FORD ED., vii, 155. (Pa., June 1797.) See FEDERALISTS.

7376. REPUBLICANS, Federalists vs. —Two parties * * * exist within the United States. They embrace respectively the following descriptions of persons. The anti-republicans consist of: 1. The old refugees and tories. 2. British merchants residing among us, and composing the main body of our merchants. 3. American merchants trading on British capital, another great portion. 4. Speculators and holders in the banks and public funds. 5. Officers of the Federal Government with some exceptions. 6. Office-hunters, willing to give up principles for places,—a numerous and noisy tribe. 7. Nervous persons, whose languid fibres have more analogy with a passive than active state of things. The republican part of our Union comprehends: 1. The entire body of landholders throughout the United States. 2. The body of laborers, not being landholders, whether in husbanding or in the arts. The latter is to the aggregate of the former party probably as 500 to 1; but their wealth is not as disproportionate, though it is also greatly superior, and is in truth the foundation of that of their antagonists. Trifling as are the numbers of the anti-republican party, there are circumstances which give them an appearance of strength and numbers. They all live in cities, together, and can act in a body and readily at all times; they give chief employment to the newspapers, and, therefore, have most of them under their command. The agricultural interest is dispersed over a great extent of country, have little means of intercommunication with each other, and feeling their own strength and will, are conscious that a single exertion of these will, at any time, crush the machinations against their government.—To C. D. EBELING. FORD ED., vii, 47. (1795.)

7377. —— ——. I trust that no section of republicans will countenance the suggestions of the federalists that there has ever been any difference at all in our political principles, or any sensible one in our views of the public interest.—To JAMES MADISON. FORD ED., ix, 242. (M., 1809.)

7378. —— ——. [It was] a contest* which was to change the condition of man over the civilized globe.—THE ANAS. FORD ED., i, 156. (1818.) See MONARCHY.

7379. REPUBLICANS, Federalist coalition with.—The gross [Chesapeake] insult lately received from the English has forced the federalists into a momentary coalition with the mass of republicans; but the moment we begin to act in the very line they have joined in approving, all will be wrong, and every act the reverse of what it should have been. Still, it is better to admit their coalescence, and leave to themselves their short-lived existence.—To THOMAS COOPER. v, 121. FORD ED., ix, 102. (W., July 1807.) See CHESAPEAKE and FEDERALISTS.

7380. REPUBLICANS, French victories and.—I think we may safely rely that the

* The contest between the Republicans and Federalists.—EDITOR.

Duke of Brunswick has retreated; and it is certainly possible enough that between famine, disease, and a country abounding with defiles, he may suffer some considerable catastrophe. The monocrats here [Philadelphia] still affect to disbelieve all this, while the republicans are rejoicing and taking to themselves the name of Jacobins, which two months ago was fixed on them by way of stigma.—To JOHN FRANCIS MERCER. iii, 495. FORD ED., vi, 147. (Pa., Dec. 1792.)

7381. REPUBLICANS, Historical misrepresentation of.—Were a reader of this period [immediately following the establishment of the Constitution] to form his idea of it from this history alone [Marshall's *Life of Washington*] he would suppose the republican party (who were in truth endeavoring to keep the government within the line of the Constitution, and prevent its being monarchised in practice) were a mere set of grumblers, and disorganizers, satisfied with no government, without fixed principles of any, and, like a British parliamentary opposition, gaping after loaves and fishes, and ready to change principles, as well as position, at any time, with their adversaries. But * * * the contests of that day were contests of principle, between the advocates of republican and those of kingly government, and had not the former made the efforts they did, our government would have been, even at this early day [1818], a very different thing from what the successful issue of those efforts have made it.—THE ANAS. FORD ED., i, 156. (1818.)

7382. ——. ——. We [the republicans] have been too careless of our own future reputation, while our tories will omit nothing to place us in the wrong.—To WILLIAM JOHNSON. vii, 277. FORD ED., x, 247. (M., 1823.)

7383. REPUBLICANS, Leadership of.—The monocrats [in Pennsylvania] have kept up the ball with respect to myself till they begin to be tired of it themselves. Their chief object was to influence the election of this State, by persuading [the people] there was a league against the government, and as it was necessary to designate a head to the league, they did me that honor.—To T. M. RANDOLPH. FORD ED., vi, 128. (Pa., 1792.)

7384. REPUBLICANS, Loyalty of.—Without knowing the views of what is called the republican party here [Philadelphia], or having any communication with them, I could undertake to assure him [President Washington] from my intimacy with that party in the late Congress, that there was not a view in the republican party as spread over the United States, which went to the frame of the government; that I believed the next Congress would attempt nothing material, but to render their own body independent; that that party were firm in their dispositions to support the government; that the maneuvers of Mr. Genet might produce some little embarrassment, but that he would be abandoned by the republicans the moment they knew the nature of his conduct.—THE ANAS. ix, 166. FORD ED., i, 257. (Aug. 1793.)

7385. ——. ——. He [President Washington] said he believed the views of the republican party were perfectly pure, but when men put a machine into motion, it is impossible for them to stop it exactly where they would choose, or to say where it will stop. That the Constitution we have is an excellent one, if we can keep it where it is; that it was, indeed, supposed there was a party disposed to change it into a monarchical form, but that he could conscientiously declare there was not a man in the United States who would set his face more decidedly against it than himself. Here, I interrupted him, by saying: "No rational man in the United States suspects you of any other disposition; but there does not pass a week, in which we cannot prove declarations dropping from the monarchical party that our government is good for nothing, is a milk and water thing which cannot support itself, we must knock it down, and set up something of more energy." He said if that was the case, he thought it a proof of their insanity, for that the republican spirit of the Union was so manifest and so solid, that it was astonishing how any one could expect to move it.—THE ANAS. ix, 166. FORD ED., i, 257. (Aug. 1793.)

7386. REPUBLICANS, New England and.—If a prospect could be once opened upon us of the penetration of truth into the Eastern States; if the people there, who are unquestionably republicans, could discover that they have been duped into the support of measures calculated to sap the very foundations of republicanism, we might still hope for salvation, and that it would come, as of old, from the East. But will that region ever awake to the true state of things? Can the Middle, Southern and Western States hold on till they awake? These are painful and doubtful questions; and if, * * * you can give me a comfortable solution of them, it will relieve a mind devoted to the preservation of our republican government in the true form and spirit in which it was established, but almost oppressed with apprehension that fraud will at length effect what force could not, and that what with currents and counter-currents, we shall, in the end, be driven back to the land from which we launched twenty years ago. Indeed, we have been but a sturdy fish on the hook of a dexterous angler, who, letting us flounce till we have spent our force, brings us up at last.—To AARON BURR. iv, 186. FORD ED., vii, 147. (Pa., June 1797.)

7387. ——. ——. The Eastern States will be the last to come over, on account of the dominion of the clergy, who had got a smell of union between Church and State, and began to indulge reveries which can never be realized in the present state of science. If, indeed, they could have prevailed on us, to view all advances in science as dangerous innovations, and to look back to the opinions and practices of our forefathers, instead of looking forward for improvement. a promising groundwork would have been laid. But I am in hopes their good sense will dictate to them, that since the mountain will not come to them, they had better go to the mountain; that they will find their interest in acquiescing in the liberty and science of their country, and that the Christian religion, when divested of the rags in which they have enveloped it, and brought to the original purity and simplicity of its benevolent institutor is a religion of all others the most friendly to liberty. science, and the freest expansion of the human mind.—To MOSES ROBINSON. iv, 379. (March 1801.)

7388. REPUBLICANS, Patronage and. —We do not mean to leave arms in the hands of active enemies.—To ALBERT GALLATIN. iv, 544. FORD ED., viii, 304. (May 1804.)

7389. ———. That I have denounced republicans by the epithet of Jacobins, and declared I would appoint none but those called moderates of both parties, and that I have avowed or entertain any predilection for those called the third party, or "Quids", is in every tittle of it false.—To WILLIAM DUANE. iv, 592. FORD ED., viii, 433. (W., 1806.) See OFFICE, OFFICES and PARTIES.

7390. REPUBLICANS, Platform of.— Divide the Treasury Department. Abolish the Bank. Repeal the Excise Law and let States raise the money. Lower impost. Treasurer to pay and receive cash not bills. Repeal irredeemable quality and borrow at 4 per cent. Exclude paper holders. Condemn report of.*—JEFFERSON MSS. FORD ED., vi, 171. (Feb. ? 1793.)

7391. REPUBLICANS, Relations to Genet.—We [the Administration] have decided unanimously to require the recall of Genet. He will sink the republican interest if they do not abandon him.—To JAMES MADISON. FORD ED., vi, 361. (Aug. 1793.) See GENET.

7392. REPUBLICANS, Rights of man and.—Whether the principles of the majority of our fellow citizens, or of the little minority still opposing them, be most friendly to the rights of man, posterity will judge; and to that arbiter I submit my own conduct with cheerfulness.—To C. F. WELLES. v, 484. (M., 1809.) See RIGHTS OF MAN.

7393. REPUBLICANS, Slandered.— They endeavored [in the elections] to conjure up the ghost of anti-federalism, and to have it believed that this and republicanism

* Paul Leicester Ford, in his edition of *Jefferson's Writings*, makes the following note : " This paper is undated, but is apparently an outline of the reforms in the government desired by Jefferson. In the absence of a definite platform of the newly formed democratic party, it is therefore of considerable importance, and is of especial interest as showing Jefferson's plans to break up the ' Treasury Junto ', by dividing the treasury, and by excluding from Congress all holders of Bank Stock. The report referred to is probably ' Hamilton's Report on the Foreign Loans of Jan. 3, 1793 ', which was an especially obnoxious one to Jefferson."—EDITOR.

were the same, and that both were Jacobinism. But those who felt themselves republicans and federalists, too, were little moved by this artifice.—To THOMAS PINCKNEY. iii, 494. FORD ED., vi, 143. (Pa., Dec. 1792.)

7394. REPUBLICANS, States rights and.—On the eclipse of federalism, although not its extinction, its leaders got up the Missouri question, under the false front of lessening the measure of slavery, but with the real view of producing a geographical division of parties, which might ensure them the next President. The people of the north went blindfolded into the snare, followed their leaders for awhile with a zeal truly moral and laudable, until they became sensible that they were injuring instead of aiding the real interests of the slaves, that they had been used merely as tools for electioneering purposes ; and that trick of hypocrisy then fell as quickly as it had been got up. To that is now succeeded a distinction, which, like that of republican and federal, or whig and tory, being equally intermixed through every State, threatens none of those geographical schisms which go immediately to a separation. The line of division now is the preservation of State rights as reserved in the Constitution, or by strained constructions of that instrument, to merge all into a consolidated government. The tories are for strengthening the Executive and General Government; the whigs cherish the representative branch, and the rights reserved by the States, as the bulwark against consolidation, which must immediately generate monarchy. And although this division excites, as yet, no warmth, yet it exists, is well understood, and will be a principle of voting at the ensuing election, with the reflecting men of both parties.—To MARQUIS LAFAYETTE. vii, 326. FORD ED., x, 281. (M., November 1823.) See CENTRALIZATION, JUDICIARY, MISSOURI QUESTION and SUPREME COURT.

7395. REPUBLICANS, Sympathy with France.—Parties seem to have taken a very well defined form in this quarter. The old tories, joined by our merchants who trade on British capital, paper dealers, and the idle rich of the great commercial towns, are with the kings. All other descriptions with the French. The war has kindled and brought forward the two parties with an ardor which our interests merely, could never excite.—To JAMES MONROE. FORD ED., vi, 281. (Pa., June 1793.) See FEDERALISTS and MONARCHY.

7396. REPUBLICANS, Unfaltering.— As long as we pursue without deviation the principles we have always professed. I have no fear of deviation from them in the main body of republicans.—To CÆSAR A. RODNEY. FORD ED., viii, 436. (W., March 1806.)

7397. REPUBLICANS, The Union and. —Our lot has been cast by the favor of heaven in a country and under circumstances highly auspicious to our peace and prosperity, and where no pretence can arise for the degrading and oppressive establishments of Europe. It is our happiness that honorable distinctions flow only from public approbation; and that finds no object in titled dignitaries and pageants. Let us then endeavor carefully to guard this happy state of things, by keeping a watchful eye over the disaffection of wealth and ambition to the republican principles of our Constitution, and by sacrificing all our local and personal interests to the cultivation of the Union, and maintenance of the authority of the laws.—R. TO A. PENNA. DEMOCRATIC REPUBLICANS. viii, 163. (1809.) See UNION.

7398. REPUBLICANS, Washington's administration and.—The object of the opposition which was made to the course of administration was to preserve the Legislature pure and independent of the Executive, to restrain the administration to republican forms and principles, and not permit the Constitution to be construed into a monarchy, and to be warped in practice into all the principles and pollutions of their favorite English model. Nor was this an opposition to General Washington. He was true to the republican charge confided to him; and has solemnly and repeatedly protested to me, in our private conversations, that he would lose the last drop of his blood in support of it, and he did this the oftener, and with the more earnestness, because he knew my suspicions of [Alexander] Hamilton's designs against it; and wished to quiet them.—THE ANAS. ix, 95. FORD ED., i, 165. (1818.) See FEDERALISTS, MONARCHY and WASHINGTON.

7399. REPUBLICS, Contending.—I would not gratify the combination of kings with the spectacle of the only two republics on earth destroying each other for two cannon; nor would I, for infinitely greater cause, add this country to that combination, turn the scale of contest, and let it be from our hands that the hopes of man receive their last stab. —OPINION ON "THE LITTLE SARAH". ix, 155. FORD ED., vi, 343. (July 1793.)

7400. REPUBLICS, Irresistible.—A republican government is slow to move, yet when once in motion, its momentum becomes irresistible.—To F. C. GRAY. vi, 438. (M., 1815.)

7401. REPUBLICS, Size of.—I suspect that the doctrine, that small States alone are fitted to be republics, will be exploded by experience, with some other brilliant fallacies accredited by Montesquieu and other political writers. Perhaps it will be found, that to obtain a just republic (and it is to secure our just rights that we resort to government at all) it must be so extensive as that local egoisms may never reach its greater part; that on every particular question, a majority may be found in its councils free from particular interests, and giving, therefore, an uniform prevalence to the principles of justice. The smaller the societies, the more violent and convulsive their schisms.—To M. D'IVERNOIS. iv, 114. FORD ED., vii, 4. (M., Feb. 1795.)

7402. —— ——. The extent [of the Republic] has saved us. While some parts were laboring under the paroxysm of delusion, others retained their senses, and time was thus given to the affected parts to recover their health. Your part of the Union [New England] is longest recovering, because the deceivers there wear a more imposing form; but a little more time and they too will recover.—To GENERAL WARREN. iv, 376. (W., 1801.)

7403. —— ——. The late chapter of our history furnishes * * * a new proof of the falsehood of Montesquieu's doctrine, that a republic can be preserved only in a small territory. The reverse is the truth. Had our territory been even a third only of what it is, we were gone.—To NATHANIEL NILES. iv, 376. FORD ED., viii, 24. (W., March 1801.)

7404. REPUTATION, Regard for.—A regard for reputation and the judgment of the world may sometimes be felt where conscience is dormant, or indolence inexcitable. —To EDWARD LIVINGSTON. vii, 404. (M., 1825.)

7405. RESIGNATION, To Divine will. —The most fortunate of us, in our journey through life, frequently meet with calamities and misfortunes which may greatly afflict us: and, to fortify our minds against the attacks of these calamities and misfortunes, should be one of the principal studies and endeavors of our lives. The only method of doing this is to assume a perfect resignation to the Divine will, to consider that whatever does happen, must happen; and that, by our uneasiness, we cannot prevent the blow before it does fall, but we may add to its force after it has fallen. These considerations, and others such as these, may enable us in some measure to surmount the difficulties thrown in our way; to bear up with a tolerable degree of patience under this burden of life; and to proceed with a pious and unshaken resignation, till we arrive at our journey's end, when we may deliver up our trust into the hands of Him who gave it, and receive such reward as to Him shall seem proportioned to our merit. Such will be the language of the man who considers his situation in this life, and such should be the language of every man who would wish to render that situation as easy as the nature of it will admit. Few things will disturb him at all: nothing will disturb him much.—To JOHN PAGE. i, 187. FORD ED., i, 349. (S., 1763.)

7406. RESISTANCE, Morality and.— When wrongs are pressed because it is believed they will be borne, resistance becomes morality.—To MADAME DE STAEL. v, 133. (W., 1807.)

7407. RESISTANCE, Spirit of.—What country can preserve its liberties if its rulers are not warned from time to time that its people preserve the spirit of resistance?—To W. S. SMITH. ii, 318. FORD ED., iv, 467. (P., 1787.)

7408. RESOLUTION, Power of.—I do not like your saying that you are unable to read the ancient print of your Livy but with the aid of your master. We are always equal to what we undertake with resolution. A little degree of this will enable you to decipher your

Livy. If you always lean on your master, you will never be able to proceed without him. It is part of the American character to consider nothing as desperate, to surmount every difficulty by resolution and contrivance. In Europe there are shops for every want; its inhabitants, therefore, have no idea that their wants can be supplied otherwise. Remote from all other aid, we are obliged to invent and to execute; to find means within ourselves, and not to lean on others. Consider, therefore, the conquering your Livy as an exercise in the habit of surmounting difficulties; a habit which will be necessary to you in the country where you are to live, and without which you will be thought a very helpless animal, and less esteemed.—To Martha Jefferson. Ford ed., iv, 373. (1787.)

7409. RESPECT, A safeguard.—Respect is a safeguard to interest.—To John Adams. i, 592. (P., 1786.)

7410. RESPECT, Strengthening.—Our national respect certainly needs strengthening in Europe.—To James Monroe. Ford ed., iv, 223. (P., 1786.)

7411. RESPECTABILITY, National.—It should ever be held in mind, that insult and war are the consequences of a want of respectability in the national character.—To James Madison. i, 531. Ford ed., iv, 192. (P., 1786.)

7412. ——— ———. An alliance* with the Emperor of Austria will give us respectability in Europe, which we have occasion for.—To Elbridge Gerry. i, 557. (P., 1786.) See Joseph II.

7413. RESPONSIBILITY, Essential principle.—In truth, man is not made to be trusted for life, if secured against all liability to account.—To M. Coray. vii, 322. (M., 1823.)

7414. RESPONSIBILITY, Free Government and.—Responsibility is a tremendous engine in a free government.—To Archibald Stuart. iii, 315. Ford ed., v, 410. (Pa., 1791.)

7415. RESPONSIBILITY, Individual.—Responsibility weighs with its heaviest force on a single head.—To Samuel Kerchival. vii, 12. Ford ed., x, 40. (M., 1816.)

7416. RESPONSIBILITY, Official.—I am for responsibilities at short periods, seeing neither reason nor safety in making public functionaries independent of the nation for life, or even for long terms of years.—To James Martin. vi, 213. Ford ed., ix, 420. (M., Sep. 1813.)

7417. ——— ———. That there should be public functionaries independent of the nation, whatever may be their demerit, is a solecism in a republic, of the first order of absurdity and inconsistency.—To William T. Barry. vii, 256. (M., 1822.)

7418. RESPONSIBILITY, People and.—It should be remembered, as an axiom of

* By alliance Jefferson meant a commercial treaty.—Editor.

eternal truth in politics, that whatever power in any government is independent, is absolute also; in theory only, at first, while the spirit of the people is up, but in practice, as fast as that relaxes. Independence can be trusted nowhere but with the people in mass. They are inherently independent of all but moral law.—To Spencer Roane. vii, 134. Ford ed., x, 141. (P.F., 1819.)

7419. RESPONSIBILITY, Shirking.—Leave no screen of a Council behind which to skulk from responsibility.—To Samuel Kerchival. vii, 12. Ford ed., x, 39. (M., 1816.)

7420. RETALIATION, Barbarous.—The English have burned our Capitol and President's House by means of their force. We can burn their St. James's and St. Paul's by means of our money, offered to their own incendiaries, of whom there are thousands in London who would do it rather than starve. But it is against the laws of civilized warfare to employ secret incendiaries. Is it not equally so to destroy the works of art by armed incendiaries? Bonaparte, possessed at times of almost every capital of Europe, with all his despotism' and power, injured no monument of art. If a nation, breaking through all the restraints of civilized character, uses its means of destruction (power, for example) without distinction of objects, may we not use our means (*our* money and *their* pauperism) to retaliate their barbarous ravages? Are we obliged to use for resistance exactly the weapons chosen by them for aggression? When they destroyed Copenhagen by superior force, against all the laws of God and 'man, would it have been unjustifiable for the Danes to have destroyed their ships by torpedoes? Clearly not; and they and we should now be justifiable in the conflagration of St. James's and St. Paul's. And if we do not carry it into execution, it is because we think it more moral and more honorable to set a good example, than follow a bad one.—To Thomas Cooper. vi, 380. (M., 1814.)

7421. RETALIATION, Burning cities.—Perhaps the British fleet will burn New York or Boston. If they do, we must burn the city of London, not by expensive fleets or Congreve rockets, but by employing an hundred or two Jack-the-painters, whom nakedness, famine, desperation, and hardened vice, will abundantly furnish from among themselves.—To William Duane. vi, 76. Ford ed., ix, 366. (M., Aug. 1812.)

7422. RETALIATION, Deplorable.—We deplore the event which shall oblige us to shed blood for blood, and shall resort to retaliation but as the means of stopping the progress of butchery.—Report to Congress. Ford ed., i, 495. (1775.)

7423. RETALIATION, Destructive.—Humane conduct on our part was found to produce no effect; the contrary therefore was to be tried. If it produces a proper lenity to our prisoners in captivity, it will have the effect we meant; if it does not, we shall return a severity as terrible as universal. * * * If, declining the tribunal of truth and reason, they choose to pervert this into a contest of cruelty and destruction, we will contend with them in that line, and measure out misery to those in our power in that multiplied proportion which the advantage of superior numbers enables us to do. * * * Iron will be retaliated by iron * * * ; prison ships by prison ships, and like for like in general.*—To COL. MATHEWS. i, 234. FORD ED., ii, 262. (1779.)

7424. RETALIATION, A duty.—Retaliation is a duty we owe to those engaged in the cause of their country, to assure them that if any unlucky circumstance, baffling the efforts of their bravery, shall put them in the power of their enemies, we will use the pledges in our hands to warrant their lives from sacrifice.—REPORT TO CONGRESS. FORD ED., i, 495. (1775.)

7425. RETALIATION, Effective.—The numbers of our countrymen betrayed into the hands of the enemy by the treachery, cowardice or incompetence of our high officers, reduce us to the humiliating necessity of acquiescing in the brutal conduct observed towards them. When, during the last war, I put Governor Hamilton and Major Hay into a dungeon and in irons for having themselves personally done the same to the American prisoners who had fallen into their hands, and was threatened with retaliation by Phillips, then returned to New York, I declared to him I would load ten of their Saratoga prisoners (then under my care and within half a dozen miles of my house) with double irons for every American they should misuse under pretence of retaliation, and it put an end to the practice. But the ten for one are now with them.—To WILLIAM DUANE. vi, 211. (M., Sep. 1813.)

7426. RETALIATION, France and.—A recent fact, proving the anxiety of France for a reconciliation with us is the following. You know that one of the armed vessels which we took from her was refitted by us, sent to cruise on them, recaptured, and carried into Guadaloupe under the name of the Retaliation. On the arrival there of Desfourneaux, the new commissioner, he sent Victor Hughes home in irons; called up our captain; told him that he found he had a regular commission as an officer of the United States; that his vessel was then lying in harbor; that he should enquire into no fact preceding his own arrival (by this he avoided noticing that the vessel was really French property) and that therefore, himself and crew were free to depart with their vessel; that as to the differences between France and the United States, commissioners were coming to settle them, and in the meantime, no injury should be done on their part. The captain insisted on being a prisoner; the other disclaimed; and so he arrived here [Philadelphia] the day before yesterday. Within an hour after this was known to the Senate, they passed a retaliation bill. This was the more remarkable, as the bill was founded expressly on the *Arret* of Oct. 29, which had been communicated by the President as soon as received, and he remarked, "that it could not be too soon communicated to the two Houses and the public". Yet he almost in the same instant received, through the same channel, Mr. King, information that the *Arret* was suspended, and though he knew we were making it the foundation of a retaliation bill, he has never yet communicated it. But the Senate knew the fact informally from the Sec-

* The practical inculcation of such a lesson produced a sensible humiliation in the conduct of the enemy, through the subsequent stages of the war. The door of British magnanimity, which was barred to the dictates of reason, justice, and national honor, was compelled, reluctantly, to yield to the cries of their own countrymen, and the fatal admonitions of experience.—RAYNER's *Life of Jefferson*, New York edition, p. 194.

retary of State, and knowing it, passed the bill.—To EDMUND PENDLETON. iv, 288. FORD ED., vii, 357. (Pa., Feb. 14, 1799.)

7427. ——— ———. Our government contemplate restoring the Frenchmen taken originally in the same vessel, and kept at Lancaster [Penna.] as prisoners. This has furnished the idea of calling her a *cartel* vessel, and pretending that she came as such for an exchange of prisoners, which is false. She was delivered free and without condition, but it does not suit to let any new evidence appear of the desire of conciliation in France.—To EDMUND PENDLETON. iv, 290. FORD ED., vii, 360. (Pa., Feb. 1799.)

7428. ——— ———. Leblanc, an agent from Desfourneaux of Guadaloupe, came in the Retaliation. You will see in the papers Desfourneaux's letter to the President. * * * The vessel and crew were liberated without condition. Nothwithstanding this, they have obliged Leblanc to receive the French prisoners, and to admit, in the papers, the terms, "in *exchange* for *prisoners* taken from us", he denying at the same time that they consider them as *prisoners*, or had any idea of *exchange*. The object of his mission was not at all relative to that; but they choose to keep up the idea of a cartel, to prevent the transaction from being used as evidence of the sincerity of the French towards a reconciliation. He came to assure us of a discontinuance of all irregularities in French privateers from Guadaloupe. He has been received very cavalierly.—To JAMES MADISON. iv, 291. FORD ED., vii, 361. (Pa., Feb. 19, 1799.)

7429. RETALIATION, Governor Hamilton's case.—I hope you will ascribe the advice of the [Governor's] Council [confining Governor Hamilton], not to want of attention to the sacred nature of public conventions, of which I hope we shall never, in any circumstances, lose sight, but to a desire of stopping the effusion of the unoffending blood of women and children, and the unjustifiable severities exercised on our captive officers and soldiers in general, by proper severities on our part.—To SIR GUY CARLETON. FORD ED., ii, 256. (1779.) See WAR, PRISONERS OF.

7430. ——— ———. On receipt of your letter of August 6th, during my absence, the Council had the irons taken off the prisoners of war. When your advice was asked, we meant it should decide with us; and upon my return to Williamsburg, the matter was taken up and the enclosed advice* given.—To GENERAL WASHINGTON. i, 230. FORD ED., ii, 258. (1779.)

* The advice was in the form of an Order of Council which was written by Governor Jefferson as follows: "The Board having been at no time unmindful of the circumstances attending the confinement of Lieutenant Governor Hamilton, Captain Lamothe and Philip Dejean, which the personal cruelties of those men, as well as the general conduct of the enemy had constrained them to advise; wishing, and willing to expect, that their sufferings may lead them to the practice of humanity, should any future turn of fortune, in their favor, submit to their discretion the fate of their fellow-creatures; that it may prove an admonition to others, meditating like cruelties, not to rely for impunity in any circumstances of distance or present security; and that it may induce the enemy to reflect what must be the painful consequences should a continuation of the same conduct on their part impel us again to severities, while such multiplied subjects of retaliation are within our power; sensible that no impression can be made on the event of the war by wreaking vengeance on miserable captives; that the great

7431. ——— ———. Governor Hamilton and his companions were imprisoned and ironed, 1st. In retaliation for cruel treatment of our captive citizens by the enemy in general. 2d. For the barbarous species of warfare which himself and his savage allies carried on in our western frontier. 3d. For particular acts of barbarity, of which he himself was personally guilty, to some of our citizens in his power. Any one of these charges was sufficient to justify the measures we took.—To Colonel Mathews. i, 233. Ford ed., ii, 262. (Wg., 1779.)

7432. RETALIATION, Humanity and. —A uniform exercise of kindness to prisoners on our part has been returned by as uniform severity on the part of our enemies. * * * It is high time * * * to teach respect to the dictates of humanity; in such a case retaliation becomes an act of humanity.— To Sir Guy Carleton. Ford ed., ii, 251. (1779.)

7433. RETALIATION, Legislative.— Legislative warfare was begun by the British parliament. * * * The stat. 12 G. 3, c. 24 for carrying our citizens *charged* with the offences it describes, to be tried in a foreign country; by foreign judges instead of a jury of their vicinage, by laws not their own, without witnesses, without friends, or the means of making them; that of the 14 G. 3, c. 39, for protecting from punishment those who should murder an American in the execution of a British law, were previous to our acts of exile, and even to the commencement of the war. Their act of 14 G. 3, c. 19, for shutting up the harbor of Boston, and thereby annihilating, with the commerce of that city, the value of its property; that of 15 G. 3, c. 10, forbidding us to export to foreign markets the produce we have hitherto raised and sold at those markets, and thereby leaving that produce useless on our hands; that of 10 G. 3, c. 5, prohibiting all exports even to British markets, and making them legal prize when taken on the high seas, was dealing out confiscation, by wholesale, on the property of entire nations, which our acts, cited by you, retaliated but on the small scale of individual confiscation. But we never retaliated the 4th section of the last mentioned act, under which multitudes of our citizens taken on board our vessels were forced by starving, by periodical whippings, and by constant chains to become the murderers of their countrymen, perhaps of their fathers and brothers. If from this legislative warfare we turn to those scenes of active hostility which wrapped our houses in flame, our families in slaughter, our property in universal devastation, is the wonder that our Legislature did so much, or so little? Compare their situation with that of the British Parliament enjoying in ease and safety all the comforts and blessings of the earth, and hearing of these distant events as of the wars of

cause which has animated the two nations against each other is not to be decided by unmanly cruelties on wretches, who have bowed their necks to the power of the victor, but by the exercise of honorable valor in the field; earnestly hoping that the enemy, viewing the subject in the same light, will be content to abide the event of that mode of decision, and spare us the pain of a second departure from kindness to our captives; confident that commiseration to our prisoners is the only possible motive to which can be candidly ascribed, in the present actual circumstances of the war, the advice we are now about to give; the Board does advise the Governor to send Lieutenant Governor Hamilton, Captain Lamothe and Philip Dejean, to Hanover Court House, there to remain at large, within reasonable limits, taking the parole in the usual manner. The Governor orders accordingly."—Editor.

Benaris, or the extermination of the Rohillas, and say with candor whether the difference of scene and situation would not have justified a contrary difference of conduct towards each other? *—To George Hammond. Ford ed., vi, 12. (Pa., 1792.)

7434. RETALIATION, Life for life.— If the [British] enemy shall put to death, torture, or otherwise ill-treat any of the hostages in their hands, or of the Canadian, or other prisoners captivated by them in the service of the United Colonies,† recourse must be had to retaliation as the sole means of stopping the progress of human butchery, and for that purpose punishments of the same kind and degree shall be inflicted on an equal number of their subjects taken by us, till they shall be taught due respect to the violated rights of nations.—Report to Congress. Ford ed., ii, 34. (June 1776.)

7435. RETALIATION, Necessary.—I shall give immediate orders for having in readiness every engine which the enemy have contrived for the destruction of our unhappy citizens, captured by them. The presentiment of these operations is shocking beyond expression. I pray heaven to avert them; but nothing in this world will do it, but a proper conduct in the enemy. In every event, I shall resign myself to the hard necessity under which I shall act.— To Gen. Washington. i, 232. Ford ed., ii, 261. (Wg., 1779.)

7436. RETALIATION, Opportunity for. —It is impossible [that the British] can be serious in attempting to bully us * * * . We have too many of their subjects in our power and too much iron to clothe them with and, I will add, too much resolution to avail ourselves of both, to fear their pretended retaliation.‡—To General Washington. i, 231. Ford ed., ii, 259. (Wg., 1779.)

7437. RETALIATION, On prisoners of war.—This question [contest with Great Britain] will not be decided by wreaking vengeance on a few helpless captives but by achieving success in the fields of war, and gathering there those laurels which grow for the warrior brave. In this light we view the object between us, in this line we have hitherto conducted ourselves for its attainment.§—Report to Congress. Ford ed., i, 494. (1775.)

7438. ——— ———. Should you think proper in these days to revive ancient barbarism and again disgrace our nature with the sacrifice, the fortune of war has put into our power subjects for multiplied retaliation. To them, to you, and to the world we declare they shall not be wretched unless their imprudence or your example shall oblige us to make them so; but we declare that their lives shall teach our enemies to respect the rights of nations. Report to Congress. Ford ed., i, 494. (Dec. 1775.)

* From Jefferson's letter to George Hammond, British Minister, on the infractions of the peace treaty. The extract was in reply to a charge made by Hammond. Alexander Hamilton thought "it may involve irritating discussion", and Jefferson struck it out.—Editor.
† Here Jefferson had written "States of America", which has been stricken out by another hand and "Colonies" written in its place.—Note in Ford Edition.
‡ Jefferson was then Governor of Virginia, and a controversy had arisen respecting the treatment of prisoners of war.—Editor.
§ Ethan Allen and others were at that time prisoners in the hands of the British army. The report was not accepted by Congress.—Editor.

7439. —— ——. It is my duty, as well as it was my promise to the Virginia captives, to take measures for discovering any change which may be made in their situation. For this purpose, I must apply for your Excellency's interposition. I doubt not but you have an established mode of knowing. at all times, through your commissary of prisoners, the precise state of those in the power of the enemy. I must, therefore, pray you to put into motion, any such means you have, for obtaining knowledge of the situation of the Virginia officers in captivity. If you should think proper, as I could wish, to take upon yourself to retaliate any new sufferings which may be imposed on them, it will be more likely to have due weight, and to restore the unhappy on both sides, to that benevolent treatment for which all should wish. —To General Washington. i, 237. Ford ed., ii, 280. (Wg., Nov. 1779.)

7440. RETALIATION, On Savages.— To do wrong is a melancholy resource, even where retaliation renders it indispensably necessary. It is better to suffer much from the scalpings, the conflagrations, the rapes and rapine of savages, than to countenance and strengthen such barbarisms by retortion. I have ever deemed it more honorable and more profitable, too. to set a good example than to follow a bad one.—To M. Correa. vi, 405. (M., 1814.)

7441. RETIREMENT, Called from.— I had folded myself in the arms of retirement, and rested all prospects of future happiness on domestic and literary objects. A single event [Mrs. Jefferson's death] wiped away all my plans, and left me a blank which I had not the spirits to fill up. In this state of mind an appointment [Minister to France] from Congress found me, requiring me to cross the Atlantic.— To M. de Chastellux. i, 322. Ford ed., iii, 65. (Am., 1782.)

7442. —— ——. I had retired after five and twenty years of constant occupation in public affairs, and total abandonment of my own. I retired much poorer than when I entered the public service, and desired nothing but rest and oblivion. My name, however, was again brought forward [for the Presidency], without concert or expectation on my part. On my salvation I declare it.—To Edward Rutledge. iv, 151. Ford ed., vii, 93. (M., Dec. 1796.)

7443. RETIREMENT, Desire for.— However ardently my retirement to my own home and my own affairs, may be wished for by others, * * * there is no one of them who feels the wish once where I do a thousand times.—To Francis Eppes. Ford ed., v, 507. (Pa., April 1792.)

7444. RETIREMENT, Happiness in.— If I can carry into retirement the good will of my fellow citizens, nothing else will be wanting to my happiness.—To James Sullivan. v, 252. (1808.)

7445. RETIREMENT, Longing for.— Oh for the day when I shall be withdrawn from [office] ; when I shall have leisure to enjoy my family, my friends, my farm and books!—To Dr. Benjamin Rush. v, 225. (W., January 1808.)

7446. —— ——. It is now among my most fervent longings to be on my farm, which, with a garden and fruitery. will constitute my principal occupation in retirement.—To Robert R. Livingston. v, 224. (W., 1808.)

7447. —— ——. My longings for retirement are so strong, that I with difficulty encounter the daily drudgeries of my duty.—To James Monroe. v, 248. Ford ed., ix, 178. (W., Feb. 1808.)

7448. —— ——. As the moment of my retirement approaches, I become more anxious for its arrival, and to begin at length to pass what yet remains to me of life and health in the bosom of my family and neighbors, and in communication with my friends, undisturbed by political concerns or passions.—To Dr. Logan. v, 405. (W., Dec. 1808.)

7449. —— ——. Five weeks more will relieve me from a drudgery to which I am no longer equal, and restore me to a scene of tranquillity, amidst my family and friends, more congenial to my age and natural inclinations. —To James Monroe. v, 420. Ford ed., ix, 244. (W., Jan. 1809.)

7450. RETIREMENT, Newspaper attacks and.— I have for some time past been under an agitation of mind which I scarcely ever experienced before, produced by a check on my purpose of returning home at the close of this session of Congress. My operations at Monticello had been all made to bear upon that point of time, my mind was fixed on it with a fondness which was extreme, the purpose firmly declared to the President, when I became assailed from all quarters with a variety of objections. Among these it was urged that my return just when I had been attacked in the public papers, would injure me in the eyes of the public, who would suppose I either withdrew from investigation, or because I had not tone of mind sufficient to meet slander. The only reward I ever wished on my retirement was to carry with me nothing like a disapprobation of the public. These representations have, for some weeks past, shaken a determination which I had thought the whole world could not have shaken. I have not yet finally made up my mind on the subject, nor changed my declaration to the President. But having perfect reliance in the disinterested friendship of some of those who have counselled and urged it strongly; believing that they can see and judge better a question between the public and myself than I can. I feel a possibility that I may be detained here [Philadelphia] into the summer.—To Martha Jefferson Randolph. iii, 506. Ford ed., vi, 163. (Pa., Jan. 1793.)

7451. —— ——. It happened unfortunately that the attack made on me in the newspapers came out soon after I began to speak freely and publicly of my purpose to retire this Spring. * * * I find that as well those who are my friends as those who are not, putting the two things together as cause and effect, conceived I was driven from office either from want of firmness or perhaps fear of investigation. Desirous that my retirement may be clouded by no imputations of this kind, I see not only a possibility, but rather a probability, that I shall postpone it for some time.—To T. M. Randolph. D. L. J., 215. (Pa., Feb. 1793.)

7452. RETIREMENT, Occupations in. —In [retirement] I shall devote myself to occupations much more congenial with my inclinations, than those to which I have been called by the character of the times into which my lot was cast. About to be relieved from this *corvée* by age and the fulfillment of the *quadragena stipendia*, what remains to me of physical activity will chiefly be employed in the amusements of agriculture. Having little practical skill, I count more on the pleasures than the profits of that occupation.—To M. Lasteyrie. v, 315. (W., 1808.)

7453. —— ——. Within a few days I retire to my family, my books and farms; and having gained the harbor myself, I shall look on my friends still buffeting the storm with anxiety indeed, but not with envy.—To Dupont de Nemours. v, 432. (W., March 1809.)

7454. —— ——. I retire from scenes of d.fficulty, anxiety, and of contending passions, to the elysium of domestic affections, and the irresponsible direction of my own affairs. Safe in port myself, I shall look anxiously at my friends still buffeting the storm, and wish you all safe in port also.—To General Armstrong. v, 434. (W., 1809.)

7455. —— ——. I shall now bury myself in the groves of Monticello, and become a mere spectator of the passing events.—To Baron Humboldt. v, 435. (W., 1809.)

7456. —— ——. I am now retired: I resign myself, as a passenger, with confidence to those at present at the helm, and ask but for rest, peace and good will.—To Samuel Kerchival. vii, 9. Ford ed., x, 37. (M., 1816.)

7457. RETIREMENT, Old age.—I am too desirous of quiet to place myself in the way of contention. Against this I am admonished by bodily decay, which cannot be unaccompanied by corresponding wane of the mind. Of this I am as yet sensible, sufficiently to be unwilling to trust myself before the public, and when I cease to be so, I hope that my friends will be too careful of me to draw me forth and present me, like a Priam in armor, as a spectacle for public compassion. I hope our political bark will ride through all its dangers; but I can in future be but an inert passenger. —To Thomas Ritchie. vii, 193. Ford ed., x, 171. (M., 1820.)

7458. RETIREMENT, Power and.—Never did a prisoner, released from his chains, feel such relief as I shall on shaking off the shackles of power. Nature intended me for the tranquil pursuits of science, by rendering them my supreme delight. But the enormities of the times in which I have lived, have forced me to take a part in resisting them, and to commit myself on the boisterous ocean of political passions. I thank God for the opportunity of retiring from them without censure, and carrying with me the most consoling proofs of public approbation.—To Dupont de Nemours. v. 432. (W., March 2, 1809.)

7459. RETIREMENT, Principle and.—At the end of the next four years I shall certainly retire. Age, inclination and principle all dictate this.—To Philip Mazzei. iv, 554. (W., July 1804.)

7460. RETIREMENT, Reasons for.—The President [Washington] said, in an affectionate tone, that he had felt much concern at an expression which dropped from me yesterday [Feb. 28, 1792], and which marked my intention of retiring [from the Secretaryship of State] when he should; that as to himself, many motives obliged him to it, * * * yet he should consider it as unfortunate, if that should bring on the retirement of the great officers of the government, and that this might produce a shock on the public mind of dangerous consequence. I told him that no man had ever had less desire of entering into public of-

fices than myself; that the circumstance of a perilous war, which had brought everything into danger, and called for all the services which every citizen could render, had induced me to undertake the administration of the government of Virginia; that I had both before and after refused repeated appointments of Congress to go abroad in that sort of office, which, if I had consulted my own gratification, would almost have been the most agreeable to me; that at the end of two years, I resigned the government of Virginia, and retired with a firm resolution never more to appear in public life; that a domestic loss, however, happened, and made me fancy that absence and a change of scene for a time might be expedient for me; that I, therefore, accepted a foreign appointment, limited to two years; that at the close of that, Dr. Franklin having left France, I was appointed to supply his place, which I had occupied, and though I continued in it three or four years, it was under the constant idea of remaining only a year or two longer; that the Revolution in France coming on, I had so interested myself in the event of that, that when obliged to bring my family home, I had still an idea of returning and awaiting the close of that, to fix the era of my final retirement; that on my arrival here I found he had appointed me to my present office [Secretary of State]; that he knew I had not come into it without some reluctance; that it was, on my part, a sacrifice of inclination to the opinion that I might be more serviceable here than in France, and with a firm resolution in my mind, to indulge my constant wish for retirement at no very distant day; that when, therefore, I had received his letter, written from Mount Vernon, on his way to Carolina and Georgia (April 1, 1791), and discovered from an expression in that, that he meant to retire from the government ere long, and as to the precise epoch there could be no doubt, my mind was immediately made up, to make that the epoch of my own retirement from those labors of which I was heartily tired. That, however, I did not believe there was any idea in any of my brethren in the administration of retiring; that, on the contrary, I had perceived at a late meeting of the trustees of the sinking fund, that the Secretary of the Treasury had developed the plan he intended to pursue, and that it embraced years in its view. He said that he considered the Treasury Department as a much more limited one, going only to the single object of revenue, while that of the Secretary of State, embracing nearly all the objects of administration, was much more important, and the retirement of the officer, therefore, would be more noticed; that though the government had set out with a pretty general good will of the public, yet that symptoms of dissatisfaction had lately shown themselves far beyond what he could have expected, and to what height these might arise in case of too great a change in the administration, could not be foreseen.—The Anas. ix, 102. Ford ed., i, 175. (Feb. 29, 1792.)

7461. —— ——. I expressed to him [Washington] my excessive repugnance to public life, the particular uneasiness of my situation in this place [Philadelphia], where the laws of society oblige me always to move exactly in the circle which I know to bear me peculiar hatred; that is to say, the wealthy aristocrats, the merchants connected closely with England, the new created paper fortunes; that thus surrounded, my words were caught, multiplied, misconstrued, and even fabricated and spread abroad to my injury; that he saw also, that there was such an opposition of views between myself and another part of the Administration, as to render it peculiarly unpleasing, and to destroy the necessary harmony.—THE ANAS. ix, 166. FORD ED., i, 256. (Aug. 1793.)

7462. RETIREMENT, Washington opposed to Jefferson's.—The President calls on me [to-day, August 6], at my house in the country, and introduces my letter of July 31, announcing that I should resign at the close of the next month. He again expressed his repentance at not having resigned himself, and how much it was increased by seeing that he was to be deserted by those on whose aid he had counted; that he did not know where he should look to find characters to fill up the offices; that mere talents did not suffice for the Department of State, but it required a person conversant in foreign affairs, perhaps acquainted with foreign courts; that without this, the best talents would be awkward and at a loss. He told me that Colonel Hamilton had three or four weeks ago written to him, informing him that private as well as public reasons had brought him to the determination to retire, and that he should do it towards the close of the next session. He said he had often before intimated dispositions to resign, but never as decisively before; that he supposed he had fixed on the latter part of next session, to give an opportunity to Congress to examine into his conduct; that our going out at times so different increased his difficulty; for if he had both places to fill at once, he might consult both the particular talents and geographical situation of our successors. He expressed great apprehension at the fermentation which seemed to be working in the mind of the public: that many descriptions of persons, actuated by different causes, appeared to be uniting; what it would end in he knew not; a new Congress was to assemble, more numerous, perhaps of a different spirit; the first expressions of their sentiments would be important; if I would only stay to the end of that, it would relieve him considerably.—THE ANAS. ix, 165. FORD ED., i, 256. (Aug. 1793.)

7463. RETIREMENT, Welcome.—The moment of my retiring [from the Secretaryship of State] is now approaching, and is to me as land was to Columbus in his first American voyage.—To DAVID HUMPHREYS. iii, 490. (Nov. 1792.)

7464. ——. I now contemplate the approach of the moment of my retirement with the fondness of a sailor who has land in view.—To THOMAS PINCKNEY. FORD ED., vi, 132. (Pa., Nov. 1792.)

7465. ——. When I came into office, it was with a resolution to retire from it as soon as I could with decency. It pretty early appeared to me that the proper moment would be the first of those epochs at which the Constitution seems to have contemplated a periodical change or renewal of the public servants. * * * I look to that period with the longing of a wave-worn mariner, who has at length the land in view, and shall count the days and hours which still lie between me and it.—To PRESIDENT WASHINGTON. iii, 467. FORD ED., vi, 108. (M., Sep. 1792.) See APPROBATION.

7466. RETRENCHMENT, Salutary.—These views of reducing our burdens are formed on the expectation that a sensible, and at the same time a salutary reduction may take place in our habitual expenditures. For this purpose,

those of the civil government, the army and navy, will need revisal.—FIRST ANNUAL MESSAGE. viii, 9. FORD ED., viii, 119. (Dec. 1801.)

7467. REVENGE, For abuse.—I shall take no other revenge [for the slanders heaped upon me] than, by a steady pursuit of economy and peace, and by the establishment of republican principles in substance and in form, to sink federalism into an abyss from which there shall be no resurrection for it.—To LEVI LINCOLN. iv, 451. FORD ED., viii, 175. (W., Oct. 1802.)

7468. REVENUE, Imports and.—Our revenue will be less than it would be were we to continue to import instead of manufacturing our coarse goods. But the increase of population and production will keep pace with that of manufactures, and maintain the quantum of exports at the present level at least; and the imports need be equivalent to them, and consequently the revenue on them be undiminished.—To DUPONT DE NEMOURS. v, 583. FORD ED., ix, 319. (M., 1811.) See DEBT (UNITED STATES), INTERNAL IMPROVEMENTS, SURPLUS and TAXATION.

7469. REVOLUTION, Completion of.—The generation which commences a revolution rarely completes it. Habituated from their infancy to passive submission of body and mind to their kings and priests, they are not qualified when called on to think and provide for themselves; and their inexperience, their ignorance and bigotry make them instruments often, in the hands of the Bonapartes and Iturbides, to defeat their own rights and purposes. This is the present situation of Europe and Spanish America.—To JOHN ADAMS. vii, 307. FORD ED., x, 269. (M., 1823.)

7470. REVOLUTION, Right of.—Prudence, indeed, will dictate that governments long established should not be changed for light and transient causes; and accordingly all experience hath shown that mankind are more disposed to suffer, while evils are sufferable, than to right themselves by abolishing the forms to which they are accustomed. But, when a long train of abuses and usurpations [begun at a distinguished period and], pursuing invariably the same object, evinces a design to reduce them under absolute despotism, it is their right, it is their duty, to throw off such government, and to provide new guards for their future security. Such has been the patient sufferance of these Colonies; and such is now the necessity which constrains them to expunge * their former systems of government.—DECLARATION OF INDEPENDENCE AS DRAWN BY JEFFERSON.

7471. REVOLUTION (American), Appeal to British people.—In defence of our persons and properties under actual violation, we took up arms. When that violence shall be removed, when hostilities shall cease on the part of the aggressors, hostilities shall cease on our part also. For the achievement of this happy event, we call for and confide in the good offices of our fellow-subjects beyond the Atlantic. Of their friendly dispositions we do not cease to hope; aware, as they must be, that they have nothing more to expect from the same common enemy, than the

* Congress struck out the words in brackets and substituted "alter" for "expunge".—EDITOR.

humble favor of being last devoured.—DEC-LARATION ON TAKING UP ARMS. FORD ED., i, 475. (July 1775.)

7472. REVOLUTION (American), Battle of Lexington.—Within this week we have received the unhappy news of an action of considerable magnitude, between the King's troops and our brethren of Boston, in which it is said five hundred of the former, with the Earl of Percy, are slain. * * * This accident * has cut off our last hope of reconciliation, and a frenzy of revenge seems to have seized all ranks of people.—To DR. WILLIAM SMALL. i, 198. FORD ED., i, 453. (May 1775.)

7473. REVOLUTION (American), Beginning of.—The question who commenced the Revolution? is as difficult as that of the first inventors of a thousand good things. For example, who first discovered the principle of gravity? Not Newton; for Galileo, who died the year that Newton was born, had measured its force in the descent of gravid bodies. Who invented the Lavoiserian chemistry? The English say Dr. Black, by the preparatory discovery of latent heat. Who invented the steamboat? Was it Gerbert, the Marquis of Worcester, Newcommen, Savary, Papin, Fitch, Fulton? The fact is, that one new idea leads to another, that to a third, and so on through a course of time until some one, with whom no one of these ideas was original, combines all together, and produces what is justly called a new invention. I suppose it would be as difficult to trace our Revolution to its first embryo. We do not know how long it was hatching in the British cabinet before they ventured to make the first of the experiments which were to develop it in the end and to produce complete parliamentary supremacy. Those you mention in Massachusetts as preceding the Stamp Act, might be the first visible symptoms of that design. The proposition of that Act in 1764, was the first here. Your opposition, therefore, preceded ours, as occasion was sooner given there than here, and the truth, I suppose, is, that the opposition in every colony began whenever the encroachment was presented to it. This question of priority is as the inquiry would be who first, of the three hundred Spartans, offered his name to Leonidas?—To DR. BENJAMIN WATERHOUSE. vii, 99. FORD ED., x, 102. (M., 1818.)

7474. ——— ———. It would * * * be as difficult to say at what moment the Revolution began, and what incident set it in motion, as to fix the moment that the embryo becomes an animal, or the act which gives him a beginning. —To JOHN ADAMS. vii, 104. FORD ED., x, 107. (M., 1818.)

7475. ——— ———. A * * * misapprehension of * * * a passage in Mr. [William] Wirt's book, for which I am quoted, has produced a * * * reclamation of the part of Massachusetts, by some of her most distinguished and estimable citizens. I had been applied to by Mr. Wirt for such facts respecting Mr. [Patrick] Henry, as my intimacy with him and participation in the transactions of the day,

* Commenting on this passage, PARTON, in his *Life of Jefferson*, says: "We may judge of the strength of the tie between the mother country and the Colonies, by the fact that so un-English a mind as Jefferson's clung with sentimental fondness to the union long after there was any reasonable hope of their preserving it." Dr. Small, Jefferson's professor and friend at William and Mary College, was then living in England.—EDITOR.

might have placed within my knowledge. I accordingly committed them to paper; and Virginia being the theatre of his action, was the only subject within my contemplation, while speaking of him. Of the resolutions and measures here, in which he had the acknowledged lead. I used the expression that " Mr. Henry certainly gave the first impulse to the ball of revolution ". (Wirt, page 41.) The expression is, indeed, general, and in all its extension, would comprehend all the sister States; but indulgent construction would restrain it, as was really meant, to the subject matter under contemplation, which was Virginia alone; according to the rule of the lawyers and a fair canon of general criticism, that every expression should be construed *secundum subjectam materiem*. Where the first attack was made, there must have been, of course, the first act of resistance, and that was in Massachusetts. Our [Virginia's] first overt act of war was Mr. Henry's embodying a force of militia from several counties, regularly armed and organized, marching them in military array and making reprisal on the King's treasury at the seat of government, for the public powder taken away by his Governor. This was in the last days of April, 1775. Your formal battle of Lexington was ten or twelve days before that, which greatly overshadowed in importance, as it preceded in time. our little affray, which merely amounted to a levying of arms against the King; and, very possibly, you had had military affrays before the regular battle of Lexington.—To SAMUEL A. WELLS. i, 116. vii, 120. FORD ED., x. 128. (M., 1819.)

— REVOLUTION (American), British cruelty in.—See CRUELTY.

7476. REVOLUTION (American), Canada and.—In a short time, we have reason to hope, the delegates of Canada will join us in Congress, and complete the American union, as far as we wish to have it completed.—To JOHN RANDOLPH. i, 202. FORD ED., i, 492. (Pa., Nov. 1775.)

7477. REVOLUTION (American), Change of government.—With respect to the State of Virginia in particular. the people seem to have laid aside the monarchical, and taken up the republican government, with as much ease as would have attended their throwing off an old, and putting on a new suit of clothes. Not a single throe has attended this important transformation. A half-dozen aristocratical gentlemen, agonizing under the loss of preeminence, have sometimes ventured their sarcasms on our political metamorphosis. They have been thought fitter objects of pity, than of punishment.—To BENJAMIN FRANKLIN. i. 204. FORD ED., ii, 131. (1777.)

7478. REVOLUTION (American), Confident of victory.—We have long been out of all fear for the event of the war.—To JOHN ADAMS. i, 207. FORD ED., ii, 157. (Wg., June 1778.)

7479. REVOLUTION (American), Consequences of.—The enquiry which has been excited among the mass of mankind by our Revolution and its consequences, will ameliorate the condition of men over a great portion of the globe.—To JOHN DICKINSON. iv, 366. FORD ED., viii, 8. (W., March 1801.)

7480. REVOLUTION (American), French alliance and.—If there could have been a doubt before as to the event of the war, it is now totally removed by the interposition of France, and the generous alliance she has entered into with us.—To ———. i, 208. FORD ED., ii, 157. (Wg., 1778.)

7481. REVOLUTION (American), Gage's perfidy.—Hostilities thus commenced [at Lexington, &c.], on the part of the ministerial army have been since by them pursued without regard to faith or fame. The inhabitants of the town of Boston, in order to procure their enlargement, having entered into treaty with General Gage, their Governor, it was stipulated that the said inhabitants, having first deposited their arms with their own magistrates, should have liberty to depart from out of the said town taking with them their other effects. Their arms they accordingly delivered in, and claimed the stipulated license of departing with their effects. But in open violation of plighted faith and honor, in defiance of the sacred obligation of treaty which even savage nations observe, their arms, deposited with their own magistrates to be preserved as their property, were immediately seized by a body of armed men under orders from the said General; the greater part of the inhabitants were detained in the town, and the few permitted to depart were compelled to leave their most valuable effects behind. We leave the world to its own reflections on this atrocious perfidy.—DECLARATION ON TAKING UP ARMS. FORD ED.. i, 471. (July 1775.)

7482. REVOLUTION (American), Hopes of reconciliation.—When I saw Lord Chatham's bill. I entertained high hope that a reconciliation could have been brought about. The difference between his terms and those offered by our Congress might have been accommodated, if entered by both parties with a disposition to accommodate. But the dignity of Parliament, it seems, can brook no opposition to its power.—To DR. WILLIAM SMALL. i, 199. FORD ED., i, 454. (May 1775.)

7483. ——— ———. Looking with fondness towards a reconciliation with Great Br'tain, I cannot help hoping that you * may be able to contribute towards expediting this good work. I think it must be evident to yourself, that the Ministry have been deceived by their officers on this side of the water, who (for what purpose I cannot tell) have constantly represented the American opposition as that of a small faction, in which the body of the people took little part. This, you can inform them, of your own knowledge, is untrue. They have taken it into their heads, too. that we are cowards, and shall surrender at d'scretion to an armed force. * * * I wish they were thoroughly and minutely acquainted with every circumstance relative to America, as it exists in truth. I am persuaded, this would go far towards disposing them to reconciliation.—To JOHN RANDOLPH. i, 200. FORD ED.. i, 482. (M., August 1775.)

7484. ——— ———. If undeceiving the Minister, as to matters of fact, may change his disposition, it will, perhaps, be in your power, by assisting to do this, to render service to the whole empire. at the most critical time, certainly, that it has ever seen. Whether Britain shall continue the head of the greatest empire on earth, or shall return to her original station in the political scale of Europe, depends, perhaps, on the resolutions of the succeeding win-

* This John Randolph was the King's Attorney General, and a son of Sir John Randolph. He sided with the Crown and went to England. Peyton Randolph was his brother.—EDITOR.

ter. God send they may be wise and salutary for us all.—To JOHN RANDOLPH. i, 201. FORD ED., i, 484. (M., August 1775.)

7485. ——— ———. One bloody campaign will probably decide. everlastingly, our future course; and I am sorry to find a bloody campaign is decided on. If our winds and waters should not combine to rescue their shores from slavery, and General Howe's reinforcements should arrive in safety, we have hopes he will be inspirited to come out of Boston and take another drubbing; and we must drub him soundly, before the sceptred tyrant will know we are not mere brutes, to crouch under his hand, and kiss the rod with which he designs to scourge us.—To JOHN RANDOLPH. i, 203. FORD ED., i, 493. (M., Nov. 1775.)

7486. REVOLUTION (American), Influence on France.—The American Revolution seems first to have awakened the thinking part of the French nation in general from the sleep of despotism in which they were sunk.—AUTOBIOGRAPHY. i, 69. FORD ED., i, 96. (1821.) See REVOLUTION, FRENCH.

7487. REVOLUTION (American), Losses in.—I think that upon the whole [our loss * in the war] has been about one-half the number lost by the Brit'sh. * * * This difference is ascribed to our superiority in taking aim when we fire; every soldier in our army having been intimate with his gun from his infancy.—To ———. i, 208. FORD ED., ii, 157. (Wg.. 1778.)

7488. REVOLUTION (American), Memory of.—The memory of the American Revolution will be immortal, and will immortalize those who record it. The reward is encouraging, and will justify all those pains which a rigorous investigation of facts will render necessary.—To HILLIARD D'AUBERTEUIL. i, 535. (P., 1786.)

7489. REVOLUTION (American), Mythical British victories.—From the kind anxiety expressed in your letter, as well as from other sources of information, we discover that our enemies have filled Europe with Thrasonic accounts of victories they had never won and conquests they were fated never to make. While these accounts alarmed our friends in Europe, they afforded us diversion.—To ———. i, 207. FORD ED., ii, 156. (Wg., 1778.)

7490. REVOLUTION (American), New England and Virginia.—Throughout the whole of the Revolution, Virginia and the four New England States acted together; indeed they made the Revolution. Their five votes were always to be counted on: but they had to pick up the remaining two for a majority, when and where they could.—DANIEL WEBSTER'S CONVERSATION WITH JEFFERSON. FORD ED., x, 329.

7491. REVOLUTION (American), Peace propositions.—Though this Congress, during the dependence of these States on the British crown with unwearied supplications sued for peace and just redress, and though they still retain a sincere disposition to peace; yet as his Britannic majesty by an obstinate perseverance in injury and a callous indifference to the sufferings and the complaints of these States, has driven them to the necessity of declaring themselves independent, this Congress bound by the voice of their constituents, which coincides with their own sentiments, have no power to enter into conference or to receive any

* From Lexington to the end of 1777.—EDITOR.

propositions on the subject of peace which do not, as a preliminary, acknowledge these States to be sovereign and independent: and that whenever this shall have been authoritatively admitted on the part of Great Britain, they shall at all times and with that earnestness which the love of peace and justice inspires, be ready to enter into conference or treaty for the purpose of stopping the effusion of so much kindred blood.—RESOLUTIONS ON PEACE PROPOSITIONS. FORD ED., ii, 90. (Aug. 1776.)

7492. REVOLUTION (American), Resources of.—The main confidence of the Colonies was in their own resources. They considered foreign aid as probable and desirable, but not essential. I believe myself, from the whole of what I have seen of our resources and perseverance, 1, that had we never received any foreign aid, we should not have obtained our independence; but that we should have made a peace with Great Britain on any terms we pleased, short of that, which would have been a subjection to the same king, a union of force in war, &c. 2. That had France supplied us plentifully with money, suppose about four millions of guineas a year, without entering into the war herself at all, we should have established our Independence; but it would have cost more time, and blood, but less money. 3. That France, aiding us as she did, with money and forces, shortened much the time, lessened the expense of blood, but at a greater expense of money to her than would have otherwise been requisite.—NOTES ON M. SOULES'S WORK. ix, 297. FORD ED., iv, 305. (P., 1786.)

7493. —— ——. The submission of the States would not have been effected but by a long course of disasters, and such, too, as were irreparable in their nature. Their resources were great, and their determination so rooted, that they would have tried the last of them.— NOTES ON M. SOULES'S WORK. ix, 297. FORD ED., iv, 305. (P., 1786.)

7494. REVOLUTION (American), Royal incendiarism.—It is a lamentable circumstance, that the only mediatory power, acknowledged by both parties, instead of leading to a reconciliation his divided people, should pursue the incendiary purpose of still blowing up the flames, as we find him constantly do:ng, in every speech and public declaration.—To DR. WILLIAM SMALL. i, 199. FORD ED., i, 454. (May 1775.) See GEORGE III.

7495. REVOLUTION (American), Separation.—There is not in the British empire a man who more cordially loves a union with Great Britain, than I do. But by the God that made me, I will cease to exist before I yield to a connection on such terms as the British Parliament propose; and in this, I think I speak the sentiments of America. We want neither inducement nor power, to declare and assert a separation. It is will, alone, which is wanting, and that is growing apace under the fostering hand of our King.—To JOHN RANDOLPH. i, 203. FORD ED., i, 493. (Pa., November 1775.)

7496. REVOLUTION (American), Spirit of.—Even those in Parliament who are called friends to America seem to know nothing of our real determinations. I observe, they pronounced in the last Parliament that the Congress of 1774 did not mean to insist rigorously on the terms they held out, but kept something in reserve to give up; and, in fact, that they would give up everything but the article of taxation. Now, the truth is far from this, as I

can affirm, and put my honor to the assertion. Their continuance in this error may, perhaps, produce very ill consequences. The Congress stated the lowest terms they thought possible to be accepted, in order to convince the world they were not unreasonable. They gave up the monopoly and regulation of trade and all acts of Parliament prior to 1764, leaving to British generosity to render these, at some time, as easy to America as the interest of Britain would admit. But this was before blood was spilt. I cannot affirm, but have reason to think these terms would not now be accepted.—To JOHN RANDOLPH. i, 200. FORD ED., i, 483. (M., 1775.)

7497. REVOLUTION (American), Treaty of peace.—The terms obtained for us are indeed great, and are so deemed by your country, a few ill-designing debtors excepted.— To JOHN JAY. i, 332. FORD ED., iii, 316. (Pa., 1783.)

—— REVOLUTION (American), Underlying causes of.—See COLONIES (AMERICAN).

7498. REVOLUTION (American), Unnatural contest.—I hope the returning wisdom of Great Britain will, ere long, put an end to this unnatural contest.—To JOHN RANDOLPH. i, 200. FORD ED., i, 482. (M., August 1775.)

7499. REVOLUTION (American), Washington and.—The moderation and virtue of a single character have probably prevented this Revolution from being closed, as most others have been, by a subversion of that liberty it was intended to establish.—To GENERAL WASHINGTON. i, 335. FORD ED., iii, 467. (A., 1784.) See COLONIES, CORNWALLIS, DECLARATION OF INDEPENDENCE, GEORGE III., PARLIAMENT, RIGHTS OF BRITISH AMERICA, WAR and WASHINGTON.

7500. REVOLUTION (French), American revolution and.—Celebrated writers of France and England had already sketched good principles on the subject of government; yet the American Revolution seems first to have awakened the thinking part of the French nation in general from the sleep of despotism in which they were sunk. The officers, too, who had been to America, were mostly young men, less shackled by habit and prejudice, and more ready to assent to the suggestions of common sense, and feeling of common rights, than others. They came back with new ideas and impressions. The press, notwithstanding its shackles, began to disseminate them; conversation assumed new freedoms. Politics became the theme of all societies, male and female, and a very extensive and zealous party was formed, which acquired the appellation of the Patriotic Party, who, sensible of the abusive government under which they lived, sighed for occasions of reforming it. This party comprehended all the honesty of the kingdom, sufficiently at leisure to think, the men of letters, the easy Bourgeois, the young nobility, partly from reflection, partly from mode; for these sentiments became matter of mode, and as such united most of the young women to the party. —AUTOBIOGRAPHY. i, 69. FORD ED., i, 96. (1821.)

7501. —— ——. The French nation has been awakened by our Revolution, they feel their strength, they are enlightened, their lights are spreading, and they will not retrograde.— To GENERAL WASHINGTON. ii, 535. (P., Dec. 1788.)

— REVOLUTION (French), Bill of rights.—See BILL OF RIGHTS.

7502. REVOLUTION (French), Clergy and nobles.—It was imagined the ecclesiastical elections would have been generally in favor of the higher clergy; on the contrary, the lower clergy have obtained five-sixths of these deputations. These are the sons of peasants, who have done all the drudgery of the service for ten, twenty, and thirty guineas a year, and whose oppressions and penury, contrasted with the pride and luxury of the higher clergy, have rendered them perfectly disposed to humble the latter. They have done it, in many instances, with a boldness they were thought insusceptible of. Great hopes have been formed that these would concur with the *Tiers Etat* in voting by persons. In fact, about half of them seem as yet so disposed; but the bishops are intriguing, and drawing them over with the address which has ever marked ecclesiastical intrigue.—To JOHN JAY. iii, 27. (P., May 1789.)

7503. —— ——. The clergy and the nobles, by their privileges and their influence, have hitherto screened their property in a great degree, from public contribution. That half of the orange, then, remains yet to be squeezed, and for this operation there is no agent powerful enough but the people. They are, therefore, brought forward as the favorites of the Court, and will be supported by them.—To JOHN JAY. ii, 561. (P., 1789.)

7504. —— ——. The Clergy will leave nothing unattempted to secure [the voting by orders in the States General]; for they see that the spirit of reformation will not confine itself to the political, but will extend to the ecclesiastical establishment also.—To JOHN JAY. ii, 561. (P., 1789.)

— REVOLUTION (French), Constitutional reforms.—See CONSTITUTION, FRENCH.

— REVOLUTION (French), Execution of Louis XVI.—See LOUIS XVI.

— REVOLUTION (French), Fall of Bastile.—See BASTILE.

7505. REVOLUTION (French), Famine and.—We have had such a winter here as is not on record. The mercury was 18½° below freezing on Reaumur's scale, and I think it was nearly two months varying between that and zero. It gave occasion for a display of the benevolent character of this nation, which, great as I had thought it, went beyond my expectations. There seems to be a very general apprehension of the want of bread this spring. Supplies are hoped from our country, and indeed they have already reduced the price of flour at Bordeaux from 36l. to 33l. the barrel.—To COUNT DE MOUSTIER. ii, 590. (P., March 1789.)

7506. —— ——. We have had such a winter as makes me shiver yet whenever I think of it. All communications, almost, were cut off. Dinners and suppers were suppressed, and the money laid out in feeding and warming the poor, whose labors were suspended by the rigor of the season.—To MADAME DE BREHAN. ii, 591. FORD ED., v, 79. (P., 1789.)

7507. —— ——. The want of bread is very seriously dreaded through the whole kingdom. Between twenty and thirty shiploads of wheat and flour have already arrived from the United States, and there will be about the same quantity of rice sent from Charleston to this country directly. * * * Paris consumes about a shipload a day (say two hundred and fifty tons).—To WILLIAM CARMICHAEL. iii, 22. (P., May 1789.)

7508. —— ——. There have been some mobs, occasioned by the want of bread, in different parts of the kingdom, in which there may have been some lives lost, perhaps a dozen or twenty. These had no professed connection, generally, with the constitutional revolution. A more serious riot happened lately in Paris, in which about one hundred of the mob were killed. This execution has been universally approved, as they seemed to have no view but mischief and plunder.—To JAMES MADISON. iii, 34. (P., May 1789.)

7509. —— ——. The want of bread had been foreseen for some time past, and M. de Montmorin had desired me to notify it in America, and that, in addition to the market price, a premium should be given on what should be brought from the United States. Notice was accordingly given, and produced considerable supplies. Subsequent information made the importations from America, during the months of March, April and May, into the Atlantic ports of France, amount to about twenty-one thousand barrels of flour, besides what went to other ports, and in other months; while our supplies to their West Indian islands relieved them also from that drain. This distress for bread continued till July.—AUTOBIOGRAPHY. i, 89. FORD ED., i, 123. (1821.)

7510. REVOLUTION (French), Financial abuses.—The discovery of the abominable abuses of public money by the late Comptroller General, some new expenses of the Court, not of a piece with the projects of reformation, and the imposition of new taxes, have, in the course of a few weeks, raised a spirit of discontent in the nation, so great and so general, as to threaten serious consequences. The parliaments in general, and particularly that of Paris, put themselves at the head of this effervescence, and direct its object to the calling of the States General, who have not been assembled since 1614. The object is to fix a constitution, and to limit expenses. The King has been obliged to hold a bed of justice, to enforce the registering the new taxes; the parliament on their side, propose to issue a prohibition against their execution. Very possibly this may bring on their exile.—To GENERAL WASHINGTON. ii, 251. (P., 1787.)

7511. REVOLUTION (French), Flight of the King.—We are now under the first impression of the news of the King's flight from Paris, and his recapture. It would be unfortunate were it in the power of any one man to defeat the issue of so beautiful a revolution. I hope and trust it is not, and that, for the good of suffering humanity all over the earth, that revolution will be established and spread through the whole world.—To SIR JOHN SINCLAIR. iii, 284. (Pa., 1791.)

7512. —— ——. You have heard of the peril into which the French Revolution is brought by the flight of their King. Such are the fruits of that form of government which heaps importance on idiots, and of which the tories of the present day are trying to preach into our favor.—To EDWARD RUTLEDGE. iii, 285. FORD ED., v, 376. (Pa., 1791.)

7513. REVOLUTION (French), History of.—As yet, we are but in the first chapter of its history.—Autobiography. i, 106. Ford ed., i, 147. (1821.)

7514. REVOLUTION (French), Imperial· imbecility.—The government has published an *Arret,* suspending all reimbursements of capital, and reducing the payments of the principal mass of demands for interest to twelve sous in the livre; the remaining eight sous to be paid with certificates. * * * The consternation is as yet too great to let us judge of the issue. It will probably ripen the public mind to the necessity of a change in their constitution, and to the substituting the collected wisdom of the whole in place of a single will, by which they have been hitherto governed. It is a remarkable proof of the total incompetency of a single head to govern a nation well, when, with a revenue of six hundred millions, they are led to a declared bankruptcy, and to stop the wheels of government, even in its most essential movements, for want of money.—To John Jay. ii, 468. (P., August 1788.)

7515. REVOLUTION (French), Influence of women.—In my opinion, a kind of influence which none of their plans of reform take into account, will elude them all; I mean the influence of women in the government. The manners of the nation allow them to visit, alone, all persons in office, to solicit the affairs of the husband, family, or friends, and their solicitations bid defiance to laws and regulations. This obstacle may seem less to those who, like our countrymen, are in the precious habit of considering right as a barrier against all solicitation. Nor can such an one, without the evidence of his own eyes, believe in the desperate state to which things are reduced in this country from the omnipotence of an influence which, fortunately for the happiness of the sex itself, does not endeavor to extend itself in our country beyond the domestic line.— To General Washington. ii, 536. (P., Dec. 1788.)

7516. REVOLUTION (French), Jefferson's relations to.—I considered a successful reformation of government in France, as insuring a general reformation through Europe, and the resurrection, to a new life, of their people, now ground to dust by the abuses of the governing powers. I was much acquainted with the leading patriots of the Assembleé. Being from a country which had successfully passed through a similar reformation, they were disposed to my acquaintance, and had some confidence in me. I urged, most strenuously, an immediate compromise; to secure what the government was now ready to yield, and trust to future occasions for what might still be wanting. It was well understood that the King would grant, at this time, 1. Freedom of the person by *habeas corpus;* 2. Freedom of conscience: 3. Freedom of the press: 4. Trial by jury: 5. A representative legislature: 6. Annual meetings: 7. The origination of laws: 8. The exclusive right of taxation and appropriation: and 9. The responsibility of ministers; and with the exercise of these powers they could obtain, in future, whatever might be further necessary to improve and preserve their constitution. They thought otherwise, however, and events have proved their lamentable error. For, after thirty years of war. foreign and domestic, the loss of millions of lives, the prostration of private happiness, and foreign subjugation of their own country for a time, they have obtained no more,

nor even that securely. They were unconscious of (for who could foresee?) the melancholy sequel of their well-meant perseverance; that their physical force would be usurped by a first tyrant to trample on the independence, and even the existence, ot other nations; that this would afford a fatal example for the atrocious conspiracy of kings against their people: would generate their unholy and homicide alliance to make common cause among themselves, and to crush, by the power of the whole, the efforts of any part, to moderate their abuses and oppressions.—Autobiography. i, 93. Ford ed., i, 129. (1821.) See Holy Alliance.

7517. ——— ———. Possibly you may remember, at the date of the *jeu de paume,* how earnestly I urged yourself and the patriots of my acquaintance, to enter then into a compact with the King, securing freedom of religion, freedom of the press, trial by jury, *habeas corpus,* and a national legislature, all of which it was known he would then yield, to go home, and let these work on the amelioration of the condition of the people, until they should have rendered them capable of more, when occasions would not fail to arise for communicating to them more. This was as much as I then thought them able to bear soberly and usefully for themselves. You thought otherwise, and that the dose might still be larger. And I found you were right; for subsequent events proved they were equal to the constitution of 1791. Unfortunately, some of the most honest and enlightened of our patriotic friends (but closet politicians merely, unpracticed in the knowledge of man), thought more could still be obtained and borne. They did not weigh the hazards of a transition from one form of government to another, the value of what they had already rescued from those hazards, and might hold in security if they pleased, nor the imprudence of giving up the certainty of such a degree of liberty, under a limited monarchy, for the uncertainty of a little more under the form of a republic. You differed from them. You were for stopping there and for securing the constitution which the National Assembly had obtained. Here, too, you were right; and from this fatal error of the republicans, from their separation from yourself and the constitutionalists, in their councils, flowed all the subsequent sufferings and crimes of the French nation. The hazards of a second change fell upon them by the way. The foreigner gained time to anarchise by gold the government he could not overthrow by arms, to crush in their own councils the genuine republicans, by the fraternal embraces of exaggerated and hired pretenders, and to turn the machine of Jacobinism from the change to the destruction of order; and, in the end, the limited monarchy they had secured was exchanged for the unprincipled and bloody tyranny of Robespierre; and the equally unprincipled and maniac tyranny of Bonaparte. You are now rid of him, and I sincerely wish you may continue so. But this may depend on the wisdom and moderation of the restored dynasty. It is for them now to read a lesson in the fatal errors of the republicans; to be contented with a certain portion of power, secured by a formal compact with the nation, rather than, grasping at more, hazard all upon uncertainty, and risk meeting the fate of their predecessor, or a renewal of their own exile.—To Marquis Lafayette. vi, 421. Ford ed., ix, 505. (M., Feb. 1815.)

7518. ——— ———. I had no apprehension that the tempest, of which I saw the beginning was to spread over such an extent of space and time.—To Comte Diodati. v, 62. (W., 1807.)

7519. REVOLUTION (French), Leaders in.—I was intimate with the leading characters of the year 1789. So I was with those of the Brissotine party who succeeded them; and have always been persuaded that their views were upright. Those who have followed them have been less known to me.—To M. DE MEUNIER. FORD ED., vii, 13. (M., 1795.)

7520. ———. When I left France at the close of '89, your revolution was, as I thought, under the direction of able and honest men. But the madness of some of their successors, the vices of others, the malicious intrigues of an envious and corrupting neighbor, the *tracasserie* of the Directory, the usurpations, the havoc, and devastations of your Attila, and the equal usurpations, depredations and oppressions of your hypocritical deliverers, will form a mournful period in the history of man, a period of which the last chapter will not be seen in your day or mine, and one which I still fear is to be written in characters of blood. Had Bonaparte reflected that such is the moral construction of the world, that no national crime passes unpunished in the long run, he would not now be in the cage of St. Helena; and were your oppressors to reflect on the same truth, they would spare to their own countries the penalties on their present wrongs which will be inflicted on them in future times. The seeds of hatred and revenge which they are now sowing with a large hand, will not fail to produce their fruits in time. Like their brother robbers on the highway, they suppose the escape of the moment a final escape, and deem infamy and future risk countervailed by present gain.—To M. DE MARBOIS. vii, 76. (M., 1817.)

7521. REVOLUTION (French), Lettres de cachet.—Though they see the evil of *lettres de cachet,* they believe they do more good on the whole. They will think better in time. —To DR. CURRIE. ii, 544. (P., 1788.)

7522. REVOLUTION (French), Liberty and.—The liberty of the whole earth was depending on the issue of the contest, and was ever such a prize won with so little innocent blood?—To WILLIAM SHORT. iii, 502. FORD ED., vi, 154. (Pa., 1793.)

— REVOLUTION (French), Marie Antoinette.—See MARIE ANTOINETTE.

7523. REVOLUTION (French), Ministerial reforms.—I hope the internal affairs of this country will be finally arranged without having cost a drop of blood. Looking on as a bystander, no otherwise interested, than as entertaining a sincere love for the nation in general, and a wish to see their happiness promoted, keeping myself clear of the particular views and passions of individuals, I applaud extremely the patriotic proceedings of the present ministry. Provincial Assemblies established, the States General called, the right of taxing the nation without their consent abandoned, *corvées* abolished, torture abolished, the criminal code reformed, are facts which will do eternal honor to their administration, in history.—To WILLIAM CARMICHAEL. ii, 466. (P., Aug. 1788.)

7524. ———. The internal good they are doing to their country makes me completely their friend.—To WILLIAM CARMICHAEL. ii, 467. (P., 1788.)

7525. REVOLUTION (French), Monarchy and parliaments.—The struggle in France is as yet * * * between the monarchy and the parliaments. The nation is no otherwise concerned, but as both parties may be induced to let go some of its abuses, to court the public favor. The danger is that the people, deceived by a false cry of liberty, may be led to take side with one party, and thus give the other a pretext for crushing them still more.— To E. RUTLEDGE. ii, 435. FORD ED., v, 42. (P., July 1788.)

7526. ———. This nation is * * * under great internal agitation. The authority of the crown on one part, and that of the parliaments on the other, are fairly at issue. Good men take part with neither, but have raised an opposition, the object of which is to obtain a fixed and temperate constitution. There was a moment when this opposition ran so high as to endanger an appeal to arms, in which case, perhaps, it would have been crushed. The moderation of government has avoided this, and they are yielding daily one right after another. They have given them Provincial Assemblies, which will be very perfect representatives of the nation, and stand somewhat in the place of our State Assemblies. They have reformed the criminal laws; acknowledged the King cannot lay a new tax, without the consent of the States General; and they will call the States General the next year. —To COLONEL MONROE. ii, 457. (P., 1788.)

7527. ———. The contest here is exactly what it was in Holland: a contest between the monarchical and aristocratical parts of the government, for a monopoly of despotism over the people. The aristocracy in Holland, seeing that their common prey was likely to escape out of their clutches, chose rather to retain its former portion, and therefore coalesced with the single head. The people remained victims. Here, I think, it will take a happier turn. The parliamentary part of the aristocracy is alone firmly united. The Noblesse and Clergy, but especially the former, are divided partly between the parliamentary and the despotic party, and partly united with the real patriots, who are endeavoring to gain for the nation what they can, both from the parliamentary and the single despotism. I think I am not mistaken in believing that the King and some of his ministers are well affected to this band; and surely, that they make great concessions to the people, rather than small ones to the parliament. They are, accordingly, yielding daily to the national reclamations, and will probably end in according a well-tempered constitution. —To M. DE CREVECOEUR. ii, 457. (P., 1788.)

7528. REVOLUTION (French), Monarchy waning.—In the course of three months, the royal authority has lost, and the rights of the nation gained as much ground by a revolution of public opinion only, as England gained in all her civil wars under the Stuarts. I rather believe, too, they will retain the ground gained because it is defended by the young and the middle aged in opposition to the old only. The first party increases, and the latter diminishes daily from the course of nature.—To JOHN ADAMS. ii, 259. (P., 1787.)

7529. REVOLUTION (French), National Assembly.—The National Assembly (for that is the name they take), having shown through every stage of these transactions a coolness, wisdom, and resolution to set fire to the four corners of the kingdom and to perish with it themselves, rather than to relinquish an iota from their plan of a total change of government, are now in complete and undisputed possession of the sovereignty. The executive and aristocracy are at their feet; the mass of the nation, the mass of the clergy, and the army are with them. They have prostrated the old government, and are now beginning to build one from the foundation.—To Thomas Paine. iii, 69. (P., July 1789.)

7530. —— ——. It is impossible to desire better dispositions towards us than prevail in the National Assembly. Our proceedings have been viewed as a model for them on every occasion; and though in the heat of debate men are generally disposed to contradict every authority urged by their opponents, ours has been treated like that of the Bible, open to explanation but not to question. I am sorry that in the moment of such a disposition, anything should come from us to check it. The placing them on a mere footing with the English will have this effect.—To James Madison. iii, 99. Ford ed., v, 110. (P., Aug. 1789.)

7531. —— ——. The difficulties which now appear threatening to my mind are those which will result from the size of the Assembly. Twelve hundred persons of any rank and of any nation assembled together would with difficulty be prevented from tumult and confusion. But when they are to compose an assembly for which no rules of debate or proceeding have been yet formed, in whom no habits of order have been yet established, and to consist moreover of Frenchmen, among whom there are always more speakers than listeners, I confess to you I apprehend some danger.—To Mr. Shippen. ii, 580. (P., March 1789.)

7532. REVOLUTION (French), National debt.—Calonné stated to * * * [the Assembly of Notables] that the annual excess of expenses beyond the revenue, when Louis XVI. came to the throne, was thirty-seven millions of livres; that four hundred and forty millions had been borrowed to reestablish the navy; that the American war had cost them fourteen hundred and forty millions (two hundred and fifty-six millions of dollars), and that the interest of these sums, with other increased expenses had added forty millions more to the annual deficit. (But a subsequent and more candid estimate made it fifty-six millions.)—Autobiography. i, 70. Ford ed., i, 97. (1821.)

7533. REVOLUTION (French), Necker recalled.—The Archbishop [of Toulouse] has been removed * * * and M. Necker called in as Director General of finance. To soften the Archbishop's dismission, a cardinal's hat is asked for him from Rome, and his nephew promised the succession to the archbishopric of Sens. The public joy, on this change of administration, was very great indeed. The people of Paris were amusing themselves with trying and burning the Archbishop in effigy, and rejoicing on the appointment of M. Necker. The commanding officer of the city guards undertook to forbid this, and not being obeyed, he charged the mob with fixed bayonets, killed two or three, and wounded many. This stopped their rejoicings for that day; but enraged at being thus obstructed in amusements wherein they had committed no disorder whatever, they collected in great numbers the next day, attacked the guards in various places, burned ten or twelve guard houses, killed two or three of the guards, and had about six or eight of their own number killed. The city was, hereupon, put under martial law, and after a while, the tumult subsided, and peace was restored.—To John Jay. ii, 471. (P., Sep. 1788.)

7534. REVOLUTION (French), Nobles and people.—With respect to the nobles, the younger members are generally for the people, and the middle-aged are daily coming over to the same side.—To John Jay. ii, 561. (P Jan. 1789.)

7535. REVOLUTION (French), Notables called.—The King has called an *Assemblée des Notables.* This has not been done for one hundred and sixty years past. Of course it calls up all the attention of the people. The objects of this Assembly are not named. Several are conjectured. T. e tolerating the Protestant religion; removing all the internal custom houses to the frontier; equalizing the gabelles on salt through the kingdom; the sale of the King's domains to raise money; or, finally, the effecting this necessary end by some other means are talked of. But in truth, nothing is known about it. This government practices secrecy so systematically, that it never publishes its purposes or its proceedings sooner or more extensively than is necessary.—To John Jay. ii, 91. (P., 1787.)

7536. —— ——. The *Assemblée des Notables* met yesterday [Feb. 22]. The King, in a short but affectionate speech, informed them of his wish to consult with them on the plans he had digested, and on the general good of his people, and his desire to imitate the head of his family, Henry IV., whose memory is so dear to the nation. The *Gardé des Sceaux* then spoke about twenty minutes, chiefly in compliment to the orders present. The Comptroller General, in a speech of about an hour, opened the budget, and enlarged on the several subjects which will be under their deliberation, * * * and the institution of Provincial Assemblies. The *Assemblée* was then divided into committees, with a prince of the blood at the head of each.—To John Jay. ii, 129. (P., 1787.)

7537. —— ——. The first step of the deputies to the *Assemblée des Notables* should be to get themselves divided into two chambers instead of seven; the noblesse and the commons separately. The second, to persuade the King, instead of choosing the deputies of the Commons himself, to summon those chosen by the people for the Provincial administrations. The third, as the *noblesse* is too numerous to be of the *Assemblée,* to obtain permission for that body to choose its own deputies. Two houses, so elected, would contain a mass of wisdom which would make the people happy, and the King great; would place him in history where no other act can possibly place him. They would thus put themselves in the track of the best guide they can follow; they would soon overtake it, become its guide in turn and lead to the wholesome modifications wanting in that model and necessary to constitute a rational government. Should they attempt more than the established habits of the people are ripe for, they may lose all, and retard indefinitely the ultimate object of their aim.—To Madame la Comtesse de Tesse. ii, 133. (N., 1787.)

7538. —— ——. The *Assemblée des Notables* has been productive of much good. The reformation of some of the most oppressive laws has taken place, and is taking place. The allotment of the State into subordinate governments, the administration of which is committed to persons chosen by the people, will work in time a very beneficial change in their constitution. The expense of the trappings of monarchy, too, is lightening. Many of the useless officers, high and low, of the King, Queen, and Princes, are struck off.—To GENERAL WASHINGTON. ii, 251. (P., 1787.)

7539. REVOLUTION (French), Principles of.—I continue eternally attached to the principles of your [the French] Revolution. I hope it will end in the establishment of some firm government, friendly to liberty, and capable of maintaining it. If it does, the world will become inevitably free. If it does not, I feel that the zealous apostles of English despotism here, will increase the number of its disciples. However, we shall still remain free. Though they may harass our spirits, they cannot make impression on our centre.—To J. P. BRISSOT DE WARVILLE. FORD ED., vi, 249. (Pa., May 1793.)

7540. REVOLUTION (French), Provincial Assemblies.—The establishment of the Provincial Assemblies was, in itself, a fundamental improvement. They would be of the choice of the people, one-third renewed every year, in those provinces where there are no States, that is to say, over about three-fourths of the kingdom. They would be partly an Executive themselves, and partly an executive council to the Intendant, to whom the executive power, in his province, had been, heretofore, entirely delegated. Chosen by the people, they would soften the execution of hard laws and, having a right of representation to the King, they would censure bad laws, suggest good ones, expose abuses, and their representations, when united, would command respect. To the other advantages might be added the precedent itself of calling the *Assemblée des Notables,* which would perhaps grow into habit. The hope was that the improvements thus promised would be carried into effect; that they would be maintained during the present [Louis XVI.] reign, and that that would be long enough for them to take some root in the constitution, so that they might come to be considered as a part of that, and be protected by time, and the attachment of the nation.—AUTOBIOGRAPHY. i, 71. FORD ED., i, 98. (1821.)

7541. REVOLUTION (French), Reform and.—If the people do not obtain now so much as they have a right to, they will in the long run. The misfortune is that they are not yet ripe for receiving the blessings to which they are entitled. I doubt, for instance, whether the body of the nation, if they could be consulted, would accept of a *habeas corpus* law, if offered them by the King.—To JAMES MADISON. ii, 506. FORD ED., v, 53. (P., Nov. 1788.)

7542. REVOLUTION (French), Riots.—We have had in Paris a very considerable riot, in which about one hundred people have been probably killed. It was the most unprovoked, and is therefore, justly, the most unpitied catastrophe of that kind I ever knew. Nor did the wretches know what they wanted, except to do mischief. It seems to have had no particular connection with the great national question now in agitation.—To WILLIAM CARMICHAEL. iii, 22. (P., May 1789.)

7543. ———— ————. Hitherto no acts of popular violence had been produced by the struggle for political reformation. Little riots, on ordinary incidents, had taken place, as at other times, in different parts of the kingdom, in which some lives, perhaps a dozen or twenty, had been lost; but in the month of April, 1788, a more serious one occurred in Paris, unconnected, indeed, with the revolutionary principle,

but making part of the history of the day. The Faubourg St. Antoiné is a quarter of the city inhabited entirely by the class of day laborers and journeymen in every line. A rumor was spread among them, that a great paper manufacturer, of the name of Reveillon, had proposed, on some occasion, that their wages should be lowered to fifteen sous a day. Inflamed at once into rage, and without inquiring into its truth, they flew to his house in vast numbers, destroyed everything in it, and in his magazines and workshops, without secreting, however, a pin's worth to themselves, and were continuing this work of devastation, when the regular troops were called in. Admonitions being disregarded, they were of necessity fired on, and a regular action ensued, in which about one hundred and twenty of them were killed, before the rest would disperse. There had rarely passed a year without such a riot, in some part or other of the Kingdom; and this is distinguished only as contemporary with the Revolution, although not produced by it.—AUTOBIOGRAPHY. i, 89. FORD ED., i, 124. (1821.)

7544. ———— ————. They were the most abandoned banditti of Paris, and never was a riot more unprovoked and unpitied. They began, under a pretence that a paper manufacturer had proposed in an assembly to reduce their wages to fifteen sous a day. They rifled his house, destroyed everything in his magazines and shops, and were only stopped in their career of mischief by the troops engaging in regular action with them and killing probably one hundred of them. Neither this nor any of the other riots has had a professed connection with the great national reformation now going on. They are such as have happened every year since I have been here, and as will continue to be produced by common incidents.—To JOHN JAY. iii, 26. (P., May 1789.)

7545. REVOLUTION (French), States General.—The States General were opened on the 5th of May, 1789, by speeches from the King, the *Gardé des Sceaux,* Lamoignon, and M. Necker. The last was thought to trip too lightly over the constitutional reformations which were expected. His notices of them in this speech were not as full as in his previous "*Rapport au Roi*". This was observed to his disadvantage; but much allowance should have been made for the situation in which he was placed, between his own counsels, and those of the ministers and party of the Court. Overruled in his own opinions, compelled to deliver, and to gloss over those of his opponents, and even to keep their secrets, he could not come forward in his own attitude. The composition of the *Assemblée,* although equivalent on the whole to what had been expected, was something different in its elements. It had been supposed, that a superior education would carry into the scale of the Commons a respectable portion of the *Noblesse.* It did so as to those of Paris, of its vicinity and of the other considerable cities, whose dearer intercourse with enlightened society had liberalized their minds, and prepared them to advance up to the measure of the times. But the Noblesse of the country, which constituted two-thirds of that body, were far in their rear. Residing constantly on their patrimonial feuds, and familiarized, by daily habit, with seigneurial powers and practices, they had not yet learned to suspect their inconsistence with reason and right. They were willing to submit to equality of taxation, but not to descend from their rank and prerogatives to be incorporated in session with the *Tiers Etat.* Among the Clergy, on the other hand, it had been apprehended that the higher orders of the hierarchy, by their wealth and connections, would have carried the elections generally; but it proved that in most cases the lower clergy had obtained the popular majorities. These consisted of the curés, sons of the peasantry, who had been employed to do all the drudgery of parochial services for ten, twenty, or thirty Louis a year; while their superiors were consuming their princely revenues in palaces of luxury and indolence. The objects for which this body was convened, being of the first order of importance, I felt it very interesting to understand the views of the parties of which it was composed, and especially the ideas prevalent as to the organization contemplated for their government. I went, therefore, daily from Paris to Versailles, and attended their debates, generally till the hour of adjournment. Those of the *Noblesse* were impassioned and tempestuous. They had some able men on both sides, and actuated by equal zeal. The debates of The Commons were temperate, rational, and inflexibly firm. As preliminary to all other business, the awful questions came on, Shall the States sit in one, or in distinct apartments? And shall they vote by heads or houses? The opposition was soon found to consist of the Episcopal order among the clergy, and two-thirds of the *Noblesse;* while the *Tiers Etat* were to a man united and determined. After various propositions of compromise had failed, the Commons undertook to cut the Gordian Knot. The Abbé Sieyés, the most logical head of the nation (author of the pamphlet "*Qu'est ce que le Tiers Etat*"? which had electrified that country, as Paine's "Common Sense" did us), after an impressive speech on the 10th of June, moved that a last invitation should be sent to the *Noblesse* and Clergy, to attend in the hall of the States, collectively or individually, for the verification of powers, to which the Commons would proceed immediately, either in their presence or absence. This verification being finished, a motion was made, on the 15th, that they should constitute themselves a National Assembly; which was decided on the 17th, by a majority of four-fifths. During the debates on this question, about twenty of the curés had joined them, and a proposition was made in the chamber of the Clergy that their whole body should join them. This was rejected at first by a small majority only; but, being afterwards somewhat modified, it was decided affirmatively, by a majority of eleven. While this was under debate and unknown to the court, to wit, on the 10th, a council was held in the afternoon at Marly, wherein it was proposed that the King should interpose by a declaration of his sentiments, in a *seance royale*. A form of declaration was proposed by Necker, which, while it censured in general the proceedings both of the Nobles and Commons, announced the King's views, such as substantially to coincide with the Commons. It was agreed to in Council, the *seance* was fixed for the 22d, the meetings of the States were till then to be suspended, and everything, in the meantime, kept secret. The members, the next morning (20th), repairing to their house, as usual, found the doors shut and guarded, a proclamation posted up for a *seance royale* on the 22d, and a suspension of their meetings in the meantime. Concluding that their dissolution was now to take place, they repaired to a building called the "Jeu de paume" (or Tennis, court) and there bound themselves by oath to each other, never to separate of their own accord, till they had settled a constitution for the nation, on a solid basis, and, if separated by force, that they would reassemble in some other

place. The next day they met in the church of St. Louis, and were joined by a majority of the clergy.—AUTOBIOGRAPHY. i, 90. FORD ED., i, 125. (1821.)

7546. —— ——. Viewing it as an opera, it was imposing.—To WILLIAM CARMICHAEL. iii, 22. (P., May 1789.)

7547. —— ——. I was present at that august ceremony. Had it been enlightened with lamps and chandeliers, it would have been almost as brilliant as the opera.—To M. DE CREVE-COEUR. iii, 43. (P., 1789.)

7548. —— ——. The States General are too numerous. I see great difficulty in preventing twelve hundred people from becoming a mob.—To WILLIAM CARMICHAEL. FORD ED., v, 73. (P., Mar. 1789.)

7549. —— ——. Should confusion * * * be prevented, I suppose the States General, with the consent of the King, will establish some of the leading features of a good constitution.—To WILLIAM CARMICHAEL. FORD ED., v, 73. (P., Mar. 1789.)

7550. REVOLUTION (French), Sympathy with.—I still hope the French Revolution will issue happily. I feel that the permanence of our own leans in some degree on that, and that a failure there would be a powerful argument to prove that there must be a failure here.—To EDWARD RUTLEDGE. iii, 285. FORD ED., v, 377. (Pa., 1791.)

7551. —— ——. The success of the French Revolution will ensure the progress of liberty in Europe, and its preservation here. The failure of that would have been a powerful argument with those who wish to introduce a king, lords, and commons here, a sect which is all head and no body.—To EDMUND PENDLETON. FORD ED., v, 358. (Pa., 1791.)

7552. —— ——. I am looking ardently to the completion of the glorious work in which France is engaged. I view the general condition of Europe as hanging on the success or failure of France. Having set such an example of philosophical arrangement within, I hope it will be extended without your limits also, to your dependents and to your friends in every part of the earth.—To MARQUIS DE CONDORCET. FORD ED., v, 379. (Pa., 1791.)

7553. —— ——. I was a sincere well-wisher to the success of the French Revolution, and still wish it may end in the establishment of a free and well-ordered republic.—To ELBRIDGE GERRY. iv, 269. FORD ED., vii, 329. (Pa., 1799.)

7554. —— ——. I have expressed to you my sentiments, because they are really those of ninety-nine in an hundred of our citizens. The universal feasts and rejoicings, which have lately been had on account of the successes of the French, showed the genuine effusions of their hearts.—To WILLIAM SHORT. iii, 502. FORD ED., vi, 154. (Pa., Jan. 1793.)

7555. —— ——. The event of the French Revolution is now little doubted of, even by its enemies. The sensations it has produced here, and the indications of them in the public papers, have shown that the form our own government was to take depended much more on the events of France than anybody had before imagined. The tide which, after our former relaxed government, took a violent course towards the opposite extreme, and seemed ready to hang everything round with the tassels and baubles of monarchy, is now getting back as we hope to a just mean, a government of laws addressed to the reason of the people, and not to their weaknesses.—To T. M. RANDOLPH. iii, 504. FORD ED., vi, 157. (Pa., Jan. 1793.)

7556. RHODE ISLAND, Adoption of Constitution.—What do you propose to do with Rhode Island [on the question of the new Federal Constitution]? As long as there is hope, we should give her time. I cannot conceive but that she will come to rights in the long run. Force, in whatever form, would be a dangerous precedent.—To E. CARRINGTON. ii, 405. FORD ED., v, 21. (P., 1788.)

7557. ———— ————. The little *vautrien*, Rhode Island, will come over [to the new Constitution] with a little time.—To M. DE LAFAYETTE. iii, 132. FORD ED., v, 152. (N.Y., 1790.)

7558. ———— ————. Rhode Island has at length acceded to the Union by a majority of two voices only in their convention.—To WILLIAM SHORT. FORD ED., v, 178. (N.Y., June 1790.)

7559. RHODE ISLAND, Characteristics of.—How happens it that Rhode Island is opposed to every useful proposition? Her geography accounts for it, with the aid of one or two observations. The cultivators of the earth are the most virtuous citizens, and possess most of the *amor patriæ*. Merchants are the least virtuous, and possess the least of the *amor patriæ*. The latter reside principally in the seaboard towns, the former in the interior country. Now, it happened that of the territory constituting Rhode Island and Connecticut, the part containing the seaports was erected into a State by itself, called Rhode Island, and that containing the interior country was erected into another State called Connecticut. For though it has a little seacoast, there are no good ports in it. Hence it happens that there is scarcely one merchant in the whole State of Connecticut, while there is not a single man in Rhode Island who is not a merchant of some sort. Their whole territory is but a thousand square miles, and what of that is in use is laid out in grass farms almost entirely. Hence they have scarcely anybody employed in agriculture. All exercise some species of commerce. This circumstance has decided the character of these two States. The remedies to this evil are hazardous. One would be to consolidate the two States into one. Another would be to banish Rhode Island from the Union. A third, to compel her submission to the will of the other twelve. A fourth, for the other twelve to govern themselves according to the new propositions, and to let Rhode Island go on by herself according to the ancient articles. But the dangers and difficulties attending all these remedies are obvious.—ANSWERS TO M. DE MEUNIER. ix, 288. FORD ED., iv, 143. (P., 1786.)

7560. RHODE ISLAND, College of.—I was honored in the month of January last with a letter * * * from the corporation of Rhode Island College to his most Christian Majesty [Louis XVI.] * * * . I turned my attention to that object which was the establishment of a professorship of the French language in the college, and the obtaining a collection of the best French authors with the aid of the king. That neither the college nor myself might be compromitted uselessly, I thought it necessary to sound previously those who were able to inform me what would be the success of the application. I was assured so as to leave no doubt, that it would not be complied with; that there had never been an instance of the king's granting such a demand in a foreign country, and that they would be cautious of setting the precedent; that in this moment, too, they were embarrassed with the difficult operation of putting down all establishments of their own, which could possibly be dispensed with, in order to bring their expenditures down to the level of their receipts. Upon such information I was satisfied that it was most prudent not to deliver the letter. * * * The king did give two colleges in America copies of the works printed in the public press, * * * of no consequence. * * * No endeavors of mine should have been spared, could they have effected their wish.—To RHODE ISLAND DELEGATES. ii, 184. (P., 1787.)

7561. RHODE ISLAND, Regeneration of.—A new subject of congratulation has arisen. I mean the regeneration of Rhode Island. I hope it is the beginning of that resurrection of the genuine spirit of New England which arises for life eternal. According to natural order, Vermont will emerge next, because least, after Rhode Island, under the yoke of hierocracy.—To GIDEON GRANGER. iv, 395. FORD ED., viii, 48. (W., 1801.)

7562. RICE, African.—I was fortunate in receiving from the coast of Africa last fall a cask of mountain rice. This I have dispersed into many hands, having sent the mass of it to South Carolina.—To BENJAMIN VAUGHAN. FORD ED., v, 332. (Pa., 1791.)

7563. ———— ————. In 1790, I got a cask of heavy upland rice, from the river Denbigh, in Africa, about lat. 9° 30′ North, which I sent to Charleston, in hopes it might supersede the culture of the wet rice, which renders South Carolina and Georgia so pestilential through the summer.—JEFFERSON'S MSS. i, 176. (M., 1821.)

7564. RICE, Chinese.—In Asia they have several distinct species of this grain. Monsieur Poivre, a former governor of the Isle of France, in travelling through several countries of Asia, observed with particular attention the objects of their agriculture, and tells us that in Cochin-China they cultivate six several kinds of rice, which he describes, three of them requiring water, and three growing on highlands. The rice of Carolina is said to come from Madagascar, and De Poivre tells us, it is the white rice which is cultivated there. This favors the probability of its being of a different species originally, from that of Piedmont; and time, culture, and climate may have made it still more different. Under this idea I thought it would be well to furnish you with some of the Piedmont rice, unhusked, but was told it was contrary to the laws to export it in that form. I took such measures as I could, however, to have a quantity brought out, and lest these should fail, I brought myself a few pounds. A part of this I have addressed to you by way of London; a part comes with this letter; and I shall send another parcel by some other conveyance to prevent the danger of miscarriage. Any one of them arriving safe may serve to put in seed, should the society think it an object.—To WILLIAM DRAYTON. ii, 196. (P., 1787.)

7565. ———— ————. The dry rice of Cochin-China has the reputation of being the whitest to the eye, best flavored to the taste, and most productive. It seems, then, to unite the good qualities of both the others known to us. Could it supplant them, it would be a great happiness, as it would enable us to get rid of those ponds of stagnant water, so fatal to human health and life. But such is the force of habit, and caprice of taste, that we could not be sure beforehand it would produce this effect. The experiment, however, is worth trying, should it only end in producing a third quality, and increasing the demand. I will endeavor to procure some to be brought from Cochin-China.—To WILLIAM DRAYTON. ii, 197. (P., 1787.)

7566. —— ——. I have considerable hopes of receiving some dry rice from Cochin-China, the young prince of that country lately gone hence [Paris], having undertaken that it shall come to me. * * * These are all but experiments. The precept, however, is wise which directs us to try all things, and hold fast that which is good.—To WILLIAM DRAYTON. ii, 347. (F., 1788.)

7567. RICE, Egyptian.—I have forwarded to you two couffes of rough rice, which I had brought from Egypt. I wish both may arrive in time for the approaching seed time, and that the trials with this and the Piedmont rice may furnish new advantages to your agriculture.—To WILLIAM DRAYTON. ii, 347. (P., 1788.)

7568. RICE, Italian.—I wished particularly to know whether it was the use of a different machine for cleaning, which brought European rice to market less broken than ours, as had been represented to me by those who deal in that article in Paris. I found several persons who had passed through the rice country of Italy, but not one who could explain to me the nature of the machine. But I was given to believe that I might see it myself immediately on entering Piedmont. I determined to go and ascertain this point, as the chance only of placing our rice above all rivalship in quality, as it is in color, by the introduction of a better machine, if a better existed * * *. I found the rice country to be in truth Lombardy, * * * and that though called Piedmont rice, not a grain is made in the country of Piedmont. I passed through the rice fields of the Vennellese and Milanese, about sixty miles, * * * and found that the machine is absolutely the same as ours. * * * It is a difference in the species of grain, of which the government of Turin is so sensible, that, as I was informed, they prohibit the exportation of rough rice on pain of death. I have taken measures, however, which I think will not fail for obtaining a quantity of it, and I bought on the spot a small parcel. * * * I propose * * * to send the rice to the society at Charleston for promoting agriculture, supposing that they will be best able to try the experiment of cultivating the rice of this quality, and to communicate the species to South Carolina and Georgia, if they find it answer.—To JOHN JAY. ii, 138. FORD ED., iv, 377. (Mar. 1787.)

7569. —— ——. I had expected to satisfy myself at Marseilles, of the cause of the differences of quality between the rice of Carolina, and that of Piedmont, which is brought in quantities to Marseilles. Not being able to do it, I made an excursion of three weeks into the rice country beyond the Alps, going through it from Vercelli to Pavia about sixty miles. I found the difference to be not in the management, as had been supposed both here and in Carolina, but in the species of rice; and I hope to enable them in Carolina to begin the cultivation of the Piedmont rice, and carry it on. hand in hand, with their own, that they may supply both qualities; which is absolutely necessary at this market.—To JOHN ADAMS. ii, 162. FORD ED., iv, 396. (P., 1787.)

7570. —— ——. At Marseilles I hoped to know what the Piedmont machine was, but I could find nobody who knew anything of it. I determined, therefore, to sift the matter to the bottom, by crossing t. e Alps into the rice country. I found their machine exactly such a one as you had described to me in Congress in the year 1775. There was but one conclusion, then, to be drawn, to wit, that the rice was of a different species, and I determined to take enough to put you in seed. They informed me, however, that its exportation in the husk was prohibited, so I could only bring off as much as my coat and surtout pockets would hold. I took measures with a muleteer to run a couple of sacks across the Apennines to Genoa, but have not great dependence on its success. The little, therefore, which I brought myself, must be relied on for fear we should get no more; and because, also, it is genuine from Vercelli, where the best is made of all the Sardinian Lombardy, the whole of which is considered as producing a better rice than the Milanese. This is assigned as the reason for the strict prohibition.—To E. RUTLEDGE. ii, 178. FORD ED., iv, 407. (P., 1787.)

7571. —— ——. Having observed that the consumption of rice in this country [France], and particularly in this capital [Paris], was very great, I thought it my duty to inform myself from what markets they draw their supplies. * * * [I found] that the dealers in Paris were in the habit of selling two qualities of rice. that of Carolina, with which they were supplied chiefly from England, and that of Piedmont; that the Carolina rice was long, slender, white and transparent, answers well when prepared with milk, sugar, &c., but not so well when prepared au gras; that that of Piedmont was shorter, thicker, and less white; but that it presented its form better when dressed au gras, was better tasted, and, therefore, preferred by good judges for those purposes. * * * [The dealers] supposed this difference of quality to proceed from a difference of management; that the Carolina rice was husked with an instrument that broke it more, and that less pains were taken to separate the broken from the unbroken grains, imagining that it was the broken grains which dissolved in oily preparations. * * * The objection to the Carolina rice, then, being that it crumbles in certain forms of preparation, and this supposed to be the effect of a less perfect machine for husking, I flattered myself I should be able to learn what might be the machine of Piedmont, when I should arrive at Marseilles. * * * At Marseilles, however, they differed as much in account of the machines, as at Paris they had differed about other circumstances. Some said it was husked between mill-stones, others between rubbers of wood in the form of mill-stones, others of cork. They concurred in one fact, however, that the machine might be seen by me immediately on crossing the Alps. This would be an affair of three weeks. I crossed them and went through the rice country from Vercelli to Pavia, about sixty miles. I found the machine to be absolutely the same with that used in Carolina. * * * In some of them, indeed, they arm each pestle with an iron tooth, consisting of nine spikes hooked together, which I do not remember in the description [of the machine] of Mr. Rutledge. I, therefore, had a tooth made, which I forward you; observing, at the same time, that as many of their machines are without teeth as with them, and of course, that the advantage is not very palpable. It seems to follow, then, that the rice of Lombardy (for though called Piedmont rice, it does not grow in that country, but in Lombardy) is of a different species from that of Carolina; different in form, in color and in quality.—To WILLIAM DRAYTON. ii, 194. (P., 1787.)

7572. RICE, Smuggling.—Poggio, a muleteer who passes every week between Vercelli and Genoa, will smuggle a sack of rough rice for me to Genoa; it being death to export it in that form.—TRAVELS IN ITALY. ix, 338. (1787.)

7573. RICE, Southern cultivation.—The upland rice which I procured fresh from Africa and sent them [the South], has been preserved and spread in the upper parts of Georgia, and I believe in Kentucky.—To JAMES RONALDSON. vi, 92. FORD ED., ix, 371. (M., Jan. 1813.)

7574. RICE, Upland vs. Swamp.—I first became informed of the existence of a rice which would grow in uplands without any more water than the common rains, by reading a book of M. de Poivre, who had been Governor of the Isle of France, who mentions it as growing there and all along the coast of Africa successfully, and as having been introduced from Cochin-China. I was at that time (1784-89) in France, and there happening to be there a Prince of Cochin-China, on his travels, and then returning home, I obtained his promise to send me some. I never received it, however, and mention it only as it may have been sent, and furnished the ground for the inquiries of Dr. De Carro, respecting my receiving it from China. When at Havre on my return from France, I found there Captain Nathaniel Cutting, who was the ensuing spring to go on a voyage along the coast of Africa. I engaged him to enquire for this. * * * He procured and sent me a thirty gallon cask of it. * * * I divided it between the Agricultural Society of Charleston and some private gentlemen of Georgia, recommending it to their care, in the hope which had induced me to endeavor to obtain it, that if it answered as well as the swamp rice, it might rid them of that source of their summer diseases. Nothing came of the trials in South Carolina, but being carried into the upper hilly parts of Georgia, it succeeded there perfectly, has spread over the country, and is now commonly cultivated; still, however, for family use chiefly, as they cannot make it for sale in competition with the rice of the swamps.—To DR. BENJAMIN WATERHOUSE. v, 393. (W., 1808.)

7575. RICHMOND (Va.), Capture of.—Is the surprise of an open and unarmed place, although called a city, and even a capital, so unprecedented as to be a matter of indelible reproach? Which of our own capitals, during the same war, was not in possession of the same enemy, not merely by surprise and for a day only, but permanently? That of Georgia? Of South Carolina? North Carolina? Pennsylvania? New York? Connecticut? Rhode Island? Massachusetts? And if others were not, it was because the enemy saw no object in taking possession of them. Add to the list in the late war (1812) Washington, the metropolis of the Union, covered by a fort, with troops and a dense population. And what capital on the continent of Europe (St. Petersburg and its regions of ice excepted), did not Bonaparte take and hold at his pleasure? Is it then just that Richmond and its authorities alone should be placed under the reproach of history, because, in a moment of peculiar denudation of resources, by the *coup de main* of an enemy, led on by the hand of fortune directing the winds and weather to their wishes, it was surprised and held for twenty-four hours? Or strange that that enemy with such advantages, should be enabled, then, to get off, without risking the honors he had achieved by burnings and destructions of property peculiar to his principles of warfare? We, at least, may leave these glories to their own trumpet.—To HENRY LEE. vii, 447. FORD ED., x, 388. (M., 1826.)

7576. RICHMOND (Va.), Street architecture.—There is one street in Richmond (from the bridge straight on towards Curries) which would be considered as handsomely built in any city of Europe.—To WILLIAM SHORT. FORD ED., v, 137. (1789.)

7577. RIDICULE, Reason and.—Resort is had to ridicule only when reason is against us.—To PRESIDENT MADISON. vi, 112. FORD ED., ix, 382. (M., 1813.)

7578. RIDICULE, Reformation and.—The most remarkable effect as yet of the convention of the Notables is the number of puns and *bon mots* it has generated. I think, were they all collected, it would make a more voluminous work than the Encyclopédie. This occasion, more than anything I have seen, convinces me that this nation is incapable of any serious effort but under the word of command. The people at large view every object only as it may furnish puns and *bon mots*; and I pronounce that a good punster would disarm the whole nation were they ever so seriously disposed to revolt. Indeed, they are gone, when a measure so capable of doing good, as the calling the Notables, is treated with so much ridicule; we may conclude the nation desperate, and in charity pray that heaven may send them good kings.—To MRS. JOHN ADAMS. FORD ED., iv, 370. (P., 1787.)

7579. RIEDESEL (Baron), Jefferson and.—I thank you for your kind congratulations; though condolations would be better suited to the occasion, not only on account of the labors of the office [Governorship] to which I am called, and its withdrawing me from retirement, but also the loss of the agreeable society I have left of which Madame Riedesel and yourself were an important part.*—To BARON DE RIEDESEL. FORD ED., ii, 245. (1779.)

7580. RIENZI (Nicolo Gabrini) Estimate of.—This poor counterfeit of the Gracchi seems to have had enthusiasm and eloquence, without either wisdom or firmness.—To F. VAN DER KEMP. FORD ED., x, 78. (M., 1817.)

7581. RIGHT, Administer.—Deal out to all equal and impartial right.—RIGHTS OF BRITISH AMERICA. i, 141. FORD ED., i, 446. (1774.)

7582. RIGHT, Doing.—I shall pursue in silence the path of right.—To GENERAL WASHINGTON. i, 337. (A., 1784.)

7583. ——— ———. My principle is to do whatever is right, and leave the consequences to Him who has the disposal of them.—To DR. GEORGE LOGAN. vi, 217. FORD ED., ix, 423. (M., 1813.)

* Baron Riedesel was then a prisoner near Charlottesville. He commanded the Hessian troops in Burgoyne's army.—EDITOR.

7584. RIGHT, Moral.—It has a great effect on the opinion of our people and the world to have the moral right on our side.—To President Madison. v, 442. Ford ed., ix, 251. (M., April 1809.)

7585. RIGHT AND WRONG.—The great principles of right and wrong are legible to every reader; to preserve them, requires not the aid of many counsellors.—Rights of British America. i, 141. Ford ed., i, 446. (1774.)

— RIGHT OF ASYLUM.—See Asylum.

7586. RIGHT OF EXPATRIATION.—Nature has given to all men the right of departing from the country in which chance * * * has placed them.—Rights of British America. i, 125. Ford ed., i, 429. (1774.) See Expatriation.

7587. RIGHT OF REPRESENTATION.—He has refused to pass * * * laws for the accommodation of large districts of people, unless those people would relinquish the right of representation in the legislature, a right inestimable to them and formidable to tyrants only.—Declaration of Independence as Drawn by Jefferson.

7588. RIGHT OF SUFFRAGE.—Let every man who fights and pays exercise his just and equal right in the election of the Legislature.—To Samuel Kerchival. vii, 11. Ford ed., x, 39. (M., 1816.) See Suffrage.

7589. RIGHTS, Advancing.—Circumstances sometimes require, that rights the most unquestionable should be advanced with delicacy.—To William Short. iii, 275. Ford ed., v, 364. (Pa., 1791.)

7590. RIGHTS, Aggression on.—No man has a natural right to commit aggression on the equal rights of another; and this is all from which the laws ought to restrain him.—To F. W. Gilmer. vii, 3. Ford ed., x, 32. (M., 1816.)

7591. RIGHTS, Aristocratic encroachments on.—Hereditary bodies * * * always existing, always on the watch for their own aggrandizement, profit of every opportunity of advancing the privileges of their order, and encroaching on the rights of the people.—To M. Coray. vii, 319. (M., 1823.)

7592. RIGHTS, Attainment of.—If we cannot secure all our rights, let us secure what we can.—To James Madison. iii, 4. Ford ed., v, 82. (P., March 1789.)

7593. RIGHTS, Availability of.—It is a principle that the right to a thing gives a right to the means without which it could not be used, that is to say, that the means follow their end.—Mississippi River Instructions. vii, 579. (1791.)

— RIGHTS, Bill of.—See Bill of Rights.

7594. RIGHTS, Defence of.—We will ever be ready to join with our fellow-subjects in every part of the British empire, in executing all those rightful powers which God has given us, for the reestablishment and guaranteeing their constitutional rights, when, where, and by whomsoever invaded.*—Resolutions of Albemarle County. Ford ed., i, 419. (July 26, 1774.)

7595. RIGHTS, Deprivation of.—The proscribing any citizen as unworthy the public confidence, by laying upon him an incapacity of being called to offices of trust or emolument, unless he profess or renounce this or that religious opinion, is depriving him injudiciously of those privileges and advantages to which, in common with his fellow citizens, he has a natural right.—Statute of Religious Freedom. Ford ed., ii, 238. (1779.)

7596. RIGHTS, Education and.—For promoting the public happiness, those persons, whom nature has endowed with genius and virtue, should be rendered by liberal education worthy to receive, and able to guard the sacred deposit of the rights and liberties of their fellow citizens; and they should be called to that charge without regard to wealth, birth or other accidental condition or circumstance.—Diffusion of Knowledge Bill. Ford ed., ii, 221. (1779.)

— RIGHTS, Equal.—See Equality and Equal Rights.

7597. RIGHTS, Establishing.—It can never be too often repeated, that the time for fixing every essential right on a legal basis is while our rulers are honest, and ourselves united.—Notes on Virginia. viii, 402. Ford ed., iii, 266. (1782.)

7598. RIGHTS, Fortifying popular.—I am particularly happy to perceive that you still manfully maintain our good old principle of cherishing and fortifying the rights and authorities of the people in opposition to those who fear them, who wish to take all power from them, and to transfer all to Washington.—To Nathaniel Macon. Ford ed., x, 378. (M., 1826.)

7599. RIGHTS, Inalienable.—We hold these truths to be self-evident that all men are created equal; that they are endowed by their Creator with inherent† and inalienable rights; that among these, are life, liberty, and the pursuit of happiness. That, to secure these rights, governments are instituted among men, deriving their just powers from the consent of the governed; that, whenever any form of government becomes destructive of these ends, it is the right of the people to alter or to abolish it, and to institute new government, laying its foundation on such principles, and organizing its powers in such form, as to them shall seem most likely to effect their safety and happiness.—Declaration of Independence as Drawn by Jefferson.

7600. RIGHTS, Infringements on.—Let no act be passed by any one legislature

* Jefferson's own county.—Editor.
† Congress struck out "inherent and" and inserted "certain".—Editor.

[Parliament] which may infringe on the rights and liberties of another.—RIGHTS OF BRITISH AMERICA. i, 141. FORD ED., i, 446. (1774.)

7601. RIGHTS, Invasions of.—He has dissolved Representative houses repeatedly [and continually]* for opposing, with manly firmness, his invasions on the rights of the people.—DECLARATION OF INDEPENDENCE AS DRAWN BY JEFFERSON.

7602. —— ——. There are rights which it is useless to surrender to the government, and which governments have yet always been found to invade. [Among] these * * * is the right of free commerce.—To DAVID HUMPHREYS. iii, 13. FORD ED., v, 89. (P., 1789.)

7603. RIGHTS, Money and.—Courtiers had rather give up power than pleasure. They will barter, therefore, the usurped prerogatives of the King for the money of the people. This is the agent by which modern nations will recover their rights.—To COMTE DE MOUSTIER. ii, 389. FORD ED., v, 12. (P., 1788.)

— RIGHTS, Natural.—See NATURAL RIGHTS.

7604. RIGHTS, The people and.—The people, especially when moderately instructed, are the only safe, because the only honest, depositaries of the public rights, and should therefore, be introduced into the administration of them in every function to which they are sufficient; they will err sometimes and accidentally, but never designedly, and with a systematic and persevering purpose of overthrowing the free principles of the government.—To M. CORAY. vii, 319. (M., 1823.)

7605. RIGHTS, Personal.—It were contrary to feeling, and indeed, ridiculous to suppose that a man had less right in himself than one of his neighbors, or indeed, than all of them put together. This would be slavery, and not that liberty which the bill of rights has made inviolable, and for the preservation of which our government has been charged. Nothing could so completely divest us of that liberty as the establishment of the opinion, that the State has a *perpetual* right to the services of all its members. This, to men of certain ways of thinking, would be to annihilate the blessing of existence, and to contradict the Giver of life, who gave it for happiness and not for wretchedness.—To JAMES MONROE. i, 319. FORD ED., iii, 58. (M., 1782.)

7606. —— ——. Every man should be protected in his lawful acts.—To ISAAC McPHERSON. vi, 175. (M., 1813.)

7607. RIGHTS, Persons and.—Rights and powers can only belong to persons, not to things, not to mere matter, unendowed with will.—To JOHN CARTWRIGHT. vii, 359. (M., 1824.)

* Congress struck out the words in brackets.—EDITOR.

7608. RIGHTS, Religion and civil.—Our civil rights have no dependence upon our religious opinions, more than our opinions in physics or geometry.—STATUTE OF RELIGIOUS FREEDOM. viii, 455. FORD ED., ii, 238. (1779.)

7609. RIGHTS, Reserved.—It had become an universal and almost uncontroverted position in the several States, that the purposes of society do not require a surrender of all our rights to our ordinary governors; that there are certain portions of right not necessary to enable them to carry on an effective government, and which experience has nevertheless proved they will be constantly encroaching on, if submitted to them; that there are also certain fences which experience has proved peculiarly efficacious against wrong, and rarely obstructive of right, which yet the governing powers have ever shown a disposition to weaken and remove. Of the first kind, for instance, is freedom of religion; of the second, trial by jury, *habeas corpus* laws, free presses. These were the settled opinions of all the States,—of that of Virginia, of which I was writing [in the Notes on Virginia], as well as of the others. The others had, in consequence, delineated these unceded portions of right, and these fences against wrong, which they meant to exempt from the power of their governors, in instruments called declarations of rights and constitutions; and as they did this by conventions, which they appointed for the express purpose of reserving those rights, and of delegating others to their ordinary legislative, executive and judiciary bodies, none of the reserved rights can be touched without resorting to the people to appoint another convention for the express purpose of permitting it. Where the constitutions, then, have been so formed by conventions, named for this express purpose, they are fixed and unalterable but by a convention or other body to be specially authorized; and they have been so formed by, I believe, all the States, except Virginia. That State concurs in all these opinions, but has run into the wonderful error that her constitution, though made by the ordinary legislature, cannot yet be altered by the ordinary legislature.—To NOAH WEBSTER. iii, 201. FORD ED., v, 254. (Pa., 1790.)

7610. RIGHTS, Safest depository of.—The mass of the citizens is the safest depositary of their own rights.—To JOHN TAYLOR. vi, 608. FORD ED., x, 31. (M., 1816.)

7611. RIGHTS, Safety of.—It would be a dangerous delusion were a confidence in the men of our choice to silence our fears fo. the safety of our rights.—KENTUCKY RESOLUTIONS. ix, 470. FORD ED., vii, 303. (1798.)

7612. RIGHTS, Securing.—It is to secure our rights that we resort to government at all.—To M. D'IVERNOIS. iv, 114. FORD ED., vii, 4. (M., Feb. 1795.)

— RIGHTS, State.—See STATE RIGHTS.

7613. RIGHTS, Suppression of.—It is impossible the world should continue long insensible to so evident a truth as that the right to have commmerce and intercourse with our neighbors is a natural right. To suppress this neighborly intercourse is an exercise of force, which we shall have a just right to remove when the superior force.—To T. M. RANDOLPH. iii, 146. FORD ED., v, 174. (N. Y., 1790.)

7614. RIGHTS, Surrendering.—The justifiable rights of our country ought not to be given up by those * * * appointed and trusted to defend them where they may be justly defended.—To ALEXANDER HAMILTON. FORD ED., vi, 9. (1792.)

7615. RIGHTS, Swallowing up.—Did his Majesty possess such a right as this [sending troops], it might swallow up all our other rights, whenever he should think proper.—RIGHTS OF BRITISH AMERICA. i, 140. FORD ED., i, 445. (1774.)

7616. RIGHTS, Unmerited praise and. —To give praise where it is not due might be well from the venal, but it would ill become those who are asserting the rights of human nature.—RIGHTS OF BRITISH AMERICA. i, 141. FORD ED., i, 446. (1774.)

7617. RIGHTS, Usurpation of.—The royal claim to wrecks, waifs, strays, treasure-trove, royal mines, royal fish, royal birds, are declared to have been usurpations on common right.—PROPOSED VA. CONSTITUTION. FORD ED., ii, 28. (June 1776.)

— **RIGHTS OF BRITISH AMERICA, A summary view of the.**—See APPENDIX.

— **RIGHTS OF CONSCIENCE.**—See CONSCIENCE.

7618. RIGHTS OF MAN, Appeal to.— The appeal to the rights of man, which had been made in the United States, was taken up by France, first of the European nations. From her, the spirit has spread over those of the South. The tyrants of the North have allied indeed against it; but it is irresistible. Their opposition will only multiply its millions of human victims; their own satellites will catch it, and the condition of man through the civilized world will be finally and greatly ameliorated. This is a wonderful instance of great events from small causes. So inscrutable is the arrangement of causes and consequences in this world, that a two-penny duty on tea, unjustly imposed in a sequestered part of it, changes the condition of all its inhabitants.—AUTOBIOGRAPHY. i, 106. FORD ED., i, 147. (1821.)

7619. RIGHTS OF MAN, Assertion of. —I hope and firmly believe that the whole world will, sooner or later, feel benefit from the issue of our assertion of the rights of man.—To BENJAMIN GALLOWAY. vi, 41. (M., 1812.)

7620. RIGHTS OF MAN, Charter of.— The Declaration of Independence, the Declaratory Charter of our rights, and of the rights of man.—To SAMUEL A. WELLS. i, 121. FORD ED., x, 131. (M., 1819.)

7621. RIGHTS OF MAN, Equal.—The equal rights of man, and the happiness of every individual, are now acknowledged to be the only legitimate objects of government. Modern times * * * have discovered the only device by which these rights can be secured, to wit: government by the people, acting not in person, but by representatives chosen by themselves, that is to say, by every man of ripe years and sound mind, who contributes either by his purse or person to the support of his country.—To M. CORAY. vii, 319. (M., 1823.)

7622. RIGHTS OF MAN, Government and.—No interests are dearer to men than those which ought to be secured to them by their form of government, and none deserve better of them than those who contribute to the amelioration of that form.—To M. RUELLE. v, 430. (W., 1809.)

7623. RIGHTS OF MAN, Immortal.— Although the horrors of the French Revolution have damped for awhile the ardor of the patriots in every country, yet it is not extinguished—it will never die. The sense of right has been excited in every breast, and the spark will be rekindled by the very oppressions of that detestable tyranny employed to quench it. The errors of the honest patriots of France, and the crimes of her Dantons and Robespierres, will be forgotten in the more encouraging contemplation of our sober example, and steady march to our object.—To BENJAMIN GALLOWAY. vi, 41. (M., 1812.)

7624. RIGHTS OF MAN, Immutable.— Nothing is unchangeable but the inherent and inalienable rights of man.—To JOHN CARTWRIGHT. vii, 359. (M., 1824.)

7625. RIGHTS OF MAN, Legal.—The laws of the land are the inheritance and the right of every man before whatever tribunal he is brought.—NOTES ON STEVENS CASE. ix, 475. (1804.)

7626. RIGHTS OF MAN, Legislators and.—Our legislators are not sufficiently apprized of the rightful limits of their power; that their true office is to declare and enforce only our natural rights and duties, and to take none of them from us.—To F. W. GILMER. vii, 3. FORD ED., x, 32. (M., 1816.)

7627. RIGHTS OF MAN, Moral and political.—That man may at length find favor with Heaven, and his present struggles issue in the recovery and establishment of his moral and political rights will be the prayer of my latest breath.—To HARRY INNES. FORD ED., vii, 383. (M., 1799.)

7628. RIGHTS OF MAN, Recognition of.—All eyes are opened, or opening, to the rights of man. The general spread of the light of science has already laid open to every view the palpable truth, that the mass of mankind has not been born with saddles on their backs, nor a favored few booted and spurred, ready to ride them legitimately, by the grace of God.*—To ROGER C. WEIGHT-MAN. vii, 450. FORD ED., x, 391. (M., June 24, 1826.)

7629. RIGHTS OF MAN, Securing.— Modern times * * * have discovered the only device by which the rights of man can be secured, to wit, government by the people, acting not in person, but by representatives chosen by themselves; that is to say, by every man of ripe years and sane mind, who contributes either by his purse or person to the support of his country.—To M. CORAY. vii, 319. (M., 1823.) See PAINE.

7630. RITTENHOUSE (David), Astronomer.— That this Commonwealth [of Virginia] may not be without so great an ornament, nor its youth such an help towards attaining astronomical science, as the mechanical representation, or model of the solar system, conceived and executed by that greatest of astronomers, David Rittenhouse, * * * the visitors [of William and Mary College] * * * shall be author zed [to purchase] one of the models.—WILLIAM AND MARY COLLEGE BILL. FORD ED., ii, 235. (1779.)

7631. ———. We have supposed Mr. Rittenhouse second to no astronomer living; that in genius he must be first, because he is self-taught. As an artist, he has exhibited as great a proof of mechanical genius as the world has ever produced. He has not indeed made a world; but he has by imitation approached nearer its Maker, than has any man who has lived from the creation to this day.—NOTES ON VIRGINIA. viii, 313. FORD ED., iii, 169. (1782.)

7632. RITTENHOUSE (David), Genius of.— The amazing mechanical representation of the solar system, which you conceived and executed, has never been surpassed by any but the work of which it is a copy. Are these powers, then, which being intended for the condition of the world are like air and light, the world's common property, to be taken from their proper pursuit to do the commonplace drudgery of governing a single State, a work which may be executed by men of an ordinary stature, such as are always and everywhere to be found?—To DAVID RITTENHOUSE. FORD ED., ii, 163. (M., 1778.)

7633. ———. I doubt not there are in your country many persons equal to the task of conducting government; but you should consider that the world has but one Rittenhouse, and that it never had one before.—To DAVID RITTENHOUSE. FORD ED., ii, 163. (1778.)

7634. ———. I have been much pleased to hear you had it in contemplation to endeavor to establish Rittenhouse in our College. This would be an immense acquisition, and would draw youth to it from every part of the continent.—To JOHN PAGE. i, 400. (P., 1785.)

7635. RITTENHOUSE (David), Invaluable friend.— Our late invaluable friend, Rittenhouse.—To DR. BENJAMIN RUSH. iv, 165. FORD ED., vii, 113. (M., 1797.)

7636. RITTENHOUSE (David), Mechanician.— Rittenhouse, as an astronomer, would stand on a line with any of his time;

* From the last letter written by Jefferson. Mr. Weightman was Mayor of Washington City, and the letter was in reply to an invitation to be present at a Fourth of July celebration at the capital. Jefferson and Adams both died on that day.—EDITOR.

and as a mechanician, he certainly has not been equaled. In this view he was truly great; but, placed alongside of Newton, every human character must appear diminutive, and none would have shrunk more feelingly from the painful parallel than the modest and amiable Rittenhouse, whose genius and merit are not the less for this exaggerated comparison of his over zealous biographer.—To JOHN ADAMS. vi, 307. (M., 1814.)

7637. RIVER, Illinois.— The Illinois is a fine river, clear, gentle, and without rapids; insomuch that it is navigable for bateaux to its source. From thence is a portage of two miles only to the Chicago, which affords a bateau navigation of sixteen miles to its entrance into Lake Michigan.—NOTES ON VIRGINIA. viii, 255. FORD ED., iii, 93. (1782.)

7638. RIVER, James.— James River itself affords a harbor for vessels of any size in Hampton Road, but not in safety through the whole winter. * * * In some future state of population, I think it possible, that its navigation may also be made to interlock with that of the Potomac, and through that to communicate by a short portage with the Ohio.—NOTES ON VIRGINIA. viii, 251. FORD ED., iii, 89. (1782.)

7639. RIVER, Kanawha.— The Great Kanawha is a river of considerable note for the fertility of its lands, and still more, as leading towards the head waters of James river. Nevertheless it is doubtful whether its great and numerous rapids will admit a navigation, but at an expense to which it will require ages to render its inhabitants equal. The great obstacles begin at what are called the great falls, ninety miles above the mouth, below which are only five or six rapids, and these passable, with some difficulty, even at low water. * * * It is said, however, that at a very moderate expense the whole current of the upper part of the Kanawha may be turned into the South Fork of Roanoke, the Alleghany there subsiding, and the two rivers approaching so near, that a canal nine miles long, and thirty feet deep, at the deepest part would draw the water of the Kanawha into this branch of the Roanoke; this canal would be in Montgomery County, the court-house of which is on the top of the Alleghanies.—NOTES ON VIRGINIA. viii, 259. FORD ED., iii, 96. (1782.)

7640. ———. The Little Kanawha * * * yields a navigation of ten miles only. Perhaps its northern branch, called Junius's Creek, which interlocks with the western of Monongahela, may one day admit a shorter passage from the latter into the Ohio.—NOTES ON VIRGINIA. viii, 259. FORD ED., iii, 97. (1782.)

7641. RIVER, Mississippi.— The Mississippi will be one of the principal channels of future commerce for the country westward of the Alleghany.—NOTES ON VIRGINIA. viii, 253. FORD ED., iii, 91. (1782.)

7642. ———. The country watered by the Mississippi and its eastern branches constitutes five-eighths of the United States, two of which five-eighths are occupied by the Ohio and its waters; the residuary streams which run into the Gulf of Mexico, the Atlantic, and the St. Lawrence, water the remaining three-eighths.—NOTES ON VIRGINIA. viii, 261. FORD ED., iii, 98. (1782.)

7643. RIVER, Missouri.— The Missouri is, in fact, the principal river, contributing more to the common stream than does the Mississippi, even after its junction with the Illinois. It is remarkably cold, muddy and rapid.—Notes on Virginia. viii, 254. Ford ed., iii, 92. (1782.)

7644. RIVER, Ohio.—The Ohio is the most beautiful river on earth. Its current gentle, waters clear, and bosom smooth and unbroken by rocks and rapids, a single instance only excepted.—Notes on Virginia. viii, 256. Ford ed., iii, 93. (1782.)

7645. RIVER, Potomac.—The passage of the Potomac through the Blue Ridge is, perhaps, one of the most stupendous scenes in nature. You stand on a very high point of land. On your right comes up the Shenandoah, having ranged along the foot of the mountain an hundred miles to seek a vent. On your left approaches the Potomac, in quest of a passage also. In the moment of their junction, they rush together against the mountain, rend it asunder, and pass off to the sea. The first glance of this scene hurries our senses into the opinion, that this earth has been created in time, that the mountains were formed first, that the rivers began to flow afterwards, that in this place, particularly, they have been dammed up by the Blue Ridge of mountains, and have formed an ocean which filled the whole valley; that continuing to rise they have at length broken over at this spot, and have torn the mountain down from its summit to its base. The piles of rock on each hand, but particularly on the Shenandoah, the evident marks of their disrupture and avulsion from their beds by the most powerful agents of nature, corroborate the impression. But the distant finishing which nature has given to the picture, is of a very different character. It is a true contrast to the foreground. It is as placid and delightful as that is wild and tremendous. For the mountain being cloven asunder, she presents to your eye, through the cleft, a small catch of smooth blue horizon, at an infinite distance in the plain country, inviting you as it were from the riot and tumult roaring around, to pass through the breach and participate of the calm below. Here the eye ultimately composes itself; and that way, too, the road happens actually to lead. You cross the Potomac above the junction, pass along its side through the base of the mountain for three miles, its terrible precipices hanging in fragments over you, and within about twenty miles reach Fredericktown, and the fine country round that. This scene is worth a voyage across the Atlantic. Yet here, as in the neighborhood of the Natural Bridge, are people who have passed their lives within half a dozen miles, and have never been to survey these monuments of a war between rivers and mountains, which must have shaken the earth itself to its centre.—Notes on Virginia. vii, 264. Ford ed., iii, 102. (1782.)

7646. RIVER, Red.—Your observations * * * have determined me to confine the ensuing mission to the ascent of the Red river to its source, and to descend the same river again, which will give an opportunity of better ascertaining that which, in truth, next to the Missouri, is the most interesting water of the Mississippi. You will accordingly receive instructions to this effect from the Secretary of War.—To Mr. Dunbar. iv, 577. (W., May 1805.)

7647. ———— ————. The work we are now doing is, I trust, done for posterity, in such a way that they need not repeat it. For this we are much indebted to you, not only for the

labor and time you have devoted to it, but for the excellent method of which you have set the example, and which I hope will be the model to be followed by others. We shall delineate with correctness the great arteries of this great country. Those who come after us will extend the ramifications as they become acquainted with them, and fill up the canvas we begin.—To Mr. Dunbar. iv, 580. (W., 1805.)

7648. RIVER, Rhone.—Nature never formed a country of more savage aspect, than that on both sides the Rhone. A huge torrent rushes like an arrow between high precipices, often of massive rock, at other times of loose stone, with but little earth. Yet has the hand of man subdued this savage scene, by planting corn where there is little fertility, trees where there is still less, and vines where there is none. On the whole, it assumes a romantic, picturesque, and pleasing air.—Travels in France. ix, 320. (1787.)

7649. RIVER, St. Croix.—A difference of opinion having arisen as to the river intended by the Plenipotentiaries [in the treaty of peace] to be the boundary between us and the dominions of Great Britain, and by them called the St. Croix, which name, it seems, is given to two different rivers, the ascertaining of this point becomes a matter of present urgency. It has heretofore been the subject of application from us to the Government of Great Britain.—To George Hammond. Ford ed., vi, 469. (Pa., Dec. 1793.)

7650. RIVER, Wabash.—The Wabash is a very beautiful river.—Notes on Virginia. viii, 258. Ford ed., iii, 95. (1782.)

7651. RIVERS, Exploration of.—I should be glad of a copy of any sketch or account you may have made of the river Platte of the passage from its head across the mountains, and of the river Cashecatungo, which you suppose to run into the Pacific. This would probably be among the first exploring journeys we undertake after a settlement with Spain, as we wish to become acquainted with all the advantageous water connections across our continent.—To Anthony G. Bettay. v, 246. (W., 1808.)

7652. RIVERS, Highways of commerce.—The principal connections of the western waters with the Atlantic are three: the Hudson River, the Potomac, and the Mississippi itself. Down the last will pass all heavy commodities. But the navigation through the Gulf of Mexico is so dangerous, and that up the Mississippi so difficult and tedious, that it is thought probable that European merchandise will not return through that channel. It is most likely that flour, timber, and other heavy articles will be floated on rafts, which will themselves be an article for sale as well as their loading, the navigators returning by land, or in light bateaux. There will, therefore, be a competition between the Hudson and Potomac rivers for the residue of the commerce of all the country westward of Lake Erie, on the waters of the Lakes, of the Ohio, and upper parts of the Mississippi.—Notes on Virginia. viii, 261. Ford ed., iii, 98. (1782.)

7653. RIVERS, Increments of.—In granting appropriations [of lands], some sovereigns have given away the increments of rivers to a greater, some to a lesser extent, and some not at all. Rome, which was not feudal, and Spain and England which were, have granted them largely; France, a feudal country, has not granted them. at all on navigable rivers. Louis XIV., therefore, was strictly correct when in his edict of 1693, he declared that the increments of rivers were incontestably his, *as a necessary consequence of the sovereignty.* That is to say, that where no special grant of them to an individual could be produced, they remained in him, as a portion of the original lands of the nation, or as new created lands, never yet granted to any individual. They are unquestionably a regalian, or national right, paramount, and pre-existent to the establishment of the feudal system. That system has no fixed principle on the subject, as is evident from the opposite practices of different feudal nations. The position. therefore, is entirely unfounded, that the right to them is derived from the feudal law.—Batture Case.   viii, 541.   (1812.)

7654. RIVERS, Obstructions in.—I think the State should reserve a right to the use of the [river] waters for navigation, and that where an individual landholder impedes that use, he shall remove that impediment, and leave the subject in as good a state as nature formed it.—To Joseph C. Cabell. vi, 541.   (M., 1816.)

7655. ———   ———. I think the power of permitting dams to be erected across our river [Fluviana], ought to be taken from the courts, so far as the stream has water enough for navigation.—To Charles Yancey. vi, 514.   Ford ed., x..1.   (M., 1816.)

7656. RIVERS, Right of navigation.—The movements of the King of Prussia to emancipate the navigation of the Vistula, and of the Emperor [of Germany] to free that of the Scheld do not, I believe, threaten the peace of Europe. * * * This assertion, then, of the natural right of the inhabitants of the upper part of a river to an innocent passage through the country below is pleasing to us. It tends to establish a principle favorable to our right of navigating the Mississippi.—To Governor Benj. Harrison. Ford ed., iii, 414. (A., March 1784.)

7657. RIVERS, Velocity of.—I shall forward your ingenious paper on the subject of the Mississippi to the Philosophical Society. To prove the value I set on it, and my wish that it may go to the public without any imperfection about it. I will take the liberty of submitting to your consideration the only passage which I think may require it. You say. "the velocity of rivers is greatest at the surface, and generally diminishes downwards". And this principle enters into some subsequent parts of the paper, and has too much effect on the phenomena of that river not to merit mature consideration. I can but suppose it at variance with the law of motion in rivers. In strict theory. the velocity of water at any given depth in a river is (in addition to its velocity at its surface) whatever a body would have acquired by falling through a space equal to that depth.—To William Dunbar. iv, 537. (W.. 1804.)

7658. ROANE (Spencer), Courage of.—Against this [consolidation] I know no one who, equally with Judge Roane himself. possesses the power and the courage to make resistance: and to him I look, and have long looked. as our strongest bulwark.—To Archibald Thweat. vii, 199. Ford ed., x, 184. (M., 1821.)

7659. ROANE (Spencer), Judge Marshall and.—On the decision of the case of Cohens *vs.* the State of Virginia, in the Supreme Court of the United States, in March, 1821, Judge Roane, under the signature of "Algernon Sidney", wrote for the Enquirer [Richmond] a series of papers on the law of that case. I considered these papers maturely as they came out, and confess that they appeared to me to pulverize every word which had been delivered by Judge Marshall, of the extra-judicial part of his opinion.—To William Johnson. vii, 294. Ford ed., x, 229. (M., 1823.)

7660. ROBESPIERRE, Atrocities of.—What a tremendous obstacle to the future attempts at liberty will be the atrocities of Robespierre!—To Tench Coxe. Ford ed., vii, 22.   (M., 1795.)

7661. ROBESPIERRE, Condemned.—Robespierre met the fate, and his memory the execration, he so justly merited. The rich were his victims, and perished by thousands.—To Madame de Stael. vi, 114. (M., May 1813.)

7662. ROCHAMBEAU (Count), Proposed bust.—Count Rochambeau has really deserved more attention than he has received. Why not set up his bust, that of Gates, Greene, Franklin, in your new capitol?—To James Madison. i, 534. Ford ed.. iv, 196. (P., 1786.)

7663. RODNEY (Cæsar A.), Affection for.—I avail myself of this occasion * * * to express all the depth of my affection for you; the sense I entertain of your faithful cooperation in my late labors, and the debt I owe for the valuable aid I received from you [in the cabinet].—To Caesar A. Rodney. v. 502. Ford ed., ix, 272.   (M., 1810.)

7664. RODNEY (Cæsar A.), Appeal to.—I am told you are the only person who can unite the greatest portion of the republican votes [in Delaware], and the only one, perhaps, who can procure the dismission of your present representative [in Congress] to that obscurity of situation where his temper and principles may be disarmed of all effect. You are, then, bound to do this good office to the rest of America. You owe to your State to make her useful to her friends, instead of being an embarrassment and a burden. Her long speeches and wicked workings at this session have added at least thirty days to its length, cost us $30,000, and filled the Union with falsehoods and misrepresentations.—To Caesar A. Rodney. Ford ed.. viii, 148. (W., 1802.)

7665. RODNEY (Cæsar A.), Retirement.—I lament the necessity which calls for your retirement, if that necessity really exists. I had looked to you as one of those calculated to give cohesion to our rope of sand.—To Caesar A. Rodney. Ford ed., viii, 296. (W., Feb. 1804.)

7666. ROGUES, Diplomacy and.—Our part of the country [Virginia] is in considerable fermentation on what they suspect to be a recent roguery of this kind. They say that while all hands were below deck mending sails. splicing ropes, and every one at his own business, and the captain in his cabin attending to his log-book and chart, a rogue of a pilot has run them into an enemy's port. But metaphor apart. there is much dissatisfaction with Mr. Jay and his treaty.—To Mann Page. iv. 120. Ford ed., vii, 25. (M., Aug. 1795.) See Jay Treaty.

7667. ROGUES, Proportion of.—I do not believe with the Rochefoucaulds and Mon-

taignes, that fourteen out of fifteen men are
rogues; I believe a great abatement from that
proportion may be made in favor of general
honesty. But I have always found that rogues
would be uppermost, and I do not know that
the proportion is too strong for the higher
orders, and for those who, rising above the
swinish multitude, always contrive to nestle
themselves into the places of power and profit.
These rogues set out with stealing the people's good opinion, and then steal from them
the right of withdrawing it, by contriving laws
and associations against the power of the people themselves.—To MANN PAGE. iv, 119. FORD
ED., vii, 24. (M., 1795.)

7668. ROGUES, Railing.—The rogues
may rail without intermission.—To DR. BENJA-
MIN RUSH. iv, 426. FORD ED., viii, 128. (W.,
1801.)

**7669. ROHAN (Cardinal de), Imprison-
ment.**—The Cardinal de Rohan and Caglios-
tro remain * * * in the Bastile; nor do their
affairs seem as yet to draw towards a conclusion. It has been a curious matter, in which
the circumstances of intrigue and detail have
busied all the tongues, the public liberty none.
—To MR. OTTO. i, 558. (P., 1786.)

**7670. ROTATION IN OFFICE, Aban-
donment of.**—I dislike, and greatly dislike
[in the new Federal Constitution] the abandonment in every instance of the principle* of
rotation in office, and most particularly in the
case of the President.—To JAMES MADISON.
ii, 330. FORD ED., iv, 477. (P., Dec. 1787.)
See PRESIDENT.

7671. —— ——. I apprehend that the
total abandonment of the principle of rotation
in the offices of President and Senator [in the
Federal Constitution] will end in abuse.—To
E. RUTLEDGE. ii, 435. FORD ED., v, 42. (P.,
1788.)

7672. —— ——. The abandoning the
principle of necessary rotation in the Senate
has, I see, been disapproved by many; in the
case of the President, by none. I readily,
therefore, suppose my opinion wrong, when
opposed by the majority, as in the former instance, and the totality, as in the latter. In
this, however, I should have done it with
more complete satisfaction, had we all judged
from the same position.—To JAMES MADISON.
ii, 447. FORD ED., v, 48. (P., July 1788.)

**7673. ROTATION IN OFFICE, Ap-
proval of.**—I am for responsibilities at short
periods, seeing neither reason nor safety in
making the public functionaries independent
of the nation for life, or even for a long term
of years. On this principle I prefer the Presidential term of four years to that of seven
years which I myself had at first suggested,
annexing to it, however, ineligibility to it
forever after; and I wish it were now annexed to the second quadrennial election of
President.—To JAMES MARTIN. vi, 213.
FORD ED., ix, 420. (M., 1813.) See THIRD
TERM.

**7674. ROTATION IN OFFICE, Defini-
tion of.**—Rotation is the change of officers

* " Necessity " of rotation in FORD EDITION.—EDI-
TOR.

required by the laws at certain epochs, and
in a certain order. Thus, in Virginia, our
justices of the peace are made sheriffs, one
after the other, each remaining in office two
years, and then yielding it to his next brother
in order of seniority. This is the just and
classical meaning of the word. But in America, we have extended it (for want of a
proper word), to all cases of officers who
must be necessarily changed at a fixed epoch,
though the successor be not pointed out in
any particular order, but comes in by free
election. By the term rotation in office, then,
we mean an obligation on the holder of that
office to go out at a certain period. In our
first confederation, the principle of rotation
was established in the office of President of
Congress, who could serve but one year in
three; and in that of a member of Congress,
who could serve but three years in six.—
To J. SARSFIELD. iii, 17. (P., 1789.)

**7675. ROTATION IN OFFICE, Restora-
tion of.**—The second amendment [to the new
Federal Constitution], which appears to me to
be essential, is the restoring the principle of
necessary rotation, particularly to the Senate
and Presidency, but most of all to the last.—
To E. CARRINGTON. ii, 404. FORD ED., v, 20.
(P., 1788.)

7676. ROWAN (A. H.), Asylum for.—
Should you choose Virginia for your asylum,
the laws of the land, administered by upright
judges, would protect you from an exercise of
power unauthorized by the Constitution of the
United States. The *Habeas Corpus* secures
every man here, alien or citizen, against everything which is not law, whatever shape it may
assume. Should this, or any other circumstance, draw your footsteps this way, I shall
be happy to be among those who may have an
opportunity of testifying, by every attention
in our power, the sentiments of esteem and
respect which the circumstances of your history
have inspired. *—To A. H. ROWAN. iv, 257.
FORD ED., vii, 281. (1798.)

7677. RULES, Forming.—The forming a
general rule requires great caution.—To PRESI-
DENT WASHINGTON. FORD ED., vi, 408. (Pa.,
1793.)

— **RULES, Jefferson's ten.**—See ADVICE.

7678. RUSH (Benjamin), Tribute to.—A
better man than Rush could not have left us;
more benevolent, more learned, of finer genius,
or more honest.—To JOHN ADAMS. vi, 120.
(M., 1813.)

7679. RUSH (Benjamin), Virtues.—His
virtues rendered him dear to all who knew
him, and his benevolence led him to do all men
every good in his power. Much he was able
to do, and much, therefore, will be missed.—
To RICHARD RUSH. FORD ED., ix, 385. (M.,
1813.)

7680. RUSSIA, Empress Catherine.—
The Empress endeavored to bully the Turk,
who laughed at her, and she is going back.—
To J. BANNISTER, JR. ii, 150. (P., 1787.) See
ALEXANDER OF RUSSIA and DASHKOFF.

* Archibald Hamilton Rowan was one of the
leaders in the rebellion in Ireland in 1798. He was
a refugee in Wilmington, Delaware, when Jefferson
wrote to him.— EDITOR.

7681. RUSSIA, United States and.— Russia' and the United States being in character and practice essentially pacific, a common interest in the rights of peaceable nations gives us a common cause in their maintenance.—To M. DASHKOFF. v, 463. (M., 1809.)

7682. RUTLEDGE (Edward), Appeal to,—Would to God yourself, General Pinckney and Major Pinckney, would come forward and aid us with your efforts. You are all known, respected, wished for; but you refuse yourselves to everything. What is to become of us if the vine and the fig tree withdraw, and leave us to the bramble and the thorn?—To EDWARD RUTLEDGE. iii, 285. FORD ED., v, 376. (Pa., 1791.)

7683. RUTLEDGE (Edward), Politics.— I have often doubted whether most to praise or to blame your line of conduct. If you had lent to your country the excellent talents you possess, on you would have fallen those torrents of abuse which have lately been poured forth on me. So far, I praise the wisdom which has descried and steered clear of a waterspout ahead. But now for the blame. There is a debt of service due from every man to his country, proportioned to the bounties which nature and fortune have measured to him. Counters will pay this from the poor of sp'rit; but from you coin was due. There is no bankrupt law in heaven, by which you may get off with shillings in the pound; with rendering to a single State what you owed to the whole confederacy. I think it was by the Roman law that a father was denied sepulture, unless his son would pay his debts. Happy for you and us, that you have a son whom genius and education have qualified to pay yours. But as you have been a good father in everything else, be so in this also. Come forward and pay your own debts. Your friends, the Pinckneys, have at length undertaken their tour. My joy at this would be complete if you were in gear with them.—To EDWARD RUTLEDGE. iv, 152. FORD ED., vii, 94. (M., 1796.)

7684. RUTLEDGE (John), Chief Justice.—The rejection of Mr. Rutledge [to be Chief Justice] by the Senate is a bold thing; because they cannot pretend any objection to him but his disapprobation of the [Jay] treaty. It is, of course, a declaration that they will receive none but tories hereafter into any department of the government.—To W. B. GILES. iv, 127. FORD ED., vii, 44. (M., Dec. 1795.)

7685. —— ——. The appointment of J. Rutledge to be Chief Justice seems to have been intended merely to establish a precedent against the descent of that office by seniority, and to keep five mouths always gaping for one sugar plum; for it was immediately negatived by the very votes which so implicitly concur with the will of the Executive.—To JAMES MONROE. FORD ED., vii, 59. (M., 1796.)

7686. SACRIFICES, Necessary.—Temporary sacrifices are necessary to save permanent rights.—To DR. WILLIAM EUSTIS. v, 411. FORD ED., ix, 236. (W., 1809.)

7687. SACRIFICES, Rewarding.—It is for the public interest to encourage sacrifices and services, by rewarding them, and they should weigh to a certain point, in the decision between candidates.—To JOHN ADAMS. i, 503. (P., 1785.)

7688. SAFETY, Rights and.—It would be a dangerous delusion were a confidence in the men of our choice to silence our fears for the safety of our rights.—KENTUCKY RESOLUTIONS. ix, 470. FORD ED., vii, 303. (1798.)

7689. SAFETY, Union and.—Our safety rests on the preservation of our Union.—To THE RHODE ISLAND ASSEMBLY. iv, 397. (W., May 1801.)

7690. SALARIES, Adequate.—Congress were pleased to order me an advance of two quarters' salary. At that time, I supposed that I might refund it, or spare so much from my expenses, by the time the third quarter became due. Probably they might expect the same. But it has been impossible. The expense of my outfit, though I have taken it up, on a scale as small as could be admitted, has been very far beyond what I had conceived. I have, therefore, not only been unable to refund the advance ordered, but been obliged to go beyond it. I wished to have avoided so much as was occasioned by the purchase of furniture. But those who hire furniture asked me forty per cent. a year for the use of it. It was better to buy, therefore; and this article, clothes, carriage, &c., have amounted to considerably more than the advance ordered. Perhaps, it may be thought reasonable to allow me an outfit. The usage of every other nation has established this, and reason really pleads for it. I do not wish to make a shilling: but only my expenses to be defrayed, and in a moderate style. On the most moderate, which the reputation or interest of those I serve would admit, it will take me several years to liquidate the advances for my outfit. I mention this to enable you to understand the necessities which have obliged me to call for more money than was probably expected, and, understanding them, to explain them to others.*—To SAMUEL OSGOOD. i, 452. (P., 1785.)

7691. SALARIES, Competent.—Render the [State] judiciary respectable by every means possible, to wit firm tenure in office, [and] competent salaries.—To ARCHIBALD STUART. iii, 315. FORD ED., v, 410. (Pa., 1791.)

7692. SALARIES, Foreign Ministers.— The bill on the intercourse with foreign nations restrains the President from allowing to Ministers Plenipotentiaries, or to Congress, more than $9,000, and $4,500 for their "personal services, and other expenses". This definition of the object for which the allowance is provided appearing vague, the Secretary of State thought it his duty to confer with the gentlemen heretofore employed as ministers in Europe, to obtain from them, in aid of his own information, an enumeration of the expenses incident to these offices, and their opinion which of them would be included within the fixed salary, and which would be entitled to be charged separately. He, therefore, asked a conference with the

* During his public life Jefferson sometimes lived on his salary, sometimes exceeded it, and only while he was Vice-President saved anything from it.— MORSE'S *Life of Jefferson*, 335.

Vice-President, who was acquainted with the residences of London and the Hague, and the Chief Justice, who was acquainted with that of Madrid. The Vice-President, Chief Justice, and Secretary of State concurred in the opinion that the salaries named by the act are much below those of the same grade at the courts of Europe, and less than the public good requires they should be. Consequently, that the expenses not included within the definition of the law, should be allowed as an additional charge.*—OPINION ON SALARIES. vii, 501. (1790.)

7693. SALARIES, Increasing.—It * * * [is] inconsistent with the principles of civil liberty, and contrary to the natural rights of the other members of the society, that any body of men therein should have authority to enlarge their own powers, prerogatives, or emoluments without restraint, the General Assembly cannot at their own will increase the allowance which their members are to draw from the public treasury for their expenses while in assembly: but to enable them to do so on application to the body of the people * * * is necesssary.—ADEQUATE ALLOWANCE BILL. FORD ED., ii, 165. (1778.)

7694. SALARIES, Legislators'.—It is just that members of General Assembly, delegated by the people to transact for them the legislative business, should, while attending that business, have their reasonable sustenance defrayed, dedicating to the public service their time and labors freely and without account: and it is also expedient that the public councils should not be deprived of the aid of good and able men, who might be deterred from entering into them by the insufficiency of their private fortunes to [meet] the extraordinary expenses they must necessarily incur.—ADEQUATE ALLOWANCE BILL. FORD ED., ii, 165. (1778.)

7695. SALARIES, Multiplication of.—I am not for a multiplication of * * * salaries merely to make partisans.—To ELBRIDGE GERRY. iv, 268. FORD ED., vii, 327. (Pa., 1799.)

7696. SALARIES, Official.—No salaries, or perquisites, shall be given to any officer but by some future act of the Legislature.—PROPOSED VA. CONSTITUTION. FORD ED., ii, 28. (June 1776.)

7697. —— ——. No salaries shall be given to the Administrator, members of the legislative houses, judges of the Court of Appeals, judges of the County Courts, or other inferior jurisdictions, privy counsellors, or delegates to the American Congress; but the reasonable expenses of the Administrator, members of the House of Representatives,

* There is an impression that we owe to Jefferson the system of paying extravagantly low salaries to high men. Not so. He was far too good a republican to favor an idea so aristocratic. Make offices desirable, he says, if you wish to get superior men to fill them. * * * There is nothing in the writings of Jefferson which gives any show of support to temptation salaries or to ignorant suffrage.—JAMES PARTON'S *Life of Jefferson*, 378.

judges of the Court of Appeals, privy counsellors, and delegates for subsistence, while acting in the duties of their office, may be borne by the public, if the Legislature shall so direct.—PROPOSED VA. CONSTITUTION. FORD ED., ii, 28. (June 1776.)

7698. SALARIES, Reduction of.—I remark [in your address to the Legislature] the phenomenon of a chief magistrate recommending the reduction of his own compensation. This is a solecism of which the wisdom of our late Congress cannot be accused.—To GOVERNOR PLUMER. vii, 19. (M., 1816.)

7699. SALT WATER, Distillation.—The obtaining fresh from salt water was for ages considered as an important desideratum for the use of navigators. The process for doing this by simple distillation is so efficacious, the erecting an extempore still with such utensils as are found on board of every ship, is so practicable, as to authorize the assertion that this desideratum is satisfied to a very useful degree. * But though this has been done for upwards of thirty years, though its reality has been established by the actual experience of several vessels which have had recourse to it, yet neither the fact nor the process is known to the mass of seamen, to whom it would be the most useful, and for whom it was principally wanted. The Secretary of State is, therefore, of opinion that since the subject has now been brought under observation, t should be made the occasion of disseminating its knowledge generally and effectually among the seafaring citizens of the United States.—REPORT TO CONGRESS. vii, 459. (1790.)

— SANCHO (Ignatius).—See NEGROES, LITERARY.

7700. SAN DOMINGO, Commerce with.—A clause in a bill now under debate for opening commerce with Toussaint and his black subjects, now in open rebellion against France will be a circumstance of high aggravation to that country, and in addition to our cruising around their islands will put their patience to a great proof.—To JAMES MONROE. iv, 265. FORD ED., vii, 321. (Pa., Jan. 1799.)

7701. —— ——. As it is acknowledged * * * that it is impossible the French should invade us since the annihilation of their power on the sea, our constituents will see in the [army and navy] preparations the utmost anxiety to guard them against even impossibilities. The Southern States do not discover the same care, however, in the bill author'zing Toussaint's subjects to a free commerce with them, and free ingress and intercourse with their black brethren in these States. However, if they are guarded against the cannibals of the terrible republic, they ought not to object to being eaten by a more civilized enemy.—To AARON BURR. FORD ED., vii, 348. (Pa., Feb. 1799.)

7702. —— ——. Toussaint's clause was retained.† Even South Carolinians in the House of Representatives voted for it. We may expect, therefore, black crews, and supercargoes.

* The House of Representatives had referred to Jefferson the petition of Jacob Isaacs of Rhode Island, who claimed to have discovered a method of converting salt water into fresh. Isaacs desired the government to buy his secret.—EDITOR.
† Jefferson referred to the exemption of San Domingo in the French non-intercourse bill.—EDITOR.

and missionaries thence into the Southern States; and when that leaven begins to work, I would gladly compound with a great part of our northern country, if they would honestly stand neuter. If this combustion can be introduced among us under any veil whatever, we have to fear it.—To JAMES MADISON. FORD ED., vii, 349. (Pa., Feb. 1799.)

7703. SAN DOMINGO, England and.— Rigaud, at the head of the people of color, maintains his allegiance [to France]. But they are only twenty-five thousand souls, against five hundred thousand, the number of the blacks. The [British] treaty made with them by Maitland is (if they are to be separated from France) the best thing for us. They must get their provisions from us. It will, indeed, be in English bottoms, so that we shall lose the carriage. But the English will probably forbid them the ocean, confine them to their island, and thus prevent their becoming an American Algiers. It must be admitted, too, that they may play them off on us when they please. Against this there is no remedy but timely measures on our part, to clear ourselves, by degrees, of the matter on which that lever can work.—To JAMES MADISON. iv, 281. FORD ED., vii, 343. (Pa., Feb. 1799.)

7704. SAN DOMINGO, Exile of aristocrats.—Genet tells me that the Patriotic party in St. Domingo had taken possession of six hundred aristocrats and monocrats, had sent two hundred of them to France, and were sending four hundred here. * * * I wish we could distribute our four hundred among the Indians, who would teach them lessons of liberty and equality.—To MARTHA JEFFERSON RANDOLPH. FORD ED., vi, 268. (Pa., 1793.)

7705. SAN DOMINGO, Fugitives from.—The situation of the St. Domingo fugitives (aristocrats as they are) calls aloud for pity and charity. Never was so deep a tragedy presented to the feelings of man. I deny the power of the General Government to apply money to such a purpose, but I deny it with a bleeding heart. It belongs to the State governments. Pray urge ours to be liberal. The Executive should hazard themselves here on such an occasion, and the Legislature when it meets ought to approve and extend it. It will have a great effect in doing away the impression of other disobligations towards France. —To JAMES MONROE. iv, 20. FORD ED., vi, 349. (Pa., July 1793.)

7706. SAN DOMINGO, Military expeditions to.—It is not permitted by the law to prohibit the departure of the emigrants to St. Domingo, according to the wish you express, any more than it is to force them away, according to that expressed by you in a former letter. Our country is open to all men, to come and go peaceably, when they choose; and your letter does not mention that these emigrants meant to depart armed, and equipped for war. Lest, however, this should be attempted, the Governors of * * * Pennsylvania and Maryland are requested * * * to see that no military expedition be covered or permitted under color of the right which the passengers have to depart from these States.—To E. C. GENET. iv, 87. FORD ED., vi, 459. (Pa., Nov. 1793.)

7707. SAN DOMINGO, Supplies to.— When the distresses in St. Domingo first broke forth, we thought we could not better evidence our friendship to that, and to the Mother country also, than to step into its relief, on your application, without waiting a formal authorization from the National Assembly. As the case was unforeseen, so it was unprovided for on their part, and we did what we doubted not they would have desired us to do, had there been time to make the application, and what we presumed they would sanction as soon as known to them. We have now been going on more than a twelve-month, in making advances for the relief of the Colony, without having, as yet, received any such sanction; for the decree of four millions of livres in aid of the Colony, besides the circuitous and informal manner by which we became acquainted with it, describes and applies to operations very different from those which have actually taken place. The wants of the Colony appear likely to continue, and their reliance on our supplies to become habitual. We feel every disposition to continue our efforts for administering to those wants; but that cautious attention to forms which would have been unfriendly in the first moment, becomes a duty to ourselves; when the business assumes the appearance of long continuance, and respectful also to the National Assembly itself, who have a right to prescribe the line of an interference so materially interesting to the Mother country and the Colony. By the estimate you were pleased to deliver me, we perceive that there will be wanting, to carry the Colony through the month of December, between thirty and forty thousand dollars, in addition to the sums before engaged to you. I am authorized to inform you, that the sum of forty thousand dollars shall be paid to your orders at the Treasury of the United States, and to assure you, that we feel no abatement in our dispositions to contribute these aids from time to time, as they shall be wanting, for the necessary subsistence of the Colony; but the want of express approbation from the National Legislature, must ere long produce a presumption that they contemplate perhaps other modes of relieving the Colony and dictate to us the propriety of doing only what they shall have regularly and previously sanctioned. —To JEAN BAPTISTE TERNANT. iii, 491. FORD ED., vi, 136. (Pa., Nov. 1792.)

7708. ———— ————. We are continuing our supplies to the island of St. Domingo, at the request of the minister of France here. We would wish, however, to receive a more formal sanction from the government of France than has yet been given. Indeed, we know of none but a vote of the late National Assembly for four millions of livres of our debt, sent to the government of St. Domingo, communicated by them to the minister here, and by him to us. And this was in terms not properly applicable to the form of our advances. We wish, therefore, for a full sanction of the past, and a complete expression of the desires of their government as to future supplies to their colonies. —To GOUVERNEUR MORRIS. FORD ED., vi, 151. (Pa., 1792.)

— SAN JUAN (Porto Rico).—See FREE PORTS.

— SARATOGA, Proposed State of.—See WESTERN TERRITORY.

7709. SARDINIA, Commerce with.—A desire of seeing a commerce commenced between the dominions of his Majesty, the King of Sardinia, and the United States of America, and a direct exchange of their respective productions, without passing through a third nation, led me into the conversation which I had the honor of having with you on that subject, and afterwards with Monsieur Tallon at Turin. * * * The articles of your produce wanted with us are brandies, wines, oils, fruits, and manufactured silks. Those wh·ch we can furnish you are ind go, potash, tobacco, flour, salt fish, furs and peltries, ships and materials for building them.—To M. Guide. ii, 146. (Ms., 1787.)

7710. SAUSSURE (Horace B.), Philosopher.—M. Saussure is one of the best philosophers of the present age. Cautious in not letting his assent run before his evidence, he possesses the wisdom which so few possess, of preferring ignorance to error. The contrary disposition in those who call themselves philosophers in this country classes them, in fact, with the writers of romance.—To William Rutledge. ii, 475. (P., 1788.)

— **SAY (Jean Baptiste).**—See Government, Works on.

7711. SCENERY, American.—The Falling Spring, the Cascade of Niagara, the passage of the Potomac through the Blue Mountains, the Natural Bridge,—it is worth a voyage across the Atlantic to see those objects, much more to paint and make them, and thereby ourse!ves, known to all ages.—To Mrs. Cosway. i', 35. Ford ed., iv, 315. (P., 1786.)

7712. SCHISM, Dangers of.—Strong in our numbers, our pos:tion and resources, we can never be endangered but by schisms at home.—R. to A. Wilmington Citizens. viii, 149. (1809.)

7713. SCHISM, Governmental.—Government, as well as religion, has furnished its schisms, its persecutions, and its devices for fattening idleness on the earnings of the people. It has its hierarchy of emperors, kings, princes, and nobles, as that has of popes, cardinals, archbishops, bishops and priests.—To Charles Clas. vi, 413. (M., 1815.)

7714. SCHISM, Self-government and.—All these schisms, small or great, only accumulate truths of the solid qualifications of our citizens for self-government.—To Thomas Leiper. Ford ed., viii, 503. (W., 1806.)

7715. SCHISM, Silence.—Frown into silence all disorganizing movements.—R. to A. Wilmington Citizens. viii 149. (1809.)

7716. SCHOOLS, Abortive.—The annual reports show that our plan of primary schools [in Virginia] is becoming completely abortive, and must be abandoned very shortly, after costing us to this day one hundred and eighty thousand dollars, and yet to cost us forty-five thousand dollars a year more until it shall be discontinued; and if a single boy has received the elements of common education, it must be in some part of the country not known to me. Experience has but too fully confirmed the early predictions of its fate.—To William T. Barry. vii, 256. (M., 1822.)

7717. SCHOOLS, European.—Why send an American youth to Europe for education? What are the objects of an useful American education? Classical knowledge, modern languages, chiefly French, Span'sh and Italian; mathematics, natural philosophy, natural history, civil history and ethics. In natural philosophy, I mean to include chemistry and agriculture; and in natural history to include botany, as well as the other branches of those departments. It is true that the habit of speaking the modern languages cannot be so well acquired in America; but every other article can be as well acquired at William and Mary College, as at any place in Europe. When college education is done with,

and a young man is to prepare h:mself for public life, he must cast his eyes (for America) either on law or physics. For the former, where can he apply so advantageously as to Mr. Wythe? For the latter, he must come to Europe; the medical class of students, therefore, is the only one which need come to Europe.—To J. Bannister. i, 467. (P., 1785.)

7718. ——. Let us view the disadvantages of sending a youth to Europe. To enumerate them all would require a volume. I will select a few. If he goes to England, he learns drinking, horse racing and boxing. These are the peculiarities of English education. The following circumstances are common to education in that and the other countries of Europe. He acquires a fondness for European luxury and dissipation, and a contempt for the simplicity of his own country; he is fascinated with the privileges of the European aristocrats, and sees, with abhorrence, the lovely equality which the poor enjoy with the rich in his own country; he contracts a partiality for aristocracy or monarchy; he forms foreign friendships which will never be useful to him, and loses the seasons of life for forming, in his own country, those friendships which, of all others, are the most faithful and permanent; * * * and * * * he returns to his own country unacquainted w·th the practices of domestic economy, necessary to preserve him from ruin, speaking and writing his native tongue as a foreigner, and, therefore, unqualified to obtain those distinctions, which eloquence of the pen and tongue ensures in a free country; for I would observe to you, that what is called style 'n writing or speaking, is formed verv early in life, while the imagination is warm, and impressions are permanent.—To J. Bannister. i, 467. (P., 1785.)

7719. ——. An American, coming to Europe for education, loses in his knowledge, in his morals, in his health, in his habits, and in his happiness. I had entertained only doubts on this head before I came to Europe; what I see and hear, since I came here, proves more than I had even suspected.—To J. Bannister. i, 468. (P., 1785.)

7720. ——. Cast your eye over America: who are the men of most learning, of most eloquence, most beloved by their countrymen and most trusted and promoted by them? They are those who have been educated among them, and whose manners, morals, and habits, are perfectly homogeneous with those of the country. * * * The consequences of foreign education are alarming to me as an American.—To J. Bannister. i, 468. (P., 1785.)

7721. ——. With respect to the schools of Europe, my mind is perfectly made up, and on full enquiry. The best in the world is Edinburgh. Latterly, too, the spirit of republicanism has become that of the students in general, and of the younger professors; so on that account it is eligible for an American. On the continent of Europe, no place is comparable to Geneva. The sciences are there more modernized than anywhere else. There, too, the spirit of republicanism is strong with the body of the inhabitants; but that of the aristocracy is strong also with a particular class: so that it is of some consequence to attend to the class of society in which a youth is made to move.—To Mr. M'Alister. iii, 313. (Pa., 1791.)

7722. SCHOOLS, Fostering genius in.—By that part of our plan [of education in Virginia] wh'ch prescribes the selection of the youths of genius from among the classes of the poor, we hope to avail the State of those talents which nature has sown as liberally among the poor as the rich, but which perish without use, if not sought for and cultivated.—NOTES ON VIRGINIA. viii, 390. FORD ED., iii, 254. (1782.) See GENIUS.

7723. SCHOOLS, Government of.—If it is believed that the elementary schools will be better managed by the Governor and Council, the Commissioners of the Literary Fund, or any other general authority of the government, than by the parents within each ward, it is a belief against all experience.—To JOSEPH C. CABELL. vi, 543. (1816.)

7724. SCHOOLS, History in.—At these [Virginia public] schools shall be taught reading, wr'ting, and common arithmetic, and the books which shall be used therein for instructing the children to read shall be such as will, at the same time, make them acquainted with Græcian, Roman, English, and American history.—DIFFUSION OF KNOWLEDGE BILL. FORD ED., ii, 223. (1779.)

7725. SCHOOLS, Trustees.—I have received your favor, informing me that the Board of Trustees for the public school in Washington had unanimously reappointed me their President. I pray you to present to them my thanks for the mark of their confidence, with assurances that I shall at all times be ready to render to the institution any services which shall be in my power.—To ROBERT BRENT. v, 196. (M., Sep. 1807.)

7726. SCHOOLS, Visitors.—I had formerly thought that visitors of the school might be chosen by the county, and charged to provide teachers for every ward, and to superintend them. I now think it would be better for every ward to choose 'ts own resident visitor, whose business it would be to keep a teacher in the ward, to superintend the school, and to call meetings of the ward for all purposes relating to it; their accounts to be settled, and wards laid oft by the courts. I think ward elections better for many reasons, one of which is sufficient, that it will keep elementary education out of the hands of fanatic'sing preachers, who, 'n county elections, would be universally chosen, and the predominant sect of the county would possess itself of all its schools.—To JOSEPH C. CABELL. vii, 189. FORD ED., x, 167. (P.F., 1820.)

7727. SCHOOLS, Wealth and.—In the elementary bill they [the Legislature] inserted a provision which completely defeated it; for they left it to the court of each county to determine for itself when this act should be carried into execution within their county. One provision of the bill was that the expenses of these schools should be borne by the inhabitants of the county, every one in proportion to his general tax rate. This would throw on wealth the education of the poor; and the justices, being generally of the more wealthy class, were unwilling to incur that burden, and I believe 't was not suffered to commence in a single county.—AUTOBIOGRAPHY. i, 48. FORD ED., i, 67. (1821.) See ACADEMY, EDUCATION, LANGUAGES, and UNIVERSITY.

7728. SCIENCE, Acquirement of.—The possession of science is, what (next to an honest heart) will above all things render you dear to your friends, and give you fame and promotion in your own country.—To PETER CARR. i, 395. (P., 1785.)

7729. SCIENCE, American field of.—What a field have we at our doors to signalize ourselves in. The Botany of America is far from being exhausted, its Mineralogy 's untouched, and its Natural History or Zoology, totally mistaken and misrepresented. As far as I have seen, there is not one single species of terrestrial birds common to Europe and America, and I question if there be a single species of quadrupeds. (Domestic animals are to be excepted.) It is for such institutions as that [Harvard] over which you preside so worthily to do justice to our country, its productions and its genius. It is the work to which the young men whom you are forming should lay their hands. We have spent the prime of our lives in procuring them the precious blessing of liberty. Let them spend theirs in showing that it is the great parent of science and of virtue; and that a nation will be great in both, always in proportion as it is free.—To DR. WILLARD. iii, 16. (P., 1789.)

7730. SCIENCE, Common property.—The field of knowledge is the common property of mankind, and any discoveries we can make in 't will be for the benefit of yours and of every other nation, as well as our own.—To HENRY DEARBORN. v, 111. FORD ED., ix, 86. (W., 1807.)

7731. SCIENCE, Delight in.—Nature intended me for the tranquil pursuits of science, by rendering them my supreme delight.—To DUPONT DE NEMOURS. v, 432. (W., March 2, 1809.)

7732. SCIENCE, Elementary works.—I have received a copy of your mathematical principles of natural philosophy, which I have looked into with all the attention which the rust of age and long continued avocations of a very different character permit me to exercise. I think them entirely worthy of approbation, both as to matter and method, and for their brevity as a text book; and I remark particularly the clearness and precision with which the propositions are enounced and, in the demonstrations, the easy form in which ideas are presented to the mind, so as to be almost intuitive and self-evident. Of Cavallo's book, which you say you are enjoined to teach [in William and Mary College], I have no knowledge, having never seen it; but its character is, I think, that of mere mediocrity; and, from my personal acquaintance with the man, I should expect no more. He was heavy, capable enough of understanding what he had read, and with memory to retain it, but without the talent of digestion or 'mprovement. But, indeed, the English generally have been very stationary in latter times, and the French, on the contrary, so active and successful, particularly in preparing elementary books, in the mathematical and natural sciences, that those who wish for instruction, without caring from what nation they get 't. resort universally to the latter language. Besides the earlier and invaluable works of Euler and Bezont, we have latterly that of Lacroix in mathematics. of Legendre in geometry, Lavoisier in chemistry, the elementary works of Haüy in physics, Biot in experimental physics and physical astronomy, Dumeril in natural history, to say nothing of many detached essays of Monge and others, and the transcendent labors of Laplace. I am informed by a high'y instructed person recently from Cambridge. that the mathematic'ans of that institution. sensible of being in the rear of those of the continent, and ascribing the cause much to their too long-continued preference of the geometrical over the analytical methods, which the French have so much cultivated and improved, have now adopted the latter; and that they have also g ven up the fluxionary, for the differential calculus. To confine a school, therefore, to the obsolete work of Cavallo, is to shut out all advances in the physical sciences which have been so great in latter times.—To PATRICK K. RODGERS. vii, 327. (M., 1824.)

7733. SCIENCE, Encouragement of.—I am for the encouraging the progress of science in all its branches; and not for raising a hue and cry against the sacred name of philosophy; for awing the human mind by stories of raw-head and bloody bones to a distrust of its own vision, and to repose implicitly on that of others; to go backward instead of forward to look for improvement: to believe that government, religion, morality, and every other science were in the highest perfection in the ages of the darkest ignorance, and that nothing can ever be devised more perfect than what was established by our forefathers.—To ELBRIDGE GERRY. iv, 269. FORD ED., vii, 328. (Pa., 1799.)

7734. SCIENCE, Mother of freedom.—Freedom, the first-born daughter of science.—To M. D'IVERNOIS. iv. 113. FORD ED., vii, 3. (M., Feb. 1795.)

7735. SCIENCE, Objects of.—The main objects of all science are the freedom and happiness of man.—To GENERAL KOSCIUSKO. v, 509. (M., 1810.)

7736. SCIENCE, Pursuit of.—On the revival of letters, learning became the universal favorite [pursuit]. And with reason, because there was not enough of it existing to manage the affairs of a nation to the best advantage, nor to advance its individuals to the happiness of which they were susceptible, by improvements in their minds, their morals, their health, and in those conveniences which contribute to the comfort and embellishment of life. All the efforts of the society, therefore, were directed to the increase of learning, and the inducements of respect, ease, and profit were held up for its encouragement. Even the charities of the nation forgot that misery was their object, and spent themselves in founding schools to transfer to science the hardy sons of the plow. To these incitements were added the powerful fascinations of great cities. These circumstances have long since produced an overcharge in the class of competitors for learned occupation, and great distress among the supernumerary candidates; and the more, as their habits of life have disqualified them for reentering into the laborious class. The evil cannot be suddenly, nor perhaps ever entirely cured: nor should I presume to say by what means it may be cured. Doubtless there are many engines which the nation might bring to bear on this object. Public opinion, and public encouragement are among these.—To DAVID WILLIAMS. iv. 513. (W., 1803.)

7737. SCIENCE, Republican government and.—Science is more important in a republican than in any other government.—To —— ——. vii, 221. (M., 1821.)

7738. —— ——. Science is important to the preservation of our republican government and it is also essential to its protection against foreign power.—To —— ——. vii, 222. (M., 1821.)

7739. SCIENCES, Distribution of the.—I have received the copy of your System of Universal Science. * * * It will be a monument of the learning of the author and of the

analyzing powers of his mind. * * * These analytical views indeed must always be ram fied according to their object. Yours is on the great scale of a methodical encyclopedia of all human sciences, taking for the basis of their distribution, matter, mind, and the union of both. Lord Bacon founded his first great division on the faculties of the mind which have cognizance of these sciences. It does not seem to have been observed by any one that the origination of this division was not with him. It had been proposed by Charron, more than twenty years before, in his book de la Sagesse. B. 1, c. 14, and an imperfect ascription of the sciences to these respective faculties was there attempted. This excellent moral work was published in 1600. Lord Bacon is said not to have entered on his great work until his retirement from public office in 1621. Where sciences are to be arranged in accommodation to the schools of an university, they will be grouped to coincide with the kindred qualifications of professors in ordinary. For a library, which was my object, their divisions and subdivisions will be made such as to throw convenient masses of books under each separate head. Thus, in the library of a physician, the books of that science, of which he has many, will be subdivided under many heads; and those of law, of which he has few, will be placed under a single one. The lawyer, again, will distribute his law books under many subdivisions, his medical under a single one. Your idea of making the subject matter of the sciences the basis of their distribution, is certainly more reasonable than that of the faculties to which they are addressed. * * * Were I to re-compose my tabular view of the sciences, I should certainly transpose a certain branch. The naturalists, you know, distribute the history of nature into three kingdoms or departments: zoology, botany, mineralogy. Ideology, or mind, however, occupies so much space in the field of science, that we might perhaps erect it into a fourth kingdom or department. But, inasmuch as it makes a part of the animal construction only, it would be more proper to subdivide zoology into physical and moral. The latter including ideology, ethics, and mental science generally, in my catalogue, considering ethics, as well as religion, as supplements to law in the government of man, I had them in that sequence. But certainly the faculty of thought belongs to animal history, is an important portion of it, and should there find its place.—To MR. WOODWARD. vii, 338. (M., 1824.)

— **SCIENTIFIC SOCIETIES.**—See SOCIETIES, SCIENTIFIC.

— **SCIPIO.**—See ORATORY.

— **SCREW PROPELLER.**—See INVENTIONS.

7740. SCULPTURE, Style.—As to the style or costume [for a statue of General Washington], I am sure the artist, and every person of taste in Europe, would be for the Roman. * * * Our boots and regimentals have a very puny effect.—To NATHANIEL MACON. vi, 535. (M., 1816.)

7741. SEAMEN, American.—The seamen which our navigation raises had better be of our own. It is neither our wish nor our interest ever to employ [those of England].—To WILLIAM SHORT. vi, 128. (M., June 1813.)

7742. SEAMEN, Distressed.—Another circumstance which claims attention, as directly affecting the very source of our navigation, is the defect or the evasion of the law providing for the return of seamen, and particularly of those belonging to vessels sold abroad. Numbers of them, discharged in foreign ports, have been thrown on the hands of our consuls, who, to rescue them from the dangers into which their distresses might plunge them, and save them to their country, have found it necessary in some cases to return them at the public charge.—SECOND ANNUAL MESSAGE. viii, 16. FORD ED., v'ii, 182. (Dec. 1802.)

7743. SEAMEN, Foreign.—Your estimate of the number of foreign seamen in our employ, renders it prudent, in my opinion, to drop the idea of any proposition not to employ them.—To ALBERT GALLATIN. v, 71. (M., April 1807.)

— **SEARCH, Right of.**—See IMPRESSMENT.

7744. SECESSION, Baleful.—Mr. New showed me your letter * * * which gave me an opportunity of observing what you said as to the effect, with you, of public proceedings, and that it was not unwise* now to estimate the separate mass of Virginia and North Carolina, with a view to their separate existence. It is true that we are completely under the saddle of Massachusetts and Connecticut, and that they ride us very hard, cruelly insulting our feelings, as well as exhausting our strength and subsistence. Their natural friends, the three other Eastern States, join them from a sort of family pride, and they have the art to divide certain other parts of the Union, so as to make use of them to govern the whole. This is not new, it is the old practice of despots; to use a part of the people to keep the rest in order. And those who have once got an ascendency, and possessed themselves of all the resources of the nation, their revenues and offices, have immense means of retaining their advantage. But our present situation is not a natural one. The republicans, through every part of the Union, say that it was the irresistible influence and popularity of General Washington played off by the cunning of Hamilton, which turned the government over to anti-republican hands, or turned the republicans chosen by the people into anti-republicans. He delivered it over to his successor in this state, and very untoward events since, improved with great artifice, have produced on the public mind the impressions we see. But, still, I repeat it, this is not the natural state. Time alone would bring round an order of things more correspondent to the sentiments of our constituents. But, are there no events impending, which will do it within a few months? The crisis with England, the public and authentic avowal of sentiments hostile to the leading principles of our Constitution, the prospect of a war, in which we shall stand alone, land tax, stamp tax, increase of public debt, &c. Be this as it may, in every free and deliberating society, there must, from the nature of man, be opposite parties, and violent dissensions and discords;

* A descendant of Mr. Taylor claimed that he wrote "it is not *usual* now", &c. See FORD EDITION.—EDITOR.

and one of these, for the most part, must prevail over the other for a longer or shorter time. Perhaps this party division is necessary to induce each to watch and debate to the people the proceedings of the other. But if on a temporary superiority of the one party, the other is to resort to a scission of the Union, no federal government can ever exist. If to rid ourselves of the present rule of Massachusetts and Connecticut, we break the Union, will the evil stop there? Suppose the New England States alone cut off, will our nature be changed? Are we not men still to the south of that, and with all the passions of men? Immediately, we shall see a Pennsylvania and a Virginia party arise in the residuary confederacy, and the public mind will be distracted with the same party spirit. What a game, too, will the one party have in their hands, by eternally threatening the other that unless they do so and so, they will join their northern neighbors. If we reduce our Union to Virginia and North Carolina, immediately the conflict will be established between the representatives of these two States, and they will end by breaking into their simple units. Seeing, therefore, that an association of men who will not quarrel with one another is a thing which never existed, from the greatest confederacy of nations down to a town meeting or a vestry; seeing that we must have somebody to quarrel with, I had rather keep our New England associates for that purpose, than to see our bickerings transferred to others. They are circumscribed within such narrow limits, and their population so full, that their numbers will ever be the minority, and they are marked, like the Jews, with such a perversity of character, as to constitute, from that circumstance, the natural division of our parties. A little patience, and we shall see the reign of witches pass over, their spells dissolved, and the people recovering their true sight, restoring their government to its true principles. It is true that, in the meantime, we are suffering deeply in spirit, and incurring the horrors of a war, and long oppressions of enormous public debt. But who can say what would be the evils of a scission, and when and where they would end? Better keep together as we are, haul off from Europe as soon as we can, and from all attachments to any portions of it; and if they show their power just sufficiently to hoop us together, it will be the happiest situation in which we can exist. If the game runs sometimes against us at home, we must have patience till luck turns, and then we shall have an opportunity of winning back the *principles* we have lost. For this is a game where principles are the stake.—To JOHN TAYLOR. iv, 245. FORD ED., vii, 263. (Pa., June 1798.)

— **SECESSION, Kentucky and.**—See KENTUCKY.

7745. SECESSION, Local discontentedness and.—Dangers of another kind [than usurpation] might more reasonably be apprehended from this perfect and distinct organization, civil and military, of the States; to wit, that certain States from local and occasional discontents, might attempt to secede from the Union. This is certainly possible and would be befriended by this regular [civil and military] organization. But it is not probable that local discontents can spread to such an extent as to be able to faze the sound parts of so extensive a Union; and if ever they should reach the majority, they would then become the regular government, acquire the ascendency in Congress, and be able to redress their own grievances by laws peaceably and constitutionally passed. And even the States in which local discontents might engender a commencement of fermentation, would be paralyzed and self-checked by that very division into parties into which we have fallen, into which all States must fall wherein men are at liberty to think, speak, and act freely, according to the diversities of their individual conformations, and which are, perhaps, essential to preserve the purity of the government, by the censorship which these parties habitually exercise over each other.—To DESTUTT TRACY. v, 571. FORD ED., ix, 309. (M., 1811.)

7746. SECESSION, Louisiana purchase and.—Whether we remain in one confederacy, or form into Atlantic and Mississippi confederacies, I believe not very important to the happiness of either part.* Those of the Western confederacy will be as much our children and descendants as those of the Eastern, and I feel myself as much identified what that country, in future time, as with this: and did I now foresee a separation at some future day, yet I should feel the duty and the desire to promote the Western interests as zealously as the Eastern, doing all the good for both portions of our future family which should fall within my power.—To DR. JOSEPH PRIESTLEY. iv, 525. FORD ED., viii, 295. (W., Jan. 1804.)

7747. SECESSION, Missouri question and.—Should time not be given, and the schism [Missouri] be pushed to separation, it will be for a short term only; two or three years' trial will bring them back, like quarreling lovers to renewed embraces, and increased affections. The experiment of separation would soon prove to both that they had mutually miscalculated their best interests. And even were the parties in Congress to secede in a passion, the soberer people would call a convention and cement again the severance attempted by the insanity of their functionaries.—To RICHARD RUSH. vii, 182. (M., 1820.)

7748. SECESSION, New England and.—I am glad of an occasion of congratulating you [William Eustis] as well as my country, on your accession to a share in the direction of our Executive councils. [Secretaryship of War.] Besides the general advantages we may promise ourselves from the employment

* The opponents of the Louisiana purchase were, at this period, predicting dire disaster to the Union because of its acquisition.—EDITOR.

of your talents and integrity in so important a station, we may hope peculiar effect from it towards restoring deeply wounded amity between your native State [Massachusetts] and her sisters. The design of the leading federalists then having direction of the State, to take advantage of the first war with England to separate the New England States from the Union, has distressingly impaired our future confidence in them. In this, as in all other cases, we must do them full justice, and make the fault all their own, should the last hope of human liberty be destined to receive its final stab from them.—To WILLIAM EUSTIS. FORD ED., ix, 236. (M., Oct. 1809.) See EUSTIS.

7749. ——— ———. Should the determination of England, now formally expressed, to take possession of the ocean, and to suffer no commerce on it but through her ports, force a war upon us, I foresee a possibility of a separate treaty between her and your Essex men, on the principles of neutrality and commerce. Pickering here, and his nephew Williams there, can easily negotiate this. Such a lure to the quietists in our ranks with you, might recruit theirs to a majority. Yet, excluded as they would be from intercourse with the rest of the Union and of Europe, I scarcely see the gain they would propose to themselves, even for the moment. The defection would certainly disconcert the other States, but it could not ultimately endanger their safety. They are adequate, in all points, to a defensive war. However, I hope your majority, with the aid it is entitled to, will save us from this trial, to which I think it possible we are advancing.—To HENRY DEARBORN. v, 607. (P.F., Aug. 1811.) See EMBARGO, FEDERALISTS, HARTFORD CONVENTION and MONARCHY.

7750. SECESSION, Suppression of.— What does this English faction with you [in New England] mean? Their newspapers say rebellion, and that they will not remain united with us unless we will permit them to govern the majority. If this be their purpose, their anti-republican spirit, it ought to be met at once. But a government like ours should be slow in believing this, should put forth its whole might, when necessary, to suppress it, and promptly return to the paths of reconciliation. The extent of our country secures it, I hope, from the vindictive passions of the petty incorporations of Greece. I rather suspect that the principal office of the other seventeen States will be to moderate and restrain the excitement of our friends with you, when they (with the aid of their brothers of the other States, if they need it), shall have brought the rebellious to their feet. They count on British aid. But what can that avail them by land? They would separate from their friends, who alone furnish employment for their navigation, to unite with their only rival for that employment. When interdicted the harbors of their quondam brethren, they will go, I suppose, to ask and share in the carrying trade of their rivals, and a dispensation with their navigation act. They think they will be happier in an association under

the rulers of Ireland, the East and West Indies, than in an independent government,
where they are obliged to put up with their
proportional share only in the direction of
affairs. But, I trust, that such perverseness
will not be that of the honest and well-meaning mass of the federalists of Massachusetts;
and that when the questions of separation and
rebellion shall be nakedly proposed to them,
the Gores and the Pickerings will find their
levees crowded with silk stocking gentry, but
no yeomanry; an army of officers without
soldiers.—To ELBRIDGE GERRY. vi, 63. FORD
ED., ix, 359. (M., 1812.)

**7751. SECESSION, War with France
and.**—It is quite impossible when we consider
all the existing circumstances, to find any reason in its favor [war against France] resulting
from views either of interest or honor, and
plausible enough to impose even on the weakest
mind; and especially, when it would be undertaken by a majority of one or two only. Whatever, then, be our stock of charity or liberality,
we must resort to other views. And those so
well known to have been entertained at Annapolis, and afterwards at the grand [Phila-
delphia] convention, by a particular set of men,
present themselves as those alone which can
account for so extraordinary a degree of impetuosity. Perhaps, instead of what was then
in contemplation, a separation of the Union,
which has been so much the topic to the eastward of late, may be the thing aimed at.—To
JAMES MADISON. iv, 222. FORD ED., vii, 220.
(Pa., March 1798.)

7752. SECRECY, Government and.—
All nations have found it necessary, that for
the advantageous conduct of their affairs, some
of their proceedings, at least, should remain
known to their executive functionary only.—
To GEORGE HAY. v, 97. FORD ED., ix, 57.
(W., 1807.)

**7753. SECRET SERVICE MONEY,
Necessary.**—That in cases of military operations some occasions for secret service money
must arise, is certain. But I think that they
should be more fully explained to the government than General Wilkinson has done, seems
also proper.—To HENRY DEARBORN. v, 322.
(W., July 1808.)

— SECRET SOCIETIES.—See SOCIETIES
(SECRET).

**7754. SECRETARIES OF LEGATION,
Training.**—I explained to you in my former
letter the principles on which [the appointment
of Mr. Sumter to be Secretary of Legation]
was made, to wit, * * * to teach for public service in future such subjects as from their
standing in society, talents, principles and fortune, may probably come into the public councils.—To ROBERT R. LIVINGSTON. FORD ED.,
vii, 30. (1801.)

7755. SECTIONALISM, Dangers of.—
The idea of a geographical line, once suggested, will brood in the minds of all those
who prefer the gratification of their ungovernable passions to the peace and union of
their country.—To M. L. HILL. vii, 155.
(M., 1820.)

7756. —— ——. All, I fear, do not see
the speck in our horizon which is to burst on
us as a tornado, sooner or later. The line

of division lately marked out between different portions of our confederacy, is such as
will never, I fear, be obliterated, and we are
now trusting to those who are against us in
position and principle, to fashion to their own
form the minds and affections of our youth.
—To GENERAL BRECKENRIDGE. vii, 204. (M.,
1821.)

**7757. SECTIONALISM, Moral and po-
litical.**—A geographical line, coinciding with
a marked principle, moral and political, once
conceived and held up to the angry passions
of men, will never be obliterated; and every
new irritation will mark it deeper and deeper.
—To JOHN HOLMES. vii, 159. FORD ED., x,
157. (M., 1820.)

7758. SECTIONALISM, Peace and.—I
am so completely withdrawn from all attention to public matters, that nothing less could
arouse me than the definition of a geographical line which, as an abstract principle, is to
become the line of separation of these States,
and to render desperate the hope that man
can ever enjoy the two blessings of peace and
self-government.—To H. NELSON. vii, 151.
FORD ED., x, 156. (M., 1820.) See APPOR-
TIONMENT and SECESSION.

**7759. SEDITION LAW, Connecticut
cases.**—With respect to the dismission of the
prosecutions for sedition in Connecticut, it is
well known to have been a tenet of the republican portion of our fellow citizens, that the Sedition law was contrary to the Constitution and
therefore void. On this ground I considered
it as a nullity wherever I met it in the course
of my duties; and on this ground I directed
nolle prosequis in all the prosecutions which
had been instituted under it, and as far as the
public sentiment can be inferred from the occurrences of the day, we may say that this
opinion had the sanction of the nation. The
prosecutions, therefore, which were afterwards
instituted in Connecticut, of which two were
against printers, two against preachers, and one
against a judge, were too inconsistent with this
principle to be permitted to go on. We were
bound to administer to others the same measure
of law, not which they had meted out to us,
but we to ourselves, and to extend to all equally
the protection of the same constitutional principles. Those prosecutions too were chiefly for
charges against myself, and I had from the beginning laid it down as a rule to notice nothing
of the kind. I believed that the long course of
services in which I had acted on the public
stage, and under the eye of my fellow citizens,
furnished better evidence to them of my character and principles, than the angry invectives
of adverse partisans in whose eyes the very acts
most approved by the majority were subjects
of the greatest demerit and censure. These
prosecutions against them, therefore, were to
be dismissed as a matter of duty.—To GIDEON
GRANGER. vi, 332. FORD ED., ix, 456. (M.,
1814.) See LIBELS.

7760. SEDITION LAW, England and.—
I enclose you a column, cut out of a London
paper, to show you that the English, though
charmed with our making their enemies our
enemies, yet blush and weep over our Sedition
law.—To JOHN TAYLOR. iv, 260. FORD ED.,
vii, 311. (M., 1798.)

**7761. SEDITION LAW, Executive vs.
Judiciary.**—You seem to think it devolved

on the judges to decide on the valid'ty of the Sedition law. But nothing in the Constitution has given them a right to decide for the Executive, more than the Executive to decide for them. Both magistrates are equally independent in the sphere of action assigned to them. The judges, believing the law constitutional, had a right to pass a sentence of fine and imprisonment; because the power was placed in their hands by the Constitution. But the Executive, believing the law to be unconstitutional, were bound to remit the execution of it; because that power has been confided to them by the Constitution. That instrument meant that, its coord'nate branches should be checks on each other. But the opinion which gives to the judges the right to decide what laws are constitutional, and what not, not only for themselves in their own sphere of action, but for the Legislature and Executive also, in their spheres, would make the judiciary a despotic branch. Nor does the opinion of the unconstitutionality, and consequent nullity of that law, remove all restraint from the overwhelming torrent of slander, which is confounding all vice and virtue, all truth and falsehood, in the United States. The power to do that is fully possessed by the several State Legislatures. It was reserved to them, and was denied to the General Government, by the Constitution, according to our construction of it. While we deny that Congress have a right to control the freedom of the press, we have ever asserted the right of the States, and their exclusive right, to do so.—To Mrs. JOHN ADAMS. iv, 561. FORD ED., viii, 311. (M., Sep. 1804.)

7762. SEDITION LAW, Unconstitutional.—I found a prosecution going on against Duane for an offence against the Senate, founded on the Sedition act. I affirm that act to be no law, because in opposition to the Constitution; and I shall treat 't as a nullity, wherever it comes in the way of my functions. —To EDWARD LIVINGSTON. FORD ED., viii, 58. (W., Nov. 1801.)

7763. ———. The ground on which I acted in the cases of Duane, Callender, and others [was] that the Sedition law was unconstitutional and null, and that my obligation to execute what was law, involved that of not suffering rights secured by valid laws to be prostrated by what was no law.—To WILSON C. NICHOLAS. v, 453. FORD ED., ix, 254. (M., 1809.) See ALIEN AND SEDITION LAWS.

7764. SELF-GOVERNMENT, America and.—Before the establishment of the American States, nothing was known to history but the man of the old world, crowded within limits either small or overcharged, and steeped in the vices which that situation generates. A government adapted to such men would be one thing; but a very different one, that for the man of these States. Here every man may have land to labor for himself, if he chooses; or, preferring the exercise of any other industry, may exact for it such compensation as not only to afford a comfortable subsistence, but wherewith to provide for a cessation from labor in old age. Every one, by his property, or by his satisfactory situation, is interested in the support of law and order. And such men may safely and advantageously reserve to themselves a wholesome control over their public affairs, and a degree of freedom, which, in the hands of the *canaille* of the cities of Europe, would be instantly per-

verted to the demolition and destruction of everything public and private. The history of the last twenty-five years of France, and of the last forty years in America, nay of its last two hundred years, proves the truth of both parts of this observation.—To JOHN ADAMS. vi, 226. FORD ED., ix, 428. (M., 1813.)

7765. SELF-GOVERNMENT, British parliament and.—The British Parliament has no right to intermeddle with our provisions for the support of civil government, or administration of justice. * * * While Parliament pursue their plan of civil government, within their own jurisdiction, we, also, hope to pursue ours without molestation.— REPLY TO LORD NORTH'S PROPOSITION. FORD ED., i, 479. (July 1775.)

7766. ———. While Parliament pursue their plan of civil government within their own jurisdiction we hope also to pursue ours without molestation.—REPLY TO LORD NORTH'S PROPOSITION. FORD ED., i, 480. (July 1775.)

7767. ———. The proposition [of Lord North] is altogether unsatisfactory * * * because they [Parliament] do not renounce the power of * * * legislating for us themselves in all cases whatsoever.—REPLY TO LORD NORTH'S PROPOSITION. FORD ED., i, 480. (July 1775.)

7768. SELF-GOVERNMENT, Classes vs. Masses.—The general spread of the light of science has already laid open to every view the palpable truth, that the mass of mankind has not been born with saddles on their backs, nor a favored few booted and spurred, ready to ride them legitimately, by the grace of God.—To ROGER C. WEIGHTMAN. vii, 450. FORD ED., x, 391. (M., June 1826.)

7769. SELF-GOVERNMENT, Connecticut and.—It would seem impossible that an intelligent people [of Connecticut] with the faculty of reading and right of thinking, should continue much longer to slumber under the pupilage of an interested aristocracy of priests and lawyers, persuading them to distrust themselves, and to let them think for them. I sincerely wish that your efforts may awaken them from this voluntary degradation of mind, restore them to a due estimate of themselves and their fellow citizens, and a just abhorrence of the falsehoods and artifices which have seduced them.—To THOMAS SEYMOUR. v, 44. FORD ED., ix, 31. (W., 1807.) See CONNECTICUT.

7770. SELF-GOVERNMENT, Education and.—Whenever the people are well informed, they can be trusted with their own government.—To DR. PRICE. ii, 533. (P., 1789.)

7771. SELF-GOVERNMENT, Europe and.—A first attempt to recover the right of self-government may fail, so may a second, a third, etc. But as a younger and more instructed race comes on, the sentiment becomes more and more intuitive, and a fourth, a fifth, or some subsequent one of the ever renewed attempts will ultimately succeed. In France, the first effort was defeated by Robespierre, the second by Bonaparte, the third by Louis XVIII. and his holy allies; another is yet to come, and all Europe, Russia excepted, has caught the spirit; and all will attain representative government, more or less perfect. * * * To attain all this, however, rivers of blood must yet flow, and years of desolation pass over; yet the object is worth rivers of blood, and years of desolation. For what inheritance so valuable, can man leave to his posterity? You and I shall look down from another world on these glorious achievements to man, which will add to the joys even of heaven.—To JOHN ADAMS. vii, 307. FORD ED., x, 270. (M., 1823.)

7772. SELF-GOVERNMENT, Experiments in.—We have no interests nor passions different from those of our fellow citizens. We have the same object, the success of representative government. Nor are we acting for ourselves alone, but for the whole human race. The event of our experiment is to show whether man can be trusted with self-government. The eyes of suffering humanity are fixed on us with anxiety as their only hope, and on such a theatre, for such a cause, we must suppress all smaller passions and local considerations.—To GOVERNOR HALL. FORD ED., viii, 156. (W., July 1802.)

7773. SELF-GOVERNMENT, French people and.—The people of France have never been in the habit of self-government, are not yet in the habit of acknowledging that fundamental law of nature, by which alone self-government can be exercised by a society, I mean the *lex majoris partis*. Of the sacredness of this law, our countrymen are impressed from their cradle, so that with them it is almost innate.—To JOHN BRECKENRIDGE. FORD ED., vii, 417. (Pa., 1800.)

7774. ——— ———. Who could have thought the French nation incapable of self-government?—To DR. JOSEPH PRIESTLEY. FORD ED., viii, 179. (W., 1802.)

7775. SELF-GOVERNMENT, Generations and.—The present generation has the same right of self-government which the past one has exercised for itself.—To JOHN H. PLEASANTS. vii, 346. FORD ED., x, 303. (M., 1824.)

7776. SELF-GOVERNMENT, Growth of.—When forced to assume self-government, we were novices in its science. Its principles and forms had entered little into our former education. We established however some, although not all its important principles.—To JOHN CARTWRIGHT. vii, 356. (M., 1824.)

7777. SELF-GOVERNMENT, Interference with.—We [the Virginia House of Burgesses] cannot, my Lord, close with the terms of that resolution [Lord North's Conciliatory Propositions] * * * because the British Parliament has no right to intermeddle with the support of civil government in the Colonies. For us, not for them, has govern-

ment been instituted here. Agreeable to our ideas, provision has been made for such officers as we think necessary for the administration of public affairs; and we cannot conceive that any other legislature has a right to prescribe either the number or pecuniary appointments of our offices. As a proof that the claim of Parliament to interfere in the necessary provisions for the support of civil government is novel, and of a late date, we take leave to refer to an Act of ou. Assembly, passed so long since as the thirty-second year of the reign of King Charles the Second, intituled, "An Act for Raising a Publick Revenue, and for the Better Support of the Government of His Majesty's Colony of Virginia". This act was brought over by Lord Culpepper, then Governor, under ' the great seal of England, and was enacted in the name of the "King's most Excellent Majesty, by and with the consent of the General Assembly".—ADDRESS TO GOVERNOR DUNMORE. FORD ED., i, 456. (1775.)

7778. SELF-GOVERNMENT, Irresistible.—Alliances, holy or hellish, may be formed, and retard the epoch of deliverance, may swell the rivers of blood which are yet to flow, but their own will close the scene, and leave to mankind the right of self-government.—To MARQUIS LAFAYETTE. vii, 324. FORD ED., x, 280. (M., 1823.)

7779. SELF-GOVERNMENT, Limitations of.—The right of self-government does not comprehend the government of others.—OFFICIAL OPINION. vii, 499. FORD ED., v, 208. (1790.)

7780. SELF-GOVERNMENT, Local.—My bill for the more general diffusion of learning had for a further object to impart to these wards those portions of self-government for which they are best qualified, by confiding to them the care of their poor, their roads, police, elections, the nomination of jurors, administration of justice in small cases, elementary exercises of militia; in short, to have made them little republics, with a warden at the head of each, for all those concerns which, being under their eye, they would better manage than the larger republics of the county or State. A general call of ward meetings by their wardens on the same day through the State, would at any time produce the genuine sense of the people on any required point, and would enable the State to act in mass, as [the New England] people have so often done, and with so much effect by their town meetings.—To JOHN ADAMS. vi, 225. FORD ED., ix, 427. (M., 1813.) See WARDS.

7781. SELF-GOVERNMENT, Louisiana and.—Although it is acknowledged that our new fellow citizens [in Louisiana] are as yet as incapable of self-government as children, yet some [in Congress] cannot bring themselves to suspend its principles for a single moment. The temporary or territorial government of that country, therefore, will encounter great difficulty.—To DE WITT CLINTON. FORD ED., viii, 283. (W., Dec. 1803.)

7782. SELF-GOVERNMENT, Maximum.—My most earnest wish is to see the republican element of popular control pushed to the maximum of its practicable exercise. I shall then believe that our government may be pure and perpetual.—To Isaac H. Tiffany. vii, 32. (M., 1816.)

7783. SELF-GOVERNMENT, Men capable of.—I have no fear but that the result of our experiment will be, that men may be trusted to govern themselves without a master. Could the contrary of this be proved, I should conclude, either that there is no God, or that he is a malevolent being.—To David Hartley. ii, 165. (P., 1787.)

7784. —— ——. I have not any doubt that the result of our experiment will be that men are capable of governing themselves without a master.—To T. B. Hollis. ii, 168. (P., 1787.)

7785. —— ——. Sometimes it is said that man cannot be trusted with the government of himself. Can he then be trusted with the government of others? Or have we found angels, in the form of kings, to govern him? Let history answer this question.—First Inaugural Address. viii, 3. Ford ed., viii, 3. (1801.)

7786. —— ——. It is a happy truth that man is capable of self-government, and only rendered otherwise by the moral degradation designedly superinduced on him by the wicked acts of his tyrant.—To M. de Marbois. vii, 77. (M., 1817.)

7787. SELF-GOVERNMENT, Natural.—From the nature of things, every society must at all times possess within itself the sovereign powers of legislation.—Rights of British America. i, 138. Ford ed., i, 443. (1774.)

7788. SELF-GOVERNMENT, Preservation of.—It behooves our citizens to be on their guard, to be firm in their principles, and full of confidence in themselves. We are able to preserve our self-government if we will but think so.—To T. M. Randolph. iv, 320. Ford ed., vii, 423. (Pa., Feb. 1800.)

7789. SELF-GOVERNMENT, Purposes of.—The provisions we have made [for our government] are such as please ourselves; they answer the substantial purposes of government and of justice, and other purposes than these should not be answered.—Reply to Lord North's Proposition. Ford ed., i, 479. (July 1775.)

7790. SELF-GOVERNMENT, Qualifications for.—Some preparation seems necessary to qualify the body of a nation for self-government.—To Dr. Joseph Priestley. Ford ed., viii, 179. (W., 1802.)

7791. SELF-GOVERNMENT, Reason and.—It is honorable for us to have produced the first legislature who had the courage to declare that the reason of man may be trusted with the formation of his own action.—To James Madison. ii, 67. Ford ed., iv, 334. (P., 1786.)

7792. SELF-GOVERNMENT, Right to.—The inhabitants of the several States of *British America* are subject to the laws which they adopted at their first settlement, and to such others as have since been made by their respective Legislatures, duly constituted and appointed with their own consent. No other Legislature whatever can rightly exercise authority over them; and these privileges they hold as the common rights of mankind, confirmed by the political constitutions they have respectively assumed, and also by several charters of compact from the Crown.—Resolution of Albemarle* County. Ford ed., i, 418. (July 26, 1774.)

7793. —— ——. Every man, and every body of men on earth, possesses the right of self-government. They receive it with their being from the hand of nature. Individuals exercise it by their single will, collections of men by that of their majority; for the law of the *majority* is the natural law of every society of men.—Official Opinion. vii, 496. Ford ed., v, 205. (1790.)

7794. SELF-GOVERNMENT, Rightful limits.—We owe every other sacrifice† to ourselves, to our federal brethren, and to the world at large, to pursue with temper and perseverance the great experiment which shall prove that man is capable of living in society, governing itself by laws self-imposed, and securing to its members the enjoyment of life, liberty, property and peace; and further to show, that even when the government of its choice shall manifest a tendency to degeneracy, we are. not at once to despair but that the will and the watchfulness of its sounder parts will reform its aberrations, recall it to original and legitimate principles and restrain it within the rightful limits of self-government.—Virginia Protest. ix, 498. Ford ed., x, 351. (M., 1825.)

7795. SELF-GOVERNMENT, Spaniards and.—I fear the Spaniards are too heavily oppressed by ignorance and superstition for self-government, and whether a change from foreign to domestic despotism will be to their advantage remains to be seen.—To Dr. Samuel Brown. vi, 165. (M., 1813.)

7796. SELF-GOVERNMENT, Study of.—I sincerely think that the prominent characters of the country where you are could not better prepare their sons for the duties they will have to perform in their new government than by sending them here [the University of Virginia] where they might become familiarized with the habits and practice of self-government. This lesson is scarcely to be acquired but in this country, and yet without it, the political vessel is all sail and no ballast.‡—To Henry Dearborn. Ford ed., x, 237. (M., 1822.)

7797. SELF-GOVERNMENT, Training for.—The qualifications for self-government

* Jefferson's own county.—Editor..
† "Except that of living under a government of unlimited powers."—Editor.
‡ General Dearborn was then Minister to Portugal. —Editor.

in society are not innate. They are the result of habit and long training.*—To EDWARD EVERETT. vii, 341. (M., 1824.)

7798. SELF-GOVERNMENT, Universal.—I wish to see all mankind exercising self-government, and capable of exercising it. —To MARQUIS LAFAYETTE. vii, 67. FORD ED., x, 85. (M., 1817.)

7799. SELF-GOVERNMENT, Usurpation and.—[The] exercises of usurped power [by Parliament] have not been confined to instances alone in which themselves were interested, but they have also intermeddled with the regulation of the internal affairs of the Colonies.—RIGHTS OF BRITISH AMERICA. i, 130. FORD ED., i, 434. (1774.)

7800. SELF-GOVERNMENT, Voluntary associations and.—If [the society] is merely a voluntary association, the submission of its members will be merely voluntary also, as no act of coercion would be permitted by the general law.—To WILLIAM LEE. vii. 57. (M., 1817.)

7801. SELF-PRESERVATION, Law of. —The law of self-preservation overrules the laws of obligation to others.—OPINION ON FRENCH TREATIES. vii, 613. FORD ED., vi, 221. (1793.)

7802. SENATE (French), Plan of.— They [the French] propose a Senate, chosen on the plan of our Federal Senate by the Provincial Assemblies, but to be for life, of a certain age (they talk of forty years), and certain wealth (four or five hundred guineas a year), but to have no other power as to laws but to remonstrate against them to the representatives, who will then determine their fate by a simple majority. This * * * is a mere council of revision like that of New York, which, in order to be something, must form an alliance with the King, to avail themselves of his veto. The alliance will be useful to both, and to the nation.—To JAMES MADISON. iii, 97. FORD ED., v, 108. (P., Aug. 1789.)

7803. SENATE (United States), Advice and consent.—When the British treaty of ——— arrived, without any provision against the impressment of our seamen, I determined not to ratify it. The Senate thought I should ask their advice. I thought that would be a mockery of them, when I was predetermined against following it, should they advise ratification.—To SPENCER ROANE. vii, 135. FORD ED., x, 142. (P.F., Sep. 1819.)

7804. ——— ———. The Constitution has made the advice of the Senate necessary to confirm a treaty, but not to reject it. This has been blamed by some; but I have never doubted its soundness.—To SPENCER ROANE. vii, 135. FORD ED., x, 142. (P.F., 1819.)

7805. SENATE (United States), Cabal in.—Mischief may be done negatively as well as positively. Of this a cabal in the Senate of the United States has furnished many proofs.—To JOHN ADAMS. vi, 224. FORD ED., ix, 426. (M., 1813.)

7806. SENATE (United States), Check on House of Representatives.—The Senate was intended as a check on the will of the Representatives when too hasty. They are not only that, but completely so on the will of the people also; and in my opinion are heaping coals of fire, not only on their persons, but on their body, as a branch of the Legislature. * * * It seems that the opinion is fairly launched into public that they should be placed under the control of a more frequent recurrence to the will of their constituents.* This seems requisite to complete the experiment, whether they do more harm or good.—To JAMES MADISON. iv, 107. FORD ED., vi, 511. (M., May 1794.)

7807. SENATE (United States), Executive and.—The President desired my opinion whether the Senate has a right to negative the *grade* he may think it expedient to use in a foreign mission as well as the *person* to be appointed. I think the Senate has no right to negative the *grade.*—OPINION ON THE POWERS OF THE SENATE. vii, 465. FORD ED., v, 161. (1790.)

7808. ——— ———. The Senate is not supposed by the Constitution to be acquainted with the concerns of the Executive Department. It was not† intended that these should be communicated to them.—OPINION ON POWERS OF SENATE. vii, 466. FORD ED., v, 162. (1790.)

7809. ——— ———. It may be objected that the Senate may by continual negatives on the *person,* do what amounts to a negative on the *grade,* and so, indirectly, defeat this right of the President. But this would be a breach of trust; an abuse of the power confided to the Senate, of which that body cannot be supposed capable.—OPINION ON THE POWERS OF THE SENATE. vii, 466. FORD ED., v, 162. (1790.) See APPOINTMENT.

7810. SENATE (United States), Executive information and.—The Secretary of State, having received a note from Mr. Strong, as chairman of a Committee of the Senate, asking a conference with him on the subject of the late diplomatic nominations to Paris, London and the Hague, he met them in the Senate chamber in the evening of the same day, and stated to them in substance * * * that he should on all occasions be ready to give to the Senate, or to any other branch of the government, whatever information might properly be communicated, and might be necessary to enable them to proceed in the line of their respective offices: that on the present occasion particularly, *as the Senate had to decide on the fitness of certain persons to act for the United States at certain*

---

* Jefferson was considering the condition of affairs in South America, and he added, " for these (habit and training), they will require time and probably much suffering ".—EDITOR.

* Jefferson was condemning the failure to pass the Non-Importation bill.—EDITOR.
† " Not " is omitted in the FORD EDITION. " It was not intended " is the reading in the original MS. —EDITOR.

courts, they would be the better enabled to decide, if they were informed of the state of our affairs at those courts, and what we had to do there. [Jefferson then explained the situation of affairs.]—THE ANAS. ix, 420. FORD ED., i, 170. (W., January 1792.)

7811. SENATE (United States), Firmness.—The Senate alone remained undismayed to the last. Firm to their purposes, regardless of public opinion, and more disposed to coerce than to court it, not a man of their majority gave way in the least.—To JAMES MADISON. iv, 330. FORD ED., vii, 447. (Pa., May 1800.)

7812. SENATE (United States), Honorable.—The Senate is the most honorable and independent station in our government, one where you can peculiarly raise yourself in the public estimation.—To WILLIAM SHORT. FORD ED., v, 244. (M., 1790.)

7813. SENATE (United States), Jefferson's address to.—To give the usual opportunity of appointing a President *pro tempore*, I now propose to retire from the chair of the Senate; and, as the time is near at hand when the relations will cease which have for some time subsisted between this honorable house and myself, I beg leave, before I withdraw, to return them my grateful thanks for all the instances of attention and respect with which they have been pleased to honor me. In the discharge of my functions here, it has been my conscientious endeavor to observe impartial justice, without regard to persons or subjects; and if I have failed in impressing this on the mind of the Senate, it will be to me a circumstance of the deepest regret. I may have erred at times. No doubt I have erred. This is the law of human nature. For honest errors, however, indulgence may be hoped. I owe to truth and justice at the same time to declare that the habits of order and decorum, which so strongly characterize the proceedings of the Senate, have rendered the umpirage of their president an office of little difficulty; that in times and on questions which have severely tried the sensibilities of the house, calm and temperate discussion has rarely been disturbed by departures from order. Should the support which I received from the Senate, in the performance of my duties here, attend me into the new station to which the public will has transferred me, I shall consider it as commencing under the happiest auspices. With these expressions of my dutiful regard to the Senate, as a body, I ask leave to mingle my particular wishes for the health and happiness of the individuals who compose it, and to tender them my cordial and respectful adieu. —SPEECH TO THE U. S. SENATE. iv, 362. FORD ED., vii, 501. (Feb. 28, 1801.)

7814. SENATE (United States), John Adams's opinions.—The system of the Senate may be inferred from their transactions heretofore, and from the following declaration made to me personally by their oracle [President Adams]: "No republic can ever be of any duration without a Senate, and a Senate deeply and strongly rooted; strong enough to bear up against all popular storms and passions. The only fault in the constitution of our Senate is, that their term of office is not durable enough. Hitherto they have done well, but probably they will be forced to give way in time." I suppose "their having done well hitherto", alluded to the stand they made on the British treaty. This declaration may be considered as their text; that they consider themselves as the bulwarks of the government, and will be rendering that the more secure, in proportion as they can assume greater powers.—To JAMES MADISON. iv, 215. FORD ED., vii, 207. (Pa., Feb. 1798.)

7815. ——— ———. President Adams and I got on the Constitution; and in the course of our conversation he said, that no republic could ever last which had not a Senate, and a Senate deeply and strongly rooted, strong enough to bear up against all popular storms and passions; that he thought our Senate as well constituted as it could have been, being chosen by the Legislatures; for if these could not support them, he did not know what could do it; that perhaps it might have been as well for them to be chosen by the State at large, as that would insure a choice of distinguished men, since none but such could be known to a whole people; that the only fault in our Senate was that it was not durable enough, that, hitherto, it had behaved very well; however, he was afraid they would give way in the end. That as to trusting to a popular assembly for the preservation of our liberties, it was the merest chimera imaginable; they never had any rule of decision but their own will, that he would as lieve be again in the hands of our old committees of safety, who made the law and executed it at the same time; that it had been observed by some writer * * * that anarchy did more mischief in one night than tyranny in an age; and that in modern times we might say with truth, that in France, anarchy had done more harm in one night, than all the despotism of their kings had ever done in twenty or thirty years. The point in which he views our Senate, as the Colossus of the Constitution, serves as a key to the politics of the Senate, who are two-thirds of them in his sentiments, and accounts for the bold line of conduct they pursue.—THE ANAS. ix, 189. FORD ED., i, 277. (Nov. 1798.)

7816. SENATE (United States), Nominations.—Should the [federalists] yield the election, I have reason to expect, in the outset, the greatest difficulties as to nominations. The late incumbents, running away from their offices and leaving them vacant, will prevent my filling them without the *previous* advice of the Senate. How this difficulty is to be got over I know not.—To JAMES MONROE. iv, 355. FORD ED., vii, 491. (W., Feb. 1801.)

7817. SENATE (United States), People and.—In the General Government, the Senate is scarcely republican at all, as not

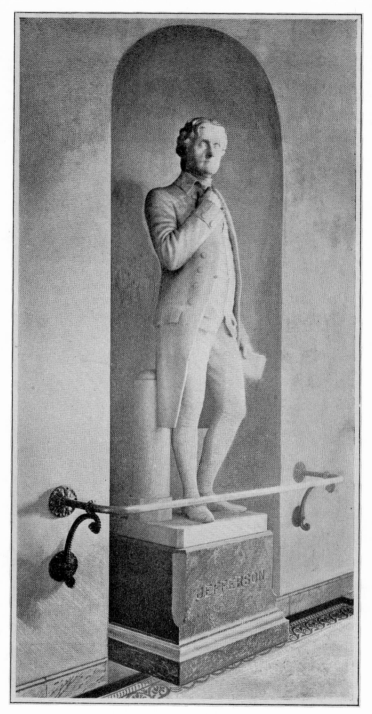

Thomas Jefferson

Age unknown

Marble statue by Hiram Powers.

Bought by the United States Government in 1855 for the sum of $10,000. It stands in a niche at the foot of the marble staircase leading to the gallery of the House of Representatives, United States Capitol.

elected by the people directly, and so long secured even against those who do elect them.—To John Taylor. vi, 607. Ford ed., x, 30. (M., 1816.)

7818. SENATE (United States), Rules of.—The rules of the [British] Parliament are probably as wisely constructed for governing the debates of a considerative body, and obtaining its true sense, as any which can become known to us; and the acquiescence of the Senate hitherto under the references to them, has given them the sanction of their approbation.—Parliamentary Manual. ix, 3. (1797.)

7819. —— ——. I have begun a sketch which those who come after me will successively correct and fill up, till a code of rules shall be formed for the use of the Senate, the effects of which may be accuracy in business, economy of time, order, uniformity, and impartiality.—Parliamentary Manual. ix, 4. (1797.)

7820. —— ——. In the old Congress [of the confederation] the mode of managing the business of the House was not only unparliamentary, but the forms were so awkward and inconvenient that it was impossible sometimes to get at the true sense of the majority. The House of Representatives of the United States are now pretty much in the same situation. In the Senate it is in our power to get into a better way. Our ground is this: The Senate have established a few rules for their government, and have subjected the decisions on these and on *all other points of order* without debate, and without appeal, to the judgment of their President. He, for his own sake, as well as theirs, must prefer recurring to some system of rules ready formed; and there can be no question that the parliamentary rules are the best known to us for managing the debates, and obtaining the sense of a deliberative body. I have, therefore, made them my rule of decision, rejecting those of the old Congress altogether, and it gives entire satisfaction to the Senate; insomuch that we shall not only have a good system there, but probably, by the example of its effects, produce a conformity in the other branch. But in the course of this business I find perplexities, * * * and so little has the parliamentary branch of the law been attended to, that I not only find no person here [Philadelphia], but not even a book to aid me. * * * You will see by the enclosed paper what they are. I know with what pain you write; therefore, I have left a margin in which you can write a simple negative or affirmative opposite every position. This is what I earnestly solicit from you, and I would not give you the trouble if I had any other resource. But you are, in fact, the only spark of parliamentary science now remaining to us. I am the more anxious, because I have been forming a Manual of Parliamentary Law, which I mean to deposit with the Senate as the standard by which I judge, and am willing to be judged.—To George Wythe. ix, 5. Ford ed., vii, 426. (Pa., Feb. 1800.) See Parliamentary Law.

7821. SENATE (United States), Wisdom.—The Senate * * * must from its constitution be a wise and steady body.—To C. W. F. Dumas. ii, 367. (A., 1788.) See Congress and Judiciary.

7822. SENATE (Virginia), Defects in.—The Senate [of Virginia] is, by its constitution, too homogeneous with the House of Delegates. Being chosen by the same electors, at the same time, and out of the same subjects, the choice falls of course on men of the same description. The purpose of establishing different houses of legislation is to introduce the influence of different interests or different principles. Thus in Great Britain it is said their constitution relies on the House of Commons for honesty, and the Lords for wisdom; which would be a rational reliance, if honesty were to be bought with money, and if wisdom were hereditary. In some of the American States, the delegates and Senators are so chosen, as that the first represent the persons, and the second the property of the State. But with us, wealth and wisdom have equal chance for admission into both houses. We do not, therefore, derive from the separation of our Legislature into two houses, those benefits which a proper complication of principles is capable of producing, and those which alone can compensate the evils which may be produced by their dissensions.—Notes on Virginia. viii, 361. Ford ed., iii, 223. (1782.)

7823. SENATE (Virginia), Election of members.—For the election of Senators, let the several counties be allotted by the Senate, from time to time, into such and so many districts as they shall find best; and let each county at the time of electing its delegates, choose senatorial electors, qualified as themselves are, and four in number for each delegate their county is entitled to send, who shall convene, and conduct themselves in such manner as the legislature shall direct, with the senatorial electors from the other counties of their district, and then choose, by ballot, one senator for every six delegates which their district is entitled to choose.—Proposed Constitution for Virginia. viii, 443. Ford ed., iii, 323. (1783.)

— SENATORS (United States), Election of.—See Constitution (Federal).

7824. SENATORS (United States), Term of office.—The term of office to our Senate, like that of the judges, is too long for my approbation.—To James Martin. vi, 213. Ford ed., ix, 420. (M., Sep. 1813.)

7825. SENECA, Moral system of.—Seneca is a fine moralist, disfiguring his work at times with some Stoicisms, and affecting too much antithesis and point, yet giving us on the whole a great deal of sound and practical morality.—To William Short. vii, 139. Ford ed., x, 144. (M., 1819.)

7826. SENILITY, Abhorrent.—Bodily decay is gloomy in prospect, but of all human contemplations the most abhorrent is body without mind.—To John Adams. vii, 27. (M., 1816.)

7827. SENILITY, Unconscious.—The misfortune of a weakened mind is an insensibility of its weakness.—To EDWARD LIVINGSTON. vii, 405. (M., 1825.)

7828. SENSE, Directed by.—The good sense of our people will direct the boat ultimately to its proper point.—To MARQUIS LAFAYETTE. FORD ED., x, 234. (M., 1822.)

7829. SENSE, National.—My chief object is to let the good sense of the nation have fair play, believing it will best take care of itself.—To DR. JOSEPH PRIESTLEY. FORD ED., viii, 181. (W., 1802.)

7830. SENSE, People and.—I am persuaded myself that the good sense of the people will always be found to be the best army.—To EDWARD CARRINGTON. ii, 99. FORD ED., iv, 359. (P., 1787.)

7831. —— ——. I have such reliance on the good sense of the body of the people, and the honesty of their leaders, that I am not afraid of their letting things go wrong to any length in any cause.—To M. DUMAS. ii, 358. (P., 1788.)

7832. —— ——. The operations which have lately taken place in America [adoption of Constitution] fill me with pleasure. They realize the confidence I had, that whenever our affairs go obviously wrong, the good sense of the people will interpose, and set them to rights. —To DAVID HUMPHREYS. iii, 12. FORD ED., v, 89. (P., 1789.)

7833. SENSE, Republicanism and.—It was by the sober sense of our citizens that we were safely and steadily conducted from monarchy to republicanism, and it is by the same agency alone we can be kept from falling back. —To ARTHUR CAMPBELL. iv, 198. FORD ED., vii, 170. (M., 1797.) See COMMON SENSE.

7834. SERVICE, Civic.—Every man is under the natural duty of contributing to the necessities of the society; and this is all the laws should enforce on him.—To F. W. GILMER. vii, 3. FORD ED., x, 32. (M., 1816.) See DUTY.

7835. SERVICE, Credit for.—The inquiries in your printed letter * * * would lead to the writing the history of my whole life, than which nothing could be more repugnant to my feelings. I have been connected, as many fellow laborers were, with the great events which happened to mark the epoch of our lives. But these belong to no one in particular, all of us did our parts, and no one can claim the transactions to himself.—To SKELTON JONES. v, 462. (M., 1809.)

7836. —— ——. I was only of a band devoted to the cause of Independence, all of whom exerted equally their best endeavors for its success, and have a common right to the merits of its acquisition. So also is the civil revolution of 1801. Very many and very meritorious were the worthy patriots who assisted in bringing back our government to its republican tack.—To WILLIAM T. BARRY. vii, 255. (M., 1822.)

7837. SERVICE, Old age and.—Had it been my good fortune to preserve at the age of seventy, all the activity of body and mind which I enjoyed in earlier life, I should have employed it now, as then, in incessant labors to serve those to whom I could be useful.— To M. DE LOMERIE. vi, 107. (M., 1813.)

7838. SERVICE, Rendering.—Nothing makes me more happy than to render any service in my power, of whatever description.—To SAMUEL OSGOOD. i, 451. (P., 1785.)

7839. SERVICE, Reward of.—If, in the course of my life, it has been in any degree useful to the cause of humanity, the fact itself bears its full reward.—To DAVID BARROW. vi, 456. FORD ED., ix, 515. (M., 1815.)

7840. SERVICE, Tours of.—You say I " must not make my final exit from public life till it will be marked with just fying circumstances which all good citizens will respect, and to which my friends can appeal ". To my fellow-citizens the debt of service has been fully and faithfully paid. I acknowledge that such a debt exists, that a tour of duty, in whatever line he can be most useful to his country, is due from every individual. It is not easy, perhaps, to say of what length exactly this tour should be, but we may safely say of what length it should not be. Not of our whole life, for instance, for that would be to be born a slave— not even of a very large portion of it. I have now been in the public service four and twenty years; one-half of which has been spent in total occupation with their affairs, and absence from my own. I have served my tour then. No positive engagement, by word or deed, binds me to the r further service. No commitment of their interests in any enterprise by me requires that I should see them through it. I am pledged by no act which gives any tribunal a call upon me before I withdraw. Even my enemies do not pretend this. I stand clear, then, of public right on all points. My friends I have not committed. No circumstances have attended my passage from office to office, which could lead them, and others through them, into deception as to the time I might remain, and particularly they and all have known with what reluctance I engaged and have continued in the present one [Secretary of State], and of my uniform determination to retire from it at an early day. If the public, then, has no claim on me, and my friends nothing to justify, the decision will rest on my own feelings alone. There has been a time when these were very different from what they are now; when perhaps the esteem of the world was of higher value in my eye than everything in it. But age, experience and reflection preserving to that only its due value, have set a higher on tranquillity.—To JAMES MADISON. iii, 577. FORD ED., vi, 290. (June 1793.) See JEFFERSON.

7841. SHAYS'S REBELLION, Conduct and motives of.—Can history produce an instance of rebellion so honorably conducted? I say nothing of its motives. They were founded in ignorance, not wickedness. God forbid we should ever be twenty years without such a rebellion. The people cannot be all, and always, well informed. The part which is wrong will be discontented in proportion to the importance of the facts they misconceive. If they remain quiet under such misconceptions, it is a lethargy, the forerunner of death to the public liberty.—To W. S. SMITH. ii, 318. FORD ED., iv, 467. (P., 1787.)

7842. SHAYS'S REBELLION, European opinion of.—The tumults in America, I expected, would have produced in Europe an unfavorable opinion of our political state. But it has not. On the contrary, the small effect of these tumults seems to have given more confidence in the firmness of our governments. The interposition of the people themselves on the side of government has had a great effect on the opinion here.—To EDWARD CARRINGTON. ii, 99. FORD ED., iv, 359. (1787.)

7843. SHAYS'S REBELLION, Excuse for.—Those people are not entirely without excuse. Before the war, those States depended on their whale oil and fish. The former was consumed in England, and much of the latter in the Mediterranean. The heavy duties on American whale oil, now required in England, exclude it from that market; and the Algerines exclude them from bringing their fish into the Mediterranean. France is opening her ports for their oil, but in the meanwhile, their ancient debts are pressing them, and they have nothing to pay with. The Massachusetts Assembly, too, in their zeal for paying their public debt had laid a tax too heavy to be paid in the circumstances of their State. The Indians seem disposed, too, to make war on us. These complicated causes determined Congress to increase their forces to 2000 men. The latter was the sole object avowed, yet the former entered for something into the measure.—To WILLIAM CARMICHAEL. ii, 81. FORD ED., iv, 345. (P., 1786.)

7844. SHAYS'S REBELLION, Government and.—I am not discouraged by this; for thus I calculate: An insurrection in one of thirteen States in the course of eleven years that they have subsisted, amounts to one in any particular State, in one hundred and forty-three years, say a century and a half. This would not be near as many as have happened in every other government that has ever existed. So that we shall have the difference between a light and a heavy government as clear gain.—To DAVID HARTLEY. ii, 165. (P., 1787.)

7845. ————. This insurrection will not weigh against the inconveniences of a government of force, such as are monarchies and aristocracies.—To T. B. HOLLIS. ii, 168. (P., 1787.)

7846. SHAYS'S REBELLION, Lessons of.—The commotions that have taken place in America, as far as they are yet known to me, offer nothing threatening. They are a proof that the people have liberty enough, and I could not wish them less than they have. If the happiness of the mass of the people can be secured at the expense of a little tempest now and then, or even of a little blood, it will be a precious purchase. *Malo libertatem periculosam quam quietem servitutem.* Let common sense and honesty have fair play, and they will soon set things to rights.—To EZRA STILES. ii, 77. (P., 1786.)

7847. SHAYS'S REBELLION, The people and.—The interposition of the people themselves on the side of the government has had a great effect on the opinion here [Europe]. I am persuaded myself that the good sense of the people will always be found to be the best army. They may be led astray for a moment, but will soon correct themselves. The people are the only censors of their governors; and even their errors will tend to keep these to the true principles of their institution. To punish these errors too severely would be to suppress the only safeguard of the public liberty. The way to prevent these irregular interpositions of the people is to give them full information of their affairs through the channels of the public papers, and to contrive that those papers should penetrate the whole mass of the people. The basis of our government being the opinion of the people, the very first object should be to keep that right; and were it left to me to decide whether we should have a government without newspapers, or newspapers without a government, I should not hesitate a moment to prefer the latter. But I should mean that every man should receive those papers, and be capable of reading them.—To EDWARD CARRINGTON. ii, 99. FORD ED., iv, 359. (P., 1787.)

7848. SHAYS'S REBELLION, Unalarmed by.—I had seen without alarm accounts of the disturbances in the East. * * * I can never fear that things will go far wrong where common sense has fair play.—To JOHN ADAMS. ii, 73. (P., 1786.)

7849. ————. The late rebellion in Massachusetts has given more alarm than I think it should have done. Calculate that one rebellion in thirteen States in the course of eleven years, is but one for each State in a century and a half. No country should be so long without one. Nor will any degree of power in the hands of government prevent insurrections. France, with all its despotism, and two or three hundred thousand men always in arms, has had three insurrections in the three years I have been here, in every one of which greater numbers were engaged than in Massachusetts, and a great deal more blood was spilt. In Turkey, which Montesquieu supposes more despotic, insurrections are the events of every day. In England, where the hand of power is lighter than here, but heavier than with us, they happen every half dozen years. Compare again the ferocious depredations of their insurgents with the order, the moderation, and the almost self-extinguishment of ours.—To JAMES MADISON. ii, 331. FORD ED., iv, 479. (P., 1787.)

7850. SHAYS'S REBELLION, Unjustifiable.—I am impatient to learn your sentiments on the late troubles in the Eastern States. So far as I have yet seen, they do not appear to threaten serious consequences. Those States have suffered by the stoppage of the channels of their commerce, which have not yet found other issues. This must render money scarce, and make the people uneasy. This uneasiness has produced acts absolutely unjustifiable; but I hope they will provoke no severities from their governments. A consciousness of those in power that their administration of the public affairs has been honest may, perhaps, produce too great a degree of indignation; and those characters, wherein fear predominates over hope, may apprehend too much from these instances of irregularity. They may conclude too hastily that nature has formed man insusceptible of any other government than that of force, a conclusion not founded in truth nor experience.—To JAMES MADISON. ii, 104. FORD ED., iv, 361. (P., 1787.)

7851. SHEEP, Profits from.—I had never before considered, with due attention, the profit from sheep. I shall not be able to put the farm into that form exactly the ensuing autumn, but against another I hope I shall.—To PRESIDENT WASHINGTON. iv, 5. FORD ED., vi, 83. (Pa., 1793.)

7852. SHEEP, Protection of.—If you return to us, bring a couple of pair of true-bred shepherd's dogs. You will add a valuable possession to a country now beginning to pay great attention to the raising of sheep.—To DUPONT DE NEMOURS. v, 433. (W., 1809.)

7853. SHEEP, Wolves and.—Sheep are subject to many diseases which carry them off in great numbers. In the middle and upper parts of Virginia they are subject to the wolf, and in all parts of it to dogs. These are great obstacles to their multiplication.—Notes on Arthur Young's Letter. Ford ed., vi, 85. (1792.)

7854. SHEEP (Merinos), Importing.— The necessity we are under, and the determination we have formed of emancipating ourselves from a dependence on foreign countries for manufactures which may be advantageously established among ourselves, has produced a very general desire to improve the quality of our wool by the introduction of the Merino race of sheep. Your sense of the duties you owe to your station will not permit me to ask, nor yourself to do any act which might compromit you with the government [Spain] with which you reside, or forfeit that confidence on their part which can alone enable you to be useful to your country. But, as far as that will permit you to give aid to the procuring and bringing away some of the valuable race, I take the liberty of soliciting you to do so. It will be an important service rendered to your country; to which you will be further encouraged by the assurance that the enterprise is solely on the behalf of agricultural gentlemen of distinguished character in Washington and its neighborhood, with a view of disseminating the benefits of their success as widely as they can. Without any interest in it myself, other than the general one, I cannot help wishing a favorable result * * * .—To George W. Irving. v, 479. (M., Nov. 1809.)

7855. SHEEP (Merinos), Present of.— I send you a Merino ram of full blood, born of my imported ewe of the race called Agueirres, by the imported ram of the Paular race which belonged to the Prince of Peace, was sold by order of the Junto of Estremadura, was purchased and sent to me, 1810, by Mr. Jarvis, our consul at Lisbon. The Paulars are deemed the finest race in Spain for size and wool taken together, the Agueirres superior to all in wool, but small.—To Archibald Stuart. Ford ed., x, 109. (M., 1818.)

7856. SHEEP (Merinos), Raising.— I thank you [President Madison] for your promised attention to my portion of the Merinos. * * * What shall we do with them? I have been so disgusted with the scandalous extortions lately practiced in the sale of these animals, and with the ascription of patriotism and praise to the sellers, as if the thousands of dollars apiece they have not been ashamed to receive were not rewards enough, that I am disposed to consider as right, whatever is the reverse of what they have done. Since fortune has put the occasion upon us, is it not incumbent upon us so to dispose this benefit to the farmers of our country, as to put to shame those who, forgetting their own wealth, and the honest simplicity of the farmers, have thought them fit objects of the shaving art, and to excite, by a better example, the condemnation due to theirs? No sentiment is more acknowledged in the family of agriculturists than that the few who can afford it should incur the risk and expense of all new improvements, and give the benefit freely to the many of more restricted circumstances. The question then recurs, what are we to do with them? I shall be willing to concur with you in any plan you shall approve, and in order that we may have some proposition to begin upon, I will throw out a first idea, to be modified or postponed to whatever you shall think better.

Give all the full-blooded males we can raise to the different counties of our State, one to each, as fast as we can furnish them. And as there must be some rule of priority for the distribution, let us begin with our own counties, which are contiguous and nearly central to the State, and proceed, circle after circle, till we have given a ram to every county. This will take about seven years, if we add to the full descendants those which will have passed to the fourth generation from common ewes. To make the benefit of a single male as general as practicable to the county, we may ask some known character in each county to have a small society formed which shall receive the animal and prescribe rules for his care and government. We should retain ourselves all the full-blooded ewes, that they may enable us the sooner to furnish a male to every county. When all shall have been provided with rams, we may in a year or two more, be in a condition to give a ewe also to every county, if it be thought necessary. * * * In the meantime, we shall not be without a profit indemnifying our trouble and expense. For if of our present stock of common ewes, we place with the ram as many as he may be competent to, suppose fifty, we may sell the male lambs of every year for such reasonable price as, in addition to the wool, will pay for the maintenance of the flock. The first year they will be half-bloods, the second three-quarters, the third seven-eighths, and the fourth full-blooded. If we take care in selling annually half the ewes also, to keep those of the highest blood, this will be a fund for kindnesses to our friends, as well as for indemnification to ourselves; and our whole State may thus, from this small stock, so dispersed, be filled in a very few years with this valuable race, and more satisfaction result to ourselves than money ever administered to the bosom of a shaver. There will be danger that what is here proposed, though but an act of ordinary duty, may be perverted into one of ostentation. but malice will always find bad motives for good actions. Shall we therefore never do good?—To President Madison. v, 522. (M., 1810.)

7857. SHELLS, Growth of.— It will not be difficult to induce me to give up the theory of the growth of shells, without their being the nidus of animals. It is only an idea, and not an opinion, with me. In the Notes [on Virginia] * * * I had observed that there were three opinions as to the origin of these shells. 1. That they have been deposited, even in the highest mountains, by an universal deluge. 2. That they, with the calcareous stones and earths, are animal remains. 3. That they grow or shoot as crystals do. I find that I could swallow the last opinion. sooner than either of the others; but I have not yet swallowed it Another opinion might have been added, that some throe of nature has forced up parts which had been the bed of the ocean. But have we any better proof of such an effort of nature. than of her shooting a lapidific juice into the form of a shell? No such convulsion has taken place in our time, nor within the annals of history: nor is the distance greater between the shooting of the lapidific juice into the form of a crystal or a diamond, which we see. and into the form of a shell, which we do not see. than between the forcing volcanic matter a little above the surface, where it is in fusion. which we see. and the forcing the bed of the sea fifteen thousand feet above the ordinary surface of the earth. which we do not see. It is not possible to believe any of these hypotheses: and, if we lean towards any of them, it should be only till some other is produced, more analagous to the known operations of nature.—To Mr. Rittenhouse. i, 515. (P., 1786.)

7858. SHELLS, Voltaire's errors.—I have lately become acquainted with a memoir on a petrifaction mixed with shells by a Monsieur de La Sauvagere, giving an exact account of what Voltaire had erroneously stated in his questions Encyclopediques, article coquilles, from whence I had transferred it into my Notes. Having been lately at Tours, I had an opportunity of enquiring into de La Sauvagere's character and the facts he states. The result was entirely in his and their favor. This fact is so curious, so circumstantially detailed, and yet so little like any known operation of nature, that it throws the mind under absolute suspense.—To Rev. James Madison. ii, 247. (P., 1787.) See Deluge.

7859. SHERIFF, Election in Virginia.—High sheriffs * * * of Counties shall be annually elected by those qualified to vote for Representatives; and no person who shall have served as high sheriff one year shall be capable of being reelected to the said office, in the same county, till he shall have been out of office five years.—Proposed Constitution for Virginia. Ford ed., ii, 20. (June 1776.)

7860. SHERIFF, Important office.—The office of sheriff is the most important of all the executive offices of the county.—To Samuel Kerchival. vii, 11. Ford ed., x, 38. (M., 1816.)

7861. SHIPPING (American), British hostility.—The British Parliament have a bill before them for allowing wheat, imported in British bottoms, to be warehoused free. In order further to circumscribe the carrying business of the United States, they now refuse to consider as an American bottom any vessel not built here. By this construction, they take from us the right of defining, by our own laws, what vessels shall be deemed ours, and naturalized here; and in the event of a war, in which we should be neutral, they put it out of our power to benefit ourselves of our neutrality, by increasing suddenly, by purchase and naturalization, our means of carriage. If we are permitted to do this by building only, the war will be over before we can be prepared to take advantage of it.—To President Washington. iii, 249. Ford ed., v, 322. (Pa., 1791.)

7862. ———— ————. Great Britain is still endeavoring to plunder us of our carrying business. The Parliament have a bill before them to admit wheat brought in British bottoms to be warehoused rent free, so that the merchants are already giving a preference to British bottoms for that commodity. Should we lose the transportation of our own wheat, it will put down a great proportion of our shipping, already pushed by British vessels out of some of the best branches of business. In order further to circumscribe our carrying, the Commissioners of the Treasury have lately determined to admit no vessel as American, unless built here. This takes from us the right of prescribing by our own laws the conditions of naturalizing vessels in our own country, and in the event of a war in which we should be neutral, prevents our increasing, by purchase, the quantity of our shipping, so as to avail ourselves of the full benefit of the neutrality of our flag. If we are to add to our own stock of shipping only as much as we can build, a war will be over before we shall be the better of it.—To James Monroe. Ford ed., v, 318. (Pa., 1791.)

7863. ———— ————. Our ships, though purchased and navigatated by their own [British] subjects, are not permitted to be used even in their trade with us. While the vessels of other nations are secured by standing laws, which cannot be altered but by the concurrent will of the three branches of the British legislature, in carrying thither any produce or manufacture of the country to which they belong, which may be lawfully carried in any vessels, ours, with the same prohibition of what is foreign, are further prohibited by a standing law (12 Car. 2, 18, sect. 3,) [the Navigation Act] from carrying thither all and any of our own domestic productions and manufactures. A subsequent act, indeed, has authorized their executive to permit the carriage of our own productions in our own bottoms, at its sole discretion; and the permission has been given from year to year by proclamation, but subject every moment to be withdrawn on that single will; in which event, our vessels having anything on board, stand interdicted from the entry of all British ports. The disadvantage of a tenure which may be so suddenly discontinued, was experienced by our merchants on a late occasion (April 12, 1792), when an official notification that this law would be strictly enforced, gave them just apprehensions for the fate of their vessels and cargoes despatched or destined for the ports of Great Britain. The minister of that court, indeed, frankly expressed his personal conviction that the words of the order went farther than was intended, and so he afterwards officially informed us; but the embarrassments of the moment were real and great, and the possibility of their renewal lays our commerce to that country under the same species of discouragement as to other countries, where it is regulated by a single legislator; and the distinction is too remarkable not to be noticed, that our navigation is excluded from the security of fixed laws, while that security is given to the navigation of others.—Foreign Commerce Report. vii, 641. Ford ed., vi, 474. (Dec. 1793.)

7864. SHIPPING (American), French decree against.—The French decree making the vessel, friendly or enemy, according to the hands by which the cargo was manufactured, has produced a great sensation among the merchants of Philadelphia. Its operation is not yet perhaps well understood; but it probably will put our shipping out of competition, because British bottoms, which can come under convoy, will alone be trusted with return cargoes. Ours, losing this benefit, would need a higher freight out, in which, therefore, they will be underbid by the British. They must then retire from the competition.—To James Madison. iv, 220. Ford ed., vii, 216. (Pa., March 1798.)

7865. SHIPPING (American), Navigation act.—Our navigation law (if it be wise to have any) should be the reverse of that of England. Instead of confining *importations* to home-bottoms, or those of the *producing* nation, I think we should confine *exportations* to home-bottoms, or to those of nations *having treaties* with us. Our exportations are heavy, and would nourish a great force of our own, or be a tempting price to the nation to whom we should offer a participation of it, in exchange for free access to all their possessions. This is an object to which our government alone is adequate, in the gross; but I have ventured to pursue it here [France], so far as the consumption of our productions by this country extends. Thus, in our arrangements relative to tobacco, none can be received here, but in French or American bottoms. This is employment for near two thousand seamen, and puts nearly that number of British out of employ.—To GENERAL WASHINGTON. ii, 536. FORD ED., v, 58. (P., 1788.)

7866. SHIPPING (American), Peculiarities of.—It is doubted whether it will be expedient to regulate the duty, payable by an American vessel entering a French port, either by her draught or the number of her masts. If by the draught of water, it will fall unequally on us as a nation; because we build our vessels sharp-bottomed, for swift sailing, so that they draw more water than those of other nations, of the same burthen. If by the number of masts, it will fall unequally on individuals; because we often see ships of one hundred and eighty tons, and brigs of three hundred and sixty. This, then, would produce an inequality among individuals of six to one. The present principle is the most just, to regulate by the burthen.—To COUNT DE MONTMORIN. ii, 172. FORD ED., iv, 399. (P., 1787.)

7867. SHIPPING (American), Protection of.—When a nation refuses to consider any vessel as ours which has not been built within our territories, we should refuse to consider as theirs, any vessel not built within their territories.—FOREIGN COMMERCE REPORT. vi, 649. FORD ED., vi, 482. (Dec. 1793.)

7868. SHIPPING (American), Simplification of duties.—It is certainly desirable that these duties should be reduced to a single one. Their names and numbers perplex and harass the merchant more than their amount; subject him to imposition, and to the suspicion of it when there is none.—To COUNT DE MONTMORIN. ii, 173. FORD ED., iv, 400. (P., 1787.)

7869. SHIPPING (American), West Indian trade.—The British allow our commodities to be taken from our own ports to the West Indies in their vessels only. Let us allow their vessels to take them to no port. The transportation of our own produce is worth seven hundred and fifty thousand pounds sterling annually, will employ 200,000 tonnage of ships, and 12,000 seamen constantly. It will be no misfortune that Great Britain obliges us to exclude her from a participation in this business. Our own shipping will grow fast under the exclusion, and till it is equal to the object the Dutch will supply us.—To JAMES MADISON. FORD ED., iv, 37. (P., 1785.) See COMMERCE, DUTIES, DISCRIMINATING, FLAG PROTECTION and NAVIGATION.

7870. SHIPS, Passports.—It has been stated in our treaties with the French, Dutch and Prussians, that when it happens that either party is at war, and the other neutral, the neutral shall give passports of a certain tenor to the *vessels belonging to their subjects*, in order to avoid dissension; and it has been thought that passports of such high import to the persons and property of our citizens should have the highest sanction; that of the signature of the President, and seal of the United States. The authority of Congress also, in the case of sea letters to East India vessels, was in favor of this sanction. It is now become a question whether these passports shall be given only to ships *owned and built* in the United States, or may be given also to those *owned* in the United States, though *built* in foreign countries. The persons and property of our citizens are entitled to the protection of our government in all places where they may lawfully go. No laws forbid a merchant to buy, own, and use a *foreign-built* vessel. She is, then, his lawful property, and entitled to the protection of his nation wherever he is lawfully using her. The laws, indeed, for the encouragement of shipbuilding, have given to home-built vessels the exclusive privilege of being registered and paying lighter duties. To this privilege, therefore, the foreign-built vessel, though owned at home, does not pretend. But the laws have not said that they withdraw their protection from the foreign-built vessel. To this protection, then, she retains her title, notwithstanding the preference given to the home-built vessel as to duties. It would be hard, indeed, because the law has given one valuable right to home-built vessels, to infer that it had taken away all rights from those foreign-built. In conformity with the idea that all the vessels of a State are entitled to its protection, the treaties before menioned have settled that passports shall be given, not merely to vessels *built* in the United States, but to the vessels belonging to them: and when one of these nations shall take a vessel, if she has not such a passport, they are to conclude she does not *belong* to the United States, and is, therefore, lawful prize; so that to refuse these passports to foreign-built vessels *belonging* to our merchants, is to give them up to capture with their cargoes. * * * France and Holland permit our vessels to be neutralized with them; not even to suffer theirs to be purchased here might give them just cause to revoke the privilege of naturalization given to ours, and would inflict on the ship-building States and artizans a severe injury. *Objection.* To protect foreign-built vessels will lessen the demand for ship-building here. *Answer.* Not all; because as long as we can build cheaper than other nations, we shall be employed in preference to others; besides, shall we permit the greatest part of the produce of our fields to rot on our hands, or lose half its value by subjecting it to high insurance, merely that our ship-builders may have brisker employ? Shall the whole mass of our farmers be sacrificed to the class of ship wrights? *Objection.* There will be collusive transfers of foreign ships to our merchants, merely to obtain for them the cover of our passports. *Answer.* The same objection lies to giving passports to home-built vessels. They may be owned, and are owned by foreigners, and may be collusively re-transferred to our merchants to obtain our passports. To lessen the danger of collusion, however, I should be for delivering passports in our own ports only. If they were to be sent blank to foreign ports, to be delivered there, the power of checking collusion would be small, and they might be employed to cover purposes of no benefit to us (which we ought not to countenance), and to throw our vessels out of business; but if issued only to vessels in our own ports, we can generally be certain that the vessel is our property; and always that the *cargo* is of our produce. State the case that it shall be found that all our shipping, home-built and foreign-built, is inadequate to the transportation of our produce to market; so that after all these are loaded, there shall yet remain produce on hand. This must be put into vessels owned by foreigners. Should these obtain collusively the protection of our passport, it will cover their *vessel*, indeed, but it will cover also our *cargo*. I repeat it, then, that if the issuing passports be continued to our ports, it will be our own *vessels* for the most part, and always our *cargoes* which will be covered by them. I am, therefore, of opinion, that passports ought to be issued to all vessels *belonging* to citizens of the United States, but only on their clearing out from our own ports, and for that voyage only.—OPINION ON SHIP PASS-PORTS. vii, 624. (May 1793.)

7871. —— ——. The most important interests of the United States hang upon this quest on. [Giving passports to foreign-built ships.] The produce of the earth is their principal source of wealth. Our *home-built* vessels would suffice for the transportation of a very small part of this produce to market, and even a part of these vessels will be withdrawn by high premiums to other lines of business. All the rest of our produce, then, must remain on our hands, or have its price reduced by a war insurance. Many descriptions of our produce will not bear this reduction and would, therefore, remain on hand. We shall lose, also, a great proportion of the profits of navigation. The great harvest for these is when other nations are at war, and our flag neutral. But if we can augment our stock of shipping only by the slow process of building, the harvest will be over while we are only preparing instruments to reap it. The moment of breeding seamen will be lost for want of bottoms to embark them in.—OPINION ON SHIP PASSPORTS. vii, 625. (May 1793.)

7872. —— ——. It has been stated in our treaties with the French, Dutch, and Prussians, that when it happens that either party is at war, and the other neutral, the neutral shall give passports of a certain tenor to the *vessels belonging to their subjects*, in order to avoid dissension; and it has been thought that passports of such high import to the persons and property of our citizens should have the highest sanction; that of the signature of the President, and seal of the United States. The authority of Congress also, in the case of sea letters to East India vessels, was in favor of this sanction. It is now become a question whether these passports shall be given only to ships *owned and built* in the United States, or may be given also to those *owned* in the United States, though *built* in foreign countries. * * * I am of opinion that passports ought to be issued to all vessels *belonging* to citizens of the United States, but only on their clearing out from our own ports, and for that voyage only.—OPINION ON SHIP PASSPORTS. vii, 624-6. (Dec. 1793.)

7873. —— ——. As our citizens are free to purchase and use *foreign-built* vessels, and these, like all their other lawful property, are entitled to the protection of their government, passports will be issued to them as freely as to *home-built* vessels. This is strictly within our treaties, the letter of which, as well as their spirit, authorizes passports to all vessels *belonging* to citizens of the United States.—To THOMAS PINCKNEY. iii, 550. FORD ED., vi, 242. (Pa., 1793.)

7874. —— ——. Before the receipt of * * * the form of your passports, it had been determined here, that passports should be issued in *our own ports* only, as well to secure us against those collusions which would be fraudulent towards our friends, and would introduce a competition injurious to our own vessels, as to induce these to remain in our own service, and thereby give to the productions of our own soil the protection of its own flag in its passage to foreign markets.—To THOMAS PINCKNEY. iii, 550. FORD ED., vi, 242. (Pa., May 1793.)

7875. —— ——. It is determined that passports shall be given in our own ports only,

and to serve but for one voyage. It has also been determined that they shall be given to all vessels *bonâ fide* owned by American citizens *wholly*, whether built here or not. Our property, whether in the form of vessels, cargoes, or anything else, has a right to pass the seas untouched by any nation, by the law of nations; and no one has a right to ask where a vessel was built, but where she is owned.—To GOUVERNEUR MORRIS. iii, 581. FORD ED., vi, 301. (Pa., June 1793.)

7876. —— ——. The most rigorous measures will be taken to prevent any vessel, not wholly and *bonâ fide* owned by American citizens, from obtaining our passports. It is much our interest to prevent the competition of other nations from taking from us the benefits we have a right to expect from the neutrality of our flag.—To GOUVERNEUR MORRIS. iii, 582. FORD ED., vi, 301. (Pa., June 1793.)

7877. SHIPS, Purchase of foreign.—As our home-built vessels are adequate to but a small proportion of our transportation, if we could not suddenly augment the stock of our shipping, our produce would be subject to war insurance in the vessels of the belligerent powers, though we remain at peace ourselves.—To THOMAS PINCKNEY. iii, 550. FORD ED., vi, 242. (Pa., May 1793.)

7878. —— ——. Had it not been in our power to enlarge our national stock of shipping suddenly in the present exigency, a great proportion of our produce must have remained on our hands for want of the means of transportation to market.—To GOUVERNEUR MORRIS. iii, 581. FORD ED., vi, 301. (Pa., June 1793.)

7879. —— ——. With respect to the increase of our shipping, our merchants have no need * * * of a permission to buy up foreign bottoms. There is no law prohibiting it, and when bought they are American property, and as such entitled to pass freely by our treaties with some nations, and by the law of nations, with all. Such accordingly, by a determination of the Executive, will receive American passports. They will not be entitled, indeed, to import goods on the low duties of *home-built* vessels, the laws having confined that privilege to these only.—To JAMES MONROE. iv, 7. FORD ED., vi, 323. (Pa., 1793.)

7880. SHIPS, Registers.—Our laws, indeed, indulge home-built vessels with the payment of a lower tonnage, and to evidence their right to this, permit them alone to take out registers from our own offices; but they do not exclude foreign-built vessels owned by our citizens from any other right.—To THOMAS PINCKNEY. iii, 550. FORD ED., vi, 242. (Pa., 1793.)

7881. —— ——. The laws of the United States confine registers to *home-built* vessels belonging to citizens: but they do not make it unlawful for citizens to own foreign-built vessels; and the treaties give the right of sea-letters to all vessels belonging to citizens. But who are citizens? The laws of registry consider a citizenship obtained by a foreigner who comes merely for that purpose, and returns to reside in his own country, as fraudulent, and deny a register to such an one, even owning home-built vessels. I consider the distinction as sound and safe, and that we ought not to give sea-letters to a vessel belonging to such a pseudo-citizen. It compromises our peace, by lending our flag to cover the goods of one of the belligerents to the injury of the other. It produces vexatious searches on the vessels of our real citizens, and gives to others the participation of our neutral advantages, which belong to the real citizen only.—To ALBERT GALLATIN. iv, 566. (1805.)

— SHIPS, Screw-propeller.—See INVENTIONS.

7882. SHIPS, Sea-letters.—Sea-letters are the creatures of treaties. No act of the ordinary Legislature requires them. The only treaties now existing with us, and calling for them, are those with Holland, Spain, Prussia, and France. In the two former, we have stipulated that when the other party shall be at war, the vessels belonging to our people shall be furnished with sea-letters; in the two latter, that the *vessels of the neutral* party shall be so furnished. France being now at war, the sea-letter is made necessary for our vessels; and consequently it is our duty to furnish them.—To ALBERT GALLATIN. iv, 566. (1805.)

7883. ——— ———. I would propose as a rule that sea-letters be given to all vessels *belonging* to citizens under whose ownership of a registered vessel such vessel would be entitled to the benefits of her register.—To ALBERT GALLATIN. iv, 567. (1805.)

7884. SHIPS, Subsidies for.—I should be happy to hear that Congress thought of establishing packets of their own between New York and Havre. * * * Could not the surplus of the Post Office revenue be applied to this? This establishment would look like the commencement of a little Navy, the only kind of force we ought to possess.—To RICHARD HENRY LEE. FORD ED., iv, 69. (P., 1785.)

7885. SHIPS, Tonnage duties.—The French complain of our tonnage duty; but it is because it is not understood. In the ports of France, we pay fees for anchorage, buoys and beacons, fees to measurers, weighers and gaugers, and in some countries for light-houses. We have thought it better that the public here should pay all these, and reimburse itself by a consolidation of them into one fee, proportioned to the tonnage of the vessel, and therefore called by that name. They complain that the foreign tonnage is higher than the domestic. If this complaint had come from the English, it would not have been wonderful, because the foreign tonnage operates really as a tax on their commerce, which, under this name, is found to pay 16½ dollars for every dollar paid by France.—To WILLIAM SHORT. iii, 275. FORD ED., v, 363. (Pa., 1791.)

7886. ——— ———. I like your idea of proportioning the tonnage of the vessel to the value (in some degree) of the property, but its bulk must also be taken into consideration.—To ALBERT GALLATIN. v, 260. (W., 1808.)

7887. SHIPS, Voyage to China.—I have the honor of enclosing to your Excellency [Count de Vergennes] a report of the voyage of an American ship, the first which has gone to China. The circumstances which induce Congress to direct this communication is the very friendly conduct of the consul of his Majesty at Macao, and of the commanders and other officers of the French vessels in those seas. It has been with singular satisfaction that Congress have seen these added to the many other proofs of the cordiality of this nation towards our citizens. It is the more pleasing, when it appears in the officers of government, because it is then viewed as an emanation of the spirit of the government. It would be an additional gratification to Congress, in this particular instance, should any occasion arise of notifying those officers, that their conduct has been justly represented to your Excellency on the part of the United States, and has met your approbation.—To COUNT DE VERGENNES. i, 456. (P., 1785.)

— SHIPS, Water for.—See SALT-WATER.

7888. SHORT (William), Attachment to.—I see with extreme concern that you have received an impression that my attachment to you has become lessened, and that you have drawn this inference from circumstances taking place while you were in Washington. What these circumstances could be is to me incomprehensible, but one thing I certainly know, that they have been misconstrued. That this change could not be previous to my retirement from the government in 1794, your appointments to France, to Holland, to Spain are proofs. And if, during my present place in the government, I have not met your desires, the public motives which have been frankly declared have given the real grounds. You think them not founded in fact; but if the testimony we receive is of different complexions, neither should wonder at the difference of conclusion drawn by the other, and I do trust that you will become sensible that there is no necessity, at least, for supposing a change in affections, which are the same now as they have ever been. Certainly I shall not, on my part, permit a difference of view on a single subject to efface the recollections and attachments of a whole life.—To WILLIAM SHORT. FORD ED., ix, 70. (W., 1807.)

7889. SHORT (William), Diplomatic services.—Mr. Short has desired me to suggest his name as that of a person willing to become a legatine secretary, should these offices be continued. I have apprised him of the possibility that they may not. You know my high opinion of his abilities and merits; I will, therefore, only add that a peculiar talent for prying into facts seems to mark his character as proper for such a business. He is young, and little experienced in business, though well prepared for it. These defects will lessen daily. Should persons be proposed less proper on the whole, you would on motives of public good, knowing his willingness to serve, give him a nomination and do justice to his character.—To JAMES MADISON. FORD ED., iii, 318. (T., May 1783.)

7890. ——— ———. A treaty of commerce between the United States of America and his Majesty the King of Prussia having been arranged with the Baron de Thulemeyer, his Majesty's envoy extraordinary at the Hague, specially empowered for this purpose, and it being inconsistent with our other duties to repair to that place ourselves for the purpose of executing and exchanging the instruments of treaty, we hereby appoint you special secretary for that purpose.—To WILLIAM SHORT. i, 372. (P., 1785.)

7891. ——— ———. The President has appointed you Minister Resident * * * at the Hague which was approved by the Senate on January 16.—To WILLIAM SHORT. iii, 322. FORD ED., v, 425. (Pa., Jan. 1792.)

7892. ——— ———. The President has joined you in a special and temporary commission with Mr. Carmichael to repair to Madrid, and there negotiate certain matters respecting the navigation of the Mississippi, and other points of common interest between Spain and us.—To WILLIAM SHORT. iii, 324. FORD ED., v, 427. (Pa., Jan. 1792.)

7893. SHORT (William), Private secretary.—I shall, on Mr. Short's return from the Hague, appoint him my private secretary, till Congress shall think proper to signify their pleasure.—To JAMES MONROE. i, 407. FORD ED., iv, 86. (P., 1785.)

7894. —— ——. His talents and character allow me to say, with confidence, [are such] that nothing will suffer in his hands [during my absence from Paris at home]. The friendly dispositions of Monsieur de Montmorin would induce him readily to communicate with Mr. Short in his present character [private secretary to Jefferson]; but should any of his applications be necessary to be laid before the Council, they might suffer difficulty; nor could he attend the diplomatic societies, which are the most certain sources of good intelligence. Would Congress think it expedient to remove the difficulties by naming him Secretary of Legation, so that he would act. of course, as Chargé des Affaires during my absence?—To JOHN JAY. ii, 514. (P., 1788.)

7895. SHORT (William), Rejected by Senate.—It is with much concern I inform you that the Senate has negatived your appointment. We thought it best to keep back the nomination to the close of the session, that the mission might remain secret as long as possible, which you know was our purpose from the beginning. It was then sent in with an explanation of its object and motives. We took for granted, if any hesitation should arise, that the Senate would take time, and that our friends in that body would make inquiries of us, and give us the opportunity of explaining and removing objections. But to our great surprise, and with an unexampled precipitancy, they rejected it at once. This reception of the last of my official communications to them could not be unfelt, nor were the causes of it spoken out by them. Under this uncertainty, Mr. Madison, on his entering into office, proposed another person (John Quincy Adams). He also was negatived, and they adjourned *sine die.* Our subsequent information was that, on your nomination, your long absence from this country, and their idea that you do not intend to return to it, had very sensible weight; but that all other motives were superseded by an unwillingness to extend our diplomatic connections, and a desire even to recall the foreign ministers we already have. All were sensible of the great virtues, the high character. the powerful influence, and valuable friendship of the Emperor. But riveted to the system of unentanglement with Europe, they declined the proposition. * * * I pray you to place him *rectus in curiâ* in this business with the Emperor, and to assure him that I carry into my retirement the highest veneration for his virtues, and fondly cherish the belief that his dispositions and power are destined by heaven to better, in some degree at least, the condition of oppressed man.—To WILLIAM SHORT v, 435. FORD ED., ix, 249. (W., March 1809.) See 261.

7896. SHORT (William), Republicanism.—I know your republicanism to be pure, and that it is no decay ot that which has embittered you against its votaries in France, but too great a sensibility at the partial evil [with] which its object has been accomplished there —To WILLIAM SHORT. iii, 503. FORD ED., vi, 155. (Pa., 1793.)

7897. SHORT (William), Talents.—I wish in the next election of delegates for Congress, Short could be sent. His talents are great, and his weight in our State must ere

long become principal.—To JAMES MADISON. FORD ED., iii, 403. (A., Feb. 1784.)

7898. —— ——. His talents and merits are such as to have placed him, young as he is, in the Supreme Executive Council of Virginia, an office which he relinquished to visit Europe. —To BARON THULEMEYER. i, 369. (P., 1785.)

7899. SIEYES (Abbe), Logical.—The Abbé Sieyes was the most logical head of the [French] nation. His pamphlet "*Qu'est ce que le Tiers Etat"?* electrified that country, as Paine's *Common Sense* did us.—AUTOBIOGRAPHY. i, 91. FORD ED., i, 127. (1821.)

7900. SILENCE, Golden.—We often repent of what we have said, but never of that which we have not.—To GIDEON GRANGER. vi, 333. FORD ED., ix, 458. (M., 1814.)

— SILVER, Intrinsic value of.—See DOLLAR and MONEY.

7901. SIMPLICITY, Government and.—I am for a government rigorously frugal and simple.—To ELBRIDGE GERRY. iv, 268. FORD ED., vii, 327. (1799.)

7902. —— ——. We have suppressed all those public forms and ceremonies which tended to familiarize the public eye to the harbingers of another form of government.— To GENERAL KOSCIUSKO. iv, 430. (W., April 1802.)

7903. —— ——. Levees are done away.— To NATHANIEL MACON. iv, 396. FORD ED., viii, 52. (W., May 1801.)

7904. SIMPLICITY, Individual.—Let us deserve well of our country by making her interests the end of all our plans, and not our own pomp, patronage and irresponsibility.—To ALBERT GALLATIN. iv, 429. FORD ED., viii, 141. (W., 1802.) See CEREMONY.

7905. SINCERITY, Language and.—Such is become the prostitution of language that sincerity has no longer distinct terms in which to express her own truths.—To GEORGE WASHINGTON. i, 325. FORD ED., iii, 298. (Pa., 1783.)

7906. SINCERITY, Valued.—Sincerity I value above all things; as between those who practice it, falsehood and malice work their efforts in vain.—To WILLIAM DUANE. iv, 590. FORD ED., viii, 431. (W., 1806.)

7907. SINCLAIR (Sir John), Benefactor.—Like our good old Franklin, your labors and science go all to the utilities of human life. —To SIR JOHN SINCLAIR. vii, 22. (M., 1816.)

7908. SINECURES, Taxation and.—We do not mean that our people shall be burdened with oppressive taxes to provide sinecures for the idle or the wicked, under color of providing for a civil list.—REPLY TO LORD NORTH'S PROPOSITION. FORD ED.. i, 480. (July 1775.)

7909. SLANDER, Anonymous.—Your favor has been received * * * with the tribute of respect due to a person, who, unurged by motives of personal friendship or acquaintance, and unaided by particular information, will so far exercise his justice as to advert to the proofs of approbation given to a public character ·by his own State and the United States, and weigh them in the scale against the fatherless calumnies he hears uttered against him. These public acts are known even to those who know nothing of my private life, and surely are better evidence to a mind disposed to truth, than slanders which no man will affirm on his own knowledge, or ever saw one who would.—To URIAH M'GREGORY. iv, 333. (M., 1800.)

7910. SLANDER, Answer to.—As to federal slanders, I never wished them to be answered but by the tenor of my life, half a century of which has been on a theatre at which the public have been spectators, and competent judges of its merit. Their approbation has taught a lesson, useful to the world, that the man who fears no truths has nothing to fear from lies. I should have fancied myself half guilty had I condescended to put pen to paper in refutation of their falsehoods, or drawn to them respect by any notice from myself.—To DR. GEORGE LOGAN. FORD ED., x, 27. (M., 1816.)

7911. ——— ———. I ascribe these hard expressions to the ardor of his zeal for the public good, and as they contain neither argument nor proof, I pass them over without observation. Indeed, I have not been in the habit of noticing these morbid ejections of spleen either with or without the names of those venting them. But I have thought it a duty on the present occasion to relieve my fellow citizens and my country from the degradation in the eyes of the world to which this informer is endeavoring to reduce it by representing it as governed hitherto by a succession of swindlers and speculators. Nor shall I notice any further endeavors to prove or to palliate this palpable misinformation. I am too old and inert to undertake minute investigations of intricate transactions of the last century; and I am not afraid to trust to the justice and good sense of my fellow-citizens on future as on former attempts to lessen me in their esteem.—To RITCHIE AND GOOCH. vii, 242. FORD ED., x, 211. (M., 1822.)

7912. SLANDER, Brutal.—I certainly have known, and still know, characters eminently qualified for the most exalted trusts, who could not bear up against the brutal hackings and hewings of these heroes of Billingsgate. I may say, from intimate knowledge, that we should have lost the services of the greatest character of our country, had he been assailed with the degree of abandoned licentiousness now practiced. The torture he felt under rare and slight attacks, proves that under those of which the federal bands have shown themselves capable, he would have thrown up the helm in a burst of indignation.—To JAMES SULLIVAN. iv, 576. FORD ED., viii, 355. (W., 1805.)

7913. SLANDER, Character vs.—For myself, when placed under the necessity of deciding in a case where on the one hand is a young and worthy person, all the circumstances of whose education and position in life pronounce her virtuous and innocent, and on the other the proneness of the world to sow and spread slander, there is no hesitation in my mind.—To ST. GEORGE TUCKER. FORD ED., vi, 425. (Pa., 1793.)

7914. SLANDER, Chrism of.—You have indeed received the federal unction of lying and slandering. But who has not? Who will ever again come into eminent office, unanointed with this chrism? It seems to be fixed that falsehood and calumny are to be their ordinary engines of opposition; engines which will not be entirely without effect. The circle of characters equal to the first stations is not too large, and

will be lessened by the voluntary retreat of those whose sensibilities are stronger than their confidence in the justice of public opinion. * * * Yet this effect of sensibility must not be yielded to. If we suffer ourselves to be frightened from our post by mere lying, surely the enemy will use that weapon; for what one so cheap to those of whose system of politics morality makes no part?—To JAMES SULLIVAN. iv, 576. FORD ED., viii, 355. (W., 1805.)

7915. SLANDER, Disregard of.—My rule of life has been never to harass the public with fendings and provings of personal slanders.—To MARTIN VAN BUREN. vii, 372. FORD ED., x, 315. (M., 1824.)

7916. SLANDER, Hamilton and.—To a thorough disregard of the honors and emoluments of office, I join as great a value for the esteem of my countrymen, and conscious of having merited it by an integrity which cannot be reproached, and by an enthusiastic devotion to their rights and liberty, I will not suffer my retirement to be clouded by the slanders of a man [Alexander Hamilton] whose history, from the moment at which history can stoop to notice him, is a tissue of machinations against the liberty of the country which has not only received and given him bread, but heaped its honors on his head.—To PRESIDENT WASHINGTON. iii, 468. FORD ED., vi, 109. (M., 1792.)

7917. SLANDER, Irritating.—I am fond of quiet, willing to do my duty, but irritable by slander, and apt to be forced by it to abandon my post.—To MRS. JOHN ADAMS. FORD ED., iv, 100. (P., 1785.)

7918. SLANDER, Newspapers and.—An editor * * * [should] set his face against the demoralizing practice of feeding the public mind habitually on slander, and the depravity of taste which this nauseous aliment induces.—To JOHN NORVELL. v, 93. FORD ED., ix, 74. (W., 1807.)

7919. SLANDER, Of patriots.—The patriot, like the Christian, must learn that to bear revilings and persecutions is a part of his duty; and in proportion as the trial is severe, firmness under it becomes more requisite and praiseworthy. It requires, indeed, self-command. But that will be fortified in proportion as the calls for its exercise are repeated.—To JAMES SULLIVAN. iv, 576. FORD ED., viii, 355. (W., 1805.)

7920. SLANDER, Political.—The federal leaders have gone too far ever to change. Their bitterness increases with their desperation. They are trying slanders now which nothing could prompt but a gall which blinds their judgments as well as their consciences. I shall take no other revenge, than, by a steady pursuit of economy and peace, and by the establishment of republican principles in substance and in form, to sink federalism into an abyss from which there shall be no resurrection for it.—To LEVI LINCOLN. iv, 451. FORD ED., viii, 175. (W., Oct. 1802.)

7921. SLANDER, Prevalent.—Defamation is becoming a necessary of life; insomuch, that a dish of tea in the morning or evening cannot be digested without this stimulant.—To JOHN NORVELL. v, 93. FORD ED., ix, 74. (W., 1807.)

7922. SLANDER, Public office and.—It is really a most afflicting consideration, that it is impossible for a man to act in any office for the public without encountering a persecution which even his retirement will not withdraw him from.—To JAMES MONROE. FORD ED., vii, 233. (Pa., 1798.)

7923. SLANDER, Punishment for.— Slanderers I have thought it best to leave to the scourge of public opinion.—To DE WITT CLINTON. v, 80. FORD ED., ix, 63. (W., 1807.)

7924. SLANDER, Secret.—Secret slanders cannot be disarmed because they are secret.—To WILLIAM DUANE. iv, 591. FORD ED., vii·, 431. (W., 1806.)

7925. SLANDER, Voluminous.—As to the volume of slanders supposed to have been cut out of newspapers and preserved [by me] it would not, indeed, have been a single volume, but an encyclopedia in bulk. But I never had such a volume; indeed, I rarely thought those libels worth reading, much less preserving and remembering.—To JOHN ADAMS. vii, 274. (M., 1823.) See ABUSE, CALUMNY, LIBELS and NEWSPAPERS.

7926. SLAVE TRADE, Abolition of.—I congratulate you [Congress] on the approach of the period at which you may interpose your authority constitutionally, to withdraw the citizens of the United States from a'l further participation in those violations of human rights which have been so long continued on the unoffending inhabitants of Africa, and which the morality, the reputation, and the best interests of our country, have long been eager to proscribe. Although no law you may pass can take prohibitory effect till the first day of the year one thousand eight hundred and eight, yet the intervening period is not too long to prevent, by timely notice, expeditions which cannot be completed before that day.—SIXTH ANNUAL MESSAGE. viii, 67. FORD ED., viii, 492. (Dec. 1806.)

7927. ―― ――. I am very sensible of the honor you propose to me of becoming a member of the society for the abolition of the slave trade. You know that nobody wishes more ardently to see an abolit'on, not only of the trade, but of the condition of slavery; and certainly nobody will be more willing to encounter every sacrifice for that object. But the influence and information of the friends to this proposition in France will be far above the need of my association. I am here as a public servant, and those whom I serve, having never yet been able to give their voice against this practice, it is decent for me to avoid too public a demonstration of my · wishes to see it abolished. Without serving the cause here, it might render me less able to serve it beyond the water. I trust you will be sensible of the prudence of those motives, therefore, which govern my conduct on this occasion.—To J. P. BRISSOT DE WARVILLE. ii, 357. FORD ED., v, 6. (P., Feb. 1788.)

7928. SLAVERY, Abolition of.—After the year 1800 of the Christian era, there shall be neither slavery nor involuntary servitude in any of the said States, * otherwise than in pun'shment of crimes, whereof the party shall have been duly convicted to have been personally guilty.—WESTERN TERRITORY REPORT. FORD ED., iii, 409. (March 1. 1784.)

* In 1784, Jefferson was chairman of a committee of Congress, appointed to devise a plan of government for the western country above the parallel of 31° north latitude The measure was defeated by one vote. In addition to the Northwestern Territory, the region embraced what afterwards became the States of Alabama, Mississippi, Tennessee and Kentucky.—EDITOR.

7929. ―― ――. The clause respecting slavery was lost by an individual vote only. Ten States were present. The four Eastern States, New York and Pennsylvania, were for the clause. Jersey would have been for it, but there were but two members, one of whom was s ck in his chambers. South Carolina, Maryland, and! Virginia! voted against it. North Carolina was divided, as would have been Virginia, had not one of its delegates been sick in bed.—To JAMES MADISON. FORD ED., iii, 471. (A., April· 25, 1784.)

7930. ―― ――. There were ten States present; six voted unanimously for it, three against it, and one was divided; and seven votes being requisite to decide the proposition affirmatively, it was lost. The voice of a single individual of the State which was divided, or of one of those which were of the negative, would have prevented this abominable crime from spreading itself over the new country. Thus we see the fate of millions unborn hanging on the tongue of one man, and heaven was silent in that awful moment! But it is to be hoped it w'll not always be silent, and that the friends to the rights of human nature will in the end prevail.—To M. DE MEUNIER. ix, 276. FORD ED., iv, 181. (P., 1786.)

7931. ―― ――. What a stupendous, what an incomprehensible machine is man! who can endure toil, famine, stripes, imprisonment, and death itself, :n vindication of his own liberty, and, the next moment, be deaf to all those motives whose power supported him through his trial, and inflict on his fellow men a bondage, one hour of which is fraught with more misery than ages of that which he rose in rebellion to oppose. *—To M. DE MEUNIER. ix, 279. FORD ED., iv, 185. (P., 1786.)

7932. ―― ――. I have long since given up the expectation of any early provision for the extinguishment of slavery among us. There are many virtuous men who would make any sacrifices to effect it, many equally virtuous who persuade themselves either that the thing is not wrong, or that it cannot be remedied, and very many with whom interest is morality. The older we grow, the larger we are disposed to believe the last party to be. But interest is really going over to the side of morality. The value of the slave is every day lessening; his burden on his master daily increasing. Interest is, therefore, preparing the disposition to be just; and this will be goaded from time to time by the insurrectionary spirit of the slaves. This is easily quelled in its first efforts; but from being local it will become general, and whenever it does, it will rise more formidable after every defeat, until we shall be forced, after dreadful scenes and sufferings, to release them in their own way, which, without such sufferings we might now model after our own convenience.—To WILLIAM A. BURWELL. FORD ED., viii, 340. (W., Jan. 1805.)

7933. ―― ――. I can say with conscious truth that there is not a man on earth who would sacrifice more than I would to relieve us from this heavy reproach in any *practicable* way. The cess'on of that kind of property, for so it is misnamed, is a bagatelle which would not cost me a second thought, if, in that way, a general emancipation and *expatriation* could be effected; and, gradually, and with due sacrifices, I think it m'ght be. But, as it is, we have the wolf by the ears, and we can

* The reference is to the passage of the slave bill by the Virginia Legislature without the emancipation amendment.—EDITOR.

neither hold h'm, nor safely let him go. Justice is in one scale and self-preservation in the other.—To John Holmes. vii, 159. Ford ed., x, 157. (M., 1820.)

7934. ——— ———. The abolition of the evil is not impossible; it ought never, therefore, to be despaired of. Every plan should be adopted, every experiment tried, wh ch may do something towards the ultimate object. That which you propose is weil worthy of trial. It has succeeded with certain portions of our white brethren, under the care of a Rapp and an Owen; and why may it not succeed with the man of color?—To Miss Fanny Wright. vii, 408. Ford ed., x. 344. (M., 1825.)

7935. SLAVERY, Abomination.—This abomination must have an end. And there is a superior bench reserved in heaven for those who hasten it.—To E. Rutledge. ii, 180. Ford ed., iv, 410. (P., 1787.)

7936. SLAVERY, Colonial condemnation.—The abolition of domestic slavery is the great object of desire 'n those Colonies, where it was, unhappily, introduced in their infant state. But previous to the enfranchisement of the slaves we have, it is necessary to exclude all further importations from Africa. Yet our repeated attempts to effect this by prohibitions, and by imposing duties which might amount to a prohibition, have been hitherto defeated by his Majesty's negative: Thus preferring the immed'ate advantages of a few British corsairs to the lasting interests of the Amer'can States, and to the rights of human nature, deeply wounded by this infamous practice.*—Rights of British America. i, 135. Ford ed.. i, 440. (1774.)

7937. SLAVERY, Constitutional inhibition.—No person hereafter coming into this country shall be held within the same in slavery under any pretext whatever.—Proposed Va. Constitution. Ford ed., ii, 26. (June 1776.)

7938. ——— ———. The General Assembly [of Virginia] shall not have power to * * * permit the introduction of any more slaves to reside in this State, or the continuance of slavery beyond the generation which shall be living on the 31st day of December, 1800; all persons born after that day being hereby declared free.—Proposed Constitution for Virginia. viii, 446. Ford ed., iii, 325. (1783.)

7939. SLAVERY, Deplorable results of.—The whole commerce between master and slave is a perpetual exercise of the most boisterous passions, the most unremitting despotism on the one part, and degrading submissions on the other. Our children see this, and learn to imitate it; for man is an imitative animal. This quality is the germ of all education in him. From his cradle to his grave he is learning to do what he sees others do. If a parent could find no motive either in his philanthropy or his self-love, for restraining the intemperance of passion towards his slave, it should always be a sufficient one that his child is present. But, generally, it is not sufficient. The parent storms, the child looks on, catches the lineaments of wrath, puts on the same airs in the circle of smaller slaves, gives a loose to the worst of passions, and thus nursed, educated, and daily exercised in tyranny, cannot but be stamped by it with odious peculiarities. The man must be a prodigy who can retain his manners and morals undepraved by such circumstances. And with what execrations should the statesman be loaded, who, permitting one-

* See note under Veto.—Editor.

half the citizens thus tc trample on the rights of the other, transforms those into despots, and these into enemies, destroys the morals of the one part, and the *amor patriæ* of the other. For if a slave can have a country in this world, it must be any other in preference to that in which he 's born to live and labor for another: in which he must lock up the faculties of his nature, contribute as far as depends on his individual endeavors to the evanishment of the human race, or entail his own miserable condition on the endless generations proceeding from him.—Notes on Virginia. viii, 403. Ford ed., iii, 266. (1782.)

7940. SLAVERY, Destructive of industry.—With the morals of the people, their industry also is destroyed. For in a warm climate, no man will labor for himself who can make another labor for him. This is so true, that of the proprietors of slaves a very small proportion indeed are ever seen to labor.—Notes on Virginia. viii, 403. Ford ed., iii, 267. (1782.)

7941. SLAVERY, Divine justice and.—Can the liberties of a nation be thought secure when we have removed their only firm basis, a conviction in the minds of the people that these liberties are of the gift of God? That they are not to be violated but with his wrath? Indeed, I tremble for my country when I reflect that God is just; that his justice cannot sleep forever; that considering numbers, nature and natural means only, a revolution of the wheel of fortune, an exchange of situation is among possible events; that it may become probable by supernatural interference! The Almighty has no attribute which can take side with us in such a contest.—Notes on Virginia. viii, 404. Ford ed., i'i, 267. (1782.)

7942. SLAVERY, Establishment in Virginia.—The first establishment [of slavery] in Virginia which became permanent, was made in 1607. I have found no mention of negroes in the Colony until about 1650. The first brought here as slaves were by a Dutch ship: after which the English commenced the trade, and continued it until the Revolutionary war. That suspended, *ipso facto*, their further importation for the present, and the business of the war pressing constantly on the legislature, this subject was not acted on finally until the year '78, when I brought in a bill to prevent their further importation. This passed without opposition, and stopped the increase of the evil by importation, leaving to future efforts its final eradication.—Autobiography. i, 38. Ford ed., i, 51. (1821.)

7943. SLAVERY, Extension of.—Of one thing I am certain, that as the passage of slaves from one State to another, would not make a slave of a single human being who would not be so without it. so their diffusion over a greater surface would make them individually happier, and proportionally facilitate the accomplishment of their emancipation, by dividing the burden on a greater number of coadjutors. An abstinence, too, from this act of power would remove the jealousy excited by the undertak'ng of Congress to regulate the condition of the different descriptions of men composing a State. This certainly is the exclusive right of every State, wh'ch nothing in the Constitution has taken from them and given to the General Government. Could Congress, for example, say that the non-freemen of Connecticut shall be freemen, or that they shall not emigrate into any other State?—To John Holmes. vii, 159. Ford ed., x, 158. (M., 1820.)

7944. SLAVERY, George III. and.—He [George III.] has waged cruel war against human nature itself, violating its most sacred rights of life and liberty in the persons of a distant people who never offended him, captivating and carrying them into slavery in another hemisphere, or to incur miserable death in their transportation thither. This piratical warfare, the opprobrium of INFIDEL powers, is the warfare of the CHRISTIAN King of Great Britain. Determined to ..eep open a market where MEN should be bought and sold, he has prostituted his negative for suppressing every leg slative attempt to prohibit or to restrain th s execrable commerce. And that this assemblage of horrors might want no fact of distinguished dye, he is now excit ng those very people to rise in arms among us, and to purchase that liberty of which he has deprived them, by murdering the people upon whom he has obtruded them: thus paying off former crimes committed against the LIBERTIES of one people, with crimes which he urges them to commit against the LIVES of another.*—DECLARATION OF INDEPENDENCE AS DRAWN BY JEFFERSON.

7945. SLAVERY, Indians and.—An inhuman practice once prevailed in this country, of making slaves of the Indians. This practice commenced with the Spaniards with the first discovery of America.—NOTES ON VIRGINIA. viii, 306. FORD ED., iii, 154. (1782.)

7946. SLAVERY, Lawfulness.—On the question of the lawfulness of slavery, that is of the right of one man to appropriate to himself the faculties of another without his consent, I certainly retain my early opinions. On that, however, of third persons to interfere between the parties, and the effect of conventional modificat ons of that pretension, we are probably nearer together.—To EDWARD EVERETT. vii, 437. FORD ED., x, 385. (M., 1826.)

7947. SLAVERY, Moral reproach of.— My sentiments on the subject of slavery of negroes have long since been in possession of the public, and time has only served to give them stronger root. The love of justice and the love of country plead equally the cause of these people, and it is a moral reproach to us that they should have pleaded it so long in vain, and should have produced not a single effort, nay I fear not much serious willingness to relieve them and ourselves from our present condition of moral and political reprobation. * * * I had always hoped that the younger generation rece ving their early impressions after the flame of liberty had been kindled in every breast, and had become, as it were, the vital spirit of every American, that the generous temperament of youth, analogous to the motion of the blood, and above the suggestions of avarice. would have sympathized with oppression wherever found, and proved their love of liberty beyond their own share of it. But my intercourse with them since my return [from Europe] has not been sufficient to ascertain that they had made towards this point the progress I had hoped.—To EDWARD COLES. FORD ED., ix, 477. (M., 1814.)

* "This clause," says Jefferson, in his Autobiography (i, 19), "was struck out in complaisance to South Carolina and Georgia, who had never attempted to restrain the importation of slaves, and who, on the contrary, still wished to continue it. Our northern brethren, also, I believe, felt a little tender under those censures; for though their people had very few slaves themselves, yet they had been pretty considerable carriers of them to others."—EDITOR.

7948. SLAVERY, Poem against.—I have received a letter from Mr. Thomas Brannagan, * * * Philadelphia, asking my subscription to the work announced in the enclosed paper.* The cause in which he embarks is so holy, the sentiments he expresses in his letter so friendly, that it is highly painful to me to hesitate on a compliance which appears so small. But that is not its true character, and it would be injurious even to his views, for me to commit myself on paper by answering his letter. I have most carefully avoided every public act or manifestation on that subject. Should an occasion ever occur in which I can interpose with decisive effect, I shall certainly know and do my duty with promptitude and zeal. But, in the meantime, it would only be disarming myself of influence to be taking small means. The subscr ption to a book on this subject is one of those little irritating measures, which, without advancing its end at all, would, by lessening the confidence and good will of a description of friends composing a large body. only lessen my powers of doing them good in the other great relations in which I stand to the public. Yet, I cannot be easy in not answering Mr. Brannagan's letter, unless he can be made sensible that it is better I should not answer it; and I do not know how to effect this, unless you would have the goodness * * * to enter into an explanation with him. —To DR. GEORGE LOGAN. FORD ED., viii, 351. (W., May 1805.)

7949. SLAVERY, Political error of.— Whatever may have been the circumstances which influenced our forefathers to permit the introduction of personal bondage into any part of these States, and to participate in the wrongs committed on an unoffending quarter of the globe, we may rejoice that such circumstances, and such a sense of them, exist no longer. It is honorable to the nation at large that their Legislature availed themselves of the first practicable moment for arresting the progress of this great moral and political error.—R. TO A. OF QUAKERS. viii, 119. (Nov. 1807.)

7950. SLAVERY, Roman.—We know that among the Romans, about the Augustan age especially, the condition of their slaves was much more deplorable than that of the blacks on the continent of America. The two sexes were confined in separate apartments, because to ra se a child cost the master more than to buy one. Cato, for a very restricted indulgence to his slaves in this particular, took from them a certain price. But in this country the slaves multiply as fast as the free inhab tants. * * * The same Cato, on a principle of economy, always sold his sick and superannuated slaves. He gives it as a standing precept to a master visiting his farm, to sell his old oxen, old wagons, old tools, old and diseased servants, and everything else become useless. * * * The American slaves cannot enumerate this among the injuries and nsults they receive. It was the common practice to expose in the island Æsculapius, in the Tiber, diseased slaves whose cure was likely to become tedious. The Emperor Claudius, by an edict, gave freedom to such of them as should recover, and first declared that if any person chose to kill rather than to expose them, it should be deemed homicide. The exposing them is a cr me of which no instance has existed with us; and were it to be followed by death, it would be punished cap-

* This refers to "Avenia; or, A Tragical Poem on the Oppression of the Human Species", an antislavery work printed in Philadelphia in 1805.—NOTE IN THE FORD EDITION.

itally. We are told of a certain Vedius Pollio, who, in the presence of Augustus, would have given a slave as food to his fish for having broken a glass. With the Romans, the regular method of taking the evidence of their slaves was under torture. Here it has been thought better never to resort to their evidence. When a master was murdered, all his slaves, in the same house, or within hearing, were condemned to death. Here punishment falls on the guilty only, and as precise proof is required against him as against a freeman. Yet notwithstanding these and other discouraging circumstances among the Romans, their slaves were often their rarest artists. They excelled, too, in science, insomuch as to be usually employed as tutors to their master's children. Epictetus, Terence, and Phœdrus, were slaves. But they were of the race of whites. It is not their condition then. but nature which has produced the distinction. Whether further observation w'll or will not verify the conjecture, that nature has been less bountiful to them in the endowments of the head, I believe that in those of the heart she will be found to have done them justice.—NOTES ON VIRGINIA. viii, 384. FORD ED., iii, 247. (1782.) See NEGROES.

7951. SLAVERY, Sectional views in 1785.—Southward of the Chesapeake, your pamphlet [against slavery] will find but few readers concurring with it in sentiment on the subject of slavery. From the mouth to the head of the Chesapeake, the bulk of the people will approve it in theory, and it will find a respectable minority ready to adopt it in practice; a minority which for weight and worth of character preponderates against the greater number, who have not the courage to divest their families of a property which, however, keeps their conscience unquiet. Northward of the Chesapeake, you may find here and there an opponent to your doctrine, as you may find here and there a robber and murderer; but in no greater number. In that part of America, there being but few slaves, they can easily disencumber themselves of them; and emancipation is put into such a train that in a few years there will be no slaves northward of Maryland. In Maryland, I do not find such a disposition to begin the redress of this enormity as in Virginia. This is the next State to which we may turn our eyes for the interesting spectacle of justice in conflict with avarice and oppression; a conflict wherein the sacred side is gaining daily recruits from the influx into office of young men grown, and growing up. These have sucked in the principles of liberty, as it were, with their mother's milk; and it is to them I look with anxiety to turn the fate of this question. Be not therefore discouraged. What you have written will do a great deal of good.—To DR. PRICE. i, 377. FORD ED., iv, 82. (P., 1785.)

7952. SLAVERY, Strictures on.—The strictures on slavery [in the Notes on Virginia] * * * I do not wish to have made public, at least till I know whether their publication would do most harm or good. It is possible, that in my own country, these strictures might produce an irritation, which would indispose the people towards [one of] the two great objects I have in view; that is, the emancipation of their slaves.*—To GENERAL CHASTELLUX. i. 339. FORD ED., iii, 71. (P., 1785.) See COLONIZATION, COLONY and MISSOURI QUESTION.

* General Chastellux had proposed to print extracts from a private copy in a French scientific paper. —EDITOR.

7953. SLAVES, Abuse of.—The check on the tenants against abusing my slaves was, by the former lease, that I might discontinue it on a reference to arbitrators. Would it not be well to retain an optional right to sue them for ill-usage of the slaves or to discontinue it by arbitration, whichever you should choose at the time?—To NICHOLAS LEWIS. FORD ED., v, 31. (P., 1788.)

7954. SLAVES, British seizure of.—The British army, after ravaging the State of Virginia, had sent off a very great number of slaves to New York. By the seventh article of the treaty of peace, they stipulated not to carry away any of these. Notwithstanding this, it was known, when they were evacuating New York, that they were carrying away the slaves, General Washington made an official demand of Sir Guy Carleton, that he should cease to send them away. He answered, that these people had come to them under promise of the King's protection, and that that promise should be fulfilled in preference to the stipulation in the treaty. The State of Virginia, to which nearly the whole of these slaves belonged, passed a law to forbid the recovery of debts due to British subjects. They declared, at the same time, they would repeal the law, if Congress were of opinion they ought to do it. But, desirous that their citizens should be discharging their debts, they afterwards permitted British creditors to prosecute their suits, and to receive their debts in seven equal and annual payments; relying that the demand for the slaves would be either admitted or denied in time to lay their hands on some of the latter payments for reimbursement.*—REPORT TO CONGRESS. ix, 240. FORD ED., iv, 127. (P., 1785.)

7955. SLAVES, Comfort of.—I am miserable till I shall owe not a shilling. The moment that shall be the case, I shall feel myself at liberty to do something for the comfort of my slaves.—To NICHOLAS LEWIS. FORD ED., iv, 343. (P., 1786.)

7956. SLAVES, Duty to.—My opinion has ever been that, until more can be done for them, we should endeavor, with those whom fortune has thrown on our hands, to feed and clothe them well, protect them from ill usage, require such reasonable labor only as is performed voluntarily by freemen, and be led by no repugnances to abdicate them, and our duties to them. The laws do not permit us to turn them loose, if that were for their good; and to commute them for other property is to commit them to those whose usage of them we cannot control.—To EDWARD COLES. FORD ED., ix, 479. (M., 1814.)

7957. SLAVES, European laborers and.—Our only blot is becoming less offensive by the great improvement in the condition and civilization of that race, who can now more advantageously compare their situation with that of the laborers of Europe. Still it is a hideous blot, as well from the heteromorph peculiarities of the race, as that, with them, physical compulsion to action must be substituted for the moral necessity which constrains the free laborers to work equally hard. We feel and deplore it morally and politically, and we look without entire despair to some redeeming means not yet specifically foreseen. I am happy in believing that the conviction of

* The extract is from a report to Congress of a conference with Count de Vergennes, Foreign Minister of France, on the subject of commerce.—EDITOR.

the necessity of removing this evil gains ground with time. Their emigration to the westward lightens the difficulty by dividing it, and renders it more practicable on the whole. And the neighborhood of a government of their color promises a more accessible asylum than that from whence they came.—To WILLIAM SHORT. vii, 310. (M., 1823.)

7958. SLAVES, Hiring out.—I observe in your letter * * * that the profits of the whole estate [of Monticello] would be no more than the hire of the few negroes hired out would amount to. Would it be better to hire more where good masters could be got? Would it be better to hire plantations and all, if proper assurance can be provided for the good usage of everything?—To NICHOLAS LEWIS. FORD ED., iv, 342. (P., 1786.)

7959. SLAVES, Importation of.—During the regal government we had, at one time, obtained a law which imposed such a duty on the importation of slaves as amounted nearly to a prohibition, when one inconsiderate assembly, placed under a peculiarity of circumstance, repealed the law. This repeal met a joyful sanction from the then reigning sovereign, and no devices, no expedients which could ever be attempted by subsequent assemblies (and they seldom met without attempting them) could succeed in getting the royal assent to a renewal of the duty. In the very first session held under the republican government, the assembly passed a law for the perpetual prohibition of the importation of slaves. This will, in some measure, stop the increase of this great political and moral evil, while the minds of our citizens may be ripening for a complete emancipation of human nature.—NOTES ON VIRGINIA. viii, 334. FORD ED., iii, 102. (1782.)

7960. ——— ———. I congratulate you on the law of your State [South Carolina] for suspending the importation of slaves, and for the glory you have justly acquired by endeavoring to prevent it forever.—To E. RUTLEDGE. ii, 180. FORD ED., iv, 410. (P., 1787.)

7961. SLAVES, Increase of.—Under the mild treatment our slaves experience, and their wholesome, though coarse food, this blot in our country increases as fast, or faster than the whites.—NOTES ON VIRGINIA. viii, 334. FORD ED., iii, 192. (1782.)

7962. SLAVES, Labor and.—An opinion is hazarded by some, but proved by none, that moral urgencies are not sufficient to induce [the negro] to labor; th t nothing can do this but physical coercion. But this is a problem which the present age alone is prepared to solve by experiment. It would be a solecism to suppose a race of animals created without sufficient foresight and energy to preserve their own existence. It is disproved, too, by the fact that they exist and have existed through all the ages of history. We are not sufficiently acquainted with all the nations of Africa to say that there may not be some in which habits of industry are established, and the arts practiced which are necessary to render life comfortable. The experiment now in progress in Santo Domingo, those of Sierra Leone and Cape Mesurado, are but beginning. Your proposition has its aspects of promise also; and should it not answer fully to calculations in figures, it may yet, in its developments, lead to happy results. —To MISS FANNY WRIGHT. vii, 408. FORD ED., x, 344. (M., 1825.)

7963. SLAVES, Manumission of.—As far as I can judge from the experiments which have been made to give liberty to, or rather, to abandon persons whose habits have been formed in slavery is like abandoning children. —To DR. EDWARD BANCROFT. FORD ED., v, 66. (P., 1789.)

7964. SLAVES, Masters and.—The inculcation [in your book] on the master of the moral duties which he owes to the slave, in return for the benefits of his service, that is to say, of food, clothing, care in sickness, and maintenance under age and disability, so as to make him in fact as comfortable and more secure than the laboring man in most parts of the world, * * * gives great merit to the work, and will, I have no doubt, produce wholesome impressions.—To CLEMENT CAINE. vi, 13. FORD ED., ix, 329. (M., 1811.)

7965. SLAVES, Metayers and.—I am decided on my final return to America to try this experiment. I shall endeavor to import as many Germans as I have grown slaves. I will settle them and my slaves, on farms of fifty acres each, intermingled, and place all on the footing of the Metayers (Medietani) of Europe. Their children shall be brought up, as others are, in habits of property and foresight, and I have no doubt but that they will be good citizens. Some of their fathers will be so; others I suppose will need government. With these all that can be done is to oblige them to labor as the laboring poor of Europe do, and to apply to their comfortable subsistence the produce of their labor, retaining such a moderate portion of it as may be a just equivalent for the use of the lands they labor, and the stocks and other necessary advances.—To DR. EDWARD BANCROFT. FORD ED., v, 67. (P., 1789.)

7966. SLAVES, Property in.—Actual property has been lawfully vested in that form [negroes] and who can lawfully take it from the possessors?—To JARED SPARKS. vii, 333. FORD ED., x, 290. (M., 1824.)

7967. SLAVES, Protection of.—In the first or second session of the Legislature after I became a member, I drew to this subject the attention of Colonel Bland, one of the oldest, ablest, and most respected members, and he undertook to move for certain moderate extensions of the protection of the laws to these people. I seconded his motion and, as a younger member, was more spared in the debate; but he was denounced as an enemy of his country, and was treated with the grossest indecorum.—To EDWARD COLES. FORD ED., ix, 477. (M., 1814.)

7968. SLAVES, Recovery of fugitive.—We have received with great satisfaction notification of the orders of his Catholic Majesty, not to permit that persons, held in slavery within the United States, introduce themselves as free persons into the Province of Florida. * * * As a consequence of the same principles of justice and friendship, we trust that your Excellency will permit, and aid the recovery of persons of the same description, who have heretofore taken refuge within your government.—To GOVERNOR QUESADA. iii, 219. FORD ED., v, 296. (Pa., 1791.)

7969. ——— ———. The governor of East Florida informs me that he has received the King's orders, not to permit, under any pretext, that persons held in slavery in the United States introduce themselves as free, into the province of East Florida. I am happy that this grievance, which had been a subject of great complaint from the citizens of Georgia, s to be removed.—To MR. VIAR. iii, 195. (M., 1790.)

7970. SLAVES, San Domingo insurrection.—If something is not done, and soon done, we shall be the murderers of our own children. The *"murmura venturos nautis prudentia ventos"* has already reached us [from San Domingo]; the revolutionary storm, now sweeping the globe, will be upon us, and happy if we make timely provision to give it an easy passage over our land. From the present state of things in Europe and America, the day which begins our combustion must be near at hand; and only a single spark is wanting to make that day to-morrow. If we had begun sooner, we might probably have been allowed a lengthier operation to clear ourselves, but every day's delay lessens the time we may take for emancipation. Some people derive hope from the aid of the confederated States. But this is a delusion. There is but one State in the Union which will aid us sincerely, if an insurrection begins, and that one may, perhaps, have its own fire to quench at the same time.— To ST. GEORGE TUCKER. iv, 196. FORD ED., vii, 168. (M., 1797.)

7971. ——— ———. As to the mode of emancipation, I am satisfied that that must be a matter of compromise between the passions, the prejudices, and the real difficulties which will each have its weight in that operation. Perhaps the first chapter of this history, which has begun in St. Domingo, and the next succeeding ones, will recount how all the whites were driven from all the other islands, may prepare our minds for a peaceable accommodation between justice, policy and necessity; and furnish an answer to the difficult question, whither shall the colored emigrants go? and the sooner we put some plan under way, the greater hope there is that it may be permitted to proceed peaceably to its ultimate effect.—To ST. GEORGE TUCKER. iv, 196. FORD ED., vii, 167. (M., 1797.)

7972. SLAVES, Thievery and.—That disposition to theft with which they have been branded, must be ascribed to their situation, and not to any depravity of the moral sense. The man in whose favor no laws of property exist, probably feels himself less bound to respect those made in favor of others. When arguing for ourselves, we lay it down as a fundamental, that laws, to be just, must give a reciprocation of right; that, without this, they are mere arbitrary rules of conduct, founded in force, and not in conscience; and it is a problem which I give to the master to solve, whether the religious precepts against the violation of property were not framed for him as well as his slave? And whether the slave may not as justifiably take a little from one who has taken all from him, as he may slay one who would slay him? That a change in the relations in which a man is placed should change his ideas of moral right or wrong, is neither new, nor peculiar to the color of the blacks. Homer tells us it was so two thousand six hundred years ago.—NOTES ON VIRGINIA. viii, 385. FORD ED., iii, 249. (1782.)

7973. SLAVES (Emancipation), Bill for.—The bill to emancipate all slaves born after the passing of the act, reported by the revisers [of the Virginia Code] did not contain this proposition; but an amendment containing it was prepared, to be offered to the Legislature

whenever the bill should be taken up, and further directing that they should continue with their parents to a certain age, then to be brought up, at the public expense, to tillage, arts, or sciences, according to their geniuses, till the females should be eighteen, and the males twenty-one years of age, when they should be colonized to such place as the circumstances of the time should render most proper, sending them out with arms, implements of household and of the handicraft arts, seeds, pairs of the useful domestic animals, &c., to declare them a free and independent people, and extend to them our alliance and protection, till they have acquired strength; and to send vessels, at the same time, to other parts of the world for an equal number of white inhabitants; to induce them to migrate hither, proper encouragements were to be proposed.—NOTES ON VIRGINIA. viii, 380. FORD ED., iii, 243. (1782.)

7974. ——— ———. The separation of infants from their mothers would produce some scruples of humanity. But this would be straining at a gnat, and swallowing a camel.— To JARED SPARKS. vii, 335. FORD ED., x, 293. (M., 1824.)

7975. SLAVES (Emancipation), Blessings of.—Who could estimate its blessed effects? I leave this to those who will live to see their accomplishment, and to enjoy a beatitude forbidden to my age. But I leave it with this admonition,—to rise and be doing. A million and a half are within our control; but six millions (which a majority of those now living will see them attain), and one million of these fighting men, will say, "we will not go".—To JARED SPARKS. vi, 335. FORD ED., x, 292. (M., 1824.)

7976. SLAVES (Emancipation), Certain.—The hour of emancipation is advancing, in the march of time. It will come; and whether brought on by the generous energy of our own minds; or by the bloody process of St. Domingo, excited and conducted by the power of our present enemy [England], if once stationed permanently within our country, and offering asylum and arms to the oppressed, is a leaf of our history not yet turned over.—To EDWARD COLES. FORD ED., ix, 478. (M., 1814.)

7977. ——— ———. It was found that the public mind would not bear the proposition [gradual emancipation], nor will it bear it even at this day (1821). Yet the day is not distant, when it must bear and adopt it, or worse will follow. Nothing is more certainly written in the book of fate, than that these people are to be free; nor is it less certain, that the two races, equally free, cannot live in the same government. Nature, habit, opinion have drawn indelible lines of distinction between them. It is still in our power to direct the process of emancipation and deportation, peaceably, and in such slow degree, as that the evil will wear off insensibly, and their place be, *pari passu*, filled up by free white laborers. If, on the contrary, it is left to force itself on, human nature must shudder at the prospect held up. We should in vain look for an example in the Spanish deportation, or deletion of the Moors. This precedent would fall far short of our case. —JEFFERSON MSS. RAYNER, 164.

7978. SLAVES (Emancipation), Defeated.—In 1769, I became a member of the legislature by the choice of the county in which I live [Albemarle], and so continued until it was closed by the Revolution. I made one effort in that body for the permission of the emancipation of slaves, which was rejected: and indeed, during the regal government, nothing liberal could expect success. Our minds were circumscribed within narrow limits, by an habitual belief that it was our duty to be subordinate to the mother country in all matters of government, to direct all our labors in subservience to her interests, and even to observe a bigoted intolerance for all religions but hers. The difficulties with our representatives were of habit and despair, not of reflection and conviction. Experience soon proved that they could bring their minds to rights on the first summons of their attention. But the King's Council, which acted as another house of legislature, held their places at will, and were in most humble obedience to that will; the Governor, too, who had a negative on our laws, held by the same tenure, and with still greater devotedness to it; and, last of all, the royal negative closed the last door to every hope of amelioration.*—AUTOBIOGRAPHY. i, 3. FORD ED., i, 5. (1821.)

7979. SLAVES (Emancipation), Gradual.—I concur entirely in your leading principles of gradual emancipation, of establishment on the coast of Africa, and the patronage of our nation until the emigrants shall be able to protect themselves.—To DR. THOMAS HUMPHREYS. vii, 57. FORD ED., x, 76. (M., 1817.)

7980. SLAVES (Emancipation), Methods of.—As to the method by which this difficult work is to be effected, if permitted to be done by ourselves, I have seen no proposition so expedient on the whole, as that of emancipation of those born after a given day, and of their education and expatriation after a given age.—To EDWARD COLES. FORD ED., ix, 478. (M., 1814.)

7981. SLAVES (Emancipation), Prayers for.—It shall have all my prayers, and these are the only weapons of an old man.— To EDWARD COLES. FORD ED., ix, 479. (M., 1814.)

7982. SLAVES (Emancipation), Preparations for.—Unhappily it is a case for which both parties require long and difficult preparation. The mind of the master is to be apprized by reflection, and strengthened by the energies of conscience, against the obstacles of self interest to an acquiescence in the rights of others; that of the slave is to be prepared by instruction and habit for self-government, and for the honest pursuits of industry and social duty. Both of these courses of preparation require time, and the former must precede the latter. Some progress is sensibly made in it; yet not so much as I had hoped and expected. But it will yield in time to temperate and steady pursuit, to the enlargement of the human mind, and its advancement in science. We are not in a world ungoverned by the laws and the power of a Superior Agent. Our efforts are in His hand, and directed by it; and He will give them their effect in his own time. Where the disease is most deeply seated, there it will be slowest in eradication. In the Northern States it was merely superficial, and easily corrected. In the Southern it is incorporated with the whole system, and requires time, patience and perseverance in the curative process. That it may finally be effected, and its process hastened, will be my last and fondest prayer.—To DAVID BARROW. vi, 456. FORD ED., ix, 515. (M., May 1815.)

* This was Jefferson's first public measure.—EDITOR.

7983. SLAVES (Emancipation), Principle and.—From those of the former generation who were in the fulness of age when I came into public life, which was while our controversy with England was on paper only, I soon saw that nothing was to be hoped. Nursed and educated in the daily habit of seeing the degraded condition, both bodily and mental, of those unfortunate beings, not reflecting that that degradation was very much the work of themselves and their fathers, few minds have yet doubted but that they were as legitimate subjects of property as their horses and cattle. The quiet and monotonous course of colonial life had been disturbed by no alarm, and little reflection on the value of liberty. And when alarm was taken at an enterprise on their own, it was not easy to carry them to the whole length of the principles which they invoked for themselves.—To EDWARD COLES. FORD ED., ix, 477. (M., 1814.)

7984. SLAVES (Emancipation), Propaganda for.—I hope you will reconcile yourself to your country and its unfortunate condition; that you will not lessen its stock of sound disposition by withdrawing your portion from the mass; that, on the contrary, you will come forward in the public councils, become the missionary of this doctrine truly Christian, insinuate and inculcate it softly but steadily, through the medium of writing and conversation; associate others in your labors, and when the phalanx is formed, bring on and press the proposition perseveringly until its accomplishment. —To EDWARD COLES. FORD ED., ix, 479. (M., 1814.)

7985. SLAVES (Emancipation), Providence and.—We must await with patience the workings of an overruling Providence, and hope that that is preparing the deliverance of these, our suffering brethren. When the measure of their tears shall be full, when their groans shall have involved heaven itself in darkness, doubtless a God of justice will awaken to their distress, and by diffusing light and liberality among their oppressors, or, at length, by His exterminating thunder, manifest His attention to the things of this world, and that they are not left to the guidance of a blind fatality.—To M. DE MEUNIER. ix, 279. FORD ED., iv, 185. (P., 1786.)

7986. SLAVES (Emancipation), Time and.—I have not perceived the growth of this disposition [to emancipate the slaves and settle them elsewhere] in the rising generation, of which I once had sanguine hopes. No symptoms inform me that it will take place in my day. I leave it, therefore, to time, and not at all without hope that the day will come, equally desirable and welcome to us as to them. Perhaps the proposition now on the carpet at Washington to provide an establishment on the coast of Africa for voluntary emigrations of people of color may be the corner stone of this future edifice.—To THOMAS HUMPHREYS. vii, 58. FORD ED., x, 77. (M., 1817.)

7987. —— ——. At the age of eighty-two, with one foot in the grave and the other uplifted to follow it, I do not permit myself to take part in any new enterprises, even for bettering the condition of man, not even in the great one which is the subject of your letter, and which has been through life that of my greatest anxieties. The march of events has not been such as to render its completion practicable within the limits of time allotted to me; and I leave its accomplishment as the work of another generation.—To Miss Fanny Wright. vii, 408. Ford ed., x, 344. (M., 1825.)

7988. SLAVES (Emancipation), Total.
—It is impossible to be temperate and to pursue this subject through the various considerations of policy, of morals, of history, natural and civil. We must be contented to hope they will force their way into every one's mind. * * * The way, I hope, is preparing, under the auspices of heaven, for a total emancipation, and that this is disposed, in the order of events, to be with the consent of the masters, rather than by their extirpation.—Notes on Virginia. vii, 404. Ford ed., iii, 267. (1782.)

7989. SLAVES (Emancipation), United States purchase of.—The bare proposition of purchase [of the slaves] by the United States generally would excite infinite indignation in all the States north of Maryland. The sacrifice must fall on the States alone which hold them; and the difficult question will be how to lessen this so as to reconcile our fellow citizens to it. Personally, I am ready and desirous to make any sacrifice which shall ensure their gradual but complete retirement from the State, and effectually, at the same time, establish them elsewhere in freedom and safety.—To Dr. Thomas Humphreys. vii, 58. Ford ed., x, 76. (M., 1817.)

7990. SLAVES (Emancipation), West Indies and.—I become daily more convinced that all the West India Islands will remain in the hands of the people of color, and a total expulsion of the whites sooner or later take place. It is high time we should foresee the bloody scenes which our children certainly, and possibly ourselves (south of the Potomac), have to wade through and try to avert them.—To James Monroe. iv, 20. Ford ed., vi, 349. (Pa., July 1793.)

7991. ———. On the subject of emancipation I have ceased to think because not to be a work of my day. The plan of converting the blacks into serfs would certainly be better than keeping them in their present position, but I consider that of expatriation to the governments of the West Indies of their own color as entirely practicable, and greatly preferable to the mixture of color here. To this I have great aversion.—To William Short. Ford ed., x, 362. (M., 1826.) See Colonization.

7992. SLEEP, Habits of.—I am not so regular in my sleep as the doctor [Dr. Rush] says he was, devoting to it from five to eight hours, according as my company or the book I am reading interests me; and I never go to bed without an hour, or half hour's, previous reading of something moral whereon to ruminate in the intervals of sleep. But whether I retire to bed early or late I am up with the sun.—To Doctor Vine Utley. vii, 117. Ford ed., x, 126. (M., 1819.)

7993. SMALL (William), Guide and friend.—Dr. Small was * * * to me as a father. To his enlightened and affectionate guidance of my studies while at college, I am indebted for everything. He was Professor of Mathematics at William and Mary, and, for some time, was in the philosophical chair. He first introduced into both schools rational and elevated courses of study, and, from an extraordinary conjunction of eloquence and logic, was enabled to communicate them to the students with great effect. He procured for me

the patronage of Mr. Wythe, and both of them the attentions of Governor Fauquier, the ablest man who ever filled the chair of government here. They were inseparable friends, and at their frequent dinners with the Governor (after his family had returned to England), he admitted me always, to make it a *partie quarree*. At these dinners I have heard more good sense, more rational and philosophical conversation, than in all my life besides. They were truly Attic societies. The Governor was musical, also, and a good performer, and associated me with two or three other amateurs in his weekly concerts. He merits honorable mention in your history if any proper occasion offers.—To Mr. Girardin. vi, 411. (M., 1815.)

7994. SMALL (William), Jefferson's early companion.—It was my great good fortune, and what probably fixed the destinies of my life, that Dr. William Small of Scotland, was then (1760) professor of mathematics [in William and Mary College], a man profound in most of the useful branches of science, with a happy talent of communication, correct and gentlemanly manners, and an enlarged and liberal mind. He, most happily for me, became soon attached to me, and made me his daily companion when not engaged in the school; and from his conversation, I got my first views of the expansion of science, and of the system of things in which we are placed.—Autobiography. i, 2. Ford ed., i, 4. (1821.)

— SMITH (Adam).—See Government, Works on.

7995. SMITH (John), Services to Virginia.—Captain Smith, who next to Sir Walter Raleigh may be considered as the founder of our Colony, has written its history. He was a member of the council, and afterwards president of the Colony; and to his efforts principally may be ascribed its support against the opposition of the natives. He was honest, sensible, and well informed; but his style is barbarous and uncouth. His history, however, is almost the only source from which we derive any knowledge of the infancy of our State.—Notes on Virginia. vii, 415. Ford ed., iii, 281. (1782.)

7996. SMITH (Robert), Estimate of.—I have seen with very great concern the late address of Mr. [Robert] Smith to the public. He has been very ill-advised, both personally and publicly. As far as I can judge from what I hear, the impression made is entirely unfavorable to him.—To President Madison. v, 600. Ford ed., ix, 325. (M., 1811.)

7997. SMITH (Samuel), Tender of office.—If you can be added to the Administration I am forming it will constitute a magistracy entirely possessed of the public confidence. * * * You will bring us the benefit of adding in a considerable degree the acquiescence, at least, of the leaders who have hitherto opposed. Your geographical situation [Maryland], too, is peculiarly advantageous, and will favor the policy of drawing our naval resources towards the States from which their benefits and production may be extended equally to all parts. * * * If you refuse, I must abandon from necessity, what I have been so falsely charged with doing from choice, the expectation of procuring to our country such benefits as may compensate the expenses of their navy.—To General Samuel Smith. Ford ed., viii, 13. (W., March 1801.)

7998. SMITH (William S.), Character of.—I learn that Mr. Adams desires to be recalled, and that Smith should be appo nted Chargé des Affaires there. * * * You can judge of Smith's abilities by his letters. They are not of the first order, but they are good. For his honesty, he is like our friend Monroe; turn his soul wrong side outwards, and there is not a speck on it. He has one foible, an excessive inflammability of temper, but he feels it when it comes on, and has resolution enough to suppress it, and to remain silent till it passes over.—To James Madison. ii, 110. Ford ed., iv, 368. (P., 1787.)

7999. SMUGGLING, Temptations to.—Contraband does not increase on lessening the temptations to it.—To Count de Vergennes. i, 389. (P., 1785.)

8000. SNAKES, Antipathy to.—There 's in man as well as in brutes an antipathy to the snake, which makes it a disgusting object wherever it is presented.—To Governor Henry Lee. Ford ed., vi, 320. (Pa., 1793.)

8001. SOCIAL INTERCOURSE, Contentment and.—Without society, and a society to our taste, men are never contented.—To James Monroe. ii, 71. (P., 1786.) See Society.

8002. SOCIAL INTERCOURSE, Harmony and.—If we can once more get social intercourse restored to its pristine harmony, I shall believe we have not lived in vain.—To Thomas Lomax. iv, 361. Ford ed., vii, 500. (W., Feb. 1801.)

8003. SOCIAL INTERCOURSE, Opinions and.—Opinions, which are equally honest on both sides, should not affect personal esteem or social intercourse.—To John Adams. vi, 146. (M., 1813.)

8004. SOCIAL INTERCOURSE, Politics and.—A difference in politics should never be permitted to enter into social intercourse, or to disturb its friendships, its charities or justice.—To H. Lee. vii, 376. Ford ed., x, 317. (M., 1824.)

8005. SOCIETIES (Communal), Experiments.—A society of seventy families, the number you name, may very possibly be governed as a single family, subsisting on their common industry, and holding all things in common. Some regulators of the family you still must have, and it remains to be seen at what period of your increasing population your simple regulations will cease to be sufficient to preserve order, peace, and justice. The experiment is interesting; I shall not live to see its issue, but I wish it success equal to your hopes.—To William Ludlow. vii, 378. (M., 1824.)

8006. SOCIETIES (Communal), Practicability.—That, on the principle of a communion of property, small societies may exist in habits of virtue, order, industry, and peace, and consequently in a state of as much happiness as heaven has been pleased to deal out to imperfect humanity, I can readily conceive, and, indeed, have seen its proofs in various small societies which have been constituted on that principle. But I do not feel authorized to conclude from these that an extended society, like that of the United States, or of an individual State, could be governed happily on the same principle. I look to the diffusion of light and education as the resource most to be

relied on for ameliorating the condition, promoting the v rtue, and advancing the happiness of man.—To C. C. Blatchly. vii, 263. (M., 1822.)

— SOCIETIES (Democratic).—See Democratic Societies.

8007. SOCIETIES (Scientific), Peaceful.—These [scientific] societies are always in peace, however their nations may be at war. Like the republic of letters, they form a great fraternity spreading over the whole earth, and their correspondence is never interrupted by any civilized nation.—To John Hollins. v, 428. (W., 1809.)

8008. SOCIETIES (Secret), Dangerous.—I acknowledge the right of voluntary associations for laudable purposes and in moderate numbers. I acknowledge, too, the expediency, for revolutionary purposes, of general associations, coextensive with the nation. But where, as in our case, no abuses call for revolution, voluntary associations so extensive as to grapple with and control the government, should such be or become their purpose, are dangerous machines, and should be frowned down in every well regulated government.—To James Madison. Ford ed., x, 207. (M., 1822.)

8009. SOCIETIES (Secret), Government and.—As revolutionary instruments (when nothing but revolution will cure the evils of the State) they [secret societies] are necessary and indispensable, and the right to use them is inalienable by the people; but to admit them as ordinary and habitual instruments as a part of the machinery of the Constitution, would be to change that machinery by introducing moving powers foreign to it, and to an extent depending solely on local views, and, therefore, incalculable. *—To William Duane. Ford ed., viii, 256. (M., 1803.) See Democratic Societies.

8010. SOCIETY, American.—In America, * * * the society of your husband, the fond cares of the children, the arrangements of the house, the improvements of the grounds, fill every moment with a healthy and an useful activity. Every exertion is encouraging, because, to present amusement, it joins the promise of some future good. The intervals of leisure are filled by the society of real friends, whose affections are not th nned to cob-web by being spread over a thousand objects. This is the picture, in the light it 's presented to my mind.—To Mrs. Bingham. ii, 117. (P., 1787.)

8011. SOCIETY, Jefferson's choice.—I have changed my circle here [Philadelphia] according to my wish, abandoning the rich and declining their dinners and parties, and associating entirely with the class of science, of whom there is a valuable society here.—To Martha Jefferson Randolph. D. L. J. 262. (Pa., 1800.)

8012. SOCIETY, Majority rule.—The fundamental law of every society [is] the *lex majoris partis*, to which we are bound to submit.—To David Humphreys. iii, 13. Ford ed., v, 90. (P., 1789.)

8013. SOCIETY, Necessity for.—I am convinced our own happiness requires that we should continue to m x with the world, and to keep pace with it as it goes; and that every

* A political committee of Philadelphia had sent a communication to Jefferson on the subject of removals from office.—Editor.

person who retires from free communication with it is severely punished afterwards by the state of mind into which he gets, and which can only be prevented by feeding our sociable principles. I can speak from experience on this subject. From 1793 to 1797, I remained closely at home, saw none but those who came there, and at length became very sensible of the ill effect it had on my own mind, and of its direct and irresistible tendency to render me unfit for society and uneasy when necessarily engaged in it. I felt enough of the effect of withdrawing from the world then to see that it led to an anti-social and misanthropic state of mind, which severely punishes him who gives in to it; and it will be a lesson I never shall forget as to myself.—To MARY JEFFERSON EPPES. D. L. J. 284. (W., March 1802.) See SOCIAL INTERCOURSE.

8014. SOCIETY, Parisian.—To what does the bustle of Paris tend? At eleven o'clock, it is day, *chez madame*. The curtains are drawn. Propped on bolsters and pillows, and her head scratched into a little order, the bulletins of the sick are read, and the billets of the well. She writes to some of her acquaintance, and receives the visits of others. If the morning is not very thronged, she is able to get out and hobble round the cage of the Palais Royal; but she must hobble quickly, for the *coiffeur's* turn is come; and a tremendous turn it is! Happy, if he does not make her arrive when dinner is half over! The torpitude of digestion a little passed, she flutters half an hour through the streets, by way of paying visits, and then to the spectacles. These finished, another half hour is devoted to dodging in and out of the doors of her every sincere friends, and away to supper. After supper, cards; and after cards, bed; to rise at noon the next day, and to tread, like a mill horse, the same trodden circle over again. Thus the days of life are consumed, one by one, without an object beyond the present moment; ever flying from the ennui of that, yet carrying it with us; eternally in pursuit of happiness, which keeps eternally before us. If death or bankruptcy happen to trip us out of the circle, it is matter for the buzz of the evening, and is completely forgotten by the next morning.—To MRS. BINGHAM. ii, 116. (P., 1787.)

— SOCIETY OF THE CINCINNATI.— See CINCINNATI SOCIETY.

8015. SOCRATES, Dæmon of.—An expression in your letter * * * that "the human understanding is a revelation from its Maker", gives the best solution that I believe can be given of the question, "what did Socrates mean by his Dæmon"? He was too wise to believe, and too honest to pretend that he had real and familiar converse with a superior and invisible being. He probably considered the suggestions of his conscience, or reason, as revelations, or inspirations from the Supreme Mind, bestowed, on important occasions, by a special superintending Providence.—To JOHN ADAMS. vi, 220. (M., 1813.)

8016. SOCRATES, Plato and.—The superlative wisdom of Socrates is testified by all antiquity, and placed on ground not to be questioned. When, therefore, Plato puts into his mouth such paralogisms, such quibbles on words, and sophisms as a schoolboy would be ashamed of, we conclude they were the whimsies of Plato's own foggy brain, and acquit Socrates of puerilities so unlike his character.—To WILLIAM SHORT. vii, 165. (M., 1820.) See PHILOSOPHY.

8017. SOLITUDE, Philosophy and.— Let the gloomy monk, sequestered from the world, seek unsocial pleasures in the bottom of his cell! Let the sublimated philosopher grasp visionary happiness, while pursuing phantoms dressed in the garb of truth! Their supreme wisdom is supreme folly; and they mistake for happiness the mere absence of pain. Had they ever felt the solid pleasure of one generous spasm of the heart, they would exchange for it all the frigid speculations of their lives.—To MRS. COSWAY. ii, 39. FORD ED., iv. 319. (P., 1786.)

8018. SOULS, Transmigration of.—It is not for me to pronounce on the hypothesis you present of a transmigration of souls from one body to another in certain cases. The laws of nature have withheld from us the means of physical knowledge of the country of spirits, and revelation has, for reasons unknown to us, chosen to leave us in the dark as we were. When I was young I was fond of the speculations which seemed to promise some insight into that hidden country, but observing at length that they left me in the same ignorance in which they had found me, I have for very many years ceased to read or to think concerning them, and have reposed my head on that pillow of ignorance which a benevolent Creator has made so soft for us, knowing how much we should be forced to use it. I have thought it better, by nourishing the good passions and controlling the bad, to merit an inheritance in a state of being of which I can know so little, and to trust for the future to Him who has been so good for the past.—To REV. ISAAC STORY. iv, 422. FORD ED., vii, 107. (W., 1801.) See IMMORTALITY.

8019. SOUTH AMERICA, Revolt in.— I enter into all your doubts as to the event of the revolution of South America. They will succeed against Spain. But the dangerous enemy is within their own breasts. Ignorance and superstition will chain their minds and bodies under religious and military despotism. I do believe it would be better for them to obtain freedom by degrees only; because that would by degrees bring on light and information, and qualify them to take charge of themselves understandingly; with more certainty, if in the meantime, under so much control as may keep them at peace with one another. Surely, it is our duty to wish them independence and self-government, because they wish it themselves, and they have the right, and we none, to choose for themselves; and I wish, moreover, that our ideas may be erroneous and theirs prove well-founded. But these are speculations which we may as well deliver over to those who are to see their development.—To JOHN ADAMS. vii, 104. FORD ED., x, 108. (M., 1818.) See SPANISH AMERICA.

8020. SOUTH CAROLINA, Fidelity.— The steady union of our fellow citizens of South Carolina is entirely in their character. They have never failed in fidelity to their country and the republican spirit of its Constitution.—To MR. LETUE. v, 384. (W., 1808.)

8021. SOUTH CAROLINA, Free government and.—I see with pleasure another proof that South Carolina is ever true to the principles of free government.—To HENRY MIDDLETON. vi, 91. (M., Jan. 1813.)

8022. SOVEREIGNTY, Infringement. —The granting military commissions within the United States by any other authority than their own, is an infringement on their sovercignty, and particularly so when granted to their own citizens to lead them to acts contrary to the duties they owe their own country.—To EDMOND CHARLES GENET. iii, 572. FORD ED., vi, 283. (Pa., June 1793.)

8023. —— ——. Mr. Hammond says the issuing the commission [to the Citoyen Genet] by M. Genet, within our territory, was an infringement of our sovereignty; therefore, the proceeds of it should be given up to Great Britain. The infringement was a matter between France and us. Had we insisted on any penalty or forfeiture by way of satisfaction to our insulted rights. it would have belonged to us, not to a third party. As between Great Britain and us, * * * we deemed we did enough to satisfy her.— To THOMAS PINCKNEY. iii. 583. FORD ED., vi, 302. (Pa., June 1793.)

8024. SOVEREIGNTY, Justice and.— The administration of justice is a branch of the sovereignty over a country, and belongs exclusively to the nation inhabiting it. No foreign power can pretend to participate in their jurisdiction, or that their citizens received there are not subject to it.—To GEORGE HAMMOND. iii, 415. FORD ED., vi, 56. (Pa., 1792.)

8025. SOVEREIGNTY, Partition of.—I see with great pleasure every testimony to the principles of pure republicanism; and every effort to preserve untouched that partition of the sovereignty which our excellent Constitution has made between the general and particular governments.—To JAMES SULLIVAN. FORD ED., v, 369. (Pa., 1791.)

8026. SPAIN, Bonaparte and.—I suppose Napoleon will get possession of Spain; but her colonies will deliver themselves to any member of the Bourbon family. Perhaps Mexico will choose its sovereign within itself. He will find them much more difficult to subdue than Austria or Prussia; because an enemy (even in peace an enemy) possesses the element over which he is to pass to get at them; and a more powerful enemy (climate) will soon mow down his armies after arrival. This will be, without any doubt, the most difficult enterprise the Emperor has ever undertaken. He may subdue the small colonies; he never can the old and strong; and the former will break off from him the first war he has again with a naval power.—To GENERAL ARMSTRONG. v, 434. (W., March 1809.)

8027. SPAIN, Common interests.—It may happen * * * that the interests of Spain and America may call for a concert of proceedings against that State (Algiers). * * * May not the affairs of the Mosquito coast, and our western posts, produce another instance of a common interest? Indeed, I meet this correspondence of interest in so many quarters, that I look with anxiety to the issue of Mr. Gardoqui's mission, hoping it will be a removal of the only difficulty at present subsisting between the two nations, or which is likely to arise.—To WILLIAM CARMICHAEL. i, 393. (P., 1785.)

8028. SPAIN, Conciliation of.—We consider Spain's possession of the adjacent country as most favorable to our interests, and should see with extreme pain any other nation substituted for them. In all communications, therefore, with their officers, conciliation and mutual accommodation are to be mainly attended to. Everything irritating to be avoided, everything friendly to be done for them.—To WILLIAM C. CLAIBORNE. FORD ED., viii, 71. (W., July 1801.)

8029. SPAIN, English alliance against. —I think you have misconceived the nature of the treaty I thought we should propose to England. I have no idea of committing ourselves immediately or independently of our further will to the war. The treaty should be provisional only, to come into force on the event of our being engaged in war with either France or Spain during the present war in Europe. In that event we should make common cause, and England should stipulate not to make peace without our obtaining the objects for which we go. to war, to wit, the acknowledgment by Spain of the rightful boundaries of Louisiana (which we should reduce to our minimum by a second article) and 2, indemnification for spoliations, for which purpose we should be allowed to make reprisal on the Floridas and *retain them* as an indemnification. Our cooperation in the war (if we should really enter into it) would be sufficient consideration for Great Britain to engage for its object; and it being generally known to France and Spain that we had entered into treaty with England, would probably ensure us a peaceable and immediate settlement of both points. But another motive much more powerful would indubitably induce England to go much further. Whatever ill-humor may at times have been expressed against us by individuals of that country, the first wish of every Englishman's heart is to see us once more fighting by their sides against France; nor could the King or his ministers do an act so popular as to enter into an alliance with us. The nation would not weigh the consideration by grains and scruples. They would consider it as the price and pledge of an indissoluble friendship. I think it possible that for such a provisional treaty they would give us their general guarantee of Louisiana and the Floridas. At any rate we might try them. A failure would not make our situation worse. If such a one could be obtained, we might await our convenience for calling up the *casus fœderis.* I think it important that England should receive an overture as early as possible. as it might prevent her listening to terms of peace. If I recollect rightly, we had instructed Monroe, when he went to Paris, to settle the deposit; if he failed in that object to propose a treaty to England immediately. We could not be more engaged to secure the deposit than we are the country now, after paying fifteen millions for it. I do expect, therefore, that. considering the present state of things as analogous to that, and virtually within his instructions, he will very likely make the proposition to England.—To JAMES MADISON. iv, 585. FORD ED., viii, 377. (M., Aug. 1805.)

8030. —— ——. A letter from Charles Pinckney of May 22 [1805], informs me that Spain refuses to settle a limit, and perseveres in withholding the ratification of the convention. He says not a word of the *status quo,* from which I conclude it has not been proposed. * * * I think the *status quo,* if not already proposed, should be immediately offered through Bowdoin. Should it even be refused, the refusal to settle a limit is not of itself a sufficient cause of war, nor is the withholding a ratification worthy of such a redress. Yet these acts show a purpose both in Spain and France which we ought to provide before the conclusion of a peace. I think, therefore, we should take into consideration whether we ought not immediately to propose to England an eventual treaty of alliance, to come into force whenever (within — years) a war shall take place with Spain or France. It may be proper for the ensuing Congress to make some preparations for such an event, and it should be in our power to show we have done the same.—To JAMES MADISON. FORD ED., viii, 374. (M., Aug. 1805.)

8031. —— ——. On a view of our affairs with Spain, * * * I wrote you * * * that I thought we should offer them the *status quo*, but immediately propose provisional alliance with England. I have not yet received the whole correspondence. But the portion of the papers now enclosed to you, confirm me in the expediency of a treaty with England, but make the offer of the *status quo* more doubtful. * * * From the papers already received I infer a confident reliance on the part of Spain on the omnipotence of Bonaparte, but a desire of procrastination till peace in Europe shall leave us without an ally.—To JAMES MADISON. iv, 583. FORD ED., viii, 375. (M., Aug. 1805.)

8032. SPAIN, Friendship with.—Under an intimate conviction of long standing in my mind, of the importance of an honest friendship with Spain, and one which shall identify her American interests with our own, I see in a strong point of view the necessity that the organ of communication which we establish near the King should possess the favor and confidence of that government. I have, therefore, destined for that mission a person whose accommodating and reasonable conduct, which will be still more fortified by instructions, will render him agreeable there, and an useful channel of communication between us. I have no doubt the new appointment by that government to this, in the room of the Chevalier d'Yrujo, has been made under the influence of the same motives.—To DON JOSEPH YZNARDI. iv, 385. FORD ED., viii, 33. (W., March 1801.)

8033. —— ——. The Chevalier d'Yrujo being intimately known to us, the integrity, sincerity, and reasonableness of his conduct having established in us a perfect confidence, in nowise diminished by the bickerings which took place between him and a former Secretary of State [Pickering], whose irritable temper drew on more than one affair of the same kind, it will be a subject of great regret if we lose him. However, if the interests of Spain require that his services should be employed elsewhere, it is the duty of a friend to acquiesce; and we shall certainly receive any successor the King may choose to send, with every possible degree of favor and friendship.—To DON JOSEPH YZNARDI. iv, 385. FORD ED., viii, 33. (W., March 1801.)

8034. SPAIN, Good faith towards.—No better proof of the good faith of the United States could have been given, than the vigor with which we have acted, and the expense incurred, in suppressing the enterprise meditated lately by Burr against Mexico. Although at first he proposed a separation of the Western country, and on that ground received encouragement and aid from Yrujo, according to the usual spirit of his government towards us, yet he very early saw that the fidelity of the Western country was not to be shaken, and turned himself wholly towards Mexico. And so popular is an enterprise on that country in this, that we had only to be still, and he would

have had followers enough to have been in the city of Mexico in six weeks.—To JAMES BOWDOIN. v, 64. FORD ED., ix, 41. (W., April 1807.)

8035. SPAIN, Good offices of.—I see with extreme satisfaction and gratitude the friendly interposition of the court of Spain with the Emperor of Morocco on the subject of the brig Betsey, and I am persuaded it will produce the happiest effects in America. Those, who are intrusted with the public affairs there, are sufficiently sensible how essential it is for our interest to cultivate peace with Spain, and they will be pleased to see a corresponding disposition in that court. The late good office of emancipating a number of our countrymen from slavery is peculiarly calculated to produce a sensation among our people, and to dispose them to relish and adopt the pacific and friendly views of their leaders towards Spain.—To W. CARMICHAEL. i, 392. (P., 1785.)

8036. SPAIN, Government of.—If anything thrasonic and foolish from Spain could add to my contempt of that government, it would be the demand of satisfaction now made by Foronda. However, respect to ourselves requires that the answer should be decent, and I think it fortunate that this opportunity is given to make a strong declaration of facts, to wit, how far our knowledge of Miranda's objects went, what measures we took to prevent anything further, the negligence of the Spanish agents to give us earlier notice, the measures we took for punishing those guilty, and our quiet abandonment of those taken by the Spaniards.—To JAMES MADISON. v, 164. FORD ED., ix, 124. (M., Aug. 1807.) See MIRANDA EXPEDITION.

8037. SPAIN, Honest, but unwise.—Spain is honest if it is not wise.—To JOHN ADAMS. FORD ED., iv, 295. (P., 1786.)

8038. SPAIN, Hostility of.—Our relations with Spain are vitally interesting. That they should be of a peaceable and friendly character has been our most earnest desire. Had Spain met us with the same dispositions, our idea was that her existence in this hemisphere and ours should have rested on the same bottom; should have swam or sunk together. We want nothing of hers, and we want no other nation to possess what is hers. But she has met our advances with jealousy, secret malice and ill-faith. Our patience under this unworthy return of disposition is now on its last trial. And the issue of what is now depending between us will decide whether our relations with her are to be sincerely friendly, or permanently hostile. I still wish and would cherish the former, but have ceased to expect it.—To JAMES BOWDOIN. FORD ED., viii, 351. (W., April 1805.)

8039. SPAIN, Incitement of Indians.—With respect to the treaties, the speech and the letter, you will see that they undertake to espouse the concerns of Indians within our limits; to be mediators of boundary between them and us; to guarantee that boundary to them; to support them with their whole power; and hazard to us intimations of acquiescence to avoid disagreeable results. They even propose to extend their intermeddlings to the northern Indians. These are pretensions so totally inconsistent with the usages established among the white nations, with respect to Indians living within their several limits, that it is believed no example of them can be produced, in times of peace; and they are presented to us in a manner wh'ch we cannot deem friendly.—To CARMICHAEL AND SHORT. iii, 366. FORD ED., vi, 272. (Pa., May 1793.)

8040. ———— ————. The papers communicated you [in October and November, 1792] made it evident that the Baron de Carondelet, the Governor of New Orleans, had industriously excited the southern Indians to war against us, and furnished them with arms and ammunition in abundance, for that express purpose. We placed this under the view of the commiss'oners of Spain here, who undertook to communicate it to their court, and also to write on the subject to the Baron de Carondelet. They have lately made us communications from both these quarters; the aspect of which, however, is by no means such as to remove the causes of our dissatisfaction. I send you these communications, consisting of treaties between Spain, the Creeks, Choctaws, Chickasaws, and Cherokees, handed us by express order from their court, a speech of Baron de Carondelet to the Cherokees, and a letter from Messrs. de Viar and Jaudenes, covering that speech, and containing in itself very serious matter. I will first observe to you, that the question stated in that letter, to have been proposed to the Cherokees, what part they would take, in the event of a war between the United States and Spain? was never proposed by authority from this government. Its instructions to its agents have, on the contrary, been explicitly to cultivate, with good faith, the peace between Spain and the Indians; and from the known prudence and good conduct of Governor Blount, to whom it is imputed, it is not believed to have been proposed by him. This proposition, then, you are authorized to disavow to the court of Madrid, in the most unequivocal terms.—To CARMICHAEL AND SHORT. iii, 566. FORD ED., vi, 271. (Pa., May 1793.)

8041. ———— ————. The consequence is that the Indians, and particularly the Creeks, finding themselves so encouraged, have passed, without the least provocation on our part, from a state of peace, which appeared to be well settled, to that of serious hostility. Their murders and depredations, which, for some months we were willing to hope were only individual aggressions, now assume the appearance of unequivocal war. Yet, such is our desire of courting and cultivating the peace of all our Indian neighbors, that instead of marching at once into their country, and taking satisfaction ourselves, we are peaceably requiring punishment of the individual aggressors; and, in the meantime, are holding ourselves entirely on the defensive. But this state of things cannot continue. Our citizens are entitled to effectual protection, and defensive measures are, at the same time, the most expensive and least effectual. If we find, then, that peace cannot be obtained by the temperate means we are still pursuing, we must proceed to those which are extreme, and meet all the consequences, of whatever nature. or from whatever quarter they may be.—To CARMICHAEL AND SHORT. iii, 567. FORD ED., vi, 272. (Pa., May 1793.)

8042. ———— ————. We have certainly been always desirous to avoid whatever might disturb our harmony with Spa'n. We should be st'll more so, at a moment when we see that nation making part of so powerful a confederacy as is formed in Europe, and under particular good understanding with England, our other neighbor. In so delicate a position, therefore, instead of expressing our sense of these things, by way of answer to Messrs. Viar and Jaudenes, the President has thought it better that

it should be done to you, and to trust to your discretion the moment, the measure, and the form of communicating it to the Court of Madrid. The actual state of Europe at the time you will receive this, the solidity of the confederacy, and especially, as between Spain and England, the temper and views of the former, or of both, towards us, the state of your negotiation, are circumstances which will enable you better to decide how far it may be necessary to soften, or even, perhaps, to suppress, the expressions of our sentiments on this subject. To your discretion, therefore, it is committed by the President, to let the Court of Spain see how impossible it 's for us to submit with folded arms, to be butchered by these savages, and to prepare them to view, with a just eye, the more vigorous measures we must pursue to put an end to their atrocities, if the moderate ones we are now taking, should fail of that effect.—To CARMICHAEL AND SHORT. iii, 567. FORD ED., vi, 272. (Pa., May 1793.)

8043. SPAIN, Invasion of.—The invasion of Spain has been the most unprecedented and unprincipled of the transactions of modern times. The crimes of its enemies, the licentiousness of its associates in defence, the exertions and sufferings of its inhabitants under slaughter and famine, and its consequent depopulation, will mark indelibly the baneful ascendency of the tyrants of the sea and continent, and characterize with blood and wretchedness the age in which they have lived.—To LE CHEVALIER DE ONIS. vi, 341. (M., 1814.)

8044. SPAIN, Loss of colonies.—I hail your country as now likely to resume and surpass its ancient splendor among nations. This might perhaps have been better secured by a just confidence in the self-sufficient strength of the peninsula itself; everything without its limits being its weakness, not its force.—To CHEVALIER DE ONIS. vi, 342. (M., April 1814.)

8045. SPAIN, Peace with.—Spain is so evidently *picking a quarrel* with us, that we see a war absolutely inevitable with her. We are making a last effort to avoid it.—To JAMES MONROE. iv, 6. FORD ED., vi, 322. (June 1793.)

8046. ———— ————. We are sending a courier to Madrid to make a last effort for the preservation of honorable peace.—To JAMES MADISON. iv, 8. FORD ED., vi, 325. (June 1793.)

8047. SPAIN, Perfidy of.—Never did a nation act towards another with more perfidy and injustice than Spain has constantly practiced against us; and if we have kept our hands off her till now, it has been purely out of respect to France, and from the value we set on the friendship of France. We expect, therefore, from the friendship of the Emperor, that he will either compel Spain to do us justice, or abandon her to us. We ask but one month to be in possession of the city of Mexico.—To JAMES BOWDOIN. v, 64. FORD ED., ix, 40. (W., April 1807.)

8048. SPAIN, Reprisal on.—While war with England is probable, everything leading to it with every other nation should be avoided, except Spain. As to her, I think it the precise moment when we should declare to the French government that we will instantly seize on the Floridas as reprisal for the spoliations denied us, and that if by a given day they are paid to us, we will restore all east of the Perdido, and hold the rest subject to amicable decision.

Otherwise, we will hold them forever as a compensation for the spoliations.—To JAMES MADISON. v, 181. FORD ED., ix, 134. (M., Sep. 1807.)

8049. SPAIN, Republicanism in.— The spirit of the Spaniard, and his deadly and eternal hatred to a Frenchman, give me much confidence that he will never submit, but finally defeat this atrocious violation of the laws of God and man, under which he is suffering; and the wisdom and firmness of the Cortes afford reasonable hope that that nation will settle down in a temperate representative government, with an executive properly subordinated to that.—To JOHN ADAMS. vii, 308. FORD ED., x, 270. (M., 1823.)

8050. SPAIN, Spanish America and.— The most advantageous relation in which Spain can stand with her American colonies is that of independent friendship, secured by the ties of consanguinity, sameness of language, religion, manners, and habits, and certain from the influence of these, of a preference in her commerce, if, instead of the eternal irritations, thwartings, machinations against their new governments, the insults and aggressions which Great Britain has so unwisely practiced towards us, to force us to hate her against our natural inclinations, Spain yields. like a genuine parent, to the forisfamiliation of her colonies, now at maturity, if she extends to them her affections, her aid, her patronage in every court and country, it will weave a bond of union indissoluble by time.—To DON V. DE TORONDA CORUNA. vi, 274. (M., Dec. 1813.)

8051. ——— ———. That Spain's divorce from its American colonies, which is now unavoidable, will be a great blessing, it is impossible not to pronounce on a review of what she was when she acquired them, and of her gradual descent from that proud eminence to the condition in which her present war found her. Nature has formed that peninsula to be the second, and why not the first nation in Europe? Give equal habits of energy to the bodies, and of science to the minds of her citizens, and where could her superior be found?—To DON V. DE TORONDA CORUNA. vi, 274. (M., Dec. 1813.)

8052. SPAIN, Spoliations and boundaries.— With Spain our negotiations for a settlement of differences have not had a satisfactory issue. Spoliations during the former war, for which she had formally acknowledged herself responsible, have been refused to be compensated, but on conditions affecting other claims in nowise connected with them. Yet the same practices are renewed in the present war, and are already of great amount. On the Mobile, our commerce passing through that river continues to be obstructed by arbitrary duties and vexatious searches. Propositions for adjusting amicably the boundaries of Louisiana have not been acceded to. While, however. the right is unsettled, we have avoided changing the state of things. by taking new posts, or strengthening ourselves in the disputed territories, in the hope that the other power would not, by a contrary conduct. oblige us to meet their example, and endanger conflicts of authority, the issue of which may not be entirely controlled. But in this hope we have now reason to lessen our confidence. Inroads have been recently made into the territories of Orleans and the Mississippi, our citizens have been seized and their property plundered in the very parts of the former which had been actually delivered up by Spain. and this by the regular officers and soldiers of that government. I have, therefore, found it necessary at length to give orders to our troops on that frontier to be in readiness to protect our citizens, and to repel by arms any similar aggressions in future.—FIFTH ANNUAL MESSAGE. viii, 48. FORD ED., viii, 390. (Dec. 3, 1805.)

8053. ——— ———. The depredations which had been committed on the commerce of the United States during a preceding war, by persons under the authority of Spain * * * made it a duty to require from that government indemnifications for our injured citizens. A convention was accordingly entered into * * * by which it was agreed that spoliations committed by Spanish subjects and carried into ports of Spain should be paid for by that nation; and that those committed by French subjects, and carried into Spanish ports should remain for further discussion. Before this convention was returned to Spain with our ratification, the transfer of Louisiana by France to the United States took place, an event as unexpected as disagreeable to Spain. From that moment she seemed to change her conduct and dispositions towards us. It was first manifested by her protest against the right of France to alienate Louisiana to us, which however was soon retracted, and the right confirmed. Then, high offence was manifested at the act of Congress establishing a collection district on the Mobile, although by an authentic declaration immediately made, it was expressly confined to our acknowledged limits. And she now refused to ratify the convention signed by her own minister under the eye of his sovereign, unless we would relinquish all consent to alterations of its terms which would have affected our claims against her for the spoliations by French subjects carried into Spanish ports. To obtain justice, as well as to restore friendship, I thought a special mission advisable, and accordingly appointed James Monroe, Minister Extraordinary and Plenipotentiary, to repair to Madrid, and in conjunction with our Minister Resident there, to endeavor to procure a ratification of the former convention and to come to an understanding with Spain as to the boundaries of Louisiana. It appeared at once that her policy was to reserve herself for events, and in the meantime to keep our differences in an undetermined state. This will be evident from the papers now communicated to you. After nearly five months of fruitless endeavor to bring them to some definite and satisfactory result our ministers ended the conferences without having been able to obtain indemnity for spoliations of any description, or any satisfaction as to the boundaries of Louisiana, other than a declaration that we had no rights eastward of the Iberville, and that our line to the west was one which would have left us but a string of land on that bank of the river Mississippi. Our injured citizens were thus left without any prospect of retribution from the wrongdoer; and as to the boundary each party was to take its own course. That which they have chosen to pursue will appear from the documents now communicated. They authorize the inference that it is their intention to advance on our possessions until they shall be repressed by an opposing force. Considering that Congress alone is constitutionally invested with the power of changing our condition from peace to war, I have thought it my duty to await their authority for using force in any degree which could be avoided. I have barely instructed the officers stationed in the neighborhood of the aggressions to protect our citizens from violence, to patrol within the borders actually delivered to us, and not to go out of them but when necessary to repel an inroad, or to rescue a citizen or his property. —Confidential Message. Ford ed., viii, 397. (Dec. 6, 1805.)

8054. —— ——. With Spain we are making a last effort at peaceable accommodation. The subject is merely a settlement of the limits of Louisiana, and our right of passing down the rivers of Florida. This negotiation is to be held at Paris, where we may have the benefit of the good offices of France, but she will be no party to the contract.—To Thomas Paine. Ford ed., viii, 436. (W., March 1806.)

8055. —— ——. Notwithstanding the efforts made here, and made professedly to assassinate the negotiation in embryo, if the good sense of Bonaparte should prevail over his temper, the present state of things in Europe may induce him to require of Spain that she should do us justice at least. That he should require her to sell us East Florida, we have no right to insist; yet there are not wanting considerations which may induce him to wish a permanent foundation for peace laid between us.—To Mr. Bidwell. v, 15. (W., July 1806.)

8056. —— ——. It is grossly false that our ministers * * * had proposed to surrender our claims to compensation for Spanish spoliations, or even for French. Their instructions were to make no treaty in which Spanish spoliations were not provided for; and although they were permitted to be silent as to French spoliations carried into Spanish ports, they were not expressly to abandon even them.— To W. A. Burwell. v, 20. Ford ed., viii, 469. (M., Sep. 1806.)

8057. —— ——. Our affairs with Spain laid dormant during the absence of Bonaparte from Paris, because we know Spain would do nothing towards settling them, but by compulsion. Immediately on his return, our terms were stated to him, and his interposition obtained. If it was with good faith, its effect will be instantaneous; if not with good faith, we shall discover it by affected delays, and must decide accordingly.—To William Short. v, 211. (W., Nov. 1807.)

8058. SPAIN, Treaty with.—Some fear our envelopment in the wars engendering from the unsettled state of our affairs with Spain, and therefore are anxious for a ratification of our treaty with her. I fear no such thing, and hope that if rat'fied by Spain, it will be rejected here. We may justly say to Spain, " When this negotiation commenced, twenty years ago, your authority was acknowledged by those you are selling to us. That authority is now renounced, and their right of self-disposal asserted. In buying them from you, then, we buy but a war-title, a right to subdue them, which you can neither convey nor we acquire. This is a family quarrel, in which we have no right to meddle. Settle it between yourselves, and we will then treat with the party whose right is acknowledged ". With whom that will be, no doubt can be entertained. And why should we revolt them by purchasing them as cattle, rather than receiving them as fellow-men? Spain has held off until she sees they are lost to her, and now thinks it better to get something than nothing for them. When she shall see South America equally desperate, she will be wise to sell that also.—To M. de Lafayette. vii, 194. Ford ed., x, 179. (M., Dec. 1820.)

8059. SPAIN, War against.—I had rather have war against Spain than not, if we go to war against England. Our southern defensive force can take the Floridas, volunteers for a Mexican army will flock to our standard, and rich pabulum will be offered to our privateers in the plunder of their commerce and coasts. Probably Cuba would add itself to our confederation.—To James Madison. v, 164. Ford ed., ix, 124. (M., Aug. 1807.) See Florida, Louisiana, Mississippi River Navigation, New Orleans and Spanish America.

8060. SPANISH AMERICA, Aid to.— Every kindness which can be shown the South Americans, every friendly office and aid within the limits of the law of nations, I would extend to them, without fearing Spain or her Swiss auxiliaries. For this is but an assertion of our own independence. But to join in their war, as General Scott proposes, and to which even some members of Congress seem to squint, is what we ought not to do as yet.—To James Monroe. vi, 550. Ford ed., x, 19. (M., Feb. 1816.)

8061. —— ——. That a war is brewing between us and Spain cannot be doubted. When that disposition is matured on both sides, and open rupture can no longer be deferred, then will be the time for our joining the South Americans, and entering into treaties of alliance with them. There will then be but one opinion, at home or abroad, that we shall be justifiable in choosing to have them with us, rather than against us. In the meantime, they will have organized regular governments, and perhaps have formed themselves into one or more confederacies; more than one, I hope, as in single mass they would be a very formidable neighbor. —To James Monroe. vi, 551. Ford ed., x, 19. (M., Feb. 1816.)

8062. —— ——. The Spanish Colonies cannot reasonably expect us to sink ourselves uselessly and even injuriously for them by a quixotic encounter of the whole world in arms. Were it Spain alone I should have no fear. But Russia is said to have seventy ships of the line; France approaching that number, and what should we be in fronting such a force? It is not for the interest of Spanish America that our Republic should be blotted out of the map, and to the rest of the world it would be an act of treason.—To President Monroe. Ford ed., x, 316. (M., July 1824.)

8063. SPANISH AMERICA, Constitution for.—For such a condition of society, the constitution you [Dupont de Nemours] have devised is probably the best imaginable. It is certainly calculated to elicit the best talents; although perhaps not well guarded against the egoism of its functionaries. But that egoism will be light in comparison with the pressure of a military despot and his army of Janizaries. Like Solon to the Athenians, you have given to your Columbians, not the best possible government, but the best they can bear. —To Dupont de Nemours. vi, 592. Ford ed., x, 25. (P.F., 1816.)

8064. SPANISH AMERICA, Ignorance in.—Another great field of political experiment is opening in our neighborhood, in Spanish America. I fear the degrading ignorance into which their priests and kings have sunk them, has disqualified them from the maintenance or even knowledge of their rights, and that much blood may be shed for little improvement in their condition. Should their new rulers honestly lay their shoulders to remove the great obstacles of ignorance, and press the remedes of education and information, they will still be in jeopardy until another generation comes into place, and what may happen in the interval cannot be predicted.—To Dupont de Nemours. v, 584. Ford ed., ix, 322. (M., 1811.)

8065. —— ——. No mortal wishes them more success than I do. But if what I have heard of the ignorance and bigotry of the mass be true, I doubt their capacity to understand and to support a free government; and fear that their emancipation from the foreign tyranny of Spain, will result in a military despotism at home. Palacios may be great; others may be great; but it is the multitude which possess force; and wisdom must yield to that.—To Dupont de Nemours. vi, 592. Ford ed., x, 25. (P.F., 1816.)

8066. SPANISH AMERICA, Independence of.—It is intimated to us, in such a way as to attract our attention, that France means to send a strong force early this spring to offer independence to the Spanish American colonies, beginning with those on the Mississippi and that she will not object to the receiving those on the East side into our confederation. Interesting considerations require that we should keep ourselves free to act in this case according to circumstances, and consequently that you should not, by any clause of treaty, bind us to guarantee any of the Spanish colonies against their own independence; nor indeed against any other nation. For, when we thought we might guarantee Louisiana on their ceding the Floridas to us, we apprehended it would be seized by Great Britain, who would thus completely encircle us with her colonies and fleets. This danger is now removed by the concert between Great Britain and Spain. And the times will soon enough give independence, and consequently free commerce to our neighbors, without our risking the involving ourselves in a war for them.*—To Carmichael and Short. iii, 534. Ford ed., vi, 206. (Pa., March 1793.)

8067. —— ——. On the question of our interest in their independence, were that alone a sufficient motive of action, much may be said on both sides. When they are free, they will drive every article of our produce from every market, by underselling it, and change the condition of our existence, forcing us into other habits and pursuits. We shall indeed, have n exchange some commerce with them, but in what I know not, for we shall have nothing to offer which they cannot raise cheaper; and their separation from Spain seals our everlasting peace with her. On the other hand, so long as they are dependent, Spain, from her jealousy, is our natural enemy, and always in either open or secret hostility with us. These countries, too, in war will be a powerful weight in her scale, and, in peace, totally shut to us. Interest, then, on the whole, would wish their independence, and justice makes the wish a duty. They have a right to be free, and we a right to aid them, as a strong man has a right to assist a weak one assailed by a robber or murderer.—To James Monroe. vi, 550. Ford ed., x, 19. (M., Feb. 1816.)

8068. —— ——. We go with you all lengths in friendly affections to the independ-

*Short and Carmichael were commissioners to negotiate a treaty with Spain. Appended to the extract are the words in President Washington's handwriting: "The above meets the approval of George Washington."—Editor.

ence of South America. But an immediate acknowledgment of it calls up other considerations. We view Europe as covering at present a smothered fire, which may shortly burst forth and produce general conflagration. From this it is our duty to keep aloof. A formal acknowledgment of the independence of her Colonies would involve us with Spain certainly, and perhaps, too, with England, if she thinks that a war would divert her internal troubles. Such a war would hurt us more than it would help our brethren of the South; and our right may be doubted of mortgaging posterity for the expenses of a war in which they will have a right to say their interests were not concerned. —To Destutt Tracy. Ford ed., x, 174. (M., 1820.)

8069. SPANISH AMERICA, Interest in.—However distant we may be, both in condition and dispositions, from taking an active part in any commotions in that country [South America], nature has placed it too near us, to make its movements altogether indifferent to our interests, or to our curiosity.—To John Jay. ii, 145. Ford ed., iv, 385. (Mar. 1787.)

8070. SPANISH AMERICA, Name for. —I wish you had called them the Columbian republics, to distinguish them from our American republics. Theirs would be the more honorable name, and they best entitled to it; for Columbus discovered their continent, but never saw ours.—To Dupont de Nemours. vi, 593. Ford ed., x, 25. (P.F., 1816.)

8071. SPANISH AMERICA, Natural divisions of.—The geography of the [Spanish-American] country seems to indicate three confederacies. 1. What is north of the Isthmus. 2. What is south of it on the Atlantic: and 3. the southern part on the Pacific. In this form, we might be the balancing power.— To James Monroe. vi, 551. Ford ed., x, 20. (M., Feb. 1816.)

8072. SPANISH AMERICA, Relations with Spain.—If the mother country [Spain] has not the magnanimity to part with the colonies in friendship, thereby making them what they would certainly be, her natural and firmest allies, these will emancipate themselves, after exhausting her strength and resources in ineffectual efforts to hold them in subjection. They will be rendered enemies of the mother country, as England has rendered us by an unremitting course of insulting injuries and silly provocations. I do not say this from the impulse of national interest, for I do not know that the United States would find an interest in the independence of neighbor nations, whose produce and commerce would rivalize ours. It could only be that kind of interest which every human being has in the happiness and prosperity of every other. But putting right and reason out of the question, I have no doubt that on calculations of interest alone, it is that of Spain to anticipate voluntarily, and as a matter of grace, the independence of her colonies, which otherwise necessity will force.—To Chevalier de Onis. vi, 342. (M., April 1814.)

8073. SPANISH AMERICA, Revolt of. —Behold another example of man rising in his might and bursting the chains of his oppressor, and in the same hemisphere. Spanish America is all in revolt. The insurgents are triumphant in many of the States, and will be so in all. But there the danger is that the cruel arts of their oppressors have enchained their minds, have kept them in the ignorance of children, and as incapable of self-government as children. If the obstacles of bigotry and priestcraft can be surmounted, we may hope that common sense will suffice to do everything else. God send them a safe deliverance.—To GENERAL KOSCIUSKO. v, 586. (M., 1811.)

8074. —— ——. That they will throw off their European dependence I have no doubt; but in what kind of government their revolution will end I am not so certain. History, I believe, furnishes no example of a priest-ridden people maintaining a free civil government. This marks the lowest grade of ignorance, of which their civil as well as religious leaders will always ava l themselves for their own purposes. The vicinity of New Spain to the United States, and their consequent intercourse, may furnish schools for the higher. and example for the lower classes of their citizens. And Mexico, where we learn from you that men of science are not wanting, may revolutionize itself under better auspices than the Southern provinces. These last, I fear, must end in military despotisms. The different castes of their inhabitants, their mutual hatreds and jealousies, their profound ignorance and bigotry, will be played off by cunning leaders, and each be made the instrument of enslaving others. * * * But in whatever governments they end they will be *American* governments, no longer to be involved in the never-ceasing broils of Europe.—To BARON VON HUMBOLDT. vi, 267. FORD ED., ix, 430. (Dec. 1813.)

8075. SPANISH AMERICA, Self-government and.—The Spanish-American countries are beginning to be interesting to the whole world. They are now becoming the scenes of political revolution, to take their stations as integral members of the great family of nations. All are now in insurrection. In several, the Independents are already triumphant, and they will undoubtedly be so in all. What kind of government will they establish? How much liberty can they bear without intoxication? Are their chiefs sufficiently enlightened to form a well-guarded government, and their people to watch their chiefs? Have they mind enough to place their domesticated Ind ans on a footing with the whites? All these questions you [Baron Humboldt] can answer better than any other. I imagine they will copy our outlines of confederation and elective government, abolish distinction of ranks, bow the neck to their priests, and persevere in intolerantism. Their greatest difficulty will be in the construction of their executive. I suspect that, regardless of the experiment of France, and of that of the United States in 1784, they will begin with a directory, and when the unavoidable schisms in that kind of executive shall drive them to something else, their great question will come on whether to substitute an executive elective for years, for life, or an hereditary one. But unless instruction can be spread among them more rapidly than experience promises, despotism may come upon them before they are qualified to save the ground they will have gained.—To BARON VON HUMBOLDT. v, 580. (M., April 1811.)

8076. —— ——. The achievement [by the Spanish Colonies] of their independence of Spain is no longer a question. But it is a very serious one, what will then become of them? Ignorance and bigotry, like other insanities, are incapable of self-government. They will fall under military despotism, and become the murderous tools of the ambition of their respective

Bonapartes; and whether this will be for their greater happiness, the rule of one only has taught you to judge. No one, I hope, can doubt my wish to see them and all mankind exercising self-government, and capable of exercising it. But the question is not what we wish, but what is practicable? As their sincere friend and brother, then, I do believe the best thing for them, would be for themselves to come to an accord with Spain, under the guarantee of France, Russia, Holland, and the United States, allowing, to Spain a nominal supremacy, with authority only to keep the peace among them, leaving them otherwise all the powers of self-government, until their experience in them, their emancipation from their priests, and advancement in information, shall prepare them for complete independence. I exclude England from this confederacy, because her selfish principles render her incapable of honorable patronage or disinterested co-operation.—To MARQUIS LAFAYETTE. vii, 67. FORD ED., x, 84. (M., 1817.)

8077. —— ——. The issue of [Spanish America's] struggles, as they respect Spain, is no longer matter of doubt. As it respects their own liberty, peace and happiness, we cannot be quite so certain. Whether the blinds of bigotry, the shackles of the priesthood, and the fascinating glare of rank and wealth, give fair play to the common sense of the mass of their people, so far as to qualify them for self-government, is what we do not know. Perhaps our wishes may be stronger than our hopes.—To F. H. ALEXANDER VON HUMBOLDT. vii, 74. FORD ED., x, 88. (M., 1817.)

8078. —— ——. I feared from the beginning that these people were not yet sufficiently enlightened for self-government; and that after wading through blood and slaughter, they would end in military tyrannies, more or less numerous. Yet, as they wished to try the experiment, I wished them success in it; they have now tried it, and will possibly find that their safest road will be an accommodation with the mother country, which shall hold them together by the single link of the same chief magistrate, leaving to him power enough to keep them in peace with one another, and to themselves the essential power of self-government and self-improvement. until they shall be sufficiently trained by education and habits of freedom, to walk safely by themselves. Representative government, native functionaries, a qualified negative on their laws, with a previous security by compact for freedom of commerce, freedom of the press, *habeas corpus* and trial by jury, would make a good beginning. This last would be the school in which their people might begin to learn the exercise of civic duties as well as rights. For freedom of religion they are not yet prepared. The scales of bigotry have not sufficiently fallen from their eyes, to accept it for themselves individually, much less to trust others with it. But that will come in time, as well as a general ripeness to break entirely from the parent stem.—To JOHN ADAMS. vii, 200. FORD ED., x, 186. (M., Jan. 1821.)

8079. SPANISH AMERICA, United States and.—I cannot help suspecting the Spanish squadron to be gone to South America, and that some disturbances have been excited there by the British. The Court of Madrid may suppose we would not see this with an unwilling eye. This may be true as to the uninformed part of our people; but those who look into futurity farther than the present moment or age, and who combine well what is, with what is to be, must see that our interests, well understood, and our wishes are, that Spain shall (not forever, but) very long retain her possessions in that quarter; and that her views and ours must, in a good degree, and for a long time, concur.—To WILLIAM CARMICHAEL. ii, 398. FORD ED., v, 23. (P., 1788.)

8080. SPECIAL LEGISLATION, Favoritism and.—To special legislation we are generally averse, lest a principle of favoritism should creep in and pervert that of equal rights. It has, however, been done on some occasions where a special national advantage has been expected to overweigh that of adherence to the general rule.—To GEORGE FLOWER. vii, 83. (P.F., 1817.)

— SPECIE.—See MONEY, METALLIC.

8081. SPECULATION, Agriculture vs.—A war wherein France, Holland, and England should be parties, seems, *primâ facie*, to promise much advantage to us. But, in the first place, no war can be safe for us which threatens France with an unfavorable issue; and in the next, it will probably embark us again into the ocean of speculation, engage us to overtrade ourselves, convert us into sea-rovers, under French and Dutch colors, divert us from agriculture, which is our wisest pursuit, because it will in the end contribute most to real wealth, good morals and happiness.—To GENERAL WASHINGTON. ii, 251. (P., Aug. 1787.)

8082. SPECULATION, A crime.—Wilson Nicholas is attacked in his election. The ground on which the attack is made is that he is a speculator. The explanations which this has produced prove it a serious crime in the eyes of the people.—To JAMES MADISON. FORD ED., vii, 1. (M., Feb. 1795.)

8083. SPECULATION, Excessive.—It is impossible to say where the appetite for gambling will stop. The land office, the Federal town, certain schemes of manufacture, are all likely to be converted into aliment for that rage.—To JAMES MONROE. iii, 268. FORD ED., v, 353. (Pa., 1791.)

8084. —— ——. The *unmoneyed* farmer, as he is termed, his cattle and crops are no more thought of here [Philadelphia*] than if they did not feed us. Scrip and stock are food and raiment here.—To T. M. RANDOLPH. FORD ED., v, 455. (Pa., 1792.)

8085. SPECULATION, In France.—All the money men [in France] are playing deeply in the stocks of the country. The spirit of "*agiotage*" (as they call it) was never so high in any country before. It will probably produce as total deprivation of morals as the system of [John] Law did. All the money of France is now employed in this, none being free even for the purposes of commerce, which suffers immensely from this cause.—To R. IZARD. ii, 206. (P., 1787.)

8086. SPECULATION, Gambling and.—The wealth acquired by speculation and

* Philadelphia was then the capital.—EDITOR.

plunder, is fugacious in its nature, and fills society with the spirit of gambling.—To GENERAL WASHINGTON. ii, 252. (P., 1787.)

8087. —— ——. A spirit of gambling in the public paper has lately seized too many of our citizens. Commerce, manufactures, the arts and agriculture will suffer from it, if not checked. Many are ruined by it; but I fear that ruin will be no more a correction in this case than in common gaming.—To DAVID HUMPHREYS. FORD ED., v, 372. (Pa., 1791.)

8088. —— ——. The credit and fate of the nation seem to hang on the desperate throws and plunges of gambling scoundrels. —To T. M. RANDOLPH. FORD ED., v, 455. (Pa., 1792.)

8089. SPECULATION, Land.—You mention that my name is used by some speculators in Western land jobbing, as if they were acting for me as well as for themselves. About the years 1776 or 1777, I consented to join Mr. Harvey and some others in an application for lands there; which scheme, however, I believe he dropped on the threshold, for I never after heard one syllable on the subject. In 1782, I joined some gentlemen in a project to obtain some lands in the western part of North Carolina. But in the winter of 1782 and 1783, while I was in expectation of going to Europe, and that the title to western lands might possibly come under the discussion of the ministers, I withdrew myself from this company. I am further assured that the members never prosecuted their views. These were the only occasions in which I ever took a single step for the acquisition of western lands, and in these I retracted at the threshold. I can with truth, therefore, declare to you, and wish you to repeat it on every proper occasion, that no person on earth is authorized to place my name in any adventure for lands on the western waters, that I am not engaged in any but the two before mentioned. I am one of eight children to whom my father left his share in the loyal company, whose interests, however, I never espoused, and they have long since received their quietus. Excepting these, I never was, nor am I now, interested in one foot of land on earth off the waters of James River.—To JAMES MADISON. FORD ED., iv, 2. (P. 1784.)

8090. SPECULATION, Morality and.—Though we shall be neutrals, and as such shall derive considerable pecuniary advantages, yet I think we shall lose in happiness and morals by being launched again into the ocean of speculation, led to overtrade ourselves, tempted to become sea-robbers, under French colors, and to quit the pursuits of agriculture, the surest road to affluence, and best preservative of morals.—To J. BLAIR. ii, 248. (P., 1787.)

8091. SPECULATION, Stocks.—I wish to God you had some person who could dispose of your paper at a judicious moment for you, and invest it in good lands. I would do anything my duty [as Secretary of State] would permit, but were I to advise your agent (who is himself a stock dealer) to sell out yours at this or that moment, it would be used as a signal to guide speculations.—To WILLIAM SHORT. iii, 343. FORD ED., v, 459. (Pa., March 1792.) See CAPITAL.

8092. SPELLING, Correct.—Take care that you never spell a word wrong. Always before you write a word, consider how it is spelled, and, if you do not remember it, turn to a dictionary. It produces great praise to a lady to spell well.—To MARTHA JEFFERSON. FORD ED., iii, 346. (A., 1783.)

8093. SPELLING, Reform of English.—A change has been long desired in English orthography, such as might render it an easy and true index of the pronunciation of words. The want of conformity between the combinations of letters, and the sounds they should represent, increases to foreigners the difficulty of acquiring the language, occasions great loss of time to children in learning to read, and renders correct spelling rare but in those who read much. In England a variety of plans and propositions has been made for the reformation of their orthography. Passing over these, two of our countrymen, Dr. Franklin and Dr. Thornton, have also engaged in the enterprise; the former proposing an addition of two or three new characters only, the latter a reformation of the whole alphabet nearly. But these attempts in England, as well as here, have been without effect. About the middle of the last century an attempt was made to banish the letter *d* from the words bridge, judge, hedge, knowledge, &c., others of that termination, and to write them as we write age, cage, sacrilege, privilege; but with little success. The attempt was also made, which you mention, * * * to drop the letter *u* in words of Latin derivation ending in o*u*r, and to write honor, candor, rigor, &c., instead of honour, candour, rigour. But the *u* having been picked up in the passage of these words from the Latin, through the French, to us, is still preserved by those who consider it as a memorial of our title to the words. Other partial attempts have been made by individual writers, · but with as little success. Pluralizing nouns in *y* and *ey*, by adding *s* only, as you propose, would certainly simplify the spelling, and be analogous to the general idiom of the language. It would be a step gained in the progress of general reformation, if it could prevail. But my opinion being requested I must give it candidly, that judging **of** the future by the past, I expect no better fortune to this than similar preceding propositions have experienced. It is very difficult to persuade the great body of mankind to give up what they have once learned, and are now masters of, for something to be learned anew. Time alone insensibly wears down old habits, and produces small changes at long intervals, and to this process we must all accommodate ourselves, and be content to follow those who will not follow us. Our Anglo-Saxon ancestors had twenty ways of spelling the word "many". Ten centuries have dropped all of them and substituted that which we now use. I now return your MS.* without being able, with the gentlemen whose letters are cited, to encourage hope as to its effect. I am bound, however, to acknowledge that this is a subject to which I have not paid much attention; and that my

* It is proposed that the plurals of words ending in *y* and *ey* be formed by adding *s* only.—EDITOR.

doubts, therefore, should weigh nothing against their more favorable expectations. That these may be fulfilled, and mine prove unfounded, I sincerely wish, because I am a friend to the reformation generally of whatever can be made better.—To JOHN WILSON. vi, 190. FORD ED., ix, 396. (M., 1813.)

8094. SPIES, Congress and.—As in time of war the enemies of these States might employ emissaries and spies to discover the views and proceedings of Congress, that body should have authority, within a certain distance of the place of their session, to arrest and deal with as they shall think proper, all persons, not being citizens of any of these States nor entitled to their protection, whom they shall have cause to suspect to be spies.—RESOLVE ON CONTINENTAL CONGRESS. FORD ED., ii¹, 464. (1784.)

8095. SPIES, Employment of.—Will it not be proper to rebut Foronda's charge [with respect to Lieutenant Pike's expedition] of this government sending a spy to Santa Fé, by saying that this government has never employed a spy in any case?—To JAMES MADISON. v, 178. (Aug. 1807.)

8096. SPIES, Jefferson and.—All my motions at Philadelphia, here [Monticello], and everywhere, are watched and recorded.—To SAMUEL SMITH. iv, 253. FORD ED., vii, 276. (M., 1798.)

— **SPIES, Treasury.**—See NEUTRALITY.

8097. SPIRIT, Party.—The happiness of society depends so much on preventing party spirit from infecting the common intercourse of life, that nothing should be spared to harmonize and amalgamate the two parties in social circles.—To WILLIAM C. CLAIRORNE. FORD ED., viii, 70. (W., 1801.)

8098. SPIRIT, Of the people.—It is the manners and spirit of the people which preserve a republic in vigor.—NOTES ON VIRGINIA. viii, 406. FORD ED., iii, 269. (1782.)

8099. SPRINGS, Medicinal.—There are several medicinal springs [in Virginia], some of which are indubitably efficacious, while others seem to owe their reputation as much to fancy and change of air and regimen, as to their real virtues.—NOTES ON VIRGINIA. viii, 279. FORD ED., iii, 121. (1782.) See MEDICINAL SPRINGS.

8100. SQUATTERS, Prohibition of.—I do not recollect the instructions to Governor [Meriwether] Lewis respecting squatters. But if he had any they were unquestionably to prohibit them rigorously. I have no doubt, if he had not written instructions, that he was verbally so instructed.—To ALBERT GALLATIN. v, 408. (W., Jan. 1809.)

8101. SQUATTERS, Removal.—The General Government have never hesitated to remove by force the squatters and intruders on the public lands. Indeed, if the nation were put to action against every squatter, for the recovery of their lands, we should have only lawsuits, not lands for sale.—BATTURE CASE. viii, 588. (1812.)

8102. STABILITY, Laudable.—Perseverance in object, though not by the most direct way, is often more laudable than perpetual changes, as often as the object shifts light.—To GOVERNOR HENRY. i, 220. FORD ED., ii, 178. (Alb., 1779.)

8103. STABILITY, Of the Republic.— The order and good sense displayed in this recovery from delusion, and in the momentous crisis which lately arose [Presidential election], really bespeak a strength of character in our nation which augurs well for the duration of our Republic; and I am much better satisfied now of its stability than I was before it was tried.—To DR. JOSEPH PRIESTLEY. iv, 374. FORD ED., viii, 22. (W., March 1801.)

8104. STAEL (Madame de), Sympathy. —[I assure you] of my sincere sympathies for the share which you bear in the afflictions of your country, and the deprivation to which a lawless will has subjected you. In return, you enjoy the dignified satisfaction of having met them, rather than be yoked with the abject, to his car; and that, in withdrawing from oppression, you have followed the virtuous example of a father whose name will ever be dear to your country and to mankind.—To MADAME DE STAEL. vi, 119. (May 1813.)

8105. STANDARD, Arbitrary.—The first question to be decided is between those who are for units of measures, weights, and coins, having a known relation to something in nature of fixed dimension, and those who are for an arbitrary standard. On this " *dice vexata quaestio* " it is useless to say a word, every one having made up his mind on a view of all that can be said. Mr. Dorsey was so kind as to send me his pamphlet, by which I found he was for the arbitrary standard of one-third of the standard yard of H. G. of England, supposed to be in the Exchequer of that nation, a fac simile of which was to be procured and lodged in Philadelphia. I confess myself to be of the other sect, and to prefer an unit bearing a given relation to some fixed subject of nature, and of preference to the pendulum, because it may be in the possession of every man, so that he may verify his measures for himself. I proposed alternative plans to Congress, that they might take the one or the other, according to the degree of courage they felt. Were I now to decide, it would be in favor of the first, with this single addition, that each of the denominations there adopted, should be divisible decimally at the will of every individual. The iron-founder deals in tons; let him take the ton for his unit, and divide it into 10ths, 100ths, and 1000ths. The dry-goods merchant deals in pounds and yards; let him divide them decimally. The land-measurer deals in miles and poles; divide them decimally, only noting over his figures what the unit is, thus:

Tons.	Lbs.	Yds.	Miles.
18.943,	18.943,	18.943,	18.943, etc.

—To THOMAS COOPER. v, 377. (W., 1808.)

8106. STANDARD, Decimal system.— Is it in contemplation with the House of Representatives to * * * arrange * * * our measures and weights [the same as the coinage] in a decimal ratio? The facility which this would introduce into the vulgar arithmetic would, unquestionably, be soon and sensibly felt by the whole mass of the people, who would thereby be enabled to compute for themselves whatever they should have occasion to buy, to sell, or to measure, which the present complicated and dif-

ficult ratios place beyond their computation for the most part.—COINAGE, WEIGHTS AND MEASURES REPORT. vii, 477. (July 1790.)

8107. ——— ———. It will give me real pleasure to see some good system of measures and weights introduced and combined with the decimal arithmetic. It is a great and difficult question whether to venture only on a half reformation, * * * or, as the French have tried with success, make a radical reform.—To J. DORSEY. v, 236. (W., 1808.)

— STANDARD, Money.—See DOLLAR and MONEY.

8108. STANDARD, Regulating.—The Administrator shall not possess the prerogative * * * of regulating weights and measures. —PROPOSED VA. CONSTITUTION. FORD ED., ii, 19. (June 1776.)

8109. STANDARD (Measures), English.—The cogent reason which will decide the fate of whatever you report is, that England has lately adopted the reference of its measures to the pendulum. It is the mercantile part of our community which will have most to do in this innovation; it is that which having command of all the presses can make the loudest outcry, and you know their identification with English regulations, practices, and prejudices. It is from this identification alone you can hope to be permitted to adopt even the English reference to a pendulum. But the English proposition goes only to say what proportion their measures bear to the second pendulum of their own latitude, and not at all to change their unit, or to reduce into any simple order the chaos of their weights and measures. That would be innovation, and innovation there is heresy and treason.—To JOHN QUINCY ADAMS. vii, 89. (M., 1817.)

8110. STANDARD (Measures), French. —Candor obliges me to confess that the element of measure, adopted by France, is not what I would have approved. It is liable to the inexactitude of mensuration as to that part of the quadrant of the earth which is to be measured, that is to say as to one-tenth of the quadrant, and as to the remaining nine-tenths they are to be calculated on conjectural data, presuming the figure of the earth which has not yet been proved. It is liable, too, to the objection that no nation but your own can come at it; because yours is the only nation within which a meridian can be found of such extent crossing the 45th degree, and terminating at both ends in a level. We may certainly say, then, that this measure is uncatholic, and I would rather have seen you depart from catholicism in your religion than in your philosophy.—To THE MARQUIS DE CONDORCET. FORD ED., v, 378. (Pa., 1791.)

8111. STANDARD (Measures), Invariable.—On the subject of weights and measures, you will have, at its threshold, to encounter the question on which Solon and Lycurgus acted differently. Shall we mould our citizens to the law, or the law to our citizens? And in solving this question their peculiar character is an element not to be neglected. Of the two only things in nature which can furnish an invariable standard, to wit, the dimensions of the globe itself, and the time of its diurnal revolution on its axis, it is not perhaps of much importance which we adopt. * * * I sincerely wish you may be able to rally us to either standard, and to give us an unit, the aliquot part of something invariable which may be applied simply and conveniently to our measures, weights and coins, and most especially that the decimal divisions may pervade the whole. The convenience of this in our moneyed system has been approved by all, and France has followed the example.—To John Quincy Adams. vii, 87. (M., 1817.)

8112. STANDARD (Measures), Method of obtaining.—To obtain uniformity in measures, weights and coins. it is necessary to find some measure of invariable length, with which, as a standard, they may be compared. There exists not in nature, as far as has been hitherto observed, a single subject or species of subject, accessible to man, which presents one constant and uniform dimension. The globe of the earth itself, indeed, might be considered as invariable in all its dimensions, and that its circumference would furnish an invariable measure; but no one of its circles, great or small, is accessible to admeasurement through all its parts, and the various trials to measure definite portions of them, have been of such various result as to show there is no dependence on that operation for certainty. Matter, then, by its mere extension, furnishing nothing invariable, its motion is the only remaining resource. The motion of the earth round its axis, though not absolutely uniform and invariable, may be considered as such for every human purpose. It is measured obviously, but unequally, by the departure of a given meridian from the sun, and its returning to it, constituting a solar day. Throwing together the inequalities of solar days, a mean interval, or day, has been found, and divided, by very general consent, into 86,400 equal parts. A pendulum, vibrating freely, in small and equal arcs, may be so adjusted in its length, as, by its vibrations, to make this division of the earth's motion into 86,400 equal parts, called seconds of mean time. Such a pendulum, then, becomes itself a measure of determinate length, to which all others may be referred to as to a standard. But even a pendulum is not without its uncertainties.—Coinage, Weights and Measures Report. vii, 473. (July 1790.)

8113. STANDARD (Measures), Odometer.—I have lately had a proof how familiar this division into dimes, cents, and mills, is to the people when transferred from their money to anything else. I have an odometer fixed to my carriage, which gives the distances in miles, dimes, and cents. The people on the road inquire with curiosity what exact distance I have found from such a place to such a place. I answer so many miles, so many cents. I find they universally and at once form a perfect idea of the relation of the cent to the mile as an unit. They would do the same as to yards of cloth, pounds of shot, ounces of silver, or of medicine. I believe, therefore, they are susceptible of this degree of approximation to a standard rigorously philosophical; beyond this I might doubt.—To Thomas Cooper. v, 378. (W., 1808.)

8114. STANDARD (Measures), Pendulum.—But why leave this adoption to the tardy will of governments who are always, in their stock of information, a century or two behind the intelligent part of mankind, and who have interests against touching ancient institutions? Why should not the college of the literary societies of the world adopt the second pendulum as the unit of measure on the authorities of reason, convenience and common consent? And why should not our Society [American Philosophical] open the proposition by a circular letter to the other learned institu-

tions of the earth? If men of science, in their publications, would express measures always in multiples and decimals of the pendulum, annexing their value in municipal measures as botanists add the popular to the botanical names of plants, they would soon become familiar to all men of instruction, and prepare the way for legal adoptions. At any rate, it would render the writers of every nation intelligible to the readers of every other, when expressing measures of things.—To Dr. Patterson. vi, 12. (M., 1811.)

8115. —— ——. In favor of the standard to be taken from the time employed in a revolution of the earth on its axis, it may be urged that this revolution is a matter of fact present to all the world, that its division into seconds of time is known and received by all the world, that the length of a pendulum vibrating seconds in the different circles of latitude is already known to all, and can at any time and in any place be ascertained by any nation or individual, and inferred by known laws from their own to the medium latitude of 45°, whenever any doubt may make this desirable; and that this is the particular standard which has at different times been contemplated and desired * by the philosophers of every nation, and even by those of France, except at the particular moment when this change was suddenly proposed and adopted, and under circumstances peculiar to the history of the moment.—To John Quincy Adams. vii, 88. (M., 1817.)

8116. —— ——. [The standard based on] the dimensions of the globe, preferred ultimately by the French, after first adopting the other [that founded on the time of the diurnal revolution of the earth on its axis], has been objected to from the difficulty, not to say impracticability, of the verification of their admeasurement by other nations. Except the portion of a meridian which they adopted for their operation, there is not another on the globe which fulfills the requisite condition. to wit, of so considerable length, that length too divided, not very unequally, by the 45th degree of latitude, and terminating at each end in the ocean. Now, this singular line lies wholly in France and Spain. Besides the immensity of expense and time which a verification would always require, it cannot be undertaken by any nation without the joint consent of these two powers. France having once performed the work, and refusing, as she may. to let any other nation reexamine it, she makes herself the sole depositary of the original standard for all nations; and all must send to her to obtain, and from time to time to prove their standards. To this, indeed, it may be answered, that there can be no reason to doubt that the mensuration has been as accurately performed as the intervention of numerous waters and of high ridges of craggy mountains would admit; that all the calculations have been free of error, their coincidences faithfully reported, and that, whether in peace or war. to foes as well as friends, free access to the original will at all times be admitted.—To John Quincy Adams. vii, 88. (M., 1817.) See Pendulum.

8117. STANDARD (Measures), Rod.—Congress having referred to me to propose a plan of invariable measures. I have considered maturely your proposition, and am abundantly

* If, conforming to this desire of other nations. we adopt the second pendulum, 3-10 of that for our foot will be the same as 1-5 or 2-10 of the second rod, because that rod is to the pendulum, as 5 to 2. This would make our foot 1-4 inch less than the present one.—Note by Jefferson.

satisfied of its utility; so that if I can have your leave, I mean to propose in my report to adopt the rod in preference to the pendulum, mentioning expressly that we are indebted to you for the idea.—To Mr. LESLIE. iii, 156. (N.Y., 1790.)

8118. STANDARD (Measures), Universal.—The pendulum is equally [with the meridian] fixed by the laws of nature, is in the possession of every nation, may be verified everywhere and by every person, and at an expense within every one's means. I am not, therefore, without a hope that the other nations of the world will still concur, some day, in making the pendulum the basis of a common system of measures, weights and coins, which applied to the present metrical systems of France and of other countries, will render them all intelligible to one another. England and th's country may give it a beginning, notwithstanding the war they are entering into. The republic of letters is unaffected by the wars of geographical divisions of the earth.—To Dr. PATTERSON. vi, 11. (M., 1811.)

8119. —— ——. I do not like the new system of French measures, because not the best, and adapted to a standard accessible to themselves exclusively, and to be obtained by other nations only from them. For, on examining the map of the earth, you will find no meridian on it but the one passing through their country, offering the extent of land on both sides of the 45th degree, and terminating at both ends in a portion of the ocean which the conditions of the problem for an universal standard of measures require. Were all nations to agree, therefore, to adopt this standard, they must go to Paris to ask it; and they might as well long ago have all agreed to adopt the French foot, the standard of which they could equally have obtained from Paris.—To Dr. PATTERSON. vi, 11. (M., 1811.)

8120. STANDARD (Weights), Avoirdupois and Troy.—It would be for their [the people's] convenience to suppress the pound and ounce troy, and the drachm and quarter avoirdupois; and to form into one series the avoirdupois pound and ounce, and the troy pennyweight and grain.—COINAGE, WEIGHTS AND MEASURES REPORT. vii, 486. (1790.)

8121. STANDARD (Weights), Basis.—Let it be established that an ounce is of the weight of a cube of rain water of one-tenth of a foot; or, rather, that it is the thousandth part of the weight of a cubic foot of rain water, weighed in the standard temperature; that the series of weights of the United States shall consist of pounds, ounces, pennyweights and grains; whereof 24 grains shall be one pennyweight; 18 pennyweights one ounce; 16 ounces one pound.—COINAGE, WEIGHTS AND MEASURES REPORT. vii, 487. (1790.)

8122. STANDARD (Weights), Ratios.—The weight of the pound troy is to that of the pound avoirdupois as 144 to 175. It is remarkable that this is exactly the proportion of the ancient liquid gallon of Guildhall of 224 cubic inches to the corn gallon of 272. It is further remarkable still that this is also the exact proportion between the specific weight of any measure of wheat and of the same measure of water. * * * This seems to have been so combined as to render it indifferent whether a thing were dealt out by weight or measure.—COINAGE, WEIGHTS AND MEASURES REPORT. vii, 484. (1790.)

8123. —— ——. Another remarkable correspondence is that between weights and measures. For 1,000 ounces avoirdupois of pure water fills a cubic foot, with mathematical exactness. What circumstances of the times, or purpose of barter or commerce, called for this combination of weights and measures, with the subjects to be exchanged or purchased, are not now to be ascertained. But a triple set of exact proportionals representing weights, measures and the things to be weighed or measured, and a relation so integral between weights and solid measures, must have been the result of design and scientific calculation and not a mere coincidence of hazard.—COINAGE, WEIGHTS AND MEASURES REPORT. vii, 485. (1790.)

8124. STATE RIGHTS, Coercion.—Respect and friendship should, I think, mark the conduct of the General towards the particular government, and explanations should be asked and time and color given them to tread back their steps before coercion is held up to their view.—OPINION ON GEORGIAN LAND GRANTS. vii, 468. FORD ED., v, 167. (1790.) See COERCION OF A STATE.

8125. STATE RIGHTS, Congress and.—Can it be thought that the Constitution intended that for a shade or two of *convenience,* more or less, Congress should be authorized to break down the most ancient and fundmental laws of the several States; such as those against Mortmain, the laws of Alienage, the rules of Descent, the acts of Distribution, the laws of Escheat and Forfeiture, the laws of Monopoly? Nothing but a necessity invincible by any other means, can justify such a prostitution of laws, which constitute the pillars of our whole system of jurisprudence. Will Congress be too straightlaced to carry the Constitution into honest effect, unless they may pass over the foundation-laws of the State government for the slightest convenience of theirs?—NATIONAL BANK OPINION. vii, 560. FORD ED., v, 289. (1791.) See BANK (U. S.), CONSTITUTIONALITY OF.

8126. —— ——. [The States] alone being parties to the [Federal] compact, * * * [are] solely authorized to judge in the last resort of the powers exercised under it, Congress being not a party, but merely the creature of the compact, and subject as to its assumptions of power to the final judgment of those by whom, and for whose use itself and its powers were all created and modified.—KENTUCKY RESOLUTIONS. ix, 469. FORD ED., vii, 301. (1798.) See KENTUCKY RESOLUTIONS.

8127. STATE RIGHTS, Constitution and.—I am firmly persuaded that it is by giving due tone to the particular governments that the general one will be preserved in vigor also, the Constitution having foreseen its incompetency to all the objects of government, and, therefore, confined it to those specially described.—To JAMES SULLIVAN. FORD ED., v, 369. (Pa., 1791.)

8128. STATE RIGHTS, Encroachments on.—Whilst the General Assembly [of Virginia] thus declares the rights retained by the States, rights which they have never yielded, and which this State will never voluntarily yield, they do not mean to raise the banner of disaffection, or of separation from their sister States, coparties with themselves to this compact. They know and value too highly the blessings of their Union as to foreign nations and questions arising among themselves, to consider every infraction of it as to be met by actual resistance. They respect too affectionately the opinions of those possessing the same rights under the same instrument, to make that difference of construction a ground of immediate rupture. They would. indeed, consider such a rupture as among the greatest calamities which could befall them; but not the greatest. There is yet one greater, submission to a government of unlimited powers. It is only when the hope of avoiding this shall have become absolutely desperate, that further forbearance could not be indulged. Should a majority of the coparties, therefore, contrary to the expectation and hope of this Assembly, prefer, at this time acquiescence in these assumptions of power by the Federal member of the government, we will be patient and suffer much under the confidence that time, ere it be too late, will prove to them also the bitter consequences in which that usurpation will involve us all. In the meantime we will breast with them, rather than separate from them, every misfortune, save that only of living under a government of unlimited powers. We owe every other sacrifice to ourselves, to our Federal brethren. and to the world at large, to pursue with temper and with perseverance the great experiment which shall prove that man is capable of living in society, governing itself by laws self-imposed, and securing to its members the enjoyment of life, liberty, property, and peace; and further to show, that even when the government of its choice shall manifest a tendency to degeneracy we are not at once to despair, but that the will and the watchfulness of its sounder parts will reform its aberrations. recall it to original and legitimate principles, and restrain it within the rightful limits of self-government.—VIRGINIA PROTEST. ix, 498. FORD ED., x, 351. (1825.)

8129. STATE RIGHTS, Freedom and. —The States should be left to do whatever acts they can do as well as the General Government.—To JOHN HARVIE. FORD ED., v, 214. (N.Y., 1790.)

8130. STATE RIGHTS, General welfare.—This Assembly [of Virginia] does disavow and declare to be most false and unfounded, the doctrine that the compact, in authorizing its Federal branch to lay and collect taxes. duties, imposts, and excises, to pay the debts and provide for the common defence and general welfare of the United States, has given them thereby a power to do whatever *they* may *think*, or pretend, would promote the general welfare. which construction would make that. of itself, a complete government,

without limitation of powers; but that the plain sense and obvious meaning were, that they might levy the taxes necessary to provide for the general welfare, by the various acts of power therein specified and delegated to them, and by no others.—VIRGINIA PROTEST. ix, 497. FORD ED., x, 350. (1825.) See GENERAL WELFARE CLAUSE.

8131. STATE RIGHTS, Home rule.—I believe the States can best govern our home concerns.—To WILLIAM JOHNSON. vii, 297. FORD ED., x, 232. (M., 1823.)

8132. ——— ———. To the State governments are reserved all legislation and administration, in affairs which concern their own citizens only.—To JOHN CARTWRIGHT. vii, 358. (M.. 1824.)

8133. STATE RIGHTS, Interior Government.—Interior government is what each State should keep to itself.—To JAMES MADISON. i, 531. FORD ED., iv, 192. (P., 1786.)

8134. STATE RIGHTS, Lines of demarcation.—I have always thought that where the line of demarcation between the powers of the General and the State governments was doubtfully or indistinctly drawn. it would be prudent and praiseworthy in both parties never to approach it but under the most urgent necessity.—To J. C. CABELL. vi, 310. FORD ED., ix, 452. (M.. 1814.)

8135. STATE RIGHTS, Metallic money and.—I recollect but one instance of control vested in the Federal over the State authorities, in a matter purely domestic, which is that of metallic tenders.—To ROBERT J. GARNETT. vii, 336. FORD ED., x, 295. (M., 1824.)

8136. STATE RIGHTS, National bank and.—The bill for establishing a National Bank undertakes * * * to form the subscribers into a corporation [and] * * * communicates to them, in their corporate capacities, a power to make laws paramount to the laws of the States; for so they must be construed, to protect the institution from the control of the State legislatures; and so, probably. they will be construed.—NATIONAL BANK OPINION. vii, 555-6. FORD ED., v, 285. (1791.) See BANK (U. S.), CONSTITUTIONALITY OF.

8137. STATE RIGHTS, Nullification. —Every State has a natural right in cases not within the compact (*casus non fœderis*) to nullify of their own authority all assumptions of power by others within their limits; without this right, they would be under the dominion, absolute and unlimited, of whosoever might exercise this right of judgment for them.—KENTUCKY RESOLUTIONS. ix, 469. FORD ED., vii, 301. (1798.)

8138. STATE RIGHTS, Preservation of.—I am for preserving to the States the powers not yielded by them to the Union and to the Legislature of the Union its constitutional share in the division of powers; and I am not for transferring all the powers of the States to the General Government, and all those of that government to the Executive branch.—To ELBRIDGE GERRY. iv, 268. FORD ED., vii, 327. (1799.) See CENTRALIZATION.

8139. —— ——. I wish to preserve [in a new constitution for Virginia] the line drawn by the Federal Constitution between the General and particular governments as it stands at present, and to take every prudent means of preventing either from stepping over it.—To ARCHIBALD STUART. iii, 314. FORD ED., v, 409. (Pa., 1791.) See CONSTITUTION (FEDERAL).

8140. STATE RIGHTS, Judiciary and. —It is of immense consequence that the States retain as complete authority as possible over their own citizens. The withdrawing themselves under the shelter of a foreign jurisdiction, is so subversive of order and so pregnant of abuse, that it may not be amiss to consider how far a law of *præmunire* should be revised and modified, against all citizens who attempt to carry their causes before any other than the State courts, in cases where those other courts have no right to their cognizance. A plea to the jurisdiction of the courts of their State, or a reclamation of a foreign jurisdiction, if adjudged valid, would be safe; but if adjudged invalid, would be followed by the punishment of *præmunire* for the attempt.—To JAMES MONROE. iv, 200. FORD ED., vii, 173. (M., 1797.) See JUDICIARY and SUPREME COURT.

8141. STATE RIGHTS, Reserved.—Nor is it admitted * * * that the people of these States, by not investing their Federal branch with all the means of bettering their condition, have denied to themselves any which may effect that purpose; since in the distribution of those means they have given to that branch those which belong to its department, and to the States have reserved separately the residue which belong to them separately. And thus by the organization of the two branches taken together, they have completely secured the first object of human association, the full improvement of their condition, and reserved to themselves all the faculties of multiplying their own blessings. —VIRGINIA PROTEST. ix, 497. FORD ED., x, 351. (1825.)

8142. STATE RIGHTS, Slavery and.— An abstinence from this act of power [prohibition of slavery in Missouri], would remove the jealousy excited by the undertaking of Congress to regulate the condition of the different descriptions of men composing a State. This certainly is the exclusive right of every State, which nothing in the Constitution has taken from them and given to the General Government. Could Congress, for example, say, that the non-freemen of Connecticut shall be freemen, or that they shall not emigrate into any other State?—To JOHN HOLMES. vii, 159. FORD ED., x, 158. (M., 1820.)

8143. STATE RIGHTS, Sovereignty.— The States should severally preserve their sovereignty in whatever concerns themselves alone, and whatever may concern another State, or any foreign nation, should be made a part of the Federal sovereignty.—To GEORGE WYTHE. ii, 267. FORD ED., iv, 445. (P., Sep. 1787.)

8144. STATE RIGHTS, Support of.— The support of the State governments in all their rights, as the most competent administrations for our domestic concerns and the surest bulwarks against anti-republican tendencies, I deem [one of the] essential principles of our government and, consequently [one] which ought to shape its administration.—FIRST INAUGURAL ADDRESS. viii, 4. FORD ED., viii, 4. (1801.)

8145. STATE RIGHTS, Surrender of.— Can it be believed, that under the jealousies prevailing against the General Government, at the adoption of the Constitution, the States meant to surrender the authority of preserving order, of enforcing moral duties and restraining vice within their own territory?—To WILLIAM JOHNSON. vii, 297. FORD ED., x, 231. (M., 1823.) See FEDERAL GOVERNMENT AND UNION (FEDERAL).

8146. STATES, Admission of new.— The 11th Article of Confederation admits Canada to accede to the Confederation at its own will, but adds that, "no other Colony shall be admitted to the same, unless such admission be agreed to by nine States". When the plan of April, 1784. for establishing new States was on the carpet, the committee who framed the report of that plan, had inserted this clause, "provided nine States agree to such admission, according to the reservation of the 11th of the Articles of Confederation". It was objected, 1. That the words of the Confederation, "no other Colony", could only refer to the residuary possessions of Great Britain, as the two Floridas, Nova Scotia, &c., not being already parts of the Union; that the law for "admitting" a new member into the Union, could not be applied to a territory which was already in the Union, as making part of a State which was a member of it. 2. That it would be improper to allow "nine" States to receive a new member, because the same reasons which rendered that number proper now, would render a greater one proper when the number composing the Union should be increased. They, therefore, struck out this paragraph, and inserted a proviso. that "the consent of so many States, in Congress, shall be first obtained, as may, at the time be competent"; thus leaving the question. whether the 11th Article applies to the admission of new States? to be decided when that admission shall be asked. (See the Journal of Congress of April 20, 1784.) Another doubt was started in this debate, viz.: whether the agreement of the nine States, required by the Confederation, was to be made by their legislatures, or by their delegates in Congress? The expression adopted. viz.: "so many States in Congress is first obtained", shows what was their sense in this matter. If it be agreed that the 11th

Article of the Confederation is not to be applied to the admission of these new States, then it is contended that their admission comes within the 13th Article, which forbids " any alteration, unless agreed to in a Congress of the United States, and afterwards confirmed by the legislatures of every State ".—ANSWERS TO M. DE MEUNIER. ix, 251. FORD ED., iv, 156. (P., 1786.) See CONFEDERATION, DEFECTS.

8147. STATES, Barriers of liberty.— The true barriers of our liberty are our State governments; and the wisest conservative power ever contrived by man, is that of which our Revolution and present government found us possessed. Seventeen distinct States, amalgamated into one as to their foreign concerns, but single and independent as to their internal administration, regularly organized with legislature and governor resting on the choice of the people, and enlightened by a free press, can never be so fascinated by the arts of one man, as to submit voluntarily to his usurpation. Nor can they be constrained to it by any force he can possess. While that may paralyze the single State in which it happens to be encamped, sixteen others, spread over a country of two thousand miles diameter, rise up on every side, ready organized for deliberation by a constitutional legislature, and for action by their governor, constitutionally the commander of the militia of the State, that is to say, of every man in it able to bear arms; and that militia, too, regularly formed into regiments and battalions, into infantry, cavalry and artillery, trained under officers general and subordinate, legally appointed, always in readiness, and to whom they are already in habits of obedience. The republican government of France was lost without a struggle, because the party of " *un et indivisible* " had prevailed; no provisional organizations existed to which the people might rally under authority of the laws, the seats of the directory were virtually vacant, and a small force sufficed to turn the legislature out of their chamber, and to salute its leader chief of the nation. But with us, sixteen out of seventeen States rising in mass, under regular organization, and legal commanders, united in object and action by their Congress, or, if that be in *duresse,* by a special convention, present such obstacles to an usurper as forever to stifle ambition in the first conception of that object.—To M. DESTUTT TRACY. v, 570. FORD ED., ix, 308. (M., 1811.)

8148. STATES, Confederation of.—The alliance between the States under the old Articles of Confederation, for the purpose of joint defence against the aggression of Great Britain, was found insufficient, as treaties of alliance generally are, to enforce compliance with their mutual stipulations; and these, once fulfilled, that bond was to expire of itself, and each State to become sovereign and independent in all things.—THE ANAS. ix, 88. FORD ED., i, 157. (1818.) See CONFEDERATION, DEFECTS.

8149. STATES, Cooperation of.—Your opinion of the propriety and advantage of a more intimate correspondence between the Executives of the several States, and that of the Union, as a central point, is precisely that which I have ever entertained; and on coming into office I felt the advantages which would result from that harmony. I had it even in contemplation, after the annual recommendation to Congress of those measures called for by the times, which the Constitution had placed within their power, to make communications in like manner to the Executives of the several States, as to any parts of them to which the legislatures might be alone competent. For many are the exercises of power reserved to the States, wherein an uniformity of proceeding would be advantageous to all. Such are quarantines, health laws, regulations of the press, banking institutions, training militia, &c., &c. But you know what was the state of the several governments when I came into office. That a great proportion of them were federal, and would have been delighted with such opportunities of proclaiming their contempt, and of opposing republican men and measures. Opportunities so furnished and used by some of the State governments, would have produced an ill effect, and would have insured the failure of the object of uniform proceeding. If it could be ventured even now (Connecticut and Delaware being still hostile) it must be on some greater occasion than is likely to arise within my time. I look to it, therefore, as a course which will probably be left to the consideration of my successor.—To JAMES SULLIVAN. v, 100. FORD ED., ix, 76. (W., 1807.)

8150. STATES, Commerce between.— Experience shows that the States never bought foreign goods of one another. The reasons are, that they would, in so doing, pay double freight and charges; and again, that they would have to pay mostly in cash, what they could obtain for commodities in Europe.—To JOHN ADAMS. i, 493. (P., 1785.)

**8151. ———— ————. What a glorious exchange would it be could we persuade our navigating fellow citizens to embark their capital in the internal commerce of our country, exclude foreigners from that, and let them take the carrying trade in exchange; abolish the diplomatic establishments, and never suffer any armed vessel of any nation to enter our ports. [Faded] things can be thought of only in times of wisdom, not of party and folly.—To EDMUND PENDLETON. FORD ED., vii, 376. (M., April 1799.)

8152. STATES, Common interests.— The interests of the States ought to be made joint in every possible instance, in order to cultivate the idea of our being one nation, and to multiply the instances in which the people shall look up to Congress as their head.—To JAMES MONROE. i, 347. FORD ED., iv, 52. (P., 1785.)

8153. STATES, Correspondence between Executives.—As to the mode of correspondence between the general and particular executives, I do not think myself a good judge. Not because my position gives me any prejudice on the occasion; for if it be possible to be certainly conscious of anything, I am conscious of feeling no difference between writing to the highest or lowest being on earth; but because I have ever thought that forms should yield to whatever should facilitate business. Comparing the two governments together, it is observable that in all those cases where the independent or reserved rights of the States are in question, the two Executives, if they are to act together, must be exactly coordinate; they are, in those cases, each the supreme head of an independent government. Such is the case in the beginning of this letter where the two Executives were to treat *de pair en pair.* In other cases, to wit, those transferred by the Constitution to the General Government, the general Executive is certainly preordinate: *e. g.,* in a question respecting the militia, and others easily to be recollected. Were these, therefore, to be a stiff adherence to etiquette, I should say- that in the former cases the correspondence should be between the two heads, and that in the latter, the Governor must be subject to receive orders from the War Department as any other subordinate officer would. And were it observed that either party set up unjustifiable pretensions, perhaps the other might be right in opposing them by a tenaciousness of his own rigorous right. But I think the practice in General Washington's administration was most friendly to business, and was absolutely equal. Sometimes he wrote to the Governors, and sometimes the heads of departments wrote. If a letter is to be on a general subject, I see no reason why the President should not write; but if it is to go into details, these being known only to the head of the department, it is better he should write directly. Otherwise, the correspondence must involve circuities. If this be practiced promiscuously in both classes of cases, each party setting examples of neglecting etiquette, both will stand on equal ground, and convenience alone will dictate through whom any particular communication is to be made. All the governors have freely corresponded with the heads of departments, except Hancock, who refused it. But his Legislature took advantage of a particular case which justified them in interfering, and they obliged him to correspond with the head of a department. General Washington sometimes wrote to them. I presume Mr. Adams did, as you mention his having written to you. On the whole, I think a free correspondence best, and shall never hesitate to write myself to the Governors even in a federal case, where the occasion presents itself to me particularly.—To Governor Monroe. iv, 401. Ford ed., viii, 59. (W., May 1801.)

8154. STATES, Counties and.—A county of a State cannot be governed by its own laws, but must be subject to those of the State of which it is a part.—To William Lee. vii, 57. (M., 1817.) See Counties.

8155. STATES, Division of authority. —The way to have good and safe government, is not to trust it all to one, but to divide it among the many, distributing to every one exactly the functions he is competent to. Let the National Government be entrusted with the defence of the nation, and its foreign and federal relations; the State governments with the civil rights, laws, police, and administration of what concerns the State generally; the counties with the local concerns of the counties, and each ward direct the interests within itself. It is by dividing and subdividing these republics from the great national one down through all its subordinations, until it ends in the administration of every man's farm by himself; by placing under every one what his own eye may superintend, that all will be done for the best.—To Joseph C. Cabell. vi, 543. (M., 1816.) See Centralization.

8156. STATES, Equality in size.—In establishing new States regard is had to a certain degree of equality in size.—To William Lee. vii, 57. (M., 1817.)

8157. STATES, Federal government and.—I [shall] consider the most perfect harmony and interchange of accommodations and good offices with the State governments, as among the first objects [of my administration].—To Governor Thomas M'Kean. iv, 350. Ford ed., vii, 487. (W., 1801.)

8158. ——— ———. Considering the General and State governments as cooperators in the same holy concerns, the interest and happiness of our country, the interchange of mutual aid is among the most pleasing of the exercises of our duty.—To W. H. Cabell. v, 114. Ford ed., ix, 87. (W., 1807.)

8159. ——— ———. The States can best govern our home concerns, and the General Government our foreign ones.—To William Johnson. vii, 297. Ford ed., x, 232. (M., 1823.)

8160. ——— ———. The extent of our country was so great, and its former division into distinct States so established, that we thought it better to confederate as to foreign affairs only. Every State retained its self-government in domestic matters, as better qualified to direct them to the good and satisfaction of their citizens, than a general government so distant from its remoter citizens, and so little familiar with the local peculiarities of the different parts.—To M. Coray. vii, 320. (M., 1823.)

8161. ——— ———. If the Federal and State governments should claim each the same subject of power, where is the common umpire to decide ultimately between them? In cases of little importance or urgency, the prudence of both parties will keep them aloof from the questionable ground; but if it can neither be avoided nor compromised, a convention of the States must be called, to ascribe the doubtful power to that department which they may think best.—To JOHN CARTWRIGHT. vii, 358. (M., 1824.) See FEDERAL GOVERNMENT.

8162. STATES, Fundamental principles of new.—The temporary and permanent governments* [shall] be established on these principles as their basis. 1. They shall forever remain a part of the United States of America. 2. In their persons, property and territory, they shall be subject to the Government of the United States in Congress assembled, and to the Articles of Confederation in all those cases in which the original States shall be so subject. 3. They shall be subject to pay a part of the Federal debts, contracted or to be contracted, to be apportioned on them by Congress, according to the same common rule and measure by which apportionments thereof shall be made on the other States. 4. Their respective governments shall be in republican forms, and shall admit no person to be a citizen, who holds any hereditary title. 5. After the year 1800 of the Christian era, there shall be neither slavery nor involuntary servitude in any of the said States, otherwise than in punishment of crimes, whereof the party shall have been duly convicted to have been personally guilty.†—WESTERN TERRITORY REPORT. FORD ED., iii, 409. (Mar. 1784.) See SLAVERY, ABOLITION.

8163. —— ——. Whenever any of the said States shall have, of free inhabitants as many as shall then be in any one of the least numerous of the thirteen original States, such State shall be admitted by its delegates into the Congress of the United States, on an

* Of the States to be formed out of the Western Territory.—EDITOR.

† Next to the Declaration of Independence (if indeed standing second to that), this document ranks in historical importance of all those drawn by Jefferson; and, but for its being superseded by the "Ordinance of 1787", would rank among all American State papers immediately after the National Constitution. * * * That it contains practically every provision which has made the latter ordinance famous, has been carefully overlooked by those who have desired to give the credit of them to Northerners. Still more have these special pleaders suppressed the fact that Jefferson proposed to interdict slavery in all the Western Territory and not merely in the Northwest Territory, as the ordinance of 1787 did. Had it been adopted as Jefferson reported it, slavery would have died a natural death, and secession would have been impossible. There is another reason, however, for the little reputation this paper has brought to Jefferson, aside from the studious suppression of its importance by the special pleaders of New England. This plan, with its limitations of slavery, though failing by only one vote of adoption in 1784, was unpopular at the South and increasingly so as slavery became more and more profitable and more and more a southern institution. As early as 1790, Jefferson's partisans were already his apologists for this document, and from that time Jefferson carefully avoided any public utterance on slavery. This change of attitude is alone sufficient explanation why Southerners acquiesced with the Northerners in the suppression of this paper, and of Jefferson's drafting of it. In Jefferson's memoranda of the services which he took pride in having rendered his country, written in 1800, he carefully omitted all mention, as also in his autobiography written in 1821. And thus it has been left to the Massachusetts orators to glorify King, Dane, and Cutler for clauses in the Ordinance of 1787, which the latter had in truth taken from the Ordinance of 1784, and which they made sectional, where Jefferson had made them national.—NOTE IN FORD EDITION, iii, 430.

equal footing with the said original States.—WESTERN TERRITORY REPORT. FORD ED., iii, 409. (1784.)

8164. STATES, Government of.—Though the experiment has not yet had a long enough course to show us from which quarter encroachments are most to be feared, yet it is easy to foresee, from the nature of things, that the encroachments of the State governments will tend to an excess of liberty which will correct itself (as in the late instance), while those of the General Government will tend to monarchy, which will fortify itself from day to day, instead of working its own cure, as all experience shows. I would rather be exposed to the inconveniences attending too much liberty, than those attending too small a degree of it. Then it is important to strengthen the State governments; and as this cannot be done by any change in the Federal Constitution (for the preservation of that is all we need contend for), it must be done by the States themselves, erecting such barriers at the constitutional line as cannot be surmounted either by themselves or by the General Government. The only barrier in their power is a wise government. A weak one will lose ground in every contest. To obtain a wise and a safe government, I consider the following changes as important: Render the legislature a desirable station by lessening the number of representatives (say to 100) and lengthening somewhat their term, and proportion them equally among the electors. Adopt also a better mode of appointing senators. Render the Executive a more desirable post to men of abilities by making it more independent of the legislature. To wit, let him be chosen by other electors, for a longer time, and ineligible forever after. Responsibility is a tremendous engine in a free government. Let him feel the whole weight of it then, by taking away the shelter of his Executive Council. Experience both ways has already established the superiority of this measure. Render the judiciary respectable by every means possible, to wit, firm tenure in office, competent salaries, and reduction of their numbers. Men of high learning and abilities are few in every country; and by taking in those who are not so, the able part of the body have their hands tied by the unable. This branch of the government will have the weight of the conflict on their hands because they will be the last appeal of reason. These are my general ideas of amendments; but, preserving the ends, I should be flexible and conciliatory as to the means.—To ARCHIBALD STUART. iii, 314. FORD ED., v, 409. (Pa., 1791.)

8165. STATES, Kentucky's appeal to.—* * * This Commonwealth * * * calls on its co-States for an expression of their sentiments on the acts concerning aliens, and for the punishment of certain crimes hereinbefore specified, plainly declaring whether these acts are or are not authorized by the Federal compact. And it doubts not that their sense will be so announced as to prove their attachment unaltered to limited government, whether general or particular. And that the rights and liberties of their co-States will be exposed to no dangers by remaining embarked in a common bottom with their own. That they will concur with this Commonwealth in considering the said acts as so palpably against the Constitution as to amount to an undisguised declaration that that compact is not meant to be the measure of the powers of the General Government, but that it will proceed in the exercise over these States, of all powers whatsoever: that they will view this as seizing the rights of the States, and consolidating them in the hands of the General Government, with a power assumed to bind the States (not merely in the cases made Federal (*casus fœderis*), but, in all cases whatsoever, by laws made, not with their consent, but by others against their consent: that this would be to surrender the form of government we have chosen, and live under one deriving its powers from its own will, and not from our authority; and that the co-States recurring to their natural right in cases not made federal, will concur in declaring these acts void, and of no force, and will each take measures of its own for providing that neither these acts, nor any others of the General Government, not plainly and intentionally authorized by the Constitution, shall be exercised within their respective territories.—KENTUCKY RESOLUTIONS. ix, 471. FORD ED., vii, 305. (1798.) See KENTUCKY RESOLUTIONS.

8166. STATES, Power of.—As long as the States exercise, separately, those acts of power which respect foreign nations, so long will there continue to be irregularities committed by some one or other of them, which will constantly keep us on an ill-footing with foreign nations.—To JAMES MADISON. i, 531. FORD ED., iv, 192. (P., February 1786.)

8167. STATES, Respect for.—I do not think it for the interest of the General Government itself, and still less of the Union at large, that the State governments should be so little respected as they have been. However, I dare say that in time all these as well as their central government, like the planets revolving round their common sun, acting and acted upon according to their respective weights and distances, will produce that beautiful equilibrium on which our Constitution is founded, and which, I believe, it will exhibit to the world in a degree of perfection, unexampled but in the planetary system itself. The enlightened statesman, therefore, will endeavor to preserve the weight and influence of every part, as too much given to any member of it would destroy the general equilibrium.—To PEREGRINE FITZHUGH. iv, 217. FORD ED., vii, 210. (Pa., 1798.)

8168. STATES, Safety of citizens.—For the ordinary safety of the citizens of the several States, whether against dangers within or without, their reliance must be on the means to be provided by their respective States.—To GOVERNOR TOMPKINS. v, 239. (W., 1808.)

8169. STATES, Sovereignty of.—The several States, now comprising the United States of America, were, from their first establishment, separate and distinct societies, dependent on no other society of men whatever. They continued at the head of their respective governments the executive Magistrate who presided over the one they had left. * * * The part which our chief magistrate took in a war waged against us by the nation among whom he resided, obliged us to discontinue him, and to name one within every State.—MISSISSIPPI RIVER INSTRUCTIONS. vii, 570. FORD ED., v, 461. (1792.)

8170 STATES, Union of.—We are so * * * sincerely disposed to render the union of the States more perfect that we shall, on all occasions, endeavor to render to our neighbors every friendly office which circumstances shall bring within the compass of our powers.—To THE PRESIDENT OF PENNSYLVANIA. iii, 17. (R., 1781.)

8171. ———— ————. Our citizens have wisely formed themselves into one nation as to others, and several States as among themselves. To the united nation belong our external and mutual relations; to each State, severally, the care of our persons, our property, our reputation, and religious freedom. This wise distribution, if carefully preserved, will prove, I trust from example, that while smaller governments are better adapted to the ordinary objects of society, larger confederations more effectually secure independence, and the preservation of republican government.—To THE RHODE ISLAND ASSEMBLY. iv, 397. (W., May 1801.) See STATE RIGHTS and UNION (FEDERAL).

8172. STATES, Vermont and Franklin.—I am anxious to hear what is done with the States of Vermont and Franklin. I think that the former is the only innovation on the system of April 23, 1784, which ought ever possibly be admitted. If Congress are not firm on that head, our several States will crumble to atoms by the spirit of establishing every little canton into a separate State. I hope Virginia will concur in that plan as to her territory South of the Ohio, and not leave to the Western country to withdraw themselves by force, and become our worst enemies instead of our best friends.—To RICHARD HENRY LEE. FORD ED., iv, 71. (P., 1785.)

8173. STATESMEN, Honesty and.—The man who is dishonest as a statesman, would be a dishonest man in any station.—To GEORGE LOGAN. FORD ED., x, 68. (P.F., 1816.)

8174. STEAM, Application of.—You asked me * * * whether the steam mill in London was turned by the steam immediately, or by the intermediate agency of water raised by the steam. When I was in London, Boulton made a secret of his mill. Therefore I was permitted to see it only superficially. I saw no water wheels, and therefore supposed none. I answered you accordingly that there were none. But when I was at Nismes, I went to see the steam mill there, and they showed 't to me in all its parts. I saw that their steam raised water, and that this water turned a wheel. I expressed my doubts of the necessity of the inter-agency of water, and that the London mill was without it. But they supposed me mistaken. Perhaps I was so. I have had no opportunity since 'of clearing up the doubt.—To CHARLES THOMSON. ii, 277. FORD ED., iv, 449. (P., 1787.)

8175. STEAM, Domestic use.—A smaller agent, applicable to our daily concerns, is infinitely more valuable than the greatest which can be used only for great objects. For these interest the few alone, the former the many. I once had an idea that it might perhaps be possible to economize the steam of a common pot, kept boiling on the kitchen fire until its accumulation should be sufficient to give a stroke, and although the strokes might not be rapid, there would be enough of them in the day to raise from an adjacent well the water necessary for daily use; to wash the linen, knead the bread, beat the hominy, churn the butter, turn the spit, and do all other household offices which require only a regular mechanical motion. The unproductive hands now necessarily employed in these, might then increase the produce of our fields. I proposed it to Mr. Rumsey, one of our greatest mechanics, who believed in its possibility. * * * but his death disappointed this hope.—To GEORGE FLEMING. vi, 505. (M., 1815.)

8176. STEAM, Engines.—It happens that of all the machines which have been employed to aid human labor, I have made myself the least acquainted with (that which is certainly the most powerful of all) the steam engine. In its original and simple form indeed, as first constructed by Newcommen and Savary, it had been a subject of my early studies; but once possessed of the principle, I ceased to follow up the numerous modifications of the machinery for employing it, of which I do not know whether England or our own country has produced the greater number.—To GEORGE FLEMING. vi, 504. (M., 1815.)

8177. STEAM, Fire engine.—You speak of a new method of raising water by steam, which, you suppose, will come into general use. I know of no new method of that kind, and suppose (as you say the account you have received of it is very imperfect) that some person has represented to you, as new, a fire engine erected at Paris, and which supplies the greater part of the town with water. But this is nothing more than the fire engine you have seen described in the books of hydraulics, and particularly in the Dictionary of Arts and Sciences, published by Owen, the idea of which was first taken from Papin's Digester. It would have been better called the steam engine. The force of the steam of water, you know, is immense. In this engine, it is made to exert itself towards the working of pumps. That of Paris is, I believe, the largest known, raising four hundred thousand cubic feet (French) of water in twenty-four hours; or, rather, I should have said, *those* of Paris, for there are two under one roof, each raising that quantity.—To PROFESSOR JAMES MADISON.* i, 446. (P., 1785.)

8178. STEAM, Grist mills.—I could write you volumes on the improvements which I find made, and making here [England], in the arts. One deserves particular notice, be-

* Professor in William and Mary College; a cousin of the President.—EDITOR.

cause it is simple, great, and likely to have extensive consequences. It is the application of steam, as an agent for working grist mills. I have visited the one lately made here. It was, at that time, turning eight pair of stones. It consumes one hundred bushels of coal a day. It is proposed to put up thirty pair of stones. I do not know whether the quantity of fuel is to be increased.—To CHARLES THOMSON. i, 542. (L., 1786.)

8179. ——— ———. In the arts, the most striking thing I saw in England, new, was the application of the principle of the steam-engine to grist mills. I saw eight pairs of stones which are worked by steam, and there are to be set up thirty pair in the same house. A hundred bushels of coal a day, are consumed at present. I do not know in what proportion the consumption will be increased by the additional gear.—To JOHN PAGE. i, 550. FORD ED., iv, 215. (P., 1786.)

8180. STEAM, Horse power vs.—You say you have not been able to learn whether, in the new mills in London, steam is the immediate mover of the machinery, or raises water to move it. It is the immediate mover. The power of this agent, though long known, is but now beginning to be applied to the various purposes of which it is susceptible. * * * I have had a conversation on the subject * * * with the famous Boulton to whom those mills belong. * * * He compares the effect of steam with that of horses in the following manner: Six horses, aided with the most advantageous combination of the mechanical powers hitherto tried, will grind six bushels of flour in an hour; at the end of which time they are all in a foam, and must rest. They can work thus six hours in the twenty-four, grinding thirty-six bushels of flour, which is six to each horse, for the twenty-four hours. His steam mill in London consumes one hundred and twenty bushels of coal in twenty-four hours, turns ten pair of stones, which grind eight bushels of flour an hour each, which is nineteen hundred and twenty bushels in the twenty-four hours. This makes a peck and a half of coal perform exactly as much as a horse in one day can perform.*—To CHARLES THOMSON. ii, 67. FORD ED., iv, 337. (P., 1786.)

8181. STEAM, Livingston's experiments.—I have received with great pleasure your favor on the subject of the steam engine. Though deterred by the complexity of that hitherto known, from making myself minutely acquainted with it, yet I am sufficiently acquainted with it to be sensible of the superior simplicity of yours, and its superior economy. I particularly thank you for the permission to communicate it to the Philosophical Society.—To ROBERT R. LIVINGSTON. iv, 295. FORD ED., vii, 367. (Pa., 1799.)

8182. STEAM, Navigation.—I hear you are applying steam in America to navigate boats, and I have little doubt, but that it will be applied generally to machines, so as to super-

* Parton, in his *Life of Jefferson*, p. 303, says: "It was Jefferson who first sent to America the most important piece of mechanical intelligence that pen ever recorded,—the success of the Watt steam engine, by means of which 'a peck and a half of coal performs as much work as a horse in a day'. He conversed at Paris with Boulton, who was Watts's partner in the manufacture of the engines, and learned from his lips this astounding fact. But it did not astound him in the least. He mentions it quietly in the postcript of a long letter; for no man yet foresaw the revolution in all human affairs which that invention was to effect."—EDITOR.

sede the use of water ponds, and, of course, to lay open all the streams for navigation. We know that steam is one of the most powerful engines we can employ; and in America, fuel is abundant.—To CHARLES THOMSON. i, 543. (L., 1786.)

8183. ——— ———. Internal navigation by steamboats is rapidly spreading through all our States, and that by sails and oars will ere long be looked back to as among the curiosities of antiquity. We count much, too, on its efficacy for harbor defence; and it will soon be tried for navigation by sea.—To BARON HUMBOLDT. vii, 75. FORD ED., x, 89. (M., 1817.)

8184. STEAM, Rumsey's ship.—Mr. Rumsey has obtained a patent in England for his navigation by the force of steam, and is soliciting a similar one here [France]. His principal merit is in the improvement of the boiler, and instead of the complicated machinery of oars and paddles, proposed by others, the substitution of so simple a thing as the reaction of a stream of water on his vessel. He is building a sea vessel at this time in England. He has suggested a great number of mechanical improvements in a variety of branches; and, upon the whole, is the most original and the greatest mechanical genius I have ever seen.—To DOCTOR WILLARD. iii, 16. (P., 1789.)

8185. STEAM, Water supply.—There is one object to which I have often wished a steam engine could be adapted. You know how desirable it is both in town and country to be able to have large reservoirs of water on the top of our houses, not only for use (by pipes) in the apartments, but as a resource against fire. * * * Could any agent be employed which would be little or no additional expense or trouble except the first purchase, it would be done. Every family has such an agent, its kitchen fire. It is small, indeed, but if its small but constant action could be accumulated so as to give a stroke from time to time which might throw ever so small a quantity of water from the bottom of a well to the top of the house (say one hundred feet), it would furnish more than would waste by evaporation, or be used by the family. I know nobody who must better know the value of such a machine than yourself, nor more equal to the invention of it.—To ROBERT R. LIVINGSTON. iv, 296. FORD ED., vii, 367. (Pa., 1799.)

— STERNE (Laurence), Writings of.—See MORAL SENSE.

8186. STEUBEN (Baron), Services of.—Baron Steuben, a zealous friend, has descended from the dignity of his proper command to direct our [Virginia] smallest movements. His vigilance has, in a great measure, supplied the want of force in preventing the enemy from crossing the [James] river, which might have been * * * fatal. He has been assiduously employed in preparing equipments for the militia as they should assemble, pointing them to a proper object, and other offices of a good commander.—To GENERAL WASHINGTON. i. 284. FORD ED., ii, 408. (R., 1781.)

8187. STEWART (Dugald), Metaphysician.—Stewart is a great man, and among the most honest living. After you left Europe he * * * came to Paris. He brought me a letter from Lord Wycombe, whom you knew. I became immediately intimate with him, calling mutually on each other and almost daily during his stay at Paris, which was of some months.

I consider him and Tracy as the ablest metaphysicians living.—To JOHN ADAMS. vii, 152. (M., 1820.)

— STRAWBERRY.—See AGRICULTURE.

8188. STRENGTH, National.—Weakness provokes insult and injury while a condition to punish often prevents them.—To JOHN JAY. i, 404. FORD ED., iv, 89. (P., 1785.)

8189. ——— ———. We confide in our strength, without boasting of it; we respect that of others, without fearing it.—To CARMICHAEL AND SHORT. iv, 17. FORD ED., vi, 338. (Pa., 1793.)

8190. STUART (Archibald), Talented.—A young man of good talents from the westward.—To JAMES MADISON. FORD ED., iii, 318. (T., May 1783.)

8191. STUART (House of), America and.—This country [American Colonies] which had been acquired by the lives, the labors, and fortunes of individual adventurers, was, by these Princes [the Stuarts], several times, parted out and distributed among the favorites and followers of their fortunes; and, by an assumed right of the Crown alone, were erected into distinct and independent governments; a measure, which, it is believed, his Majesty's prudence and understanding would prevent him from imitating at this day; as no exercise of such power, of dividing and dismembering a country, has ever occurred in his Majesty's realm of England, though now of very ancient standing; nor could it be justified or acquiesced under there, or in any part of his Majesty's empire.—RIGHTS OF BRITISH AMERICA. i, 127. FORD ED., i, 431. (1774.)

8192. STUART (House of), Crimes.—The treasonable crimes [of the Stuarts] against their people brought on them the exertion of those sacred and sovereign rights of punishment, reserved in the hands of the people for cases of extreme necessity, and judged by the constitution unsafe to be delegated to any other judicature.—RIGHTS OF BRITISH AMERICA. i, 127. FORD ED., i, 431. (1774.)

8193. STUART (House of), Evil influence.—It is not in the history of modern England or among the advocates of the principles or practices of her government, that the friend of freedom, or of political morality, is to seek instruction. There has, indeed, been a period, during which both were to be found, not in her government, but in the band of worthies who so boldly and ably reclaimed the rights of the people, and wrested from their government theoretic acknowledgments of them. This period began with the Stuarts, and continued but one reign after them. Since that, the vital principle of the English constitution is *corruption*, its practices the natural results of that principle, and their consequences a pampered aristocracy, annihilation of the substantial middle class, a degraded populace, oppressive taxes, general pauperism, and national bankruptcy.—To JOHN F. WATSON. vi, 346. (M., 1814.)

8194. STUART (House of), Hume and.—Hume spared nothing to wash the Stuarts white, and to palliate their misgovernment. For this purpose he suppressed truths, advanced falsehoods, forged authorities, and falsified records.—To ——— ———. vii, 412. (M., 1825.)

8195. STUDY, In old age.—I was a hard student until I entered on the business of life, the duties of which leave no idle time to those disposed to fulfil them ; and now, retired, and at the age of seventy-six, I am again a hard student.—To Dr. Vine Utley. vii, 116. Ford ed., x, 126. (M., 1819.)

8196. STUDY, Young men and.—A part of my occupation, and by no means the least pleasing, is the direction of the studies of such young men as ask it. They place themselves in the neighboring village and have the use of my library and counsel, and make a part of my society. In advising the course of their reading, I endeavor to keep their attention fixed on the main objects of all science, the freedom and happiness of man. So that coming to bear a share in the councils and government of their country, they will keep ever in view the sole objects of all legitimate government.—To General Kosciusko. v, 509. (M., 1810.)

— **STYLOGRAPH.**—See Inventions.

8197. SUBMISSION, To parliament.—Submission to their parliament was no part of our Constitution, nor ever in idea, if history may be credited.*—Declaration of Independence as Drawn by Jefferson.

8198. SUBSERVIENCE, Americans and.—We owe gratitude to France, justice to England, good-will to all, and subservience to none.—To Arthur Campbell. iv, 198. Ford ed., vii, 170. (M., 1797.)

— **SUBSIDIES.**—See Bounties.

8199. SUBSISTENCE, Discoveries and.—Every discovery which multiplies the subsistence of man must be a matter of joy to every friend of humanity.—To Monsieur L Hommande. ii, 236. (P., 1787.)

8200. SUFFRAGE, Ark of safety.—The elective franchise, if guarded as the ark of our safety, will peaceably dissipate all combinations to subvert a Constitution, dictated by the wisdom, and resting on the will of the people.—To Benjamin Waring. iv, 378. (W., March 1801.)

8201. SUFFRAGE, Bribery and.—I believe we may lessen the danger of buying and selling votes, by making the number of voters too great for any means of purchase; I may further say that I have not observed men's honesty to increase with their riches.— To Jeremiah Moor. Ford ed., vii, 454. (M., Aug. 1800.)

8202. SUFFRAGE, Education and.—There is one provision [in the new constitution of Spain] which will immortalize its inventors. It is that which, after a certain epoch, disfranchises every citizen who cannot read and write. This is new, and is the fruitful germ of the improvement of everything good, and the correction of everything imperfect in the present constitution.—To Chevalier de Onis. vi, 342. (M., 1814.)

8203. —— ——. In the constitution of Spain, as proposed by the late Cortes, there was a principle entirely new to me, * * * that no person, born after that day, should ever acquire the rights of citizenship until he

* Struck out by Congress.—Editor.

could read and write. It is impossible sufficiently to estimate the wisdom of this provision. Of all those which have been thought of for securing fidelity in the administration of the government, constant ralliance to the principles of the Constitution, and progressive amendments with the progressive advances of the human mind, or changes in human affairs, it is the most effectual. Enlighten the people generally, and tyranny and oppressions of body and mind will vanish like evil spirits at the dawn of day. * * * The constitution of the Cortes had defects enough; but when I saw in it this amendatory provision, I was satisfied all would come right in time, under its salutary operation.—To Dupont de Nemours. vi, 592. Ford ed., x, 24. (P.F., 1816.) See Constitution, Spanish.

8204. —— ——. By the bill [in the revision of the Virginia Code] for a general education, the people would be qualified to understand their rights, to maintain them, and to exercise with intelligence their parts in self-government.—Autobiography. i, 49. Ford ed., i, 69. (1821.)

8205. SUFFRAGE, Exercise of.—Should things go wrong at any time, the people will set them to rights by the peaceable exercise of their elective rights.—To Wilson C. Nicholas. v, 5. Ford ed., viii, 435. (W., 1806.)

8206. SUFFRAGE, General.—When the Constitution of Virginia was formed I was in attendance at Congress. Had I been here, I should probably have proposed a general suffrage; because my opinion has always been in favor of it. Still, I find some very honest men who, thinking the possession of some property necessary to give due independence of mind, are for restraining the elective franchise to property.—To Jeremiah Moor. Ford ed., vii, 454. (M., Aug. 1800.)

8207. SUFFRAGE, Instrument of reform.—The rational and peaceable instrument of reform, the suffrage of the people.— To Spencer Roane. vii, 133. Ford ed., x, 140. (P.F., 1819.)

8208. SUFFRAGE, Property qualification.—All male persons of full age and sane mind, having a freehold estate in one-fourth of an acre of land in any town, or in twenty-five acres of land in the country, and all persons resident in the colony, who shall have paid, scot and lot, to government the last two years, shall have right to give their vote in the election of their respective representatives.—Proposed Va. Constitution. Ford ed., ii, 14. (June 1776.)

8209. —— ——. All free male citizens, of full age and sane mind, who for one year before shall have been resident in the county, or shall through the whole of that time have possessed therein real property to the value of ——, or shall for the same time have been enrolled in the militia, and no others, shall have a right to vote for delegates for the * * * county, and for senatorial electors for the district. They shall give their votes personally, and *vivâ voce.*—Proposed Va. Constitution. viii, 444. Ford ed., iii, 323. (1783.)

8210. —— ——. In the scheme of constitution for Virginia which I prepared in 1783, * * * I found [the suffrage] on a year's residence in the country, or the possession of property in it, or a year's enrollment in its militia.—To Jeremiah Moor. Ford ed., vii, 454. (M., Aug. 1800.)

8211. SUFFRAGE, Restricted.—It has been thought that corruption is restrained by confining the right of suffrage to a few of the wealthier of the people; but it would be more effectually restrained by an extension of that right to such numbers as would bid defiance to the means of corruption.—Notes on Virginia. viii, 391. Ford ed., iii, 255. (1782.)

8212. SUFFRAGE, Taxes and militia duty.—Every male citizen of the commonwealth, liable to taxes or to militia duty in any county, shall have a right to vote for representatives for that county to the legislature.—Notes for a Constitution. Ford ed., vi, 520. (1794.) See Voting.

8213. SUGAR, Maple.—What a blessing to substitute a sugar [maple] which requires only the labor of children for that which is said to render the slavery of the blacks necessary.—To Benjamin Vaughan. iii, 158. (N.Y., 1790.)

8214. —— ——. I am sorry to hear my sugar maples have failed. I shall be able, however, to get here [Philadelphia] any number I may desire. * * * It is too hopeful an object to be abandoned.—To T. M. Randolph. Ford ed., v, 508. (Pa., 1792.)

8215. —— ——. I should think the sugar-maple more worthy of experiment [in France than the sugar cane]. There is no part of France of which the climate would not admit this tree. I have never seen a reason why every farmer should not have a sugar orchard, as well as an apple orchard. The supply of sugar for his family would require as little ground, and the process of making it is as easy as that of cider. Mr. Micheaux, your botanist here, could send you plants as well as seeds, in any quantity from the United States.—To M. Lasteyrie. v, 314. (W., July 1808.)

8216. SUGAR, The poor and.—Sugar and coffee being articles of food for the poorer class, a small increase of price places them above the reach of this class.—To Marquis Lafayette. i, 597. Ford ed., iv, 257. (P., 1786.)

— **SUICIDE.**—See Murder, Self.

8217. SUMTER (Thomas), Description of.—I think I have selected a governor for Louisiana. as perfect in all points as we can expect. Sound judgment, standing in society, knowledge of the world, wealth, liberality, familiarity with the French language, and having a French wife. You will perceive I am describing Sumter. I do not know a more proper character for the place.—To James Madison. Ford ed., viii, 260. (M., July 1803.)

8218. SUN, Almighty physician.—The sun,—my almighty physician.—To James Monroe. Ford ed., iv, 41. (P., 1785.)

8219. SUN-DIAL, Calculations for a.—While much confined to the house by my rheumatism, I have amused myself w th calculating the hour lines of an horizontal d al for the latitude of this place [Poplar Forest]. * * * As I do not know that anybody here has taken this trouble before, I have supposed a copy would be acceptable to you.—To Mr. Clay. vi, 7. (P.F., 1811.)

8220. SUPREME COURT, Appointments to.—The appointment of a successor to Judge Patterson was bound up by rule. The last judiciary system requiring a judge for each district, rendered it proper that he should be of the district. This has been observed in both the appointments to the Supreme Bench made by me. Where an office is local we never go out of the limits for the officer.—To Cæsar A. Rodney. Ford ed., viii, 497. (W., Dec. 1806.)

8221. SUPREME COURT, Centralization and.—The great object of my fear is the Federal Judiciary. That body, like gravity, ever acting, with noiseless foot, and unalarming advance, gaining ground step by step, and holding what it gains, is engulfing insidiously the special governments into the jaws of that which feeds them.—To Spencer Roane. vii, 212. Ford ed., x, 189. (M., 1821.)

8222. —— ——. There is no danger I apprehend so much as the consolidation of our Government by the noiseless, and therefore unalarming, instrumentality of the Supreme Court. This is the form in which federalism now arrays itself, and consolidation is the present principle of distinction between republicans and the pseudo-republicans but real federalists.—To William Johnson. vii, 278. Ford ed., x, 248. (M., 1823.)

8223. SUPREME COURT, Individual opinions.—A most condemnable practice of the Supreme Court to be corrected is that of cooking up a decision in caucus and delivering it by one of their members as the opinion of the Court, without the possibility of our knowing how many, who, and for what reasons each member concurred. This completely defeats the possibility of impeachment by smothering evidence. A regard for character in each being now the only hold we can have of them, we should hold fast to it. They would, were they to give their opinions *seriatim* and publicly, endeavor to justify themselves to the world by explaining the reasons which led to their opinion.—To James Pleasants. Ford ed., x, 199. (M., Dec. 1821.)

8224. —— ——. There is a subject respecting the practice of the Court of which you are a member which has long weighed on my mind. * * * It is the habitual mode of making up and delivering the opinions. You know that from the earliest ages of the English law, from the date of the Year-Books, at least, to the end of the Second George, the judges of England, in all but self-evident cases, delivered their opinions *seriatim*, with the reasons and authorities which governed their decisions. If they sometimes consulted together, and gave a general opinion, it was so rarely as not to excite either alarm or notice. Besides the light which their separate arguments threw on the subject, and the instruction communicated by their several modes of reasoning, it showed whether the judges were unanimous or divided, and gave accordingly more or less weight to the judgment as a precedent. It sometimes happened, too, that when there were three opinions against one, the reasoning of the one was so much the most cogent as to become afterwards the law of the land. When Lord Mansfield came to the bench he introduced the habit of caucusing opinions. The judges met at their chambers, or elsewhere, secluded from the presence of the public, and made up what was to be delivered as the opinion of the court. On the retirement of Mansfield, Lord Kenyon put an end to the practice, and the judges returned to that of *seriatim* opinions, and practice it habitually to this day I believe. I am not acquainted with the late Reporters, do not possess them, and state the fact from the information of others. To come now to ourselves, I know nothing of what is done in other States, but in this [Virginia] our great and good Mr. Pendleton was, after the Revolution, placed at the head of the Court of Appeals. He adored Lord Mansfield, and considered him as the greatest luminary of law that any age had ever produced, and he introduced into the court over which he presided, Mansfield's practice of making up opinions in secret, and delivering them as the oracle of the court, in mass. Judge Roane, when he came to that bench, broke up the practice, refused to hatch judgments, in conclave, or to let others deliver opinions for him. At what time the *seriatim* opinions ceased in the Supreme Court of the United States, I am not informed. They continued I know to the end of the 3d Dallas in 1800, later than which I have no Reporter of that court. About that time the present Chief-Justice [Marshall] came to the bench. Whether he carried the practice of Mr. Pendleton to it, or who, or when I do not know; but I understand from others it is now the habit of the Court, and I suppose it is true from the cases sometimes reported in the newspapers, and others which I casually see, wherein I observed that the opinions were uniformly prepared in private. Some of these cases, too, have been of such importance, of such difficulty, and the decisions so grating to a portion of the public as to have merited the fullest explanation from every judge, *seriatim*, of the reasons which had produced such convictions on his mind. It was interesting to the public to know whether these decisions were really unanimous, or might not perhaps be of four against three, and, consequently, prevailing by the preponderance of one voice only. The Judges, holding their offices for life, are under two responsibilities only. 1. Impeachment. 2. Individual reputation. But this practice completely withdraws them from both. For no-

body knows what opinion any individual member gave in any case, nor even that he who delivers the opinion, concurred in it himself. Be the opinion, therefore, ever so impeachable, having been done in the dark, it can be proved on no one. As to the second guarantee, personal reputation, it is shielded completely. The practice is certainly convenient for the lazy, the modest and the incompetent. It saves them the trouble of developing their opinion methodically and even of making up an opinion at all. That of *seriatim* argument shows whether every judge has taken the trouble of understanding the case, of investigating it minutely, and of forming an opinion for himself, instead of pinning it on another's sleeve. It would certainly be right to abandon this practice in order to give to our citizens one and all, that confidence in their judges which must be so desirable to the judges themselves, and so important to the cement of the Union. During the administration of General Washington, and while E. Randolph was Attorney General, he was required by Congress to digest the judiciary laws into a single one, with such amendments as might be thought proper. He prepared a section requiring the judges to give their opinions *seriatim*, in writing to be recorded in a distinct volume. Other business prevented this bill from being taken up, and it passed off; but such a volume would have been the best possible book of reports, and the better as unincumbered with the hired sophisms and perversions of counsel.—To WILLIAM JOHNSON. FORD ED., x, 223. (M., Oct. 1822.)

8225. —— ——. I rejoice in the example you set of *seriatim* opinions. Some of your brethren will be encouraged to follow it occasionally, and in time, it may be felt by all as a duty, and the sound practice of the primitive court be again restored. Why should not every judge be asked his opinion, and give it from the bench, if only by yea or nay? Besides ascertaining the fact of his opinion, which the public have a right to know, in order to judge whether it is impeachable or not, it would show whether the opinions were unanimous or not, and thus settle more exactly the weight of their authority.—To WILLIAM JOHNSON. vii, 298. FORD ED., x, 232. (M., 1823.)

8226. —— ——. I must comfort myself with the hope that the judges will see the importance and the duty of giving their country the only evidence they can give of fidelity to its Constitution and integrity in the administration of its laws; that is to say, by every one's giving his opinion *seriatim* and publicly on the cases he decides. Let him prove by his reasoning that he has read the papers, that he has considered the case, that in the application of the law to it, he uses his own judgment independently and unbiased by party views and personal favor or disfavor. Throw himself in every case on God and his country; both will excuse him for error and value him for his honesty. The very idea of cooking up opinions in conclave, begets suspicions that something passes which fears the public ear. and this, spreading by degrees, must produce at some time abridgment of tenure, facility of removal, or some other modification which may promise a remedy. For, in truth, there is at this time more hostility to the Federal Judiciary than to any other organ of the government.— To WILLIAM JOHNSON. vii, 278. FORD ED., x, 248. (M., 1823.)

8227. SUPREME COURT, Marshall's opinions.—This practice of Judge Marshall, of travelling out of his case to prescribe what the law would be in a moot case not before the court, is very irregular and very censurable. I recollect another instance, and the more particularly, perhaps, because it in some measure bore on myself. Among the midnight appointments of Mr. Adams, were commissions to some Federal justices of the peace for Alexandria. These were signed and sealed by him, but not delivered. I found them on the table of the Department of State, on my entrance into office. and I forbade their delivery. Marbury, named in one of them. applied to the Supreme Court for a mandamus to the Secretary of State . (Mr. Madison) to deliver the commission intended for him. The Court determined at once, that being an original process, they had no cognizance of it; and, therefore, the question before them was ended. But the Chief Justice went on to lay down what the law would be, had they jurisdiction of the case, to wit: that they should command the delivery. The object was clearly to instruct any other court having the jurisdiction, what they should do if Marbury should apply to them. Besides the impropriety of this gratuitous interference, could anything exceed the perversion of law? For, if there is any principle of law never yet contradicted, it is that delivery is one of the essentials to the validity of a deed. Although signed and sealed, yet as long as it remains in the hands of the party himself, it is in *fieri* only, it is not a deed, and can be made so only by its delivery. In the hands of a third person it may be made an escrow. But whatever is in the Executive officers is certainly deemed to be in the hands of the President; and in this case, was actually in my hands, because, when I countermanded them, there was as yet no Secretary of State. Yet this case of "Marbury *vs.* Madison" is continually cited by bench and bar, as if it were settled law, without any animadversion on its being an *obiter* dissertation of the Chief Justice. It may be impracticable to lay down any general formula of words which shall decide at once, and with precision, in every case, this limit of jurisdiction. But there are two canons which will guide us safely in most of the cases. First. The capital and leading object of the Constitution was to leave with the States all authorities which respected their own citizens only, and to transfer to the United States those which respected citizens of foreign or other States; to make us several as to ourselves, but one as to all others. In the latter case, then, constructions should lean to the general jurisdiction, if the words will bear it; and in favor of the States in the former, if possible to be so construed. And indeed, between citizens and citizens of the same State, and under their own laws, I know but a single case in which a jurisdiction is given to the General Government. That is, where anything but gold or silver is made a lawful tender, or the obligation of contracts is any otherwise impaired. The separate legislatures had so often abused that power, that the citizens themselves chose to trust it to the General, rather than to their own special authorities. Secondly. On every question of construction, carry ourselves back to the time when the Constitution was adopted, recollect the spirit manifested in the debates, and instead of trying what meaning may be squeezed out of the text, or invented against it, conform to the probable one in which it was passed. Let us try Cohen's case by these canons only, referring always, however, for full argument, to the essays before cited. 1. It was between a citizen and his own State, and under a law of his State. It was a domestic case, therefore, and not a foreign one. 2. Can it be believed, that under the jealousies prevailing against the General Government, at the adoption of the Constitution, the States meant to surrender the authority of preserving order, of enforcing moral duties and restraining vice, within their own territory? And this is the present case. that of Cohen being under the ancient and general law of gaming. Can any good be effected by taking from the States the moral rule of their citizens, and subordinating it to the General authority, or to one of their corporations, which may justify forcing the meaning of words, hunting after possible constructions, and hanging inference on inference, from heaven to earth, like Jacob's ladder? Such an intention was impossible, and such a licentiousness of construction and inference, if exercised by both governments, as may be done with equal right, would equally authorize both to claim all power, general and particular, and break up the foundations of the Union. Laws are made for men of ordinary understanding, and should, therefore, be construed by the ordinary rules of common sense. Their meaning is not to be sought for in metaphysical subtleties, which may make anything mean anything or nothing. at pleasure. It should be left to the sophisms of advocates, whose trade it is, to prove that a defendant is a plaintiff, though dragged into court, *torto collo*, like Bonaparte's volunteers, into the field in chains, or that a power has been given, because it ought to have been given, *et alia talia*. The States supposed that by their Tenth Amendment, they had secured themselves against constructive powers. They were not lessened yet by Cohen's case, nor aware of the slipperiness of the eels of the law. I ask for no straining of words against the General Government nor yet against the States. I believe the

States can best govern our home concerns, and the General Government our foreign ones. I wish, therefore, to see maintained that wholesome distribution of powers established by the Constitution for the limitation of both; and never to see all offices transferred to Washington, where, further withdrawn from the eyes of the people, they may more secretly be bought and sold as at market. But the Chief Justice says, "there must be an ultimate arbiter somewhere". True, there must; but does that prove it is either party? The ultimate arbiter is the people of the Union, assembled by their deputies in convention, at the call of Congress, or of two-thirds of the States. Let them decide to which they mean to give an authority claimed by two of their organs. And it has been the peculiar wisdom and felicity of our Constitution, to have provided this peaceable appeal, where that of other nations is at once to force.—To WILLIAM JOHNSON.* vii, 293. FORD ED., x, 230. (M., 1823.) See MARSHALL.

8228. SUPREME COURT, Questions of constitutionality.—It is a very dangerous doctrine to consider the judges as the ultimate arbiters of all constitutional questions. It is one which would place us under the despotism of an oligarchy. * * * The Constitution has erected no such single tribunal, knowing that to whatever hands confided, with the corruptions of time and party, its members would become despots. It has more wisely made all the departments coequal and cosovereign within themselves.—To WILLIAM C. JARVIS. vii, 178. FORD ED., x, 160. (M., 1820.

8229. ——   ——. If the Legislature fails to pass laws for a census, for paying the Judges and other officers of government, for establishing a militia, for naturalization as prescribed by the Constitution, or if they fail to meet in Congress, the Judges cannot issue their mandamus to them; if the President fails to supply the place of a judge, to appoint other civil or military officers, to issue requisite commissions, the Judges cannot force him. They can issue their mandamus or distringas to no executive or legislative officer to enforce the fulfilment of their official duties any more than the President or Legislature may issue orders to the Judges or their officers. Betrayed by English example, and unaware, as it should seem, of the control of our Constitution in this particular, they have at times overstepped their limit by undertaking to command executive officers in the discharge of their executive duties; but the Constitution, in keeping the three departments distinct and independent, restrains the authority of the Judges to judiciary organs, as it does the Executive and Legislative to executive and legislative organs. The Judges certainly have more frequent occasion to act on constitutional questions, because the laws of *meum* and *tuum* and of criminal action,

*Associate Justice William Johnson, of South Carolina, appointed by Jefferson to the Supreme Court bench, March, 1804.—EDITOR.

forming the great mass of the system of law, constitute their particular department. When the legislative or executive functionaries act unconstitutionally, they are responsible to the people in their elective capacity. The exemption of the Judges from that is quite dangerous enough.—To WILLIAM C. JARVIS. vii, 178. FORD ED., x, 160. (M., 1820.)

8230. SUPREME COURT, Republicanism and.—At length, we have a chance of getting a republican majority in the Supreme Judiciary. For ten years has that branch braved the spirit and will of the nation, after the nation had manifested its will by a complete reform in every branch depending on them. The event is a fortunate one, and so timed as to be a God-send to me. I am sure its importance to the nation will be felt, and the occasion employed to complete the great operation they have so long been executing, by the appointment of a decided republican, with nothing equivalent about him.—To ALBERT GALLATIN. v, 549. FORD ED., ix, 284. (M., 1810.)

8231. ——   ——. The misfortune of Bidwell removes an able man from the competition. Can any other bring equal qualifications to those of [Levi] Lincoln? I know he was not deemed a profound common lawyer; but was there ever a profound common lawyer known in one of the Eastern States? There never was, nor never can be, one from those States. The basis of their law is neither common nor civil; it is an original, if any compound can be so called. Its foundation seems to have been laid in the spirit and principles of Jewish law, incorporated with some words and phrases of common law, and an abundance of notions of their own. This makes an *amalgam sui generis,* and it is well known that a man, first and thoroughly initiated into the principles of one system of law, can never become pure and sound in any other. Lord Mansfield was a splendid proof of this. Therefore, I say, there never was, nor can be a profound common lawyer from those States. Sullivan had the reputation of preeminence there as a common lawyer, but we have his History of Land Titles, which gives us his measure. Mr. Lincoln is, I believe, considered as learned in their laws as any one they have. Federalists say that Parsons is better. But the criticalness of the present nomination puts him out of the question. As the great mass of the functions of the new judge are to be performed in his own district, Lincoln will be most unexceptionable and acceptable there; and on the Supreme bench equal to any who can be brought thence. Add to this his integrity, political firmness, and unimpeachable character, and I believe no one can be found to whom there will not be more serious objections.—To ALBERT GALLATIN. v, 550. FORD ED., ix, 285. (M., Sep. 1810.)

3232. ——   ——. Bidwell's disgrace withdraws the ablest man of the section in which Cushing's successor must be named. The pure integrity, unimpeachable conduct, talents and republican firmness of [Levi] Lincoln, leave him now, I think, without a rival. He is thought not an able *common* lawyer. But there is not and never was an able one in the New England States. Their system is *sui generis,* in which the common law is little attended to. Lincoln is one of the ablest in their system, and it is among them he is to execute the great portion of his duties.—To CÆSAR A. RODNEY. v, 547. (M., Sep. 1810.)

8233. —— ——. The death of [Associate Justice] Cushing is opportune, as it gives an opening for at length getting a republican majority on the Supreme Bench. Ten years has the anti-civism of that body been bidding defiance to the spirit of the whole nation, after they had manifested their will by reforming every other branch of government. I trust the occasion will not be lost. * * * Nothing is more material than to complete the reformation of the government by this appointment, which may truly be said to be putting the keystone into the arch.—To CÆSAR A. RODNEY. v, 547. (M., Sep. 1810.)

8234. —— ——. A circumstance of congratulation is the death of Cushing. The nation ten years ago declared its will for a change in the principles of the administration of their affairs. They have changed the two branches depending on their will, and have steadily maintained the reformation in those branches. The third, not dependent on them, has so long bid defiance to their will, erecting themselves into a political body, to correct what they deem the errors of the nation. The death of Cushing gives an opportunity of closing the reformation by a successor of unquestionable republican principles. Our friend, Lincoln, has, of course, presented himself to your recollection. I know you think lightly of him as a lawyer; and I do not consider him as a correct common lawyer, yet as much so as any one which ever came, or ever can come from one of the Eastern States. Their system of jurisprudence made up from the Jewish law, a little dash of common law, and a great mass of original notions of their own, is a thing *sui generis,* and one educated in that system can never so far eradicate early impressions as to imbibe thoroughly the principles of another system. It is so in the case of other systems of which Lord Mansfield is a splendid example. Lincoln's firm republicanism, and known integrity, will give complete confidence to the public in the long desired reformation of their judiciary. Were he out of the way, I should think Granger prominent for the place. His abilities are great; I have entire confidence in his integrity, though I am sensible that J.[ohn] R.[andolph] has been able to lessen the confidence of many in him. But that I believe he would soon reconcile to him, if placed in a situation to show himself to the public, as he is, and not as an enemy has represented him. As the choice must be of a New Englander, to exercise his functions for New England men, I confess I know of none but these two characters. Morton is really a republican, but inferior to both the others

in every point of view. Blake calls himself republican, but never was one at heart. His treachery to us under the Embargo should put him by forever. Story and Bacon are exactly the men who deserted us on that measure, and carried off the majority. The former, unquestionably a tory, and both are too young. I say nothing of professing federalists. Granger and Morton have both been interested in Yazooism. The former, however, has long been clear of it. I have said thus much because I know you must wish to learn the sentiments of others, to hear all, and then do what on the whole you perceive to be best.—To PRESIDENT MADISON. FORD ED., ix, 282. (M., Oct. 1810.)

8235. —— ——. I consider the substituting, in the place of Cushing, a firm, unequivocating republican, whose principles are born with him, and not an occasional ingraftment, as necessary to complete that great reformation in our government to which the nation gave its fiat ten years ago. They have completed and maintained it steadily in the two branches dependent on them, but the third, unfortunately and unwisely, made independent not only of the nation, but even of their own conduct, have hitherto bid defiance to the public will, and erected themselves into a political body with the assumed functions of correcting what they deem the errors of the nation.—To GIDEON GRANGER. FORD ED., ix, 286. (M., Oct. 1810.)

8236. SUPREME COURT, State rights and.—There are two measures which if not taken, we are undone. First,* to check these unconstitutional invasions of State rights by the Federal judiciary. How? Not by impeachment, in the first instance, but by a strong protestation of both houses of Congress that such and such doctrines, advanced by the Supreme Court, are contrary to the Constitution; and if afterwards they relapse into the same heresies, impeach and set the whole adrift. For what was the government divided into three branches, but that each should watch over the others and oppose their usurpations?—To NATHANIEL MACON. FORD ED., x, 192. (M., Aug. 1821.)

8237. —— ——. The Legislative and Executive branches may sometimes err, but elections and dependence will bring them to rights. The Judiciary branch is the instrument which, working like gravity, without intermission, is to press us at last into one consolidated mass. * * * If Congress fails to shield the States from dangers so palpable and so imminent, the States must shield themselves, and meet the invader foot to foot.—To ARCHIBALD THWEAT. vii, 199. FORD ED., x, 184. (M., 1821.)

8238. —— ——. You request me confidentially, to examine the question, whether the Supreme Court has advanced beyond its constitutional limits, and trespassed on those of the State authorities? I do not undertake it, because I am unable. Age and the

* For the "second" one, see No. 2066. – EDITOR.

wane of mind consequent on it, have disqualified me from investigations so severe, and researches so laborious. And it is the less necessary in this case, as having been already done by others with a logic and learning to which I could add nothing. On the decision of the case of *Cohen* vs. *The State of Virginia,* in the Supreme Court of the United States, in March, 1821, Judge Roane, under the signature of "Algernon Sidney", wrote for the [Richmond] *Enquirer* a series of papers on the law of that case. I considered these papers maturely as they came out, and confess that they appeared to me to pulverize every word which had been delivered by Judge Marshall, of the extra-judicial part of his opinion; and all was extra-judicial, except the decision that the act of Congress had not purported to give to the Corporation of Washington the authority claimed by their lottery law, of controlling the laws of the States within the States themselves. But, unable to claim that case, he could not let it go entirely, but went on gratuitously to prove, that notwithstanding the Eleventh Amendment of the Constitution. a State *could* be brought as a defendant, to the bar of his court; and again, that Congress might authorize a corporation of its territory to exercise legislation within a State, and paramount to the laws of that State. I cite the sum and result only of his doctrines, according to the impression made on my mind at the time, and still remaining. If not strictly accurate in circumstance, it is so in substance. This doctrine was so completely refuted by Roane, that if he can be answered, I surrender human reason as a vain and useless faculty, given to bewilder, and not to guide us. And I mention this particular case as one only of several, because it gave occasion to that thorough examination of the constitutional limits between the General and State jurisdictions, which you have asked for. There were two other writers in the same paper, under the signatures of " Fletcher of Saltoun ", and " Somers ", who, in a few essays, presented some very luminous and striking views of the question. And there was a particular paper which recapitulated all the cases in which it was thought the Federal Court had usurped on the State jurisdictions. * * * The subject was taken up by our [Virginia] Legislature of 1821-'22, and two drafts of remonstrances were prepared and discussed. As well as I remember, there was no difference of opinion as to the matter of right; but there was as to the expediency of a remonstrance at that time, the general mind of the States being then under extraordinary excitement by the Missouri question; and it was dropped on that consideration. But this case is not dead. it only sleepeth. The Indian chief said he did not go to war for every petty injury by itself, but put it into his pouch. and when that was full, he then made war. Thank heaven, we have provided a more peaceable and rational mode of redress.—To JUDGE WILLIAM JOHNSON. vii, 293. FORD ED., x, 229. (M., June 1823.)

— **SURGERY.**—See MEDICINE.

8239. SURPLUS, Accumulation of.—
[We] have left us in the treasury eight millions and a half of dollars. A portion of this sum may be considered as a commencement of accumulation of the surpluses of revenue, which, after paying the instalments of debts as they shall become payable, will remain without any specific object. It may partly, indeed, be applied toward completing the defence of the exposed points of our country, on such a scale as shall be adapted to our principles and circumstances. This object is doubtless among the first entitled to attention, in such a state of our finances, and it is one which, whether we have peace or war, will provide security where it is due. Whether what shall remain of this, with the future surpluses, may be usefully applied to purposes already authorized, or more usefully to others requiring new authorities, or how otherwise they shall be disposed of, are questions calling for the notice of Congress, unless indeed they shall be superseded by a change in our public relations now awaiting the determinations of others.—SEVENTH ANNUAL MESSAGE. viii, 88. FORD ED., ix, 165. (Oct. 1807.)

8240. SURPLUS, Congress and.—The probable accumulation of the surpluses of revenue * * * merits the consideration of Congress. Shall it lie unproductive in the public vaults? Shall the revenue be reduced? Or shall it rather be appropriated to the improvements of roads, canals, rivers, education, and other great foundations of prosperity and union, under the powers which Congress may already possess, or such amendments of the Constitution as may be approved by the States?—EIGHTH ANNUAL MESSAGE. viii, 110. FORD ED., ix, 224. (Nov. 1808.)

8241. SURPLUS, Disposition of.—When both of these branches of revenue [Mediterranean fund and Salt tax] shall * * * be relinquished, there will still ere long be an accumulation of moneys in the treasury beyond the instalments of public debt which we are permitted by contract to pay. They cannot. then, without a modification assented to by the public creditors, be applied to the extinguishment of this debt, and the complete liberation of our revenues—the most desirable of all objects; nor, if our peace continues, will they be wanting for any other existing purpose. The question, therefore, now comes forward,—to what other objects shall these surpluses be appropriated, and the whole surplus of impost, after the entire discharge of the public debt, and during those intervals when the purposes of war shall not call for them? Shall we suppress the impost and give that advantage to foreign over domestic manufactures? On a few articles of more general and necessary use, the suppression in due season will doubtless be right, but the great mass of the articles on which impost is paid is foreign luxuries, purchased by those only who are rich enough to afford themselves the use of them. Their patriotism would certainly prefer its continuance and application to the great purposes of the public education, roads, rivers, canals, and such other objects of public improvement as it may be thought proper to add to the constitutional enumeration of federal powers. By these operations new channels of communication will be opened between the States; the lines of separation will disappear, their interests will be identified. and their Union cemented by new and indissoluble ties.—SIXTH ANNUAL MESSAGE. viii, 68. FORD ED., viii, 493. (Dec. 1806.)

8242. SURPLUS, Taxation and.—Sound principles will not justify our taxing the industry of our fellow citizens to accumulate treasure for wars to happen we know not when, and which might not perhaps happen but from the temptations offered by that treasure.—FIRST ANNUAL MESSAGE. viii, 9. FORD ED., viii. 119. (1801.)

8243. SURVEYING, Method of platting.—You requested for the use of your school, an explanation of a method of platting the courses of a survey, which I mentioned to you as of my own practice. This is so obvious and simple, that as it occurred to myself, so I presume it has to others, although I have not seen 't stated in any of the books. For drawing parallel lines, I use the triangular rule, the hypothenusal side of which being applied to the side of a common straight rule, the triangle slides on that, as thus, always parallel to itself. Instead of drawing meridians on his paper, let the pupil draw a parallel of latitude, or east and west line, and note in that a point for his first station, then applying to it his protractor, lay off the first course. and distance in the usual way to ascertain his second station. For the second course, lay the triangular rule to the east and west line, or first parallel, holding the straight or guide rule firmly against its hypothenusal side. Then slide up the triangle (for a northerly course) to the point of his second station, and pressing it firmly there, lay the protractor to that, and mark off the second course, and distance as before, for the third station. Then lay the triangle to the first parallel again, and sliding it as before to the point of the third station, then apply to it the protractor for the third course and distance, wh'ch gives the fourth station; and so on. When a course is southwardly, lay the protractor, as before, to the northern edge of the triangle, but prick its reversed course, which reversed again in drawing, gives the true course. When the station has got so far from the first parallel, as to be out of the reach of the parallel rule sliding on its hypothenuse, another parallel must be drawn by laying the edge, or longer leg of the triangle to the first parallel as before, app'ying the guide-rule to the end, or short leg (instead of the hypothenuse), as in the margin, and sliding the triangle up to the point for the new parallel. I have found this, in practice, the quickest and most correct method of platting which I have ever tried, and the neatest also, because it

disfigures the paper with the fewest unnecessary lines.—To MR. GIRARDIN. vi, 338. (M., 1814.)

8244. SWARTWOUT (Samuel), Character of.—The distribution of so atrocious a libel as the pamphlet "Aristides", and still more the affirming its contents to be true as Holy Writ, presents a shade in the morality of Mr. Swartwout, of which his character had not before been understood to be susceptible. Such a rejection of all regard to truth, would have been sufficient cause against receiving him into the corps of executive officers at first; but whether it is expedient after a person is appointed, to be as nice on a question of removal requires great consideration.—To DE WITT CLINTON. FORD ED., viii, 322. (W., Oct. 1804.)

— SYLVANIA, Proposed state of.— See WESTERN TERRITORY.

8245. SYMPATHY, For the afflicted.— What more sublime delight than to mingle tears with one whom the hand of heaven hath smitten! To watch over the bed of sickness, and to beguile its tedious and its painful moments! To share our bread with one whom misfortune has left none! This world abounds indeed with misery; to lighten its burthen, we must divide it with one another.—To MRS. COSWAY. ii, 38. FORD ED., iv, 318. (P., 1786.)

8246. SYMPATHY, Of friends.—When languishing under disease, how grateful is the solace of our friends! How are we penetrated with their assiduities and attentions! How much are we supported by their encouragement and kind offices! When heaven has taken from us some object of our love, how sweet is it to have a bosom whereon to recline our heads. and into which we may pour the torrent of our tears! Grief, with such a comfort, is almost a luxury!—To MRS. COSWAY. ii, 38. FORD ED., iv, 318. (P., 1786.)

8247. TALENTS, Hidden.—The object [of my educational bill] is to bring into action that mass of talents which lies buried in poverty in every country, for want of the means of development, and thus give activity to a mass of mind, which, in proportion to our population, shall be the double or treble of what it is in most countries.—To M. CORREA. vii, 94. (P.F., 1817.)

8248. TALENTS, Public councils and. —Talents in our public councils are at all times important.—To CÆSAR A. RODNEY. FORD ED., viii, 296. (W., 1804.)

8249. TALENTS, Republics and.—I hold it to be one of the distinguishing excellences of elective over hereditary successions, that the talents which nature has provided in sufficient proportion. should be selected by the society for the government of their affairs. rather than that this should be transmitted through the loins of knaves and fools, passing from the debauches of the table to those of the bed.—To PRESIDENT WASHINGTON. iii, 466. FORD ED., vi, 107. (M., 1792.)

8250. TALENTS, Science and.—Talents and science are sufficient motives with me in appointments to which they are fitted.—To PRESIDENT WASHINGTON. iii, 466. FORD ED., vi, 107. (M., 1792.)

8251. TALENTS, Useful.—The times do not admit of the inactivity of such talents as yours.—To James Madison. Ford ed., vii, 244. (Pa., 1798.) See Ability, Education, Genius and Schools.

8252. TALLEYRAND, Connection with X. Y. Z. plot.—There were interwoven with these overtures* some base propositions on the part of Talleyrand, through one of his agents, to sell his interest and influence with the Directory towards smoothing difficulties with them, in consideration of a large sum (fifty thousand pounds sterling) ; and the arguments to which his agent resorted to induce compliance with this demand, were very unworthy of a great nation (could they be imputed to them), and calculated to excite disgust and indignation in Americans generally, and alienation in the republicans particularly, whom they so far mistake, as to presume an attachment to France and hatred to the federal party, and not the love of their country, to be their first passion. —To James Madison. iv, 232. Ford ed., vii, 235. (Pa., April 1798.)

8253. TALLEYRAND, Corrupt.—The Envoys have been assailed by swindlers, whether with or without the participation of Talleyrand is not very apparent. The known corruption of his character renders it very possible he may have intended to share largely in the £50,000 demanded. But that the Directory knew anything of it, is neither proved nor probable. On the contrary, when the Portuguese ambassador yielded to like attempts of swindlers, the conduct of the Directory in imprisoning him for an attempt at corruption, as well as their general conduct, really magnanimous, places them above suspicion.—To Peter Carr. iv, 235. Ford ed., vii, 238. (Pa., April 1798.)

8254. TALLEYRAND, Hostility of.—I am told that Talleyrand is personally hostile to us. This, I suppose, has been occasioned by the X. Y. Z. history. He should consider that that was the artifice of a party, willing to sacrifice him to the consolidation of their power. This nation has done him justice by dismissing them ; * * * those in power are precisely those who disbelieved that story ; saw in it nothing but an attempt to deceive our country ; that we entertain towards him personally the most friendly dispositions.†—To M. Dupont de Nemours. iv, 436. (April 1802.)

8255. TARIFF, Burdens of.—I wish it were possible to increase the impost on any articles affecting the rich chiefly, to the amount of the sugar tax, so that we might relinquish that at the next session. But this must depend on our receipts keeping up. As to the tea and coffee tax, the people do not regard it. The next tax which an increase of revenue should enable us to suppress, should be the salt tax, perhaps ; indeed, the production of that article at home is already undermining that tax.—To Albert Gallatin. Ford ed., viii, 171. (M., Sep. 1802.)

8256. ——— ———. The revenue on the consumption of foreign articles, is paid cheerfully by those who can afford to add foreign luxuries to domestic comforts, being collected on our seaboards and frontiers only, and in-

* See X. Y. Z. PLOT.—EDITOR.
† Jefferson requested that these representations be made to Talleyrand.—EDITOR.

corporated with the transactions of our mercantile citizens, it may be the pleasure and pride of an American to ask, what farmer, what mechanic, what laborer, ever sees a tax-gatherer of the United States?—Second Inaugural Address. viii, 41. Ford ed., viii, 343. (1805.)

8257. ——— ———. These revenues will be levied entirely on the rich, the business of household manufacture being now so established that the farmer and laborer clothe themselves entirely. The rich alone use imported articles, and on these alone the whole taxes of the General Government are levied. The poor man, who uses nothing but what is made in his own farm or family, or within his own country, pays not a farthing of tax to the General Government, but on his salt ; and should we go into that manufacture also, as is probable, he will pay nothing. Our revenues liberated by the discharge of the public debt, and its surplus applied to canals, roads, schools, &c., the farmer will see his government supported, his children educated, and the face of his country made a paradise by the contributions of the rich alone, without his being called on to spend a cent from his earnings.*—To General Kosciusko. v, 586. (M., 1811.)

8258. TARIFF, Confederation and.—Congress, on the 18th of April, 1783, recommended to the States to invest them with a power, for twenty-five years, to levy an impost of five per cent. on all articles imported from abroad.—To M. de Meunier. ix, 256. Ford ed., iv, 161. (P., 1786.)

8259. TARIFF, Debts and.—The principal objection [to assumption] now is that all the debts, general and State, will have to be raised by tax on imposts, which will thus be overburdened ; whereas had the States been left to pay the debts themselves, they could have done it by taxes on land and other property, which would thus have lightened the burden on commerce.—To Dr. Gilmer. iii, 167. (N.Y., 1790.)

8260. TARIFF, Direct taxation and.—Would it not have been better [in the new Federal Constitution] to assign to Congress exclusively the articles of imposts for Federal purposes, and to have left direct taxation exclusively to the States? I should suppose the former fund sufficient for all probable events, aided by the land office.—To E. Carrington. ii, 334. Ford ed., iv, 482. (P., 1787.)

8261. TARIFF, Discriminating.—Between nations who favor our productions and navigation and those who do not favor them, one distinction alone will suffice : one set of moderate duties for the first, and a fixed advance on these as to some articles, an prohibitions as to others, for the last.—Foreign Commerce Report. vii, 650. Ford ed., vi, 483. (Dec. 1793.)

8262. TARIFF, Excessive.—It is really an extraordinary proposition that the agri-

* Jefferson wrote a similar letter to Dupont de Nemours.—EDITOR.

cultural, mercantile, and navigating classes shall be taxed to maintain that of manufactures.—To THOMAS COOPER. FORD ED., x, 285. (M., 1823.)

8263. —— ——. Congress has done nothing remarkable except the passing a tariff bill by squeezing majorities, very revolting to a great portion of the people of the States, among whom it is believed it would not have received a vote but of the manufacturers themselves. It is considered as a levy on the labors and efforts of the other classes of industry to support that of manufactures, and I wish it may not draw on our surplus, and produce retaliatory impositions from other nations.—To RICHARD RUSH. FORD ED., x, 304. (M., 1824.)

8264. TARIFF, Incidental protection.— As to the tariff, I should say put down all banks, admit none but *a metallic circulation,* that will take its proper level with the like circulation in other countries, and then our manufacturers may work in fair competition with those of other countries, and the import duties which the government may lay for the purposes of revenue will so far place them above equal competition.—To CHARLES PINCKNEY. vii, 180. FORD ED., x, 162. (M., 1820.)

8265. TARIFF, Paper money.— The long succession of years of stunted crops, of reduced prices, the general prostration of the farming business, under levies for the support of manufacturers, &c., with the calamitous fluctuations of value in our paper medium, has kept agriculture in a state of abject depression, which has peopled the Western States by silently breaking up those on the Atlantic, and glutted the land market, while it drew off its bidders. In such a state of things, property has lost its character of being a resource for debts. Highland in Bedford, which, in the days of our plethory, sold readily for from fifty to one hundred dollars the acre (and such sales were many then), would not now sell for more than from ten to twenty dollars, or one-quarter or one-fifth of its former price.—To JAMES MADISON. vii, 434. FORD ED., x, 377. (M., February 1826.)

8266. TARIFF, Patriotism and.— Shall we suppress the impost and give that advantage to foreign over domestic manufactures? On a few articles of more general and necessary use, the suppression in due season will doubtless be right, but the great mass of the articles on which impost is paid is foreign luxuries, purchased by those only who are rich enough to afford themselves the use of them. Their patriotism would certainly prefer its continuance and application to the great purposes of the public education, roads, rivers, canals, and such other objects of public improvement as it may be thought proper to add to the constitutional enumeration of Federal powers.—SIXTH ANNUAL MESSAGE. viii, 68. FORD ED., viii, 493. (1806.)

8267. TARIFF, Prohibitory.— Duties of from ten to twenty per cent. on articles of heavy carriage, prevent their importation. They eat up all the profits of the merchant, and often subject him to loss. This has been much the case with respect to turpentine, tar and pitch, which are principal articles of remittance from the State of North Carolina. It is hoped that it will coincide with the views of the government * * * to suppress the duties on these articles, which of all others can bear them least.—To COUNT DE MONTMORIN. ii, 175. FORD ED., iv, 402. (P., 1787.)

8268. TARIFF, Protective.— Where a nation imposes high duties on our productions, or prohibits them altogether, it may be proper for us to do the same by theirs; first burdening or excluding those productions which they bring here in competition with our own of the same kind; selecting next, such manufactures as we take from them in greatest quantity, and which, at the same time, we could the soonest furnish to ourselves, or obtain from other countries; imposing on them duties lighter at first, but heavier and heavier, afterwards, as other channels of supply open. Such duties, having the effect of indirect encouragement to domestic manufactures of the same kind, may induce the manufacturer to come himself into these States, where cheaper subsistence, equal laws, and a vent of his wares, free of duty, may ensure him the highest profits from his skill and industry. And here, it would be in the power of the State governments to co-operate essentially, by opening the resources of encouragement which are under their control, extending them liberally to artists in those particular branches of manufacture for which their soil, climate, population and other circumstances have matured them, and fostering the precious efforts and progress of *household* manufacture, by some patronage suited to the nature of its objects, guided by the local informations they possess, and guarded against abuse by their presence and attentions. The oppressions on our agriculture, in foreign ports, would thus be made the occasion of relieving it from a dependence on the councils and conduct of others, and of promoting arts, manufactures and population at home.—FOREIGN COMMERCE REPORT. vii, 648. FORD ED., vi, 481. (Dec. 1793.)

8269. TARIFF, Public improvements and.— Of the two questions of the tariff and public improvements, the former, perhaps, is not yet at rest, and the latter will excite boisterous discussions. It happens that both these measures fall in with the western interests, and it is their secession from the agricultural States which gives such strength to the manufacturing and consolidating parties, on these two questions. The latter is the most dreaded, because thought to amount to a determination in the Federal Government to assume all powers non-enumerated as well as enumerated in the Constitution, and by giving a loose to construction, make the text say whatever will relieve them from the bridle of the States. These are all difficulties for your

day; I shall give them the slip.—To RICHARD
RUSH. vii, 380. FORD ED., x, 322. (M.,
1824.)

8270. TARIFF, Reciprocal.—There
might have been mentioned a third* species
of arrangement, that of making special agreements on every special subject of commerce,
and of settling a tariff of duty to be paid
on each side, on every particular article; but
this would require in our Commissioners [to
Spain] a very minute knowledge of our commerce; as it is impossible to foresee every
proposition, of this kind, which might be
brought into discussion, and to prepare them
for it by information and instruction from
hence. Our commerce, too, is, as yet, rather
in a course of experiment, and the channels in
which it will ultimately flow are not sufficiently known to enable us to provide for it
by special agreement. Nor have the exigencies of our new government, as yet, so far
developed themselves, as that we can know
to what degree we may, or must have recourse
to commerce, for the purpose of revenue. No
common consideration, therefore, ought to induce us, as yet, to arrangements of this kind.
Perhaps nothing should do it, with any nation,
short of the privileges of natives, in all their
possessions, foreign and domestic.—MISSIS-
SIPPI RIVER INSTRUCTIONS. vii, 589. FORD
ED., v, 479. (March 1792.)

8271. TARIFF, Revenue and.—The
powers of the government for the collection
of taxes are found to be perfect, so far as they
have been tried. This has been as yet only by
duties on consumption. As these fall principally on the rich, it is a general desire to
make them contribute the whole money we
want, if possible. And we have a hope that
they will furnish enough for the expenses of
Government and the interest of our whole
public debt, foreign and domestic.—To COMTE
DE MOUSTIER. iii, 200. (Pa., 1790.)

8272. ——— ———. The imports are not a
proper object to bear all the taxes of a State.
—To JOHN HARVIE. FORD ED., v, 214. (N.Y.,
1790.)

8273. TARIFF, Salt and.—The duties
composing the Mediterranean fund will cease
by law at the end of the present season. Considering, however, that they are levied chiefly
on luxuries, and that we have an impost on
salt, a necessary of life, the free use of which
otherwise is so important, I recommend to
your consideration the suppression of the
duties on salt, and the continuance of the
Mediterranean fund, instead thereof, for a
short time, after which that also will become
unnecessary for any purpose now within contemplation. SIXTH ANNUAL MESSAGE. viii,
67. FORD ED., viii, 493. (1806.)

**8274. TARIFF, Specific and ad valo-
rem duties.**—There must be something more
in this increase of revenue than the *natural
and war* increase; *depreciation* to a small de-

* The first was that of exchanging the privileges
of *native citizens;* and the second, those of the *most
favored nation.*—EDITOR.

gree in other countries, a sensible one in this,
and a great one in England, must make a
part of it, and is a lesson to us to prefer ad
valorem to fixed duties. The latter require
often retouching, or they become delusive.—
To ALBERT GALLATIN. FORD ED., viii, 357.
(May 1805.)

8275. TARIFF, States and.—Several
States have passed acts for vesting Congress
with the whole regulation of their commerce,
reserving the revenue arising from these regulations to the disposal of the State in which
it is levied; * * * but the Assembly of
Virginia, apprehensive that this disjointed
method of proceeding may fail in its effect,
or be much retarded, passed a resolution on
the 21st of January, 1786, appointing commissioners to meet others from the other
States, whom they invite into the same measure, to digest the form of an act for investing
Congress with such powers over their commerce as shall be thought expedient, which
act is to be reported to their several Assemblies for their adoption.—To M. DE MEUNIER.
ix, 257. FORD ED., iv, 162. (P., 1786.) See
DEBT, DRAWBACKS, DUTIES, EXCISE LAW,
FREE TRADE, GENERAL WELFARE CLAUSE, IN-
TERNAL IMPROVEMENTS, MANUFACTURES, PRO-
TECTION, SURPLUS, and TAXATION.

**8276. TARLETON (Colonel Bannas-
tre), Raid on Monticello.**—Colonel Tarleton, with his regiment of horse, was detached
by Lord Cornwallis to surprise Mr. Jefferson
(whom they thought still in office) [as Gov-
ernor] and the Legislature now sitting in Char-
lottesv:lle. The Speakers of the two houses, and
some other members of the Legislature, were
lodging with Mr. Jefferson at Monticello. Tarleton, early in the morning, when within ten
miles of that place, detached a company of
horse to secure him and his guests, and proceeded himself rapidly with h's main body to
Charlottesville, where he hoped to find the
Legislature unapprized of his movement. Notice of it, however, had been brought, both to
Monticello and Charlottesvil'e, about sunrise.
The Speakers, w:th their colleagues returned to
Charlottesville, and with the other members of
the Legislature, had barely time to get out of
his way. Mr. Jefferson sent off h's family to
secure them from danger, and was himself still
at Monticello making arrangements for his own
departure, when a Lieutenant Hudson arrived
there at half speed, and informed him that the
enemy were then ascending the hill at Monticello. He departed immediately, and knowing
that he would be pursued if he took the high
road, he plunged into the woods of the adjoining mountain, where, being at once safe, he proceeded to overtake his family. This is the famous adventure of Carter's Mountain, which
has been so often resounded through the
slanderous chronicles of federalism. But they
have taken care never to detail the facts, lest
these should show that this favorite charge
amounted to nothing more than that he did not
remain in his house, and there singly fight a
whole troop of horse, or suffer himself to be
taken prisoner. Having accompanied his family one day's journey, he returned to Monticello. Tarleton had retired after eighteen
hours' stay in Charlottesville. Mr. Jefferson
then rejoined his family, and proceeded with
them to an estate he had in Bedford, about
eighty miles southwest, where, riding on his

farm sometime after, he was thrown from his horse, and disabled from riding on horseback for a considerable time. But Mr. Turner finds it more convenient to give him this fall in his retreat from Tarleton, which had happened some weeks before, as a proof that he withdrew from a troop of horse with a precipitancy which Don Quixote would not have practiced.—INVASION OF VA. MEMORANDUM. ix, 223. (M., 1781.)

8277. —— ——. I did not suffer by Colonel Tarleton. On the contrary, he behaved very genteelly with me. On his approach to Charlottesville, which is within three miles of my house at Monticello, he dispatched a troop of his horse, under Captain McLeod, with the double object of taking me prisoner, with the two Speakers of the Senate and Delegates, who then lodged with me, and of remaining in *vidette*, my house command:ng a view of ten or twelve counties round about. He gave strict orders to Captain McLeod to suffer nothing to be injured. The troop failed in one of their objects, as we had notice of their coming, so that the two Speakers had gone off about two hours before their arrival at Monticello, and myself with my family, about five m:nutes. Captain McLeod preserved everything with sacred care.—To DR. WILLIAM GORDON. ii, 425. FORD ED., v, 38. (P., 1788.) See CORNWALLIS.

8278. TASTE, Control of.—Taste cannot be controlled by law.—NOTES ON A MONEY UNIT. i, 168. FORD ED., iii, 451. (1784.)

8279. TAXATION, Basis of.—The taxes with which we are familiar, class themselves readily according to the basis on which they rest. 1. Capital. 2. Income. 3. Consumption. These may be considered as commensurate; Consumption being generally equal to Income, and Income the annual profit of Capital. A government may select any one of these bases for the establishment of its system of taxation, and so frame it as to reach the faculties of every member of the society, and to draw from him his equal proportion of the public contributions; and, if this be correctly obtained, it is the perfection of the function of taxation. But, when once a government has assumed its basis, to select and tax special articles from either of the other classes, is double taxation. For example, if the system be established on the basis of Income, and his just proportion on that scale has been already drawn from every one, to step into the field of Consumption, and tax special articles in that, as broadcloth or homespun, wine or whiskey, a coach or a wagon, is doubly taxing the same article. For that portion of Income with which these articles are purchased, having already paid its tax as Income, to pay another tax on the thing it purchased, is paying twice for the same thing, it is an aggrievance on the citizens who use these articles in exoneration of those who do not, contrary to the most sacred of the duties of a government, to do equal and impartial justice to all its citizens. How far it may be the interest and the duty of all to submit to this sacrifice on other grounds; for instance, to pay for a time an impost on the importation of certain articles, in order to encourage their manufac-

ture at home, or an excise on others injurious to the morals or health of the citizens, will depend on a series of considerations of another order, and beyond the proper limits of this note. * * * To this a single observation shall yet be added. Whether property alone, and the whole of what each citizen possesses, shall be subject to contribution, or only its surplus after satisfying his first wants, or whether the faculties of body and mind shall contribute also from their annual earnings, is a question to be decided. But, when decided, and the principle settled, it is to be equally and fairly applied to all. To take from one, because it is thought that his own industry and that of his fathers' has acquired too much, in order to spare to others, who, or whose fathers have not exercised equal industry and skill, is to violate arbitrarily the first principle of association, " the guarantee to every one of a free exercise of his industry, and the fruits acquired by it ". If the overgrown wealth of an individual be deemed dangerous to the State, the best corrective is the law of equal inheritance to all in equal degree; and the better, as this enforces a law of nature, while extra-taxation violates it.—NOTE IN DESTUTT TRACY'S POLITICAL ECONOMY. vi, 573. (1816.)

8280. TAXATION, Commerce, property and.—I am principally afraid that commerce will be overloaded by the assumption [of the State debts], believing that it would be better that property should be duly taxed.—To MR. RANDOLPH. iii, 185. (N.Y., 1790.)

8281. TAXATION, Control over.—The Congress * * * are of opinion that the Colonies of America possess the exclusive privilege of giving and granting their own money; that this involves the right of deliberating whether they will make any gift, for what purpose it shall be made, and what shall be the amount of the gift, and that it is a high breach of this privilege, for any body of men, extraneous to their constitutions to prescribe the purposes for which money shall be levied on them; to take to themselves the authority of judging of their conditions, circumstances and situation, of determining the amount of the contributions to be levied. As they possess a right of appropriating their gifts, so are they entitled, at all times, to inquire into their application, to see that they be not wasted among the venal and corrupt, for the purpose of undermining the civil rights of the givers, nor yet be diverted to the support of standing armies, inconsistent with their freedom and subversive of their quiet.—REPLY TO LORD NORTH'S CONCILIATORY PROPOSITION. FORD ED., i, 477. (July 1775.)

8282. TAXATION, Debt and.—Taxation follows public debt, and in its train wretchedness and oppression.—To SAMUEL KERCHIVAL. vii, 14. FORD ED., x, 42. (M., 1816.)

8283. TAXATION, Direct.—Would it not have been better [in the new Federal Constitution] * * * to have left direct taxation exclusively to the States?—To E. Car-RINGTON. ii, 334. FORD ED., iv, 482. (P., 1787.)

8284. —— ——. I will add one question to what I have said there [letter to Mr. Madison]. Would it not have been better to assign to Congress exclusively the article of imposts for Federal purposes, and to have left direct taxation exclusively to the States? I should suppose the former fund sufficient for all probable events, aided by the land office.—To EDWARD CARRINGTON. ii, 334. FORD ED., iv, 482. (P., Dec. 1787.)

8285. —— ——. I have no doubts that the States * * * could have availed themselves of resources for this government [Assumption] which are cut off from the General Government by the prejudices existing against direct taxation in their hands.—To JOHN HARVIE. FORD ED., v, 214. (N.Y., 1790.)

8286. —— ——. The disgusting particularities of the direct tax.—To EDMUND PENDLETON. iv, 275. FORD ED., vii, 338. (Pa., 1799.)

8287. TAXATION, Direct and indirect. —It is uncertain what will be the fate of the proposed tax on horses. Besides its partiality, it is infinitely objectionable as foisting in a *direct* tax under the name of an indirect one. —To T. M. RANDOLPH. FORD ED.; vi, 149. (Pa., 1792.)

8288. —— ——. A proposition has been made to Congress to begin sinking the public debt by a tax on pleasure horses; that is to say, on all horses not employed for the draught or farm. It is said there is not a horse of that description eastward of New York. And as to call this a *direct tax* would oblige them to proportionate it among the States according to the census, they choose to class it among the *indirect* taxes.—To DR. GEORGE GILMER. iii, 494. FORD ED., vi, 146. (Pa., 1792.)

8289. TAXATION, Equalization of.— To equalize and moderate the public contributions, that while the requisite services are invited by due remuneration, nothing beyond this may exist to attract the attention of our citizens from the pursuits of useful industry, nor unjustly to burthen those who continue in those pursuits— * * * [is one of the] functions of the General Government on which you have a right to call.—REPLY TO VERMONT ADDRESS. iv, 418. (W., 1801.)

8290. TAXATION, Exports and.—I have read with attention and satisfaction the pamphlet you have sent me. It is replete with sound views, some of which will doubtless be adopted. Some may be checked by difficulties. None more likely to be so than the proposition to amend the Constitution, so as to authorize Congress to tax exports. The provision against this in the framing of that instrument, was a *sine quâ non* with the States of peculiar productions, such as rice, indigo, cotton and tobacco, to which may now be added sugar. A jealousy prevailing that to

the few States producing these articles, the justice of the others might not be a sufficient protection in opposition to their interest, they moored themselves to this anchor. Since the hostile dispositions lately manifested by the Eastern States, they would be less willing than before to place themselves at their mercy; and the rather as the Eastern States have no exports which can be taxed equivalently. It is possible, however, that this difficulty might be got over; but the subject looking forward beyond my time, I leave it to those to whom its burthens and benefits will belong.—To A. C. MITCHELL. vi, 483. (M., 1815.)

8291. TAXATION, Extravagant.—If anything could revolt our citizens against the war, it would be the extravagance with which they are about to be taxed. It is strange indeed that at this day, and in a country where English proceedings are so familiar, the principles and advantages of funding should be neglected, and expedients resorted to. Their new bank, if not abortive at its birth, will not last through one campaign; and the taxes proposed cannot be paid. How can a people who cannot get fifty cents a bushel for their wheat, while they pay twelve dollars a bushel for their salt, pay five times the amount of taxes they ever paid before? Yet that will be the case in all the States south of the Potomac. Our resources are competent to the maintenance of the war if duly economized and skillfully employed in the way of anticipation. However, we must suffer, I suppose, * * * and consider now, as in the Revolutionary war, that although the evils of resistance are great, those of submission would be greater. We must meet, therefore, the former as the casualties of tempests and earthquakes, and like them necessarily resulting from the constitution of the world.—To WILLIAM SHORT. vi, 400. (M., Nov. 1814.)

8292. TAXATION, Federal Government and.—I thought at first that the power of taxation [given in the new Federal Constitution] might have been limited. A little reflection soon convinced me it ought not to be. —To F. HOPKINSON. ii, 586. FORD ED., v, 76. (P., March 1789.)

8293. TAXATION, French.—It is confidently believed * * * that the stamp tax and land tax will be repealed, and other means devised of accommodating their receipts and expenditures. Those supposed to be in contemplation are a rigorous levy of the old tax of the *deux vingtièmes* on the rich, who had in a great measure withdrawn their property from it, as well as on the poor, on whom it had principally fallen.—To JOHN JAY. ii, 272. (P., 1787.)

8294. —— ——. The right of taxation includes the idea of * * * equalizing the taxes on the clergy and nobility as well as the commons. The two former orders do not pay one-third of the proportion *ad valorem*, which the last pay.—To DR. CURRIE. ii, 544. (P., 1788.)

8295. —— ——. The clergy and nobles [in France], by their privileges and influence, have kept their property in a great measure untaxed.—To Dr. Price. ii, 556. (P., Jan. 1789.)

8296. —— ——. Nor should we wonder at * * * [the] pressure [for a fixed constitution in 1788-9] when we consider the monstrous abuses of power under which * * * [the French] people were ground to powder; when we pass in review * * * the oppressions of the tithes, the tailles, the corvées, the gabelles, the farms and the barriers.—Autobiography. i, 86. Ford ed., i, 118. (1821.)

8297. —— ——. [We] should not wonder at * * * [the] pressure [for a fixed constitution in 1788-9] when we consider the monstrous abuses of power under which * * * [the French] people were ground to powder; when we pass in review the weight of their taxes and the inequality of their distribution.—Autobiography. i, 86. Ford ed., i, 118. (1821.)

8298. TAXATION, Internal.—Many of the opposition [to the new Federal Constitution] wish to take from Congress the power of internal taxation. Calculation has convinced me that this would be very mischievous.—To William Carmichael. ii, 550. (P., Dec. 1788.)

8299. —— ——. All are willing to add a bill of rights [to the Federal Constitution] but they fear the power of internal taxation will be abridged.—To William Short. ii, 542. (P., 1788.)

8300. TAXATION, Luxuries.—The government which steps out of the ranks of the ordinary articles of consumption to select and lay under disproportionate burdens a particular one, because it is a comfort, pleasing to the taste, or necessary to the health, and will, therefore, be bought, is, in that particular, a tyranny.—To Samuel Smith. vii, 285. Ford ed., x, 252. (M., 1823.)

8301. TAXATION, Oppressive English.—No earthly consideration could induce my consent to contract such a debt as England has by her wars for commerce, to reduce our citizens by taxes to such wretchedness, as that laboring sixteen of the twenty-four hours, they are still unable to afford themselves bread, or barely to earn as much oatmeal or potatoes as will keep soul and body together. And all this to feed the avidity of a few millionary merchants, and to keep up one thousand ships of war for the protection of their commercial speculations.—To William Crawford. vii, 7. Ford ed., x, 35. (M., 1816.)

8302. —— ——. If we run into such debts, as that we must be taxed in our meat and in our drink, in our necessaries and our comforts, in our labors and our amusements, for our callings and our creeds, as the people of England are, our people, like them, must come to labor sixteen hours in the twenty-four, give the earnings of fifteen of these to the government for their debts and daily expenses; and the sixteenth being insufficient to afford us bread, we must live, as they now do, on oatmeal and potatoes; have no time to think, no means of calling the mismanagers to account; but be glad to obtain subsistence by hiring ourselves to rivet their chains on the necks of our fellow-sufferers. * * * And this is the tendency of all human governments. A departure from principle in one instance becomes a precedent for a second; that second for a third; and so on, till the bulk of the society is reduced to be mere automatons of misery, to have no sensibilities left but for sinning and suffering. Then begins, indeed, the *bellum omnium in omnia,* which some philosophers observing to be so general in this world, have mistaken it for the natural instead of the abusive state of man. And the fore horse of this frightful team is public debt. Taxation follows that, and in its train wretchedness and oppression.—To Samuel Kerchival. vii, 14. Ford ed., x, 41. (M., 1816.)

8303. TAXATION, Parliamentary.—We [Virginia House of Burgesses] cannot, my Lord, close with the terms of that Resolution [Lord North's Conciliatory Proposition]. * * * because to render perpetual our exemption from an unjust taxation, we must saddle ourselves with a perpetual tax, adequate to the expectations, and subject to the disposal of Parliament alone; Whereas, we have a right to give our money, as the Parliament do theirs, without coercion, from time to time, as public exigencies may require. We conceive that we alone are the judges of the condition, circumstances, and situation of our people, as the Parliament are of theirs. It is not merely the mode of raising, but the freedom of granting our money, for which we have contended. Without this, we possess no check on the royal prerogative; and what must be lamented by dutiful and loyal subjects, we should be stripped of the only means, as well of recommending this country to the favors of our most gracious Sovereign, as of strengthening those bonds of amity with our fellow-subjects, while we would wish to remain indissoluble.—Address to Governor Dunmore. Ford ed., i, 456. (1775.)

8304. —— ——. By several acts of Parliament * * * they [the Ministers] have undertaken to give and grant our money without our consent—a right of which we have ever had the exclusive exercise.—Declaration on Taking up Arms. Ford ed., i, 467. (July 1775.)

8305. —— ——. Congress are of opinion * * * that the suspension of the exercise of their [Parliament's] pretended power of taxation being expressly made commensurate with the continuing of our gifts, these must be perpetual to make that so: whereas no experience has shown that a gift of perpetual revenues secures a perpetual return of duty or of kind dispositions. On the contrary, the parliament itself, wisely attentive to this observation, are in the established practice of granting their own money from year to year only.—REPLY TO LORD NORTH'S PROPOSITION. FORD ED., i, 478. (July 1775.)

8306. ———— ————. A proposition to give our money, when accompanied with large fleets and armies, seems addressed to our fears rather than to our freedom.—REPLY TO LORD NORTH'S PROPOSITION. FORD ED., i, 479. (July 1775.)

8307. ———— ————. We think the attempt unnecessary and unwarrantable to raise upon us, by force or by threats, our proportional contributions to the common defence, when all know and themselves acknowledge. we have fully contributed whenever called to contribute, in the character of freemen.—REPLY TO LORD NORTH'S PROPOSITION. FORD ED., i, 479. (July 1775.)

8308. ———— ————. The proposition [of Lord North] is altogether unsatisfactory because it imports only a suspension of the mode, not a renunciation of the pretended right to tax us. —REPLY TO LORD NORTH'S PROPOSITION. FORD ED., i, 480. (July 1775.)

8309. ———— ————. We had been so long in the habit of seeing the British consider us merely as objects for the extension of their *commerce,* and of submitting to every duty or regulation imposed with that view, that we had ceased to complain of them. But when they proposed to consider us as objects of *taxation,* all the States took the alarm.— NOTES ON M. SOULÉS'S WORK. ix, 295. FORD ED., iv, 302. (P., 1786.)

8310. **TAXATION, Politics and.**—The principle of the present [federalist] majority is *excessive expense,* money enough to fill all their maws, or it will not be worth the risk of their supporting. * * * Paper money would be perilous even to the paper men. Nothing then but excessive taxation can get us along; and this will carry reason and reflection to every man's door, and particularly in the hour of election.—To JOHN TAYLOR. iv, 259. FORD ED., vii, 310. (M., 1798.)

8311. **TAXATION, Problem of.**—Taxation is the most difficult function of government, and that against which their citizens are most apt to be refractory. The general aim is, therefore, to adopt the mode most consonant with the circumstances and sentiments of the country.—PREFACE TO TRACY'S POLITICAL ECONOMY. vi, 570. (1816.)

8312. **TAXATION, Public opinion and.** —The purse of the people is the real seat of sensibility. It is to be drawn upon largely, and they will then listen to truths which could not excite them through any other organ.—To A. H. ROWAN. iv, 257. FORD ED., vii, 281. (M., 1798.)

8313. ———— ————. All the [party] passions are boiling over, and one who keeps himself cool and clear of the contagion, is so far below the point of ordinary conversation, that he finds himself isolated in every society.

However, the fever will not last. War, land tax and stamp tax, are sedatives which must cool its ardor. They will bring on reflection, and that, with information, is all which our countrymen need, to bring themselves and their affairs to rights.—To JAMES LEWIS, JR. iv, 241. FORD ED., vii, 250. (Pa., May 1798.)

8314. **TAXATION, Redress of grievances and.**—The privilege of giving or withholding our moneys is an important barrier against the undue exertion of prerogative, * * * and all history shows how efficacious its intercession [is] for redress of grievances and reestablishment of rights, and how improvident would be the surrender of so powerful a mediator.—REPLY TO LORD NORTH'S PROPOSITION. FORD ED., i, 477. (July 1775.)

8315. **TAXATION, Regulation of.**—Our properties, within our own territories, shall [not] be taxed or regulated by any power on earth, but our own.—RIGHTS OF BRITISH AMERICA. i, 142. FORD ED., i, 447. (1774.)

8316. **TAXATION, Religion and.**—The restoration of the rights of conscience [in Virginia by the Revised Code] relieved the people from taxation for the support of a religion not theirs; for the [Church of England] Establishment was truly of the religion of the rich, the dissenting sects being entirely composed of the less wealthy people.—AUTOBIOGRAPHY. i. 49. FORD ED., i, 69. (1821.)

8317. **TAXATION, Representation and.** —Preserve inviolate the fundamental principle, that the people are not to be taxed but by representatives chosen immediately by themselves.—To JAMES MADISON. ii, 328. FORD ED., iv, 475. (P., 1787.)

8318. ———— ————. There are certain principles in which the constitutions of our several States all agree, and which all cherish as vitally essential to the protection of the life, liberty, property and safety of the citizen. [One is] the exclusive right of legislation and taxation in the representatives of the people. —To M. CORAY. vii, 323. (M., 1823.)

8319. **TAXATION, Revolution from unjust.**—So inscrutable is the arrangement of causes and consequences in this world, that a two-penny duty on tea, unjustly imposed in a sequestered part of it, changes the condition of all its inhabitants.—AUTOBIOGRAPHY. i, 106. FORD ED.. i, 147. (1821.)

8320. **TAXATION, Simplest system.**— The simplest system of taxation yet adopted is that of levying on the land and the laborer. But it would be better to levy the same sums on the produce of that labor when collected in the barn of the farmer; because then if through the badness of the year he made little, he would pay little. It would be better yet to levy only on the surplus of this product above his own wants. It would be better, too, to levy it not in his hands, but in those of the merchant purchaser; because though the farmer would in fact pay it, as the merchant purchaser would deduct it from the original price of his produce, yet the farmer would not be sensible that he paid it. This idea would no doubt meet its difficulties and objections when it should come to be reduced to practice; yet I suspect it would be practical and expedient. * * * What a comfort to the farmer to be allowed to supply his own wants before he should be liable to pay anything, and then only pay on his surplus.—To JAMES MADISON. FORD ED., iv, 16. (P., Dec. 1784.)

8321. TAXATION, Uniformity of.—The public contributions should be as uniform as practicable from year to year, that our habits of industry and of expense may become adapted to them; and that they may be duly digested and incorporated with our annual economy.—To J. W. EPPES. vi, 198. FORD ED., ix, 398. (P.F., Sep. 1813.)

8322. TAXATION, War and.—War requires every resource of taxation and credit.—To GENERAL WASHINGTON. ii, 533. FORD ED., v, 57. (P., 1788.)

8323. —— ——. Calculation has convinced me that circumstances may arise, and probably will arise, wherein all the resources of taxation will be necessary for the safety of the State.—To GENERAL WASHINGTON. ii, 533. FORD ED., v, 56. (P., Dec. 1788.)

8324. —— ——. Sound principles will not justify our taxing the industry of our fellow citizens for wars to happen we know not when, and which might not perhaps happen but from temptations offered by that treasure.—FIRST ANNUAL MESSAGE. viii, 9. FORD ED., viii, 119. (1801.)

8325. TAXES, Abolition of internal.—Other circumstances, combined with the increase of numbers, have produced an augmentation of revenue arising from consumption, in a ratio far beyond that of population alone; and though the changes of foreign relations now taking place so desirable for the world, may for a season affect this branch of revenue, yet, weighing all probabilities of expense, as well as of income, there is reasonable ground of confidence that we may now safely dispense with all the internal taxes—comprehending excises, stamps, auctions, licenses, carriages, and refined sugars, to which the postage on newspapers may be added, to facilitate the progress of information: and that the remaining sources of revenue will be sufficient to provide for the support of the government, to pay the interest of the public debts, and to discharge the principals in shorter periods than the laws or the general expectation had contemplated. War, indeed, and untoward events, may change this prospect of things, and call for expenses which the imposts could not meet; but sound principles will not justify our taxing the industry of our fellow-citizens to accumulate treasure for wars to happen we know not when, and which might not perhaps happen but from the temptations offered by that treasure.—FIRST ANNUAL MESSAGE. viii, 9. FORD ED., viii, 119. (1801.)

8326. —— ——. You will perhaps have been alarmed, as some have been, at the proposition to abolish the whole of the internal taxes. But it is perfectly safe. They are under a million of dollars, and we can economize the government two or three millions a year. The impost alone gives us ten or eleven millions annually, increasing at a compound ratio of six and two-thirds per cent. per annum, and consequently doubling in ten years. But leaving that increase for contingencies, the present amount will support the government, pay the interest of the public debt, and discharge the principal in fifteen years. If the increase proceeds, and no contingencies demand it, it will pay off the principal in a shorter time. Exactly one half of the public debt, to wit, thirty-seven millions of dollars, is owned in the United States. That capital, then, will be set afloat, to be employed in rescuing our commerce from the hands of foreigners, or in agriculture, canals, bridges, or other useful enterprises. By suppressing at once the whole internal taxes, we abolish three-fourths of the offices now existing, and spread over the land.—To JOHN DICKINSON. iv, 425. (W., Dec. 1801.)

8327. —— ——. The economies of the [first] session of the first Congress, convened since republicanism has recovered its ascendency, * * * have enabled us to suppress all the internal taxes, and still to make such provision for the payment of their public debt as to discharge that in eighteen years.—To GENERAL KOSCIUSKO. iv, 430. (W., April 1802.)

8328. —— ——. The suppression of unnecessary offices, of useless establishments and expenses, enabled us to discontinue our internal taxes. These, covering our land with officers, and opening our doors to their intrusions, had already begun that process of domiciliary vexation which, once entered, is scarcely to be restrained from reaching successively every article of produce and property. If among these taxes some minor ones fell which had not been inconvenient, it was because their amount would not have paid the officers who collected them, and because, if they had any merit, the State authorities might adopt them, instead of others less approved. The remaining revenue on the consumption of foreign articles, is paid cheerfully by those who can afford to add foreign luxuries to domestic comforts, being collected on our seaboards and frontiers only, and incorporated with the transactions of our mercantile citizens, it may be the pleasure and pride of an American to ask, what farmer, what mechanic, what laborer, ever sees a tax-gatherer of the United States? These contributions enable us to support the current expenses of the government, to fulfill contracts with foreign nations, to extinguish the native right of soil within our limits, to extend those limits, and to apply such a surplus to our public debts, as places at a short day their final redemption; and that redemption once effected, the revenue thereby liberated may, by a just repartition among the States, and a corresponding amendment of the Constitution, be applied, *in time of peace,* to rivers, canals, roads, arts, manufactures, education, and other great objects within each State. *In time of war,* if injustice, by ourselves or others, must sometimes produce war, increased as the same revenue will be increased by population and consumption, and aided by other resources reserved for that crisis, it may meet within the year all the expenses of the year, without encroaching on the rights of future generations, by burdening them with the debts of the past. War will then be but a suspension of useful works, and a return to a state of peace, a return to the progress of improvement.—SECOND INAUGURAL ADDRESS. viii, 40. FORD ED., viii, 343. (1805.)

8329. TAXES, Consent and.—He [George III.] has endeavored to pervert the exercise of the kingly office in Virginia into a detestable and unsupportable tyranny * * * by combining with others to subject us to a foreign jurisdiction, giving his assent to their pretended acts of legislation * * * for imposing taxes on us without our consent.—PROPOSED VA. CONSTITUTION. FORD ED., ii, 10. (June 1776.)

8330. ———. He has combined with others * * * for imposing taxes on us without our consent.—DECLARATION OF INDEPENDENCE AS DRAWN BY JEFFERSON.

8331. ———. From the * * * origin [of the controversy with Great Britain] to this day, there never was a time when these States intimated a disposition to give away *in perpetuum* their essential right of judging whether they should give or withhold their money, for what purposes they should make the gift, and what should be its continuance.—RESOLUTIONS ON PEACE PROPOSITIONS. FORD ED., ii, 91. (Aug. 28, 1776.)

8332. TAXES, Consumption and.—The objects of finance in the United States have hitherto been very simple; merely to provide for the support of the government on its peace establishment, and to pay the debt contracted in the Revolutionary war. The means provided for these objects were ample, and resting on a consumption which little affected the poor, may be said to have been felt by none.—To J. W. EPPES. vi, 194. FORD ED., ix, 395. (P.F., Sep. 1813.)

8333. TAXES, Exact division of.—It will be said that, though, for taxes, there may always be found a divisor which will apportion them among the States according to numbers exactly, without leaving any remainder, yet, for representatives, there can be no such common ratio, or divisor, which, applied to the several numbers, will divide them exactly, without a remainder or fraction. I answer, then, that taxes must be divided *exactly,* and representatives *as nearly as the nearest ratio* will admit.—OPINION ON APPORTIONMENT BILL. vii, 596. FORD ED., v, 495. (1792.)

8334. TAXES, Excessive.—Our taxes are now a third and will soon be half of our whole exports; and when you add the expenses of the State Governments we shall be found to have got to the plenum of taxation in ten short years of peace. Great Britain, after centuries of wars and revolutions, had at the commencement of the present war taxed only to the amount of two-thirds of her exports.—To ARCHIBALD STUART. iv, 284. FORD ED., vii, 351. (Pa., Feb. 1799.)

8335. TAXES, Excise.—The excessive unpopularity of the excise and bank bills in the South, I apprehend, will produce a stand against the Federal Government.—To WILLIAM SHORT. FORD ED., v, 296. (Pa., March 1791.)

8336. ———. I hope the death blow to that most vexatious and unproductive of all taxes [excise] was given at the commencement of my administration, and believe its revival would give the deathblow to any administration whatever.—To DUPONT DE NEMOURS. v, 583. FORD ED., ix, 320. (M., 1811.)

8337. ———. If the excise tax could be collected from those who buy to sell again, so as to prevent domiciliary visits by the officers, I think it would be acceptable. and, I am sure, a wholesome tax.—To MR. NELSON. vi, 47. (M., April 1812.)

8338. TAXES, Imposition of.—No tax should ever be yielded for a longer term than that of the Congress wanting it, except when pledged for the reimbursement of a loan.—To J. W. EPPES. vi, 195. FORD ED., ix, 395. (P.F., Sep. 1813.)

8339. TAXES, Income.—Taxes on consumption like those on capital or income, to be just, must be uniform.—To SAMUEL SMITH. vii, 285. FORD ED., x, 252. (M., 1823.) See TAXATION, BASIS OF.

8340. TAXES, Land.—I am suggesting an idea on the subject of taxation which might, perhaps, facilitate much that business, and reconcile all parties. That is * * * to lay a land tax, leviable in 1798, &c. But if by the last day of 1798, any State shall bring its *whole* quota into the Federal Treasury, the tax shall be suspended one year for that State. If by the end of the next year they bring another year's tax, it shall be suspended a second year as to them, and so *toties quoties* forever. If they fail, the Federal collectors will go on, of course, to make their collection. In this way, those who prefer excises may raise their quota by excises, and those who prefer land taxes may raise by land taxes, either on the Federal plan, or on any other of their own which they like better. This would tend, I think, to make the General Government popular, and to render the State Legislatures useful allies and associates instead of rivals, and to mollify the harsh tone of government which has been asserted. I find the idea pleasing to most of those to whom I have suggested it. It will be objected to by those who are for consolidation.—To PEREGRINE FITZHUGH. FORD ED., vii, 136. (Pa., June 1797.)

8341. —— ——. I think that the matter of finances, which has set the people of Europe to thinking, is now advanced to that point with us, that the next step (and it is an unavoidable one), a land tax, will awaken our constituents, and call for inspection into past proceedings.—To St. George Tucker. iv, 197. Ford ed., vii, 169. (M., 1797.)

8342. —— ——. It had been expected that we must have laid a land tax this session [of Congress]. However, it is thought we can get along another year without it.—To Peregrine Fitzhugh. iv, 217. Ford ed., vii, 210. (Pa., Feb. 1798.)

8343. —— ——. A land tax is the decided resource of many [of the federalists], perhaps of a majority.—To James Madison. Ford ed., vii, 243. (Pa., April 1798.)

8344. —— ——. The federalists talk * * * of a land tax. This will probably not be opposed. The only question will be, how to modify it. On this there may be a great diversity of sentiment. One party will want to make it a new source of patronage and expense.—To James Madison. iv, 234. Ford ed., vii, 237. (Pa., April 1798.)

8345. —— ——. The land tax is now on the carpet to raise two millions of dollars; yet I think they must at least double it, as the expenses of the provisional army were not provided for in it, and will require of itself four millions a year.—To James Monroe. iv, 242. Ford ed., vii, 156. (Pa., May 1798.)

8346. —— ——. In most of the middle and southern States some land tax is now paid into the State treasury, and for this purpose the lands have been classed and valued, and the tax assessed according to that valuation. In these an excise is most odious. In the eastern States land taxes are odious, excises less unpopular.—To Dupont de Nemours. v, 583. Ford ed., ix, 321. (M., April 1811.)

8347. TAXES, Legislation and.—Taxes should be continued by annual or biennial reenactments.—To J. W. Eppes. vi, 195. Ford ed., ix, 395. (P.F., Sep. 1813.)

8348. —— ——. Taxes should be continued by annuel or biennial reenactments, because a constant hold, by the nation, of the strings of the public purse, is a salutary restraint from which an honest government ought not to wish, nor a corrupt one to be permitted to be free.—To J. W. Eppes. vi, 195. Ford ed., ix, 395. (P.F., Sep. 1813.)

8349. TAXES, Necessary wants and.—Taxes should be proportioned to what may be annually spared by the individual.—To James Madison. Ford ed., iv, 15. (P., Dec. 1784.)

8350. TAXES, Paper money and.—Every one, through whose hands a bill passed, lost on that bill what it lost in value, during the time it was in his hands. This was a real tax on him; and * * * the most op-

pressive of all, because the most unequal of all, —To M. de Meunier. ix, 260. Ford ed., iv, 165. (P., 1786.)

8351. TAXES, Politics and suppression of.—Bitter men are not pleased with the suppression of taxes. Not daring to condemn the measure, they attack the motive; and too disingenuous to ascribe it to the honest one of freeing our citizens from unnecessary burthens and unnecessary systems of office, they ascribe it to a desire of popularity. But every honest man will suppose honest acts to flow from honest principles, and the rogues may rail without intermission.—To Dr. Benjamin Rush. iv, 426. Ford ed., viii, 128. (W., 1801.)

8352. TAXES, Resources of internal.—Whenever we are destined to meet events which shall call forth all the energies of our countrymen, we have * * * the comfort of leaving for calls like these the extraordinary resources of loans and internal taxes.—Second Annual Message. viii, 19. Ford ed., viii, 185. (Dec. 1802.)

8353. TAXES, Sinecures and.—We do not mean that our people shall be burdened with oppressive taxes to provide sinecures for the idle or the wicked, under color of providing for a civil list.—Reply to Lord North's Proposition. Ford ed., i, 480. (July 1775.)

8354. TAXES, Stamp.—To the stamp tax I have not seen a man who is not totally irreconcilable. * * * Yet, although a very disgusting pill, I think there can be no question the people will swallow it, if their representatives determine on it.—To Mr. Nelson. vi, 47. (M., April 1812.)

8355. TAXES, Unnecessary.—To impose on our citizens no unnecessary burden, * * * [is one of] the landmarks by which we are to guide ourselves in all our proceedings.—Second Annual Message. viii, 21. Ford ed., viii, 187. (Dec. 1802.)

8356. TAXES, War and.—The report of the Committee of Finance proposes taxes to the amount of twenty millions. This is a dashing proposition. But, if Congress pass it, I shall consider it sufficient evidence that their constituents generally can pay the tax. No man has greater confidence than I have in the spirit of the people, to a rational extent. Whatever they can, they will. But, without either market or medium, I know not how it is to be done. All markets abroad, and all at home are shut, to us; so that we have been feeding our horses on wheat. Before the day of collection, bank notes will be but as oak leaves; and of specie. there is not within all the United States, one half of the proposed amount of the taxes. I had thought myself as bold as was safe in contemplating, as possible, an annual taxation of ten millions, as fund for emissions of treasury notes; and when further emissions should be necessary, that it would be better to enlarge the time, than the tax for redemption. Our position, with respect to our enemy, and our markets. distinguish us from all other nations; inasmuch, as a state of war, with us annihilates in an instant all our surplus produce, that on which we depended for many comforts of life. This renders particularly expedient the throwing a part of the burdens of war on times of peace and commerce.—To JAMES MONROE. vi, 395. FORD ED., ix, 493. (M., Oct. 1814.)

8357. —— ——. Instead of taxes for the whole year's expenses, which the people cannot pay, a tax to the amount of the interest and a reasonable portion of the principal will command the whole sum, and throw a. part of the burdens of war on times of peace and prosperity.—To WILLIAM SHORT. vi, 401. (M., 1814.)

8358. TAXES, Wasted.—If there be anything amiss in the present state of our affairs, as the formidable deficit lately unfolded to us indicates, I ascribe it to the inattention of Congress to their duties, to their unwise dissipation and waste of the public contributions. They seemed, some little while ago, to be at a loss for objects whereon to throw away the supposed fathomless funds of the treasury. * * * I am aware that in one of their most ruinous vagaries the people were themselves betrayed into the same phrenzy with their representatives. The deficit produced, and a heavy tax to supply it, will, I trust, bring both to their sober senses.—To THOMAS RITCHIE. vii, 191. FORD ED., x, 170. (M., 1820.)

8359. TAX-GATHERERS, Cost of.—Our tax-gatherers in Virginia cost as much as the whole civil list besides.—To JAMES MADISON. FORD ED., iv, 16. (P., 1784.)

8360. TAX-GATHERERS, Discontent and.—The tax-gatherer has already excited discontent.—To JAMES MADISON. iv, 261. FORD ED., vii, 313. (Pa., Jan. 1799.)

8361. TAYLOR (John), Political principles.—Colonel Taylor and myself have rarely, if ever, differed in any political principle of importance. Every act of his life, and every word he ever wrote, satisfies me of this.— To THOMAS RITCHIE. vii, 191. FORD ED., x, 170. (M., 1820.)

8362. —— ——. Colonel Taylor's book of "Constructions Construed" * * * is the most logical retraction of our governments to the original and true principles of the Constitution creating them, whi h has appeared since the adoption of that instrument. I may not perhaps concur in all its opinions, great and small, for no two men ever thought alike on so many points. But on all important questions, it contains the true political faith, to which every catholic republican should steadfastly hold. It should be put into the hands of all our functionaries, authoritatively, as a standing instruction and true exposition of our Constitution, as understood at the time we agreed to it.—To SPENCER ROANE. vii, 213. FORD ED., x, 189. (M., 1821.)

8363. TEA, Duty on.—So inscrutable is the arrangement of causes and consequences in this world, that a two-penny duty on tea, unjustly imposed in a sequestered part of it, changes the condition of all its inhabitants.— AUTOBIOGRAPHY. i, 106. FORD ED., i, 147. (1821.) See BOSTON PORT BILL.

8364. TEACHERS, Appreciation of.—Respect and gratitude [are] due to those who devote their time and efforts to render the youths of every successive age fit governors for the next.—To HUGH L. WHITE. v, 522. (M., 1810.)

8365. TEMPER, Southern.—Our Southern sun has been accused of sometimes sublimating the temper too highly.—To E. RUTLEDGE. iii, 166. FORD ED., v, 197. (N.Y., 1790.)

8366. TEMPER, Smooth.—Nothing enables a man to get along in business so well as a smooth temper.—ANAS. FORD ED., i, 337. (1808.)

8367. TEMPERANCE, At table.—In the pleasures of the table [the French] are far before us, because, with good taste they unite temperance. They do not terminate the most sociable meals by transforming themselves into brutes.—To MR. BELLINI. i, 445. (P., 1785.)

8368. TEMPERANCE, France and.—I have never yet seen a man drunk in France, even among the lowest of the people.—To MR. BELLINI. ', 445. (P., 1785.)

8369. TEMPERANCE, Principles of.—I have received and read with thankfulness and pleasure your denunciation of the abuses of tobacco and wine. Yet, however sound in its principles, I expect it will be but a sermon to the wind. You will find it * * * difficult to inculcate these sanative precepts on the sensualities of the present day.—To DR. BENJAMIN WATERHOUSE. vii, 252. FORD ED., x, 219. (M., 1822.)

—— TEMPERATURE.—See CLIMATE.

8370. TENANTS, For Monticello.—The subject [obtaining tenants] is one I have very much at heart, for I find I am not fit to be a farmer with the kind of labor we have, and also subject to such long avocation.—To S. T. MASON. FORD ED., vii, 396. (M., Oct. 1799.)

8371. TENANTS, Seeking.—You promised to endeavor to send me some tenants. I am waiting for them. * * * Tenants of any size may be accommodated with the number of fields suited to their force. Only send me good people.—To S. T. MASON. FORD ED., vii, 283. (M., 1798.)

8372. TERNANT (J. B.), Hamilton and.—Ternant has at length openly hoisted the flag of monarchy by going into deep mourning for his prince [Louis XVI.]. I suspect he thinks a cessation of his visits to me a necessary accompaniment to this pious duty. A connection between him and Hamilton seems to be springing up.—To JAMES MADISON. iii, 520. FORD ED., vi, 193. (Pa., 1793.)

8373. TERNANT (J. B.), Medal for.—The President of the United States, in a letter addressed to the Primary Executive Council of the French Republic, has expressed his sense of your merit, and his entire approbation of your conduct while here. He has also charged me to convey to yourself the same sentiments on his part. It is with pleasure I obey this charge, in bearing witness to the candor and integrity of your conduct with us, and to the share you may justly claim in the cultivation of harmony and good understanding between the two nations * * *. As testimony of the regard of the United States, we shall take an early occasion to ask your acceptance of a medal and chain of gold on their part.—To JEAN BAPTISTE TERNANT. FORD ED., vi, 263. (Pa., 1793.)

8374. TERNANT (J. B.), Shifting affiliations.—When Ternant received certain account of his appointment, thinking he had nothing further to hope from the Jacobins, he that very day found out something to be offended at in me (in which I had been made *ex officio* the ostensible agent in what came from another quarter, and he has never been undeceived), attached himself intimately to Hamilton, put on mourning for the King, and became a perfect counter-revolutioner. A few days ago, he received a letter from Genet, giving him a hope they will employ him in the army. On this, he tacked about again, became a Jacobin, and refused to present the Viscount Noailles, and some other French aristocrats arrived here. However, he will hardly have the impudence to speak to me again.—To JAMES MONROE. iii, 549. FORD ED., vi, 240. (Pa., May 1793.)

8375. TERNANT (J. B.), Soldier.—Ternant established a solid reputation in Europe by his conduct when Generalissimo of one of the United Provinces, during their late disturbances; and it is generally thought that if he had been put at the head of the principal province, instead of the Rhingrave de Salm, he would have saved that cause.—To JOHN JAY. ii, 572. (P., 1789.)

8376. TERRITORY, Acquisition of.—I know that the acquisition of Louisiana has been disapproved by some, from a candid apprehension that the enlargement of our territory would endanger its Union. But who can limit the extent to which the federative principle may operate effectively?—SECOND INAUGURAL ADDRESS. viii, 41. FORD ED., viii, 344. (1805.) See LOUISIANA.

— TERRITORY, Acquisition of Canada.—See CANADA.

8377. TERRITORY, Admission of new States.—I am aware of the force of the observations you make on the power given by the Constitution to Congress, to admit new States into the Union, without restraining the subject to the territory then constituting the United States. But when I consider that the limits of the United States are precisely fixed by the treaty of 1783, that the Constitution expressly declares itself to be made for the United States, I cannot help believing the intention was to permit Congress to admit into the Union new States, which should be formed out of the territory for which, and under whose authority alone, they were then acting. I do not believe it was meant that they might receive England, Ireland, Holland, &c., into it, which would be the case on your construction.—To WILSON C. NICHOLAS. iv, 505. FORD ED., viii, 247. (M., Sep. 1803.)

8378. TERRITORY, Alienation of.—The power to alienate the *unpeopled* territories of any State, is not among the enumerated powers given by the Constitution to the General Government, and if we may go out of that instrument, and *accommodate to exigencies which may arise* by alienating the *unpeopled* territory of a State, we may accommodate ourselves a little more by alienating

that which is *peopled,* and still a little more by selling the *people* themselves. A shade or two more in the degree of exigency is all that will be requisite, and of that degree we shall ourselves be the judges. However, may it not be hoped that these questions are forever laid to rest by the * * * amendment * * * to the Constitution, declaring expressly that "the powers not delegated to the United States by the Constitution are reserved to the States respectively"? And if the General Government has no power to alienate the territory of a State, it is too irresistible an argument to deny ourselves the use of it on the present occasion.*—To ALEXANDER HAMILTON. FORD ED., v, 443. (1792.)

8379. ——— ———. A disastrous war might, by necessity, supersede this stipulation [the provision of the Constitution guaranteeing every State against the invasion of its territory] (as necessity is above all law), and oblige them to abandon a part of a State; but nothing short of this can justify or obtain such an abandonment.—MISSISSIPPI RIVER INSTRUCTIONS. vii, 573. FORD ED., v, 464. (1792.)

8380. ——— ———. We have neither the right nor the disposition to alienate an inch of what belongs to any member of our Union.—MISSISSIPPI RIVER INSTRUCTIONS. vii, 586. FORD ED., v, 476. (1792.)

8381. ——— ———. [President Washington, at a Cabinet meeting, submitted the question]: "Will it be expedient to relinquish to the Indians the right of soil of any part of the land north of the Ohio, if essential to peace?" The Secretaries of the Treasury and War, and the Attorney General are of opinion it will be expedient to make such relinquishment if essential to peace, provided it do not include any lands sold or reserved for special purposes (the reservations for trading places excepted). The Secretary of State is of opinion that the Executive and Senate have authority to stipulate with the Indians, and that if essential to peace, it will be expedient to stipulate that we will not settle any lands between those already sold or reserved for special purposes, and the lines heretofore validly established with the Indians.—OPINION ON INDIAN WAR. FORD ED., vi, 191. (Feb. 1793.)

8382. ——— ———. I considered [at a Cabinet meeting] that the Executive, with either or both branches of the Legislature, could not alien any part of our territory; that by the law of nations it was settled, that the unity and indivisibility of the society was so fundamental, that it could not be dismembered by the constituted authorities, except, 1, where *all power* was delegated to them (as in the case of despotic governments), or 2, where it was expressly delegated; that neither of these delegations had been made to our General Government and, therefore, that it had no right to dismember or alienate any portion of territory once ultimately consolidated with us; and that we could no more cede to the Indians

* The navigation of the Mississippi River was the subject under consideration.—EDITOR.

than to the English or Spaniards, as it might, according to acknowledged principles, remain as irrevocably and eternally with the one as the other. But I thought, that as we had a right to sell and settle lands once comprehended within our lines, so we might forbear to exercise that right, retaining the property till circumstances should be more favorable to the settlement, and this I agreed to do in the present instance, if necessary for peace.—THE ANAS. ix, 137. FORD ED., i, 219. (Feb. 1793.)

8383. —— ——. The Cabinet met * * * on the subject of your [President Washington's] circular letter, and agreed on all points, except as to the power of ceding territory, on which point there remained the same difference of opinion as when the subject was discussed in your presence.—To PRESIDENT WASHINGTON. FORD ED., vi, 212. (Pa., April 1793.)

8384. ——. The negotiators at Ghent are agreed in everything except as to a rag of Maine, which we cannot yield nor they seriously care about.—To MRS. TRIST. D. L. J. 359. (M., Dec. 1814.)

8385. **TERRITORY, Annexation of Canada.**—That Bonaparte would give us the Floridas to withhold intercourse with the residue of the [Spanish] colonies cannot be doubted. But that is no price; because they are ours in the first moment of the first war; and until a war they are of no particular necessity to us. But, although with difficulty, he will consent to our receiving Cuba into our Union, to prevent our aid to Mexico and the other provinces. That would be a price, and I would immediately erect a column on the southernmost limit of Cuba and inscribe on it a *ne plus ultra* as to us in that direction. We should then have only to include the north in our Confederacy, which would be, of course, in the first war, and we should have such an empire for liberty as she has never surveyed since the creation; and I am persuaded no Constitution was ever before so well calculated as ours for extensive empire and self-government.—To PRESIDENT MADISON. v, 444. (M., April 1809.) See CANADA.

8386. **TERRITORY, British acquisition of American.**—The consequences of their [the British] acquiring all the country on our frontier, from the St. Croix to the St. Mary's, are too obvious to you to need development. You will readily see the dangers which would then environ us. We wish you, therefore, to intimate to them that we cannot be indifferent to enterprises of this kind; that we should contemplate a change of neighbors with extreme uneasiness; and that a due balance on our borders is not less desirable to us, than a balance of power in Europe has always appeared to them. We wish to be neutral, and we will be so, *if they will execute the treaty* [of peace] *fairly, and attempt no conquests adjoining us.* The first condition is just; the second imposes no hardship on them. They cannot complain that the other dominions of

Spain would be so narrow as not to leave them room enough for conquest.*—To GOUVERNEUR MORRIS. iii, 182. FORD ED., v, 224. (N.Y., 1790.)

8387. —— ——. It was evident to me that the British had it in view to claim a slice on our north-western quarter, that they may get into the Mississippi; indeed, I thought it presented as a sort of make-weight with the posts to compensate the great losses their citizens had sustained by the infractions [of the treaty of peace] charged on us.—THE ANAS. ix, 428. FORD ED., i, 196. (June 1792.)

8388. **TERRITORY, Cession of Northwest.**—The territories contained within the charters erecting the Colonies of Maryland, Pennsylvania, North and South Carolina, are hereby ceded, released, and forever confirmed to the people of those Colonies respectively, with all the rights of property, jurisdiction and government, and all other rights whatsoever which might at any time, heretofore, have been claimed by this colony [Virginia]. The western and northern extent of this country shall in all other respects stand as fixed by the charter of —— until. by act of the Legislature, one or more Territories shall be laid off westward of the Alleghany mountains for new colonies, which colonies shall be established on the same fundamental laws contained in this instrument, and shall be free and independent of this Colony and of all the world.—PROPOSED VA. CONSTITUTION. FORD ED., ii, 25. (June 1776.) See WESTERN TERRITORY.

8389. —— ——. The General Assembly shall have power to sever from this State all or any parts of its territory westward of the Ohio, or of the meridian of the mouth of the Great Kanawha.—PROPOSED CONSTITUTION FOR VIRGINIA. viii, 446. FORD ED., iii, 325. (1783.)

8390. —— ——. I do myself the honor of transmitting to your Excellency a resolution of the General Assembly of this Commonwealth, entered into in consequence of the resolution of Congress of September 6th, 1780. on the subject of confederation. I shall be rendered very happy if the other States of the Union, equally impressed with the necessity of that important convention, shall be willing to sacrifice equally to its completion. This single event, could it take place shortly, would overweigh every success which the enemy [England] have hitherto obtained, and render desperate the hopes to which those successes have given birth.—To THE PRESIDENT OF CONGRESS. i, 287. FORD ED., ii, 423. (R., January 17, 1781.)

8391. **TERRITORY, Constitution and.** —No constitution was ever before so well calculated as ours for extensive empire and self-government.—To PRESIDENT MADISON. v, 444. (M., April 1809.)

* Morris was then informal agent of the United States in London. It was feared that England would wrest Louisiana from Spain.—EDITOR.

— **TERRITORY, Constitution and acquisition of foreign.**—See LOUISIANA.

8392. TERRITORY, Cuba.—I candidly confess that I have ever looked on Cuba as the most interesting addition which could ever be made to our system of States.—To PRESIDENT MONROE. vii, 316. FORD ED., x, 278. (M., 1823.) See CUBA.

8393. TERRITORY, Disputed.—The Colony of Virginia does not entertain a wish that one inch should be added to theirs from the territory of a sister Colony * * *. The decision, whatever it be, will not annihilate the lands. They will remain to be occupied by Americans, and whether these be counted in the members of this or that of the United States will be thought a matter of little moment.—LETTER TO PENNSYLVANIA CONVENTION. FORD ED., ii, 65. (July 1776.)

8394. TERRITORY, Dissensions and.— The larger our association, the less will it be shaken by local passions.—SECOND INAUGURAL ADDRESS. viii, 41. FORD ED., viii, 344. (1805.)

8395. — —. It seems that the smaller the society the bitterer the dissensions into which it breaks. Perhaps this observation answers all the objections drawn by Mr. [John] Adams from the small republics of Italy. I believe ours is to owe its permanence to its great extent, and the smaller portion comparatively, which can ever be convulsed at one time by local passions.—To GOVERNOR ROBERT WILLIAMS. v, 209. FORD ED., ix, 167. (W., 1807.)

8396. — —. The extent of our territory secures it, I hope, from the vindictive passions of the petty incorporations of Greece. —To ELBRIDGE GERRY. vi, 63. FORD ED., ix, 360. (M., 1812.)

8397. — —. I see our safety in the extent of our confederacy, and in the probability that in the proportion of that the sound parts will always be sufficient to crush out local poison.—To HORATIO G. SPAFFORD. vi, 335. (M., 1814.)

8398. — —. I still believe that the western extension of our territory will ensure its duration, by overruling local factions, which might shake a smaller association.—To HENRY DEARBORN. vii, 215. FORD ED., x, 192. (M., 1821.)

8399. TERRITORY, European influence in American.—We consider their interests [Cuba and Mexico] and ours as the same, and that the object of both must be to exclude all European influence from this hemisphere. —To GOVERNOR CLAIBORNE. v, 381. FORD ED., ix, 213. (W., Oct. 1808.)

8400. TERRITORY, Expansion of.— Our confederacy must be viewed as the nest from which all America, North and South, is to be peopled. We should take care, too, not to think it for the interest of that great Continent to press too soon on the Spaniards. Those countries cannot be in better hands. My fear is that they are too feeble to hold

them till our population can be sufficiently advanced to gain it from them piece by piece. —To ARCHIBALD STUART. i, 518. FORD ED., iv, 188. (P., 1786.)

8401. — —. However our present interests may restrain us within our own limits, it is impossible not to look forward to distant times, when our rapid multiplication will expand itself beyond those limits, and cover the whole northern, if not the southern continent, with a people speaking the same language, governed in similar forms, and by similar laws * * *.—To JAMES MONROE. iv, 420. FORD ED., viii, 105. (W., Nov. 1801.)

8402. TERRITORY, Good government and.—Our present federal limits are not too large for good government, nor will the increase of votes in Congress produce any ill effect. On the contrary, it will drown the little divisions at present existing there.—To ARCHIBALD STUART. i, 518. FORD ED., iv, 188. (P., Jan. 1786.)

8403. TERRITORY, Holding foreign.— The Constitution has made no provision for our holding foreign territory, still less for incorporating foreign nations into our Union. The Executive in seizing the fugitive occurrence [Louisiana purchase] which so much advances the good of their country, have done an act beyond the Constitution. The Legislature in casting behind them metaphysical subtleties, and risking themselves like faithful servants, must ratify and pay for it, and throw themselves on their country for doing for them unauthorized, what we know they would have done for themselves had they been in a situation to do it. It is the case of a guardian, investing the money of his ward in purchasing an important adjacent territory; and saying to him when of age, I did this for your good; I pretend to no right to bind you: you may disavow me, and I must get out of the scrape as I can. I thought it my duty to risk myself for you. But we shall not be disavowed by the nation, and their act of indemnity will confirm and not weaken the Constitution, by more strongly marking out its lines.—To JOHN C. BRECKENRIDGE. iv, 500. FORD ED., viii, 244. (M., Aug. 1803.)

8404. TERRITORY, Naval defence and. —Nothing should ever be accepted which would require a navy to defend it.—To PRESIDENT MADISON. v, 445. (M., April 1809.)

8405. TERRITORY, Pacific.—On the waters of the Pacific, we can found no claim in right of Louisiana. If we claim that country at all, it must be on Astor's settlement near the mouth of the Columbia, and the principle of the *jus gentium* of America, that when a civilized nation takes possession of the mouth of a river in a new country, that possession is considered as including all its waters.—To JOHN MELISH. vii, 51. (M., 1816.)

8406. TERRITORY, Preservation of.— Were we to give up half our territory [Mississippi region] rather than engage in a just war to preserve it, we should not keep the other half long.—INSTRUCTIONS TO WILLIAM CARMICHAEL. ix, 412. FORD ED., v, 226. (1790.)

— **TERRITORY, Purchase of Florida.**— See FLORIDA.

8407. TERRITORY, Purchases of Indian.—To be prepared against the occupation of Louisiana by a powerful and enterprising people [the French], it is important that, setting less value on interior extension of purchases from the Indians, we bend our whole views to the purchase and settlement of the country on the Mississippi, from its mouth to its northern regions, that we may be able to present as strong a front on our western as on our eastern border, and plant on the Mississippi itself the means of its own defence. We now own from 31° to the Yazoo, and hope this summer to purchase what belongs to the Choctaws from the Yazoo up to their boundary, supposed to be about opposite the mouth of Arkansas. We wish at the same time to begin in your quarter, for which there is at present a favorable opening. The Cahokias extinct, we are entitled to their country by our paramount sovereignty. The Peorias, we understand, have all been driven off from their country, and we might claim it in the same way; but as we understand there is one chief remaining, who would, as the survivor of the tribe, sell the right, it is better to give him such terms as will make him easy for life, and take a conveyance from him. The Kaskaskias being reduced to a few families, I presume we may purchase their whole country for what would place every individual of them at his ease, and be a small price to us,—say by laying off for each family, wherever they would choose it, as much land as they could cultivate, adjacent to each other, enclosing the whole in a single fence, and giving them such an annuity in money or goods forever as would place them in happiness; and we might take them also under the protection of the United States. Thus possessed of the rights of these tribes, we should proceed to the settling of their boundaries with the Pottawatamies and Kickapoos, claiming all doubtful territory, but paying them a price for the relinquishment of their concurrent claim, and even prevailing on them, if possible, to *cede*, for a price, such of their own unquestioned territory as would give us a convenient northern boundary. Before broaching this, and while we are bargaining with the Kaskaskias, the minds of the Pottawatamies and Kickapoos should be soothed and conciliated by liberalities and sincere assurances of friendship. Perhaps by sending a well-qualified character to stay some time in Duquoin's village, as if on other business, and to sound him and introduce the subject by degrees to his mind and that of the other heads of families, inculcating in the way of conversation, all those considerations which prove the advantages they would receive by a cession on these terms, the object might be more easily and effectually obtained than by abruptly proposing it to them at a formal treaty. Of the means, however, of obtaining what we wish, you will be the best judge; and I have given you this view of the system which we suppose will best promote the interests of the Indians and ourselves, and finally consolidate our whole country into one nation only; that you may be enabled the better to adapt your means to the object, for this purpose we have given you a general commission for treating.—To GOVERNOR HARRISON. iv, 473. (W., Feb. 1803.)

8408. —— ——. The crisis is pressing: whatever can now be obtained must be obtained quickly. The occupation of New Orleans, hourly expected, by the French, is already felt like a light breeze by the Indians. You know the sentiments they entertain of that nation; under the hope of their protection they will immediately stiffen against cessions of lands to us. We had better, therefore, do at once what can now be done. This letter is to be considered as private. * * * You will perceive how sacredly it must be kept within your own breast, and especially how improper to be understood by the Indians. For their interests and their tranquillity, it is best they should see only the present age of their history.—To GOVERNOR HARRISON. iv, 474. (W., Feb. 1803.)

8409. —— ——. As a means of increasing the security, and providing a protection for our lower possessions on the Mississippi, I think it also all important to press on the Indians, as steadily and strenuously as they can bear, the extension of our purchases on the Mississippi from the Yazoo upwards; and to encourage a settlement along the whole length of that river, that it may possess on its own banks the means of defending itself, and presenting as strong a frontier on our western as we have on our eastern border. We have, therefore, recommended to Governor Dickinson taking, on the Tombigbee, only as much as will cover our actual settlements, to transfer the purchase from the Choctaws to their lands westward of the Big Black, rather than the fork of Tombigbee and Alabama, which has been offered by them in order to pay their debt to Ponton and Leslie. I have confident expectations of purchasing this summer a good breadth on the Mississippi, from the mouth of the Illinois down to the mouth of the Ohio, which would settle immediately and thickly; and we should then have between that settlement and the lower one, only the uninhabited lands of the Chickasaws on the Mississippi; on which we could be working at both ends. You will be sensible that the preceding views, as well those which respect the European powers as the Indians, are such as should not be formally declared, but be held as a rule of action to govern the conduct of those within whose agency they lie; and it is for this reason that instead of having it said to you in an official letter, committed to records which are open to many, I have thought it better that you should learn my views from a private and confidential letter, and be enabled to act upon them yourself, and guide others into them.— To GOVERNOR CLAIBORNE. iv, 487. (W., May 1803.)

8410. —— ——. Another important acquisition of territory has also been made since the last session of Congress. The friendly tribe of Kaskaskia Indians, with which we have never had a difference, reduced by the wars and wants of savage life to a few individuals unable to defend themselves against the neighboring tribes, has transferred its country to the United States, reserving only for its members what is sufficient to maintain them in an agricultural way. The considerations stipulated are that we shall extend to them our patronage and protection, and give them certain annual aids in money, in implements of agriculture, and other articles of their choice. This country, among the most fertile within our limits, extending along the Mississippi from the mouth of the Illinois to and up the Ohio, though not so necessary as a barrier since the acquisition of the other bank, may yet be well worthy of being laid open to immediate settlement, as its inhabitants may descend with rapidity in support of the lower country should future circumstances expose that to foreign enterprise.—THIRD ANNUAL MESSAGE. viii, 25. FORD ED., viii, 269. (Oct. 1803.)

8411. —— ——. On this side the Mississippi, an important relinquishment of native title has been received from the Delawares. That tribe, desiring to extinguish in their people the spirit of hunting, and to convert superfluous lands into the means of improving what they retain, have ceded to us all the country between the Wabash and the Ohio, south of, and including the road from the rapids towards Vincennes, for which they are to receive annuities in animals and implements for agriculture, and in other necessaries. This acquisition is important, not only for its extent and fertility. but as fronting three hundred miles on the Ohio, and near·half that on the Wabash. The produce of the settled countries descending those rivers will no longer pass in review of the Indian frontier but in a small portion, and with the cession heretofore made with the Kaskaskias, nearly consolidates our possessions north of the Ohio, in a very respectable breadth, from Lake Erie to the Mississippi. The Piankeshaws having some claim to the country ceded by the Delawares, t has been thought best to quiet that by fair purchase also.—FOURTH ANNUAL MESSAGE. viii, 37. FORD ED., viii, 330. (Nov. 1804.)

8412. —— ——. The northern [Indian] tribes have sold to us: the lands between the Connecticut Reserve, and the former Indian boundary; and those on the Ohio, from the same boundary to the Rapids, and for a considerable depth inland. The Chickasaws and Cherokees have sold us their country between the two districts of and adjacent to the two districts of Tennessee, and the Creeks, the residue of their lands in the fork of Ocmulgee, up to the river which we expect is by this time ceded by are important, inasmuch as they consolidate disjointed parts of our settled country, and render their intercourse secure; and the second particularly so, as with the small point on the river which we expect is by this time ceded by the Piankeshaws. it completes our possession of the whole of both banks of the Ohio, from its source to near its mouth, and the navigation of that river is thereby rendered forever safe to our citizens settled and settling on its extensive waters.—FIFTH ANNUAL MESSAGE. viii, 52. FORD ED., viii, 394. (Dec. 1805.)

8413. TERRITORY, Republicanism and. —The late chapter* of our history * * * furnishes a new proof of the falsehood of Montesquieu's doctrine, that a republic can be preserved only in a small territory. The reverse is the truth. Had our territory been even a third only of what it is, we were gone. But while frenzy and delusion, like an epidemic, gained certain parts the residue remained sound and untouched, and held on till their brethren could recover from the temporary delusion.—To NATHANIEL NILES. iv, 376. FORD ED., viii, 24. (W., March 1801.)

8414. —— ——. While smaller governments are better adapted to the ordinary objects of society, larger confederations more effectually secure independence, and the pres-

* The Presidential contest in the House of Representatives.—EDITOR.

ervation of republican government.—To THE RHODE ISLAND ASSEMBLY. iv, 397. (W., May 1801.)

8415. —— ——. I have much confidence that we shall proceed successfully for ages to come, and that, contrary to the principle of Montesquieu, it will be seen that the larger the extent of country, the more firm its republican structure, if founded, not on conquest, but in principles of compact and equality. My hope of its duration is built much on the enlargement of the resources of life going hand in hand with the enlargement of territory, and the belief that men are disposed to live honestly, if the means of doing so are open to them.—To M. DE MARBOIS. vii, 77. (M., 1817.)

8416. TERRITORY, Seizure.—I consider war between France and England as unavoidable. * * * In this conflict, our neutrality will be cheaply purchased by a cession of the island of New Orleans and the Floridas; because taking part in the war, we could so certainly seize and securely hold them and more. And although it would be unwise in us to let such an opportunity pass of obtaining the necessary accession to our territory even by force, if not obtainable otherwise, yet it is infinitely more desirable to obtain it with the blessing of neutrality rather than the curse of war.—To GOVERNOR CLAIBORNE. iv, 487. (W., May 1803.)

8417. —— ——. You have thought it advisable sooner to take possession of adjacent territories. But we know that they are ours the first moment that any war is forced upon us for other causes, that we are at hand to anticipate their possession, if attempted by any other power, and, in the meantime, we are lengthening the term of our prosperity, liberating our revenues, and increasing our power.—To GENERAL ARMSTRONG. v, 433. (W., March 1809.)

8418. TERRITORY, Spanish pretensions.—I say nothing of the claims of Spain to our territory north of the thirty-first degree, and east of the Mississippi. They never merited the respect of an answer [to Spain]; and * * * it has been admitted at Madrid that they were not to be maintained.—To WILLIAM CARMICHAEL. iii, 173. FORD ED., v, 217. (N.Y., 1790.)

8419. TESTS, Religious.—The proscribing any citizen as unworthy the public confidence, by laying upon him an incapacity of being called to offices of trust or emolument. unless he profess or renounce this or that religious opinion, is depriving him injudiciously of those privileges and advantages, to which in common with his fellow citizens, he has a natural right.—STATUTE OF RELIGIOUS FREEDOM. FORD ED., ii, 238. (1779.)

8420. —— ——. All men shall be free to profess, and by argument to maintain, their opinion in matters of religion; and * * * the same shall in no wise diminish, enlarge, or affect their civil capacities.—STATUTE OF RELIGIOUS FREEDOM. FORD ED., ii, 239. (1799.)

— **THANKSGIVING.**—See FAST DAYS.

8421. THEATRES, Utility of.—I have never expressed an objection to the part of your plan relative to the theatre. The utility of this in America is a great question on which I may be allowed to have an opinion; but it is not for me to decide on it, nor to object to the proposal of establishing one at Richmond. The only objection to your plan which I have ever made, is that * * * I feared it was too extensive for the poverty of the country. You remove the objection by observing it is to extend to several States. Whether professors itinerant from one State to another may succeed, I am unable to say, having never known an experiment of it. The fear that these professors may be disappointed in their expectations, has determined me not to meddle in the business at all.—To M. DE QUESNAY. i, 346. (P., 1788.)

8422. THEORY, Demolishing.—Theories are more easily demolished than rebuilt.—To REV. JAMES MADISON. ii, 430. (P., 1788.)

8423. THEORY, Imagination and.—The moment a person forms a theory, his imagination sees, in every object, only the traits which favor that theory.—To CHARLES THOMSON. ii, 276. FORD ED., iv, 447. (P., 1787.)

8424. THEORY, Victims of.—Men come into business at first with visionary principles. It is practice alone which can correct and conform them to the actual current of affairs. In the meantime, those to whom their errors were first applied have been their victims.—To JAMES MADISON. ii, 408. FORD ED., v, 16. (P., 1788.)

8425. THIRD TERM, Age and.—I owe you much thankfulness for the favorable opinion you entertain of my services, and the assurance expressed that they would again be acceptable in the Executive chair. But I was sincere in stating age as one of the reasons of my retirement from office, beginning then to be conscious of its effects, and now much more sensible of them. Senile inertness is not what is to save our country; the conduct of a war requires the vigor and enterprise of younger heads. All such undertakings, therefore, are out of the question with me, and I say so with the greater satisfaction when I contemplate the person to whom the Executive powers were handed over.—To THOMAS C. FLOURNOY. vi, 82. (M., Oct. 1812.)

8426. THIRD TERM, Constitution and. —Your approbation of the reasons which induced me to retire from the honorable station in which my countrymen had placed me, is the proof of your devotion to the principles of our Constitution. These are wisely opposed to all perpetuations of power, and to every practice which may lead to hereditary establishments.—REPLY TO ADDRESS. v, 473. (M., 1809.)

8427. THIRD TERM, Dangers of.—My opinion originally was that the President of the United States should have been elected

for seven years, and forever ineligible afterwards. I have since become sensible that seven years is too long to be irremovable, and that there should be a peaceable way of withdrawing a man in midway who is doing wrong. The service for eight years, with a power to remove at the end of the first four, comes nearly to my principle as corrected by experience; and it is in adherence to that, that I determine to withdraw at the end of my second term. The danger is that the indulgence and attachments of the people will keep a man in the chair after he becomes a dotard, that reelection through life shall become habitual, and election for life follow that. General Washington set the example of voluntary retirement after eight years. I shall follow it. And a few more precedents will oppose the obstacle of habit to any one after awhile who shall endeavor to extend his term. Perhaps it may beget a disposition to establish it by an amendment of the Constitution. I believe I am doing right, therefore, in pursuing my principle. I had determined to declare my intention, but I have consented to be silent on the opinion of friends, who think it best not to put a continuance out of my power in defiance of all circumstances. There is, however, but one circumstance which could engage my acquiescence in another election; to wit, such a division about a successor, as might bring in a monarchist. But that circumstance is impossible.—To JOHN TAYLOR. iv, 565. FORD ED., viii, 339. (W., Jan. 1805.)

8428. ——— ———. If some period be not fixed, either by the Constitution or by practice, to the services of the First Magistrate, his office, though nominally elective, will, in fact, be for life; and that will soon degenerate into an inheritance.—To MR. WEAVER. v, 89. (W., June 1807.)

8429. ——— ———. That there are in our country a great number of characters entirely equal to the management of its affairs, cannot be doubted. Many of them, indeed, have not had opportunities of making themselves known to their fellow citizens; but many have had, and the only difficulty will be to choose among them. These changes are necessary, too, for the security of republican government. —To MR. WEAVER. v, 89. (W., June 1807.)

8430. THIRD TERM, Determination to refuse.—Believing that a definite period of retiring from this station will tend materially to secure our elective form of government; and sensible, too, of that decline which advancing years bring on, I have felt it a duty to withdraw at the close of my present term of office; and to strengthen by practice a principle which I deem salutary.—To ABNER WATKINS. viii, 125. (W., Dec. 1807.)

8431. THIRD TERM, Duty and.—That I should lay down my charge at a proper season, is as much a duty as to have borne it faithfully.—To MR. WEAVER. v, 88. (W., June 1807.)

8432. ——— ———. Having myself highly approved the example of an illustrious predecessor, in voluntarily retiring from a trust, which, if too long continued in the same hands, might become a subject of reasonable uneasiness and apprehension, I could not mistake my own duty when placed in a similar situation.—R. TO A. CONNECTICUT REPUBLICANS. viii, 140. (1808.)

8433. THIRD TERM, Irksome.—At the end of my present term, of which two years are yet to come, I propose to retire from public life, and to close my days on my patrimony of Monticello, in the bosom of my family. I have hitherto enjoyed uniform health; but the weight of public service begins to be too heavy for me. and I long for the enjoyment of rural life, among my books, my farms and my family. Having performed my *quadragena stipendia,* I am entitled to my discharge, and should be sorry, indeed, that others should be sooner sensible than myself when I ought to ask it. I have, therefore, requested my fellow citizens to think of a successor for me, to whom I shall deliver the public concerns with greater joy than I received them. I have the consolation, too, of having added nothing to my private fortune, during my public service, and of retiring with hands as clean as they are empty.—To COMTE DIODATI. v, 62. (W., March 1807.)

8434. THIRD TERM, Jefferson urged to accept.—I am panting for retirement, but am as yet nearly two years from that goal. The general solicitations I have received to continue another term give me great consolation, but considerations public as well as private determine me inflexibly on that measure.—To MARQUIS DE LAFAYETTE. FORD ED., ix, 67. (W., May 1807.)

8435. THIRD TERM, Massachusetts and.—I derive great personal consolation from the assurances in your friendly letter, that the electors of Massachusetts would still have viewed me with favor as a candidate for a third Presidential term. But the duty of retirement is so strongly impressed on my mind, that it is impossible for me to think of that.—To JAMES SULLIVAN. v, 252. (W., March 1808.)

8436. THIRD TERM, Opposed to.—I am for responsibilities at short periods, seeing neither reason nor· safety in making public functionaries independent of the nation for life, or even for long terms of years. On this principle I prefer the Presidential term of four years, to that of seven years, which I myself had at first suggested, annexing to it, however, ineligibility forever after; and I wish it were now annexed to the second quadrennial election of President.—To JAMES MARTIN. vi, 213. FORD ED., ix, 420. (M., Sep. 1813.)

8437. THIRD TERM, Physical decline and.—My determination to retire is the result of mature reflections, and on various considerations. Not the least weighty of these is that a consciousness that a decline of physical faculties cannot leave those mental en-

tirely unimpaired; and it will be happy for me if I am the first who shall become sensible of it. As to a successor, there never will be a time when it will not produce some difficulty, and never less, I believe, than at present. That some of the federalists should prefer my continuance to the uncertainty of a successor, I can readily believe. There are among them men of candor, who do not join in the clamor and condemnation of everything, nor pretend that even chance never throws us on a right measure. There are some who know me personally, and who give a credit to my intentions, which they deny to my understanding; some who may fear a successor, preferring a military glory of a nation to the prosperity and happiness of its individuals. But to the mass of that political sect, it is not the less true, the 4th of March, 1809, will be a day of jubilee, but it will be a day of greater joy to me. I never did them an act of injustice, nor failed in any duty to them imposed by my office.—To WILLIAM SHORT. FORD ED., ix, 50. (W., May 1807.)

8438. THIRD TERM, Precedent against.—The reeligibility of the President for life [in the new Constitution], I quite disapproved.* * * My fears of that feature were founded on the importance of the office, on the fierce contentions it might excite among ourselves, if continuable for life, and the dangers of interference, either with money or arms, by foreign nations, to whom the choice of an American President might become interesting. Examples of this abounded in history; in the case of the Roman Emperors, for instance; of the Popes, while of any significance; of the German Emperors; the Kings of Poland and the Deys of Barbary. I had observed, too, in the Feudal history, and in the recent instance, particularly, of the Stadtholder of Holland, how easily offices, or tenures for life, slide into inheritances. My wish, therefore, was, that the President should be elected for seven years, and be ineligible afterwards. This term I thought sufficient to enable him. with the concurrence of the Legislature. to carry through and establish any system of improvement he should propose for the general good. But the practice adopted, I think is better, allowing his continuance for eight years, with a liability to be dropped at half way of the term, making that a period of probation. That his continuance should be restrained to seven years, was the opinion of the Convention at an earlier stage of its session, when it voted that term, by a majority of eight against two, and by a simple majority that he should be ineligible a second time. This opinion was confirmed by the House so late as July 26, referred to the Committee of Detail, reported favorably by them, and changed to the present form by final vote, on the last day but one only of their session.* Of this

* This is an evident error. On September 4th, the committee of eleven reported a clause making the term four years, which was adopted by the convention on the 6th, and not altered thereafter.—NOTE IN FORD EDITION.

change, three States expressed their disapprobation; New York, by recommending on amendment, that the President should not be eligible a third time, and Virginia and North Carolina that he should not be capable of serving more than eight, in any term of sixteen years; and although this amendment has not been made in form, yet practice seems to have established it. The example of four Presidents voluntarily retiring at the end of their eighth year, and the progress of public opinion, that the principle is salutary, have given it in practice the force of precedent and usage; insomuch, that, should a President consent to be a candidate for a third election, I trust he would be rejected, on this demonstration of ambitious views.—AUTOBIOGRAPHY. i, 79. FORD ED., i, 109. (1821.)

8439. THIRD TERM, Retirement and.—A retirement from the exercise of my present charge is equally for your good and my own happiness.—R. TO A. PENNSYLVANIA CITIZENS. v, 262. (W., 1808.)

8440. THIRD TERM, Rotation in office and.—I am sensible of the kindness of your rebuke on my determination to retire from office at a time when our country is laboring under difficulties truly great. But if the principle of rotation be a sound one, as I conscientiously believe it to be with respect to this office. no pretext should ever be permitted to dispense with it, because there never will be a time when real difficulties will not exist, and furnish a plausible pretext for dispensation. You suppose I am "in the prime of life for rule". I am sensible I am not; and before I am so far declined as to become insensible of it, I think it right to put it out of my own power. I have the comfort, too, of knowing that the person whom the public choice has designated to receive the charge from me, is so eminently qualified as a safe depositary by the endowments of integrity, understanding, and experience. On a review, therefore, of my reasons for retirement, I think you cannot fail to approve them.—To HENRY GUEST. v, 407. (W., January 1809.)

8441. —— ——. In no office can rotation be more expedient; and none less admits the indulgence of age.—R. TO A. PHILADELPHIA CITIZENS. viii, 145. (1809.)

8442. THIRD TERM, Vermont and.—I received the *address* of the Legislature of Vermont, bearing date the 5th of November, 1806, in which, with their approbation of the general course of my administration, they were so good as to express their desire that I would consent to be proposed again, to the public voice, on the expiration of my present term of office. Entertaining, as I do, for the Legislature of Vermont those sentiments of high respect which would have prompted an immediate answer, I was certain, nevertheless, they would approve a delay which had for its object to avoid a premature agitation of the public mind, on a subject so interesting as the election of the Chief Magistrate. That I should lay down my charge at a proper period, is as much a duty as to have borne it faithfully. If some termination to the services of the Chief Magistrate be not fixed by the Constitution, or supplied by practice, his office, nominally for years, will, in fact, become for life; and history shows how easily that degenerates into an inheritance. Believing that a representative government, responsible at short intervals of election, is that which produces the greatest sum of happiness to mankind, I feel it a duty to do no act which shall essentially impair that principle; and I should unwillingly be the person who, disregarding the sound precedent set by an illustrious predecessor, should furnish the first example of prolongation beyond the second term of office. Truth, also, requires me to add, that I am sensible of that decline which advancing years bring on; and feeling their physical, I ought not to doubt their mental effect. Happy if I am the first to perceive and to obey this admonition of nature, and to solicit a retreat from cares too great for the wearied faculties of age.—R. TO A. VERMONT LEGISLATURE. viii, 121. (Dec. 1807.)

—— THRESHING MACHINE.—See INVENTIONS.

8443. TIFFIN (H. D.), Fidelity.—I have seen with the greatest satisfaction that among those who have distinguished themselves by their fidelity to their country, on the occasion of the enterprise of Mr. Burr, yourself and the Legislature of Ohio have been the most eminent. The promptitude and energy displayed by your State have been as honorable to itself as salutary to its sister States; and in declaring that you have deserved well of your country, I do but express the grateful sentiment of every faithful citizen in it. The hand of the people has given the mortal blow to a conspiracy which. in other countries, would have called for an appeal to armies, and has proved that government to be the strongest of which every man feels himself a part. It is a happy illustration, too, of the importance of preserving to the State authorities all that vigor which the Constitution foresaw would be necessary. not only for their own safety, but for that of the whole.—To GOVERNOR H. D. TIFFIN. v, 37. FORD ED., ix, 21. (W., 1807.)

8444. TIME, Waste of.—Determine never to be idle. No person will have occasion to complain of the want of time who never loses any. It is wonderful how much may be done, if we are always doing.—To MARTHA JEFFERSON. FORD ED., iv, 387. (Mar. 1787.)

8445. TITLE, President's.—The Senate and Representatives differed about the title of the President. The former wanted to style him, "His Highness, George Washington. President of the United States, and Protector of Their Liberties". The latter insisted, and prevailed, to give no title but that of office, to wit, "George Washington, President of the United States". I hope the terms of Excellency, Honor, Worship, Esquire, forever disappear from among us, from that moment. I wish that of Mr. would follow them.—To WILLIAM CARMICHAEL. iii, 88. (P., 1789.)

8446. —— ——. The President's title, as proposed by the Senate, was the most superlatively ridiculous thing I ever heard of.—To JAMES MADISON. FORD ED., v, 104. (P., 1789.)

8447. —— ——. I will presume to suggest to Mr. [John Quincy] Adams the question whether he should not send back Onis's letters in which he has the impudence to qualify you by the term " His Excellency "? An American gentleman in Europe can rank with the first nobility because we have no titles which stick him at any particular place in their line. So the President of the United States, under that designation ranks with the emperors and kings; but add Mr. Onis's courtesy of " His Excellency " and he is then on a level with Mr. Onis himself, with the governors of provinces, and even of every petty fort in Europe, or the colonies.—To PRESIDENT MONROE. FORD ED., x, 123. (M., 1819.)

8448. TITLES, Adulatory.—The new government has shown genuine dignity, in my opinion, in exploding adulatory titles. They are the offerings of abject baseness, and nourish that degrading vice in the people.— To JAMES MADISON. iii, 100. FORD ED., v, 112. (P., 1789.)

8449. TITLES, Granting.—The Administrator [of Virginia] shall not possess the prerogative * * * of creating dignities or granting rights of precedence.—PROPOSED VA. CONSTITUTION. FORD ED., ii, 19. (June 1776.)

8450. TITLES, Hereditary.—[The proposed new States] shall admit no person to be a citizen, who holds any hereditary title.— WESTERN TERRITORY REPORT. FORD ED., iii, 409. (1784.)

8451. —— ——. The clause respecting hereditary honors was struck out, not from an approbation of such honors, but because it was thought an improper place to encounter them.—To JAMES MADISON. FORD ED., iii, 471. (A., April 1784.)

8452. TOBACCO, Culture of.—It is a culture productive of infinite wretchedness. Those employed in it are in a continual state of exertion beyond the power of human nature to support. Little food of any kind is raised by them; so that the men and animals on these farms are badly fed, and the earth is rapidly impoverished.—NOTES ON VIRGINIA. viii, 407. FORD ED., iii, 271. (1782.)

8453. TOBACCO, Differential duties.— The difference of duty on tobacco carried to France in French and American bottoms, has excited great uneasiness. We presume the National Assembly must have been hurried into the measure without being allowed time to reflect on its consequences. A moment's consideration must convince anybody, that no nation upon earth ever submitted to so enormous an assault on the transportation of their own produce. Retaliation, to be equal, will have the air of extreme severity and hostility.—To M. LA MOTTE. iii, 289. (Pa., 1791.)

8454. —— ——. I take for granted the National Assembly were surprised into the mea-

sure by persons whose avarice blinded them to the consequences, and hope it will be repealed before our legislature shall be obliged to act on it. Such an attack on our carriage of our own productions, and such a retaliation would illy prepare the minds of the two nations for a liberal treaty as wished for by the real friends of both.—To JOSEPH FENWICK. FORD ED., v, 380. (Pa., 1791.)

8455. TOBACCO, European use of.—The European nations can do well without all our commodities except tobacco.—To JOHN ADAMS. i, 488. (P., 1785.)

8456. TOBACCO, Monopoly in France.— I take the liberty of offering to your attention some papers * * * written by * * * merchants of L'Orient, and others, some of whom are citizens of the United States, and all of them concerned in the trade between the two countries. This has been carried on by an exchange of the manufactures and produce of France for the produce of the United States, and principally for tobacco, which, though on its arrival here, confined to a single purchaser, has been received equally from all sellers. In confidence of a continuance of this practice, the merchants of both countries were carrying on their commerce of exchange. A late contract by the Farm has, in a great measure, fixed in a single mercantile house the supplies of tobacco wanted for this country. This arrangement found the established merchants with some tobacco on hand, some on the seas coming to them, and more still due. By the papers now enclosed, it seems that there are six thousand four hundred and eight hogsheads in the single port of L'Orient. Whether the government may interfere, as to articles furnished by the merchants after they had notice of the contract before mentioned, must depend on principles of policy. But those of justice seem to urge that, for commodities furnished before such notice, they should be so far protected, as that they may wind up without loss, the transactions in which the new arrangement found them actually engaged.—To COUNT DE VERGENNES. i, 547. (P., 1786.)

8457. —— ——. My hopes on that subject (suppression of the monopoly in the purchase of tobacco in France), are not desperate, but neither are they flattering.—To T. PLEASANTS. i, 563. (P., 1786.)

8458. —— ——. My letters from New York inform me that * * * the monopoly of the purchase of tobacco for France, which had been obtained by Robert Morris, had thrown the commerce of that article in agonies. He had been able to reduce the price in America from 40| to 22|6, lawful the hundred weight, and all other merchants being deprived of that medium of remittance, the commerce between America and that country, so far as it depended on that article, which was very capitally too, was absolutely ceasing. An order has been obtained, obliging the Farmers General to purchase from such other merchants as shall offer fifteen thousand hogsheads of tobacco at thirty-four, thirty-six and thirty-eight livres the hundred, according to the quality, and to grant to the sellers in other respects the same terms as they had granted to Robert Morris. As this agreement with Morris is the basis of this order, I send you some copies of it, which I will thank you to give to any American (not British) merchants in London who may be in that line. During the year this contract has subsisted, Virginia and Maryland have lost £400,000 by the

reduction of the price of their tobacco.—To
John Adams. i, 586. Ford ed., iv, 252. (P.,
1786.)

8459. ——. ——. During the former government of France (the monarchy), our tobacco was under a monopoly, but paid no duties.
* * * The first National Assembly * * *
emancipated tobacco from its monopoly, but
subjected it to duties of eighteen livres, fifteen
sous the qu'ntal, carried in their own vessels,
and five livres carried in ours—a difference
more than equal to the freight of the article.—
Foreign Commerce Report. vii, 640. Ford
ed., vi, 474. (Dec. 1793.) See Monopoly.

8460. TOBACCO, Oppressions by merchants.—Long experience has proved to us
that there never was an instance of a man's
getting out of debt, who was once in the hands
of a tobacco merchant, and bound to consign his
tobacco to him. It is the most delusive of all
snares. The merchant feeds the inclination
of his customer to be credited till he gets the
burthen of debt so increased that he cannot
throw it off at once; he then begins to give
him less for his tobacco, and ends with giving
him what he pleases for it.—To Mrs. Paradise.
Ford ed., iv, 288. (P., 1786.)

8461. TOBACCO, Price of.—I am offered
at Monticello four shillings above the present
market price. * * * You know I have an
established privilege of being considerably above
the market. * * * The quality of last year's
crop is inferior, but still mine preserving its
comparative superiority, stands on its usual
ground with respect to others.—To James
Brown. Ford ed., vii, 6. (M., 1795.)

8462. TOLERATION, Political.—I feel
extraordinary gratification in addressing this
letter to you, with whom shades of difference
in political sentiment have not prevented the
interchange of good opinion, nor cut off the
friendly offices of society and good correspondence. This political tolerance is the more
valued by me, who consider social harmony
as the first of human felicities, and the happiest moments, those which are given to the
effusions of the heart.—To Governor John
Henry. Ford ed., iii, 159. (P., 1797.)

8463. ——. ——. During the contest of
opinion [Presidential election] through which
we have passed, the animation of discussion
and of exertions has sometimes worn an aspect which might impose on strangers, unused to think freely, and to speak and to write
what they think; but, this being now decided
by the voice of the nation, announced, according to the rules of the Constitution, all will,
of course, arrange themselves under the will
of the law, and unite in common efforts for
the common good. All, too, will bear in mind
this sacred principle, that, though the will
of the majority is in all cases to prevail, that
will, to be rightful, must be reasonable; that
the minority possess their equal rights, which
equal laws must protect, and to violate which
would be oppression. Let us, then, fellow-citizens, unite with one heart and one mind;
let us restore to social intercourse that harmony and affection without which liberty and
even life itself are but dreary things. And let
us reflect, that, having banished from our land
that religious intolerance under which man-

kind so long bled and suffered, we have yet
gained little, if we countenance a political intolerance as despotic, as wicked, and capable
of as bitter and bloody persecutions. During
the throes and convulsions of the ancient
world; during the agonizing spasms of infuriated man, seeking, through blood and
slaughter, his long-lost liberty, it was not
wonderful that the agitation of the billows
should reach even this distant and peaceful
shore; that this should be more felt and
feared by some, and less by others; that this
should divide opinions as to measures of
safety. But every difference of opinion is not
a difference of principle. We have called by
different names brethren of the same principle. We are all republicans; we are all federalists. If there be any among us who
would wish to dissolve this Union, or to
change its republican form, let them stand,
undisturbed, as monuments of the safety with
which error of opinion may be tolerated
where reason is left free to combat it. * * *
Let us, then, with courage and confidence,
pursue our own federal and republican principles—our attachment to our Union and
representative government.—First Inaugural Address. viii, 2. Ford ed., viii, 2.
(1801.)

8464. TONTINE, Raising money by.—
The raising money by Tontine, more practiced
on the continent of Europe than in England, is
liable to the same objection [as funding], of
encroachment on the independent rights of
posterity; because the annuities not expiring
gradually, with the lives on which they rest,
but all on the death of the last survivor only,
they will, of course, overpass the term of a
generation, and the more probably as the subjects on whose lives the annuities depend, are
generally chosen of the ages, constitutions, and
occupations most favorable to long life.—To
J. W. Eppes. vi, 197. Ford ed., ix, 397.
(P.F., 1813.)

8465. TORIES, Confederacy and.—The
tories would, at all times, have been glad to
see the confederacy dissolved, even by particles at a time, in hopes of their attaching
themselves again to Great Britain.—Answers
to M. de Meunier. ix, 251 Ford ed., iv,
156. (P., 1786.)

8466. TORIES, Definition of.—A tory
has been properly defined to be a traitor in
thought, but not in deed. The only description by which the laws have endeavored to
come at them, was that of non-jurors, or persons refusing to take the oath of fidelity to
the State.—Notes on Virginia. viii, 396.
Ford ed., iii, 260. (1782.)

8467. TORIES, Nature and.—Nature has
made some men monarchists and tories by
their constitution, and some, of course, there
always will be.—To Albert Gallatin. vii,
80. Ford ed., x, 92. (M., 1817.)

8468. TORIES, Taxation of.—Persons of
this description were at one time subjected
to double taxation, at another to treble, and
lastly were allowed retribution, and placed on
a level with good citizens.—Notes on Virginia. viii, 396. Ford ed., iii, 260. (1782.)

8469. TORIES, Whigs and.—It has ever appeared to me, that the difference between the whig and the tory of England is, that the whig deduces his rights from the Anglo-Saxon source, and the tory from the Norman. —To JOHN CARTWRIGHT. vii, 356. (M., 1824.)

8470. TORPEDOES, Defensive value.— I consider your torpedoes as very valuable means of the defence of harbors, and have no doubt that we should adopt them to a considerable degree. Not that I go the whole length (as I believe you do) of considering them as solely to be relied on. Neither a nation nor those entrusted with its affairs, could be justifiable, however sanguine its expectations, in trust'ng solely to an engine not yet sufficiently tried, under all the circumstances which may occur, and against which we know not as yet what means of parrying may be devised. If, indeed, the mode of attaching them to the cable of a ship be the only one proposed, modes of prevention cannot be difficult. But I have ever looked to the submarine boat as most to be depended on for attaching them, and though I see no mention of it in your letter, or your publications, I am in hopes it is not abandoned as impracticable. I should wish to see a corps of young men trained to this service. It would belong to the engineers if at hand, but being naut'cal, I suppose we must have a corps of naval engineers, to practice and use them.—To ROBERT FULTON. v, 165. FORD ED., ix, 125. (M., Aug. 1807.)

8471. —— ——. Although no public servant could justify the risking the safety of an important seaport, solely on untried means of defence, yet I have great confidence in those proposed by you as additional to the ordinary means.—To ROBERT FULTON. v, 341. (M., Aug. 1808.)

8472. TORPEDOES, Experiments with. —Mr. Fulton writes to me under a great desire to prepare a decisive experiment of his torpedo at Washington, for the meeting of Congress. This means of harbor-defence has acquired such respectability, from its apparent merit, from the attention shown it by other nat'ons, and from our own experiments at New York, as to entitle it to a full experiment from us. He asks only two workmen for one month from us, which he estimates at $130 only. But should it cost considerably more I should really be for granting it, and would accord'ngly recommend it to you. This sum is a mere trifle as an encroachment on our appropriation.—To ROBERT SMITH. v, 337. (M., Aug. 1808.)

8473. TORPEDOES, Success of.—Your torpedoes will be to cities what vaccination has been to mankind. It extinguishes their greatest danger.—To ROBERT FULTON. v, 517. (M., 1810.)

8474. TORTURE, Forbidden.—The General Assembly shall not have power to * * * prescribe torture in any case whatever.*—PROPOSED VA. CONSTITUTION. viii, 445. FORD ED., iii, 325. (1783.)

8475. TORTURE, In France.—Nor should we wonder at * * * [the] pressure [for a fixed constitution in 1788-9] when we consider the monstrous abuses of power under which * * * [the French] people were

* Heresy was then punishable by burning in Virginia.—EDITOR.

ground to powder; when we pass in review * * * the atrocities of the rack.—AUTOBIOGRAPHY. i, 86. FORD ED., i, 118. (1821.)

8476. TOULOUSE (Archbishop of), Character of.—The Archbishop of Toulouse is made minister principal, a virtuous, patriotic, and able character.—To JOHN ADAMS. ii, 258. (P., 1787.)

8477. TOULOUSE (Archbishop of), Garde des sceaux and.—The *Garde des sceaux* is considered as the Archbishop of Toulouse's bull dog, braving danger like that animal. His talents do not pass mediocrity.— To JAMES MADISON. ii, 444. FORD ED., v, 43. (P., 1788.)

8478. TOULOUSE (Archbishop of), Influence with Queen.—It may not be uninstructive to give you the origin and nature of his influence with the Queen [Marie Antoinette]. When the Duke de Choiseul proposed the marriage of the Dauphin with this lady, he thought it proper to send a person to Vienna to perfect her in the language. He asked his friend, the Archbishop of Toulouse, to recommend to him a proper person. He recommended a certain abbé. The abbé, from his first arrival in Vienna, either tutored by his patron, or prompted by gratitude. impressed on the Queen's mind the exalted talents and merit of the Archbishop, and continually represented h'm as the only man fit to be placed at the helm of affairs. On his return to Paris. being retained near the person of the Queen, he kept him constantly in her view. The Archbishop was named of the Assemblee des Notables, had occasion enough there to prove his talents, and Count de Vergennes, his great enemy, dying opportunely, the Queen got him 'nto place. He uses the abbé even yet for instilling all his notions into her mind.—To JOHN JAY. ii, 310. FORD ED., iv, 463. (P., 1787.)

8479. —— ——. The Archbishop continues well with his patroness [Marie Antoinette]. Her object is a close connection with her brother. I suppose he convinces her that peace will furnish the best occasion of cementing that connection.—To JOHN JAY. ii, 310. FORD ED., iv, 463. (P., 1787.)

8480. TOULOUSE (Archbishop of), Minister.—The Archbishop of • Toulouse * * * is a good and patriotic minister for peace, and very capable in the department of finance. At least he is so in theory. I have heard his talents for execution censured.—To JOHN JAY. ii, 294. (P., 1787.)

8481. TOULOUSE (Archbishop of), Talents.—That he has imposing talents, and patriotic dispositions, I think is certain. Good judges think him a theorist only, little acquainted with the details of business, and spoiling all his plans by a bungled execution.—To JOHN JAY. ii, 310. FORD ED., iv, 464. (P., 1787.)

— TOWNS.—See WARD GOVERNMENT.

8482. TRACY (Comte de), Books of.— Destutt Tracy is, in my judgment, the ablest living writer on intellectual subjects, or the operations of the understanding. His three octavo volumes on Ideology, which constitute the foundation of what he has since written, I have not entirely read; because I am not fond of reading what is merely abstract, and unapplied immediately to some useful sc'ence. Bonaparte, with his repeated derisions of Ideologists (squ'nting at this author), has by this time felt that true wisdom does not lie in mere practice without principle. The next work Tracy wrote was the " Commentary on Montesquieu ", never published in the original, because not safe; but translated and published in Philadelphia, yet without the author's name. He has since permitted his name to be mentioned. Although called a commentary, it is, in truth, an elementary work on the principles of government, comprised in about three hundred pages octavo. He has lately published a third work, on " Political Economy ", comprising the whole subject within about the same compass; in which all its principles are demonstrated with the severity of Euclid, and, like him, without ever using a superfluous word. I have procured this to be translated, and have been four years endeavoring to get it printed; but as yet, without success. In the meantime, the author has published the original in France, which he thought unsafe while Bonaparte was in power. * * * He has his fourth and last work now in the press at Paris, closing as he conceives, the circle of metaphysical sciences. This work, which is on ethics, I have not seen, but suspect I shall differ from it in its foundation, although not in its deductions. I gather from his other works that he adopts the principle of Hobbes, that justice is founded in contract solely, and does not result from the construction of man.— To JOHN ADAMS. vii, 38. (M., 1816.)

8483. ———. Tracy comprehends under the word " Ideology " all the subjects which the French term *Morale,* as the correlation to *Physique.* His works on Logic, Government, Political Economy and Morality, he considers as making up the circle of ideological subjects, or of those which are within the scope of the understanding, and not of the senses. His Logic occupies exactly the ground of Locke's work on the Understanding. The translation of that on Political Economy is now printing; but it is no translation of mine. I have only had the correction of it, which was, indeed, very laborious. *Le premier jet* having been by some one who understood neither French nor English, it was impossible to make it more than faithful. But it is a valuable work.—To JOHN ADAMS. vii, 55. FORD ED., x, 72. (M., 1817.)

8484. TRACY (Comte de), Infirmity of. —The Tracy I mentioned to you is the one connected by marriage with Lafayette's family. * * * He writes me that he is become blind, and so infirm that he is no longer able to compose anything; so that we are to consider his works as now closed.—To JOHN ADAMS. vii, 43. (M., 1816.)

8485. TRADE, Carrying.—I think it essential to exclude the English from the carriage of American produce.—To JAMES MONROE. FORD ED., iv, 41. (P., 1785.) See CARRYING TRADE, COMMERCE, MARKETS, NAVIGATION and SHIPS.

8486. TRADE, Destroying.—He [George III.] has endeavored to pervert the exercise of the kingly office in Virginia into a detestable and insupportable tyranny * * * by combining with others to subject us to a foreign jurisdiction, giving his assent to their pretended acts of legislation * * * for cutting off our trade with all parts of the world.—PROPOSED VA. CONSTITUTION. FORD ED. ii, 10. (June 1776.)

8487. ——— ———. He has combined, with others, * * * for cutting off our trade

with all parts of the world.—DECLARATION OF INDEPENDENCE AS DRAWN BY JEFFERSON.

8488. TRADE, Monopolizing.—It is not just that the colonies should be required to oblige themselves to other contributions while Great Britain possesses a monopoly of their trade. This of itself lays them under heavy contribution. To demand, therefore, an additional contribution in the form of a tax is to demand the double of their equal proportion. If we contribute equally with other parts of the empire, let us, equally with them, enjoy free commerce with the whole world; but while the restrictions on our trade shut to us the resources of wealth, is it just, we should bear all other burdens equally with those to whom every resource is open?—REPLY TO LORD NORTH'S PROPOSITION. FORD ED., i, 479. (July 1775.)

8489. TRADE, Restraining.—The proposition [of Lord North] is altogether unsatisfactory * * * because it does not propose to repeal the several acts of Parliament, passed for the purposes of restraining the trade * * * of the Eastern colonies.—REPLY TO LORD NORTH'S PROPOSITION. FORD ED., i, 480. (July 1775.)

8490. TRADE, Restrictions on.—Some of the colonies having thought proper to continue the administration of their government in the name and under the authority of his Majesty, King Charles I. whom, notwithstanding his late deposition by the Commonwealth of England, they continued in the sovereignty of their State, the Parliament for the Commonwealth, took the same in high offence, and assumed upon themselves the power of prohibiting their trade with all other parts of the world, except the Island of Great Britain. This arbitrary act, however, they soon recalled, and by solemn treaty entered into on the 12th day of March, 1651, between the said Commonwealth, by their Commissioners, and the Colony of Virginia by their House of Burgesses, it was expressly stipulated by the eighth article of the said treaty, that they should have " free trade as the people of England do enjoy to all places and with all nations, according to the laws of that Commonwealth ". But * * * upon the restoration of his Majesty, King Charles II., their rights of free commerce fell once more a victim to arbitrary power; and by several acts of his reign, as well as of some of his successors, the trade of the Colonies was laid under such restrictions, as show what hopes they might form from the justice of a British Parliament, were its uncontrolled power admitted over these States.—RIGHTS OF BRITISH AMERICA. i, 127. FORD ED., i, 432. (1774.)

8491. ——— ———. We cannot, my lord, close with the terms of that resolution [Lord North's conciliatory Proposition] because on our agreeing to contribute our proportion towards the common defence, they do not propose to lay open to us a free trade with all the world: whereas, to us it appears just that those who bear equally the burdens of government should equally participate of its benefits; either be contented with the monopoly of our trade, which brings greater loss to us and benefit to them than the amount of our proportional contributions to the common defence; or, if the latter be preferred, relinquish the former, and not propose, by holding both, to exact from us double contributions.—ADDRESS TO LORD DUNMORE. FORD ED., i, 457. (R., 1775.)

8492. TRADE, Right to.—No man has a natural right to the trade of a money lender but he who has the money to lend.—To J. W. EPPES. vi, 141. FORD ED., ix, 394. (M., 1813.)

8493. TRADE MARKS, Recommended. —The Secretary of State, to whom was referred by the House of Representatives the petition of Samuel Breck and others, proprietors of a sail-cloth manufactory in Boston, praying that they may have the exclusive privilege of using particular marks for designating the sailcloth of their manufactory, has had the same under consideration, and thereupon reports: That it would, in his opinion, contribute to fidelity in the execution of manufactures, to secure to every manufactory an exclusive right to some mark on its wares, proper to itself. This should be done by general laws, extending equal right to every case to which the authority of the Legislature should be competent. These cases are of divided jurisdiction: Manufactures made and consumed within a State being subject to State legislation, while those which are exported to foreign nations, or to another State, or into the Indian Territory, are alone within the legislation of the General Government. That it will, therefore, be reasonable for the General Government to provide in this behalf by law for those cases or manufacture generally, and those only which relate to commerce with foreign nations, and among the several States, and with the Indian tribes. This may be done by permitting the owner of every manufactory, to enter in the records of the court of the district wherein his manufactory is, the name with which he chooses to mark or designate his wares, and rendering it penal in others to put the same mark to any other wares.— REPORT ON TRADE MARKS. vii, 563. (December 1791.)

8494. TRANQUILLITY, Basis of.— Tranquillity of mind depends much on ourselves, and greatly on due reflection " how much pain have cost us the evils which have never happened ".—To WILLIAM SHORT. vi, 402. (M., 1814.)

8495. TRANQUILLITY, Love of.—I cherish tranquillity too much to suffer political things to enter my mind at all.—To PRESIDENT WASHINGTON. iv, 106. FORD ED., vi, 510. (M., May 1794.)

8496. TRANQUILLITY, National.— That love of order and obedience to the laws, which so remarkably characterize the citizens of the United States, are sure pledges of internal tranquillity.—To BENJAMIN WARING. iv, 378. (W., 1801.)

8497. TRANQUILLITY, Old age and.— Tranquillity is the old man's milk. I go to enjoy it in a few days, and to exchange the roar and tumult of bulls and bears, for the prattle of my grandchildren and senile rest.—To EDWARD RUTLEDGE. iv, 191. FORD ED., vii, 155. (Pa., 1797.)

8498. ———. My object at present is peace and tranquillity, neither doing nor saying anything to be quoted, or to make me the subject of newspaper disquisitions.—To DAVID HOWELL. v, 554. (M., 1810.)

8499. ———. The *summum bonum* with me is now truly epicurean, ease of body and tranquillity of mind.—To JOHN ADAMS. vi, 143. (M., 1813.)

8500. ———. Tranquillity is the *summum bonum* of age. I wish, therefore, to offend no man's opinion, nor to draw disquieting animadversions on my own. While duty required it, I met opposition with a firm and fearless step. But loving mankind in my individual relations with them, I pray to be permitted to depart in their peace; and like the superannuated soldier, " *quadragenis stipendiis emeritis* ", to hang my arms on the post.—To SPENCER ROANE. vii, 136. FORD ED., x, 142. (P.F., 1819.)

8501. ———. There is a time for things; for advancing and for retiring; for a Sabbath of rest as well as for days of labor, and surely that Sabbath has arrived for one near entering on his 80th year. Tranquillity is the *summum bonum* of that age. I wish now for quiet, to withdraw from the broils of the world, to soothe the enmities, and to die in the peace and good will of all mankind.—To ARCHIBALD THWEAT. FORD ED., x, 185. (M., 1821.)

8502. ———. Tranquillity is the last and sweetest asylum of age.—To SPENCER ROANE. vii, 211. FORD ED., x, 188. (M., 1821.)

8503. ———. At the age of eighty, tranquillity is the greatest good of life, and the strongest of our desires that of dying in the good will of all mankind.—To JAMES SMITH. vii, 270. (M., 1822.)

— TRANSMIGRATION OF SOULS.— See SOULS, TRANSMIGRATION OF.

8504. TRAVEL, Advice as to.—The people you will naturally see the most of will be tavern keepers, *valets de place*, and postillions. These are the hackneyed rascals of every country. Of course they must never be considered when we calculate the national character.— TRAVELLING HINTS. ix, 404. (1788.)

8505. ———. To pass once along a public road through a country, and in one direction only, to put up at its tavern, and get into conversation with the idle, drunken individuals who pass their time lounging in these taverns, is not the way to know a country, its inhabitants, or manners.—To PROFESSOR EBELING. FORD ED., vii, 45. (1795.)

8506. TRAVEL, Philanthropy and.— From the first olive fields of Pierrelatte to the orangeries of Hières, has been continued rapture to me. I have often wished for you [Lafayette]. I think you have not made this journey. It is a pleasure you have to come, and an improvement to be added to the many you have already made. It will be a great comfort to you to know, from your own inspection, the condition of all the provinces of your own country, and it will be interesting to them, at some future day, to be known to you. This is, perhaps, the only moment of your life in which you can acquire that knowledge. And to do it most effectually, you must be absolutely *incognito*; you must ferret the people out of their hovels as I have done, look into their kettles, eat their bread, loll on their beds under pretense of resting yourself, but in fact to find if they are soft. You will feel a sublime pleasure in the course of this investigation, and a sublimer one hereafter, when you shall be able to apply your knowledge to the softening of their beds, or the throwing a morsel of meat into their kettle of vegetables.—To MARQUIS DE LAFAYETTE. ii, 136. (Ne., 1787.)

8507. —— ——. I am never satiated with rambling through the fields and farms [in France], examining the culture and cultivators, with a degree of curiosity which makes some take me to be a fool, and others to be much wiser than I am.—To MARQUIS DE LAFAYETTE. ii, 135. (Ne., 1787.)

8508. —— ——. The politics of each country [is] well worth studying so far as respects internal affairs. Examine its influence on the happiness of the people. Take every possible occasion for entering into the houses of the laborers, and especially at the moments of their repast; see what they eat, how they are clothed, whether they are obliged to work too hard; whether the government or their landlord takes from them an unjust proportion of their labor; on what footing stands the property they call their own, their personal liberty, &c., &c.—TRAVELLING HINTS. ix, 405. (1788.)

8509. TRAVEL, Reflection during.—I think one travels more usefully when alone, because he reflects more.—To J. BANNISTER, JR. ii, 151. (P., 1787.)

8510. TRAVEL, Tours of political.— With respect to the tour my friends have proposed that I should make in that quarter, I have not made up a final opinion. The course of life which General Washington had run, civil and military, the services he had rendered, and the space he therefore occupied in the affections of his fellow citizens, take from his examples the weight of precedents for others; because no others can arrogate to themselves the claims which he had on the public homage. To myself, therefore, it comes as a new question, to be viewed under all the phases it may present. I confess that I am not reconciled to the idea of a Chief Magistrate parading himself through the several States, as an object of public gaze, and in quest of applause which, to be valuable, should be purely voluntary. I had rather acquire silent good will by a faithful discharge of my duties, than owe expressions of it to my putting myself in the way of receiving them.—To JAMES SULLIVAN. v. 101. FORD ED., ix, 77. (W., June 1807.)

8511. —— ——. A journey to Boston or Portsmouth, after I shall be a private citizen, would much better harmonize with my feelings, as well as duties; and, founded in curiosity, would give no claims to an extension of it. I should see my friends, too, more at our mutual ease, and be left more exclusively to their society.—To JAMES SULLIVAN. v, 102. FORD ED., ix. 78. (W., June 1807.)

8512. TRAVEL, Wisdom, happiness and.—Travelling makes men wiser, but less happy. When men of sober age travel, they gather knowledge, which they may apply usefully for their country; but they are subject ever after to recollections mixed with regret; their affections are weakened by being extended over more objects; and they learn new habits which cannot be gratified when they return home.—To PETER CARR. ii, 241. FORD ED., iv, 432. (P., 1787.)

8513. TRAVEL, Young men and.— Young men, who travel, * * * do not acquire that wisdom for which a previous foundation is requisite, by repeated and just observations at home. The glare of pomp and pleasure is analogous to the motion of the blood; it absorbs all their affection and attention, and they are torn from it as from the only good in this world, and return to their home as to a place of exile and condemnation. Their eyes are forever turned back to the object they have lost, and its recollection poisons the residue of their lives. * * * A habit of idleness, an inability to apply themselves to business is acquired, and renders them useless to themselves and their country. These observations are founded in experience. There is no place where your pursuit of knowledge will be so little obstructed by foreign objects as in your own country, nor any, wherein the virtues of the heart will be less exposed to be weakened. Be good, be learned, and be industrious, and you will not want the aid of travelling to render you precious to your country, dear to your friends, happy within yourself.—To PETER CARR. ii, 241. FORD ED., iv, 433. (P., 1787.)

8514. TRAVELERS, Entertaining.—It is the general interest of our country that strangers of distinction passing through it should be made acquainted with its best citizens, and those most qualified to give favorable impressions of it.—To MR. HITE. iv, 146. (M., 1796.)

8515. TREASON, Executions for.—It may be mentioned as a proof, both of the lenity of our government, and unanimity of its inhabitants, that though this [Revolutionary] war has now raged near seven years, not a single execution for treason has taken place.—NOTES ON VIRGINIA. viii, 396. FORD ED., iii, 260. (1782.)

8516. TREASON, Patriotism vs.—Treason, when real, merits the highest punishment. But most codes extend their definitions of treason to acts not really against one's country. They do not distinguish between acts against the government, and acts against the oppressions of the government. The latter are virtues; yet have furnished more victims to the executioner than the former. Real treasons are rare; oppressions frequent. The unsuccessful strugglers against tyranny have been the chief martyrs of treason laws in all countries. Reformation of government with our neighbors* [being] as much wanting now as reformation of religion is, or ever was anywhere, we should not wish then to give up to the executioner the patriot who fails, and flees to us.—REPORT ON SPANISH CONVENTION. iii, 353. FORD ED., v, 483. (1792.)

8517. TREASON, Punishment for.— Treasons, taking the simulated with the real, are sufficiently punished by exile.—REPORT ON SPANISH CONVENTION. iii, 353. FORD ED., v, 483. (1792.)

8518. TREASON, Security against.— The framers of our Constitution certainly supposed they had guarded, as well their government against destruction by treason, as their citizens against oppression, under pre-

* The Spanish provinces.—EDITOR.

tence of it; and if these ends are not attained, it is of importance to enquire by what means, more effectual, they may be secured.—Seventh Annual Message. viii, 88. Ford ed., ix, 164. (1807.)

8519. TREASON, Suspected.—Having received information that divers citizens of this Commonwealth [Virginia], in the counties of James and York, have lately committed acts some of which amount to high treason and others to misprision of treason; and that some, though they may have been able to disguise and conceal their transactions as that legal evidence cannot be obtained by which they may be subjected to prosecution, * * * yet have so conducted themselves as to furnish the most pregnant circumstances of suspicion that they have been guilty of those offences, or are disaffected to the Independence of the United States, and will, whenever they shall have opportunity, aid or advise the measures of the public enemy, which persons, in the critical situation of this Commonwealth, it is indispensably necessary to punish for their crimes by way of example to others and to disable from doing mischief; I must, therefore, * * * desire and authorize you to make enquiry into the premises, and where you shall have probable cause to believe that any persons have been guilty of treason, or misprision of treason; that there is legal evidence to commit them thereof; and that an examining court can be had on them in the county where the offence was committed before there shall be any danger of rescue by the enemy, you have them delivered to the warrant of a justice of the peace, in order that they may be prosecuted in the usual forms of law; and that you aid in their safe conveyance to the public jail in Richmond, if they be ordered to be conveyed. But where you shall be of opinion that legal evidence cannot be obtained, that an examining court cannot be procured in the county before there will be danger of a rescue by the enemy, and that there are pregnant circumstances of suspicion that they have been guilty of the offences of treason or misprision of treason; or where there shall be pregnant causes of suspicion that persons in these counties are disaffected to the Independence of the United States; and when occasion serves, aid or advise the operations of the enemy; that in those cases, you apprehend such persons, and send them in safe custody to the jail of Richmond county. * * * They shall be treated by those into whose hands they shall be committed with no insult or rudeness unnecessary for their safe custody.—To Colonel James Innes. Ford ed., iii, 27. (R., May 1781.)

8520. TREASURY, Conduct of.—There is a point * * * on which I should wish to keep my eye, and to which I should aim to approach by every tack which previous arrangements force upon us. That is, to form into one consolidated mass all the moneys received into the treasury, and to the several expenditures, giving them a preference of payment according to the order in which they should be arranged. As for example. 1. The interest of the public debt. 2. Such portions of the principal as are exigible. 3. The expenses of government. 4. Such other portions of principal as, though not exigible, we are still free to pay when we please. The last object might be made to take up the residuum of money remaining in the treasury at the end of every year, after the three first

objects were complied with, and would be the barometer whereby to test the economy of the administration. It would furnish a simple measure by which every one could mete their merit, and by which every one could decide when taxes were deficient or superabundant.—To Albert Gallatin. iv, 428. Ford ed., viii, 140. (W., 1802.)

8521. TREASURY, Hamilton and.—This constellation of great men in the Treasury department was of a piece with the rest of Hamilton's plans. He took his own stand as a lieutenant general, surrounded by his major generals, and stationed his brigadiers and colonels under the name of supervisors, inspectors, &c., in the different States. Let us deserve well of our country by making her interests the end of all our plans, and not our own pomp, patronage, and irresponsibility.—To Albert Gallatin. iv, 429. Ford ed., viii, 141. (W., 1802.)

8522. TREASURY, Necessity for.—Every circumstance we hear induces us to believe that it is the want of will, rather than of ability, to furnish contributions which keeps the public treasury so poor. The Algerines will probably do us the favor to produce a sense of the necessity of a public treasury and a public force on that element where it can never be dangerous.—To David Humphreys. ii, 10. (P., 1786.)

8523. TREASURY, Organization of.—We shall now get rid of the commissioner of the internal revenue, and superintendent of stamps. It remains to amalgamate the comptroller and auditor into one, and reduce the register to a clerk of accounts; and then the organization will consist, as it should at first, of a keeper of money, a keeper of accounts, and the head of the department.—To Albert Gallatin. iv, 429. Ford ed., viii, 141. (W., 1802.)

— TREASURY, Patronage.—See Post-office.

8524. TREASURY, Separate department.—The act of September 2d, 1789, establishing a Department of Treasury, should be so amended as to constitute the office of the Treasurer of the United States a separate department, independent of the Secretary of the Treasury.—Giles Treasury Resolutions. Ford ed., vi, 171. (1793.)

— TREASURY NOTES.—See National Currency.

8525. TREATIES, Binding force of.—The moral duties which exist between individual and individual in a state of nature, accompany them into a state of society, and the aggregate of the duties of all the individuals composing the society constitutes the duties of that society towards any other; so that between society and society the same moral duties exist as did between the individuals composing them, while in an unassociated state, and their Maker not having released them from those duties on their forming themselves into a nation.—OPINION ON FRENCH TREATIES. vii, 613. FORD ED., vi, 220. (1793.)

8526. —— ——. Compacts between nation and nation are obligatory on them by the same moral law which obliges individuals to observe their compacts. There are circumstances, however, which sometimes excuse the non-performance of contracts between man and man; so are there also between nation and nation. When performance, for instance, becomes impossible, non-performance is not immoral. So if performance becomes *self-destructive* to the party, the law of self-preservation overrules the laws of obligation in others. For the reality of these principles I appeal to the true fountains of evidence, the head and heart of every rational and honest man. It is there nature has written her moral laws, and where every man may read them for himself. He will never read there the permission to annul his obligations for a time, or forever, whenever they become "dangerous, useless, or disagreeable", certainly not when merely *useless* or *disagreeable,* as seems to be said in an authority which has been quoted,* Vattel. 2. 197, and though he may, under certain degrees of *danger,* yet the danger must be imminent, and the degree great. Of these, it ': true, that nations are to be judges for themselves; since no nation has a right to sit in judgment over another. But the tribunal of our consciences remains, and that also of the opinion of the world. These will revise the sentence we pass in our own case, and as we respect these, we must see that in judging ourselves we have honestly done the part of impartial and rigorous judges.—OPINION ON FRENCH TREATIES. vii, 613. FORD ED., vi, 220. (1793.)

8527. —— ——. It is not the *possibility of danger* which absolves a party from his contract, for that possibility always exists, and in every case. * * * If possibilities would void contracts, there never could be a valid contract, for possibilities hang over everything. Obligation is not suspended till the danger is become real, and the moment of it so imminent, that we can no longer avoid decision without forever losing the opportunity to do it.—OPINION ON FRENCH TREATIES. vii, 614. FORD ED., vi, 222. (1793.)

8528. —— ——. I deny that the most explicit declaration made at this moment, that we acknowledge the obligation of the [French] treaties, could take from us the right of non-compliance at any future time, when compliance would involve us in great and inevitable danger.—OPINION ON FRENCH TREATIES. vii, 617. FORD ED., vi, 224. (1793.)

8529. —— ——. The doctrine of Grotius, Puffendorf and Wolf is that "treaties remain obligatory, notwithstanding any change in the form of government, except in the single case, where the preservation of that form was the object of the treaty". There, the treaty ex-

* By Alexander Hamilton.—EDITOR.

tinguishes, not by the election or declaration of the party remaining in *statu quo,* but independently of that, by the evanishment of the object. Vattel lays down, in fact, the same doctrine, that treaties continue obligatory, notwithstanding a change of government by the will of the other party; that to oppose that will would be a wrong; and that the ally remains an ally, notwithstanding the change. So far he concurs with all the previous writers:—but he then adds what they had not said, nor would say,—"but if this change renders the alliance *useless,* dangerous or *disagreeable* to it, it is free to renounce it". (Vattel. 2. 197.) It was unnecessary for him to have specified the exception of *danger* in this particular case, because that exception exists in all cases, and its extent has been considered; but when he adds that, because a contract is become merely *useless* or *disagreeable* we are free to renounce it,—he is in opposition to Grotius, Puffendorf and Wolf, who admit no such license against the obligation of treaties, and he is in opposition to the morality of every honest man, to whom we may safely appeal to decide whether he feels himself free to renounce a contract the moment it becomes merely *useless* or *disagreeable* to him.—OPINION ON FRENCH TREATIES. vii, 619. FORD ED., vi, 227. (1793.)

8530. TREATIES, Construction of.— Where the missionary of one government construes differently from that to which he is sent, the treaties and laws which are to form a common rule of action for both, it would be unjust in either to claim an exclusive right of construction. Each nation has an equal right to expound the meaning of their common rule; and reason and usage have established, in such cases, a convenient and well-understood train of proceeding. It is the right and duty of the foreign missionary to urge his own constructions, to support them with reasons, which may convince, and in terms of decency and respect which may reconcile the government of the country to a concurrence. It is the duty of that government to listen to his reasonings with attention and candor, and to yield to them when just. But if it shall still appear to them that reason and right are on their side, it follows of necessity, that exercising the sovereign powers of the country, they have a right to proceed on their own constructions and conclusions as to whatever is to be done within their limits. The minister then refers the case to his own government, asks new instructions, and, in the meantime, acquiesces in the authority of the country. His government examines his constructions, abandons them if wrong, insists on them if right, and the case then becomes a matter of negotiation between the two nations.—To GOUVERNEUR MORRIS. iv, 44. FORD ED., vi, 388. (Aug. 1793.)

8531. TREATIES, Embarrassing.— It is against our system to embarrass ourselves with treaties, or to entangle ourselves at all with the affairs of Europe.—To PHILIP MAZZEI. iv, 553. (W., July 1804.)

8532. —— ——. Our system is to have no treaties with any nation, as far as can be avoided. The treaty with England has, therefore, not been renewed, and all overtures for treaty with other nations have been declined. We believe, that with nations as with individuals, dealings may be carried on as advantageously, perhaps more so, while their continuance depends on a voluntary good treatment, as if fixed by a contract, which, when it becomes injurious to either, is made, by forced constructions, to mean what suits them, and becomes a cause of war instead of a bond of peace.—To PHILIP MAZZEI. iv, 552. (W., 1804.)

8533. —— ——. We are infinitely better off without treaties of commerce with any nation.—To PRESIDENT MADISON. vi, 453. FORD ED., ix, 513. (M., March 1815.)

8534. TREATIES, Infractions of.—On the breach of any article of a treaty by the one party, the other has its election to declare it dissolved in all its articles, or to compensate itself by withholding execution of equivalent articles; or to waive notice of the breach altogether.—To GEORGE HAMMOND. iii, 391. FORD ED., vi, 33. (1792.)

8535. —— ——. When one party breaks any stipulation of a treaty, the other is free to break it also, either in the whole, or in equivalent parts at its pleasure.—To GEORGE HAMMOND. iii, 424. FORD ED., vi, 64. (1792.)

8536. —— ——. If, in withholding a compliance with any part of the treaties, we do it without just cause or compensation, we give to France a cause of war, and so become associated in it on the other side.—OPINION ON FRENCH TREATIES. vii, 618. FORD ED., vi, 225. (1793.)

8537. TREATIES, Laws of the land.—Treaties are legislative acts. A treaty is a law of the land. It differs from other laws only as it must have the consent of a foreign nation, being but a contract with respect to that nation. In all countries, I believe, except England, treaties are made by the legislative power; and there, also, if they touch the laws of the land, they must be approved by Parliament. * * * An act of Parliament was necessary to validate the American treaty of 1783.—PARLIAMENTARY MANUAL. ix, 80.

8538. TREATIES, Nations and.—I consider the people who constitute a society or nation as the source of all authority in that nation; as free to transact their common concerns by any agents they think proper; to change these agents individually, or the organization of them in form or function whenever they please; that all the acts done by those agents under the authority of the nation, are the acts of the nation, are obligatory on them and enure to their use, and can in no wise be annulled or affected by any change

in the form of the government, or of the persons administering it.—OPINION ON FRENCH TREATIES. vii, 612. FORD ED., vi, 220. (April 1793.)

8539. —— ——. The treaties between the United States and France were not treaties between the United States and Louis Capet, but between the two nations of America and France; and the nations remaining in existence, though both of them have since changed their forms of government, the treaties are not annulled by these changes.—OPINION ON FRENCH TREATIES. vii, 613. FORD ED., vi, 220. (April 1793.)

8540. TREATIES, Opposition to European.—I am not for linking ourselves by new treaties with the quarrels of Europe; entering that field of slaughter to preserve their balance, or joining in the confederacy of kings to war against the principles of liberty.—To ELBRIDGE GERRY. iv, 268. FORD ED., vii, 328. (Pa., 1799.)

8541. —— ——. We wish to let every treaty we have drop off without renewal. * * * The interest which European nations feel, as well as ourselves, in the mutual patronage of commercial intercourse, is a sufficient stimulus on both sides to ensure that patronage. A treaty, contrary to that interest, renders war necessary to get rid of it.—To WILLIAM SHORT. iv, 415. FORD ED., viii, 98. (W., 1801.)

8542. TREATIES, Power to make.—The States of America before their present Union possessed completely, each within its own limits, the exclusive right to * * * [make treaties and] by their act of Union, they have as completely ceded [it] to the General Government. Art. 2d. Section 1st. " The President shall have power, by and with the advice and consent of the Senate, to make treaties, provided two-thirds of the Senators present concur." Section 10th, " No State shall enter into any treaty, alliance, or confederation. No State shall, without the consent of Congress, * * * enter into any agreement of compact with another State, or with a foreign power * * * ." These paragraphs of the Constitution, declaring that the General Government shall have, and that the particular ones shall not have, the right of * * * treaty, are so explicit that no commentary can explain them further, nor can any explain them away.—OPINION ON GEORGIAN LAND GRANTS. vii, 468. FORD ED., v, 166. (1790.)

8543. —— ——. Consulted verbally by the President [Washington] on whom a committee of the Senate are to wait * * * to know whether he will think it proper to redeem our Algerine captives, and make a treaty with the Algerines, on the single vote of the Senate, without taking that of the Representatives. * * * The subsequent approbation of the Senate being necessary to validate a treaty, they expect to be consulted beforehand, if the case admits. So the subsequent act of the Representatives being necessary where money is given, why should not they expect to be consulted in like manner, when the case admits? A treaty is a law of the land. But prudence will point out this difference to be attended to in making them; viz., where a treaty contains such articles only as will go into execution of themselves, or be carried into execution by the judges, they may be safely made; but where there are articles which require a law to be passed afterwards by the legislature, great caution is requisite. Therefore [I am] against hazarding this transaction without the sanction of both houses. The President concurred.—THE ANAS. ix, 106. FORD ED., i, 183. (March 1792.)

8544. —— ——. The subsequent approbation of the Senate being necessary to validate a treaty, [the Senate] expect to be consulted beforehand, if the case admits. So the subsequent act of the Representatives being necessary where money is given, why should not they expect to be consulted in like manner, when the case admits? A treaty is a law of the land. But prudence will point out this difference to be attended to in making them; viz., where a treaty contains such articles only as will go into execution of themselves, or be carried into execution by the judges, they may be safely made; but where there are articles which require a law to be passed afterwards by the Legislature, great caution is requisite. For example, the consular convention with France required a very small legislative regulation. This convention was unanimously ratified by the Senate. Yet the same identical men threw by the law to enforce it ,at the last session, and the Representatives at this session have placed it among the laws which they may take up or not, at their own convenience, as if that was a higher motive than the public faith. I am, therefore, against hazarding this transaction without the sanction of both Houses.*—THE ANAS. ix, 106. FORD ED., i, 184. (March 1792.)

8545. —— ——. President Washington wished to redeem our captives at Algiers and to make peace with them on paying an annual tribute. The Senate were willing to approve this, but unwilling to have the lower house applied to previously to furnish the money; they wished the President to take the money from the treasury, or open a loan for it. They thought that to consult the Representatives on one occasion would give them a handle always to claim it, and would let them into a participation of the power of making treaties, which the Constitution had given exclusively to the President and Senate. They said, too, that if the particular sum was voted by the Representatives, it would not be a secret. The President had no confidence in the secrecy of the Senate, and did not choose to take money from the treasury or to borrow. But he agreed he

* The transaction was the making a treaty with the Algerines, and providing for the redemption of the Algerine prisoners, which involved the raising of a loan.—EDITOR.

would enter into the provisional treaties with the Algerines, not to be binding on us till ratified here. I prepared questions for consultation with the Senate, and added, that on the return of the provisional treaty, and after they should advise the ratification, he would not have the seal put to it till the *two* Houses should vote the money. He asked me, if the treaty stipulating a sum and ratified by him, with the advice of the Senate, would not be good under the Constitution, and obligatory on the Representatives to furnish the money? I answered it certainly would, and that it would be the duty of the Representatives to raise the money; but that they might decline to do what was their duty, and I thought it might be incautious to commit himself by a ratification with a foreign nation, where he might be left in the lurch in the execution; it was possible, too, to conceive a treaty, which it would not be their duty to provide for. He said he did not like throwing too much into democratic hands, that if they would not do what the Constitution called them to do, the government would be at an end, and must *then assume another form.*—THE ANAS. ix, 114. FORD ED., i, 190. (April 1792.)

8546. —— ——. I had observed, that wherever the agency of either or both Houses would be requisite subsequent to a treaty, to carry it into effect, it would be prudent to consult them previously, if the occasion admitted: that thus it was, we were in the habit of consulting the Senate previously, when the occasion permitted, because their subsequent ratification would be necessary; that there was the same reason for consulting the lower House previously, where they were to be called on afterwards, and especially in a case of money, as they held the purse strings, and would be jealous of them.—THE ANAS. ix, 115. FORD ED., i, 191. (April 1792.)

8547. —— ——. [Alexander] Hamilton laid down this position* with great positiveness: That the Constitution having given power to the President and Senate to make treaties, they might make a treaty of neutrality which should take from Congress the right to declare war in that particular case, and that under the form of a treaty they might exercise any powers whatever, even those exclusively given by the Constitution to the House of Representatives. Randolph opposed this position, and seemed to think that where they undertook to do acts by treaty (as to settle a tariff of duties), which were exclusively given to the Legislature, that an act of the Legislature would be necessary to confirm them, as happens in England, when a treaty interferes with duties established by law. I insisted that in giving to the President and Senate a power to make treaties, the Constitution meant only to authorize them to carry into effect, by way of treaty, any powers they might constitutionally exercise. I was sensible of the weak points in this po-

* At a Cabinet meeting to consider the Neutrality Proclamation.—EDITOR.

sition, but there were still weaker in the other hypothesis; and if it be impossible to discover a rational measure of authority to have been given by this clause, I would rather suppose that the cases which my hypothesis would leave unprovided, were not thought of by the convention, or if thought of, could not be agreed on, or were thought on and deemed unnecessary to be invested in the government. Of this last description, were treaties of neutrality, treaties offensive and defensive, &c. In every event, I would rather construe so narrowly as to oblige the nation to amend, and thus declare what powers they would agree to yield, than too broadly, and indeed, so broadly as to enable the Executive and Senate to do things which the Constitution forbids.—THE ANAS. ix, 181. FORD ED., i, 268. (Nov. 1793.)

8548. —— ——. According to the rule established by usage and common sense, of construing one part of the instrument by another, the objects on which the President and Senate may exclusively act by treaty are much reduced, but the field on which they may act with the sanction of the Legislature, is large enough; and I see no harm in rendering their sanction necessary, and not much harm in annihilating the whole treaty-making power, except as to making peace.—To JAMES MADISON. iv, 135. FORD ED., vii, 69. (M., March 1796.)

8549. —— ——. If you [House of Representatives] decide in favor of your right to refuse cooperation in any case of treaty, I should wonder on what occasion it is to be used, if not on one where the rights, the interests, the honor and faith of our nation are so grossly sacrificed; where a faction has entered into a conspiracy with the enemies of their country to chain down the Legislature at the feet of both; where the whole mass of your constituents have condemned this work in the most unequivocal manner, and are looking to you as their last hope to save them from the effects of the avarice and corruption of the first agent, the revolutionary machinations of others, and the incomprehensible acquiescence of the only honest man who has assented to it. I wish that his honesty and his political errors may not furnish a second occasion to exclaim, " curse on his virtues, they have undone his country".—To JAMES MADISON. iv, 135. FORD ED., vii, 69. (M., March 1796.)

8550. —— ——. I was glad to hear it admitted on all hands in discussion [in the Senate], that laws of the United States, subsequent to a treaty, control its operation, and that the Legislature is the only power which can control a treaty. Both points are sound beyond doubt.—To JAMES MADISON. iv, 244. FORD ED., vii, 261. (Pa., May 1798.)

8551. —— ——. To what subject the treaty-making power extends, has not been defined in detail by the Constitution; nor are we entirely agreed among ourselves. 1. It is admitted that it must concern the foreign na-

tion, party to the contract, or it would be a mere nullity *res inter alia acta*. 2. By the general power to make treaties, the Constitution must have intended to comprehend only those objects which are usually regulated by treaty, and cannot be otherwise regulated. 3. It must have meant to except out of these the rights reserved to the States; for surely the President and Senate cannot do by treaty what the whole government is interdicted from doing in any way. 4. And also to except those subjects of legislation in which it gave a participation to the House of Representatives. This last exception is denied by some, on the ground that it would leave very little matter for the treaty power to work on. The less the better say others. The Constitution thought it wise to restrain the Executive and Senate from entangling and embroiling our affairs with those of Europe. Besides, as the negotiations are carried on by the Executive alone, the subjecting to ratification of the Representatives such articles as are within their participation, is no more inconvenient than to the Senate. But the ground of this exemption is denied as unfounded. For examine, *e. g.*, the treaty of commerce with France, and it will be found that out of thirty-one articles, there are not more than small portions of two or three of them which would not still remain as subjects of treaties, untouched by these exceptions.—PARLIAMENTARY MANUAL. ix, 80.

8552. —— ——. The property and sovereignty of all Louisiana * * * have on certain conditions been transferred to the United States by instruments bearing date the 30th of April last. When these shall have received the constitutional sanction of the Senate, they will without delay be communicated to the Representatives also, for the exercises of their functions, as to those conditions which are within the powers vested by the Constitution in Congress.—THIRD ANNUAL MESSAGE. viii, 24. FORD ED., viii, 268. (Oct. 1803.)

8553. —— ——. Whatever of the enumerated objects is proper to be executed by way of a treaty, the President and Senate may enter into the treaty.—To WILSON C. NICHOLAS. iv, 506. FORD ED., viii, 248. (M., 1803.)

8554. —— ——. A writer in the *National Intelligencer* of Feb. 24, 1816, who signs himself " B.", is endeavoring to shelter under the cloak of General Washington, the present enterprise of the Senate to wrest from the House of Representatives the power. given them by the Constitution, of participating with the Senate in the establishment and continuance of laws on specified subjects. Their aim is, by associating an Indian chief, or foreign government, in form of a treaty. to possess themselves of the power of repealing laws become obnoxious to them, without the assent of the third branch. although that assent was necessary to make it a law. We are then to depend for the secure possession of our laws, not on our immediate representatives chosen by ourselves, and amenable to ourselves every other year, but on Senators chosen by the Legislatures, amenable to them only, and that but at intervals of six years, which is nearly the common estimate for a term for life. But no act of that sainted worthy, no thought of General Washington, ever countenanced a change of our Constitution so vital as would be the rendering insignificant the popular, and giving to the aristocratical branch of our government, the power of depriving us of our laws. The case for which General Washington is quoted is that of his treaty with the Creeks, wherein was a stipulation that their supplies of goods should continue to be imported duty free. * * * General Washington's stipulation in that treaty was nothing more than that our laws should not levy duties where we have no right to levy them, that is, in foreign ports, or foreign countries. * * * The same writer quotes from a note in Marshall's *History,* an opinion of Mr. Jefferson, given to General Washington on the same occasion of the Creek treaty. Two or three little lines only of that opinion are given us, which do indeed express the doctrine in broad and general terms. Yet we know how often a few words withdrawn from their place may seem to bear a general meaning, when their context would show that their meaning must have been limited to the subject with respect to which they were used. If we could see the whole opinion, it might probably appear that its foundation was the peculiar circumstances of the Creek nation. We may say, too, on this opinion, as on that of a judge whose positions beyond the limits of the case before him are considered as *obiter* sayings, never to be relied on as authority. In July '90, moreover, the Government was but just getting under way. The duty law was not passed until the succeeding month of August. This question of the effect of a treaty was then of the first impression; and none of us, I suppose, will pretend that on our first reading of the Constitution we saw at once all its intentions, all the bearings of every word of it, as fully and as correctly as we have since understood them, after they have become subjects of public investigation and discussion; and I well remember the fact that, although Mr. Jefferson had retired from office before Mr. Jay's mission, and the question on the British treaty, yet during its discussion we were well assured of his entire concurrence in opinion with Mr. Madison and others who maintained the rights of the House of Representatives, so that, if on a *primâ facie* view of the question, his opinion had been too general, on stricter investigation, and more mature consideration, his ultimate opinion was with those who thought that the subjects which were confided to the House of Representatives in conjunction with the President and Senate, were exceptions to the general treaty power given to the President and Senate alone (according to the general rule that an instrument is to be so construed as to reconcile and give meaning and effect to all its parts); that whenever a treaty stipulation interferes with a law of the three branches, the consent of the third branch is necessary to give it effect; and that there is to this but the single exception of the question of war and peace. There the Constitution expressly requires the concurrence of the three branches to commit us to the state of war, but permits two of them, the President and Senate, to change it to that of peace, for reasons as obvious as they are wise. I think, then, I may affirm in contradiction to B., that the present attempt of the Senate is not sanctioned by the opinion either of General Washington or of Mr. Jefferson.—JEFFERSON MSS. vi, 557. (March 1816.)

8555. —— ——. When the British treaty of 18— arrived, without any provision against the impressment of our seamen, I determined not to ratify it. The Senate thought I should ask their advice. I thought that would be a mockery of them, when I was predetermined against following it, should they advise its ratification. The Constitution had made their advice necessary to confirm a treaty, but not to reject it. This has been blamed by some; but I have never doubted its soundness.—To SPENCER ROANE. vii, 135. FORD ED., x, 142. (P.F., 1819.)'

8556. TREATIES, Preliminary.—I consider a preliminary treaty as establishing certain heads of agreement, and a truce till these and others can be definitely arranged; as suspending acts of hostility, and as not changing the legal character of the *enemy* into that of a *friend.*—To ALEXANDER HAMILTON. FORD ED., vi, 10. (Pa., 1792.)

8557. TREATIES, Ratification of.—It has been the usage of the Executive, when it communicates a treaty to the Senate for their ratification, to communicate also the correspondence of the negotiations. This, having been omitted in the case of the Prussian treaty, was asked by a vote of the House of February 12, 1800, and was obtained. And in December, 1800, the Convention of that year, between the United States and France, with the report of the negotiations by the envoys, but not their instructions, being laid before the Senate, the instructions were asked for, and communicated by the President.—PARLIAMENTARY MANUAL. ix, 81.

8558. TREATIES, Regulation of commerce by.—Treaties are very imperfect machines for regulating commerce in detail.—To M. DE MEUNIER. ix, 287. FORD ED., iv, 142. (P., 1786.)

8559. —— ——. It is desirable, in many instances, to exchange mutual advantages by legislative acts rather than by treaty; because the former, though understood to be in consideration of each other, and therefore greatly respected, yet when they become too inconvenient, can be dropped at the will of either party; whereas stipulations by treaty are forever irrevocable but by joint consent let a change of circumstances render them ever so bothersome.— REPORT ON TONNAGE LAW. FORD ED., v, 273. (1791.)

8560. TREATIES, Repeal of.—A treaty made by the President, with the concurrence of two-thirds of the Senate, is a law of the land, and a law of superior order, because it not only repeals past laws, but cannot itself be repealed by future ones.*—OFFICIAL OPINION. vii, 505. FORD ED., v, 216. (1790.)

8561. TREATIES, Rescinding.—Treaties being declared, equally with the laws of the United States, to be the supreme law of the land, it is understood that an act of the Legislature alone can declare them infringed and rescinded. This was accordingly the process adopted in the case of France, 1798.— PARLIAMENTARY MANUAL. ix, 81.

8562. TREATIES, Self-liberation from. —Reason which gives * * * [the] right of self-liberation from a contract in certain cases, has subjected it to certain just limitations. 1. The danger which absolves us must be great, inevitable and imminent. * * * 2. A second limitation on our right of releasing ourselves is that we are to do it from so much of the treaties only as is bringing great and inevitable danger on us, and not from the residue, allowing the other party a right at the same time, to determine whether on our non-compliance with that part, they will declare the whole void. This right they would have, but we should not. * * * 3. A third limitation is that when a party, from necessity or danger, withholds compliance with that part of a treaty, it is bound to make compensation where the nature of the case admits and does not dispense with it.†—OPINION ON FRENCH TREATIES. vii, 614. FORD ED., vi, 221. (1793.)

8563. TREATIES, Short.—Your observations on the expediency of making short treaties are most sound. Our situation is too changing and too improving, to render an unchangeable treaty expedient for us.—TO E. RUTLEDGE. iii, 165. FORD ED., v, 196. (N.Y., 1790.)

8564. TREATIES OF COMMERCE, British.—In February, 1786, Mr. Adams wrote to me [at Paris], pressingly to join him

---

* Jefferson, at a later period, modified this opinion in the following note : " Unless with the consent or default of the other contracting party. It may well be doubted, too, and perhaps denied, that the treaty power can control a law. The question here proposed was then of the first impression. Subsequent investigations have proved that the contrary position is the more general truth."—EDITOR.

† The question under consideration, when this opinion was given, was " whether the United States had the right to renounce their treaties with France, or to hold them suspended till the government of that country shall be established". Alexander Hamilton took the ground that as France was a monarchy when the United States entered into an alliance with it, and had since declared itself to be a republic,which might issue in a military despotism and thereby render the alliance " dangerous ", to the United States, we had the right either to renounce the treaty or to declare it suspended until a settled government had been formed. Jefferson opposed this view, maintaining that the danger to be apprehended was not sufficient in sound morality to justify the United States in declaring the treaty null.—EDITOR.

---

in London immediately, as he thought he discovered there some symptoms of better disposition towards us. Colonel [William Stephens] Smith, his Secretary of Legation, was the bearer of his urgencies for my immediate attendance. I, accordingly, left Paris on the 1st of March and, on my arrival in London, we agreed on a very summary form of treaty, proposing an exchange of citizenship for our citizens, our ships, and our productions generally, except as to office.—AUTOBIOGRAPHY. i, 63. FORD ED., i, 88. (1821.)

8565. ——— ———. On my presentation as usual to the King and Queen, at their levées, it was impossible for anything to be more ungracious than their notice of Mr. Adams and myself. I saw at once that the ulcerations in the narrow mind of that mulish being left nothing to be expected on the subject of my attendance ; and on the first conference with the Marquis of Carmarthen, his Minister of Foreign Affairs, the distance and disinclination which he betrayed in his conversation, the vagueness and evasions of his answers to us. confirmed me in the belief of their aversion to have anything to do with us. We delivered him, however, our *projét.* Mr. Adams not despairing as much as I did of its effect. We afterwards, by one or more notes, requested his appointment of an interview and conference. which, without directly declining, he evaded by pretences of other pressing occupations for the moment. After staying there seven weeks. till within a few days of the expiration of our commission, I informed the minister by note that my duties at Paris required my return to that place, and that I should with pleasure be the bearer of any commands to his Ambassador there. He answered that he had none, and wishing me a pleasant journey, I left London the 26th, and arrived at Paris the 30th of April. —AUTOBIOGRAPHY. i, 64. FORD ED., i, 89. (1821.)

8566. ——— ———. There is no doubt what the determination [of the British Court with respect to a treaty] will be ; but it will be useful to have it ; as it may put an end to all further expectations on our side the water, and show that the time is come for doing whatever is to be done by us for counteracting the unjust and greedy designs of this country [England]. —TO JOHN JAY. i, 539. FORD ED., iv, 200. (L., March 1786.)

8567. ——— ———. I am quite at a loss what you will do with England. To leave her in possession of our posts, seems inadmissible ; and yet to take them, brings on a state of things for which we seem not to be in readiness. Perhaps a total suppression of her trade, or an exclusion of her vessels from the carriage of our produce, may have some effect ; but I believe not very great. Their passions are too deeply and too universally engaged in opposition to us. The ministry have found means to persuade the nation that they are richer than they were while we participated of their commercial privileges. We should try to turn our trade into other channels. I am in hopes this country [France] will endeavor to give it more encouragement.—TO ELBRIDGE GERRY. i, 557. (P., 1786.)

8568. ——— ———. I am sorry the British are sending a minister to attempt a treaty. They never made an equal commercial treaty with any nation, and we have no right to expect to be the first. It will place you between the injunctions of true patriotism and the clamors of a faction devoted to a foreign interest, in preference to that of their own country. It will confirm the English, too, in their practice of whipping us into a treaty. They did it in Jay's case, were near doing it in Monroe's, and on failure of that, have applied the scourge with tenfold vigor, and now come on to try its effect. But it is the moment when we should prove our consistency, by recurring to the principles we dictated to Monroe, the departure from which occasioned our rejection of his treaty, and by protesting against Jay's treaty being ever quoted or looked at, or even mentioned. That form will forever be a mill-stone round our necks unless we now rid ourselves of it once for all. The occasion is highly favorable, as we never can have them more in o power.—To PRESIDENT MADISON. v, 443. (M., April 1809.)

— **TREATIES OF COMMERCE,** Confederation and.—See CONFEDERATION.

8569. TREATIES OF COMMERCE, Efforts to negotiate.—Without urging, we [Franklin, Adams and Jefferson] sounded the ministers of the several European nations at the Court of Versailles, on their dispositions towards mutual commerce, and the expediency of encouraging it by the protection of a treaty. Old Frederick of Prussia met us cordially and without hesitation, and appointing the Baron de Thulemeyer, his Minister at The Hague, to negotiate with us, we communicated to him our projet, which, with little alteration by the King, was soon concluded. Denmark and Tuscany entered also into negotiations with us. Other powers appearing indifferent we did not think it proper to press them. * * * The negotiations, therefore, begun with Denmark and Tuscan we protracted designedly until our powers had expired; and abstained from making new propositions to others having no colonies; because our commerce being an exchange of raw for wrought materials, is a competent price for admission into the colonies of those possessing them: but were we to give it, without price, to others, all would claim it without price on the ordinary ground of *gentis amicissimæ.*—AUTOBIOGRAPHY. i, 62. FORD ED., i, 87. (1821.)

8570. —— ——. The European powers seemed in fact to know little about us but as rebels, who had been successful in throwing off the yoke of the mother country. They were ignorant of our commerce, which had been always monopolized by England, and of the exchange of articles it might offer advantageously to both parties. They were inclined, therefore, to stand aloof until they could see better what relations might be usefully instituted with us.—AUTOBIOGRAPHY. i, 62. FORD ED., i, 88. (1821.)

8571. —— ——. On the conclusion of peace [with Great Britain], Congress, sensible of their right to assume independence, would not condescend to ask its acknowledgment from other nations, yet were willing, by some of the ordinary international transactions, to receive what would imply that acknowledgment. They appointed commissioners, therefore. to propose treaties of commerce to the principal nations of Europe. I was then a member of Congress, was of the committee appointed to prepare instructions for the commissioners, was, as you suppose, the draughtsman of those actually agreed to, and was joined with your father and Dr. Franklin, to carry them into execution. But the stipulations making part of these instructions, which respected privateering, blockades. contraband. and freedom of the fisheries, were not original conceptions of mine. They

had before been suggested by Dr. Franklin, in some of his papers in possession of the public, and had, I think, been recommended in some letter of his to Congress. I happen only to have been the inserter of them in the first public act which gave the formal sanction of a public authority. We accordingly proposed our treaties, containing these stipulations, to the principal governments of Europe. But we were then just emerged from a subordinate condition; the nations had as yet known nothing of us, and had not yet reflected on the relations which it might be their interest to establish with us. Most of them, therefore, listened to our propositions with coyness and reserve; old Frederick [the Great] alone closing with us without hesitation. The negotiator of Portugal, indeed, signed a treaty with us, which his government did not ratify, and Tuscany was near a final agreement. Becoming sensible, however, ourselves, that we should do nothing with the greater powers, we thought it better not to hamper our country with engagements to those of less significance, and suffered our powers to expire without closing any other negotiations. Austria soon after became desirous of a treaty with us, and her ambassador pressed it often on me; but our commerce with her being no object. I evaded her repeated invitations. Had these governments been then apprized of the station we should so soon occupy among nations, all, I believe, would have met us promptly and with frankness. These principles would then have been established with all, and from being the conventional law with us alone, would have slid into their engagements with one another, and become general.

These are the facts within my recollection. They have not yet got into written history; but their adoption by our southern brethren will bring them into observance, and make them. what they should be, a part of the law of the world, and of the reformation of principles for which they will be indebted to us.—To JOHN QUINCY ADAMS. vii, 436. FORD ED., x, 383. (M., March 1826.)

8572. TREATIES OF COMMERCE, Favored nation principle.—I know of no investigation, at the instance of any nation, of the extent of the clause giving the rights of the most favored nation but from the import of the words themselves, and from the clause that a privilege granted to any other nation shall immediately become common, freely where freely granted, or *yielding the compensation* where a compensation is given, I have no doubt that if any one nation will admit our goods free in consideration of our doing the same by them, no other nation can claim an exception from duties in our ports without yielding us the same in theirs.—To JAMES MONROE. FORD ED., iv, 19. (P., Dec. 1784.)

8573. —— ——. When the first article of our instructions of May 7th, 1784, was under debate in Congress, it was proposed that neither party should make the other pay. in their ports, greater duties, than they paid in the ports of the other. One objection to this was its impracticability; another, that it would put it out of our power to lay such duties on alien importation as might encourage importation by natives. Some members. much attached to English policy, thought such a distinction should actually be established. Some thought the power to do it should be reserved, in case any peculiar circumstances should call for it, though under the present. or, perhaps, any probable circumstances, they did not think it would be good policy ever to exercise it. The footing *gentis amicissimæ* was, therefore, adopted, as you see in the instruction. As far as my enquiries enable me to judge, France and Holland make no distinction of duties between aliens and natives. I also rather believe that the other States of Europe make none, England excepted, to whom this policy, as that of her navigation act, seems peculiar. The question then is, should we disarm ourselves of the power to make this distinction against all nations, in order to purchase an exception from the alien duties in England only; for if we put her importations on the footing of native, all other nations with whom we treat will have a right to claim the same. I think we should, because against other nations, who make no distinction in their ports between us and their own subjects, we ought not to make a distinction in ours. And if the English will agree, in like manner, to make none, we should, with equal reason, abandon the right as against them. I think all the world would gain, by setting commerce at perfect liberty. I remember this proposition to put foreigners and natives on the same footing was considered; and we were all three, Dr. Franklin as well as you and myself, in favor of it. We finally, however, did not admit it, partly from the objection you mention, but more still on account of our instructions. But though the English proclamation had appeared in America at the time of framing these instructions, i think its effect, as to alien duties, had not yet been experienced, and therefore was not attended to. If it had been noted in the debate, I am sure that the annihilation of our whole trade would have been thought too great a price to pay for the reservation of a barren power, which a majority of the members did not propose ever to exercise, though they were willing to retain it. Stipulating for equal rights for foreigners and natives, we obtain more in foreign ports than our instructions required, and we only part with, in our own ports, a power of which sound policy would probably forever forbid the exercise. Add to this, that our treaty will be for a very short term, and if any evil be experienced under it, a reformation will soon be in our power. I am, therefore, for putting this among our original propositions to the court of London. If it should prove an insuperable obstacle with them, or if it should stand in the way of a greater advantage, we can but abandon it in the course of the negotiation.—To JOHN ADAMS. i, 370. FORD ED., iv, 79. (P., July 1785.)

8574. ——— ———. Though treaties, which merely exchange the rights of the most favored nations, are not without all inconvenience, yet they have their conveniences also. It is an important one that they leave each party free to make what internal regulations they please, and to give what preferences they find expedient to native merchants, vessels, and productions.—MISSISSIPPI RIVER INSTRUCTIONS. vii, 587. FORD ED., v, 477. (1792.)

8575. ——— ———. It will probably be urged, because it was urged on a former occasion, that, if Spain *grants** to us the right of navigating the Mississippi, other nations will become entitled to it by virtue of treaties giving them the rights to the *most favored nation.* * * * When those treaties were made, no nations could be under

* This extract is from Jefferson's Instructions to the Commissioners with respect to the navigation of the Mississippi river. It should not be inferred from the use of the word "grants" that Jefferson admitted the Spanish pretension to the control of the lower part of the river. He maintained, on the contrary, that we had an inherent right and also treaty rights to the navigation.--EDITOR.

contemplation but those then existing, or those, at most, who might exist under similar circumstances. America did not then exist as a nation; and the circumstances of her position and commerce, are so totally dissimilar to everything then known, that the treaties of that day were not adapted to any such being. They would better fit even China than America; because, as a manufacturing nation, China resembles Europe more. When we solicited France to admit our whale oils into her ports, though she had excluded all foreign whale oils, her Minister made the objection now under consideration, and the foregoing answer was given. It was found to be solid; and whale oils of the United States are in consequence admitted, though those of Portugal and the Hanse towns and of all other nations, are excluded. Again, when France and England were negotiating their late treaty of commerce, the great dissimilitude of our commerce (which furnishes raw materials to employ the industry of others, in exchange for articles whereon industry has been exhausted) from the commerce of the European nations (which furnishes things ready wrought only) was suggested to the attention of both negotiators, and that they should keep their nations free to make particular arrangements with ours, by communicating to each other only the rights of the most favored *European* nation. Each was separately sensible of the importance of the distinction; and as soon as it was proposed by the one, it was acceded to by the other, and the word *European* was inserted in their treaty. It may fairly be considered, then, as the rational and received interpretation of the diplomatic term, "*gentis amicissimæ*", that it has not in view a nation, unknown in many cases at the time of using the term, and so dissimilar in all cases, as to furnish no ground of just reclamation to any other nation.—MISSISSIPPI RIVER INSTRUCTIONS. vii, 583. FORD ED., v, 473. (1792.)

8576. TREATIES OF COMMERCE, Instructions respecting.—Whereas, instructions bearing date the 29th day of October, 1783, were sent to the Ministers Plenipotentiary of the United States of America at the Court of Versailles, empowered to negotiate a peace, or to any one or more of them, for concerting drafts or propositions for treaties of amity and commerce with the commercial powers of Europe: Resolved, That it will be advantageous to these United States to conclude such treaties with Russia, the Court of Vienna, Prussia, Denmark, Saxony, Hamburg, Great Britain, Spain, Portugal, Genoa, Tuscany, Rome, Naples, Venice, Sardinia, and the Ottoman Porte. Resolved, That in the formation of these treaties the following points be carefully stipulated: 1st. That each party shall have a right to carry their own produce, manufactures, and merchandise in their own bottoms to the ports of the other, and thence the produce and merchandise of the other, paying, in both cases, such duties only as are paid by the most favored nation, freely, where it is freely granted to such nation, or paying the compensation where such nation does the same. 2. That with the nations holding territorial possessions in America, a direct and similar intercourse be admitted between the United States and such possessions; or if this cannot be obtained, then a direct and similar intercourse between the United States and certain free ports within such possessions; that if this neither can be obtained, permission be stipulated to bring from such possessions, in their own bottoms, the produce and merchandise thereof to their States directly; and for these States to carry in their own bottoms the r produce and merchandise to such possessions directly. 3. That these United States be considered in all such treaties, and in every case arising under them, as one nation, upon the principles of the Federal constitution. 4. That it be proposed, though not indispensably required, that if war should hereafter arise between the two contracting parties, the merchants of either country, then residing in the other, shall be allowed to remain nine months to collect their debts and settle their affairs, and may depart freely, carrying off all their effects, without molestation or hinderance, and all fishermen, all cultivators of the earth, and all artisans or manufacturers, unarmed and inhabiting unfortified towns, villages or places, who labor for the common subsistence and benefit of mankind, and peaceably following their respective employments, shall be allowed to continue the same, and shall not be molested by the armed force of the enemy, in whose power, by the events of war, they may happen to fall; but if anything is necessary to be taken from them, for the use of such armed force, the same shall be paid for at a reasonable price; and all merchants and traders, exchanging the products of different places, and thereby rendering the necessaries, conveniences, and comforts of human life more easy to obtain and more general, shall be allowed to pass free and unmolested; and neither of the contracting powers shall grant or issue any commission to any private armed vessels empowering them to take or destroy such trading ships, or interrupt such commerce. 5. And in case either of the contracting parties shall happen to be engaged in war with any other nation, it be further agreed, in order to prevent all the difficulties and misunderstandings that usually arise respecting the merchandise heretofore called contraband, such as arms, ammunition and military stores of all kinds, that no such articles, carrying by the ships or subjects of one of the parties to the enemies of the other, shall, on any account, be deemed contraband, so as to induce confiscation, and a loss of property to individuals. Nevertheless, it shall be lawful to stop such ships and detain them for such length of time as the captors may think necessary, to prevent the inconvenience or damage that might ensue, from their proceeding on their voyage, paying, however, a reasonable compensation for the loss such arms shall occasion to the proprietors; and it shall be further allowed to use in the service of the captors, the who'e or any part of the military stores so detained, paying the owners the full value of the same, to be ascertained by the current price at the place of its destination. But if the other contracting party will not consent to discontinue the confiscation of contraband goods, then that it be stipulated, that if the master of the vessel stopped, will deliver out the goods charged to be contraband, he shall be admitted to do it, and the vessel shall not in that case be carried into any port; but shall be allowed to proceed on her voyage. 6. That in the same case, when either of the contracting parties shall happen to be engaged in war with any other power, all goods, not contraband, belonging to the subjects of that other power, and shipped in the bottoms of the party hereto, who is not engaged in the war, shall be entirely free. And that to ascertain what shall constitute the blockade of any place or port, it shall be understood to be in such predicament, when the assailing power shall have taken such a station as to expose to imminent danger any ship or ships, that would attempt to sail in or out of the said port; and that no vessel of the party, who is not engaged in the said war, shall be stopped without a material and well grounded cause; and in such cases justice shall be done, and an indemnification given, without loss of time to the persons aggrieved, and thus stopped without sufficient cause. 7. That no right be st'pulated for aliens to hold real property within these States, this being utterly inadmissible by their several laws and policy; but when on the death of any person holding real estate within the territories of one of the contracting parties, such real estate would by their laws descend on a subject or citizen of the other, were he not disqualified by alienage, then he shall be allowed reasonable time to dispose of the same, and withdraw the proceeds without molestation. 8. That such treaties be made for a term not exceeding ten years from the exchange of ratification. 9. That these instructions be considered as supplementary to those of October 29th, 1783; and not as revoking, except when they contradict them. That where in treaty with a particular nation they can procure particular advantages, to the specification of which we have been unable to descend, our object in these instructions having been to form out'ines only and general principles of treaty with many nations, it is our expectation they will procure them, though not pointed out in these instructions; and where they may be able to form treaties on principles which, in their judgment, will be more beneficial to the United States than those herein directed to be made their basis, they are permitted to adopt such principles. That as to the duration of treaties, though we have proposed to restrain them to the term of ten years, yet they are at liberty to extend the same as far as fifteen years with any nation which may pertinaciously insist thereon. And that it will be agreeable to us to have supplementary treaties with France, the United Netherlands and Sweden, which may bring the treaties we have entered into with them as nearly as may be to the principles of those now directed; but that this be not pressed, if the proposal should be found disagreeable. *Resolved*, That treaties of amity, or of amity and commerce, be entered into with Morocco, and the Regencies of Algiers, Tunis and Tripoli, to continue for the same term of ten years, or for a term as much longer as can be procured. That our Ministers, to be commissioned for treating with foreign nations, make known to the Emperor of Morocco the great satisfaction which Congress feel from the amicable disposition he has shown towards these States, and his readiness to enter into alliance with them. That the occupations of the war, and distance of our situation have prevented our meeting his friendship so early as we wished. But the powers are now delegated to them for entering into treaty with him, in the execution of which they are ready to proceed, and that as to the expenses of his Minister, they do therein what is for the honor and interest of the United States. Resolved, That a commission be issued to Mr. J. Adams, Mr. B. Frank'in, and Mr. T. Jefferson, giving powers to them, or the greater part of them, to make and receive propositions for such treaties of amity and commerce, and to negotiate and sign the same, transmitting them to Congress for their final ratification; and that such commission be in force for a term not exceeding two years.—TREATY INSTRUCTIONS OF CONGRESS. ix, 226. FORD ED., iii, 489. (May 7, 1784.)

8577. TREATIES OF COMMERCE, Objects of.—My wish to enter treaties with the other powers of Europe arises more from a desire of bringing all our commerce under the jurisdiction of Congress. than from any other views. Because, according to my idea, the commerce of the United States with those countries, not under treaty with us, is under the jurisdiction of each State separately; but that of the countries, which have treated with us, is under the jurisdiction of Congress with the two fundamental restraints only which I have before noted.—To JOHN ADAMS. i, 360. (P., 1785.)

8578. TREATIES OF COMMERCE, Portugal.—Considering the treaty with Portugal among the most interesting to the United States, I some time ago took occasion * * * to ask of the Portuguese Ambassador if he had yet received from his Court an answer to our letter. He told me he had not; but that he would make it the subject of another letter. Two days ago, his Secretaire d'Ambassade called on me with a letter from his Minister to the Ambassador. * * * By this [extract from the letter], it would seem that this power is more disposed to pursue a track of negotiation similar to that which Spain has done. I consider this answer as definitive of all further measures under our commission to Portugal.—To JOHN JAY. i, 458. (P., 1785.)

— **TREATY, Jay.**—See JAY TREATY.

8579. TREATY (British peace), Ratification of.—The definitive treaty of peace which had been signed at Paris on the 3rd of September, 1783, and received here, could not be ratified without a House of nine States. On the 23d of December, therefore, we [the Congress sitting at Annapolis] addressed letters to the several Governors, stating the receipt of the definitive treaty; that seven States only were in attendance, while nine were necessary to its ratification; and urging them to press on their delegates the necessity of their immediate attendance. And on the 26th, to save time, I moved that the Agent of Marine (Robert Morris) should be instructed to have ready a vessel at this place, at New York, and at some Eastern port, to carry over the ratification of the treaty when agreed to. It met the general sense of the House, but was opposed by Dr. [Arthur] Lee, on the ground of expense, which it would authorize the Agent to incur for us; and, he said, it would be better to ratify at once, and send on the ratification. Some members had before suggested that seven States were competent to the ratification. My motion was therefore postponed, and another brought forward by Mr. Read, of South Carolina, for an immediate ratification. This was debated the 26th and 27th. [Jacob] Read [of South Carolina], Lee, [Hugh] Williamson and Jeremiah Chase, urged that the ratification was a mere matter of form, that the treaty was conclusive from the moment it was signed by the ministers; that, although the Confederation requires the assent of *nine States* to *enter into* a treaty, yet, that its conclusion could not be called *entrance into it;* that supposing nine States requisite, it would be in the power of five States to keep us always at war; that nine States had virtually authorized the ratification, having ratified the provisional treaty, and instructed their ministers to agree to a definitive one in the same terms, and the present one was, in fact, substantially, and almost verbatim, the same; that there now remain but sixty-seven days for the ratification, for its passage across the Atlantic, and its exchange; that there was no hope of our soon having nine States present; in fact, that this was the ultimate point of time to which we could venture to wait; that if the ratification was not in Paris by the time stipulated, the treaty would become void; that if ratified by seven States, it would go under our

seal, without its being known to Great Britain that only seven had concurred; that it was a question of which they had no right to take cognizance, and we were only answerable for it to our constituents; that it was like the ratification which Great Britain had received from the Dutch, by the negotiations of Sir William Temple. On the contrary, it was argued by Monroe, Gerry, Howel, Ellery and myself, that by the modern usage of Europe, the ratification was considered as the act which gave validity to a treaty, until which, it was not obligatory. * That the commission to the ministers reserved the ratification to Congress; that the treaty itself stipulated that it should be ratified; that it became a second question, who were competent to the ratification? That the confederation expressly required nine States to enter into any treaty; that, by this, that instrument must have intended, that the assent of nine States should be necessary, as well to the *completion* as to the *commencement* of the treaty, its object having been to guard the rights of the Union in all those important cases where nine States are called for; that, by the contrary construction, seven States, containing less than one-third of our whole citizens, might rivet on us a treaty, commenced indeed under commission and instructions from nine States, but formed by the minister in express contradiction to such instructions, and in direct sacrifice of the interests of so great a majority; that the definitive treaty was admitted not to be a verbal copy of the provisional one, and whether the departures from it were of substance or not, was a question on which nine States alone were competent to decide; that the circumstances of the ratification of the provisional articles by nine States, the instructions of our ministers to form a definitive one by them, and their actual agreement in substance, do not render us competent to ratify in the present instance; if these circumstances are in themselves a ratification, nothing further is requisite than to give attested copies of them in exchange for the British ratification; if they are not, we remain where we were, without a ratification by nine States, and incompetent ourselves to ratify; that it was but four days since the seven States, now present, unanimously concurred in a resolution, to be forwarded to the Governors of the absent States, in which they stated as a cause for urging on their delegates, that nine States were necessary to ratify the treaty: that in the case of the Dutch ratification, Great Britain had courted it, and therefore was glad to accept it as it was; that they knew our Constitution, and would object to a ratification by seven; that, if that circumstance was kept back, it would be known hereafter, and would give them ground to deny the validity of a ratification into which they should have been surprised and cheated, and it would be a dishonorable prostitution of our seal; that there is a hope of nine States; that if the treaty would become null, if not ratified in time, it would not be saved by an imperfect ratification; but that, in fact, it would not be null, and would be placed on better ground, going in unexceptional form, though a few days too late, and rested on the small importance of this circumstance, and the physical impossibilities which had prevented a punctual compliance in point of time; that this would be approved by all nations, and by Great Britain herself, if not determined to renew the war, and if so determined, she would never want excuses, were this out of the way. Mr. Read gave notice, he should call for the yeas and nays; whereon

* Vattel L. 2 § 156. L. 4, § 77. 1. Mably Droi D'Europe, 86.—NOTE BY JEFFERSON.

those 'n opposition, prepared a resolution, expressing po'ntedly the reasons of their dissent irom his motion. It appearing, however, that his proposition could not be carried, it was thought better to make no entry at all. Massachusetts alone would have been for it; Rhode Island, Pennsylvania and Virginia against it. Delaware, Maryland and North Carolina would have been d'vided. * * * Those who thought seven States competent to the ratification, being very restless under the loss of their motion. I proposed on the 3rd of January, to meet them on middle ground, and therefore moved a resolution, which premised that there were but seven States present, who were unanimous for the ratification, but that they differed in opinion on the question of competency; that those, however, in the negative were unwill'ng that any powers wh'ch it might be supposed they possessed, should remain unexercised for the restoration of peace, provided it could be done, saving their good faith, and without importing any opinion of Congress, that seven States were competent, and resolving that the treaty be rat'fied so far as they had power; that it should be transmitted to our ministers, w'th instructions to keep it uncommunicated; to endeavor to obtain three months longer for exchange of ratifications; that they should be informed that so soon as nine States shall be present, a ratification by nine shall be sent them: if this should get to them before the ultimate point of time for exchange, they were to use it, and not the other; if not, they were to offer the act of the seven States in exchange, informing them the treaty had come to hand while Congress was not in session; that but seven States were as yet assembled, and these had unanimously concurred in the ratification. This was debated on the 3rd and 4th *; and on the 5th, a vessel being to sail for England, from Annapolis, the House directed the President to write to our ministers accordingly. January 14. Delegates from Connecticut having attended yesterday, and another from South Carolina coming in this day, the treaty was ratified without a dissenting voice; and three instruments of ratification were ordered to be made out, one of which was sent by Colonel Harmer, another by Colonel Franks, and the third transmitted to the Agent of Marine, to be forwarded by any good opportunity.—AUTOBIOGRAPHY. i, 55. FORD ED., i, 77. (1821.)

8580. TREATY (British peace), Violations of.—In the 7th article [of the treaty of peace], it was stipulated, that his Britannic majesty should withdraw his armies, garrisons, and fleets, without carrying away any negroes, or other property of the American inhabitants. This stipulation was known to the British commanding officers, before the 19th of March, 1783, as *provisionally* agreed; and on the 5th of April they received official notice from their court of the conclusion and ratificat'on of the preliminary articles between France, Spain, and Great Britain, which gave activity to ours, as appears by the letter of Sir Guy Carleton to General Washington, dated April 6, 1783. From this time, then, surely no negroes could be carried away without a violation of the treaty. Yet we find that so early as May 6, a *large* number of them had already been embarked for Nova Scotia, of which, as contrary to an express stipulation in the treaty, General Washington declared to him his sense and his surprise. In the letter of Sir Guy Carleton of May 12, he admits the fact; palliates it by saying he had no

* A note in the FORD EDITION says Jan. 4th was a Sunday, and that Congress was not in session.—EDITOR.

right " to deprive the negroes of that liberty he found them *possessed* of; that it was unfriendly to suppose that the King's minister could stipulate to be guilty of a notorious breach of the public faith towards the negroes; and that, *if it was his intention, it must be adjusted by compensation*, restoration being utterly impracticable, where inseparable from a breach of public faith ". But surely, Sir, an officer of the King is not to question the validity of the King's engagements, nor violate his solemn treaties, on his own scruples about the public faith. Under this pretext, however, General Carleton went on in daily infractions, embarking, from time to time, between his notice of the treaty and the 5th of April, and the evacuation of New York, November 25, 3,000 negroes, of whom our commissioners had inspection, and a very large number more, in public and private vessels, of whom they were not permitted to have inspection. Here, then, was a direct, unequivocal, and avowed violation of this part of the 7th article, in the first moments of its being known; an article which had been of extreme solicitude on our part; on the fulfilment of which depended the means of paying debts, in proportion to the number of laborers withdrawn; and when in the very act of violation we warn, and put the commanding officer on his guard, he says directly he will go through with the act, and leave it to his court to adjust it by compensation.—To GEORGE HAMMOND. iii, 387. FORD ED., vi, 30. (Pa., May 1792.)

8581. —— ——. By the 7th article [of the treaty of peace], his Britannic majesty stipulates that he will, *with all convenient speed*, withdraw his garrisons from every *post* within the United States. " When no precise term ", says a writer on the Law of Nations (Vattel, L. 4. c. 26), " has been marked for the accomplishment of a treaty, and for the execution of each of its articles, good sense determines that every point should be executed *as soon as possible*. This is, without doubt, what was understood. The term in the treaty, *with all convenient speed*, amounts to the same thing, and clearly excludes all unnecessary delay. The general pacification being signed on the 20th of January, some time would be requisite for the orders for evacuation to come over to America, for the removal of stores, property and persons, and finally for the act of evacuation. The larger the post, the longer the time necessary to remove all its contents; the smaller, the sooner done. Hence, though General Carleton received his orders to evacuate New York in the month of April, the evacuation was not completed till late in November. It had been the principal place of arms and stores: the seat, as it were, of their general government, and the asylum of those who had fled to them. A great quantity of shipping was necessary, therefore, for the removal, and the General was obliged to call for a part from foreign countries. These causes of delay were duly respected on our part. But the posts of Michillimackinac, Detroit, Niagara, Oswego, Oswegatchie, Point-au-Fer, Dutchman's Point, were not of this magnitude. The orders for evacuation, which reached General Carleton, in New York, early in April, might have gone, in one month more, to the most remote of these posts. Some of them might have been evacuated in a few days after, and the largest in a few weeks. Certainly they might all have been delivered, without any *inconvenient* speed in the operations, by the end of May, from the known facility furnished by the lakes, and the water connecting them; or by crossing immediately over into their own territory, and availing themselves of the season for making new establishments there, if that was intended. Or whatever time might, in event, have been necessary for their evacuation, certainly the order for it should have been given from England, and might have been given as early as that from New York. Was any order ever given? Would not an *unnecessary delay* of the order, producing an equal delay in the evacuation, be an infraction of the treaty? Let us investigate this matter *. * * * Now is it not fair to conclude, if the order was not arrived on the 13th of August, 1783, if it was not arrived on the 10th of May, 1784, nor yet on the 13th of July, in the same year, that, in truth, the order had never been given? and if it had never been given, may we not conclude that it never had been intended to be given? From what moment is it we are to date this infraction? From that, at which, with convenient speed, the order to evacuate the upper posts might have been given. No legitimate reason can be assigned, why that order might not have been given as early, and at the same time, as the order to evacuate New York; and *all delay, after this, was in contravention of the treaty.*—To George Hammond. iii, 388. Ford ed., vi, 31. (Pa., 1792.)

8582. ———— ————. Was this delay merely innocent and unimportant as to us, setting aside all considerations but of interest and safety? 1. It cut us off from the fur-trade, with before the war had been always of great importance as a branch of commerce, and as a source of remittance for the payment of our debts to Great Britain; for the injury of withholding our posts, they added the obstruction of all passage along the lakes and their communications. 2. It secluded us from connection with the Northwestern Indians, from all apportunity of keeping up with them friendly and neighborly intercourse, brought on us consequently, from their known dispositions, constant and expensive war, in which numbers of men, women, and children, have been, and still are, daily falling victims to the scalping knife, and to which there will be no period, but in our possession of the posts which command their country.—To George Hammond. iii, 391. Ford ed., vi, 33. (Pa., 1792.)

8583. ———— ————. It may safely be said that the treaty was violated in England before it was known in America, as soon as it was known, and that, too, in points so essential, as that, without them, it would never have been concluded.—To George Hammond. iii, 391. Ford ed., vi, 33. (Pa., 1792.)

8584. TREES, Birds and.—What would I not give that the trees planted nearest round the house at Monticello were full-grown!—To Martha Jefferson Randolph. D. L. J. 222. (Pa., 1793.) See Mocking Bird.

8585. TREES, Cork.—I have been long endeavoring to procure the cork tree from Europe but without success. A plant which I brought with me from Paris died after languishing some time.—To James Ronaldson. vi, 92. Ford ed., ix, 370. (M., 1813.)

8586. TREES, Fig and mulberry.—The culture of the fig and mulberry is by women and children, and therefore earnestly to be desired in countries where there are slaves. In these, the women and children are often employed in labors disproportioned to their sex and age.

* Jefferson here quotes the official replies of the British officers commanding different posts to the request for their surrender that they had not received the evacuation order.—Editor.

By presenting to the master objects of culture, easier and equally beneficial, all temptation to misemploy them would be removed, and the lot of this tender part of our species be much softened.—To William Drayton. ii, 199. (P., 1787.)

8587. TREES, Peach.—I thank you for your experiment on the peach tree. It proves my speculation practicable, as it shows that five acres of peach trees at twenty-one feet apart will furnish dead wood enough to supply a fireplace through the winter, and may be kept up at the trouble of only planting about seventy peach stones a year. Suppose this extended to ten fire-places, it comes to fifty acres of ground, five thousand trees, and the replacing about seven hundred of them annually by planting so many stones. If it be disposed at some little distance, say in a circular annulus from one hundred to three hundred yards from the house, it would render a cart almost useless.—To T. M. Randolph. Ford ed., v, 416. (Pa., 1792.)

— TRIAL BY JURY.—See Jury.

8588. TRIBUTE, War and.—We prefer war in all cases to tribute under any form, and to any people whatever.—To Thomas Barclay. iii, 262. (Pa., 1791.)

8589. TRIPOLI, European powers and.—There is reason to believe the example we have set, begins already to work on the dispositions of the powers of Europe to emancipate themselves from that degrading yoke. Should we produce such a revolution there, we shall be amply rewarded for all that we have done.—To Judge Tyler. iv, 574. (M., March 1805.)

8590. TRIPOLI, Expedition against.—I have never been so mortified as at the conduct of our foreign functionaries on the loss of the Philadelphia. They appear to have supposed that we were all lost now, and without resource; and they have hawked us *in forma pauperis* begging alms at every court in Europe. This self-degradation is the more unpardonable as, uninstructed and unauthorized, they have taken measures which commit us by moral obligations which cannot be disavowed. The most serious of these is with the First Consul of France, the Emperor of Russia and Grand Seigneur. The interposition of the two first has been so prompt, so cordial, so energetic, that it is impossible for us to decline the good offices they have done us. From the virtuous and warm-hearted character of the Emperor, and the energy he is using with the Ottoman Porte, I am really apprehensive that our squadron will, on its arrival, find our prisoners all restored. If this should be the case, it would be ungrateful and insulting to these three great powers, to chastise the friend (Tripoli) whom they had induced to do us voluntary justice. Our expedition will in that case be disarmed, and our just desires of vengeance disappointed, and our honor prostrated. To anticipate these measures, and to strike our blow before they shall have had their effect, are additional and cogent motives for getting off our squadron without a moment's avoidable delay.—To Robert Smith. Ford ed., viii, 301. (M., April 1804.)

8591. ———— ————. Five fine frigates have left the Chesapeake * * * for Tripoli, which, in addition to the force now there, will, I trust, recover the credit which Commodore Morris's two years' sleep lost us, and for which he has been broke. I think they will make Tripoli sensible, that they mistake their interest in choosing war with us; and Tunis also, should she have declared war as we expect, and almost wish.—To PHILIP MAZZEI. iv, 553. (W., July 1804.)

8592. TRIPOLI, Grounds for war.—The war with Tripoli stands on two grounds of fact. 1st. It is made known to us by our agents with the three other Barbary States, that they only wait to see the event of this, to shape their conduct accordingly. If the war is ended by additional tribute, they mean to offer us the same alternative. 2dly. If peace was made, we should still, and shall ever, be obliged to keep a fr gate in the Mediterranean to overawe rupture, or we must abandon that market. Our intention in sending Morris with a respectable force, was to try whether peace could be forced by a coercive enterprise on their town. His inexecution of orders baffled that effort. Having broke him, we try the same experiment under a better commander. If, in the course of the summer, they cannot produce peace, we shall recall our force, except one frigate and two small vessels, which will keep up a perpetual blockade. Such a blockade will cost us no more than a state of peace, and will save us from increased tributes, and the disgrace attached to them.—To JUDGE TYLER. iv, 574. (M., March 1805.)

8593. TRIPOLI, War with.—Tripoli * * * had come forward with demands unfounded either in right or in compact, and had permitted itself to denounce war, on our failure to comply before a given day. The style of the demand admitted but one answer. I sent a small squadron of frigates into the Mediterranean with assurances to that power of our sincere desire to remain in peace, but with orders to protect our commerce against the threatened attack. The measure was seasonable and salutary. The Bey had already declared war in form. His cruisers were out. Two had arrived at Gibraltar. Our commerce in the Mediterranean was blockaded, and that of the Atlantic in peril. The arrival of our squadron dispelled the danger. One of the Tripolitan cruisers * * * engaged the small schooner Enterprise, commanded by Lieutenant Sterret. * * * was captured after a heavy slaughter of her men, without the loss of a single one on our part. * * * Unauthorized by the Constitution, without the sanction of Congress, to go beyond the line of defence, the vessel being disabled from committing further hostilities, was liberated with its crew.—FIRST ANNUAL MESSAGE. viii, 7. FORD ED., viii, 116. (Dec. 1801.)

8594. TROUBLE, Borrowing.—Are there so few inquietudes tacked to this momentary life of ours, that we must need be loading ourselves with a thousand more?—To JOHN PAGE. i. 183. FORD ED., i, 343. (F., 1762.)

8595. TRUMBULL (John), Artist.—Our countryman Trumbull is here [Paris], a young painter of the most promising talents. He brought with him his Battle of Bunker Hill and Death of Montgomery to have them engraved here, and we may add, to have them sold; for like Dr. Ramsey's history. they are too true to suit the English palate.—To F. HOPKINSON. FORD ED., iv, 272. (P., 1786.) See CORNWALLIS.

8596. TRUST, Public.—When a man assumes a public trust, he should consider himself as public property.—To BARON VON HUMBOLDT. RAYNER, BOSTON EDITION, 356. (W., 1807.)

8597. TRUTH, Error vs.—Truth is the proper and sufficient antagonist to error, and has nothing to fear from the conflict, unless by human interposition disarmed of her natural weapons, free argument and debate; errors ceasing to be dangerous when it is permitted freely to contradict them.—STATUTE OF RELIGIOUS FREEDOM. FORD ED., ii, 239. (1779.)

8598. ——— ———. Truth being as cheap as error, it is as well to rectify it for our own satisfaction.—To JOHN ADAMS. vii, 309. FORD ED., x, 272. (M., 1823.)

8599. TRUTH, Eternal.—Truth and reason are eternal. They have prevailed. And they will eternally prevail; however, in times and places they may be overborne for a while by violence—military, civil, or ecclesiastical.—To REV. MR. KNOX. v, 503. (M., 1810)

8600. TRUTH, Falsehood and.—The firmness with which the people have withstood the late abuses of the press, the discernment they have manifested between truth and falsehood, show that they may safely be trusted to hear everything true and false, and to form a correct judgment between them.— To JUDGE TYLER. iv, 549. (W., 1804.)

8601. TRUTH, Following.—Here [the University of Virginia] we are not afraid to follow truth wherever it may lead, nor to tolerate any error so long as reason is left free to combat it.—To MR. ROSCOE. vii, 196. (M., 1820.)

8602. TRUTH, Greatness of.—Truth is great and will prevail if left to herself.—STATUTE OF RELIGIOUS FREEDOM. viii, 455. FORD ED., ii, 239. (1779.)

8603. TRUTH, Harmless.—Truth between candid minds can never do harm.—To JOHN ADAMS. iii, 270. FORD ED., v, 354. (Pa., 1791.)

8604. TRUTH, Importance of.—It is of great importance to set a resolution, not to be shaken, never to tell an untruth. There is no vice so mean, so pitiful, so contemptible; and he who permits himself to tell a lie once, finds it much easier to do it a second and a third time, till at length it becomes habitual; he tells lies without attending to it, and truths without the world's believing him. This falsehood of the tongue leads to that of the heart, and in time depraves all its good dispositions.—To PETER CARR. i, 396. (P., 1785.)

8605. TRUTH, Lies and.—The man who fears no truths has nothing to fear from lies. —To DR. GEORGE LOGAN. FORD ED., x, 27. (M., 1816.)

8606. TRUTH, Newspapers and.—The restraining the press *to truth,* as the present laws do, is the only way of making it useful. —To WILLIAM SHORT. v, 362. (M., 1808.)

8607. TRUTH, Only safe guide.—In all cases, follow truth as the only safe guide, and eschew error, which bewilders us in one false consequence after another, in endless succession.—To JOHN ADAMS. vii, 149. FORD ED., x, 153. (M., 1819.)

8608. TRUTH, Primary object.—Truth is the first object.—To DR. MAESE. v, 413. (W., 1809.)

8609. TRUTH, Propagation of.—Nor was it less uninteresting to the world, that an experiment should be fairly and fully made, whether freedom of discussion, unaided by power, is not sufficient for the propagation and protection of truth.—SECOND INAUGURAL ADDRESS. viii, 43. FORD ED., viii, 346. (1805.)

8610. TRUTH, Reason and.—No experiment can be more interesting than that we are now trying, and which we trust will end in establishing the fact, that man may be governed by reason and truth. Our first object should therefore be, to leave open to him all the avenues to truth. The most effectual hitherto found, is the freedom of the press. It is, therefore, the first shut up by those who fear the investigation of their actions.—To JUDGE TYLER. iv, 548. (W., 1804.)

8611. TRUTH, Refreshing.—We, who are retired from the business of the world, are glad to catch a glimpse of truth, here and there as we can, to guide our path through the boundless field of fable in which we are bewildered by public prints, and even by those calling themselves histories. A word of truth to us is like the drop of water supplicated from the tip of Lazarus's finger. It is as an observation of latitude and longitude to the mariner long enveloped in clouds, for correcting the ship's way.—To JOHN QUINCY ADAMS. vii, 87. (M., 1817.)

8612. TRUTH, Self-evident.—We hold these truths to be self-evident: that all men are created equal; that they are endowed by their Creator with inherent* and inalienable rights; that among these, are life, liberty, and the pursuit of happiness.—DECLARATION OF INDEPENDENCE AS DRAWN BY JEFFERSON.

8613. TRUTH, Self-reliant.—It is error alone which needs the support of government. Truth can stand by itself.—NOTES ON VIRGINIA. viii, 401. FORD ED., iii, 264. (1782.)

8614. TRUTH, Strength of.—Truth will do well enough if left to shift for herself. She seldom has received much aid from the power of great men to whom she is rarely known and seldom welcome. She has no need of force to procure entrance into the minds of men.—NOTES ON RELIGION. FORD ED., ii, 102. (1776?)

8615. TRUTH, Suppression of.—Truths necessary for our own character, must not be suppressed out of tenderness to its calumniators.—To PRESIDENT MADISON. vi, 452. FORD ED., ix, 512. (M., 1815.)

8616. TRUTH, Unfeared.—There is not a truth on earth which I fear or would dis-

* Congress struck out "inherent and" and inserted "certain".—EDITOR.

guise.—To WILLIAM DUANE. iv, 591. FORD ED., viii, 431. (W., 1806.)

8617. —— ——. There is not a truth on earth which I fear should be known.—To THOMAS SEYMOUR. v, 43. FORD ED., ix, 30. (W., 1807.)

8618. —— ——. I feel no falsehood and fear no truth.—To ISAAC HILLARD. v, 551. (M., 1810.)

8619. —— ——. There is not a truth existing which I fear, or would wish unknown to the whole world.—To HENRY LEE. vii, 448. FORD ED., x, 389. (M., May 15, 1826.)

8620. TRUXTUN (Thomas), Medal for.—I have considered the letter of the director of the mint stating the ease with which the errors of Commodore Truxtun's medal may be corrected on the medal itself and the unpracticability of doing it on the die. * * * A second law would be required to make a second die or medal. * * * It certainly may be as well or better done by the graver, and with more delicate traits. I remember it was the opinion of Doctor Franklin that where only one or a few medals were to be made it was better to have them engraved. The medal being corrected, the die becomes immaterial, that has never been delivered to the party, the medal itself being the only thing voted to him. I say this on certain grounds, because I think this and Preble's are the only medals given by the United States which have not been made under my immediate direction. The dies of all those given by the old Congress, and made at Paris, remain to this day deposited with our bankers at Paris. That of General Lee, made in Philadelphia, was retained in the mint.—To JACOB CROWNINSHIELD. v, 300. (1808.)

8621. TUDE (M. A. de la), Imprisonment.—De la Tude comes sometimes to take family soup with me, and entertains me with anecdotes of his five and thirty years' imprisonment. How fertile is the mind of man, which can make The Bastile and dungeon of Vincennes yield interesting anecdotes! You know this [imprisonment] was for making four verses on Madame du Pompadour. *—To MRS. COSWAY. ii, 42. FORD ED., iv, 322. (P., 1786.)

8622. TURKEY, Decline of army.—The Turks have lost their warlike spirit, and their troops cannot be induced to adopt the European arms.—To JAMES MONROE. i, 358. FORD ED., iv, 65. (P., 1785.)

8623. TURKEY, Greeks and.—It has been thought that the two imperial courts [Austria and Russia] have a plan of expelling the Turks from Europe. It is really a pity so charming a country should remain in the hands of a people, whose religion forbids the admission of science and the arts among them. We should wish success to the object of the two empires, if they meant to leave the country in possession of the Greek inhabitants. We might then expect, once more, to see the language of Homer and Demosthenes a living language. For I am persuaded the modern Greek would easily get back to its classical models. But this is not intended. They only propose to put the Greeks under other masters: to substitute one set of barbarians for another.—To DR. STILES. i, 365. (P., 1785.)

* Jefferson gives the verses as follows: "Sans esprit, sans sentiment, "Sans etre belle, ni neuve, "En France on peut avoir le premier amant "Pompadour en est l'epreuve".—EDITOR.

8624. TURKEY, Humanity and.—A lover of humanity would wish to see that charming country from which the Turks exclude science and freedom, in any hands rather than theirs, and in those of the native Greeks rather than any others. The recovery of the r ancient language would not be desperate, could they recover their ancient liberty. But those who wish to remove the Turks, wish to put themselves in their places. This would be exchanging one set of barbarians for another only.—To RICHARD HENRY LEE. FORD ED., iv, 72. (P., 1785.)

8625. TURKEY, Russia, Austria and.—It is believed that the Emperor [of Austria] and the Empress [of Russia] have schemes in contemplation for driving the Turks out of Europe. Were this with a view to reestablish the native Greeks in the sovereignty of their own country, I could wish them success, and to see driven from that delightful country a set of barbarians with whom an opposition to all science is an article of religion. * * * But these powers have in object to divide the country between themselves. This is only to substitute one set of barbarians for another, breaking, at the same time, the balance among the European powers.—To JOHN PAGE. i, 400. (P., 1785.)

8626. TURKEY, Terra incognita.—I cannot think but that it would be desirable to all commercial nations to have Turkey and all its dependencies driven from the seacoast into the interior parts of Asia and Africa. What a field would thus be restored to commerce! The finest parts of the old world are now dead 'n a great degree to commerce, to arts, to sciences, and to society. Greece, Syria, Egypt, and the northern coast of Africa, constituted the whole world almost for the Romans, and to us they are scarcely known, scarcely accessible at all.—To JOHN BROWN. ii, 396. FORD ED., v, 18. (P., 1788.) See CONSTANTINOPLE.

8627. TYLER (John), Judge.—Judge John Tyler is an able and well read lawyer, about 59 years of age. He was popular as a judge, and is remarkably so as a governor, for his incorruptible integrity, which no circumstances have ever been able to turn from its course. It will be difficult to find a character of firmness enough to preserve his independence on the same bench with Marshall. Tyler, I am certain, would do it, * * * and be a counterpoint to the rancorous hatred which Marshall bears to the government of his country, and * * * the cunning and sophistry within which he is able to enshroud himself.—To PRESIDENT MADISON. FORD ED., ix, 275. (1810.)

8628. TYLER (John), Patriot.—The concurrence of a veteran patriot, who from the first dawn of the Revolution to this day has pursued unchangeably the same honest course, cannot but be flattering to his fellow laborers.—To GOVERNOR TYLER. v, 425. (W., Feb. 1809.)

8629. TYPHUS FEVER, Treatment of.—While I was in Paris, both my daughters were taken with what we formerly called a nervous fever, now a typhus. * * * Dr. Gem, * * * never gave them a single dose of physic. He told me it was a disease which tended with certainty to wear itself off, but so slowly that the strength of the patient might first fail if not kept up; that this alone was the object to be attended to by nourishment and stimulus. He forced them to eat a cup of rice, or panada, or gruel, or of some of the farinaceous substances of easy digestion every two hours, and to drink a glass of Madeira.

The youngest took a pint of Madeira a day without feeling it, and that for many weeks. For costiveness, injections were used; and he observed that a single dose of medicine taken into the stomach and consuming any of the strength of the patient was often fatal. * * * I have had this fever in my family three or four times since, * * * and have carried between twenty and thirty patients through without losing a single one, by a rigorous observance of Dr. Gem's plan and principle. Instead of Madeira I have used toddy or French brandy.—To JAMES MADISON. FORD ED., x, 181. (M., 1821.)

8630. TYRANNY, Absolute.—The history of the present King of Great Britain is a history of *unremitting* injuries and usurpations, *among which appears no solitary, fact to contradict the uniform tenor of the rest, but all have* in direct object the establishment of an absolute tyranny over these States.*—DECLARATION OF INDEPENDENCE AS DRAWN BY JEFFERSON.

8631. TYRANNY, British.—That rapid and bold succession of injuries which is likely to distinguish the present from all other periods of American history.—RIGHTS OF BRITISH AMERICA. i, 130. FORD ED., i, 435. (1774.)

8632. TYRANNY, Despotism and.—But why should we enumerate their injuries in detail? By one act they have suspended the powers of one American legislature, and by another have declared they may legislate for us themselves in all cases whatsoever. These two acts alone form a basis broad enough whereon to erect a despotism of unlimited extent.—DECLARATION ON TAKING UP ARMS. FORD ED., i, 469. (July 1775.)

8633. TYRANNY, Eternal hostility to.—I have sworn upon the altar of God eternal hostility against every form of tyranny over the mind of man.—To DR. BENJAMIN RUSH. iv, 336. FORD ED., vii, 460. (M., 1800.)

8634. TYRANNY, Fear and.—Fear is the only restraining motive which may hold the hand of a tyrant.—RIGHTS OF BRITISH AMERICA. i, 131. FORD ED., i, 436. (1774.)

8635. TYRANNY, Foundation for.—Future ages will scarcely believe that the hardiness of one man adventured, within the short compass of twelve years only, to lay a foundation so broad and so undisguised for tyranny over a people fostered and fixed in the principles of freedom.†—DECLARATION OF INDEPENDENCE AS DRAWN BY JEFFERSON.

8636. TYRANNY, George III.—A prince whose character is thus marked by every act which may define a tyrant is unfit to be the ruler of a people *who mean to be free.‡*—DECLARATION OF INDEPENDENCE AS DRAWN BY JEFFERSON.

8637. TYRANNY, Guarding against.—The time to guard against corruption and tyranny is before they shall have gotten hold

* Congress struck out the words in italics.—EDITOR.
† Struck out by Congress.—EDITOR.
‡ Congress struck the words in italics and inserted "free" before "people".—EDITOR.

of us. It is better to keep the wolf out of the fold, than to trust to drawing his teeth and talons after he shall have entered.—NOTES ON VIRGINIA. viii, 363. FORD ED., iii, 225. (1782.)

8638. TYRANNY, Insurrection against.—The general insurrection of the world against its tyrants will ultimately prevail by pointing the object of government to the happiness of the people, and not merely to that of their self-constituted governors.— To MARQUIS LAFAYETTE. FORD ED., x, 233. (M., 1822.)

8639. TYRANNY, Political.—If there be a God, and He is just, His day will come. He will never abandon the whole race of man to be eaten up by the leviathans and mammoths of a day.—To MARQUIS LAFAYETTE. FORD ED., x, 302. (M., 1811.)

8640. TYRANNY, Rebellion against.— Rebellion to tyrants is obedience to God.— MOTTO ON JEFFERSON'S SEAL, *Domestic Life of Jefferson, title page.* See LANGUAGES, PURISM.

8641. TYRANNY, Spirit of.—Bodies of men, as well as individuals, are susceptible of the spirit of tyranny.—RIGHTS OF BRITISH AMERICA. i, 128. FORD ED., i, 433. (1774.)

8642. TYRANNY, Systematic.—Single acts of tyranny may be ascribed to the accidental opinion of a day; but a series of oppressions, begun at a distinguished period, and pursued unalterably through every change of ministers, too plainly prove a deliberate, systematical plan of reducing us to slavery.—RIGHTS OF BRITISH AMERICA. i, 130. FORD ED., i, 435. (1774.)

8643. UMPIRE, Impartial.—No man having a natural right to be the judge between himself and another, it is his natural duty to submit to the umpirage of an impartial third.—To F. W. GILMER. vii, 3. FORD ED., x, 32. (M., 1816.)

8644. UNEARNED INCREMENT, Definition.—If [the public lands are] sold in lots at a fixed price, as first proposed, the best lots will be sold first; as these become occupied, it gives a value to the interjacent ones, and raises them, though of inferior quality, to the price of the first.—To JAMES MONROE. i, 347. FORD ED., iv, 53. (P., 1785.)

8645. UNGER (John Louis de), Courtesies to.—The very small amusements which it has been in my power to furnish, in order to lighten some of your heavy hours, by no means merited the acknowledgment you make. Their impression must be ascribed to your extreme sensibility rather than to their own weight.—To LIEUTENANT DE UNGER.* ii, 278. FORD ED., ii, 373. (R., 1780.)

8646. UNGER (John Louis de), Invited to America.—Should your fondness for philosophy resume its merited ascendency, is it impossible to hope that this unexplored country may tempt your residence by holding out ma-

* One of the Saratoga prisoners in Virginia.—EDITOR.

terials wherewith to bu'ld a fame, founded on the happiness and not the calamities of human nature?—To LIEUTENANT DE UNGER. i, 278. FORD ED., ii, 374. (R., 1780.)

8647. UNIFORMITY, Mental.—The varieties in the structure and action of the human mind, as in those of the body, are the work of our Creator, against which it cannot be a religious duty to erect the standard of uniformity.—To JAMES FISHBACK. v, 471. (M., 1809.)

8648. UNIFORMITY, Physical and moral.—It is a singular anxiety which some people have that we should all think alike. Would the world be more beautiful were all our faces alike? were our tempers, our talents, our tastes, our forms, our wishes, aversions and pursuits cast exactly in the same mould? If no varieties existed in the animal, vegetable or mineral creation, but all moved strictly uniform, catholic and orthodox, what a world of physical and moral monotony would it be. These are the absurdities into which those run who usurp the throne of God, and dictate to Him what He should have done. May they with all their metaphysical riddles appear before that tribunal with as clean hands and hearts as you and I shall. There, suspended in the scales of eternal justice, faith and works will show their worth by their weight. —To CHARLES THOMSON. FORD ED., x, 76. (M., 1817.)

8649. UNIFORMITY, Religious.—Is uniformity attainable? Millions of innocent men, women and children, since the introduction of Christianity, have been burnt, tortured, fined and imprisoned; yet we have not advanced one inch towards uniformity.— NOTES ON VIRGINIA. viii, 401. FORD ED., iii, 265. (1782.)

8650. UNION (The Federal), Anchor of hope.—I have been happy in believing * * * that whatever follies we may be led into as to foreign nations, we shall never give up our Union, the last anchor of our hope, and that alone which is to prevent this heavenly country from becoming an arena of gladiators.—To ELBRIDGE GERRY. iv, 173. FORD ED., vii, 122. (Pa., May 1797.)

8651. UNION (The Federal), Attempts to disrupt.—Not less worthy of your indignation have been the machinations of parricides who have endeavored to bring into danger the Union of these States, and to subvert, for the purposes of inordinate ambition, a government founded in the will of its citizens, and directed to no object but their happiness.—R. TO A. NORTH CAROLINA LEGISLATURE. viii, 125. (1808.)

8652. ———. Surrounded by such difficulties and dangers, it is really deplorable that any should be found among ourselves vindicating the conduct of the aggressors; cooperating with them in multiplying embarrassments to their own country, and encouraging disobedience to the laws provided for its safety. But a spirit which should go further, and countenance the advocates for a dissolution of the Union, and for setting in hostile array one portion of our citizens against another, would require to be viewed under a more serious aspect. It would prove indeed that it is high time for every friend to his country, in a firm and decided manner, to express his sentiments of the measures which government has adopted to avert the impending evils, unhesitatingly to pledge himself for the support of the laws, liberties and independence of his country; and with the * * * republicans of Connecticut, to resolve that, for the preservation of the Union, the support and enforcement of the laws, and for the resistance and repulsion of every enemy, they will hold themselves in readiness and put at stake, if necessary, their lives and fortunes, on the pledge of their sacred honor.—R. TO A. CONNECTICUT REPUBLICANS. viii, 169. (1809.)

8653. ———— ————. The times do certainly render it incumbent on all good citizens, attached to the rights and honor of their country, to bury in oblivion all internal differences, and rally around the standard of their country in opposition to the outrages of foreign nations. All attempts to enfeeble and destroy the exertions of the General Government, in vindication of our national rights, or to loosen the bands of union by alienating the affections of the people, or opposing the authority of the laws at so eventful a period, merit the discountenance of all.—To GOVERNOR TOMPKINS. viii, 153. (1809.)

8654. UNION (The Federal), Benefits of.—Union for specified national purposes, and particularly * * * [for] those specified in * * * [the] * * * Federal compact * * * [is] friendly to the peace, happiness and prosperity of all the States.—KENTUCKY RESOLUTIONS. ix, 468. FORD ED., vii, 300. (1798.)

8655. UNION (The Federal), Bond of.— The sacred bond which unites these States together.—R. TO A. PHILADELPHIA CITIZENS. viii, 144. (1809.)

8656. UNION (The Federal), Cement of the.—The cement of this Union is in the heart-blood of every American. I do not believe there is on earth a government established on so immovable a basis.—To MARQUIS DE LAFAYETTE. vi, 425. FORD ED., ix, 509. (M., 1815.)

8657. UNION (The Federal), Cherish.— [Our] Union cannot be too much cherished.— REPLY TO ADDRESS. viii, 114. (1802.)

8658. ———— ————. Cherish every measure which may foster our brotherly Union and perpetuate a constitution of government, destined to be the primitive and precious model of what is to change the condition of man over the globe.—To EDWARD LIVINGSTON. vii, 344. FORD ED., x, 301. (M., 1824.)

8659. UNION (The Federal), Constitution and.—We must take care that * * * no objection to the new form [Constitution] produces a schism in our Union. This would

be an incurable evil, because near friends falling out, never reunite cordially; whereas, all of us going together, we shall be sure to cure the evils of our new Constitution before they do great harm.—To A. DONALD. ii, 356. (P., 1788.)

8660. UNION (The Federal), Constitutional encroachments and.—When obvious encroachments are made on the plain meaning of the Constitution, the bond of Union ceases to be the equal measure of justice to all its parts.—To ARCHIBALD STUART. FORD ED., v, 454. (Pa., 1792.)

8661. UNION (The Federal), Cultivate. —Our lot has been cast by the favor of heaven and under circumstances highly auspicious to our peace and prosperity, and where no pretence can arise for the degrading and oppressive establishments of Europe. It is our happiness that honorable distinctions flow only from public approbation; and that finds no object in titled dignitaries and pageants. Let us, then, endeavor carefully to guard this happy state of things, by keeping a watchful eye over the disaffection of wealth and ambition to the republican principles of our Constitution, and by sacrificing all our local and personal interests to the cultivation of the Union, and maintenance of the authority of the laws.—R. TO A. PENNA. DEMOCRATIC-REPUBLICANS. viii, 163. (1809.)

8662. UNION (The Federal), Dissolution of.—I can scarcely contemplate a more incalculable evil than the breaking of the Union into two or more parts.—To PRESIDENT WASHINGTON. iii, 363. FORD ED., vi, 4. (1792.)

8663. ———— ————. I have been among the most sanguine in believing that our Union would be of long duration. I now doubt it much, and see the event at no great distance, and the direct consequence of this question; [Missouri] not by the line which has been so confidently counted on,—the laws of nature control this,—but by the Potomac, Ohio and Missouri, or, more probably, the Mississippi upwards to our northern boundary. My only comfort and confidence is, that I shall not live to see this; and I envy not the present generation the glory of throwing away the fruits of their fathers' sacrifices of life and fortune, and of rendering desperate the experiment which was to decide ultimately whether man is capable of self-government. This treason against human hope will signalize their epoch in future history as the counterpart of the medal of their predecessors.—To WILLIAM SHORT. vii, 158. (M., 1820.)

8664. ———— ————. Were we to break to pieces, it would damp the hopes and the efforts of the good, and give triumph to those of the bad through the whole enslaved world. As members, therefore, of the universal society of mankind, and standing in high and responsible relation with them, it is our sacred duty to suppress passion among ourselves, and not to blast the confidence we have inspired of proof that a government of reason is better than one of force.—To RICHARD RUSH. vii, 183. (M., 1820.)

8665. UNION (The Federal), Europe and.—Let us cling in mass to our country and to one another, and bid defiance, as we can if united, to the plundering combinations of the old world.—To DR. GEORGE LOGAN. vii, 20. (M., 1816.)

8666. UNION (The Federal), Expansion and.—Our present federal limits are not too large for good government, nor will the increase of votes in Congress produce any ill effect. On the contrary, it will drown the little divisions at present existing there. Our confederacy must be viewed as the nest, from which all America, North and South, is to be peopled. We should take care, too, not to think it for the interest of that great Continent to press too soon on the Spaniards. Those countries cannot be in better hands. My fear is, that they are too feeble to hold them till our population can be sufficiently advanced to gain it from them, piece by piece. The navigation of the Mississippi we must have. This is all we are as yet ready to receive.—To ARCHIBALD STUART. i, 578. FORD ED., iv, 188. (P., Jan. 1786.)

8667. UNION (The Federal), Family of States.—I sincerely wish that the whole Union may accommodate their interests to each other, and play into their hands mutually as members of the same family, that the wealth and strength of any one part should be viewed as the wealth and strength of the whole.—To HUGH WILLIAMSON. FORD ED., vii, 201. (Pa., Feb. 1798.)

8668. UNION (The Federal), Foreign plots against.—The request of a communication of any information, which may have been received at any time since the establishment of the present [Federal] Government, touching combinations with foreign nations for dismembering the Union, or the corrupt receipt of money by any officer of the United States, from the agents of foreign governments, can be complied with but in a partial degree. It is well understood that, in the first or second year of the presidency of General Washington, information was given to him relating to certain combinations with the agents of a foreign government for the dismemberment of the Union; which combinations had taken place before the establishment of the present Federal Government. This information, however, is believed never to have been deposited in any public office, or left in that of the President's secretary, these having been duly examined, but to have been considered as personally confidential, and therefore, retained among his private papers. A communication from the Governor of Virginia to General Washington, is found in the office of the President's secretary, which, though not strictly within the terms of the request of the House of Representatives, is communicated, inasmuch as it may throw some light on the subjects of the correspond-

ence of that time, between certain foreign agents and citizens of the United States. In the first or second year of the administration of President Adams, Andrew Ellicott, then employed in designating, in conjunction with the Spanish authorities the boundaries between the territories of the United States and Spain, under the treaty with that nation, communicated to the Executive of the United States papers and information respecting the subjects of the present inquiry, which were deposited in the office of State. Copies of these are now transmitted to the House of Representatives, except of a single letter and a reference from the said Andrew Ellicott, which being expressly desired to be kept secret, is, therefore, not communicated, but its contents can be obtained from him in a more legal form, and directions have been given to summon him to appear as a witness before the court of inquiry. [Wilkinson court of inquiry.] A paper " on the commerce of Louisiana ", bearing date of the 18th of April, 1798, is found in the office of State, supposed to have been communicated by Mr. Daniel Clark, of New Orleans. then a subject of Spain, and now of the House of Representatives of the United States, stating certain commercial transactions of General Wilkinson, in New Orleans; an extract from this is now communicated, because it contains facts which may have some bearing on the questions relating to him. The destruction of the War Office, by fire, in the close of 1800, involved all information it contained at that date. The papers already described, therefore, constitute the whole information on the subjects, deposited in the public offices, during the preceding administrations, as far as has yet been found; but it cannot be affirmed that there may be no others, because the papers of the office being filed, for the most part, alphabetically, unless aided by the suggestion of any particular name which may have given such information, nothing short of a careful examination of the papers in the offices generally, could authorize such affirmation. About a twelvemonth after I came to the administration of the government, Mr. Clark gave some verbal information to myself, as well as to the Secretary of State, relating to the same combination for the dismemberment of the Union. He was listened to freely, and he then delivered the letter of Governor Gagoso, addressed to himself, of which a copy is now communicated. After his return to New Orleans, he forwarded to the Secretary of State other papers, with a request, that, after perusal, they should be burned. This. however, was not done, and he was so informed by the Secretary of State, and that they would be held subject to his order. These papers have not yet been found in the office. A letter, therefore, has been addressed to the former chief clerk, who may, perhaps, give information respecting them. As far as our memories enable us to say, they related only to the combinations before spoken of, and not at all to the corrupt receipt of money by any officer of the United States; consequently, they respected what was considered as a dead matter, known to the preceding administrations, and offering nothing new to call for investigations, which those nearest the dates of the transactions had not thought proper to institute. In the course of the communications made to me on the subject of the conspiracy of Aaron Burr, I sometimes received letters, some of them anonymous, some under names true or false, expressing suspicions and insinuations against General Wilkinson. But only one of them and that anonymous, specified any particular fact, and that fact was one of those which had already been communicated to a former administration. No other information within the purview of the request of the House is known to have been received by any department of the Government from the establishment of the present Federal Government. That which has recently been communicated to the House of Representatives, and by them to me, is the first direct testimony ever made known to me, charging General Wilkinson with the corrupt receipt of money; and the House of Representatives may be assured that the duties which this information devolves on me shall be exercised with rigorous impartiality. Should any want of power in the court to compel the rendering of testimony, obstruct that full and impartial inquiry, which alone can establish guilt or innocence, and satisfy justice, the legislative authority only will be competent to the remedy.*—SPECIAL MESSAGE. viii, 90. (Jan. 1808.)

8669. UNION (The Federal), Love for. —Sincere love I shall forever strive to cultivate with all our sister States.—To THE PRESIDENT OF CONGRESS. FORD ED., ii, 298. (Wg., 1780.)

8670. UNION (The Federal), Massachusetts federalists and.—The design of the leading federalists, then having direction of the State [Massachusetts], to take advantage of the first war with England to separate the Northeast States from the Union has distressingly impaired our future confidence in them. In this, as in all other cases, we must do them full justice, and make the fault all their own, should the last hope of human liberty be destined to receive its final stab from them.—To DR. WILLIAM EUSTIS. FORD ED., ix, 237. (M., Oct. 1809.)

8671. UNION (The Federal), Miseries of secession.—What would you think of a discourse on the benefit of the Union and miseries which would follow a separation of the States, to be exemplified in the eternal and wasting wars of Europe, in the pillage and profligacy to which these lead, and the abject oppression and degradation to which they reduce its inhabitants? Painted by your vivid pencil, what could make deeper impres-

* In a subsequent message Jefferson informed Congress that the Clark letters had been found, and transmitted some extracts from them. As to combinations with foreign agents for the dismemberment of the Union they contained nothing new,"nor have we found any intimation of the corrupt receipt of money by any officer of the United States from any foreign nation".—EDITOR.

sions, and what impressions could come more home to our concerns, or kindle a livelier sense of our present blessings?—To MR. OGILVIE. v, 605. (M., 1811.)

8672. UNION (The Federal), Nourish.— Possessed of the blessing of self-government, and of such a portion of civil liberty as no other civilized nation enjoys, it now behooves us to guard and preserve them by a continuance of the sacrifices and exertions by which they were acquired, and especially to nourish that Union which is their sole guarantee.— R. TO A. NEW LONDON PLYMOUTH SOCIETY. viii, 166. (1809.)

8673. UNION (The Federal), Pennsylvania, Virginia and.—I wish and hope you may consent to be added to our [Virginia] Assembly itself. There is no post where you can render greater services, without going out of your State. Let but this block stand firm on its basis, and Pennsylvania do the same, our Union will be perpetual, and our General Government kept within the bounds and form of the Constitution.—To JAMES MADISON. iv 162. FORD ED., vii, 110. (M., Jan. 1797.)

8674. UNION (The Federal), Rock of safety.—A solid Union is the best rock of our safety.—To C. W. F. DUMAS. iii, 260. (Pa., 1791.)

8675. ——— ———. To cherish the Federal Union as the only rock of our safety, * * * [is one of] the landmarks by which we are to guide ourselves in all our proceedings.— SECOND ANNUAL MESSAGE. viii, 21. FORD ED., viii, 187. (Dec. 1802.)

8676. UNION (The Federal), Safety in. —It is a momentous truth, and happily of universal impression on the public mind, that our safety rests on the preservation of our Union.—To THE RHODE ISLAND ASSEMBLY. iv, 397. (W., May 1801.)

8677. ——— ———. I trust the Union of these States will ever be considered as the palladium of their safety, their prosperity and glory, and all attempts to sever it, will be frowned on with reprobation and abhorrence. —To GOVERNOR TOMPKINS. viii, 153. (1809.)

8678. UNION (The Federal), Sectional ascendency.—If on a temporary superiority of one party, the other is to resort to a scission of the Union, no federal government can ever exist.—To JOHN TAYLOR. iv, 246. FORD ED., vii, 264. (Pa., 1798.)

8679. UNION (The Federal), Self-government and.—I regret that I am now to die in the belief, that the useless sacrifice of themselves by the generation of 1776, to acquire self-government and happiness to their country, is to be thrown away by the unwise and unworthy passions of their sons, and that my only consolation is to be, that I live not to weep over it. If they would but dispassionately weigh the blessings they will throw away, against an abstract principle more likely to be effected by union than by scission, they would pause before they would perpetrate this act of suicide on themselves, and of treason against the hopes of the world.—To JOHN HOLMES. vii, 160. FORD ED., x, 158. (M., 1820.)

8680. UNION (The Federal), Sheet anchor.—The sheet anchor of our peace at home and safety abroad.—FIRST INAUGURAL ADDRESS. viii, 4. FORD ED., viii, 4. (1801.)

8681. —— ——. To preserve the republican form and principles of our Constitution, and cleave to the salutary distribution of powers which that has established, are the two sheet anchors of our Union. If driven from either, we shall be in danger of foundering.—To WILLIAM JOHNSON. vii, 298. FORD ED., x, 232. (M., 1823.)

8682. UNION (The Federal), State rights and.—I am for preserving to the States the powers not yielded by them to the Union, and to the Legislature of the Union its constitutional share in the division of powers; and I am not for transferring all the powers of the States to the General Government, and all those of that Government to the Executive branch.—To ELBRIDGE GERRY. iv, 268. FORD ED., vii, 327. (Pa., 1799.)

8683. UNION (The Federal), Strength.—If there be any among us who would wish to dissolve this Union, or to change its republican form, let them stand undisturbed as monuments of the safety with which error of opinion may be tolerated where reason is left free to combat it. I know, indeed, that some honest men fear that a republican government cannot be strong; that this Government is not strong enough. But would the honest patriot, in full tide of successful experiment, abandon a Government which has so far kept us free and firm, on the theoretic and visionary fear that this Government, the world's best hope, may by possibility want energy to preserve itself? I trust not. I believe this, on the contrary, the strongest government on earth. I believe it is the only one where every man, at the call of the laws, would fly to the standard of the law, and would meet invasions of the public order as his own personal concern. Sometimes it is said that man cannot be trusted with the government of himself. Can he, then, be trusted with the government of others? Or have we found angels, in the forms of kings, to govern him? Let history answer this question.—FIRST INAUGURAL ADDRESS. viii, 2. FORD ED., viii, 3. (1801.)

8684. UNION (The Federal), War and.—If we engage in a war during our present passions, and our present weakness in some quarters, our Union runs the greatest risk of not coming out of that war in the shape in which it enters it.—To ELBRIDGE GERRY. iv, 188. FORD ED., vii, 150. (M., June 1797.)

8685. UNION (The Federal), Washington and.—I can scarcely contemplate a more incalculable evil than the breaking of the Union into two or more parts. Yet when we review the mass which opposed the original coalescence, when we consider that it lay chiefly in the Southern quarter, that the Legislature have availed themselves of no occasion of allaying it, but on the contrary whenever the Northern and Southern prejudices have come into conflict, the latter have been sacrificed and the former soothed; that the owers of the [public] debt are in the Southern and the holders of it in the Northern division; that the anti-federal champions are now strengthened in argument by the fulfilment of their predictions; that this has been brought about by the monarchical federalists themselves, who, having been for the new government merely as a stepping stone to monarchy, have themselves adopted the very constructions of the Constitution, of which, when advocating its acceptance before the tribunal of the people, they declared it insusceptible; that the republican federalists, who espoused the same government for its intrinsic merits, are disarmed of their weapons; that which they denied as prophecy, having now become true history, who can be sure that these things may not proselyte the small number which was wanting to place the majority on the other side? And this is the event at which I tremble, and to prevent which I consider your [President Washington] continuing at the head of affairs as of the last importance. The confidence of the whole Union is centred in you. Your being at the helm, will be more than answer to every argument which can be used to alarm and lead the people in any quarter into violence and secession. North and South will hang together, if they have you to hang on; and, if the first correction of a numerous representation [in Congress] should fail in its effect, your presence will give time for trying others not inconsistent with the Union and peace of the States.—To PRESIDENT WASHINGTON. iii, 363. FORD ED., vi, 4. (Pa., May 1792.)

8686. UNION (The Federal), Western interests and.—Our true interest will be best promoted by making all the just claims of our fellow citizens, wherever situated, our own; by urging and enforcing them with the weight of our whole influence; and by exercising in * * * , every * * * instance, a just government in their concerns, and making common cause even where our separate interest would seem opposed to theirs. No other conduct can attach us together; and on this attachment depends our happiness.—To JAMES MONROE. i, 605. FORD ED., iv, 263. (P., 1786.)

8687. —— ——. This measure [dividing the Western country into fewer and smaller States] with the disposition to shut up the Mississippi, gives me serious apprehensions of the severance of the Eastern and Western parts of our confederacy. It might have been made the interest of the Western States to remain united with us, by managing their interests honestly, and for their own good. But, the moment we sacrifice their interests to our own, they will see it is better to govern themselves. The moment they resolve to do this, the point is settled. A forced connection is

neither our interest, nor within our power.—
To James Madison. ii, 66. Ford ed., iv, 333.
(P., Dec. 1786.)

8688. ——— ———. I fear, from an expression in your letter, that the people of Kentucky
think of separating, not only from Virginia
(in which they are right), but also from the
Confederacy. I own, I should think this a
most calamitous event, and such an one as
every good citizen on both sides should set
himself against.—To Archibald Stuart. i,
518. Ford ed., iv, 188. (P., Jan. 1786.)

8689. ——— ———. Whether we remain in
one confederacy, or break into Atlantic and
Mississippi confederacies, I believe not very
important to the happiness of either part.
Those of the western confederacy will be as
much our children and descendants as those
of the eastern, and I feel myself as much
identified with that country, in future time,
as with this; and did I now foresee a separation at some future day, yet I should feel the
duty and the desire to promote the western
interests as zealously as the eastern, doing all
the good for both portions of our future
family which should fall within my power.—
To Dr. Joseph Priestley. iv, 525. Ford
ed., viii, 295. (W., Jan. 1804.) See Centralization, Colonies, Confederation, Constitution, Federal Government and United
States.

8690. UNITED STATES, Assumption
of title.—We, therefore, the representatives
of the United States of America, in General Congress assembled, do in the name,
and by the authority of the good people of these States reject and renounce
all allegiance and subjection to the kings
of Great Britain and all others who may
hereafter claim by, through, or under them;
we utterly dissolve all political connection
which may heretofore have subsisted between us and the people or parliament of
Great Britain: and finally we do assert and
declare these Colonies to be free and independent States; and that as free and independent States, they have full power to levy
war, conclude peace, contract alliances, establish commerce, and to do all other acts and
things which independent States may of right
do. And for the support of this declaration,
we mutually pledge to each other our lives,
our fortunes, and our sacred honor.*—
Declaration of Independence as Drawn by
Jefferson.

* Congress changed the above so as to make it read
"We, therefore, the representatives of the United
States of America in General Congress assembled, appealing to the Supreme Judge of the World
for the rectitude of our intentions, do in the name,
and by the authority of the good people of these
Colonies, solemnly publish and declare, that these
united Colonies are, and of right ought to be, free
and independent States: that they are absolved
from all allegiance to the British crown, and that all
political connection between them and the state of
Great Britain is, and ought to be, totally dissolved:
and that as free and independent States, they
have full power to levy war, conclude peace, contract
alliances, establish commerce, and to do all other
acts and things which independent States may of
right do. And for the support of this Declaration,

8691. UNITED STATES, Benign influence.—The station which we occupy among
the nations of the earth is honorable, but
awful. Trusted with the destinies of this
solitary republic of the world, the only monument of human rights, and the sole depositary
of the sacred fire of freedom and self-government, whence it is to be lighted up in
other regions of the earth, if other regions of
the earth shall ever become susceptible of its
benign influence. All mankind ought then,
with us, to rejoice in its prosperous, and
sympathize in its adverse fortunes, as involving everything dear to man. And to what
sacrifices of interest, or convenience, ought
not these considerations to animate us? To
what compromises of opinion and inclination,
to maintain harmony and union among ourselves, and to preserve from all danger this
hallowed ark of human hope and happiness.
—R. to A. Citizens of Washington. viii,
157. (1809.)

8692. UNITED STATES, Continental
influence.—When our strength shall permit
us to give the law of our hemisphere it
should be that the meridian of the mid-Atlantic should be the line of demarcation between peace and war, on this side of which
no act of hostility should be committed, and
the lion and the lamb lie down in peace together.—To Dr. Crawford. vi, 33. (1812.)

8693. UNITED STATES, Destinies of.—
A rising nation, spread over a wide and
fruitful land, traversing all the seas with the
rich productions of their industry, engaged in
commerce with nations who feel power and
forget right, advancing rapidly to destinies
beyond the reach of mortal eye,—when I contemplate these transcendent objects, and see
the honor, the happiness, and the hopes of
this beloved country committed to the issue
and the auspices of this day, I shrink from
the contemplation, and humble myself before
the magnitude of the undertaking.—First Inaugural Address. viii, 1. Ford ed., viii, 2.
(1801.)

8694. UNITED STATES, Disputed territory.—Spain sets up a claim to possessions
within the State of Georgia, founded on her
having rescued them by force from the British, during the late war. The following view
of the subject seems to admit no reply: The
several States, now comprising the United
States of America, were, from their first establishment, separate and distinct societies,
dependent on no other society of men whatever. They continued at the head of their respective governments the executive magistrate who presided over the one they had left,
and thereby secured, in effect, a constant
amity with that nation. In this stage of their
government, their several boundaries were
fixed; and particularly the southern boundary
of Georgia, the only one now in question, was
established at the 31st degree of latitude from
the Apalachicola westwardly; and the west-
with a firm reliance on the protection of Divine
Providence, we mutually pledge to each other our
lives, our fortunes, and our sacred honor."—Editor.

ern boundary, originally the Pacific Ocean, was, by the Treaty of Paris, reduced to the middle of the Mississippi. The part which our chief magistrate took in a war waged against us by the nation among whom he resided, obliged us to discontinue him, and to name one within every State. In the course of this war, we were joined by France as an ally, and by Spain and Holland as associates having a common enemy. Each sought that common enemy wherever they could find him. France, on our invitation, landed a large army within our territories, continued it with us two years, and aided us in recovering sundry places from the possession of the enemy. But she did not pretend to keep possession of the places rescued. Spain entered into the remote western part of our territory, dislodged the common enemy from several of the posts they held therein, to the annoyance of Spain; and perhaps thought it necessary to remain in some of them, as the only means of preventing their return. We, in like manner, dislodged them from several posts in the same western territory, to wit: Vincennes, Cahokia, Kaskaskia, &c., rescued the inhabitants, and retained constantly afterwards both them and the territory under our possession and government. At the conclusion of the war, Great Britain, on the 30th of November, 1782, by treaty acknowledged our Independence, and our boundary, to wit, the Mississippi to the West, and the completion of the 31st degree, &c., to the South. In her treaty with Spain, concluded seven weeks afterwards, to wit, January 20th, 1783, she ceded to her the two Floridas (which had been defined in the proclamation of 1763), and Minorca; and by the eighth article of the treaty, Spain agreed to *restore without compensation,* all the territories conquered by her, and not included in the treaty either under the head of cessions or restitutions, that is to say, all except Minorca and the Floridas. According to this stipulation, Spain was expressly bound to have delivered up the possessions she had taken within the limits of Georgia, to Great Britain, if they were conquests on Great Britain, who was to deliver them over to the United States; or rather she should have delivered them over to the United States themselves, as standing, *quoad hoc,* in the place of Great Britain. And she was bound by natural right to deliver them to the same United States on a much stronger ground, as the real and only proprietors of those places which she had taken possession of, in a moment of danger, without having had any cause of war with the United States, to whom they belonged, and without having declared any; but on the contrary, conducting herself in other respects as a friend and associate.—(*Vattel,* L. 3, 122.) —Mississippi River Instructions. vii, 570. Ford ed., v, 461. (1792.)

8695. ——. Should Spain pretend * * * that there was a secret article of treaty between the United States and Great Britain, agreeing if, at the close of the [Revolutionary] war, the latter should retain the Floridas, that then the southern boundary of

Georgia should be the completion of the 32d degree of North latitude, the commissioners [appointed to negotiate with Spain to secure the free navigation of the Mississippi], may safely deny all knowledge of the fact, and refuse conference on any such postulatum. Or, should they find it necessary to enter into any argument on the subject, they will, of course, do it hypothetically; and in that way may justly say, on the part of the United States: "Suppose that the United States, exhausted by a bloody and expensive war with Great Britain, might have been willing to have purchased peace by relinquishing, under a particular contingency, a small part of their territory, it does not follow that the same United States, recruited and better organized, must relinquish the same territory to Spain without striking a blow. The United States, too, have irrevocably put it out of their power to do it, by a new Constitution, which guarantees every State against the invasion of its territory. A disastrous war, indeed, might, by necessity, supersede this stipulation (as necessity is above all law), and oblige them to abandon a part of a State; but nothing short of this can justify, or obtain such an abandonment.—Mississippi River Instructions. vii, 572. Ford ed., v, 463. (1792.)

8696. ——. It is an established principle, that conquest gives only an inchoate right, which does not become perfect till confirmed by the treaty of peace, and by a renunciation or abandonment by the former proprietor. Had Great Britain been that former proprietor, she was so far from confirming to Spain the right to the territory of Georgia, invaded by Spain, that she expressly relinquished to the United States any right that might remain in her; and afterwards completed that relinquishment by procuring and consolidating with it the agreement of Spain herself to restore such territory without compensation. It is still more palpable that a war existing between two nations, as Spain and Great Britain, could give to neither the right to seize and appropriate the territory of a third, which is even neutral, much less which is an associate in the war, as the United States were with Spain. See, on this subject, *Grotius,* L. 3, c. 6 § 26. *Puffendorf,* L. 8, c. 6. § 17, 23. *Vattel,* L. 3 § 197. 198.—Mississippi River Instructions. vii. 572. Ford ed., v, 463. (1792.)

8697. ——. A disastrous war might. by necessity, supersede this stipulation [the provision of the Constitution guaranteeing every State against the invasion of its territory] (as necessity is above all law), and oblige them to abandon a part of a State; but nothing short of this can justify, or obtain such an abandonment.—Mississippi River Instructions. vii, 573. Ford ed., v, 464. (1792.)

8698. UNITED STATES, Enduring.— When the General Government shall become incompetent [to the objects of government specially assigned to it] instead of flying to monarchy or that tranquillity which it is the

Thomas Jefferson

Age unknown

Reproduced from an engraving by Neagle after the painting by Otis.

nature of slavery to hold forth, the true remedy would be a subdivision, as you observe. But it is to be hoped that by a due poise and partition of powers between the General and particular governments we have found the secret of extending the benign blessing of Republicanism over still greater tracts of country than we possess, and that a subdivision may be avoided for ages, if not forever.—To JAMES SULLIVAN. FORD ED., v, 369. (Pa., 1791.)

8699. —— ——. I have much confidence that we shall proceed successfully for ages to come, and that, contrary to the principle of Montesquieu, it will be seen that the larger the extent of country, the more firm its republican structure, if founded, not on conquest. but in principles of compact and equality. My hope of its duration is built much on the enlargement of the resources of life going hand in hand with the enlargement of territory, and the belief that men are disposed to live honestly, if the means of doing so are open to them.—To M. DE MARBOIS. vii, 77. (M., 1817.)

8700. UNITED STATES, England and.—These two nations [the United States and England], holding cordially together, have nothing to fear from the united world. They will be the models for regenerating the condition of man, the sources from which representative government is to flow over the whole earth.—To J. EVELYN DENISON. vii, 415. (M., 1825.)

8701. UNITED STATES, Esteemed.—I shall rejoin myself to my native country, with new attachments, and with exaggerated esteem for its advantages; for though there is less wealth there, there is more freedom, more ease, and less misery.—To BARON GEISMER. i, 427. (P., 1785.)

8702. UNITED STATES, European powers and.—While there are powers in Europe which fear our views, or have views on us, we should keep an eye on them, their connections and oppositions, that in a moment of need we may avail ourselves of their weakness with respect to others as well as ourselves, and calculate their designs and movements on all the circumstances under which they exist.—To E. CARRINGTON. ii, 335. FORD ED., iv, 483. (P., 1787.)

8703. UNITED STATES, Foreign policy.—We must make the interest of every nation stand surety for their justice, and their own loss to follow injury to us, as effect follows its cause. As to everything except commerce, we ought to divorce ourselves from them all.—To EDWARD RUTLEDGE. iv, 191. FORD ED., vii, 154. (Pa., 1797.)

8704. —— ——. The less we have to do with the amities or enmities of Europe the better.—To THOMAS LEIPER. vi, 465. FORD ED., ix, 520. (M., 1815.) See ALLIANCE and POLICY.

8705. UNITED STATES, Freedom from turmoil.—How happy is it for us that we are beyond the reach of those storms which are eternally desolating Europe. We have indeed a neighbor with whom misunderstandings are possible; but they must be the effect of interests ill calculated. Nothing is more demonstrable than is the unity of their and our interest for ages to come.—To WILLIAM CARMICHAEL. FORD ED., v, 74. (P., 1789.)

8706. —— ——. Our difficulties are indeed great, if we consider ourselves alone. But when viewed in comparison to those of Europe, they are the joys of Paradise. In the eternal revolution of ages, the destinies have placed our portion of existence amidst such scenes of tumult and outrage, as no other period, within our knowledge, had presented. Every government but one on the continent of Europe, demolished, a conqueror roaming over the earth with havoc and destruction, a pirate spreading misery and ruin over the face of the ocean. Indeed, ours is a bed of roses. And the system of government which shall keep us afloat amidst the wreck of the world, will be immortalized in history. We have, to be sure, our petty squabbles and heart burnings, and we have something of the blue devils at times, as to these Rawheads and Bloodybones who are eating up other nations. But happily for us, the Mammoth cannot swim, nor the Leviathan move on dry land; and if we will keep out of their way, they cannot get at us. If, indeed, we choose to place ourselves within the scope of their tether, a gripe of the paw, or flounce of the tail. may be our fortune. But a part of our nation chose to declare against this, in such a way as to control the wisdom of the government. I yielded with others to avoid a greater evil. But from that moment, I have seen no system which could keep us entirely aloof from these agents of destruction.—To DR. WALTER JONES. v, 510. FORD ED., ix, 274. (M., March 1810.)

8707. UNITED STATES, Future greatness.—I do believe we shall continue to grow, to multiply and prosper until we exhibit an association, powerful, wise and happy beyond what has yet been seen by men.—To JOHN ADAMS. vi, 37. FORD ED., ix, 333. (M., 1812.)

8708. —— ——. Not in our day, but at no distant one, we may shake a rod over the heads of all [the European nations], which may make the stoutest of them tremble. But I hope our wisdom will grow with our power, and teach us, that the less we use our power, the greater will it be.—To THOMAS LEIPER. vi, 465. FORD ED., ix, 520. (M., 1815.)

8709. —— ——. We are destined to be a barrier against the returns of ignorance and barbarism. Old Europe will have to lean on our shoulders, and to hobble along by our side. under the monkish trammels of priests and kings, as she can. What a Colossus shall we be when the southern continent comes up to our mark! What a stand will it secure as a ralliance for the reason and freedom of the globe!—To JOHN ADAMS. vii, 27. (M.. 1816.)

8710. UNITED STATES, Guardian of liberty.—The eyes of the virtuous all over the earth are turned with anxiety on us as the only depositaries of the sacred fire of liberty.—To JOHN HOLLINS. v, 597. (M., 1811.)

8711. UNITED STATES, Independence of.—The several States, now comprising the United States of America, were, from their first establishment, separate and distinct societies, dependent on no other society of men whatever. They continued at the head of their respective governments the executive magistrate who presided over the one they had left, and thereby secured in effect a constant amity with that nation. * * * The part which our chief magistrate took in a war, waged against us by the nation among whom he resided, obliged us to discontinue him, and to name one within every State.—MISSISSIPPI RIVER INSTRUCTIONS. vii, 571. FORD ED., v, 461. (March 1792.)

— **UNITED STATES, Inviolability of territory.**—See TERRITORY, ALIENATION OF.

8712. UNITED STATES, Manufacturing nation.—Our enemy [Great Britain] has indeed the consolation of Satan on removing our first parents from Paradise; from a peaceable and agricultural nation, he makes us a military and maufacturing one.—To WILLIAM SHORT. vi, 400. (M., 1814.) See MANUFACTURES and PROTECTION.

— **UNITED STATES, National capital.**—See WASHINGTON CITY.

8713. UNITED STATES, Natural interests.—The American hemisphere * * * is endowed by nature with a system of interests and connections of its own.—R. TO A. PITTSBURG REPUBLICANS. viii, 142. (1808.) See MONROE DOCTRINE and POLICY.

8714. UNITED STATES, Permanence.—Looking forward with anxiety to the future destinies [of my countrymen] I trust that, in their steady character unshaken by difficulties, in their love of liberty, obedience to law, and support of the public authorities, I see a sure guarantee of the permanence of our Republic; and retiring from the charge of their affairs, I carry with me the consolation of a firm persuasion that heaven has in store for our beloved country long ages to come of prosperity and happiness.—EIGHTH ANNUAL MESSAGE. viii, 110. FORD ED., ix, 225. (Nov. 1808.)

8715. UNITED STATES, Praise for.—There is not a country on earth where there is greater tranquillity; where the laws are milder, or better obeyed; where every one is more attentive to his own business or meddles less with that of others; where strangers are better received, more hospitably treated, and with a more sacred respect.—To MRS. COSWAY. ii, 36. FORD ED., iv, 316. (P., 1786.)

8716. UNITED STATES, Prosperity.—When you witnessed our first struggles in the War of Independence, you little calculated, more than we did, on the rapid growth and prosperity of this country; on the practical demonstration it was about to exhibit, of the happy truth that man is capable of self-government, and only rendered otherwise by the moral degradation designedly superinduced on him by the wicked acts of his tyrants.—To M. DE MARBOIS. vii, 77. (M., 1817.)

8717. UNITED STATES, Safety of.—Our safety rests in the preservation of our Union.—To THE RHODE ISLAND ASSEMBLY. iv, 397. (W., May 1801.) See UNION.

8718. UNITED STATES, Slanders on.—Nations, like individuals, wish to enjoy a fair reputation. It is, therefore, desirable for us that the slanders on our country, disseminated by hired or prejudiced travellers, should be corrected; but politics, like religion, holds up the torches of martyrdom to the reformers of error. Nor is it in the theatre of Ephesus alone that tumults have been excited when the crafts were in danger. You must be cautious, therefore, in telling unacceptable truths beyond the water.—To MR. OGILVIE. v, 605. (M., 1811.)

8719. UNITED STATES, Superiority over Europe.—I sincerely wish you may find it convenient to come here [Europe]; the pleasure of the trip will be less than you expect, but the utility greater. It will make you adore your own country, its soil, its climate, its equality, liberty, laws, people, and manners. My God! how little do my countrymen know what precious blessings they are in possession of, and which no other people on earth enjoy. I confess I had no idea of it myself. While we shall see multiplied instances of Europeans going to live in America, I will venture to say, no man now living will ever see an instance of an American removing to settle in Europe, and continuing there. Come, then, and see the proofs of this, and on your return add your testimony to that of every thinking American, in order to satisfy our countrymen how much it is to their interest to preserve, uninfected by contagion, those peculiarities in their government and manners, to which they are indebted for those blessings.—To JAMES MONROE. i, 352. FORD ED., iv, 59. (P., 1785.)

8720. UNITED STATES, Supremacy.—To the overwhelming power of England, I see but two chances of limit. The first is her bankruptcy, which will deprive her of the *golden* instrument of all her successes. The other is that ascendency which nature destines for us by immutable laws. But to hasten this consummation, we must exercise patience and forbearance. For twenty years to come we should consider peace as the *summum bonum* of our country. At the end of that period we shall be twenty millions in number. and forty in energy, when encountering the starved and rickety paupers and dwarfs of English workshops.—To M. DUPONT DE NEMOURS. vi, 508. (M., Dec. 1815.)

8721. UNITED STATES, Title of inhabitants.—You have properly observed (in your book on the commerce of France and the United States) that we can no longer be called Anglo-Americans. That appellation now describes only the inhabitants of Nova Scotia, Canada, &c. I had applied that of Federo-Americans to our citizens, as it would not be so decent for us to assume to ourselves the flattering appellation of free Americans.—To M. DE WARVILLE. ii, 12. FORD ED., iv, 281. (P., 1786.)

8722. UNITED STATES, Troubles and triumphs.—A letter from you calls up recollections very dear to my mind. It carries me back to the times when, beset with difficulties and dangers, we were fellow-laborers in the same cause, struggling for what is most valuable to man, his right of self-government. Laboring always at the same oar, with some wave ever ahead, threatening to overwhelm us, and yet passing harmless under our bark, we knew not how we rode through the storm with heart and hand, and made a happy port. Still we did not expect to be without rubs and difficulties; and we have had them. First, the detention of the Western posts, then the coalition of Pilnitz, outlawing our commerce with France, and the British enforcement of the outlawry. In your day, French depredations; in mine, English, and the Berlin and Milan decrees: now the English orders of Council, and the piracies they authorize. When these shall be over, it will be the impressment of our seamen or something else; and so we have gone on, and so we shall go on, puzzled and prospering beyond example in the history of man.—To JOHN ADAMS. vi, 36. FORD ED., ix, 333. (M., Jan. 1812.)

8723. UNITED STATES, Western territory.—[The proposed new States of the Western territory] shall forever remain a part of the United States of America.—WESTERN TERRITORY REPORT. FORD ED., iii, 409. (1784.) See CENTRALIZATION, CONFEDERATION, COLONIES, CONSTITUTION, FEDERAL GOVERNMENT and UNION.

8724. UNITY, Duty of.— Sole depositaries of the remains of human liberty, our duty to ourselves, to posterity, and to mankind, calls on us by every motive which is sacred or honorable, to watch over the safety of our beloved country during the troubles which agitate and convulse the residue of the world, and to sacrifice to that all personal and local considerations.—R. TO A. NEW YORK LEGISLATURE. viii, 167. (1809.)

8725. UNITY, National.—If we are forced into a war we mus give up differences of opinion and unite as one man to defend our country.—To GENERAL KOSCIUSKO. iv. 295. (Pa., 1799.)

8726. —— ——. The times do certainly render it incumbent on all good citizens, attached to the rights and honor of their country, to bury in oblivion all internal differences, and rally around the standard of their country in opposition to the outrages of foreign nations. All attempts to enfeeble and destroy the exertions of the General Government, in vindication of our national rights, or to loosen the bands of Union by alienating the affections of the people, or opposing the authority of the laws at so eventful a period, merit the discountenance of all.—To GOVERNOR TOMPKINS. viii, 153. (Feb. 1809.)

8727. UNITY, Strength in.—If the well-known energies and enterprise of our countrymen * * * are embodied by an union of will, and by a confidence in those who direct it, our nation, so favored in its situation, has nothing to fear from any quarter.—REPLY TO ADDRESS. v, 262. (W., 1808.)

8728. UNIVERSITY (National), Proposed establishment.—Education is here placed among the articles of public care, not that it would be proposed to take its ordinary branches out of the hands of private enterprise, which manages so much better all the concerns to which it is equal : but a public institution can alone supply those sciences which, though rarely called for, are yet necessary to complete the circle, all the parts of which contribute to the improvement of the country, and some of them to its preservation. The subject is now proposed for the consideration of Congress, because, if approved by the time the State Legislatures shall have deliberated on this extension of the Federal trusts, and the laws shall be passed, and other arrangements made for their execution, the necessary funds will be on hand and without employment. I suppose an amendment to the Constitution, by consent of the States, necessary, because the objects now recommended are not among those enumerated in the Constitution, and to which it permits the public moneys to be applied. The present consideration of a national establishment for education, particularly, is rendered proper by the circumstance, also, that if Congress, approving the proposition, shall yet think it more eligible to found it on a donation of lands, they have it now in their power to endow it with those which will be among the earliest to produce the necessary income. This foundation would have the advantage of being independent on war, which may suspend other improvements by requiring for its own purposes the resources destined for them.—SIXTH ANNUAL MESSAGE. viii, 68. FORD ED., viii, 494. (Dec. 1806.)

8729. —— ——. The desire of peace is very much strengthened in me by that which I feel in favor of the great subjects of your and Mr. Fulton's letters. I had fondly hoped to set those enterprises into motion with the last Legislature I shall meet. But the chance of war is an unfortunate check. I do not, however, despair that the proposition of amendment may be sent down this session to the [State] Legislatures. But it is not certain. There is a snail paced gait for the advance of new ideas on the general mind, under which we must acquiesce. A forty years' experience of popular assemblies has taught me that you must give them time for every step you take. If too hard pushed, they balk, and the machine retrogrades.—To JOEL BARLOW. v, 216. FORD ED., ix, 168. (W., Dec. 1807.)

8730. UNIVERSITY OF VIRGINIA, Aim of.—Our aim [is] the securing to our country a full and perpetual institution for all the useful sciences; one which will restore us to our former station in the confederacy. * * * Patience and perseverance on our part will secure the blessed end. If we shrink, it is gone forever.—To GENERAL BRECKENRIDGE. vii, 239. (M., 1822.)

8731. UNIVERSITY OF VIRGINIA, Basis of.—This institution of my native State, the hobby of my old age, will be based on the illimitable freedom of the human mind, to explore and to expose every subject susceptible of its contemplation.—To DESTUTT TRACY. FORD ED., x, 174. (M., 1820.)

8732. ———. This institution (University of Virginia) will be based on the illimitable freedom of the human mind. For here we are not afraid to follow truth wherever it may lead, nor to tolerate any error so long as reason is left free to combat it.—To MR. ROSCOE. vii, 196. (M., 1820.)

8733. UNIVERSITY OF VIRGINIA, Discipline.—The rock which I most dread is the discipline of the institution, and it is that on which most of our public schools labor. The insubordination of our youth is now the greatest obstacle to their education. We may lessen the difficulty, perhaps, by avoiding too much government, by requiring no useless observances, none which shall merely multiply occasions for dissatisfaction, disobedience and revolt by referring to the more discreet of themselves the minor discipline, the graver to the civil magistrate, as in Edinburgh.—To GEORGE TICKNOR. vii, 301. (M., 1823.)

8734. UNIVERSITY OF VIRGINIA, Elective studies.—I am not fully informed of the practices at Harvard, but there is one from which we shall certainly vary, although it has been copied, I believe, by nearly every college and academy in the United States. That is, the holding the students all to one prescribed course of reading, and disallowing exclusive application to those branches only which are to qualify them for the particular vocations to which they are destined. We shall, on the contrary, allow them uncontrolled choice in the lectures they shall choose to attend, and require elementary qualification only, and sufficient age. Our institution will proceed on the principle of doing all the good it can without consulting its own pride or ambition; of letting every one come and listen to whatever he thinks may improve the condition of his mind.—To GEORGE TICKNOR. vii, 300. (M., 1823.)

8735. UNIVERSITY OF VIRGINIA, Future of.—I contemplate the University of Virginia as the future bulwark of the human mind in this hemisphere.—To DR. THOMAS COOPER. vii, 172. (M., 1820.)

8736. ———. I had hoped that we should open with the next year an institution on which the fortunes of our country may de-

pend more than may meet the general eye.—To GENERAL BRECKENRIDGE. vii, 204. (M., 1821.)

8737. ———. I hope the University of Virginia will prove a blessing to my own State, and not unuseful perhaps to some others.—To EDWARD LIVINGSTON. vii, 405. (M., 1825.)

8738. UNIVERSITY OF VIRGINIA, Government and.—I fear not to say that within twelve or fifteen years from this time, a majority of the rulers of our State will have been educated here. They shall carry hence the correct principles of our day, and you may count assuredly that they will exhibit their country in a degree of sound respectability it has never known, either in our days, or those of our forefathers.—To W. B. GILES. vii, 429. FORD ED., x, 357. (M., 1825.)

8739. UNIVERSITY OF VIRGINIA, Historical course.—In modern history, there are but two nations with whose course it is interesting to us to be intimately acquainted, to wit: France and England. For the former, Millot's General History of France may be sufficient to the period when 1 Davila commences. He should be followed by Perefixe, Sully, Voltaire's Louis XIV. and XV., Lacretelles XVIIIme. Siècle, Marmontel's Regence, Foulongion's French Revolution, and Madame de Stael's, making up by a succession of particular history, the general one which they want.—To ———. vii, 412. (M., 1825.)

8740. ———. Hume, with Brodie, should be the last histories of England to be read [in the University of Virginia course]. If first read, Hume makes [his reader] an English tory, whence it is an easy step to American toryism. But there is a history by Baxter, in which, abridging somewhat by leaving out some entire incidents as less interesting now than when Hume wrote, he has given the rest in the identical words of Hume, except that when he comes to a fact falsified, he states it truly, and when to a suppression of truth, he supplies it, never otherwise changing a word. It is, in fact, an editic expurgation of Hume. Those who shrink from the volume of Rapin, may read this first, and from this lay a first foundation in a basis of truth.—To ———. vii, 414. (M., 1825.)

8741. UNIVERSITY OF VIRGINIA, Jefferson's last service.—Our University is the last of my mortal cares, and the last service I can render my country.—To J. CORREA. vii, 183. FORD ED., x, 163. (M., 1820.)

8742. ———. It is the last act of usefulness I can render, and could I see it open I would not ask an hour more of life.—To SPENCER ROANE. vii, 212. FORD ED., x, 189. (M., 1821.)

8743. ———. The University of Virginia is the last object for which I shall obtrude myself on the public observation.—To EDWARD LIVINGSTON. vii, 405. (M., 1825.)

8744. ———. I am closing the last scenes of my life by fashioning and fostering an establishment for the instruction of those who are to come after us. I hope its influence on their virtue, freedom, fame, and happiness will be salutary and permanent.—To A. B. WOODWARD. vii, 406. FORD ED., x, 342. (M., 1825.)

8745. UNIVERSITY OF VIRGINIA, Necessity for.—I have wondered at the change of political principles which has taken place in many in this State [Virginia], however much less than in others. I am still more alarmed to see, in the other States, the general political dispositions of those to whom is confided the education of the rising generation. Nor are all the academies of this State free from grounds of uneasiness. I have great confidence in the common sense of mankind in general; but it requires a great deal to get the better of notions which our tutors have instilled into our minds while incapable of questioning them, and to rise superior to antipathies strongly rooted. However, I suppose when the evil rises to a certain height, a remedy will be found, if the case admits any other than the prudence of parents and guardians.—To JEREMIAH MOOR. FORD ED., vii, 455. (M., Aug. 1800.)

8746. —— ——. How many of our youths Harvard now has, learning the lessons of anti-Missourianism, I know not; but a gentleman lately from Princeton, told me he saw there the list of the students at that place, and that more than half were Virginians. These will return home, no doubt, deeply impressed with the sacred principles of our Holy Alliance of restrictionists.—To JOSEPH C. CABELL. vii, 202. (M., 1821.)

8747. —— ——. The reflections that the boys of this age are to be the men of the next; that they should be prepared to receive the holy charge which we are cherishing to deliver over to them; that in establishing an institution of wisdom for them, we secure it to all our future generations; that in fulfilling this duty, we bring home to our own bosoms the sweet consolation of seeing our sons rising under a luminous tuition, to destinies of high promise; these are considerations which will occur to all; but all, I fear, do not see the speck in our horizon which is to burst on us as a tornado, sooner or later. The line of division lately marked out between different portions of our confederacy is such as will never, I fear, be obliterated, and we are now trusting to those who are against us in position and principle, to fashion to their own form the minds and affections of our youth. If, as has been estimated, we send three hundred thousand dollars a year to the northern seminaries, for the instruction of our own sons, then we must have there five hundred of our sons, imbibing opinions and principles in discord with those of their own country. This canker is eating on the vitals of our existence, and if not arrested at once, will be beyond remedy. We are now certainly furnishing recruits to their school.—To GENERAL BRECKENRIDGE. vii, 204. (M., 1821.)

8748. **UNIVERSITY OF VIRGINIA, Novelties in.**—There are some novelties in [the University of Virginia]. Of that of a professorship of the principles of government, you express your approbation. They will be founded in the rights of man. That of agriculture, I am sure, you will approve; and that also of Anglo-Saxon. As the histories and laws left us in that type and dialect, must be the text books of the reading of the learners, they will imbibe with the language their free principles of government.—To JOHN CARTWRIGHT. vii, 361. (M., 1824.)

8749. **UNIVERSITY OF VIRGINIA, Opposition to.**—An opposition [to the University] has been got up. That of our *alma mater*, William and Mary, is not of much weight. She must descend into the secondary rank of academies of preparation for the Uni-

versity. The serious enemies are the priests of the different religious sects, to whose spells on the human mind its improvement is ominous. Their pulpits are now resounding with denunciations against the appointment of Dr. Cooper whom they charge as a monetheist in opposition to their tritheism.—To WILLIAM SHORT. vii, 157. (M., 1820.) See COOPER.

8750. —— ——. You say my "handwriting and my letters have great effect at Richmond". I am sensible of the kindness with which this encouragement is held up to me. But my views of their effect are very different. When I retired from the administration of public affairs, I thought I saw some evidence that I retired with a good degree of public favor, and that my conduct in office had been considered by one party at least with approbation and with acquiescence by the other. But the attempt [University of Virginia], in which I have embarked so earnestly to procure an improvement in the moral condition of my native State, although, perhaps, in other States it may have strengthened good dispositions, it has assuredly weakened them within our own. The attempt ran foul of so many local interests, of so many personal views, and so much ignorance, and I have been considered as so particularly its promoter, that I see evidently a great change of sentiment towards myself. I cannot doubt its having dissatisfied with myself a respectable minority, if not a majority of the House of Delegates. I feel it deeply and very discouragingly. Yet I shall not give way. I have ever found in my progress through life that, acting for the public, if we do always what is right, the approbation denied in the beginning will surely follow us in the end. It is from posterity we are to expect remuneration for the sacrifices we are making for their service, of time, quiet and good will. And I fear not the appeal. The multitude of fine young men whom we shall redeem from ignorance, who will feel that they owe to us the elevation of mind, of character and station they will be able to attain from the result of our efforts, will insure their remembering us with gratitude.—To JOSEPH C. CABELL. vii, 394. (M., 1825.)

8751. **UNIVERSITY OF VIRGINIA, Personal sacrifices for.**—I know well your devotion to your country, and your foresight of the awful scenes coming on her, sooner or later. With this foresight, what service can we ever render her equal to this? [Support of the University of Virginia.] What object of our lives can we propose so important? What interest of our own which ought not to be postponed to this? Health, time, labor, on what in the single life which nature has given us, can these be better bestowed than on this immortal boon to our country? The exertions and the mortifications are temporary: the benefit eternal. If any member of our college of visitors could justifiably withdraw from this sacred duty, it would be myself, * * * but I will die in the last ditch, and so, I hope, you will, my friend, as well as our firm-breasted brothers and colleagues, Mr. Johnson and General Breckenridge. Nature will not give you a second life wherein to atone for the omissions of this. Pray then, dear and very dear Sir, do not think of deserting us, but view the sacrifices which seem to stand in your way, as the lesser duties, and such as ought to be postponed to this, the greatest of all. Continue with us in these holy labors, until having seen their accomplishment, we may say with old Simeon, "*nunc dimittis, Domine*".—To JOSEPH C. CABELL. vii, 202. (M., 1821.)

8752. UNIVERSITY OF VIRGINIA, Political principles.—In the selection of our law professor [for the University of Virginia], we must be rigorously attentive to his political principles. You will recollect that before the Revolution Coke-Littleton was the universal elementary book of law students, and a sounder whig never wrote, nor of profounder learning in the orthodox doctrines of the British constitution, or in what were called English liberties. You remember, also, that our lawyers were then all whigs. But when his black-letter text, and uncouth but cunning learning got out of fashion, and the honied Mansfieldism of Blackstone became the student's hornbook, from that moment, that profession (the nursery of our Congress), began to slide into toryism, and nearly all the young brood of lawyers now are of that hue. They suppose themselves, indeed, to be whigs because they no longer know what whigism or republicanism means. It is in our seminary that that vestal flame is to be kept alive; it is thence it is to spread anew over our own and the sister States. If we are true and vigilant in our trust, within a dozen or twenty years a majority of our own Legislature will be from one school, and many disciples will have carried its doctrines home with them to their several States, and will have leavened thus the whole mass.—To JAMES MADISON. vii, 433. FORD ED., x, 376. (M., 1826.)

8753. UNIVERSITY OF VIRGINIA, Proctorship.—The establishment of a proctor is taken from the practice of Europe, where an equivalent officer is made a part, and is a very essential one, of every such institution; and as the nature of his functions requires that he should always be a man of discretion, understanding, and integrity, above the common level, it was thought that he would never be less worthy of being trusted with the powers of a justice, within the limits of institution here, than the neighboring justices generally are; and the vesting him with the conservation of the peace within that limit, was intended, while it should equally secure its object, to shield the young and unguarded student from the disgrace of the common prison, except where the case was an aggravated one. A confinement to his own room was meant as an act of tenderness to him, his parents and friends; in fine, it was to give them a complete police of their own, tempered by the paternal attentions of their tutors. And, certainly, in no country is such a provision more called for than in this, as has been proved from times of old, from the regular annual riots and battles between the students of William and Mary with the town boys, before the Revolution, *quorum pars fui,* and the many and more serious affrays of later times. Observe, too, that our bill proposes no exclusion of the ordinary magistrate, if the one attached to the institution is thought to execute his power either partially or remissly.—To JOSEPH C. CABELL. vi, 537. (M., 1816.)

8754. UNIVERSITY OF VIRGINIA, Professors.—Our wish is to procure natives [for professorships] where they can be found * * * of the first order of requirement in their respective lines; but, preferring foreigners of the first order to natives of the second, we shall certainly have to go for several of our professors to countries more advanced in science than we are.—To JOHN ADAMS. vii, 130. FORD ED., x, 139. (M., 1819.)

8755. ———— ————. No secondary character will be received among them. Either the ablest which America or Europe can furnish, or none

at all. They will give us the selected society of a great city separated from the dissipations and levities of its ephemeral insects.—To WILLIAM SHORT. vii, 141. FORD ED., x, 145. (M., 1819.)

8756. ———— ————. Our intention is that its professors shall be of the first order in their respective lines which can be procured on either side of the Atlantic.—To ALBERT GALLATIN. FORD ED., x, 236. (M., 1822.)

8757. ———— ————. A man is not qualified for a professor, knowing nothing but merely his own profession. He should be otherwise well educated as to the sciences generally; able to converse understandingly with the scientific men with whom he is associated, and to assist in the councils of the faculty on any subject of science on which they may have occasion to deliberate. Without this, he will incur their contempt, and bring disreputation on the institution.—To JOSEPH C. CABELL. vii, 331. (M., 1824.)

8758. ———— ————. I have the most unlimited confidence that in the appointment of professors to our nursling institution, every individual of my associates will look with a single eye to the sublimation of its character, and adopt, as our sacred motto, *"detur digniori"*. In this way it will honor us, and bless our country.—To JOSEPH C. CABELL. vii, 331. (M., 1824.)

8759. ———— ————. In some departments of science we believe Europe to be in advance before us, and that it would advance ourselves were we to draw from thence instructors in these branches, and thus to improve our science, as we have done our manufactures, by borrowed skill. I have been much squibbed for this, perhaps by disappointed applicants for professorships, to which they were deemed incompetent.—To JOHN ADAMS. vii, 388. (M., 1825.)

8760. ———— ————. I have no reason to regret the measure taken of procuring professors from abroad where science is so much ahead of us. You witnessed some of the puny squibs of which I was the butt on that account. They were probably from disappointed candidates, whose unworthiness had occasioned their applications to be passed over. The measure has been generally approved in the South and West; and by all liberal minds in the North. It has been peculiarly fortunate, too, that the professors brought from abroad were as happy selections as could have been hoped, as well for their qualifications in science as correctness and amiableness of character. I think the example will be followed, and that it cannot fail to be one of the efficacious means of promoting that cordial good will, which it is so much the interest of both nations to cherish. These teachers can never utter an unfriendly sentiment towards their native country; and those into whom their instructions will be infused, are not of ordinary significance only; they are exactly the persons who are to succeed to the government of our country, and to rule its future enmities, its friendships and fortunes. As it is our interest to receive instruction through this channel, so I think it is yours to furnish it; for these two nations holding cordially together, have nothing to fear from the united world. They will be the models for regenerating the condition of man, the sources from which representative government is to flow over the whole earth.—To J. EVELYN DENISON. vii, 415. (M., 1825.)

8761. UNIVERSITY OF VIRGINIA, Scope.—Our views are catholic for the improvement of our country by science.—To George Ticknor. vii, 301. (M., 1823.)

8762. UNIVERSITY OF VIRGINIA, Studies.—A material question is what is the whole term of time which the students can give to the whole course of instruction? I should say that three years should be allowed to general education, and two, or rather three, to the particular profession for which they are destined. We [University of Virginia] receive our students at the age of sixteen, expected to be previously so far qualified in the languages, ancient and modern, as that one year in our schools shall suffice for their last polish. A student then with us may give his first year here to languages and mathematics; h s second to mathematics and physics; his third to physics and chemistry, with the other objects of that school. I particularize this distribution merely for illustration, and not as that which either is, or perhaps ought to be established. This would ascribe one year to languages, two to mathematics, two to physics, and one to chemistry and its associates.—To Dr. John P. Emmett. vii, 442. (M., 1826.)

8763. UNIVERSITY OF VIRGINIA, Text books.—In most public seminaries textbooks are prescribed to each of the several schools, as the *norma docendi* in that school; and this is generally done by authority of the trustees. I should not propose this generally in our University, because I believe none of us are so much at the heights of science in the several branches, as to undertake this, and therefore that it will be better left to the professors until occasion of interference shall be given. But there is one branch in which we are the best judges, in which heresies may be taught, of so interesting a character to our own State and to the United States, as to make it a duty in us to lay down the principles which are to be taught. It is that of government. Mr. Gilmer being withdrawn, we know not who his successor may be. He may be a Richmond lawyer, or one of that school of quondam federalism, now consolidation. It is our duty to guard against such principles being disseminated among our youth, and the diffusion of that poison, by a previous prescription of the texts to be followed in their discourses.—To ——. vii, 397. (M., 1825.)

8764. UNIVERSITY OF VIRGINIA, Theology.—I agree with you that a professorship of theology should have no place in our institution.—To Thomas Cooper. vi, 389. (M., 1814.)

8765. —— ——. In our University there is no professorship of divinity. A handle has been made of this to disseminate an idea that this is an nistitution, not merely of no religion, but against all religion. Occasion was taken at the last meeting of the Visitors, to bring forward an idea that might silence this calumny, which weighed on the minds of some honest friends to the institution. In our annual report to the Legislature, after stating the constitutional reasons against a public establishment of any religious instruction, we suggest the expediency of encouraging the different religious sects to establish, each for itself, a professorship of their own tenets, on the confines of the University, so near as that their students may attend the lectures there, and have the free use of our library, and every other accommodation we can give them; preserving, however, their

independence of us and of each other. This fills the chasm objected to ours, as a defect in an institution professing to give instruction in *all* useful sciences. I think the invitation will be accepted, by some sects from candid intentions, and by others from jealousy and rivalship. And by bringing the sects together, and mixing them with the mass of other students, we shall soften their asperities, liberalize and neutralize their prejudices, and make the general religion a religion of peace, reason and morality.—To Dr. Thomas Cooper. vii, 267. Ford ed., x, 243. (M., 1822.) See Education, Languages and Schools.

8766. USURPATION, Appeal against.—We have appealed to their [British people] native justice and magnanimity, as well as to the ties of our common kindred, to disavow these usurpations which were likely to interrupt our connection and correspondence. They, too, have been deaf to the voice of justice and of consanguinity.*—Declaration of Independence as Drawn by Jefferson.

8767. USURPATION, Parliamentary.—The act passed in the 4th year of his Majesty's reign [George III.], entitled "An Act for granting certain duties in the British Colonies and Plantations in America, &c."; one other act passed in the 5th year of his reign, entitled, "An Act for granting and applying certain stamp duties and other duties in the British Colonies and Plantations in America, &c."; one other act passed in the 6th year of his reign, entitled, "An Act for the better securing the dependency of his Majesty's dominions in America upon the Crown and Parliament of Great Britain"; and one other act, passed in the 7th year of his reign, entitled, "An Act for granting duties on paper, tea, &c.", form that connected chain of parliamentary usurpation, which has been the subject of frequent applications to his Majesty, and the Houses of Lords and Commons of Great Britain * * * .—Rights of British America. i, 130. Ford ed., i, 435. (1774.)

8768. VACATIONS, Health and.—The diseases of the season incident to most situations on the tide waters, now begin to show themselves here [Washington], and to threaten some of our members [of the cabinet] together with the probability of a uniform course of things in the Chesapeake [affair], induce us to prepare for leaving this place during the two sickly months, as well for the purposes of health as to bestow some little attention to our private affairs, which is necessary at some time of every year. Our respective stations will be fixed and known, so that everything will find us at them, with the same certainty as if they were here; and such measures of intercourse will be established as that the public business will be carried on at them, with all the regularity and dispatch necessary.—To W. H. Cabell. v, 144. Ford ed., ix, 91. (W., July 1807.)

8769. —— ——. In consideration of the unhealthy season now approaching at this as

*Congress changed so as to read: "We have appealed to their native justice and magnanimity, and we have conjured them, by the ties of our common kindred, to disavow these usurpations, which would inevitably interrupt our connection and correspondence. They, too, have been deaf to the voice of justice and of consanguinity."—Editor.

other places on the tide-waters, and which we have always retired from about this time, the members of the Administration, as well as myself, shall leave this place [Washington] in three or four days, not to return till the sickly term is over, unless something extraordinary should reassemble us.—To COLONEL TATHAM. v. 145. (W., July 1807.)

8770. VACATIONS, Presidential.—I consider it as a trying experiment for a person from the mountains to pass the two bilious months on the tide-water. I have not done it these forty years, and nothing should nduce me to do it. As it is not possible but that the Administration must take some portion of time for their own affairs, I think it best they should select that season for absence. General Washington set the example of those two months; Mr. Adams extended them to eight months. I should not suppose our bringing it back to two months a ground for grumbling, but, grumble who will, I will never pass those two months on tide-water.—To ALBERT GALLATIN. FORD ED., viii, 95. (M., Sep. 1801.)

8771. VACATIONS, Public officials and.—One reason for suggesting the discontinuance of the daily post was, that it was not kept up by contract, but at the expense of the United States. But the principal reason was to avoid giving ground for clamor. The general idea is, that those who receive annual compensations should be constantly at their posts. Our constituents might not in the first moment consider 1st, that we have property to take care of, which we cannot abandon for temporary salaries; 2nd, that we have health to take care of, which at this season cannot be preserved at Washington; 3d, that while at our separate homes our public duties are fully executed, and at much greater personal labor than while we are together when a short conference saves a long letter.—To JAMES MADISON. v, 181. FORD ED., ix, 134. (M., Sep. 1807.)

8772. VACCINATION, Utility of.—I am happy to see that vaccination is introduced, and likely to be kept up, in Philadelphia; but I shall not think it exhibits all its utility until experience shall have hit upon some mark or rule by which the popular eye may distinguish genuine from spurious virus. It was with this view that I wished to discover whether time could not be made the standard, and supposed, from the little experience I had, that matter, taken at eght times twenty-four hours from the time of insertion, could always be in the proper state. As far as I went I found it so; but I shall be happy to learn what the immense field of experience in Philadelphia will teach us on that subject.—To DR. BENJAMIN RUSH. iv, 425. FORD ED., viii, 126. (W., Dec. 1801.)

— VALUE, Intrinsic.—See DOLLAR and MONEY.

8773. VANITY, Personal.—I have not the vanity to count myself among those whom the State would think worth oppressing with perpetual service.—To JAMES MONROE. i, 320. FORD ED., iii, 59. (M., 1782.)

8774. VAN RENSSELAER (General S.), Failure of.—Will not Van Rensselaer be broke for cowardice and incapacity? To advance such a body of men across a river without securing boats to bring them off in case of disaster, has cost us seven hundred men; and to have taken no part himself in such an action, and against such a general could be nothing but cowardice.—To PRESIDENT MADISON. FORD ED., ix, 370. (M., Nov. 1812.)

8775. VATTEL (Emmerich von), Character of.—Let us appeal to enlightened and disinterested judges. No one is more so than Vattel.—To E. C. GENET. iii, 588. FORD ED., vi, 309. (Pa., 1793.)

8776. ———. ———. Vattel is one of the most zealous and constant advocates for the preservation of good faith in all our dealings.—OPINION ON FRENCH TREATIES. vii, 620. FORD ED., vi, 228. (1793.)

8777. VEGETABLES, Cultivating.—The wealthy people [in Virginia] are attentive to the raising of vegetables, but very little so to fruits. The poorer people attend to neither, living principally on milk and animal diet. This is the more inexcusable, as the climate requires indispensably a free use of vegetable food, for health as well as comfort.—NOTES ON VIRGINIA. viii, 393. FORD ED., iii, 257. (1782.)

8778. VEGETABLES, Jefferson's diet.—I live so much like other people, that I might refer to ordinary life as the history of my own. I have lived temperately, eating little animal food, and that not as an aliment, so much as a condiment for the vegetables, which constitute my principal diet. I double, however, the Doctor's [Rush's] glass and a half of wine, and even treble it with a friend; but halve its effects by drinking the weak wines only. The ardent wines I cannot drink, nor do I use ardent spirits in any form. Malt liquors and cider are my table drinks, and my breakfast is of tea and coffee. I have been blest with organs of digestion which accept and concoct, without ever murmuring, whatever the palate chooses to consign to them, and I have not yet lost a tooth by age.—To DR. VINE UTLEY. vii, 116. FORD ED., x, 125. (M., 1819.)

8779. VEGETATION, Electricity, light and.—Dr. Ingenhouse, you know, discovered as he supposed, from experiment, that vegetation might be promoted by occasional streams of the electrical fluid to pass through a plant, and that other physicians had received and confirmed this theory. He now, however, retracts it, and finds by more decisive experiments that the electrical fluid can neither forward nor retard vegetation. Uncorrected still of the rage of drawing general conclusions from partial and equivocal observations, he hazards the opinion that light promotes vegetation. I have heretofore supposed from observation, that light affects the color of living bodies, whether vegetable or animal; but that either the one or the other receives nutriment from that fluid, must be permitted to be doubted of, till better confirmed by observation. It is always better to have no ideas than false ones: to believe nothing than to believe what is wrong. In my mind, theories are more easily demolished than rebuilt.—To REV. JAMES MADISON. ii, 430. (P., 1788.)

8780. VENISON, Philosophy and.—You have sent me a noble animal, legitimated by superior force as a monarch of the forest; and he has incurred the death which his brother legitimates have so much more merited; like them, in death, he becomes food for a nobler race, he for man, they for worms that will revel on them; but he dies innocent, and with death all his fears and pains are at an end; they die loaded with maledictions, and liable to a sentence and sufferings which we will leave to the justice of heaven to award. In plain English, we shall heartily feast on him, and thank you heartily as the giver of the feast.—To JOHN FRY. FORD ED., x, 284. (M., 1823.)

8781. VERGENNES (Count de), Assistants.—Reyneval and Hennin are the two eyes of Count de Vergennes. The former is the more important character, because possessing the most of the confidence of the Count. He is rather cunning than wise, his views of things being neither great nor liberal. He governs himself by principles which he has learned by rote, and is fit only for the details of execution. His heart is susceptible of little passions, but not of good ones. He is brother-in-law to M. Gerard, from whom he received disadvantageous impressions of us, which cannot be effaced. He has much duplicity. Hennin is a philosopher, sincere, friendly, liberal, learned, beloved by everybody; the other by nobody. I think it a great misfortune that the United States are in the department of the former.—To JAMES MADISON. ii, 109. FORD ED., iv, 368. (P., 1787.)

8782. VERGENNES (Count de), Great and good.—He is a great and good minister, and an accident to him might endanger the peace of Europe.—To EDWARD CARRINGTON. i, 99. FORD ED., iv, 359. (P., 1787.)

8783. ———— ————. His loss would at all times have been great; but it would be immense during the critical poise of European affairs existing at this moment.—To JOHN JAY. ii, 113. (P., 1787.)

8784. VERGENNES (Count de), Monarchist.—Vergennes is a great minister in European affairs, but has very imperfect ideas of our institutions, and no confidence in them. His devotion to the principles of pure despotism renders him unaffectionate to our governments. But his fear of England makes him value us as a make-weight. He is cool, reserved in political conversations, but free and familiar on other subjects, and a very attentive, agreeable person to do business with. It is impossible to have a clearer, better organized head, but age has chilled his heart.—To JAMES MADISON. ii, 108. FORD ED., iv, 366. (P., 1787.)

8785. VERGENNES (Count de), Reputation.—The Count de Vergennes had the reputation with the diplomatic corps of being wary and slippery in his diplomatic intercourse; and so he might be with those whom he knew to be slippery and double-faced themselves. As he saw that I had no indirect views, practiced no subtleties, meddled in no intrigues, pursued no concealed object, I found him as frank, as honorable, as easy of access to reason, as any man with whom I had ever done business; and I must say the same for his successor, Montmorin, one of the most honest and worthy of human beings.—AUTOBIOGRAPHY. i, 64. FORD ED., i, 90. (M., 1821.)

8786. VERMONT, Separation from New York.—The four northernmost States wish Vermont to be received into the Union. The middle and southernmost States are rather opposed to it. But the great difficulty arises with New York which claims that territory. In the beginning every individual of that State revolted at the idea of giving them up. Congress, therefore, only interfered from time to time to prevent the two parties from coming to an open rupture. In the meanwhile the minds of the New Yorkers have been familiarizing to the idea of a separation, and it will not be long before they will consent to it.—ANSWERS TO M. DE MEUNIER. ix, 284. FORD ED., iv, 140. (P., 1786.) See OFFICES, UNCONSTITUTIONAL.

8787. VETERINARY COLLEGES, Advantages.—The advantages of the veterinary institution proposed, may perhaps be doubted. If it be problematical whether physicians prevent death where the disease, unaided, would have terminated fatally,—oftener than they produce it, where order would have been restored to the system by the process, if uninterrupted, provided by nature, and in the case of a man who can describe the seat of his disease, its character, progress, and often its cause, what might we expect in the case of the horse, mule, &c., yielding no sensible and certain indications of his disease? They have long had these institutions in Europe; has the world received as yet one iota of valuable information from them? If it has, it is unknown to me. At any rate, it may be doubted whether, where so many institutions of obvious utility are yet wanting, we should select this one to take the lead.—To JOEL BARLOW. v, 402. (W., 1808.)

8788. VETERINARY COLLEGES, Utility.—I know nothing of the veterinary institution of London * * *. I know well the Veterinary school of Paris, of long standing, and saw many of its publications during my residence there. They were classically written, announced a want of nothing but certainty as to their facts, which granted, the hypotheses were learned and plausible. The coach-horses of the rich of Paris were availed of the institution; but the farmers even of the neighborhood could not afford to call a veterinary doctor to their plough horses in the country, or to send them to a livery stable to be attended in the city. On the whole, I was not a convert to the utility of the Institution.—To DR. BENJAMIN RUSH. vi, 105. (M., 1813.)

8789. ———— ————. That there are certain diseases of the human body, so distinctly pronounced by well-articulated symptoms, and recurring so often, as not to be mistaken, wherein experience has proved that certain substances applied, will restore order, I cannot doubt. * * * But there are also a great mass of indistinct diseases, presenting themselves under no form clearly characterized, nor exactly recognized as having occurred before, and to which of course, the application of no particular substance can be known to have been made, nor its effect on the case experienced. These may be called unknown cases, and they may in time be lessened by the progress of observation and experiment. Observing that there are in the construction of the animal system some means provided unknown to us, which have a tendency to restore order, when disturbed by accident, called by physicians the *vis medicatrix naturæ*. I think it safer to trust to this power in the unknown cases, than to uncertain conjectures built on the ever-changing hypothetical systems of medicine. Now in the Veterinary department all are unknown cases. Man can tell his physician the seat of his pain, its nature, history, and sometimes its cause, and can follow his directions for the curative process; but the poor dumb horse cannot signify where his pain is, what it is, or when or whence it came, and resists all process for its cure. If in the case of man, then, the benefit of medical interference in such cases admits of question, what must it be in that of the horse? And to what narrow limits is the real importance of the veterinary art reduced?—To DR. BENJAMIN RUSH. vi, 105. (M., 1813.)

8790. VETO, Abuse of.—He (George III.) has endeavored to pervert the exercise of the kingly office in Virginia into a detestable and insupportable tyranny, by putting his negative on laws the most wholesome and necessary for the public good.—PROPOSED VA. CONSTITUTION. FORD ED., ii, 8. (June 1776.)

8791. VETO, By council.—The governor, two councillors of State, and a judge from each of the superior courts of chancery, common law, and admiralty, shall be a council to revise all bills which shall have passed both houses of Assembly, in which council the governor, when present, shall preside. Every bill, before it becomes a law, shall be represented to this council, who shall have a right to advise its rejection, returning the bill, with their advice and reasons in writing, to the house in which it originated, who shall proceed to reconsider the said bill. But if after such reconsideration, two-thirds of the house shall be of opinion that the bill should pass finally, they shall pass it and send it, with the advice and written reasons of the said Council of Revision, to the other house, wherein if two-thirds also shall be of opinion it should pass finally, it shall thereupon become law; otherwise it shall not.—PROPOSED VA. CONSTITUTION. viii, 451. FORD ED., iii, 330. (1783.)

8792. VETO, Congressional.—The negative, proposed to be given to Congress on all the acts of the several legislatures, is now, for the first time, suggested to my mind. _Primâ facie_ I do not like it. It fails in an essential character, that the hole and the patch should be commensurate. But this proposes to mend a small hole by covering the whole government. Not more than one out of one hundred State acts concerns the Confederacy. This proposition, then, in order to give them one degree of power, which they ought to have, gives them ninety-nine more which they ought not to have, upon a presumption that they will not exercise the ninety-nine. But upon every act, there will be a preliminary question, does this concern the Confederacy? And was there ever a proposition so plain as to pass Congress without a debate? Their decisions are almost always wise; they are like pure metal. But you know of how much dross this is the result.—To JAMES MADISON. ii, 152. FORD ED., iv, 390. (P., June 1787.)

8793. VETO, Denial of.—.The Administrator shall have no negative on the bills of the Legislature.—PROPOSED VA. CONSTITUTION. FORD ED., ii, 18. (June 1776.)

8794. VETO, Discretion in use of.—If the pro and con for and against a bill hang so even as to balance the President's judgment, a just respect for the wisdom of the Legislature would naturally decide the balance in favor of their opinion. It is chiefly for cases where they are clearly misled by error, ambition, or interest, that the Constitution has placed a check in the negative of the President.—NATIONAL BANK OPINION. vii, 560. FORD ED., v, 289. (1791.)

8795. VETO, Effects of non-use.—The non-user of his negative begins already to excite a belief that no President will ever

venture to use it; and has, consequently, begotten a desire to raise up barriers in the State legislatures against Congress, throwing off the control of the Constitution.— OPINION ON APPORTIONMENT BILL. vii, 601. FORD ED., v, 500. (1792.)

8796. VETO, Executive.—I like the negative given [in the Federal Constitution] to the Executive, with a third of either house; though I should have liked it better had the Judiciary been associated for that purpose, or invested with a similar and separate power.* —To JAMES MADISON. ii, 329. FORD ED., iv, 475. (P., 1787.)

8797. VETO, First Presidential.—He [President Washington] sent it [veto of the Apportionment bill] to the House of Representatives. A few of the hottest friends of the bill expressed passion but the majority were satisfied and both in and out of doors it gave pleasure to have at length an instance of the negative being exercised. —THE ANAS. ix, 115. (1792.)

8798. VETO, Inhuman.—He [George III.] has endeavored to pervert the exercise of the kingly office in Virginia into a detestable and insupportable tyranny * * * by prompting our negroes to rise in arms among us; those very negroes whom, by an inhuman use of his negative, he had refused us permission to exclude by law.—PROPOSED VA. CONSTITUTION. FORD ED., ii, 11. (June 1776.)

8799. VETO, King's.—By the Constitution of Great Britain, as well as of the several American States, his Majesty possesses the power of refusing to pass into a law, any bill which has already passed the other two branches of the legislature. His Majesty, however, and his ancestors, conscious of the impropriety of opposing their single opinion to the united wisdom of two houses of Parliament, while their proceedings were unbiased by interested principles, for several ages past have modestly declined the exercise of this power, in that part of his empire called Great Britain. But by change of circumstances, other principles than those of justice simply, have obtained an influence on their determinations. The addition of new States to the British Empire has produced an addition of new, and, sometimes, opposite interests. It is now, therefore, the great office of his Majesty, to resume the exercise of his negative power, and to prevent the passage of laws by any one legislature of the Empire, which might bear injuriously on the rights and interests of another. Yet this will not excuse the wanton exercise of this power, which we have seen his Majesty practice on the laws of the American legislatures. For the most trifling reasons, and, sometimes for

* This extract from the Ford edition is in Jefferson's own words. In the Congress edition, they are as follows: "I like the negative given to the Executive, conjointly with a third of either house; though I should have liked it better had the judiciary been associated for that purpose, or invested separately with a similar power."—EDITOR.

† This was the first instance of the exercise of the veto power under the Constitution.—EDITOR.

no conceivable reason at all, his Majesty has rejected laws of the most salutary tendency. The abolition of domestic slavery is the great object of desire* in those Colonies, where it was, unhappily, introduced in their infant state. But previous to the enfranchisement of the slaves we have, it is necessary to exclude all further importations from Africa. Yet our repeated attempts to effect this. by prohibitions, and by imposing duties which might amount to a prohibition, have been hitherto defeated by his Majesty's negative: Thus preferring the immediate advantages of a few British corsairs to the lasting interests of the American States, and to the rights of human nature, deeply wounded by this infamous practice. Nay, the single interposition of an interested individual against a law was scarcely ever known to fail of success, though, in the opposite scale were placed the interests of a whole country. This is so shameful an abuse of a power, trusted with his Majesty for other purposes, as if not reformed, would call for some legal restrictions.—RIGHTS OF BRITISH AMERICA. i, 134. FORD ED., i, 439. (1774.)

8800. —— ——. The royal negative closed the last door [in the Virginia House of Burgesses] to every hope of amelioration. [Regarding Slavery.]—AUTOBIOGRAPHY. i, 3. FORD ED., i, 5. (1821.)

8801. VETO, Prostituted.—Determined to keep open a market where MEN should be bought and sold, he has prostituted his negative for suppressing every legislative attempt to prohibit or to restrain this execrable commerce.†—DECLARATION OF INDEPENDENCE AS DRAWN BY JEFFERSON.

8802. VETO, Protection by.—The negative of the President is the shield provided by the Constitution to protect against the invasions of the Legislature: 1. The right of the Executive. 2. Of the Judiciary. 3. Of the States and State Legislatures.—NATIONAL BANK OPINION. vii, 560. FORD ED., v, 289. (1791.)

8803. VETO, Qualified.—I approved, from the first moment, of the great mass of what is in the new Constitution; * * * the qualified negative on laws given to the Executive, which, however, I should have liked better if associated with the judiciary also, as in New York.—To F. HOPKINSON. ii, 586. FORD ED., v, 76. (P., March 1789.)

8804. VETO, Satisfactory use.—The negative of the President can never be used more pleasingly to the public than in the protection of the Constitution.—OPINION ON APPORTIONMENT BILL. vii, 601. FORD ED., v, 500. (1792.)

* " In asserting," says Parton in his *Life of Jefferson*, "that the great object of desire in the Colonies was the abolition of slavery, he expressed rather the feeling of his own set,—the educated and high-minded young Whigs of the Southern Colonies, than the sentiments of the great body of the slaveholders. He could boast that the first act of his own life had been an attempt in that direction."—EDITOR.
† Struck out by Congress.—EDITOR.

8805. VETO, Suspensive.—The National Assembly [of France] have determined that the King shall have a *suspensive and iterative* veto; that is, after negativing a law, it cannot be presented again till after a new election. If he negatives it then, it cannot be presented a third time till after another new election. If it be then presented, he is obliged to pass it. This is perhaps justly considered as a more useful negative than an absolute one, which a King would be afraid to use.—To JOHN JAY. iii, 115. (P., 1789.)

8806. VICE, Knowledge and.—Although I do not, with some enthusiasts, believe that the human condition will ever advance to such a state of perfection as that there shall no longer be pain or vice in the world, yet I believe it susceptible of much improvement, and most of all, in matters of government and religion; and that the diffusion of knowledge among the people is to be the instrument by which it is to be effected.—To DUPONT DE NEMOURS. vi, 592. FORD ED., x, 25. (P.F., 1816.)

8807. VICE-PRESIDENCY, Acceptance of.—The idea that I would accept the office of President, but not that of Vice-President of the United States, had not its origin with me. I never thought of questioning the free exercise of the right of my fellow citizens to marshal those whom they call into their service according to their fitness, nor ever presumed that they were not the best judges of that. Had I indulged a wish in what manner they should dispose of me, it would precisely have coincided with what they have done.—To JAMES SULLIVAN. iv, 168. FORD ED., vii, 116. (M., Feb. 9, 1797.)

8808. VICE-PRESIDENCY, Candidates for.—I presume there will not be a vote against General Washington [for President] in the United States. It is more doubtful who will be Vice-President. The age of Dr. Franklin, and the doubt whether he would accept, are the only circumstances that admit a question, but that he would be the man. After these two characters of first magnitude, there are so many which present themselves equally, on the second line, that we cannot see which of them will be singled out. John Adams, Hancock, Jay, Madison, Rutledge, will all be voted for.—To WILLIAM CARMICHAEL. ii, 465. (P., Aug. 1788.)

8809. VICE-PRESIDENCY, Ceremony and.—I hope I shall be made a part of no ceremony whatever. I shall escape into the city as covertly as possible. If Governor Mifflin should show any symptoms of ceremony, pray contrive to parry them.—To JAMES MADISON. iv, 167. FORD ED., vii, 116. (M., Jan. 1797.)

8810. VICE-PRESIDENCY, Duties of.—As to duty. the Constitution will know me only as the member of the Legislative body; and its principle is. that of a separation of Legislative, Executive and Judiciary functions, except in cases specified. If this principle be not expressed in direct terms, it is clearly the spirit of the Constitution and it ought to be so commented and acted on by every friend of free government.—To JAMES MADISON. iv, 161. FORD ED., vii, 108. (M., Jan. 1797.)

8811. VICE-PRESIDENCY, Easy and honorable.—The second office of the* government is honorable and easy; the first is but a splendid misery.—To ELBRIDGE GERRY. iv, 171. FORD ED., vii, 120. (Pa., 1797.)

8812. VICE-PRESIDENCY, Jefferson and.—I was not aware of any necessity of going on to Philadelphia immediately, yet I had determined to do it, as a mark of respect to the public, and to do away the doubts which have spread, that I should consider the second office as beneath my acceptance.—To JAMES MADISON. iv, 161. FORD ED., vii, 107. (M., Jan. 1797.)

8813. —— ——. I know not from what source an idea has spread itself * * * that I would accept the office of President of the United States, but not of Vice-President. When I retired from the office I last held, no man in the Union less expected than I did ever to have come forward again; and, whatever has been insinuated to the contrary, to no man in the Union was the share which my name bore in the late contest more unexpected than it was to me. If I had contemplated the thing beforehand, and suffered my will to enter into action at all on it, it would have been in a direction exactly the reverse of what has been imputed to me; but I had no right to a will on the subject, much less to control that of the people of the United States in arranging us according to our capacities. Least of all could I have any feelings which would revolt at taking a station secondary to Mr. Adams. I have been secondary to him in every situation in which we ever acted together in public life for twenty years past. A contrary position would have been the novelty, and his the right of revolting at it. Be assured, then, that if I had had a fibre in my composition still looking after public office, it would have been gratified precisely by the very call you are pleased to announce to me, and no other.—To JOHN LANGDON. iv, 163. FORD ED., vii, 111. (M., Jan. 1797.)

8814. —— ——. Since I am called out, an object of great anxiety to me is that those with whom I am to act, shutting their minds to the unfounded abuse of which I have been the subject, will view me with the same candor with which I shall certainly act.—To JOHN LANGDON. iv, 164. FORD ED., vii, 112. (M., Jan. 1797.)

8815. VICE-PRESIDENCY, Notification of election.—I suppose that the choice of Vice-President has fallen on me * * * I believe it belongs to the Senate to notify the Vice-President of his election. I recollect to have heard, that on the first election of President and Vice-President, gentlemen of considerable office were sent to notify the parties chosen. But this was the inauguration

*" This " government in FORD EDITION.—EDITOR

of our new government, and ought not to be drawn into example. At the second election, both gentlemen were on the spot and needed no messengers. On the present occasion, the President will be on the spot, so that what is now to be done respects myself alone; and considering that the season of notification will always present one difficulty, that the distance in the present case adds a second, not inconsiderable, and which may in future happen to be sometimes much more considerable, I hope the Senate will adopt that method of notification, which will always be least troublesome and most certain. The channel of the post is certainly the least troublesome, is the most rapid, and, considering also that it may be sent by duplicates and triplicates, is unquestionably the most certain. Enclosed to the postmaster at Charlottesville, with an order to send it by express, no hazard can endanger the notification. Apprehending, that should there be a difference of opinion on this subject in the Senate, my ideas of self-respect might be supposed by some to require something more formal and inconvenient, I beg leave to avail myself of your friendship to declare, if a different proposition should make it necessary, that I consider the channel of the post-office as the most eligible in every respect, and that it is to me the most desirable; which I take the liberty of expressing, not with a view of encroaching on the respect due to that discretion which the Senate have a right to exercise on the occasion, but to render them the more free in the exercise of it, by taking off whatsoever weight the supposition of a contrary desire in me might have on the mind of any member.—To HENRY TAZEWELL. iv, 160. FORD ED., vii, 106. (M., Jan. 1797.)

8816. VICE-PRESIDENCY, Oath of office.—I have turned to the Constitution and laws, and find nothing to warrant the opinion that I might not have been qualified here [Monticello] or wherever else I could meet with a Senator; any member of that body being authorized to administer the oath, without being confined to time or place, and consequently to make a record of it, and to deposit it with the records of the Senate. However, I shall come on, on the principle which had first determined me—respect to the public.—To JAMES MADISON. iv, 167. FORD ED., vii, 116. (M., 1797.)

8817. VICE-PRESIDENCY, Preference for.—It seems possible * * * that you may see me in Philadelphia about the beginning of March, exactly in that character which, if I were to reappear at Philadelphia, I would prefer to all others; for I change the sentiment of Clorinda to "L'alte temo, l'humile non sdegno".—To MR. VOLNEY. iv, 158. (M., Jan. 1797.)

8818. VICE-PRESIDENCY, Pride and. —As to the second [office], it is the only office in the world about which I am unable to decide in my own mind whether I had rather have it, or not have it. Pride does not enter into the estimate; for I think with the

Romans that the general of to-day should be a soldier to-morrow if necessary. I can particularly have no feelings which would revolt at a secondary position to Mr. Adams. I am his junior in life, was his junior in Congress, his junior in the diplomatic line, his junior lately in the civil government.—To JAMES MADISON. iv, 155. FORD ED., vii, 98. (M., Jan. 1797.)

8819. VICE-PRESIDENCY, Tranquil and unoffending.—I thank you for your congratulations on the public call on me to undertake the second office in the United States, but still more for the justice you do me in viewing as I do the *escape* from the first. I have no wish again to meddle in public affairs, being happier at home than I can be anywhere else. Still less do I wish to engage in an office where it would be impossible to satisfy either friends or foes, and least of all at a moment when the storm is about to burst, which has been conjuring up for four years past. If I am to act, however, a more tranquil and unoffending station could not have been found for me, nor one so analogous to the dispositions of my mind. It will give me philosophical evenings in the winter, and rural days in summer.—To DR. BENJAMIN RUSH. iv, 165. FORD ED., vii, 113. (M., Jan. 1797.)

8820. ——— ———. I am so much attached to my domestic situation, that I would not have wished to leave it at all. However, if I am to be called from it, the shortest absences and most tranquil station suit me best. —To JAMES SULLIVAN. iv, 168. FORD ED., vii, 117. (M., 1797.)

8821. VIGILANCE, Eye of.—Be not weary of well doing. Let the eye of vigilance never be closed.—To SPENCER ROANE. vii, 212. FORD ED., x, 189. (M., 1821.)

8822. VINCENNES, Danger from Indians.—I have the pleasure to enclose you the particulars of Colonel Clark's success against Vincennes. * * * I fear it will be impossible for Colonel Clark to be so strengthened as to enable him to do what he desires. Indeed, the express who brought this letter, gives us reason to fear Vincennes is in danger from a large body of Indians collected to attack it, and said, when he came from Kaskaskias, to be within thirty leagues of the place.—To GENERAL WASHINGTON. i, 221. FORD ED., ii, 240. (Wg., 1779.)

8823. VINCENNES, Loyalty of.—I have ever considered them as sober, honest, and orderly citizens, submissive to the laws, and faithful to the nation of which they are a part. And should occasion arise of proving their fidelity in the cause of their country, I count on their aid with as perfect assurance as on that of any other part of the United States.—To WILLIAM M'INTOSH. v, 242. (W., 1808.)

8824. VINDICATION, Appeal for.—I should have retired at the end of the first four years, but that the immense load of tory calumnies which have been manufactured respecting me, and have filled the European market, have obliged me to appeal once more to my country for justification. I have no fear but that I shall receive honorable testimony by their verdict on these calumnies. At the end of the next four years I shall certainly retire. Age, inclination, and principle all dictate this.—To PHILIP MAZZEI. iv, 553. D. L. J., 310. (July 1804.)

8825. VINDICATION, Seeking.—A desire to leave public office, with a reputation not more blotted than it has deserved, will oblige me to emerge at the next session of our Assembly and, perhaps, to accept of a seat in it. But as I go with a single object, I shall withdraw when that shall be accomplished.— To EDMUND RANDOLPH. i, 313. FORD ED., iii, 50. (M., 1781.)

8826. VINE, Cultivation of.—The vine is the parent of misery. Those who cultivate it are always poor, and he who would employ himself with us in the culture of corn, cotton, &c., can procure, in exchange for them, much more wine, and better, than he could raise by its direct culture.—To GEORGE WYTHE. ii, 266. FORD ED., iv, 443. (P., 1787.) See WINES.

8827. VIRGINIA, American Revolution and.—An inquiry into the exertions of Virginia in the common cause during the period of her exemption from military invasion would be proper for the patriotic historian, because her character has been very unjustly impeached by the writers of other States, as having used no equal exertions at that time. I know it to be false; because having all that time been a member of the Legislature, I know that our whole occupation was in straining the resources of the State to the utmost, to furnish men, money, provisions and other necessaries to the common cause. The proofs of this will be found in the journals and acts of the Legislature, in executive proceedings and papers, and in the auditor's accounts. Not that Virginia furnished her quota of *requisitions* of either men or money; but that she was always above par, in what was *actually* furnished by the other States.—To SKELTON JONES. v, 461. (M., 1809.)

8828. VIRGINIA, British invasion.— On the 31st of December, a letter from a private gentleman to General Nelson came to my hands, notifying, that in the morning of the preceding day, twenty-seven sail of vessels had entered the capes; and from the tenor of the letter we had reason to expect, within a few hours, further intelligence; whether they were friends or foes, their force and other circumstances. We immediately dispatched General Nelson to the lower country, with powers to call on the militia in that quarter, or to act otherwise as exigencies should require; but waited further intelligence before we would call for militia from the middle or upper country. No further intelligence came until the 2d instant, when the former was confirmed; it was ascertained they had advanced up James River in Warrasqueak bay. All arrangements were immediately taken for calling in a sufficient body of militia for opposition. In the night of the 3d, we received advice that they were at anchor opposite Jamestown. We then supposed Williamsburg to be their object. The wind, however, which had hitherto been unfavorable, shifted fair, and the tide being also in their favor, they ascended the river to Kennon's that evening and, with the next tide, came up to Westover, having on their way taken possession of some works we had at Hood's by which two or three of their vessels received some damage but which were of necessity abandoned by the small garrison of fifty men placed there, on the enemy's landing to invest the works. Intelligence of their having quitted the station at Jamestown, from which we supposed they meant to land for Williamsburg, and of their having got in the evening to Kennon's, reached us the next morning at five o'clock, and was the first indication of their meaning to penetrate towards this place (Richmond) or Petersburg. As the orders for drawing militia here had been given but two days, no opposition was in readiness. Every effort was therefore necessary, to withdraw the arms and other military stores, records, &c., from this place. Every effort was, accordingly, exerted to convey them to the foundry five miles, and to a laboratory six miles, above this place, till about sunset of that day, when we learned the enemy had come to an anchor at Westover that morning. We then knew that this, and not Petersburg was their object, and began to carry across the river everything remaining here, and to remove what had been transported to the foundry and laboratory to Westham, the nearest crossing, seven miles above this place, which operation was continued till they had approached very near. They marched from Westover at two o'clock in the afternoon of the 4th, and entered Richmond at one o'clock in the afternoon of the 5th. A regiment of infantry and about thirty horse continued on, without halting, to the foundry. They burned that, the boring mill, the magazine and two other houses, and proceeded to Westham: but nothing being in their power there, they retired to Richmond. The next morning, they burned some buildings of public and private property, with what stores remained in them, destroyed a great quantity of private stores and, about twelve o'clock, retired towards Westover, where they encamped within the neck the next day. The loss sustained is not yet accurately known. As far as I have been able to discover, it consisted, at this place, of about three hundred muskets, some soldiers' clothing to a small amount, some quartermaster's stores, of which one hundred and twenty sides of leather was the principal article, part of the artificer's tools, and three wagons. Besides which, five brass four pounders which we had sunk in the river, were discovered to them, raised and carried off. At the foundry we lost the greater part of the papers belonging to the Auditor's office, and of the books and papers of the Council office. About five or six tons of powder, as we conjecture, was thrown into the canal, of which there will be a considerable saving by remanufacturing it. The roof of the foundry was burned, but the stacks of chimneys and furnaces not at all injured. The boring mill was consumed. Within less than forty-eight hours from the time of their landing, and nineteen from our knowing their destination, they had penetrated thirty-three miles, done the whole injury, and retired.—To GENERAL WASHINGTON. i, 282. FORD ED., ii, 405. (M., 1809.)

8829. —— ——. Their numbers, from the best intelligence I have had, are about fifteen hundred infantry; and, as to their cavalry, accounts vary from fifty to one hundred and twenty; the whole commanded by the parricide Arnold. Our militia, dispersed over a large tract of country, can be called in but slowly. On the day the enemy advanced to this place, two hundred only were embodied. They were of this town and its neighborhood and were too few to do anything. At this time they are assembled in pretty considerable numbers on the south side of James River, but are not yet brought to a point. On the north side are two or three small bodies, amounting in the whole,

to about nine hundred men. The enemy were, at four o'clock yesterday evening, still remaining in their encampment at Westover and Berkeley Neck. In the meanwhile, Baron Steuben, a zealous friend, has descended from the dignity of his proper command to direct our smallest movements. His vigilance has in a great measure supplied the want of force in preventing the enemy from crossing the river, which might have been very fatal. He has been assiduously employed in preparing equipments for the militia as they should assemble, pointing them to a proper object, and other offices of a good commander. Should they loiter a little longer, and he be able to have a sufficient force, I still flatter myself they will not escape with total impunity. To what place they will point their next exertions, we cannot even conjecture. The whole country on the tide waters and some distance from them is equally open to similar insult.—To GENERAL WASHINGTON. i, 284. FORD ED., ii, 408. (January 1781.)

8830. VIRGINIA, Conventions in.— These were at first chosen anew for every particular session. But in March, 1775, they recommended to the people to choose a convention which should continue in office a year. This was done, accordingly, in April, 1775, and in July following that convention passed an ordinance for the election of delegates in the month of April annually. It is well known, that in July, 1775, a separation from Great Britain and establishment of republican government, had never yet entered into any person's mind. A convention, therefore, chosen under that ordinance, cannot be said to have been chosen for the purposes which certainly did not exist in the minds of those who passed it. Under this ordinance, at the annual election in April, 1776, a convention for the year was chosen. Independence, and the establishment of a new form of government, were not even the objects of the people at large. One extract from the pamphlet called *Common Sense* had appeared in the Virginia papers in February, and copies of the pamphlet itself had got in a few hands. But the idea had not been opened to the mass of the people in April, much less can it be said that they had made up their minds in its favor. So that the electors of April, 1776, no more than the legislators of July, 1775, not thinking of independence and a permanent republic, could not mean to vest in these delegates powers of establishing them, or any authorities other than those of the ordinary legislature. So far as a temporary organization of government was necessary to render our opposition energetic, so far their organization was valid. But they received in their creation no powers but what were given to every legislature before and since. They could not, therefore, pass an act transcendent to the powers of other legislatures.—NOTES ON VIRGINIA. viii, 363. FORD ED., iii, 225. (1782.) See VIRGINIA CONSTITUTION, REPEALABILITY.

8831. VIRGINIA, Division of counties. —In what terms reconcilable to Majesty, and at the same time to truth, shall we speak of a late instruction to the Governor of the Colony of Virginia, by which he is forbidden to assent to any law for the division of a county, unless the new county will consent to have no representative in Assembly? That Colony has as yet affixed no boundary to the westward. Their western counties, therefore, are of an indefinite extent. Some of them are actually seated many hundred miles from their eastern limits. Is it possible, then, that his Majesty can have bestowed a single thought on the situation of those people, who, in order to obtain justice for injuries, however great or small, must, by the laws of that Colony, attend their county court, at such a distance, with all their witnesses, monthly, till their litigation be determined?—RIGHTS OF BRITISH AMERICA. i, 136. FORD ED., i, 441. (1774.)

8832. VIRGINIA, Love for.—My native State is endeared to me by every tie which can attach the human heart.—R. TO A. VIRGINIA ASSEMBLY. vi'i, 148. (1809.)

8833. VIRGINIA, Political opposition in.—Better that any one [of the other States] take the lead [against consolidation] than Virginia, where opposition is considered as commonplace, and a mere matter of form and habit.—To C. W. GOOCH. vii, 430. (M., 1826.)

8834. VIRGINIA CONSTITUTION, Amendments to.—That it is really important to provide a constitution for our State cannot be doubted; as little can it be doubted that the ordinance called by that name has important defects. But before we attempt it, we should endeavor to be as certain as is practicable that in the attempt we should not make bad worse. I have understood that Mr. Henry has always been opposed to this undertaking; and I confess that I consider his talents and influence such as that, were it decided that we should call a convention for the purpose of amending, I should fear he might induce that convention either to fix the thing as at present, or change it for the worse. Would it not, therefore, be well that means should be adopted for coming at his ideas of the changes he would agree to, and for communicating to him those which we should propose? Perhaps he might find ours not so distant from his, but that some mutual sacrifices might bring them together. I shall hazard my own ideas to you as hastily as my business obliges me. I wish to preserve the line drawn by the Federal Constitution between the General and particular governments as it stands at present, and to take every prudent means of preventing either from stepping over it. Though the experiment has not yet had a long enough course to show us from which quarter encroachments are most to be feared, yet it is easy to foresee, from the nature of things, that the encroachments of the State governments will tend to an excess of liberty which will correct itself (as in the late instance), while those of the General Government will tend to monarchy, which will fortify itself from day to day, instead of working its own cure, as all experience shows. I would rather be exposed to the inconveniences attending too much liberty than those attending too small a degree of it. Then it is important to strengthen the State governments; and as this cannot be done by any change in the Federal Constitution (for the preservation of that is all we need contend for), it must be done by the States themselves, erecting such barriers at the constitutional line as cannot be surmounted either by themselves or by the General Government. The only barrier in their power is a wise government. A weak one will lose ground in every contest. To obtain a wise and an able

government, I consider the following changes as important. Render the Legislature a desirable station by lessening the number of representatives (say to 100) and lengthening somewhat their term, and proportion them equally among the electors; adopt, also, a better mode of appointing senators. Render the Executive a more desirable post to men of abilities by making it more independent of the Legislature; to wit, let him be chosen by other electors, for a longer time. and ineligible forever after. Responsibility is a tremendous engine in a free government. Let him feel the whole weight of it then, by taking away the shelter of his executive council. Experience both ways has already established the superiority of this measure. Render the Judiciary respectable by every possible means, to wit, firm tenure in office, competent salaries, and reduction of their numbers. Men of high learning and abilities are few in every country; and by taking in those who are not so, the able part of the body have their hands tied by the unable. This branch of the government will have the weight of the conflict on their hands, because they will be the last appeal of reason. These are my general ideas of amendments; but, preserving the ends, I should be flexible and conciliatory as to the means.—To ARCHIBALD STUART. iii, 314. FORD ED., v, 408. (Pa., Dec. 1791.)

8835. VIRGINIA CONSTITUTION, Bill of rights.—The fact is unquestionable that the Bill of Rights, and the Constitution of Virginia, were originally drawn by George Mason, one of our really great men, and of the first order of greatness.—To AUGUSTUS B. WOODWARD. vii, 405. FORD ED., x, 341. (M., 1825.)

8836. VIRGINIA CONSTITUTION, Equal rights and.—The basis of our [Virginia] Constitution is in opposition to the principle of equal political rights, refusing to all but freeholders any participation in the natural right of self-government. It is believed, for example, that a very great majority of the militia, on whom the burthen of military duty was imposed in the late war, were unrepresented in the legislature, which imposed this burthen on them. However nature may by mental or physical disqualifications have marked infants and the weaker sex for the protection, rather than the direction of government, yet among the men who either pay or fight for their country, no line of right can be drawn. The exclusion of a majority of our freemen from the right of representation is merely arbitrary, and an usurpation of the minority over the majority; for it is believed that the non-freeholders compose the majority of our free and adult male citizens. And even among our citizens who participate in the representative privilege, the equality of political right is entirely prostrated by our constitution. Upon which principle of right or reason can any one justify the giving to every citizen of Warwick as much weight in the government as to twenty-two equal citizens in Loudon and similar inequalities among the other counties? If these fundamental principles are of no importance in actual government, then no principles are important.—To John Hambden Pleasants. vii, 345. Ford ed., x, 303. (M., 1824.)

8837. VIRGINIA CONSTITUTION, Improvements on.—The other States, who successively formed constitutions for themselves also, had the benefit of our (Virginia's) outline, and have made on it, doubtless, successive improvements. One in the very outset, and which has been adopted in every subsequent constitution, was to lay its foundation in the authority of the nation. To our convention no special authority had been delegated by the people to form a permanent Constitution, over which their successors in legislation should have no powers of alteration. They had been elected for the ordinary purposes of legislation only, and at a time when the establishment of a new government had not been proposed or contemplated. Although, therefore, they gave to this act the title of a Constitution, yet it could be no more than an act of legislation subject, as their other acts were, to alteration by their successors. It has been said, indeed, that the acquiescence of the people supplied the want of original power. But it is a dangerous lesson to say to them, " whenever your functionaries exercise unlawful authority over you, if you do not go into actual resistance, it will be deemed acquiescence and confirmation". How long had we acquiesced under usurpations of the British parliament? Had that confirmed them in right, and made our revolution a wrong? Besides, no authority has yet decided whether this resistance must be instantaneous; when the right to resist ceases, or whether it has yet ceased? Of the twenty-four States now organized, twenty-three have disapproved our doctrine and example, and have deemed the authority of their people a necessary foundation for a constitution.—To John Hambden Pleasants. vii, 344. Ford ed., x, 302. (M., April 1824.)

8838. VIRGINIA CONSTITUTION, Preamble to.—The history of the Preamble to the [first] Constitution of Virginia is this: I was then at Philadelphia with Congress; and knowing that the convention of Virginia was engaged in forming a plan of government, I turned my mind to the same subject, and drew a sketch or outline of a Constitution, with a preamble, which I sent to Mr. Pendleton, president of the convention, on the mere possibility that it might suggest something worth incorporation into that before the convention. He informed me afterwards by letter, that he received it on the day on which the committee of the whole had reported to the house the plan they had agreed to; that that had been so long in hand, so disputed inch by inch, and the subject of so much altercation and debate; that they were worried with the contention it had produced, and could not from mere lassitude, have been

induced to open the instrument again; but that, being pleased with the preamble to mine, they adopted it in the house, by way of amendment to the report of the committee; and thus my preamble became tacked to the work of George Mason. The Constitution, with the preamble, was passed on the 29th of June, and the Committee of Congress had only the day before that reported to that body the draught of the Declaration of Independence. The fact is, that that preamble was prior in composition to the Declaration; and both having the same object, of justifying our separation from Great Britain, they used necessarily the same materials of justification, and hence their similitude.—To A. B. Woodward. vii, 405. Ford ed., x, 341. (M., 1825.)

8839. VIRGINIA CONSTITUTION, Repealability of.—If the present Assembly pass an act, and declare it shall be irrevocable by subsequent assemblies, the declaration is merely void, and the act repealable, as other acts are. So far, and no farther authorized, they [the first Virginia convention] organized the government by the ordinance entitled a Constitution or form of government. It pretends to no higher authority than the other ordinances of the same session; it does not say that it shall be perpetual; that it shall be unalterable by other legislatures; that it shall be transcendent above the powers of those who they knew would have equal power with themselves. Not only the silence of the instrument is a proof they thought it would be alterable, but their own practice also; for this very convention, meeting as a House of Delegates in General Assembly with the Senate in the autumn of that year, passed acts of assembly in contradiction to their ordinance of government; and every assembly from that time to this has done the same. I am safe, therefore, in the position that the Constitution itself is alterable by the ordinary legislature. Though this opinion seems founded on the first elements of common sense, yet is the contrary maintained by some persons. First, because, say they, the conventions were vested with every power necessary to make effectual opposition to Great Britain. But to complete this argument, they must go on, and say further, that effectual opposition could not be made to Great Britain without establishing a form of government perpetual and unalterable by the Legislature; which is not true. An opposition which at some time or other was to come to an end, could not need a perpetual constitution to carry it on; and a government amendable as its defects should be discovered, was as likely to make effectual resistance, as one that should be unalterably wrong. Besides, the assemblies were as much vested with all powers requisite for resistance as the Conventions were. If, therefore, these powers included that of modelling the form of government in the one case, they did so in the other. The assemblies then as well as the conventions may model the government; that is, they may alter the ordinance of government. Second, they urge, that if the convention had meant that this instrument should be alterable, as their other ordinances were, they would have called it an ordinance; but they have called it a *constitution,* which, *ex vi termini,* means " an act above the power of the ordinary legislature." I answer that *constitutio, constitutum, statutum, lex,* are convertible terms. * * * Thirdly. But, say they, the people have acquiesced, and this has given it an authority superior to the laws. It is true that the people did not rebel against it; and was that a time for the people to rise in rebellion? Should a prudent acquiescence, at a critical time, be construed into a confirmation of every illegal thing done during that period? Besides, why should they rebel? At an annual election they had chosen delegates for the year, to exercise the ordinary powers of legislation, and to manage the great contest in which they were engaged. These delegates thought the contest would be best managed by an organized government. They, therefore, among others, passed an ordinance of government. They did not presume to call it perpetual and unalterable. They well knew they had no power to make it so; that our choice of them had been for no such purpose, and at a time when we could have no such purpose in contemplation. Had an unalterable form of government been meditated, perhaps we should have chosen a different set of people. There was no cause, then, for the people to rise in rebellion. But to what dangerous lengths will this argument lead? Did the acquiescence of the Colonies under the various acts of power exercised by Great Britain in our infant state, confirm these acts, and so far invest them with the authority of the people as to render them unalterable, and our present resistance wrong? On every unauthoritative exercise of power by the legislature must the people rise in rebellion, or their silence be construed into a surrender of that power to them? If so, how many rebellions should we have had already? One certainly for every session of assembly. The other States in the Union have been of opinion that to render a form of government unalterable by ordinary acts of Assembly, the people must delegate persons with special powers. They have accordingly chosen special conventions to form and fix their governments. The individuals then who maintain the contrary opinion in this country, should have the modesty to suppose it possible that they may be wrong, and the rest of America right. But if there be only a possibility of their being wrong, if only a plausible doubt remains of the validity of the ordinance of government, is it not better to remove that doubt by placing it on a bottom which none will dispute? If they be right we shall only have the unnecessary trouble of meeting once in convention. If they be wrong, they expose us to the hazard of having no fundamental rights at all. True it is, this is no time for deliberating on forms of government. While an enemy is within our bowels, the first object is to expel him. But when this shall be done, when peace shall be established, and leisure given us for intrenching

within good forms the rights for which we have bled, let no man be found indolent enough to decline a little more trouble for placing them beyond the reach of question. —Notes on Virginia. viii, 364. Ford ed., iii, 226. (1782.) See Virginia, Conventions.

8840. VIRGINIA CONSTITUTION, Representation under.—The first Constitution [of Virginia] was formed when we were new and inexperienced in the science of government. It was the first, too, which was formed in the whole United States. No wonder, then, that time and trial have discovered very capital defects in it. The majority of the men in the State, who pay and fight for its support, are unrepresented in the Legislature, the roll of freeholders entitled to vote, not including generally the half of those on the roll of the militia, or of the tax-gatherers. Among those who share the representation, the shares are very unequal. Thus the county of Warwick, with only one hundred fighting men, has an equal representation with the county of Loudon, which has one thousand seven hundred and forty-six. So that every man in Warwick has as much influence as seventeen men in Loudon.—Notes on Virginia. viii, 359. Ford ed., iii, 222. (1782.)

8841. VIRGINIA CONSTITUTION, Republican heresies in.—Inequality of representation in both houses of our Legislature, is not the only republican heresy in this first essay of our revolutionary patriots at forming a constitution. For let it be agreed that a government is republican in proportion as every member composing it has his equal voice in the direction of its concerns (not indeed in person, which would be impracticable beyond the limits of a city, or a small township, but) by representatives chosen by himself, and responsible to him at short periods, and let us bring to the test of this canon every branch of our Constitution. In the Legislature, the House of Representatives is chosen by less than half the people, and not at all in proportion to those who do choose. The Senate are still more disproportionate, and for long terms of irresponsibility. In the Executive, the Governor is entirely independent of the choice of the people, and of their control; his Council equally so, and at best but a fifth wheel to a wagon. In the Judiciary, the judges of the highest courts are dependent on none but themselves. In England, where judges were named and removable at the will of an hereditary executive, from which branch most misrule was feared, and has flowed, it was a great point gained, by fixing them for life, to make them independent of that executive. But in a government founded on the public will, this principle operates in an opposite direction, and against that will. There, too, they are still removable on a concurrence of the executive and legislative branches. But we have made them independent of the nation itself. They are irremovable, but by their own body, for any depravities of conduct, and even by their own body for the imbecilities of dotage. The justices of the inferior courts are self-chosen, are for life, and perpetuate their own body in succession forever, so that a faction once possessing themselves of the bench of a county, can never be broken up, but hold their county in chains, forever indissoluble. Yet these justices are the real executive as well as judiciary, in all our minor and most ordinary concerns. They tax us at will; fill the office of sheriff, the most important of all the executive officers of the county; name nearly all our military leaders, which leaders, once named, are removable but by themselves. The juries, our judges of all fact, and of law when they choose it, are not selected by the people, nor amenable to them. They are chosen by an officer named by the court and executive. Chosen, did I say? Picked up by the sheriff from the loungers of the court yard, after everything respectable has retired from it. Where, then, is our republicanism to be found? Not in our Constitution certainly, but merely in the spirit of our people. That would oblige even a despot to govern us republicanly. Owing to this spirit, and to nothing in the form of our Constitution, all things have gone well. But this fact, so triumphantly misquoted by the enemies of reformation, is not the fruit of our Constitution, but has prevailed in spite of it. Our functionaries have done well, because generally honest men. If any were not so, they feared to show it.—To SAMUEL KERCHIVAL. vii, 10. FORD ED., x, 38. (M., 1816.)

8842. VIRGINIA CONSTITUTION, Revision of.—Let us [Virginia] provide in our Constitution for its revision at stated periods. What these periods should be, nature herself indicates. By the European tables of mortality, of the adults living at any one moment of time, a majority will be dead in about nineteen years. At the end of that period, then, a new majority is come into place; or, in other words, a new generation. Each generation is as independent of the one preceding, as that was of all which had gone before. It has, then, like them, a right to choose for itself the form of government it believes most promotive of its own happiness; consequently, to accommodate to the circumstances in which it finds itself, that received from its predecessors; and it is for the peace and good of mankind, that a solemn opportunity of doing this every nineteen or twenty years, should be provided by the constitution; so that it may be handed on, with periodical repairs, from generation to generation, to the end of time, if anything human can so long endure.—To SAMUEL KERCHIVAL. vii, 15. FORD ED., x, 42. (M., 1816.)

8843. VIRGINIA CONSTITUTION, War power.—The power of declaring war and concluding peace, of contracting alliances, of issuing letters of marque and reprisal, of raising and introducing armed forces, of building armed vessels, forts, or strongholds, of coining money or regulating its value, of regulating weights and measures, we leave to

be exercised under the authority of the Confederation; but in all cases respecting them which are out of the said Confederation, they shall be exercised by the Governor, under the regulation of such laws as the Legislature may think it expedient to pass.—PROPOSED CONSTITUTION FOR VIRGINIA. viii, 446. FORD ED., iii, 326. (1783.)

8844. VIRTUE, Agriculture and.—I think our governments will remain virtuous for many centuries; as long as they are chiefly agricultural; and this will be as long as there shall be vacant lands in any part of America.*—To JAMES MADISON. FORD ED., iv, 479 (P., Dec. 1787.)

8845. ———. That there is much vice and misery in the world, I know; but more virtue and happiness I believe, at least in our part of it; the latter being the lot of those employed in agriculture in a greater degree than of other callings.—To ABBE SALIMANKIS. v, 516. (M., 1810.)

8846. VIRTUE, Ambition and.—It is a sublime truth that a bold, unequivocal virtue is the best handmaid even to ambition.—To JOHN JAY. iii, 52. (P., 1789.)

8847. VIRTUE, Aristocracy of.—Nature has wisely provided an aristocracy of virtue and talent for the direction of the interests of society, and scattered it with equal hand through all its conditions.—AUTOBIOGRAPHY. i, 36. FORD ED., i, 49. (1821.)

8848. VIRTUE, Essence of.—Virtue does not consist in the act we do, but in the end it is to effect. If it is to effect the happiness of him to whom it is directed, it is virtuous, while in a society under different circumstances and opinions, the same act might produce pain, and would be vicious. The essence of virtue is in doing good to others, while what is good may be one thing in one society, and its contrary in another.—To JOHN ADAMS. vii, 40. (M., 1816.)

8849. VIRTUE, Happiness and.—Without virtue, happiness cannot be.—To AMOS J. COOK. vi, 532. (M., 1816.)

8850. VIRTUE, Interest and.—Virtue and interest are inseparable.—To GEORGE LOGAN. FORD ED., x, 69. (P.F., 1816.)

8851. VIRTUE, Not hereditary.—Virtue is not hereditary.—To WILLIAM JOHNSON. vii, 291. FORD ED., x, 227. (M., 1823.)

8852. VIRTUE, Practice of.—Encourage all your virtuous dispositions, and exercise them whenever an opportunity arises; being assured that they will gain in strength by exercise, as a limb of the body does, and that exercise will make them habitual. From the practice of the purest virtue, you may be assured you will derive the most sublime com-

* In the Congress edition, Vol. 2, p. 332, this extract has been " edited " so as to read : " I think we shall be so [virtuous] as long as agriculture is our principal object, which will be the case, while there remain vacant lands in any part of America."—EDITOR.

forts in every moment of life, and in the moment of death.—To PETER CARR. i, 396. (P., 1785.)

8853. VIRTUE, Principles of.—Everything is useful which contributes to fix in the principles and practices of virtue. When any original act of charity or of gratitude, for instance, is presented either to our sight or imagination, we are deeply impressed with its beauty, and feel a strong desire in ourselves of doing charitable and grateful acts also.—To ROBERT SKIPWITH. FORD ED., i, 396. (M., 1771.)

8854. VIRTUE, Public office and.—For promoting the public happiness, those persons, whom nature has endowed with genius and virtue, should be rendered by liberal education worthy to receive, and able to guard the sacred deposit of the rights and liberties of their fellow citizens; and they should be called to that charge without regard to wealth, birth or other accidental condition or circumstance.—DIFFUSION OF KNOWLEDGE BILL. FORD ED., ii, 221. (1779.)

— **VISION.**—See OPTICS.

8855. VOLNEY (Comte de), Alien law and.—Volney has in truth been the principal object aimed at by the [Alien] law.—To JAMES MADISON. iv, 239. FORD ED., vii, 248. (Pa., May 1798.) See ALIEN AND SEDITION LAWS.

8856. VOLNEY (Comte de), Opposed to war.—Volney and a shipload of French sail [soon]. * * * It is natural to expect they go under irritations calculated to fan the flame. Not so Volney. He is most thoroughly impressed with the importance of preventing war, whether considered with reference to the interests of the two countries, of the cause of republicanism, or of man on the broad scale.—To JAMES MADISON. iv, 245. FORD ED., vii, 262. (Pa., May 1798.)

8857. VOLUNTEERS, Organizing.—I have encouraged the acceptance of volunteers, * * * [who] have offered themselves with great alacrity in every part of the Union.* They are ordered to be organized * * *.—SEVENTH ANNUAL MESSAGE. viii, 87. FORD ED., ix, 162. (Oct. 1807.) See ARMY and MILITIA.

8858. VOTES, Traffic in.—I believe we may lessen the danger of buying and selling votes, by making the number of voters too great for any means of purchase.—To JEREMIAH MOOR. FORD ED., vii, 454. (M., Aug. 1800.)

8859. VOTING, Courtesy to age.—Older electors presenting themselves should be received to vote before the younger ones, and the Legislature shall provide for the secure and convenient claim and exercise of this privilege of age.—NOTES FOR A CONSTITUTION FOR VIRGINIA. FORD ED., vi, 521. (1794.)

8860. VOTING, Viva voce.—All free male citizens of full age and sane mind * * * shall have a right to vote for delegates. * * * They shall give their votes personally, and *viva voce.*—PROPOSED VIRGINIA CONSTITUTION. viii, 444. FORD ED., iii, 323. (1783.)

* To oppose Burr's treason.—EDITOR.

8861. WABASH PROPHET, Pretensions of.—The Wabash Prophet is more rogue than fool, if to be a rogue is not the greatest of all follies. He arose to notice while I was in the administration, and became, of course, a proper subject of inquiry for me. * * * His declared object was the reformation of his red brethren, and their return to their pristine manner of living. He pretended to be in constant communication with the Great Spirit; that he was instructed by Him to make known to the Indians that they were created by Him distinct from the whites, of different natures, for different purposes, and placed under different circumstances, adapted to their nature and destinies: that they must return from all the ways of the whites to the habits and opinions of their forefathers; they must not eat the flesh of hogs, of bullocks, of sheep, &c., the deer and buffalo having been created for their food; they must not make bread of wheat but of Indian corn; they must not wear linen nor woollen, but dress like their fathers in the skins and furs of animals; they must not drink ardent spirits, and I do not remember whether he extended his inhibitions to the gun and gunpowder, in favor of the bow and arrow. I concluded from all this that he was a visionary, enveloped in the clouds of their antiquities, and vainly endeavoring to lead back his brethren to the fancied beatitudes of their golden age. I thought there was little danger of his making many proselytes from the habits and comfort they had learned from the whites, to the habits and privations of savageism, and no great harm if he did. We let him go on, therefore, unmolested. But his followers increased till the English thought him worth corruption and found him corruptible. I suppose his views were then changed; but his proceedings in consequence of them were after I left the administration, and are, therefore, unknown to me.—To JOHN ADAMS. vi, 49. FORD ED., ix, 346. (M., 1812.)

8862. WALSH (Robert), English critics and.—The malevolence and impertinence of Great Britain's critics and writers really called for the rod, and I rejoiced when I heard it was in hands so able to wield it with strength and correctness. Your work will furnish the first volume of every future American history; the Anti-Revolutionary part especially.—To ROBERT WALSH. FORD ED., x, 155. (M., 1820.)

8863. ————. After the severe chastisement given by Mr. Walsh in his American Register to English Scribblers, which they well deserved and I was delighted to see, I hoped there would be an end of this inter-crimination, and that both parties would prefer the course of courtesy and conciliation, and I think their considerate writers have since shown that disposition, and that it would prevail if equally cultivated by us.—To C. J. INGERSOLL. FORD ED., x, 325. (M., 1824.)

8864. WAR, Abhorrent.—I abhor war and view it as the greatest scourge of mankind.—To ELBRIDGE GERRY. iv, 173. FORD ED., vii, 122. (Pa., 1797.)

8865. WAR, America and.—The insulated state in which nature has placed the American continent should so far avail it that no spark of war kindled in the other quarters of the globe should be wafted across the wide oceans which separate us from them.—To BARON HUMBOLDT. vi, 268. FORD ED., ix, 431. (M., 1813.)

8866. WAR, Americans in.—Whenever an appeal to force shall take place, I feel a perfect confidence that the energy and enterprise displayed by my fellow citizens in the pursuits of peace, will be equally eminent in those of war.—To General Shee. v, 33. (W., 1807.)

8867. WAR, Avoidance of.—To remove as much as possible the occasions of making war, it might be better for us to abandon the ocean altogether, that being the element whereon we shall be principally exposed to jostle with other nations; to leave to others to bring what we shall want, and to carry what we can spare. This would make us invulnerable to Europe, by offering none of our property to their prize, and would turn all our citizens to the cultivation of the earth. It might be time enough to seek employment for them at sea, when the land no longer offers it.—Notes on Virginia. viii, 413. Ford ed., iii, 279. (1782.)

8868. ———. How much better is it for neighbors to help than to hurt one another; how much happier must it make them. If you will cease to make war on one another, if you will live in friendship with all mankind, you can employ all your time in providing food and clothing for yourselves and your families. Your men will not be destroyed in war, your women and children will lie down to sleep in their cabins without fear of being surprised by their enemies and killed or carried away. Your numbers will be increased instead of diminished, and you will live in plenty and in quiet.—Address to Mandar Nation. viii, 201. (1806.)

8869. ———. To cherish and maintain the rights and liberties of our citizens, and to ward from them the burthens, the miseries, and the crimes of war, by a just and friendly conduct towards all nations * * * [are] among the most obvious and important duties of those to whom the management of their public interests * * * [are] confided.—Reply to Baptist Address. viii, 119. (1807.)

8870. ———. It is much to be desired that war may be avoided, if circumstances will admit. Nor in the present maniac state of Europe, should I estimate the point of honor by the ordinary scale. I believe we shall on the contrary, have credit with the world, for having made the avoidance of being engaged in the present unexampled war, our first object.—To President Madison. v, 438. (M., March 1809.)

8871. WAR, Bankruptcy and.—Bankruptcy is a terrible foundation to begin a war on against the conquerors of the universe. —To James Monroe. Ford ed., vii, 241. (Pa., 1798.)

8872. WAR, Bribery vs.—I hope we shall drub the Indians well this summer, and then change our plan from war to bribery. We must do as the Spaniards and English do, keep them in peace by liberal and constant presents. They find it the cheapest plan, and

so shall we. The expense of this summer's expedition would have served for presents for half a century. In this way, hostilities being suspended for some length of time, a real affection may succeed on our frontiers to that hatred now existing there. Another powerful motive is that in this way we may leave no pretext for raising or continuing an army. Every rag of an Indian depredation will, otherwise, serve as a ground to raise troops with those who think a standing army and a public debt necessary for the happiness of the United States, and we shall never be permitted to get rid of either.—To James Monroe. Ford ed., v, 319. (Pa., 1791.)

8873. ———. I hope we shall give the Indians a good drubbing this summer, and then change our tomahawk into a golden chain of friendship. The most economical as well as the most humane conduct towards them is to bribe them into peace, and to retain them in peace by eternal bribes. The expedition this year would have served for presents on the most liberal scale for one hundred years; nor shall we otherwise ever get rid of an army, or of our debt. The least rag of Indian depredation will be an excuse to raise troops for those who love to have troops, and for those who think that a public debt is a good thing.—To Charles Carroll. iii, 246. (Pa., 1791.)

8874. WAR, Commerce and.—This exuberant commerce * * * brings us into collision with other powers in every sea, and will force us into every war of the European powers.—To Benjamin Stoddert. v, 426. Ford ed., ix, 245. (W., 1809.)

8875. WAR, Commerce vs.—War is not the best engine for us to resort to; nature has given us one *in our commerce,* which, if properly managed, will be a better instrument for obliging the interested nations of Europe to treat us with justice.—To Thomas Pinckney. iv, 177. Ford ed., vii, 129. (Pa., May 1797.)

8876. WAR, Contracts in.—I have the highest idea of the sacredness of those contracts which take place between nation and nation at war, and would be the last on earth to do anything in violation of them.—To General Washington. i, 228. Ford ed., ii, 247. (1779.)

8877. WAR, Debt and.—We wish to avoid the necessity of going to war, till our revenue shall be entirely liberated from debt. Then it will suffice for war, without creating new debt or taxes.—To Governor Claiborne. v, 381. Ford ed., ix, 213. (W., Oct. 1808.)

8878. WAR, Deprecated.—Wars with any European powers are devoutly to be deprecated.—Notes on Virginia. viii, 412. Ford ed., iii, 278. (1782.)

8879. WAR, Distresses of.—I desire to see the necessary distresses of war alleviated in every possible instance.—To Baron de Riedesel. i, 240. Ford ed., ii, 302. (R., 1780.)

8880. WAR, Embargo vs.—I have ever been anxious to avoid a war with England, unless forced by a situation more losing than war itself. But I did believe we could coerce her to justice by peaceable means, and the Embargo, evaded as it was, proved it would have coerced her had it been honestly executed.—To Henry Dearborn. v, 529. Ford ed., ix, 278. (M., July 1810.)

8881. WAR, Evils of.—The evils of war are great in their endurance, and have a long reckoning for ages to come.—R. to A. Pittsburg Republicans. viii, 142. (1808.)

8882. WAR, Executives and.—We have received a report that the French Directory has proposed a declaration of war against the United States to the Council of Ancients, who have rejected it. Thus we see two nations, who love one another affectionately, brought by the ill temper of their executive administrations, to the very brink of a necessity to imbrue their hands in the blood of each other.—To Aaron Burr. iv, 187. Ford ed., vii, 148, (Pa., June 1797.)

8883. WAR, Genius for.—I see the difficulties and defects we have to encounter in war, and should expect disasters if we had an enemy on land capable of inflicting them. But the weakness of our enemy there will make our first errors innocuous, and the seeds of genius which nature sows with even hand through every age and country, and which need only soil and season to germinate, will develop themselves among our military men. Some of them will become prominent, and seconded by the native energy of our citizens, will soon, I hope, to our force add the benefits of skill.—To William Duane. vi, 75. Ford ed., ix, 365. (M., Aug. 1812.)

8884. WAR, Holy.—If ever there was a holy war, it was that which saved our liberties and gave us independence.—To J. W. Eppes. vi, 246. Ford ed., ix, 416. (M., 1813.)

8885. ——— ———. The war of the Revolution will be sanctioned by the approbation of posterity through all future ages.—To J. W. Eppes. vi, 194. Ford ed., ix, 395. (P.F., Sep. 1813.)

8886. WAR, Honor and.—We are alarmed here [Virginia] with the apprehensions of war, and sincerely anxious that it may be avoided; but not at the expense either of our faith or honor.—To Tench Coxe. iv, 105. Ford ed., vi, 508. (M., May 1794.)

8887. WAR, Indian allies in.—[I argued in cabinet] against employing Indians in war. [It was] a dishonorable policy.—The Anas. Ford ed., i, 183. (1792.)

8888. WAR, Injury.—If nations go to war for every degree of injury, there would never be peace on earth.—To Madame de Stael. v, 133. (W., 1807.)

8889. WAR, Insult and.—I think it to our interest to punish the first insult; because an insult unpunished is the parent of many others.—To John Jay. i, 405. Ford ed., iv, 89. (P., 1785.)

8890. ——— ———. It is an eternal truth that acquiescence under insult is not the way to escape war.—To H. Tazewell. iv, 121. Ford ed., vii, 31. (M., 1795.)

8891. WAR, Interest and.—Never was so much false arithmetic employed on any subject, as that which has been employed to persuade nations that it is their interest to go to war. Were the money which it has cost to gain, at the close of a long war, a little town, or a little territory, the right to cut wood here, or to catch fish there, expended in improving what they already possess, in making roads, opening rivers, building ports, improving the arts, and finding employment for their idle poor, it would render them much stronger, much wealthier and happier. This I hope will be our wisdom.—Notes on Virginia. viii, 413. Ford ed., iii, 279. (1782.)

8892. WAR, Justifiable.—On the final and formal declarations of England, that she never would repeal her Orders of Council as to us, until those of France should be repealed as to other nations as well as us, and that no practicable arrangement against her impressment of our seamen could be proposed or devised, war was justly declared, and ought to have been declared.—To J. W. Eppes. vi, 196. Ford ed., ix, 396. (P.F., Sep. 1813.)

8893. WAR, Losses in Revolutionary.—I think that upon the whole [our loss during the war] has been about one-half the number lost by the British; in some instances more, but in others less. This difference is ascribed to our superiority in taking aim when we fire; every soldier in our army having been intimate with his gun from his infancy.—To ——— ———. i, 208. Ford ed., ii, 157. (Wg., 1778.)

8894. WAR, Markets and.—To keep open sufficient markets is the very first object towards maintaining the popularity of the war.—To President Madison. vi, 78. (M., Aug. 1812.)

8895. WAR, Monarchies and.—War is not the most favorable moment for divesting the monarchy of power. On the contrary, it is the moment when the energy of a single hand shows itself in the most seducing form.—To H. S. Crevecœur. ii, 458. (P., 1788.)

8896. WAR, Moral duty.—When wrongs are pressed because it is believed they will be borne, resistance becomes morality.—To Madame de Stael. v, 133. (W., 1807.)

8897. WAR, One enough.—I have seen enough of one war never to wish to see another.—To John Adams. iv, 104. Ford ed., vi, 505. (M., 1794.)

8898. ——— ———. I think one war enough for the life of one man; and you and I have gone through one which at least may lessen our impatience to embark in another. Still, if it becomes necessary, we must meet it like men, old men indeed, but yet good for something.—To John Langdon. Ford ed., ix, 201. (M., 1808.)

8899. —— ——. One war, such as that of our Revolution, is enough for one life.—To M. Correa. vi, 407. (M., 1814.)

8900. WAR, Opposition to.—No country, perhaps, was ever so thoroughly against war as ours. These dispositions pervade every description of its citizens, whether in or out of office.—To Gouverneur Morris. Ford ed., vi, 217. (Pa., April 1793.)

8901. WAR, Paroles.—By the law of nations, a breach of parole can only be punished by strict confinement. No usage has permitted the putting to death a prisoner for this cause. I would willingly suppose that no British officer had ever expressed a contrary purpose. It has, however, become my duty to declare that should such a threat be carried into execution, it will be deemed as putting prisoners to death in cold blood, and shall be followed by the execution of so many British prisoners in our possession. I trust, however, that this horrid necessity will not be introduced by you, and that you will, on the contrary, concur with us in endeavoring, as far as possible, to alleviate the inevitable miseries of war by treating captives as humanity and natural honor require. The event of this contest will hardly be affected by the fate of a few miserable captives in war.*—Ford ed., ii, 511. (R., March 1781.)

8902. WAR, Peace vs.—The evils which of necessity encompass the life of man are sufficiently numerous. Why should we add to them by voluntarily distressing and destroying one another? Peace, brothers, is better than war. In a long and bloody war, we lose many friends and gain nothing.—Address to Indians. viii, 185. (1802.)

8903. —— ——. The cannibals of Europe are going to eating one another again. A war between Russia and Turkey is like the battle of the kite and snake. Whichever destroys the other, leaves a destroyer the less for the world. This pugnacious humor of mankind seems to be the law of his nature, one of the obstacles to too great multiplication provided in the mechanism of the Universe. The cocks of the henyard kill one another up. Bears, bulls, rams, do the same. And the horse, in his wild state, kills all the young males, until worn down with age and war, some vigorous youth kills him, and takes to himself the harem of females. I hope we shall prove how much happier for man the Quaker policy is, and that the life of the feeder is better than that of the fighter; and it is some consolation that the desolation by these maniacs of one part of the earth is the means of improving it in other parts. Let the latter be our office, and let us milk the cow, while the Russian holds her by the horns, and the Turk by the tail.—To John Adams. vii, 244. Ford ed., x, 217. (M., 1822.)

8904. WAR, Power to declare.—The Administrator [of Virginia] shall not possess the prerogative * * * of declaring war or concluding peace.—Proposed Va. Constitution. Ford ed., ii, 19. (June 1776.)

8905. —— ——. We have already given, in example, one effectual check to the dog of war, by transferring the power of declaring war from the Executive to the legislative body, from those who are to spend to those who are to pay. I should be pleased to see this second obstacle [that no generation shall contract debts greater than may be paid during the course of its own existence], held out by us also, in the first instance.—To James Madison. iii, 108. Ford ed., v, 123. (P., 1789.) See Generations.

8906. —— ——. The States of America before their present Union possessed completely, each within its own limits, the exclusive right to * * * [make war and] by their act of Union, they have as completely ceded [it] to the General Government. Art. 1st. Section 8th, "The Congress shall have power to declare war, to raise and support armies". Section 10th, * * * "No State shall without the consent of Congress, keep troops or ships of war in time of peace, enter into any agreement or compact with another State or with a foreign power, or engage in war, unless actually invaded or in such danger as will not admit of delay". These paragraphs of the Constitution, declaring that the General Government shall have, and that the particular ones shall not have, the right of war * * * are so explicit that no commentary can explain them further, nor can any explain them away.—Opinion on Georgian Land Grants. vii, 468. Ford ed., v, 166. (1790.)

8907. —— ——. The question of declaring war is the function equally of both Houses.—The Anas. ix, 123. Ford ed., i, 206. (1792.)

8908. —— ——. I thought [the paper] should be laid before both houses [of Congress], because it concerned the question of declaring war, which was the function equally of both houses.—The Anas. ix, 123. Ford ed., i, 206. (1792.)

8909. —— ——. The question of war, being placed by the Constitution with the Legislature alone, respect to that made it my duty to restrain the operations of our militia to those merely defensive; and considerations involving the public satisfaction, and peculiarly my own, require that the decision of that question, whichever way it be, should be pronounced definitely by the Legislature themselves.*—Paragraph for President's Message. Ford ed., vi, 144. (1792.)

8910. —— ——. I opposed the right of the President to declare anything future on the question, Shall there or shall there not be war?—The Anas. ix, 178. Ford ed., i, 266. (1793.)

---

* Addressed "To the Commanding Officer of the British Force at Portsmouth". That officer was Major-General Benedict Arnold.—Editor.

* This is not dated, but was probably written in December, 1792. The message was entirely different.—Note in Ford edition.

8911. —— ——. As the Executive cannot decide the question of war on the affirmative side, neither ought it to do so on the negative side, by preventing the competent body from deliberating on the question.*—To JAMES MADISON. iii, 519. FORD ED., vi, 192. (1793.)

8912. —— ——. If Congress are to act on the question of war, they have a right to information [from the Executive].—To JAMES MONROE. FORD ED., vii, 221. (Pa., March 1798.)

8913. —— ——. We had reposed great confidence in that provision of the Constitution which requires two-thirds of the Legislature to declare war. Yet it can be entirely eluded by a majority's taking such measures as will bring on war.—To JAMES MONROE. FORD ED., vii, 222. (Pa., March 1798.)

8914. —— ——. We see a new instance of the inefficiency of constitutional guards. We had relied with great security on that provision which requires two-thirds of the Legislature to declare war. But this is completely eluded by a majority's taking such measures as will be sure to produce war.—To JAMES MADISON. iv, 222. FORD ED., vii, 220. (Pa., 1798.)

8915. —— ——. The power of declaring war being with the Legislature, the Executive should do nothing necessarily committing them to decide for war.†—To VICE-PRESIDENT CLINTON. v, 116. FORD ED., ix, 100. (W., 1807.)

8916. WAR, Preferable.—War may become a less losing business than unresisted depredation.—To PRESIDENT MADISON. v, 438. (M., March 1809.)

8917. WAR, Premeditated.—That war with us had been predetermined may be fairly inferred from the diction of Berkley's order, the Jesuitism of which proves it ministerial from its being so timed as to find us in the midst of Burr's rebellion as they expected, from the contemporaneousness of the Indian excitements, and of the wide and sudden spread of their maritime spoliations.—To THOMAS PAINE. v, 189. FORD ED., ix, 137. (M., Sep. 1807.)

8918. WAR, Preparations for.—Considering war as one of the alternatives which Congress may adopt on the failure of proper satisfaction for the outrages committed on us by Great Britain, I have thought it my duty to put into train every preparation for that which the executive powers * * * will admit of.—To JOHN NICHOLAS. v, 168. (M., 1807.)

8919. WAR, Prevention of.—The power of making war often prevents it, and in our case would give efficacy to our desire of peace. —To GENERAL WASHINGTON. ii, 533. FORD ED., v, 57. (P., 1788.)

* Not to convene Congress in special session would be, in Jefferson's opinion, to "prevent" deliberation.—EDITOR.
† This extract, Jefferson explained to Clinton, defined one of the principles that controlled his action in the issuance of his proclamation after the attack on the Chesapeake.—EDITOR.

8920. WAR, Principles and.—I do not believe war the most certain means of enforcing principles. Those peaceable coercions which are in the power of every nation, if undertaken in concert and in time of peace, are more likely to produce the desired effect. —To ROBERT R. LIVINGSTON. iv, 411. FORD ED., viii, 91. (M., 1801.)

— **WAR, Prisoners of.**—See 8966.

8921. WAR, Punishment by.—War is as much a punishment to the punisher as to the sufferer.—To TENCH COXE. iv, 105. FORD ED., vi, 508. (M., May 1794.)

8922. WAR, Quixotic.—War against Bedlam would be just as rational as against Europe, in its present condition of total demoralization. When peace becomes more losing than war, we may prefer the latter on principles of pecuniary calculation. But for us to attempt, by war, to reform all Europe, and bring them back to principles of morality, and a respect for the equal rights of nations, would show us to be only maniacs of another character. We should, indeed, have the merit of the good intentions as well as of the folly of the hero of La Mancha.—To WILLIAM WIRT. v, 595. FORD ED., ix, 319. (M., May 1811.)

8923. WAR, Readiness for.—Whatever enables us to go to war, secures our peace. —To JAMES MONROE. FORD ED., v, 198. (N.Y., 1790.)

8924. WAR, Reason and.—The large strides of late taken by the legislature of Great Britain towards establishing over these Colonies their absolute rule, and the hardiness of the present attempt to effect by force of arms what by law or right they could never effect, render it necessary for us also to change the ground of opposition, and to close with their last appeal from reason to arms.—DECLARATION ON TAKING UP ARMS. FORD ED., i, 462. (July 1775.)

8925. WAR, Redress of wrongs by.—The answer to the question: "Is it common for a nation to obtain a *redress* of wrongs by war"? you will, of course, draw from history. In the meantime, reason will answer it on grounds of probability, that where the wrong has been done by a weaker nation, the stronger one has generally been able to enforce redress; but where by a stronger nation, redress by war has been neither obtained nor expected by the weaker. On the contrary, the loss has been increased by the expenses of the war in blood and treasure. Yet it may have obtained another object equally securing itself from future wrong. It may have retaliated on the aggressor losses of blood and treasure far beyond the value to him of the wrong he has committed, and thus have made the advantage of that too dear a purchase to leave him in a disposition to renew the wrong in future.—To REV. MR. WORCESTER. vi, 539. (M., 1816.)

8926. WAR, Resort to.—The lamentable resource of war is not authorized for evils of imagination, but for those actual injuries only, which would be more destructive of our well-being than war itself.—REPLY TO ADDRESS. iv, 388. (W., 1801.)

8927. WAR, Retaliation in.—England may burn New York by her ships and congreve rockets, in which case we must burn the city of London by hired incendiaries, of which her starving manufacturers will furnish abundance. A people in such desperation as to demand of their government *aut panem, aut furcam,* either bread or the gallows, will not reject the same alternative when offered by a foreign hand. Hunger will make them brave every risk for bread.—To GENERAL KOSCIUSKO. vi, 68. FORD ED., ix, 362. (M., June 1812.)

8928. WAR, Revolutionary.—The circumstances of our [Revolutionary] war were without example. Excluded from all commerce, even with neutral nations, without arms, money or the means of getting them abroad, we were obliged to avail ourselves of such resources as we found at home. Great Britain, too, did not consider it as an ordinary war, but a rebellion; she did not conduct it according to the rules of war, established by the law of nations, but according to her acts of parliament, made from time to time, to suit circumstances. She would not admit our title even to the *strict rights* of ordinary war.—To GEORGE HAMMOND. iii, 369. FORD ED., vi, 16. (Pa., May 1792.) See REVOLUTION (AMERICAN).

8929. WAR, Secretaryship of.—I much regretted your acceptance of the War Department. Not that I know a person who I think would better conduct it. But conduct it ever so wisely, it will be a sacrifice of yourself. Were an angel from heaven to undertake that office, all our miscarriages would be ascribed to him. Raw troops, no troops, insubordinate militia, want of arms, want of money, want of provisions all will be charged to want of management in you. * * * Not that I have seen the least disposition to censure you. On the contrary, your conduct on the attack of Washington has met the praises of every one, and your plan for regulars and militia, their approbation. But no campaign is as yet opened. No generals have yet an interest in shifting their own incompetence on you, no army agents their rogueries.—To JAMES MONROE. vi, 410. FORD ED., ix, 498. (M., 1815.)

8930. WAR, Security against.—The justest dispositions possible in ourselves, will not secure us against war. It would be necessary that all other nations were just also. Justice, indeed, on our part, will save us 'from those wars which would have been produced by a contrary disposition. But how can we prevent those produced by the wrongs of other nations? By putting ourselves in a position to punish them. Weakness provokes insult and injury, while a condition to punish often prevents them. This reasoning leads to the necessity of some naval force; that being the only weapon by which we can reach an enemy.—To JOHN JAY. i, 404. FORD ED., iv, 89. (P., 1785.)

8931. WAR, Taxation and.—War requires every resource of taxation and credit.—To GENERAL WASHINGTON. ii, 533. FORD ED., v, 57. (P., 1788.)

8932. WAR, Taxation for.—Sound principles will not justify our taxing the industry of our fellow citizens to accumulate treasure for wars to happen we know not when, and which might not perhaps happen but from the temptations offered by that treasure.—FIRST ANNUAL MESSAGE. viii, 9. FORD ED., viii, 119. (1801.)

8933. WAR, Unfeared.—We love and we value peace; we know its blessings from experience. We abhor the follies of war, and are not untried in its distresses and calamities. Unmeddling with the affairs of other nations, we had hoped that our distance and our dispositions would have left us free, in the example and indulgence of peace with all the world. We had, with sincere and particular dispositions, courted and cultivated the friendship of Spain. We have made to it great sacrifices of time and interest, and were disposed to believe she would see her interests also in a perfect coalition and good understanding with us. Cherishing still the same sentiments, we have chosen, in the present instance, to ascribe the intimations in this letter [of the Spanish Commissioners] to the particular character of the writers, displayed in the peculiarity of the style of their communications, and therefore, we have removed the cause from them to their sovereign, in whose justice and love of peace we have confidence. If we are disappointed in this appeal, if we are to be forced into a contrary order of things, our mind is made up. We shall meet it with firmness. The necessity of our position will supersede all appeal to calculation now, as it has done heretofore. We confide in our strength, without boasting of it; we respect that of others without fearing it. If we cannot otherwise prevail on the Creeks to discontinue their depredations, we will attack them in force. If Spain chooses to consider our defence against savage butchery as a cause of war to her, we must meet her also in war, with regret, but without fear; and we shall be happier to the last moment, to repair with her to the tribunal of peace and reason. The President charges you to communicate the contents of this letter to the Court at Madrid, with all the temperance and delicacy which the dignity and character of that Court render proper; but with all the firmness and self-respect which befit a nation conscious of its rectitude, and settled in its purpose.—To CARMICHAEL AND SHORT. iv, 16. FORD ED., vi, 337. (Pa., June 1793.)

8934. ——— ———. Should the lawless violences of the belligerent powers render it necessary to return their hostilities, no nation has less to fear from a foreign enemy.—R. TO A. VIRGINIA REPUBLICANS. viii, 168. (1809.)

8935. WAR, Unity in.—It is our duty still to endeavor to avoid war; but if it shall actually take place, no matter by whom brought on, we must defend ourselves. If our house be on fire, without inquiring whether it was fired from within or without, we must try to extinguish it. In that, I have no doubt, we shall act as one man.—To JAMES LEWIS, JR. iv, 241. FORD ED., vii, 250. (Pa., May 1798.)

8936. ——— ———. If we are forced into war [with France], we must give up political differences of opinion, and unite as one man to defend our country. But whether at the close of such a war, we should be as free as we are now, God knows.—To GEN. KOS-CIUSKO. iv, 295. (Pa., 1799.)

8937. WAR, Unprepared for.—We are now at the close of our second campaign with England. During the first we suffered several checks, from the want of capable and tried officers; all the higher ones of the Revolution having died off during an interval of thirty years of peace. But this second campaign has been more successful, having given us all the Lakes and country of Upper Canada, except the single post of Kingston, at its lower extremity.—To DON V. TORONDA CORUNA. vi, 275. (M., Dec. 1813.)

8938. WAR, Unprofitable.—The most successful war seldom pays for its losses.—To EDMUND RANDOLPH. i, 435. (P., 1785.)

8939. WAR, Weakness provokes.—It should ever be held in mind that insult and war are the consequences of a want of respectability in the national character.—To JAMES MADISON. i, 531. FORD ED., iv, 192. (P., 1786.) See ARMY, GENERALS and REVOLUTION.

8940. WARDS, Advantages of.—My partiality for the division of counties into wards is not founded in views of education solely, but infinitely more as the means of a better administration of our government, and the eternal preservation of its republican principles. The example of this most admirable of all human contrivances in government, is to be seen in our Eastern States; and its powerful effect in the order and economy of their internal affairs, and the momentum it gives them as a nation, is the single circumstance which distinguishes them so remarkably from every other national association.—To GOVERNOR NICHOLAS. vi, 566. (M., 1816.)

8941. WARDS, Good government and.—I have long contemplated a division of our own State into hundreds or wards, as the most fundamental measure for securing good government, and for instilling the principles and exercise of good government into every fibre of every member of our commonwealth.—To JOSEPH C. CABELL. vi, 301. (M., 1814.)

8942. WARDS, Primary schools and.—One of the principal objects in my endeavors to get our counties divided into wards, is the establishment of a primary school in each [of them].—To JOHN TAYLOR. vii, 17. FORD ED., x, 51. (M., 1816.)

8943. WARDS, Size of.—I hope [the convention to amend the Virginia Constitution] will adopt the subdivision of our counties into wards. The former may be estimated at an average of twenty-four miles square; the latter should be about six miles square each, and would answer to the hundreds of your Saxon Alfred. * * * The wit of men cannot devise a more solid basis for a free, durable, and well-administered republic.—To JOHN CARTWRIGHT. vii, 357. (M., 1824.)

8944. WARDS, Vital principle.—These wards, called townships in New England, are the vital principles of their governments, and have proved themselves the wisest invention ever devised by the wit of man for the perfect exercise of self-government, and for its preservation.—To SAMUEL KERCHIVAL. vii, 13. FORD ED., x, 41. (M., 1816.) See COUNTIES.

8945. WAR OF 1812, Acrimonious.—The exasperation produced * * * by the late war * * * is great with you [Great Britain], as I judge from your newspapers; and greater with us, as I see myself. The reason lies in the different degrees in which the war has acted on us. To your people it has been a matter of distant history only, a mere war in the carnatic; with us it has reached the bosom of every man, woman and child. The maritime ports have felt it in the conflagration of their houses and towns, and desolation of their farms; the borderers in the massacres and scalpings of their husbands, wives and children; and the middle parts in their personal labors and losses in defence of both frontiers, and the revolting scenes they have there witnessed. It is not wonderful, then, if their irritations are extreme. Yet time and prudence on the part of the two governments may get over these.—To SIR JOHN SINCLAIR. vii, 23. (M., 1816.)

8946. WAR OF 1812, Benefits of.—The British war has left us in debt; but that is a cheap price for the good it has done us. The establishment of the necessary manufactures among ourselves, the proof that our government is solid and can stand the shock of war, and is superior even to civil schism, are precious facts for us; and of these the strongest proofs were furnished, when, with four Eastern States tied to us, as dead to living bodies, all doubt was removed as to the achievements of the war, had it continued. But its best effect has been the complete suppression of party. The federalists who were truly American, and their great mass was so, have separated from their brethren who were mere Anglomen, and are received with cordiality into the republican ranks.—To MARQUIS DE LAFAYETTE. vii, 66. FORD ED., x, 83. (M., 1817.)

8947. ——— ———. The war [of 1812] has done us * * * the further [good] of assuring the world, that although attached to peace from a sense of its blessings, we will meet war when it is made necessary.—To MARQUIS DE LAFAYETTE. vii, 67. FORD ED., x, 84. (M., 1817.)

8948. WAR OF 1812, British expectations in.—Earl Bathhurst [in his speech in Parliament] shuffles together chaotic ideas merely to darken and cover the views of the ministers in protracting the war; the truth being, that they expected to give us an exemplary scourging, to separate us from the States east of the Hudson, take for their Indian allies those west of the Ohio, placing three hundred thousand American citizens under the government of the savages, and to leave the residuum a powerless enemy, if not submissive subjects. I cannot conceive what is the use of your Bedlam when such men are out of it. And yet that such were their views we have in evidence, under the hand of their Secretary of State in Henry's case, and of their Commissioners at Ghent.—To Mr. Maury. vi, 471. (M., June 1815.)

8949. WAR OF 1812, Causes of.—It is incomprehensible to me that the Marquis of Wellesley * * * [should] say that "the aggression which led to the war, was from the United States, not from England". Is there a person in the world who, knowing the circumstances, thinks this? The acts which produced the war were. 1st. the impressment of our citizens by their ships of war. and, 2d, the Orders of Council forbidding our vessels to trade with any country but England, without going to England to obtain a special license. On the first subject the British minister declared to our Charge, Mr. Russel, that this practice of their ships of war would not be discontinued, and that no admissible arrangement could be proposed; and as to the second, the Prince Regent, by his proclamation of April 21st, 1812, declared in effect solemnly that he would not revoke the Orders of Council *as to us*, on the ground that Bonaparte had revoked his decrees *as to us;* that, on the contrary, we should continue under them until Bonaparte should revoke *as to all the world*. These categorical and definite answers put an end to negotiation, and were a declaration of a continuance of the war in which they had already taken from us one thousand ships and six thousand seamen. We determined then to defend ourselves, and to oppose further hostilities by war on our side also. Now, had we taken one thousand British ships and six thousand of her seamen without any declaration of war, would the Marquis of Wellesley have considered a declaration of war by Great Britain as an aggression on her part? They say we denied their maritime rights. We never denied a single one. It was their taking our citizens, native as well as naturalized, for which we went into war, and because they forbade us to trade with any nation without entering and paying duties in their ports on both the outward and inward cargo. Thus, to carry a cargo of cotton from Savannah to St. Mary's, and take returns in fruits, for example, our vessel was to go to England, enter and pay a duty on her cottons there. return to St. Mary's, then go back to England to enter and pay a duty on her fruits. and then return to Savannah, after crossing the Atlantic four times, and paying tributes on both cargoes to England, instead of the direct passage of a few hours. And the taking ships for not doing this, the Marquis says, is no aggression.—To Mr. Maury. vi, 470. (M., June 1815.)

8950. WAR OF 1812, Conquest and.—The war, undertaken, on both sides, to settle the questions of impressment, and the Orders of Council, now that these are done away by events, is declared by Great Britain to have changed its object, and to have become a war of conquest, to be waged until she conquers from us our fisheries, the province of Maine, the Lakes, States and territories north of the Ohio, and the navigation of the Mississippi; in other words, till she reduces us to unconditional submission. On our part, then, we ought to propose, as a counterchange of object. the establishment of the meridian of the mouth of the

Sorel northwardly, as the western boundary of all her possessions.—To President Madison. vi, 391. Ford ed., ix, 489. (M., Oct. 1814.)

8951. WAR OF 1812, Declaration of.—War was declared on June 18th, thirty years after the signature of our peace in 1782. * * * It is not ten years since Great Britain began a series of insults and injuries which would have been met with war in the threshold by any European power. This course has been unremittingly followed up by increased wrongs, with glimmerings, indeed, of peaceable redress, just sufficient to keep us in quiet, till she has had the impudence at length to extinguish even these glimmerings by open avowal. This would not have been borne so long, but that France has kept pace with England in iniquity of principle, although not in the power of inflicting wrongs on us. The difficulty of selecting a foe between them has spared us many years of war, and enabled us to enter into it with less debt, more strength and preparation.—To General Kosciusko. vi, 67. Ford ed., ix, 361. (M., June 1812.)

8952. ———— ————. [The declaration of war was] accompanied with immediate offers of peace on simply doing us justice. These offers were made through Russel, through Admiral Warren, through the government of Canada, and the mediation proposed by her best friend Alexander, and the greatest enemy of Bonaparte. was accepted without hesitation.—To Dr. George Logan. vi, 216. Ford ed., ix, 422. (M., Oct. 1813.)

8953. WAR OF 1812, Grounds of.—The essential grounds of the war were, first, the Orders of Council; and, secondly, the impressment of our citizens (for I put out of sight from the love of peace the multiplied insults on our government and aggressions on our commerce, with which our pouch, like the Indian's, had long been filled to the mouth). What immediately produced the declaration was, 1st, the proclamation of the Prince Regent that he would never repeal the Orders of Council as to us, until Bonaparte should have revoked his decrees as to all other nations as well as ours; and 2d, the declaration of his minister to ours that no arrangement whatever could be devised, admissible in lieu of impressment. It was certainly a misfortune that *they* did not know themselves at the date of this silly and insolent proclamation, that within one month they would repeal the Orders. and that *we*, at the date of our declaration, could not know of the repeal which was then going on one thousand leagues distant. Their determinations, as declared by themselves, could alone guide us, and they shut the door on all further negotiation, throwing down to us the gauntlet of war or submission as the only alternatives. We cannot blame the government for choosing that of war, because certainly the great majority of the nation thought it ought to be chosen.—To William Short. vi. 398. (M., Nov. 1814.)

8954. WAR OF 1812, Hartford convention and.—The negotiators at Ghent are agreed now on every point save one, the demand and cession of a portion of Maine. This, it is well known, cannot be yielded by us, nor deemed by them an object for continuing a war so expensive, so injurious to their commerce and manufactures, and so odious in the eyes of the world. But it is a thread to hold by until they can hear the result, not of the Congress of Vienna, but of Hartford. When they shall know as they will know, that nothing will be done there, they will let go their hold, and complete the peace of the world, by agreeing to the *status ante bellum*. Indemnity for the past, and security for the future, which was our motto at the beginning of this war, must be adjourned to another, when, disarmed and bankrupt, our enemy shall be less able to insult and plunder the world with impunity.—To M. Correa. vi, 407. (M., 1814.) See Hartford Convention.

8955. WAR OF 1812, Justifiable.— [Great Britain threw] down to us the gauntlet of war or submission as the only alternatives. We cannot blame the government for choosing that of war, because certainly the great majority of the nation thought it ought to be chosen, not that they were to gain by it in dollars and cents; all men know that war is a losing game to both parties. But they know, also, that if they did not resist encroachment at some point, all will be taken from them, and that more would then be lost even in dollars and cents by submission than resistance. It is the case of giving a part to save the whole, a limb to save life. It is the melancholy law of human societies to be compelled sometimes to choose a great evil in order to ward off a greater; to deter their neighbors from rapine by making it cost them more than honest gains. * * * Had we adopted the other alternative of submission, no mortal can tell what the cost would have been. I consider the war then as entirely justifiable on our part, although I am still sensible it is a deplorable misfortune to us.—To William Short. vi, 399. (M., Nov. 1814.)

8956. WAR OF 1812, Lessons of.—I consider the war as made * — * for just causes, and its dispensation as providential, inasmuch as it has exercised our patriotism and submission to order, has planted and invigorated among us arts of urgent necessity, has manifested the strong and the weak parts of our republican institutions, and the excellence of a representative democracy compared with the misrule of kings, has rallied the opinions of mankind to the natural rights of expatriation, and of a common property in the ocean, and raised us to that grade in the scale of nations which the bravery and liberality of our citizen soldiers, by land and by sea, the wisdom of our institutions and their observance of justice, entitled us to in the eyes of the world.—To Mr. Wendover. vi, 444. (M., 1815.)

8957. WAR OF 1812, Markets and.— To keep the war popular, we must keep open the markets. As long as good prices can be had, the people will support the war cheerfully.—To James Ronaldson. vi, 93. Ford ed., ix, 372. (M., Jan. 1813.)

8958. WAR OF 1812, Misrepresented.— England has misrepresented to all Europe this ground of the war [of 1812]. She has called it a new pretension, set up since the repeal of her Orders of Council. She knows there has never been a moment of suspension of our reclamation against it, from General Washington's time inclusive, to the present day; and that it is distinctly stated in our declaration of war, as one of its principal causes.—To Madame de Stael. vi, 118. (M., May 1813.)

8959. —— ——. She has pretended we have entered into the war to establish the principle of " free bottoms, free goods ", or to protect her seamen against her own rights over them. We contend for neither of these.— To Madame de Stael. vi, 118. (May 1813.)

8960. —— ——. She pretends we are partial to France; that we have observed a

fraudulent and unfaithful neutrality between her and her enemy. She knows this to be false, and that if there has been any inequality in our proceedings towards the belligerents, it has been in her favor. Her ministers are in possession of full proofs of this. Our accepting at once, and sincerely, the mediation of the virtuous Alexander, their greatest friend, and the most aggravated enemy of Bonaparte, sufficiently proves whether we have partialities on the side of her enemy. I sincerely pray that this mediation may produce a just peace.—To Madame de Stael. vi, 119. (May 1813.)

8961. WAR OF 1812, Prolongation of. —As soon as we heard of her partial repeal of her Orders of Council, we offered instantly to suspend hostilities by an armistice, if she would suspend her impressments, and meet us in arrangements for securing our citizens against them. She refused to do it, because impracticable by any arrangement, as she pretends; but, in truth, because a body of sixty to eighty thousand of the finest seamen in the world, which we possess, is too great a resource for manning her exaggerated navy, to be relinquished, as long as she can keep it open. Peace is in her hand, whenever she will renounce the practice of aggression on the persons of our citizens. If she thinks it worth eternal war, eternal war we must have. She alleges that the sameness of language, of manners, of appearance, renders it impossible to distinguish us from her subjects. But because we speak English, and look like them, are we to be punished? Are free and independent men to be submitted to their bondage?—To Madame de Stael. vi, 118. (May 1813.)

8962. WAR OF 1812, Provocation.— Nothing but the total prostration of all moral principle could have produced the enormities which have forced us at length into the war. On one hand, a ruthless tyrant, drenching Europe in blood to obtain through future time the character of the destroyer of mankind; on the other, a nation of buccaneers, urged by sordid avarice, and embarked in the flagitious enterprise of seizing to itself the maritime resources and rights of all other nations, have left no means of peace to reason and moderation. And yet there are beings among us who think we ought still to have acquiesced. As if while full war was waging on one side, we could lose by making some reprisal on the other.—To Henry Middleton. vi, 91. (M., Jan. 1813.)

8963. WAR OF 1812, Reparation and. —The sword once drawn, full justice must be done. " Indemnification for the past and security for the future" should be painted on our banners. For one thousand ships taken, and six thousand seamen impressed, give us Canada for indemnification, and the only security they can give us against their Henrys, and the savages, and agree that the American flag shall protect the persons of those sailing under it, both parties exchanging engagements that neither will receive the seamen of the other on board their vessels. This done, I should be for peace with England, and then war with France. One at a time is enough, and in fighting the one we need the harbors of the other for our prizes.—To Mr. Wright. vi, 78. (M., Aug. 1812.)

8964. WAR OF 1812, Victory and defeat.— Perhaps this Russian mediation may cut short the history of the present war, and leave to us the laurels of the sea, while our enemies are bedecked with those of the land.

This would be the reverse of what has been expected, and perhaps of what was to be wished. —To WILLIAM DUANE. vi, 110. (M., April 1813.)

8965. —— ——. I rejoice exceedingly that our war with England was single-handed. In that of the Revolution, we had France, Spain, and Holland on our side, and the credit of its success was given to them. On the late occasion, unprepared, and unexpecting war, we were compelled to declare it, and to receive the attack of England, just issuing from a general war, fully armed, and freed from all other enemies, and have not only made her sick of it, but glad to prevent by peace, the capture of her adjacent possessions, which one or two campaigns more would infallibly have made ours. She has found that we can do her more injury than any other enemy on earth, and henceforward will better estimate the value of our peace. —To THOMAS LEIPER. vi. 466. FORD ED., ix, 521. (M. 1815.) See IMPRESSMENT.

8966. WAR (Prisoners of), Comfort of. —Is an enemy so execrable, that, though in captivity, his wishes and comforts are to be disregarded and even crossed? I think not. It is for the benefit of mankind to mitigate the horrors of war as much as possible. The practice, therefore, of modern nations, of treating captive enemies with politeness and generosity, is not only delightful in contemplation, but really interesting to all the world, friends, foes and neutrals.—To GOVERNOR HENRY. i, 218. FORD ED., ii, 176. (Alb., 1779.)

8967. WAR (Prisoners of), Exchange of.—I am sorry to learn that the negotiations for the exchange of prisoners have proved abortive, as well from a desire to see the necessary distresses of war alleviated in every possible instance, as that I am sensible how far yourself and family are interested in it. Against this, however, is to be weighed the possibility that we may again have a pleasure we should otherwise, perhaps, never have had—that of seeing you again.*—To GENERAL DE RIEDESEL. i, 241. FORD ED., ii, 303. (R., 1780.)

8968. WAR (Prisoners of), Health of.— The health [of the British prisoners] is also of importance. I would not endeavor to show that their lives are valuable to us, because it would suppose a possibility, that humanity was kicked out of doors in America, and interest only attended to.—To GOVERNOR HENRY. i, 218. FORD ED., ii, 175. (Alb., 1779.)

8969. WAR (Prisoners of), Relief of.— Be assured there is nothing consistent with the honor of your country which we shall not, at all times, be ready to do for the relief of yourself and companions in captivity. We know that ardent spirit and hatred for tyranny, which brought you into your present situation, will enable you to bear up against it with the firmness which has distinguished you as a soldier, and to look forward with pleasure to the day when events shall take place against which the wounded spirits of your enemies will find no comfort, even from reflections on the most refined of the cruelties with which they have

* General Riedesel, commander of the Hessian troops, captured at Saratoga, was among the prisoners sent to Albemarle, in 1779, and, with many of his fellow officers, was a frequent guest at Monticello. They all expressed their deep obligations to Jefferson for the courtesies extended to them and the efforts made by him to lighten the hardships of their captivity.—EDITOR.

glutted themselves.*—To COLONEL GEORGE MATTHEWS. i, 235. FORD ED., ii, 264. (Wg., 1779.)

8970. WAR (Prisoners of), Treatment of.—We think ourselves justified in Governor Hamilton's strict confinement on the general principle of national retaliation. * * * Governor Hamilton's conduct has been such as to call for exemplary punishment on him personally. In saying this I have not so much in view his particular cruelties to our citizens, prisoners with him, * * * as the general nature of the service he undertook at Detroit, and the extensive exercise of cruelties which it involved. Those who act together in war are answerable for each other. No distinction can be made between principal and ally by those against whom the war is waged. He who employs another to do a deed makes the deed his own. If he calls in the hand of the assassin or murderer, himself becomes the assassin or murderer. The known rule of warfare of the Indian savages is an indiscriminate butchery of men, women and children. These savages, under this well known character, are employed by the British nation as allies in the war against the Americans. Governor Hamilton undertakes to be the conductor of the war. In the execution of that undertaking, he associates small parties of the whites under his immediate command with large parties of the savages, and sends them to act, sometimes jointly, and sometimes separately, not against our forts or armies in the field, but the farming settlements on our frontiers. Governor Hamilton is himself the butcher of men, women and children. I will not say to what length the fair rules of war would extend the right of punishment against him; but I am sure that confinement under its strictest circumstances, for Indian devastation and massacre must be deemed lenity.—To SIR GUY CARLETON. FORD ED., ii, 249. (1779.)

8971. WASHINGTON (City), Appropriations.—We cannot suppose Congress intended to tax the people of the United States at large, for all the avenues in Washington and roads in Columbia.—To ROBERT BRENT. v, 50. FORD ED., ix, 33. (W., 1807.)

8972. WASHINGTON (City), Attachment to.—It is with sincere regret that I part with the society in which I have lived here. It has been the source of much happiness to me during my residence at the seat of government, and I owe it much for its kind dispositions. I shall ever feel a high interest in the prosperity of the city, and an affectionate attachment to its inhabitants.—R. TO A. CITIZENS OF WASHINGTON. viii, 158. (March 4, 1809.)

8973. WASHINGTON (City), British capture of.—In the late events at Washington I have felt so much for you that I cannot withhold the expression of my sympathies. For although every reasonable man must be sensible that all you can do is to order, that execution must depend on others, and failures be imputed to them alone; yet I know that when such failures happen they afflict even those who have done everything they could to prevent them. Had General Washington himself been now at the head of our affairs, the same event would probably have happened. We all remember the disgraces which befell us in his time in a trifling war with one or two petty tribes of Indians, in which two armies

* Colonel Matthews was an American officer in the hands of the British. Jefferson was Governor of Virginia.—EDITOR.

were cut off by not half their numbers. Every one knew, and I personally knew, because I was then of his council, that no blame was imputable to him, and that his officers alone were the cause of the disasters. They must now do the same justice.—To PRESIDENT MADISON. vi, 385. (M., Sep. 1814.)

8974. —— ——. [The incendiarism at Washington] enlists the feelings of the world on our side; and the advantage of public opinion is like that of the weather-gauge in a naval action. In Europe, the transient possession of our capital can be no disgrace. Nearly every capital there was in possession of its enemy; some often and long. But diabolical as they paint that enemy, he burned neither public edifices nor private dwellings. It was reserved for England to show that Bonaparte, in atrocity, was an infant to their ministers and their generals. They are taking his place in the eyes of Europe, and have turned into our channel all its good will. This will be worth the million of dollars their conflagration will cost us. —To JAMES MONROE. vi, 408. FORD ED., ix, 496. (M., Jan. 1815.)

8975. —— ——. The embarrassments at Washington in August last, I expected would be great in any state of things; but they proved greater than expected. I never doubted that the plans of the President were wise and sufficient. Their failure we all impute, 1, to the insubordinate temper of Armstrong; and 2, to the indecision of Winder. However, it ends well. It mortifies ourselves and so may check, perhaps, the silly boasting spirit of our newspapers.—To JAMES MONROE. vi, 408. FORD ED., ix, 496. (M., Jan. 1815.)

8976. —— ——. I set down the *coup de main* at Washington as more disgraceful to England than to us.—To W. H. CRAWFORD. vi, 418. FORD ED., ix, 502. (M., 1815.)

8977. —— ——. The transaction has helped rather than hurt us, by arousing the general indignation of our country, and by marking to the world of Europe, the Vandalism and brutal character of the English government. It has merely served to immortalize their infamy.—To MARQUIS LAFAYETTE. vi, 424. FORD ED., ix, 508. (M., 1815.) See CAPITOL.

8978. WASHINGTON (City), Building line.—I doubt much whether the obligation to build the houses at a given distance from the street, contributes to its beauty. It produces a disgusting monotony; all persons make this complaint against Philadelphia. The contrary practice varies the appearance, and is much more convenient to the inhabitants.—FEDERAL CAPITAL OPINION. vii, 513. FORD ED., v, 253. (1790.)

8979. WASHINGTON (City), Foundation of.—As to the future residence of Congress, I can give you an account only from the information of others, all this having taken place before my arrival [in Philadelphia]. Congress, it seems, thought it best to generalize their first determination by putting questions on the several rivers on which it had been proposed that they should fix their residence. The Hudson river, the Delaware, and the Potomac, were accordingly offered to the vote. The first obtained scarcely any votes; the Delaware obtained seven. This, of course, put the Potomac out of the way; and the Delaware being once determined on, there was scarcely any difference of opinion as to the particular spot. The Falls met the approbation of all the States pres-

ent, except Pennsylvania, which was for Germantown, and Delaware, which was for Wilmington. As to the latter, it appeared that she had been induced to vote for the Delaware on the single idea of getting Congress to Wilmington, and that being disappointed in this, they would not wish them on that river at all, but would prefer Georgetown to any other place. This being discovered, the Southern delegates, at a subsequent day, brought on a reconsideration of the question, and obtained a determination that Congress should sit one-half of their time at Georgetown, and that till all accommodations should be provided there, Annapolis should be substituted in its place. This was considered by some as a compromise; by others as only unhinging the first determination and leaving the whole matter open for discussion at some future day. It was in fact a rally, and making a drawn battle of what had at first appeared to be decided against us.—To GOVERNOR BENJAMIN HARRISON. FORD ED., iii, 340. (Pa., Nov. 1783.)

8980. —— ——. I take the following to be the disposition of the several States: The four Eastern States are for any place in preference to Philadelphia, the more northern it is, however, the more agreeable to them. New York and New Hampshire are for the Falls of Delaware. Pennsylvania is for Germantown first, and next for the Falls of Delaware. It is to be noted that Philadelphia had no attention as a permanent seat. Delaware is for Wilmington; but for Georgetown in preference to the Falls of Delaware, or any other situation which [may] attract the trade of their river. Maryland is for Annapolis, and the smallest hope for this will sacrifice a certainty for Georgetown. Virginia, every place southward of Potomac being disregarded by the States as every place north of the Delaware, saw it would be useless to consider her interests as to more southern positions. The Falls of Potomac will probably, therefore, unite the wishes of the whole State. If this fails, Annapolis and the Falls of De'aware are then the candidates. Were the convenience of the delegates alone to be considered, or the general convenience to government in their transaction of business with Congress, Annapolis would be preferred without hesitation. But those who respect commercial advantages more than the convenience of individuals, will probably think that every position on the bay of Chesapeake, or any of its waters, is to be dreaded by Virginia, as it may attract the trade of that bay and make us, with respect to Maryland, what Delaware State is to Pennsylvania. Considering the residence of Congress, therefore, as it may influence trade, if we cannot obtain it on the Potomac, it seems to be our interest to bring it past all the waters of the Chesapeake bay. The three Southern States are for the most southern situation. It should be noted that New Hampshire and Georgia were absent on the decisions of these questions, but considering their interests would be directly opposite, it was thought their joint presence or absence would not change the result. From the preceding state of the views of the several members of our Union, your Excellency will be enabled to judge what will be the probable determination on any future revision of the present plan. The establishment of new States will be friendly or adverse to Georgetown according to their situation. If a State be first laid off on the Lakes, it will add a vote to the northern scale; if on the Ohio, it will add one to the southern.—To GOVERNOR BENJAMIN HARRISON. FORD ED., iii, 342. (Pa., Nov. 1783.)

8981. —— ——. The General Assembly shall have power * * * to cede to Congress one hundred square miles of territory in any other part of this State, exempted from the jurisdiction and government of this State, so long as Congress shall hold their sessions therein, or in any territory adjacent thereto, which may be tendered to them by any other State.—PROPOSED CONSTITUTION FOR VIRGINIA. viii, 446. FORD ED., iii, 325. (1783.)

8982. —— ——. Georgetown languishes. The smile is hardly covered now when the federal towns are spoken of. I fear that our chance is at this time desperate. Our object, therefore, must be, if we fail in an effort to remove to Georgetown, to endeavor then to get to some place off the waters of the Chesapeake where we may be ensured against Congress considering themselves as fixed.—To JAMES MADISON. FORD ED., iii, 400. (A., Feb. 1784.)

8983. —— ——. The remoteness of the Falls of Potomac from the influence of any overgrown commercial city recommends [that place for the] permanent seat of Congress.—NOTES ON PERMANENT SEAT OF CONGRESS. FORD ED., iii, 458. (April 1784.)

8984. —— ——. Philadelphia. In favor of it. 1. Its unrivalled conveniency for transacting the public business, and accommodating Congress. 2. Its being the only place where all the public offices, particularly that of Finance could be kept under the inspection and control of, and proper intercourse with Congress. 3. Its conveniency for foreign ministers, to which, *ceteris paribus,* some regard would be expected. 4. The circumstances which produced a removal from Philadelphia; which rendered a return, as soon as the insult had been expiated, expedient for supporting in the eyes of foreign nations the appearance of internal harmony, and preventing an appearance of resentment in Congress against the State of Pennsylvania, or city of Philadelphia, an appearance which was very much strengthened by some of their proceedings at Princeton—particularly by an unnecessary and irregular declaration not to return to Philadelphia. In addition to these overt reasons, it was concluded by sundry of the members, who were most anxious to fix Congress permanently at the Falls of the Potomac, that a temporary residence in Philadelphia would be most likely to prepare a sufficient number of votes for that place in preference to the Falls of Delaware, and to produce a reconsideration of the vote in favor of the latter. Against Philadelphia were alleged. 1. The difficulty and uncertainty of getting away from it at the time limited. 2. The influence of a large commercial and wealthy city on the public councils. In addition to these objections, the hatred against Mr. Morris, and the hope of accelerating his final resignation were latent motives with some, as perhaps envy of the prosperity of Philadelphia, and dislike of the support of Pennsylvania to obnoxious recommendations of Congress were with others.—NOTES ON PERMANENT SEAT OF CONGRESS. FORD ED., iii, 459. (April 1784.)

8985. —— ——. I like your removal to New York, and hope Congress will continue there, and never execute the idea of building their Federal town. Before it could be finished, a change in members of Congress, or the admission of new States, would remove them somewhere else. It is evident that when a sufficient number of the Western States come in, they will remove it to Georgetown. In the meantime, it is our interest that it should re-

main where it is, and give no new pretensions to any other place.—To JAMES MONROE. i, 347. FORD ED., iv, 52. (P., 1785.)

8986. —— ——. Philadelphia was first proposed, and had six and a half votes. The half vote was Delaware, one of whose members wanted to take a vote on Wilmington. Then Baltimore was proposed and carried, and afterwards rescinded, so that the matter stood open as ever on the 10th of August; but it was allowed the dispute lay only between New York and Philadelphia, and rather thought in favor of the last.—To WILLIAM SHORT. ii, 480. FORD ED., v, 49. (P., Sep. 1788.)

8987. —— ——. On the question of residence, the compromise proposed is to give it to Philadelphia for fifteen years, and then permanently to Georgetown by the same act. This is the best arrangement we have now any prospect of, and therefore the one to which all our wishes are at present pointed. If this does not take place, something much worse will; to wit, an unqualified assumption [of the State debts]. and the permanent seat on the Delaware.—To T. M. RANDOLPH. FORD ED., v, 186. (N.Y., 1790.)

8988. WASHINGTON (City), Future of.—That the improvement of this city must proceed with sure and steady steps, follows from its many obvious advantages, and from the enterprising spirit of its inhabitants, which promises to render it the fairest seat of wealth and science.—R. TO A. CITIZENS OF WASHINGTON. viii, 158. (1809.)

8989. WASHINGTON (City), Houses.—In Paris it is forbidden to build a house beyond a given height, and it is admitted to be a good restriction. It keeps down the price of ground, keeps the houses low and convenient, and the streets light and airy. Fires are much more manageable where houses are low.—FEDERAL CAPITOL OPINION. vii, 513. FORD ED., v, 253. (1790.)

8990. —— ——. I cannot help again suggesting one regulation formerly suggested, to wit: To provide for the extinguishment of fires, and the openness and convenience of the town, by prohibiting houses of excessive height; and making it unlawful to build on any one's purchase any house with more than two floors between the common level of the earth and the eaves.—FEDERAL CAPITAL OPINION. vii, 561. (March 1791.)

8991. WASHINGTON (City), Lots.—The lots [should] be sold i, breadths of fifty feet; their depths to extend to the diagonal of the square.—FEDERAL CAPITAL OPINION. vii, 513. FORD ED., v, 253. (1790.)

8992. WASHINGTON (City), Plans of.—I shall send you * * * two dozen plans of the city of Washington, which you are desired to display, not for sale, but for public inspection, wherever they may be most seen by those descriptions of people worthy and likely to be attracted to it, dividing the plans among the cities of London and Edinburgh chiefly, but sending them also to Glasgow, Bristol, and Dublin.—To THOMAS PINCKNEY. iii, 500. (Pa., 1792.)

8993. —— ——. I sent you * * * a dozen plans of the city of Washington in the Federal territory, hoping you would have them displayed to public view where they would be most seen by those descriptions of men worthy and likely to be attracted to it. Paris, Lyons, Rouen, and the seaport towns of Havre, Nantes, Bourdeaux and Marseilles would be proper places to send some of them.—To GOUVERNEUR MORRIS. iii, 523. FORD ED., vi, 201. (Pa., 1793.)

8994. WASHINGTON (City), Residence in.—On the subject of your location for the winter, it is impossible in my view of it, to doubt on the preference which should be given to this place. Under any circumstances it could not but be satisfactory to you to acquire an intimate knowledge of our political machine, not merely of its organization, but the individuals and characters composing it, their general mode of thinking, and of acting openly and secretly. Of all this you can learn no more at Philadelphia than of a diet of the empire. None but an eyewitness can really understand it, and it is quite as important to be known to them, and to obtain a certain degree of their confidence in your own right. In a government like ours, the standing of a man well with this portion of the public must weigh against a considerable difference of other qualifications.—To WILLIAM SHORT. v, 210. (W., Nov. 1807.)

8995. WASHINGTON (City), Streets.—I should propose the streets [of the Federal capital] to be at right angles, as in Philadelphia, and that no street be narrower than one hundred feet with footways of fifteen feet. Where a street is long and level, it might be one hundred and twenty feet wide. I should prefer squares of at least two hundred yards every way.—FEDERAL CAPITAL OPINION. vii, 512. FORD ED., v, 253. (1790.)

8996. WASHINGTON (George), Advice and.—His mind has been so long used to unlimited applause that it could not brook contradiction, or even advice offered unasked. To advice, when asked, he is very open.—To ARCHIBALD STUART. FORD ED., vii, 101. (M., Jan. 1797.)

8997. WASHINGTON (George), Attacks on.—The President is extremely affected by the attacks made and kept up on him in the public papers. I think he feels those things more than any person I ever yet met with. I am sincerely sorry to see them.—To JAMES MADISON. iii, 579. FORD ED., vi, 293. (June 1793.)

8998. —— ——. [At a cabinet meeting] [Secretary] Knox in a foolish, incoherent sort of a speech, introduced the pasquinade lately printed, called the funeral of George Washington and James Wilson [Associate Justice of the Supreme Court]; King and Judge, &c., where the President was placed on a guillotine. The President was much inflamed; got into one of those passions when he cannot command himself; ran on much on the personal abuse which had been bestowed on him; defied any man on earth to produce one single act of his since he had been in the government, which was not done on the purest motives; that he had never repented but once the having slipped the moment of resigning his office, and that was every moment since, that *by God* he had rather be in his grave than in his present situation; that **he** had rather be on his farm than to be made *Emperor of the world*, and yet they were charging him with wanting to be a King. That that *rascal Freneau* sent him three of his papers every day, as if he thought he would become the distributor of his papers; that he could see in this, nothing but an impudent design to in-

sult him: he ended in this high tone.*—THE ANAS. ix, 164. FORD ED., i, 254. (Aug. 1793.)

8999. WASHINGTON (George), Ceremony and.—I remember an observation of yours, made when I first went to New York, that the satellites and sycophants that surrounded him [Washington] had wound up the ceremonials of the government to a pitch of stateliness which nothing but his personal character could have supported, and which no character after him could ever maintain. It appears now that even his will be insufficient to justify them in the appeal of the times to common sense as the arbiter of everything. Naked, he would have been sanctimoniously reverenced; but enveloped in the rags of royalty, they can hardly be torn off without laceration. It is the more unfortunate that this attack is planted on popular ground, on the love of the people to France and its cause, which is universal.—To JAMES MADISON. iii, 579. FORD ED., vi, 293. (June 1793.)

9000. WASHINGTON (George), Cincinnati and.—I have wished to see you standing on ground separated from it [the Society of the Cincinnati]; and that the character which will be handed to future ages at the head of our Revolution, may, in no instance, be compromitted in subordinate altercations.—To GENERAL WASHINGTON. i, 333. FORD ED., iii, 465. (1784.) See CINCINNATI SOCIETY.

9001. WASHINGTON (George), Confidence in.—Without pretensions to that high confidence you reposed in our first and greatest revolutionary character, whose preeminent services had entitled him to the first place in his country's love, and destined for him the fairest page in the volume of faithful history, I ask so much confidence only as may give firmness and effect to the legal administration of your affairs.—FIRST INAUGURAL ADDRESS. viii, 5. FORD ED., viii, 5. (1801.)

9002. WASHINGTON (George), Crown refused.—The alliance between the States under the old Articles of Confederation, for the purpose of joint defence against the aggressions of Great Britain, was found insufficient, as treaties of alliance generally are, to enforce compliance with their mutual stipulations; and these, once fulfilled, that bond was to expire of itself, and each State to become sovereign and independent in all things. Yet it could not but occur to every one, that these separate independencies, like the petty States of Greece, would be eternally at war with each other, and would become at length the mere partisans and satellites of the leading powers of Europe. All then must have looked to some further bond of union, which would insure internal peace, and a political system of our own, independent of that of Europe. Whether all should be consolidated into a single government, or each remain independent as to internal matters, and the whole form a single nation as to what was foreign only, and whether that national government should be a monarchy or a republic, would of course divide opinions according to the constitutions, the habits, and the circumstances of each individual. Some officers of the army, as it has always been said and believed (and Steuben and Knox have ever been named as the leading agents), trained to monarchy by military habits, are understood to have proposed to General Washington to decide this great question by the army before its disbandment, and

* Genet's case was under consideration at the meeting of the cabinet.—EDITOR.

to assume himself the crown, on the assurance of their support. The indignation with which he is said to have scouted this parricide proposition was equally worthy of his virtue and his wisdom.—THE ANAS. ix, 88. FORD ED., i, 157. (1818.)

9003. WASHINGTON (George), Errors of.—He errs as other men do, but errs with integrity.—To W. B. GILES. iv, 125. FORD ED., vii, 41. (M., 1795.)

9004. ———. I wish that his honesty and his political errors may not furnish a second occasion to exclaim " curse on his virtues, they have undone his country ".—To JAMES MADISON. iv, 136. FORD ED., vii, 69. (M., 1796.)

9005. ———. The President [Washington] is fortunate to get off just as the [bank and paper] bubble is bursting, leaving others to hold the bag. Yet, as his departure will mark the moment when the difficulties begin to work, you will see that they will be ascribed to the new administration, and that he will have his usual good fortune of reaping credit from the good acts of others, and leaving to them that of his errors.—To JAMES MADISON. FORD ED., vii, 104. (M., Jan. 1797.)

9006. WASHINGTON (George), Estimate of.—His mind was great and powerful, without being of the very first order; his penetration strong, though not so acute as that of a Newton, Bacon, or Locke; and as far as he saw, no judgment was ever sounder. It was slow in operation, being little aided by invention or imagination, but sure in conclusion. Hence the common remark of his officers, of the advantage he derived from councils of war, where, hearing all suggestions, he selected whatever was best; and certainly no general ever planned his battles more judiciously. But if deranged during the course of the action, if any member of his plan was dislocated by sudden circumstances, he was slow in readjustment. The consequence was that he often failed in the field, and rarely against an enemy in station, as at Boston and York. He was incapable of fear, meeting personal dangers with the calmest unconcern. Perhaps the strongest feature in his character was prudence, never acting until every circumstance, every consideration, was maturely weighed; refraining if he saw a doubt, but, when once decided, going through with his purpose, whatever obstacles opposed. His integrity was most pure, his justice the most inflexible I have ever known, no motives of interest or consanguinity, of friendship or hatred, being able to bias his decision. He was, indeed, in every sense of the words, a wise, a good, and a great man. His temper was naturally irritable and high toned; but reflection and resolution had obtained a firm and habitual ascendency over it. If ever, however, it broke its bonds, he was most tremendous in his wrath. In his expenses he was honorable, but exact; liberal in contributions to whatever promised utility; but frowning and unyielding on all visionary projects, and all unworthy calls on his charity. His heart was not warm in its affections; but he exactly calculated every man's value, and gave him a solid esteem proportioned to it. His person was fine, his stature exactly what one would wish, his deportment easy, erect and noble; the best horseman of his age, and the most graceful figure that could be seen on horseback. Although in the circle of his friends, where he might be unreserved with safety, he took a free share in conversation, his colloquial talents were not above mediocrity, possessing

neither copiousness of ideas, nor fluency of words. In public, when called on for a sudden opinion, he was unready, short and embarrassed. Yet he wrote readily, rather diffusely, in an easy and correct style. This he had acquired by conversation with the world, for his education was merely reading, writing, and common arithmetic, to which he added surveying at a later day. His time was employed in action chiefly, reading little, and that only in agriculture and English history. His correspondence became necessarily extensive, and, with journalizing his agricultural proceedings, occupied most of his leisure hours within doors. On the whole, his character was, in its mass, perfect, in nothing bad, in few points indifferent; and it may truly be said, that never did nature and fortune combine more perfectly to make a man great, and to place him in the same constellation with whatever worthies have merited from man an everlasting remembrance. For his was the singular destiny and merit, of leading the armies of his country successfully through an arduous war for the establishment of its independence; of conducting its councils through the birth of a government, new in its forms and principles, until it had settled down into a quiet and orderly train; and of scrupulously obeying the laws through the whole of his career, civil and military, of which the history of the world furnishes no other example. How, then, can it be perilous for you to take such a man on your shoulders? I am satisfied the great body of republicans think of him as I do. We were, indeed, dissatisfied with him on his ratification of the British treaty. But this was short-lived. We knew his honesty, the wiles with which he was encompassed, and that age had already begun to relax the firmness of his purposes; and I am convinced he is more deeply seated in the love and gratitude of the republicans, than in the Pharisaical homage of the federal monarchists. For he was no monarchist from preference of his judgment. The soundness of that gave him correct views of the rights of man, and his severe justice devoted him to them. He has often declared to me that he considered our new Constitution as an experiment on the practicability of republican government, and with what dose of liberty man could be trusted for his own good; that he was determined the experiment should have a fair trial, and would lose the last drop of his blood in support of it. * * * I felt on his death with my countrymen, that verily a great man hath fallen this day in Israel.—To DR. WALTER JONES. vi, 286. FORD ED., ix, 448. (M., Jan. 1814.)

9007. WASHINGTON (George), Fame of.—Washington's fame will go on increasing until the brightest constellation in yonder heavens shall be called by his name.—DOMESTIC LIFE OF JEFFERSON. 358.

9008. ———. Our first and greatest revolutionary character, whose preeminent services have entitled him to the first place in his country's love, and destined for him the fairest page in the volume of faithful history.—FIRST INAUGURAL ADDRESS. viii, 5. FORD ED., viii, 5. (1801.)

9009. ———. The moderation of his desires, and the strength of his judgment, enabled him to calculate correctly, that the right to that glory which never dies is to use power for the support of the laws and liberties of our country, not for its destruction; and his will accordingly survive the wreck of everything now living.—To EARL OF BUCHAN. iv, 494. (W., 1803.)

9010. WASHINGTON (George), Farewell address of.—With respect to his [President Washington's] Farewell Address, to the authorship of which, it seems, there are conflicting claims, I can state to you some facts. He had determined to decline reelection at the end of his first term, and so far determined, that he had requested Mr. Madison to prepare for him something valedictory, to be addressed to his constituents on his retirement. This was done, but he was finally persuaded to acquiesce in a second election, to which no one more strenuously pressed him than myself, from a conviction of the importance of strengthening, by longer habit, the respect necessary for that office, which the weight of his character only could effect. When, at the end of this second term, his Valedictory came out, Mr. Madison recognized in it several passages of his draft; several others, we were both satisfied, were from the pen of Hamilton, and others from that of the President himself. These he probably put into the hands of Hamilton to form into a whole, and hence it may all appear in Hamilton's handwriting, as if it were all of his composition.—To WILLIAM JOHNSON. vii, 292. FORD ED., x, 228. (M., 1823.)

9011. WASHINGTON (George), Federalists and.—General Washington, after the retirement of his first cabinet, and the composition of his second, entirely federal, * * * had no opportunity of hearing both sides of any question. His measures, consequently, took the hue of the party in whose hands he was. These measures were certainly not approved by the republicans; yet they were not imputed to him but to the counsellors around him; and his prudence so far restrained their impassioned course and bias, that no act of strong mark, during the remainder of his administration, excited much dissatisfaction. He lived too short a time after, and too much withdrawn from information, to correct the views into which he had been deluded; and the continued assiduities of the party drew him into the vortex of their intemperate career; separated him still farther from his real friends, and excited him to actions and expressions of dissatisfaction, which grieved them, but could not loosen their affections from him. They would not suffer the temporary aberration to weigh against the immeasurable merits of his life; and although they tumbled his seducers from their places, they preserved his memory embalmed in their hearts with undiminished love and devotion; and there it will forever remain embalmed, in entire oblivion of every temporary thing which might cloud the glories of his splendid life. It is vain, then, for Mr. Pickering and his friends to endeavor to falsify his character, by representing him as an enemy to republicans and republican principles, and as exclusively the friend of those who were so; and had he lived longer, he would have returned to his ancient and unbiased opinions, would have replaced his confidence in those whom the people approved and supported, and would have seen that they were only restoring and acting on the principles of his own first administration.—To MARTIN VAN BUREN. vii, 371. FORD ED., x, 314. (M., 1824.)

9012. ——— ———. The federalists, pretending to be the exclusive friends of General Washington, have ever done what they could to sink his character, by hanging theirs on it, and by representing as the enemy of republicans him, who, of all men, is best entitled to the appellation of the father of that republic which they were endeavoring to subvert, and the repub-

licans to maintain. They cannot deny, because the elections proclaimed the truth, that the great body of the nation approved the republican measures.—To MARTIN VAN BUREN. vii, 371. FORD ED., x, 314. (M., 1824.)

9013. ——— ———. From the moment * * * of my retiring from the administration, the federalists got unchecked hold of General Washington. His memory was already sensibly impaired by age, the firm tone of mind for which he had been remarkable, was beginning to relax, its energy was abated; a listlessness of labor, a desire for tranquillity had crept on him, and a willingness to let others act, and even think for him. Like the rest of mankind, he was disgusted with the atrocities of the French Revolution, and was not sufficiently aware of the difference between the rabble who were used as instruments of their perpetration, and the steady and rational character of the American people, in which he had not sufficient confidence. The opposition too of the republicans to the British treaty, and zealous support of the federalists in that unpopular, but favorite measure of theirs, had made him all their own. Understanding, moreover, that I disapproved of that treaty, and copiously nourished with falsehoods by a malignant neighbor of mine [Henry Lee, " Light-Horse Harry "], who ambitioned to be his correspondent, he had become alienated from myself personally, as from the republican body generally of his fellow citizens; and he wrote the letters to Mr. Adams and Mr. Carroll, over which, in devotion to his imperishable fame, we must forever weep as monuments of mortal decay.—THE ANAS. ix, 99. FORD ED., i, 168. (1818.)

9014. WASHINGTON (George), Influence of.—You will have seen by the proceedings of Congress the truth of what I always observed to you, that one man outweighs them all in influence over the people, who have supported his judgment against their own and that of their representatives. Republicanism must lie on its oars, resign the vessel to its pilot, and themselves to the course he thinks best for them.—To JAMES MONROE. iv, 140. FORD ED., vii, 80 (M., June 1796.)

9015. WASHINGTON (George), Jefferson and.—I learn that he [General H. Lee] has thought it worth his while to try to sow tares between you and me, by representing me as still engaged in the bustle of politics, and in turbulence and intrigue against the government. I never believed for a moment that this could make any impression on you, or that your knowledge of me would not overweigh the slander of an intriguer, dirtily employed in sifting the conversations of my table, where alone he could hear of me; and seeking to atone for his sins against you by sins against another, who had never done him any other injury than that of declining his confidences. Political conversations I really dislike, and therefore avoid where I can without affectation. But when urged by others, I have never conceived that having been in public life requires me to belie my sentiments, or even to conceal them. When I am led by conversation to express them, I do it with the same independence here which I have practiced everywhere, and which is inseparable from my nature. But enough of this miserable tergiversator, who ought, indeed, either to have been of more truth, or less trusted by his country.—To PRESIDENT WASHINGTON. iv, 142. FORD ED., vii, 82. (M., 1796.)

9016. WASHINGTON (George), Just.—General Washington was always just in ascribing to every officer the merit of his own works.—NOTES ON M. SOULES'S WORK. ix, 301. FORD ED., iv, 309. (P., 1786.)

9017. WASHINGTON (George), Loved and venerated.—He possessed the love, the veneration, and confidence of all.—THE ANAS. FORD ED., i, 155. (1818.)

9018. WASHINGTON (George), Marshall's life of.—The party feelings of General Washington's biographer [Marshall] to whom after his death the collection of [Washington's papers] was confided, have culled from it a composition as different from what General Washington would have offered, as was the candor of the two characters during the period of the war. The partiality of this pen is displayed in lavishments of praise on certain military characters, who had done nothing military, but who afterwards, and before he wrote, had become heroes in party, although not in war; and in his reserve on the merits of others, who rendered signal services indeed, but did not earn his praise by apostatizing in peace from the republican principles for which they had fought in war. It shows itself too in the cold indifference with which a struggle for the most animating of human objects is narrated. No act of heroism ever kindles in the mind of this writer a single aspiration in favor of the holy cause which inspired the bosom, and nerved the arm of the patriot warrior. No gloom of events, no lowering of prospects ever excites a fear for the issue of a contest which was to change the condition of man over the civilized globe. The sufferings inflicted on endeavors to vindicate the rights of humanity are related with all the frigid insensibility with which a monk would have contemplated the victims of an auto da fé. Let no man believe that General Washington ever intended that his papers should be used for the suicide of the cause for which he had lived, and for which there never was a moment in which he would not have died. The abuse of these materials is chiefly, however, manifested in the history of the period immediately following the establishment of the present Constitution. * * * Were a reader of this period to form his idea of it from this history alone, he would suppose the republican party (who were, in truth, endeavoring to keep the government within the line of the Constitution, and prevent its being monarchized in practice) were a mere set of grumblers, and disorganizers, satisfied with no government, without fixed principles of any, and, like a British parliamentary opposition, gaping after loaves and fishes, and ready to change principles, as well as position, at any time, with their adversaries. But a short review of facts omitted, or uncandidly stated in this history will show that the contests of that day were contests of principle between the advocates of republican and those of kingly government, and that had not the former made the efforts they did, our government would have been, even at this early day, a very different thing from what the successful issue of those efforts have made it.*—THE ANAS. FORD ED., i, 155. (1818.)

9019. WASHINGTON (George), Medallion of.—That our own nation should entertain sentiments of gratitude and reverence for the great character who is the subject of your medallion, is a matter of duty. His disinterested and valuable services to them have rendered it so; but such a monument to his memory by the member of another community, proves a zeal

* In the Congressional edition this extract is omitted except the last sentence.—EDITOR.

for virtue in the abstract, honorable to him who inscribes it, as to him whom it commemorates. * * * This testimonial in favor of the first worthy of our country will be grateful to the feelings of our citizens generally.—To DANIEL ECCLESTON. v, 213. (W., 1807.)

9020. WASHINGTON (George), Memory of.—His memory will be adored while liberty shall have votaries, his name will triumph over time and will in future ages assume its just station among the most celebrated worthies of the world.—NOTES ON VIRGINIA. viii, 312. FORD ED., iii, 168. (1782.)

9021. WASHINGTON (George), National monument to.—In a former letter I enclosed you an idea of Mr. Lee's for an immediate appropriation of a number of lots to raise a sum of money for erecting a national monument in the city of Washington. It was scarcely to be doubted but that you would avoid appropriations for matters of ornament till a sufficient sum should be secured out of the proceeds of your sales to accomplish the public buildings, bridges and such other objects as are essential. Mr. Caracchi, the artist, who had proposed to execute the monument, has had hopes that a subscription set on foot for that purpose, would have sufficed to effect it. That hope is now over, and he is about to return to Europe. He is unquestionably an artist of the first class. He has had the advantage of taking the President's person in plaster, equal to every wish in resemblance and spirit. It is pretty certain that the equestrian statue of the President can never be executed by an equal workman, who has had equal advantages, and the question is whether a prudent caution will permit you to enter into any engagement now, taking time enough before the term of payment to have accomplished the more material objects of the public buildings, &c. He says to execute the equestrian statue, with the cost of the materials, in marble, will be worth twenty thousand guineas; that he would begin it on his return, if four or five years hence you can engage to pay him twenty thousand dollars, and the same sum annually afterwards, till the whole is paid, before which time the statue will be ready. It is rather probable that within some time Congress would take it off your hands, in compliance with an ancient vote of that body. The questions for your consideration are, whether, supposing no difficulty as to the means, you think such a work might be undertaken by you? Whether you can have so much confidence in the productiveness of your funds as to engage for a residuum of this amount, all the more necessary objects being first secured, and that this may be within the time first proposed? And, in fine, which will preponderate in your minds, the hazard of undertaking this now, or that of losing the aid of the artist? The nature of this proposition will satisfy you that it has not been communicated to the President, and of course would not be, unless a previous acceptance on your part, should render it necessary to obtain his sanction. Your answer is necessary for the satisfaction of Mr. Caracchi, at whose instance I submit the proposal to you, and who, I believe, will only wait here the return of that answer.—To THE COMMISSIONERS OF WASHINGTON. iii, 346. (1702.)

9022. WASHINGTON (George), Oath of office.—Knox, Randolph and myself met at Knox's where Hamilton was also to have met, to consider the time, manner and place of the President's swearing in.* Hamilton had been

* On the occasion of Washington's second inauguration.—EDITOR.

there before [us] and had left his opinion with Knox, to wit, that the President should ask a judge to attend him in his own house to administer the oath, in the presence of the heads of Departments, which oath should be deposited in the Secretary of State's office. I concurred in this opinion. E. Randolph was for the President's going to the Senate chamber to take the oath, attended by the Marshal of the United States who should then make proclamation, &c. Knox was for this and for adding the House of Representatives to the presence, as they would not yet be departed. Our individual opinions were written to be communicated to the President out of which he might form one.—THE ANAS. ix, 139. FORD ED., i, 221. (Feb. 1793.)

9023. WASHINGTON (George), Opinions of.—His opinions merit veneration and respect; for few men have lived whose opinions were more unbiased and correct. Not that it is pretended he never felt bias. His passions were naturally strong; but his reason, generally stronger.—THE ANAS. FORD ED., i, 155. (1818.)

9024. WASHINGTON (George), Opposition to administration.—I told the President [Washington] that in my opinion there was only a single source of the discontents [with the administration]. Though they had indeed appeared to spread themselves over the War Department also, yet I considered that as an overflowing only from their real channel, which would never have taken place, if they had not first been generated in another Department, to wit, that of the Treasury. That a system had there been contrived, for deluging the States with paper money instead of gold and silver, for withdrawing our citizens from the pursuits of commerce, manufactures, buildings, and other branches of useful industry, to occupy themselves and their capitals in a species of gambling destructive of morality, and which had introduced its poison into the government itself. That it was a fact, as certainly known as that he and I were then conversing, that particular members of the Legislature, while those laws were on the carpet, had feathered their nests with paper, had then voted for the laws, and constantly since lent all the energy of their talents, and instrumentality of their offices to the establishment and enlargement of this system; that they had chained it about our necks for a great length of time, and in order to keep the game in their hands had, from time to time, aided in making such legislative constructions of the Constitution, as made it a very different thing from what the people thought they had submitted to; that they had now brought forward a proposition, far beyond every one yet advanced, and to which the eyes of many were turned, as the decision which was to let us know, whether we live under a limited or an unlimited government. He asked me to what proposition I alluded? I answered to that in the Report on Manufactures, which, under color of *giving bounties* for the encouragement of particular manufactures, meant to establish the doctrine, that the power given by the Constitution to collect taxes to provide for the *general welfare* of the United States, permitted Congress to take everything under their management which *they* should deem for the *public welfare*, and which is susceptible of the application of money; consequently, that the subsequent enumeration of their powers was not the description to which resort must be had, and did not at all constitute the limits of their authority; that this was a very different question from that of the bank, which was thought an

incident to an enumerated power; that, therefore, this decision was expected with great anxiety; that, indeed, I hoped the proposition would be rejected, believing there was a majority in both Houses against it, and that if it should be, it would be considered as a proof that things were returning into their true channel; and that, at any rate, I looked forward to the broad representation which would shortly take place, for keeping the general Constitution on its true ground; and that this would remove a great deal of the discontent which had shown itself.—THE ANAS. ix, 104. FORD ED., i, 176. (Feb. 29, 1792.)

9025. ———— ————. The President said Governor Lee had that day informed him of the general discontent prevailing in Virginia, of which he never had had any conception, much less sound information; that it appeared to him very alarming. * * * I confirmed him in the fact of the great discontents in the South; that they were grounded on seeing that their judgments and interests were sacrificed to those of the Eastern States on every occasion, and their belief that it was the effect of a corrupt squadron of voters in Congress, at the command of the Treasury; and they see that if the votes of those members who had an interest distinct from, and contrary to the general interest of their constituents, had been withdrawn, as in decency and honesty they should have been, the laws would have been the reverse of what they are on all the great questions. I instanced the new Assumption carried in the House of Representatives by the Speaker's vote. On this subject he made no reply.—THE ANAS. ix, 130. FORD ED., i, 215. (Feb. 7, 1793.)

9026. ———— ————. The object of the opposition which was made to the course of administration was to preserve the Legislature pure and independent of the Executive, to restrain the Administration to republican forms and principles, and not permit the Constitution to be construed into a monarchy, and to be warped, in practice, into all the principles and pollutions of their favorite English model. Nor was this an opposition to General Washington. He was true to the republican charge confided to him; and has solemnly and repeatedly protested to me, in our conversations that he would lose the last drop of his blood in support of it; and he did this the oftener and with the more earnestness, because he knew my suspicions of Hamilton's designs against it, and wished to quiet them. For he was not aware of the drift or of the effect of Hamilton's schemes. Unversed in financial projects and calculations and budgets, his approbation of them was bottomed on his confidence in the man.—THE ANAS. ix, 95. FORD ED., i, 165. (1818.)

9027. WASHINGTON (George), Popularity of.—Such is the popularity of President Washington that the people will support him in whatever he will do or will not do, without appealing to their own reason, or to anything but their feelings towards him.—To ARCHIBALD STUART. FORD ED., vii, 101. (M., Jan. 1797.)

9028. WASHINGTON (George), President.—Though we [in Paris] have not heard of the actual opening of the new Congress, and consequently have not official information of your election as President of the United States, yet, as there never could be a doubt entertained of it, permit me to express here my felicitations, not to yourself, but to my country. Nobody who has tried both public and private life, can doubt that you were much happier on the banks of the Potomac than you will be at New York. But there was nobody so well qualified as yourself to put our new machine into a regular course of action ; nobody, the authority of whose name could have so effectually crushed opposition at home, and produced respect abroad. I am sensible of the immensity of the sacrifice on your part. Your measure of fame was full to the brim ; and, therefore, you have nothing to gain. But there are cases where it is a duty to risk all against nothing, and I believe this was exactly the case. We may presume, too, according to every rule of probability, that after doing a great deal of good, you will be found to have lost nothing but private repose.—To GENERAL WASHINGTON. iii, 30. FORD ED., v, 94. (P., May 1789.)

9029. WASHINGTON (George), Presidential reeligibility and.—The perpetual reeligibility of the same President will probably not be cured during the life of General Washington. His merit has blinded our countrymen to the danger of making so important an officer reeligible. I presume there will not be a vote against him in the United States.—To WILLIAM CARMICHAEL. ii, 465. (P., Aug. 1788.)

9030. WASHINGTON (George), Prudent.—The prudence of the President is an anchor of safety to us.—To NICHOLAS LEWIS. FORD ED., v, 282. (Pa., 1791.)

9031. WASHINGTON (George), Republicanism of.—It is fortunate that our first Executive Magistrate is purely and zealously republican. We cannot expect all his successors to be so, and therefore, should avail ourselves the present day to establish principles and examples which may fence us against future heresies preached now, to be practiced hereafter.— To HARRY INNES. iii, 224. FORD ED., v, 300. (Pa., 1791.)

9032. ———— ————. General Washington was himself sincerely a friend to the republican principles of our Constitution. His faith perhaps in its duration, might not have been as confident as mine ; but he repeatedly declared to me. that he was determined it should have a fair chance for success, and that he would lose the last drop of his blood in its support, against any attempt which might be made to change it from its republican form. He made these declarations the oftener, because he knew my suspicions that Hamilton had other views, and he wished to quiet my jealousies on this subject.—To MARTIN VAN BUREN. vii, 371. FORD ED., x, 314. (M., 1824.)

9033. WASHINGTON (George), Republicans and.—I have long thought it was best for the republican interest to soothe him by flattering where they could approve his measures, and to be silent where they disapprove, that they may not render him desperate as to their affections, and entirely indifferent to their wishes, in short to lie on their oars while he remains at the helm, and let the bark drift as his will and a superintending Providence shall direct.—To ARCHIBALD STUART. FORD ED., vii, 102. (M., Jan. 1797.)

9034. WASHINGTON (George), Second term.—When you first mentioned to me your purpose of retiring from the government, though I felt all the magnitude of the event, I was in a considerable degree silent. I knew that, to such a mind as yours, persuasion was idle and impertinent ; that before forming your decision you had weighed all the reasons for and against the measure, had made up your mind on full view of them, and that there could be little hope of changing the result. Pursuing my reflections, too, I knew we were some day to try to walk alone, and if the essay should be made while you should be alive and looking on, we should derive confidence from that circumstance, and resource, if it failed. The public mind, too, was calm and confident, and therefore in a favorable state for making the experiment. Had no change of circumstances intervened, I should not, with any hopes of success, have now ventured to propose to you a change of purpose. But the public mind is no longer confident and serene ; and that from causes in which you are no ways personally mixed. Though these causes have been hackneyed in the public papers in detail, it may not be amiss, in order to calculate the effect they are capable of producing, to take a view of them in the mass, giving to each the form, real or imaginary, under which they have been presented. It has been urged, then, that the public debt, greater than we can possibly pay before other causes of adding new debt to it will occur, has been artificially created by adding together the whole amount of the debtor and creditor sides of accounts, instead of only taking their balances, which could have been paid off in a short time ; that this accumulation of debt has taken forever out of our power those easy sources of revenue which, applied to the ordinary necessities and exigencies of government, would have answered them habitually, and covered us from habitual murmurings against taxes and taxgatherers, reserving extraordinary calls for those extraordinary occasions which would animate the people to meet them ; that though the calls for money have been no greater than we must expect generally, for the same or equivalent exigencies, yet we are already obliged to strain the impost till it produces clamor, and will produce evasion and war on our own citizens to collect it, and even to resort to an *excise* law of most odious character with the people, partial in its operation, unproductive unless enforced by arbitrary and vexatious means, and committing the authority of the government in parts where resistance is most probable and coercion least practicable. They cite propositions in Congress, and suspect other projects on foot still to increase the mass of debt. They say, that by borrowing at two-thirds of the interest, we might have paid off the principal in two-thirds of the time ; but that from this we are precluded by its being made irredeemable but in small portions and long terms ; that this irredeemable quality was given it for the avowed purpose of inviting its transfer to foreign countries. They predict that this transfer of the principal, when completed, will occasion an exportation of three millions of dollars annually for the interest, a drain of coin, of which as there have been no examples, no calculation can be made of its consequences : that the banishment of our coin will be complicated by the creation of ten millions of paper money, in the form of bank bills now issuing into circulation. They think that the ten or twelve per cent. annual profit paid to the lenders of this paper medium taken out of the pockets of the people. who would have had without interest the coin it is banishing ; that all the capital employed in paper speculation is barren and useless, producing. like that on a gaming table, no accession to itself. and is withdrawn from commerce and agriculture, where it would have produced addition to the common mass : that it nourishes in our citizens habits of vice and idleness, instead of industry and morality ; that it has furnished effectual means of corrupting such a portion of the Legislature as turns the balance between the honest voters, whichever way it is directed: that this corrupt squadron, deciding the voice of the Legislature, have manifested their dispositions to get rid of the limitations imposed by the Constitution on the general Legislature, limitations, on the faith of which, the States acceded to that instrument: that the ultimate object of all this is to prepare the way for a change from the present republican form of government to that of a monarchy, of which the English constitution is to be the model: that this was contemplated by the convention is no secret, because its partisans have made none of it. To effect it then was impracticable, but they are still eager after their object, and are predisposing everything for its ultimate attainment. So many of them have got into the Legislature, that, aided by the corrupt squadron of paper dealers, who are at their devotion, they make a majority in both houses. The republican party, who wish to preserve the government in its present form, are fewer in number; they are fewer even when joined by the two. three, or half dozen anti-federalists, who, though they dare not avow it, are still opposed to any general government; but, being less so to a republican than a monarchical one, they naturally join those whom they think pursuing the lesser evil. Of all the mischiefs objected to the system of measures before mentioned, none is so afflicting and fatal to every honest hope, as the corruption of the Legislature. As it was the earliest of these measures, it became the instrument for producing the rest, and will be the instrument for producing in future a king, lords and commons, or whatever else those who direct it may choose. Withdrawn such a distance from the eye of their constituents, and these so disposed as to be inaccessible to public information, and particularly to that of the conduct of their own representatives, they will form the most corrupt government on earth, if the means of their corruption be not prevented. The only hope of safety now hangs on the numerous representation which is to come forward the ensuing year. Some of the new members will be, probably, either in principle or interest, with the present majority; but it is expected that the great mass will form an accession to the republican party. They will not be able to undo all which the two preceding Legislatures, and especially the first, have done. Public faith and right will oppose this. But some parts of the system may be rightfully reformed, a liberation from the rest unremittingly pursued as fast as right will permit, and the door shut against similar commitments of the nation. Should the next Legislature take this course, it will draw upon them the whole monarchical and paper interest; but the latter, I think, will not go all lengths with the former, because creditors will never, of their own accord, fly off entirely from their debtors; therefore, this is the alternative least likely to produce convulsion. But should the majority of the new members be still in the same principles with the present, and show that we have nothing to expect but a continuance of the same practices, it is not easy to conjecture what would be the result, nor what means would be resorted to for correction of the evil. True wisdom would direct that they should be temperate and peaceable; but the division of sentiment and interest happens unfortunately to be so geographical, that no mortal man can say that what is most wise and temperate would prevail against what is most easy and obvious? I can scarcely contemplate a more incalculable evil than the breaking of the Union into two or more parts. Yet when we consider the mass which opposed

the original coalescence; when we consider that it lay chiefly in the Southern quarter; that the Legislature have availed themselves of no occasion of allaying it, but on the contrary whenever Northern and Southern prejudices have come into conflict, the latter have been sacrificed and the former soothed; that the owers of the debt are in the Southern, and the holders of it in the Northern division: that the antifederal champions are now strengthened in argument by the fulfillment of their predictions; that this has been brought about by the monarchical federalists themselves, who, having been for the new government merely as a stepping stone to monarchy, have themselves adopted the very constructions of the Constitution, of which, when advocating its acceptance before the tribunal of the people, they declared it unsusceptible; that the republican federalists who espoused the same government for its intrinsic merits, are disarmed of their weapons; that which they denied as prophecy, having now become true history, who can be sure that these things may not proselyte the small number which was wanting to place the majority on the other side? And this is the event at which I tremble, and to prevent which I consider your continuance at the head of affairs as of the last importance. The confidence of the whole Union is centered in you. Your being at the helm will be more than an answer to every argument which can be used to alarm and lead the people in any quarter, into violence and secession. North and South will hang together if they have you to hang on; and if the first correction of a numerous representation should fail in its effect, your presence will give time for trying others, not inconsistent with the Union and peace of the States. I am perfectly aware of the oppression under which your present office lays your mind, and of the ardor with which you pant for domestic life. But there is sometimes an eminence of character on which society have such peculiar claims as to control the predilections of the individual for a particular walk of happiness, and restrain him to that alone arising from the present and future benedictions of mankind. This seems to be your condition, and the law imposed on you by Providence in forming your character, and fashioning the events on which it was to operate; and it is to motives like these, and not to personal anxieties of mine or others who have no right to call on you for sacrifices, that I appeal, and urge a revisal of it, on the ground of change in the aspect of things. Should an honest majority result from the new and enlarged representation; should those acquiesce whose principles or interest they may control, your wishes for retirement would be gratified with less danger, as soon as that shall be manifest, without awaiting the completion of the second period of four years. One or two sessions will determine the crisis; and I cannot but hope that you can resolve to add more to the many years you have already sacrificed to the good of mankind. The fear of suspicion that any selfish motive of continuance in office may enter into this solicitation on my part, obliges me to declare that no such motive exists. It is a thing of mere indifference to the public whether I retain or relinquish my purpose of closing my tour with the first political renovation of the government. I know my own measure too well to suppose that my services contribute anything to the public confidence, or the public utility. Multitudes can fill the office in which you have been pleased to place me, as much to their advantage and satisfaction. I have, therefore, no motive to consult but my own inclination, which is bent irresistibly on the tranquil enjoyment of my family, my farm and my books. I should repose among them, it is true, in far greater security, if I were to know that you remained at the watch; and I hope it will be so. To the inducements urged from a view of our domestic affairs, I will add a bare mention, of what indeed need only to be mentioned, that weighty motives for your consideration are to be found in our foreign affairs. I think it probable that both the Spanish and English negotiations, if not completed before your purpose is known, will be suspended from the moment it is known, and that the latter nation will then use double diligence in fomenting the Indian war.—To PRESIDENT WASHINGTON. iii, 360. FORD ED., vi, 1. (Pa., May 1792.)

9035. —— ——. My letter to the President [May 23, 1792], directed to him at Mount Vernon, came to him here [Philadelphia]. He told me of this, and that he would take occasion of speaking with me on the subject. He did so this day [July 10]. He began by observing that he had put it off from day to day, because the subject was painful, to wit, his remaining in office, which that letter solicited. He said that the declaration he had made when he quitted his military command, of never again acting in public life, was sincere. That, however, when he was called on to come forward to set the present government in motion, it appeared to him that circumstances were so changed, as to justify a change in his resolution; he was made to believe that in two years all would be well in motion, and he might retire. At the end of two years he found some things still to be done. At the end of the third year, he thought it was not worth while to disturb the course of things, as in one year more his office would expire, and he was decided then to retire. Now he was told there would still be danger in it. Certainly, if he thought so, he would conquer his longing for retirement. But he feared it would be said his former professions of retirement had been mere affectation, and that he was like other men, when once in office he could not quit it. He was sensible, too, of a decay of his hearing; perhaps his other faculties might fall off, and he not be sensible of it. That with respect to the existing causes of uneasiness, he thought there were suspicions against a particular party, which had been carried a great deal too far; there might be *desires,* but he did not believe there were *designs* to change the form of government into a monarchy; that there might be a few who wished it in the higher walks of life, particularly in the great cities, but that the main body of the people in the eastern States were as steadily for republicanism as in the southern. That the pieces lately published, and particularly in Freneau's paper, seemed to have in view the exciting opposition to the government. That this had taken place in Pennsylvania as to the Excise law, according to information he had received from General Hand. That they tended to produce a separation of the Union, the most dreadful of all calamities, and that whatever tended to produce a resort to monarchical government. He considered those papers as attacking him directly, for he must be a fool indeed to swallow the little sugar plums here and there thrown out to him. That in condemning the administration of the government, they condemned him, for if they thought there were measures pursued contrary to his sentiment, they must conceive him too careless to attend to them, or too stupid to understand them. That though, indeed, he had signed many acts which he did not approve in all their

parts, yet he had never put his name to one which he did not think, on the whole, was eligible. That as to the Bank, which had been an act of so much complaint, until there was some infallible criterion of reason, a difference of opinion must be tolerated. He did not believe the discontents extended far from the seat of government. He had seen and spoken with many people in Maryland and Virginia in his late journey. He found the people contented and happy. He wished, however, to be better informed on this head. If the discontent were more extensive than he supposed, it might be that the desire that he should remain in the government was not general.—THE ANAS. ix, 116. FORD ED., i, 198. (July 1792.)

9036. —— ——. President Washington said [in conversation with me] that as yet he was quite undecided whether to retire in March or not. His inclinations led him strongly to do it. Nobody disliked more the ceremonies of his office, and he had not the least taste or gratification in the execution of its functions. That he was happy at home alone, and that his presence there was now peculiarly called for by the situation of Major Washington, whom he thought irrecoverable, and should he get well, he would remove into another part of the country, which might better agree with him. That he did not believe his presence necessary; that there were other characters who would do the business as well or better. Still, however, if his aid was thought necessary to save the cause to which he had devoted his life principally, he would make the sacrifice of a longer continuance. That he, therefore, reserved himself for future decision, as his declaration would be in time if made a month before the day of election. He had desired Mr. Lear to find out from conversation, without appearing to make the inquiry, whether any other person would be desired by anybody. He had informed him, he judged from conversations that it was the universal desire he should continue, and he believed that those who expressed a doubt of his continuance, did it in the language of apprehension, and not of desire. But this, says he, is only from the north; it may be very different in the south. I thought this meant as an opening to me to say what was the sentiment in the south, from which quarter I come. I told him, that as far as I knew, there was but one voice there, which was for his continuance. —THE ANAS. ix, 120. FORD ED., i, 202. (Oct. 1792.)

9037. WASHINGTON (George), Statue of.—There could be no question raised as to the sculptor who should be employed [to execute Washington's statue]; the reputation of Monsieur Houdon of this city [Paris] being unrivalled in Europe. He is resorted to for the statues of most of the sovereigns in Europe. On conversing with him, Doctor Franklin and myself became satisfied that no statue could be executed so as to obtain the approbation of those to whom the figure of the original is known, but on an actual view by the artist. Of course no statue of General Washington, which might be a true evidence of his figure to posterity, could be made from his picture. Statues are made every day from portraits; but if the person be living, they are always condemned by those who know him for a want of resemblance, and this furnishes a conclusive presumption that similar representations of the dead are equally unfaithful. Monsr. Houdon, whose reputation is such as to make it his principal object, was so anxious to be the person who should hand down the figure of the General to future ages, that without hesitating a moment, he offered to abandon his business here, to leave the statues of Kings unfinished, and to go to America to take the true figure by actual inspection and mensuration. We believe, from his character, that he will not propose any very considerable sum for making this journey; probably two or three hundred guineas, as he must necessarily be absent three or four months, and his expenses will make at least a hundred guineas of the money. When the whole merit of the piece was to depend on this previous expenditure, we could not doubt your approbation of the measure; and that you would think with us that things which are just or handsome should never be done by halves. We shall regulate the article of expense as economically as we can with justice to the wishes of the world. This article, together with the habit, attitude, devices, &c., are now under consideration, and till they be decided on, we cannot ultimately contract with Monsr. Houdon. We are agreed in one circumstance, that the size shall be precisely that of life. Were we to have executed a statue in any other case, we should have preferred making it somewhat larger than life; because as they are generally a little elevated they appear smaller, but we think it important that some one monument should be preserved of the true size as well as figure, from which all other countries (and our own at any future day when they shall desire it), may take copies, varying them in their dimensions as may suit the particular situation in which they wish to place them. The duty as well as the glory of this presentation we think belongs peculiarly to Virginia. We are sensible that the eye alone considered will not be quite as well satisfied; but connecting the consideration that the whole, and every part of it presents the true size of the life, we suppose the beholders will receive a greater pleasure on the whole.—To THE GOVERNOR OF VIRGINIA. FORD ED., iv, 26. (P., 1785.)

9038. —— ——. I am happy to find * * * that the modern dress for your statue would meet your approbation. I found it strongly the sentiment of West, Copley, Trumbull, and Brown, in London; after which, it would be ridiculous to add, that it was my own. I think a modern in an antique dress as just an object of ridicule as a Hercules or Marius with a periwig and a chapeau bras.—To GENERAL WASHINGTON. ii, 250. (P., 1787.)

9039. —— ——. The marble statue of General Washington in the Capitol at Richmond, with its pedestal, cost in Paris 24,000 livres or 1,000 Louis d'ors. It is of the size of life, and made by Houdon, reckoned one of the first statuaries in Europe. Besides this, we paid Houdon's expenses coming to and returning from Virginia to take the General's likeness, which, as well as I recollect, were about 500 guineas, and the transportation of the statue to Virginia with a workman to put it up, the amount of which I never heard.—To MR. PARKER. iv, 309. (Pa., 1800.) See HOUDON.

9040. WATERHOUSE (Dr.), Marine hospital appointment.—When the appointment of Dr. Waterhouse to the care of the marine hospital was decided on, no other candidate had been named to me as desiring the place. The respectable recommendations I had received, and his station as professor of medicine in a college of high reputation, sufficiently warranted his abilities as a physician, and to these was added a fact well known, that to his zeal, the United States were indebted for the introduction of a great blessing,—vaccination, which has extirpated one of the most loathsome

and mortal diseases which has afflicted humanity some years, probably, sooner than would otherwise have taken place. It was a pleasure, therefore, as well as a duty, in dispensing the public favors, to make this small return for the great service rendered our country by Dr. Waterhouse.—To JOSEPH B. VARNUM. v, 222. (W., 1807.)

9041. —— ——. Dr. Waterhouse has been appointed to the Marine Hospital of Boston, as you wished. It was a just though small return for his merit, in introducing the vaccination earlier than we should have had it. His appointment makes some noise there and here, being unacceptable to some; but I believe that schismatic divisions in the medical fraternity are at the bottom of it.—To DR. BENJAMIN RUSH. v, 225. (W., 1808.)

9042. —— ——. You have the blessings of all the friends of human happiness for the great peril from which they are rescued.—To DR. BENJAMIN WATERHOUSE. FORD ED., ix, 532. (M., 1815.)

9043. WEAKNESS, National.—Weakness provokes insult and injury, while a condition to punish often prevents them.—To JOHN JAY. i, 404. FORD ED., iv, 89. (P., 1785.)

9044. WEALTH, Acquirement of.—Wealth acquired by speculation and plunder is fugacious in its nature, and fills society with the spirit of gambling.—To GENERAL WASHINGTON. ii, 252. (P., 1787.)

9045. WEALTH, Aristocracy of.—An aristocracy of wealth [is] of more harm and danger than benefit to society.—AUTOBIOGRAPHY. i, 36. FORD ED., i, 49. (1821.)

9046. WEALTH, Checks on.—Our young Republic * * * should prevent its citizens from becoming so established in wealth and power, as to be thought worthy of alliance by marriage with the nieces, sisters, &c., of Kings.—To DAVID HUMPHREYS. ii, 253. (P., 1787.)

9047. WEALTH, Croakings of.—Do not be frightened into the surrender of [true principles] by the alarms of the timid, or the croakings of wealth against the ascendency of the people.—To SAMUEL KERCHIVAL. vii, 11. FORD ED., x, 39. (M., 1816.)

9048. WEALTH, Dominion of.—Our experience so far, has satisfactorily manifested the competence of a republican government to maintain and promote the best interests of its citizens; and every future year, I doubt not, will contribute to settle a question on which reason, and a knowledge of the character and circumstances of our fellow citizens, could never admit a doubt, and much less condemn them as fit subjects to be consigned to the dominion of wealth and force.—R. TO A. CONNECTICUT REPUBLICANS. viii, 140. (1808.)

9049. WEALTH, Freedom vs.—Though there is less wealth in America [than there is in Europe], there is more freedom, more ease, and less misery.—To BARON GEISMER. i, 427. (P., 1785.)

9050. —— ——. There is no such thing in this country as what would be called wealth in Europe. The richest are but a little at ease, and obliged to pay the most rigorous attention to their affairs to keep them together. I do not mean to speak here of the Beaujons of America; for we have some of those though happily they are but ephemeral. —To M. DE MEUNIER. FORD ED., vii, 13. (M., 1795.)

9051. WEALTH, Greediness for.—Our greediness for wealth, and fantastical expense. have degraded, and will degrade, the minds of our maritime citizens. These are the peculiar vices of commerce.—To JOHN ADAMS. vii, 104. FORD ED., x, 107. (M., 1818.)

9052. WEALTH, Liberty and.—What a cruel reflection that a rich country cannot long be a free one.—TRAVELS IN FRANCE. ix, 319. (1787.)

9053. WEALTH, Overgrown.—If the overgrown wealth of an individual be deemed dangerous to the State, the best corrective is the law of equal inheritance to all in equal degree; and the better, as this enforces a law of nature, while extra-taxation violates it.— NOTE IN TRACY'S POLITICAL ECONOMY. vi, 575. (1816.)

9054. WEALTH, Protection of.—Enough wealthy men will find their way into every branch of the legislature to protect themselves.—To JOHN ADAMS. vi, 224. FORD ED., ix, 426. (M., 1813.)

9055. WEALTH, Public office and.— For promoting the public happiness those persons, whom nature has endowed with genius and virtue, should be rendered by liberal education worthy to receive, and able to guard the sacred deposit of the rights and liberties of their fellow citizens; and they should be called to that charge without regard to wealth * * * or other accidental condition or circumstance.—DIFFUSION OF KNOWLEDGE ·BILL. FORD ED., ii, 221. (1779.)

9056. WEATHER, Contemporary observations.—As soon as I get into the house [in New York] I have hired, * * * I will propose to you to keep a diary of the weather here, and wherever you shall be, exchanging observations from time to time. I should like to compare the two climates by cotemporary observations. My method is to make two observations a day, the one as early as possible in the morning. the other from 3 to 4 o'clock, because I have found 4 o'clock the hottest and daylight the coldest point of the 24 hours. I state them in an ivory pocket book in the following form, and copy them out once a week. * * * The first column is the day of the month, and the second the thermometer in the morning. The fourth do. in the evening. The third the weather in the morning. The fifth do. in the afternoon. The sixth is for miscellanies, such as the appearance of birds, leafing and flowering of trees, frosts remarkably late or early, Aurora Borealis, &c. * * * I distinguish weather into fair or cloudy, according as the sky is more or less than half covered with clouds.—To T. M. RANDOLPH. FORD ED., v, 159. (N.Y., 1790.)

9057. WEATHER, Daily observations. —I make my daily observations as early as possible in the morning. and again about four o'clock in the afternoon, these generally showing

the maxima of cold and heat in the course of 24 hours.—To —— ——. i, 208. FORD ED., ii, 158. (Wg., 1778.)

9058. WEATHER, Extreme cold.—It is so cold that the ink freezes in my pen, so that my letter will scarcely be legible. * * * In the winter of 1779-80, the mercury in Fahrenheit's thermometer fell at Williamsburg once to six degrees above zero. In 1783-84, I was at Annapolis without a thermometer, and I do not know that there was one in that State; I heard from Virginia, that the mercury was again down to six degrees. In 1789-90, I was at Paris. The mercury here was as low as eighteen degrees below zero, of Fahrenheit. These have been the most remarkable cold winters ever known in America. We are told. however, that in 1762, at Philadelphia, it was twenty-two degrees below zero; in December, 1793, it was three degrees below zero there by my thermometer. On the 31st of January, 1796, it was one and three-fourth degrees above zero at Monticello. I shall, therefore, have to change the maximum of our cold, if ever I revise the Notes on Virginia; as six degrees above zero was the greatest which had ever been observed.—To MR. VOLNEY. iv, 157. (M., Jan. 1797.)

9059. WEATHER, Moon and.—I do not know that the coincidence has ever been remarked between the new moon and the greater degrees of cold, or the full moon and the lesser degrees; or that the reflected beams of the moon attemper the weather at all. On the contrary, I think I have understood that the most powerful concave mirror presented to the moon, and throwing its focus on the bulb of a thermometer, does not in the least affect it.—To DR. HUGH WILLIAMSON. iv, 346. FORD ED., vii, 479. (W., 1801.)

9060. WEATHER, Parisian.—From my observations (I guess, because I have not calculated their result carefully) the sun does not shine here [Paris] more than five hours of the twenty-four through the whole year.—To JAMES MADISON. FORD ED., v, 105. (P., 1789.)

9061. WEBSTER (Daniel), Future of.— I am much gratified by the acquaintance made with Mr. Webster. He is likely to become of great weight in our government.—To JAMES MONROE. FORD ED., x, 327. (M., 1824.)

9062. WEBSTER (Noah), Estimate of. —Though I view Webster as a mere pedagogue, of very limited understanding and very strong prejudices and party passions, yet as editor of a paper and as of the New Haven association, he may be worth striking.—To JAMES MADISON. FORD ED., viii, 80. (M., Aug. 1801.)

— **WEIGHTS, Standard of.**—See STANDARD (WEIGHTS).

9063. WELFARE, Public.—To preserve the peace of our fellow citizens, promote their prosperity and happiness, reunite opinion, cultivate a spirit of candor, moderation, charity and forbearance toward one another, are objects calling for the efforts and sacrifices of every good man and patriot. Our religion enjoins it; our happiness demands it; and no sacrifice is requisite but of passions hostile to both.—To THE RHODE ISLAND ASSEMBLY. iv, 397. (W., 1801.)

— **WELFARE CLAUSE, General.**—See GENERAL WELFARE CLAUSE.

9064. WEST AND SOUTH, Free government in.—It seems to me that in proportion as commercial avarice and corruption advance on us from the north and east, the principles of free government are to retire to the agricultural States of the south and west, as their last asylum and bulwark. With honesty and self-government for her portion, agriculture may abandon contentedly to others the fruits of commerce and corruption.—To HENRY MIDDLETON. vi, 91. (M., Jan. 1813.)

9065. —— ——. I fear, with you, all the evils which the present lowering aspect of our political horizon so ominously portends. That at some future day, which I hoped to be very distant, the free principles of our government might change with the change of circumstances was to be expected. But I certainly did not expect that they would not over-live the generation which established them. And what I still less expected was, that my favorite Western country was to be made the instrument of change. I had ever and fondly cherished the interests of that country, relying on it as a barrier against the degeneracy of public opinion from our original and free principles. But the bait of local interests, artfully prepared for their palate, has decoyed them from their kindred attachments, to alliances alien to them.—To CLAIBORNE W. GOOCH. vii, 430. (M., January 1826.)

9066. WEST INDIES, British.—I think that the trade with Great Britain is a ruinous one to ourselves; and that nothing would be an inducement to tolerate it, but a free commerce with their West Indies; and that this being denied to us, we should put a stop to the losing branch. The question is, whether they are right in their prognostications that we have neither resolution nor union enough for this.—To T. PLEASANTS. i, 563. (P., 1786.)

9067. WEST INDIES, Coalition with French.—In policy, if not in justice, the National Assembly [of France] should be disposed to avoid oppression, which, falling on us, as well as on their colonies, might tempt us to act together.—To WILLIAM SHORT. iii, 276. FORD ED., v, 364. (Pa., 1791.)

9068. WEST INDIES, Commerce with.—The commerce with the English West Indies is valuable and would be worth a sacrifice to us. But the commerce with the British dominion in Europe is a losing one and deserves no sacrifice. Our tobacco they must have from whatever place we make its deposit, because they can get no other whose quality so well suits the habits of their people. It is not a commodity like wheat which will not bear a double voyage. Were it so, the privilege of carrying it directly to England might be worth something.—To JAMES MADISON. FORD ED., iv, 37. (P., 1785.)

9069. —— ——. Our commerce is in agonies at present, and these would be relieved by opening the British ports in the West Indies.—To JOHN ADAMS. i, 436. (P., 1785.)

9070. —— ——. The merchants of this country [France] are very clamorous against our admission into the West Indies, and ministers are afraid for their places.—To JAMES MONROE. FORD ED., iv, 31. (P., 1785.)

9071. —— ——. The effecting treaties with the powers holding positions in the West Indies, I consider as the important part of our business. It is not of great consequence whether the others treat or not. Perhaps trade may go on with them well enough without.—To JAMES MONROE. FORD ED., iv, 31. (1785.)

9072. —— ——. Access to the West Indies is indispensably necessary to us. Yet how gain it, when it is the established system of these nations [France and England] to exclude all foreigners from their colonies? The only chance seems to be this: our commerce to the mother countries is valuable to them. We must endeavor, then, to make this the price of an admission into their West Indies, and to those who refuse the admission, we must refuse our commerce, or load theirs by odious discriminations in our ports.—To JAMES MONROE. i, 351. FORD ED., iv, 58. (P., 1785.)

9073. —— ——. To nations with which we have not yet treated, and who have possessions in America, we may offer a free vent of their manufactures in the United States, for a full or modified admittance into those possessions. But to France, we are obliged to give that freedom for a different compensation: to wit, for her aid in effecting our independence. It is difficult, therefore, to say what we have now to offer her, for an admission into her West Indies. Doubtless, it has its price; but the question is what this would be, and whether worth our while to give it. Were we to propose to give to each other's citizens all the rights of natives, they would of course count what they should gain by this enlargement of right, and examine whether it would be worth to them as much as their monopoly of their West India commerce. If not, that commercial freedom which we wish to preserve, and which indeed is so valuable, leaves us little to offer. An expression in my letter to the Count de Vergennes * * * wherein I hinted that both nations might, perhaps, come into the opinion that the condition of *natives* might be a better ground of intercourse for their citizens, than that of the *most favored* nation, was intended to furnish an opportunity to the minister of parleying on that subject, if he was so disposed, and to myself, of seeing whereabouts they would begin, that I might communicate it to Congress, and leave them to judge of the expediency of pursuing the subject. But no overtures have followed.*—REPORT TO CONGRESS. ix, 243. FORD ED., iv, 129. (P., 1785.)

9074. —— ——. Our commerce with the West Indies had never admitted amelioration during my stay in France. The temper of that period did not allow even the essay, and it was as much as we could do to hold the ground given us by the Marshal de Castries' *Arret*, admitting us to their colonies with salted provisions, &c.—To GOUVERNEUR MORRIS. iii, 448. FORD ED., vi, 80. (Pa., 1792.)

9075. WEST INDIES, Confederation of.—Could Napoleon obtain, at the close of the present war, the independence of all the West India islands, and their establishment in a separate confederacy, our quarter of the globe would exhibit an enrapturing prospect into futurity. You will live to see much of this. I shall follow, however, cheerfully my fellow laborers, contented with having borne a part in beginning this beatific reformation.—To BARON HUMBOLDT. v, 581. (M., April 1811.)

* Report of a Conference with Count de Vergennes, Foreign Minister of France, on the question of Commerce.—EDITOR.

9076. WEST INDIES, Dominion of.— Whenever jealousies are expressed as to any supposed views of ours on the dominion of the West Indies, you cannot go farther than the truth in asserting we have none. If there be one principle more deeply rooted than any other in the mind of every American, it is that we should have nothing to do with conquest. As to commerce, indeed, we have strong sensations. In casting our eyes over the earth, we see no instance of a nation forbidden, as we are, by foreign powers, to deal with our neighbors, and obliged with them to carry into another hemisphere, the mutual supplies necessary to relieve mutual wants. * * * An exchange of surpluses and wants between neighbor nations, is both a right and a duty under the moral law, and measures against right should be mollified in their exercise, if it be wished to lengthen them to the greatest term possible.—To WILLIAM SHORT. iii, 275. FORD ED., v, 363. (Pa., 1791.)

9077. WEST INDIES, French.—A jealousy of our taking. away the French carrying trade is the principal reason which obstructs our admission into their West India Islands.— To M. LIMOZIN. ii. 339. (P., 1787.)

9078. WEST INDIES, French concession.—France gives us an access to her West Indies, which, though not all we wish, is yet extremely valuable to us.—To JOHN ADAMS. i, 487. (P., 1785.)

9079. —— ——. France has explained herself generously. She does not mean to interrupt our prosperity by calling for our guarantee. On the contrary, she wishes to promote it by giving us, in all her possessions, all the rights of her native citizens, and to receive our vessels as her vessels.—To JAMES MONROE. FORD ED., vi, 281. (Pa., 1793.)

9080. WEST INDIES, Interposition in. —As to the guarantee of the French Islands, whatever doubts may be entertained of the moment at which we ought to interpose, yet I have no doubt but that we ought to interpose at a proper time, and declare both to England and France, that these Islands are to rest with France, and that we will make a common cause with the latter for that object.—To JAMES MADISON. iv, 103. FORD ED., vi, 502. (M., April 1794.)

9081. WEST INDIES, Liberty in French.—The emancipation of their islands is an idea prevailing in the minds of several members of the National Assembly, particularly those most enlightened and most liberal in their views. Such a step by this country would lead to other emancipations or revolutions in the same quarter.—To JOHN JAY. iii, 96. (P., 1789.)

9082. WEST INDIES, Monopoly of.—I observed [to the Count de Montmorin] that it would be much against our interest that any one power should monopolize all the West India islands.—To JOHN JAY. iii, 96. (P., 1789.)

9083. WEST INDIES, Negroes in.— What are you doing for your colonies? They will be lost if not more effectually succored. Indeed, no future efforts you can make will ever be able to reduce the blacks. All that can be done, in my opinion, will be to compound with them, as has been done formerly in Jamaica. We have been less zealous in aiding them, lest your government should feel any jealousy on our account. But, in truth, we as sincerely wish their restoration and their connection with you, as you do yourselves. We

are satisfied that neither your justice nor their distresses will ever again permit their being forced to seek at dear and distant markets those first necessaries of life which they may have at cheaper markets, placed by nature at their door, and formed by her for their support.—To GENERAL LAFAYETTE. iii, 450. FORD ED., vi, 78. (Pa., 1792.)

9084. —— ——. I become daily more convinced that all the West India Islands will remain in the hands of the people of color, and a total expulsion of the whites sooner or later take place. It is high time we should foresee the bloody scenes which our children certainly, and possibly ourselves (south of the Potomac). have to wade through, and try to avert them.— To JAMES MONROE. iv, 20. FORD ED., vi, 349. (P., July 1793.)

9085. —— ——. Inhabited already by a people of their own race and color; climates congenial with their natural constitution; insulated from the other descriptions of men; nature seems to have formed these islands to become the receptacle of the blacks transplanted into this hemisphere.—To JAMES MONROE. iv, 421. FORD ED., viii, 105. (W., 1801.)

9086. WEST INDIES, Opening the.— Your communications to the Count de Moustier, whatever they may have been, cannot have done injury to my endeavors here [Paris], to open the West Indies to us. On this head, the ministers are invincibly mute, though I have often tried to draw them into the subject. I have, therefore, found it necessary to let it lie, till war, or other circumstance, may force it on. Whenever they are at war with England. they must open the Islands to us, and perhaps during that war they may see some price which might make them agree to keep them always open.— To GENERAL WASHINGTON. ii, 536. FORD ED., v, 57. (P., 1788.)

9087. WEST INDIES, Portuguese.— Portugal [in making a commercial treaty with us] will probably restrain us to their dominions in Europe. We must expressly include the Azores, Madeiras and Cape de Verde islands, some of which are deemed to be in Africa. We should also contend for an access to their possessions in America * * * .—To JOHN ADAMS. i, 495. (P., 1785.)

9088. WEST INDIES, Prosperity of.— Our wishes are cordial for the reestablishment of peace and commerce in those colonies, and to give such proofs of our good faith both to them and the mother country [France] as to suppress all that jealousy which might oppose itself to the free exchange of our *mutual productions,* so essential to the prosperity of those colonies, and to the preservation of our agricultural interest. This is our true interest and our true object, and we have no reason to conceal views so justifiable, though the expression of them may require that the occasions be proper, and the terms chosen with delicacy.— To GOUVERNEUR MORRIS. iii, 339. FORD ED., v, 450. (Pa., 1792.)

9089. WEST INDIES, Proximity.—Our vicinity to their West India possessions. and to the fisheries is a bridle which a small naval force, on our part, would hold in the mouths of the most powerful of * * * the [European] countries.—To JOHN JAY. i, 405. FORD ED., iv, 90. (P., 1785.)

9090. WEST INDIES, San Domingo.—I expressed to [the San Domingo deputies] freely my opinion * * * that as to ourselves there was one case which would be peculiarly alarming to us, to wit, were there a danger of their falling under any other power [than France].—To WILLIAM SHORT. iii, 304. FORD ED., v, 395. (Pa., Nov. 1791.)

— **WEST POINT, Academy.**—See ACADEMY (MILITARY).

9091. WESTERN EXPLORATION, Michaux expedition.—The chief objects of your journey are to find the shortest and most convenient route of communication between the United States and the Pacific ocean, within the temperate latitudes, and to learn such particulars as can be obtained of the country through which the Missouri passes, its productions, inhabitants, and other interesting circumstances. As a channel of communication between these States and the Pacific ocean, the Missouri, so far as it extends, presents itself under circumstances of unquestioned preference. * * * It would seem by the latest maps as if a river called the Oregon interlocked with the Missouri for a considerable distance, and entered the Pacific ocean not far southward from Nootka Sound. But the [Philosophical] Society are aware that these maps are not to be trusted, so far as to be the ground of any positive instruction to you. * * * You will in the course of your journey, take notice of the country you pass through, its general face, soil, rivers, mountains, its productions—animal, vegetable, and mineral—so far as they may be new to us, and may also be useful or very curious.* —To ANDRE MICHAUX. ix, 434. FORD ED., vi, 159. (Jan. 1793.)

9092. WESTERN POSTS, British retention of.—I had a good deal of conversation with the Count de Vergennes on the situation of affairs between England and the United States, and particularly on their refusal to deliver up our posts. I observed to him that the obstructions thrown in the way of the recovery of their debts were the effect and not the cause, as they pretended, of their refusal to deliver up the posts; that the merchants interested in these debts showed a great disposition to make arrangements with us; that the article of time we could certainly have settled, and probably that of the interest during the war, but that the minister, showing no disposition to have these matters arranged, I thought it a sufficient proof that this was not the true cause of their retaining the posts. He concurred as to the justice of our requiring time for the payment of our debts; said nothing which showed a difference of opinion as to the article of interest, and seemed to believe fully that their object was to divert the channel of the fur trade before they delivered up the posts, and expressed a strong sense of the importance of that commerce to us. I told him I really could not foresee what would be the event of this detention; that the situation of the British funds, and desire of their minister to begin to reduce the national debt, seemed to indicate that they could not wish a war. He thought so, but that neither were we in a condition to go to war. I told him I was yet uninformed what Congress proposed to do on this subject but that we should certainly always count on the good offices of France, and I was sure that the offer of them would suffice to induce Great Britain to do us justice. He said that surely we might always count on the friendship of

* This expedition was started by private subscriptions under the patronage of the American Philosophical Society. Jefferson was a large subscriber to the fund.—EDITOR.

France. I added that, by the treaty of alliance, she was bound to guarantee our limits to us as they should be established at the moment of peace. He said they were so, "*mais qu'il nous etoit necessaire de les constater*". I told him there was no question what our boundaries were; that the English themselves admitted they were clear beyond all question. I feared, however, to press this any further, lest a reciprocal question should be put to me.—To JOHN JAY. i, 575. FORD ED., iv, 228. (P., 1786.)

9093. WESTERN POSTS, Demand for surrender.—The President * * * authorized Mr. Gouverneur Morris to enter into conference with the British ministers in order to discover their sentiments on their * * * retention of the western posts contrary to the treaty of peace. * * * The letters of Mr. Morris * * * [to the President] state the communications, oral and written, which have passed between him and the ministers; and from these the Secretary of State draws the following inference: That the British court is decided not to surrender the posts in any event; and that they will urge as a pretext that though our courts of justice are now open to British subjects, they were so long shut after the peace as to have defeated irremediably the recovery of debts in many cases. They suggest, indeed, the idea of an indemnification on our part. But, probably, were we disposed to admit their right to indemnification, they would take care to set it so high as to insure a disagreement. * * * The Secretary of State is of opinion * * * that the demands of the posts * * * should n t be again made till we are in readiness to do ourselves the justice which may be refused.—OFFICIAL REPORT. vii, 517. FORD ED., v, 261. (December 1790.)

9094. WESTERN TERRITORY, Acceptance of cession.—On receiving the act of Assembly for the Western cession, our delegation agreed on the form of a deed; we then delivered to Congress a copy of the act, and the form of the deed we were ready to execute whenever they should think proper to declare they would accept it. They referred the act and deed to a committee, who reported the act of Assembly to comport perfectly with the propositions of Congress, and that the deed was proper in its form, and that Congress ought to accept the same. On the question to agree to the report of the Committee, eight States being present, Jersey was in the negative, and South Carolina and Pennsylvania divided (being represented each by two members). Of course there were five ayes only and the report fell. We determined on consultation that our proper duty was to be still, having declared we were ready to execute, we would leave it to them to come forward and tell us they were ready to accept. We meddled not at all, therefore, and showed a perfect indifference. New Hampshire came to town which made us nine States. A member proposed that we should execute the deed and lay it on the table, which after what had been done by Congress would be final, urging the example of New York which had executed their deed, laid it on the table, where it remained eighteen months before Congress accepted it. We replied, "No", if the lands are not offered for sale the ensuing spring, they will be taken from us all by adventurers; we will, therefore, put it out of our power, by the execution of a deed, to sell them ourselves, if Congress will not. A member from Rhode Island then moved that Congress should accept. Another from Jersey proposed as an amendment a proviso that it should not amount to an 'acknowledgment of our right. We told them we were not authorized to admit any conditions or provisions; that their acceptance must be simple, absolute and unqualified, or we could not execute. On the question there were six ayes; Jersey, " No "; South Carolina and Pennsylvania divided. The motion dropped, and the House proceeded to other business. About an hour after, the dissenting Pennsylvanian asked and obtained leave to change his " no " into " aye "; the vote then passed and we executed the deed. We have desired an exemplification of it under the Seal of the States. * * * This shows the wisdom of the Assembly in not taking any new conditions, which would certainly have defeated their accommodating intentions.—To GOVERNOR BENJ. HARRISON. FORD ED., iii, 411. (A., March 1784.)

9095. WESTERN TERRITORY, Deed of cession.—To all who shall see these presents we [here name the delegates] the underwritten delegates for the Commonwealth of Virginia in the Congress of the United States of America send greeting:

Whereas the General Assembly of the Commonwealth of Virginia at their sessions begun on the 20th day of October, 1783, passed an " Act entituled ' An Act to authorize the delegates, &c.'—in these words following to wit, ' Whereas the Congress, &c.' [reciting the act verbatim].

And whereas the said General Assembly by their Resolution of June 6th, 1783, had constituted and appointed us the said A. B. C. &c., delegates to represent the said Commonwealth in Congress for one year from the first Monday in November then next following, which resolution remains in full force.

Now, therefore, know ye that we the said A. B. C. &c., by virtue of the power and authority, committed to us by the act of the said General Assembly of Virginia before recited, and in the name and for and on behalf of the said Commonwealth, do by these presents convey, transfer, assign, and make over unto the United States in Congress assembled, for the benefit of the said States, Virginia inclusive, all right, title and claim as well of soil as of jurisdiction which the said Commonwealth hath to the territory or tract of country within the limits of the Virginia charter, situate, lying, and being to the Northwest of the river Ohio, to and for the uses and purposes and on the conditions of the said recited act. In testimony whereof we have hereunto subscribed our names and affixed our seals in Congress the —— day of —— in the year of our Lord 1784, and of the Independence of the United States the eighth.—DEED OF CESSION. FORD ED., iii, 406. (March 1, 1784.)

9096. WESTERN TERRITORY, Division into States.—With respect to the new States, were the question to stand simply in this form: How may the ultramontane territory be disposed of, so as to produce the greatest and most immediate benefit to the inhabitants of the maritime States of the Union? The plan would be more plausible, of laying it off into two or more States only. Even on this view, however, there would still be something to be said against it, which might render it at least doubtful. But that is a question which good faith forbids us to receive into discussion. This requires us to state the question in its just form: How may the territories of the Union be disposed of, so as to produce the greatest degree of happiness to their inhabitants? With respect to the maritime States, little or nothing remains to be done. With respect, then, to the

ultramontane States, will their inhabitants be happiest, divided into States of thirty thousand square miles, not quite as large as Pennsylvania, or into States of one hundred and sixty thousand square miles, each, that is to say, three times as large as Virginia within the Alleghany? They will not only be happier in States of a moderate size, but it is the only way in which they can exist as a regular Society. Considering the American character in general, that of those people particularly, and the energetic nature of our governments, a State of such extent as one hundred and sixty thousand square miles, would soon crumble into little ones. These are the circumstances which reduce the Indians to such small societies. They would produce an effect on our people, similar to this. They would not be broken into such small pieces, because they are more habituated to subordination, and value more a government of regular law. But you would surely reverse the nature of things, in making small States on the ocean, and large ones beyond the mountains. If we could, in our consciences, say, that great States beyond the mountains will make the people happiest, we must still ask, whether they will be contented to be laid off into large States? They certainly will not: and, if they decide to divide themselves, we are not able to restrain them. They will end by separating from our confederacy, and becoming its enemies. We had better, then, look forward, and see what will be the probable course of things. This will surely be a division of that country into States of a small, or, at most, of a moderate size. If we lay them off into such, they will acquiesce; and we shall have the advantage of arranging them so as to produce the best combinations of interest. What Congress has already done in this matter is an argument the more in favor of the revolt of those States against a different arrangement, and of their acquiescence under a continuance of that. Upon this plan, we treat them as fellow citizens; they will have a just share in their own government; they will love us, and pride themselves in an union with us. Upon the other, we treat them as subjects; we govern them, and not they themselves; they will abhor us as masters, and break off from us in defiance. I confess to you, that I can see no other turn that these two plans would take. But I respect your opinion, and your knowledge of the country too much, to be ever confident in my own.—To JAMES MONROE. i, 587. FORD ED., iv, 246. (P., 1786.)

9097. ———— ————. I find Congress have reversed their division of the Western States and proposed to make them fewer and larger. This is reversing the natural order of things. A tractable people may be governed in large bodies; but, in proportion as they depart from this character, the extent of their government must be less. We see into what small divisions the Indians are obliged to reduce their societies.—To JAMES MADISON. ii, 66. FORD ED., iv, 333. (P., 1786.)

9098. WESTERN TERRITORY, Government for.—The Committee appointed to prepare a plan for the temporary Government of the Western Territory have agreed to the following resolutions: Resolved, that the territory ceded or to be ceded by individual States to the United States whensoever the same shall have been purchased of the Indian inhabitants and offered for sale by the United States shall be formed into distinct States bounded in the following manner as nearly as such cessions will admit, that is to say: Northwardly and

Southwardly by parallels of latitude so that each State shall comprehend from South to North two degrees of latitude beginning to count from the completion of thirty-one degrees North of the equator, but any territory Northwardly of the 47th degree shall make part of the State next below, and Eastwardly and Westwardly they shall be bounded, those on the Mississippi by that river on one side and the meridian of the lowest point of the rapids of Ohio on the other ; and those adjoining on the East by the same meridian on their Western side, and on their Eastern by the meridian of the Western cape of the mouth of the Great Kanawha. And the territory eastward of this last meridian between the Ohio, Lake Erie and Pennsylvania shall be one State. That the settlers within the territory so to be purchased and offered for sale shall, either on their own petition or on the order of Congress, receive authority from them, with appointments of time and place for their free males of full age to meet together for the purpose of establishing a temporary government, to adopt the constitution and laws of any one of these States, so that such laws nevertheless shall be subject to alteration by their ordinary legislature, and to erect, subject to a like alteration counties or townships for the election of members for their legislature. That such temporary government shall only continue in force in any State until it shall have acquired 20,000 free inhabitants, when, giving due proof thereof to Congress, they shall receive from them authority with appointments of time and place to call a convention of representatives to establish a permanent Constitution and Government for themselves. Provided, that both the temporary and permanent Governments be established on these principles as their basis. 1. That they shall forever remain a part of the United States of America. 2. That in their persons, property and territory, they shall be subject to the Government of the United States in Congress assembled, and to the Articles of Confederation in all those cases in which the original States shall be so subject. 3. That they shall be subject to pay a part of the federal debts contracted or to be contracted, to be apportioned on them by Congress, according to the same common rule and measure by which apportionments thereof shall be made on the other States. 4. That their respective Governments shall be in republican forms, and shall admit no person to be a citizen, who holds any hereditary title. 5. That after the year 1800 of the Christian era, there shall be neither slavery nor involuntary servitude in any of the said States, otherwise than in punishment of crimes, whereof the party shall have been duly convicted to have been personally guilty. That whenever any of the said States shall have, of free inhabitants as many as shall then be in any one the least numerous of the thirteen original States, such State shall be admitted by its delegates into the Congress of the United States, on an equal footing with the said original States : After which the assent of two-thirds of the United States in Congress assembled shall be requisite in all those cases, wherein by the Confederation the assent of nine States is now required. Provided the consent of nine States to such admission may be obtained according to the eleventh of the Articles of Confederation. Until such admission by their delegates into Congress, any of the said States, after the establishment of their temporary Government, shall have authority to keep a sitting Member in Congress, with a right of debating, but not of voting. That the territory Northward of the 45th degree, that is to say of the completion of 45°

from the Equator and extending to the Lake of the Woods, shall be called SYLVANIA. That of the territory under the 45th and 44th degrees, that which lies Westward of Lake Michigan shall be called MICHIGANIA, and that which is Eastward thereof, within the peninsula formed by the lakes and waters of Michigan, Huron, St. Clair and Erie, shall be called CHERRONESUS, and shall include any part of the peninsula which may extend above the 45th degree. Of the territory under the 43d and 42d degrees, that to the Westward through which the Assenisipi or Rock river runs shall be called ASSENISIPIA, and that to the Eastward in which are the fountains of the Muskingum, the two Miamis of Ohio, the Wabash, the Illinois, the Miami of the lake and Sandusky rivers, shall be called METROPOTAMIA. Of the territory which lies under the 41st and 40th degrees Western, through which the river Illinois runs, shall be called ILLINOIA ; that the next adjoining to the Eastward SARATOGA, and that between this last and Pennsylvania and extending from the Ohio to Lake Erie shall be called WASHINGTON. Of the territory which lies under the 39th and 38th degrees to which shall be added so much of the point of land within the fork of the Ohio and Mississippi as lies under the 37th degree, that to the Westward within and adjacent to which are the confluences of the rivers Wabash, Shawanee, Tennessee, Ohio, Illinois, Mississippi and Missouri, shall be called POLYPOTAMIA, and that to the Eastward, farther up the Ohio, otherwise called the Pelisipi, shall be called PELISIPIA. That the preceding articles shall be formed into a charter of Compact, shall be duly executed by the President of the United States in Congress assembled, under his hand and the seal of the United States, shall be promulgated, and shall stand as fundamental constitutions between the thirteen original States, and those now newly described, unalterable but by the joint consent of the United States in Congress assembled, and of the particular State within which such alteration is proposed to be made.—REPORT ON GOVERNMENT FOR WESTERN TERRITORY. FORD ED., iii, 407. (March 1, 1784.)

9099. —— ——. The committee to whom was recommitted the report of a plan for a temporary government of the Western Territory have agreed to the following resolutions : Resolved. That so much of the territory ceded or to be ceded by individual States to the United States as is already purchased or shall be purchased of the Indian inhabitants and offered for sale by Congress, shall be divided into distinct States, in the following manner, as nearly as such cessions will admit : that is to say, by parallels of latitude, so that each State shall comprehend from South to North two degrees of latitude beginning to count from the completion of thirty-one degrees North of the Equator ; and the meridian of longitude, one of which shall pass through the lowest point of the rapids of Ohio, and the other through the Western Cape of the mouth of the Great Kanawha, but the territory Eastward of this last meridian, between the Ohio, Lake Erie, and Pennsylvania shall be one State, whatsoever may be its comprehension of latitude. That which may lie beyond the completion of the 45th degree between the sd. meridians shall make part of the State adjoining it on the South, and that part of the Ohio which is between the same meridians coinciding nearly with the parallel of 39° shall be substituted so far in lieu of that parallel as a boundary line. That the settlers on any territory so purchased and offered for sale, either on their own petition, or on the order of Congress, receive authority from them, with appointments of time and place for their free males of full age, within the limits of their State to meet together for the purpose of establishing a temporary government, to adopt the constitution and laws of any one of the original States, so that such laws nevertheless shall be subject to alteration by their ordinary legislature; and to erect, subject to a like alteration, counties or townships for the election of members for their legislature. That such temporary government shall only continue in force in any State until it shall have acquired 20,000 free inhabitants. when giving due proof thereof to Congress, they shall receive from them authority with appointment of time and place to call a convention of representatives to establish a permanent Constitution and Government for themselves. Provided that both the temporary and permanent governments be established on these principles as their basis. 1. They shall forever remain a part of this confederacy of the United States of America. 2. That in their persons, property, and territory, they shall be subject to the Government of the United States in Congress assembled, and to the articles of Confederation in all those cases in which the original States shall be so subject. 3. That they shall be subject to pay a part of the federal debts contracted or to be contracted, to be apportioned on them by Congress, according to the same common rule and measure, by which apportionments thereof shall be made on the other States. 4. That their respective Governments shall be in republican forms and shall admit no person to be a citizen who holds any hereditary title. 5. That after the year 1800 of the Christian era, there shall be neither slavery nor involuntary servitude in any of the sd States, otherwise than in punishment of crimes whereof the party shall have been convicted to have been personally guilty. That whensoever any of the sd States shall have, of free inhabitants, as many as shall be in any one the least numerous. of the thirteen original States, such State shall be admitted by its delegates into the Congress of the United States on an equal footing with the said original States: provided nine States agree to such admission according to the reservation of the 11th of the Articles of Confederation, and in order to adapt the sd Articles of Confederation to the State of Congress when its numbers shall be thus increased, it shall be proposed to the Legislatures of the States originally parties thereto, to require the assent of two-thirds of the United States in Congress assembled in all those cases wherein by the said Articles the assent of nine States is now required; which being agreed to by them shall be binding on the new States. Until such admission by their delegates into Congress, any of the said States after the establishment of their temporary government shall have authority to keep a sitting member in Congress, with a right of debating, but not of voting. That the preceding articles shall be duly executed by the President of the United States in Congress assembled, under his hand and the seal of the United States, shall be promulgated and shall stand as fundamental constitutions between the thirteen original States and each of the several States now newly described, unalterable but by the joint consent of the United States in Congress assembled, and of the particular State within which such alteration is proposed to be made. That measures not inconsistent with the principles of the Confederation, and necessary for the preservation of peace and good order among the settlers in any of the said new States until they shall assume a temporary government as aforesaid, may from time to time be taken by the United States in Congress assembled.—WESTERN TERRITORY REPORT. FORD ED., iii, 429. (March 22, 1784.)

9100. WESTERN TERRITORY, Inhabitants.—I wish to see the Western country in the hands of people well disposed, who know the value of the connection between that and the maritime States and who wish to cultivate it. I consider their happiness as bound up together, and that every measure should be taken which may draw the bands of union tighter. It will be an efficacious one to receive them into Congress, as I perceive they are about to desire. If to this be added an honest and disinterested conduct in Congress, as to everything relating to them, we may hope for a perfect harmony.—To JOHN BROWN. ii, 395. FORD ED., v, 16. (P., 1788.)

9101. ——. In availing our western brethren of those circumstances which occur for promoting their interests, we only perform that duty which we owe to every portion of our Union, under circumstances equally favorable; and, impressed with the inconveniences to which the citizens of Tennessee are subjected by a want of contiguity in the portions composing their State, I shall be ready to do for their relief, whatever the general Legislature may authorize, and justice to our neighbors permit.—R. TO A. TENNESSEE LEGISLATURE. viii, 115. (1803.)

9102. WESTERN TERRITORY, Separation from Virginia.—I suppose some people on the western waters who are ambitious to be governors, &c., will urge a separation by authority of Congress. But the bulk of the people westward are already thrown into great ferment by the report of what is proposed, to which I think they will not submit. This separation is unacceptable to us in form only, and not in substance. On the contrary, I may safely say it is desired by the eastern part of our country whenever their western brethren shall think themselves able to stand alone. In the meantime, on the petition of the western counties, a plan is digesting for rendering their access to government more easy.—To JAMES MADISON. i, 316. FORD ED., iii, 53. (M., 1782.)

9103. ——. I hope our country will of herself determine to cede still further to the meridian of the mouth of the Great Kanawha. Further she cannot govern; so far is necessary for her own well being.—To GEORGE WASHINGTON. FORD ED., iii, 421. (A., 1784.)

9104. WESTERN TERRITORY, Slavery in.—I am glad to find we have 4,000,000 acres west of Chafalaya. How much better to have every 160 acres settled by an able-bodied militiaman, than by purchasers with their hordes of negroes, to add weakness instead of strength.—To ALBERT GALLATIN. v, 222. (Dec. 1807.)

— WESTERN TERRITORY, Trade of. —See MONOPOLY.

9105. WHALE OIL, Candles.—A Mr. Barrett has arrived here [Paris] from Boston with letters of recommendation from Governor Bowdoin, Cushing and others, * * * to get the whale business put on a general bottom, instead of the particular one which had been settled, the last year, for a special company. * * * I propose to Mr. Barrett that he should induce either his State, or individuals, to send a sufficient number of boxes of the spermaceti candle to give one to every leading house in Paris; I mean to those who lead the *ton;* and, at the same time to deposit a quantity for sale here and advertise them in the *petites affiches.*—To John Adams. i, 498. (P., 1785.)

9106. WHALE OIL, Duties on.—The result [of applications to the French government] was to put us on the footing of the Hanseatic towns, as to whale oil, and to reduce the duties to * * * about a guinea and a half the ton. But the oil must be brought in American or French ships, and the indulgence is limited to one year. However, as to this, I expressed to Count de Vergennes my hopes that it would be continued; and should a doubt arise, I should propose at the proper time, to claim it under the treaty on the footing *gentis amicissimæ.*—To John Adams. i, 498. (P., 1785.)

9107. —— ——. It being material that the reduction of the duties on whale oil, which would expire with the close of this year, should be revised in time for the whalemen to take measures in consequence, we have applied for a continuance of the reduction, and even for an abolition of all duties.—To John Jay. i, 584. (P., 1786.)

9108. WHALE OIL, England and.—I hope that England will, within a year or two, be obliged to come here [France] to buy whale oil for her lamps.—To John Adams. i, 502. (P., 1785.)

9109. WHALE OIL, Lafayette and.— The importation of our whale oil is, by the successful endeavors of M. de Lafayette, put on a good footing for this year.—To Mr. Otto. i, 559. (P., 1786.)

9110. WHALE OIL, Markets for.—I am trying here [Paris] to get contracts for the supplying the cities of France with whale oil by the Boston merchants. It would be the greatest relief possible to that State, whose commerce is in agonies, in consequence of being subjected to alien duties on their oil, in Great Britain, which has, heretofore, been their only market. Can anything be done in this way in Spain? Or do they light their streets there in the night?—To William Carmichael. i, 475. (P., 1785.)

9111. WHALING, Encouragement of. —To obtain leave for our whaling vessels to refit and refresh on the coast of the Brazils [is] an object of immense importance to that class of our vessels. We must acquiesce under such modifications as they [Portugal] may think necessary for regulating this indulgence, in hopes to lessen them in time, and to get a *pied a terre* in that country.—To John Adams. i, 495. (P., 1785.)

9112. WHEAT, British prohibition of. —The prohibition of our wheat in England would, of itself, be of no great moment, because I do not know that it is much sent there. But it is the publishing a libel on our wheat, sanctioned with the name of Parliament, and which can have no object but to do us injury, by spreading a groundless alarm in those countries of Europe where our wheat is constantly and kindly received. It is a mere assassination. If the insect they pretend to fear be the Hessian fly, it never existed in the grain. If it be the weevil, our grain always had that; and the experience of a century has proved that either the climate of England is not warm enough to hatch the egg and continue the race, or that some other unknown cause prevents any evil from it. —To Mr. Vaughan. iii, 38. (P., 1789.)

9113. WHEAT, Cultivation of.—The cultivation of wheat is the reverse in every circumstance of that of tobacco. Besides clothing the earth with herbage, and preserving its fertility, it feeds the laborers plentifully, requires from them only a moderate toil, except in the season of harvest, raises great numbers of animals for food and service, and diffuses plenty and happiness among the whole. We find it easier to make a hundred bushels of wheat than a thousand weight of tobacco, and they are worth more when made.—Notes on Virginia. viii, 407. Ford ed., iii, 271. (1782.)

9114. WHEAT, Weevils and.—The weevil is a formidable obstacle to the cultivation of wheat with us. But principles are already known which must lead to a remedy. Thus a certain degree of heat, to wit, that of the common air in summer, is necessary to hatch the eggs. If subterranean granaries, or others, therefore, can be contrived below that temperature, the evil will be cured by cold. A degree of heat beyond that which hatches the egg we know will kill it. But in aiming at this we easily run into that which produced putrefaction. To produce putrefaction, however, three agents are requisite, heat, moisture, and the external air. If the absence of any one of these be secured, the other two may safely be admitted. Heat is the one we want. Moisture then, or external air, must be excluded. The former has been done by exposing the grain in kilns to the action of fire, which produces heat, and extracts moisture at the same time; the latter, by putting the grain into hogsheads, covering it with a coating of lime, and heading it up: In this situation its bulk produced a heat sufficient to kill the egg; the moisture is suffered to remain indeed, but the external air is excluded. A nicer operation yet has been attempted; that is, to produce an intermediate temperature of heat between that which kills the egg, and that which produces putrefaction. The threshing the grain as soon as it is cut, and laying it in its chaff in large heaps, has been found very nearly to hit this temperature, though not perfectly, nor always. The heap generates heat sufficient to kill most of the eggs, whilst the chaff commonly restrains it from rising into putrefaction. But all these methods abridge too much the quantity which the farmer can manage, and enable other countries to undersell him, which are not infested with this insect.—Notes on Virginia. viii, 407. Ford ed., iii, 271. (1782.)

— WHEATLEY (Phyllis).—See Negroes, Literary.

— WHEELS (Wooden).—See Inventions.

9115. WHIGS, Loyalty of.—I do not believe there has ever been a moment, when a single whig in any one State, would not have shuddered at the very idea of a separation of their State from the Confederacy.—Answers to M. de Meunier. ix, 251. Ford ed., iv, 155. (P., 1786.)

9116. WHIGS, Principles of.—Before the Revolution we were all good English Whigs, cordial in their free principles, and in their jealousies of their executive magistrate. These jealousies are very apparent in all our State constitutions.—Autobiography. i, 81. Ford ed., i, 112. (1821.)

9117. WHIGS, Tories and.—It has ever appeared to me, that the difference between the whig and tory of England is, that the whig deduces his rights from the Anglo-Saxon source, and the tory from the Norman.—To JOHN CARTWRIGHT. vii, 355. (M., 1824.)

9118. WHISKY, Commutation.—Rum and other spirits we [Virginia] can furnish to a greater amount than you require * * * and shall be glad to commute into that article some others which we have not, particularly sugar, coffee and salt.—To GENERAL GATES. i, 260. (R., 1780.)

9119. —— ——. [As to] your application for spirits, there is not a hogshead belonging to the State, but very great quantities are in the hands of the Continental commissaries. I have special returns of upwards of twenty thousand gallons delivered them by the Commissioners * * * and [there are] no doubt great quantities of which there is no return. * * * I would observe to you that Baron Steuben informed me in conversation that spirit would be allowed as a part of the daily ration, but only on particular occasions.—To GENERAL NELSON. FORD ED., ii, 436. (R., 1781.)

9120. WHISKY, Indians and.—I am happy to hear that you have been so favored by the Divine Spirit as to be made sensible of those things which are for your good and that of your people, and of those which are hurtful to you; and particularly that you and they see the ruinous effects which the abuse of spirituous liquors has produced upon them. It has weakened their bodies, enervated their minds, exposed them to hunger, cold, nakedness, and poverty, kept them in perpetual broils, and reduced their population. I do not wonder, then, brother, at your censures, not only on your own people, who have voluntarily gone into these fatal habits, but on all the nations of white people who have supplied their calls for this article. But these nations have done to you only what they do among themselves. They have sold what individuals wish to buy, leaving to every one to be the guardian of his own health and happiness. Spirituous liquors are not in themselves bad; they are often found to be an excellent medicine for the sick; it is the improper and intemperate use of them, by those in health, which makes them injurious. But as you find that your people cannot refrain from an ill use of them, I greatly applaud your resolution not to use them at all. We have too affectionate a concern for your happiness to place the paltry gain on the sale of these articles in competition with the injury they do you. And as it is the desire of your nation, that no spirits should be sent among them, I am authorized by the great council of the United States to prohibit them. I will sincerely cooperate with your wise men in any proper measures for this purpose, which shall be agreeable to them.—To BROTHER HANDSOME LAKE. viii, 187. (1802.)

9121. WHISKY, Loathsome effects.—The loathsome and fatal effects of whisky, destroying the fortunes, the bodies, the minds, and morals of our citizens.—To WILLIAM H. CRAWFORD. FORD ED., x, 113. (M., 1818.)

9122. WHISKY, Military supplies.—We approve of your accommodating * * * the Maryland troops with spirits. They really deserve the whole, and I wish we had means of transportation for much greater quantities which we have on hand and cannot convey. This article we could furnish plentifully to you and them.—To GENERAL EDWARD STEVENS. i, 253. FORD ED., ii, 339. (R., 1780.)

9123. WHISKY, Sale to Indians.—The Indians are becoming very sensible of the baneful effects produced on their morals, their health and existence, by the abuse of ardent spirits, and some of them earnestly desire a prohibition of that article from being carried among them. The Legislature will consider whether the effectuating that desire would not be in the spirit of benevolence and liberality which they have hitherto practiced toward these our neighbors, and which has had so happy an effect toward conciliating their friendship.—SPECIAL MESSAGE. viii, 22. (Jan. 1802.)

9124. —— ——. We have taken measures to prevent spirituous liquors being carried into your country, and we sincerely rejoice at this proof of your wisdom. Instead of spending the produce of your hunting in purchasing this pernicious drink, which produces poverty, broils and murders, it will be now employed in procuring food and clothing for your families, and increasing instead of diminishing your numbers.—ADDRESS TO MIAMIS AND DELAWARES. viii, 191. (1803.)

9125. —— ——. Perceiving the injurious effects produced by the Indians' inordinate use of spirituous liquors, Congress passed laws authorizing measures against the vending or distributing such liquors among them. Their introduction by traders was accordingly prohibited, and for some time was attended with the best effects. I am informed, however, that latterly the Indians have got into the practice of purchasing such liquors themselves in the neighboring settlements of whites, and of carrying them into their towns, and that in this way our regulations so salutary to them, are now defeated. I must, therefore, request your Excellency to submit this matter to the consideration of your Legislature. I persuade myself that in addition to the moral inducements which will readily occur, they will find it not indifferent to their own interests to give us their aid in removing, for their neighbors, this great obstacle to their acquiring industrious habits, and attaching themselves to the regular and useful pursuits of life; for this purpose it is much desired that they should pass effectual laws to restrain their citizens from vending, and distributing liquors to the Indians.—To —— ——. v. 407. (W., Dec. 1808.)

9126. —— ——. The French and afterwards the English kept the hatchet always in your hand, exposing you to be killed in their quarrels, and then gave you whisky that you might quarrel and kill one another.—INDIAN ADDRESS. viii, 235. (1809.)

9127. —— ——. I have not filled you with whisky, as the English do, to make you promise, or give up what is against your interest, when out of your senses.—INDIAN ADDRESS. viii, 240. (1809.)

9128. —— ——. What do the English for you? They furnish you with plenty of whisky, to keep you in idleness, drunkenness and poverty.—INDIAN ADDRESS. viii, 233. (1809.)

9129. —— ——. If we feared you, if we were your enemies, we should have furnished you plentifully with whisky.—INDIAN ADDRESS. viii, 233. (1809.)

9130. WHISKY, Tax on.—I shall be glad if an additional tax of one-fourth of a dollar a gallon on whisky shall enable us to meet all our engagements with punctuality. Viewing that tax as an article in a system of excise, I was once glad to see it fall with the rest of the system, which I considered as prematurely and unnecessarily introduced. It was evident that our existing taxes were *then* equal to our existing debts. It was clearly foreseen, also, that the surplus from excise would only become aliment for useless offices, and would be swallowed in idleness by those whom it would withdraw from useful industry. Considering it only as a fiscal measure, this was right. But the prostration of body and mind which the cheapness of this liquor is spreading through the mass of our citizens, now calls the attention of the legislator on a very different principle. One of his important duties is as guardian of those who, from causes susceptible of precise definition, cannot take care of themselves. Such are infants, maniacs, gamblers, drunkards. The last, as much as the maniac, requires restrictive measures to save him from the fatal infatuation under which he is destroying his health, his morals, his family, and his usefulness to society. One powerful obstacle to his ruinous self-indulgence would be a price beyond his competence. As a sanitary measure, therefore, it becomes one of duty in the public guardians. Yet I do not think it follows necessarily that imported spirits should be subjected to similar enhancement, until they become as cheap as those made at home. A tax on whisky is to discourage its consumption; a tax on foreign spirits encourages whisky by removing its rival from competition. The price and present duty throw foreign spirits already out of competition with whisky, and accordingly they are used but to a salutary extent. You see no persons besotting themselves with imported spirits, wines, liquors, cordials, &c. Whisky claims to itself alone the exclusive office of sotmaking. Foreign spirits, wines, teas, coffee, cigars, salt, are articles of as innocent consumption as broadcloths and silks; and ought, like them, to pay but the average *ad valorem* duty of other imported comforts. All of them are ingredients in our happiness, and the government which steps out of the ranks of the ordinary articles of consumption to select and lay under disproportionate burdens a particular one, because it is a comfort, pleasing to the taste, or necessary to health, and will therefore, be bought, is, in that particular, a tyranny.—To SAMUEL SMITH. vii, 284. FORD ED., x, 251. (M., 1823.)

9131. WHISKY INSURRECTION, Commencement.—The people in the western parts of Pennsylvania have been to the excise officer, and threatened to burn his house, &c. They were blackened and otherwise disguised, so as to be unknown. He has resigned, and Hamilton says there is no possibility of getting the law executed, and that probably the evil will spread. A proclamation is to be issued, and another instance of my being forced to appear to approve what I have condemned uniformly from its first conception.—To JAMES MADISON. iii, 563. FORD ED., vi, 261. (Pa., May 1793.)

9132. WHISKY INSURRECTION, Hamilton and.—The servile copyist of Mr. Pitt [Alexander Hamilton] thought he. too. must have his alarms, his insurrections and plots against the Constitution. * * * Hence the example of employing military force for civil purposes, when it has been impossible to produce a single fact of insurrection, unless that term be entirely confounded with occasional riots, and when ordinary process of law had been resisted indeed in a few special cases but by no means generally, nor had its effect been duly tried. But it answered the favorite purposes of strengthening government and increasing public debt; and, therefore, an insurrection was announced and proclaimed, and armed against, but could never be found. And all this under the sanction of a name which has done too much good not to be sufficient to cover harm also. What is equally astonishing is that by the pomp of reports, proclamations, armies, &c., the mind of the Legislature itself was so fascinated as never to have asked where, when, and by whom. this insurrection has been produced? The original of this scene in another country was calculated to excite the indignation of those whom it could not impose on; the mimicry of it here is too humiliating to excite any feeling but shame.—To JAMES MONROE. FORD ED., vii, 16. (M., May 1795.)

9133. WHISKY INSURRECTION, Military and.—The information of our [Virginia's] militia, returned from the westward. is uniform, that though the people there let them pass quietly, they were objects of their laughter, not of their fear; that one thousand men could have cut off their whole force in a thousand places of the Alleghany; that their detestation of the excise law is universal, and has now associated to it a detestation of the government; and that a separation which was perhaps a very distant and problematical event, is now near, and certain, and determined in the mind of every man.—To JAMES MADISON. iv, 112. FORD ED., vi, 518. (M., Dec. 1794.)

9134. WHISKY INSURRECTION, Proclamation against.—The proclamation on the proceedings against the laws for raising a revenue on distilled spirits, I return with my signature. I think if, instead of the words. " to render laws dictated by weighty reasons of public exigency and policy as acceptable as possible ", it stood, " to render the laws as acceptable as possible ", it would be better. I see no other particular expressions which need alteration.—To PRESIDENT WASHINGTON. iii, 471. FORD ED., vi, 113. (M., Sep. 1792.)

9135. ——— ———. I am sincerely sorry to learn that such proceedings have taken place; and I hope the proclamation will lead the persons concerned into a regular line of application which may end either in an amendment of the law, if it needs it, or in their conviction that it is right.—To PRESIDENT WASHINGTON. iii, 471. FORD ED., vi, 114. (M., Sep. 1792.)

9136. WILKINSON (James), Burr's conspiracy.—I have ever and carefully restrained myself from the expression of any opinion respecting General Wilkinson, except in the case of Burr's conspiracy, wherein, after he had got over his first agitations, we believed his decision firm, and his conduct zealous for the defeat of the conspiracy, and although injudicious, yet meriting, from sound intentions. the support of the nation. As to the rest of his life, I have left it to his friends and his enemies, to whom it furnishes matter enough for disputation. I classed myself with neither.—To JAMES MONROE. vi, 35. FORD ED., ix, 332. (M., Jan. 1812.)

9137. WILKINSON (James), Commended.—I sincerely congratulate you on your safe arrival at Richmond, against the impudent surmises and hopes of the band of conspirators, who, because they are as yet permitted to walk abroad, and even to be in the character of witnesses until such a measure of evidence shall be collected as will place them securely at the bar of justice, attempt to cover their crimes under noise and insolence. You have indeed had a fiery trial at New Orleans, but it was soon apparent that the clamorous were only the criminal, endeavoring to turn the public attention from themselves and their leader upon any other object.—To GENERAL WILKINSON. v, 109. FORD ED., ix, 5. (W., June 1807.)

9138. WILKINSON (James), Confidence in.—I am thoroughly sensible of the painful difficulties of your situation, expecting an attack from an overwhelming force, unversed in law, surrounded by suspected persons, and in a nation tender as to everything infringing liberty, and especially from the military. You have doubtless seen a good deal of malicious insinuation in the papers against you. This, of course, begot suspicion and distrust in those unacquainted with the line of your conduct. We, who knew it, have not failed to strengthen the public confidence in you; and I can assure you that your conduct, as now known, has placed you on ground extremely favorable with the public. Burr and his emissaries found it convenient to sow a distrust in your mind of our dispositions towards you; but be assured that you will be cordially supported in the line of your duties.—To GENERAL WILKINSON. v, 39. FORD ED., ix, 4. (W., Feb. 1807.)

9139. WILKINSON (James), Injustice for.—Your enemies have filled the public ear with slanders, and your mind with trouble on that account. The establishment of their guilt will let the world see what they ought to think of their clamors; it will dissipate the doubts of those who doubted for want of knowledge, and will place you on higher ground in the public estimate and public confidence. No one is more sensible than myself of the injustice which has been aimed at you.—To GENERAL WILKINSON. v, 110. FORD ED., ix, 6. (W., June 1807.)

9140. WILKINSON (James), Plans against Burr.—Although we at no time believed Burr could carry any formidable force out of the Ohio, yet we thought it safest that you should be prepared to receive him with all the force which could be assembled, and with that view our orders were given; and we were pleased to see that without waiting for them, you adopted nearly the same plan yourself, and acted on it with promptitude; the difference between yours and ours proceeding from your expecting an attack by sea, which we knew was impossible, either by England or by a fleet under Truxtun, who was at home; or by our own navy, which was under our eye. Your belief that Burr would really descend with six or seven thousand men, was no doubt founded on what you knew of the numbers which could be raised in the western country for an expedition to Mexico, *under the authority of the government;* but you probably did not calculate that the want of that authority would take from him every honest man, and leave him only the desperadoes of his party, which in no part of the United States can ever be a numerous body.—To GENERAL WILKINSON. v, 39. FORD ED., ix, 4, (W., Feb. 1807.)

9141. WILKINSON (James), Suspicions.—General Wilkinson, being expressly declared by Burr to General Eaton, to be engaged with him in his design as his Lieutenant, or first in command, and suspicions of infidelity in Wilkinson being now become very general, a question is proposed [in cabinet] what is proper to be done as to him on this account, as well as for his disobedience of orders received by him June 11, at St. Louis, to descend with all practicable dispatch to New Orleans, to mark out the site of certain defensive works there, and then repair to take command at Natchitoches, on which business he did not leave St. Louis till September.—THE ANAS. FORD ED., i, 319. (Oct. 1806.)

9142. WILLIAM AND MARY COLLEGE, Aid for.—The late change in the form of our government, as well as the contest of arms in which we are at present engaged, calling for extraordinary abilities both in council and field, it becomes the peculiar duty of the Legislature, at this time, to aid and improve [William and Mary] Seminary, in which those who are to be the future guardians of the rights and liberties of their country may be endowed with science and virtue, to watch and preserve the sacred deposit.—WILLIAM AND MARY COLLEGE BILL. FORD ED., ii, 233. (1779.)

9143. WILLIAM AND MARY COLLEGE, Attachment for.—To William and Mary, as my *alma mater,* my attachment has been ever sincere, although not exclusive.—To PATRICK K. RODGERS. vii, 328. (M., 1824.)

9144. WILLIAM AND MARY COLLEGE, Changes.—Being elected, in 1779, one of the Visitors of William and Mary College, a self-electing body, I effected, during my residence in Williamsburg [as Governor of the State] that year, a change in the organization of that institution, by abolishing the Grammar school, and the two professorships of Divinity and Oriental languages, and substituting a professorship of Law and Police, one of Anatomy, Medicine and Chemistry, and one of Modern Languages; and the charter confining us to six professorships, we added the Law of Nature and Nations, and the Fine Arts to the duties of the Moral professor, and Natural History to those of the professor of Mathematics and Natural Philosophy.—AUTOBIOGRAPHY. i, 50. FORD ED., i, 69. (1821.)

9145. WILLIAM AND MARY COLLEGE, Church establishment.—The College of William and Mary was an establishment purely of the Church of England; the Visitors were required to be all of that Church; the professors to subscribe its Thirty-nine Articles; its students to learn its catechism; and one of its fundamental objects was declared to be to raise up ministers for that Church. The religious jealousies, therefore, of all the dissenters took alarm lest this might give an ascendancy to the Anglican sect, and refused acting on that bill. Its local eccentricity, too, and unhealthy autumnal climate, lessened the general inclination towards it.—AUTOBIOGRAPHY. i, 48. FORD ED., i, 67. (M., 1821.)

9146. WILLIAM AND MARY COLLEGE, Rivalry.—When the college [of William and Mary] was located at the middle plantation in 1693, Charles City was a frontier county, and there were no inhabitants above the falls of the rivers, sixty miles only higher up. It was, therefore, a position nearly central to the population, as it then was; but when the frontier became extended to the Sandy river, three hundred miles west of Williamsburg, the public convenience called, first for a removal of the seat of government, and latterly, not for a removal of the college, but for the establishment of a new one in a more central and healthy location; not disturbing the old one in its possessions or functions, but leaving them unimpaired for the benefit of those to whom it is convenient. And indeed, I do not foresee that the number of its students is likely to be much affected; because I presume that, at present, its distance and autumnal climate prevent its receiving many students from above the tidewaters, and especially from above the mountains. This is, therefore, one of the cases where the lawyers say there is *damnum absque injuriâ;* and they instance, as in point, the settlement of a new schoolmaster in the neighborhood of an old one. At any rate, it is one of those cases wherein the public interest rightfully prevails, and the justice of which will be yielded by none, I am sure, with more dutiful and candid acquiescence than the enlightened friends of our ancient and venerable institution. The only rivalship, I hope, between the old and the new (the University of Virginia) will be in doing the most good possible in their respective sections of country.—To PATRICK K. RODGERS. vii, 328. (M., 1824.)

9147. WILLIAM AND MARY COLLEGE, Unfavorable location.—We have in Virginia a college (William and Mary) just well enough endowed to draw out the miserable existence to which a miserable constitution has doomed it. It is moreover eccentric in its position, exposed to all bilious diseases as all the lower country is, and. therefore, abandoned by the public care, as that part of the country itself is in a considerable degree by its inhabitants. —To JOSEPH PRIESTLEY. iv, 312. FORD ED., vii, 407. (Pa., 1800.) See UNIVERSITY OF VIRGINIA.

9148. WINDS, Systematic observations on.—I am sorry you have received so little information on the subject of our winds. I had once (before our Revolution-war) a project on the same subject. As I had then an extensive acquaintance over this State [Virginia], I meant to have engaged some person in every county of it, giving them each a thermometer, to observe that and the winds twice a day, for one year, to wit, at sunrise and at four p. m. (the coldest and the warmest point of the twenty-four hours), and to communicate their observations to me at the end of the year. I should then have selected the days in which it appeared that the winds blew to a centre within the State, and have made a map of them, and seen how far they had analogy with the temperature of the air. I meant this to be merely a specimen to be communicated to the Philosophical Society at Philadelphia, in order to engage them, by means of their correspondents, to have the same thing done in every State. and through a series of years. By seizing the days when the winds centred in any part of the United States, we might, in time, have come to some of the causes which determine the direction of the winds, which I suspect to be very various. But this long-winded project was prevented by the war * * * and since that I have been far otherwise engaged. I am sure you will have viewed the subject from much higher ground, and I shall be glad to learn your views in some of the hours of *delassement,* which I hope we are yet to pass together.—To MR. VOLNEY. iv, 159. (M., 1797.)

9149. WINES, Making.—The culture of the vine is not desirable in lands capable of producing anything else. It is a species of gambling, and desperate gambling, too, wherein, whether you make much or nothing, you are equally ruined. The middling crop alone is the saving point, and that the seasons seldom hit. Accordingly, we see much wretchedness among this class of cultivators. Wine, too, is so cheap in these countries [of Europe], that a laborer with us, employed in the culture of any other article, may exchange it for wine, more and better than he could raise himself. It is a resource for a country the whole of whose good soil is otherwise employed. and which still has some barren spots, and surplus of population to employ on them. There the vine is good, because it is something in the place of nothing. It may become a resource to us at a still later period; when the increase of population shall increase our productions beyond the demand for them, both at home and abroad. Instead of going on to make an useless surplus of them, we may employ our supernumerary hands on the vine.—To WILLIAM DRAYTON. ii, 198. (P., 1787.)

9150. —— ——. An experiment was made in Virginia by a Mr. Mazzei, for the raising vines and making wines. He was an Italian, and brought over with him about a dozen laborers of his own country, bound to serve him four or five years. We had made up a subscription for him of £2,000 sterling, and he began his experiment on a piece of land adjoining mine. His intention was, before the time of his people should expire, to import more from Italy. He planted a considerable vineyard, and attended to it with great diligence for three years. The war then came on, the time of his people soon expired, some of them enlisted, others chose to settle on other lands and labor for themselves; some were taken away by the gentlemen of the country for gardeners, so that there did not remain a single one with him, and the interruption of navigation prevented his importing others. In this state of things he was himself employed by the State of Virginia to go to Europe as their agent to do some particular business. He rented his place to General Riedesel, whose horses in one week destroyed the whole labor of three or four years; and thus ended an experiment which, from every appearance, would in a year or two more have established the practicability of that branch of culture in America.—To ALBERT GALLATIN. iii, 505. (Pa., 1793.)

9151. —— ——. We could, in the United States, make as great a variety of wines as are made in Europe, not exactly of the same kinds, but doubtless as good. Yet I have ever observed to my countrymen, who think its introduction important, that a laborer cultivating wheat, rice, tobacco, or cotton here, will be able with the proceeds, to purchase double the quantity of the wine he could make.—To M. LASTEYRIE. v, 314. (W., 1808.)

9152. WINES, Sobriety and.—I am persuaded that were the duty on cheap wines put on the same ratio with the dear, it would wonderfully enlarge the field of those who use wine, to the expulsion of whisky. The introduction of a very cheap wine into my neighborhood, within two years past, has quadrupled in that time the number of those who keep wine, and will ere long increase them tenfold. This would be a great gain to the treasury, and to the sobriety of our country.—To ALBERT GALLATIN. v, 86. FORD ED., ix, 69. (W., June 1807.)

9153. WINES, Tax on.—I rejoice, as a moralist, at the prospect of a reduction of the duties on wine, by our national Legislature. It is an error to view a tax on that liquor as merely a tax on the rich. It is a prohibition of its use to the middling class of our citizens, and a condemnation of them to the poison of whisky, which is desolating their houses. No nation is drunken where wine is cheap: and none sober, where the dearness of wine substitutes ardent spirits as the common beverage. It is, in truth, the only antidote to the bane of whisky. Fix but the duty at the rate of other merchandise, and we can drink wine here as cheap as we do grog; and who will not prefer it? Its extended use will carry health and comfort to a much enlarged circle. Every one in easy circumstances (as the bulk of our citizens are) will prefer it to the poison to which they are now driven by their government. And the treasury itself will find that a penny apiece from a dozen, is more than a groat from a single one. This reformation, however, will require time.—To M. DE NEUVILLE. vii, 110. (M., 1818.)

9154. ——— ———. I think it a great error to consider a heavy tax on wines, as a tax on luxury. On the contrary, it is a tax on the health of our citizens. It is a legislative declaration that none but the richest of them shall be permitted to drink wine, and, in effect, a condemnation of all the middling and lower conditions of society to the poison of whisky. * * * Surely it is not from the necessities of our treasury that we thus undertake to debar the mass of our citizens the use of not only an innocent gratification, but a healthy substitute instead of a bewitching poison. This aggression on the public taste and comfort has been ever deemed among the most arbitrary and oppressive abuses of the English government. It is one which, I hope, we shall never copy.—To WILLIAM H. CRAWFORD. FORD ED., x, 112. (M., 1818.) See LIFE, JEFFERSON'S HABITS OF.

9155. WIRT (William), Seat in Congress.—I pray you that this letter may be sacredly secret, because it meddles in a line wherein I should myself think it wrong to intermeddle, were it not that it looks to a period when I shall be out of office, but others might think it wrong notwithstanding that circumstance. I suspected, from your desire to go into the army, that you disliked your profession, notwithstanding that your prospects in it were inferior to none in the State. Still, I know that no profession is open to stronger antipathies than that of the law. The object of this letter, then, is to propose to you to come into Congress. Th t is the great commanding theatre of this nation, and the threshold to whatever department of office a man is qualified to enter. With your reputation, talents, and correct views, used with the necessary prudence, you will at once be placed at the head of the republican body in the House of Representatives; and after obtaining the standing which a little time will ensure you, you may look, at your own will, into the military, the judiciary, diplomatic, or other civil departments, with a certainty of being in either whatever you please. And in the present state of what may be called the eminent talents of our country, you may be assured of being engaged through life in the most honorable employments. If you come in at the next election, you will begin your course with a new administration. That administration will be opposed by a faction, small in numbers, but governed by no principle but the most envenomed malignity. They will endeavor to batter down the Executive before it will have time, by its purity

and correctness, to build up a confidence with the people, founded on experiment. By supporting them you will lay for yourself a broad foundation in the public confidence, and indeed you will become the Colossus of the republican government of your country. * * * Perhaps I ought to apologize for the frankness of this communication. It proceeds from an ardent zeal to see this government (the idol of my soul) continue in good hands, and from a sincere desire to see you whatever you wish to be.—To WILLIAM WIRT. v, 233. (W., Jan. 1808.)

9156. WISDOM, Hereditary.—Wisdom is not hereditary.—To WILLIAM JOHNSON. vii, 291. FORD ED., x, 227. (M., 1823.)

9157. WISDOM, Honesty and.—A wise man, if nature has not formed him honest, will yet act as if he were honest; because he will find it the most advantageous and wise part in the long run.—To JAMES MONROE. FORD ED., iv, 40. (P., 1785.)

9158. WISTAR (Caspar), Philosophical society and.—I rejoice in the election of Dr. Wistar [to the presidency of the Philosophical Society], and trust that his senior standing in the Society will have been considered as a fair motive of preference of those whose merits, standing alone, would have justly entitled them to the honor, and who, as juniors, according to the course of nature, may still expect their turn.—To JOHN VAUGHAN. vi, 417. (M., 1815.)

— WOMEN, Appointment to office.— See OFFICES.

9159. WOMEN, Barbarism and.—The [Indian] women are submitted to unjust drudgery. This, I believe, is the case with every barbarous people. With such, force is law. The stronger sex, therefore, imposes on the weaker. * * * Were we in equal barbarism, our females would be equal drudges. —NOTES ON VIRGINIA. viii, 305. FORD ED., iii, 153. (1782.)

9160. WOMEN, Civilization and.—It is an honorable circumstance for man, that the first moment he is at his ease, he allots the internal employments to his female partner, and takes the external on himself. And this circumstance, or its reverse, is a pretty good indication that a people are, or are not at their ease. Among the Indians, this indication fails from a particular cause; every Indian man is a soldier or warrior, and the whole body of warriors constitute a standing army, always employed in war or hunting. To support that army, there remain no laborers but the women. Here, then, is so heavy a military establishment, that the civil part of the nation is reduced to women only. But this is a barbarous perversion of the natural destination of the two sexes—TRAVELS IN LORRAINE. ix, 396. (1787.)

9161. WOMEN, Domestic life.—You think that the pleasures of Paris more than supply its want of domestic happiness; in other words, that a Parisian is happier than an American. You will change your opinion, and come over to mine in the end. Recollect the women of this capital [Paris], some on foot, some on horses, and some in carriages, hunting pleasure in the streets, in routs and assemblies, and forgetting that they have left it behind them in their nurseries; compare them with our own countrywomen occupied in the tender and tranquil amusements of domestic life, and confess that it is a comparison of Americans and angels.—To Mrs. WILLIAM BINGHAM. FORD ED., v, 9. (P., 1788.)

9162. —— ——. American women have the good sense to value domestic happiness above all other, and the art to cultivate it beyond all other. There is no part of the earth where so much of this is enjoyed as in America.—To Mrs. WILLIAM BINGHAM. FORD ED., v, 9. (P., 1788.)

— **WOMEN, Education.**—See EDUCATION, FEMALE.

9163. WOMEN, Government and.— However nature may by mental or physical disqualifications have marked infants and the weaker sex for the protection, rather than the direction of government, yet among the men who either pay or fight for their country, no line of right can be drawn.—To JOHN H. PLEASANTS. vii, 345. FORD ED., x, 303. (M., 1824.)

9164. WOMEN, Horseback riding.—A lady should never ride a horse which she might not safely ride without a bridle.—To MARY JEFFERSON. FORD ED., v, 328. (Pa., 1791.)

9165. WOMEN, Labor and.—I observe women and children carrying heavy burdens, and laboring with the hoe. This is an unequivocal indication of extreme poverty. Men, in a civilized country, never expose their wives and children to labor above their force and sex, as long as their own labor can protect them from it.—TRAVELS IN FRANCE. ix, 313. (1787.)

9166. —— ——. The women here [Lorraine] as in Germany, do all sorts of work. While one considers them as useful and rational companions, one cannot forget that they are also objects of our pleasures; nor can they ever forget it. While employed in dirt and drudgery, some tag of a ribbon, some ring, or bit of bracelet, earbob or necklace, or something of that kind, will show that the desire of pleasing is never suspended in them.— TRAVELS IN LORRAINE. ix, 396. (1787.)

9167. WOMEN, Natural equality of.— It is civilization alone which replaces women in the enjoyment of their natural equality. That first teaches us to subdue the selfish passions, and to respect those rights in others which we value in ourselves.—NOTES ON VIRGINIA. viii, 305. FORD ED., iii, 153. (1782.)

9168. WOMEN, Needlework.—In the country life of America, there are many moments when a woman can have recourse to nothing but her needle for employment. In a dull company, and in dull weather, for instance, it is ill-mannered to read, ill manners to leave them; no card-playing there among genteel people—that is abandoned to black-

guards. The needle is, then, a valuable resource. Besides, without knowing how to use it herself, how can the mistress of a family direct the work of her servants?—To MARTHA JEFFERSON. FORD ED., iv, 373. (1787.)

9169. WOMEN, Politics and.—All the world is now politically mad. Men, women, children talk nothing else, and you know that naturally they talk much, loud and warm. Society is spoiled by it, at least for those who, like myself, are but lookers on. You, too, [in America] have had your political fever. But our good ladies, I trust, have been too wise to wrinkle their foreheads with politics. They are contented to soothe and calm the minds of their husbands returning ruffled from political debate.—To Mrs. WILLIAM BINGHAM. FORD ED., v, 9. (P., 1788.)

9170. WOMEN, Tenderness for.— Women are formed by nature for attentions, not for hard labor. A woman never forgets one of the numerous train of little offices which belong to her. A man forgets often.— TRAVELS IN FRANCE. ix, 397. (1787.)

9171. WORDS, Use of.—I am not scrupulous about words when they are once explained. —To GEORGE HAMMOND. iii, 515. FORD ED., vi, 187. (Pa., 1793.)

9172. WORLD, End of.—I hope you will have good sense enough to disregard those foolish predictions that the world is to be at an end soon. The Almighty has never made known to anybody at what time He created it; nor will He tell anybody when He will put an end to it, if He ever means to do it. As to preparations for that event, the best way for you is to be always prepared for it. The only way to be so is, never to say or do a bad thing. If ever you are about to say anything amiss, or to do anything wrong, consider beforehand you will feel something within you which will tell you it is wrong, and ought not to be said or done. This is your conscience, and be sure and obey it. Our Maker has given us all this faithful internal monitor, and if you always obey it you will always be prepared for the end of the world; or for a much more certain event, which is death. This must happen to all; it puts an end to the world as to us; and the way to be ready for it is never to do a wrong act.—To MARTHA JEFFERSON. D. L. J. 70. (1783.)

9173. WORTH, American appreciation of.—I know no country where * * * public esteem is so attached to worth, regardless of wealth [as it is in America].—To Mrs. CHURCH. FORD ED., vi, 455. (G., 1793.)

9174. WORTH, Esteem for moral.—My anxieties on this subject will never carry me beyond the use of fair and honorable means, of truth and reason; nor have they ever lessened my esteem for moral worth, nor alienated my affections from a single friend, who did not first withdraw himself. Whenever this happened, I confess I have not been insensible to it; yet have ever kept myself open to a return of their justice.—To Mrs. JOHN ADAMS. iv, 562. FORD ED., viii, 312. (M., 1804.)

9175. WRETCHEDNESS, Life and.— The Giver of life gave it for happiness and not for wretchedness.—To JAMES MONROE. i, 319. FORD ED., iii, 59. (M., 1782.)

9176. WRIGHT (Frances), Works of.—Miss Wright had before favored me with the first edition of her American work; but her " Few Days in Athens ", was entirely new, and has been a treat to me of the highest order. The matter and manner of the dialogue is strictly ancient; and the principles of the sects are beautifully and candidly explained and contrasted; and the scenery and portraiture of the interlocutors are of higher finish than anything in that line left us by the ancients; and like Ossian, if not ancient, it is equal to the best morsels of antiquity. I augur, from this instance, that Herculaneum is likely to furnish better specimens of modern than of ancient genius; and may we not hope more from the same pen?—To MARQUIS LAFAYETTE. vii, 326. FORD ED., x, 282. (M., 1823.)

9177. WRITING, For newspapers.—I have preserved through life a resolution, set in a very early part of it, never to write in a public paper without subscribing my name to it, and to engage openly an adversary who does not let himself be seen, is staking all against nothing.—To EDWARD RANDOLPH. iii, 470. (1792.)

9178. WRITING, Illegible.—I return you Mr. Coxe's letter which has cost me much time at two or three different attempts to decipher it. Had I such a correspondent, I should certainly admonish him that, if he would not so far respect my time as to write to me legibly, I should so far respect it myself as not to waste it in decomposing and recomposing his hieroglyphics.—To JAMES MADISON. FORD ED., x, 275. (M., 1823.)

9179. WRONG, Correction of.—A conviction that we are right accomplishes half the difficulty of correcting wrong.—To ARCHIBALD THWEAT. vii, 199. FORD ED., x, 184. (M., 1821.)

9180. WRONG, Opposition to foreign.—I doubt not your aid * * * towards carrying into effect the measures of your country, and enforcing the sacred principle, that in opposing foreign wrong there must be but one mind.—R. TO A. N. Y. TAMMANY SOCIETY. viii, 127. (Feb. 1808.)

9181. WRONG, Resistance to.—We have borne patiently a great deal of wrong, on the consideration that if nations go to war for every degree of injury, there would never be peace on earth. But when patience has begotten false estimates of its motives, when wrongs are pressed because it is believed they will be borne, resistance becomes morality. —To MADAME DE STAEL. v, 133. (W., 1807.)

9182. WRONG, Restrain.—We * * * owe it to mankind, as well as to ourselves, to restrain wrong by resistance, and to defeat those calculations of which justice is not the basis.—SEVENTH ANNUAL MESSAGE. viii. FORD ED., ix, 146.

9183. WRONG, Submission to.—We love peace, yet spurn a tame submission to wrong.—R. TO A. N. Y. TAMMANY SOCIETY. viii, 127. (1808.)

9184. WRONGS, Republican vs. Monarchical.—Compare the number of wrongs committed with impunity by citizens among us, with those committed by the sovereigns in other countries, and the last will be found most numerous, most oppressive on the mind, and most degrading to the dignity of man.— ANSWERS TO M. DE MEUNIER. ix, 292. FORD ED., iv, 147. (P., 1786.)

9185. WYTHE (George), Ability of.—The pride of William and Mary College is Mr. Wythe, one of the Chancellors of the State, and Professor of Law. He is one of the greatest men of the age, having held without competition the first place at the bar of our General Court for twenty-five years, and always distinguished by the most spotless virtue.—To RALPH IZARD. ii, 428. (P., 1788.)

9186. WYTHE (George), American Revolution and.—George Wythe was one of the very few (for I can barely speak of them in the plural number) * * * who. from the commencement of the [Revolutionary] contest, hung our connection with Great Britain on its true hook, that of a common king. His unassuming character, however, made him appear as a follower, while his sound judgment kept him in a line with the freest spirit.—To WILLIAM WIRT. vi, 368. FORD ED., ix, 469. (M., 1814.)

9187. —— ——. On the dawn of the Revolution, instead of higgling on half-way principles, as others did who feared to follow their reason, he took his stand on the solid ground that the only link of political union between us and Great Britain, was the identity of our Executive; that that nation and its Parliament had no more authority over us than we had over them, and that we were coordinate nations with Great Britain and Hanover.—To JOHN SAUNDERSON. i, 113. (M., 1820.)

9188. WYTHE (George), Cato of America.—No man ever left behind him a character more venerated than George Wythe. His virtue was of the purest tint; his integrity inflexible and his justice exact; of warm patriotism, and, devoted as he was to liberty and the natural and equal rights of man, he might truly be called the Cato of his country, without the avarice of the Roman, for a more disinterested person never lived.*—To JOHN SAUNDERSON. i, 114. (M., 1820.)

9189. WYTHE (George), Honor of his age.—The honor of his own, and the model of future times.—To JOHN SAUNDERSON. i, 114. (M., 1820.)

9190. WYTHE (George), Lectures of.—Your favor gave me the first information that the lectures of my late master and friend exist in MS. * * * His mind was too accurate, his reasoning powers too strong, to have committed anything to paper materially incorrect. It is unfortunate that there should be *lacunæ* in them. But you are mistaken in supposing I could supply them. It is now thirty-seven years since I left the bar, and have ceased to think on subjects of law; and the constant occupation of my mind by other concerns has obliterated from it all but the strongest traces of the science. Others, I am sure, can be found equal to it, and none more so than Judge Roane. It is not my time or trouble which I wish to spare on this occasion. They are due, in any extent, to the memory of one who was

* George Wythe was one of the signers of the Declaration. Jefferson, Chief Justice Marshall and Henry Clay were among his law pupils.—EDITOR.

my second father. My incompetence is the real obstacle; and in any other circumstance connected with the publication, in which I can be useful to his fame, and the public instruction, I shall be most ready to do my duty.—To JOHN TYLER. FORD ED., ix, 288. (M., 1810.)

9191. WYTHE (George), Mentor and friend.—Mr. Wythe continued to be my faithful and beloved mentor in youth, and my most affectionate friend through life. In 1767, he led me into the practice of the law at the bar of the General Court, at which I continued until the Revolution shut up the courts of justice.—AUTOBIOGRAPHY. i, 3. FORD ED., i, 4. (1821.)

9192. WYTHE (George), Supporter of Jefferson.—Mr. Wythe, while speaker [of the Virginia Legislature] in the two sessions of 1777, * * * was an able and constant associate [ot mine] in whatever was before a committee of the whole. His pure integrity, judgment and reasoning powers, gave him great weight.—AUTOBIOGRAPHY. i, 41. FORD ED., i, 56. (1821.)

9193. WYTHE (George), Virtuous.—One of the most virtuous of characters, and whose sentiments on the subject of slavery are unequivocal.—To DR. PRICE. i, 377. FORD ED., iv, 83. (P., 1785.)

9194. ——— ———. The exalted virtue of the man will be a polar star to guide you in all matters which may touch that element of his character. But on that you will receive imputation from no man; for, as far as I know, he never had an enemy.—To JOHN SAUNDERSON. i, 112. (M., 1820.)

— XENOPHON.—See PHILOSOPHY.

9195. X. Y. Z. PLOT, Artful misrepresentation of.—The most artful misrepresentations of the contents of these papers have been published, and have produced such a shock in the republican mind, as has never been seen since our independence. We are to dread the effects of this dismay till their fuller information.*—To JAMES MADISON. iv, 233. FORD ED., vii, 236. (Pa., April 1798.)

9196. X. Y. Z. PLOT, Astonishment over.—The public mind appears still in a state of astonishment. There never was a moment in which the aid of an able pen was so important to place things in their just attitude. On this depend the inchoate movement in the eastern mind, and the fate of the elections in that quarter. * * * I would not propose to you such a task on any ordinary occasion. But be assured that a well-digested analysis of these papers would now decide the future turn of things, which are at this moment on the creen.—To JAMES MADISON. iv, 234. FORD ED., vii, 237. (Pa., April 1798.)

9197. X. Y. Z. PLOT, Delusion through.—There is a most respectable part of our State [Virginia] who have been enveloped in the X. Y. Z. delusion, and who destroy our

* In 1797, Charles Cotesworth Pinckney, Elbridge Gerry and John Marshall were sent on an extraordinary mission to the French Republic, the Directory being then in power. Shortly after their arrival in Paris, they received letters from unofficial persons signed X, Y, and Z, intimating that, as a preliminary to the negotiation, it would be necessary to expend a large sum of money in the way of bribes to the members of the Government. These demands were not acceded to, and the federalists made skilful political use of the incident in their warfare against the republicans.—EDITOR.

unanimity for the present moment. This disease of the imagination will pass over, because the patients are essentially republican. Indeed, the doctor is now on his way to cure it, in the guise of a tax gatherer. But give time for the medicine to work, and for the repetition of stronger doses, which must be administered.—To JOHN TAYLOR. iv, 259. FORD ED., vii, 309. (M., 1798.)

9198. ——— ———. There is real reason to believe that the X. Y. Z. delusion is wearing off, and the public mind beginning to take the same direction it was getting into before that measure. Gerry's dispatches will tend strongly to open the eyes of the people. Besides this several other impressive circumstances will be bearing on the public mind. The Alien and Sedition laws as before, the direct tax, the additional army and navy, an usurious loan to set these follies on foot. a prospect of heavy additional taxes as soon as they are completed, still heavier taxes if the government forces on the war recruiting officers lounging at every court-house and decoying the laborer from his plow.—To JAMES MONROE. iv, 265. FORD ED., vii, 320. (Pa., Jan. 1799.)

9199. ——— ———. The violations of the Constitution, propensities to war, to expense, and to a particular foreign connection [Great Britain], which we have lately seen, are becoming evident to the people, and are dispelling that mist which X. Y. Z. had spread before their eyes.—To EDMUND PENDLETON. iv, 287. FORD ED., vii, 356. (Pa., Feb. 1799.)

9200. X. Y. Z. PLOT, Federalists and.—When Pinckney, Marshall, and Dana were nominated to settle our differences with France, it was suspected by many, from what was understood of their dispositions, that their mission would not result in a settlement of differences, but would produce circumstances tending to widen the breach, and to provoke our citizens to consent to a war with that nation, and union with England. Dana's resignation and your appointment gave the first gleam of hope of a peaceable issue to the mission. For it was believed that you were sincerely disposed to accommodation; and it was not long after your arrival there, before symptoms were observed ot that difference of views which had been suspected to exist. In the meantime, however, the aspect of our government towards the French Republic had become so ardent, that the people of America generally took the alarm. To the southward, their apprehensions were early excited. In the eastern States also, they at length began to break out. Meetings were held in many of your towns, and addresses to the government agreed on in opposition to war. The example was spreading like a wildfire. Other meetings were called in other places, and a general concurrence of sentiment against the apparent inclinations of the government was imminent; when, most critically for the government, the [X. Y. Z.] despatches of October 22d, prepared by your colleague Marshall, with a view to their being made public, dropped into their laps. It was truly a godsend to them. and they made the most of it. Many thousands of copies were printed and dispersed gratis, at the public expense; and the zealots for war cooperated so heartily, that there were instances of single individuals who printed and dispersed ten or twelve thousand copies at their own expense. The odiousness of the corruption supposed in those papers excited a general and high indignation among the people. Unexperienced in such maneuvers, they did not permit themselves even to suspect that the turpitude of private swindlers might mingle itself unobserved, and give its own hue to the communications of the French government, of whose participation there was neither proof nor probability. It served, however, for a time, the purpose intended. The people, in many places, gave a loose to the expressions of their warm indignation, and of their honest preference of war to dishonor The fever was long and successfully kept up, and in the meantime, war measures as ardently crowded. Still, however, as it was known that your colleagues were coming away, and yourself to stay. though disclaiming a separate power to conclude a treaty, it was hoped by the lovers of peace, that a project of treaty would have been prepared, *ad referendum,* on principles which would have satisfied our citizens, and overawed any bias of the government towards a different policy. But the expedition of the Sophia, and, as was supposed, the suggestions of the person charged with your dispatches, and his probable misrepresentations of the real wishes of the American people, prevented these hopes. They had then only to look forward to your return for such information, either through the Executive, or from yourself, as might present to our view the other side of the medal. The despatches of October 22d, 1797, had presented one face. That information, to a certain degree, is now received, and the public will see from your correspondence with Talleyrand, that France, as you testify, "was sincere and anxious to obtain a reconciliation, not wishing us to break the British treaty. but only to give her equivalent stipulations; and in general was disposed to a liberal treaty". And they will judge whether Mr. Pickering's report shows an inflexible determination to believe no declarations the French government can make, nor any opinion which you, judging on the spot and from actual view. can give of their sincerity, and to meet their designs of peace with operations of war.—To ELBRIDGE GERRY. iv, 270. FORD ED., vii, 330. (Pa., Jan. 1799.)

9201. X. Y. Z. PLOT, French government and.—You know what a wicked use has been made of the French negotiation; and particularly the X. Y. Z. dish cooked up by Marshall, where the swindlers are made to appear as the French government. Art and industry combined have certainly wrought out of this business a wonderful effect on the people. Yet they have been astonished more than they have understood it, and now that Gerry's correspondence comes out, clearing the French government of that turpitude, and showing them "sincere in their dispositions for peace, not wishing us to break the British treaty, and willing to arrange a liberal one with us", the people will be disposed to suspect they have been duped. But these communications are too voluminous for them, and beyond their reach. A recapitulation is now wanting * * * . Nobody in America can do it so well as yourself * * * . If the understanding of the people could be rallied to the truth on this subject, by exposing the dupery practiced on them, there are so many other things about to bear on them favorably for the resurrection of their republican spirit, that a reduction of the administration to constitutional principles cannot fail to be the effect.—To EDMUND PENDLETON. iv, 274. FORD ED., vii, 337. (Pa., 1799.)

9202. X. Y. Z. PLOT, War and.—Young E. Gerry informed me some time ago that he had engaged a person to write the life of his father, and asked for any materials I could fur-

nish. I sent him some letters, but in searching for them I found two, too precious to be trusted by mail, of the date of 1801, January 15 and 20, in answer to one I had written him January 26, 1799, two years before. It furnishes authentic proof that in the X. Y. Z. mission to France, it was the wish of Pickering, Marshall, Pinckney and the Federalists of that stamp, to avoid a treaty with France and to bring on war, a fact we charged on them at the time and this lette proves, and that their X. Y. Z. report was cooked up to dispose the people to war. Gerry, their colleague, was not of their sentiment, and this is his statement of that transaction. During the two years between my letter and his answer, he was wavering between Mr. Adams and myself, between his attachment to Mr. Adams personally on the one hand, and to republicanism on the other; for he was republican, but timid and indecisive. The event of the election of 1800-1, put an end to his hesitations.—To JAMES MADISON. FORD ED., x, 245. (M., Jan. 1823.)

9203. YAZOO LANDS, Speculation in.—Arthur Campbell * * * says the Yazoo bargain is likely to drop with the consent of the purchasers. He explains it thus: They expected to pay for the lands in public paper at par, which they had bought at half a crown a pound. Since the rise in the value of the public paper, they have gained as much on that as they would have done by investing it in the Yazoo lands; perhaps more, as it puts a large sum of specie at their command, which they can turn to better account. They are, therefore, likely to acquiesce under the determination of the government of Georgia to consider the contract as forfeited by non-payment.—To PRESIDENT WASHINGTON. iii, 251. FORD ED., v, 324. (Pa., 1791.)

9204. YAZOO LANDS, Title to.—I * * * return the petition of Mr. Moultrie on behalf of the South Carolina Yazoo Company. Without noticing that some of the highest functions of sovereignty are assumed in the very papers which he annexes as his justification, I am of opinion that the government should formally maintain this ground; that the Indians have a right to the occupation of their lands, independent of the States within whose chartered lines they happen to be; that until they cede them by treaty or other transaction equivalent to a treaty, no act of a State can give a right to such lands; that neither under the present Constitution, nor the ancient confederation, had any State or person a right to treat with the Indians, without the consent of the General Government; that that consent has never been given to any treaty for the cession of the lands in question: that the government is determined to exert all its energy for the patronage and protection of the rights of the Indians, and the preservation of peace between the United States and them; and that if any settlements are made on lands not ceded by them, without the previous consent of the United States, the government will think itself bound, not only to declare to the Indians that such settlements are without the authority or protection of the United States, but to remove them also by the public force.—To HENRY KNOX. iii, 280. FORD ED., v, 370. (Pa., 1791.)

9205. YELLOW FEVER, Cities and.—[As to] the town which you have done me the honor to name after me. and to lay out according to an idea I had formerly expressed to you, I am thoroughly persuaded that it will be found handsome and pleasant, and I do believe it to be the best means of preserving the cities of America from the scourge of the yellow fever, which being peculiar to our country, must be derived from some peculiarity in it. That peculiarity I take to be our cloudless skies. In Europe, where the sun does not shine more than half the number of days in the year which it does in America, they can build their town in a solid block with impunity; but here a constant sun produces too great an accumulation of heat to admit that. Ventilation is indispensably necessary. Experience has taught us that in the open air of the country the yellow fever is not only not generated, but ceases to be infectious.—To Governor Harrison. iv, 471. (W., 1803.)

9206. ―― ――. I have supposed it practicable to prevent its generation by building our cities on a more open plan. Take, for instance, the checker board for a plan. Let the black squares only be building squares, and the white ones be left open, in turf and trees. Every square of houses will be surrounded by four open squares, and every house will front an open square. The atmosphere of such a town would be like that of the country, insusceptible of the miasmata which produce yellow fever. I have proposed that the enlargements of the city of New Orleans * * * shall be on this plan.—To C. F. Volney. iv, 572. (W., 1805.)

9207. ―― ――. I really wish effect to the hints in my letter to you for so laying off the additions to the city of New Orleans, as to shield it from yellow fever. My confidence in the idea is founded in the acknowledged experience that we have never seen the *genuine* yellow fever extend itself into the country, or even to the outskirts or open parts of a close-built city. In the plan I propose, every square would be surrounded, on every side, by open and pure air, in fact, be a separate town with fields or open suburbs around it.—To Governor Claiborne. v, 520. (M., 1810.)

9208. YELLOW FEVER, Infectious.— On the question whether the yellow fever is infectious or endemic, the medical faculty is divided into two parties, and it certainly is not the office of the public functionary to denounce either party as Dr. Rush proposes. Yet, so far as they are called on to act, they must form for themselves an opinion to act on. In the early history of the disease, I did suppose it to be infectious. Not reading any of the party papers on either side, I continued in this supposition until the fever at Alexandria brought facts under my own eye, as it were, proving it could not be communicated but *in a local atmosphere*, pretty exactly circumscribed. With the composition of this atmosphere we are unacquainted. We know only that it is generated *near the water side, in close built cities, under warm climates*. According to the rules of philosophizing when one sufficient cause for an effect is known, it is not within the economy of nature to employ two. If local atmosphere suffices to produce the fever, miasmata from a human subject are not necessary and probably do not enter into the cause. Still, it is not within my province to decide the question; but as it may be within yours to require the performance of quarantine or not, I execute a private duty in submitting Dr. Rush's letter to your consideration.—To Governor Page. Ford ed., viii, 316. (M., 1804.)

9209. YELLOW FEVER, Origin.—Facts appear to have established that it is originated here by a local atmosphere, which is never gen-

erated but in the lower, closer, and dirtier parts of our large cities, and in the neighborhood of the water; and that, to catch the disease, you must enter the local atmosphere. Persons having taken the disease in the infected quarter, and going into the country, are nursed and buried by their friends, without an example of communicating it. * * * It is certainly an epidemic, not a contagious disease.—To C. F. Volney. iv, 570. (W., 1805.)

9210. YELLOW FEVER, Quarantine and.—In the course of the several visitations by this disease [yellow fever], it has appeared that it is strictly local, incident to the cities and on the tide waters only; incommunicable in the country, either by persons under the disease or by goods carried from diseased places; that its access is with the autumn, and that it disappears with the early frost·. These restrictions, within narrow limits of time and space, give security even to our maritime cities, during three-fourths of the year, and to the country always. Although from these facts it appears unnecessary, yet to satisfy the fears of foreign nations. and cautions on their part not to be complained of in a danger whose limits are yet unknown to them, I have strictly enjoined on the officers at the head of the customs to certify with exact truth for every vessel sailing for a foreign port, the state of health respecting this fever which prevailed at the place from which she sailed. Under every motive from character and duty to certify the truth, I have no doubt they have faithfully executed this injunction. Much real injury has, however, been sustained from a propensity to identify with this endemic, and to call by the same name, fevers of very different kinds, which have always been known at all times and in almost all countries, and never have been placed among those deemed contagious. As we advance in our knowledge of this disease, as facts develop the source from which individuals receive it, the State authorities charged with the care of the public health. and Congress with that of the general commerce, will become able to regulate with effect their respective functions in these departments. The burden of quarantines is at home as well as abroad; their efficacy merits examination. Although the health laws of the States should be found to need no present revisal by Congress, yet commerce claims that their attention be ever awake to them.—Fifth Annual Message. viii, 46. Ford ed., viii, 387. (Dec. 1805.)

― YEOMANRY, Beggared.—See Embargo, 2589.

9211. YORKTOWN, Gratitude to France.—If in the minds of any, the motives of gratitude to our good allies were not sufficiently apparent, the part they have borne in this action [Yorktown] must amply evince them.—To General Washington. i, 314. Ford ed., iii, 51. (M., 1781.)

9212. YOUNG MEN, Education.—I am not a friend to placing young men in populous cities [for their education] because they acquire there habits and partialities which do not contribute to the happiness of their after life.—To Dr. Wistar. v, 104. Ford ed., ix, 79. (W., 1807.)

9213. ―― ――. A part of my occupation, and by no means the least pleasing, is the direction of the studies of such young men as ask it. They place themselves in the neighboring village and have the use of my library and counsel, and make a part of my society. In advising the course of their reading, I endeavor to keep their attention fixed on the main objects of all science, the freedom and happiness of man. So that coming to bear a share in the councils and government of their country, they will keep ever in view the sole objects of all legitimate government.—To GENERAL KOSCIUSKO. v, 509. (M., 1810.)

9214. YOUNG MEN, Enthusiasm of.— Bonaparte will conquer the world if they [the European powers] do not learn his secret of composing armies of young men only, whose enthusiasm and health enable them to surmount all obstacles.—To MR. BIDWELL. v, 16. (W., 1806.)

9215. YOUNG MEN, Future rulers.— They [the students of the University of Virginia] are exactly the persons who are to succeed to the government of our country, and to rule its future enmities, its friendships and fortunes.—To J. EVELYN DENISON. vii, 415. (M., 1825.)

9216. YOUNG MEN, Patronizing.—I have written to you in the style to which I have been always accustomed with you, and which perhaps it is time I should lay aside. But while old men are sensible enough of their own advance in years, they do not sufficiently recollect it in those whom they have seen young.—To WILLIAM SHORT. iii, 503. FORD ED., vi, 156. (Pa., 1793.)

9217. YOUNG MEN, Public life and.— Wythe's school is numerous. They hold weekly courts and assemblies in the Capitol. The professors join in it, and the young men dispute with elegance, method and learning. This single school, by throwing from time to time new hands well principled, and well-informed into the Legislature, will be of infinite value.—To JAMES MADISON. FORD ED., ii, 322. (R., 1780.)

9218. YOUNG MEN, Reform and.— The [French] officers, who had been to America, were mostly young men, less shackled by habit and prejudice, and more ready to assent to the suggestions of common sense and feeling of common rights, than others. They come back [to France] with new ideas and impressions.—AUTOBIOGRAPHY. i, 69. FORD ED., i, 96. (1821.)

9219. YOUNG MEN, Self-government and.— Three sons, and hopeful ones too, are a rich treasure. I rejoice when I hear of young men of virtue and talents, worthy to receive, and likely to preserve the splendid inheritance of self-government, which we have acquired and shaped for them.—To JUDGE TYLER. iv, 549. (W., 1804.)

9220. ——— ———. The sentiments you express * * * are particularly solacing to those who, having labored faithfully in establishing the right of self-government, see in the rising generation. into whose hands it is passing, that purity of principle, and energy of character, which will protect and preserve it through their day. and deliver it over to their sons as they receive it from their fathers. —R. TO A. PITTSBURG YOUNG REPUBLICANS. viii, 141. (1808.)

9221. YOUNG MEN, Slavery and.—I look to the rising generation, and not to the one now in power, for these great reformations. [Respecting slavery.]—To GENERAL CHASTELLUX. i, 340. FORD ED., iii, 71. (P., 1785.)

9222. ——— ———. The college of William and Mary * * * is the place where are collected together all the young men of Virginia under preparation for public life. * * * I am satisfied if you could resolve to address an exhortation to those young men, with all that eloquence of which you are master. that its influence on the future decision of this important question [slavery] would be great, perhaps decisive.—To DR. PRICE. i, 377. FORD ED., iv, 83. (P., 1785.)

9223. ——— ———. [In Virginia] * * * the sacred side [in the conflict with slavery] is gaining daily recruits from the influx into office of young men grown and growing up. These have sucked in the principles of liberty, as it were, with their mothers' milk; and it is to them I look with anxiety to turn the fate of this question.—To DR. PRICE. i, 377. FORD ED., iv, 83. (P., 1785.)

9224. YOUNG MEN, Surrender to.—I leave the world and its affairs to the young and energetic, and resign myself to their care, of whom I have endeavored to take care when young.—To CHARLES PINCKNEY. vii, 180. FORD ED., x, 162. (M., 1820.)

9225. YOUNG WOMEN, Power of.—All the handsome young women [of Paris] are for the *Tiers État*, and this is an army more powerful in France than the 200,000 men of the King.—To DAVID HUMPHREYS. iii, 11. FORD ED., v, 87. (P., 1789.)

9226. ZEAL, Fervent.— Fervent zeal is all which I can be sure of carrying into their [Congress] service.—To JOHN JAY. i, 339. (P., 1785.)

9227. ZEAL, Resources of.— Utterly indeed, should I despair, did not the presence of many whom I here see remind me. that in the high authorities provided by our Constitution, I shall find resources of wisdom, of virtue. and of zeal, on which to rely under all difficulties.—FIRST INAUGURAL ADDRESS. viii, 1. FORD ED., viii, 2. (1801.)

9228. ZEAL, Ridicule and.—I fear that my zeal will make me expose myself to ridicule * * * but this risk becomes a duty by the bare possibility of doing good.—To DR. RAMSAY. ii, 216. (P., 1787.)

APPENDIX

CONTENTS

APPENDIX

REPLY TO LORD NORTH'S CONCILIATORY PROPOSITION

The Congress proceeding to take into their consideration a resolution of the House of Commons of Great Britain, referred to them by the several Assemblies of New Jersey, Pennsylvania, and Virginia, which resolution is in these words: " That it is the opinion, &c.," are of opinion:

That the Colonies of America possess the exclusive privilege of giving and granting their own money; that this involves the right of deliberating whether they will make any gift, for what purposes it shall be made, and what shall be the amount of the gift; and that it is a high breach of this privilege for any body of men, extraneous to their constitutions, to prescribe the purposes for which money shall be levied on them; to take to themselves the authority of judging of their conditions, circumstances, and situation, of determining the amount of the contribution to be levied:

That, as they possess a right of appropriating their gifts, so are they entitled at all times to inquire into their application, to see that they be not wasted among the venal and corrupt for the purpose of undermining the civil rights of the givers, nor yet be diverted to the support of standing armies, inconsistent with their freedom, and subversive of their quiet. To propose, therefore, as this resolution does, that the moneys, given by the Colonies, shall be subject to the disposal of Parliament alone, is to propose, that they shall relinquish this right of inquiry, and put it in the power of others, to render their gifts ruinous, in proportion as they are liberal:

That this privilege of giving, or withholding our moneys, is an important barrier against the undue exertion of prerogative, which, if left altogether without control, may be exercised to our great oppression; and all history shows how efficacious its intercession for redress of grievances, and reestablishment of rights, and how improvident would be the surrender of so powerful a mediator.

We are of opinion:

That the proposition contained in this resolution is unreasonable and insidious; unreasonable, because if we declare we accede to it, we declare without reservation we will purchase the favor of Parliament, not knowing, at the same time, at what price they will please to estimate their favor. It is insidious, because individual colonies, having bid and bidden again, till they find the avidity of the seller unattainable by all their powers, are then to return into opposition, divided from their sister Colonies, whom the minister will have previously detached by a grant of easier terms, or by an artful procrastination of a definitive answer:

That the suspension of the exercise of their pretended power of taxation being expressly made commensurate with the continuing of our gifts, these must be perpetual to make that so; whereas no experience has shown that a gift of perpetual revenue secures a perpetual return of duty, or of kind dispositions. On the contrary, the Parliament itself, wisely attentive to this observation, are in the established practice of granting their own money from year to year only.

Though desirous and determined to consider, in the most dispassionate view every advance towards reconciliation, made by the British Parliament, let our brethren of Britain reflect what could have been the sacrifice to men of free spirits, had even fair terms been proffered by freemen when attended as these were, with circumstances of insult and defiance. A proposition to give our money, when accompanied with large fleets and armies, seems addressed to our fears, rather than to our freedom. With what patience, would they have received articles of treaty, from any power on earth, when borne on the point of the bayonet, by military plenipotentiaries?

We think the attempt unnecessary and unwarrantable to raise upon us, by force or by threats, our proportional contributions to the common defence, when all know, and themselves acknowledge, we have fully contributed, whenever called to contribute, in the character of freemen.

We are of opinion it is not just that the Colonies should be required to oblige themselves to other contributions, while Great Britain possesses a monopoly of their trade. This does of itself lay them under heavy contribution. To demand, therefore, an additional contribution in the form of a tax, is to demand the double of their equal proportion. If we are to contribute equally with the other parts of the empire, let us equally with them enjoy free commerce with the whole world. But while the restrictions on our trade shut to us the resources of wealth, is it just we should bear all other burthens, equally with those to whom every resource is open?

We conceive, that the British Parliament has no right to intermeddle with our provisions for the support of civil government, or administration of justice; that the provisions we have made are such as please ourselves. They answer the substantial purposes of government, and of justice, and other purposes than these should not be answered. We do not mean that our people shall be burthened with oppressive taxes to provide sinecures for the idle or wicked, under color of providing for a civil list. While Parliament pursue their plan of civil government within their own jurisdiction, we hope, also, to pursue ours without molestation.

We are of opinion the proposition is altogether unsatisfactory because it imports only a suspension, not a renunciation of the right to tax us; because, too, it does not propose to repeal the several acts of Parliament, passed for the purposes of restraining the trade, and altering the form of government of one of the Eastern Colonies; extending the boundaries, and changing the government and religion of Quebec; enlarging the jurisdiction of the Courts of Admiralty and Vice-admiralty; taking from us the rights of trial by jury of the vicinage in cases affecting both life and prosperity; transporting us into other countries to be tried for criminal offences; exempting, by mock trial, the murderers of Colonists from punishment; and for quartering soldiers upon us, in times of profound peace. Nor do they renounce the power of suspending our own legislatures, and of legislating for us themselves in all cases whatsoever. On the contrary, to show they mean no discontinuance of injury, they pass acts, at the very time of holding out this proposition, for restraining the commerce and fisheries of the Province of New England; and for interdicting the trade of the other Colonies, with all foreign nations. This proves unequivocally, they mean not to relinquish the exercise of indiscriminate legislation over us.

Upon the whole, this proposition seems to have been held up to the whole world to deceive it into a belief that there is no matter in dispute between us but the single circumstance of the mode of levying taxes, which mode they are so good as to give up to us, of course that the Colonies are unreasonable if they are not, thereby, perfectly satisfied; whereas, in truth, our adversaries not only still claim a right of demanding *ad libitum,* and of taxing us themselves to the full amount of their demands if we do not fulfil their pleasure, which leaves us without anything we can call property, but, what is of more importance, and what they keep in this proposal out of sight, as if no such point was in contest, they claim a right of altering our charters, and established laws which leave us without the least security for our lives or liberties.

The proposition seems, also, calculated more particularly to lull into fatal security our well-affected fellow subjects on that other side of the water, till time should be given for the operation of those arms which a British minister pronounced would instantaneously reduce the *" cowardly "* sons of America to unreserved submission. But, when the world reflects how inadequate to justice are the vaunted terms, when it attends to the rapid and bold succession of injuries, which, during a course of eleven years, have been aimed at these Colonies, when it reviews the pacific and respectful expostulations, which, during that whole time, have been made the sole arms we oppose to them, when it observes, that our complaints were either not heard at all, or were answered with new and accumulated injuries; when it recollects, that the minister himself declared on an early occasion, " that he would never treat with America, till he had brought her to his feet "; and that an avowed partisan of ministry has, more lately, denounced against America the dreadful sentence *" Delenda est Carthago ";* and that this was done in the presence of a British senate, and being unreproved by them, must be taken to be their own sentiments, when it considers the great armaments with which they have invaded us and the circumstances of cruelty, with which these have commenced and prosecuted hostilities; when these things, we say, are laid together, and attentively considered, can the world be deceived into an opinion that we are unreasonable, or can it hesitate to believe with us, that nothing but our own exertions, may defeat the ministerial sentence of death, or submission? *—FORD ED., i, 476. (July 25, 1775.)

* This is Jefferson's draft. Congress made several verbal alterations.—EDITOR.

COMMITTEES OF CORRESPONDENCE

A court of inquiry held in Rhode Island in 1762, with a power to send persons to England to be tried for offences committed here,* was considered at our session [Virginia House of Burgesses] of the spring of 1773, as demanding attention. Not thinking our old and leading members up to the point of forwardness and zeal which the times required, Mr. [Patrick] Henry, Richard Henry Lee, Francis L. Lee, Mr. [Dabney] Carr and myself agreed to meet in the evening, in a private room of the Raleigh [tavern], to consult on the state of things. * * * We were all sensible that the most urgent of all measures was that of coming to an understanding with all the other Colonies to consider the British claims as a common cause to all, and to produce a unity of action; and, for this purpose, that a Committee of Correspondence in each Colony would be the best instrument for intercommunication; and that their first measure would probably be, to propose a meeting of deputies from every Colony, at some central place, who should be charged with the direction of the measures which should be taken by all. * * * The consulting members proposed to me to move * * * [the resolutions agreed upon], but I urged that it should be done by Mr. [Dabney] Carr, my friend and brother-in-law, then a new member, to whom I wished an opportunity should be given of making known to the house his great worth and talents. It was so agreed; he moved them, they were agreed to *nem. con.*, and a Committee of Correspondence appointed, of whom Peyton Randolph, the Speaker, was chairman. The Governor (then Lord Dunmore) dissolved us, but the Committee met the next day, prepared a circular letter to the Speakers of the other Colonies, enclosing to each a copy of the resolutions, and left it in charge with their chairman to forward them by expresses.—AUTOBIOGRAPHY. i, 5. FORD ED., 7. (1821.)

The next event which excited our sympathies for Massachusetts, was the Boston port bill, by which that port was to be shut up on the 1st of June, 1774. This arrived while we [Virginia House of Burgesses] were in session in the spring of that year. The lead in the House, on these subjects, being no longer left to the old members, Mr. Henry, R. H. Lee, Francis L. Lee, three or four other members, whom I do not recollect, and myself, agreeing that we must boldly take an unequivocal stand in the line with Massachusetts, determined to meet and consult on the proper measures in the council chamber, for the benefit of the library in that room. We were under conviction of the necessity of arousing our people from the lethargy into which they had fallen, as to passing events; and thought that the appointment of a day of general fasting and prayer would be most likely to call up and alarm their attention. No example of such a solemnity had existed since the days of our distresses in the war of '55, since which a new generation had grown up. With the help, therefore, of Rushworth, whom we rummaged over for the revolutionary precedents and forms of the Puritans of that day, preserved by him, we cooked up a resolution, somewhat modernizing their phrases, for appointing the 1st day of June, on which the port bill was to commence, for a day of fasting, humiliation, and prayer, to implore Heaven to avert from us the evils of civil war, to inspire us with firmness in support of our rights, and to turn the hearts of the King and Parliament to moderation and justice. To give greater emphasis to our proposition, we agreed to wait the next morning on Mr. [Robert Carter] Nicholas, whose grave and religious character was more in unison with the tone of our resolution, and to solicit him to move it. We accordingly went to him in the morning. He moved it the same day; the 1st of June was proposed; and it passed without opposition. The Governor dissolved us as usual. * * * We returned home, and in our several counties invited the clergy to meet assemblies of the people on the 1st of June † to perform the ceremonies of the day, and to address to them discourses suited to the occasion. The people met generally, with anxiety and alarm in their countenances, and the effect of the day, through the whole colony, was like a shock of electricity, arousing every man, and placing him erect and solidly on his centre.—AUTOBIOGRAPHY. i, 6. FORD ED., i, 9. (1821.)

The Governor dissolved us as usual. We retired to the Apollo, agreed to an association, and instructed the Committee of Correspondence to propose to the corresponding committees of the other Colonies, to appoint deputies to meet in Congress at such place, *annually*, as should be convenient, to direct, from time to time, the measures required by the general interest: and we declared that an attack on any one Colony, should be considered as an attack on the whole. This was in May [27, 1774]. We further recommended to the several counties to elect deputies to meet at Williamsburg, the 1st of August, ensuing, to consider the state of the Colony, and particularly to appoint delegates to a general Congress, should that measure be acceded to by the committees of correspondence generally. It was acceded to; Philadelphia was appointed for the place, and the 5th of September for the time of meeting.—AUTOBIOGRAPHY. i, 7. FORD ED., i, 11. (1821.)

Respecting the question, whether Committees of Correspondence originated in Virginia or Massachusetts? * * * You suppose me to have claimed it for Virginia; but certainly I have never made such a claim. The idea, I suppose, has been taken up from what is said in WIRT'S *Life of Patrick Henry*, page 87, and from an inexact attention to its precise terms. It is there said, "this House (of Burgesses, of Virginia) had the merit of originating that powerful engine of resistance, Corresponding Committees *between the Legislatures and the different Colonies*". That the fact, as here expressed is true, your letter bears witness, when it says, that the resolutions of Virginia, for this purpose, were transmitted to the speakers of the different assemblies, and by that of Massachusetts, was laid, at the next session, before that body, who appointed a committee for the specified object: adding, "thus, in Massachusetts, there were two Committees of Correspondence, one chosen by the people, the other appointed by the House of Assembly: in the former, Massachusetts preceded Virginia; in the latter, Virginia preceded Massachusetts". To the origination of committees for the interior correspondence between the counties and towns of a State, I know of no claim on the part of Virginia; and

---

* This was the famous "Gaspee" inquiry, the date being a slip for 1772.—NOTE IN FORD EDITION.
† The invitation read June 23d.
‡ The name of a public room in the Raleigh tavern.

certainly none was ever made by myself. I perceive, however, one error, into which memory had led me. Our Committee for national correspondence, was appointed in March, '73, and I well remember, that going to Williamsburg, in the month of June following, Peyton Randolph, our chairman, told me that messengers bearing dispatches between the two States, had crossed each other by the way, that of Virginia carrying our propositions for a committee of national correspondence, and that of Massachusetts, bringing, as my memory suggested, a similar proposition. But here I must have misremembered; and the resolutions brought us from Massachusetts, were probably those you mention of the town-meeting of Boston, on the motion of Mr. Samuel Adams, appointing a committee " to state the rights of the colonists, and of that province in particular, and the infringements of them; to communicate them to the several towns, as the sense of the town of Boston, and to request, of each town, a free communication of its sentiments on the subject." I suppose, therefore, that these resolutions were not received, as you think, while the House of Burgesses was in session in March, 1773, but a few days after we rose, and were probably what was sent by the messenger, who crossed ours by the way. They may, however, have been still different. I must, therefore, have been mistaken in supposing, and stating to Mr. Wirt, that the proposition of a committee for national correspondence was nearly simultaneous in Virginia and Massachusetts.—To SAMUEL A. WELLS. i, 115. FORD ED., X, 127. (M., 1819.)

A SUMMARY VIEW OF THE RIGHTS OF BRITISH AMERICA*

Resolved, That it be an instruction to the said deputies, when assembled in General Congress, with the deputies from the other States of British America, to propose to the said Congress, that an humble and dutiful address be presented to his Majesty, begging leave to lay before him, as Chief Magistrate of the British Empire, the united complaints of his Majesty's subjects in America: complaints which are excited by many unwarrantable encroachments and usurpations, attempted to be made by the legislature of one part of the empire, upon the rights which God, and the laws have given equally and independently to all. To represent to his Majesty that these, his States, have often individually made humble application to his imperial throne, to obtain, through its intervention, some redress of their injured rights; to none of which was ever even an answer condescended. Humbly to hope that this, their joint address, penned in the language of truth, and divested of those expressions of servility, which would persuade his Majesty that we are asking favors, and not rights, shall obtain from his Majesty a more respectful acceptance: and this his Majesty will think we have reason to expect, when he reflects that he is no more than the chief officer of the people, appointed by the laws, and circumscribed with definite powers, to assist in working the great machine of government, erected for their use, and, consequently, subject to their superintendence; and, in order that these, our rights, as well as the invasions of them, may be laid more fully before his Majesty, to take a view of them, from the origin and first settlement of these countries.

To remind him that our ancestors, before their emigration to America, were the free inhabitants of the British dominions in Europe, and possessed a right, which nature has given to all men, of departing from the country in which chance, not choice, has placed them of going in quest of new habitations, and of there establishing new societies, under such laws and regulations as, to them, shall seem most likely to promote public happiness. That their Saxon ancestors had, under this universal law. in like manner, left their native wilds and woods in the North of Europe, had possessed themselves of the Island of Britain, then less charged with inhabitants. and had established there that system of laws which has so long been the glory and protection of that country. Nor was ever any claim of superiority or dependence asserted over them, by that mother country from which they had migrated; and were such a claim made, it is believed his Majesty's subjects in Great Britain have too firm a feeling of the rights derived to them from their ancestors, to bow down the sovereignty of their State before such visionary pretensions.

And it is thought that no circumstance has occurred to distinguish, materially, the British from the Saxon emigration. America was conquered, and her settlements made and firmly established, at the expense of individuals, and not of the British public. Their own blood was spilt in acquiring lands for their settlement, their own fortunes expended in making that settlement effectual. For themselves they fought, for themselves they conquered, and for themselves alone they have right to hold. No shilling was ever issued from the public treasures of his Majesty, or his ancestors, for their assistance, till of very late times, after the Colonies had become established on a firm and permanent footing. That then, indeed, having become valuable to Great Britain for her commercial purposes, his Parliament was pleased to lend them assistance against an enemy who would fain have drawn to herself the benefits of their commerce, to the great aggrandizement of herself, and danger of Great Britain. Such assistance, and in such circumstances, they had often before given to Portugal and other allied States, with whom they carry on a commercial intercourse. Yet these States never supposed, that by calling in her aid, they thereby submitted themselves to her sovereignty. Had such terms been proposed. they would have rejected them with disdain, and trusted for better, to the moderation of their enemies, or to a vigorous exertion of their own force. We do not, however, mean to underrate those aids, which, to us, were doubtless valuable, on whatever principles granted; but we would show that they cannot give a title to that authority which the British Parliament would arrogate over us; and that may amply be repaid by our giving to the inhabitants of Great Britain such exclusive privileges in trade as may be advantageous to them, and, at the same time, not too restrictive to ourselves. That settlement having been thus effected in the wilds of America, the emigrants thought proper to adopt that system of laws, under which they had hitherto lived in the mother country, and to continue their union with her, by submitting themselves to the same common sovereign, who was thereby made the central link, connecting the several parts of the empire thus newly multiplied.

But that not long were they permitted, however far they thought themselves removed from the hand of oppression, to hold undisturbed the rights thus acquired at the hazard of their lives and loss of their fortunes. A family of princes was then on the British throne, whose treasonable crimes against their people, brought on them, afterwards, the exertion of those sacred and sovereign rights of punishment, reserved in the hands of the people for cases of extreme necessity, and judged by the constitution unsafe to be delegated to any other judicature. While every day brought forth some new and unjustifiable exertion of power over their subjects on that side of the water, it was not to be expected that those here, much less able at that time to oppose the designs of despotism, should be exempted from injury. Accordingly, this country which had been acquired by the lives, the labors, and fortunes of individual adventurers, was by these Princes, several times, parted out and distributed among the favorites and followers of their fortunes; and, by an assumed right of the Crown alone, were erected into distinct and independent governments; a measure which, it is believed, his Majesty's prudence and understanding would prevent him from imitating at this day; as no exercise of such power, of dividing

---

*The SUMMARY VIEW was not written for publication. It was a draft I had prepared for a petition to the King, which I meant to propose in my place as a member of the convention of 1774. Being stopped on the road by sickness, I sent it on to the Speaker, who laid it on the table for the perusal of the members. It was thought too strong for the times, and to become the act of the convention, but was printed by subscription of the members, with a short preface written by one of them. If it had any merit, it was that of first taking our true ground, and that which was afterwards assumed and maintained.—TO JOHN W. CAMPBELL. v, 465. FORD ED., ix, 258. (M., Aug. 1809.)

and dismembering a country, has ever occurred in his Majesty's realm of England, though now of very ancient standing; nor could it be justified or acquiesced under there, or in any part of his Majesty's empire.

That the exercise of a free trade with all parts of the world, possessed by the American colonists, as of natural right, and which no law of their own had taken away or abridged, was next the object of unjust encroachment. Some of the colonies having thought proper to continue the administration of their government in the name and under the authority of his Majesty, King Charles the First, whom, notwithstanding his late deposition by the Commonwealth of England, they continued in the sovereignty of their State, the Parliament, for the Commonwealth, took the same in high offence, and assumed upon themselves the power of prohibiting their trade with all other parts of the world except the Island of Great Britain. This arbitrary act, however, they soon recalled, and by solemn treaty entered into on the 12th day of March, 1651, between the said Commonwealth, by their Commissioners, and the colony of Virginia by their House of Burgesses, it was expressly stipulated by the eighth article of the said treaty, that they should have " free trade as the people of England do enjoy to all places and with all nations, according to the laws of that Commonwealth "? But that, upon the restoration of his Majesty, King Charles the Second, their rights of free commerce fell once more a victim to arbitrary power : and by several acts of his reign, as well as of some of his successors, the trade of the colonies was laid under such restrictions, as show what hopes they might form from the justice of a British Parliament, were its uncontrolled power admitted over these States.* History has informed us, that bodies of men as well as individuals, are susceptible of the spirit of tyranny. A view of these acts of Parliament for regulation, as it has been affectedly called, of the American trade, if all other evidences were removed out of the case, would undeniably evince the truth of this observation. Besides the duties they impose on our articles of export and import, they prohibit our going to any markets Northward of Cape Finisterre, in the kingdom of Spain, for the sale of commodities which Great Britain will not take from us, and for the purchase of others, with which she cannot supply us; and that, for no other than the arbitrary purpose of purchasing for themselves, by a sacrifice of our rights and interests, certain privileges in their commerce with an allied State, who, in confidence, that their exclusive trade with America will be continued, while the principles and power of the British Parliament be the same, have indulged themselves in every exorbitance which their avarice could dictate or our necessity extort; have raised their commodities called for in America, to the double and treble of what they sold for, before such exclusive privileges were given them, and of what better commodities of the same kind would cost us elsewhere; and, at the same time, given us much less for what we carry thither, than might be had at more convenient ports. That these acts prohibit us from carrying, in quest of other purchasers, the surplus of our tobaccos, remaining after the consumption of Great Britain is supplied; so that we must leave them with the British merchant, for whatever he will please to allow us, to be by him re-shipped to foreign markets, where he will reap the benefits of making sale of them for full value.

That, to heighten still the idea of Parliamentary justice, and to show with what moderation they are like to exercise power, where themselves are to feel no part of its weight, we take leave to mention to his Majesty, certain other acts of the British Parliament, by which they would prohibit us from manufacturing, for our own use, the articles we raise on our own lands, with our own labor. By an act passed in the fifth year of the reign of his late Majesty, King George the Second, an American subject is forbidden to make a hat for himself, of the fur which he has taken, perhaps, on his own soil; an instance of despotism, to which no parallel can be produced in the most arbitrary ages of British history. By one other act, passed in the twenty-third year of the same reign, the iron which we make, we are forbidden to manufacture; and, heavy as that article is, and necessary in every branch of husbandry, besides commission and insurance, we are to pay freight for it to Great Britain, and freight for it back again, for the purpose of supporting, not men, but machines, in the island of Great Britain. In the same spirit of equal and impartial legislation, is to be viewed the act of Parliament, passed in the fifth year of the same reign, by which American lands are made subject to the demands of British creditors, while their own lands were still continued unanswerable for their debts; from which, one of these conclusions must necessarily follow, either that justice is not the same thing in America as in Britain, or else, that the British Parliament pay less regard to it here than there. But, that we do not point out to his Majesty the injustice of these acts, with intent to rest on that principle the cause of their nullity; but to show that experience confirms the propriety of those political principles, which exempt us from the jurisdiction of the British Parliament. The true ground on which we declare these acts void, is, that the British Parliament has no right to exercise authority over us.

That these exercises of usurped power have not been confined to instances alone, in which themselves were interested; but they have also intermeddled with the regulation of the internal affairs of the Colonies. The act of the 9th of Anne for establishing a post office in America, seems to have had little connection with British convenience, except that of accommodating his Majesty's ministers and favourites with the sale of a lucrative and easy office.

That thus have we hastened through the reigns which preceded his Majesty's, during which the violations of our rights were less alarming, because repeated at more distant intervals, than that rapid and bold succession of injuries, which is likely to distinguish the present from all other periods of American story. Scarcely have our minds been able to emerge from the astonishment into which one stroke of Parliamentary thunder has involved us, before another more heavy and more alarming is fallen on us. Single acts of tyranny may be ascribed to the accidental opinion of a day; but a series of oppressions, begun at a distinguished period, and pursued unalterably through every change of ministers, too plainly prove a deliberate, systematical plan of reducing us to slavery.

* 12 C. 2 c. 18   15 C. 2 c. 11.   25 C. 2 c. 7.   7. 8 W. M. c. 22.   11 W. 34 Anne   6 C 2 c. 13.—NOTE BY JEF-FERSON.

Act for grant-
ing certain
duties.
Stamp act.
Act declaring
right of Par-
liament over
the Colonies.
Act for grant-
ing duties on
paper, tea, &c.
Act suspend-
ing legislature
of New York.

That the act passed in the fourth year of his Majesty's reign, entitled " An Act
One other act passed in the fifth year of his reign entitled " An Act
One other act passed in the sixth year of his reign, entitled " An Act
And one other act, passed in the seventh year of his reign, entitled " An Act
From that connected chain of Parliamentary usurpation, which has already
been the subject of frequent application to his Majesty, and the Houses of
Lords and Commons of Great Britain; and, no answers having yet been conde-
scended to any of these, we shall not trouble his Majesty with a repetition of the
matters they contained.

But that one other act passed in the same seventh year of his reign, having
been a peculiar attempt. must ever require peculiar mention. It is entitled
"An Act

One free and independent Legislature, hereby takes upon itself to suspend the powers of
another, free and independent as itself; thus exhibiting a phenomenon unknown in nature, the
creator and creature of its own power. Not only the principles of common sense, but the common feelings of human nature must be surrendered up, before his Majesty's subjects here,
can be persuaded to believe that they hold their political existence at the will of a British Parliament. Shall these governments be dissolved, their property annihilated, and their people
reduced to a state of nature, at the imperious breath of a body of men whom they never saw.
in whom they never confided, and over whom they have no powers of punishment or removal,
let their crimes against the American public be ever so great? Can any one reason be assigned,
why one hundred and sixty thousand electors in the island of Great Britain, should give law
to four millions in the States of America, every individual of whom is equal to every individual
of them in virtue, in understanding, and in bodily strength? Were this to be admitted, instead
of being a free people, as we have hitherto supposed, and mean to continue ourselves, we should
suddenly be found the slaves, not of one, but of one hundred and sixty thousand tyrants;
distinguished, too, from all others, by this singular circumstance, that they are removed from
the reach of fear, the only restraining motive which may hold the hand of a tyrant.

That, by "An Act [14 G. 3.] to discontinue in such manner, and for such time as are
therein mentioned, the landing and discharging, lading or shipping of goods, wares and merchandise, at the town and within the harbor of Boston, in the province of Massachusetts Bay,
in North America', which was passed at the last session of the British Parliament, a large and
populous town, whose trade was their sole subsistence, was deprived of that trade, and involved
in utter ruin. Let us for a while, suppose the question of right suspended, in order to examine
this act on principles of justice. An act of Parliament had been passed, imposing duties on
teas, to be paid in America, against which act the Americans had protested, as inauthoritative.
The East India Company, who, till that time, had never sent a pound of tea to America on
their own account, step forth on that occasion, the asserters of Parliamentary right, and send
hither many shiploads of that obnoxious commodity. The masters of their several vessels,
however, on their arrival in America, wisely attended to admonition, and returned with their
cargoes. In the province of New England alone, the remonstrances of the people were disregarded, and a compliance, after being many days waited for, was flatly refused. Whether in
this, the master of the vessel was governed by his obstinacy, or his instructions, let those who
know, say. There are extraordinary situations which require extraordinary interposition.
An exasperated people, who feel that they possess power, are not easily restrained within
limits strictly regular. A number of them assembled in the town of Boston, threw the tea into
the ocean, and dispersed without doing any other act of violence. If in this they did wrong,
they were known, and were amenable to the laws of the land; against which, it could not be
objected, that they had ever, in any instance, been obstructed or diverted from the regular
course, in favor of popular offenders. They should, therefore, not have been distrusted on this
occasion. But that ill-fated colony had formerly been bold in their enmities against the house
of Stuart, and were now devoted to ruin, by that unseen hand which governs the momentous
affairs of this great empire. On the partial representations of a few worthless ministerial de-
pendants, whose constant office it had been to keep that government embroiled, and who, by
their treacheries, hope to obtain the dignity of British knighthood, without calling for a party
accused, without asking a proof, without attempting a distinction between the guilty and the
innocent, the whole of that ancient and wealthy town, is in a moment reduced from opulence
to beggary. Men who had spent their lives in extending the British commerce, who had invested, in that place, the wealth their honest endeavors had merited, found themselves and
their families, thrown at once on the world for subsistence by its charities. Not the hundredth
part of the inhabitants of that town, had been concerned in the act complained of; many of
them were in Great Britain, and in other parts beyond sea; yet all were involved in one
indiscriminate ruin, by a new executive power, unheard of till then, that of a British Parliament.
A property of the value of many millions of money, was sacrificed to revenge, not repay, the
loss of a few thousands. This is administering justice with a heavy hand indeed! And when
is this tempest to be arrested in its course? Two wharves are to be opened again when his
Majesty shall think proper; the residue. which lined the extensive shores of the bay of Boston,
are forever interdicted the exercise of commerce. This little exception seems to have been
thrown in for no other purpose, than that of setting a precedent for investing his Majesty with
legislative powers. If the pulse of his people shall beat calmly under this experiment, another
and another will be tried, till the measure of despotism be filled up. It would be an insult on
common sense, to pretend that this exception was made, in order to restore its commerce to
that great town. The trade. which cannot be received at two wharves alone, must of necessity
be transferred to some other place; to which it will soon be followed by that of the two wharves.
Considered in this light, it would be an insolent and cruel mockery at the annihilation of the
town of Boston.

By the act for the suppression of riots and tumults in the town of Boston [14 G. 3.], passed
also in the last session of Parliament, a murder committed there, is, if the Governor pleases,
to be tried in the court of King's Bench, in the island of Great Britain, by a jury of Middlesex.
The witnesses, too, on receipt of such a sum as the Governor shall think it reasonable for them

to expend, are to enter into recognizance to appear at the trial. This is, in other words, taxing them to the amount of their recognizance; and that amount may be whatever a governor pleases. For who, does his Majesty think, can be prevailed on to cross the Atlantic for the sole purpose of bearing evidence to a fact? His expenses are to be borne, indeed, as they shall be estimated by a governor; but who are to feed the wife and children whom he leaves behind, and who have had no other subsistence but his daily labor? Those epidemical disorders, too, so terrible in a foreign climate, is the cure of them to be estimated among the articles of expense, and their danger to be warded off by the almighty power of a Parliament? And the wretched criminal, if he happen to have offended on the American side, stripped of his privilege of trial by peers of his vicinage, removed from the place where alone full evidence could be obtained, without money, without counsel, without friends, without exculpatory proof, is tried before judges predetermined to condemn. The cowards who would suffer a countryman to be torn from the bowels of their society, in order to be thus offered a sacrifice to Parliamentary tyranny, would merit that everlasting infamy now fixed on the authors of the act! A clause, for a similar purpose, had been introduced into an act passed in the twelfth year of his Majesty's reign, entitled, "An Act for the better securing and preserving his Majesty's dockyards, magazines, ships, ammunition and stores"; against which, as meriting the same censures, the several Colonies have already protested.

That these are the acts of power, assumed by a body of men foreign to our constitutions, and unacknowledged by our laws; against which we do, on behalf of the inhabitants of British America, enter this, our solemn and determined protest. And we do earnestly entreat his Majesty, as yet the only mediatory power between the several States of the British empire, to recommend to his Parliament of Great Britain, the total revocation of these acts, which, however nugatory they may be, may yet prove the cause of further discontents and jealousies among us.

That we next proceed to consider the conduct of his Majesty, as holding the executive powers of the laws of these States, and mark out his deviations from the line of duty. By the Constitution of Great Britain, as well as of the several American States, his Majesty possesses the power of refusing to pass into a law, any bill which has already passed the other two branches of the Legislature. His Majesty, however, and his ancestors, conscious of the impropriety of opposing their single opinion to the united wisdom of two Houses of Parliament, while their proceedings were unbiased by interested principles, for several ages past, have modestly declined the exercise of this power, in that part of his empire called Great Britain. But, by change of circumstances, other principles than those of justice simply, have obtained an influence on their determinations. The addition of new States to the British empire has produced an addition of new, and, sometimes, opposite interests. It is now, therefore, the great office of his Majesty to resume the exercise of his negative power, and to prevent the passage of laws by any one legislature of the empire, which might bear injuriously on the rights and interests of another. Yet this will not excuse the wanton exercise of this power, which we have seen his Majesty practice on the laws of the American Legislature. For the most trifling reasons, and, sometimes for no conceivable reason at all, his Majesty has rejected laws of the most salutary tendency. The abolition of domestic slavery is the great object of desire in those Colonies, where it was, unhappily, introduced in their infant state. But previous to the enfranchisement of the slaves we have, it is necessary to exclude all further importations from Africa. Yet our repeated attempts to effect this, by prohibitions, and by imposing duties which might amount to a prohibition, having been hitherto defeated by his Majesty's negative; thus preferring the immediate advantages of a few British corsairs, to the lasting interests of the American States, and to the rights of human nature, deeply wounded by this infamous practice. Nay, the single interposition of an interested individual against a law was scarcely ever known to fail of success, though, in the opposite scale, were placed the interests of a whole country. That this is so shameful an abuse of a power, trusted with his Majesty for other purposes, as if, not reformed, would call for some legal restrictions.

While equal inattention to the necessities of his people here, has his Majesty permitted our laws to lie neglected, in England, for years, neither confirming them by his assent, nor annulling them by his negative; so that, such of them as have no suspending clause, we hold on the most precarious of all tenures, his Majesty's will; and such of them as suspend themselves till his Majesty's assent be obtained, we have feared might be called into existence at some future and distant period, when time and change of circumstances shall have rendered them destructive to his people here. And, to render this grievance still more oppressive, his Majesty, by his instructions, has laid his Governors under such restrictions, that they can pass no law, of any moment, unless it have such suspending clause; so that, however immediate may be the call for legislative interposition, the law cannot be executed, till it has twice crossed the Atlantic, by which time the evil may have spent its whole force.

But in what terms reconcilable to Majesty, and at the same time to truth, shall we speak of a late instruction to his Majesty's Governor of the Colony of Virginia, by which he is forbidden to assent to any law for the division of a county, unless the new county will consent to have no representative in Assembly? That Colony has as yet affixed no boundary to the westward. Their western counties, therefore, are of an indefinite extent. Some of them are actually seated many hundred miles from their eastern limits. Is it possible, then, that his Majesty can have bestowed a single thought on the situation of those people, who, in order to obtain justice for injuries, however great or small, must, by the laws of that Colony, attend their county court at such a distance, with all their witnesses, monthly, till their litigation be determined? Or does his Majesty seriously wish, and publish it to the world, that his subjects should give up the glorious right of representation, with all the benefits derived from that, and submit themselves the absolute slaves of his sovereign will? Or is it rather meant to confine the legislative body to their present numbers, that they may be the cheaper bargain, whenever they shall become worth a purchase?

One of the articles of impeachment against Tresilian, and the other Judges of Westminster Hall, in the reign of Richard the Second, for which they suffered death, as traitors to their country, was, that they had advised the King, that he might dissolve his Parliament at any time;

and succeeding kings have adopted the opinion of these unjust judges. Since the establishment, however, of the British constitution, at the glorious Revolution, on its free and ancient principles, neither his Majesty, nor his ancestors, have exercised such a power of dissolution in the island of Great Britain; * and when his Majesty was petitioned by the united voice of his people there, to dissolve the present Parliament, who had become obnoxious to them, his ministers were heard to declare, in open Parliament, that his Majesty possessed no such power by the constitution. But how different their language, and his practice, here! To declare, as their duty required, the known rights of their country, to oppose the usurpation of every foreign judicature, to disregard the imperious mandates of a minister or governor, have been the avowed causes of dissolving Houses of Representatives in America. But if such powers be really vested in his Majesty, can he suppose they are there placed to awe the members from such purposes as these? When the representative body have lost the confidence of their constituents, when they have notoriously made sale of their most valuable rights, when they have assumed to themselves powers which the people never put into their hands, then, indeed, their continuing in office becomes dangerous to the State, and calls for an exercise of the power of dissolution. Such being the cause for which the representative body should, and should not, be dissolved, will it not appear strange, to an unbiased observer, that that of Great Britain was not dissolved, while those of the Colonies have repeatedly incurred that sentence?

But your Majesty, or your Governors, have carried this power beyond every limit known or provided for by the laws. After dissolving one House of Representatives, they have refused to call another, so that, for a great length of time, the Legislature provided by the laws, has been out of existence. From the nature of things, every society must, at all times, possess within itself the sovereign powers of legislation. The feelings of human nature revolt against the supposition of a State so situated, as that it may not, in any emergency, provide against dangers which, perhaps, threaten immediate ruin. While those bodies are in existence to whom the people have delegated the powers of legislation, they alone possess, and may exercise, those powers. But when they are dissolved, by the lopping off of one or more of their branches, the power reverts to the people, who may use it to unlimited extent, either assembling together in person, sending deputies, or in any other way they may think proper. We forbear to trace consequences further; the dangers are conspicuous with which this practice is replete.

That we shall, at this time also, take notice of an error in the nature of our land holdings, which crept in at a very early period of our settlement. The introduction of the Feudal tenures into the kingdom of England, though ancient, is well enough understood to set this matter in a proper light. In the earlier ages of the Saxon settlement, feudal holdings were certainly altogether unknown, and very few, if any, had been introduced at the time of the Norman Conquest. Our Saxon ancestors held their lands, as they did their personal property, in absolute dominion, disencumbered with any superior, answering nearly to the nature of those possessions which the feudalist termed allodial. William the Norman, first introduced that system generally. The lands which had belonged to those who fell in the battle of Hastings, and in the subsequent insurrections of his reign, formed a considerable proportion of the lands of the whole kingdom. These he granted out, subject to feudal duties, as did he also those of a great number of his new subjects, who, by persuasions or threats, were induced to surrender them for that purpose. But still, much was left in the hands of his Saxon subjects, held of no superior, and not subject to feudal conditions. These, therefore, by express laws, enacted to render uniform the system of military defence, were made liable to the same military duties as if they had been feuds; and the Norman lawyers soon found means to saddle them, also, with the other feudal burthens. But still they had not been surrendered to the king, they were not derived from his grant, and therefore they were not holden of him. A general principle was introduced, that " all lands in England were held either mediately or immediately of the Crown "; but this was borrowed from those holdings which were truly feudal, and only applied to others for the purposes of illustration. Feudal holdings were, therefore, but exceptions out of the Saxon laws of possession, under which all lands were held in absolute right. These, therefore, still form the basis or groundwork of the Common law, to prevail wheresoever the exceptions have not taken place. America was not conquered by William the Norman, nor its lands surrendered to him or any of his successors. Possessions there are, undoubtedly, of the allodial nature. Our ancestors, however, who migrated hither, were laborers, not lawyers. The fictitious principle, that all lands belong originally to the king, they were early persuaded to believe real, and accordingly took grants of their own lands from the Crown. And while the Crown continued to grant for small sums and on reasonable rents, there was no inducement to arrest the error, and lay it open to public view. But his Majesty has lately taken on him to advance the terms of purchase and of holding, to the double of what they were; by which means, the acquisition of lands being rendered difficult, the population of our country is likely to be checked. It is time, therefore, for us to lay this matter before his Majesty, and to declare, that he has no right to grant lands of himself. From the nature and purpose of civil institutions, all the lands within the limits, which any particular party has circumscribed around itself, are assumed by that society, and subject to their allotment; this may be done by themselves assembled collectively, or by their legislature, to whom they may have delegated sovereign authority; and, if they are allotted in neither of these ways, each individual of the society, may appropriate to himself such lands as he finds vacant, and occupancy will give him title.

That, in order to enforce the arbitrary measures before complained of, his Majesty has, from time to time, sent among us large bodies of armed forces, not made up of the people here, nor raised by the authority of our laws. Did his Majesty possess such a right as this, it might swallow up all our other rights, whenever he should think proper. But his Majesty has no right to land a single armed man on our shores; and those whom he sends here are

---

* On further inquiry, I find two instances of dissolutions before the Parliament would, of itself, have been at an end, viz.: the Parliament called to meet August 24, 1698, was dissolved by King William, December 19, 1700, and a new one was called to meet February 6, 1701, which was also dissolved, November 11, 1701, and a new one met December 30, 1701.—NOTE BY JEFFERSON.

liable to our laws, for the suppression and punishment of riots, routs, and unlawful assemblies, or are hostile bodies invading us in defiance of law. When, in the course of the late war, it became expedient that a body of Hanoverian troops should be brought over for the defence of Great Britain, his Majesty's grandfather, our late sovereign, did not pretend to introduce them under any authority he possessed. Such a measure would have given just alarm to his subjects of Great Britain, whose liberties would not be safe if armed men of another country, and of another spirit, might be brought into the realm at any time, without the consent of their legislature. He, therefore, applied to Parliament, who passed an act for that purpose, limiting the number to be brought in, and the time they were to continue. In like manner is his Majesty restrained in every part of the empire. He possesses indeed the executive power of the laws in every State; but they are the laws of the particular State, which he is to administer within that State, and not those of any one within the limits of another. Every State must judge for itself, the number of armed men which they may safely trust among them, of whom they are to consist, and under what restrictions they are to be laid. To render these proceedings still more criminal against our laws, instead of subjecting the military to the civil power, his Majesty has expressly made the civil subordinate to the military. But can his Majesty thus put down all law under his feet? Can he erect a power superior to that which erected himself? He has done it indeed by force; but let him remember that force cannot give right.

That these are our grievances, which we have thus laid before his Majesty, with that freedom of language and sentiment which becomes a free people, claiming their rights as derived from the laws of nature, and not as the gift of their Chief Magistrate. Let those flatter, who fear; it is not an American art. To give praise where it is not due might be well from the venal, but it would ill beseem those who are asserting the rights of human nature. They know, and will, therefore, say, that kings are the servants, not the proprietors of the people. Open your breast, Sire, to liberal and expanded thought. Let not the name of George the Third, be a blot on the page of history. You are surrounded by British counsellors, but remember that they are parties. You have no ministers for American affairs, because you have none taken from among us, nor amenable to the laws on which they are to give you advice. It behooves you, therefore, to think and to act for yourself and your people. The great principles of right and wrong are legible to every reader; to pursue them, requires not the aid of many counsellors. The whole art of government consists in the art of being honest. Only aim to do your duty, and mankind will give you credit where you fail. No longer persevere in sacrificing the rights of one part of the empire to the inordinate desires of another; but deal out to all equal and impartial right. Let no act be passed by any one legislature which may infringe on the rights and liberties of another. This is the important post in which fortune has placed you, holding the balance of a great, if a well-poised empire. This, Sire, is the advice of your great American council, on the observance of which may perhaps depend your felicity and future fame, and the preservation of that harmony which alone can continue, both to Great Britain and America, the reciprocal advantages of their connection. It is neither our wish nor our interest to separate from her. We are willing, on our part, to sacrifice everything which reason can ask, to the restoration of that tranquillity for which all must wish. On their part, let them be ready to establish union on a generous plan. Let them name their terms, but let them be just. Accept of every commercial preference it is in our power to give, for such things as we can raise for their use, or they make for ours. But let them not think to exclude us from going to other markets to dispose of those commodities which they cannot use, nor to supply those wants which they cannot supply. Still less, let it be proposed, that our properties, within our territories, shall be taxed or regulated by any power on earth, but our own. The God who gave us life, gave us liberty at the same time: the hand of force may destroy, but cannot disjoin them.

This, Sire, is our last, our determined resolution. And that you will be pleased to interpose, with that efficacy which your earnest endeavors may insure, to procure redress of these our great grievances, to quiet the minds of your subjects in British America against any apprehensions of future encroachment, to establish fraternal love and harmony through the whole empire, and that that may continue to the latest ages of time, is the fervent prayer of all British America.—i, 124. FORD ED., i, 426. (1774.)

DECLARATION OF INDEPENDENCE *

A Declaration by the Representatives of the United States of America, in *General* Congress assembled.

When, in the course of human events, it becomes necessary for one people to dissolve the political bands which have connected them with another, and to assume among the powers of the earth the separate and equal station to which the laws of nature and of nature's God entitle them, a decent respect to the opinions of mankind requires that they should declare the causes which impel them to the separation.

We hold these truths to be self evident: that all men are created equal; that they are endowed by their creator with [*inherent and*] inalienable rights; certain that among these are life, liberty, and the pursuit of happiness; that to secure these rights, governments are instituted among men, deriving their just powers from the consent of the governed; that whenever any form of government becomes destructive of these ends, it is the right of the people to alter or to abolish it, and to institute new government, laying its foundation on such principles, and organizing its powers in such form, as to them shall seem most likely to effect their safety and happiness. Prudence, indeed, will dictate that governments long established should not be changed for light and transient causes; and accordingly all experience hath shown that mankind are more disposed to suffer while evils are sufferable, than to right themselves by abolishing the forms to which they are accustomed. But when a long train of abuses and usurpations, [*begun at a distinguished period and*] pursuing invariably the same object, evinces a design to reduce them under absolute despotism, it is their right, it is their duty to throw off such government, and to provide new guards for their future security. Such has been the patient sufferance of these colonies: and such is now the necessity which constrains them to [*expunge*] their former systems of government. The history of the present king alter of Great Britain is a history of [*unremitting*] injuries and usurpations [*among which appears no solitary fact to contradict the uniform tenor of the rest, but* repeated *all have*] in direct object the establishment of an absolute tyranny over these all having states. To prove this, let facts be submitted to a candid world [*for the truth of which we pledge a faith yet unsullied by falsehood.*]

He has refused his assent to laws the most wholesome and necessary for the public good.

He has forbidden his governors to pass laws of immediate and pressing importance, unless suspended in their operation till his assent should be obtained; and, when so suspended, he has utterly neglected to attend to them.

He has refused to pass other laws for the accommodation of large districts of people, unless those people would relinquish the right of representation in the legislature, a right inestimable to them, and formidable to tyrants only.

He has called together legislative bodies at places unusual, uncomfortable, and distant from the depository of their public records, for the sole purpose of fatiguing them into compliance with his measures.

He has dissolved representative houses repeatedly [*and continually*] for opposing with manly firmness his invasions on the rights of the people.

He has refused for a long time after such dissolutions to cause others to be elected, whereby the legislative powers, incapable of annihilation, have returned to the people at large for their exercise, the state remaining, in the meantime, exposed to all the dangers of invasion from without and convulsions within.

He has endeavored to prevent the population of these states; for that purpose obstructing the laws for naturalization of foreigners, refusing to pass

---

* The parts struck out by Congress are printed in italics and enclosed in brackets those inserted by Congress are placed in the margin. In paragraph 2, line 2, the edition of JEFFERSON'S WRITINGS, printed by Congress, and also the FORD EDITION give " *inalienable rights* " as the text in the engrossed copy of the Declaration. In the first draft of the instrument Jefferson wrote " *unalienable* ", which he changed to " *inalienable* " in the draft reported to Congress. In the United States *Statutes At Large* the word is " *unalienable* ". The Hon. John Hay, Secretary of State, gives a certification of the text in the following letter:

DEPARTMENT OF STATE,
WASHINGTON, *May* 4, 1900.

JOHN P. FOLEY, ESQ.,
Brooklyn, N. Y.:

SIR—In response to your letter, * * * I have to advise you that the text of the Declaration of Independence (the original MS.) as signed by the delegates, reads, at the point of your inquiry—" unalienable rights ", while the text of Jefferson's MS. draft, as amended in committee by Franklin and Adams, reads " inalienable rights ". The latter is the paper printed in Ford's edition of Jefferson's Writings, in *fac simile*. * * *

JOHN HAY.

—EDITOR.

others to encourage their migrations hither, and raising the conditions of new appropriations of lands.

obstructed by

He has [*suffered*] the administration of justice [*totally to cease in some of these states*] refusing his assent to laws for establishing judiciary powers.

He has made [*our*] judges dependent on his will alone for the tenure of their offices, and the amount and payment of their salaries.

He has erected a multitude of new offices [*by a self-assumed power*], and sent hither swarms of officers to harass our people and eat out their substance.

He has kept among us in times of peace standing armies [*and ships of war*] without the consent of our legislatures.

He has affected to render the military independent of, and superior to, the civil power.

He has combined with others to subject us to a jurisdiction foreign to our constitutions and unacknowledged by our laws, giving his assent to their acts of pretended legislation for quartering large bodies of armed troops among us; for protecting them by a mock trial from punishment for any murders which they should commit on the inhabitants of these States; for cutting off our trade with all parts of the world; for imposing taxes on us without our

in many cases

consent; for depriving us [   ] of the benefits of trial by jury; for transporting us beyond seas to be tried for pretended offences; for abolishing the free system of English laws in a neighboring province, establishing therein an arbitrary government, and enlarging its boundaries, so as to render it at once an example and fit instrument for introducing the same absolute rule into these

colonies

[*states*]; for taking away our charters, abolishing our most valuable laws, and altering fundamentally the forms of our governments; for suspending our own legislatures, and declaring themselves invested with power to legislate for us in all cases whatsoever.

by declaring us out of his protection, and waging war against us

He has abdicated government here [*withdrawing his governors, and declaring us out of his allegiance and protection*].

He has plundered our seas, ravaged our coasts, burnt our towns, and destroyed the lives of our people.

scarcely paralleled in the most barbarous ages, and totally

He is at this time transporting large armies of foreign mercenaries to complete the works of death, desolation and tyranny already begun with circumstances of cruelty and perfidy [   ] unworthy the head of a civilized nation.

He has constrained our fellow citizens taken captive on the high seas, to bear arms against their country, to become the executioners of their friends and brethren, or to fall themselves by their hands.

excited domestic insurrection among us, and has

He has [   ] endeavored to bring on the inhabitants of our frontiers, the merciless Indian savages, whose known rule of warfare is an undistinguished destruction of all ages, sexes and conditions [*of existence*].

[*He has incited treasonable insurrections of our fellow citizens, with the allurements of forfeiture and confiscation of our property.*

He has waged cruel war against human nature itself, violating its most sacred rights of life and liberty in the persons of a distant people who never offended him, captivating and carrying them into slavery in another hemisphere, or to incur miserable death in their transportation thither. This piratical warfare, the opprobrium of INFIDEL *powers, is the warfare of the* CHRISTIAN *king of Great Britain. Determined to keep open a market where* MEN *should be bought and sold, he has prostituted his negative for suppressing every legislative attempt to prohibit or to restrain this execrable commerce. And that this assemblage of horrors might want no fact of distinguished dye, he is now exciting those very people to rise in arms among us, and to purchase that liberty of which he has deprived them, by murdering the people upon whom he also obtruded them: thus paying off former crimes committed against the* LIBERTIES *of one people, with crimes which he urges them to commit against the* LIVES *of another*].

In every stage of these oppressions we have petitioned for redress in the most humble terms: our repeated petitions have been answered only by repeated injuries.

free

A prince whose character is thus marked by every act which may define a tyrant is unfit to be the ruler of a [   ] people [*who mean to be free. Future ages will scarcely believe that the hardiness of one man adventured, within the short compass of twelve years only, to lay a foundation so broad and undisguised for tyranny over a people fostered and fixed in principles of freedom*].

an unwarantable us

Nor have we been wanting in attentions to our British brethren. We have warned them from time to time of attempts by their legislature to extend [*a*] jurisdiction over [*these our states*]. We have reminded them of the circumstances of our emigration and settlement here [*no one of which could warrant so strange a pretension: that these were effected at the expense of our own blood and treasure, unassisted by the wealth or the strength of Great Britain; that in constituting indeed our several forms of government, we had adopted one com-*

mon king, thereby laying a foundation for perpetual league and amity with them; but that submission to their parliament was no part of our constitution, nor ever in idea, if history may be credited: and], we [ ] appealed to their native justice and magnanimity [*as well as to*] the ties of our common kindred to disavow these usurpations which [*were likely to*] interrupt our connection and correspondence. They too have been deaf to the voice of justice and of consanguinity [*and when occasions have been given them, by the regular course of their laws, of removing from their councils the disturbers of our harmony, they have, by their free election, re-established them in power. At this very time too, they are permitting their chief magistrate to send over not only soldiers of our common blood, but Scotch and foreign mercenaries to invade and destroy us. These facts have given the last stab to agonizing affection, and manly spirit bids us to renounce forever these unfeeling brethren. We must endeavor to forget our former love for them, and hold them as we hold the rest of mankind, enemies in war, in peace friends. We might have been a free and a great people together; but a communication of grandeur and of freedom, it seems, is below their dignity. Be it so, since they will have it. The road to happiness and to glory is open to us too. We will tread it apart from them, and*], acquiesce in the necessity which denounces our [*eternal*] separation [ ]!

have

and we have conjured them by

would inevitably

we must therefore

and hold them as we hold the rest of mankind, enemies in war, in peace friends.

We, therefore, the representatives of the United States of America in General Congress assembled, do in the name, and by the authority of the good people of these [*states reject and renounce all allegiance and subjection to the kings of Great Britain and all others who may hereafter claim by, through or under them; we utterly dissolve all political connection which may heretofore have subsisted between us and the people or parliament of Great Britain: and finally we do assert and declare these colonies to be free and independent states*], and that as free and independent states, they have full power to levy war, conclude peace, contract alliances, establish commerce, and to do all other acts and things which independent states may of right do.

And for the support of this declaration, we mutually pledge to each other our lives, our fortunes, and our sacred honor

We, therefore, the representatives of the United States of America in General Congress assembled, appealing to the Supreme Judge of the world for the rectitude of our intentions, do in the name, and by the authority of the good people of these colonies, solemnly publish and declare, that these united colonies are, and of right ought to be free and independent states: that they are absolved from all allegiance to the British crown, and that all political connection between them and the state of Great Britain is, and ought to be, totally dissolved; and that as free and independent states, they have full power to levy war, conclude peace, contract alliances, establish commerce, and to do all other acts and things which independent states may of right do.

And for the support of this declaration, with a firm reliance on the protection of Divine Providence, we mutually pledge to each other our lives, our fortunes, and our sacred honor.—i, 19. FORD ED., ii, 42.

PREAMBLE TO THE VIRGINIA CONSTITUTION

Whereas, the delegates and representatives of the good people of Virginia, in convention assembled, on the twenty-ninth day of June, in the year of our Lord one thousand seven hundred and seventy-six, reciting and declaring, that whereas George the Third, King of Great Britain and Ireland, and Elector of Hanover, before that time intrusted with the exercise of the kingly office in the government of Virginia, had endeavored to pervert the same into a detestable and insupportable tyranny, by putting his negative on laws the most wholesome and necessary for the public good; by denying his governors permission to pass laws of immediate and pressing importance, unless suspended in their operation for his assent, and when so suspended, neglecting to attend to them for many years; by refusing to pass certain other laws unless the persons to be benefited by them would relinquish the inalienable right of representation in the legislature; by dissolving legislative assemblies, repeatedly and continually, for opposing with manly firmness his invasions of the rights of the people; when dissolved by refusing to call others for a long space of time, thereby leaving the political system without any legislative head; by endeavoring to prevent the population of our country, and for that purpose obstructing the laws for naturalization of foreigners; by keeping among us, in time of peace, standing armies and ships of war; by affecting to render the military independent of and superior to the civil power; by combining with others to subject us to a foreign jurisdiction, giving his assent to their pretended acts of legislation for quartering large bodies of armed troops among us; for cutting off our trade with all parts of the world; for imposing taxes on us without our consent; for depriving us of the benefit of trial by jury; for transporting us beyond the seas for trial for pretended offences; for suspending our own legislatures, and declaring themselves invested with power to legislate for us in all cases whatsoever; by plundering our seas, ravaging our coasts, burning our towns, and destroying the lives of our people; by inciting insurrection of our fellow-subjects with the allurements of forfeiture and confiscation; by prompting our negroes to rise in arms among us—those very negroes whom, by an inhuman use of his negative, he had refused us permission to exclude by law; by endeavoring to bring on the inhabitants of our frontiers the merciless Indian savages, whose known rule of warfare is an undistinguished destruction of all ages, sexes and conditions of existence; by transporting hither a large army of foreign mercenaries to complete the work of death, desolation and tyranny, then already begun, with circumstances of cruelty and perfidy unworthy the head of a civilized nation; by answering our repeated petitions for redress with a repetition of our injuries; and finally, by abandoning the helm of government and declaring us out of his allegiance and protection—by which several acts of misrule, the government of this country, as before exercised under the crown of Great Britain, was totally dissolved—did, therefore, having maturely considered the premises, and viewing with great concern the deplorable condition to which this once happy country would be reduced unless some regular, adequate mode of civil policy should be speedily adopted, and in compliance with the recommendation of the general Congress, ordain and declare a form of government of Virginia.—POORE'S FEDERAL AND STATE CONSTITUTIONS.

DEBATES ON THE ARTICLES OF CONFEDERATION

On Friday, July 12 [1776], the committee appointed to draw the Articles of Confederation reported them, and, on the 22d, the House resolved themselves into a committee to take them into consideration. On the 30th and 31st of that month, and 1st of the ensuing, those articles were debated which determined the proportion, or quota, of money which each state should furnish to the common treasury, and the manner of voting in Congress. The first of these articles was expressed in the original draught in these words. " Art. XI. All charges of war and all other expenses that shall be incurred for the common defence, or general welfare, and allowed by the United States assembled, shall be defrayed out of a common treasury, which shall be supplied by the several colonies in proportion to the number of inhabitants of every age, sex, and quality, except Indians not paying taxes, in each colony, a true account of which, distinguishing the white inhabitants, shall be triennially taken and transmitted to the Assembly of the United States."

Mr. Chase moved that the quotas should be fixed, not by the number of inhabitants of every condition, but by that of the " white inhabitants." He admitted that taxation should be always in proportion to property, that this was, in theory, the true rule; but that, from a variety of difficulties, it was a rule which could never be adopted in practice. The value of the property in every State, could never be estimated justly and equally. Some other measure for the wealth of the State must therefore be devised, some standard referred to, which would be more simple. He considered the number of inhabitants as a tolerably good criterion of property, and that this might always be obtained. He therefore thought it the best mode which we could adopt, with one exception only: he observed that negroes are property, and as such, cannot be distinguished from the lands or personalties held in those States where there are few slaves; that the surplus of profit which a Northern farmer is able to lay by, he invests in cattle, horses, &c., whereas a Southern farmer lays out the same surplus in slaves. There is no more reason, therefore, for taxing the Southern States on the farmer's head, and on his slave's head, than the Northern ones on their farmer's heads and the heads of their cattle; that the method proposed would, therefore, tax the Southern States according to their numbers and their wealth conjunctly, while the Northern would be taxed on numbers only; that negroes, in fact, should not be considered as members of the State, more than cattle, and that they have no more interest in it.

Mr. John Adams observed, that the numbers of people were taken by this article, as an index of the wealth of the State, and not as subjects of taxation; that, as to this matter, it was of no consequence by what name you called your people, whether by that of freemen or of slaves; that in some countries the laboring poor were called freemen, in others they were called slaves; but that the difference as to the state was imaginary only. What matters it whether a landlord, employing ten laborers on his farm, gives them annually as much money as will buy them the necessaries of life, or gives them those necessaries at short hand? The ten laborers add as much wealth annually to the State, increase its exports as much in the one case as the other. Certainly five hundred freemen produce no more profits, no greater surplus for the payment of taxes, than five hundred slaves. Therefore, the State in which are the laborers called freemen, should be taxed no more than that in which are those called slaves. Suppose by an extraordinary operation of nature or of law, one-half the laborers of a State could in the course of one night be transformed into slaves; would the State be made the poorer or the less able to pay taxes? That the condition of the laboring poor in most countries, that of the fishermen particularly of the Northern States, is as abject as that of slaves. It is the number of laborers which produces the surplus for taxation, and numbers, therefore, indiscriminately, are the fair index of wealth; that it is the use of the word " property " here, and its application to some of the people of the State, which produces the fallacy. How does the Southern farmer procure slaves? Either by importation or by purchase from his neighbor. If he imports a slave, he adds one to the number of laborers in his country, and proportionably to its profits and abilities to pay taxes; if he buys from his neighbor, it is only a transfer of a laborer from one farm to another, which does not change the annual produce of the State, and therefore, should not change its tax: that if a Northern farmer works ten laborers on his farm, he can, it is true, invest the surplus of ten men's labor in cattle; but so may the Southern farmer, working ten slaves; that a State of one hundred thousand freemen can maintain no more cattle, than one of one hundred thousand slaves. Therefore, they have no more of that kind of property; that a slave may indeed, from the custom of speech, be more properly called the wealth of his master, than the free laborer might be called the wealth of his employer; but as to the State, both were equally its wealth, and should, therefore, equally add to the quota of its tax.

Mr. Harrison proposed, as a compromise, that two slaves should be counted as one freeman. He affirmed that slaves did not do as much work as freemen, and doubted if two effected more than one; that this was proved by the price of labor; the hire of a laborer in the Southern colonies being from 8 to £ 12, while in the Northern it was generally £ 24.

Mr. Wilson said, that if this amendment should take place, the Southern colonies would have all the benefit of slaves, whilst the Northern ones would bear the burthen: that slaves increase the profits of a State, which the Southern States mean to take to themselves; that they also increase the burthen of defence, which would of course fall so much the heavier on the Northern: that slaves occupy the places of freemen, and eat their food. Dismiss your slaves, and freemen will take their places. It is our duty to lay every discouragement on the importation of slaves; but this amendment would give the *jus trium liberorum* to him who would import slaves; that other kinds of property were pretty equally distributed through all the colonies: there were as many cattle, horses and sheep, in the North as the South, and South as the North; but not so as to slaves: that experience has shown that those colonies have been always able to pay most, which have the most inhabitants, whether they be black or white; and the practice of the Southern colonies has always been to make every farmer pay poll taxes upon all his laborers, whether they be black or white. He acknowledges, indeed, that freemen work the most; but they consume the most also. They do not produce a greater surplus for taxation. The slave is neither fed nor clothed so expensively as a freeman. Again, white women are exempted from labor generally, but negro women are not. In this, then, the Southern States have an advantage as the article now stands. It has sometimes been said, that slavery is necessary, because the commodities they raise would be too dear for market if cultivated by freemen; but now it is said that the labor of the slave is the dearest.

Mr. Payne urged the original resolution of Congress, to proportion the quotas of the States to the number of souls.

Dr. Witherspoon was of opinion, that the value of lands and houses was the best estimate of the wealth of a nation, and that it was practicable to obtain such a valuation. This is the true barometer of wealth. The one now proposed is imperfect in itself, and unequal between the States. It has been objected that negroes eat the food of freemen, and, therefore, should be taxed; horses also eat the food of freemen; therefore they also should be taxed. It has been said too, that in carrying slaves into the estimate of the taxes the State is to pay, we do no more than those States themselves do, who always take slaves into the estimate of the taxes the individual is to pay. But the cases are not parallel. In the Southern colonies slaves pervade the whole colony; but they do not pervade the whole continent. That as to the original resolution of Congress, to proportion the quotas according to the souls, it was temporary only, and related to the moneys heretofore emitted: whereas we are now entering into a new compact, and therefore stand on original ground.

August 1. The question being put, the amendment proposed was rejected by the votes of New Hampshire, Massachusetts, Rhode Island, Connecticut, New York, New Jersey, and Pennsylvania, against those of Delaware, Maryland, Virginia, North and South Carolina. Georgia was divided.

The other article was in these words. "Art. XVII. In determining questions, each colony shall have one vote."

July 30, 31, August 1. Present forty-one members. Mr. Chase observed this article was the most likely to divide us, of any one proposed in the draught then under consideration: that the larger colonies had threatened they would not confederate at all, if their weight in Congress should not be equal to the numbers of people they added to the confederacy; while the smaller ones declared against a union, if they did not retain an equal vote for the protection of their rights. That it was of the utmost consequence to bring the parties together, as, should we sever from each other, either no foreign power will ally with us at all, or the different States will form different alliances, and thus increase the horrors of those scenes of civil war and bloodshed, which in such a state of separation and independence, would render us a miserable people. That our importance, our interests, our peace required that we should confederate, and that mutual sacrifices should be made to effect a compromise of this difficult question. He was of opinion, the smaller colonies would lose their rights, if they were not in some instances allowed an equal vote; and, therefore, that a discrimination should take place among the questions which would come before Congress. That the smaller States should be secured in all questions concerning life or liberty, and the greater ones, in all respecting property. He therefore, proposed, that in votes relating to money, the voice of each colony should be proportioned to the number of its inhabitants.

Dr. Franklin thought, that the votes should be so proportioned in all cases. He took notice that the Delaware counties had bound up their delegates to disagree to this article. He thought it a very extraordinary language to be held by any State, that they would not confederate with us, unless we would let them dispose of our money. Certainly, if we vote equally, we ought to pay equally; but the smaller States will hardly purchase the privilege at this price. That had he lived in a State where the representation, originally equal, had become unequal by time and accident, he might have submitted rather than disturb government; but that we should be very wrong to set out in this practice, when it is in our power to establish what is right. That at the time of the Union between England and Scotland, the latter had made the objection which the smaller States now do; but experience had proved that no unfairness had ever been shown them: that their advocates had prognosticated that it would again happen, as in times of old, that the whale would swallow Jonas, but he thought the prediction reversed in event, and that Jonas had swallowed the whale; for the Scotch had in fact got possession of the government, and gave laws to the English. He reprobated the original agreement of Congress to vote by colonies, and, therefore, was for their voting, in all cases, according to the number of taxables.

Dr. Witherspoon opposed every alteration of the article. All men admit that a confederacy is necessary. Should the idea get abroad that there is likely to be no union among us, it will damp the minds of the people, diminish the glory of our struggle, and lessen its importance: because it will open to our view future prospects of war and dissension among ourselves. If an equal vote be refused, the smaller States will become vassals to the larger; and all experience has shown that the vassals and subjects of free States are the most enslaved. He instanced the Helots of Sparta, and the provinces of Rome. He observed that foreign powers, discovering this blemish, would make it a handle for disengaging the smaller States from so unequal a confederacy. That the colonies should in fact be considered as individuals; and that, as such, in all disputes, they should have an equal vote; that they are now collected as individuals making a bargain with each other, and, of course, had a right to vote as individuals. That in the East India Company they voted by persons, and not by their proportion of stock. That the Belgic confederacy voted by provinces. That in questions of war the smaller States were as much interested as the larger, and therefore, should vote equally; and indeed, that the larger States were more likely to bring war on the confederacy, in proportion as their frontier was more extensive. He admitted that equality of representation was an excellent principle, but then it must be of things which are co-ordinate; that is, of things similar, and of the same nature: that nothing relating to individuals could ever come before Congress; nothing but what would respect colonies. He distinguished between an incorporating and a federal union. The union of England was an incorporating one; yet Scotland had suffered by that union: for that its inhabitants were drawn from it by the hopes of places and employments: nor was it an instance of equality of representation; because, while Scotland was allowed nearly a thirteenth of representation, they were to pay only one-fortieth of the land tax. He expressed his hopes, that in the present enlightened state of men's minds, we might expect a lasting confederacy, if it was founded on fair principles.

John Adams advocated the voting in proportion to numbers. He said that we stand here as the representatives of the people: that in some States the people are many, in others they are few; that therefore, their vote here should be proportioned to the numbers from whom it comes. Reason, justice and equity never had weight enough on the face of the earth, to govern the councils of men. It is interest alone which does it, and it is interest alone which can be trusted: that therefore the interests within doors, should be the mathematical representatives of the interests without doors: that the individuality of the colonies is a mere sound. Does the individuality of a colony increase its wealth or numbers? If it does, pay equally. If it does not add weight in the scale of the confederacy, it cannot add to their rights, nor weigh in argument. A. has £50, B. £500, C. £1000 in partnership. Is it just they should equally dispose of the moneys of the partnership? It has been said, we are independent individuals making a bargain together. The question is not what we are now, but what we ought to be when our bargain shall be made. The confederacy is to make us one individual only; it is to form us like separate parcels of metal, into one common mass. We shall no longer retain our separate individuality, but become a single individual as to all questions submitted to the confederacy. Therefore, all those reasons, which prove the justice and expediency of equal representation in other assemblies, hold good here. It has been objected that a proportional vote will endanger the smaller States. We answer that an equal vote will endanger the larger. Virginia, Pennsylvania, and Massachusetts, are the three greater colonies. Consider their distance, their difference of produce, of interests, and of manners, and it is apparent they can never have an interest or inclination to combine for the oppression of the smaller: that the smaller will naturally divide on all questions with the larger. Rhode Island, from its relation, similarity and intercourse, will generally pursue the same objects with Massachusetts; Jersey, Delaware, and Maryland, with Pennsylvania.

Dr. Rush took notice, that the decay of the liberties of the Dutch republic proceeded from three causes. 1. The perfect unanimity requisite on all occasions. 2. Their obligation to consult their constituents. 3. Their voting by provinces. This last destroyed the equality of representation, and the liberties of Great Britain also are sinking from the same defect. That a part of our rights is deposited in the hands of our legislatures. There, it was admitted, there should be an equality of representation. Another part of our rights is deposited in the hands of Congress: why is it not equally necessary there should be an equal representation there? Were it possible to collect the whole body of the people together, they would determine the questions submitted to them by their majority. Why should not the same majority decide when voting here, by their representatives? The larger colonies are so providentially divided in situation, as to render every fear of their combining visionary. Their interests are different, and their circumstances dissimilar. It is more probable they will become rivals, and leave it in the power of the smaller States to give preponderance to any scale they please. The voting by the number of free inhabitants, will have one excellent effect, that of inducing the colonies to discourage slavery, and to encourage the increase of their free inhabitants.

Mr. Hopkins observed, there were four larger, four smaller, and four middle-sized colonies. That the four largest would contain more than half the inhabitants of the confederated States, and therefore, would govern the others as they should please. That history affords no instance of such a thing as equal representation. The Germanic body votes by States. The Helvetic body does the same; and so does the Belgic confederacy. That too little is known of the ancient confederations, to say what was their practice.

Mr. Wilson thought, that taxation should be in proportion to wealth, but that representation should accord with the number of freemen. That government is a collection or result of the wills of all: that if any government could speak the will of all, it would be perfect; and that, so far as it departs from this, it becomes imperfect. It has been said that Congress is a representation of States, not of individuals. I say, that the objects of its care are all the individuals of the States. It is strange that annexing the name of " State " to ten thousand men, should give them an equal right with forty thousand. This must be the effect of magic, not of reason. As to those matters which are referred to Congress, we are not so many States; we are one large State. We lay aside our individuality, whenever we come here. The Germanic body is a burlesque on government; and their practice, on any point, is a sufficient authority and proof that it is wrong. The greatest imperfection in the constitution of the Belgic confederacy is their voting by provinces. The interest of the whole is constantly sacrificed to that of the small States. The history of the war in the reign of Queen Anne sufficiently proves this. It is asked, shall nine colonies put it into the power of four to govern them as they please? I invert the question, and ask, sha'l two millions of people put it in the power of one million to govern them as they please? It is pretended, too, that the smaller colonies will be in danger from the greater. Speak in honest language and say, the minority will be in danger from the majority. And is there an assembly on earth, where this danger may not be equally pretended? The truth is, that our proceedings will then be consentaneous with the interests of the majority, and so they ought to be. The probability is much greater, that the larger States will disagree, than that they will combine. I defy the wit of man to invent a possible case, or to suggest any one thing on earth, which shall be for the interests of Virginia, Pennsylvania and Massachusetts, and which will not also be for the interest of the other States.

These articles, reported July 12, '76, were debated from day to day, and time to time, for two years, were ratified July 9, '78, by ten States, by New Jersey on the 26th of November of the same year, and by Delaware on the 23d of February following. Maryland alone held off two years more, acceding to them March 1, '81, and thus closing the obligation.—i, 26. FORD ED., i, 38.

A BILL FOR ESTABLISHING RELIGIOUS FREEDOM

SECTION 1. Well aware that the opinions and belief of men depend not on their own will, but follow involuntarily the evidence proposed to their minds; that Almighty God hath created the mind free, and manifested His supreme will that free it shall remain by making it altogether insusceptible of restraint: that all attempts to influence it by temporal punishments or burthens, or by civil incapacitations, tend only to beget habits of hypocrisy and meanness, and are a departure from the plan of the Holy Author of our religion, who being Lord both of body and mind, yet chose not to propagate it by coercions on either, as was in his Almighty power to do, but to exalt it by its influence on reason alone: that the impious presumption of legislature and ruler, civil as well as ecclesiastical, who, being themselves but fallible and uninspired men, have assumed dominion over the faith of others, setting up their own opinions and modes of thinking as the only true and infallible, and as such endeavoring to impose them on others, hath established and maintained false religions over the greatest part of the world, and through all time: That to compel a man to furnish contributions of money for the propagation of opinions which he disbelieves and abhors is sinful and tyrannical; that even the forcing him to support this or that teacher of his own religious persuasion, is depriving him of the comfortable liberty of giving his contributions to the particular pastor whose morals he would make his pattern, and whose powers he feels most persuasive to righteousness; and is withdrawing from the ministry those temporary rewards, which, proceeding from an approbation of their personal conduct, are an additional incitement to earnest and unremitting labors for the instruction of mankind, that our civil rights have no dependence on our religious opinions, any more than our opinions in physics or geometry; and therefore the proscribing any citizen as unworthy the public confidence by laying upon him an incapacity of being called to office of trust or emolument, unless he profess or renounce this or that religious opinion, is depriving him injudiciously of those privileges and advantages to which, in common with his fellow citizens, he has a natural right; that it tends also to corrupt the principles of that very religion it is meant to encourage, by bribing with a monopoly of worldly honors and emoluments, those who will externally profess and conform to it; that though indeed these are criminals who do not withstand such temptation, yet neither are those innocent who lay the bait in their way; that the opinions of men are not the object of civil government, nor under its jurisdiction; that to suffer the civil magistrate to intrude his powers into the field of opinion, and to restrain the profession or propagation of principles on supposition of their ill tendency is a dangerous fallacy which at once destroys all religious liberty, because, he being of course judge of that tendency, will make his opinions the rule of judgment, and approve or condemn the sentiments of others only as they shall square with or differ from his own; that it is time enough for the rightful purposes of civil government for its officers to interfere when principles break out into overt acts against peace and good order; and finally, that truth is great and will prevail if left to herself; that she is the proper and sufficient antagonist to error, and has nothing to fear from the conflict unless, by human interposition, disarmed of her natural weapons, free argument and debate; errors ceasing to be dangerous when it is permitted freely to contradict them:

SECT. II. We, the General Assembly of Virginia, do enact that no man shall be compelled to frequent or support any religious worship, place, or ministry whatsoever, nor shall be enforced, restrained, molested, or burthened in his body or goods, or shall otherwise suffer on account of his religious opinions or belief; but that all men shall be free to profess, and by argument to maintain, their opinions in matters of religion, and that the same shall in no wise diminish, enlarge, or affect their civil capacities.

SECT. III. And though we well know that this Assembly, elected by the people for the ordinary purposes of legislation only, have no power to restrain the acts of succeeding Assemblies, constituted with powers equal to our own, and that, therefore, to declare this act to be irrevocable would be of no effect in law; yet we are free to declare, and do declare, that the rights hereby asserted are of the natural rights of mankind, and that if any act shall be hereafter passed to repeal the present or to narrow its operations, such act will be an infringement of natural right.—viii, 454. FORD ED., ii, 237. (1786.)

KENTUCKY RESOLUTIONS

1. *Resolved,* That the several States composing the United States of America, are not united on the principle of unlimited submission to their General Government; but that, by a compact under the style and title of a Constitution for the United States, and of Amendments thereto, they constituted a General Government for special purposes,—delegated to that government certain definite powers, reserving, each State to itself, the residuary mass of right to their own self-government; and that whensoever the General Government assumes undelegated powers, its acts are unauthoritative, void, and of no force: that to this compact each State acceded as a State, and is an integral party, its co-States forming, as to itself, the other party: that the Government created by this compact was not made the exclusive or final judge of the extent of the powers delegated to itself; since that would have made its discretion, and not the Constitution, the measure of its powers: but that, as in all other cases of compact among powers having no common judge, each party has an equal right to judge for itself, as well of infractions as of the mode and measure of redress.

2. *Resolved,* That the Constitution of the United States, having delegated to Congress a power to punish treason, counterfeiting the securities and current coin of the United States, piracies, and felonies committed on the high seas, and offences against the law of nations, and no other crimes whatsoever; and it being true as a general principle, and one of the amendments to the Constitution having also declared, that " the powers not delegated to the United States by the Constitution, nor prohibited by it to the States, are reserved to the States respectively, or to the people ", therefore the act of Congress, passed on the 14th day of July, 1798, and intituled " An Act in addition to the act intituled ' An Act for the punishment of certain crimes against the United States ' ", as also the act passed by them on the —— day of June, 1789, intituled " An Act to punish frauds committed on the Bank of the United States " (and all their other acts which assume to create, define, or punish crimes, other than those so enumerated in the Constitution), are altogether void, and of no force: and that the power to create, define, and punish such other crimes is reserved, and, of right, appertains solely and exclusively to the respective States, each within its own territory.

3. *Resolved,* That it is true as a general principle, and is also expressly declared by one of the amendments to the Constitution, that " the powers not delegated to the United States by the Constitution, nor prohibited by it to the States, are reserved to the States respectively, or to the people "; and that no power over the freedom of religion, freedom of speech, or freedom of the press being delegated to the United States by the Constitution, nor prohibited by it to the States, all lawful powers respecting the same did of right remain, and were reserved to the States or the people; that thus was manifested their determination to retain to themselves the right of judging how far the licentiousness of speech and of the press may be abridged without lessening their useful freedom, and how far those abuses which cannot be separated from their use should be tolerated, rather than the use be destroyed. And thus also they guarded against all abridgment by the United States of the freedom of religious opinions and exercises, and retained to themselves the right of protecting the same, as this State, by a law passed on the general demand of its citizens, had already protected them from all human restraint or interference. And that in addition to this general principle and express declaration, another and more special provision has been made by one of the amendments to the Constitution, which expressly declares, that " Congress shall make no law respecting an establishment of religion, or prohibiting the free exercise thereof, or abridging the freedom of speech, or of the press "; thereby guarding in the same sentence, and under the same words, the freedom of religion, of speech, and of the press: insomuch, that whatever violated either. throws down the sanctuary which covers the others, and that libels, falsehoods, and defamation, equally with heresy and false religion, are withheld from the cognizance of Federal tribunals. That, therefore, the act of Congress of the United States, passed on the 14th day of July, 1798, intituled " An Act in addition to the act intituled ' An Act for the punishment of certain crimes against the United States ' " which does abridge the freedom of the press, is not law, but is altogether void, and of no force.

4. *Resolved,* That alien friends are under the jurisdiction and protection of the laws of the State wherein they are; that no power over them has been delegated to the United States, nor prohibited to the individual States, distinct from their power over citizens. And it being true as a general principle, and one of the amendments to the Constitution having also declared, that " the powers not delegated to the United States by the Constitution, nor prohibited by it to the States, are reserved to the States respectively, or to the people ", the act of the Congress of the United States, passed on the —— day of July, 1798, intituled " An Act concerning aliens ", which assumes powers over alien friends, not delegated by the Constitution, is not law, but is altogether void, and of no force.

5. *Resolved,* That in addition to the general principle, as well as the express declaration, that powers not delegated are reserved, another and more special provision, inserted in the Constitution from abundant caution, has declared that " the migration or importation of such persons as any of the States now existing shall think proper to admit, shall not be prohibited by the Congress prior to the year 1808 ": that this Commonwealth does admit the migration of alien friends, described as the subject of the said act concerning aliens: that a provision against prohibiting their migration, is a provision against all acts equivalent thereto, or it would be nugatory: that to remove them when migrated, is equivalent to a prohibition of their migration, and is, therefore, contrary to the said provision of the Constitution, and void.

6. *Resolved,* That the imprisonment of a person under the laws of this Commonwealth, on his failure to obey the simple *order* of the President to depart out of the United States, as is undertaken by said act intituled " An Act concerning aliens " is contrary to the Constitution, one amendment to which has provided that " no person shall be deprived of liberty without due process of law "; and that another having provided that " in all criminal prosecutions the accused shall enjoy the right to public trial by an impartial jury, to be informed of the nature and cause of the accusation, to be confronted with the witnesses against him, to have compulsory process for obtaining witnesses in his favor, and to have the assistance of counsel for his

defence ", the same act, undertaking to authorize the President to remove a person out of the United States, who is under the protection of the law, on his own suspicion, without accusation, without jury, without public trial, without confrontation of the witnesses against him, without hearing witnesses in his favor, without defence, without counsel, is contrary to the provision also of the Constitution, is therefore not law, but utterly void, and of no force: that transferring the power of judging any person, who is under the protection of the laws, from the courts to the President of the United States, as is undertaken by the same act concerning aliens, is against the article of the Constitution which provides that "the judicial power of the United States shall be vested in courts, the judges of which shall hold their offices during good behavior "; and that the said act is void for that reason also. And it is further to be noted, that this transfer of judiciary power is to that magistrate of the General Government who already possesses all the Executive and a negative on all Legislative powers.

7. *Resolved,* That the construction applied by the General Government (as is evidenced by sundry of their proceedings) to those parts of the Constitution of the United States which delegate to Congress a power "to lay and collect taxes, duties, imposts and excises, to pay the debts, and provide for the common defence and general welfare of the United States", and "to make all laws which shall be necessary and proper for carrying into execution the powers vested by the Constitution in the government of the United States, or in any department or officer thereof", goes to the destruction of all limits prescribed to their power by the Constitution: that words meant by the instrument to be subsidiary only to the execution of limited powers, ought not to be so construed as themselves to give unlimited powers, nor a part to be so taken as to destroy the whole residue of that instrument: that the proceedings of the General Government under color of these articles, will be a fit and necessary subject of revisal and correction, at a time of greater tranquillity, while those specified in the preceding resolution call for immediate redress.

8. *Resolved,* That a committee of conference and correspondence be appointed, who shall have in charge to communicate the preceding resolutions to the Legislatures of the several States: to assure them that this Commonwealth continues in the same esteem of their friendship and union which it has manifested from that moment at which a common danger first suggested a common union: that it considers union, for specified national purposes, and particularly to those specified in their late Federal compact, to be friendly to the peace, happiness and prosperity of all the States: that faithful to that compact, according to the plain intent and meaning in which it was understood and acceded to by the several parties, it is sincerely anxious for its preservation: that it does also believe, that to take from the States all the powers of self-government and transfer them to a general and consolidated government, without regard to the special delegations and reservations solemnly agreed to in that compact, is not for the peace, happiness or prosperity of these States: and that, therefore, this Commonwealth is determined, as it doubts not its co-States are, to submit to undelegated, and consequently unlimited powers in no man, or body of men on earth: that in cases of an abuse of the delegated powers, the members of the General Government, being chosen by the people, a change by the people would be the constitutional remedy; but, where powers are assumed which have not been delegated, a nullification of the act is the rightful remedy: that every State has a natural right in cases not within the compact (*casus non fœderis*), to nullify of their own authority all assumptions of power by others within their limits: that without this right, they would be under the dominion, absolute and unlimited, of whosoever might exercise this right of judgment for them: that nevertheless, this Commonwealth, from motives of regard and respect for its co-States, has wished to communicate with them on the subject: that with them alone it is proper to communicate, they alone being parties to the compact, and solely authorized to judge in the last resort of the powers exercised under it, Congress being not a party, but merely the creature of the compact, and subject as to its assumptions of power to the final judgment of those by whom, and for whose use itself and its powers were all created and modified: that if the acts before specified should stand, these conclusions would flow from them; that the General Government may place any act they think proper on the list of crimes, and punish it themselves whether enumerated or not enumerated by the Constitution as cognizable by them; that they may transfer its cognizance to the President, or any other person, who may himself be the accuser, counsel, judge, and jury, whose *suspicions* may be the evidence, his *order* the sentence, his *officer* the executioner, and his breast the sole record of the transaction: that a very numerous and valuable description of the inhabitants of these States being, by this precedent, reduced, as outlaws, to the absolute dominion of one man, and the barrier of the Constitution thus swept away from us all, no rampart now remains against the passions and the powers of a majority in Congress to protect from a like exportation, or other more grievous punishment, the minority of the same body, the legislatures, judges, governors, and councillors of the States, nor their other peaceable inhabitants, who may venture to reclaim the constitutional rights and liberties of the States and people, or who for other causes, good or bad, may be obnoxious to the views, or marked by the suspicions of the President, or be thought dangerous to his or their election, or other interests, public or personal: that the friendless alien has indeed been selected as the safest subject of a first experiment; but the citizen will soon follow, or rather, has already followed, for already has a Sedition Act marked him as its prey: that these and successive acts of the same character, unless arrested at the threshold, necessarily drive these States into revolution and blood, and will furnish new calumnies against republican government, and new pretexts for those who wish it to be believed that man cannot be governed but by a rod of iron: that it would be a dangerous delusion were a confidence in the men of our choice to silence our fears for the safety of our rights: that confidence is everywhere the parent of despotism—free government is founded in jealousy, and not in confidence: it is jealousy and not confidence which prescribes limited constitutions, to bind down those whom we are obliged to trust with power: that our Constitution has accordingly fixed the limits to which, and no further, our confidence may go; and let the honest advocate of confidence read the Alien and Sedition Acts, and say if the Constitution has not been wise in fixing limits to the government it created, and whether we should be wise in destroying those limits. Let him say what the government is, if it be not a tyranny, which the men of our choice have conferred on our President, and the President of our choice has assented to, and accepted over the friendly strangers to whom the

mild spirit of our country and its laws have pledged hospitality and protection: that the men of our choice have more respected the bare *suspicions* of the President, than the solid right of innocence, the claims of justification, the sacred force of truth, and the forms and substance of law and justice. In questions of power, then, let no more be heard of confidence in man, but bind him down from mischief by the chains of the Constitution. That this Commonwealth does, therefore, call on its co-States for an expression of their sentiments on the acts concerning aliens, and for the punishment of certain crimes herein before specified, plainly declaring whether these acts are or are not authorized by the Federal compact. And it doubts not that their sense will be so announced as to prove their attachment unaltered to limited government, whether general or particular. And that the rights and liberties of their co-States will be exposed to no dangers by remaining embarked in a common bottom with their own. That they will concur with this Commonwealth in considering the said acts as so palpably against the Constitution as to amount to an undisguised declaration that that compact is not meant to be the measure of the powers of the General Government, but that it will proceed in the exercise over these States, of all powers whatsoever: that they will view this as seizing the rights of the States, and consolidating them in the hands of the General Government, with a power assumed to bind the States (not merely in the cases made Federal (*casus fœderis*) but) in all cases whatsoever, by laws made, not with their consent, but by others against their consent; that this would be to surrender the form of government we have chosen, and live under one deriving its powers from its own will, and not from our authority; and that the co-States, recurring to their natural right in cases not made Federal, will concur in declaring these acts void, and of no force, and will each take measures of its own for providing that neither these acts, nor any others of the General Government not plainly and intentionally authorized by the Constitution, shall be exercised within their respective territories.

9. *Resolved,* That the said committee be authorized to communicate by writing or personal conferences, at any times or places whatever, with any person or persons who may be appointed by any one or more co-States to correspond or confer with them; and that they lay their proceeding before the next session of Assembly.—ix, 464. Ford ed., vii, 289. (1798.)

FIRST INAUGURAL ADDRESS

March 4, 1801

Friends and fellow-citizens:

Called upon to undertake the duties of the first executive office of our country, I avail myself of the presence of that portion of my fellow-citizens which is here assembled, to express my grateful thanks for the favor with which they have been pleased to look toward me, to declare a sincere consciousness that the task is above my talents, and that I approach it with those anxious and awful presentiments which the greatness of the charge and the weakness of my powers so justly inspire. A rising nation, spread over a wide and fruitful land; traversing all the seas with the rich productions of their industry; engaged in commerce with nations who feel power and forget right; advancing rapidly to destinies beyond the reach of mortal eye,—when I contemplate these transcendent objects, and see the honor, the happiness, and the hopes of this beloved country committed to the issue and the auspices of this day, I shrink from the contemplation, and humble myself before the magnitude of the undertaking. Utterly, indeed, should I despair, did not the presence of many whom I here see remind me that in the other high authorities provided by our Constitution I shall find resources of wisdom, of virtue, and of zeal, on which to rely under all difficulties. To you, then, gentlemen, who are charged with the sovereign functions of legislation, and to those associated with you, I look with encouragement for that guidance and support which may enable us to steer with safety the vessel in which we are all embarked, amid the conflicting elements of a troubled world.

During the contest of opinion through which we have passed, the animation of discussion and of exertions has sometimes worn an aspect which might impose on strangers, unused to think freely, and to speak and to write what they think; but, this being now decided by the voice of the nation, announced according to the rules of the Constitution, all will, of course, arrange themselves under the will of the law, and unite in common efforts for the common good. All, too, will bear in mind this sacred principle, that, though the will of the majority is in all cases to prevail, that will, to be rightful, must be reasonable; that the minority possess their equal rights, which equal laws must protect, and to violate which would be oppression. Let us, then, fellow-citizens, unite with one heart and one mind; let us restore to social intercourse that harmony and affection without which liberty and even life itself are but dreary things. And let us reflect that having banished from our land that religious intolerance under which mankind so long bled and suffered, we have yet gained little if we countenance a political intolerance as despotic, as wicked, and capable of as bitter and bloody persecutions. During the throes and convulsions of the ancient world, during the agonizing spasms of infuriated man, seeking through blood and slaughter his long-lost liberty, it was not wonderful that the agitation of the billows should reach even this distant and peaceful shore; that this should be more felt and feared by some and less by others; that this should divide opinions as to measures of safety. But every difference of opinion is not a difference of principle. We have called by different names brethren of the same principle. We are all republicans; we are all federalists. If there be any among us who would wish to dissolve this Union, or to change its republican form, let them stand, undisturbed, as monuments of the safety with which error of opinion may be tolerated where reason is left free to combat it. I know, indeed, that some honest men fear that a republican government cannot be strong; that this Government is not strong enough. But would the honest patriot, in the full tide of successful experiment, abandon a Government which has so far kept us free and firm, on the theoretic and visionary fear that this Government, the world's best hope, may, by possibility, want energy to preserve itself? I trust not. I believe this, on the contrary, the strongest Government on earth. I believe it is the only one where every man, at the call of the law, would fly to the standard of the law, and would meet invasions of the public order as his own personal concern. Sometimes it is said that man cannot be trusted with the government of himself. Can he, then, be trusted with the government of others? Or have we found angels in the form of kings to govern him? Let history answer this question.

Let us, then, with a courage and confidence, pursue our own federal and republican principles, our attachment to our Union and representative government. Kindly separated by nature and a wide ocean from the exterminating havoc of one quarter of the globe; too high-minded to endure the degradations of the others; possessing a chosen country, with room enough for our descendants to the hundredth and thousandth generation; entertaining a due sense of our equal right to the use of our own faculties, to the acquisitions of our industry, to honor and confidence from our fellow-citizens, resulting not from birth but from our actions, and their sense of them; enlightened by a benign religion, professed, indeed, and practiced in various forms, yet all of them inculcating honesty, truth, temperance, gratitude, and the love of man; acknowledging and adoring an overruling Providence, which, by all its dispensations, proves that it delights in the happiness of man here, and his greater happiness hereafter; with all these blessings, what more is necessary to make us a happy and prosperous people? Still one thing more, fellow-citizens,— a wise and frugal Government, which shall restrain men from injuring one another, which shall leave them otherwise free to regulate their own pursuits of industry and improvement, and shall not take from the mouth of labor the bread it has earned. This is the sum of good government, and this is necessary to close the circle of our felicities.

About to enter, fellow-citizens, on the exercise of duties which comprehend every thing dear and valuable to you, it is proper that you should understand what I deem the essential principles of our Government, and, consequently, those which ought to shape its administration. I will compress them within the narrowest compass they will bear, stating the general principle, but not all its limitations. Equal and exact justice to all men, of whatever state or persuasion, religious or political; peace, commerce, and honest friendship with all nations, entangling alliances with none; the support of the State governments in all their rights, as the most competent administrations for our domestic concerns, and the surest bulwarks against anti-republican tendencies; the preservation of the General Government in its whole constitutional vigor, as the sheet-anchor of our peace at home and safety abroad; a jealous care of the right of election by the people,—

a mild and safe corrective of abuses which are lopped by the sword of revolution, where peaceable remedies are unprovided; absolute acquiescence in the decisions of the majority,— the vital principle of republics, from which is no appeal but to force, the vital principle and immediate parent of despotism; a well-disciplined militia,—our best reliance in peace and for the first moments of war, till regulars may relieve them; the supremacy of the civil over the military authority; economy in the public expense, that labor may be lightly burdened; the honest payment of our debts and sacred preservation of the public faith; encouragement of agriculture, and of commerce as its handmaid; the diffusion of information and arraignment of all abuses at the bar of public reason; freedom of religion; freedom of the press; freedom of person under the protection of the *habeas corpus;* and trial by juries impartially selected. These principles form the bright constellation which has gone before us, and guided our steps through an age of revolution and reformation. The wisdom of our sages and the blood of our heroes have been devoted to their attainment. They should be the creed of our political faith, the text of civic instruction, the touch-stone by which to try the services of those we trust; and should we wander from them in moments of error or of alarm, let us hasten to retrace our steps, and to regain the road which alone leads to peace, liberty, and safety.

I repair, then, fellow-citizens, to the post you have assigned me. With experience enough in subordinate offices to have seen the difficulties of this, the greatest of all, I have learned to expect that it will rarely fall to the lot of imperfect man to retire from this station with the reputation and the favor which bring him into it. Without pretensions to that high confidence reposed in our first and greatest revolutionary character, whose pre-eminent services had entitled him to the first place in his country's love, and destined for him the fairest page in the volume of faithful history, I ask so much confidence only as may give firmness and effect to the legal administration of your affairs. I shall often go wrong, through defect of judgment. When right, I shall often be thought wrong by those whose positions will not command a view of the whole ground. I ask your indulgence for my own errors, which will never be intentional; and your support against the errors of others, who may condemn what they would not if seen in all its parts. The approbation implied by your suffrage is a consolation to me for the past; and my future solicitude will be to retain the good opinion of those who have bestowed it in advance, to conciliate that of others by doing them all the good in my power, and to be instrumental to the happiness and freedom of all.

Relying, then, on the patronage of your good will, I advance with obedience to the work, ready to retire from it whenever you become sensible how much better choice it is in your power to make. And may that Infinite Power which rules the destinies of the universe, lead our councils to what is best, and give them a favorable issue for your peace and prosperity.— viii, 1. FORD ED., viii, 1. (March 4, 1801.)

SECOND INAUGURAL ADDRESS

March 4, 1805

Proceeding, fellow-citizens, to that qualification which the Constitution requires before my entrance on the charge again conferred upon me, it is my duty to express the deep sense I entertain of this new proof of confidence from my fellow-citizens at large, and the zeal with which it inspires me so to conduct myself as may best satisfy their just expectations.

On taking this station, on a former occasion, I declared the principles on which I believed it my duty to administer the affairs of our commonwealth. My conscience tells me that I have, on every occasion, acted up to that declaration, according to its obvious import, and to the understanding of every candid mind.

In the transaction of your foreign affairs, we have endeavored to cultivate the friendship of all nations, and especially of those with which we have the most important relations. We have done them justice on all occasions, favor where favor was lawful, and cherished mutual interests and intercourse on fair and equal terms. We are firmly convinced, and we act on that conviction, that with nations, as with individuals, our interests soundly calculated, will ever be found inseparable from our moral duties; and history bears witness to the fact, that a just nation is taken on its word, when recourse is had to armaments and wars to bridle others.

At home, fellow-citizens, you best know whether we have done well or ill. The suppression of unnecessary offices, of useless establishments and expenses, enabled us to discontinue our internal taxes. These, covering our land with officers, and opening our doors to their intrusions, had already begun that process of domiciliary vexation, which, once entered, is scarcely to be restrained from reaching, successively, every article of produce and property. If, among these taxes some minor ones fell which had not been inconvenient, it was because their amount would not have paid the officers who collected them, and because, if they had any merit, the State authorities might adopt them instead of others less approved.

The remaining revenue, on the consumption of foreign articles, is paid cheerfully by those who can afford to add foreign luxuries to domestic comforts. Being collected on our seaboard and frontiers only, and incorporated with the transactions of our mercantile citizens, it may be the pleasure and pride of an American to ask, what farmer, what mechanic, what laborer, ever sees a tax-gatherer of the United States? These contributions enable us to support the current expenses of the Government; to fulfil contracts with foreign nations; to extinguish the native right of soil within our limits; to extend those limits; and to apply such a surplus to our public debts as places at a short day their final redemption; and, that redemption once effected, the revenue thereby liberated may, by a just repartition among the States, and a corresponding amendment of the Constitution, be applied, *in time of peace,* to rivers, canals, roads, arts, manufactures, education, and other great objects, within each State. *In time of war,* if injustice by ourselves or others must sometimes produce war, increased, as the same revenue will be increased by population and consumption, and aided by other resources reserved for that crisis, it may meet, within the year all the expenses of the year, without encroaching on the rights of future generations, by burdening them with the debts of the past. War will then be but a suspension of useful works; and a return to a state of peace, a return to the progress of improvement.

I have said, fellow-citizens, that the income reserved had enabled us to extend our limits; but that extension may possibly pay for itself before we are called on, and, in the mean time, may keep down the accruing interest; in all events, it will repay the advances we have made. I know that the acquisition of Louisiana has been disapproved by some, from a candid apprehension that the enlargement of our territory would endanger its union. But who can limit the extent to which the federative principle may operate effectively? The larger our association, the less will it be shaken by local passions; and, in any view, is it not better that the opposite bank of the Mississippi should be settled by our own brethren and children, than by strangers of another family? With which shall we be most likely to live in harmony and friendly intercourse?

In matters of religion, I have considered that its free exercise is placed by the Constitution independent of the powers of the General Government. I have therefore undertaken, on no occasion, to prescribe the religious exercises suited to it, but have left them as the Constitution found them, under the direction and discipline of State and Church authorities acknowledged by the several religious societies.

The aboriginal inhabitants of these countries I have regarded with the commiseration their history inspires. Endowed with the faculties and the rights of men, breathing an ardent love of liberty and independence, and occupying a country which left them no desire but to be undisturbed, the stream of overflowing population from other regions directed itself on these shores. Without power to divert, or habits to contend against, they have been overwhelmed by the current, or driven before it. Now reduced within limits too narrow for the hunter state, humanity enjoins us to teach them agriculture and the domestic arts, to encourage them to that industry which alone can enable them to maintain their place in existence, and to prepare them, in time, for that state of society which to bodily comforts adds the improvement of the mind and morals. We have, therefore, liberally furnished them with the implements of husbandry and household use; we have placed among them instructors in the arts of first necessity; and they are covered with the ægis of the law against aggressors from among ourselves.

But the endeavors to enlighten them on the fate which awaits their present course of life, to induce them to exercise their reason, follow its dictates, and change their pursuits with the change of circumstances, have powerful obstacles to encounter. They are combated by the habits of their bodies, prejudice of their minds, ignorance, pride, and the influence of interested and crafty individuals among them, who feel themselves something in the present order of things, and fear to become nothing in any other. These persons inculcate a sanctimonious reverence for the customs of their ancestors; that whatsoever they did must be done through all time; that reason is a false guide, and to advance under its counsel in their physical, moral, or political conditions, is perilous innovation; that their duty is to remain as their Creator made them—ignorance being safety, and knowledge full of danger. In short, my friends, among them is seen the action and counteraction of good sense and bigotry. They, too, have their anti-philosophers, who find an interest in keeping things in their present state, who dread reformation, and exert all their faculties to maintain the ascendency of habit over the duty of improving our reason and obeying its mandates.

In giving these outlines, I do not mean, fellow-citizens, to arrogate to myself the merit of the measures; that is due, in the first place, to the reflecting character of our citizens at large, who, by the weight of public opinion, influence and strengthen the public measures. It is due to the sound discretion with which they select from among themselves those to whom they confide the legislative duties. It is due to the zeal and wisdom of the characters thus selected, who lay the foundations of public happiness in wholesome laws, the execution of which alone remains for others. And it is due to the able and faithful auxiliaries whose patriotism has associated with me in the executive functions.

During this course of administration, and in order to disturb it, the artillery of the press has been levelled against us, charged with whatsoever its licentiousness could devise or dare. These abuses of an institution so important to freedom and science are deeply to be regretted, inasmuch as they tend to lessen its usefulness and to sap its safety. They might, indeed, have been corrected by the wholesome punishments reserved and provided by the laws of the several States against falsehood and defamation; but public duties more urgent press on the time of public servants, and the offenders have therefore been left to find their punishment in the public indignation.

Nor was it uninteresting to the world, that an experiment should be fairly and fully made, whether freedom of discussion, unaided by power, is not sufficient for the propagation and protection of truth? Whether a government, conducting itself in the true spirit of its constitution, with zeal and purity, and doing no act which it would be unwilling the whole world should witness, can be written down by falsehood and defamation? The experiment has been tried. You have witnessed the scene. Our fellow-citizens have looked on cool and collected. They saw the latent source from which these outrages proceeded. They gathered around their public functionaries; and, when the Constitution called them to the decision by suffrage, they pronounced their verdict, honorable to those who had served them, and consolatory to the friend of man, who believes he may be intrusted with his own affairs.

No inference is here intended that the laws provided by the State against false and defamatory publications should not be enforced. He who has time, renders a service to public morals and public tranquillity in reforming these abuses by the salutary coercions of the law. But the experiment is noted to prove that, since truth and reason have maintained their ground against false opinions, in league with false facts, the press, confined to truth, needs no other legal restraint. The public judgment will correct false reasonings and opinions, on a full hearing of all parties; and no other definite line can be drawn between the inestimable liberty of the press and its demoralizing licentiousness. If there be still improprieties which this rule would not restrain, its supplement must be sought in the censorship of public opinion.

Contemplating the union of sentiment now manifested so generally, as auguring harmony and happiness to our future course, I offer to our country sincere congratulations. With those, too, not yet rallied to the same point, the disposition to do so is gaining strength. Facts are piercing through the veil drawn over them; and our doubting brethren will at length see that the mass of their fellow-citizens, with whom they cannot yet resolve to act, as to principles and measures, think as they think, and desire what they desire; that our wish, as well as theirs, is, that the public efforts may be directed honestly to the public good, that peace be cultivated, civil and religious liberty unassailed, law and order preserved, equality of rights maintained, and that state of property, equal or unequal, which results to every man from his own industry, or that of his father's. When satisfied of these views, it is not in human nature that they should not approve and support them. In the meantime, let us cherish them with patient affection; let us do them justice, and more than justice, in all competitions of interest,—and we need not doubt that truth, reason, and their own interests, will at length prevail—will gather them into the fold of their country, and will complete their entire union of opinion which gives to a nation the blessing of harmony, and the benefit of all its strength.

I shall now enter on the duties to which my fellow-citizens have again called me, and shall proceed in the spirit of those principles which they have approved. I fear not that any motives of interest may lead me astray. I am sensible of no passion which could seduce me, knowingly, from the path of justice; but the weaknesses of human nature, and the limits of my own understanding, will produce errors of judgment sometimes injurious to your interests. I shall need, therefore, all the indulgence I have heretofore experienced, the want of it will certainly not lessen with increasing years. I shall need, too, the favor of that Being in whose hands we are; who led our forefathers, as Israel of old, from their native land, and planted them in a country flowing with all the necessaries and comforts of life; who has covered our infancy with His providence, and our riper years with His wisdom and power; and to whose goodness I ask you to join with me in supplications, that He will so enlighten the minds of your servants, guide their councils, and prosper their measures, that whatsoever they do shall result in your good, and shall secure to you the peace, friendship, and approbation of all nations.—viii, 40. FORD ED., viii, 341. (March 4, 1805.)

ADDRESS OF THE GENERAL ASSEMBLY OF VIRGINIA

The " Valedictory Address of the General Assembly of Virginia ", which was agreed to on the 7th of February, 1809, gives a good idea of the high estimation in which Jefferson was held by his party, and the great majority of his countrymen, when he retired from the Presidency. It is as follows :—

"Sir.—The General Assembly of your native State cannot close their session, without acknowledging your services in the office which you are just about to lay down, and bidding you a respectful and affectionate farewell.

" We have to thank you for the model of an administration conducted on the purest principles of republicanism ; for pomp and state laid aside ; patronage discarded ; internal taxes abolished ; a host of superfluous officers disbanded ; the monarchic maxim that ' a national debt is a national blessing ', renounced, and more than thirty-three millions of our debt discharged ; the native right to nearly one hundred millions of acres of our national domain extinguished ; and, without the guilt or calamities of conquest, a vast and fertile region added to our country, far more extensive than her original possessions, bringing along with it the Mississippi and the port of Orleans, the trade of the West to the Pacific ocean, and in the intrinsic value of the land itself, a source of permanent and almost inexhaustible revenue. These are points in your administration which the historian will not fail to seize, to expand, and teach posterity to dwell upon with delight. Nor will he forget our peace with the civilized world, preserved through a season of uncommon difficulty and trial ; the good will cultivated with the unfortunate aborigines of our country, and the civilization humanely extended among them ; the lesson taught the inhabitants of the coast of Barbary, that we have the means of chastising their piratical encroachments, and awing them into justice ; and that theme, on which, above all others, the historic genius will hang with rapture, the liberty of speech and of the press, preserved inviolate, without which genius and science are given to man in vain.

" In the principles on which you have administered the government, we see only the continuation and maturity of the same virtues and abilities, which drew upon you in your youth the resentment of Dunmore. From the first brilliant and happy moment of your resistance to foreign tyranny, until the present day, we mark with pleasure and with gratitude the same uniform, consistent character, the same warm and devoted attachment to liberty and the Republic, the same Roman love of your country, her rights, her peace, her honor, her prosperity.

" How blessed will be the retirement into which you are about to go ! How deservedly blessed will it be ! For you carry with you the richest of all rewards, the recollection of a life well spent in the service of your country, and proofs the most decisive, of the love, the gratitude, the veneration of your countrymen.

" That your retirement may be as happy as your life has been virtuous and useful ; that our youth may see, in the blissful close of your days, an additional inducement to form themselves on your model, is the devout and earnest prayer of your fellow-citizens who compose the General Assembly of Virginia."—RAYNER'S *Life of Jefferson*, p. 494.

ADDRESS TO THE INHABITANTS OF ALBEMARLE CO., IN VIRGINIA

Returning to the scenes of my birth and early life, to the society of those with whom I was raised, and who have been ever dear to me, I receive, fellow-citizens and neighbors, with inexpressible pleasure, the cordial welcome you were so good as to give me. Long absent on duties which the history of a wonderful era made incumbent on those called to them, the pomp, the turmoil, the bustle and splendor of office; have drawn but deeper sighs for the tranquil and irresponsible occupations of private life, for the enjoyment of an affectionate intercourse with you, my neighbors and friends, and the endearments of family love, which nature has given us all, as the sweetner of every hour. For these I gladly lay down the distressing burthen of power, and seek, with my fellow-citizens, repose and safety under the watchful cares, the labors and perplexities of younger and abler minds. The anxieties you express to administer to my happiness, do, of themselves, confer that happiness; and the measure will be complete, if any endeavors to fulfil my duties in the several public stations to which I have been called, have obtained for me the approbation of my country. The part which I have acted on the theatre of public life, has been before them; and to their sentence I submit it; but the testimony of my native county, of the individuals who have known me in private life, to my conduct in its various duties and relations, is the more grateful, as proceeding from eye-witnesses and observers, from triers of the vicinage. Of you, then, my neighbors, I may ask, in the face of the world, " whose ox have I taken, or whom have I defrauded? Whom have I oppressed, or of whose hand have I received a bribe to blind mine eyes therewith "? On your verdict I rest with conscious security. Your wishes for my happiness are received with just sensibility, and I offer sincere prayers for your own welfare and prosperity.—To THE INHABITANTS OF ALBEMARLE COUNTY, VA. v, 439. FORD ED., ix, 250. (M., April 3, 1809.)

DECLARATION AND PROTEST OF THE COMMONWEALTH OF VIRGINIA*

We, the General Assembly of Virginia, on behalf, and in the name of the people thereof, do declare as follows:

The States of North America which confederated to establish their independence of the government of Great Britain, of which Virginia was one, became, on that acquisition free and independent States, and as such, authorized to constitute governments, each for itself, in such form as it thought best.

They entered into a compact (which is called the Constitution of the United States of America), by which they agreed to unite in a single government as to their relations with each other, and with foreign nations, and as to certain other articles particularly specified. They retained at the same time, each to itself, the other rights of independent government, comprehending mainly their domestic interests.

For the administration of their Federal branch, they agreed to appoint, in conjunction, a distinct set of functionaries, legislative, executive and judiciary, in the manner settled in that compact; while to each, severally, and of course remained its original right of appointing, each for itself, a separate set of functionaries, legislative, executive and judiciary, also, for administering the domestic branch of their respective governments.

These two sets of officers, each independent of the other, constitute thus a *whole* of government, for each State separately; the powers ascribed to the one, as specifically made federal, exercised over the whole, the residuary powers, retained to the other, exercisable exclusively over its particular State, foreign herein, each to the others, as they were before the original compact.

To this construction of government and distribution of its powers, the Commonwealth of Virginia does religiously and affectionately adhere, opposing, with equal fidelity and firmness, the usurpation of either set of functionaries of the rightful powers of the other.

But the Federal branch has assumed in some cases, and claimed in others, a right of enlarging its own powers by constructions, inferences, and indefinite deductions from those directly given, which this Assembly does declare to be usurpations of the powers retained to the independent branches, mere interpolations into the compact, and direct infractions of it.

They claim, for example, and have commenced the exercise of a right to construct roads, open canals, and effect other internal improvements within the territories and jurisdictions exclusively belonging to the several States, which this Assembly does declare has not been given to that branch by the constitutional compact, but remains to each State among its domestic and unalienated powers, exercisable within itself and by its domestic authorities alone.

This Assembly does further disavow and declare to be most false and unfounded, the doctrine that the compact, in authorzing its Federal branch to lay and collect taxes, duties, imposts and excises, to pay the debts and provide for the common defence and general welfare of the United States, has given them thereby a power to do whatever *they* may think, or pretend, would promote the general welfare, which construction would make that, of itself, a complete government, without limitation of powers; but that the plain sense and obvious meaning were, that they might levy the taxes necessary to provide for the general welfare, by the various acts of power therein specified and delegated to them, and by no others.

Nor is it admitted, as has been said, that the people of these States, by not investing their Federal branch with all the means of bettering their condition, have denied to themselves any which may effect that purpose; since, in the distribution of these means they have given to that branch those which belong to its department, and to the States have reserved separately the residue which belong to them separately. And thus by the organization of the two branches taken together, have completely secured the first object of human association, the full improvement of their condition, and reserved to themselves all the faculties of multiplying their own blessings.

Whilst the General Assembly thus declares the rights retained by the States, rights which they have never yielded, and which this State will never voluntarily yield, they do not mean to raise the banner of dissatisfaction, or of separation from their sister States, co-parties with themselves to this compact. They know and value too highly the blessings of their Union as to foreign nations and questions arising among themselves, to consider every infraction as to be met by actual resistance. They respect too affectionately the opinions of those possessing the same rights under the same instrument, to make every difference of construction a ground of immediate rupture. They would, indeed, consider such a rupture as among the greatest calamities which could befall them; but not the greatest. There is yet one greater, submission to a government of unlimited powers. It is only when the hope of avoiding this shall have become absolutely desperate, that further forbearance could not be indulged. Should a majority of the co-parties, therefore, contrary to the expectation and hope of this Assembly, prefer, at this time, acquiescence in these assumptions of power by the Federal member of the government, we will be patient and suffer much, under the confidence that time, ere it be too late, will prove to them also the bitter consequences in which that usurpation will involve us all. In the meanwhile, we will breast with them, rather than separate from them, every misfortune, save that only of living under a government of unlimited powers. We owe every other sacrifice to ourselves, to our federal brethren, and to the world at large, to pursue with temper and with perseverance the great experiment which shall prove that man is capable of living in society, governing itself by laws self-imposed, and securing to its members the enjoyment of life, liberty, property, and peace; and further to show, that even when the govern-

---

* This paper was entitled by Jefferson, "The Solemn Declaration and Protest of the Commonwealth of Virginia, on the Principles of the Constitution of the United States of America, and on the violations of them". Jefferson sent it to Madison in December, 1825, with an explanatory letter (vii, 422. FORD ED., x, 348) in which he said: "It may intimidate the wavering. It may break the western coalition, by offering the same thing in a different form. It will be viewed with favor in contrast with the Georgia opposition, and fear of strengthening that. It will be an example of a temperate mode of opposition in future and similar cases."—EDITOR.

ment of its choice shall manifest a tendency to degeneracy, we are not at once to despair but that the will and the watchfulness of its sounder parts will reform its aberrations, recall it to original and legitimate principles, and restrain it within the rightful limits of self-govern-ment. And these are the objects of this Declaration and Protest.

Supposing, then, that it might be for the good of the whole, as some of its co-States seem to think, that the power of making roads and canals should be added to those directly given to the Federal branch, as more likely to be systematically and beneficially directed, than by the independent action of the several States, this Commonwealth, from respect to these opinions, and a desire of conciliation with its co-States, will consent, in concurrence with them, to make this addition, provided it be done regularly by an amendment of the compact, in the way established by that instrument, and provided also, it be sufficiently guarded against abuses, compromises, and corrupt practices, not only of possible, but of probable occurrence.

And as a further pledge of the sincere and cordial attachment of this Commonwealth to the Union of the whole, so far as has been consented to by the compact called " The Con-stitution of the United States of America " (constructed according to the plain and ordinary meaning of its language, to the common intendment of the time, and of those who framed it) ; to give also to all parties and authorities, time for reflection and consideration, whether, under a temperate view of the possible consequences, and especially of the constant obstruc-t'ons which an equivocal majority must ever expect to meet, they will still prefer the assump-tion of this power rather than its acceptance from the free will of their constituents ; and to preserve peace in the meanwhile, we proceed to make it the duty of our citizens, until the Legislature shall otherwise and ultimately decide, to acquiesce under those acts of the Federal branch of our government which we have declared to be usurpations, and against which, in point of right, we do protest as null and void, and never to be quoted as precedents of right.

We, therefore, do enact, and Be It Enacted by the General Assembly of Virginia, That all citizens of this Commonwealth, and persons and authorities within the same, shall pay full obedience at all times to the acts which may be passed by the Congress of the United States, the object of which shall be the construction of post roads, making canals of navigation, and maintaining the same in any part of the United States, in like manner as if said acts were *totidem verbis*, passed by the Legislature of this Commonwealth.—ix, 496. Ford ed., x, 349. (Dec. 24, 1825.)

ESTRANGEMENT AND RECONCILIATION OF JEFFERSON AND ADAMS

[To Mrs. John Adams.]

Dear Madam,—The affectionate sentiments which you have had the goodness to express in your letter of May 20, towards my dear departed daughter, have awakened in me sensibilities natural to the occasion, and recalled your kindness to her, which I shall ever remember with gratitude and friendship. I can assure you with truth, they had made an indelible impression on her mind, and that to the last, on our meetings after long separations, whether I had heard lately of you, and how you did, were among the earliest of her enquiries. In giving you this assurance I perform a sacred duty for her, and, at the same time, am thankful for the occasion furnished me, of expressing my regret that circumstances should have arisen, which have seemed to draw a line of separation between us. The friendship with which you honored me has ever been valued, and fully reciprocated; and although events have been passing which might be trying to some minds, I never believed yours to be of that kind, nor felt that my own was. Neither my estimate of your character, nor the esteem founded in that, has ever been lessened for a single moment, although doubts whether it would be acceptable may have forbidden manifestations of it.

Mr. Adams's friendship and mine began at an earlier date. It accompanied us through long and important scenes. The different conclusions we had drawn from our political reading and reflections, were not permitted to lessen personal esteem; each party being conscious they were the result of an honest conviction in the other. Like differences of opinion existing among our fellow citizens, attached them to one or the other of us, and produced a rivalship in their minds which did not exist in ours. We never stood in one another's way; for if either had been withdrawn at any time, his favorers would not have gone over to the other, but would have sought for some one of homogeneous opinions. This consideration was sufficient to keep down all jealousy between us, and to guard our friendship from any disturbance by sentiments of rivalship; and I can say with truth, that one act of Mr. Adams's life, and one only, ever gave me a moment's personal displeasure. I did consider his last appointments to office as personally unkind. They were from among my most ardent political enemies, from whom no faithful cooperation could ever be expected; and laid me under the embarrassment of acting through men whose views were to defeat mine, or to encounter the odium of putting others in their places. It seemed but common justice to leave a successor free to act by instruments of his own choice. If my respect for him did not permit me to ascribe the whole blame to the influence of others, it left something for friendship to forgive, and after brooding over it for some little time, and not always resisting the expressing of it, I forgave it cordially, and returned to the same state of esteem and respect for him which had so long subsisted. Having come into life a little later than Mr. Adams, his career has preceded mine, as mine is followed by some other; and it will probably be closed at the same distance after him which time originally placed between us. I maintain for him, and shall carry into private life, an uniform and high measure of respect and good will, and for yourself a sincere attachment. * * *—To Mrs. John Adams. iv, 545. Ford ed., viii, 306. (W., June 1804.)

[To Mrs. John Adams.]

Dear Madam,—Your favor of the 1st inst. was duly received, and I would not have again intruded on you, but to rectify certain facts which seem not to have been presented to you under their true aspects.* My charities to Callender are considered as rewards for his calumnies. As early, I think, as 1796, I was told in Philadelphia that Callender, the author of the " Political Progress of Britain ", was in that city, a fugitive from persecution for having written that book, and in distress. I had read and approved the book; I considered him as a man of genius, unjustly persecuted. I knew nothing of his private character, and immediately expressed my readiness to contribute to his relief, and to serve him. It was a considerable time after, that, on application from a person who thought of him as I did, I contributed to his relief, and afterwards repeated the contribution. Himself I did not see till long after, nor ever more than two or three times. When he first began to write, he told some useful truths in his coarse way; but nobody sooner disapproved of his writing than I did, or wished more that he would be silent. My charities to him were no more meant as encouragements to his scurrilities, than those I give to the beggar at my door are meant as rewards for the vices of his life, and to make them chargeable to myself. In truth, they would have been greater to him, had he never written a word after the work for which he fled from Britain . * * *

But another fact is, that " I liberated a wretch who was suffering for a libel against Mr. Adams ". I do not know who was the particular wretch alluded to; but I discharged every person under punishment or prosecution under the Sedition law, because I considered, and now consider, that law to be a nullity, as absolute and as palpable as if Congress had ordered us to fall down and worship a golden image; and that it was as much my duty to arrest its execution in every stage, as it would have been to have rescued from the fiery furnace those who should have been cast into it for refusing to worship the image. It was accordingly done in every instance, without asking what the offenders had done, or against whom they had offended, but whether the pains they were suffering were inflicted under the pretended Sedition law. It was certainly possible that my motives for contributing to the relief of Callender, and liberating sufferers under the Sedition law, might have been to protect, encourage, and reward slander; but they may also have been those which inspire ordinary charities to objects of distress, meritorious or not, or the obligation of an oath to protect the Constitution, violated by an unauthorized act of Congress. Which of these were my motives, must be decided by a

* Mrs. Adams, in replying to the preceding letter, put forward Jefferson's patronage of Editor Callender as an offset to the midnight appointments. See Callender.—Editor.
+ Quotation 59 gives the part of the letter omitted at this point.—Editor.

regard to the general tenor of my life. On this I am not afraid to appeal to the nation at large, to posterity, and still less to that Being who sees Himself our motives, who will judge us from His own knowledge of them, and not on the testimony of *"Porcupine"* or Fenno.

You observe, there has been one other act of my administration personally unkind, and suppose it will readily suggest itself to me. I declare on my honor, Madam, I have not the least conception what act is alluded to. I never did a single one with an unkind intention. * * *—To Mrs. John Adams. iv, 555. Ford ed., viii, 308. (July 1804.)

[To Mrs. John Adams.]

Your letter, Madam, of the 18th of August, has been some days received, but a press of business has prevented the acknowledgment of it; perhaps, indeed, I may have already trespassed too far on your attention. With those who wish to think amiss of me, I have learned to be perfectly indifferent; but where I know a mind to be ingenuous, and to need only truth to set it to rights, I cannot be as passive. The act of personal unkindness alluded to in your former letter, is said in your last to have been the removal of your eldest son from some office to which the judges had appointed him. I conclude, then, he must have been a commissioner of bankruptcy. But I declare to you, on my honor, that this is the first knowledge I have ever had that he was so. It may be thought, perhaps, that I ought to have enquired who were such, before I appointed others. But it is to be observed, that the former law permitted the judges to name commissioners occasionally only, for every case as it arose, and not to make them permanent officers. Nobody, therefore, being in office, there could be no removal. The judges, you well know, have been considered as highly federal; and it was noted that they confined their nominations exclusively to federalists. The Legislature, dissatisfied with this, transferred the nomination to the President, and made the offices permanent. The very object in passing the law was, that he should correct, not confirm, what was deemed the partiality of the judges. I thought it, therefore, proper to inquire, not whom they had employed, but whom I ought to appoint to fulfil the intentions of the law. In making these appointments, I put in a proportion of federalists, equal, I believe, to the proportion they bear in numbers through the Union generally. Had I known that your son had acted, it would have been a real pleasure to me to have preferred him to some who were named in Boston, in what was deemed the same line of politics. To this I should have been led by my knowledge of my integrity, as well as my sincere dispositions towards yourself and Mr. Adams *. * * * The candor manifested in your letter, and which I ever believed you to possess, has alone inspired the desire of calling your attention, once more, to those circumstances of fact and motive by which I claim to be judged. I hope you will see these intrusions on your time to be, what they really are, proofs of my great respect for you. I tolerate with the utmost latitude the right of others to differ from me in opinion without imputing to them criminality. I know too well the weakness and uncertainty of human reason to wonder at its different results. Both of our political parties, at least the honest part of them, agree conscientiously in the same object—the public good; but they differ essentially in what they deem the means of promoting that good. One side believes it best done by one composition of the governing powers; the other, by a different one. One fears most the ignorance of the people; the other, the selfishness of rulers independent of them. Which is right, time and experience will prove. We think that one side of this experiment has been long enough tried, and proved not to promote the good of the many; and that the other has not been fairly and sufficiently tried. Our opponents think the reverse. With whichever opinion the body of the nation concurs, that must prevail. My anxieties on this subject will never carry me beyond the use of fair and honorable means, of truth and reason; nor have they ever lessened my esteem for moral worth, nor alienated my affections from a single friend, who did not first withdraw himself. Whenever this has happened, I confess I have not been insensible to it; yet have ever kept myself open to a return of their justice. I conclude with sincere prayers for your health and happiness, that yourself and Mr. Adams may long enjoy the tranquillity you desire and merit, and see in the prosperity of your family what is the consummation of the last and warmest of human wishes.—To Mrs. John Adams. iv, 560. Ford ed., viii, 310. (M., Sep. 11, 1804.)

[To Dr. Benjamin Rush.]

I receive with sensibility your observations on the discontinuance of friendly correspondence between Mr. Adams and myself, and the concern you take in its restoration. This discontinuance has not proceeded from me, nor from the want of sincere desire and of effort on my part, to renew our intercourse. You know the perfect coincidence of principle and of action, in the early part of the Revolution, which produced a high degree of mutual respect and esteem between Mr. Adams and myself. Certainly no man was ever truer than he was, in that day, to those principles of rational republicanism which, after the necessity of throwing off our monarchy, dictated all our efforts in the establishment of a new government. And although he swerved, afterwards, towards the principles of the English constitution, our friendship did not abate on that account †. * * *

You remember the machinery which the federalists played off, about that time, to beat down the friends to the real principles of our Constitution, to silence by terror every expression in their favor, to bring us into war with France and alliance with England, and finally to homologize our Constitution with that of England. Mr. Adams, you know, was overwhelmed with feverish addresses, dictated by the fear, and often by the pen, of the *bloody buoy,* and was seduced by them into some open indications of his new principles of

---

* The part of the letter omitted here is printed in this volume under the title, Sedition Law, Executive vs. Judiciary.—Editor.

† For omitted clause, see quotation 89.—Editor.

government, and in fact, was so elated as to mix with his kindness a little superciliousness towards me. Even Mrs. Adams, with all her good sense and prudence, was sensibly flushed. And you recollect the short suspension of our intercourse, and the circumstance which gave rise to it which you were so good as to bring to an early explanation, and have set to rights, to the cordial satisfaction of us all *. * * *

Two or three years after, having had the misfortune to lose a daughter, between whom and Mrs. Adams there had been a considerable attachment, she made it the occasion of writing me a letter, in which, with the tenderest expression of concern at this event, she carefully avoided a single one of friendship towards myself, and even concluded it with the wishes " of her who *once* took pleasure in subscribing herself your friend, Abigail Adams ". Unpromising as was the complexion of this letter, I determined to make an effort towards removing the cloud from between us. · This brought on a correspondence which I now enclose for your perusal, after which be so good as to return it to me, as I have never communicated it to any mortal breathing, before. I send it to you, to convince you I have not been wanting either in the desire, or the endeavor to remove this misunderstanding. Indeed, I thought it highly disgraceful to us both, as indicating minds not sufficiently elevated to prevent a public competition from affecting our personal friendship. I soon found from the correspondence that conciliation was desperate, and yielding to an intimation in her last letter, I ceased from further explanation†. * * *

I have gone into these details, that you might know everything which had passed between us, might be fully possessed of the state of facts and dispositions, and judge for yourself whether they admit a revival of that friendly intercourse for which you are so kindly solicitous. I shall certainly not be wanting in anything on my part which may second your efforts, which will be the easier with me, inasmuch as I do not entertain a sentiment of Mr. Adams, the expression of which could give him reasonable offence.—To Dr. BENJAMIN RUSH. v, 558. FORD ED., ix, 299. (M., Jan. 1811.)

[To Dr. Benjamin Rush.]

I communicated to you the correspondence which had parted Mrs. Adams and myself, in proof that I could not give friendship in exchange for such sentiments as she had recently taken up towards myself, and avowed and maintained in her letters to me. Nothing but a total renunciation of these could admit a reconciliation, and that could be cordial only in proportion as the return to ancient opinions was believed sincere. In these jaundiced sentiments of hers I had associated Mr. Adams, knowing the weight which her opinions had with him, and notwithstanding she declared in her letters that they were not communicated to him. A late incident has satisfied me that I wronged him as well as her, in not yielding entire confidence to this assurance on her part. Two of the Mr. —— ——, my neighbors and friends, took a tour to the northward during the last summer. In Boston they fell into company with Mr. Adams. and * * * passed a day with him at Braintree. He spoke out to them everything which came uppermost, * * * and seemed most disposed to dwell on those things which happened during his own administration. He spoke of his *masters,* as he called his Heads of departments, as acting above his control, and often against his opinions. Among many other topics, he adverted to the unprincipled licentiousness of the press against myself, adding, " I always loved Jefferson, and still love him ".

This is enough for me. I only needed this knowledge to revive towards him all the affections of the most cordial moments of our lives. Changing a single word only in Dr. Franklin's character of him, I knew him to be always an honest man, often a great one, but sometimes incorrect and precipitate in his judgments; and it is known to those who have ever heard me speak of Mr. Adams, that I have ever done him justice myself, and defended him when, assailed by others, with the single exception as to political opinions. But with a man possessing so many other estimable qualities, why should we be dissocialized by mere differences of opinion in politics, in religion, in philosophy, or anything else? His opinions are as honestly formed as my own. Our different views of the same subject are the result of a difference in our organization and experience. I never withdrew from the society of any man on this account, although many have done it from me; much less should I do it from one with whom I had gone through, with hand and heart, so many trying scenes. I wish, therefore, but for an apposite occasion to express to Mr. Adams my unchanged affections for him. There is an awkwardness which hangs over the resuming a correspondence so long discontinued, unless something could arise which should call for a letter. Time and chance may perhaps generate such an occasion, of which I shall not be wanting in promptitude to avail myself. From this fusion of mutual affections, Mrs. Adams is, of course, separated. It will only be necessary that I never name her. In your letters to Mr. Adams, you can, perhaps suggest my continued cordiality towards him, and knowing this, should an occasion of writing first present itself to him, he will, perhaps, avail himself of it, as I certainly will, should it first occur to me. No ground for jealousy now existing, he will certainly give fair play to the natural warmth of his heart.—To Dr. BENJAMIN RUSH. vi, 30. FORD ED., ix, 299. (P.F., Dec. 1811.)

* Quotations 77, 78, 83 and 88 give the continuation of the text.—EDITOR.
† Quotations 72 and 60, read consecutively, supply the omission in the text.—EDITOR.

TOPICAL INDEX

WITH CROSS-REFERENCES